NAVAL WEAPONS
OF WORLD WAR TWO

The old and the new: the big gun, represented by the 320mm/44cal main armament of the Italian battleship *Andrea Doria* (top); and the aircraft carrier, in the form of the American CVL *Cabot* and the CV *Ticonderoga*, leading a line of battleships.

Elio Ando' (top) and CPL

NAVAL WEAPONS OF WORLD WAR TWO

JOHN CAMPBELL

Naval
Institute
Press

First published in Great Britain 1985 by
Conway Maritime Press Ltd
24 Bride Lane, Fleet Street
London EC4Y 8DR

Published and distributed in the United States of America by the Naval Institute Press, Annapolis, Maryland 21402

Library of Congress Catalog Card
No 85-62422

ISBN 0-87021-459-4

This edition is authorized for sale only in the United States and its territories and possessions, and Canada

Manufactured in the United Kingdom

CONTENTS

GREAT BRITAIN

UNITED STATES OF AMERICA

JAPAN

GERMANY

FRANCE

ITALY

SOVIET UNION

OTHER COUNTRIES

ACKNOWLEDGEMENTS AND SOURCES

This book is the result of several years of research and it is not possible to quote all sources or indeed to mention all those who have so willingly helped. Some of those who gave the greatest assistance are no longer in their former positions. For British weapons the principal sources have been handbooks, lists, reports and summaries written in the war and immediate post-war periods. Among special items may be noted the Torpedo School reports, Confidential Admiralty Fleet Orders (CAFOs), Range Tables, Range and Elevation Scales, Gun Mounting Appropriation Lists, List of Change, Ordnance Board minutes and other papers, and Gun Registers. Also to be noted are the large collection of unsorted Elswick drawings in the National Maritime Museum and the numerous actual weapons and ordnance stores in the Naval Ordnance Museum, Priddy's Hard.

Special thanks are due to Mr David Brown, head of the Naval Historical Branch, to the late Captain Michael Beeching and Lieutenant-Commander Mike Wilson of that Branch, to Mr Alan Francis and Miss Helen White of the Naval Historical Library, to Mr David Lyon and Mr Michael Dandridge of the National Maritime Museum and to Mr Cyril Susans, Mr Arthur Ingham and Mr Stanley Hackman of the Naval Ordnance Museum. Also to be mentioned are the Cumbria Archives for Vickers drawings, Mr Munday of the Air Historical Branch for data on airborne weapons, Lieutenant-Commander Pike of HMS *Excellent* and Mr Peter Hodges for much help on fire-control.

For the weapons of foreign navies, information will be found in the above material but mostly from other sources. For the USA special thanks are due to Dr Norman Friedman, the author of *US Naval Weapons*, particularly for help with the omnibus edition of the gun catalogue *OP 127*. There is no omnibus gun mounting catalogue, but the 1945 edition of *OP 1112* is in the Naval Historical Branch. Mr Craig Hatcher of Encinitas, California provided data on range tables as did Mr Nathan Okun on projectiles.

For Japan the US Naval Technical Mission Reports, some in the Naval Historical Branch and some in the Imperial War Museum are the main source and special thanks are due to the Naval Historical Branch staff mentioned above and to Mr Philip Reed of the Imperial War Museum. Information was also obtained from Terasaki *Kaigun Hojutsu Shi* on Japanese guns.

In the case of Germany special thanks are due to Mr Bob Coppock of the Naval Historical Branch for help with their large collection of German material and also to Mr Philip Reed of the Imperial War Museum. Mr Antony Preston lent me his copy of the Cordes Report, essential for the understanding of German gunnery development.

For other navies an important source is the German intelligence summary 'Waffentechnische - Nachrichten aus fremden Marinen' in the Naval Historical Branch. For France much information was provided by the Centre d'Archives de l'Armement and by Sciences et Techniques de l'Armement, and for Italy by the Naval Attaché and from Bagnasco *Le Armi delle Navi Italiane*. There is important data on Italian torpedoes in the CAFOs and on guns in the Ordnance Board minutes, National Maritime Museum and Imperial War Museum. With Russia Lieutenant-Colonel Charles E Somers USA (Retd) was of great help as was Karl-Erik Westerlund for Sweden.

In conclusion special thanks are due to Mrs Molly Westmore for typing the book and for her patience and skill in dealing with very small and at times nearly illegible handwriting.

PUBLISHER'S NOTE

ORGANISATION

This book is organised by country, with the information within each national section following a standard order for ease of reference. Thus for each country, general prefatory remarks are followed by chapters on Guns, Torpedoes, Anti-submarine weapons, Mines, and aerial weapons (Bombs, Rockets and Guided Missiles). These in turn are divided into a technical introduction and a list of weapons, which is sub-divided by the relevant categories, all of which are given on the Contents page. Guns, which form the vast majority of the book, are listed in order of size (largest first) with the newest weapons preceding older marks. The final section on 'Other Countries' follows much the same pattern, except that the primary division is by weapon-type, sub-divided into countries (in alphabetical order).

ILLUSTRATIONS

Collecting, collating and editing the drawings and photographs for this book was a mammoth task and the publishers are indebted to a large number of individuals and organisations who helped out most willingly. For the sake of completeness, it was necessary to re-use a number of drawings from previous Conway publications, and for permission to do this we are grateful to Peter Hodges, John Lambert, John Roberts, Al Ross, Erwin Sieche, Ross Watton and David Westwood. New drawing work was carried out most skillfully by Przemyslaw Budzbon and John Lambert (larger scale copies of many of John Lambert's illustrations are available through the David MacGregor Plans Service, 99 Lonsdale Road, London SW13 9DA, UK).

Copies of official drawings were kindly supplied by Commander Canisius of Den Helder Naval Museum (for the Netherlands), Robert Dumas (for France), Norman Friedman (for the USA), Karl-Erik Westerlund (for Bofors weapons), and Mike Whitley (for Germany) and we are pleased to acknowledge the considerable research effort involved.

However, we must pay particular tribute to Gino Chesi, who made available the magnificent drawings of Italian Weapons produced by the Associazione Navimodellisti Bolognesi. Credited *ANB* after the captions, these and many other large-scale drawings are available from Casella Postale 976, 40100 Bologna, Italy.

Assistance with photographs came from all over the world, the following individuals being especially generous: Elio Ando', D K Brown, Przemyslaw Budzbon, Ian Buxton, Aldo Fraccaroli, Pierre Hervieux, John Lambert, Jacques Navarret, Robert Scheina, Marek Twardowski, Karl-Erik Westerlund and Mike Whitley.

Some gaps in the illustration remain, and many of the official drawings do not reproduce as well as could be wished, but thanks to this truly international effort, the pictorial coverage now matches the encyclopedic text.

ABBREVIATIONS AND GLOSSARY

Many of the weapons introductory sections give fuller descriptions of the items noted below. Readers should also turn to these introductions for an explication of particular systems of designation, as used for example by Germany and Japan.

AA Anti-aircraft

ABU Auto barrage unit (noted in section on British HA fire-control)

AFCC Admiralty fire-control clock (noted in section on British LA fire-control)

AFCT Admiralty fire-control table (noted in section on British LA fire-control)

AGTU Admiralty gyro transmission unit (noted in section on British LA fire-control)

AMC Armed merchant cruiser

Amplidyne generator A US rotating electrical power amplifier, generally similar to the British metadyne noted later in the glossary

APC Armour-piercing capped shell

AP Armour-piercing shell

AR Anti-radar shell, containing radar reflecting material

Arbor The shaft supporting a depth charge in a depth charge thrower, and in later designs acting as a non-expendable piston

A/S Anti-submarine

Autofrettage, autofretted Literally 'self-hooping', 'self-hooped'. A process of expanding a partly-machined hollow gun forging, usually a barrel or liner, by applying hydraulic pressure to the interior surface. The elastic limit is increased, particularly that of the inner part, while the less strained outer part applies a compressive force to the inner as if a hoop or tube had been shrunk-on. The process often enabled steels with low alloy content to be used

B Barbette. Used at one time to denote British turret mountings

BD Between decks. Used for gun mountings located on the deck below that over which the guns fire

Ballistic cap A thin metal ogive or cone fixed to the nose of a shell to reduce its air-resistance

Ballistic height corrector (noted in section on British HA fire-control)

Base-ring mounting A mounting on a platform supported by a hollow ball or roller race, smaller than but similar to that supporting a turret

BM Breech mechanism

Bourrelet An accurately machined or ground surface immediately in rear of the shell head, providing a front bearing surface

BTH British Thomson Houston Company

BL Originally breech-loading as opposed to muzzle-loading; later applied to guns with bag charges

Boat tailing Tapering part of the shell in rear of the driving band to reduce air-resistance particularly at lower velocities

Casemate mountings Mountings suited for enclosed casemates or batteries

Clarkson's cases Flash-proof non-expendable cases sometimes used for transporting bag charges for 6in guns between magazine and gun

Coaster gear Similar to a bicycle free-wheel gear (noted in section on Japanese 46cm mounting)

Common, special common, shell Common shell was originally black powder filled and intended for the attack of lightly armoured or unarmoured targets. Later TNT or similar fillings were used. (Special Common is noted in section on US Projectiles)

Converter A fire-control instrument for converting one system of co-ordinates to another. Also a rotating electrical machine for transforming the characteristics of the supply (noted in section on German HA and LA fire-control)

Copper choking Reduction of the bore of a gun by copper deposits from the driving bands

Corrections (Tilt, Dip, Displacement) (noted in section on British LA fire-control)

CP Centre pivot. Applied to gun mountings rotating on a ball or roller race round a fixed pivot

CPC, CPBC Common pointed capped shell. Common pointed ballistic capped shell, known from 1946 as SAPBC

CRBF Close-range blind fire (noted in section on British close-range HA fire-control)

crh The radius of a shell head in calibres. 5/10crh, or similar expressions, means a radius of 10 calibres but the head length of a 5crh shell

CT Conning-tower

D (explosive) Ammonium picrate, the standard USN filling for armour-piercing shell

DAMS Defensively armed merchant ships. First World War term

DEMS Defensively equipped merchant ships. Second World War term

DCT, DT Director control tower, Director tower. DCT also depth charge thrower

DFCT Dreyer fire-control table

DINA Bis-nitroxyethylnitramine (noted in section on US propellants)

Dipole An antenna consisting of a single wire, usually half a wavelength long and fed at the centre

Doppler effect The change in apparent frequency of sound or electromagnetic waves emitted or reflected by a moving object

Dopp MPLC Twin central pivot mounting (German)

Dumaresq A simple course and speed resolver used to estimate rates

EFC Equivalent full charges. In British practice a half charge for heavy guns was reckoned as 1/16 of a full charge in calculating gun life

Elswick three-motion short-arm mechanism A type of screw breech-mechanism favoured in Britain and Japan for certain heavy guns. It had the advantage of much reduced slam compared with the Vickers 'pure couple' mechanism, but was superseded after the First World War by the Asbury roller cam mechanism

EMF Electromotive force

EM(M) gear Magnetic coils to hold the P sight gyro vertical (noted in section on British LA fire-control)

Equilibriator Spring, compressed air or hydraulic buffers added to a gun mounting to compensate for the weight of the barrel when the cradle trunnions are much in rear of the centre of gravity of the elevating parts. Much more frequent in army guns

FCB Fire-control box (noted in section on British LA and HA fire-control)

Fixed/separate ammunition For QF guns. In fixed ammunition the shell was pressed into the mouth of the cartridge case and formed a single permanent unit, while in separate the shell and cartridge were independant units.

FKC Fuze keeping clock (noted in section on British HA fire-control)

Flame-back The emission of burning gases when the breech of a gun is opened before the barrel has been cleared by air or water blast or when the charge has not ignited properly

Follow-the-pointer gear A system of data transmission where the pointer of a dial driven from the relevant control is matched by an operator moving a second pointer connected or transmitting to the corresponding indicator.

FuMO An abbreviation of the German term (*Funkmessortung*) for naval radar

Fuzes The most important development was the VT (variable time) or proximity fuze (noted in sections on US and British projectiles). Other shell fuzes can be classified as percussion, with or without delay; time depending on the burning of a variable length of gunpowder composition; and mechanical time depending on a clockwork mechanism. Time and percussion fuzes, originally for field gun shrapnel, were rare in naval shells. The position (base and/or nose) and types of fuze used in the more recent shells are noted in the projectile sections of the major navies

Gaine (booster) An explosive container detonated by the fuze and in turn detonating the main shell fitting

g-c Gun-cotton. High nitrogen nitrocellulose used as the explosive in old types of mines and torpedoes. Generally used wet

GLC, GXLC Gyro level corrector; gyro cross-level corrector (noted in section on British HA fire-control)

GRU, GRUB, GRUDOU, GRUS Gyro Rate Unit; Gyro Rate Unit Box; Gyro Rate Unit Deflection Oil Unit; Gyro Rate Unit Stabliser (all noted in section on British HA fire-control)

Gyro stable vertical (noted in section on US fire-control)

HA High angle

HACS High angle control system (noted in section on British HA fire-control)

Helm compensating gear (noted in section on British LA fire-control)

HE High explosive, often applied to shell with large percentage weights of explosive

HADFAS HA director forward area sight (noted in section on British HA fire-control)

HDML Harbour defence motor launch

HF/DF High frequency direction finder

Hornrings Rings shrunk onto German heavy guns to which the piston rods of the recoil and run-out cylinders were attached (see, for example, the 40.6cm SKC/34)

Hydrostatic flooder (noted in description of German UMB mine)

K devices Dye stuffs located inside the ballistic cap of a shell so that the splashes of a particular ship could be identified in concentrated firing

Kenyon doors An alternative to shell bogies only fitted to some British 15in mountings (noted under 15in Mk 1 gun)

Kst MPLC Coast central pivot mounting (German)

LA Low angle

Lands, rifling The raised areas between two rifling grooves. The bore diameter of a gun was measured over the lands

LCG(L) Landing craft gun (large)

LCS(M) Landing craft support (medium)

Lobing Continuously switching a radar beam between two or more positions (lobes). Comparison between the returns gives increased directional accuracy

Loose liner, loose barrel construction Building a gun with a small clearance between the outer diameter of the liner or barrel and the inner diameter of the next outer part. When firing, the gas pressure expands the liner or barrel elastically, but otherwise the clearance remains and it is easy to change the liner or barrel after removal of locking devices

Magnetostriction hydrophone A hydrophone depending on the alteration in the magnetic properties of some nickel alloys when subject to changes in mechanical pressure produced by an acoustic diaphragm

Magslips The British pattern of 'synchro' (noted in section on British LA fire-control)

MC, MD, SC Cordite (noted in section on British propellants)

Metadyne A system of electrical power amplification originally developed by Metropolitan-Vickers for underground railway traction. A DC metadyne generator is turned by a constant speed electric motor, and no current is produced unless the field windings are fed by an amplified error signal converted to DC from magslips. The signal power is amplified by the metadyne generator by a factor of up to about 10,000, and the DC current of the same polarity as the signal is fed to the armature of the mounting elevating or training motor, the field coils having a constant DC supply from the mains. The motors only run when fed by the generator and turned in either direction depending on the polarity of the current. Torque is proportional to the error signal. Separate metadyne generators were used for elevation and training, often driven by the same constant speed motor. The principle was also applied to some fuze setting machines

mil A unit of angular measurement, equal to 1/6400 of a circle. It may be assumed approximately to subtend a distance of 1/1000 of the range

MG Machine gun

ML Motor launch

MMS Motor minesweeper

MTB Motor torpedo boat

MGB Motor gunboat

MNBDO Mobile naval base defence organisation

Monel metal Monel metal is a corrosion-resistant alloy mainly of nickel and copper

Monobloc A gun built from a single tube apart from the breech-ring and mechanism

MPLC German central pivot mounting – *Mittel-pivot-laffette*, C being followed by the last two figures of the nominal date (noted in German introduction)

MF/DF Medium frequency direction finder

MV Muzzle velocity

NC Nitrocellulose

N Nitrogen

NG Nitroglycerin

N (Cordite N) A British army flashless propellant (noted in section on US propellants)

NF, NQFP, NFQ, NH, FNHP Flashless propellants (noted in section on British propellants)

NVNC New Vickers non-cemented armour (noted in section on Japanese projectiles)

Obturator A device for sealing the breech of a gun, more specifically a screw breech BL. In the usual De Bange system the mushroom head of the vent axial was driven back on firing against a pad which was forced into a conical seating. Pad compositions vary but originally a mixture of asbestos, tallow and wax was used, pressed into shape and protected by a cover of canvas or asbestos-wire cloth.

P Pedestal gun mounting. The mounting has a pivot which rotates inside a ball or roller race carried in a fixed pedestal

Pantograph linkage rammer A method used by the Italians, of keeping the rammer in line with the bore as the gun elevated

Paraboloid antenna Radar antenna in the form obtained by rotating a parabola about its axis

Paravane A fish-shaped body with cable cutters, streamed on each side of the forefoot to protect a ship against moored mines by cutting the moorings. The first mine cable was cut in November 1915. Also towed on each quarter by high speed minesweepers

Parkerising Treatment of steel in a phosphate solution which gives limited protection against rust

PETN The explosive pentaerythritol tetranitrate

Pl, Sl Applied to the foremost port and starboard gun mountings, P2 being the next aft on the port side, etc

Plate normal The direction at right angles to the plate surface

Polyrods Elementary radiators scanned by phase-switching used in the US Mk 8 radar

Pom-pom A term applied to the British 2pdr Mk II and Mk VIII guns. It originated with the 37mm 1pdr used in the Boer War, and was supposed to indicate the sound made by such automatic guns when firing

Potentiometer Basically an instrument for measuring potential difference by means of a resistor under constant potential and a movable contact

Precessional torque Torque applied to the gimbals of a gyro causing the latter to precess – that is for the rotor axis to tend to realign itself parallel to the axis of an applied external force

PRF Pulse Repetition Frequency, the rate at which radar pulses repeat in pulses/second

'Probertised' chamber A gun chamber with a long taper known as a 'leed' before the full depth of the rifling was reached. It had advantages with very high velocity guns particularly if the shell had a forward centring band

Push-pull gear A mechanism operating forwards and backwards usually in a straight line

QF Quick-firer or quick-firing gun. A gun with the propellant charge in whole or in part in a metal case (noted in British guns introduction)

Quickmatch A thread or wick of textile material impregnated with a fast-burning explosive composition

Radome Weather-proof cover for a radar set, largely transparent at the frequency used by the set

Range-keeper The US equivalent of the British fire-control table (noted in section on US fire-control)

RDX (cyclonite) The explosive cyclomethylene trinitramine

Recuperator cylinder Alternative term for run-out cylinder

RF Range-finder

RFA Royal fleet auxiliary

RGF (Woolwich) Royal gun factory

ROF Royal ordnance factory

rpm Rounds per minute. Also revolutions per minute for torpedo engines, gyros and other revolving objects

RP50 An electrical system of remote power control with power amplification by metadyne

RPC Remote power control. Systems where the power training and/or elevation of a gun mounting is directly controlled from director or fire-control table. Also applied to the third axis in some triaxial mountings and to directors controlled from the fire-control table

S Submarine

SA Semi-automatic, applied to a gun when the breech opens automatically after firing

SAP Semi armour-piercing shell

SAPC Semi armour-piercing capped shell

SAPBC Semi armour-piercing ballistic capped shell

Screw box liner The USN term for breech bush, the component into which a screw breech block screws on closing and which is itself permanently located in the breech end of a gun

Second look, random look, reverse look US terms for various magnetic mine firing programmes, respectively at second activation, first activitation and with dead periods of 0.5 to over 10.5 secs

Selsyn The type of synchro favoured by the US Navy

Sights Various types of sights and director telescopes are noted in the British, USA, Japanese and German fire-control sections. The main developments were in the use of gyros for stabilisation and for rate measurements in sights for close-range AA guns and directors. The weight actually controlled by the gyro was reduced as far as possible to lessen extraneous effects

Speed/rate Speed is used in the conventional sense, while rate is the rate of change of the target's range. It can also be used in such terms as 'vertical rate' or 'angular rate' to indicate rate of change of height or bearing

STAAG Stabilised tachymetric anti-aircraft gun, applied to certain 40mm Bofors not in service in the RN until after the war

Star (illuminating) shell Contains a parachute except in obsolescent types and container of illuminating composition. The shell is burst at the appropriate height and range to illuminate a night action

Stator The active fixed part of rotating electro-magnetic machines and some turbines

Steel choking Reduction of the bore of a gun from concentrated longitudinal stresses. It was particularly frequent in guns with the inner A tube located by forward shoulders and caused much trouble before the First World War

Sterilisers Devices to de-activate a mine after a given period of time

Strengthened bolt actuating Part of the breech mechanism of British 4in QF Mk 'A' V and Mk 'A' V* guns

Striker gear The firing pin and associated mechanism used in percussion firing

Sub-calibre gun A relatively small gun adapted to fit inside a larger one, or in some navies clamped outside, and used for firing-drills to save expense and wear

Super-elevation The gun elevation above the line of sight necessary to compensate for gravity

Swashplate engine An engine with the pistons working on an adjustable oscillating plate. Usually hydraulic

Tallboy console A cabinet containing elevation and training control units and continuous prediction unit (noted in section on British HA fire-control)

Thermite An incendiary composition mainly consisting of aluminium powder and iron oxide

Tracking The process of following a target, usually by radar and before opening fire

TS Transmitting station

Tachymetric, non-tachymetric HA fire-control based on measurement of the target speed (tachymetric)

Thyratron RPC A system of remote power control employing thyratrons for power amplification (noted in section on German fire-control)

TIC Time interval compensation gear

TIR Time interval receiving unit (noted in section on British LA fire-control)

TNA The explosive trinitroanisole

TNT The explosive trinitrotoluene

Triaxial Applied to gun mountings with the usual axes of training and elevation and a third keeping the trunnions parallel to the horizon. Also applied to directors and sights

TT Torpedo tubes

UD Upper deck

Vent axial A component of screw breeches. The mushroom head forced the obturation pad into its seating on firing and the hollow stem which passed through the breech block took the firing tube

VT fuze Variable time or proximity fuze (noted in section on US and British projectiles)

VH Vickers hardened armour (noted in section on Japanese projectiles)

Vickers 'pure couple' A single motion screw breech mechanism, much used by the British in First World War guns

Walking pipes Jointed pipes supplying hydraulic power to the moving parts of a turret mounting

Welin block A screw breech block with stepped threads and very widely used

Windshield An alternative term for ballistic cap

W/T Wireless telegraphy. Early British term for radio

GREAT BRITAIN

At first sight British naval armaments, more than those of any other navy, seem to have been suited to the basic needs of the war with little apparent regard for the future. However desirable such economy of effort might be, further study gives rise to a strong suspicion that the Royal Navy did not get its proper share of the design, development and production facilities available. Improved systems of AA fire-control were thus delayed until after the war, and this was the field in which the Navy was weakest, because of the pre-war adoption of an inherently defective system. Against surface gunnery targets the position was much better, and British torpedoes of the fuel/air type were surpassed only by the Japanese (who used oxygen in place of air), though no British electric torpedo entered service during the war. Mines appear to have been adequate, and anti-submarine weapons, once the actual requirements had been determined, were among the best of the period. Airborne anti-ship weapons were generally satisfactory, the defect here being the scarcity of high-performance aircraft for naval purposes.

The huge resources of the United States provided considerable assistance, and much more would have been welcome, particularly in the AA field, where the USN was far ahead in the later years of World War II.

In conclusion, it must be noted that British naval weapons of 1939, whatever their deficiencies, were more likely to be effective in action than those of the far more spectacular fleet of 1914.

Glasgow and *Gambia* post war showing twin 4in QF Mk XVI and single Bofors. A greater supply of both weapons would have enhanced the chances of survival for British warships during the war.
CPL

NAVAL GUNS

Naval guns and mountings are described at length in most cases, with briefer notes on the less important. Coast defence was an Army or sometimes in emergency a Royal Marine responsibility, but several guns were used both at sea and on land, and this is noted in the descriptions of them. Regular coastal-defence mountings were at least nominally distinct, but many emergency batteries used naval mountings; these are also noted.

IDENTIFICATION

Guns were divided into BL and QF and the original meaning of these terms was 'breech loading', as distinct from muzzle loading, and 'quick firing' which indicated a rapidly working breech mechanism accompanied by a brass cartridge case, though instances can be found where the brass case was not used. Long before the Second World War these terms had altered their meaning: BL indicated the use of a bag – that is, fabric covered – propellant charge and QF the use of a metal cartridge case. Except in ammunition books and lists, QF guns were not usually divided into those using fixed and separate ammunition.

Individual guns were distinguished by the diameter of the bore in inches or, in many smaller guns, by the nominal weight of the projectile in pounds (lb), as 'pounder', abbreviated to 'pdr', followed by BL or QF and the Mark number, sometimes with one or more 'stars' (asterisks) indicating minor modifications, though there was little consistency in the addition of a star or the creation of a new Mark. Occasionally letters were used instead of stars. A few automatic guns were identified by the bore diameter in millimetres and sometimes the parent company's name, such as Hotchkiss, Bofors or Oerlikon. On occasions when a gun was of markedly different type from previous ones of the same bore diameter, it might be distinguished by the weight in hundredweight (cwt), and the same practice had also been used in the past to reduce confusion over such guns as the First World War 3in (*76mm*). It should be remembered that BL and QF guns of the same bore were numbered in separate Mark series, and that Army guns were usually included in the appropriate naval series which often accounts for missing Marks such as 6in (*152mm*) BL Marks XIX and XXI.

Gun mountings, which came under a different organisation from guns, were classified as 'barbette' and 'turret' or as 'transferable' mountings, though the application of this had not always been logical, and there were several borderline cases. They were identified by Mark numbers and stars which by 1939 were usually in a continuous series for each calibre of gun, though 4in (*102mm*) submarine mountings were a notable exception. The principal letters used were: B – barbette; P – pedestal; CP – centre pivot; HA – high angle; LA – low angle; S – submarine; BD – between decks; UD – upper deck; RPC – remote power control. Occasionally letters were used in place of stars. Army coast-defence mountings were numbered in separate series.

Other special identification symbols for guns and mountings are explained as they occur in the descriptions.

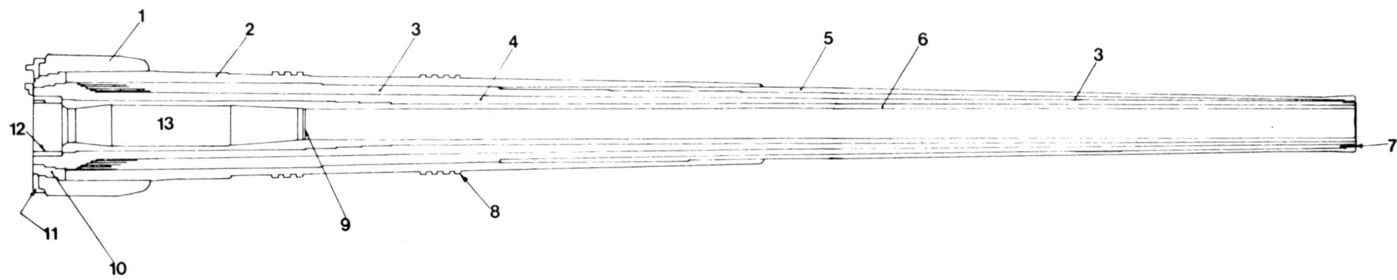

GUN DESIGN

British naval guns in service of 5.5in (*140mm*) calibre and upwards were BL, as were some of the older 4.7in (*120mm*) and 4in (*102mm*) guns, and in these bore and chamber lengths were measured from the top of the mushroom head of the vent axial. Apart from the above, service guns of 5.25in (*133mm*) and under were QF with sliding breech blocks except for a few with the interrupted screw type. Chamber lengths were taken to the base of the seated shot and rifling lengths from the beginning of the groove in a new gun. The muzzle velocities given are for new guns at a charge temperature of 80°F (*26.7°C*) and, unless stated, ranges are for this muzzle velocity. It should be noted that British range tables were usually drawn up for a lower velocity than the above, but there is no constant ratio between range table and new gun velocities, so that the table ranges have been carefully adjusted by the velocity correction tables, known as range and elevation scales, to obtain the new gun values. Many of the older range tables seriously exaggerate the range at 20° elevation and above, and the later and more reliable tables have been used.

Most recent naval guns were either of Vickers-Armstrong design modified to a greater or lesser extent by the Ordnance authorities, or designed by the latter, though the two best automatic guns, the Bofors and Oerlikon, were not British in origin. The old wire-wound construction, which was far better than is often supposed, was superseded in about 1929 by a highly satisfactory built-up construction with the minimum of component parts. From late 1941 the Vickers-Armstrong practice for their foreign designs of using $^{24}/_{27}$ths of the yield point as the maximum permissible stress in the steel was adopted instead of the earlier $^{20}/_{27}$ths, which allowed weight to be

15in Mk 1 gun in section. This is typical of British full length wire-wound construction, though in later designs the wire was wound in a single length with one start and finish, known as taper winding. The B tube and jacket could also be combined in a single forging. As was normal in British heavy guns an inner A tube is fitted.

1 Breech ring
2 Jacket
3 Wire
4 A tube
5 B tube
6 Inner A tube
7 Stop ring
8 Collars for fitting in cradle
9 Start of rifling
10 Shrunk collar
11 Breech frame
12 Breech bush
13 Chamber

John Roberts

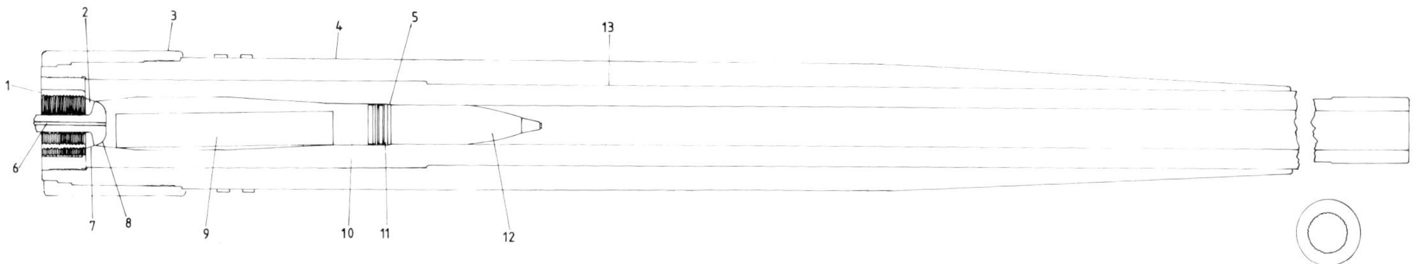

6in BL Mk XXIII gun in section showing built-up construction, without inner A tube.
John Lambert

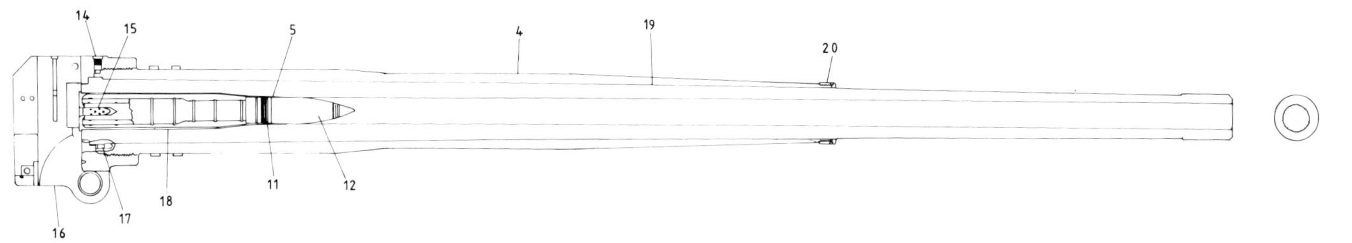

4in QF Mk XVI* gun in section, showing loose barrel construction.

1 Breech bush
2 Obturator pad
3 Breech ring
4 Jacket
5 Commencement of the rifling
6 Tube flash channel
7 Seat of obturation
8 Vent axial
9 Charge
10 Chamber
11 Driving band
12 Projectile
13 A tube
14 Positioning stop
15 Primer
16 Removable breech ring
17 Screw securing loose barrel
18 Cartridge case
19 Loose barrel
20 Sealing collar

John Lambert

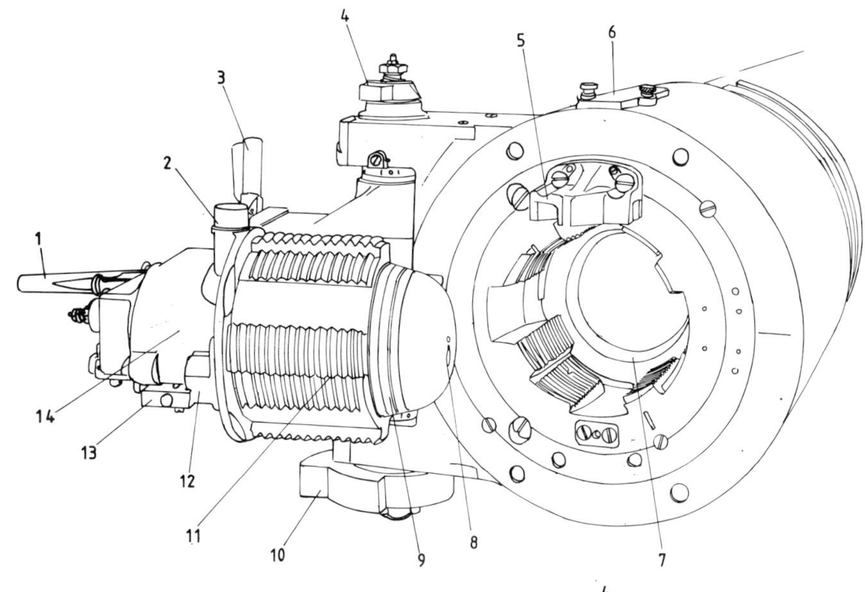

Asbury breech mechanism of 6in BL Mk XXIII.

1 Breech mechanism lever
2 Roller
3 Lock handlever
4 Air blast cam
5 Cam rotating breech screw
6 Cover for clinometer plane
7 Obturator seating
8 Vent axial
9 Obturator pad
10 Loading tray safety cam
11 Breech screw
12 Safety cam
13 Retracting bar
14 Carrier
15 Lever withdrawing sleeve
16 Electric lock
17 Lock guide bolt
18 Link actuating lock
19 Control arc
20 Hang fire latch
21 Half-cock push

John Lambert

reduced. There were also considerable factors of safety in most instances. Loose barrels were used in recent guns from 5.25in (*133mm*) downwards, unless a monobloc construction was employed, and designs were prepared up to 16in (*406mm*), but loose liners were limited to some 4in (*102mm*) and 3in (*76mm*) guns. Many barrels from 5.25in (*133mm*) down were autofretted.

British heavy guns were designed for regularity, accuracy and relatively long life, with an adequate but unspectacular muzzle velocity which could have been increased if cord charges had been replaced by those of tubular grain. In general they were highly satisfactory, but it seems that this was not always the case with those of smaller calibre. The much used 4in (*102mm*) QF Mark XVI had neither long barrel life nor particularly high accuracy, which was attributed to a shell with too short a parallel section leading to poor centring at the muzzle. In the Army 3.7in (*94mm*)/65cal Mark VI AA gun, the use of a 'Probertised' chamber with long leed, shells with forward and rear bands and a short unrifled length at the muzzle, achieved a barrel life of about 500 EFC with cool propellant and a muzzle velocity of 3500f/s (*1067m/s*), but no similar naval gun was in service during the war.

Uniform twist rifling was standard in later naval guns of British design, though increasing twist was probably desirable in those firing fixed ammunition. The rifling lands were also narrow in most designs and it appears that some driving bands were unnecessarily massive.

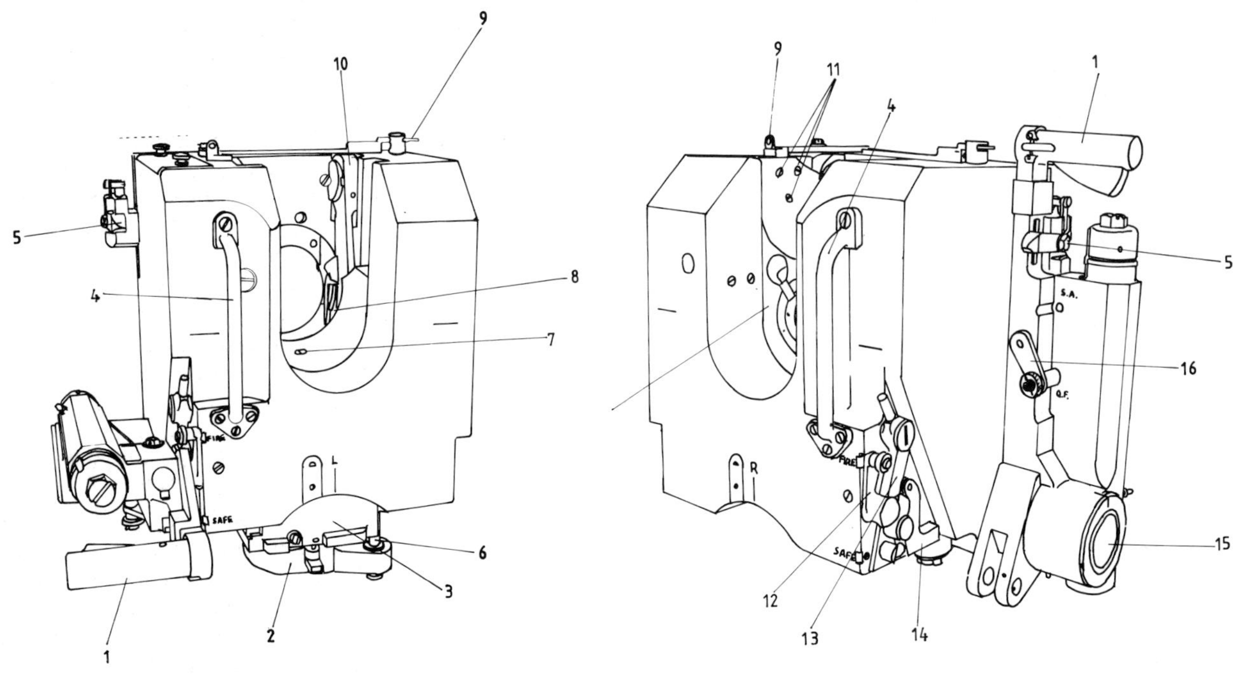

Vertical sliding block breech mechanism of 4in QF Mk XVI* gun.

1 Breech mechanism lever
2 Breech block yoke
3 Breech block
4 Loading handle
5 BM lever latch
6 Counterbalance rod
7 Preserving screw [lifting eye]
8 Extractor
9 Trigger
10 Catch retaining breech block open
11 Preserving screw [breech block arm, sub-calibre]
12 Safety lever
13 Intermediate safety lever
14 Recocking shaft actuating lever
15 Actuating shaft
16 Locking lever

John Lambert

GUN MOUNTINGS

Most naval gun mountings were of Vickers-Armstrong design, the principal exception being those made by Marine Mountings for coastal craft, and some of the more modern turrets gave considerable trouble when first introduced. In the 8in (*203mm*), over-ambitious staff requirements were partly to blame and, in all, complicated interlocks and other precautions had been introduced to avoid the disastrous results of propellant flash as demonstrated at Jutland in 1916. Because of financial and then wartime stringencies, sufficiently detailed design and development proved impossible and highly skilled crews became scarcer. The various mountings are described in the following pages but some general notes are useful here. Most mountings were oil hydraulically powered with self-contained units driven by electric motors, though other means of driving the hydraulic gear were used, and 15in (*381mm*) and 14in (*356mm*) turrets were powered from a ring main using a water-base fluid. Electrically powered naval mountings without hydraulic drive were limited to those of 4.5in (*114mm*) and below fitted with RP 50 series gear, except for the Hazemeyer Bofors, the only triaxial mounting in service, which was not of British design.

RPC, remote power control, was restricted in application by a lack of manufacturing capacity and was limited to the elevation and training of a number of 5.25in, (*133mm*), 4.5in (*113mm*), 4in (*102mm*), 40mm Bofors and 2pdr (*40mm*) pom-pom mountings, though it was later installed for training *Vanguard*'s 15in (*381mm*) turrets.

In British systems, the misalignment of gun and director was detected by Magslips and the amplified signal from these operated a servo valve in the hydraulic RP 10 series or controlled a metadyne generator in the electric RP 50 series. The hydraulic RP 41 system, in which the amplified signal controlled the tilt angle of the A (pump) end of the hydraulic drive, was introduced to service in the post-war 4.5in (*114mm*) Mk VI mounting.

PROPELLANTS

British propellant had a poor reputation after the 1914–18 War, due both to spontaneous magazine explosions (of which the worst blew up the *Vanguard* in Scapa Flow in July 1917), and to the loss of the battlecruisers *Indefatigable*, *Queen Mary* and *Invincible*, as well as the armoured cruisers *Defence* and *Black Prince*, from magazine explosions which followed shell hits at Jutland. Much work was done on these problems in the 1920s, and the spontaneous explosions were traced beyond any reasonable doubt to the presence in the nitrocellulose of dust impurities 0.005in (*0.13mm*) or less in diameter with a high content of iron pyrites (iron disulphide). The sulphur in the pyrites slowly oxidised to sulphuric acid, which corroded the nitrocellulose with local evolution of heat sufficient to cause spontaneous ignition and explosion. The source of the contamination was easy to find in pyritic coal dust, untarred cinder paths and dumps of pyrites, and the cure was obvious.

Unless the German practice of enclosing at least part of the charge in a brass cartridge case was adopted for all guns, magazine explosions resulting from shell hits on turret or barbette could be avoided only by changing the details of the ammunition supply to the guns so as to reduce as far as possible the probability of the flash of ignited propellant reaching a magazine. Various improvements were made in BL charges between the wars, principally concerning igniters. In 8in (*203mm*) and 6in (*152mm*) guns it was found possible to eliminate igniters if 1in (*25mm*) tubes were used with a suitable vent channel, and though it was not practicable to extend this to heavy guns, improvements in intended (and less chance of unintended) ignition were achieved by concentrated igniters with three-ply non-removable covers using ½in (*13mm*) tubes. Concentrated igniters were contained in a recess in the end of the cartridge and the three-ply covers consisted of two layers of cashmere with 0.001in (*0.025mm*) tinfoil between. In 14in (*356mm*) and 15in (*381mm*) guns two of the four quarter-charges each had a concentrated igniter containing 4lbs (*1.814kg*) G 12 (known previously as RFG^2) black powder. In 16in (*406mm*) there was one such igniter on two of the six part charges, but the black powder was increased to 5lb (*2.268kg*) per igniter in 1943. These improvements were not introduced with any great speed, as *Rodney*, all the surviving *Queen Elizabeth* class, *Revenge*, *Ramillies*, *Erebus* and six 8in cruisers were still without them in January 1942. In order to prevent copper deposits in the bore, tinfoil was introduced as a component of all BL and QF charges.

According to 1939 Proportion Books, Cordite MC was still listed as an alternative propellant for some guns, but SC (introduced in 1927) was the standard. MC was a First World War development of MD, differing principally in the use of cracked mineral jelly, while SC was an entirely different solventless propellant.

Propellant	NC(%N)	NG	MJ	Cen	CV	Tok°
MC	65(13.1)	30	5	—	1025	3215
SC	49.5(12.2)	41.5	—	9	970	3090

NC(%N) = nitrocellulose (% nitrogen); NG = nitroglycerin; MJ = mineral jelly; Cen = Centralite, symmetrical diphenyl diethyl urea; CV = calorific value; Tok° = Temperature uncooled degrees Kelvin

SC was far better stabilised than NC and could be made accurately to size, while MC shrank *c*25% in solvent removal. It lost much of its rigidity at over 80°F and though 'cooler' than MC was still a 'hot' propellant by Second World War standards. Because of the presence of calcium in the small amount of chalk which was incorporated to counteract traces of residual acid, the flash of SC was notoriously bright. It was nearly always used as cord, but 6pdr (*57mm*) Hotchkiss, 3pdr (*47mm*) Hotchkiss and 2pdr (*40mm*) Mk VIII had a hotter version, HSC or HSCK (with potassium cryolite), in tube form. HSC differed from SC in having 47% NG and 3.5% Centralite with Calorific value 1175 and Tok° 3625.

Flashless propellant was an urgent necessity for star shell and it was highly desirable for at least a proportion of the charges of all guns, though increased smoke was a disadvantage. A good flashless propellant, NF, known earlier as NFQ, was developed with the composition 55% picrite (nitroguanidine), 16.5% nitrocellulose (12.1%N), 21% nitroglycerin, 7.5% centralite, and also 0.3% cryolite. The calorific value was only 753 and Tok° *c*2425, so that gun life would be much increased. NF was not easy to make, and the basic initial material for picrite, calcium carbide, required large supplies of cheap electricity for its manufacture, so that the only picrite production plant in the British Empire was at Welland in Canadian territory near Niagara Falls. Its output of 575 tons a week was only 19% of the peak forecast. NF was used in most guns from 5.25in (*133mm*) down to the more powerful of the 4in (*102mm*) as slotted tube for full charges, but reduced star-shell charges in these and full charges for other 4in and most smaller guns employed cord, while ribbon was used in the 4.5in (*113mm*) 8cwt (*406kg*) gun.

With heavier guns than 5.25in (*133mm*), full flashless charges became too bulky for existing turret fittings, and it became more difficult to ensure the absence of flash, increasing additions of such materials as potassium sulphate becoming necessary as the calibre rose. Flashlessness was a requirement for the proposed 16in (*406mm*) Mk IV, but at the end of the war only the 6in (*152mm*) Mk XXIII had been issued with such charges and they were reduced flash or 'non-blinding' rather than flashless. NQFP was used in cord form and this differed from NF in having 4.5% more nitrocellulose and 4.5% less centralite, with 2% potassium sulphate and a calorific value of *c*880. A similar composition without potassium sulphate was used in ribbon form in Bofors guns.

Nitrocellulose propellant in flake or tube form was standard in Oerlikons, and United States Dupont NH propellants of nitrocellulose dinitrotoluene type were at one period in the war used extensively in multi-tube form for 5.25in (*133mm*) to 4in (*102mm*) guns. The composition was 86%NC (13.15%N), 10% DNT, 3% dibutyl phthalate, 1% diphenylamine, while FNHP (differing in 2% less NC and 2% more dibutyl phthalate with 0.8% potassium sulphate) was a common propellant in 40mm Bofors, the respective calorific values being *c*790 and 750 and Tok° 2680 and 2510. The short multi-tube grain was found to be convenient for filling strongly necked cases such as in 4.5in (*113mm*) fixed ammunition.

British propellant and turret precautions had a good safety record in the Second World War. The loss of the *Hood* was due to different causes from those which destroyed the battlecruisers at Jutland. In the *Hood* a 15in (*380mm*) shell is thought to have burst in the after 4in (*102mm*) QF magazines, causing them to explode with at least partial subsequent explosion of the after turret magazines. No tests had ever been done in Britain to assess the effect of a heavy shell bursting in a QF magazine, but USN war experience in *Boise* and *Savannah* indicated that the only hope was for the magazine to be sufficiently opened to the sea by the shell or bomb for water to flood in before the gas pressure from ignited charges rose sufficiently to cause an explosion.

PROJECTILES

The specifications for British heavy APC shell were issued by the Admiralty, but the shape of the cavity, type of cap, overall length within a maximum limit, and chemical analysis of the steels used for shell and cap, as well as the methods of forging and heat treatment, were the responsibility of the contractors, either Hadfield's or Firth Brown. The usual fairly high carbon nickel chromium steel was used for shell and cap and in both hardened decrementally from head to base. In contrast with American and German practice, 'sheath hardening', with the area near the apex of the cavity left relatively soft, was not employed and the hardness was more or less uniform across a section of the shell in that position. The shell proper had a 1.4 calibre radius head (crh), and the cap together with windshield or ballistic cap accounted for about 11.5-13% of the total shell weight. Firth Brown favoured knob and ring types of cap while Hadfield's used rounded or roughly conical forms with latterly a flattened front. The ballistic cap was 6/12crh in 14in (*356mm*) shells and in those for the 16in (*406mm*) Mks II and III which did not enter service. It was 6/ ∞ in shells for the 16in (*406mm*) Mk I and 5/10 in later 15in (*381mm*) shells, though older shells were 3.05/4crh. Recent shells had the Hadfield recessed base, with relieved adaptor screwing into the shell some distance above the base, so that the fuze was separated by an annulus from the bottom part of the shell wall and had less chance of being damaged in oblique impact.

The usual burster was Shellite (70% trinitrophenol, 'Lyddite'; 30% dinitrophenol), the amount being 2.5% of the total weight, but shells for the 16in (*406mm*) Mk I had block TNT and, as the density of the filling was lower, the amount did not exceed *c*2.3%. To enable ships to distinguish their own shell splashes, 'K' shell was introduced in late 1942-43, containing bags of coloured dye inside the ballistic cap with a small burster and nose fuze to ensure dispersion. The idea had been developed some years previously by the French Navy.

The most important plate proof test was the low velocity limit for perforating 12in (*30cm*) carburised armour at 30° to the normal with cavity intact and the shell in fit condition to burst. The velocities were 1700f/s (*518m/s*) for shells for the 16in (*406mm*) Mk I, and 1750f/s (*533m/s*) for 14in (*356mm*) and 15in (*381mm*). In the case of shells for the 16in (*406mm*) Mks II and III, a 14in (*35cm*) carburised plate at 30° and 1770f/s (*539m/s*) were the intended conditions. Occasionally specifications were relaxed, as for some 14in (*356mm*) in 1940, when the velocity was raised to 1900f/s (*579m/s*). There was also a high velocity limit, usually in the range 2100-2300f/s (*640-701m/s*), above which shells were expected to break up at 30° impact.

In 1944 it was decided to make some changes in AP shell design, though these were not carried through. It was realised for the first time that the assumption that a shell which did not ricochet continued in a straight line on striking water was entirely false, a fact that might have been learnt at any time from the Shoeburyness ranges, and designs to give a long, straight underwater trajectory were put in hand, as they had been earlier in Japan. It was also considered that the policy of having APC made primarily for the attack of vertical armour was unsound, as most actions had been chasing ones, in which impact on side armour would be very oblique. This neglected barbette and turret face armour and, in any case, might have been entirely erroneous against the Japanese. However, it became approved policy to develop new APC primarily for the attack of deck armour and, for ranges where the trajectory was too flat, to use a new HE piercing shell designed to go through a 2in (*50mm*) deck and burst with maximum

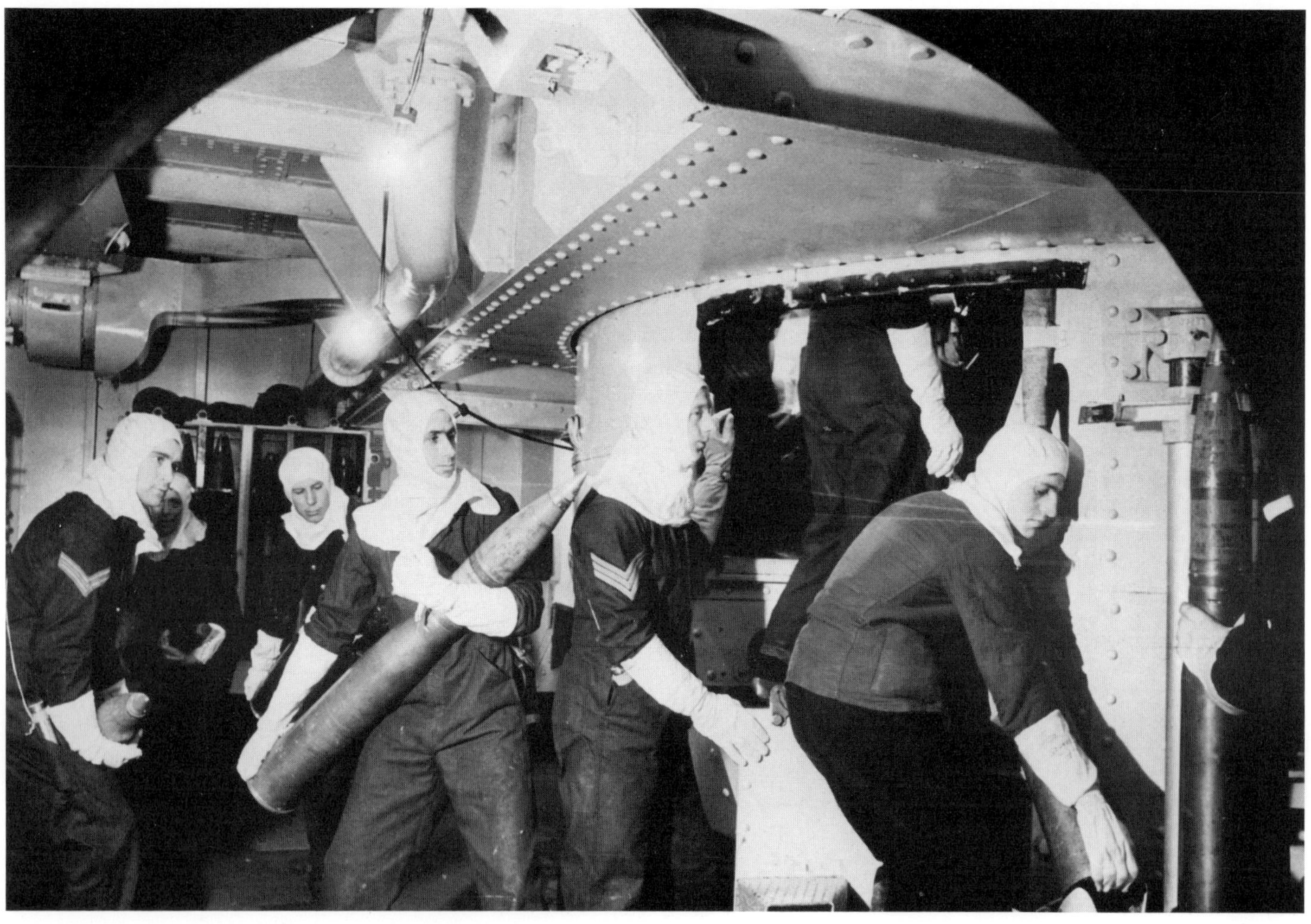

4.5in twin Mk II BD mounting in *Illustrious* showing ammunition passers handling fixed rounds. The hoists were separate from the mountings
CPL

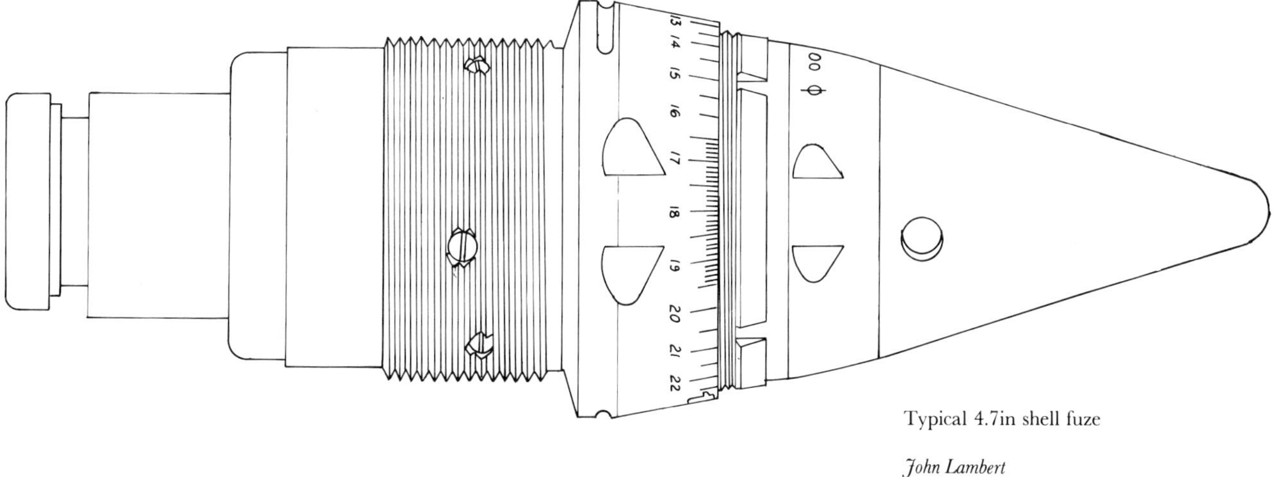

Typical 4.7in shell fuze

John Lambert

effect beyond it. The battleship outfit would become 24% APC, 36% HE piercing and 40% HE, instead of 95% or so APC unless on bombardment duty. For perforating heavy deck armour at greater angles than 30° to the normal, a blunter shell head than 1.4crh was needed, perhaps in the form of a truncated cone. This, however, increased the chance of shearing the threads holding the adaptor, due, it was thought to the violent elastic recovery of the shell as the first pressure wave on hitting returned from the base as a tensile wave.

SAP shell was available for most guns from 8in (*203mm*) down to 12pdr (*76mm*) and initially *Hood* and *Repulse* had some old CPC refilled with TNT. It was known as SAPC in 8in (*203mm*) and during the war as CPBC in 6in (*152mm*), changed in 1946 to SAPBC. The 8in shell resembled major-calibre APC except that the bursting charge of block TNT, TNT/beeswax or Shellite amounted to 4.27-4.7%. The low velocity, 30° to normal, plate proof figures were 4in (*10cm*) carburised plate at 1250f/s (*381m/s*). Shells of 6in and smaller were without a true AP cap and did not have relieved adaptors, while those of 5.25in (*133mm*) and below had the American-type 'K' device, which had no nose fuze and spread the dye through holes in the ballistic cap after the hole covers had been removed on impact with the sea. Bursters were TNT or, in the 112lb (*50.8kg*) 6in (*152mm*), TNT/beeswax and the amount was usually 3.5 - 4.3%, though in some 100lb (*45.4kg*) 6in (*152mm*) it reached 6.2%. Low velocity, 30° to normal, plate proof figures were 3in (*7.5cm*) noncarburised at 1200f/s (*366m/s*) for 6in and 2.5in (*6.3cm*) for 5.25in at the same velocity.

All the shells so far noted were base fuzed, usually with some form of ballistic cap, but HE shell which was made for all guns was nearly always nose fuzed, with the shell head giving approximately the same form as the corresponding ballistic cap. The principal exceptions were the first 16in (*406mm*), later withdrawn, where there was a ballistic cap with the fuze inside at the apex of the shell proper, 15in (*381mm*) which had nose and base fuzes, and the special short shells for the 4.5in (*113mm*)/8cwt (*406kg*) which were base fuzed. The burster usually amounted to 6-10% though there were lower exceptions and the 4.5in/8cwt had shells with 34%. TNT used as RDX ('cyclonite', cyclomethylene trinitramine)/TNT was mostly limited by the shortage of RDX to 4.7-4in (*120-102mm*) guns likely to engage surfaced submarines.

By far the greatest development in HE shells for AA fire was the introduction in the latter part of the war of radio proximity fuzes known as VT - variable time - which eliminated fuze setting. They were used in 5.25-4in (*133-102mm*) guns as available, but all were produced in the USA and supplied under Lend-Lease. At low angles of sight they were affected by waves, particularly if the sea was rough, and a shell too distant to be influenced by the target gave no burst to indicate by how much it was missing, but these failings were far outweighed by the advantages. With time fuzes, when range errors predominate, a good forward effect is needed, but with VT the main effect of the burst should be sideways, and redesign of 5.25in (*133mm*) and 4in (*102mm*) shells was started, with RDX/TNT as the burster and also replacing TNT in 4.5in (*114mm*).

Star shell was available for 5.25in (*133mm*) to 12pdr (*76*mm) guns, and at the end of the war the policy was to design star shell for guns over 4in (*102mm*) that could be fired with full charges.

'Shark', fired by 4in (*102mm*) guns, is described with other anti-submarine weapons.

Close range AA, 40 - 20mm, was usually fired HE with 6.35-11.7% bursters generally TNT, though RDX compositions were later introduced. SAP was available and 20mm shells often included incendiary bodies. Tracers in 20mm Oerlikon HE reduced the burster to *c*3.5%.

In the earlier part of the war, tracer was considered essential to supplement the mediocre performance of available AA fire-control equipment, but by 1945 opinion had changed and, although the huge stocks of tracer ammunition meant that close range outfits varied from 1 in 8 to all tracer, the intention was to phase tracer gradually out. Tracer in large AA was also to be abandoned on the grounds of interference with VT fuzes, but dark ignition night tracer with optional functioning was to be used in shells intended for the attack of surface targets.

Driving bands were usually single and made of copper, though a few shells had cupro-nickel. Double bands were to be found among 8in (*203mm*), and 6in (*152mm*) 100lb (*45.4kg*) and 112lb (*50.8kg*) shells for Mk XXII and XXIII guns. Streamlining of the base - 'boat tailing' - was not favoured in British naval shells though the 40mm Bofors had it.

DEVELOPMENT OF FIRE-CONTROL

Against surface targets, British systems were generally good, the most obstinate problems being excessive cross-roll when firing ahead or astern. Against aircraft, a non-tachymetric system had been adopted before the war. This was likely to give good results only with experienced crews against slow aircraft, and none of the tachymetric additions resulted in satisfactory systems. Greatly improved equipment was under development, but too late for use during hostilities. In March 1946 the Director of the Gunnery Division analysed the overall gunnery efficiency with existing equipment of ships built or building, compared with new equipment then available or due in time for the modernisation programme expected to begin in 1948. Out of a possible 10 marks the assessment was: *Vanguard* 6½, *King George V* class 2–3, 8in cruisers 1–2, 6in cruisers 1–3, 5.25in cruisers 1–2½, later 'C' and earlier 'Battle' destroyers 5, later 'Battle' and *Daring* class 8, earlier destroyers 1–2. The US Mk 37 Director was used to control the 5.25in of *Vanguard* and the 4.5in of the later Battles, while ships of the *Daring* class were to have the British Mk VI Director with Flyplane predictor.

LOW-ANGLE CONTROL

The most complete systems were required by the main armament of capital ships, but in *Barham*, *Malaya*, the five *Royal Sovereigns*, *Repulse* and *Hood*, little had been done to bring directors (or fire-control tables) up to date. The main director position in these ships was on the tripod foremast, while the second, armoured, director was on the CT roof. This director had a weight of 30.5 tons (*31t*) due to the 6in (*15cm*) maximum hood which was rotated by hydraulic power independently of the sights. The aloft director had a light canopy and was trained by hand. The usual weight was about 2.4 tons (*2.44t*). In all examples, the sights were set for elevation and deflection (like gun sights), which was unnecessary and could interfere with maintenance of the line of sight. Improvements were made in *Nelson* and *Rodney*, where the director sights were not disturbed by changes in elevation and deflection, and the gunnery control tower was combined with the director as a director-control tower (DCT). These towers weighed 24 tons (*24.4t*) and were trained by electric motors with hydraulic drive at up to 9°/sec as were most later DCTs. They were protected by 2-1in (*50–25mm*) plating and were located on the bridge tower and abaft the mainmast. There was also a director tower (DT), on the CT roof. This had a 5in (*13cm*) maximum armoured hood with weight and power training as in the DCTs. It was removed from *Nelson* in 1944–45.

In *Warspite*, *Renown*, *Valiant* and *Queen Elizabeth*, the DCT was located on the bridge tower and the old armoured DT was moved to the after superstructure. This pattern of DCT weighed 14.5 tons (*14.7t*).

The *King George V* class had the forward DCT on the bridge tower, with an armoured DCT on the after superstructure. Respective weights with 274 radar aerials were 18 tons (*18.3t*) and 41 tons (*41.7t*). The armoured DCT was protected by 3in (*75mm*), with 2in (*50mm*) on the 12ft (*3.66m*) diameter ring bulkhead.

In *Vanguard*, the forward and after DCTs were generally similar and located as above. They were protected by 2in (*50mm*) plating and weighed 33.1 tons (*33.6t*). Maximum training speed was 10°/sec and both DCTs had RP 40 remote power control training from the fire-control table. This was an electrically controlled hydraulic system accompanied by the use of power amount instead of velocity local power control. During their last wartime refits, the four surviving *King George V* class also had RP 40 installed for their forward DCTs, but in *Howe* the process did not get beyond conversion to power amount local control.

The most important feature of the director system was the stabilised gyro sight. In the 'P' sight in the *King George V* class and *Vanguard*, the whole elevating part of the sight, including the brackets for the layer's and trainer's binoculars, was stabilised, while in the sights in the *Nelson* class and reconstructed 15in (*38cm*) ships only prisms in the optical system were stabilised. The 'P' sight gyro only controlled the relay valve of a powerful oil motor, while in earlier sights the gyro operated the firing gear directly. This relieved the 'P' gyro of some external influences which gave rise to precessional torques, and EM (M) gear (see below) gave much improved horizon seeking, so that it was possible to omit the former adjustments which corrected topple, altered the plane of stabilisation, and corrected wander, allowing the director layer to concentrate on firing the guns. Optical properties were much improved by using X7 night-sight type binoculars with only six glass-air surfaces instead of sixteen.

Limitations were that firing under blind fire conditions must be within ±30° roll from the vertical, and that the gyro was still considerably affected by large or rapid alterations of course. No method of eliminating these errors was devised during the war, though they were greatly reduced by helm compensating gear. To meet heavy roll conditions without appreciable lag, there was velocity compensation of the power follow-up for stabilisation purposes.

In EM (M) gear the gyro was held vertically by magnetic coils energised through mercury switches fitted on the gyro or its gimbals. The helm compensating gear added during the war was a constrained gyro which cut out the current to mercury switches when the ship altered course. Adjustments could be made to prevent the gear coming into play during a yaw. When engaging *Scharnhorst*, *Duke of York* maintained a fairly consistant 4° yaw, and a routine was established of firing at the end of the yaw in TS control.

To allow for the roll of the ship between closing the firing circuit and shot ejection, and for the vertical linear velocity component of the roll to which the shell is subject, time interval compensation (TIC)

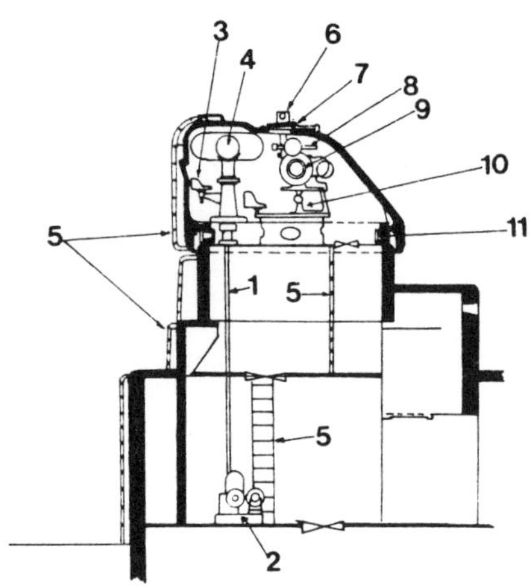

Armoured director tower as fitted on CT of *Hood*, shown in section.

1 Training drive shaft
2 Training motor
3 Rangetaker's seat
4 30ft rangefinder
5 Ladders
6 Periscopes
7 Manhole cover
8 Telescopic sights
9 Setting dials
10 Tripod type director
11 Roller path

John Roberts

Development of British capital ship forward control positions from *Hood* through *Nelson* and *King George V* to *Vanguard*.

HOOD, AFTER 1939 REFIT
1 Distant reading thermograph added *c*1935–36
2 Type 75 W/T aerial added during 1936 refit
3 Combined anemometer and wind vane
4 Syren fitted on reduced platform
5 9ft rangefinder
6 Searchlight platform removed
7 Air defence position added during 1936 refit
8 Extension to Admiral's bridge
9 0.5in MG mounting added during 1934 refit
10 Submarine lookouts
11 12ft rangefinder moved down from fore top during 1934 refit
12 Signalling lamp
13 20in signalling searchlight
14 Pom-pom director, moved down from fore top during 1936 refit
15 Upper compass platform enlarged
16 Air defence position added during 1936 refit
17 HACS director Mk II added (port and starboard)
18 Admiral's signal platform extended

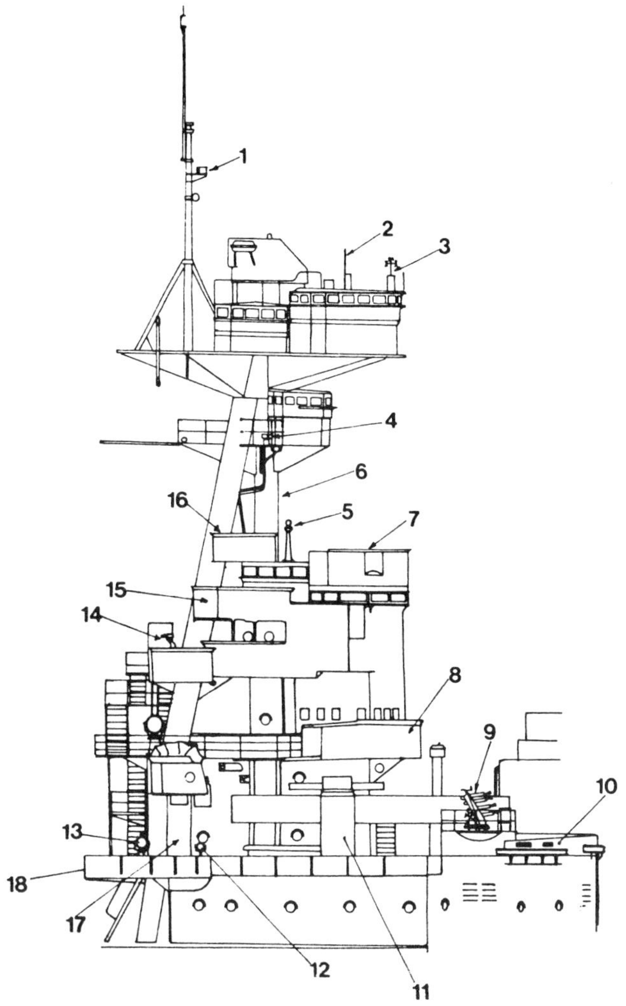

RODNEY, 1928
1 AA control platform
2 12ft high angle rangefinder
3 Bearing sight
4 High angle director
5 Dumaresq
6 Main director control tower with 15ft rangefinder
7 Secondary armament director control tower with 12ft rangefinder
8 9ft rangefinder
9 Director platform
10 Compass platform
11 Revolving armoured director hood
12 Conning tower
13 Searchlight platform
14 18in searchlights
15 Captain's bridge
16 Bearing sights
17 Admiral's bridge
18 Torpedo sights
19 Searchlight control
20 High angle calculating position
21 Short range W/T aerial

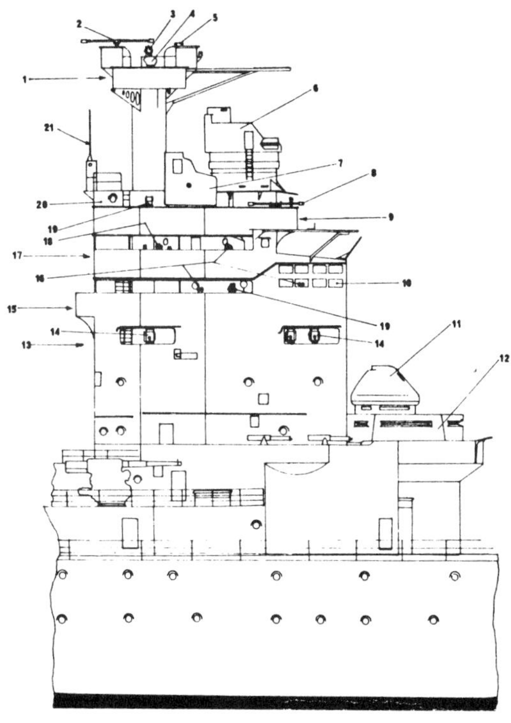

gear was fitted. This comprised a constrained gyro measuring the rate of change of level angle and transmitting to the time interval receiving (TIR) unit in the sight. The time varied between 78 and 162 milliseconds. The firing switch was mechanically operated at the instant when there was no angular difference between sight-elevation and director-setting drives, and the moment of contact could be advanced by TIC unit or director-setting handwheel. To avoid shell wave interference when the guns were closer than 14 calibres, the firing of one gun was delayed by 15 milliseconds.

The 'P' sight had elevation limits of +65° and -20°. There were combined eye-shooting and open sights for close AA barrages and target detection, and a back-laying periscope so that the back horizon could be used in blind fire if the front were obscured. For any roll experienced in battleships, the error in the stabilised binocular crosswires was less than ±2′.

For visual laying at a surface target, the layer kept the stabilised horizontal cross-wire on target, correcting small gyro departures from the horizontal by an adjustment knob. The layer could hunt the roll with the handwheel of the director-

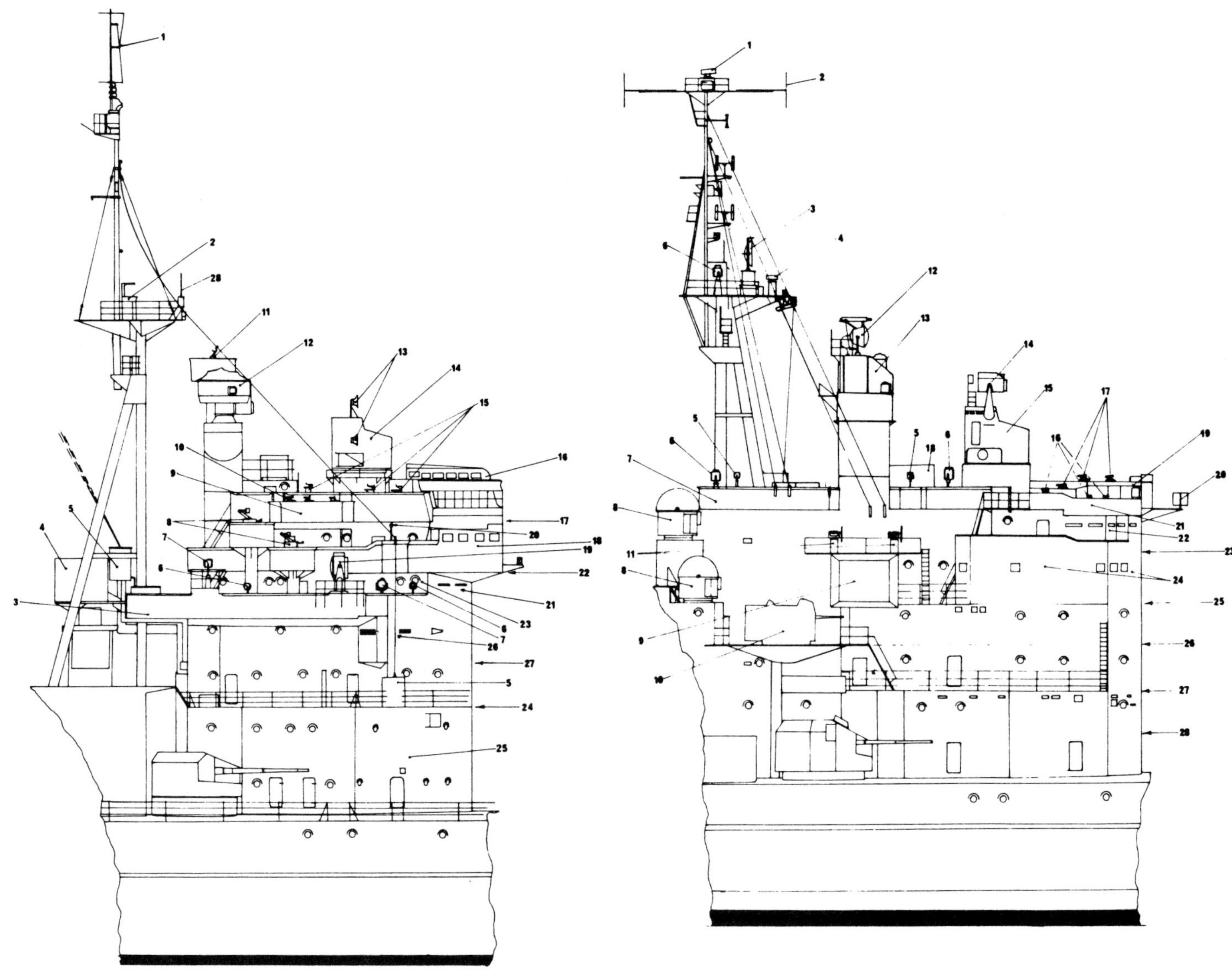

KING GEORGE V, 1940
1 Transmitting aerial for Type 279 air warning radar
2 Crowsnest
3 Signal (flag) deck
4 Radar office
5 W/T aerial screen
6 Signalling lamp
7 12in signalling searchlight
8 Pom-pom directors
9 Air-look-out position (ALO)
10 ALO sights
11 Director for UP mounting on B turret
12 HA/LA directors with 15ft rangefinders
13 Radar aerials for Type 284 gunnery radar
14 Main armament director control tower with 15ft rangefinder
15 Bearing sights for target indication, star shell, etc
16 Compass platform and charthouse
17 Upper bridge
18 Admiral's bridge
19 44in searchlight
20 9ft rangefinder
21 Conning tower
22 Lower bridge
23 Charthouse
24 No 1 platform (crew space etc)
25 Lower section of bridge containing stores, recreation space, galley, etc
26 Surface look-out
27 No 2 platform (officers' accommodation, navigating office and surface look-out)
28 Short range W/T aerial

VANGUARD, 1946
1 Aerial for Type 293 air/surface target indication radar
2 TBS ('Talk-Between-Ships') aerials
3 Aerial for Type 277 air/surface warning radar
4 Aerial for Type 930 navigation radar
5 Signal lamps
6 18in signalling searchlights
7 Signal (flag) deck
8 CRBF (Close Range Blind Fire) directors
9 Boiler room vent
10 Bofors mounting
11 Saluting guns
12 Aerials for Type 275 gunnery radar
13 Secondary armament HA/LA directors with 15ft rangefinders
14 Aerial for Type 274 gunnery radar
15 Main armament director control tower with 30ft rangefinder
16 ALO sights
17 Bearing sights for target indication, etc
18 W/T office
19 Compass platform
20 MF/DF aerial
21 Air-look-out (ALO) position
22 Conning tower and charthouse
23 Conning tower platform
24 Admiral's conning position
25 Admiral's bridge
26 No 1 platform (officers' accommodation)
27 Boat deck
28 Shelter deck

John Roberts

setting unit, not strictly a part of the sight, thus firing at any desired point of the roll. Forecasting was automatic from TIC and TIR, and if the layer was pressing the firing circuit pistol set at 'Gyro' the guns fired automatically when the zero mark of the director setting scales collimator crossed the horizontal binocular cross-wire plus or minus the amount forecast. If the director-setting handwheel was moved just before firing, pointer-following errors occurred at the guns, and the layer also warned the trainer before firing.

If TIC was not working, the forecast was made by moving the stabilised line of sight above or below the target with the sight elevation adjustment handwheel, and if the motion of the ship was insufficient to ensure the firing circuits making, the pistol was put to 'Director' and the guns were fired by the layer.

The sight was put to 'Director' if stabilisation broke down. The layer then used the director-setting handwheel to keep the horizontal cross-wire and the zero of the collimator (locked together) on target, and forecast by hunting the roll and firing before the line of sight was dead on target.

For blind firing at a surface target, the sight was stabilised and the dip to the horizon set on the angle of sight dial. Sight elevation adjustments could be made by layer or trainer, and if the RP 40 training was not keeping 'on' the trainer could make line corrections, which was done in blind fire by the radar trainer in the transmitting station. Prior to fitting RP 40, blind training from the fire-control table or radar training tube in the transmitting station was by follow the pointer dial in the DCT, or by the radar training tube in the latter.

In *Vanguard*, cross-level was determined by the gyro sight and gun plane converters in the transmitting station, but in the *King George V* class and some older ships a different system was used. The cross-level instrument in the DCT had a rotatable mirror which enabled a graticule in the periscope to be laid on the horizon and thus measured the cross-level angle. As the effect on gun training was much greater at high elevation, a cam rotated for range was incorporated. For the 14in(*356mm*) guns in the *King George V* class there was no error in this correction between 6500yd (*5940m*) and 35,300yd(*32,280m*) for a ±10° cross-roll and very little from 1300yd(*1190m*) to 36,000yd(*32,920m*).

In unskilled hands the gear could be a menace. The horizon had to be followed smoothly and continuously, and a large correction made just before firing could not be followed in time by the turrets, which caused serious errors. In heavy weather it was better to abandon the cross-level gear and leave it to the director layer to try and fire when the ship was upright.

Inclinometers originallly fitted in the DCTs of the *King George V* class and older ships were abandoned.

From 1941 optical range-finders were gradually replaced by gunnery radar sets, though they continued as a secondary means. Coincidence instruments were favoured and the largest were 42ft (*12.8m*) in the quadruple turrets of the *King George V* class and 41ft (*12.5m*) in the triple turrets of *Nelson* and *Rodney*. RFs on DT or DCT were from 15ft (*4.57m*) to 30ft (*9.14m*).

Gunnery radar sets provided the best means of range and rate determination against visible targets. They were equally efficient against blind targets and could determine the target bearing. They were also capable of spotting the fall of salvos for range but not for line. The original gunnery sets worked in the 'L' (50cm) band. A prototype was tried in *Nelson* in June 1940 and could detect to 24,000yd (*21,950m*). This went into production as the Type 284, and was first installed in *King George V* with separate receiving and transmitting trough aerials - 21ft (*19.2m*) long with 24 dipoles - on the forward DCT. By early 1942 it had been fitted to all battleships and battlecruisers except *Royal Oak* and *Barham*, sunk previously. The aerials, which were in some cases 12ft 6in (*11.4m*) long, were located on the forward DCT or DT except in *Hood*, where they were on the mast-head DT. Against the *Bismarck*, *King George V* was able to range to 25,100yd (*22,950m*) and spot to at least 13,600yd (*12,440m*) for the 25 minutes during which the set was working.

Considerable improvements made in 1941-42 resulted in the Type 284M. Power was increased and pulse length reduced, while bearing accuracy was improved by beamswitching and one aerial was made unnecessary by the use of common-aerial working. In her action with the *Scharnhorst*, *Duke of York*'s 284M was able to detect at 34,000yd (*31,090m*), hold for bearing at 25,800yd (*23,590m*) and spot fall of shot for range at 21,500yd (*19,660m*).

The 'S' (10cm) band Type 274 developed in 1942-43 was a great improvement, being able to spot salvos to 34,000yd (*31,090m*) for range, which gave a good margin, since a time of flight of fifty seconds, equivalent to less than 30,000yd (*27,430m*) for all British heavy guns, was considered the limit for accurate fire control. The aerial, which was stabilised for level, was a double 'cheese' of 14ft (*4.27m*) aperture with beamswitching applied to the upper 'cheese' (receiver). It was carried on the forward and after DCTs of *Anson* and *Duke of York* by the end of the war, and also in *Vanguard*, but installed in *King George V* and *Howe* only on the forward DCT, the after one being equipped for the previous 50cm sets. Of older battleships only *Nelson* had Type 274.

The 274 set gave an indication for line in spotting but *Vanguard* as completed also had a Type 930, which it was hoped would provide plan spotting. This worked in the 'X' (3cm) band and only one seems to have been made. Very large and cumbersome, it was replaced by a Type 931, developed in Canada and working in the 'K' (1.5cm)

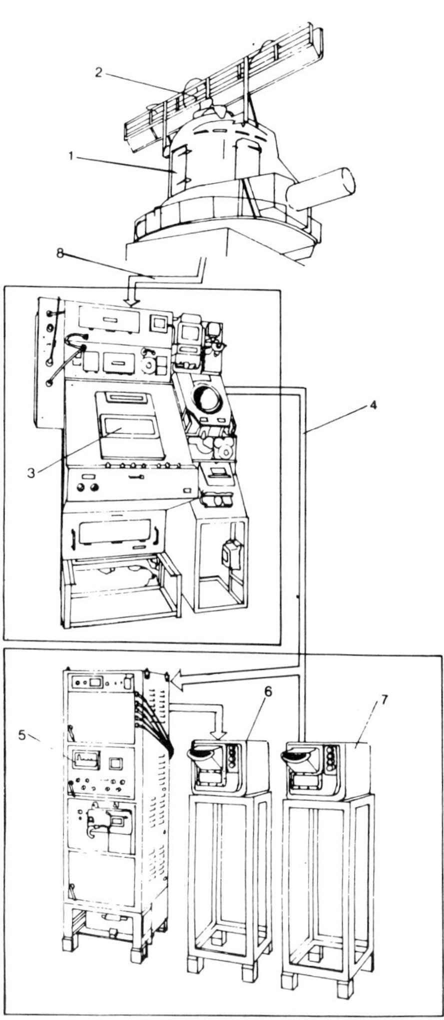

Type 284 main armament radar with displays in transmitting station.

1 Director control tower
2 Radar aerial
3 Ranging display (panel L12), normally removed when display panels fitted in TS
4 Radar signals to displays in TS
5 Ranging display (panel L24)
6 Spotting tube
7 Training tube
8 Radar signals to radar office

In addition to the equipment shown above, the TS was fitted with a second ranging display (panel L18 - part of the Type 273QR) for use as a stand-by or with the after gunnery radar set.

John Roberts

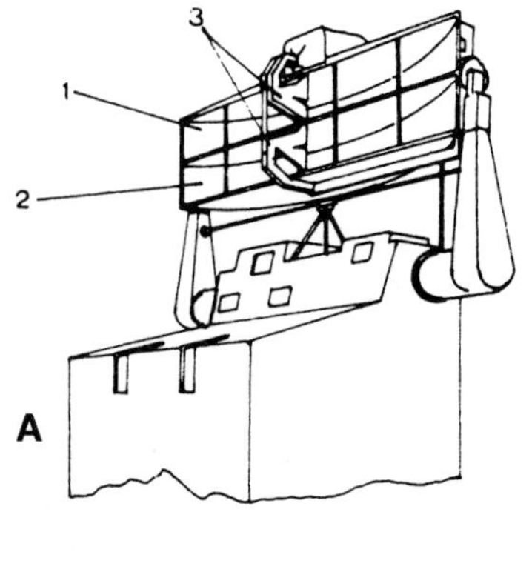

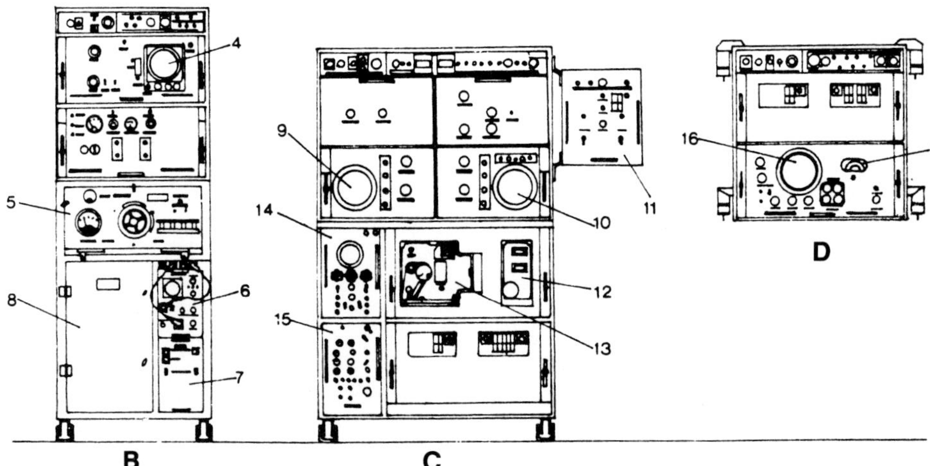

Type 274 10cm main armament radar equipment.

A Director control tower: (1) receiving aerial, (2) transmitting aerial, (3) waveguides.
B Radar panels 3AW and L30: (4) local indicator, (5) panel 3AW control unit, (6) wave monitor, (7) trigger unit, (8) modulator.
C Radar panel L31: (9) ranging tube, (10) spotting tube, (11) video filter unit, (12) spotting box, (13) RTU (range transmission unit) Mk VII, (14) wave monitor, (15) oscillator.
D Radar panel L32; (16) coarse bearing tube, (17) fine bearing meter.

The L31 and L32 panels were located in the transmitting station along with the AFCT, L32 being hung from the deckhead while L31 was deck mounted. The panels could also be employed with the surface warning radar.

John Roberts

band. Only about twelve reached the Royal Navy and they are believed to have given promising results, but details are lacking. In favourable circumstances it was possible to assess target inclination. Rain would have been a problem in the 'K' band. The aerial was below that for the 274 on the forward DCT and was stabilised with it. Details for the main LA gunnery sets were:

Type	**284**	**284M**	**274**
Frequency (MHz)	600	600	3296
Peak power (kW)	25	150	400
Pulse (microseconds)	2	1	0.5
Range (yards)	24,000 ± 120	30,000 ± 25	40,000 ± 25
Range (metres)	21,950 ± 110	27,430 ± 23	36,580 ± 23
Horizontal beam width (degrees)	8	8	2
Bearing accuracy (minutes of arc)	± 30	±5	±3

Azimuth was taken from the ship's gyro compass but, unless the compass was at the centre of roll, would be measured in a plane that oscillated about the horizon. This was overcome by the Admiralty Gyro Transmission Unit (AGTU), in which slave gyros monitored by a transmission of limited power from the gyro compass made the necessary corrections. As far as is known, *Vanguard* was the only battleship to have this.

Other variables were wind speed and direction, non-standard ballistics depending on air temperature and pressure, gun wear, propellant temperature and alterations in ballistic coefficient for different shells, and drift (sometimes corrected for latitude). There were also corrections to be made for director and turret roller paths that were not exactly horizontal (tilt), for vertical distances between guns and director (dip), and the distance that each mounting was separated laterally from some datum in the ship (displacement). Tilt, dip and displacement required corrections to elevation, while convergence was a training correction that allowed for the lateral distance between the datum director, other directors, and each mounting.

The necessary calculations to ensure that elevation and deflection as passed to the guns were correct for hitting the target at the time when the salvo would fall were carried out by the fire-control table in the transmitting station. In the course of World War II, this last increased greatly in importance relative to the director, as had been foreseen after the First World War. The various Marks of fire-control table were mechanical calculators depending on cams, gear trains, racks, slotted wheels, friction drives and other such devices, and the results were indicated on dials, counters and plots. The tables were powered by motors, in the more recent designs usually oil or compressed air, and alternatively by hand. Unreconstructed 15in (*38cm*) ships had various modifications of the Dreyer FCT Mk IV* except for *Hood* with Mk V. Further tables of better mechanical design were known as Admiralty Fire-Control Tables (AFCT). *Nelson* and *Rodney* had MkI, the four reconstructed 15in ships Mk VII, the *King George V* class Mk IX, and *Vanguard* Mk X. Missing Marks were mostly for cruisers. The substitution of range-finders by radar as the primary source of range measurements made the RF plot, originally the essential part of the FCT, virtually redundant if radar was working. The target echo was followed manually on the radar range tubes against a calibrated scale, as automatic following was fitted only in *Vanguard.* Ranges from other radar sets could also be displayed on the ranging tubes.

The range measured continuously by radar, with spotting corrections and those for own, target and wind speeds, and also for non-standard ballistics, gave gun range. This was converted to quadrant elevation by a flat cam or similar device. Clock range was also generated by the AFCT. This consisted of an initial range setting kept up to date by integration of the range rate, calculated from own and estimated target course and speed. Spotting corrections when added to this gave the so-called true range which, if radar range failed, was the best available value of the geometric range. By comparison of radar range with true or clock range, the accuracy of the target course and speed settings could be checked and suggested modifications obtained. Corrections for line were applied as azimuth deflections.

No battleship in service during World War II had RPC for her turrets, and errors in matching the pointers of the follow-the-pointer dials twice reached 25′ in training during *Duke of York*'s action with *Scharnhorst.*

The latest type of electrical data transmission, by Magslips, did not enter service until 1938. These were instruments of the type known as 'synchros'. They worked on 50-volt, 50-cycle AC, and the transmitter rotor winding excited by the AC supply induced EMFs in the stator windings which varied as the rotor was moved mechanically. The stator windings of the transmitter were connected to exactly similar stator windings in the receiver, and the varying EMF in the transmitter stator was reproduced in the receiver stator, so that the receiver rotor aligned itself with that of the transmitter. The accuracy was about ±1° in 360°; to reduce it to an acceptable figure of about ±1′, a fine transmitter geared down to rotate once for every 5° or so was included with a suitable receiver as well as the 360° coarse unit. This system, known as 'Indicator Magslip', was used where little torque was required from the receiver. In other cases Power Magslip was used. The transmitter and receiver, the latter known as a 'hunter', operated the sensitive valve of an oil motor, while a re-setter driven mechnically from the oil motor re-centred the hunter electrically, which closed the valve and stopped the oil motor as soon as the re-setter had been rotated through exactly the same amount as the transmitter was originally offset. The nominal accuracy was ±15′ over 360°, but if the transmission was geared down 18-1, a figure of ±1′ was obtained over 20°, with a 360° coarse indicator Magslip transmitter and receiver to show which particular 20° sector applied.

LA Fire-Control in cruisers was similar in principle. All 8in (*203mm*) cruisers had directors with 'undisturbed' sights, as in *Nelson*, but otherwise there was considerable variation. *Canberra*, *Devonshire*, *Shropshire* and *Sussex* retained the original fore DT weighing 4.5 tons (*4.6t*) and after DT of 3.6 tons (*3.7t*). The fore DT could train at 9°/sec, as with other power driven units, but the after DT was hand trained at up to 6°/sec. *Dorsetshire*, *Norfolk*, *York* and *Exeter* also retained their original towers, but though the after DT was as above there was a powered DCT forward weighing 11.2 tons (*11.4t*). Of reconstructed ships, *Cumberland* and *Suffolk* retained their original fore DT, but the after DT was converted into a hand-trained DCT weighing 5 tons (*5.1t*). *Australia*, *Berwick*, *Cornwall*, *Kent* and *London* had a later type of powered DCT forward weighing up to 16.4 tons (*16.7t*) with 284 radar, while the original fore DT was converted to a 5.5 ton (*5.6t*) DCT and mounted aft with its former power training.

From *Leander* onwards all 6in (*152mm*) cruisers had a powered DCT forward weighing from 13.5 tons (*13.7t*) to 17.5 tons

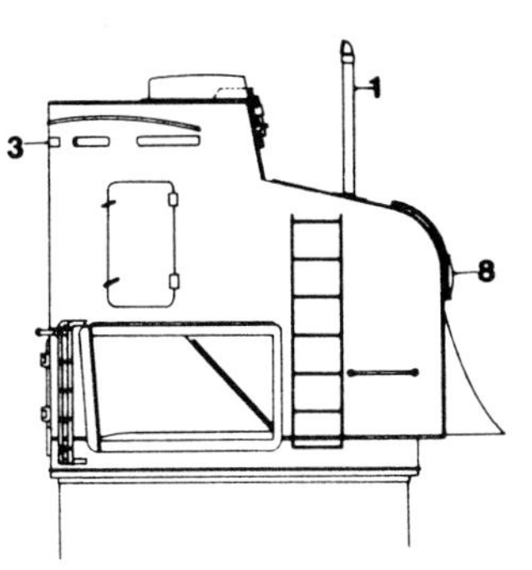

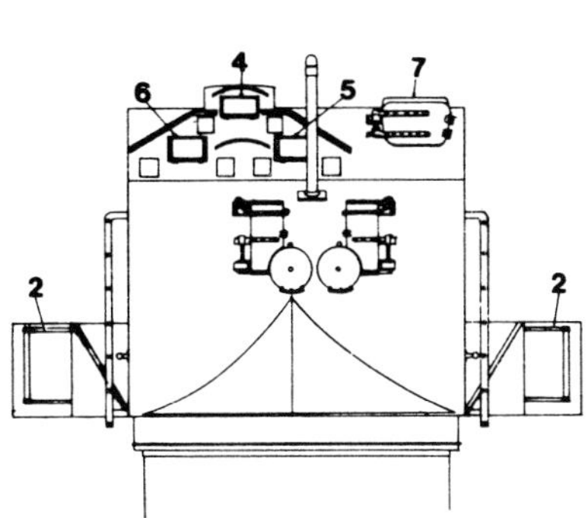

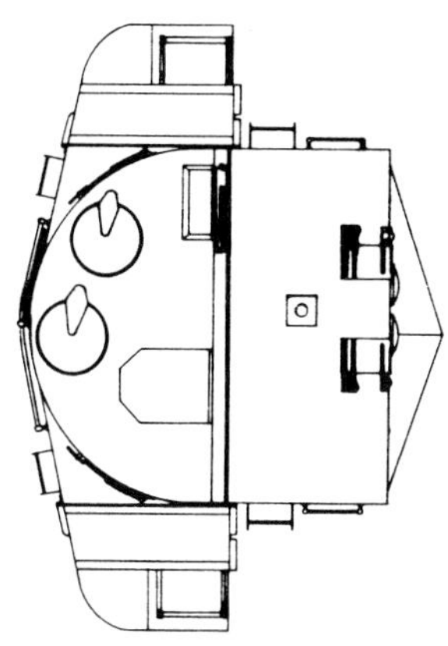

Typical 6in cruiser director control tower as fitted in 1939, shown in profile, front elevation and plan.

1 Dial sight Type GB 2 (forward DCT only)
2 15ft rangefinder
3 Rear windows
4 Control officer's lookout
5 Rate officer's lookout
6 Spotting officer's lookout
7 Inclinometer lookout
8 Kent clear view screen, for gyro director sight

Ross Watton

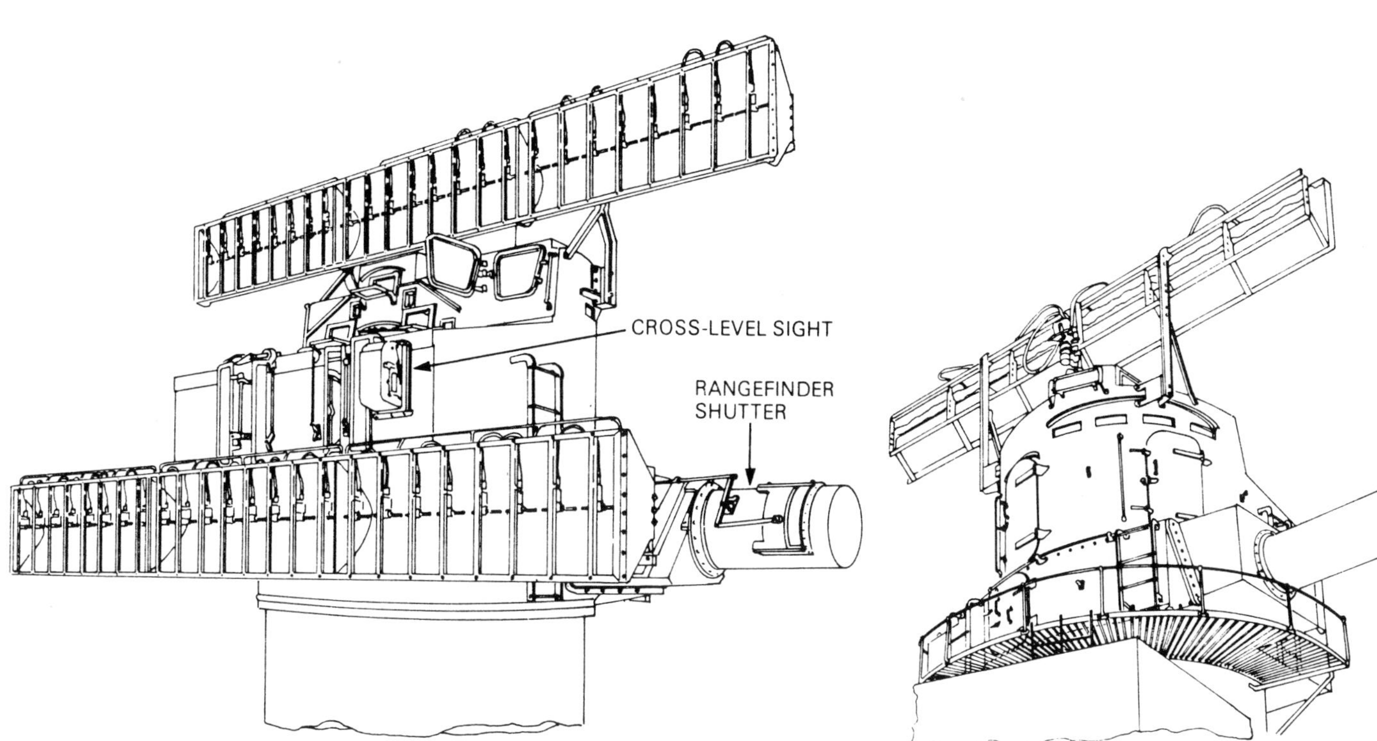

Cruiser DCT with early Type 284 radar aerial
Peter Hodges

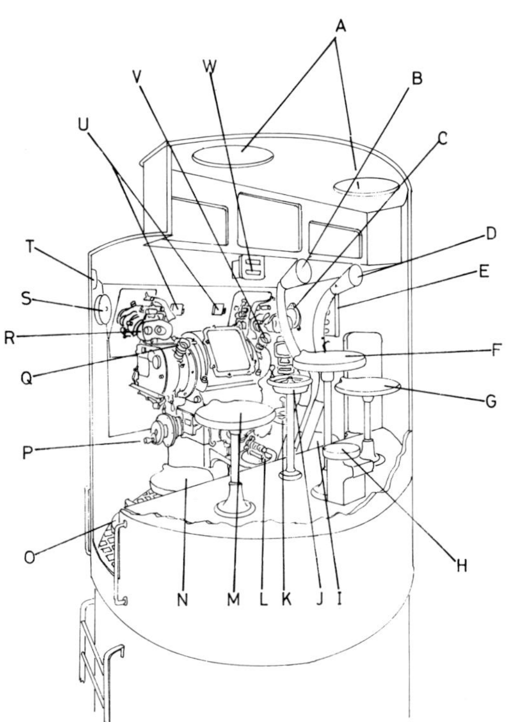

Destroyer DCT in section. This type was fitted for surface fire-control in the majority of fleet destroyers

A Look out hatches
B Voice pipe to Transmitting Station
C Fire gong
D Voice pipe to Captain and Rangetaker
E Gun ready lamp box
F Control Officer's seat
G Spotting Officer's seat
H Gyro compass bearing receiver
I Trainer's seat
J Control Officer's training handwheel
K Trainer's handwheel
L Firing circuit changeover switch and firing pistol
M Rate Officer's seat
N Layer's seat
O Cross-level operator's seat
P Director elevation handwheel
Q Eyepiece of layer's stabilised sight
R Layer's stabilised sight binoculars
S Check fire bell
T 'Fall of shot' warning rattler
U Stabilised sighting port 'Clear view' screen switches
V Eyepiece of trainer's stabilised sight
W Combined range and deflection receiver
Peter Hodges

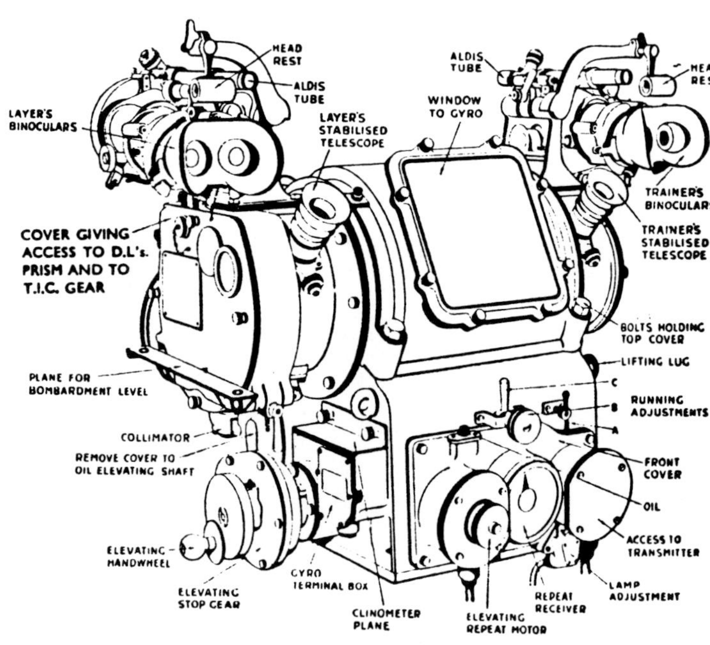

Gyro Director Sight, Type H, Mk I. One of the earlier types of gyro sight for surface targets and fitted in the DCT of 'C' and 'D' class destroyers.
MoD

(*17.8t*), the latter figure including 274 radar. After DCTs of similar type were in *Gloucester*, *Liverpool* (until removed), *Manchester*, *Belfast* and *Edinburgh*, but otherwise it was usual for the after HA director to act for the main armament, though the *Leander* and *Sydney* classes, *Arethusa*, *Galatea*, *Southampton*, and *Newcastle* had, at least originally, a simple sight transmitting training only. The four-turret *Fiji* class had a position at the rear of 'X'. The 5.25in (*133mm*) cruisers of the *Dido* type all had a powered DCT forward weighing 15.3–17.2 tons (*15.5–17.5t*), the higher figure including 284 radar. The after HA director also controlled the 5.25in (*133mm*) in surface fire.

RP 40 training of the DCT from the AFCT was fitted in *Swiftsure*, *Ontario* and *Superb* as completed and also in *Newfoundland*, *Kenya*, *Mauritius*, *Liverpool* (fore only) and *Sheffield*. *Norfolk* was to have been fitted, but only the change to power amount local control was carried out.

'P' gyro sights were introduced in the *Fiji* and *Dido* classes with a prototype tried in *Southampton*, and in late refits *Liverpool*, *Birmingham* and possibly *Glasgow* had them fitted. TIC gear was used as in battleships but the total time was 40–82 milliseconds.

Cross-level was a problem, as in battleships, though it was easier for the lighter turrets to follow the training corrections. A prototype unit with a gyro stabilising the sight and automatic transmission to gun training was installed in *Superb*, but the design was intended for the RP 10 5.25in (*133mm*) of the later *Dido* class though not fitted during the war. Inclinometers were abandoned, and optical range-finders gradually became obsolescent. Turret RFs were 22ft (*6.7m*) or 23ft (*7.0m*) where fitted, and in DCTs mostly 15ft (*4.6m*) or 22ft (*6.7m*).

The development of gunnery radar sets in cruisers was similar to that in battleships. At the end of the war or shortly afterwards, Type 274 was in *Glasgow*, *Sheffield*, *Liverpool*, *Belfast* (2), *Bermuda*, *Jamaica*, *Kenya*, *Mauritius*, *Newfoundland*, *Ontario*, *Swiftsure*, and *Superb*. It was also fitted in *Norfolk* and *Leander*. Type 931 was listed in *Kenya* and *Mauritius* after the war. AGTU for gyro-compass correction was fitted post-war to *Bermuda*, *Jamaica* and *Sheffield*.

An unfortunate change in cruiser fire-control tables was made in the 1930s for reasons of economy and alterations were found to be necessary. The older AFCTs comprised Mk II in the *Kent* class, *Australia* and *Canberra*, Mk III in other 8in (*203mm*) cruisers, Mk IV in *Leander* and Mk IV* in *Achilles*, *Neptune* and *Orion*, and these generally resembled Mk I in *Nelson* and *Rodney*. AFCT Mk V in *Ajax*, the *Sydney* class, *Arethusa*, *Galatea*, *Penelope*, *Southampton*, and *Newcastle* had an improved clock, but only a speed-across plot and a very small-scale range plot, which was later enlarged. Later 6in (*152mm*) cruisers up to and including *Superb*, and 5.25in (*133mm*) cruisers had AFCT Mk VI and VI* respectively, in which a partial return was made to some features of the earlier type. The *Tiger* class as originally designed would have had Mk VI, but the proposed triple turret *Neptunes* were to have AFCT Mk X as in *Vanguard*, altered to suit ballistics.

There were three different systems of surface fire-control in fleet destroyers, the first in the 'A' and 'B' classes, the second in the 'C' to 'K' classes, 4.7in (*120mm*) 'Tribals', 'N' class and 'Q' to 'V' classes, and the third in the 4.7in (*120mm*) 'L' and 'M' classes. In the first type there were a pedestal director sight and AFCC (fire-control clock) with separate 9ft (*2.74m*) RF.

The second type had a hand trained DCT weighing up to 3.5 tons (*3.56t*) con-

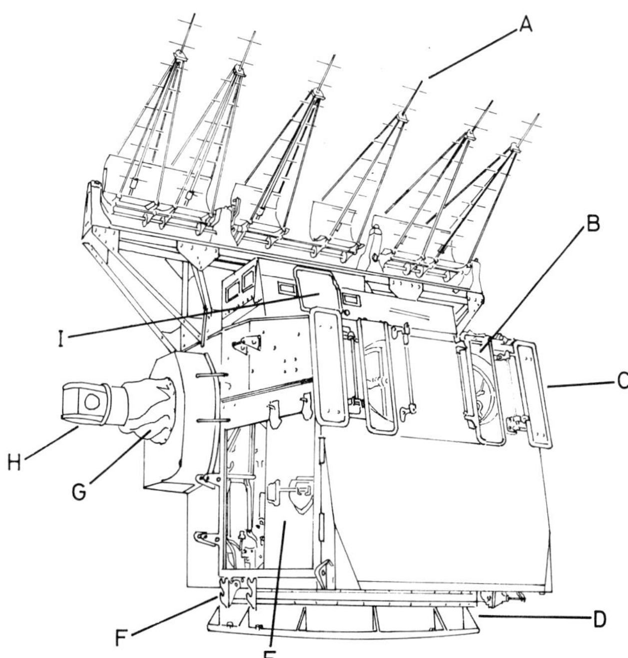

Mk IV Type TP HA/LA DCT with Type 285 radar fitted in 'Z' and 'Ca' class destroyers, and hydraulically powered.

A Radar Type 285 aerial array
B Layer's sighting port
C Sighting port door
D Training Base
E Right hand sliding access door
F Hangers for access ladder
G Flexible gaiter
H Rangefinder
I Control Officer's sight port

Peter Hodges

taining a gyro sight. It could be trained at 10½°/sec or perhaps 18°/sec if the Control Officer helped. The sight was 'undisturbed', and director setting and line of sight training were transmitted to the AFCC. This resembled an AFCT without plots, and transmitted elevation and training to the guns. The earlier classes had, at least originally, a separate RF as in the first type, but the Tribals and 'Q' to 'V' classes had a RF/director which functioned as a 12ft (*3.66m*) RF in surface fire and also as an HA director. A somewhat similar fitting in the 'J', 'K' and 'N' classes known as the three-man Mk I director replaced the RF originally in these.

In the third type, there was a Mk IV Type TP HA/LA director on the lines of the DCTs in battleships and cruisers, and incorporating a stabilised 12ft (*3.66m*) RF. It was power trained except in *Laforey*, *Lookout* and *Marne* originally, and had a 'P' Mk III sight. Otherwise, surface fire-control was similar to that of the second type. The DCT was also used in HA fire with the angle of sight transmitted to the fuze-keeping clock (FKC) in 12′ of arc steps, and the control officer had angle of presentation binoculars as in HA directors.

TIC gear was installed from the 'C' class onwards, with a time range of 33–52 milliseconds, and XL gear of a similar type to that in heavier ships was fitted in the 'E' and later classes. Surface gunnery radar was not fitted, but later ships and most of the earlier ones that survived had Type 285 HA gunnery sets installed as they became available. With the aerial fixed at about 10° elevation, satisfactory ranges were obtainable against surface targets.

In many cases, surface fire-control was a secondary function of the HA director. The 5.25in (*133mm*) guns in the *King George V* class were controlled by AFCC operating from the HA directors and Control tables, and in *Vanguard* control was by the US Mk 37 directors and computers. TIC gear in the *King George V* class provided for a time interval of 52 milliseconds.

In battleships and aircraft carriers with 4.5in (*113mm*) guns up to and including *Indomitable* and also in the cruisers *Charybdis* and *Scylla* control was similar to that in the *King George V* class. The 6in (*152mm*) cruisers *Birmingham*, *Glasgow*, *Sheffield* and the first eight *Fijis* had only one DCT and the after HA director could control the main armament either through the AFCT or AFCC. In the 5.25in (*133mm*) cruisers there was no AFCC, and the HA directors could control in surface fire through the AFCT or the LA part of their HA control tables.

In *Implacable* and *Indefatigable* there was an interim modified small ship system with fuze-keeping clocks (FKC), the HA directors controlling the 4.5in (*113mm*) in surface fire through fire-control boxes (FCB), which were in effect reduced AFCCs, but with mechanical input. In the last three *Fijis* and *Swiftsure*, *Ontario* and *Superb* FCB replaced AFCC and the two last ships had FKCs instead of HA control tables.

The first 'Battles' and the 'W', 'Z' and 'Ca' classes had AFCC with FKCs but 4in (*102mm*) ships had FCBs of various marks though the *Abdiel* class fast minelayers and *Black Swan* type sloops had AFCC. HA directors and their associated HA equipment are described below, as is the K director fitted in the 'Z' and 'Ca' classes though this was more correctly a dual purpose unit.

HIGH-ANGLE CONTROL

Fire-control against aircraft was far more difficult than that against ships. The target's speed and rate were much greater while motion was in three dimensions. Also, corrections due to roll and pitch of the firing ship became greater as the gun's elevation increased and at near 90° became impossible for biaxial mountings. Triaxial or quadraxial mountings provided a solution, but the mechanical difficulties were great in the larger AA weapons, and the only such mounting in service during World War II was the twin Hazemeyer Bofors introduced from the Dutch navy. A triaxial director was used in the USN Mk 37 system but the light cruiser *Delhi*, re-armed in America, was the only British ship to have this during the war.

A further problem was fuze setting, which required a time difference in the calculations.

The type of equipment stabilisation generally used in the war was altitude-azimuth, which endeavoured to achieve dry-land conditions. One gyro measured level and another cross-level, while stabilisation in azimuth was derived from the navigational compass. The system was subject to considerable errors except under the most favourable conditions; for example, corrections calculated in the horizontal plane were applied in the deck plane.

In British biaxial stabilised systems, the relevant units were the Gyro Level Corrector (GLC), Gyro Cross-Level Corrector (GXLC) and Cross-Level Calculating Unit. The GLC had a gyro with vertical spin axis and was continuously trained so that the outer gimbal axis was at 90° to the plane of sight. When the deck tilted, the level angle was measured by the rotation of the outer gimbal axis and transmitted to the director sight elevation. The GXLC had a similar gyro and was continuously trained so that the outer gimbal axis remained in the plane of sight. The XL angle was measured by the rotation of the outer gimbal axis and transmitted to the Cross L Calculating Unit which also received director elevation. The director XL training correction was transmitted to director training after combination with allowances for yaw and alterations of course from the master compass. Director training, less the XL correction, was transmitted as 'original director training' for training the GXLC.

Differences between gun and director sight level angle were ignored, but gun XL training correction was calculated from gun elevation and XL angle. On subtraction of director XL training correction, the gun canted trunnion training correction was obtained.

In the 'Battle' class destroyers with Mk VI directors the XL corrector and calculating unit were combined as a Gyro Cross-Level Calculator in the transmitting station. Gun canted trunnion correction was ignored in AA fire, but not in surface fire.

The foregoing simple type of stabilisation did not provide a complete solution, but was usually sufficient to keep the target in the field of view so that the layer and trainer could make corrections. GLCs were fitted in many ships, but GXLCs were generally limited to the most important and recent units. No pom-pom directors had any stabilisation.

Range-finders (usually known as 'height-finders', though slant range was the distance measured) remained as a safeguard after the introduction of AA gunnery radar. The directors for the heavier AA guns had a 15ft (*4.6m*) or, in older installations, 12ft (*3.7m*) coincidence instrument, while a 4ft (*1.2m*) RF was used for pom-pom directors. Although the superiority of stereoscopic RFs was arguable for surface fire, they were better for AA, but the Admiralty disliked the special care of the rangetakers' stereoscopic vision that was erroneously thought to be necessary.

The following notes on radar are concerned with AA gunnery sets, and Air Warning and Target Indication are omitted. The first long-range set Type 285, was tried in the *Southdown* in late 1940. A five or six 'Yagi' aerial array was used, according to the space available, two or three for transmitting and three for receiving. The set worked in the 'L' (50cm) band and was originally not very satisfactory, in part because of the deficiencies of the then AA computing system. In an attempt to improve this, Auto Barrage Units (ABU) were introduced. These caused barrage salvos to be fired automatically so that the shell bursts occurred when the target reached the selected range set between 1000yd and 5000. Fire had to be withheld until the target was at 5000yd or less, and there was only one chance to destroy it. Type 285M/P, introduced in 1942, was a considerable improvement. Transmitter power was increased and beam switching applied in the horizontal plane, while common-aerial working also improved the bearing accuracy and it was possible to display thousand-yard sections of the range instead of the full distance. Range and rate were determined, and the bearing of an unseen target could be given - but not the line of sight, which made it necessary to use an optical director sight.

The much better Type 275, working in the 'S' (10cm) band, had conical scanning equivalent to beamswitching in elevation and azimuth. Separate aerials were used with two 4ft (*1.2m*) parabolic dishes in nacelles on either side of the Mk VI director and the feed to the receiver aerial offset to produce a conical scan. Blind tracking was achieved, the line of sight being determined by this set, but there was no auto-follow in wartime or immediate post war units, and manual radar following had to be used at the Tallboy console. This contained Elevation and Training Control Units (ECU, TCU) for remote control of the Mk VI director, and also a Continuous Prediction Unit (CPU) which had some resemblance to ABU, but four separate barrage salvos could be fired. The Mk VI director with 275 radar had little war service, the earliest installations being in the refitted *Anson*, in *Ontario* and *Superb* and in the first 'Battles'. The type 275 was also used with the US Mk 37 director in *Vanguard*.

Another 'L' band set, the Type 283, had a twin 'Yagi' aerial, and was used with a Barrage Director and a type of ABU to enable the 8in (*203mm*) and 6in (*152mm*) of cruisers to be used against aircraft. It was intended to apply the system to the heavy guns of battleships. Barrage directors were of simple type, previously tried without ABU in *Shropshire*, *Nelson* and *Rodney*. Their predecessor was the Augmenting Table, which provided data from the HACS for the LA system.

The Type 282 radar for close range use with pom-pom directors was also an 'L' (50cm) band set with two 'Yagi' aerials introduced in 1940-41. It suffered from electrical troubles among others and, more

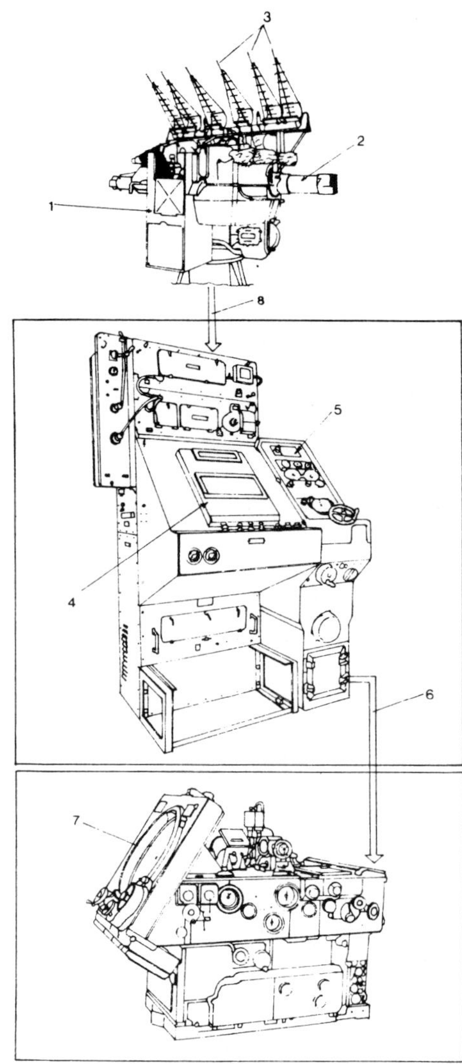

Type 285 radar as used with HACS Mk III.

1 HACS director
2 Rangefinder
3 'Yagi' aerials
4 Ranging display (panel L12) of radar set
5 Range transmission unit (RTU)
6 Range information transmitted to HACS in high angle control position (HACP)
7 HACS Mk III - a mechanical computer which processed the fire control information for AA weapons
8 Radar signals to radar office

In its later development, two ranging displays (Panels L24 and L22) together with a spotting tube were fitted in the HACP and the ranging panel in the radar set was removed

John Roberts

Details of AA Gunnery Sets

Type	**285**	**285M/P**	**275**
Frequency (MHz)	600	600	3100
Peak Power (kW)	25	150	500
Pulse (microseconds)	2	1	0.5
Range (yards)	18000 ± 150	18000 ± 25	30000 ± 25
Range (metres)	16460 ± 137	16460 ± 23	27430 ± 23
Horizontal Beam Width (degrees)	18	9.5	5
Vertical Beam Width (degrees)	43	43	5
Accuracy (minutes of arc)	—	± 15H	± 10H and V

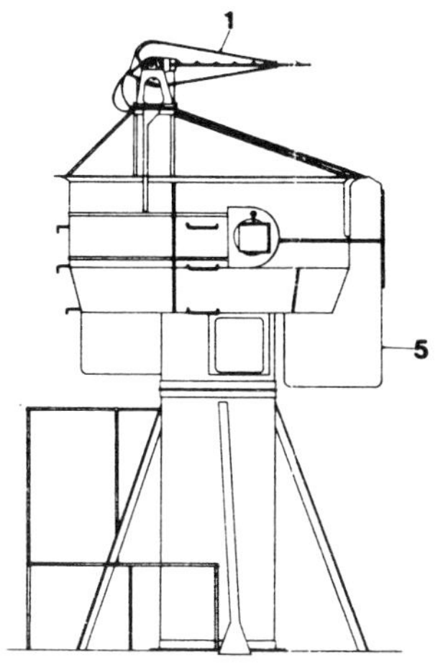

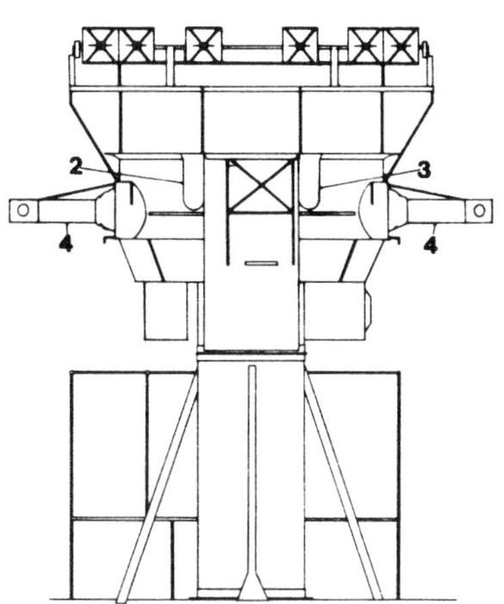

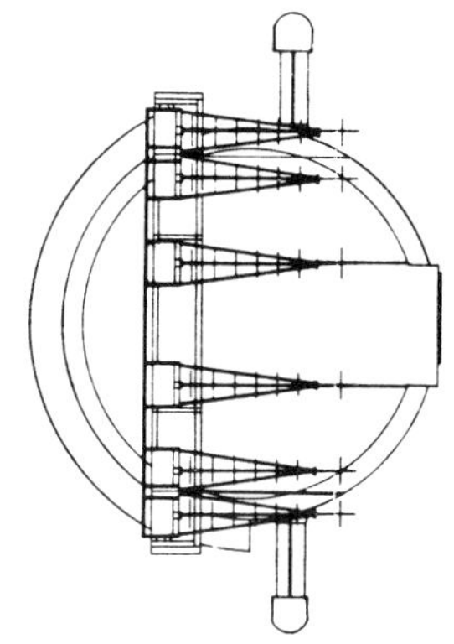

Typical 4in HA director tower with Type 285 radar as fitted in 1942, shown in profile, front elevation and plan.

1 Type 285 radar
2 Trainer's sighting port
3 Layer's sighting port
4 15ft HA rangefinder
5 Rangetaker's legspace

Ross Watton

Details of Type 282 and 282M Radars

Type	**282**	**282M**
Frequency (MHz)	600	600
Peak Power (kW)	25	160
Pulse (microseconds)	2	1
Range (yards)	5000 ± 50	6000 ± 50
Range (metres)	4570 ± 46	5490 ± 46
Horizontal Beam Width (degrees)	40	29
Vertical Beam Width (degrees)	43	43
Accuracy (minutes of arc)	—	90 H

fundamentally, from the 40° wide beam, which meant that the range operator might well be on a different target from that at which the director was pointing.

The much improved Type 282M of 1942 had increased power, common aerial working and beam switching in the horizontal plane; it was a useful range-finder for pom-pom directors and, in a modified version, for the self-contained Hazemeyer twin Bofors.

The 'X' (3cm) band Type 262 giving automatic lock on and subsequent following at up to 5000yd (*4570m*), did not enter service until after the war.

The control system in use for the larger AA guns in the early part of World War II depended on the target's travelling at constant speed in a straight line at constant height. In these conditions it was not necessary to measure range continuously if target bearing and angle of sight were continuously available. With the advent of 275 radar, it was possible to assume that height was not necessarily constant, though changing at constant rate, since in this case slant range, target bearing, and angle of sight, as well as their rates, had to be measured continuously. Assumptions of constant speed with constant rates of change in height and course, or of movement with constant vector acceleration, belong to the post-war period.

The early type of Mk IV HA director and Mk IV HA Control System (HACS) were the latest in service in 1939. The layer and trainer had telescopes with undisturbed lines of sight, and director setting and training were transmitted. Training was hydraulic or, alternatively, by hand, and elevation was by hand, supplemented by hydraulic drive from the level corrector. The height finder could move independently of the layer.

The control officer, kept on target by layer and trainer, aligned a graticule in his binoculars with the target aircraft and transmitted the fuselage angle of presentation. If one imagines a clock dial in the plane through the target at right angles to the line of sight with its centre on the future line of sight, the fuselage angle of presentation is then the hour angle at which the target appears to enter the dial. The control officer also estimated the target speed.

The setting of the clockwork time fuze was in the sequence: future range, ballistic corrections, fuze range, height, time of flight, set back correction, fuze number. Future range was found by plotting present range against time, and after a period equalling the dead time - predicting fuze to firing salvo - and time of flight, the plot reached future range.

The present range pricker made dots every half-second on the range plot, which gave the observed plot, and a mean or generated range plot was made by the plot operator, a second pricker making dashes every 1½ seconds. With the advent of 285 radar a third pricker plotted continuous ranges as a series of small holes. Fuze data were transmitted continuously.

Deflection was deduced from the image of a ring on a screen. The ring was tilted by a drive from the future angle of sight and the image on the screen gave an ellipse of the required shape. The size of the ellipse was adjusted by moving the projection unit by an amount calculated by dividing the target speed by the average projectile velocity. The angle of presentation transmitted by the control officer moved a pointer on the screen indicating the target's direction of travel. With present target position on the circumference of the ellipse and future position at the centre, the vertical and lateral deflections were given by the distance of the present position from the centre, measured parallel with the ellipse axes. Lateral deflection was corrected to deflection in azimuth by conversion gear, and corrections for own ship's movement, convergence and drift were applied to deflection.

The ballistic height corrector for muzzle velocity, projectile shape and air temperature and density overcorrected, so that the fuze numbers were set back by the set-back correction, and the rate unit continued the generated plot if the height finder failed or the target was obscured. Tilt correction was applied at the director, dip at the tangent elevation drum, but wind only by the control officer offsetting the graticule in his binoculars.

Barrages could be fired with fuzes set at 1500yd(*1370m*) and aiming off by the control officer with the HA director forward area sight (HADFAS). The gunnery report of *Illustrious* on the attacks of January 1941 in which the eight available 4.5in(*113mm*) fired about three thousand HE shells at an average of twelve per gun per minute, states that HADFAS was of no use against dive bombers. In barrage fire the control officers looked straight at the dive bombers and used the vertical and lateral deflection handwheels to 'hose-pipe' bursts on the target.

Important additions to the HACS were the Gyro Rate Unit (GRU), Gyro Rate Unit Box (GRUB) and Gyro Rate Unit Deflection Oil Unit (GRUDOU). These are not to be confused with the post-war

Gyro Rate Unit Stabiliser (GRUS) applied to stabilised line-of-sight systems, such as Flyplane.

GRU was a constrained gyro fitted in the director with the axis of rotation initially parallel to the director line of sight and measured the angular velocity of the target relative to the ship. GRU transmitted vertical and lateral rates and angle of presentation to GRUB in the HA transmitting station. Typically maximum precession rate was 6°/sec with an error of ±6′/sec or 5% of the true rate, whichever was the greater. Full accuracy was not reached at lower rates than 2.5°/sec and at 15′/sec the error might reach 20%. GRU was thus most to be relied upon at short ranges. Accuracy was affected by cross-roll.

GRUB enabled the observed angle of presentation and target ground speed to be applied to the HA table, whether the observed values were from GRU or control officer's estimates. Under windless conditions and with GRUB controlling, any form of spotting correction was far more likely to do harm than good, but GRUB had no wind corrector and the control officer might have to override. He also had to inform the GRUB operators of any observed alteration of target's course, warning them that a new setting of the presentation follow up handwheel was necessary.

If the target was seen to climb or dive, continuous operation of presentation follow up and target speed handwheels was ordered by the control officer. The design of GRUB assumed straight and level flight and it could generate fresh rates automatically only as long as level flight was maintained. GRU could still measure vertical and lateral rates if the target was not in level flight and GRUB could be set to give these rates by fictitious speed and target plan inclination. These in turn gave deflections acceptable for small angles of climb and dive.

GRUDOU gave deflection in barrage fire at 1000yd (*910m*) to 5000yd (*4570m*) in conjunction with range solutions from ABU or CPU. The accuracy was no greater than necessary for this application, and rates were received from GRU.

With the addition of GRU, the director Mark became IVG and IVGB with the further addition of cross-level stabilisation, scooter control, rate aided training and hydraulic elevation. With 285 radar Mk IVGB weighed 5½ tons (*5590kg*). Most Mk IV directors had been altered to IVGB by the end of the war.

Directors of the Mk IV series were fitted in *King George V*, *Prince of Wales*, *Renown*, *Queen Elizabeth*, *Valiant*, *Ark Royal*, *Illustrious*, *Victorious*, *Formidable*, *Aurora*, *Birmingham*, *Glasgow*, *Sheffield*, *Gloucester* class, *Belfast* class, *Fiji* class, *Swiftsure* and all 5.25in (*133mm*) cruisers as well as *Charybdis* and *Scylla*.

Mk V series directors which differed only in the position of the RF, were intended to give less cramped conditions for the crew than Mk IV. They were designed for radar, and had binocular layer's and trainer's sights. Additional fittings were as in Mk IVGB. Weight with 285 radar was 8 tons (*8130 kg*). There was no corresponding new HACS table and the directors were in *Anson* (originally), *Duke of York*, *Howe*, and *Indomitable*.

The Mk V* (M) Director was fully Metadyne powered, and within the limits of 285M/P radar could be trained from the Tallboy console. There was no HACS table, the director being used with a fuze keeping clock (FKC). This system was in *Implacable* and *Indefatigable*.

This director was followed by the MkVI, which was a complete redesign that incorporated 275 radar and also a target selector sight placed at the centre of the

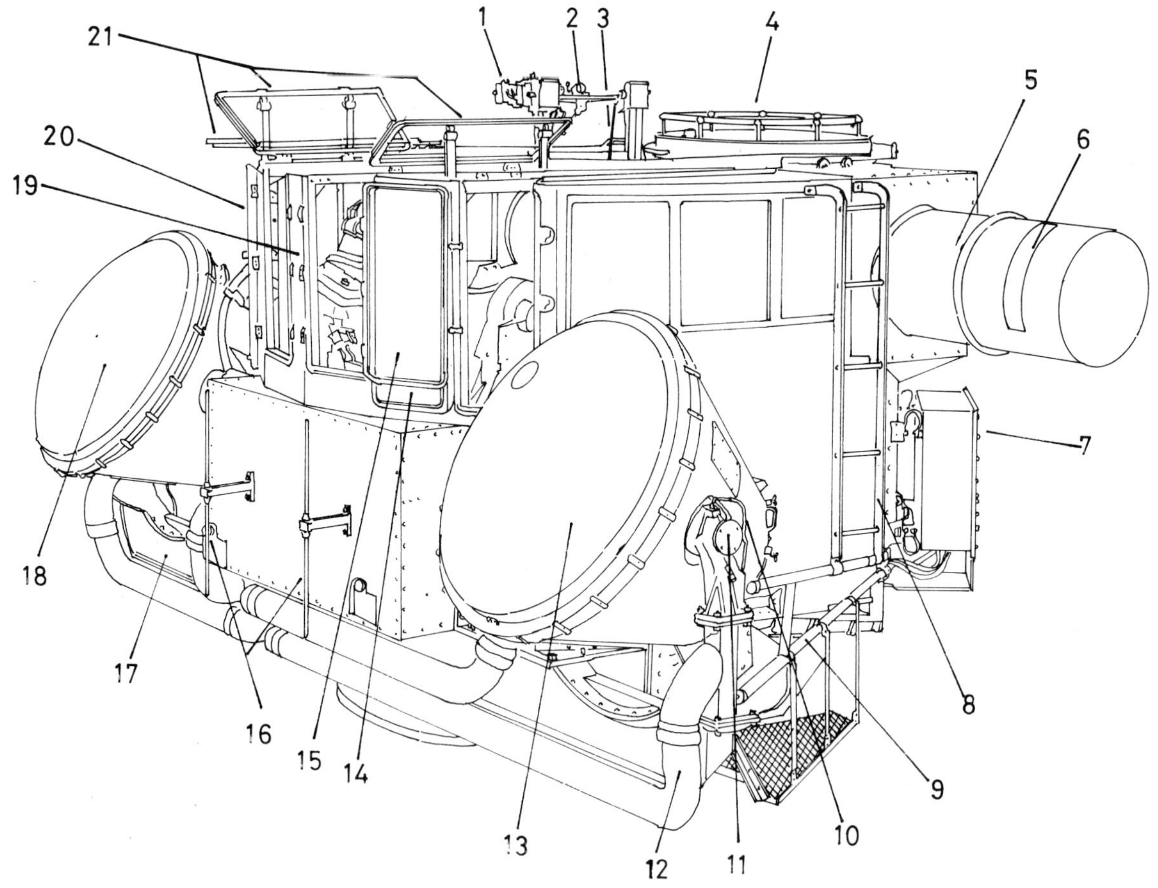

Mk VI HA/LA DCT with 275 radar. This entered service late in the war and was limited to *Anson* as refitted, *Ontario*, *Superb* and the earlier 'Battle' class

1 Elevation transmission unit of independent searcher sight
2 Searcher sight binoculars (shown at 90° to Director Line of Sight)
3 Searcher sight elevation link from elevation handle to binocular platform
4 Searcher sight hatch in open position
5 Fixed rangefinder shield
6 Slot for lens of Rangefinder Type UL Mk II
7 Nacelle blower motor starter
8 Roof access ladder
9 Nacelle trunnion access platform support tube
10 Forced lubrication pipe to trunnion bearing
11 Nacelle trunnion end cap
12 Nacelle air blower pipe
13 Radar Type 275 Receiver nacelle
14 Layer's window, fully open
15 Control Officer's window, fully open, over layer's window
16 Twin IFF dipole aerials
17 Nacelle trunnions support beam
18 Radar Type 275 Transmitter nacelle
19 Rate Officer's position
20 Trainer's and Rate Officer's windows, fully open
21 Roof windows, fully open

Peter Hodges

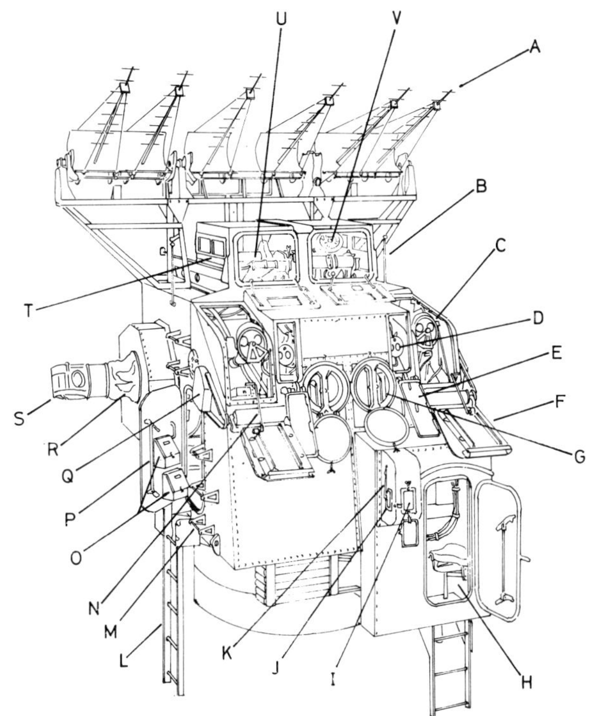

Mk I Type 'K' HA/LA DCT with Type 285 radar fitted in 'Z' and 'Ca' class destroyers, and hydraulically powered.

A Radar Type 285 aerial array
B Hand-grip
C Layer's HA binocular sight
D Layer's unstabilised LA binocular sight
E Unstabilised sighting port door
F Folding HA sighting port door
G Layer's stabilised sighting port
H Cross level operator's position
I Port providing light to cross level sight
J Cross level sighting port
K Manual sighting port wiper
L Access ladder
M Access rungs
N Closing lever for HA sighting port doors
O Communication headset stowage boxes
P Link between access door securing clips
Q HA sighting port door counterbalance weight
R Flexible gaiter
S Rangefinder
T Sliding hood over control and Rate Officer's position
U Rate Officer's binocular mounting plate
V Control Officer's Angle of Presentation binoculars

Peter Hodges

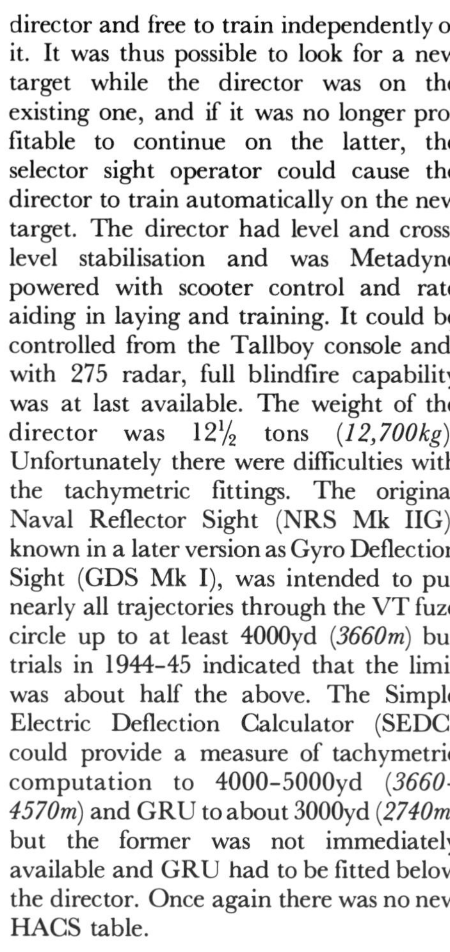

director and free to train independently of it. It was thus possible to look for a new target while the director was on the existing one, and if it was no longer profitable to continue on the latter, the selector sight operator could cause the director to train automatically on the new target. The director had level and cross-level stabilisation and was Metadyne powered with scooter control and rate aiding in laying and training. It could be controlled from the Tallboy console and, with 275 radar, full blindfire capability was at last available. The weight of the director was 12½ tons (*12,700kg*). Unfortunately there were difficulties with the tachymetric fittings. The original Naval Reflector Sight (NRS Mk IIG), known in a later version as Gyro Deflection Sight (GDS Mk I), was intended to put nearly all trajectories through the VT fuze circle up to at least 4000yd (*3660m*) but trials in 1944-45 indicated that the limit was about half the above. The Simple Electric Deflection Calculator (SEDC) could provide a measure of tachymetric computation to 4000-5000yd (*3660-4570m*) and GRU to about 3000yd (*2740m*) but the former was not immediately available and GRU had to be fitted below the director. Once again there was no new HACS table.

Of the ships fitted with Mark VI during the war, *Anson*, as refitted, had HACS, *Ontario*, *Superb* and the earlier 'Battles' FKC. Postwar lists show SEDC in the last and GRU in the others.

The USN Mark 37 Director, described under that navy, was only fitted to the AA Cruiser *Delhi* during the war, when she was rearmed in the USA with 5in (*127mm*) guns. It had been hoped to obtain 82 of these excellent directors, but the model was only fitted postwar to *Vanguard*, *Eagle*, *Ark Royal* and the last eight 'Battles'. It was heavy, the version in *Vanguard* with 275 radar weighing 16½ tons (*16,760kg*).

As previously noted the HA directors also had a LA function in many instances. Of ships with Mk IV to VI HA directors, battleships and aircraft carriers had four and cruisers three except for *Aurora* and all the *Dido* class with two, while 'Battle' class destroyers had one.

The earlier hand-trained HA directors of the Mk I to III series resembled Mk IV in principle as did their associated HA Tables.

The Fuze-Keeping Clock (FKC) was originally intended for sloops and destroyers. It worked on the same principles and with the same target assumptions as the HACS table, but there was no plot and the FKC was not a self contained unit, calculating only the special corrections for AA fire, and otherwise fed by the associated AFCC or FCB. As there was no plot, fuze settings depended on the rate clock in the FKC, the latter calculating future range.

Most ships with FKCs were fitted with some type of RF director, but in addition to the Mk V* (M) and Mk VI HA/LA directors already noted, there were the K Type Mk I HA/LA DCT in 'Z' and 'Ca' destroyers, the Mk IV Type TP DCT, and the three-man Mk I director, both described under LA Control. The K DCT, which weighed 8½ tons (*8640kg*) with 285 radar, was hydraulically powered and had scooter control. It had separate LA (gyro) and HA layer's and trainer's sights. GLC and GXLC were fitted and also LA cross-level gear. Within the limits of its radar, it could be trained by the Tallboy TCU.

RF directors transmitted director elevation and training as well as range and angle of presentation and were used in some ships simply as RFs in LA fire. There were two main types, one with electrical transmission to an AFCC and the other with mechanical transmission to a FCB. In the latter the transmitting station was located in a vulnerable position immediately below the director.

CLOSE-RANGE HA CONTROL

The policy at the beginning of World War II, at least in cruisers and larger ships, was to have one director with self-contained calculator for each multiple pom-pom mounting. It was not however until 1940 that eyeshooting principles were abandoned with the introduction of the Mk IV Director, in which lateral and vertical angular rates were measured by GRU and combined with time of flight in the calculator to give lateral and vertical deflections. The director, which was hand worked in laying and training, weighed 36cwt (*1830kg*) or with later additions 52cwt (*2640kg*), had no stabilisation and required a crew of eight. It was essential that the GRU and director operators used the same point of aim. RPC between director and mounting, fitted to many but not all by the end of the war, was also highly important to avoid pointer errors which were often excessive with high speed aircraft at close range.

Radar aerials suitable for beam switching were fitted to new directors from December 1942 and on overhaul to 21 older ones. With improved type 282 the present range was determined and the rate of the target generated, from which a function was calculated and combined with angular rates to give deflections. Convergence, tangent elevation and dip corrections were added by the calculator mechanism.

Local scooter power control for joystick aiming by the control officer was fitted to new directors from February 1944 and retrospectively to 30 more. This enabled the control officer to put the layer's and trainer's binoculars on any target with minimum delay. In mass attacks the director could be aimed off by eyeshooting, thus avoiding loss of time while gyro rates were developed.

Optical RFs (4ft, *1.22m*) were removed from May 1944 from new directors and retrospectively from 30 others. Range and rate were obtained by radar, and, in its absence, it had been found better to fire at a fixed range setting, as optical ranges were too difficult to obtain accurately. The crew was reduced to seven.

Remote scooter control from the radar office for training only in blind fire was installed in new directors from November 1944 and retrospecively to 29 more.

The mechanical calculator provided vertical and lateral deflections, wind rates, and convergences, but approximations were made and the figures were correct only within certain target speeds and ranges.

The Mk IV could give good results in calm weather if well maintained with a good crew, but performance fell off rapidly in bad weather. Maintenance of the calculating unit and GRU were difficult, a large crew was needed and had to be highly trained to produce accurate deflections from GRU in the absence of any stabilisation, so that a replacement director was overdue by the end of the war.

Earlier marks of pom-pom directors with eyeshooting were widely used during the war.

The gunnery report of *Illustrious* on the attacks of January 1941 is of interest. Her 40 remaining Mk VIII AHV pom-poms had fortunately had their crank journals just modified and dressed up, so that they worked very well and in nearly every action each mounting fired its full load of 154 rounds per gun in continuous fire. Altogether about 30,000 rounds were expended. The five-man directors – Mk III* – then fitted are described as useless against mass dive bombers, and the space better used for Oerlikons.

The USN Mk 51 Director introduced to Britain in 1943 with the American twin and quadruple Bofors was more in line with requirements than the Mk IV pom-pom director. It was essentially a Mk 14 gyro sight on a pedestal mounting with a crew of one. Vertical and lateral rates were measured by two spring-constrained gyros and converted to deflections by a function of the estimated present and future range, there being no RF or radar. The director was manually operated with handle-bar control and hydraulic damping and transmission to the RPC of the mounting for elevation; training was by power synchros (Magslips). Weight was 710lb (*322kg*). The virtue of the Mk 51 was its simplicity made possible by design for short or very short ranges. The above gyro sight was a rate-measuring device and entirely distinct from those in LA DCTs.

Owing to an inadequate supply of Mk 51, a British version was produced. It was known as the Simple Tachymetric Director (STD) Mk I, or as the 'Austerity' Director. This was first indended for the Mk XI Bofors gun in the twin RP 50 Mk V mounting, but could be used with any mounting with RPC and/or Magslip receivers. The Mk 14 sight was soon superseded by the British Type 6 Mk II, with maximum deflection reduced from 24° to 11½°. Wind corrections could be made at the price of doubling the crew to two. Weight, with Type 6 sight, was 1120lb (*508kg*). The overall performance was considered to be about the same as or a little better than the Mk IV pom-pom director and 1945 policy was for it to replace the latter as opportunity occurred.

The Hazemeyer Mk IV Bofors had its own self-contained tachymetric director with the layer and trainer tracking the target. The wind analyser worked in

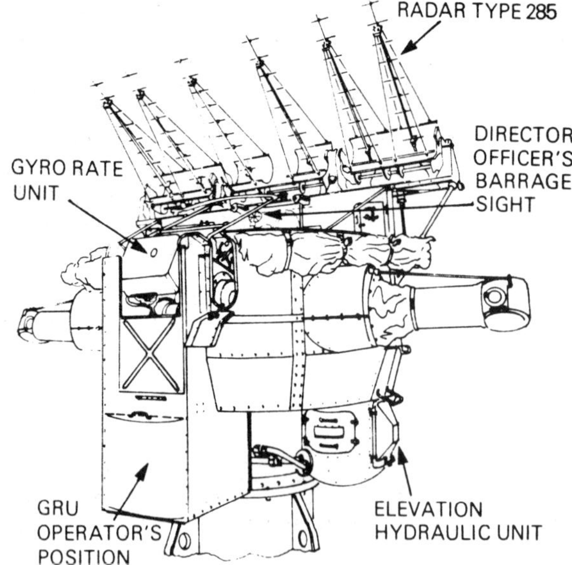

HACS Mk IV director, about 1943
Peter Hodges

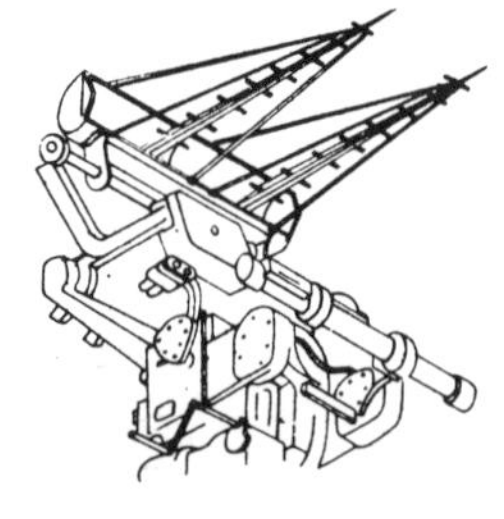

Type 282 radar fitted to a pom-pom director.

azimuth only. Later versions (Mk IV*) had 282 P(2) radar with beam switching and lateral tracking by the auxiliary trainer. The calculator was hand worked. The Close Range Blind Fire Director (CRBF) with 262 radar and full blind fire capability, intended for the six-barrel Bofors mounting or (in its self-contained version) for STAAG, was too late for the war.

In the absence of Mk 51 or STD directors, Mk 14 or Type 6 gyro sights fitted on the gun mounting improved the efficiency of close-range AA weapons against kamikazes by a factor of four or five compared with eyeshooting and were fitted as supply permitted, to ships of the Pacific Fleet, or those intended to join it, in 1945.

HEAVY CALIBRE GUNS

Originally intended for the four 'G3' battlecruisers cancelled under the Washington treaty, this gun was mounted in triple Mk I turrets in *Nelson* and *Rodney*. It was the last British heavy wire-wound gun. Construction comprised a tapered inner A tube with two rear locating shoulders, the foremost 554.4in (*14,081.8mm*) from the muzzle, A tube, full length taper wound wire, B tube, and overlapping jacket and breech ring. There was the usual shrunk collar on the rear of the A tube. A breech bush located in the A tube took the Welin type breech block operated by hydraulic Asbury mechanism, the weight being only 2 tons (*2032kg*). Altogether 29 guns were made, Nos 1-10 by Elswick, Nos 11-18 by Vickers, Nos 19-23 by Beardmore, and Nos 24-29 by RGF. It may be of interest to record that an 18in (*457mm*) Mk I, No 1, originally in *Furious*'s Y turret, had been lined to a 16in (*406mm*) Mk I for trial purposes and was still in existence. Its original weight including BM was 149 tons (*151,391kg*). As shown in the notes to the table below, the guns were not uniform, though the differences in performance between Mk I and Mk II rifling were thought to decrease with wear. As completed both ships had Mk I rifling in all guns, the three short chamber guns Nos 3, 4, 24 being in *Nelson*'s A turret. These were not changed to guns with Mk II rifling until March 1945, while B and X turrets had been changed to this rifling in May 1944. In *Rodney*, A turret was changed to Mk II rifling in February 1942, B had two Mk II and one Mk I rifling from December 1937, and X always had Mk I rifling. Such differences were totally at variance with the usual British policy for heavy guns in important ships, particularly when combined with differences in wear as shown in the table of *Rodney*'s guns when she engaged *Bismarck*.

Originally a muzzle velocity of 2715f/s (*828m/s*) was intended but at 2670f/s (*814m/s*) wear was rapid, accuracy insufficient and the rifling was damaged by hammering of the short bodied, long-headed shell, so that stripping occurred. These defects were remedied by reducing the muzzle velocity, and some recovery in performance would have been obtained with a proposed 2250lb (*1021kg*) shell, but financial stringencies in the early 1930s prevented any change.

The propellant charge was divided into sixths and originally only APC shells were carried unless HE were required for bombardment but from mid 1943 five time-fuzed HE were carried per gun with 95 APC. The original bombardment HE had the fuze at the nose of the shell proper inside the ballistic cap, which led to failure in detonation, and all were withdrawn in 1943 after *Rodney*'s bombardment of Djebel Santon at Oran in the North African landings. The later HE shell had a true nose fuze and was also of better ballistic shape.

The triple turret design was a break with previous British practice, the main intention being to prevent magazine explosions of the kind which had destroyed three battlecruisers at Jutland. The turrets were hydraulically powered using light mineral oil instead of the usual water-based liquid. It is believed that this was done to avoid corrosion in the pusher hoists. There was one pump per turret driven by a 750HP steam engine, but each turret could draw on the other pumps, which were located in the fixed structure with accumulators in the pump rooms and in the turrets. The guns were on individual slides with front and rear saddles, usually called cradles, and compressed air runout was employed. Elevation was by hydraulic cylinder and piston connected to the slide with limits of +40° -3°. Each turret had two 400HP

16in (406mm) Mark I

Gun Data

Bore	16in	406.4mm	
Weight incl BM	108 tons	109,733kg	
Length oa	742.2in	18,852mm	46.39cal
Length bore	720in	18,288mm	45.0cal
Length chamber	125.5in	3187.7mm	
Volume chamber	35,205in^3	576.9dm^3	
Length rifling	588.95in	14,959.3mm	
Grooves	(80) 0.135in deep × 0.377	3.43 × 9.576mm	
Lands	0.2512in	6.380mm	
Twist	Uniform 1 in 30		
Weight projectile	2048lb	929kg	
Propellant charge	495lb SC 280	224.5kg	
Muzzle velocity	2614f/s	797m/s	
Working pressure	20 tons/in^2	3150kg/cm^2	
Approx life	250 EFC		
Max range (APC)	39,780 yd/40°	36,375m/40°	

The above figures are for guns with Mk II rifling. Mk I rifling was 586.964in (14,908.9mm) long and had 96 grooves, 0.124 × 0.349in (*3.15 × 8.865mm*), with lands 0.1745in (*4.432mm*). MV was 2586f/s (*788m/s*) and range 39,090yd (*35,745m*). Guns Nos 3,4 and 24 had chambers of the same volume but 118.5in (*3009.9mm*) long, and the length of the Mk I rifling was 592.4in (*15,047mm*).

With the later type of HE shell, ranges were 41,690yd (*38,120m*) with Mk II rifling and 40,890yd (*37,390m*) with Mk I.

Range and Elevation Data for APC shell, 2525 f/s (770m/s) MV

Range (yd)	**(m)**	**Elevation**	**Descent**	**Time of flight (sec)**	**Striking V (f/s)**	**(m/s)**
5000	4570	2°20.4′	2°31′	6.32	2248	685
10,000	9140	5°7.3′	5°51′	13.42	1996	608
15,000	13,720	8°25.9′	10°12′	21.45	1778	542
20,000	18,290	12°31.0′	16°30′	31.05	1606	490
25,000	22,860	17°29.3′	24°38′	41.87	1486	453
30,000	27,430	23°43.6′	33°29′	54.65	1431	436
35,000	32,000	32°24′	43°40′	70.95	1453	443
37,500	34,290	39°13′	50°28′	82.84	1503	458

Gun Mounting Data

Revolving weight	1464-1483 tons	1487-1507t
Roller path diameter	33ft mean	10.06m mean
Barbette int diameter	37ft 6in	11.43m
Distance apart gun axes	98in	2.489m
Recoil distance	44.6in	113cm
Max elevating speed	10°/sec designed	
Max training speed	4°/sec designed	
Firing cycle	30 sec designed, actual 35-40 sec	
Turret shield	face 15.68in; sides 10.78-8.82in; rear 8.82in; roof 7.105in	398mm; 274-224mm; 224mm; 180mm

16in Mk I guns in *Rodney*. The barrel in the right lower corner is that of a 4.7in QF Mk VIII HA gun. *CPL*

swashplate training engines, only one in use at a time, and these drove through a worm and gear train.

In the magazines, which were located below the shell rooms, the charges were placed on roller tracks running to waiting trays in the corners and then passed through flashtight sliding chopper doors to waiting trays at each corner of the handing room. From here they were carried by hand to flashtight tilting scuttles on the revolving structure. Each of the three cordite hoists was served by two tilting scuttles (each holding a half charge), and the scuttles were brought into line with a flashtight hopper containing two brass canisters. The charge was rammed into the canisters which were then tilted vertically in the hopper and hoisted up. The cordite hoists were powered by hydraulic rams with wire lift and pulleys, giving a ninefold multiplication of movement.

In the shell rooms, shells were moved by gantry crane to rammer trays and pushed through chopper doors in the watertight bulkhead separating shell room and shell handing room to four pivoted trays, which revolved into position for ramming the shell on one of four shell bogies, interconnected by rods to prevent collision. The shell was tilted from horizontal to vertical on the bogie and brought into line with one of three revolving scuttles. From there it moved to one of the three pusher shell hoists. As usual, the bogies were locked to the revolving structure during the transfer of shells from bogies to hoists. There were no auxiliary hoists for shells or charges.

Loading was at +3° with telescopic chain rammers at the rear of the turret. The shell hoist was in line with the bore and the shell came up vertically into a bucket, while the cordite hoists were to the right of the left gun and to the left of the other two, and the charges in their canisters went into a vertical flashtight bucket. The canisters remained there until loading was completed, when they were sent down for the next charge. After the breech was opened, the shell and cordite buckets were tilted horizontal, the shell was rammed through the bucket, the shell and cordite trays traversed together until the first and then the second half charge was in line and rammed. All trays were then traversed back and tilted vertical. There were flashtight doors at the top of each shell hoist and at intervals throughout the length of the cordite hoists.

The turrets gave much trouble initially, and several modifications had to be made in the shell handing rooms and elsewhere, while a vertical guide roller race was added just below the main horizontal one. The interconnected shell bogies made it necessary to load all three guns together and, as full salvos caused increased dispersion, it was better to fire double salvos of five and four guns accepting the reduction in maximum rate of fire. By 1939 the turrets were considered reliable and proved far more so than the 14in against the *Bismarck*.

Data for guns in *Rodney* during action with *Bismarck*

Position	Gun No	EFC at 4 May 1941	Mean wear at 4 May 1941	EFC at 30 May 1941	Mean wear at 30 May 1941	Shells fired 4-30 May 1941
Left A	12	129 8/16	0.4175in (*10.6mm*)	165 8/16	0.445in (*11.3mm*)	36
Centre A	14	118 2/16	0.3935in (*10.0mm*)	168 2/16	0.445in (*11.3mm*)	50
Right A	16	127 10/16	0.424in (*10.8mm*)	149 10/16	0.436in (*11.1mm*)	22
Left B	1	25	0.1075in (*2.7mm*)	70	0.250in (*6.4mm*)	45
Centre B	23	20 10/16	0.113in (*2.9mm*)	67 10/16	0.2635in (*6.7mm*)	47
Right B	25	17 4/16	0.085in (*2.2mm*)	69 4/16	0.256in (*6.5mm*)	52
Left X	28	41 12/16	0.2785in (*7.1mm*)	85 12/16	0.321in (*8.2mm*)	44
Centre X	21	30 12/16	0.1555in (*3.9mm*)	72 12/16	0.270in (*6.9mm*)	42
Right X	26	55	0.3515in (*8.9mm*)	99	0.350in (*8.9mm*)	44

Nos 1 and 25 had Mk II rifling. Mean wear is taken at 1 in (*25.4mm*) from commencement of rifling, and it would seem that errors occurred in measuring No 26. The total number of shells fired 4-30 May 1941 is 382, while expenditure against *Bismarck* is given as 380.

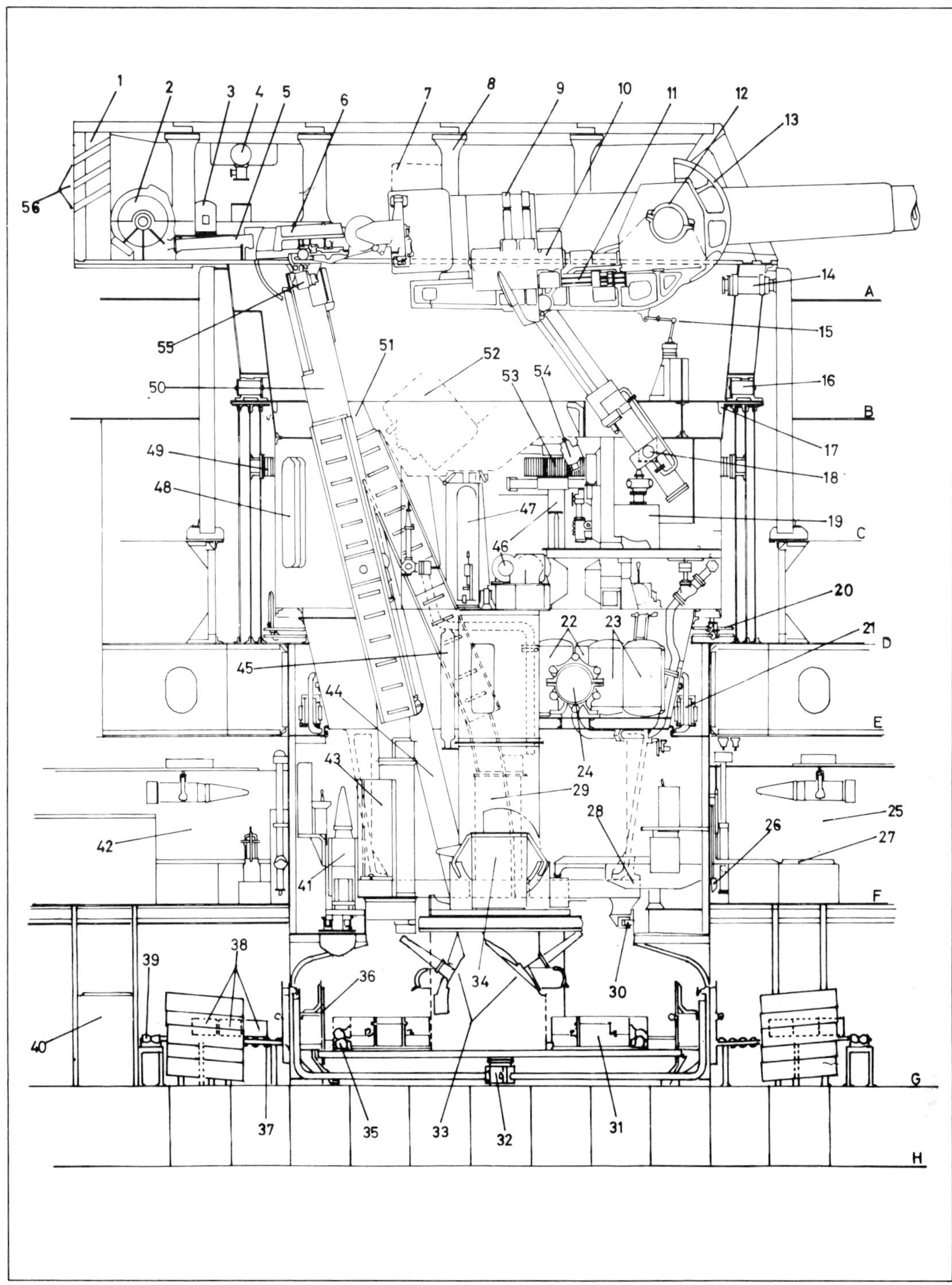

16in Mk I triple mounting designed for maximum safety of ammunition.

1 Counterbalance weight
2 Rammer engine casing
3 Churn levers
4 Rangefinder
5 Telescopic rammer tube casing
6 Tilting tray
7 Position of breech at full depression (-3°)
8 Gunhouse roof support pillar
9 Rear collars
10 Recoil cylinder
11 Sliding pipes for hydraulics, air blast and washout squirt to breech
12 Trunnion cap
13 Mantlet plate
14 Locking bolt
15 Walking pipes to elevating structure
16 Training base roller
17 Turret clip
18 Elevating cylinder trunnion
19 Exhaust tank
20 Steam heating pipes
21 Cable winding gear
22 Washout squirt tanks
23 Turret drenching tanks
24 Hydraulic accumulator
25 Shell room (X turret)
26 Watertight door
27 Shell room rammer tray
28 Pivoting tray
29 Revolving shell scuttle
30 Trunk guide roller
31 Cordite swinging tray
32 Central pivot
33 Cordite cage tilting cylinders
34 Shell bogie in horizontal position
35 Cordite rammer engine
36 Flash door
37 Cordite roller-conveyor
38 Triple cordite charges
39 Athwartships cordite roller-conveyor
40 Cordite stowage bay
41 Shell bogie (tilted upright)
42 Shell room (A turret)
43 Revolving shell scuttle
44 Cordite hoist trunk
45 Washout squirt air bottles
46 Training engine and drive shaft
47 Shell striking down trunk
48 Air blast bottles
49 Training rack
50 Centre gun shell hoist trunk
51 Left gun shell hoist trunk
52 Breech in full recoil at maximum elevation (+40°)
53 Drive pinion and twin training pinion
54 Elevation buffer stop
55 Tilting engine
56 Gunhouse vents

A Upper (forecastle) deck
B Main deck
C Middle deck
D Beam line
E Lower deck
F Platform deck
G Inner bottom
H Outer bottom

Peter Hodges

These guns were intended for the *Lion*, *Temeraire*, *Conqueror* and *Thunderer* which were suspended in 1939 and later cancelled. They would have been in Mk II triple turrets, and in the event no turrets and only four guns, two of each Mark, were completed. The construction comprised a tapered inner A tube, A tube, jacket, breech ring of rectangular external shape, a breech bush located in the A tube, and a shrunk collar on the tube. There were two locating shoulders on the inner A tube, the foremost 555in (*14,097mm*) from the muzzle. The A tube forging was the largest gun forging ever made in Britain and weighed about 64 tons (*65t*), while the finished A tube weighed 44.5 tons (*45.2t*). The only difference between Mk II and Mk III was that the former had three rear and two forward shoulders where the jacket was located on the A tube, and the latter two rear and three forward. A Welin breech block was used with hydraulic Asbury type mechanism, and the weight was 2.65 tons (*2693kg*). In general the gun resembled an enlarged 14in Mk VII.

A new APC shell considerably heavier at 2375lb (*1077kg*) than that for the Mk I gun, was developed, but the HE shell was the same as the later shell for the previous gun. The propellant charge was in sixths.

The Mk II triple mounting was to be on the general lines of the 14in quadruple with +40° -3° elevation and shells limited to 73in (*1854.2mm*) in length. Loading was at +5°.

16in (406mm) Marks II, III

Bore	16in	406.4mm	
Weight incl BM	118.74 tons	120,645kg	
Length oa	743.3in	18,880mm	46.46cal
Length bore	720in	18,288mm	45.0cal
Length chamber	129.4in	3286.8mm	
Volume chamber	34,022in^3	557.5dm^3	
Length rifling	583.47in	14,820.1mm	
Grooves	(80) 0.131in deep x 0.377	3.33 x 9.576mm	
Lands	0.2512in	6.380mm	
Twist	Uniform 1 in 30		
Weight projectile	2375lb APC	1077kg	
Propellant charge	520lb SC 350	235.9kg	
Muzzle velocity	*c*.2483f/s	757m/s	
Working pressure	20.5tons/in^2	3230kg/cm^2	
Approx life	Not determined		
Max range (APC)	40,560yd/40°	37,090m/40	

Including balance weights, 131.09 tons (*133,194kg*). With 2048lb (*929kg*) HE shell, MV and range approximately as for 16in Mk I gun with Mk II rifling.

Range and Elevation Data for APC shell, 2400f/s (731.5m/s) MV

Range (yd)	(m)	Elevation	Descent	Time of flight (secs)	Striking V(f/s)	(m/s)
5000	4570	2°33.9′	2°43′	6.56	2187	667
10,000	9140	5°30.3′	6°15′	13.81	1982	604
15,000	13,720	8°57.1′	10°46′	21.96	1804	550
20,000	18,290	13°4.7′	16°40′	31.28	1647	502
25,000	22,860	18°3.7′	23°57′	41.98	1544	471
30,000	27,430	24°9.8′	32°14′	54.32	1498	457
35,000	32,000	32°3′	41°27′	69.49	1517	462
38,000	34,750	39°28′	48°27′	82.34	1573	479

Gun Mounting Data

Revolving weight	*c*1600 tons	*c*1626t
Roller path diameter	34ft mean	10.36m
Barbette int diameter	38ft 6in	11.73m
Distance apart gun axes	102in	2.5908m
Recoil distance	47in	119.4cm
Max elevating speed	*c*8°/sec	
Max training speed	*c*2°/sec	
Firing cycle	30 sec	
Turret shield	face 14.7in; sides 9.8-6.86; rear 6.86; roof 5.88in	373mm; 249-174mm; 174mm; 149mm

16in (406mm) Mark IV

This, the last British heavy gun, was intended for a projected redesign of the *Lion* and *Temeraire*. It was to have been mounted in triple turrets with several novel features. The specification called for a bore length of 45 calibres, a new gun muzzle velocity of 2450f/s (*747m/s*) minimum at 70°F, and a design pressure of 24 tons/in^2 (*3780kg/cm^2*) to allow for firing across the Straits of Dover with supercharges and special shells. The gun was to have a loose barrel and a screw breech block opening upwards. It was to be flashless with full charges of suitable propellant. The projectile was limited to 78in (*1981.2mm*) and the weight was to be determined by the best base-fuzed HE bombardment shell that could be designed within this length. This shell would cause maximum damage against 3in (*76mm*) or thinner armour. The APC was to be of the same weight with optimum performance against deck armour and effective against heavy side armour.

For preliminary trials one of the two 16in Mk IIIs was relined with a 27,000in^3 (*442.5dm^3*) chamber for flashless trials, and an autofrettaged loose barrel was ordered for the other, though this conversion could not have been used at anywhere near the full designed pressure.

A Vickers-Armstrong design of 6 July 1945, which may well not have been the final one, shows a loose barrel to be autofretted at 32 tons/in^2 (*5040kg/cm^2*) in order to obtain a yield point of 45 tons/in^2 (*7090kg/cm^2*), and weighing 35.1 tons (*35,663kg*). The A tube ended 188in (*4775.2mm*) from the muzzle and there were a jacket, breech ring and removable breech bush weighing 1.263 tons (*1283kg*). Gun weight including BM was 117.85 tons (*119,741kg*), overall length 743.3in (*18,880mm*) and the 26,000in^3 (*426dm^3*) chamber was 113.4in (*2880.4mm*) long. The propellant charge was expected to be about 610lb (*277kg*) of nitroguanidine type.

Only limited work seems to have done on the triple mounting. The breech blocks would have opened upwards, presumably during run-out, and shell and charge were to be rammed in one stroke, with a coaxial rammer. The firing cycle was planned at 20 sec and the gun axes 102in (*2.591m*) apart. A surviving sketch design, which shows an earlier horizontally opening breech block, has a mean roller path diameter of 34ft (*10.36m*). Elevation limits are +45° to -3° with loading at +3°, and elevation is by arc and pinion. The complete charges, in sixths, are stowed horizontally in tubes in the magazines and rammed into a large tilting and training bucket which brings them into line with the three endless-chain charge hoists. Shells, which are to have polished bases, are stowed vertically in the shell rooms, rammed to a shell ring and from there to buckets at the base of the three pusher shell hoists where they are inclined from vertical to the angle of the hoists. In the gunhouse, shells are tipped into loading trays, but it is not shown how complete charges are transferred to the tubular interior of the coaxial rammers, which look like those in the 8in (*203mm*) twin turrets. The charge hoists come up in rear of the shell hoists and there seems very little space for the complete charge to be tilted.

An earlier and much more spacious design with loading at any angle to +45° required a mean roller path diameter of 39ft (*11.89m*) and had separate hoists for HE and APC shells and separate shell and charge rammers.

Forward 15in, *Warspite* 1944
CPL

15in (381mm) Mark I

Gun Data

Bore	15in	381mm	
Weight incl BM	100 tons	101,605kg	
Length oa	650.4in	16,520mm	43.36 cal
Length bore	630in	16,002mm	42.0cal
Length chamber	107.68in	2735.1mm	
Volume chamber	30,650in^3	502.3dm^3	
Length rifling	516.33in	13,114.8mm	
Grooves	(76) 0.1245in deep × 0.445	3.16 × 11.30mm	
Lands	0.175in	4.445mm	
Twist	Uniform 1 in 30		
Weight projectile	1938lb	879kg	
Propellant charge	432lb SC 280	196kg	
Muzzle velocity	2458f/s	749m/s	
Working pressure	20tons/in^2	3150kg/cm^2	
Approx life	335 EFC		
Max range	33,550yd/30°	30,680m/30°	

At 20° elevation range was 26,650yds (*24,370m*). With 1920lb (*871kg*) shell, MV was 2467f/s (*752m/s*) and ranges 24,350yd/20° (*22,265m*), 30,180yd/30° (*27,595m*). 486lb (*220.4kg*) SC 300 supercharges gave 2638f/s (*804m/s*) with 1938lb (*879kg*) shell and ranges 29,930yd/20° (*27,370m*), 37,870yd/30° (*34,630m*).

This famous old gun performed excellently in World War I and its origins date to 1911. It was still carried by many ships in twin turret mountings of the following Marks: I in *Barham, Malaya, Royal Sovereign, Royal Oak, Revenge, Ramillies*, two turrets in *Resolution*, two turrets in *Repulse, Marshal Soult, Terror, Roberts*; I/N in *Queen Elizabeth, Warspite, Valiant, Abercrombie*; I/N RP 12 in *Vanguard*; I* – two turrets in *Resolution*, one turret in *Repulse* and *Erebus*; I*/N in *Renown*; II in *Hood*. Important differences between turrets of the same Mark are given below.

The gun was of the then standard wire-wound construction. The tapered inner A tube had four locating shoulders, the foremost 474.3in (*12,047.2mm*) from the muzzle, and there were A tube, full-length multi-start wire, B tube, and overlapping jacket and breech ring. The breech bush screwed into the A tube, which also had a rear shrunk collar. The Welin screw breech block was operated by hydraulic Vickers 'pure-couple' mechanism and the weight was 2.85 tons (*2896kg*). It may be noted that, if the A tube forging of the second experimental gun E597 had not failed, a full-length jacket without B tube and Elswick 3 motion short arm breech mechanism would probably have been adopted since E597 included both these features, but the delay was inadmissible.

Altogether 186 guns were made including the two experimental ones, 36 by Armstrong at Elswick and 12 at Openshaw, 37 by Beardmore, 19 by Coventry Ordnance, 49 by Vickers and 33 by the RGF. Of these 179 were available for the RN in September 1939. There were five mounted for coast defence at Singapore and from June 1942, two at Wanstone near Dover which were both changed four times. The coast defence mountings allowed +50° or 55° elevation and extreme range with 5/10 crh shells and supercharges as later used at Wanstone, was about 44,150yd (*40,370m*).

The propellant charge was in quarters, and there were two distinct types of shell, the later with a 5/10 crh head, usually known as 6 crh, and weighing 1938lb (*879kg*), and the earlier with a 3.05/4 crh, usually known as 4 crh, and weighing 1920lb (*871kg*). Originally 6 crh shells were limited to *Warspite, Renown, Valiant* and *Queen Elizabeth*, with the addition of *Barham* by mid 1940. Their use was extended to other ships from late 1941 to mid 1943. Neither *Hood* nor *Repulse* seems ever to have had them. APC and HE shells were available in both lengths, but CPC only as 4crh. Initially battleships and *Renown* carried shellite-filled APC only, but *Hood* and *Repulse* had 20% CPC with TNT filling. In the latter years of the war five APC were replaced in all by time-fuzed HE, and if required for bombardment purposes HE could always be carried instead of all or part of the APC. In monitors about 30% of the outfit comprised APC or TNT filled CPC and the balance HE, with time-fuzed HE later replacing five APC (though in the earlier part of the war more APC or CPC were included). Supercharges in quarters were authorised for *Malaya* and the four surviving *Royal Sovereigns* in late 1941 at the rate of twenty per gun, but it is doubtful if they were ever used. They could also have been fired by *Vanguard*, not completed until after the war.

The twin turret mountings were developed from the 12in(*305mm*) BV in *Vengeance* completed in April 1902, via a number of 12in (*305mm*) and 13.5in (*343mm*) mountings. The Mk I mounting is described below followed by the differences in other Marks, except that shield thicknesses are given with the data table.

The turrets were hydraulically powered from a ring main using a water/soluble oil mixture. The guns were on individual slides with front and rear saddles or cradles, and hydraulic power was used for run-out. Elevation was by hydraulic cylinder connected to the slide with limits of +20°/–5° except in *Marshal Soult, Terror*

15in Mk I mounting modified for 30° elevation, known as Mk I/N.

1 Cabinet
2 Rangefinder hood
3 Cordite compartment of gunloading cage
4 Cordite dropping lever
5 Breech-screw
6 Lever actuating lock, on carrier
7 Alternative breech hand-drive
8 'Spoon tray' in position over breech threads
9 Recoil piston tail-rod
10 Balance weight
11 'Kicking strap'
12 Locking-bolt lever
13 Recoil cylinder
14 Rear collars on gun
15 Saddle cap
16 Front collars
17 Trunnion arm
18 Elevation walking pipes
19 Training roller
20 Elevation cylinder
21 Cordite rammer
22 Shell rammer
23 Training walking pipes
24 Cordite hoppers

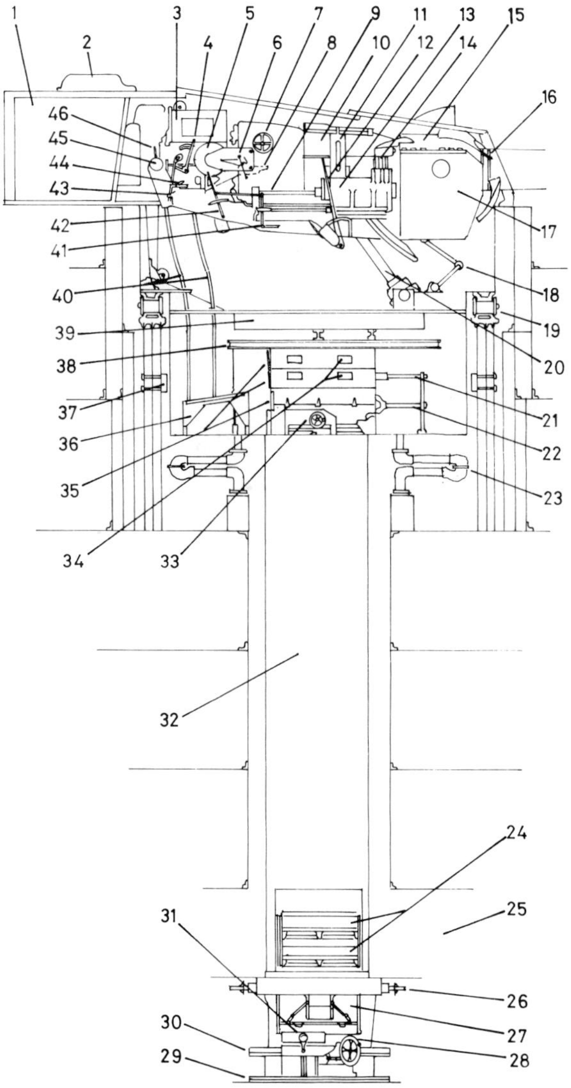

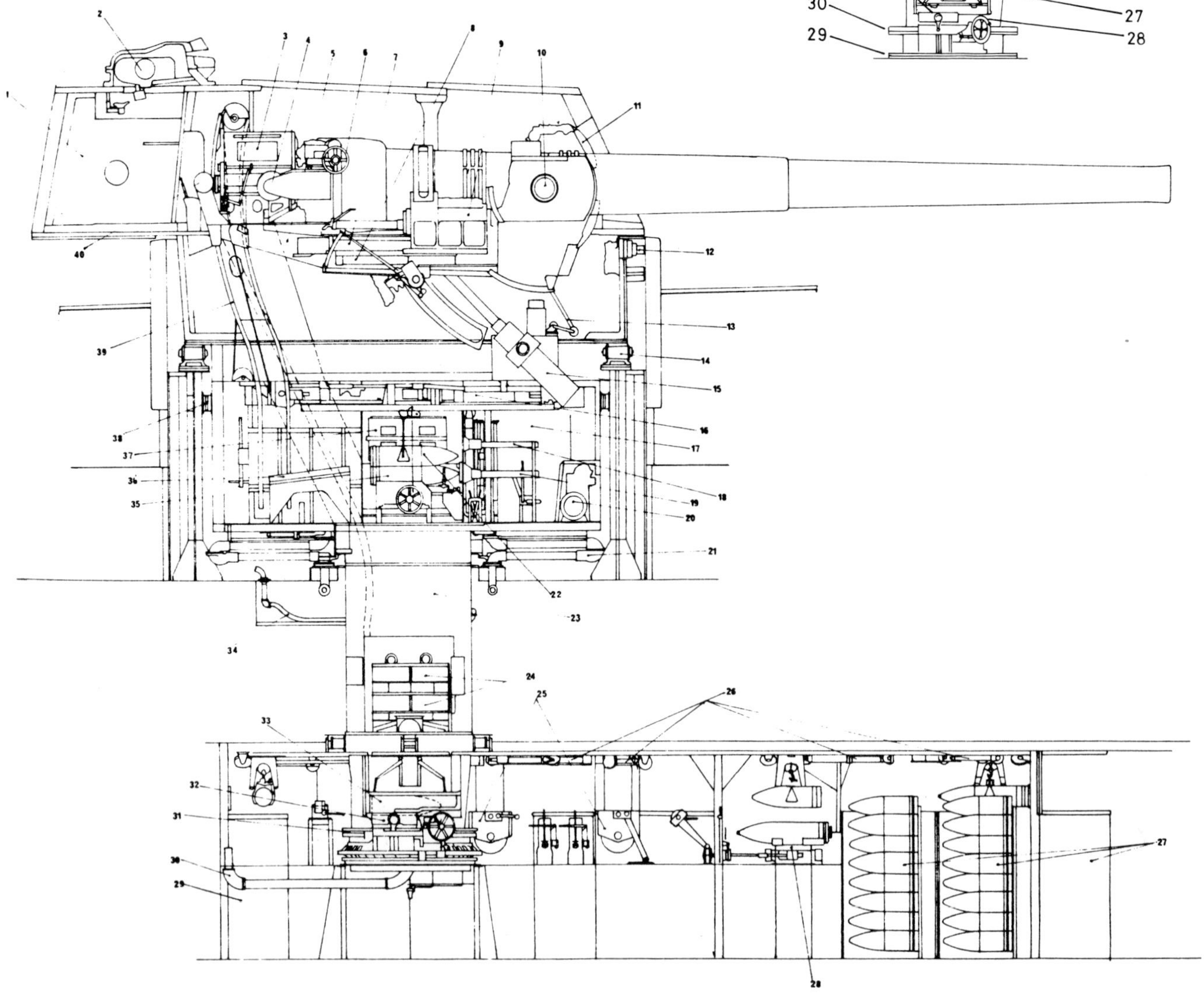

25 Cordite handing room
26 Trunk guide rollers
27 Shell door
28 Shell bogie training hand wheel
29 'Fixed' rack on shell room deck
30 'Moving' rack on trunk
31 Shell traversing handle
32 Main ammunition trunk
33 Shell carrier
34 Inspection windows in flashtight cordite 'waiting' position
35 Automatic flash doors
36 Shell waiting tray
37 Training rack (training gear not visible in this section)
38 Overhead rail in working chamber for secondary shell supply
39 Envelope of cage lifting press
40 Gunloading cage rail
41 Interlocking linkage to breech lever
42 Breech worker's lever
43 Rammer lever
44 Rammer foot-pedal
45 Chain rammer engine
46 Gun 'wash-out squirt' lever

Peter Hodges

15in Mk II mounting, only in *Hood*. 'Y' is shown.

1 Officers' cabinet
2 Rangefinder
3 Gun loading cage
4 Breech (open)
5 Loading arm (attached to gun slide)
6 Breech operating hand wheel
7 Run-out cylinder
8 Chain rammer casing
9 Gun cradle and recoil cylinder
10 Trunnion
11 Splinter shield to gunport
12 Turret training locking bolt
13 Walking pipes (hydraulic power to elevating structure)
14 Roller path
15 Elevating cylinder
16 Ammunition hoist lifting gear
17 Working chamber
18 Cordite rammers (hoist to cage)
19 Shell rammer (hoist to cage)
20 Electric pump
21 Walking pipes (hydraulic power from fixed to revolving structure)
22 Shell suspended from radial transport rail (ready use)
23 Trunk (containing shell and cordite hoists)
24 Cordite hoppers
25 Shell traversing winches
26 Hydraulic shell lifting and traversing gear
27 Shell bins
28 Shell traversing bogie
29 Shell bin
30 Electric cables
31 Shell bogie ring
32 Revolving shell bogie
33 Shell on bogie
34 Flexible voice pipe (fixed to revolving structure)
35 Shell waiting position
36 Shell waiting tray (ready use)
37 Cordite waiting position
38 Training rack
39 Gun loading cage rails
40 Rammer motor

Elevation 30°. Shell room is reversed on drawing, for compactness, with forward end facing aft.

John Roberts

Range and Elevation Data for 1938lb (879kg) shell, 2400f/s (731.5m/s) MV

Range (yd)	(m)	Elevation	Descent	Time of flight (sec)	Striking V (f/s)	(m/s)
5000	4570	2°35.7′	2°50′	6.58	2144	653
10,000	9140	5°39.4′	6°35′	14.11	1909	582
15,000	13,720	9°19.5′	11°40′	22.64	1709	521
20,000	18,290	13°46.3′	18°20′	32.52	1556	474
25,000	22,860	19°14.2′	26°17′	43.80	1461	445
30,000	27,430	26°8.9′	35°39′	57.28	1433	437
32,500	29,720	30°33′	40°43′	65.41	1446	441

Range and Elevation Data for 1920lb (871kg) shell, 2400f/s (731.5m/s) MV

Range (yd)	(m)	Elevation	Descent	Time of flight (sec)	Striking V (f/s)	(m/s)
5000	4570	2°38.9′	2°57′	6.71	2074	632
10,000	9140	5°56.7′	7°18′	14.63	1776	541
15,000	13,720	10°7.1′	13°33′	23.99	1537	468
20,000	18,290	15°30.1′	22°15′	35.12	1377	420
25,000	22,860	22°29.0′	32°39′	48.70	1317	401
29,000	26,520	30°4′	41°59′	62.06	1326	404

Range and Elevation Data for 1938lb (879kg) shell, 2575f/s (785m/s) MV

Range (yd)	(m)	Elevation	Descent	Time of flight (sec)	Striking V(f/s)	(m/s)
5000	4570	2°14.8′	2°26′	6.15	2312	705
10,000	9140	4°52.4′	5°41′	13.06	2063	629
15,000	13,720	7°59.2′	10°1′	20.91	1852	564
20,000	18,290	11°40.7′	15°29′	29.79	1683	513
25,000	22,860	16°6.6′	22°13′	39.86	1560	475
30,000	27,430	21°23.7′	29°56′	51.27	1497	456
35,000	32,000	27°55.7′	38°15′	64.59	1496	456
36,500	33,380	30°16.0′	40°54′	69.20	1507	459

Gun Mounting Data for Mark I/N Mounting

Revolving weight	*c*815 tons	*c*828t
Roller path diameter	27ft mean	8.23m
Barbette int diameter	30ft 6in	9.30m
Distance apart gun axes	98in	2.49m
Recoil distance	46in	117cm
Max elevating speed	5°/sec	
Max training speed	2°/sec	
Firing cycle	30 sec	
Turret shield	face 12.74in; sides 10.78in; rear 10.78in; roof 4.9in	324mm; 274mm; 274mm; 124mm

Revolving weight for Mk I mountings was *c*770 tons (*782t*) and for Mk II *c*880 tons (*894t*). The figure for the Mk I/N RP 12 in *Vanguard* was 855 tons (*869t*). The following differences in shield thickness include all types of 15in mountings:

Face 14.7in (*373mm*) *Hood*; 8.82in (*224mm*) *Renown*, *Repulse*; sides 11.76–10.78in (*299–274mm*) *Hood*, 8.82–6.86in (*224–174mm*) *Vanguard*, *Renown*, *Repulse*; roof 5.88in (*149mm*) *Vanguard*, *Abercrombie*, 4.165in (*106mm*) *Royal Sovereign* class, *Malaya*, *Renown*, *Repulse*, *Erebus*.

and *Roberts* where the slide trunnions were raised $25\frac{1}{2}$in(*64.8cm*) to allow +30° to +2°. *Roberts* had the turret previously in *Marshal Soult*, and *Terror* that removed from *Marshal Ney* in 1916. Training was by one of two swashplate engines driving through worm and gear train.

Magazines were located above shell rooms and quarter-charges were delivered to the handing room via revolving scuttles and then placed by hand in cordite hoppers on the main turret truck. Each hopper had two trays, each holding two quarter-charges which rolled into the hoist cage when the trays were tilted. As there was no shell handing room, shells were carried by overhead hydraulic or hand gear to one of two shell bogies which were then locked to the trunk and the shell entered into the hoist cage by a traversing trolley on the bogie. A shell door then closed the trunk opening. The shell cage picked up the cordite cage and in the working chamber the shell was transferred to the waiting position by a traversing shell carrier and the two half-charges tipped into the totally enclosed upper compartments of the waiting position. From there, shell and charge were rammed into the gun loading cage of the upper hoist, and on arrival at the gun the shell was loaded, followed by the first and then the second half charges dropping one after another into line with the gun axis. Auxiliary hoists for charges and shells were provided, the former running from handing room to gunhouse.

In the 30° mountings loading was at +5°, but in the others the chain rammer was carried on an extension of the slide so that loading was possible over the full range of +20° to -5°, though to avoid slow run-out it was usually at about +5° or less.

Mk I* differed only in the use of Kenyon doors instead of shell bogies. The shell was traversed from an overhead rail on the fixed structure to one on the trunk and was lowered and slid into the tray door and thence into the hoist cage, the tray door covering the opening in the trunk when closed. *Erebus* had one of the turrets originally built for *Furious* in case the 18in (*457mm*) guns were unsatisfactory, and this had been altered to give +30° +2° elevation as in two of the Mk I turrets.

The next mounting in chronological order was Mk II. This had a higher gunhouse and deeper turntable, allowing +30° to -5° elevation with loading at +20° to -5° and pneumatic run-out was fitted. The turret shield was more heavily armoured, the sighting ports were cut in the face instead of having roof hoods, and flash precautions were improved.

Mk I/N and Mk I*/N were the earlier Marks modified as far as possible to Mk II standards without new gunhouses and turntables. Pneumatic run-out was fitted, and raising the slide trunnions 8.75in (*22.2cm*) and moving them back 7.25in (*18.4cm*), combined with the same movement forward of guns and slides relative to the trunnions, made it possible to obtain +30° to -4½° elevation with loading at up to 20° for the price of a 12-ton balance weight fixed over the rear collars on each gun. *Abercrombie* had what was originally the other Mk I* turret for *Furious* and, in addition to the modifications above, the Kenyon doors were replaced by shell bogies, a shell handing room was built with shells transferred from the shell room via four rammer trays, and flashtight scuttles were added to the hoppers on the main trunk in the magazine handing room. The flash doors on the gun loading cage were also redesigned.

The Mk I/N RP12 turrets in *Vanguard* were originally the Mark I* in *Courageous* and *Glorious* removed on their conversion to aircraft carriers. The modifications noted for *Abercrombie* were carried out with alterations to the cordite hoppers on the trunk, and to enable the hydraulic RP 12 remote power training control system to be used the worm in the training drive was replaced by bevel and additional spur gears. In addition the magazines were located below the shell rooms in *Vanguard* and, to avoid major changes in the loading arrangements, the turret trunk ended at the shell handing room with the magazine handing room above, while the magazines were connected to their handing rooms by fixed hoists, four each in A and B turrets and three each in X and Y. In the magazines half-charges were taken from their cases and pushed by hand on roller conveyors to top and bottom hoppers on the fixed hoist trunk and rammed into the hoist cage. In the handing rooms the half-charges were rammed into hoppers and tipped out via scuttles to trays. They were then placed by hand on roller conveyors and pushed to loading trays where they were loaded into power worked flashtight revolving hoppers and thence into the main hoist cage.

This last version was never tested in action, but the 15in (*381mm*) twin turret was the best liked of British heavy gun mountings.

14in (356mm) Mark VII

Gun Data

Bore	14in	355.6mm	
Weight incl BM	78.988 tons	80256kg	
Length oa	650.85in	16,531.6mm	46.49cal
Length bore	630in	16,002m	45.0cal
Length chamber	108.54in	2756.9mm	
Volume chamber	22,000in³	360.5dm³	
Length rifling	515.68in	13,098.3mm	
Grooves	(72) 0.117in deep × 0.3665in	2.97 × 9.309mm	
Lands	0.2444in	6.208mm	
Twist	Uniform 1 in 30		
Weight projectile	1590lb	721kg	
Propellant charge	338.25lb SC 300	153.4kg	
Muzzle velocity	2483f/s	757m/s	
Working pressure	20.5tons/in²	3230kg/cm²	
Approx life	375 EFC		
Max range	38,560yd/40°	35,260m/40°	

The above weight is for guns Nos 91-136, Nos 61-90 weighed 79.588 tons (*80,865kg*). With balance-weights Nos 91-136 were 91.488 tons (*92,956kg*) and Nos 61-90 90.588 (*92,042kg*).

Range and Elevation Data for 2400f/s (731.5m/s) MV

Range (yd)	(m)	Elevation	Descent	Time of flight (sec)	Striking V (f/s)	(m/s)
5000	4570	2°35.0′	2°48′	6.59	2160	658
10,000	9140	5°36.7′	6°30′	14.06	1927	587
15,000	13,720	9°15.8′	11°33′	22.57	1726	526
20,000	18,290	13°43.2′	18°12′	32.41	1563	476
25,000	22,860	19°14.9′	26°23′	43.86	1459	445
30,000	27,430	26°11.0′	35°37′	57.43	1432	436
35,000	32,000	35°58′	46°5′	74.97	1482	452
36,500	33,380	40°42′	50°27′	83.20	1523	464

This gun was mounted in twin Mk II and quadruple Mk III turrets in the five ships of the *King George V* class. It was the first 14in gun to be adopted as standard by the RN, previous Marks having been taken over with the Chilean battleship *Almirante Latorre* building in England, obtained from the USA or introduced as Army railway guns. The construction was based on that of the experimental 12in (*305mm*) Mk XIV, comprising tapered inner A tube, A tube, jacket, breech ring of rectangular external shape, breech bush located in the A tube and a shrunk collar on this tube. The inner A tube had two locating shoulders, the foremost 490.1in (*12,448.5mm*) from the muzzle. Later guns had a breech ring of different shape, and a Mk VII* has been found in one list. It is thought that this refers to a projected loose barrel design that was never made. The usual Welin breech block and hydraulic Asbury type mechanism were used, the weight being 1.85 tons (*1880kg*). Including two trial guns a total of 78 were made, 24 by ROF, 39 by Vickers-Armstrong, Elswick, and 15 by Beardmore.

In addition to its use afloat, two of the above total were mounted at Dover in 1940, one in No 26 Proof Structure and the other in an 18in (*457mm*) monitor mounting which had been adapted for proof purposes. With a very heavy supercharge of 486lb (*220.4kg*) SC 500, a muzzle velocity of 2850f/s (*869m/s*) could be reached with standard shells and an extreme range of *c*51,000yd (*46,630m*) obtained at 45° elevation. They were used for cross-channel firing but the mountings were not suitable for rapidly moving ship targets.

The propellant charges, including the above supercharge, were in quarters, and initially only APC were carried unless HE were required for bombardment, but in mid 1943 five of the 100 APC per gun were replaced by time fuzed HE. The twin and quadruple mountings were based more on the 15in (*381mm*) than on the 16in (*406mm*) Mk I, and except for the difference in the number of guns were virtually identical, though the quadruple turret was not a double twin as in French designs. They were hydraulically powered from a ring main using water/soluble oil as the fluid. For the first time in a British heavy turret, the guns recoiled in cast steel cradles and not on slides, a feature first tried with the 12in (*305mm*) Mk XIV. Compressed air run-out was employed and elevation was by hydraulic cylinder and piston connected to the rear of the cradle with limits of +40° to -3°. Each gun was independently elevated, as in other British heavy turrets. Training was by one of two swashplate engines, 160BHP in the quadruple and 70BHP in the twin, driving through worm and gear trains. As in the altered 16in (*406mm*), a vertical-guide roller race was located just below the main horizontal one in both two and four gun mountings.

Magazines were below the shell rooms and, in the former, quarter charges were run on roller chutes into a hydraulically operated flashtight cage which raised them the short distance to handing room level. There were four such lifts in A and B magazines, but only two in Y, where the other two were replaced by flashtight double-door scuttles for reasons of level. In the handing room the quarter-charges rolled (or, where there were scuttles, slid) to open waiting trays. From there they were carried to cordite hoppers, mounted one per gun on a circular platform attached to the hoist trunk, and by means of power rotated scuttles and chain rammers transferred to the lower hoist cage, each tube of which took one half-charge.

In the shell rooms shells were moved by over-

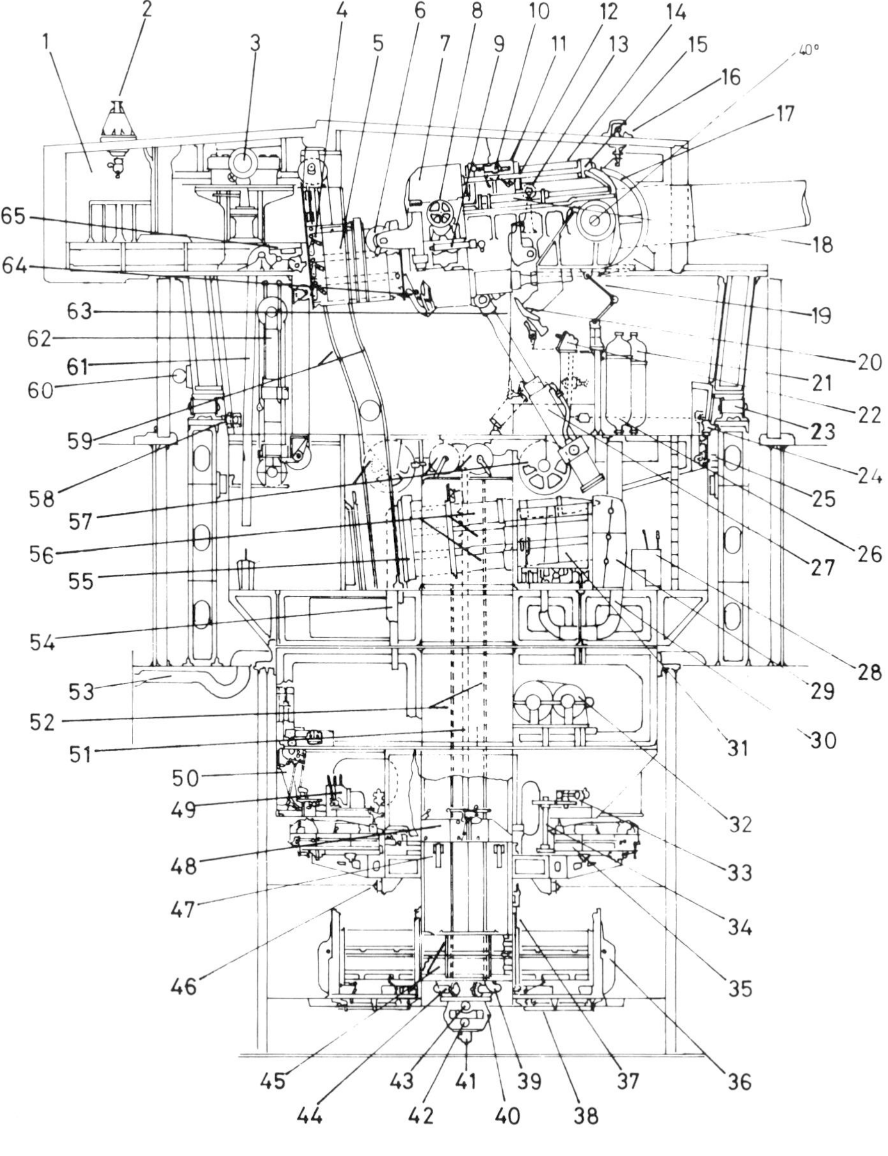

14in Mk III quadruple mounting. Ammunition supply differed widely from that in the 16in Mk I triple.

1 Navigating compartment ('A' mounting only)
2 Navigator's periscope
3 Rangefinder
4 Flash door linkage
5 Gunloading cage
6 Breech-screw (open)
7 Upper balance weight
8 Manual breech-operating hand wheel
9 Power breech-operating cylinder
10 Automatic recuperator gland pressure intensifier
11 Recuperator cylinder
12 Right-hand recuperator tie-rod
13 Power elevation control wheel
14 Recuperator ram
15 Recuperator ram crosshead
16 Look-out periscope
17 Mantlet plate
18 Telescopic air-blast and hydraulic supply sliding pipes to breech mechanism
19 Hydraulic walking pipes to elevating mass
20 Elevation cut-off cam
21 High-pressure air cylinders
22 Elevation buffer
23 Training roller
24 Training clip
25 Safety firing cam rail
26 Cut-off linkage from safety firing cams
27 Elevation cylinder
28 Rammer and traverser control console
29 Rammer, 'traverser to gunloading cage'
30 Retracted chain-rammer casing
31 Traverser
32 Training gear
33 On-mounting shell-ring hydraulic motor
34 Shell-ring power drive
35 Revolving shell-ring
36 Cordite rammers
37 Cordite hopper flash doors
38 Rammer/flash door linkages
39 On-mounting pressure supply
40 Centre-pivot swivel connection
41 High-pressure air supply
42 Off-mounting pressure connection
43 Off-mounting exhaust connection
44 On-mounting exhaust line
45 Cordite cage
46 Trunk guide rollers
47 Spring-loaded shell cage stops
48 Shell cage
49 On-mounting rammer, shell-ring traverse and locking-bolt control console
50 Retracted chain rammer casing
51 Cage lifting cables
52 Ammunition lift rails
53 Electric cables to 'winding' platforms
54 Retracted chain rammer casing
55 Rammer, 'ammunition cage to traverser'
56 Bridge trays
57 Ammunition cage winches
58 Vertical guide roller
59 Gunloading cage rails
60 Training buffer
61 Gunloading rammer casing
62 Gunloading cage lifting press
63 Link rod from elevation control hand wheel
64 Breech thread protection tray operating linkage
65 Gunloading rammer

Peter Hodges

Gun Mounting Data for two-gun Mark II mounting

Revolving weight	898 tons	912t
Roller path diameter	26ft mean	7.92m
Barbette int diameter	29ft 6in	8.99m
Distance apart gun axes	96in	2.44m
Recoil distance	45in	114cm
Max elevating speed	8°/sec	
Max training speed	2°/sec	
Firing cycle	30 sec	
Turret shield	face 12.74in; sides 8.82-6.86in; rear 6.86in; roof 5.88in	324mm; 224-174mm; 174mm; 149mm

Gun Mounting Data for four-gun Mark III mounting

Revolving weight	1550 tons	1575t
Roller path diameter	35ft 6in mean	10.82m
Barbette int diameter	40ft	12.19m
Distance apart gun axes	96in	2.44m
Recoil distance	45in	114cm
Max elevating speed	8°/sec	
Max training speed	2°/sec	
Firing cycle	30 sec	
Turret sheild	face 12.74in; sides 8.82-6.86in; rear 6.86in; roof 5.88in	324mm; 224-174mm; 174mm; 149mm

head gear and rammed through openings normally closed by watertight doors, over hinged trays to the revolving shell ring in the shell handing room. The shell ring held 16 trays in four groups at 90° apart – eight trays in four groups in twin turrets. To load from the shell room it was unclutched from the mounting, clutched to the operating gear on the ship, rotated to the required position for loading and locked to the ship. It was then disconnected from the ship, clutched to the mounting operating gear and rotated to bring a group of shells opposite the flash doors on the trunk, to which it was locked. The shells were rammed into the top cages of the lower hoists. Shell arresters, subsequently strengthened by hydraulic buffers, were fitted. The shell ring was driven by a 24BHP hydraulic engine through flexible coupling, friction clutch, worm and pinions, with allowance for eccentricity and a 1in (*25mm*) rise or fall in the ship relative to the mounting when it was connected to the ship, and by a similar engine and drive without eccentricity and level allowances when connected to the mounting.

The lower hoists were operated by winches with two drums of different diameter on the same shaft so that the cordite cage caught up the shell cage, and they arrived in the working chamber together. Here shells and half charges were rammed into traversers which ran on rails across the working chamber until they were in line with the gun loading cage of the particular gun into which shell and half-charges were rammed through bridge trays. The upper hoists raised the gun loading cages until the shell was in line with the gun axis at the loading angle of +5° and, after the shell was rammed, the cage was twice slightly raised to bring the two half-charges successively into line for ramming.

Flash precautions were very extensive and the turrets should have been highly satisfactory. Unfortunately, through lack of experienced personnel and time for detail design and development, and a shortage of highly trained crews, serious defects occurred in action. Thus, against the *Bismarck*, trouble with the shell rings and associated fittings in *Prince of Wales* and *King George V* and the imperfect functioning of several other components meant that *Prince of Wales* fired only 55 of a possible 74 shells in the first action, and *King George V* fired 339 shells compared with the 380 of *Rodney*. In the later action against *Scharnhorst*, *Duke of York* achieved only *c*68% of her possible output because of the failure of bridge tube flash doors in the working chamber to close completely and also the collapse of shell arresters in the lower hoist.

Forward 14in Mk VII guns *Duke of York*. The spacing between the guns in the quadruple turret is uniform, unlike that in French turrets.
IWM

Of the 206 wire-wound guns originally made and mounted in the *Orion*, *King George V*, *Iron Duke* and *Lion* classes, *Queen Mary* and *Tiger*, 54 were in existence and 12 of them had fired less than 20 EFC. There were three twin Mk II** turrets still in the demilitarised *Iron Duke*, while two turrets removed from her and four from *Tiger* were in store at Rosyth. A total of four guns with slides and cradles (saddles) from *Tiger*'s former turrets, had been sold to Turkey for coast defence but none were delivered.

The Dover area defences were augmented by three guns on railway mountings and three more were linered to 8in (*203mm*) as not very successful super-velocity guns – a remarkable waste of effort. With 400lb (*181.4kg*) SC 390 supercharges and special 8/16crh 1250lb (*567kg*) shells, the railway guns had a muzzle velocity of 2950f/s (*899m/s*) and a range of 48,900yd (*44,710m*) at the 40° maximum elevation of the railway mounting.

13.5in (343mm) Mark V

Gun Data

Bore	13.5in	342.9mm	
Weight incl BM	76.125 tons	77,347kg	
Length oa	625.9in	15,897.9mm	46.36cal
Length bore	607.5in	15,430.5mm	45.0cal
Length chamber	92.13in	2340.1mm	
Volume chamber	19650in^3	322dm^3	
Weight projectile	1400lb	635kg	
Propellant charge	299lb SC 280	135.6kg	
Muzzle velocity	2491f/s	759m/s	
Max range	23,740yd/20°	21,710m/20°	

MEDIUM CALIBRE BREECH-LOADING GUNS

Twelve of the original 45 Mk XI guns had been kept from the *Lord Nelson* and *Minotaur* classes for possible small monitors, but all mountings were scrapped in 1938 and the guns followed in 1943-44. The 9.2in Mk X was no longer a naval gun, though it was the standard Army coast defence gun. None of the mountings allowed more than 35° elevation. the exact bore in both was 9.2in (*233.68mm*).

With supercharges the muzzle velocity of Mk X was raised to 2872f/s (*875m/s*) and with 5/10 crh shells this gave a 35° range of *c*32,600yd (*29,810m*).

9.2in (234mm) Mark X, Mark XI

Gun Data 9.2in (234mm) Mark X

Weight incl BM	28.313 tons	28,767kg	
Length bore			46.66cal
Weight projectile	380lb	172.4kg	
Muzzle velocity	2748f/s	838m/s	

Gun Data 9.2in (234mm) Mark XI

Weight incl BM	28.375tons	28,830kg	
Length bore			50.15cal
Weight projectile	380lb	172.4kg	
Muzzle velocity	2890f/s	881m/s	

This gun was mounted in twin turrets in all British 8in cruisers, the *Kent* class having Mk I, the *London* class Mk I*, the *Norfolk* class and *York* Mk II and *Exeter* Mk II* mountings. There were three types of gun, all interchangeable. Mk VIII was of full length wire construction with inner A tube, A tube, wire, B tube, overlapping jacket, breech ring and breech bush. Mk VIII* had no inner A tube, and on relining became Mk VIII, but Mk VIII** had no wire and comprised inner A tube, A tube, jacket to 170in (*4318mm*) from muzzle, breech ring, breech bush. Guns with inner A tubes had two locating shoulders, the foremost 323.5in (*8216.9mm*) from the muzzle. All had Welin screw breech blocks and hydraulic or hand Asbury mechanism, the weight being 840lb (*381kg*).

In all, 168 guns were made including two experimental prototypes which were built without wire. Of the others the last 26 were Mk VIII*, but due to trouble with A tubes many guns were originally Mk VIII instead of VIII*, and a list of 14 January 1932 gives only 70 of the latter. During the war six of the above Mk VIII** were mounted in the Folkestone-Dover area on single 70° mountings for coast defence.

The propellant charge was in halves and it was found possible to dispense with igniters if 1in (*25mm*) tubes were used. The original specified muzzle velocity was 2900f/s (*884m/s*) but this was reduced in the interests of accuracy and life. SAPC shells were carried with 20HE per gun, or more if required.

The requirements for the Mk I mounting were over ambitious. It was to have AA capability with elevating speed of 10°/sec and training speed of 8°/sec, but accurate control was impossible with the former, and the latter overloaded the pumps. There was one hydraulic pump per turret mounted on the revolving structure and driven by a 120BHP electric motor, and also one in A and one in X shell rooms for powered fittings in shell room and shell handing room. Mineral oil was used as the pressure medium to avoid corrosion in the pusher hoists, which were most inaccessible. This also allowed weight to be saved by the replacement of bronze by steel. The guns were in individual tubular forged cradles, compressed air run-out was employed, and there was a 4.2 ton (*4267kg*) balance ring on each gun. Elevation was by a 13BHP swashplate engine driving through gearing and worm toothed arcs on the underside of the cradle. To improve control, 4 to 1 reduction gear was introduced, which with later elevating brakes reduced the speed to 4°/sec. Elevation limits were +70° to -3°. Each turret had two 40BHP swashplate engines of which only one was normally used at a time, driving through worm and gearing, and capable of training at 8°/sec, but limited to 6°/sec by the demand on the pump, or to only 2°/sec during loading operations.

Magazines and shell rooms were on the same level. Charges were passed to the handing room through flashtight revolving scuttles and placed on waiting trays attached to the hoist trunk. This contained a cordite hoist for each gun, and each hoist had two cages so that, while one was being unloaded between the breech ends of the guns, the other cage was loading in the handing room. Charges were horizontal when hoisted.

Since it was thought undesirable to bend the pusher shell hoists in two planes, the shell handing room was a deck above the shell room to obviate the need for this. In the shell room, shells were handled by powered overhead gear. At each side there was a transporter hoist of pusher or one shot type which delivered shells to the shell ring in the shell handing room. The shell ring was hydraulically powered and ran on

8in (203mm) Mark VIII

Gun Data

Bore	8in	203.2mm	
Weight incl BM	17.20 tons	17,476kg	
Length oa	413.1in	10,492.7mm	51.64cal
Length bore	400.007in	10,160.18mm	50.00cal
Length chamber	50.104in	1272.64mm	
Volume chamber	3646in^3	59.75dm^3	
Length rifling	346.296in	8795.92mm	
Grooves	(48) 0.055in deep x 0.376	1.40 x 9.55mm	
Lands	0.1476in	3.749mm	
Twist	Uniform 1 in 30		
Weight projectile	256lb	116.1kg	
Propellant charge	66lb SC 205	29.94kg	
Muzzle velocity	2805f/s	855m/s	
Working pressure	20.5 tons/in^2	3230kg/cm^2	
Approx life	550 EFC		
Max range	30,650yd/45°	28,030m/45°	

The above is for Mk VIII and Mk VIII* guns. Mk VIII** weighed 17.25 tons (*17,527kg*).

Range and Elevation Data for 2725f/s (830.5 m/s) MV

Range (yd)	(m)	Elevation	Descent	Time of flight (sec)	Striking V (f/s)	(m/s)
5000	4570	2°11.0′	2°31′	6.15	2154	657
10,000	9140	5°14.1′	7°15′	14.14	1683	513
15,000	13,720	9°47.3′	15°49′	24.66	1322	403
20,000	18,290	16°34.0′	28°31′	38.35	1169	356
25,000	22,860	26°44′	43°7′	55.88	1164	355
29,000	26,520	41°28′	56°37′	78.58	1240	378

Gun Mounting Data

Revolving weight	183-187 tons	186-190t
Roller path diameter	18ft mean	5.49m
Barbette int diameter	20ft 6in	6.25m
Distance apart gun axes	84in	2.13m
Recoil distance	24in	61cm
Max elevating speed	4-5½°/sec	
Max training speed	5-6°/sec	
Firing cycle	11 sec	
Turret shield	1in	25mm

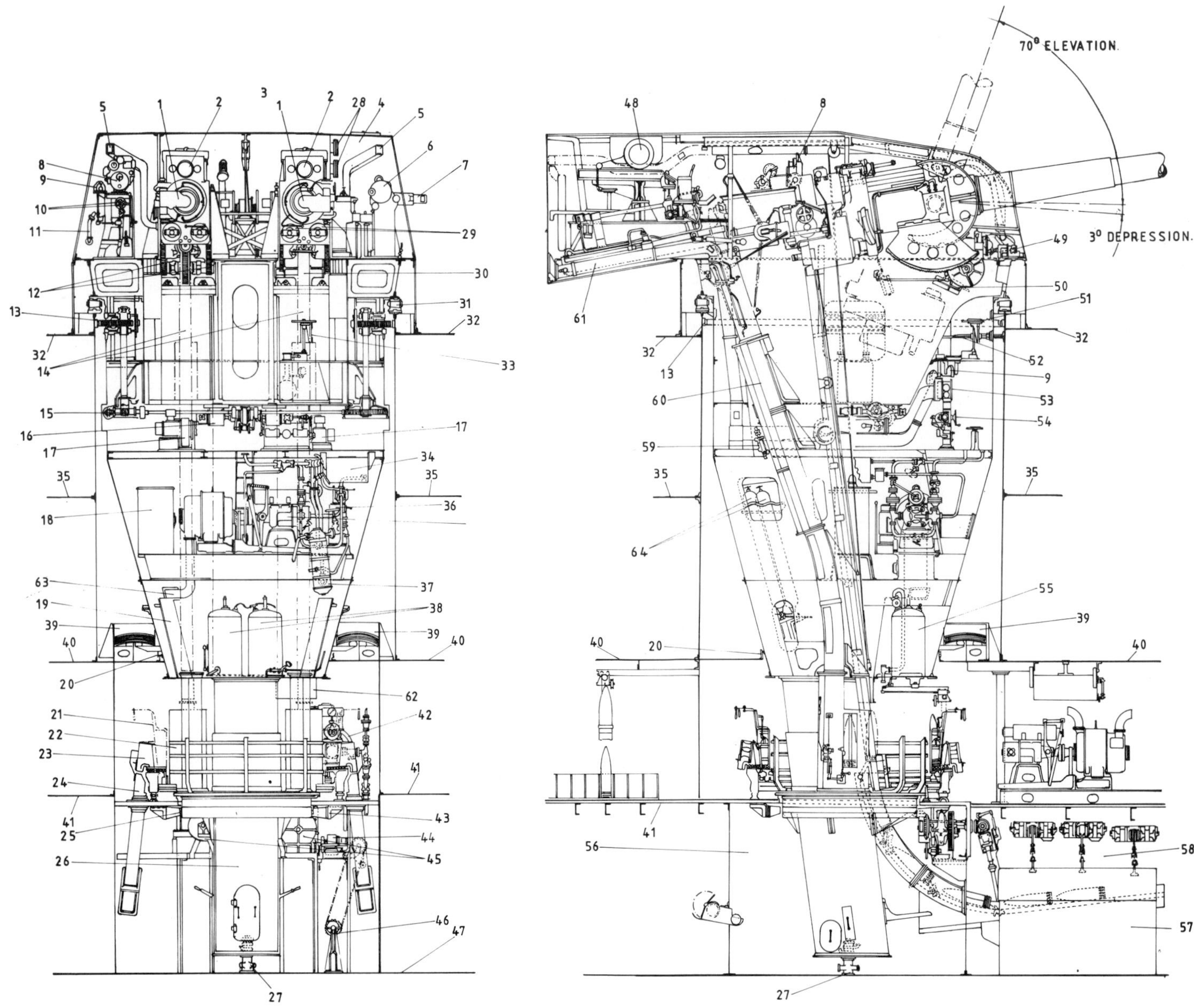

8in twin Mk I turret mounting.

1 Breech
2 Run-out cylinder
3 Auxiliary shell winch
4 Silent cabinet
5 Vent
6 Range elevation and deflection unit
7 Local director sight
8 Elevation receiver
9 Barrage receiver
10 Elevation controls
11 Voice pipe
12 Elevating arcs
13 Training rack
14 Shell hoist
15 Training gear
16 Swashplate training engine
17 Ventilating fan
18 Pump motor starter
19 Valve panel
20 Flashtight apron
21 Revolving shell bogie
22 Shell hoist scuttle
23 Shell ring
24 Transporter hoist
25 Guide roller
26 Cordite hoist
27 Centre pivot
28 Telephones
29 Recoil cylinder
30 Elevating gear
31 Turntable rollers
32 Upper deck
33 Drive to training receiver
34 Tank supplying swashplate pump
35 Main deck
36 Motor generator
37 Serck oil cooler
38 Tanks for washout squirts
39 Cable troughs
40 Lower deck
41 Platform deck
42 Swashplate pumping engine
43 Shell ring roller track
44 Swashplate engine for transporter and shell ring
45 Operating gear for shell room machinery
46 Hand operating gear for transport and shell ring
47 Magazine flat
48 Rangefinder
49 Elevating motor
50 70° elevation buffer
51 Drive to training receivers
52 Depression control rods
53 Main training receiver
54 Director training control handwheel
55 Gun washout tanks
56 Cordite handling room
57 Shell bin
58 Shell room
59 Pusher hoist cut-off valves
60 Pusher hoist casing
61 Ventilation intake
62 Tank supplying swashplate engine
63 Air duct
64 High pressure air bottles

John Lambert

a roller path bolted to the deck of the shell handing room. It had 30 compartments, each capable of holding one shell in a vertical position. Two hand-operated shell bogies which could be locked at any one of the 30 compartments or to the hoist trunk delivered shells to the pusher hoists, of which there was one per gun. The purpose of the shell ring was to reduce the distance travelled by the shell bogies.

In the gunhouse, charges were rammed by hand from hoist cage to the cordite compartment of the hollow rammer, while shells were deposited in rear of the guns in shell tilting trays which incorporated a telescopic loading tray. The hollow rammer slewed about a pivot from cordite hoist to gun and, after ramming of the shell from the loading tray, the charge was rammed in the same stroke by a coaxial ram. The loading angle was +10°.

The Mk I* mounting differed in having a 3 to 1 reduction gear in the elevation drive which allowed a rate of 5½°/sec, and 55 more shells could be accommodated per turret as more shell room space had been provided.

Important changes were made in the Mk II mounting. Each turret had two hydraulic pumps driven by a common 165BHP motor and there was a smaller motor and pump on the fixed structure for each turret. Elevation was by cylinder and piston working on an arm attached to the cradle forward of the trunnions, and it was also normal to use both training engines together, the maximum training speed being 5°/sec. Loading was at +6°, and the hollow rammer traversed horizontally from hoist to gun instead of slewing about a pivot. It was also found possible to bend the pusher shell hoists in two planes so that the transporter hoists were eliminated and the shell handing room was made common with the magazine handing room. Each shell room had two power driven endless-band conveyors, the lower for the R gun and the upper for the L, which placed shells on fixed loading trays in the shell handing room. The shells were then pushed by hand into power-operated pivoted buckets and, when these locked to the pusher shell hoists, the latter picked the shells up. The charge hoists differed in that the cage held the charge vertically and was tilted to the 6° loading angle at the top of the hoist. The transfer rammer from cage to main hollow rammer was power operated.

In Mk II* mountings AA capability was abandoned and elevation altered to +50° to -3°.

8in (203mm) Marks IX and X

These guns were intended for the triple turrets of projected cruisers which, because of various wartime pressures, never got beyond sketch design stage. The Mk IX* would have had A tube, jacket, breech ring and breech bush screwing into the jacket, with a slightly modified Mk VIII breech mechanism. On relining with an inner A tube, it was to become Mk IX. One gun was ordered from Vickers-Armstrong in April 1941 but was abandoned on the introduction of the new design rules in favour of the much lighter Mk X* which, when relined with an inner A tube, would have become Mk X. Apart from weight, construction was to be as in Mk IX* but a new design of breech mechanism was to be used. The order was cancelled in October 1942.

Some preliminary design work was done on the triple mounting.

Gun Data

Bore	8in	203.2mm	
Weight incl BM	17.038 tons	17,311kg	
Length oa	413.25in	10,496.55mm	51.66cal
Length bore	400in	10,160mm	50.0cal
Length chamber	58.35in	1482.09mm	
Volume chamber	4300in^3	70.46dm^3	
Weight projectile	290lb	131.54kg	
Propellant charge	72.25lb SC 205	32.77kg	
Muzzle velocity	2670f/s	814m/s	
Max range	31,300yd/45°	28,620m/45°	

Above weight is for Mk IX and Mk IX*. Mk X and Mk X* weighed *c*12.5 tons (*c*12,700kg).

Range and Elevation Data for 2600f/s (792.5ms) MV

Range (yd)	(m)	Elevation	Descent	Time of flight (sec)	Striking V (f/s)	(m/s)
10,000	9140	5°23′	6°59′	14.3	1716	523
15,000	13,720	9°53′	14°57′	24.4	1396	425.5
20,000	18,290	16°16′	26°15′	37.1	1223	373
25,000	22,860	25°24′	39°59′	53.6	1198	365
30,000	27,430	43°51′	57°9′	81.9	1291	393.5

7.5in (190mm) Mark VI

This gun was originally mounted in the five ships of the *Hawkins* class in single CP Mk V mountings, but only *Frobisher* and *Hawkins* carried it in the war. It was identical internally except for narrower rifling grooves and wider lands to the Mk I gun in the *Hampshire* class armoured cruisers, but was of improved construction, with tapered inner A tube, A tube, full-length wire, full-length jacket, breech ring, shrunk collar and breech bush. The one locating shoulder on the inner A tube was 274.5in (*6972.3mm*) from the muzzle, and there was a Welin screw breech block with hand-operated Asbury mechanism, the weight being 535lb (*242.7kg*). The propellant charge was in halves and SAPC and HE shells were carried.

As all 44 guns were still in existence, there were a large number of spares and during the war seven went to the Dutch West Indies, three to Canada and five to Mozambique, all for coast defence. There was also for a time a three-gun battery at South Shields.

The CP Mk V mounting was basically a hand-operated centre pivot mounting with additional power training and elevation provided by a 10HP electric motor and hydraulic pump. Elevation was +30° to -5° and loading was possible up to +10°. Run-out was by springs, and the total weight including gun and 1in (*25mm*) open-backed shield, 45.975 tons (*46,713kg*).

Gun Data

Bore	7.5in	190.5mm	
Weight incl BM	13.789 tons	14,010kg	
Length oa	349.2in	8869.7mm	46.56cal
Length bore	337.5in	8572.5mm	45.00cal
Length chamber	54.66in	1388.4mm	
Volume chamber	4500in^3	73.7dm^3	
Length rifling	278.5in	7073.9mm	
Grooves	(44 or 45) 0.0555in deep × 0.38	1.41 × 9.65mm	
Lands	0.1555 or 0.1436in	3.95 or 3.647mm	
Twist	Uniform 1 in 30		
Weight projectile	200lb	90.7kg	
Propellant charge	61.875lb SC 150	28.07kg	
Muzzle velocity	2770f/s	844m/s	
Working pressure	18 tons/in^2	2830kg/cm^2	
Approx life	650 EFC		
Max range	21,110yd/30°	19,300m/30°	

Range and Elevation Data for 2700f/s (823m/s) MV

Range (yd)	(m)	Elevation	Descent	Time of flight (sec)	Striking V (f/s)	(m/s)
5000	4570	2°29.9′	3°19′	6.84	1799	548
10,000	9140	7°3.3′	12°32′	17.25	1218	371
15,000	13,720	15°21′	27°33′	32.11	1038	316
20,000	18,290	27°59′	44°35′	51.14	1071	326
20,500	18,750	29°37′	46°21′	53.46	1078	329

7.5in Mk VI guns in *Frobisher*.
CPL

A total of 25 of these guns comprising four Mk II, one Mk II** and 20 Mk V had been kept for possible use in small monitors. Mk II** and Mk V were originally in the *Minotaur* and *Achilles* classes of armoured cruisers and Mk II had been transferred to the RN from Indian coast defence. It had been intended to adapt Mk III mountings, originally in *Swiftsure*, for these guns, but the mountings were scrapped in 1938-39 and the guns followed in 1943-34, except for four used for experimental purposes. Exact bore was 190.5mm.

Gun Data 7.5in Mk II

Weight incl BM	14.563 tons	14,797kg	
Length bore			50cal
Weight projectile	200lb	90.7kg	
Muzzle velocity	2827f/s	862m/s	

Gun Data 7.5in Mk**, Mk V

Weight incl BM	15.063 tons	15,305 kg	
Length bore			50cal
Weight projectile	200lb	90.7kg	
Muzzle velocity	2827f/s	862m/s	

6in (152mm) BL Mark XXIII

This gun was in the later 6in cruisers of the period. The *Leander*, *Perth* and *Arethusa* classes had twin Mk XXI mountings, the *Southampton* and *Gloucester* classes triple Mk XXII and the *Belfast*, *Fiji*, *Ceylon*, *Swiftsure* classes and the *Superb* triple Mk XXIII mountings. It was initially proposed that the *Belfast* class should have quadruple mountings and the triple RP 10 Mk XXIV was intended for the *Tiger* class as originally designed.

The Mk XXIII gun comprised an A tube, jacket to 115in (*2921mm*) from the muzzle, breech ring and breech bush screwed into the jacket. A Welin screw breech block was used with hand-operated Asbury mechanism, the weight being 434lb (*197kg*). If relined with a tapered inner A tube with two locating shoulders, the foremost 252.0in (*6400.8mm*) from the muzzle, the gun became Mk XXIII*. A modified gun for the proposed quadruple turrets was to have had power-worked breech mechanism and loading. In all 469 guns were made.

The propellant charge was in one bag and later flashless NQFP charges were supplied if ordered. Shells were CPBC with some HE or mostly the latter if required for bombardment.

The twin Mk XXI was a short trunk turret powered by a 65HP electric motor and hydraulic pump using oil and mounted on the revolving structure. The guns were in

Gun Data

Bore	6in	152.4mm	
Weight incl BM	6.906 tons	7017kg	
Length oa	309.8in	7869mm	51.63cal
Length bore	300in	7620mm	50.0cal
Length chamber	41.0in	1041.4mm	
Volume chamber	1750in^3	28.7dm^3	
Length rifling	255.36in	6486.1mm	
Grooves	(36) 0.046in deep × 0.3759	1.17 × 9.548mm	
Lands	0.1477in	3.752mm	
Twist	Uniform 1 in 30		
Weight projectile	112lb	50.8kg	
Propellant charge	30lb SC 150 or 32lb NQFP 128	13.6kg, 14.5kg	
Muzzle velocity	2758f/s	841m/s	
Working pressure	20.5 tons/in^2	3230kg/cm^2	
Approx life	1100 EFC, with NQFP 2200		
Max range	25,480yd/45°	23,300m/45°	

Range and Elevation Data for 2700f/s (823m/s) MV

Range (yd)	(m)	Elevation	Descent	Time of flight (sec)	Striking V (f/s)	(m/s)
5000	4570	2°22.7′	3°0′	6.57	1939	591
10,000	9140	6°14.9′	9°57′	15.94	1371	418
15,000	13,720	13°6′	23°38′	29.42	1098	335
20,000	18,290	24°7′	39°52′	47.16	1087	331
24,500	22,400	41°4′	56°27′	71.41	1159	353

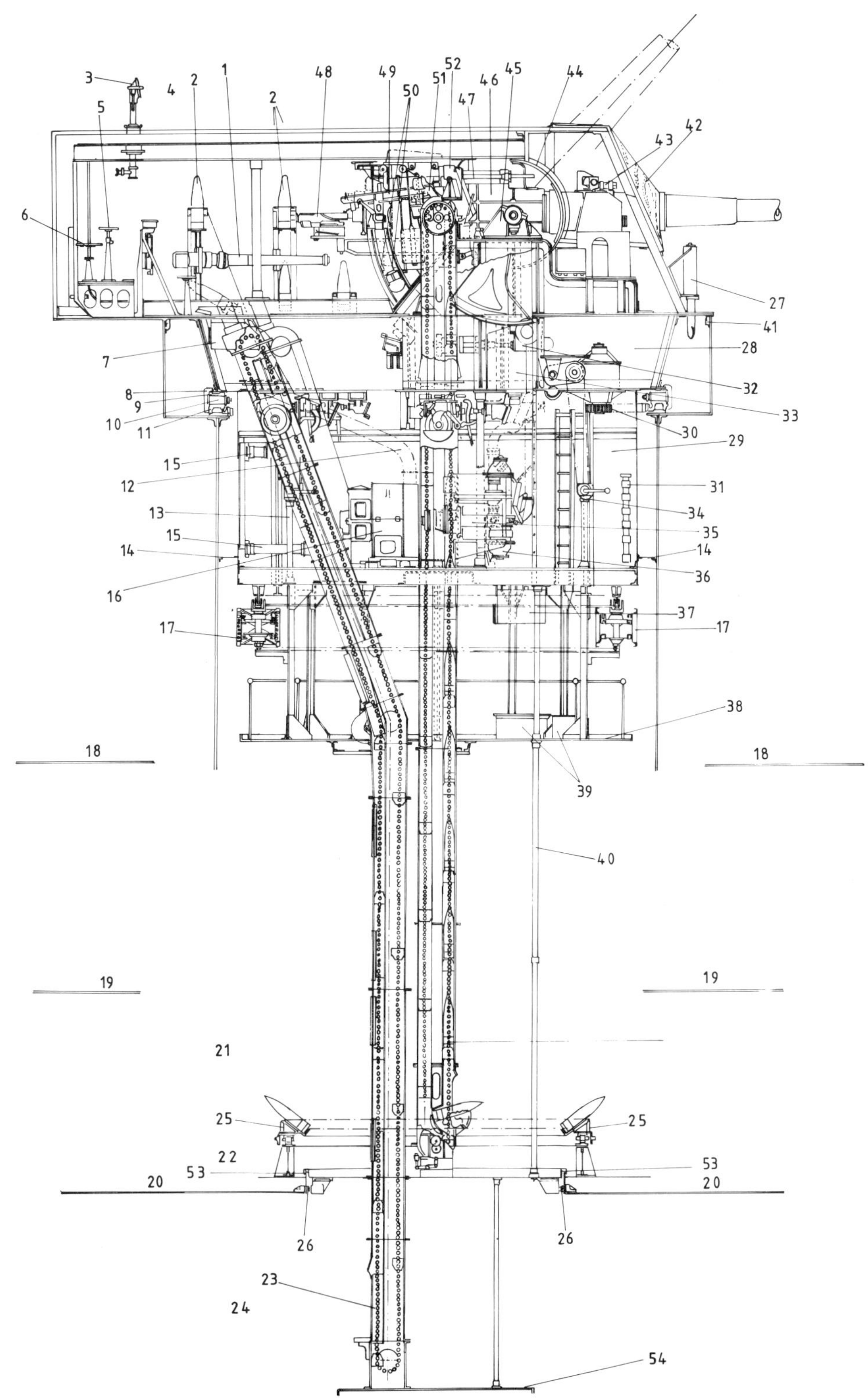

6in triple Mk XXIII turret mounting.

1 Sub-calibre gun
2 Ready use shells
3 Monocular periscope
4 Telephone standard
5 OLO seat
6 OLO platform
7 Gun wash-out tank
8 Turntable clip
9 Upper roller path
10 Roller
11 Lower roller path
12 Ventilating duct
13 Cordite hoist hand gear
14 Baffle plate
15 Cordite hoist vents
16 Motor for pump
17 Whyham cable gear
18 Upper deck
19 Lower deck
20 Platform deck
21 Shell room
22 Shell loading platform
23 Cordite hoist
24 Magazine handling room
25 Revolving shell ring
26 Spring guide rollers
27 Safety depression gear (A & B mountings only)
28 Turntable compartment
29 Working chamber
30 Training gear
31 Pressure valve stack
32 Elevating gear
33 Make up feed tank
34 Hand training gear
35 Pump
36 Serck oil cooler
37 Reserve oil tank
38 Access platform
39 Battery boxes
40 Tubular tie bar
41 Leather apron
42 Canvas blast bag
43 Local director sights
44 Splinter protection plate
45 Trunnion bracket
46 Gun cradle
47 Recuperator cylinder
48 Gun loading tray
49 Intermediate loading tray
50 Guide rails for tray
51 Fixed tray
52 Shell tilting bucket
53 Flashtight apron
54 Platform at base of cordite hoists
John Lambert

individual cast steel cradles and compressed air run-out was used. There was a balancing ring on each gun. Elevation was by a swash-plate engine driving, through worm and pinions, an arc attached to the cradle. Alternatively hand gear could be used. The limits were +60° -5°. There were two training engines with worm and pinion drive and usually both were used together as control was better, though maximum speed was less than with one. Hand training could be used.

There was one magazine for the forward and one for the after turrets with handing rooms for each turret, and charges in flash resistant cardboard containers (not removed until just before loading) were passed through vertical revolving scuttles and placed in fixed electrically driven endless-chain hoists. There was one of these per turret (not Y) and 16 charges were supplied per minute to the ammunition lobby. In Y turret this was on the deck above the handing room and the hoist was replaced by two hand-ups. Each turret had a shell room on the same level as the magazines, and a fixed electric endless-chain hoist supplied 16 shells per minute to the ammunition lobby. This was on the fixed structure and the upper hydraulic endless-chain hoists, one shell and one charge per gun, which revolved with the turret, were loaded here by hand, shells being slid round on a fixed chute.

In the gunhouse the shell hoists came up close to the centre line of the turret and about 4ft (*1.22m*) in rear of the inner cradle trunnions, with the charge hoists about 7ft (*2.13m*) further in rear. Shells were transferred via tilting bucket, fixed tray, and intermediate tray to the loading tray pivoted on an arm from the cradle, and hand rammed, while charges were placed on the loading tray and hand loaded. Loading angle limits were +12½° to -5°.

The triple Mk XXII was also a short trunk turret and had many features as in Mk XXI. The trunnions of the centre gun's cradle were set back 30in (*76cm*) to reduce shell interference. The pump motor was increased to 103HP and the elevation limits altered to +45° -5°. There were a magazine and handing room to each turret, and duplex electric endless-chain fixed hoists could deliver 32 charges a minute to the upper handing room one deck below the gunhouse floor. Here they were passed to the cordite gallery still in the fixed structure and extending round the working chamber. Charges were carried by hand round the gallery and passed to men in the cordite pockets 5ft (*1.52m*) above on the revolving structure and thence via hand-ups to the gunhouse. Each turret had a shell room on the same level as the magazine, and duplex hoists (as above) could deliver 32 shells a minute to the fixed shell handing room immediately below the working chamber. The three upper hydraulic endless-chain shell hoists entered the shell handing room and there was a platform attached to the hoists and revolving with them and the turret on which the men loading the hoists stood. Shells were passed to them from a circular chute fed by the lower hoists. Spring guide rollers bore against the platform edge.

In the gunhouse the L and R hoists came up about 4ft (*1.22m*) in rear of the inner trunnions of the cradles and the C hoist near the L with the hand-ups about 10ft (*3.05m*) in rear of the trunnions. Loading was as in Mk XXI with an extension on the fixed tray for the centre gun, as it was further from its hoist than was the case with the others.

Two comments which probably apply to all three Marks, were that the preferred loading angle was +7° to +5° and that the gunlayer usually followed the pointer from the director by hand, changing to power elevation for larger movements.

The triple Mk XXIII differed from Mk XXII in being a long trunk turret with entirely different ammunition supply, though it was similar in other respects apart from a further increase in the pump motor to 114BHP. Each turret had a magazine and handing room with a shell room one deck above. Charges were passed by hand from the magazine in cardboard containers as in the other 6in(*152mm*) turrets through the usual flashtight revolving scuttles and loaded into the hydraulic endless chain hoists which ran direct to the gunhouse. There was one charge hoist per gun and maximum supply rate was 12 per minute for each hoist. The hoist loaders stood on a platform revolving with the turret and supported from a similar platform for the shell loaders. In the shell room, shells were passed by hand to an electrically powered revolving shell ring on the fixed structure holding 56 shells inclined with noses upwards and outwards. From here they were passed by hand to the loading trays of the shell hoists, the hoist loaders standing on a platform. Spring guide rollers bore against this platform edge. There was one shell hoist per gun of similar type to the charge hoists and with the same delivery rate. As in Mk XXI and Mk XXII, shells and charges were vertical in the hoists.

The centre gun was set back 30in (*76cm*) as in Mk XXII and the L and C shell hoists came up 39in (*1m*) in rear of the L cradle inner trunnions and the R shell hoist the same distance from those of the R cradle. The L and R charge hoists came up about 7ft 4in (*2.24m*) and the C hoist about 9ft (*2.74m*) in rear of the line of the shell hoists. Loading was as in Mk XXI and Mk XXII.

In the RP 10 Mk XXIV triple, a return would have been made to a limited AA capacity with 60° elevation. Barbette and roller path diameters were unchanged.

A sketch drawing of the proposed quadruple mounting for the *Belfast* class shows a roller path diameter of 19ft (*5.79m*) with the guns in two pairs. The gun axes in each pair are only 27.5in (*69.85cm*) apart with 46.5in (*118.1cm*) between the inner axes of the pairs. Estimated weight is 229 tons (*232.75t*).

Gun Mounting Data for two-gun Mark XXI mounting

Revolving weight	*c*95 tons	*c*96.5t
Roller path diameter	13ft 9in mean	4.19m
Barbette int diameter	17ft 6in	5.33m
Distance apart gun axes	84in	2.13m
Recoil distance	16.5in	42cm
Max elevating speed	10°/sec	
Max training speed	5-7°/sec	
Firing cycle	7.5-10 sec	
Turret shield	1in	25mm

Gun Mounting Data for three-gun Mark XXII mounting

Revolving weight	*c*150 tons (*Southampton*)	*c*152t
Roller path diameter	19ft mean	5.79m
Barbette int diameter	23ft 6in	7.16m
Distance apart gun axes	78in	1.98m
Recoil distance	16.5in	42cm
Max elevating speed	10°/sec	
Max training speed	5-7°/sec	
Firing cycle	7.5-10 sec	
Turret shield	1in (*Southampton*);	25mm
	3.9in face, 2in remainder (*Gloucester*)	100mm, 50mm

Gun Mounting Data for three-gun Mark XXIII mounting

Revolving weight	*c*175 tons	*c*178*t*
Roller path diameter	19ft mean	5.79m
Barbette int diameter	23ft 6in	7.16m
Distance apart gun axes	78in	1.98m
Recoil distance	16.5in	42cm
Max elevating speed	10°/sec	
Max training speed	5-7°/sec	
Firing cycle	7.5-10 sec	
Turret shield	3.9in face, 2in remainder (*Belfast*)	100mm, 50mm
	2in face, roof, 1in remainder (*Fiji* and later)	50mm, 25mm

Nelson in 1947 showing 6in BL Mk XXII guns in twin Mk XVIII turret mountings, 4.7in QF Mk VIII guns in shielded HA XII mountings and after main DCT. *CPL*

Though of much heavier construction, this gun was internally similar to the Mk XXIII. It was only carried by *Nelson* and *Rodney* in twin Mk XVIII mountings. Mk XXII* comprised A tube, taper wound wire, full-length jacket, breech ring and breech bush screwed into the A tube with Welin screw breech block and hand-operated pure-couple mechanism, the weight being 364lb (*165kg*). On relining with a tapered inner A tube having three locating shoulders, the foremost 233.25in (*5924.5mm*) from the muzzle, it became Mk XXII. Some time later Mk XXII** was introduced. It was built without wire but with an inner A tube distinguished by the position of the foremost shoulder, 240.0in (*6096mm*) from the muzzle. A total of 40 guns were made, including two experimental, and of these six were Mk XXII**.

Ammunition intially differed from that for the Mk XXIII gun in that the shells were 100lb and the SC charges 31lb, but from about 1942 it was the same as in Mk XXIII except that flashless charges do not appear to have been provided.

The Mk XVIII mounting generally resembled the Mk XXI and could elevate from +60° to -5°, but telescopic power rammers were used at a fixed loading angle of 5° and the rate of fire was well below that for the Mk XXI mounting. The hydraulic pump was driven by a 50BHP electric motor and there was only one training engine. The ammunition supply also differed. There was a lower magazine with one handing room. Two hoists supplied the working spaces of P1 and S1 turrets; an upper magazine with two handing rooms and four hoists supplied the working spaces of the other four turrets. A shell room above was equipped with six hoists. The charge hoists were endless chain and the shell hoists pusher, both electrically powered, while the upper hoists, one shell and one charge per gun, were hydraulic pusher. Charges were issued from the magazines in Clarkson's cases and travelled in them until just before loading. As these cases were not expendable, they were returned to the working space via a tube and to the magazines by the down side of the lower hoists and return flashtight scuttles. Flash precautions were very thorough in this mounting.

6in (152mm) BL Mark XXII

Gun Data

Bore	6in	152.4mm	
Weight incl BM	9.0125 tons	9157kg	
Length oa	309.728in	7867.1mm	51.62cal
Length bore	300in	7620mm	50.0cal
Length chamber	40.809in	1036.5mm	
Volume chamber	1750in^3	28.7dm^3	
Length rifling	255.555in	6491mm	
Grooves	36. 0.046in deep × 0.3759	1.17 × 9.548mm	
Lands	0.1477in	3.752mm	
Twist	Uniform 1 in 30		
Weight projectile	100lb	45.36kg	
Propellant charge	31lb SC 150	14.06kg	
Muzzle velocity	2960f/s	902m/s	
Working pressure	20.5 tons/in^2	3230kg/cm^2	
Approx life	700 EFC		
Max range	25,800yd/45°	23,590m/45°	

The above weight is for Mk XXII and Mk XXII* guns; Mk XXII** weighed 9.023 tons (*9168kg*).

Range and Elevation Data for 2900f/s (884m/s) MV

Range (yd)	(m)	Elevation	Descent	Time of flight (sec)	Striking V (f/s)	(m/s)
5000	4570	2°5.2′	2°48′	6.20	2029	618
10,000	9140	5°37.2′	9°13′	15.22	1390	424
15,000	13,720	12°5.4′	23°2′	28.55	1094	333
20,000	18,290	22°54′	39°46′	46.14	1056	322
25,000	22,860	42°37′	59°0′	74.92	1148	350

Gun Mounting Data

Revolving weight	*c*85 tons	*c*86t
Rolier path diameter	14ft mean	4.27m
Barbette int diameter	17ft 9in	5.41m
Distance apart gun axes	78in	1.98m
Recoil distance	16.5in	42cm
Max elevating speed	8°/sec	
Max training speed	*c*5°/sec	
Firing cycle	12 sec	
Turret shield	1½-1in	38-25mm

6in (152mm) BL Mark XII

This gun introduced in the light cruiser *Birmingham*, completed in January 1914, was still widely used. At some time during World War II it was mounted as follows (though removed from several ships by 1945): PIX in *Barham, Malaya, Warspite, Royal Sovereign* class, *Cockchafer* (1944); PXIII, *Adelaide*; PXIII*, *Caledon* class, *Cardiff, Ceres, Effingham, Aphis, Cockchafer* (1945); PXIII**, *Capetown, Colombo*; CPXIV, *Dauntless, Emerald* classes, *Scarab*; Mk XVI, *Diomede* (one gun until 1942-43); Mk XVII, *Enterprise* (two guns in twin mounting).

The gun is also recorded in 18 AMCs mostly in PVII* mountings but some in PVII, PXIII**, CPXIV, as well as in a few large liners and DEMS. It was also used for emergency coast MNBDO defence batteries in PXIII*, PXIII** if MNBDO or otherwise in PVII, PVII* or PIX.

The Mk XII gun was built with a tapered inner A tube, A tube, wire, full length jacket, breech ring and breech bush screwing into the A tube. A Welin screw block was used with 'pure-couple' hand-worked mechanism, the weight being 364lb (*165kg*). There were three locating shoulders on the inner A tube, the foremost 203.47in (*5168.14mm*) from the muzzle.

Mk XIIA had a modified chamber with parallel front end, while XIIB had the modified chamber and a bore of 5.985in(*152.02mm*) to reduce clearance. Originally 463 guns were made of which 431 remained to the Navy in 1939. Where practicable it was preferred not to mix XIIB guns with XII and XIIA.

Supercharges are recorded only for *Aphis* and the AMC *Canton*, which had PVII* mountings, and these fired 6crh HE, with CPBC also in *Canton*. Other ships had 4crh shells, CPBC and HE, or CPC and HE in battleships and AMCs. It is possible that 6crh CPBC and HE were later issued to AMCs *Alcantara* and *Monowai* but without supercharges.

The Mk XVII mountings resembled Mk XVIII for the Mk XXII gun differing in a 40HP pump motor, +40° to -5° elevation and shell and charge hoists with no breaks. Mk XVI was a single hydraulic mounting with enclosed 'weatherproof' shield and +40° to -10° elevation, while details of the hand-worked P and CP mountings are given in the table.

Gun Data

Bore	5.985in	152.02mm	
Weight incl BM	6.8875 tons	6998kg	
Length oa	279.728in	7105.09mm	46.74cal
Length bore	270in	6858mm	45.11cal
Length chamber	40.81in	1036.6mm	
Volume chamber	1770in^3	29.0dm^3	
Length rifling	226.065in	5742.05mm	
Grooves	(36) 0.0535 in deep × 0.3759in	1.36 × 9.548mm	
Lands	0.1477in	3.752mm	
Twist	Uniform 1 in 30		
Weight projectile	100lb	45.36kg	
Propellant charge	27.81lb SC 122	12.61kg	
Muzzle velocity	2807f/s	856m/s	
Working pressure	20 tons/in^2	3150kg/cm^2	
Approx life	670 EFC		
Max range	15,660yd/20°	14,320m/20°	
	18,750yd/30°	17,145m/30°	
	20,620yd/40°	18,855m/40°	

Above data is for Mk XIIB firing 4crh shells. Mk XII and Mk XIIA differed in having 6.0in (*152.4mm*) bore, length overall 46.62 cal, length bore 45.0 cal, depth rifling grooves 0.046 in (*1.17mm*), MV 2800f/s (*853m/s*) and range down 40-50yd (*37-46m*). Mk XII also differed in chamber length 36.2in (*919.5mm*) and rifling length 230.56in (*5856.2mm*). With 100lb (*45.36kg*) 6crh shells and 34.25lb (*15.54kg*) SC 150 supercharges, MV was 3070f/s (*936m/s*) and ranges 20,020yd/20° (*18,310m*), 23,770yd/30° (*21,735m*).

Gun Mounting Data

Mounting	**Elevation**	**Weight inc gun less shield**		**Max thickness shield**		**Weight shield**	
		(tons)	**(kg)**	**(in)**	**(mm)**	**(tons)**	**(kg)**
PVII	+20°-7°	14.125	14,352	3in	76mm	5.00	5080
PVII*	+20° -7°	13.900	14,123	0.25	6.3	0.90	914
PIX	+14° -7°	13.375	13,590	2.94	75	2.65	2693
PXIII	+30° -7°	14.525	14,758	2.75	70	5.50	5588
PXIII*	+30° -7°	14.812	15,050	0.25	6.3	1.14	1158
PXIII**	+30° -7°	14.675	14,910	0.25	6.3	1.14	1158
CPXIV	+30° -5°	14.820	15,058	1.5in	38	4.75	4826

Some PIX mountings in coast defence batteries had 17½° maximum elevation. The above weight for CPXIV is with compressed air run-out. With springs the figure was 0.487 tons (*495kg*) more.

6in (152mm) BL Marks XI, XIII, XVI, XVII

These were all 50-calibre guns. Mk XI, introduced in the *Black Prince* (completed in January 1906), was in auxiliary warships and a few armed liners and DEMS, its principal use afloat being in PVI mountings in 14 Ocean Boarding Vessels. Mk XIII, originally in *Agincourt*, was in the gunboats *Aphis* and *Ladybird* in PXI mountings until 1941 when the former was rearmed and the latter sunk. Mk XVI, originally in *Erin*, was not mounted afloat, but Mk XVII introduced for *Canada* and *Eagle* was still in the latter in PXII* mountings. Mk XVII, the only one in a major warship in the Second World War, resembled Mk XII in construction, but the screw breech block had the rear part parallel and the front conical, with hand-worked Elswick sliding hinge mechanism, the weight being 399lb (*181kg*).

The total of Mk XI and Mk XI*, which differed in constructional details, was originally 177, of which 126 remained for Royal Navy use in 1939. All 24 Mk XIII and 19 Mk XVI guns were still available, but 14 of the 29 Mk XVII had been returned to Chile with the *Almirante Latorre* ex-*Canada*. Twenty-six Mk XI had been mounted in Australian coast defences pre-war,

Gun Data Mark XI, XI*

Bore	6in	152.4mm	
Weight incl BM	8.588 tons	8726kg	
Length oa	309.728in	7867.1mm	51.62cal
Lenght bore	300in	7620mm	50.0cal
Length chamber	(34).3in	871.22mm	
Volume chamber	2030in^3	33.27dm^3	
Weight projectile	100lb	45.36kg	
Propellant charge	33.05lb SC 150	14.99kg	
Muzzle velocity	2937f/s	895m/s	
Max range	14,310yd/15°	13,085m/15°	

Gun Data Mark XIII

Bore	6in	152.4mm	
Weight incl BM	8.777 tons	8918kg	
Length oa	310.425in	7884.8mm	51.74cal
Length bore	300in	7620mm	50.0cal
Length chamber	(31).683in	804.75mm	
Volume chamber	1550in^3	25.40dm^3	
Weight projectile	100lb	45.36kg	
Propellant charge	24.44lb SC 140	11.09kg	
Muzzle Velocity	2770f/s	844m/s	
Max range	13,475yd/15°	12,320m/15°	

and many others went into emergency coast-defence batteries in PV or PVI mountings, as did Mk XIII in PXI and Mk XVI in PX mountings.

Shells carried afloat were 4crh CPBC and HE in *Eagle* and CPC and HE in others.

Most PV mountings had their maximum elevation increased from 13° to 20°, while PVI, PX, PXI allowed 15°. PXII* allowed +20° -7° and weighed 13.625 tons (*13844kg*) with gun but without shield. The latter was 3in(*76mm*) maximum and weighed 7.20 tons (*7316kg*).

Gun Data Mark XVI

Bore	6in	152.4mm	
Weight incl BM	8.144 tons	8275kg	
Length oa	310.07in	7875.8mm	51.68cal
Length bore	300in	7620mm	50.0cal
Length chamber	44.433in	1128.6mm	
Volume chamber	1910in^3	31.30dm^3	
Weight projectile	100lb	45.36kg	
Propellant charge	(32).91lb SC 150	14.93kg	
Muzzle velocity	3000f/s	914m/s	
Max range	14,640yd/15°	13,385m/15°	

Gun Data Mark XVII

Bore	6in	152.4mm	
Weight incl BM	8.716 tons	8856kg	
Length oa	310.425in	7884.8mm	51.74cal
Length bore	300in	7620mm	50.0cal
Length chamber	33.75in	857.25mm	
Volume chamber	1650in^3	27.04dm^3	
Weight projectile	100lb	45.36kg	
Propellant charge	28.13lb SC 140	12.76kg	
Muzzle velocity	2905f/s	885m/s	
Max range	16,190yd/20°	14,800m/20°	

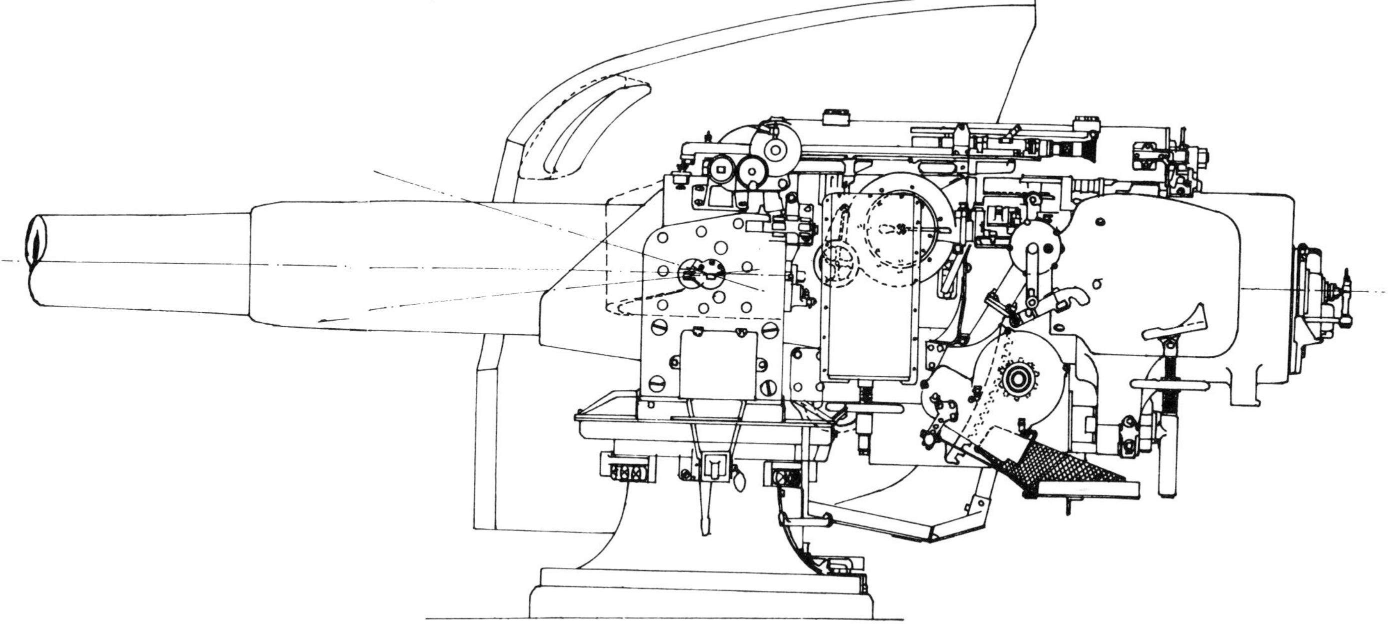

6in BL Mk XI gun in PVI mounting.
John Roberts

This elderly gun, introduced in the *Cressy* (completed in May 1901), was at some time in the war carried in PVIII mountings in *Iron Duke* and in PIII mountings in *Aphis, Cicala, Cockchafer, Cricket, Gnat, Mantis, Moth, Scarab* and *Tarantula*. In PIII, PIV or PVII mountings, it was also recorded in 47 AMCs, a few other auxiliary warships and many armed liners and DEMS.

In construction Mk VII differed from MK XII by being partially wire-wound, the forward part of the wire being replaced by a B tube with the jacket extending over part of the B tube and the wire. There was also a locating shoulder near the muzzle on the inner A tube. A Welin screw breech block and hand-worked skew gear mechanism were used. The weight amounted to 359lb (*163kg*).

A total of 901 guns is shown in the Naval Registers of which 629 remained in 1939. Many guns on PIII, PIV or PVIII mountings went for emergency coast-defence, but Mk VII was also a standard Army coast-defence gun and these are not included in the totals above. Mk VII*, relined with a high strength alloy steel inner A tube and with a much improved performance, was purely an Army gun, as was Mk XXIV, a loose barrel gun with the same ballistics as Mk VII*.

6in (152mm) BL Mark VII

Gun Data

Bore	6in	152.4mm	
Weight incl BM	7.398 tons	7517kg	
Length oa	279.228in	7092.4mm	46.54cal
Length bore	269.5in	6845.3mm	44.92cal
Length chamber	32.74in	831.6mm	
Volume chamber	1715in^3	28.10dm^3	
Weight projectile	100lb	45.36kg	
Propellant charge	23.13lb SC 103	10.49kg	
Muzzle velocity	2573f/s	784m/s	
Max range	14,600yd/20°	13,350m/20°	

With 28.17lb (*12.78kg*) SC 140 charge, MV was 2775f/s (*846m/s*) and 20° range 15,800 yd (*14,450m*). If 6crh 112lb (*50.8kg*) shells were fired with 28.25lb (*12.81kg*) SC 150 charge, MV was 2640f/s (*805m/s*) and 20° range 17,870yd (*16,340m*). Mk VII* fired 100lb (*45.36kg*) 6crh shells with 29.88lb (*13.56kg*) SC 140 charge and had MV 2890f/s (*881m/s*) and 45° range 25,100 yd (*22,950m*).

Heavy 28.17lb (*12.78kg*) charges were carried by *Iron Duke* and the *Aphis* class but AMCs usually had light 23.13lb (*10.49kg*) charges. Special 28.25lb (*12.81kg*) charges with 112lb shells were later supplied to *Alcantara, Carnarvon Castle, Cheshire* and *Worcestershire*, all of which had PIII mountings. Otherwise ships had 4crh CPC and/or HE with some shrapnel in the *Aphis* class.

PVIII mountings allowed only 14° maximum elevation, but PIII and PIV virtually all had 20° in ships though some in emergency coast-defence batteries had the original 15°.

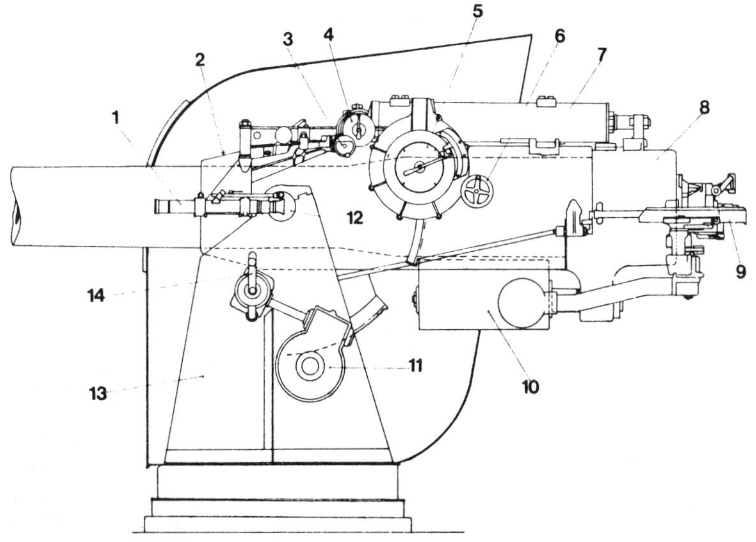

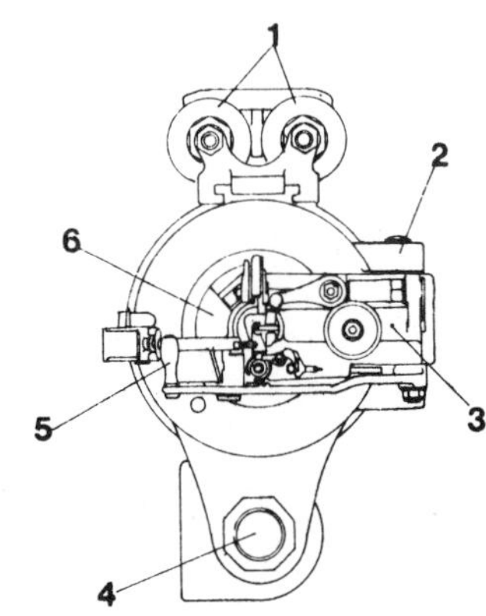

5.5in BL Mk I gun in CP II mounting.

MOUNTING
1 Gun layer's telescopic sight
2 Cradle
3 Deflection handwheel
4 Deflection dial
5 Range dial
6 Range setting handwheel
7 Recuperator spring case
8 Breech
9 Loading tray
10 Recoil cylinder
11 Elevating gear
12 Trunnion
13 Trunnion bracket
14 Elevating crank

GUN BREECH
1 Recuperators
2 Carrier hinge
3 Carrier
4 Recoil cylinder
5 Breech operating lever
6 Breech block

John Roberts

5.5in (140mm) BL Mark I

This gun, designed by Coventry Ordnance Works, was introduced with the former Greek light cruisers *Birkenhead* and *Chester*. It was the only gun taken over in such a manner ever to be adopted for further manufacture. In the Second World War it was at some time carried by *Hood* in CPII mountings and by *Hermes* and the AMCs *Laurentic* and *Montclare* in PI*.

It was of wire-wound construction with tapered inner A tube without forward shoulders, A tube, full-length wire, B tube, overlapping jacket, breech ring and breech bush. The Welin screw block was operated by hand-worked Holmstrom mechanism, the weight being 399lb (*181kg*).

A total of 81 guns were made out of 246 originally ordered, and 79 were extant in 1939. Surplus guns were mounted in emergency coast defence batteries on PI, PI*, PI** and CPII mountings.

CPC and HE shells were carried by all ships.

Gun Data

Bore	5.5in	139.7mm	
Weight incl BM	6.230 tons	6330kg	
Length oa	284.728in	7232.09mm	51.77cal
Length bore	275in	6985.0mm	50.0cal
Length chamber	36.46in	926.08mm	
Volume chamber	1500in³	24.58dm³	
Weight projectile	82lb	37.19kg	
Propellant charge	22.54lb SC 115	10.22kg	
Muzzle velocity	2790f/s	850m/s	
Max range	17,770yd/30°	16,250m/30°	

The PI mounting allowed +15° to -7° elevation, PI* and PI** +25° to -7° and CPII +30° to -5°. The last named weighed 14.33 tons (*14,560kg*) including gun but without shield which was 1.5in (*38mm*) max and weighed 4.25 tons (*4318kg*).

4.7in (120mm) BL Marks I, II

These guns were carried by the surviving ships of the *Scott* class in CPVI mountings, by *Keppel*, *Broke* and modified 'W' class destroyers in CPVI*, and by *Amazon* and *Ambuscade* in CPVI**. They were also mounted in the French destroyers *Mistral* and *Ouragan*, the aircraft transports *Athene* and *Engadine*, in six LCG(L)3 and in ten LCG(L)4. Mk I was of wire-wound construction with tapered inner A tube and full-length jacket, Mk I* was the same with no inner A tube, while Mk II had a monobloc barrel, breech ring and breech bush only. All were interchangeable and had Welin breech blocks with Vickers mechanism, the weight being 168lb (*76kg*).

Altogether 187 Mk I and I* were completed out of 776 ordered and 176 remained in 1939. A total of 32 Mk IIs were ordered in August 1940 and all were completed.

Flashless charges were later supplied if ordered, and SAP and HE shells were carried with, subsequently, 40/50 star shells per ship (or 150/200 on escort duty).

Gun Data

Bore	4.724in	120mm	
Weight incl BM	3.125 tons	3175kg	
Length oa	219.78in	5582.4mm	46.52cal
Lengh bore	212.58in	5399.5mm	45.0cal
Length chamber	25.80in	655.3mm	
Volume chamber	665in³	10.90dm³	
Weight projectile	50lb	22.68kg	
Propellant charge	11.45lb SC103 or 13.78lb NF/S(164-048)	5.19kg, 6.25kg	
Muzzle velocity	2669f/s	814m/s	
Max range	15,800yd/30°	14,450m/30°	

Above weight for Mk I and Mk I* guns; Mk II weighed 3.138 tons (*3188kg*).

All mountings allowed +30° to -9½° elevation, the weight with gun but without shield being 7.40-7.53 tons (*7519-7651kg*). The abbreviated 0.25in (*6.3mm*) shield weighed 0.40-0.51 tons (*406-518kg*).

Support landing ships showing a variety of weapons including 4.7in BL and single pom-poms.
By courtesy of John Lambert

LIGHT CALIBRE BREECH-LOADING GUNS

This widely used gun was designed as a BL version of the QF Mk V for the triple mountings in *Renown* and *Repulse* as it was more suitable for director firing and, in addition to triples in the *Courageous* class, it was carried during World War I in single mountings by monitors, sloops, minesweepers and in over 1200 DEMS. During World War II it was still in Mk I triple mountings in *Repulse* and in single CPI mountings in most 'Flower' type corvettes, some *Bathurst* class minesweepers, the gunboats *Scarab* and *Cockchafer* in 1940–43, surviving First World War sloops and minesweepers, 'Dance' class and some other trawlers, RFA oilers and a variety of ships including many DEMS.

Mk IX was of wire-wound construction with tapered inner A tube and full length jacket. Mk IX* differed in having no inner A tube, while Mk IX**, which also had no inner A, had a B tube and overlapping shorter jacket, as well as the older type of multi-start wire winding. With a tapered inner A tube this became IX***. Lastly, Mk IX**C covered some guns with the start of the breech screw thread 180° out of

4in (102mm) BL Mark IX

Gun Data

Bore	4in	101.6mm	
Weight incl BM	2.125 tons	2159kg	
Length oa	184.6in	4688.8mm	46.15cal
Length bore	177.4in	4506mm	44.35cal
Length chamber	25.493in	647.52mm	
Volume chamber	470.3in^3	7.707dm^3	
Length rifling	149.415in	3795.14mm	
Grooves	(32) 0.037in deep × 0.27	0.94 × 6.86mm	
Lands	0.1227in	3.117mm	
Twist	Uniform 1 in 30		
Weight projectile	31lb	14.06kg	
Propellant charge	7.914lb SC 103 or 9.39lb NF/S 164-048	3.59kg, 4.255kg	
Muzzle velocity	2642f/s	805ms	
Working pressure	18.5 tons/in^2	2910kg/cm^2	
Approx life	3600 EFC with NF/S 14400		
Max range	13,840yd/30°	12,660m/30°	

The older type of chamber was 25.255in(*641.48mm*) long, 468.3in^3 (*7.674dm^3*) volume, with rifling length 149.725in(*3803.02mm*).

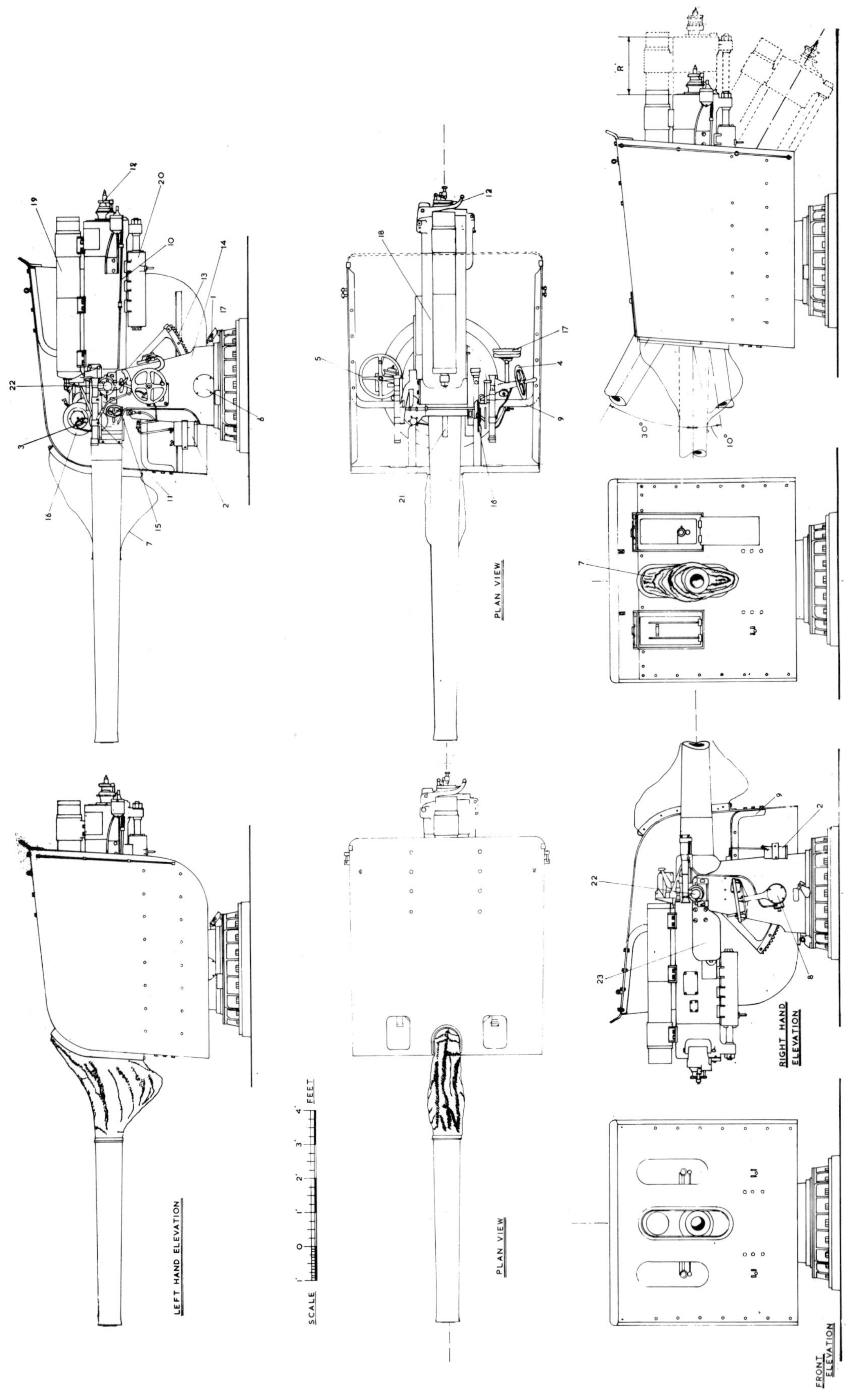
LEFT HAND ELEVATION
PLAN VIEW
PLAN VIEW
RIGHT HAND ELEVATION
FRONT ELEVATION
SCALE
FEET

4in BL Mk IX gun in CPI mounting.

1 Training stop
2 Battery box
3 Dial lamp
4 Elevating handwheel
5 Training handwheel
6 Access plate to elevating gear
7 Canvas blast bag
8 Access plate to training gear
9 Bracket for supporting shield
10 Firing pull rod
11 Telescope holder
12 Breech mechanism lever
13 Elevating arc
14 Pedestal
15 Range handwheel
16 Range dial
17 Body rest
18 Cradle
18 Spring case
20 Recoil cylinder
21 Gun key
22 Trunnion cap
23 Body shield

John Lambert

Gun Mounting data

Mounting	Elevation	Weight inc guns less shield (tons)	(kg)	Max thickness shield (in)	(mm)	Weight shield (tons)	(kg)
Mk I Triple	+30°–10°	17.475	17,755	0.25	6.3	0.975	991
CPI	+30°–10°	4.721	4797	0.25	6.3	0.718	730

place. All had Welin blocks with Vickers mechanism, the weight being 140lb (*63.5kg*).

The total number made was 2382, of which 2193 were in existence in September 1939. Some of these were mounted in coast defence and other emergency batteries during the war.

A proportion of flashless charges were later carried if ordered. Shells were 3crh SAP and/or HE with shrapnel in some. Up to 100 star shells per ship were issued in the later years.

The triple mounting was hand worked and not very satisfactory. The guns were in separate cradles but, if desired, the elevating gears could be connected and all three elevated by one gun-layer. The gun axes were 42in (*106.7cm*) apart. Details of it and of CPI are given in the table.

4in (102mm) BL Mark VIII

Introduced in the *Swift* and in pre First World World War destroyers, this gun was limited to DEMS, apart from one RFA oiler. Mountings comprised PIII, III*, V, VII. A total of 246 were made of which 194 remained in 1939. SAP and/or HE 3crh shells were carried with some shrapnel. Mountings allowed +20° to -10° elevation.

Gun Data

Bore	4in	101.6mm	
Weight incl BM	1.296 tons	1317kg	
Length oa	166.4in	4226.6mm	41.6cal
Length bore	159.2in	4043.7mm	39.8cal
Length chamber	15.9in	404.37mm	
Volume chamber	298in^3	4.88dm^3	
Weight projectile	31lb	14.06kg	
Propellant charge	5.54lb SC 103	2.513kg	
Muzzle velocity	2287f/s	697m/s	
Max range	10,210yd/20°	9340m/20°	

4in (102mm) BL Mark VII

This gun was introduced in the *Bellerophon*, completed in February 1909, but in the Second World War it was limited to DEMS, apart from two LCSs. Mountings comprised PII, II*, IV*, IV**, VI, VIII and guns Mk VII, VII**, VII***, differing in details of construction. A total of 600 guns were made, of which 482 remained in 1939. A considerable number were used in coast defence and other emergency batteries. Shells were 3crh, and SAP and/or HE with some shrapnel were carried. Mountings allowed +15° to -10° elevation or to -7° in PII, II*, VI.

Gun Data

Bore	4in	101.6mm	
Weight incl BM	2.092 tons	2126kg	
Length oa	208.45in	5294.6mm	52.11cal
Length bore	201.25in	5111.75mm	50.31cal
Length chamber	27.45in	697.23mm	
Volume chamber	600in^3	9.83dm^3	
Weight projectile	31lb	14.06kg	
Propellant charge	9.69lb SC 103	4.395kg	
Muzzle velocity	2864f/s	873m/s	
Max range	11,600yd/15°	10,610m/15°	

MEDIUM CALIBRE QUICK-FIRING GUNS

6in (152mm) QF Mark V

Gun Mounting Data

Revolving weight	202–204 tons	205 to 207t
Roller path diameter	22ft mean	6.71m
Barbette int diameter	26ft 8in	8.13m
Distance apart gun axes	91.5in	2.324m

Later known as 6in N5, this gun belongs to the post-war period, but its development dates back to 1944 after some abortive work in 1942–43. It was clear by 1944 that a 6in(*152mm*) BL gun had become an anachronism and any new gun should be QF with separate ammunition loaded at one stroke. Originally intended for triple Mk XXV mountings in the projected *Neptune* class, it was to have been mounted in twin Mk XXVI mountings in the *Minotaur* class designs of 1947. This project was abandoned, along with much else, and the first two experimental guns were not completed until 1949. After extensive trials ashore and in the trials cruiser *Cumberland*, the 6in (*152mm*) gun in Mk XXVI mounting was eventually introduced in the *Tiger*, completed in March 1959, 15 years after the start of the gun's development. In its final form it was a 50-calibre loose barrel gun with hydraulically operated horizontal sliding breech block, firing a 129.75lb (*58.85kg*) shell at 2520f/s (*768m/s*). The firing cycle was 3sec. A muzzle velocity 2640f/s (*805m/s*) was originally envisaged but was reduced to obtain a more curved trajectory and better effect on decks.

A drawing for the proposed Mk XXV mounting shows each gun in a separate cradle with electric training and elevation via hydraulic drive and pinions working on the training rack and elevation arcs. Loading was by hydraulic rammer at any angle between the limits of +80° to -5°. There was one pusher cartridge hoist per gun, fed from a cartridge ring holding 21 cartridges, and a double pusher shell hoist per gun, one for HA and one for LA shells. These were fed from their respective revolving shell rings, one above the other and each holding 72 shells. Used cartridge cases were ejected via a chute through flaps in the gunhouse face.

5.25in (133mm) QF Mark I

Gun Data

Bore	5.25in	133.35mm	
Weight incl BM	4.293 tons	4362kg	
Length oa	275.5in	6997.7mm	52.48cal
Length bore	262.5in	6667.5mm	50.0cal
Length chamber	30.6in	777.24mm	
Volume chamber	894in^3	14.65dm^3	
Length rifling	228.45in	5802.6mm	
Grooves	(36) 0.0465in deep × 0.3053	1.18 × 7.755mm	
Lands	0.1528in	3.881mm	
Twist	Uniform 1 in 30		
Weight projectile	80lb	36.3kg	
Propellant charge	18.05lb SC140 or 21lb NF/S198-054	8.19kg, 9.53kg	
Muzzle velocity	2672f/s	814m/s	
Working pressure	20.5 tons/in^2	3230kg/cm^2	
Approx life	750 EFC, with NF/S 2000		
Max range	24,070yd/45°	22,010m/45°	
Ceiling	46,500ft/70°	14,170m/70°	

Gun Mounting Data

Revolving weight	84–96 tons	85.3–97.5t
Roller path diameter	15ft 1½in mean	4.61m
Distance apart gun axes	96in	2.44m
Recoil distance	24in	61cm
Max elevating speed	10°/sec	
Max training speed	10°/sec	
Firing cycle	5–6 sec, actual *c*8 sec	
Turret shield	½in	13mm

Above data for Mk II mounting; Mk I weighed 77.5 tons(*78.7t*) and had a 1in(*25mm*) shield. Figures include crew and ammunition on revolving structure.

This gun, the largest QF in service with the Royal Navy during the War, was carried in Mk I twin mountings by the *King George V* class, and by 9 of the first 11 *Didos* in Mk II twin mountings, the exceptions being *Scylla* and *Charybdis* with 4.5in (*114mm*) guns. It was also in RP 10 Mk II mountings in the last five *Didos* (*Spartan* class) and, late in the war, the two after mountings in *Argonaut* were converted to RP 10, as were the Mk I mountings in *Anson*. The later RP 10 Mk 1* mounting was in *Vanguard*. The *Lion* class as originally designed would also have had 5.25in (*133mm*) guns. Ship trials were carried out in *Iron Duke* in 1939. Altogether 267 guns were made, of which six were lent to the Army.

The construction comprised an autofretted loose barrel, jacket to 99in (*2515mm*) from muzzle, removable breech ring and sealing collar. To change barrels it was necessary to remove the gun from the gunhouse. The horizontal sliding breech block had hand-operated mechanism with SA opening, the weight being 473lb (*214.5kg*). The loose barrel weighed 1.654 tons (*1681kg*).

The propellant charge was in a brass case 30.8in (*782mm*) long and weighing 41lb (*18.6kg*) with SC charge. Later in the war flashless charges were standard. SAP and HE were carried and, by 1945, 25% of the HE were to have VT proximity fuzes, the proportion rising to 50% with availability. The allowance of star shell was 400 per battleship and 250 per light cruiser. Up to 200 AR (anti-radar) shells per ship were later carried in the Pacific and the Indian Ocean.

There is some confusion over later 5.25in (*133mm*) guns. Mk II was an Army version of Mk I with stronger breech ring and block for 22tons/in^2 (*3460kg/cm^2*) and muzzle velocity of 2850f/s (*869m/s*) at the price of much reduced life. It was in single mountings allowing 70° elevation and was intended for coast defence and AA, though only three guns in the Tyne defences fulfilled the former role. Mk III was an abortive version of Mk II with forward banded shells and 'Probertised' chamber, and Mks V and V/I were as Mk II but altered to suit improved AA mountings. The remaining version, Mk IV, was an improved Mk I for the Navy with an upward opening breech block on the lines of that in the 4.5in (*113mm*) Mk V. Two experimental guns were ordered in January 1944. Apart from a higher rate of fire, performance was to be as in Mk I, but later sketch drawings of the Mk III twin mounting belong to the post war era with a rate of fire of 70 rounds per gun per minute and fixed ammunition.

The Mk I and Mk II mounts were respectively short and long trunk versions. They were powered by an 80 BHP (peak 160BHP) electric motor and oil hydraulic pump mounted on the revolving structure, and the guns were in individual cast steel cradles. Compressed air run-out was used and the recuperator cylinders and balance weights were on arms attached to the cradles. Elevation was by a hydraulic motor for each gun driving an arc on the cradle through worm and pinion with alternative hand gear. Limits were +70° to -5°. Training was by a single hydraulic motor with two worm and pinion drives or by alternative hand gear.

The ammunition supply in the *King George V* class was different for end and middle turrets. In P and S Nos 1 and 4, fixed electric endless-chain hoists for LA shell, HA shell, and cartridges ran from shell rooms and magazines to lobbies on the deck below the mounting. Here shells and cartridges were fed into chutes leading to

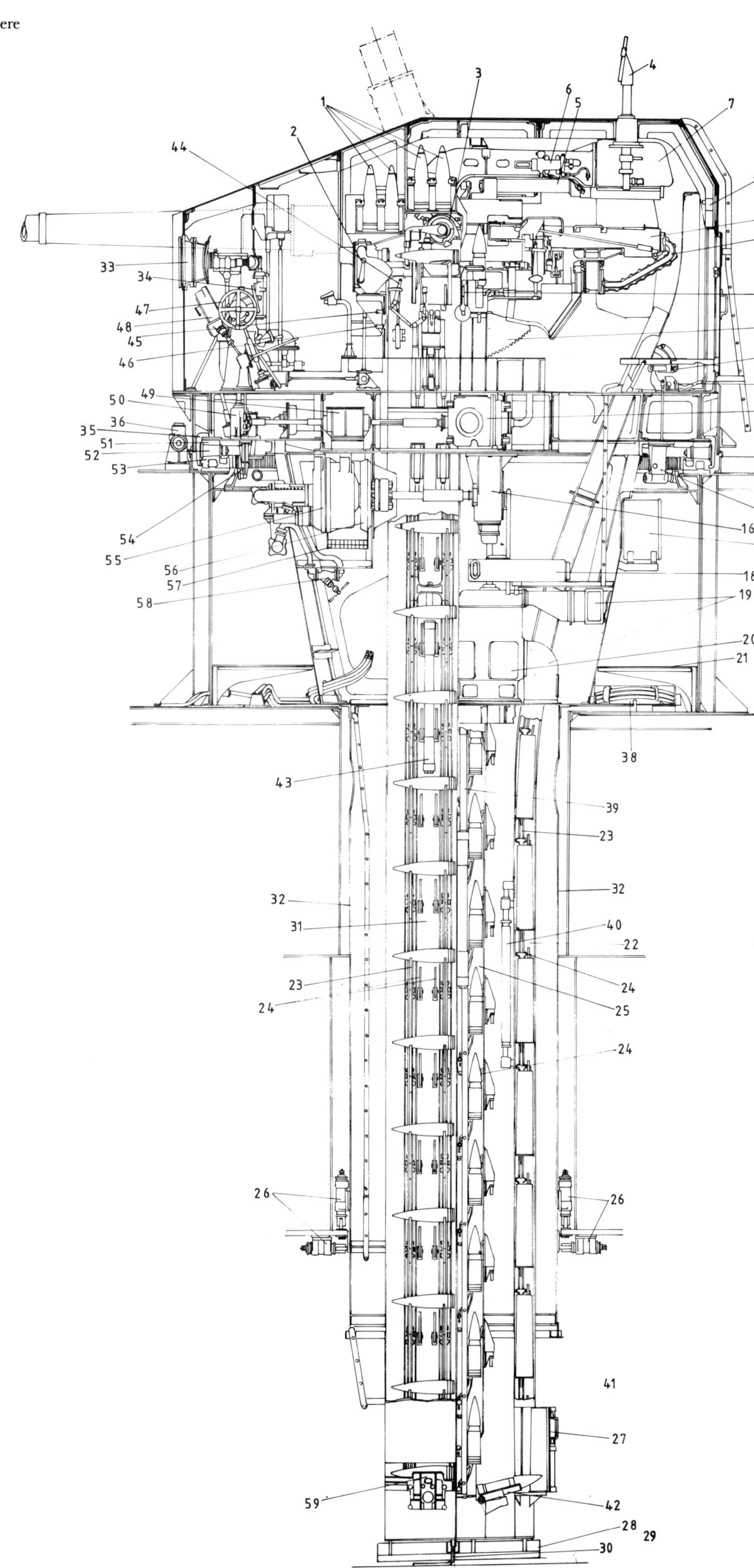

5.25in twin Mk II long trunk mounting. There were separate hoists for LA and HA shells.

1 Ready use shells
2 Fuze setting machine
3 Trunnion bracket
4 Monocular periscope
5 Recuperator
6 Intensifier
7 Balance weight
8 Teleflex indicator
9 Elevating arc
10 Stop switch for motor
11 Gun loading tray
12 Power rammer chain
13 Training motor
14 Leather apron
15 Training housing stop
16 Spiral bevel gear box
17 Automatic starter box
18 Oil tank for gear box
19 Ventilating ducts for motor
20 Electric motor for pump
21 Empty cylinder platform
22 Cordite hoist
23 Moving pawl
24 Fixed pawl
25 LA shell hoist
26 Spring guide roller
27 Cordite door
28 Save-all
29 Magazine flat
30 Air supply pipe
31 HA shell hoist
32 Gun trunk
33 Sight port window
34 Power elevating
35 Turn-table clip
36 Training buffer
37 Cordite hoist control lever
38 Platform supporting cable lead in gear
39 Ram for pusher hoist LA shell
40 Ram for cordite hoist
41 Combined magazine and shell room
42 LA hoist loading tray
43 Cylinder for pusher hoist HA shell
44 Extension hoist lever
45 HA hoist control lever
46 LA hoist control lever
47 Hand elevating gear
48 Elevation receiver
49 Training clutch gear box
50 Hand training gear
51 Upper roller path
52 Roller
53 Lower roller path
54 Training cut-off gear
55 Newton pump
56 Cooler fan
57 Cooler
58 By-pass valve
59 HA hoist loading tray

John Lambert

circular rings round the mounting at working chamber level, whence cartridges were passed by hand-ups to the gunhouse and HA and LA shells raised by hydraulic pusher hoists for each gun. The HA hoists raised the shell horizontally to a hand-controlled extension hoist near the inner trunnions and it then rolled into the fuze setting tray and was passed by hand to the loading tray. The LA hoists came up in rear of the HA hoists and the shell was raised vertically to be passed by hand to the loading tray. In P and S Nos 2 and 3, there were two sets of fixed lower hoists with a break and transfer via chutes on the lower deck. The shell hoists of the lower set were dredger type, with the shells horizontal and not vertical as in the endless-chain hoists. Otherwise, supply was the same.

In Mk II mountings there was a trunk down to the combined magazine and shell room, containing two HA and two LA shell hoists and two cartridge hoists. All hoists were hydraulic pusher delivering shells to the gunhouse as in Mk I mountings, HA shells being horizontal, while the cartridge hoists came up towards the back of the gunhouse.

In both marks the loading tray contained the hydraulic and hand rammers and rotated round a supporting tube extending from the cradle via the power ram cylinder. There was a balance weight so that the loading tray was moved by hand. Shell and cartridge were rammed together and loading was at any angle of elevation. However, gunhouses were cramped, and there was too much manual work in them for the designed rate of fire to be maintained.

In RP 10 mountings vertical rollers were added to steady the turret, the drives in the elevating and training gear were altered with reversible worms for smoothness, and the loading tray was converted to power operation with an automatic ramming link. Maximum elevating and training speeds were increased to 20°/sec.

The RP 10 Mk I* mounting, which was not in service during the war, had a larger gunhouse with 2½in (*6.3mm*) maximum shield, the motor and hydraulic pump were moved to the fixed structure, and in P and S Nos 2 and 3 turrets in *Vanguard* the break in the fixed hoists was raised to the middle deck. The HA and LA upper hoists were transposed with Mk VII Metadyne fuze-setting machines above the new HA Hoists. Joystick local control was fitted, and revolving weight was 95 tons (*96.5t*).

Vanguard at Capetown in February 1947. The twin 5.25in and six-barrelled Bofors are well shown, as are the main armament directors, the US Mk 37 for the 5.25in with Type 275 radar and the CRBF director for the after Bofors.
CPL

This was the only gun of the above calibre to fire shells of modern design with 5/10crh heads and increased weight. It was carried in twin Mk XX mountings by four of the 'L' class destroyers, *Laforey*, *Lightning*, *Lookout* and *Loyal*, and by the eight of the 'M' class. A total of 87 guns were made. Construction resembled that of the 5.25in Mk I with autofretted loose barrel, jacket to 85in (*2159mm*) from muzzle, removable breech ring and sealing collar. The loose barrel weighed 1.400 tons (*1422kg*), and the horizontal sliding breech block with hand mechanism and SA opening 375lb (*170kg*).

The brass case for the propellant charge was 28.195in (*716.2mm*) long and with SC charge weighed 32.25lb (*14.63kg*). Flashless charges were carried as ordered later in the war. SAP and HE shells were provided and by 1945 25% of the HE were to have VT fuzes, the figure rising to 50% with availability. For attacking surfaced submarines 60 HE with RDX/TNT fillings and 230 P fuzes were supplied for each

4.7in (120mm) QF Mark XI

Gun Data

Bore	4.724in	120mm	
Weight incl BM	3.351 tons	3405kg	
Length oa	247.7in	6291.6mm	52.43cal
Length bore	236.2in	5999.5mm	50.0cal
Length chamber	28.0in	711.2mm	
Volume chamber	670in³	10.98dm³	
Length rifling	204.88in	5203.95mm	
Grooves	(38) 0.0365in deep × 0.27	0.927 × 6.86mm	
Lands	0.1205in	3.061mm	
Twist	Uniform 1 in 30		
Weight projectile	62lb	28.12kg	
Propellant charge	12.81lb SC 122 or 15.38lb NF/S 198-054	5.81kg, 6.98kg	
Muzzle velocity	2538f/s	774m/s	
Working pressure	20.5 tons/in²	3230kg/cm²	
Approx life	800 EFC with NF/S 3200		
Max range	21,240yd/45°	19,420m/45°	

ship by 1945 and the star shell allowance was from 150 to 200 per ship.

The Mk XX mounting was powered by a 45 BHP (peak 102BHP) electric motor and oil hydraulic pump on the fixed structure but was in part hand operated. The guns were in individual cast steel cradles and run-out was by compressed air. The recuperator cyclinders and balance weights were on arms attached to the cradles. Elevation was by hand through worm and pinions working on an arc fixed to the cradle and was separate for each gun, the limits being +50° to -10°. Training was by a hydraulic motor with two worm and pinion drives, or by hand. There were two shell and two cartridge hydraulic pusher hoists per gunhouse in a single fixed trunk, the turntable rotating about them.

Gun Mounting Data

Revolving weight	37.363 tons	37.963t
Roller path diameter	10ft 7in	3.23m
Distance apart gun axes	96in	2.44m
Recoil distance	26.5in	67.3cm
Max training speed	10°/sec	
Firing cycle	6 sec	
Shield	¼in	6mm

The weight figure includes crew and ammunition on the revolving structure.

Shell and cartridge were placed by hand on the tilting tray of the fuze setter and slid to the loading tray. This contained the hydraulic and hand rammers and was rotated about its supporting tube from the cradle by hand, a balancing spring being fitted. Shell and cartridge were rammed together at any angle of elevation.

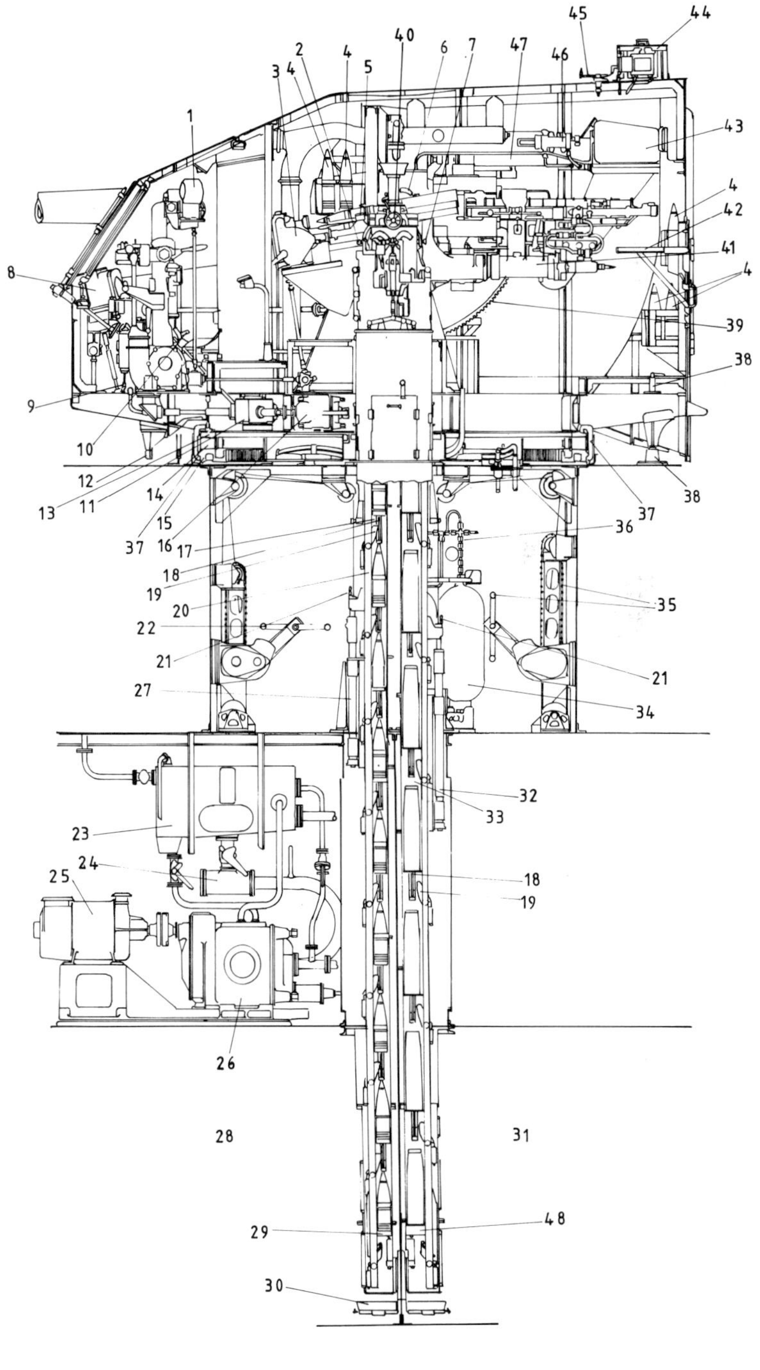

4.7in twin Mk XX mounting for QF Mk XI guns.

1 Fuze receiver
2 Shell hoist control lever
3 Fuze setting machine
4 Ready use shells
5 Tilting tray
6 Trunnion bracket
7 Cordite hoist control lever
8 Training receiver
9 Training cut off gear
10 Hand and power lever
11 Training clutch gear box
12 Training buffer stop
13 Upper roller path
14 Roller
15 Lower roller path
16 Training motor
17 Shell hoist
18 Fixed pawl
19 Moving pawl
20 Moving pawl POD
21 Clutch lever - hand and power
22 Hand operated shell hoist
23 Oil tank
24 Strainer
25 Motor
26 Pump
27 Operating cylinder for shell hoist
28 Shell room
29 Shell hoist loading tray
30 Drip tray
31 Magazine
32 Operating cylinder for cordite hoist
33 Cordite hoist
34 Air cylinder
35 Hand operated cordite hoist
36 Air blast
37 Turntable clip
38 Training housing stop
39 Elevating arc
40 Teleflex indicator
41 Gun loading tray
42 Lookout platform
43 Balance weight
44 Lookout hood
45 Safety trainer's sight
46 Intensifier
47 Recuperator
48 Cordite hoist loading tray

John Lambert

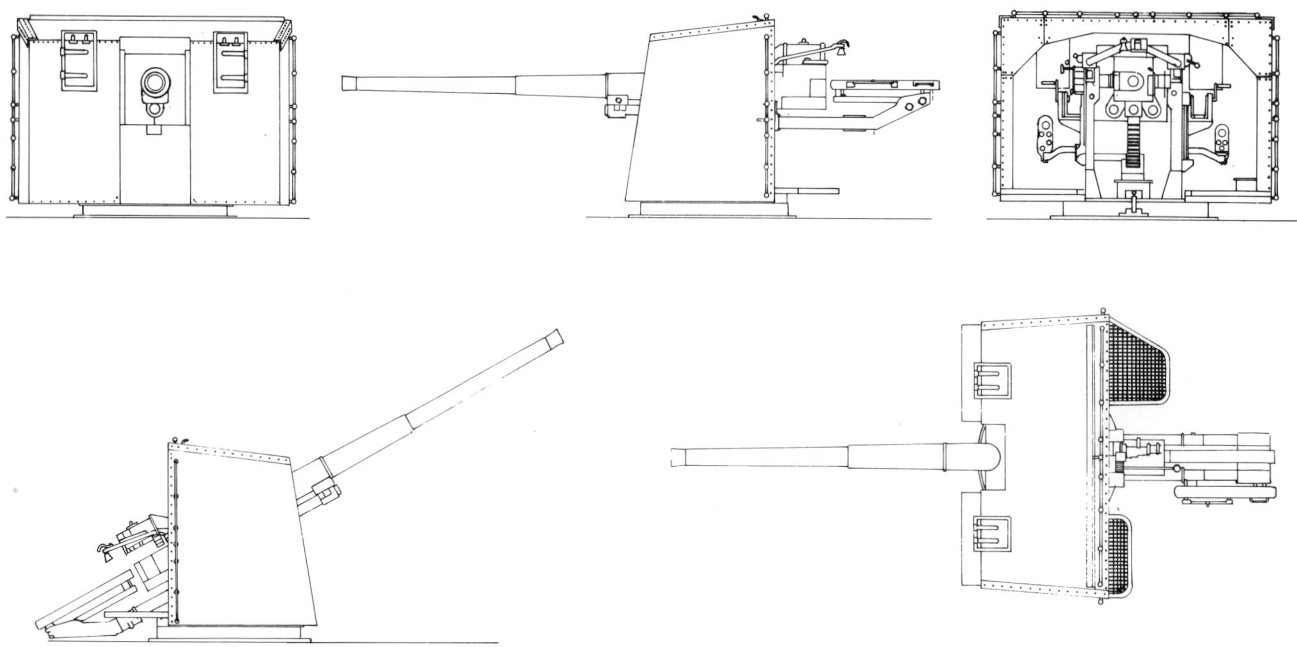

4.7 QF Mk IX gun in CPXIV mounting.
John Lambert

The Mk IX gun, essentially a separate ammunition QF version of the 4.7in (*120mm*) BL, was first tried in the *Mackay* in a clumsy 60° CPXIII mounting and later also in *Bulldog*. During the war the Mk IX gun was mounted as follows:

CPXIV 'A', 'B', 'C', 'D' class destroyers *Saguenay* class, sloops *Leith, Wellington, Deptford, Indus, Enchantress*. The later, lightened version was in the sloops only. There were also four CPXVI interchangeable with CPXIV and converted from the submarine (S) XVI. Only one, lost in *Acasta*, was used afloat.
CPXVII 'E', 'F', 'G' class destroyers
CPXVIII 'H', 'I', 'Q', 'R' class destroyers including ex-Brazilian and ex-Turkish, also *Onslow, Offa, Onslaught, Oribi.*
CPXXII 'S' (less *Savage*), 'T', 'U', 'V', 'W' class destroyers.

Mountings uncertain LCG (L)3 Nos 1-20, depot ship *Barracuda*, DEMS *Rochester Castle*.

Mk XII was ballistically identical to Mk IX but designed for the powered twin CPXIX mounting. It was tried in *Hereward* and during the war mounted in the 'Tribal' class including the Australian and first four Canadian units, as well as in 'J', 'K', 'N' class destroyers.

Detailed identification was complicated. Mk IX variants used in the war were:
Mk IX A tube, jacket to 80in (*2032mm*) from muzzle, breech ring. Horizontal sliding breech block, hand operated with SA opening.
Mk IXA loose barrel conversion, removable breech ring.
Mk IX* differences in breech ring and SA gear.
Mk IX** differences in breech ring to suit CP XVIII mounting.
Mk IXA** loose barrel conversion, removable breech ring.
Mk IXB** new loose barrel guns. Differ from IX**A in breech ring/jacket connection, removable breech ring.
Prefixes used were: C, percussion firing only; D, EMF and percussion; F, EMF, later type breech block; G, DEF and percussion.

4.7in (120mm) QF Marks IX and XII

Gun Data

Bore	4.724in	120mm	
Weight incl BM	2.963/2.984 tons	3011/3032kg	
Length oa	220.62in	5603.75mm	46.70cal
Length bore	212.58in	5399.5mm	45.0cal
Length chamber	30.55in	775.97mm	
Volume chamber	628in^3	10.29dm^3	
Length rifling	179.2225in	4552.25mm	
Grooves	(38) 0.037in deep x 0.27	0.94 x 6.86mm	
Lands	0.1205in	3.061mm	
Twist	Uniform 1 in 30		
Weight projectile	50lb	22.68kg	
Propellant charge	11.58lb SC 109 or 13.13lb NF/S 164-048	5.25kg, 5.96kg	
Muzzle velocity	2650f/s	808m/s	
Working pressure	20 tons/in^2	3150kg/cm^2	
Approx life	1400 EFC with NF/S 4200		
Max range	16,970yd/40°	15,520m/40°	

Above data for Mk IX and sub-marks. Mk XII and sub-marks weighed 3.238-3.245 tons (*3290-3297kg*) and had length oa 224.08in (*5691.63mm*, 47.43cal).

Gun Mounting Data Twin CPXIX

Total weight	25.489 tons	25.898t
Distance apart gun axes	38in	96.5cm
Recoil distance	26.5in	67.3cm
Max elevating speed	10°/sec	
Max training speed	10°/sec	
Firing cycle	5 sec	
Shield	2.55 tons	2591kg

Gun Mounting Data Single CP Mountings

Mounting	**Elevation**		**Weight incl gun less shield**		**Max thickness shield**		**Weight shield**	
			tons	**kg**	**in**	**mm**	**tons**	**kg**
CPXIV	+30°	-10°	8.642	8781	0.144	3.7	0.85	864
CPXVII	+40°	-10°	8.829	8971	0.125	3.2	0.85	864
CPXVIII	+40°	-10°	9.544	9697	0.125	3.2	1.163	1182
CPXXII	+55°	-10°	11.580	11,766	0.375	9.5	1.813	1842

Later CPXIV mountings weighed 8.129 tons (*8259kg*). CPXVII mountings only elevated to 29½° unless the gun-well covers were lowered. Firing cycles were normally 5-6 sec in CPXXII and 6-8 sec in the others.

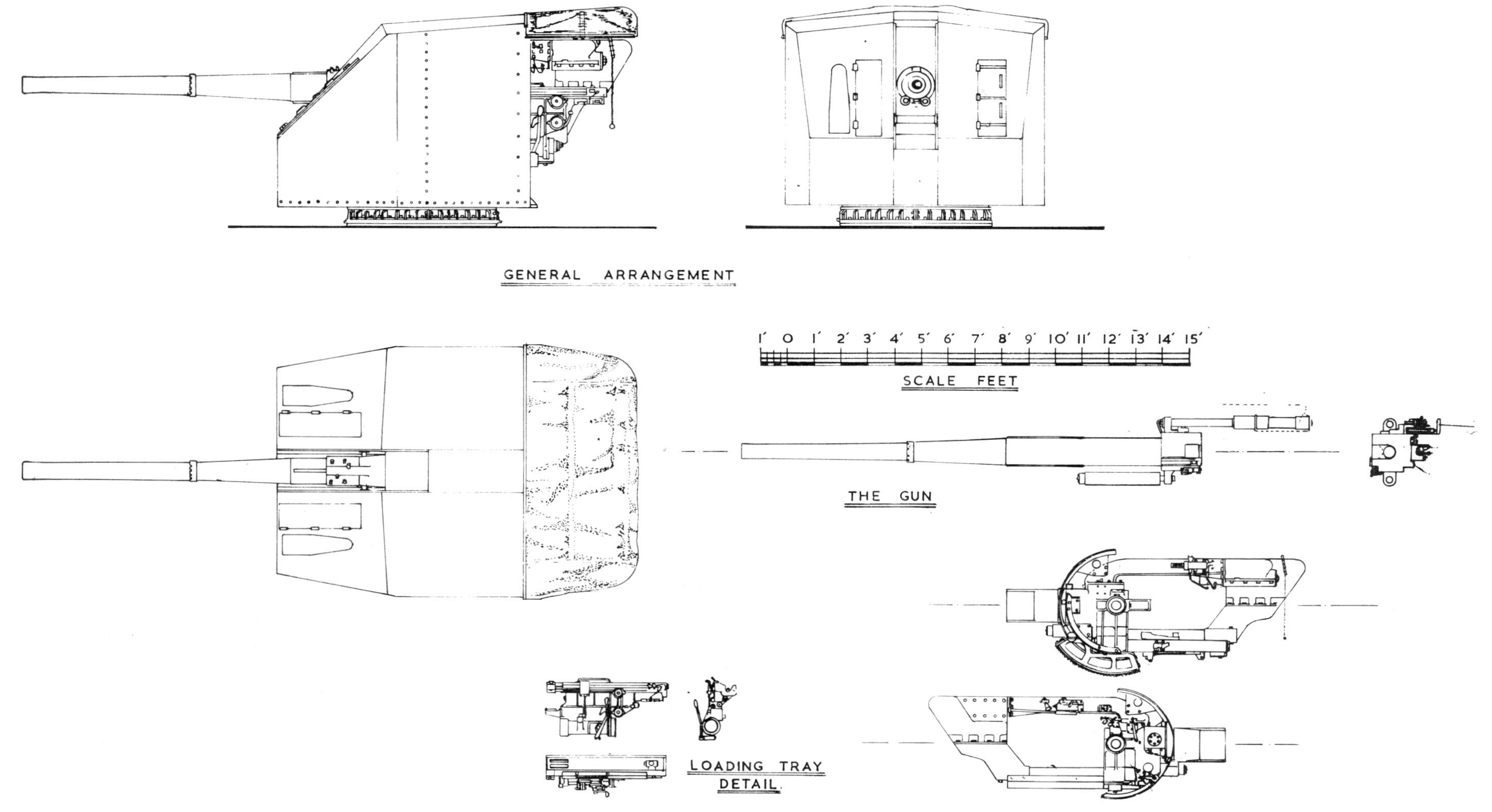

4.7in QF Mk IX gun in CPXXII mounting.
John Lambert

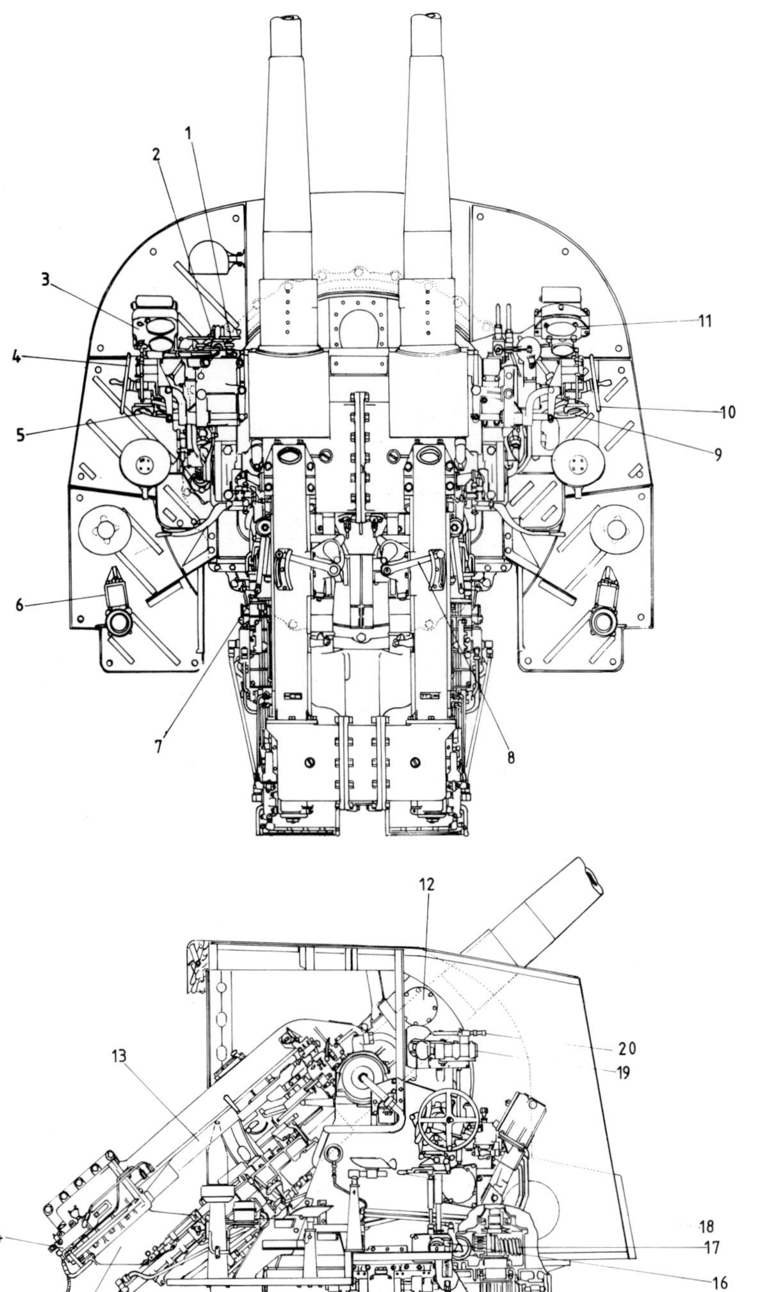

4.7in QF Mk XII guns in twin CPXIX mounting.

1 Deflection handwheel
2 Range handwheel
3 Elevation receiver type E Mark I*
4 Hand elevating
5 Power elevating
6 Fuze receiver
7 Breech mechanism lever
8 Change-over lever in semi-automatic position
9 Power training
10 Hand training
11 Training receiver type D Mark IV
12 Recoil cylinder filling tank
13 Recuperator
14 Intensifier
15 Training buffer stop
16 Pedal for training stop cut off
17 Training drive and roller path [in section]
18 Clutch lever - training
19 Monocular telescope
20 Aldis telescope
21 Trunnion bearing [in section]
22 Shield
23 Clutch lever - elevating
24 Firing CO lever [RG - both guns - LG]
25 Firing pedal
26 Safety depression gear
27 Safety depression cam
28 Locking bolt
29 Drain well
30 Drain cock
31 Drain valve
32 Cables
33 Interceptor
34 Loading tray
35 Rammer lever in 'withdrawn' position
36 Firing handle
37 Recoil cylinder
38 Elevating drive and pinion [in section]
39 Voice pipe
40 Pressure stop valve
41 Non-return valve
42 Pressure drain valve
43 Exhaust drain valve
44 Balance weight

John Lambert

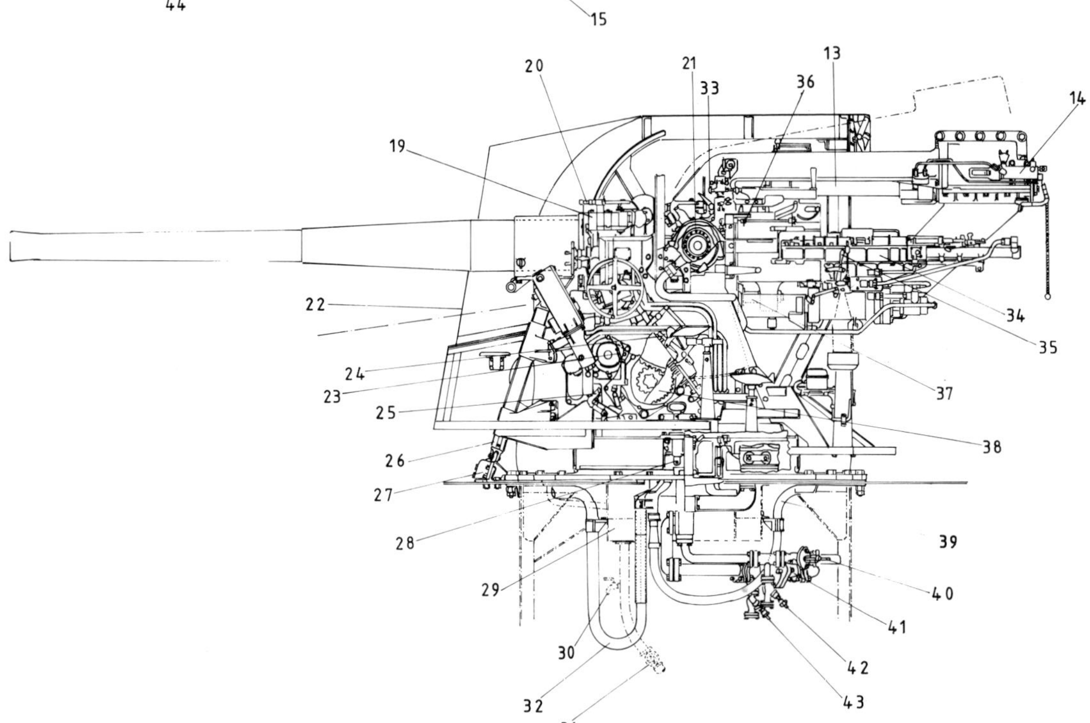

Mk XII was simpler:
Mk XII as Mk IX in general construction but removable breech ring.
Mk XII* No step in rear part of A tube, breech rings to suit.
Mk XIIB loose barrel conversion.

All loose barrels weighed 1.225 tons(*1245kg*) but breech mechanisms in Mk IX varied from 252lb (*114kg*) to 266lb (*121kg*) and in Mk XII from 392lb (*178kg*) to 395lb (*179kg*). Total numbers made were 742 Mk IX and 372 Mk XII.

The brass case for the propellant was 30.922in (*785.4mm*) long and with SC weighed 30.5lb (*13.8kg*). As ordered a proportion of flashless charges were later carried. Shells were SAP and HE. Towards the end of the war in fleet destroyers 25% of HE had VT fuzes, and the proportion rose to 50% with availability. An allowance of 10 HE per gun with RDX/TNT fillings and 230 P fuzes was later issued for attacking surfaced submarines. Star shell varied from 50 to 200 per ship.

The single CP mountings were all hand worked, except that CP XXII had a spring-operated rammer, cocked by the recoil. But it and CP XXIII had arms attached to the cradle carrying the recuperator cylinder and balance weight.

The twin CP XIX mountings in the 'Tribal' class were in two groups, each powered by a 140 HP steam turbine and oil hydraulic pump, but in the 'J', 'K', 'N' classes there was a 70HP electric motor and pump to each mounting. All were on the fixed structure. The cradles were bolted together and run-out was by compressed air. Recuperator cylinders and balance weights were carried by arms projecting from the cradles.

The guns were elevated together, a hydraulic motor driving arcs fixed to the cradles by a common shaft, itself driven by bevel gears, worm and pinions. Limits were +40° to -10°. Training was also by hydraulic motor with similar worm and gear drive. Hoists were independent of the mounting, and there was a hand-operated loading tray with balance spring rotating about a shaft attached to the cradle and containing hydraulic and hand rammers. Shell and cartridge were rammed together at any angle of elevation. Fuze setting was by hand.

4.7in twin CPXIX mounting in *Warramunga* *CPL*

4.7in (120mm) QF Mark VIII

This was the largest calibre fixed ammunition gun ever in service in the RN, though the round was considerably lighter than the 4.5in (*114mm*). It was carried in the power-worked HA XII mounting by *Nelson, Rodney, Courageous, Glorious, Albatross* and *Adventure* only.

Construction comprised a tapered inner A tube with locating shoulder 158.95in (*4037.3mm*) from the muzzle, A tube, part length wire, jacket and breech ring. The breech mechanism had a horizontal sliding block operated by hand with SA opening and weighed 263lb (*119kg*). The prefixes E and F referring to DEF and EMF are occasionally to be found. In all 84 guns were made.

The fixed round with SC weighed 76lb (*34.5kg*) with a maximum length of 44.26in (*1124.2mm*). SAP and HE were carried in 1939, but only HE in the *Nelson* class and *Albatross*. By the end of the war, rounds with flashless charges were issued as ordered, and in the *Nelson* class half the HE shells were to have VT proximity fuzes with an allowance of 400 star shell per ship.

The HA XII mounting was of the usual CP type with +90° to -5° elevation, but a 9HP electric motor and hydraulic pump were fitted on the mounting to provide elevation and training speeds of 10°/sec, twice those by hand. There was also a power rammer carried by the loading tray rocking arm. Recoil was 18in (*46cm*) and run-out by springs. The minimum firing cycle was about 5 sec, though 4 sec is recorded, but rammers were unreliable at this speed. One mounting in *Rodney* had rack type rammer gear, which limited elevation to 77°. Total weight was 12.089 tons (*12.283t*) without the shields later fitted in *Nelson* and *Rodney*.

Gun Data

Bore	4.724in	120mm	
Weight incl BM	3.087 tons	3137kg	
Length oa	197in	5003.8mm	41.70cal
Length bore	188.96in	4799.6mm	40.0cal
Length chamber	23.42in	594.87mm	
Volume chamber	454in^3	7.44dm^3	
Length rifling	161.735in	4108.07mm	
Grooves	(38) 0.037in deep × 0.27	0.94 × 6.86mm	
Lands	0.1205in	3.061mm	
Twist	Uniform 1 in 30		
Weight projectile	50lb	22.68kg	
Propellant charge	9.19lb SC 103 or 10.94lb NF/S 164-048	4.17kg, 4.96kg	
Muzzle velocity	2457f/s	749m/s	
Working pressure	20.5 tons/in^2	3230kg/cm^2	
Approx life	1050/1200 EFC with NF/S 3500		
Max range	16,160yd/45°	14,780mm/45°	
Ceiling	32,000ft/90°	9750m/90°	

This gun was ordered during the First World War for manufacture in Japan as armament for DAMS. It was of separate ammunition screw breech design, outdated even when new. Out of 620 guns, 24 had been lost in transit and 525 remained in 1939. In World War II it was mounted in a few auxiliary warships, but mostly in DEMS, and some large liners including *Aquitania*. It was also in emergency coast defence batteries. CP or HE shells were supplied and the brass case with charge weighed 26.5lb (*12kg*). Mountings were PV or PX with +20° to -10° elevation.

4.7in (120mm) QF Mark V*

Gun Data

Bore	4.724in	120mm	
Weight incl BM	2.65 tons	2693kg	
Length oa	212.6in	5400mm	45.00cal
Length bore	207.5in	5270.5mm	43.92cal
Length chamber	26.3in	668.0mm	
Volume chamber	489.6in^3	8.023dm^3	
Weight projectile	50lb	22.68kg	
Propellant charge	8.648lb SC 103	3.92kg	
Muzzle velocity	2330f/s	710m/s	
Max range	11,960yd/20°	10,940m/20°	

4.5in (114mm) QF Marks I, III, IV

Gun Data

Bore	4.45in	113.03mm	
Weight incl BM	2.814 tons	2859 kg	
Length oa	211.75in	5378.45mm	47.58cal
Length bore	200.25in	5086.35mm	45.0cal
Length chamber	25.06/25.15in	636.52/638.8mm	
Volume chamber	600in^3	9.83dm^3	
Length rifling	170.92in	4341.37mm	
Grooves	(32) 0.037in deep × 0.291	0.94 × 7.39mm	
Lands	0.1459in	3.706mm	
Twist	Uniform 1 in 25		
Weight projectile	55lb	24.95kg	
Propellant charge	11.035lb SC 122 or 13.63lb NF/S 198-054	5.005 kg, 6.18kg	
Muzzle velocity	2449f/s	746m/s	
Working pressure	20.5 tons/in^2	3230kg/cm^2	
Approx life	750 EFC with NF/S 1500 to 1725		
Max range	20,750yd/45°	18,970m/45°	
Ceiling	41,000ft/80°	12,500m/80°	

The above weight is for Mk I and Mk III guns; Mk IV weighed 2.759 tons (*2803kg*).

Gun Mounting Data Mark II mounting

Weight	37.95 tons	38.56t
Roller path diameter	9ft 5in mean	2.87m
Distance apart gun axes	38in	96.5cm
Recoil distance	18in	46cm
Max elevating speed	10°/sec	
Max training speed	15°/sec	
Firing cycle	5 sec	
Turret shield	0.5in	13mm

Although the gun was always known as 4.5in, the actual bore was 4.45in (*113.03mm*). Mks I and III were interchangeable, differing only in details of the firing mechanism, while Mk IV was ballistically identical, but modified to suit converted 4.7in (*120mm*) CP XXII mountings. The Mk I gun was in *Ark Royal, Forth, Maidstone* together with three guns in *Queen Elizabeth*, five in *Valiant* and four in *Renown* only. The 4.5in gun was mounted as follows during the war and immediate post-war period:

Mk I and Mk III guns in MkII BD mounts. *Queen Elizabeth, Valiant, Renown, Illustrious, Victorious, Formidable, Indomitable.*
Mk III guns in RP 10 Mk II BD mountings**. *Implacable, Indefatigable.*
Mk I and Mk III guns in Mk III UD mountings. *Ark Royal, Scylla, Charybdis, Forth, Maidstone, Tyne, Hecla, Adamant.*
Mk III guns in RP 10 Mk IV mountings. *Savage*, first sixteen 'Battle' class destroyers.
Mk III guns in RP 10 Mk IV* mountings. Last eight 'Battle' class destroyers.
Mk IV guns in Mk V mountings. *Savage*, 'Z', 'Ca' class destroyers.
Mk IV guns in RP 50 Mk V mountings. 'Ch', 'Co', 'Cr' class destroyers.
Mk IV guns in RP 50 Mk V* mountings. Last eight 'Battle' class destroyers.

Construction of production guns comprised an autofretted loose barrel, jacket, removable breech ring and sealing collar. Guns had to be dismounted to change barrels. The breech mechanism in Mks I and III was very similar to that in the 4.7in(*120mm*) Mk XII but in Mk I all electric firing was obtained by eliminating the percussion elements while Mk III was designed for electric firing only. All three Marks had horizontal sliding breech blocks with hand-operated mechanism and SA opening. The BM weights were 395lb (*179kg*) in Mks I and III, and 296lb (*134kg*) in Mk IV. Loose barrels weighed 0.975 tons (*991kg*).

In all five experimental guns, 46 Mk I, 524 Mk III and 199 Mk IV were made, not including any Mk IVs ordered after the war.

Fixed ammunition was fired by guns in Mk II, II** and III mountings. The round had a maximum length of 49in (*1245mm*) and weighed up to 91.75lb (*41.6kg*). As all mountings required some manhandling of ammunition, this was too long and heavy, and there was a tendency for shells to separate from the cases, so that guns in other mountings fired separate ammunition, the brass case being 25.35in (*643.9mm*) long and weighing 38.5lb (*17.5kg*) maximum with charge.

Originally SAP and HE were carried by battleships and aircraft carriers and HE only by depot ships. By the end of the war most charges were flashless, if available, and SAP and HE were carried by all except aircraft carriers, which had HE only. Except in depot ships, 25% of the HE were to have VT proximity fuzes, rising to 50% as available, and in destroyers 10 rounds per gun were RDX/TNT filled HE with 230P fuzes for use against surfaced submarines. Star shell allowances were from 150 to 400 per ship but depot ships had none.

The Mk II gun was an Army AA weapon, a few batteries also having a coast defence function, and was generally similar to the Navy guns. It was entirely distinct from the 4.5in medium field gun which was BL and a true 4.5in (*114.3mm*) bore. Mk V was strictly a post-war gun, although much development was carried out during the war. It was first tried at sea in the destroyer *Saintes* in 1947. It used separate ammunition and was identical ballistically to the earlier guns but had a vertical sliding breech block hydraulically operated and a firing cycle of 2.5-3 sec. As recoil and run-out cylinders were incorporated in the breech ring and the BM was much heavier, the total gun weight was 3.315 tons (*3.368t*) including BM.

The Mk II mounting had a distinctive appearance with a low shield showing above deck. It was powered by a 46 HP motor and oil hydraulic pump on the fixed structure. The two cradles were bolted together and run-out was by compressed air. Recuperator cylinders and balance weights were carried on arms attached to the cradles. The elevation arcs were driven by pinions on a common shaft, powered by a hydraulic motor through bevel gears and worm and wheel, and the training pinion was similarly powered. Elevation limits were +80° to -5°. The ammunition hoists were independent of the mounting and comprised one or two endless-chain hoists and an endless-chain

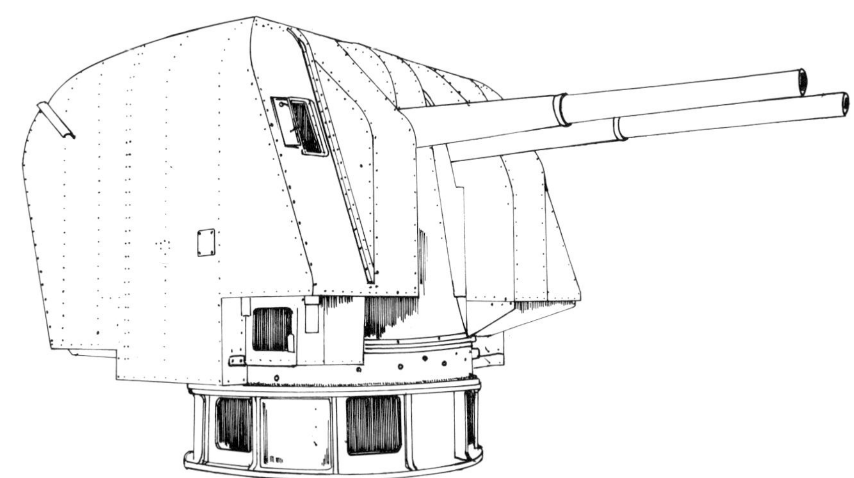
4.5in twin Mk III UD mounting
John Lambert

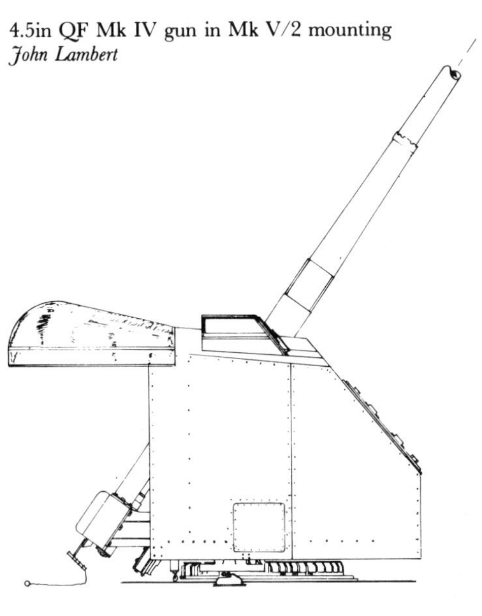
4.5in QF Mk IV gun in Mk V/2 mounting
John Lambert

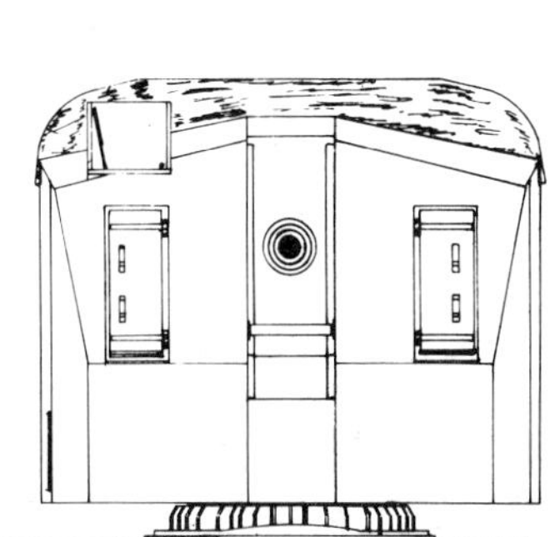

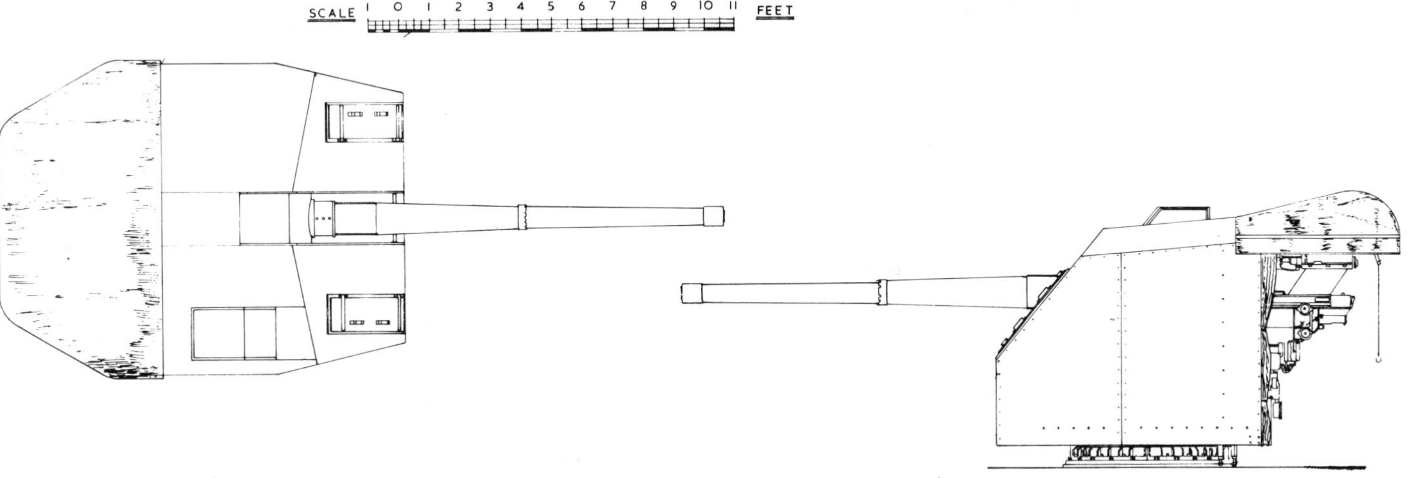

conveyor, all electrically powered. There was a revolving scuttle holding three rounds vertically at each side of the mounting at the rear, and rounds were passed to the R or L fuze setting machine and hence to the respective loading tray. This was rotated by hand about a tubular shaft from the cradle and contained the hydraulic and hand rammers. Loading was at any angle of elevation.

RP 10 Mk II** differed, apart from the RP gear, in having a vertical roller race to limit jump, no worms in the power elevation, and training drives and power-operated loading trays. It had maximum elevation and training speeds of 20°/sec and weighed 43.119 tons (*43.811t*).

Mk III mountings were similar to Mk II but had open back shields weighing only 2.625 tons (*2667kg*) compared with 9.088 tons (*9234kg*) for the Mk II gunhouse. There were no revolving scuttles on the mounting and the roller path mean diameter was smaller at 7ft 9in (*2.36m*). Weight was 29.738 tons (*30.215t*).

RP 10 Mk IV resembled RP 10 Mk** but was a turret mounting with revolving trunk. Each gun had hydraulic pusher shell and cartridge hoists on the revolving structure and extending one deck down where they were fed by hand from the fixed electric endless-chain hoists. Shells were delivered to the gunhouse horizontally and passed via the fuze setting machines to the loading trays, while cartridges came up vertically in rear. There was only a single elevating arc, and joystick local control was fitted. The weight was increased to 45.579 tons (*46.310t*) of which 11.2 tons (*11,380kg*) was due to the 0.5in (*13mm*) gunhouse. RP 10 Mk IV* differed in having Mk VII Metadyne fuze setting machines and was fitted for use with USN computer system.

Mk V mountings were converted 4.7in (*120mm*) CP XXII with 18in (*46cm*) recoil instead of 26.5in (*67.3cm*) and a firing cycle of 4.3 sec. There was also a reduction of 0.345 tons (*351kg*) in total weight less shield and of 0.122 tons (*124kg*) in the shield.

RP 50 Mk V had electric training and elevation with Metadyne RPC and maximum speeds of 20°/sec for both. Joystick local control was fitted and gun and mounting less shield weighed 13.106 tons (*13316kg*) with 1.913 tons

The 4.5in Mk II gun in RP 10 Mk IV mounting.

A Captain of turret's lookout hood
B Exhaust fan trunking
C Trainer's sighting port door
D HP air bottle for air blast
E Right gun shell hoist trunking
F Shell 'legend' at foot of shell hoist, to ensure correct projectile position, nose to the rear
G Waiting shell
H Automatic shell release, synchronised with hoist movement
I Right gun shell and cordite hoist operator's platform
J Waiting cartridge
K Single-stroke cartridge hoist
L Fixed mounting training base
M Left gun shell and cordite hoist structures
N Right hand gunhouse access door
1 Original gundeck level in Mk II mountings
2 Revised gundeck level for Mk IV mountings

Peter Hodges

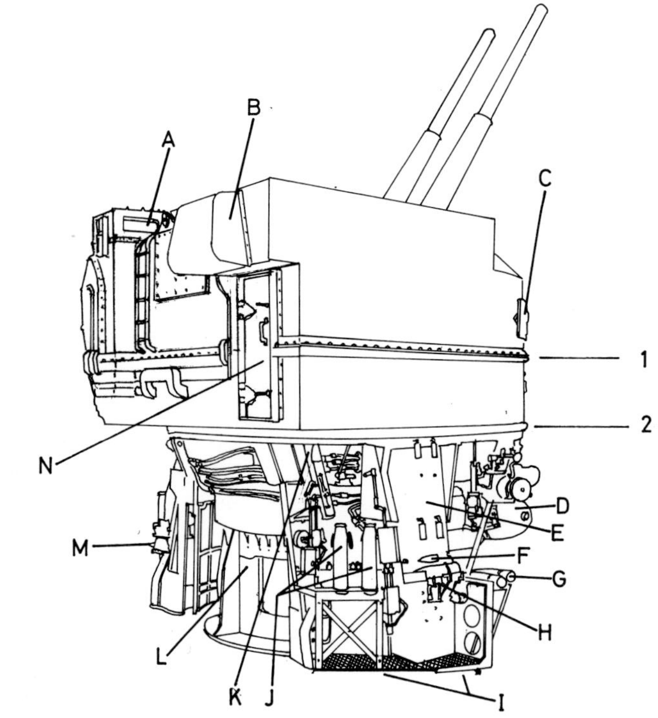

4.5in RP 41 twin Mk VI* mounting in post-war *Daring* class.

1 Air bottle
2 Metadyne set for fuze setting
3 5in trunnion locking bolt
4 Elevating cut off gear
5 Shell hoists
6 Elevating control unit
7 Lever for turntable securing bolt
8 Amplifier assembly
9 Ready use shell racks
10 Access door
11 Access for lifting gear
12 Extended cartridge chute
13 Vent doors
14 Roof ladder
15 Gas proof cowl
16 Elevating cylinder
17 12.5in exhaust fan
18 Cartridge hoist
19 7.5in vent fan
20 Turntable floor

John Lambert

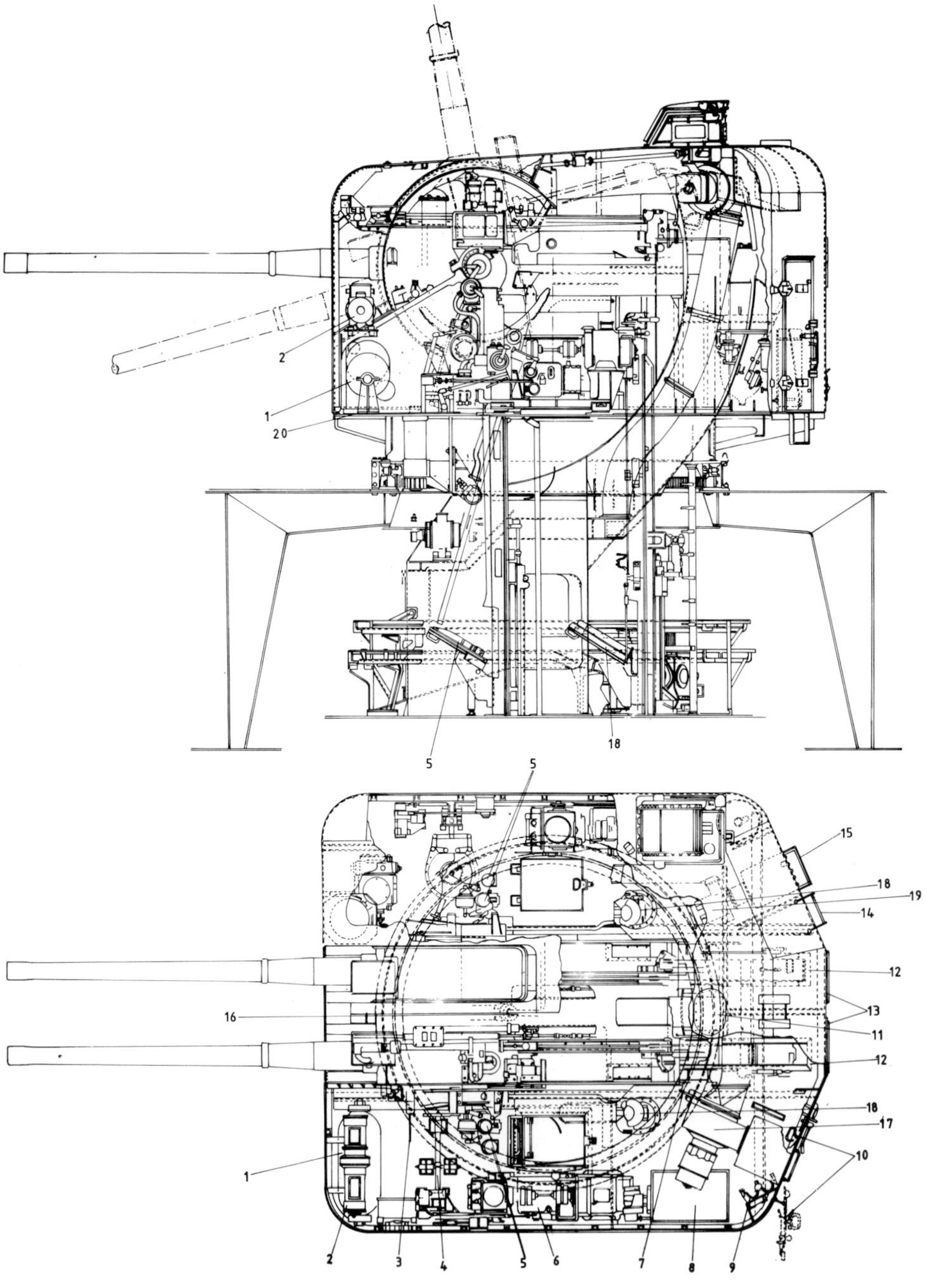

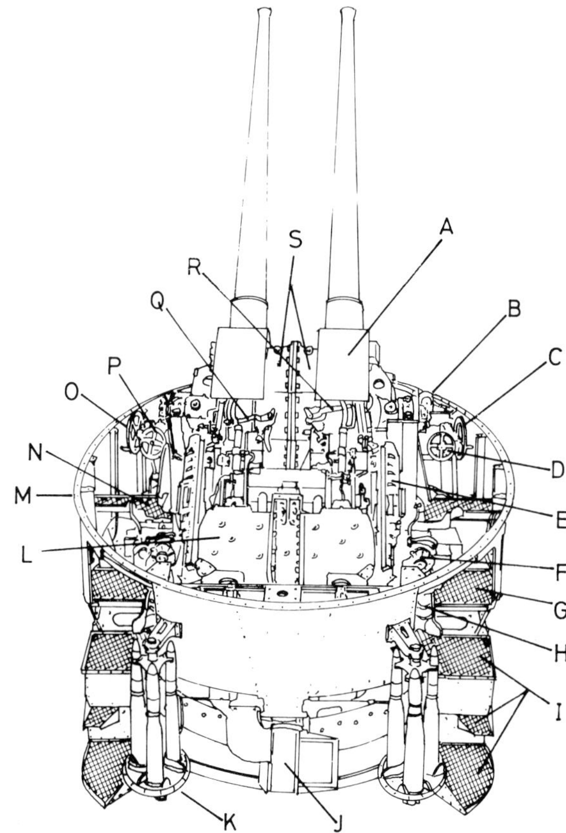

The 4.5in Mk II BD mounting.

A Mantlet plate
B Training receiver
C Trainer's manual handwheel
D Trainer's power drive handwheel
E Right gun loading tray
F Right gun fuze setting machine
G Gunhouse deck level
H Fuze setting tray
I Loading access steps
J Ventilation fan and trunking
K Revolving three-round scuttle
L Balance weight
M Securing flange for upper portion of gunhouse (at gundeck level)
N Breech-worker's platform
O Layer's manual handwheel
P Layer's power drive handwheel
Q Left gun QF/SA lever in 'Quick-fire' position
R Right gun QF/SA lever in 'Semi-automatic' position
S Left and right sections of common gun cradle

Peter Hodges

(*1944kg*) for the shield.

RP 50 Mk V* was fitted for use with USN computer system and had spring-powered loading trays. Further modifications were later introduced for modernised 'Ca' class destroyers and for 'Tribal' frigates.

Of other mountings Mk I was a single UD mounting not in service, RP 10 Mk II*, with a single elevating arc, was intended for the *Albion* class but omitted in these ships as completed, and RP 10 Mk II*** was in *Eagle* and *Ark Royal* when eventually in service. This had separate ammunition with shell and cartridge rails round the mounting space in the gun-bay. Shells were raised by short pusher hoist and cartridges passed up by hand. Mk VII Metadyne fuze setters were located at the top of the hoists and joystick local control was fitted. Weight rose to 49.395 tons (*50.188t*).

The Mk V gun, standard in many post-war ships, was in RP 41 Mk VI mountings and later variants. These were true turrets with three upper and three lower hoists per gun for AA shells, other shells and cartridges. RP 41 Mk VII, intended for the *Malta* class aircraft carriers and probably for the final *Lion* battleship design, would have differed principally in a roller path of 14ft (*4.27m*) diameter instead of 11ft(*3.3m*).

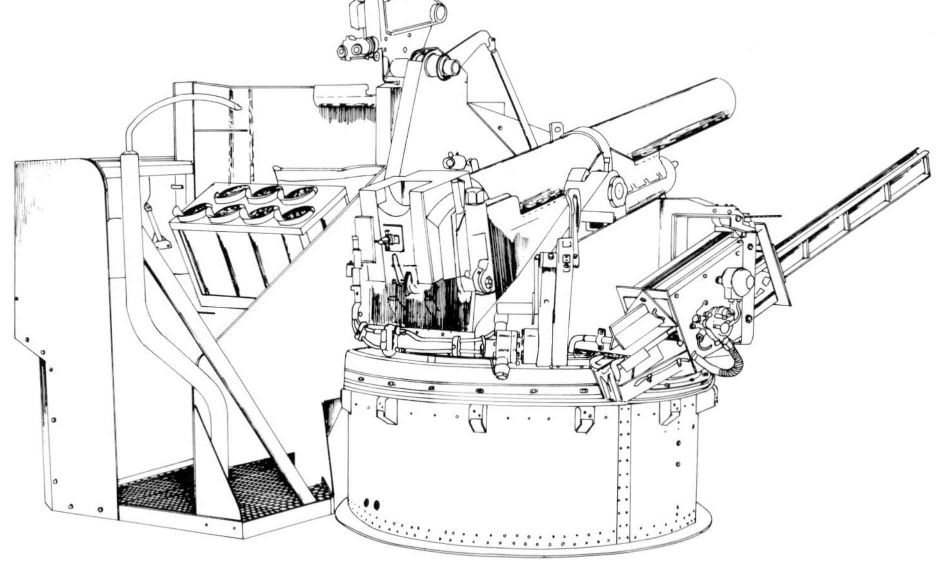

4.5in 8cwt QF Mk I gun in Mk I mounting with rocket flare launcher to right.
John Lambert

This gun was developed for MTBs but was not ready for service until just after the war. The 8cwt Mk I mounting was power worked and in a list shortly after the war is recorded in *MTB 509, 520, 528, 538, 2014, 2017, 5007, 5008*. The hand-worked Mk II mounting with 30° elevation was cancelled.

The gun was of simple construction with barrel, removable breech ring and vertical sliding breech block with SA opening. A total of 98 guns, but only 36 mountings, were made.

Fixed ammunition was fired with base-fuzed HE shell, the round weighing 22lb (*10kg*) with a length of 19in (*483mm*). The mounting was

4.5in (114mm) 8cwt (406kg) QF Mark I

Gun Data

Bore	4.45in	113.03mm	
Weight incl BM	0.400 tons	0.406t	
Length oa	89.06in	2262.1mm	20.01cal
Length bore	84.0in	2133.6mm	18.88cal
Length chamber	8.82in	224.03mm	
Volume chamber	137.5in^3	2.253dm^3	
Weight projectile	14.69lb	6.66kg	
Propellant charge	1.148lb NQ/R 014 x 048	0.521kg	
Muzzle velocity	1500f/s	457m/s	

hydraulically powered from a pump driven by the auxiliary or main engines or in emergency from a manual pump on the mounting. The built-up cradle was trough shaped and run-out was by springs. Elevation was by cylinder and ram, and training by hydraulic motor and spur pinions with a horizontal rather than a vertical rack. Elevation limits were +12° to -10°. The usual upper and lower roller paths with live rollers were replaced by rollers with their axis pins secured to a rotating ring and there were also vertical rollers. The ready-use rack held seven rounds. The gun was on the centre line of the mounting with the aimer on the left side with a shield also on this side protecting him and the scooter control valve box. The right side of the mounting accommodated a 2in (*51mm*) rocket flare unit.

The mounting with gun weighed 1.738 tons (*1766kg*) and could train at 25 to 30°/sec. Recoil was 29-30in (*74-76cm*) and the gun was sighted to 3300yd (*3018m*) at 9° 58′. The firing cycle was 6 sec.

LIGHT CALIBRE QUICK-FIRING GUNS

4in (102mm) QF Marks XVI, XXI

Gun Data

Bore	4in	101.6mm	
Weight incl BM	2.010 tons	2042kg	
Length oa	190.5in	4838.7mm	47.63cal
Length bore	180in	4572mm	45.0cal
Length chamber	26.03in	661.16mm	
Volume chamber	511.8in^3	8.387dm^3	
Length rifling	149.52in	3797.81mm	
Grooves	(32) 0.037in deep × 0.27	0.94 × 6.86mm	
Lands	0.1227in	3.117mm	
Twist	Uniform 1 in 30		
Weight projectile	35lb	15.88kg	
Propellant charge	9.023lb SC 103 or 10.5lb NF/S 164-048	4.093kg, 4.763kg	
Muzzle velocity	2660f/s	811m/s	
Working pressure	20.5 tons/in^2	3230kg/cm^2	
Approx life	600 EFC, with NF/S 1800		
Max range	19,850yd/45°	18,150m/45°	
Ceiling	39,000ft/80°	11,890m/80°	

The above weight is for Mk XVI*; Mk XVI weighed 2.007 tons (*2039kg*) and Mk XXI 1.517 tons (*1541kg*).

By far the most important of these was Mk XVI in twin Mk XIX mountings, to be found in the following ships during the war:

As AA armament *Barham, Malaya, Warspite, Royal Sovereign* class, *Hood; Roberts, Abercrombie*; all 8in (*203mm*) cruisers except *Canberra, York; Danae, Dragon, Effingham, Leander* class, *Perth* class (except *Sydney), Arethusa, Southampton, Gloucester, Belfast, Fiji, Ceylon, Swiftsure* classes, *Superb*; most 'Tribal' class destroyers; AMCs *Canton, Corfu.*

As main armament AA principal function *Furious, Unicorn, Activity, Campania, Nairana, Vindex, Pretoria Castle; Caledon, Curaçoa, Cairo, Calcutta, Carlisle, Colombo; Abdiel* class; *Ghurka, Lance, Legion, Lively*, last four Canadian 'Tribal' class, *Petard, Wallace*, some 'V' and 'W' classes, all 'Hunts'; most sloops, 'Bay' class and many Canadian and some Australian frigates, auxiliary AA ships, some landing ships, depot ships, netlayers.

The Mk XVI gun in single Mk XX mounting was only in Australian ships - *Parramatta, Warrego*, 'River' class frigates, some *Bathurst* class minesweepers and the landing ship *Kanimbla.*

Mark XXI in single Mk XXIV mounting was intended for later 'Loch' class frigates and 'Castle' class corvettes but was only in *Loch Veyatie* completed after the war.

The original Mk XVI had an A tube, jacket to 63.5in (*1612.9mm*) from muzzle and removable breech ring. The vertical sliding breech block was hand operated with SA opening downwards. Most of these were converted to Mk XVI* on repair and the great majority of guns were made to this pattern, originally to have been called Mk XVIII. This differed in having the A tube replaced by an autofretted loose barrel with a sealing collar at the front of the jacket. The loose barrel weighed 0.85 tons (*864kg*) and the BM in both 336lb (*152.4kg*).

Mk XXI was a lighter version built to the revised design rules with an autofretted monobloc barrel and removable breech ring. The BM was as above.

The total of Mk XVI and XVI* made was 2555, of which only one had been stricken before the war while 238 Mk XXI were completed. Of the total 604 Mk XVI* and 135 Mk XXI were made in Canada and 45 Mk XVI* in Australia.

Fixed ammunition was fired, the round being up to 45.125in (*1146.2mm*) in length and 66.75lb (*30.28kg*) in weight. In the latter part of the war most charges were flashless if available. Most shells were HE and (except in depot ships by the end of the war) 25% were to have VT proximity fuzes, rising to 50% with availability. By this time escort ships had 10 HE per gun with RDX/TNT fillings and 230 P fuzes against surfaced submarines, and also in many cases 12-22 Shark per ship. SAP was also usually carried but not in capital ships, aircraft carriers, most cruisers and 'Tribal' destroyers. From 30 to 400 star shell per ship were provided.

The Mk XIX mounting was a normal hand-worked HA CP with the two guns in a common cradle, each having its own recoil and compressed air run-out system. The gun axes were 21in (*53.3cm*) apart. The balance weights were located on the guns in front of the breech ring. Elevation was +80° to -10°, recoil 15in (*38cm*) and firing cycle 5 sec. The total weight including guns varied with the type of fuze setter and with the size of the 0.125in (*3.2mm*) shield from 14 tons to 15.5 tons (*14,225-15,749kg*).

The single Mk XX mounting was similar but weighed 9.85 tons (*10,008kg*) and the single Mk XXIV, which also had 80° elevation, is listed with a 4-second firing cycle and weighed 8.5 tons (*8636kg*). No shield is given for this last mounting.

During the war a number of Mk XIX mountings were fitted with RPC, there being three Metadyne types, RP 50, RP 51 and RP 52. All had the elevating and training motors on the mounting and driving through worm and gears. In RP 51 the Metadyne sets were also on the mounting, but in the other two on the fixed structure. RP 50 had maximum elevating and training speeds of 15°/sec, while in RP 51 and RP 52 the figure was 20°/sec. The two last mentioned also had joystick local control. Weights of mounting including guns and shield, increased to 16.58-17.54 tons (*16.85-17.82t*).

A list of 1948 records RP mountings in the following ships:

RP 50 Mk XIX *Abercrombie, Roberts; Shropshire; Delhi* (ex-*Achilles*), *Birmingham, Belfast, Gambia, Jamaica, Nigeria, Newfoundland, Quebec* (ex-*Uganda*).

RP 51 Mk XIX *Apollo, Manxman;* 'Weapon' class (completed 1947-8), *Petard*, some 'Hunts', later sloops, some 'Bay' class frigates.

RP 52 Mk XIX *Cumberland, Australia, Devonshire, Sussex, Norfolk; Hobart, Glasgow, Sheffield, Liverpool, Bermuda, Kenya, Mauritius, Ceylon, Ontario, Swiftsure, Superb.*

4in twin Mk XIX mounting.

1 Recuperator
2 Trunnion rollers
3 Range dial
4 Deflection dial
5 Depression stop
6 Sight arc
7 Elevating arc
8 Geared sight
9 Elevating wormwheel
10 Elevating receiver
11 Elevating handle
12 Training wormwheel
13 Safety depression control gear
14 Clip
15 Upper roller path
16 Lower roller path
17 Live roller ring
18 Training pinion
19 Vertical rollers
20 Hydraulic buffer
21 Fuze setting machine
22 PE coil cylinder
23 Balance weight
24 SA & QF gear
25 BM lever
26 Interceptor
27 Breechworker's firing lever
28 Recoil cylinder compensating tank
29 Training drive

John Lambert

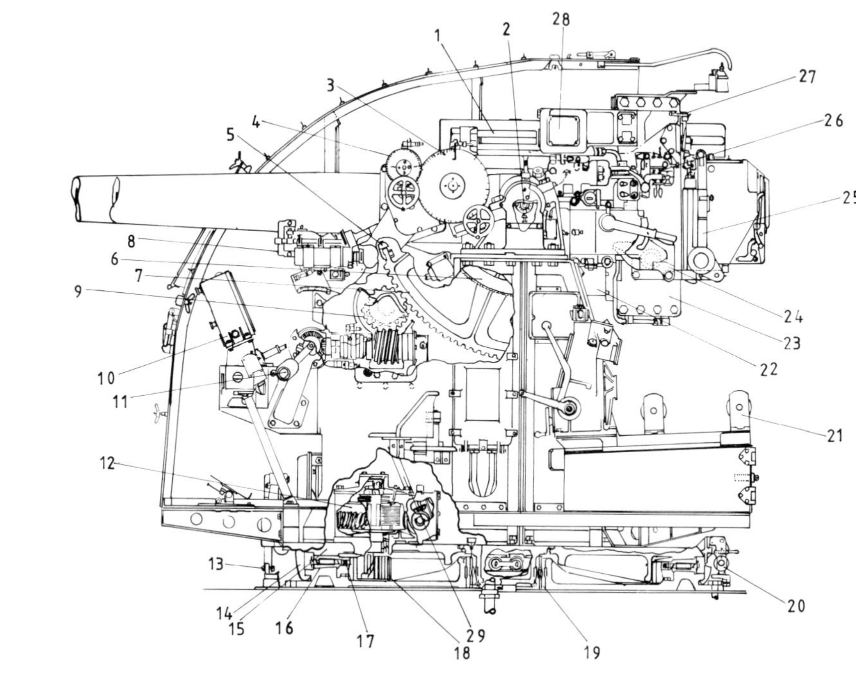

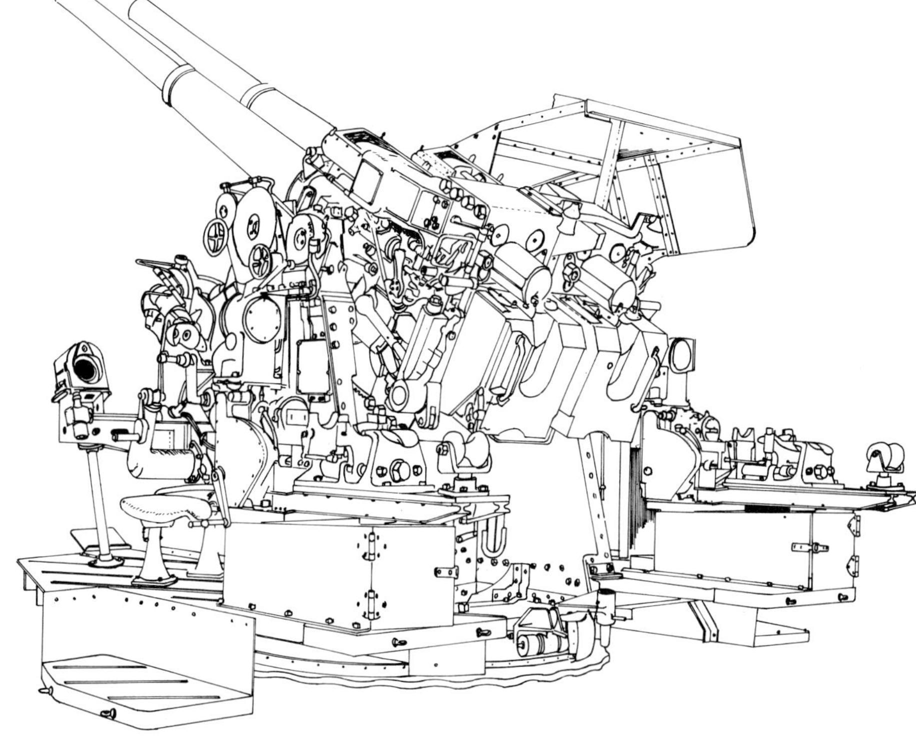

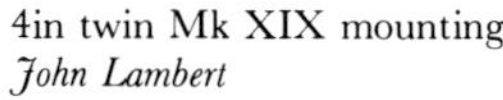
4in twin Mk XIX mounting.
John Lambert

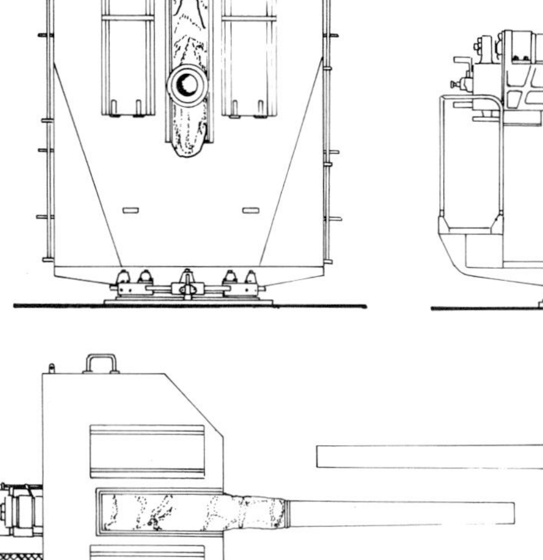

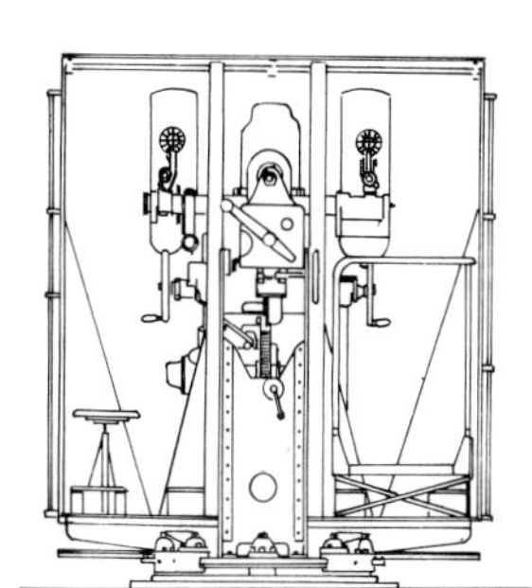

4in QF Mk XIX gun in CP Mk XXIII mounting.
John Lambert

Introduced in the *Arethusa* (completed in August 1914) on 20° PX mountings, this gun was still the standard single 4in AA, and a considerable number of new guns were made during the war. On HA Mk III, III*, III**, IV mountings it was in *Repulse, Eagle, Hermes, Canberra, York* and *Sydney* up to their loss and, until replaced by Mk XVI guns, in *Devonshire, Shropshire, Sussex, Exeter, Achilles, Arethusa, Galatea*. It was in many other ships including AA cruisers *Coventry, Curlew*, four 'O' and all 'P' class destroyers (until *Petard* rearmed) as main armament, 'Loch' class frigates, *Algerine* class minesweepers. In nearly all the ships of these last three classes mountings were Mk III**. LA guns on CPII mountings were carried by some of the old 'V' and 'W' destroyers and by a few sloops, patrol vessels and river gunboats. For a time, there was also one in *Bonaventure, Charybdis, Dido, Phoebe* and *Scylla* as a star-shell gun.

Mk V was a wire-wound gun with tapered inner A tube, A tube, taper wound wire, full-length jacket and breech ring. There was a horizontal sliding breech block with SA opening. Mk V* had no inner A tube, and the prefix 'A' to both these Marks indicated a strengthened bolt actuating. Experiments were made with a thin Italian Pittoni loose liner, but in Mk V**, which became standard for repaired guns in 1937, a heavy autofretted loose liner was used with a muzzle bush on the jacket and a removable breech ring. Mk V*** differed in detail and had a sealing ring instead of the muzzle bush. The liner could also be changed on board in Mk V***, as could the loose barrel in the final Mk VC, which otherwise had a jacket to 63.5in (*1612.9mm*) from the muzzle, removable breech ring and sealing collar. The BM weighed 168-176lb (*76-80kg*), the loose liner in Mk V**, V*** 1.238 tons (*1258kg*), which was heavier than the loose barrel in Mk VC at 1.214 tons (*1233kg*).

Altogether 283 Mk VC guns and 637 of earlier patterns were made. The earlier guns include 83 transferred from the Army, but not those retained for AA or coast defence use in the First World War. Of the 637, there were still 601 extant in 1939.

Fixed ammunition was fired by HA guns and by LA in most ships other than 'V' and 'W' destroyers, which fired separate ammunition. The largest fixed round weighed 56lb (*25.4kg*) and was 44.375in (*1127mm*) long. The separate cartridge with SC charge was 22.5lb (*10.2kg*) and 27.914in (*709mm*). Flashless charges were later carried if authorised, and SAP, HE, shrapnel and star shells were provided. 'O' and 'P' class destroyers, 'Loch' frigates and *Algerine* minesweepers carried the same variety of ammunition as escort ships with Mk XVI guns. 4.38/6 crh HE shells for AA guns considerably improved performance.

The various single hand-worked HA mountings differed in fuze setting, sights and

4in (102mm) QF Mark V

Gun Data

Bore	4in	101.6mm	
Weight incl BM	2.171 tons	2206kg	
Length oa	187.8in	4770.1mm	46.95cal
Length bore	180in	4572mm	45.0cal
Length chamber	26.975in	685.17mm	
Volume chamber	447in^3	7.325dm^3	
Length rifling	149.725in	3803.02mm	
Grooves	(32) 0.037in deep × 0.27	0.94 × 6.86mm	
Lands	0.1227in	3.117mm	
Twist	Uniform 1 in 30		
Weight projectile	31lb	14.06kg	
Propellant charge	6.078lb SC 061 or 7.313lb NF/S 116-036	2.757kg, 3.317kg	
Muzzle velocity	2387f/s	728m/s	
Working pressure	18.5 tons/in^2	2910kg/cm^2	
Approx life	850 EFC, with NF/S 3200		
Max range	16,430yd/44°	15,020m/44°	
Ceiling	31,000ft/80°	9450m/80°	

Above figures are for QF Mk VC guns firing fixed AA ammunition with 4.38/6 crh shells. Mark V and V* guns weighed 2.138 tons (*2172kg*), while V** and V*** guns which weighed 2.155 tons (*2190kg*), were 0.3in (*7.62mm*) shorter in overall, bore and rifling length.

Differences with separate ammunition

Length chamber	28.105in	711.58mm
Volume chamber	464in^3	7.604dm^3
Propellant charge	7.914lb SC 103 or 9.375lb NF/S 164-048	3.59kg, 4.252kg
Muzzle velocity	2642f/s	805m/s
Approx life	600 EFC, with NF/S 2400	
Max range	13840yd/30°	12660m/30°

Separate ammunition not used in HA guns. With fixed LA ammunition the chamber dimensions were as for HA guns and the propellant charge was 8.055lb SC 103 (*3.654kg*) or 9.563lb (*4.338kg*) NF/S 164-048. The above range is for 3 crh shells.

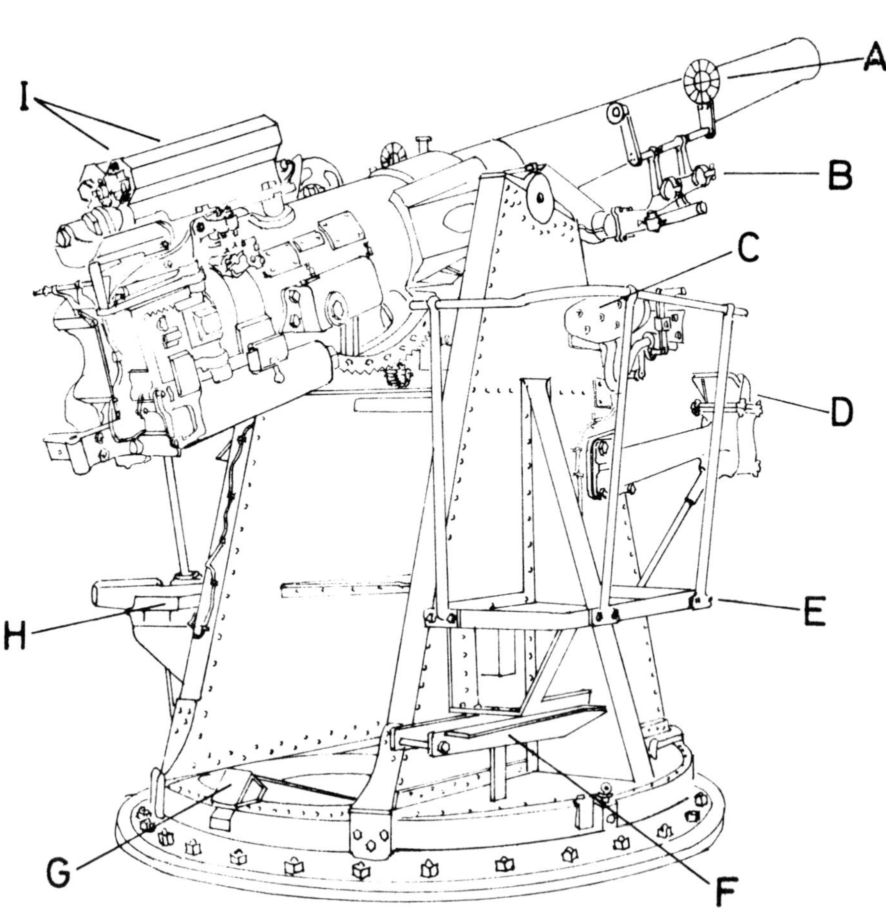

4in QF Mk V in HA Mk III mounting.

A Trainer's open sight
B Trainer's telescope clamps
C Trainer's body rest
D Training receiver
E Trainer's platform
F Support for breech worker's platform
G Spent cartridge deflector
H Sight setter's platform
I Hydro-pneumatic recuperator

Peter Hodges

run-out, the latter being by springs in Mk III** and by compressed air in Mk III, III*, IV. Elevation was +80° to -5°, recoil 15in (*38cm*) and firing cycle 3-4 seconds. Weights including gun were 6.696-7.05 tons (*6.803-7.163t*). Shields if fitted, added 1.638-2.0 tons (*1664-2032kg*). The CP II mounting allowed +30° to -10° elevation and with gun and spray shield weighed 5.308 tons (*5.393t*).

4in (102mm) QF Mark IV

Gun Data

Bore	4in	101.6mm	
Weight incl BM	1.225 tons	1245kg	
Length oa	166.6in	4231.6mm	41.65cal
Length bore	160in	4064mm	40.0cal
Length chamber	19.25/19.38in	488.95/492.25mm	
Volume chamber	287in^3	4.70dm^3	
Weight projectile	31lb	14.06kg	
Propellant charge	5.133/5.188lb SC 103	2.328/2.353kg	
	or 5.563lb NF 059		
	or 6.00lb NF 070	2.523kg, 2.722kg	
Muzzle velocity	2177f/s	664m/s	
Max range	11.580yd/30°	10,590m/30°	

The above range is for 3 crh shells.

This gun was introduced in the rearmed scout cruiser *Foresight* in mid 1913. In the Second World War it was carried in PIX or CPIII and IIIc mountings by numerous ships including old destroyers and sloops, some *Bangor* class minesweepers, merchant aircraft carriers, special service vessels (decoy ships), ABVs, trawlers and DEMS.

The Mk IV was a part wire-wound gun with horizontal sliding breech block and SA opening. Of the 1141 guns made, 979 remained in 1939. A number were mounted in emergency coast and land defences during the war.

Separate ammunition was generally used, fixed having been provided for submarines in which the gun was no longer mounted. The cartridge case weighed 16.25lb (*7.37kg*) with SC charge and was 19.839in (*503.9mm*) long. Flashless charges were later available and SAP, HE, shrapnel and star shells carried. Late in the war escort ships had the same variety of projectiles as those with other marks of 4in QF.

PIX mountings allowed +20° to -10° elevation and CPIII and IIIc +30° to -10°. Respective weights including gun and shield were 3.015, 4.020 and 3.970 tons (*3063, 4085, 4034kg*). CPIIIc differed only in that the gun was moved back in the cradle and the latter moved forward to improve balance.

4in (102mm) QF Mark XIX

Gun Data

Bore	4in	101.6mm	
Weight incl BM	1.288 tons	1309kg	
Length oa	166.6in	4231.6mm	41.65cal
Length bore	161.84in	4110.74mm	40.46cal
Length chamber	17.51in	444.75mm	
Volume chamber	265.9in^3	4.357dm^3	
Length rifling	139.88in	3552.95mm	
Grooves	(32) 0.037in deep × 0.27	0.94 × 6.86mm	
Lands	0.1227in	3.117mm	
Twist	Uniform 1 in 30		
Weight projectile	35lb	15.88kg	
Propellant charge	1.875lb SC048 or	0.850kg, 1.013kg	
	2.234lb NF042		
Muzzle velocity	1300f/s	396m/s	
Working pressure	8.25 tons/in^2	1300kg/cm^2	
Approx life	2000 EFC, with NF 8000		
Max range	9700yd/40°	8870m/40°	

This low velocity gun, intended primarily for use against surfaced submarines, was carried in CP Mk XXIII and XXIII* mountings by many 'River' class frigates, 'Castle' class and some 'Flower' class corvettes, some *Bathurst* class minesweepers, 'Military' class trawlers, various auxiliary warships, RFA oilers and, in XXIII** mountings, by many DEMS. It was also mounted as a star shell gun in the 'Battle' class destroyers *Armada, Barfleur, Camperdown, Hogue, Trafalgar*. In all 2023 guns were made including 1006 in Canada and 219 in Australia.

The gun was of simple construction with monobloc barrel and shrunk-on breech ring. The horizontal sliding block BM weighed 85lb (*38.6kg*). Fixed ammunition was fired, the heaviest round weighing 50.06lb (*22.71kg*) with a length of 35.875in (*911.2mm*). Flashless

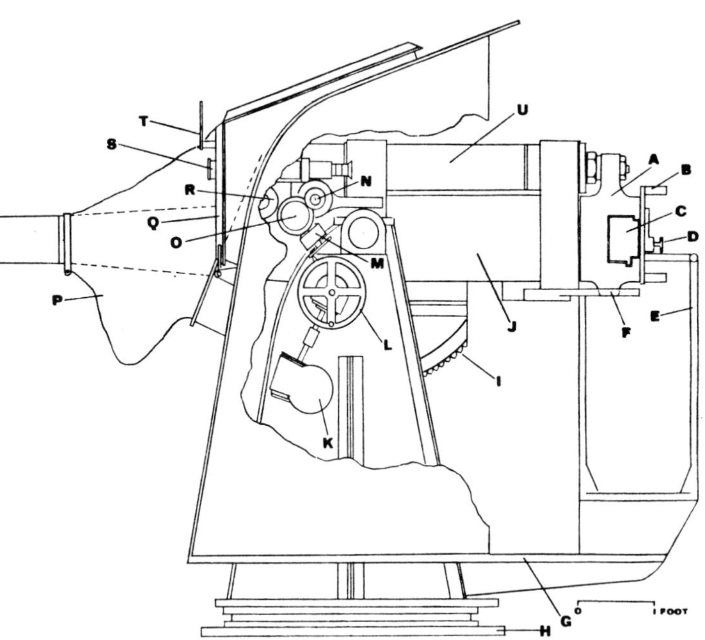

4in QF Mk XIX in CP Mk XXIII mounting.

A Breech ring
B Breech operating lever
C Breech block
D Striker re-cocking handle
E Breech-worker's platform guard rail
F Guide for gun in recoil
G Mounting platform
H Mounting base
I Elevating arc
J Gun cradle
K Elevation wormwheel gearbox
L Layer's handwheel
M Range-setting drive
N Deflection-setting handwheel
O Deflection dial
P Canvas blast bag
Q Sighting port
R Range dial
S Layer's telescope
T Open barrage sight
U Combined run-out spring and recoil buffer cover

Peter Hodges

charges were later issued as ordered to ships other than DEMS, and HE and shrapnel shells provided with, in escort ships, 10 rounds per gun of HE with RDX/TNT filling and 230 P fuze, star shells and 12 to 18 Shark per ship. Battle class destroyers carried 160 star shells only. The hand-worked mountings allowed +60° to -10° elevation, differing in details of shield and sights. Recoil was 16.5in (*42cm*), run-out by springs and weight with gun and shield 4.512-5.105 tons (*4584-5187kg*). The firing cycle is given as 4 sec.

4in (102mm) QF Marks XII, XXII

Gun Data

Bore	4in	101.6mm	
Weight incl BM	1.297 tons	1318kg	
Length oa	165.4in	4201.2mm	41.35cal
Length bore	160in	4064mm	40.0cal
Length chamber	18.74in	476mm	
Volume chamber	288in^3	4.72dm^3	
Length rifling	138.175in	3509.65mm	
Grooves	(32) 0.037in deep × 0.27	0.94 × 6.86mm	
Lands	0.1227in	3.117mm	
Twist	Uniform 1 in 25		
Weight projectile	35lb	15.88kg	
Propellant charge	4.578lb NF059	2.077kg	
Muzzle velocity	1873f/s	571m/s	
Working pressure	16 tons/in^2	2520kg/cm^2	
Approx life	8000EFC		
Max range	10,450yd/20°	9560m/20°	

Above data is for Mk XXII; Mk XII and Mk XII* guns measured 166.6in (*4231.6mm*) oa, had uniform 1 in 30 rifling and weighed respectively 1.313 tons (*1334kg*) and 1.331 tons (*1352kg*). With 31lb (*14.06kg*) shell and 5.188lb (*2.353kg*) SC 103 charge, MV was 2160f/s (*658m/s*), life 2000 EFC and range 11490yd/20° (*10510m*) for 4.38/6 crh HE.

Mks XII, XII* and XXII formed an interchangeable series of guns, based on Mk IV but specially adapted for SI mountings in submarines. The first Mk XII was issued to *L33* in October 1919 and in the Second World War these Marks were mounted in the three surviving 'L' class and in the 'O', 'P', 'R', *Thames, Porpoise*, 'T' and later 'S' classes, as well as the earlier boats of the 'A' class completed post-war. Most wartime guns were Mk XII or XII*, Mk XXII being only in *Talent* (ex-*Tasman*), *Tapir, Tarn, Templar, Trusty, Sanguine* and *Spearhead* of boats completed during the war.

Mk XII had a tapered inner A tube, A tube, wire for about half the length, jacket for rather over half-length, and breech ring, while Mks XII* and XXII had a monobloc barrel and breech ring with a thin fabricated sleeve 63.3in (*1607.8mm*) long with two guides, shrunk to the barrel. Mk XXII had a muzzle swell and rectangular breech ring, while XII* had no muzzle swell and the breech ring was shaped. All had horizontal sliding block BM with no SA gear. The weights were: XII, 224lb (*101.6kg*); XII*, 234lb (*106.1kg*); XXII, of simplified design, 109lb (*49.4kg*).

Totals of 60 Mk XII of which 58 were extant in 1939, 52 Mk XII* and 46 Mk XXII were made.

Fixed ammunition was fired, rounds with the newer heavy shell issued in late 1944-45 weighing up to 52.3lb (*23.7kg*) with a maximum length of 36.75in (*933.5mm*) while figures for the lighter type were 47.5lb (*21.5kg*) and 35.874in (*911.2mm*). Towards the end of the war flashless charges were used with SAP, HE, 10 rounds of HE with RDX/TNT filling and 230 P fuze, and 10 star shell. All heavy HE was to have RDX/TNT filling.

The SI hand-worked mounting allowed +20° to -3° elevation and had 36in (*91.4cm*) recoil. Run-out was by compressed air. The firing cycle was about 4.6 seconds and weight including gun and shield up to 5.016 tons (*5096kg*).

The Mk XXIII gun of 33.04 calibre bore in the 30° SII mounting was not issued to the 'A' class until August 1946.

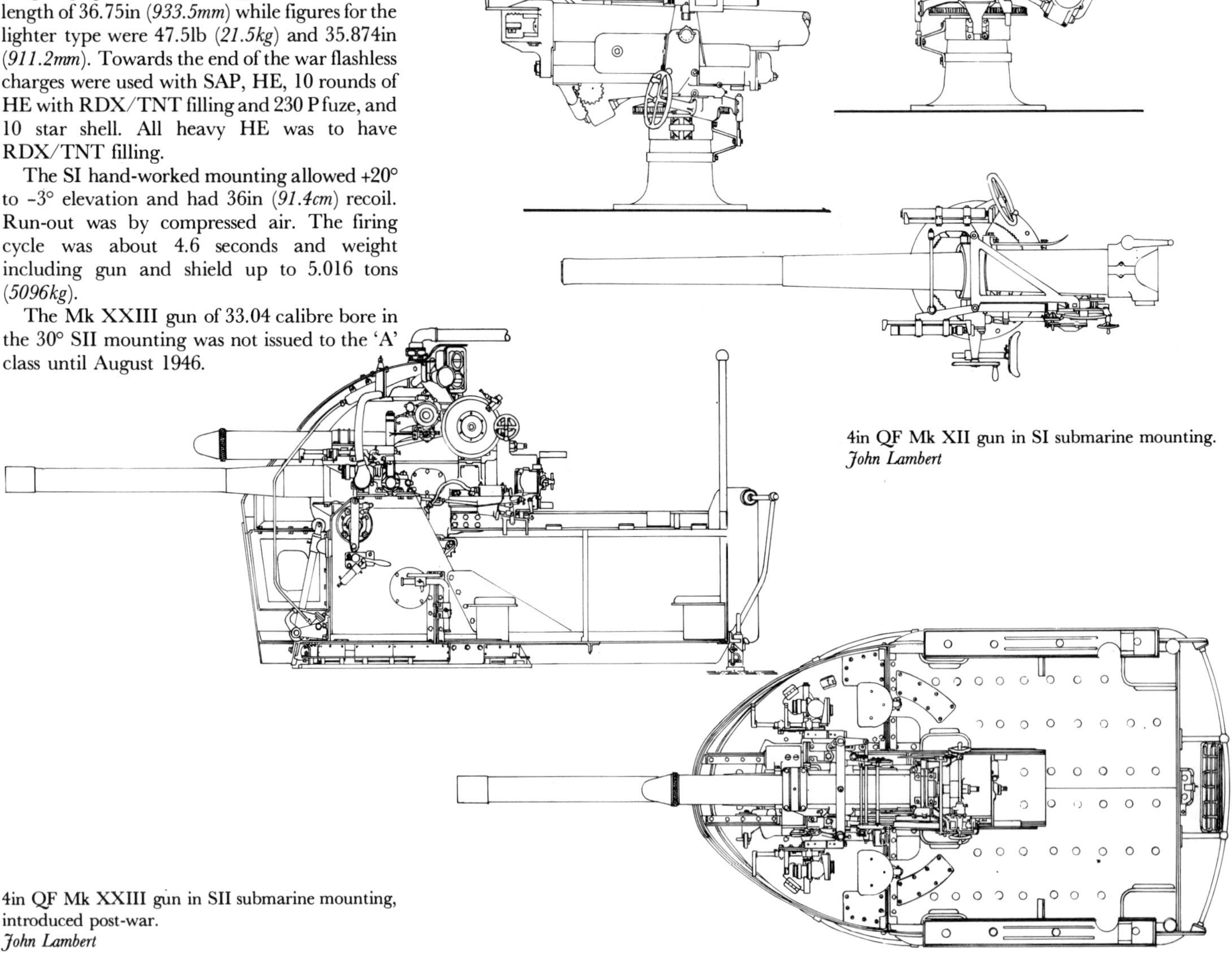

4in QF Mk XII gun in SI submarine mounting.
John Lambert

4in QF Mk XXIII gun in SII submarine mounting, introduced post-war.
John Lambert

This was the Vickers Mk M* gun mounted only in *P614* and *P615* originally for Turkey. It was generally similar to Mk XII* but differed as given below, and also in a lighter BM of 132lb (*60kg*). The mounting allowed +30° to -10° elevation

4in (102mm) QF Mark XX

Weight incl BM	1.246 tons	1266kg
Length chamber	20.73in	526.54mm
Volume chamber	295in^3	4.834dm^3
Length rifling	136.055in	3455.80mm
Weight projectile	31lb	14.06kg
Propellant charge	6.563lb NF/S 164-048	2.977kg
Muzzle velocity	2219f/s	676m/s
Max range	13970yd/30°	12770m/30°

25pdr (88mm) QF Mark II and **17pdr** (76mm) QF Mark III

These army type guns were carried in 17pdr/25pdr Mks I and II (naval) mountings by LCG(M) landing craft. From the gun records 25pdrs were mounted in 49 and 17pdrs in 15 of these craft.

The 25pdr Mk II was the well known field gun of 3.45in (*87.6mm*) bore with loose barrel, jacket and breech ring, while the 17pdr Mk III was the Mk I anti-tank gun with the semi-automatic gear removed and was of 3in (*76.2mm*) bore with monobloc barrel, breech ring and muzzle brake. Both had vertical sliding breech blocks. The naval Gun Registers list 215 of the 25pdrs and 58 of the 17pdrs.

The 25pdr fired separate ammunition with army HE and smoke shells, and the 17pdr fixed ammunition with army APC or HE, the latter with reduced charge. The APC round weighed 35½lb (*16.1kg*) and was 32.3in (*817.9mm*) long.

The Mk I and II mountings only differed in training gear, and would take either gun with its cradle, recoil and run-out systems. They were hand worked and weighed about 12 tons (*12.2t*). The shield was 2½-1½in (*63.5-38mm*) and elevation limits +30° to -10° for the 25pdr and +15° -10° for the 17pdr.

Brief details of the 25pdr were: weight including BM, 0.446 tons (*453kg*), bore 26.78 cals, MV 1790f/s (*546m/s*) with the heaviest of a series of charges. For the 17pdr figures were: weight including BM, 0.825 tons (*838kg*); bore 55.15 cal; MV 3015f/s (*919m/s*).

It was proposed in 1943 to adapt some 25pdrs to fire fixed ammunition and mount them on 3in (*76mm*) CPV mountings in submarines. This project was abandoned in favour of a new 30.5 calibre 3.5in (*88.9mm*) QF Mk I in CP I mountings, but this was in turn cancelled in 1946.

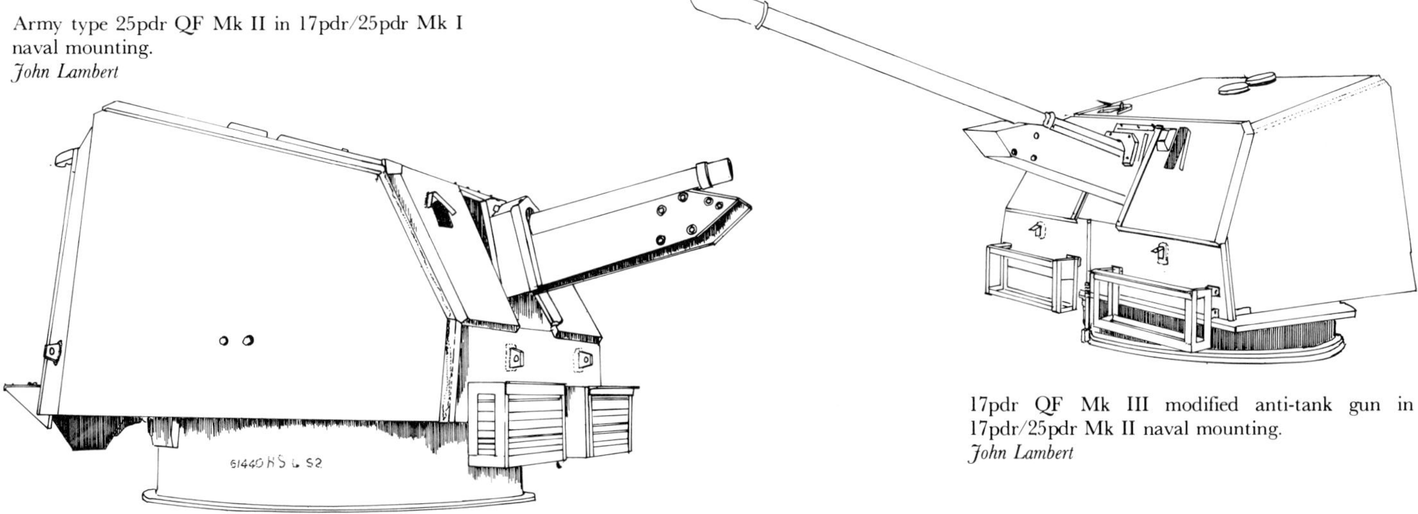

Army type 25pdr QF Mk II in 17pdr/25pdr Mk I naval mounting.
John Lambert

17pdr QF Mk III modified anti-tank gun in 17pdr/25pdr Mk II naval mounting.
John Lambert

3in (76mm)/20cwt (1016kg) QF Marks I, II, III, IV

This series of AA guns was introduced in early 1914 in *Iron Duke*. The mountings for the different Marks of gun were respectively HA Mk II or IIA, Mk III, MK IV, Mk IVA, and in the Second World War they were in a variety of ships including destroyers up to the 'I' class, some minesweepers, auxiliary warships and some DEMS. Mark I guns on CPV mountings were in many 'S' and 'U' class submarines.

The various marks and sub-marks mounted afloat were:

Mk I A tube, full length wire, full-length jacket, breech ring, vertical sliding breech block with SA gear.
Mk I* Rifled 1 in 40 instead of 1 in 30. To be used only in absolute necessity.
Mk IB Loose liner, full-length jacket, removable breech ring.
Mk IC Similar to IB but differs in details of loose liner - converted Mk I guns.
Mark IC* Four guns with muzzle bush instead of loose liner sealing ring.
Mk IE Monobloc barrel, screwed and shrunk breech ring.
Mk SIE As Mk IE but SA fittings removed, balance weight added, chamber slightly modified, some parts stainless steel.

Gun Data

Bore	3in	76.2mm	
Weight incl BM	1.004 tons	1020kg	
Length oa	140.0in	3556mm	46.67cal
Length bore	135.0in	3429mm	45.0cal
Length chamber	15.525in	394.34mm	
Volume chamber	152.9in^3	2.506dm^3	
Length rifling	117.385in	2981.58mm	
Grooves	(20) 0.0375in deep × 0.3137	0.953 × 7.968mm	
Lands	0.1575in	4.001mm	
Twist	Uniform 1 in 30		
Weight projectile	17.5lb	7.94kg	
Propellant charge	2.105lb SC048 or 2.719lb NF052	0.955kg, 1.233kg	
Muzzle velocity	2024f/s	617m/s	
Working pressure	18 tons/in^2	2830kg/cm^2	
Approx life	1440 EFC, with NF 5760		
Max range	12,920yd/40°	11,810m/40°	
Ceiling	*c*25,500ft/90°	7770m/90°	

Above data for Mk IE and SIE. For other marks weights were between the above and 0.982 tons (*998kg*), length oa 139.8-140.25in (*3550.9-3562.4mm*), length bore from the above to 134.8in (*3423.9mm*), and length rifling 117.185-117.585in (*2976.5-2986.66mm*). The most recent performance figures were for 17½lb (*7.94kg*) shell as given above. Shells used during the war were however from 16-17lb (*7.26-7.71kg*) with muzzle velocities up to 2100f/s (*640m/s*).

Mk II As Mk I but different breech ring lugs to suit Mk III mounting. No SA gear.
Mk III Emergency First World War design with parallel screw breech block and two-motion BM.
Mk IV As Mk III but different breech ring, Welin block and Asbury type BM.
Mk IVA Two guns converted to loose liners.

The BM weights were for Mk I and sub-marks 159lb (*72.1kg*), Mk II 116lb (*52.6kg*), Mk III 99lb (*44.9kg*), Mk IV 91lb (*41.3kg*).

The 3in/20cwt was used extensively on land in World War I and there were some transfers between Army and Royal Navy. The totals on naval books, with sub-marks included in the principal mark, are: Mk I 596, Mk II 198, Mk III 44, Mk IV 144, and by September 1939 43, 14, 17 and 33 respectively had been lost or stricken.

All guns fired fixed ammunition with, in the latter part of the war, flashless propellant for submarines. These had HE with some star shell and other ships mostly HE and shrapnel. The heaviest round weighed 28.3lb (*12.8kg*) and was 30.25in (*768.4mm*) long.

The PV mounting weighed 2.3 tons (*2337kg*) with gun, elevated from +40° (+30° in a few) to -10°, had 13in (*33cm*) recoil and a firing cycle of about 4.6 sec. The various HA mountings weighed 2.77-2.83 tons (*2814-2875kg*) with gun and elevated to +90° with depression varying between 0 and 10°. HA Mk III was originally designed as a disappearing mounting for large submarines but the hydro-pneumatic gear for this had been removed. Recoil in all HA mountings was 11in (*28cm*).

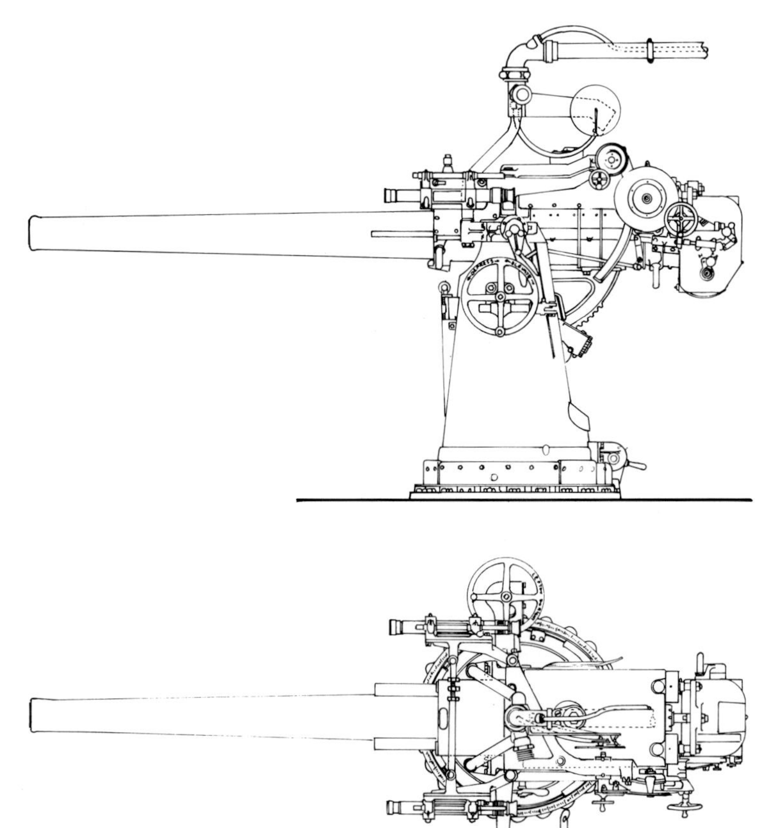

3in/20cwt QF Mk I series gun in CPV mounting.
John Lambert

A Mk II gun on a Mk III mounting.
John Lambert

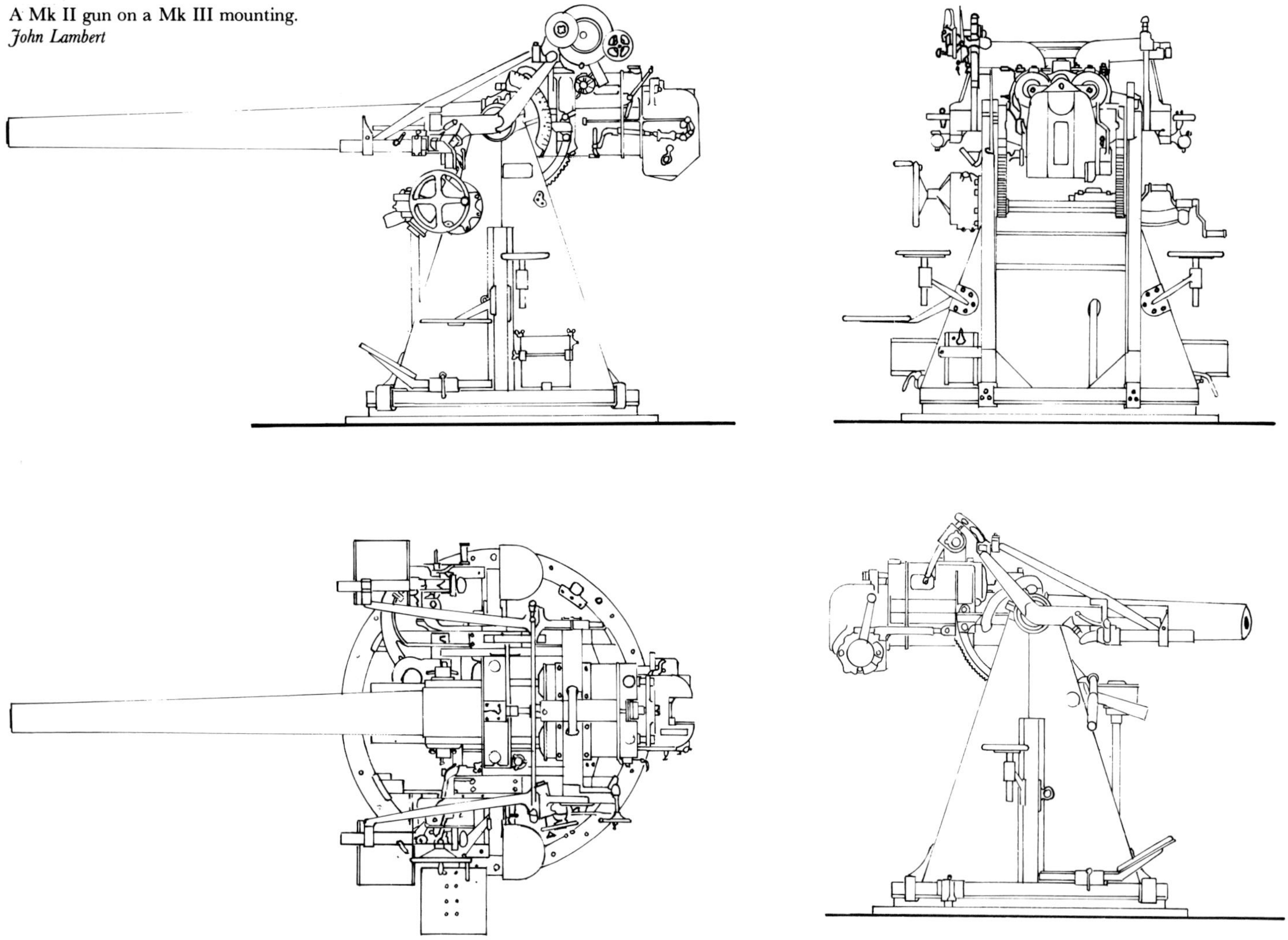

12pdr (76mm)/12cwt (610kg) QF Marks I, II, V

Gun Data

Bore	3in	76.2mm	
Weight incl BM	0.600 tons	610kg	
Length oa	123.6in	3139.4mm	41.2cal
Length bore	120.0in	3048mm	40.0cal
Length chamber	15.477in	393.12mm	
Volume chamber	121.7in^3	1.994dm^3	
Length rifling	103.035in	2617.09mm	
Grooves	(16) 0.0375in deep × 0.365	0.953 × 9.27mm	
Lands	0.224in	5.69mm	
Twist	Uniform 1 in 30		
Weight projectile	12.94lb	5.87kg	
Propellant charge	2.094lb SC061 or 2.75lb NF059	0.950kg, 1.247kg	
Muzzle velocity	2235f/s	681m/s	
Working pressure	16tons/in^2	2520kg/cm^2	
Approx life	2700 EFC, with NF 10800		
Max range	11,750yd/40°	10,740m/40°	
Ceiling	19,000ft/70°	5790m/70°	

Some guns still had increasing twist rifling 1 in 120 to 1 in 28, or straight for 18.0in (*457.2mm*) and then increasing to 1 in 30 at muzzle.

These 3in (*76.2mm*) 40 calibre guns were introduced to the navy in 1894 in the 27-knot destroyers. A variety of mountings were in existence in 1939, principally PI* with HA VIII, some PI and SII and a few PIII and PV, and these were supplemented by many HA/LA IX during the war. These were to be found in some 'U' class submarines, old destroyers, many other warships, RFAs and DEMS. Destroyers, submarines and most other ships had HA/LA IX mountings as available.

Mk I guns were built with an A tube, B tube, jacket and C hoop shrunk over the B tube/jacket join. Mk II was a First World War gun with B tube and jacket combined and a breech ring added or, in some, a breech bush, and the Second World War Mark V had a monobloc barrel and breech ring. All had hand-operated screw BM with the front part of the block conical in Mks I and II and cylindrical in Mk V. In all the weight was 56lb (*25.4kg*). Mks I*, II* had a cartridge retaining catch for HA fire and Mks IA, IIA and V this and extractors to give complete extraction. The prefix A to Mk V indicated lanyard instead of

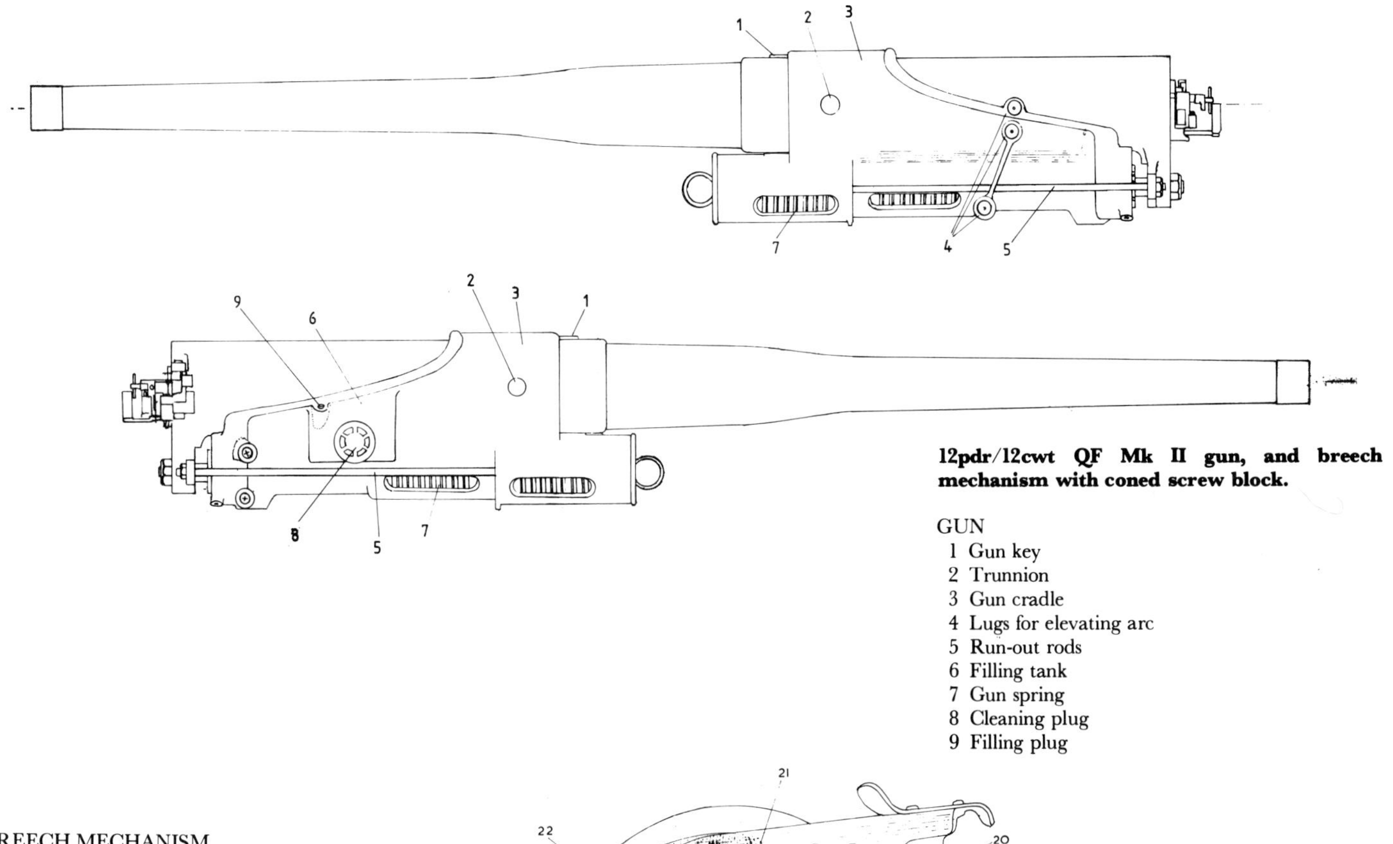

12pdr/12cwt QF Mk II gun, and breech mechanism with coned screw block.

GUN
1 Gun key
2 Trunnion
3 Gun cradle
4 Lugs for elevating arc
5 Run-out rods
6 Filling tank
7 Gun spring
8 Cleaning plug
9 Filling plug

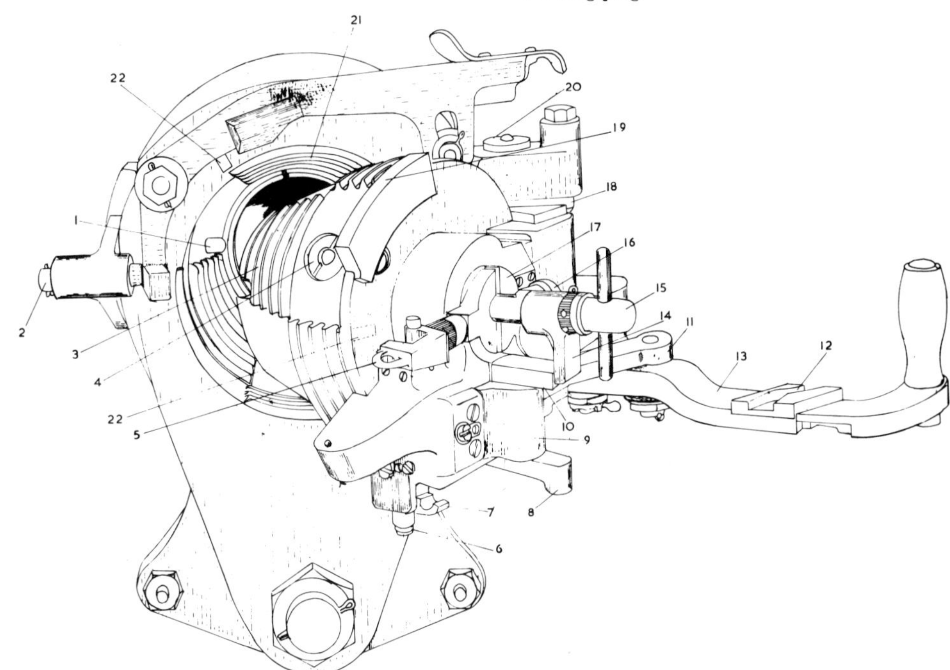

BREECH MECHANISM
1 Catch retaining cartridge
2 Spring and plunger
3 Breech screw
4 Radial fixing screw
5 Trigger head
6 Volute spring
7 Catch retaining BM lever closed
8 Safety stop
9 Carrier
10 Cocking cam
11 Link actuating breech screw
12 Cam groove
13 BM lever
14 Striker head
15 Re-cocking handle
16 Stop bracket
17 Nut retaining striker
18 Catch retaining carrier open
19 Cam
20 Carrier hinge pin
21 Extractor
22 Indicating marks

John Lambert

palm firing.

There was some exchange of guns between the Royal Navy and coast defence, the total of Mks I and II on naval books being 4737, of which 2646 remained in 1939, while 3494 Mk V were built including 1588 in Canada. All fired separate ammunition, the filled case weighing up to 9.5lb (*4.3kg*) with a length of 15.75in (*40cm*). Flashless charges were later available, and shells comprised SAP, CP, HE, shrapnel and star, submarines having HE and star.

All mountings were hand worked and PI* and the original HA VIII were trained by the gunlayer's body weight against a training bar. Recoil was 9.6-10in (*24-25cm*) and firing cycle about 4sec.

HA/LA IX* covered mountings modified for gunlayer firing with Mks IA and IIA guns and IX** those similarly modified with Mk V and AV guns. Two surviving Canadian HA/LA IX** mountings converted from PI* each weigh 2.95 tons (*2997kg*) including gun and 0.425 tons (*432kg*) shield 0.4in (*10mm*) thick.

Gun Mounting Data

Mounting	Weight incl gun (tons)	(kg)	Elevation	Comments
PI*	1.233	1253	+30°-10°	Some converted to HA/LA IX-IX**
HA VIII	2.10	2134	+90°-10°	Most converted to HA VIII* with hand wheel training.
HA/LA IX	2.45	2489	+70°-10°	(See below)

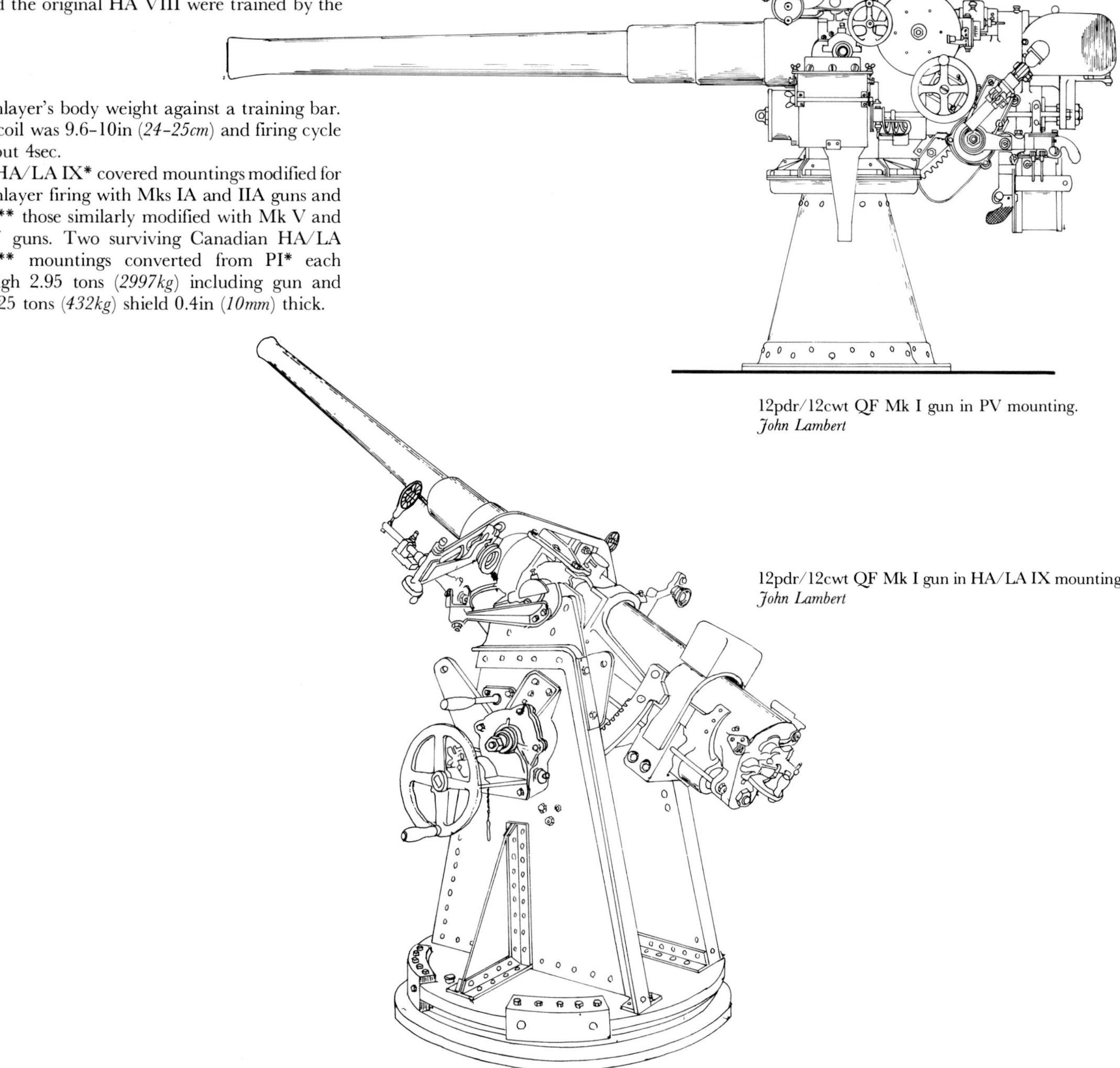

12pdr/12cwt QF Mk I gun in PV mounting.
John Lambert

12pdr/12cwt QF Mk I gun in HA/LA IX mounting.
John Lambert

This was a coast-defence gun intended for use against motor torpedo boats and other small craft. In modified twin Mk I mountings it was later carried by *Campbell*, *Mackay*, *Montrose*, *Whitshed*, *Wivern*, *Worcester*, *Walpole*, and *Windsor* against German motor torpedo boats off the English coast, and a total of 22 guns were transferred to the Royal Navy. The construction comprised an A tube, part length jacket and breech ring with SA vertical sliding breech block. Fixed ammunition was fired with HE shells, half having tracer. The coast-defence mounting was hand worked and allowed +80° to -10° elevation so that firing at low flying aircraft was possible. Recoil was 12in (*30.5cm*), and rate of fire 36 rounds per gun per minute. The naval mounting was distinguished by a more extensive shield.

6pdr (57mm)/10cwt (508kg) QF Mark I

Gun Data

Bore	2.244in	57mm	
Weight incl BM	1060lb	481kg	
Length oa	109.72in	2786.9mm	48.89cal
Length bore	105.47in	2678.9mm	47.0cal
Length chamber	16.5in	419.1mm	
Volume chamber	73.5in^3	1.204dm^3	
Weight projectile	6.28/6.54lb	2.849/2.966kg	
Propellant charge	1.27lb N 045	0.576kg	
Muzzle velocity	2386/2356f/s	727/718m/s	
Max range	11,300yd	10,330m	

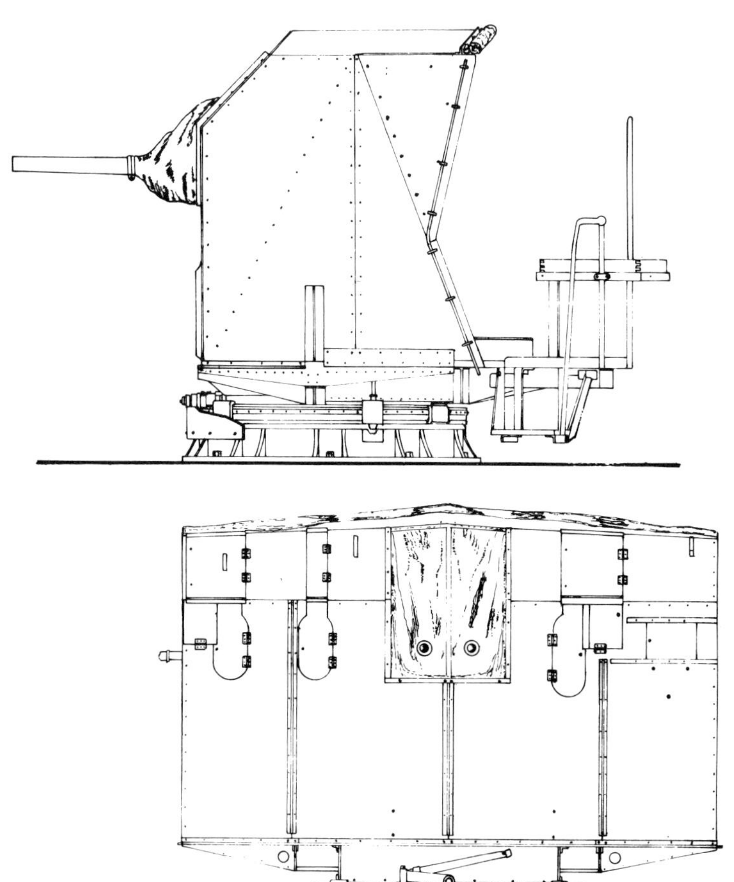

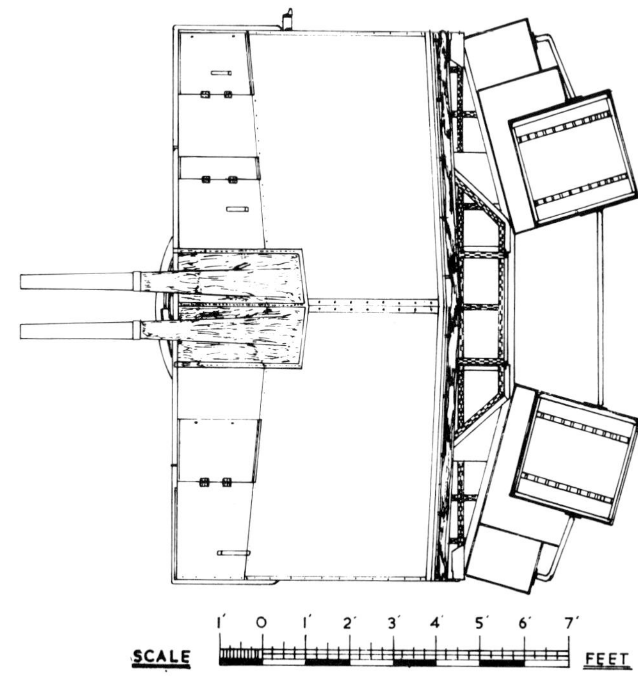

6pdr/10cwt QF Mk I guns in modified twin Mk I mounting
John Lambert

These guns were originally known as 6pdr Hotchkiss and were introduced in 1884 for use against torpedo boats. Many were later used as subcalibre guns and by 1939 there were only 51 mountings left. New non-recoil and Mk VI, VI* and VI** mountings were hurriedly made and, in these, the guns had a new lease of life in MTBs, MLs, 'Flower' class corvettes and many other ships. The 'Flower' class usually had non-recoil mountings and coastal forces the Mk VI series.

The Mk I gun had a barrel and short jacket, which took the trunnions and vertical sliding breech block, with a locking hoop screwed to the front of the jacket. The original Mk I* differed in the recocking lever, but from 1890 all guns were altered to Mk I*, the nomenclature reverting to Mk I. The new Mk I* covered converted subcalibre guns, Mk I*** converted First World War single tube guns, and Mk II former army guns with different fittings. Altogether 3984 guns were in naval lists, but at least 2344 had been lost or stricken by 1939. Nearly all surviving guns were Mk I.

Fixed ammunition was fired, later with a proportion of flashless charges. HE or AP projectiles were provided, the complete round weighing *c*9.5lb (*4.3kg*) with a maximum length of 20.265in (*51.473cm*).

The new non-recoil mountings allowed 38° maximum elevation and Mk VI, VI* and VI** 70°. The last two marks were modified for coastal forces.

6pdr (57mm)/8cwt (406kg) QF Marks I, II

Gun Data

Bore	2.244in	57mm	
Weight incl BM	849lb	385kg	
Length oa	97.63in	2479.8mm	43.51cal
Length bore	89.76in	2279.9mm	40.0cal
Length chamber	10.26in	260.6mm	
Volume chamber	46in^3	0.754dm^3	
Weight projectile	6lb	2.72kg	
Propellant charge	0.55lb HSCT 134-055 or 0.70lb NF029	0.249kg,0.318kg	
Muzzle velocity	1765f/s	538m/s	
Max range	9400yd	8600m	

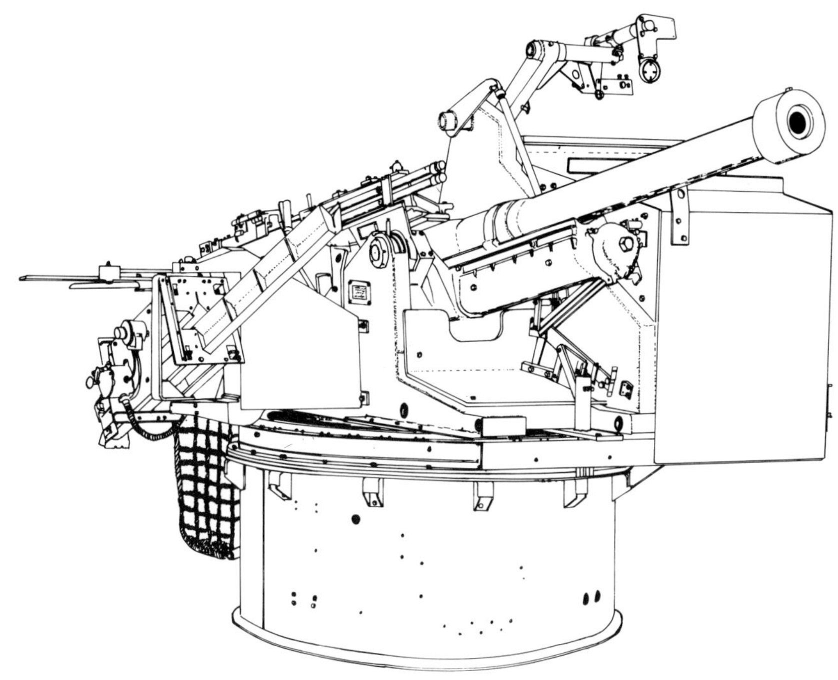

6pdr/7cwt QF Mk IIA modified anti-tank gun in Mk VII mounting.
John Lambert

6pdr (57mm)/7cwt(356kg) QF Marks IIA, V

The 6pdr Mk IIA was a modification of the Mk II anti-tank gun fitted with Molins auto-loading gear and carried by many MTBs in power operated Mark VII mountings. A proposal to mount the Mk II gun without Molins gear on Mk VIII pedestal mountings in submarines reached only the prototype stage, and the Mk V gun in Valentine tank turrets, known as Mk IX mountings, was limited to LCS(L)2 Nos 251-260. Construction was simple with monobloc barrel, removable breech ring and SA vertical sliding breech block, the BM weighing 88lb (*39.9kg*). Altogether 587 Mk IIA, 118 unmodified Mk II and 11 Mk V guns are shown on naval books. MTBs carried HE rounds with flashless propellant, the complete round weighing 12.25lb (*5.56kg*) and being up to 24.85in (*631mm*) long, but LCS(L)s had army APC and HE.

The Mk VII mounting weighed 1.719 tons (*1747kg*) including gun and auto-loader and was hydraulically powered with a maximum training speed of 40°/second. The hydraulic pump was driven by the main or auxiliary engines and was not on the mounting. Elevation was +12° to -10° and recoil 29-30in (*74-76cm*). A total of seven rounds, one in the gun and six in the auto-loader, were in the feed system and when six had been fired the seventh round, then in the gun, could not be fired - a measure to prevent the feed running out of ammunition. The ready-use rack on the mounting held a further twelve rounds. The trigger had to be pressed and released to fire each round and rate of fire was 40 rounds per minute. The Mk IX mounting allowed +17° to -8° elevation and had 2.6-2.4in (*65-60mm*) armour on the turret.

Gun Data

Bore	2.244in	57mm	
Weight incl BM	760lb	345kg	
Length oa	100.95in	2564.1mm	44.99cal
Length bore	96.2in	2443.5mm	42.87cal
Length chamber	16.2in	411.5mm	
Volume chamber	100in^3	1.639dm^3	
Length rifling	78.18in	1985.77mm	
Grooves	(24) 0.02in deep × 0.22	0.51 × 5.59mm	
Lands	0.0737in	1.872mm	
Twist	Uniform 1 in 30		
Weight projectile	6lb	2.72kg	
Propellant charge	1.305lb NF 029	0.592kg	
Muzzle velocity	2150f/s	655m/s	
Working pressure	20.5tons/in^2	3230kg/cm^2	
Approx life	4000 EFC		
Max range	6200yd/12°	5670m/12°	

The above figures are for the Mk IIA gun firing HE shell in Mk VII mountings. As an anti-tank gun, the Mk II achieved a muzzle velocity up to 2845f/s (*867m/s*) with 6.28lb APC, while that of the Mk V, which had the same chamber and a 16in (*406.4mm*) longer barrel, was 2965f/s (*904m/s*) with the same APC. The Mk V weighed 720lb (*327kg*) including BM and the bore was 50.0 calibres.

6pdr (57mm)/6cwt (305kg) QF Marks I, II

First World War tank guns of which 163 were transferred to the Royal Navy and used in minor auxiliary warships. By far the majority, if not all, were Mk II, which was of built-up construction whereas Mk I had a monobloc barrel and breech ring. Both had vertical sliding breech blocks. The actual weight, including BM, was 651lb (*295kg*) for Mk I and 630lb (*286kg*) for Mk II, both having a bore of 23.23cal, and chambers as in the 8cwt (*406kg*) gun. Muzzle velocity was about 1360f/s (*415m/s*). The mounting appears to have been known as 6pdr Mk II in naval lists. Maximum elevation was 20°. These guns must not be confused with the 6 pdr/6 cwt QF Mk III, an experimental automatic high velocity army AA gun of 1941-47.

3½ pdr (47mm) automatic gun

This experimental AA gun was cancelled in 1946 after two prototypes had been made by Vickers-Armstrong. Both were water cooled, the barrel recoiling through the water jacket in one and with it in the other. The automatic mechanism does not appear to have been fully developed. The bore was 75cal and the chamber volume 50.0in^3 (*0.819dm^3*). With a 3.5lb (*1.59kg*) projectile and 1.352lb (*0.613kg*) NF/S 093-031 charge, muzzle velocity was *c*3350f/s (*1021m/s*).

3pdr (47mm) Hotchkiss QF Marks I, II

These guns were introduced in 1886 for mounting where 6pdr (*57mm*) guns were considered to be too heavy. Many were later used as subcalibre and as saluting guns. The last use meant that 550 Mk I and 91 Mk I* mountings survived with 31 HA Mk IV, and these were supplemented by new Mk V and a few Mk VI mountings and conversions of Mk I and I* to 50° elevation. The 3pdr Hotchkiss was carried by MLs and many minor auxiliary warships. HA Mk IV mountings were limited to harbour-defence craft and Mk VI to APVs.

The construction of the Mk I gun was similar to that of the 6pdr (*57mm*) Hotchkiss Mk I, and Mks I* and II had the same meaning as the corresponding Marks in the larger gun. Of a total of 2950 guns on naval books at least 1002 had been lost or stricken by 1939. Nearly all surviving guns were Mk I.

HE rounds were carried, some later being flashless, with in the earlier part of the war also common shell. The complete round weighed *c*6.7lb (*3.04kg*) with a maximum length of 21.357in (*54.247cm*)

The unconverted Mk I and I* mountings allowed 25° maximum elevation, converted mountings 50°, Mk V 70° and Mk VI, which had rubber recoil buffers, 60°.

Gun Data

Bore	1.850in	47mm	
Weight incl BM	528lb	239.5kg	
Length oa	80.635in	2048.1mm	43.59cal
Length bore	74.06in	1881.1mm	40.03cal
Length chamber	13.606in	345.6mm	
Volume chamber	43in^3	0.705dm^3	
Weight projectile	3.30lb	1.497kg	
Propellant charge	0.465lb HSCT 134-055 0.602lb NF 029	0.211kg, 0.273kg	
Muzzle velocity	1884f/s	574m/s	
Max range	Tables to 6500yd/20°41′	5944m/20° 41′	

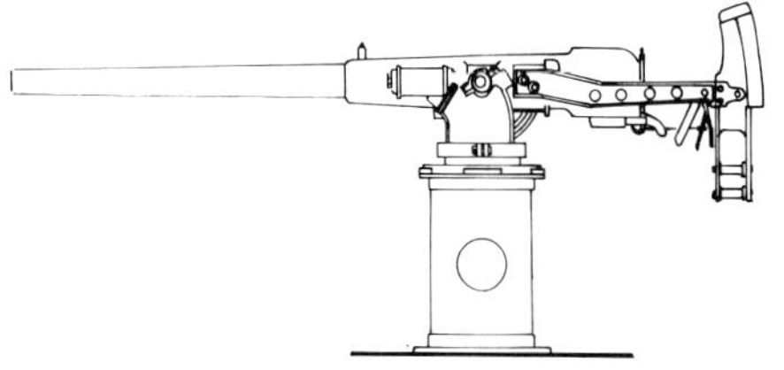

3pdr Hotchkiss in Mk I mounting.
John Lambert

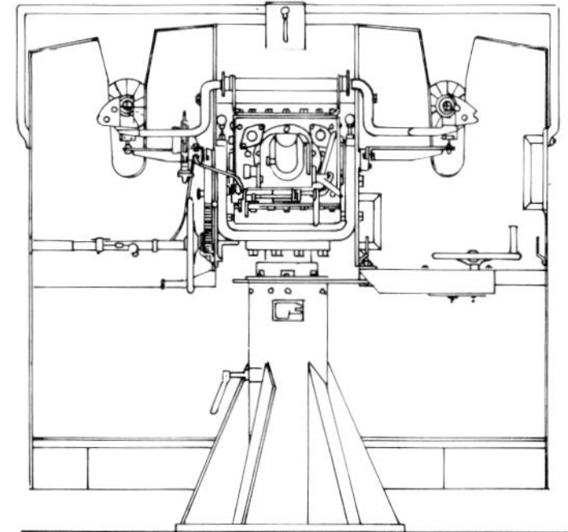

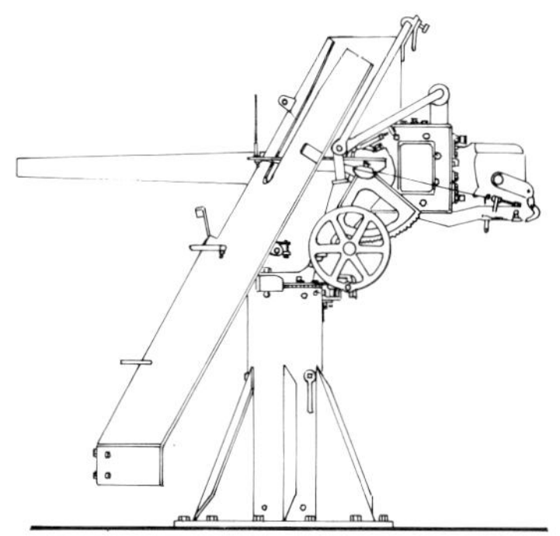

3pdr Hotchkiss in Mk V mounting.
John Lambert

3pdr Hotchkiss in Mk VI* mounting.
John Lambert

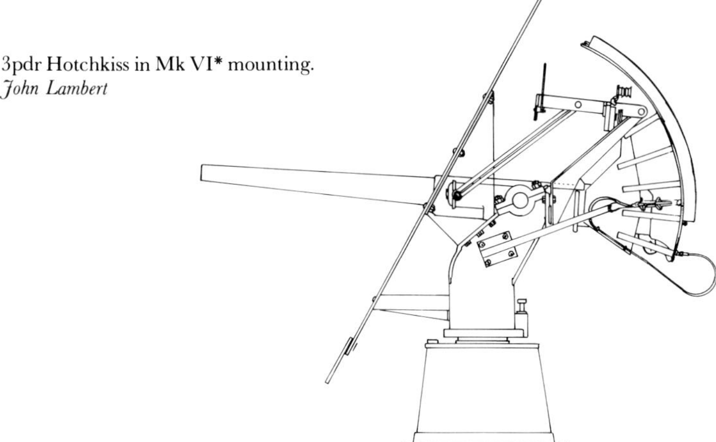

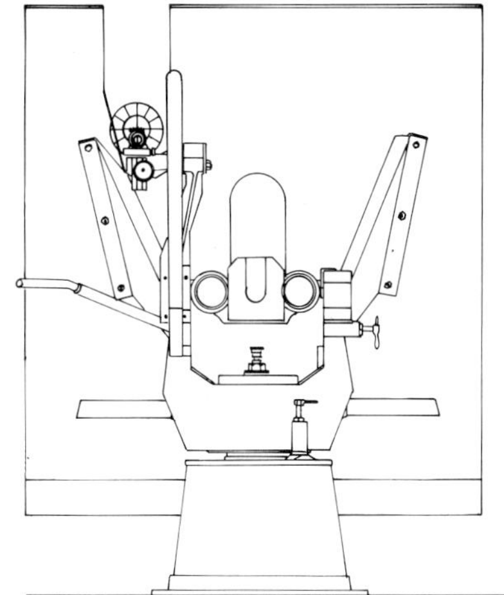

AUTOMATIC GUNS

40mm (1.575in) Bofors, various QF Marks

Gun Data

Bore	1.575in	40mm	
Weight of gun	1120–1163lb	508–528kg	
Weight of barrel	227–230lb	103–104kg	
Length gun	145.3–145.5in	3690.6–3695.7mm	
Length bore	88.578in	2249.88mm	56.25cal
Length chamber	10.335in	262.51mm	
Volume chamber	28.661in^3	0.4697dm^3	
Length rifling	75.85in	1926.6mm	
Grooves	(16) 0.0236in deep x 0.22	0.60 x 5.59mm	
Lands	0.0892in	2.66mm	
Twist	Increasing 1 in 45 to 1 in 30		
Weight projectile	1.97lb	0.894kg	
Propellant charge	0.719lb FNH/PO22	0.326kg	
Muzzle velocity	2890f/s	881m/s	
Working pressure	19.68 tons/in^2	3100kg/cm^2	
Approx life	10,000 EFC		
Max range	10,750yd/2800f/s	9830mm/853m/s	
Ceiling	23,500ft/2800f/s	7160mm/853m/s	

Serious British interest in these, the best of Second World War light AA guns, was first shown by the Army in 1933 and was followed by an order for 100 guns from Bofors in 1937, prior to manufacture being established in England. These land service guns were air cooled on single mountings and, apart from rescued guns temporarily carried in the evacuation of Norway, are first recorded in the Royal Navy in 1941, the ships being *Prince of Wales, Nelson, Manchester* and *Erebus*. The army mountings were known in the Navy as LS Mk III and records for June 1942 give a total of 314, of which 301 were in DEMS. By the end of the war these figures, which are undoubtedly erroneous to some extent, had risen to 1392 with 568 in DEMS. They were to be found in every type of warship, the largest total being 14 in the escort carrier *Trouncer* with 12 in *Indomitable* and *Ocean* and 11 in *Colossus* and *Vengeance*.

Of mountings modified to some extent for naval use, there were 500 Mk III CN at the end of the war, 291 being in DEMS. There were very few in major warships, but five each are recorded for *Bulolo* and *Maidstone*. Mk III* with gyro sights is not recorded afloat at the end of the war, and RPLS Mk III and Toadstool are also not listed. The first production order for Mk VII mountings, which were more fully adapted for naval service, is dated 29 May 1945, though one experimental mounting had been ordered on 17 March. Boffin, which was a twin power-worked Oerlikon Mk V or VC mounting adapted to take a single Bofors, was in many important ships by the end of the war, a list of July 1945 giving 161 afloat in fleet and light fleet aircraft carriers, cruisers, destroyers and a few other ships. The greatest number was 12 in *Glory* with 10 in *Colossus, Vengeance* and *Venerable*. Lastly there were some US Army guns in single US Mk 3 mountings, end-of-war figures giving a total of 141 of which those afloat were mostly in LSTs.

However effective the foregoing were, close-range naval AA required a water-cooled gun in at least a twin mounting as the major weapon. This role was generally filled by the 2pdr (*40mm*) pom-pom in four and eight barrel mountings but, if control and mountings were of equal efficiency, the Bofors was reckoned to be twice as effective as the pom-pom against torpedo planes, though not much better against very close targets such as kamikazes.

The first British water cooled Bofors, the Mk IV gun in the twin Mk IV Hazemeyer triaxal mounting, had its origins with the arrival in Britain of the Dutch minelayer *Willem van der Zaan* in 1940. It may be noted that Hazemeyer were a Dutch subsidiary of Siemens Halske. The British versions were mounted in many of the newer destroyers, *Hobart, Apollo, Ariadne*, the AA cruisers *Colombo* and *Caledon* and some sloops, the first issue of guns being to *Whimbrel* in November 1942.

The much simpler twin biaxial RP 50 Mk V mounting taking the Mk XI gun was introduced in 1945, the first issue of guns being to the 'Hunt' class *Meynell* on 3 February. It was also in a few sloops, the 'Bay' class frigates and some LSTs. The greatest number of either mounting was four in the first 'Battle' destroyers.

The six-barrel biaxial RP 50 Mk VI

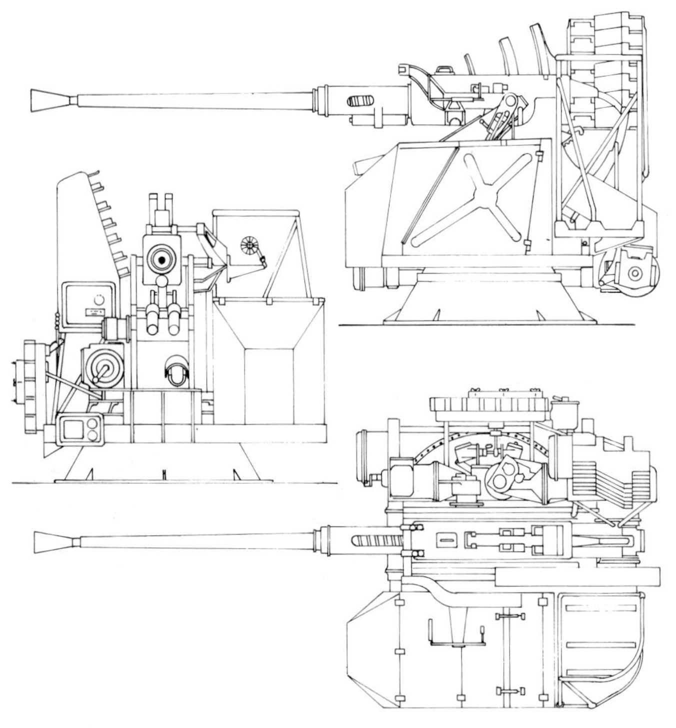

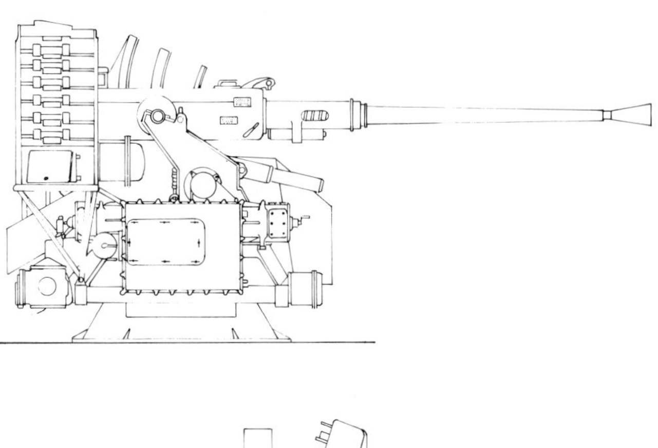

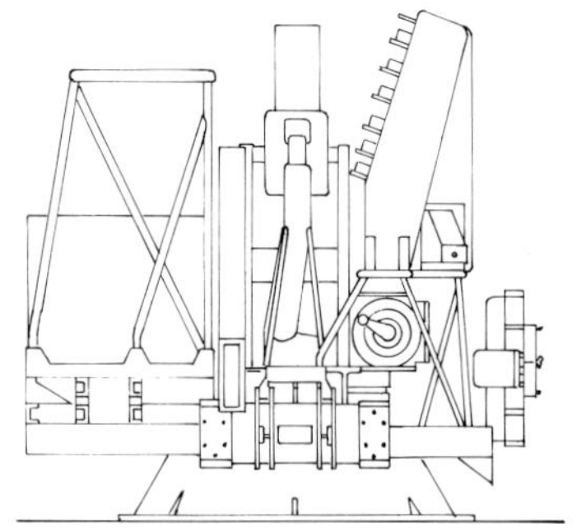

40mm Bofors NI in Mk IX mounting, which entered service post war
John Lambert

40mm Bofors on Mk V Boffin mounting.

1 Ammunition stowage
2 Shot guides
3 Sight link
4 Layer's cab
5 Fixed structure
6 Loader's platform
7 Gyro sight Mk XIV and open sight

Ross Watton

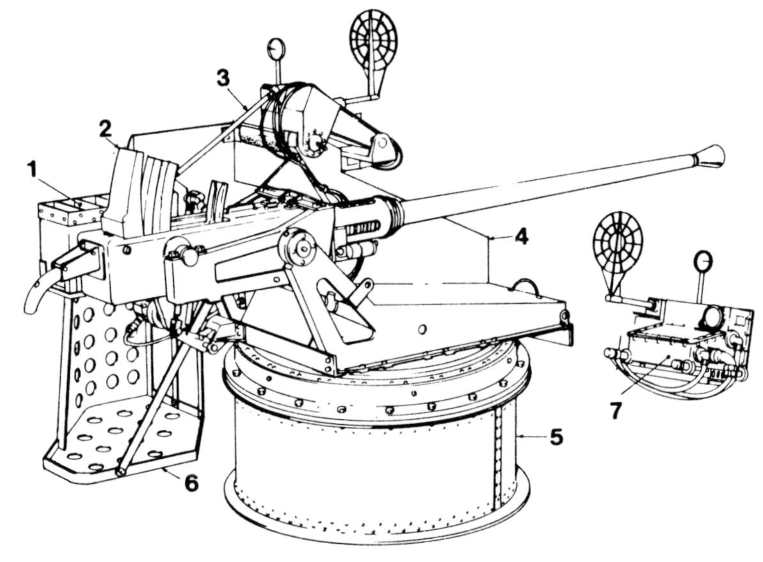

40mm Bofors Mk IV guns in twin triaxial Hazemeyer Mk IV mounting.
John Lambert

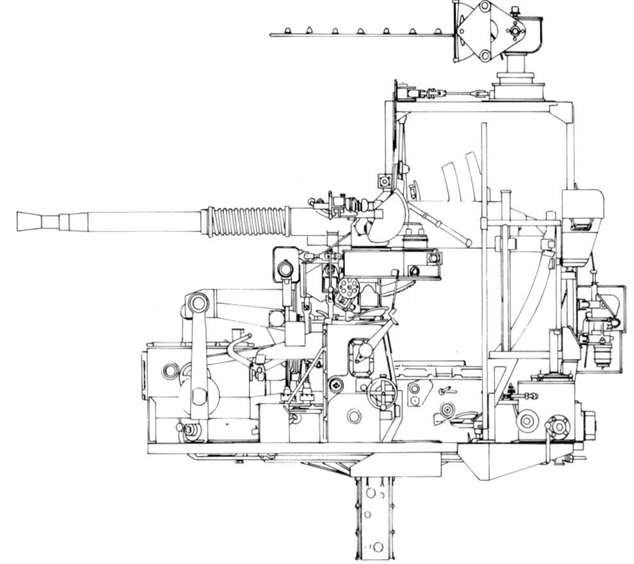

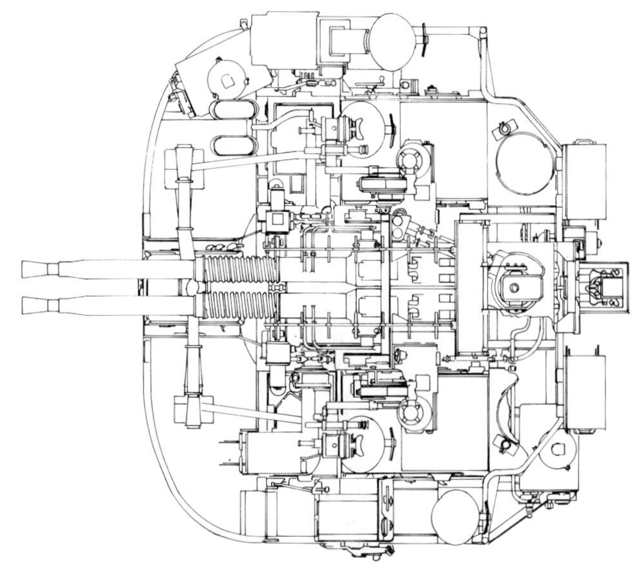

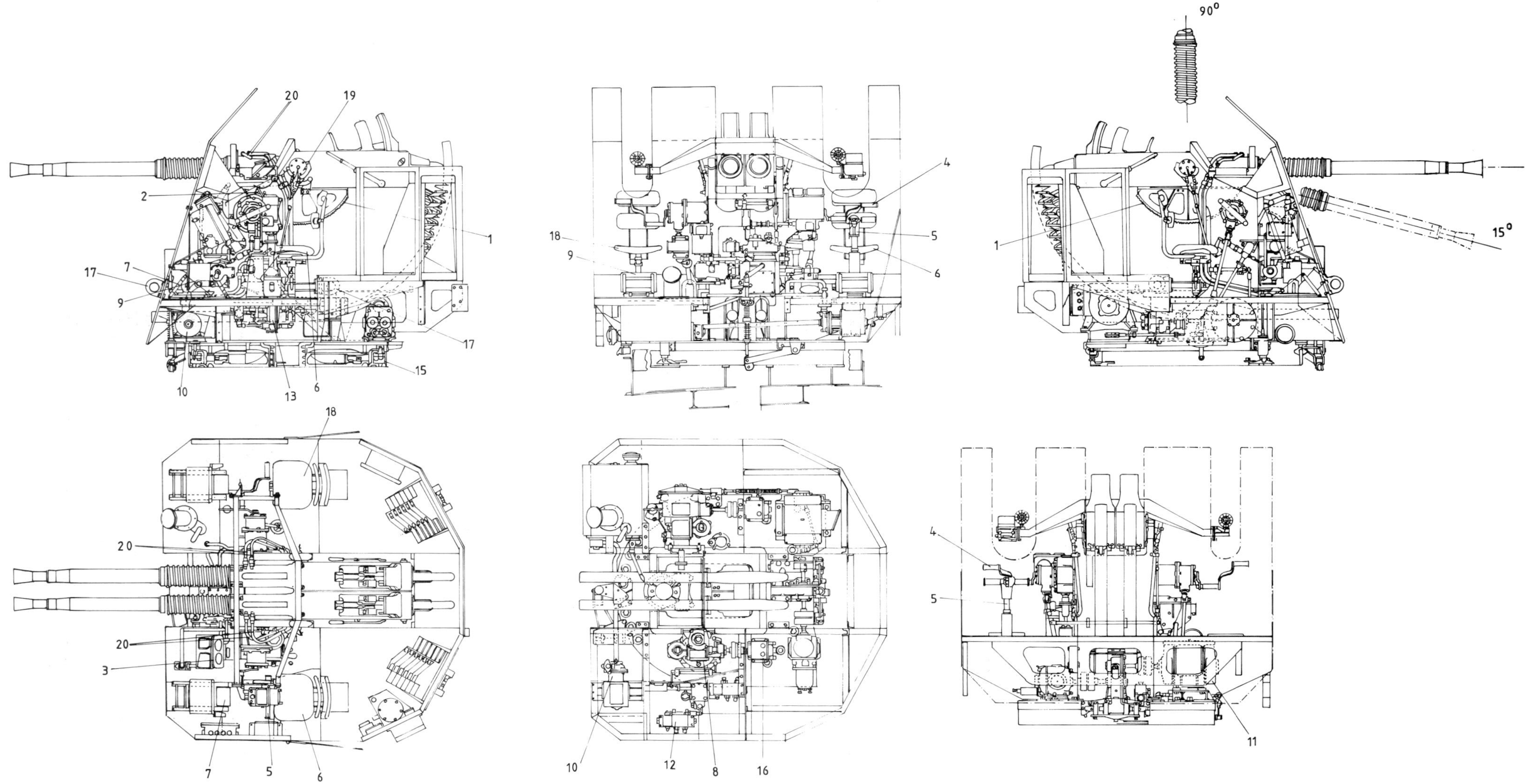

40mm Bofors Mk XI guns in twin RP 50 Mk V mounting.

1 Elevating arc
2 Elevation locking bolt
3 Elevation receiver
4 Elevating handles
5 Joystick
6 Gunlayer's seat
7 Firing pedal
8 Main gear box
9 Gunlayer's adjustable foot rest
10 Coolant pump motor
11 Joystick controllers
12 Resetter box
13 Reduction gear box
14 Clip rollers
15 Training buffer
16 Elevation driving motor
17 Lifting eye
18 Trainer's seat
19 Firing arm bracket
20 Cooling water hose connections

John Lambert

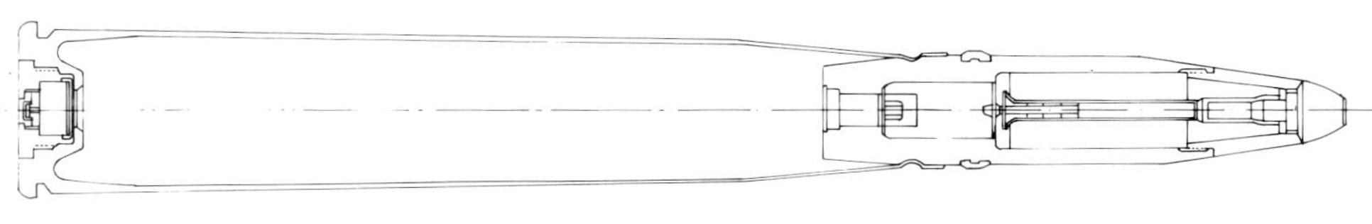

40mm Bofors HE tracer round.
John Lambert

mounting with Mk IX guns and the twin pseudo-triaxial STAAG with Mk X guns were not in service until after the war, while the single STAAG and twin triaxial Buster (Mk VIII guns) were abandoned. Fortunately the USN was able to provide a number of their Mk I (left hand) and Mk II (right hand) guns in RP biaxial twin Mk I and quad Mk II mountings. The quad mounting was first installed in June 1943 in *Phoebe* and by the end of the war was also in *Nelson*, the four *King George V* class, *Indomitable, Victorious, Uganda, Newfoundland, Birmingham, Ajax* and *Cleopatra*. It had apparently been removed from *Arethusa*. The usual number was two mountings per ship but *Cleopatra* and *Pheobe* had three each and *Nelson* and *Birmingham* four.

The twin mounting was introduced with the *Attacker* class of Lend-Lease escort carriers in January 1943 and was also in the *Ameer* class, *Archer*, the 'Colony' class frigates and some 'Captain' class. It was in *Victorious, Indomitable, Australia, Ariadne, Opossum*, a few LSTs and the liners *Queen Elizabeth* and *Queen Mary*. The later escort carriers had eight mountings each, and *Australia* is believed to have had ten after her 1945 refit.

In spite of the different Mk Nos, all Bofors guns in Royal Navy use were basically similar. They were recoil operated with a monobloc barrel and detachable breech ring, breech casing and automatic loader, the last term referring to the 'machine gun' mechanism. There was a vertical sliding breech block which began to open 5 milliseconds after recoil began and was fully open after 30 milliseconds, the full recoil period being about 100. Rate of fire was 120 per minute though 140–150 was attained with the gun horizontal. The firing gear controlled the rammer only and not the striker. The ammunition was in four-round clips and the gun accommodated eight rounds, though ten could be loaded with two loose rounds between the clips. There was no automatic replenishment until the six-barrel mounting and the cancelled Buster and the loading number had to feed further clips by hand. It was thought that 24 rounds might be fired continuously with a skilful loader. Single shots could be fired by all wartime guns, though not in Mks VIII, IX and X.

The basic air cooled Mks I, I*, III differed in details of the automatic loader, Mk III taking simplified types while Mk I* took these or the original as in Mk I. The Canadian-made IC and I*C were very similar to the basic marks, and the Australian I* was identical to the British made gun. The American marks are described under that country.

The water cooled guns Mks IV, VIII, IX, X and XI all had water jackets with circulating pumps, and differed in detail from one another as required by their particular mountings.

The total number of air cooled guns in the wartime Navy is not known. The above gun mounting figures total 2103, plus 141 ex USA, while the end-of-war gun summaries give 1772 plus 167 ex USA. Stock figures for July 1946 total 2793 guns and the register for US Mk I air cooled guns lists 378. Figures for water cooled guns are reliable, end-of-war totals being 442 Mk IV, 342 Mk XI and 393 each of US Mk I and Mk II.

The usual ammunition was HE tracer, the round weighing 4.88lb (*2.21kg*) with a length of 17.75in (*45.1cm*). The shells were self destructing at 3000–3500yd (*2700–3200m*) though this could be increased to 7000yd (*6400m*) in some. SAP rounds were also available.

Brief particulars of the various single mountings were:

LS Mk III. Hand-operated Army mountings. Many were fitted for electrically powered oil hydraulic elevation and training, not suited to ships' power supply.

RPLS Mk III. Army mounting with remote power control from Kerrison predictor.

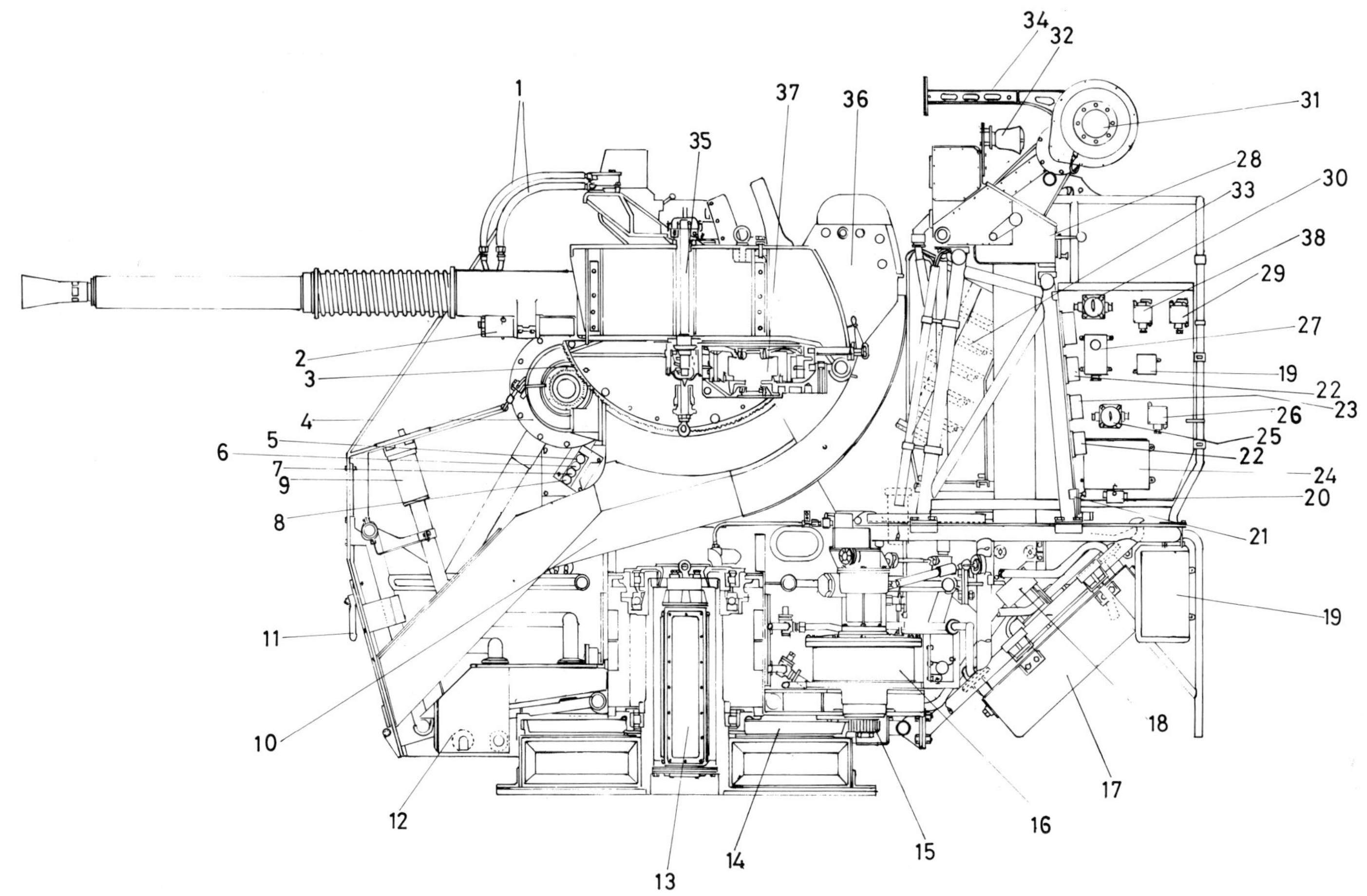

40mm Bofors Mk X guns in twin pseudo-triaxial STAAG Mk 2* mounting which entered service post war.

1 Cooling water to barrels
2 Recoil buffer
3 Elevation quadrant
4 Elevating motor
5 Range
6 Acceleration
7 Range rate
8 Mounting bearing
9 Main oil tank filling
10 Cartridge chute
11 Door clamp
12 Main oil tank
13 Centre pivot
14 Training rack
15 Training pinion
16 Training motor
17 Oil and water cooler
18 Fan motor
19 Junction box
20 Telephone plug socket
21 Hand training clutch
22 Water heater switch
23 Oil heater switch
24 Telephone stowage box
25 Ready use rack illumination
26 Ready use rack illumination distribution box
27 CO's illumination dimmer
28 CO's panel
29 Master illumination
30 Auto level switch
31 Auto level unit
32 Armament broadcast loudspeaker
33 Ready use ammunition rack
34 Open sight
35 Lateral deflection pivot
36 Balance weight
37 Lateral deflection motor
38 Gyro main alternator starter

John Lambert

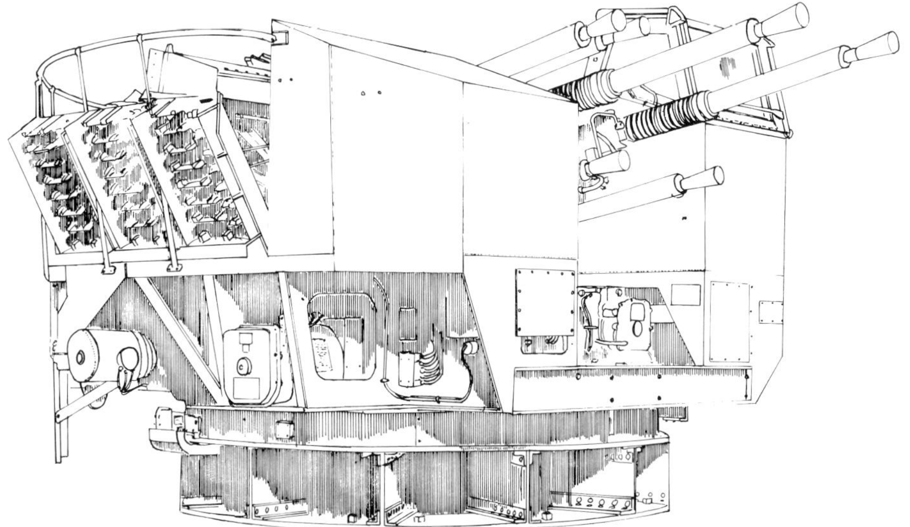

40mm Bofors Mk IX guns in 6-barrelled RP 50 Mk VI mounting which entered service post-war. *John Lambert*

Mk III CN. Hand-operated, similar to Army mounting, but with shield and slightly modified for naval service.
Mk III*. Hand-operated Army mountings adapted for naval service with Type 6 gyro sights for layer and trainer.
Toadstool. Army mountings with joystick controlled power operation using Army components. One Type 6 gyro sight.
Boffin. Oerlikon Twin Mark V or VC (Canadian) 'turret' type, oil hydraulically powered, shielded mounting converted to take one Bofors instead of two Oerlikons. Gyro sight.
Mk VII. Army mountings adapted for Navy with light alloy structures and weather shield, Type 6 gyro sight and electro-hydraulic power operation. Motor and pump on revolving structure and scooter control fitted. Diameter of deck ring and holding down arrangements as in Oerlikon Twin Mk V and 2pdr (*40mm*) Mk XVI*.

The American mountings are described with other USN weapons. Of the British twin mountings RP 50 Mk V was a simple design with training base and sections of the elevating and training power drives as in the 2pdr (*40mm*) RP 50 Mk VII quadruple mounting. A Type 6 gyro-sight was fitted for the joystick operator if RPC was not in use. Canadian mountings differed in a heavier metadyne generator.

The Mk IV triaxial mounting had the trunnions at the top of an oscillating carriage which was moved about a centre-line pivot by a spur quadrant and pinion at the bottom, the pinion being driven via a worm and wheel gearbox. Elevation and training were through worm and wheel and pinions working on elevating arc or training rack. The mounting was powered on the Ward Leonard system and the level and cross-level gyros were used to drive the control gear and not the mounting direct. Yaw and course data were supplied by the ships' gyro compasses. The target movement was obtained by the layer and trainer tracking with their sights and this provided the basic data for the self-contained Hazemeyer tachometric control system. Type 282P(2) radar was also fitted. The later Mk IV* mounting differed in details of the control and gyros. This mounting was advanced for its day but somewhat delicate for destroyers or sloops, and the later self-contained STAAG and Buster designs were very much heavier. The cancelled Buster was about 20 tons (*20,320kg*), an excessive amount for a pair of Bofors. The six-barrelled biaxial RP 50 Mk VI was intended for large ships where stabilisation was less necessary.

Recoil in all mountings was 8-8.7in (*20-22cm*). Elevation limits were +90° to -5° in army mountings, about +70° to -10° in Boffin, +90° to -10° in Mk IV and +90° to -15° in RP 50 Mk V. Cross-level limits in Mk IV were ±14°, the control cutting out at ±12°. Maximum elevating speed in this mounting was 25°/sec, though elevating and training control were limited to a little over 10°/sec. In RP 50 Mk V maximum training speed was 35°/sec with 28°/sec for elevating or 35°/sec in Canadian mountings. In RP 50 Mk VI both figures were 30°/sec and in STAAG 36°/sec. Weights including guns were: LS Mk III, 1.20 tons (*1220kg*); Mk VII 1.40 tons (*1420kg*); Mk IV 7.047 tons (*7160kg*); Mk V 6.397 tons (*6500kg*); Mk VI 21.24 tons (*21,580kg); STAAG* Mk II* 15.0 tons (*15,240kg*).

2pdr (40mm) QF Mark VIII

Gun Data

Bore	1.575in	40mm	
Weight of gun	784-918lb	356-416kg	
Weight of barrel	125lb	56.7kg	
Length gun	115.6in	2936.2mm	
Length bore	62in	1574.8mm	39.37cal
Length chamber	5.382in	136.7mm	
Volume chamber	9.98in^3	0.1635dm^3	
Length rifling	54.84in	1392.94mm	
Grooves	(12) 0.0141 in deep × 0.322	0.358 × 8.18mm	
Lands	0.894in	2.271mm	
Twist	Uniform 1 in 30		
Weight projectile	1.684lb	0.764kg	
Propellant charge	0.2793lb HSCT/K 134-055	0.1267kg	
Muzzle velocity	2400f/s	732m/s	
Working pressure	16.5 tons/in^2	2600kg/cm^2	
Approx life	5000 EFC		
Max range	6800yd/2300f/s	6220m/701m/s	
Ceiling	13000ft/2300f/s	3960m/701m/s	

Above figures are for HV ammunition. LV differed in projectile 2.0lb (*0.907kg*) charge of same propellant 0.243lb (*0.110kg*), MV 2040f/s (*622m/s*), Working pressure 15.5 tons/in^2 (*2440kg/cm^2*).

This recoil operated, water cooled, belt fed gun was a redesign of the earlier Mk II to suit eight-barrel mountings. An extemporary arrangement of six Mk II guns on a common base was tried in *Dragon* in 1921-22, and as a result design work on experimental multiple mountings was started by Armstrong and Vickers. The Armstrong version was the more complex and was designed for continuous fire, unlike the Vickers mounting. It was subsequently abandoned in favour of the latter. A mock-up was examined at Vickers, Dartford, in July 1923 but because of Treasury parsimony it was not until 1927 that satisfactory trials were carried out at Eastney, followed by sea trials in *Tiger* in 1928 and the issue of the first eight-barrel service mounting to *Valiant* at the end of 1930. During 1931, *Nelson, Rodney* and *Revenge* received one mounting and *Hood* two, to be followed in 1932 by two each in *Furious* and *Royal Sovereign* and one in *Renown*. At first known as the M mounting, this became Mk V and was succeeded by the generally similar Mk VI. Both had controlled fire guns but in 1939 automatic fire was introduced, the mountings becoming Mks VA and VIA.

A serious defect of the original Mk VIII guns was the low muzzle velocity of 2040f/s (*622m/s*) and after work on an eight-barrel 1½pdr Mk V of 1.36in (*34.54mm*) bore and 2600f/s (*792m/s*) muzzle velocity had been abandoned in early 1937, as it came out heavier than the eight-barrel 2pdr (*40mm*), it was found possible to increase the muzzle velocity of the latter to an eventual 2400f/s (*732m/s*). Mountings with these guns were distinguished by a star added to the Mark.

During the war remote power control, either hydraulic, RP 10, RP 11, or Metadyne, RP 50, was introduced for Mk VIA* mountings, this being accompanied by the addition of a cooling water circulation system.

At the outbreak of war eight-barrel

2pdr pom-pom eight-barrelled Mk VIA* mounting in *Illustrious* in summer 1940, viewed from front. The guns are AHV.
CPL

2pdr pom-pom eight-barrelled Mk VIA* mounting viewed from left hand side.
By courtesy of John Lambert

mountings were in battleships, battlecruisers, some large cruisers, *Coventry*, *Curlew* and *Adventure*, the greatest number being four Mk VI in *Warspite* and *Ark Royal*. Numbers increased during the war and by September 1945 as many as eight mountings were in the *King George V* class with up to six in fleet carriers, *Nelson* and *Sussex*. In some ships mountings were mixed, *Anson* having one Mk VIA*, three RP 10, Mk VIA* and four RP 50, Mk VIA*.

The eight-barrel mounting was too heavy for many ships and in 1935–36 a quadruple mounting to be known as Mk VII was successfully tried in the destroyer *Crusader*. During World War II this type of mounting was widely used in the smaller carriers, cruisers, destroyers and many other ships, and in addition as a supplementary kamikaze defence in some ships with eight-barrel mountings. All quadruple mountings had controlled fire guns, Mk VII* indicating high muzzle velocity, while RP 50 Mk VII* and Mk VII*P were later introduced, the latter being a self-contained powered mounting. Both had water circulation systems. By September 1945 six RP 50 mountings were in each of the *Colossus* class, *Glasgow* and *Liverpool*, and six Mk VII*P in *Duke of York*, *Anson* and *Howe*.

A large number of single mountings were also made, Mk VIII with low velocity guns, and Mk VIII* with high velocity, both automatic fire, were hand worked and mounted in older destroyers, the 'Hunt' class, corvettes, some frigates and a variety of other ships. Mk VIII* was far the more common. Mk XVI was a later power-worked single mounting mostly in coastal forces. Automatic high velocity guns were fitted and most mountings were converted to Mk XVI* with gyro sights and were carried by *Ocean* and some cruisers and destroyers as anti-kamikaze weapons.

There were also some former land service single and twin mountings, but it is doubtful if the former were used afloat and the 57 twins never were.

Differences between the various Mk VIII guns were indicated as follows: CLV, controlled low velocity; CHV, controlled high velocity; CHV(U), as CHV with modifications to latch, locking crank; ALV, automatic low velocity; AHV, automatic high velocity; CHV^{W}, AHV^{W} – W indicated modifications to cooling jacket to suit water circulation.

In addition the different positions in the eight-barrel mounting required right and left hand outer and inner guns (RHO, LHO, RHI, LHI). Quadruple mountings had R and L hand upper and lower guns and singles used RHI. In outer guns and in upper guns in quadruple mountings, the connecting block in the gun which took the barrel, buffer cylinders and ejector tube was lengthened by 13in (*33cm*) to allow the ammunition feed for inner and lower guns to pass through.

The Mk VIII gun had a monobloc barrel and the lock (breech block) moved parallel with the gun axis. Unlike most British guns, the Mk VIII had a very small chamber and an expansion ratio thought to be too large. The ammunition was in 14-round steel-linked belts which could be hooked together to give up to 140 rounds per gun in the eight-barrel mountings. With

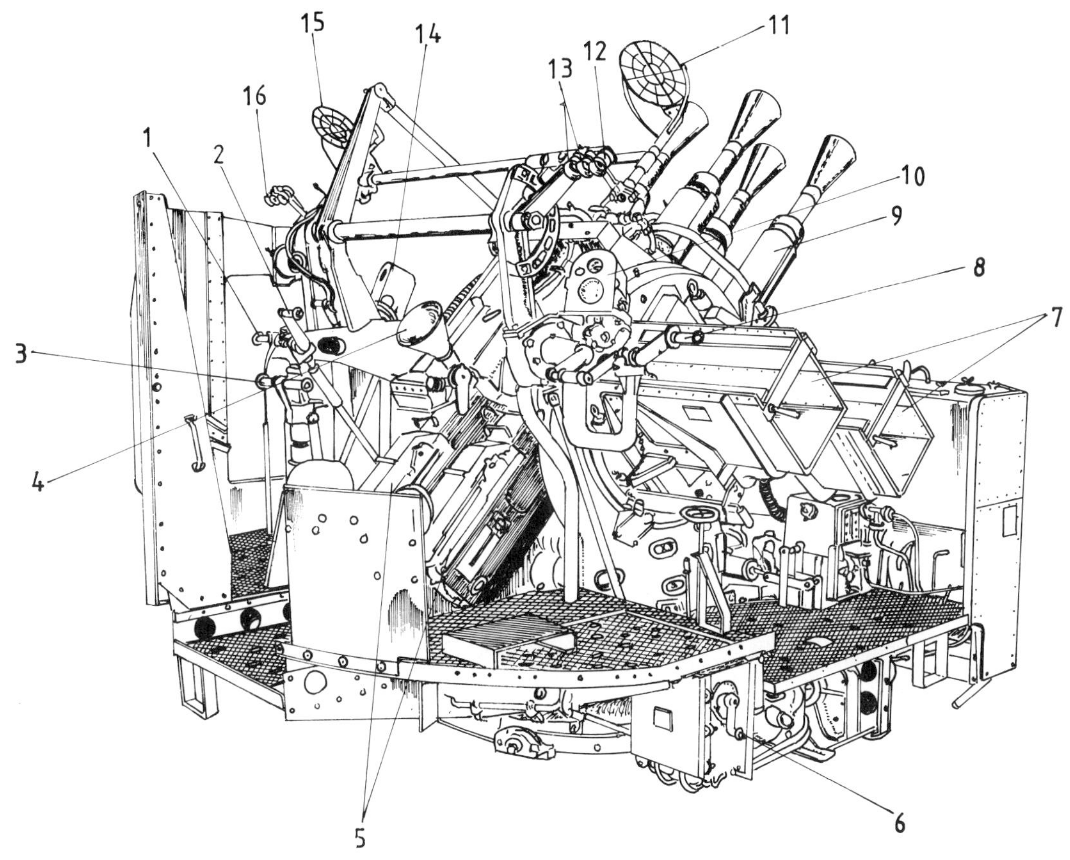

2pdr pom-pom quadruple Mk VII*P mounting.

1 Elevating handwheel
2 Firing handles
3 Joystick laying and training
4 Water filler and stopcock
5 Gun mechanisms
6 Starter for power motor
7 Ammunition feedrails
8 Training handwheel
9 Barrel heater
10 Training receiver
11 Trainer's fore sight
12 Trainer's back sight
13 Blank eyepieces
14 Elevation receiver
15 Layer's fore sight
16 Layer's back sight

John Lambert

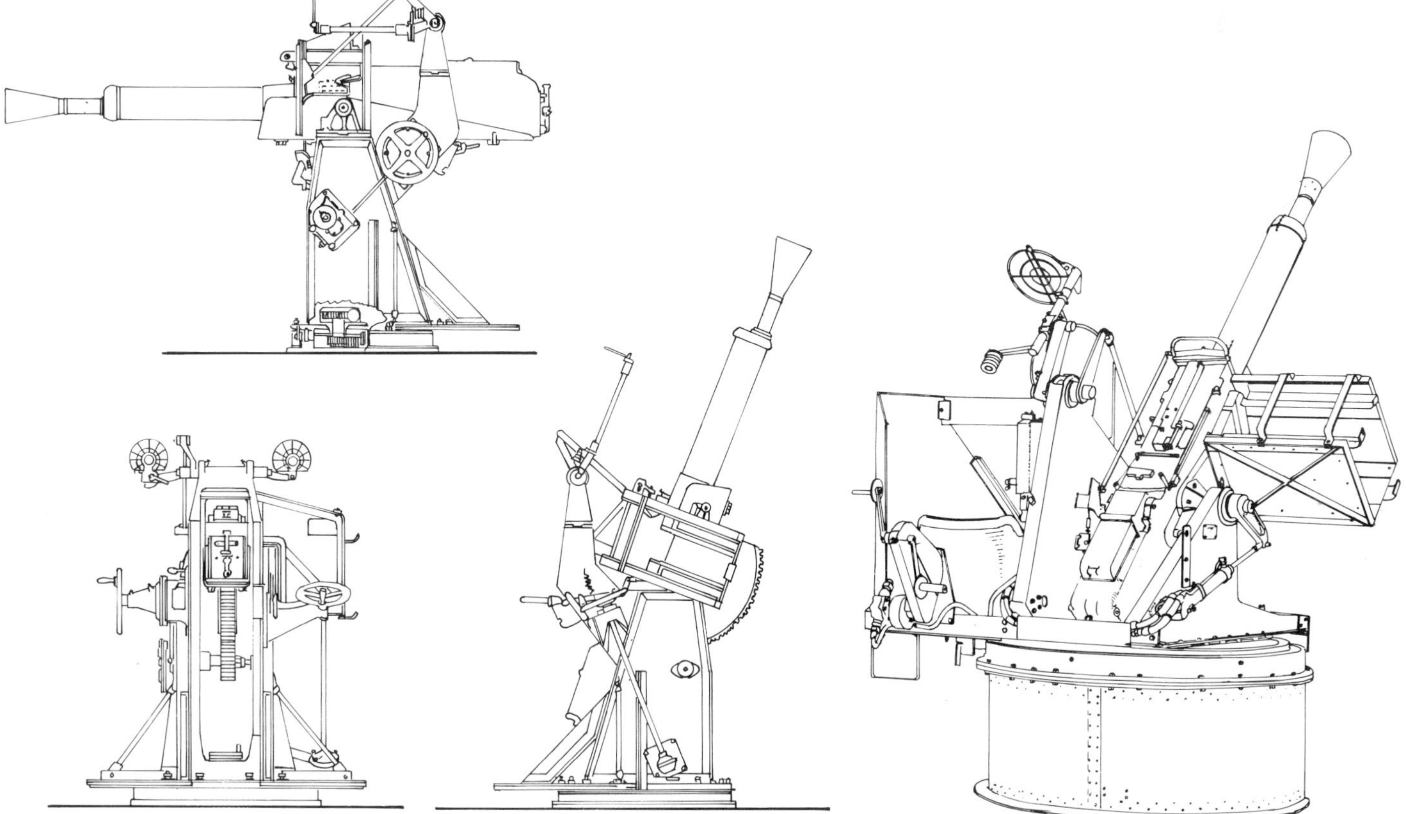

2pdr QF Mk VIII pom-pom in single Mk VII* or VIII* mounting.
John Lambert

2pdr QF Mk VIII pom-pom in single Mk XVI powered mounting.
John Lambert

automatic fire the rate was 115 rounds per minute and with controlled fire, when the mechanism was interrupted before the round was actually fired, 96 to 98 rounds per minute.

The naval gun registers list a total of 6691 guns made in Britain, including 12 prototypes, 843 made in Canada and 219 ex land service which were scrapped in 1944–45.

The usual ammunition was HE or HE tracer, the complete round weighing 3lb (*1.36kg*) with a maximum length of 11.995in (*30.47cm*). SAP and AP were also issued to some ships.

Some general features of the various mountings have been given above. The Mk V series differed from the Mk VI in having a lighter carriage and different controlled-fire gear, later rendered inoperative or removed. Both were powered by a self-contained electro-hydraulic system driven by an 11 HP motor. RP mountings also had local joystick control and maximum elevating and training speeds were increased from 15°/sec to 20–25°/sec. Gyro sights for local kamikaze defence are believed to have been fitted to the mounting on B turret in *Anson* and *Duke of York*. Elevation was +80° to -10° in all and weights were: Mk VA*, 15.038 tons (*15,279kg*); Mk VIA*, 15.678 tons (*15,930kg*) – if controlled fire gear removed 15.552 tons (*15,802kg*); RP 10, RP 11 Mk VIA*, 20.25 tons (*20,575kg*); RP 50 Mk VIA* 18.25 (*18,543kg*).

Of the quadruple mountings Mks VII and VII* were hand elevated and trained, VII*P had a self-contained electro-hydraulic power system with dual joystick control, and RP 50 mountings also had local joystick control. Maximum elevating and training speeds were 25°/sec in powered mountings and elevation +80° to -10° in all. Gyro sights were to be fitted to Mk VII*P mountings in *Anson, Duke of York, Implacable* and probably in some other ships.

Weights were: Mk VII*, 8.575 tons (*8713kg*); Mk VII*P, 11.013 tons (*11,190kg*); RP 50 Mk VII*, 10.000 tons (*10,160kg*).

The single Mk VIII and VIII* mountings were hand worked while Mk XVI was hydraulically powered by an off-mounting pump driven by the coastal craft's main or auxiliary engines. In Mark XVI* an electric motor was provided to drive the hydraulic pump. Gyro sights were fitted to this mounting and both it and Mk XVI had scooter control. Maximum training speeds were 40°/sec and elevating 25°/sec. The range of elevation in both Mk VIII and XVI was +70° to -10°.

Weights were: Mk VIII* 1.780 tons (*1809kg*) including 0.5in (*13mm*) 0.275 tons (*279kg*) shield; Mk XVI 1.10 tons (*1118kg*) including 0.10 tons (*102kg*) shield; Mk XVI* 1.379 tons (*1401kg*) including 0.10 tons (*102kg*) shield.

2pdr (40mm) various QF Marks

Mk II introduced in March 1915, was of generally similar type to Mk VIII and had the same barrel, but the automatic mechanism was lighter and less robust, the total weight with cooling water being 550lb (*249kg*). Ballistics were as for the low velocity Mk VIII, but a 25-round fabric belt was used and the rate of fire was 200 per minute. Mk II was originally far from satisfactory, and Mk II* was modified to improve the gun's functioning, while Mk II*C was converted to fire 14-round steel-linked belts.

The original hand-worked HA Mk II mounting allowed +80° to -5° elevation and weighed 1568lb (*711kg*) with gun. Mk II* later known as II*C, was converted for the Mk II*C gun and was 55lb (*25kg*) heavier. These mountings were principally in the older destroyers, HDMLs and other coastal craft. There was also a powered Mk XV resembling Mk XVI for the Mk VIII gun, but only 28 were made and the surviving 23 were scrapped by early 1944.

In all 785 guns were made of which 577 were still extant in 1939.

Mks IX, X.
These army 50-calibre tank and anti-tank guns differed only in that Mk IX had an autofretted barrel. They had removable breech rings and SA vertical sliding block BM. Weight with BM was 287lb (*130kg*) and with a 2.72lb (*1.23kg*) AP shot, MV was 2650f/s (*808m/s*). A total of 14 guns were on naval books of which five were mounted in Daimler armoured car turrets in LCS (L) 201–205.

Mk XI.
Converted 25-calibre HA sub-calibre guns with single tube barrel, breech ring and horizontal radial shaped breech block. Weight with BM was about 132lb (*60kg*) and with a 2lb (*0.907kg*) projectile MV was *c*1200f/s (*366m/s*). The Mk IX mounting of pedestal type had rubber buffers to absorb recoil and was fitted with a shield. Maximum elevation was 70°. A total of 180 guns were converted and mounted as emergency scatter guns in HDMLs and small auxiliaries. Case shot was originally provided as well as more conventional ammunition.

Mk XII.
Converted 39.37-calibre LA sub-calibre guns with single-tube barrel, screwed and shrunk breech ring and horizontal sliding block. Weight with BM was about 170lb (*77kg*) and ballistics as for the low velocity Mk VIII gun. Mounting and usage were as in Mk XI, and 115 guns were converted.

Mk XIV.
SA 50.8-calibre guns designed by Rolls Royce and, originally at least, not very satisfactory. The gun had a monobloc barrel, breech ring and breech body in which the breech block moved longitudinally. Casings and cradle were of aluminium alloy, and ballistics as in the HV Mk VIII gun. The Mk XIV mounting of pedestal type with shield allowed +60° to -12° elevation and recoil was $17\frac{1}{2}$in (*44.5cm*). The weight was 1036lb (*470kg*) of which gun and cradle accounted for 336lb (*152kg*). It was mainly carried by MLs and a total of 602 guns were made.

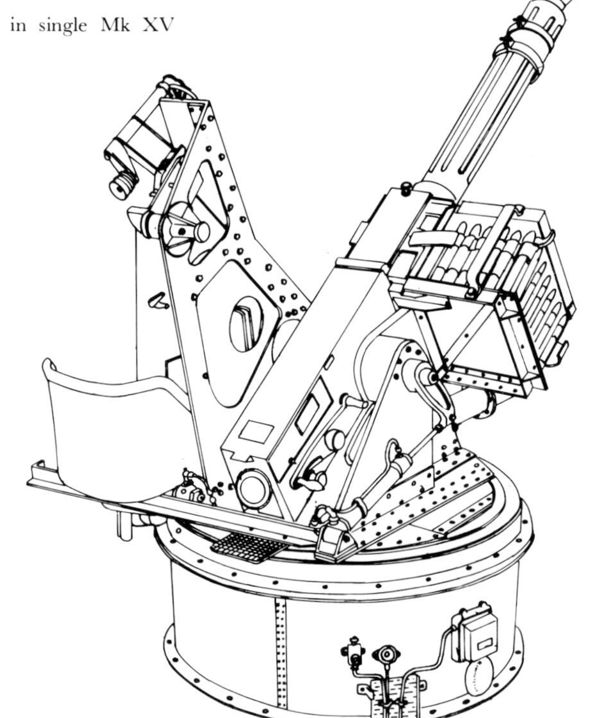

2pdr QF Mk II*C pom-pom in single Mk XV powered mounting.
John Lambert

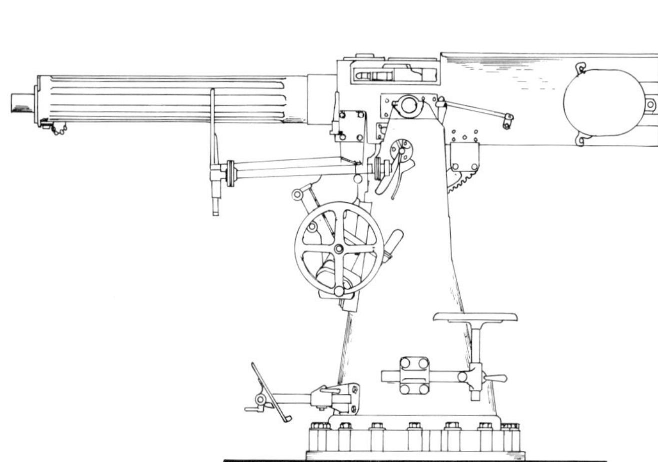

2pdr QF Mk II pom-pom in single Mk II mounting.
John Lambert

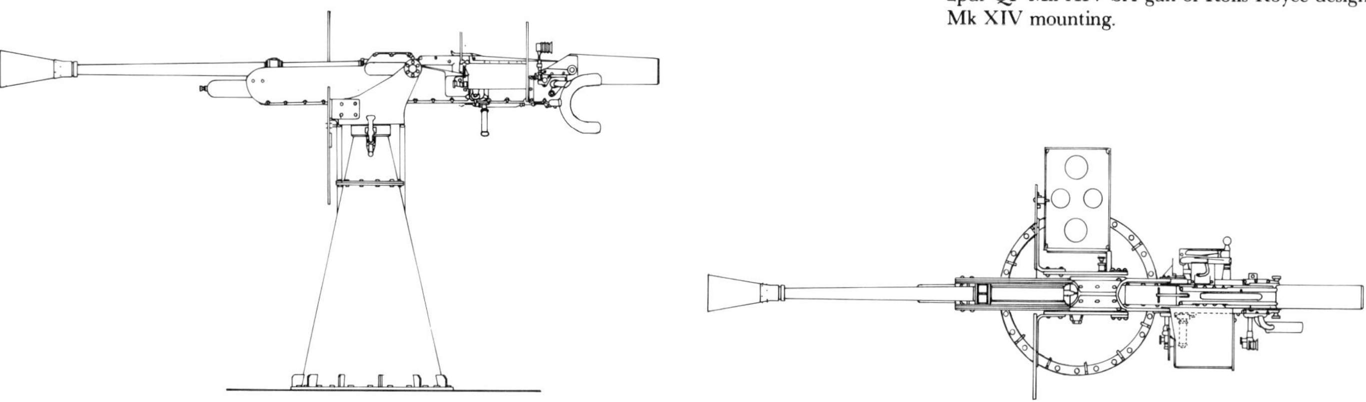

2pdr QF Mk XIV SA gun of Rolls Royce design in Mk XIV mounting.

These air cooled magazine fed blow-back guns were at first imported from Switzerland pending the establishment of manufacturing facilities in America and England. Firing explosive shells, the Oerlikon was a great improvement on the 0.5in (*12.7mm*) Vickers with solid bullets, and was eventually carried by almost every type of ship. Though highly successful it was being superseded in many larger ships by the 40mm (*1.575in*) Bofors towards the end of World War II as its shell was unlikely to destroy a kamikaze soon enough.

Introduced in 1939 the guns were mainly on single free-swinging mountings. Adjustable column mountings included Mks I, IA, II, IIUS, IVUS, VIUS, of which Mk IVUS was the most common, and fixed pedestal mountings Mks IIA, IIIA, VUS, VRCN, VIIA and XUS, Mk IIIA being the most plentiful. Special mountings for submarines were Mks IIA S/M and VIIA* S/M, and for coastal craft Mks IIIA Dwarf and VIIIA. Twin, hand-worked mountings were mostly for coastal craft and comprised Mk IX twin, XIA twin and XIIA twin with a prototype, XIA S/M twin, for submarines. Powered twin mountings were Twin Mk V and Twin Mk VC, and the cancelled quadruple mounting was to have been Mk XIV.

Between 60 and 70 guns were eventually carried in some capital ships, mostly in a variety of single mountings, though *Renown* and *Queen Elizabeth* had 20 powered twin mountings each in September 1944, and similar numbers of these mountings were in some fleet aircraft carriers at this time, *Victorious* having 23.

20mm (0.787in) Oerlikon, various Marks

Gun Data

Bore	0.7874in	20mm	
Weight of gun	141–150lb	64–68kg	
Weight of barrel	48lb	21.8kg	
Length gun	87in	2210mm	
Length bore	55.118in	1400mm	70.0cal
Length chamber	*c*3.97in	*c*100.8mm	
Volume chamber	2.127in^3	34.855cm^3	
Length rifling	49.061in	1246.15mm	
Grooves	(9) 0.015in deep × 0.205	0.38 × 5.207mm	
Lands	0.068in	1.73mm	
Twist	Uniform 1 in 36		
Weight projectile	0.272lb	0.123kg	
Propellant charge	0.0628lb NC flake or tube	0.0285kg	
Muzzle velocity	2750f/s	838m/s	
Working pressure	20 tons/in^2	3150kg/cm^2	
Approx life	9000 EFC		
Max range	4800yd/2725f/s	4390m/831m/s	
Ceiling	10,000ft/2725f/s	3050m/831m/s	

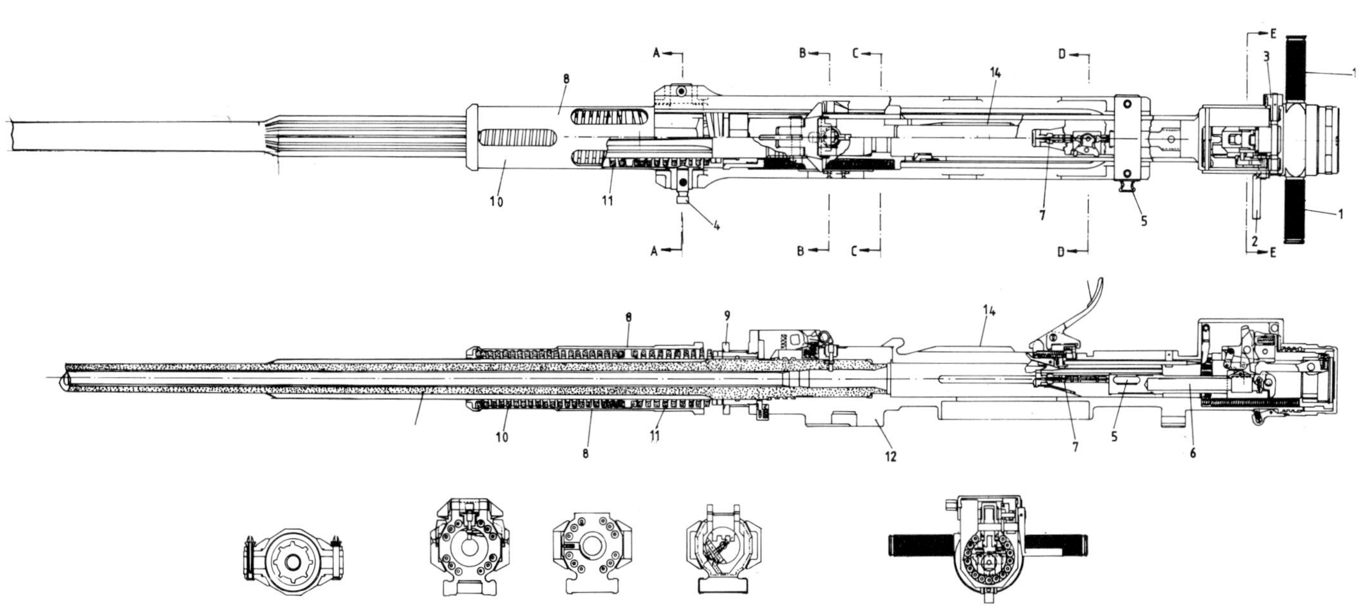

20mm Oerlikon gun sectioned in plan and elevation.

1 Hand grip
2 Trigger
3 Safety catch
4 Cocking stud
5 Breech cotter
6 Bolt
7 Striker
8 Barrel spring casing
9 Buffer
10 Left barrel spring
11 Right barrel spring
12 Breech
13 Barrel
14 Magazine support shoulder

The sections from left to right are through A-A, B-B, C-C, D-D and E-E on the plan view.

John Lambert

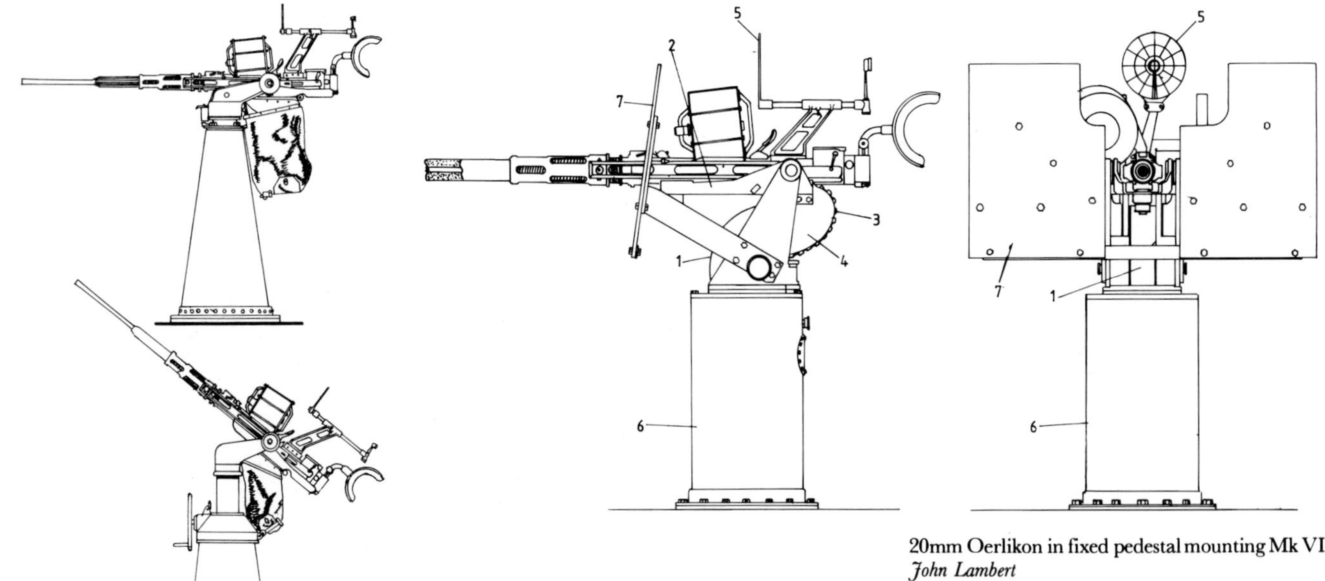

SCALE 1′ 0′ 1′ 2′ 3′ FEET

Left: 20mm Oerlikon in adjustable column mounting Mk I and fixed mounting Mk IIA.
John Lambert

20mm Oerlikon in fixed pedestal mounting Mk VIIA.
John Lambert

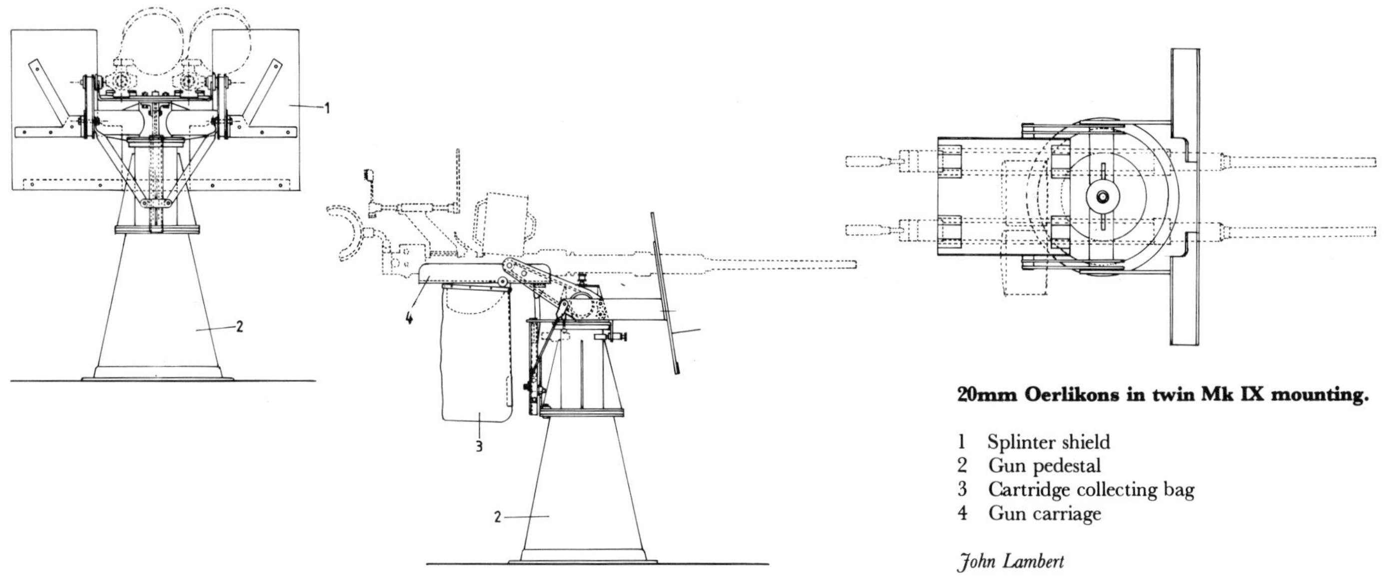

20mm Oerlikons in twin Mk IX mounting.

1 Splinter shield
2 Gun pedestal
3 Cartridge collecting bag
4 Gun carriage

John Lambert

The Oerlikon gun was contrary to normal British practice in its functioning and also required cartridges lubricated with anti-freeze grease. The explosion pressure blew the empty case back against the breech, forcing it to the rear against the barrel springs, and the breech was not locked at firing, the round being fired before it was fully home in the chamber and the neck of the case swelling to form a gas seal. The rate of fire was 465 to 480 rounds a minute, and the magazine held 60 rounds driven along the internal spiral track by a spring. Of the various marks in British naval service, Mk I was the original Swiss-made gun and Mks II, IIUS and IVUS the British and American versions. The differences between Mk I and the others, which were very similar, were mainly in the arrangement of the buffer springs, and the same was the case with the later Mk VII which had a single heavy buffer spring. The Mk I gun also differed from the others in allowing single shots.

The detailed Gun Registers have apparently not survived, but from the Mounting Appropriation Lists of September 1945 the total number of guns in the British and Dominion navies was about 55000.

Ammunition comprised HE and HE incendiary both tracer and non-tracer while SAP was also available. The complete round weighed about 8.5ozs (*241gm*) and was up to 7.18in (*182.4mm*) long.

Of the various mountings, the Mk XIV quadruple would have had belt-fed guns, each able to fire 150 rounds continuously, but was abandoned in favour of twin Bofors.

The Twin Mk V and Canadian Mk VC mountings were powered by an electro-hydraulic off mounting unit except in coastal craft where the pump was driven by the main or auxiliary engines, and had joystick control with gyro sights in the later mountings. Elevation was +70° to -10° and weight less ammunition 1.228 tons (*1248kg*) or 1.149 tons (*1167kg*) less gyro sight. These weights include the electric motor and pump and also the shield which protected the gunlayer and control valve box. The gun axes were 13in (*33cm*) apart.

Of the hand-worked twins, Mk IX was free swinging and normally used against surface or low flying targets as it was difficult to control at high angles if the ship had appreciable motion. Elevation was +85° to -10° and weight with 0.5in (*13mm*) shield 1260lb (*572kg*). Mk XIA had floating cradles and was elevated by hand gearing and arc, though with free training. There was a violent throw off on opening fire which made gyro sights impossible. Elevation was +80° to -12½°. Only one of Mk XIA S/M for submarines is listed and the same is the case for Mk XIIA, though more of these were made subsequently. This was an improved Mk XIA designed to take a gyro sight and with separation of the gun axes reduced from 13½in (*34cm*) to 7½in (*19cm*). Weight is given as 1.25 tons (*1270kg*).

Of the adjustable column single mountings Mks I, II, IIUS, IVUS were very similar to the original Swiss design, while Mk IA and VIUS had the height adjusted by pedal-operated hydraulic gear. Of the pedestal mountings, Mks IIA, IIIA, and VIIA, the last was distinguished by cam, chain and weight balancing gear, while Mks VRCN and XUS had fabricated-steel tripod pedestals and Mk V US a heavy cast-iron one. Elevation was mostly +85° to -5°, the main exception being Mk VIIA with +85° to -15° or +75° to -15° in some. Weights were 1146-1680lb (*520-762kg*) including a 0.5in (*13mm*) 224lb (*102kg*) shield.

The submarine mountings Mk IIAS/M and VIIA* S/M had no shields but had provision for extra greasing with some stainless steel parts, while Mk IIIA Dwarf for coastal craft had a shortened pedestal and was lightened where possible. Mk VIIIA was a light mounting with +20° to -15° elevation and weighed only 616lb (*279kg*) with 0.5in (*13mm*) shield.

Finally there were single mobile mountings with detachable wheels, the Haszard RM type and the HB Mk I.

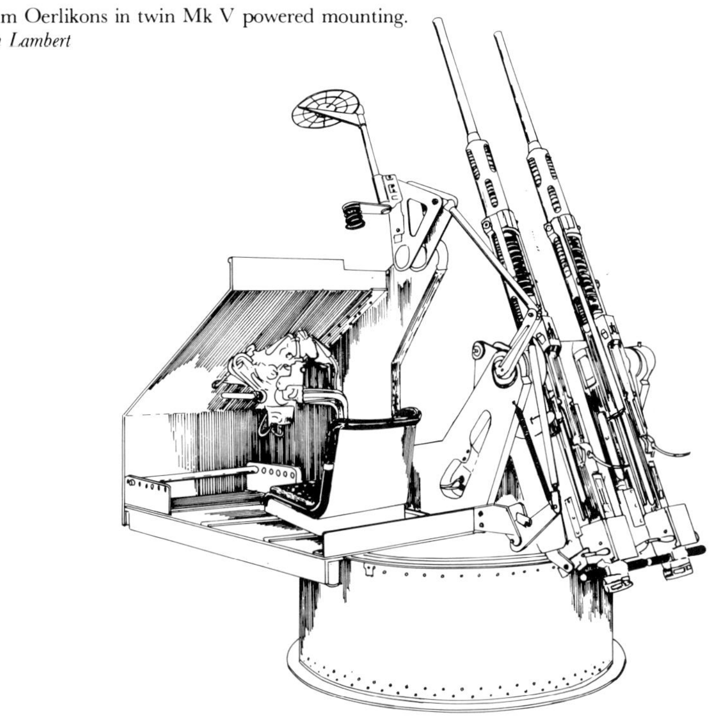

20mm Oerlikons in twin Mk V powered mounting. *John Lambert*

Left: The prototype 20mm Oerlikon quadruple Mk XIV mounting. Unlike in the US Mk 15 the guns have been adapted to belt feed. *Author's collection*

A selection of 20mm projectiles shown in section.

A Projectile/Tracer
B HE/Incendiary
C HE/Incendiary/Tracer
D Shell/HE/Tracer

1 Weighting
2 Borax
3 Tracer composition
4 Priming composition
5 Closing disc
6 Base plug
7 Percussion fuze
8 Rear disc
9 Detonator
10 Paper discs
11 HE filling
12 Waxed cloth disc
13 Incendiary filling
14 Base plate
15 Boxcloth washer

John Lambert

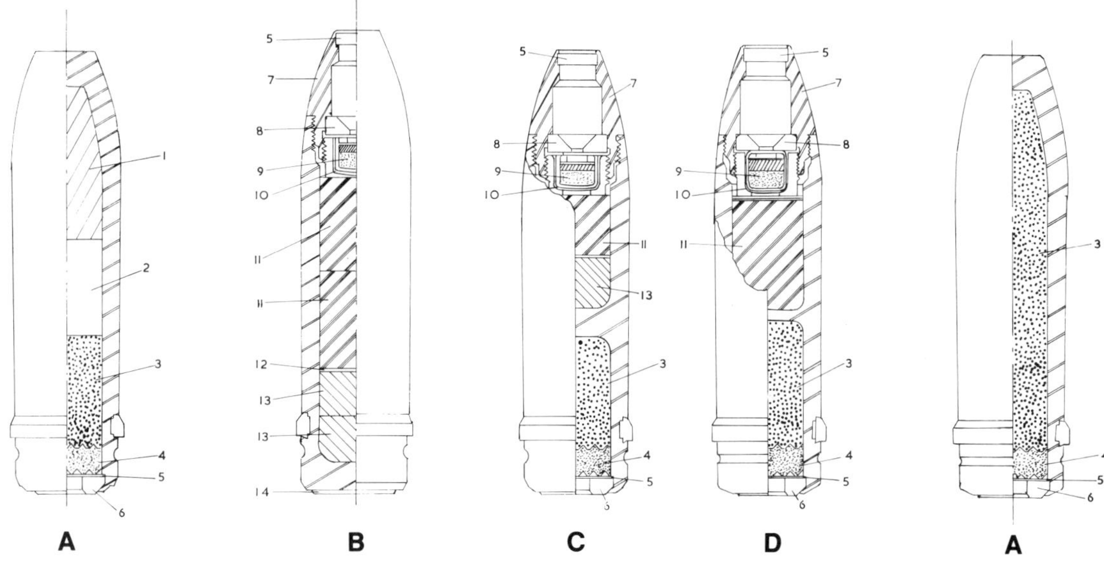

Other close range guns, 1in (5mm) and below

None of these was of much importance after the first years of the war. The 20mm (*0.7874in*) Hispano, much liked by the RAF, was not rugged enough for use in ships. It was an air-cooled, gas-operated gun with higher muzzle velocity and rate of fire than the Oerlikon, 2900f/s (*884m/s*) maximum, and 650 rpm in Mks I and II, which were those mounted afloat. A spring driven 60-round magazine was used, replaced in 1941 at least as far as airborne guns were concerned, by belt feed. A list of June 1942 gives one single mounting in RFA *Blue Ranger* and 184 in DEMS.

The 20mm (*0.7874in*) Polsten was a simplified Oerlikon with 30-round magazine, and a considerable number were on offer from the army in 1944, but no records of this gun's use afloat have been found.

A prototype 0.661in (*16.79mm*) gun and six-barrel mounting was ordered from Vickers-Armstrong in 1935 but cancelled in 1938. It was to fire 3oz (*85gm*) bullets at 3125f/s (*952m/s*), and a rate of fire of 300 rounds per gun per minute was expected with feed rails instead of belts.

The 0.5in (*12.7mm*) Vickers Mk III was the standard 'last resort' AA gun prior to the Oerlikon and was introduced in 1932. It was a recoil-operated, water-cooled gun with link-belt feed, and was in quadruple Mk I, I**, II, II* and III mountings. In large ships there were usually four mountings, though *Ark Royal* had eight, in cruisers there were two to four and in destroyers two. The twin Mk IV mounting was mainly in MLs, MMS, some *Bangor* class minesweepers, and trawlers, while the powered twin Mk V and VC were in MTB, LCS(M) and a few destroyers and corvettes. There were also Mk VI single and Scarff ring mountings.

The Mk III No 1 gun used in the quadruple mountings weighed 65lb (*29.5kg*) with cooling water, and had a bore length of 62.2 calibres. The bullet weighed 1.326oz (*37.6gm*) and muzzle velocity was 2520f/s (*768m/s*). The 200-round link belts were coiled in drums and rate of fire was 650-700 rpm per gun or 450 with a delay pawl. The No 2 and 3 guns in hand-worked twin and single mountings were similar but had shoulder pieces.

The quadruple mountings had the guns vertically above each other in separate linked trunnions. Elevation was +70° to -10° in Mks I, I** and +80° to -10° in the others, and weights without ammunition were from 2190lb (*993kg*) to 2888lb (*1310kg*). Training and elevation were by hand wheel and gearing. Twin mountings had +70° to -10° elevation, Mk IV weighing 1592lb (*722kg*) and the powered turret type Mk V 1041lb (*472kg*). In the latter the belt feed ran through the hollow inner trunnions and maximum training and elevating speeds were 72°/sec and 50°/sec. The hydraulic pump was off mounting and driven from the engines in MTBs. American-made Mk VC mountings had the water cooled version of the 0.50in (*12.7mm*) Browning M2 as alternative guns, and these, or the heavy-barrel air-cooled type in various American mountings, were in many DEMS and some escort vessels. The M2 is described in the US section and was a heavier, more powerful gun than the Vickers, firing a 1.6oz (*45.4gm*) bullet at 2930f/s (*893m/s*).

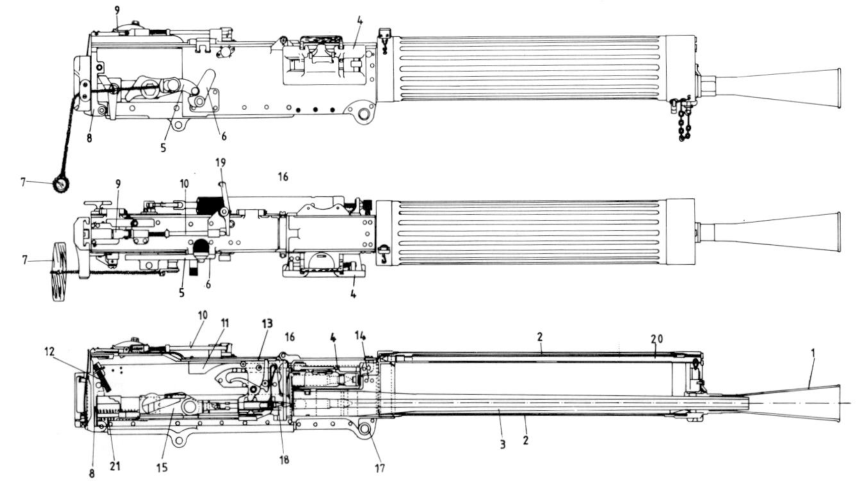

0.5in Vickers water-cooled machine gun in right side and plan view and in section.

1 Flash eliminator
2 Water jacket
3 Gun barrel
4 Feed block
5 Crank handle
6 Check lever
7 Loading cocking lanyard
8 Rear crosspiece
9 Safety catch
10 Firing rod
11 Extractor guides
12 Shock absorbing spring
13 Trigger bar
14 Trunnion block
15 Crank
16 Front cover hinge pin
17 Front joint pin
18 Firing pin
19 Trigger bar lever
20 Steam tube
21 Buffer spring

John Lambert

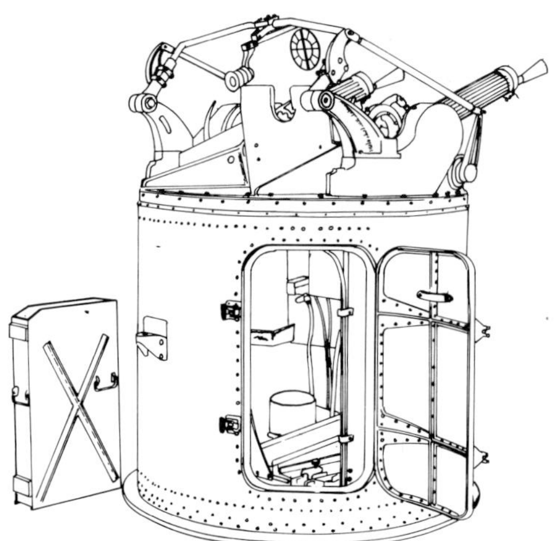

0.5in Vickers machine guns in twin Mk V powered mounting.
John Lambert

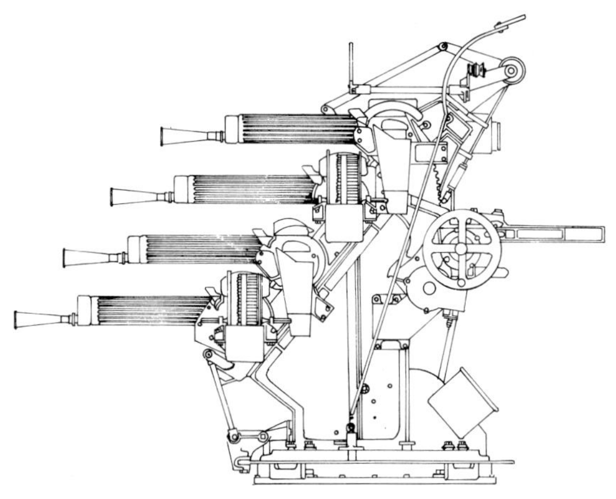

0.5in Vickers machine guns in quadruple Mk III mounting.
John Lambert

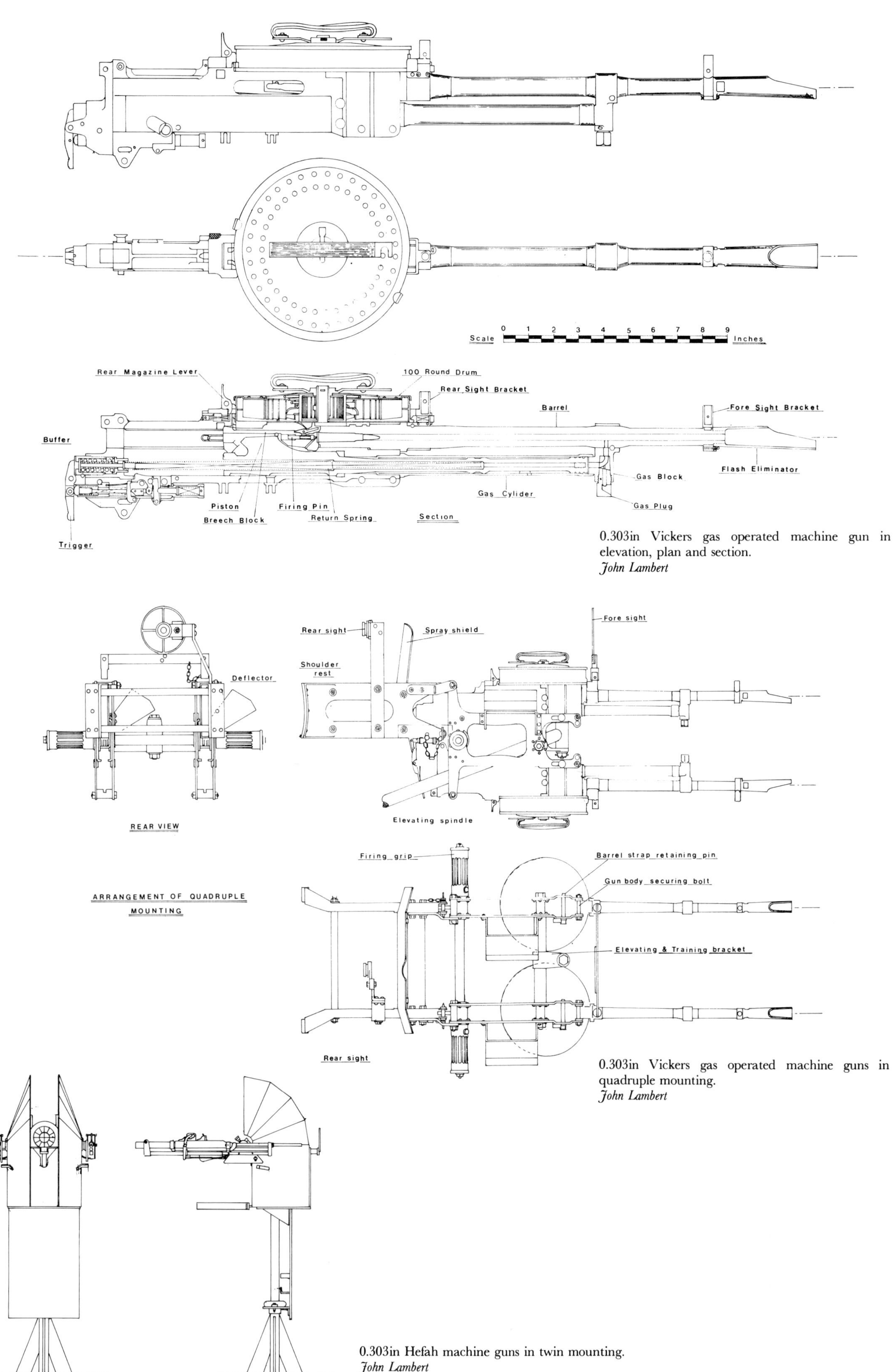

0.303in Vickers gas operated machine gun in elevation, plan and section.
John Lambert

0.303in Vickers gas operated machine guns in quadruple mounting.
John Lambert

0.303in Hefah machine guns in twin mounting.
John Lambert

Rifle calibre machine guns were in single, twin or occasionally quadruple mountings. The most important was the 0.303in (*7.7mm*) gas-operated, air-cooled Vickers which had a 100 or later 96-round magazine and a rate of fire of 950–1000 rpm. Other gas-operated, air-cooled 0.303in guns with magazine feed were the Lewis, Bren and Hefah, while the Hotchkiss had strip or belt feed. Recoil-operated, water-cooled, belt-fed 0.303in guns included the Browning, Vickers and Maxim. Browning and Lewis guns were also to be found with the US 0.30in (*7.62mm*) bore and the Marlin, which was a gas-operated air-cooled belt-fed gun, was apparently only used as 0.30in. Muzzle velocity varied a little with barrel length, but the British figure can be taken as 2440f/s (*744m/s*) with a 174gr (*11.3gm*) bullet, and the US 2700–2800f/s (*823–853m/s*) with a 151gr (*9.8gm*) bullet.

Finally two weapons which were not machine guns, the Boys anti-tank rifle of 0.55in (*14mm*) bore, carried by some minesweepers for sinking floating mines, and the 1in (*25.4mm*) Elswick C rifle. This was a conversion of the B aiming rifle for a four-legged light mounting allowing 40° elevation, and 300 mountings were made for harbour defence craft. The gun was essentially a 1in Nordenfelt barrel with screw breech block and carrier.

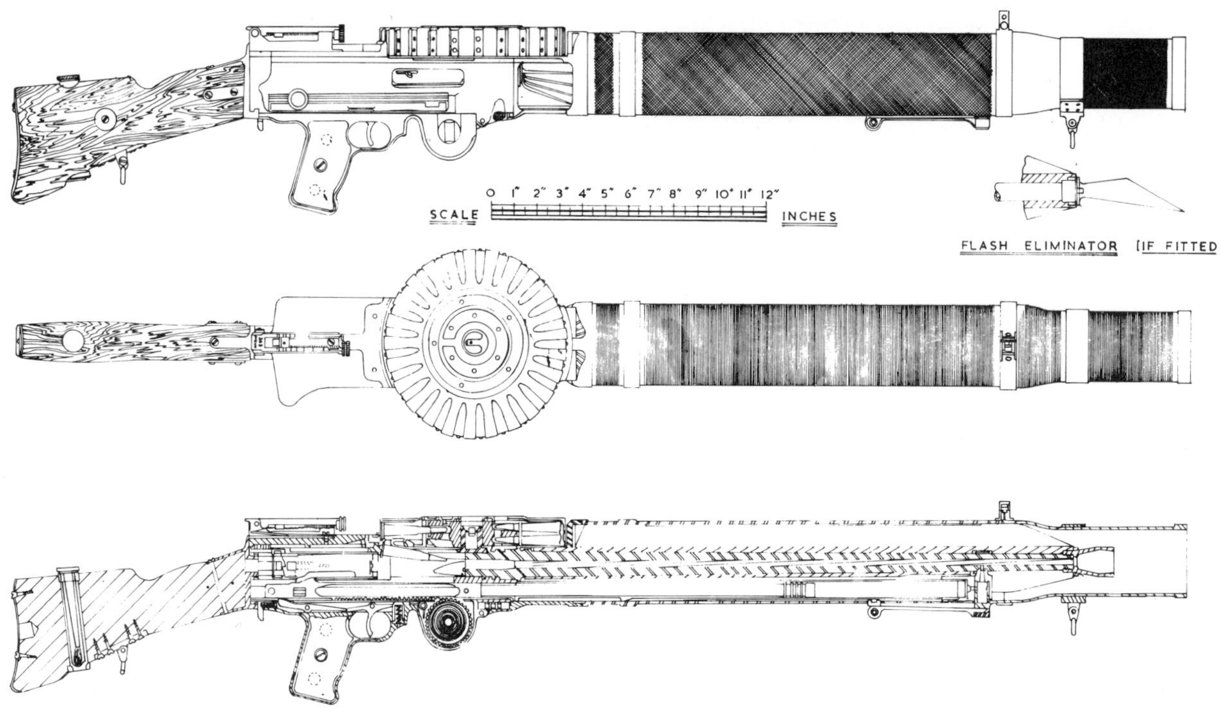

0.303in Lewis gun in elevation, plan and section. *John Lambert*

TORPEDOES

Britain held the lead in torpedoes for much of the period between the two World Wars, but was overtaken by the Japanese, with their use of pure oxygen – though Britain remained first among other navies, which all favoured air. This success was mainly due to the adoption of the Brotherhood burner-cycle engine (described below) in the mid 1920s. During the Second World War the principal defect was found to be in the magnetic exploder which, though satisfactory at Taranto in 1940, was not generally reliable and was not replaced in service by an improved design before the end of 1943. Lack of adequate production was also a serious failing initially. Even though output roughly balanced gross expenditure, distribution failed to meet requirements and local shortages of certain types persisted for some time. Thus several obsolescent Marks had still to be used, even in the more recent ships, until supply improved. Fortunately there were *c*7100 torpedoes in existence in September 1939, but only 3000 were of types still in production.

Torpedoes were made at the Royal Naval Torpedo Factory at Greenock and Alexandria, near Dumbarton, the Vickers-Armstrong (formerly Whitehead) works at Weymouth and later also at Bournemouth and Staines. Other firms included Morris Motors and Bliss (USA) as well as BTH, Stone Platt, Templeton & Nairn and Bullards (USA) while 500 18in (*45cm*) were ordered in Australia. Production per month was about 80 at the start of World War II and for the first 18 months ran at just below 100, rising to 200 after two years. Production overtook expenditure in early 1942 and the total number exceeded the requirements for outfits and reserves in early 1944 when production was at its peak of nearly 800 a month. The various types were not correctly proportioned, however. Monthly requirements, already diminishing, had fallen to 190 in April 1945 and to 40 by the end of the war. The total fired in action was *c*7770 and almost exactly the same number were lost in ships, depots and in transit.

In addition to the above, the destroyers lent in 1940 had the old USN Bliss-Leavitt Mk 8 subsequently used by some MTBs and, later, other USN torpedoes, as the airborne Mk 13 and the homing Mk 24 Mine, known as 'Fido', were supplied. Very few Mk 13 were used in action by the RN, but 204 Mk 24 were expended by Allies other than the USA, and mostly by Britain. Some Whitehead torpedoes for other navies are noted under 21in (*53.3cm*) Mk X and a few French torpedoes were also used.

Figures compiled shortly after the war give the following for hits and probable hits:

Firing vessel	Torpedoes fired	Certain hits	Probable hits	%Certain & probable
Capital ships	12	-	1	8.3
Cruisers	94	16	4	21.3
Destroyers	606	86	12	16.2
MTB and SGB	1328	318	37	26.7
Submarines	5121	1040	95	22.2
Naval aircraft	609	167	37	33.5
Total	7770	1627	186	23.3

Torpedo development was centered at the Torpedo Experimental Establishment, Greenock, formerly the Torpedo Experiment and Design Department. Several good projects, far more practical than the science-fiction tainted Zonal of the late 1940s, were put on one side under the original belief that it would be a short war, and others suffered from lack of a service requirement, though it is not unknown for the latter to change to an urgent need when too late for effective satisfaction. Work on homing torpedoes (noted below) was also carried out by the RAF at Halton and Titchfield and by GEC at Wembley in collaboration with TEE.

Turbines were kept under review between the wars, but consumption of expendables was large unless the inlet gases were at unusually high temperature and the four-cylinder radial Brotherhood engine was preferred. More efficient oxidants than natural air were investigated, and it is ironical that work on oxygen enriched air in the 1920s caused the Japanese to develop their far more effective pure-oxygen system. To avoid ignition risks the British used 50% alcohol/water as the fuel with air enriched to 56-60% oxygen by volume. Such torpedoes were in the *Nelson* class and most 8in cruisers, but they were not liked on account of the complications of oxygen, and their performance was far below that of the later Japanese versions. The torpedoes for cruisers were converted to natural air early in the war.

The burner-cycle engine was in effect a semi-diesel. Typically air at *c*840lb/in^2 (*59kg/cm^2*), was heated to *c*1000°C by burning a small amount of the kerosene type fuel, traditionally Broxburn Lighthouse Shale oil though five commercial brands of kerosene were found to work as well, atomised into the air. The oxygen content was only slightly depleted by this, and the hot gas was fed into the engine via four poppet valves. More fuel was injected into each cylinder a little before top dead centre and its spontaneous ignition supplied the power. There were four main exhaust ports in the cylinder liner and two auxiliary ones in the piston crown, the gases leaving through the hollow propellor shaft. This system was very efficient and could be adapted for other oxidants such as hydrogen peroxide or nitric acid. The first burner-cycle torpedo in service, the 21in (*53.3cm*) Mk VIII, dated to 1927 and was issued to the 'P' class submarines completed in 1930-31. Very good power/weight ratios could be achieved even with air. The standard four-cylinder radial for 21in (*53.3cm*) torpedoes had cylinders 4.5 × 4.4in (*114.3* × 111.8mm) with swept volume 280in^3 (*4588cm^3*) and 1939 figures of 400 BHP maximum at 1360 rpm and 320 rated at 1200 rpm for a weight of 210lb (*95kg*). By the end of the war 465BHP could be attained, and an experimental eight-cylinder two-row radial of the same cylinder dimensions gave 817 BHP for 440lb (*200kg*) in 1939. This last was never in service though development was slowly continued during the war.

Similarly the four-cylinder radial for 18in - actually 45cm (*17.7in*) - torpedoes had cylinders 4in (*101.6mm*) × 3.75in (*95.3mm*) with swept volume 188in^3 (*3081cm^3*) and 225 maximum BHP at 1230 rpm for a weight of 120lb (*54kg*). Suitable strengthening in 1939 could increase the output to 270 maximum BHP at 1340 rpm.

Of the various oxidants investigated up to 1939, nitric acid containing 44% oxygen in concentrated, or 62% in pure, form seems to have given most promise with methanol or benzol as fuel. A prototype short range 21in (*53.3cm*) torpedo which was expected to reach 60kts with 750 BHP, was 90% complete at the outbreak of war but the 'short war belief' prevented running.

Hydrogen peroxide had been considered as an oxidant in 1923 but instability and procurement difficulties were against it, and it was not until work in Germany and the USA had been studied after the war that development of the 21in (*53.3cm*) Mk 12, originally known as Ferry and then as Fancy was taken in hand. Several were issued in 1954 but after an explosion wrecked the submarine *Sidon* and another occurred on the Arrochar range, interest waned and the requirement was cancelled in early 1959.

In addition to these high performance developments, experiments were carried out in 1942 on a jet-propelled torpedo which attained 800yds (*730m*)/24kts. It was thought that this could have been much improved but there was no requirement at the time. Another investigation begun in 1942 was into the use of a solid mono-fuel charge in a sealed container inserted in the torpedo and feeding directly to the engine inlet valves. Temperature and pressure were to be controlled by the composition and shape of the charge. The first tests in January 1945 used a former wet-heater engine from a 21in (*53.3cm*) Mk V with an ammonium nitrate/guanidine nitrate charge catalysed by ammonium dichromate, and with ammonium oxalate injection to reduce engine corrosion. Work was, however, stopped after the first successes through lack of support and it was left to the USN Mark 46/0 to introduce solid torpedo propellants to service in 1963.

The Royal Navy had no great interest in electric torpedoes in 1939 on account of their relatively poor performance, and there was no particular demand for tracklessness. Work began on low priority in 1940 after the first pieces of the German G7e had been received, and in 1942 BTH Rugby were asked to start production of what became the 21in (*53.3cm*) Mk XI as there was then a requirement for trackless torpedoes in the Mediterranean. The first torpedo was ready for trials in May 1943 but production which had been envisaged at 80 and then 100 per month from BTH, with the same from Stone, Platt, was cut back to a total of 25 each month in August 1944, the date when the first production torpedo was actually delivered. Some Mk XI torpedoes were transferred to the Far East but the war ended before they were in use. An RAF-designed 22.4in (*56.9cm*) electric torpedo was abandoned before production.

Pattern running had been available well before 1939 for destroyer torpedoes in the form of W gear, and preliminary work on data for homing torpedoes was begun before the war but was stopped for lack of a requirement. It was restarted in 1942 with Bowler, an active homing version of the 18in - 17.7in (*45cm*) - airborne torpedo and intended to improve the chances of hitting in attacks from ahead which were much safer for the aircraft than attacks from the beam. It was cancelled, as premature turns could be induced by explosion of another torpedo or by charges in the water.

Trumper, another active homer, was based on the 21in (*53.3cm*) Mks VIII and IX and was developed in collaboration with GEC, Wembley. The design was settled in 1943, and the quartz crystal transmitters and mosaic receiver crystals were contained in an oil-filled dome fitted to a flattened Mk VIII nose. Two stacks of crystals were paired to give a single broad bean of *c*60°. The target was kept on the edge of the beam to give a lead angle of about 30° and some protection from towed counter-measures and the ship's wake. A preferred side could be selected according to the angle of attack, and when the torpedo was within 170yd (*155m*) it turned 40° to hit. Trumper was on sea trials when the war ended but did not progress much further.

A 1942 active homer project by a RAF

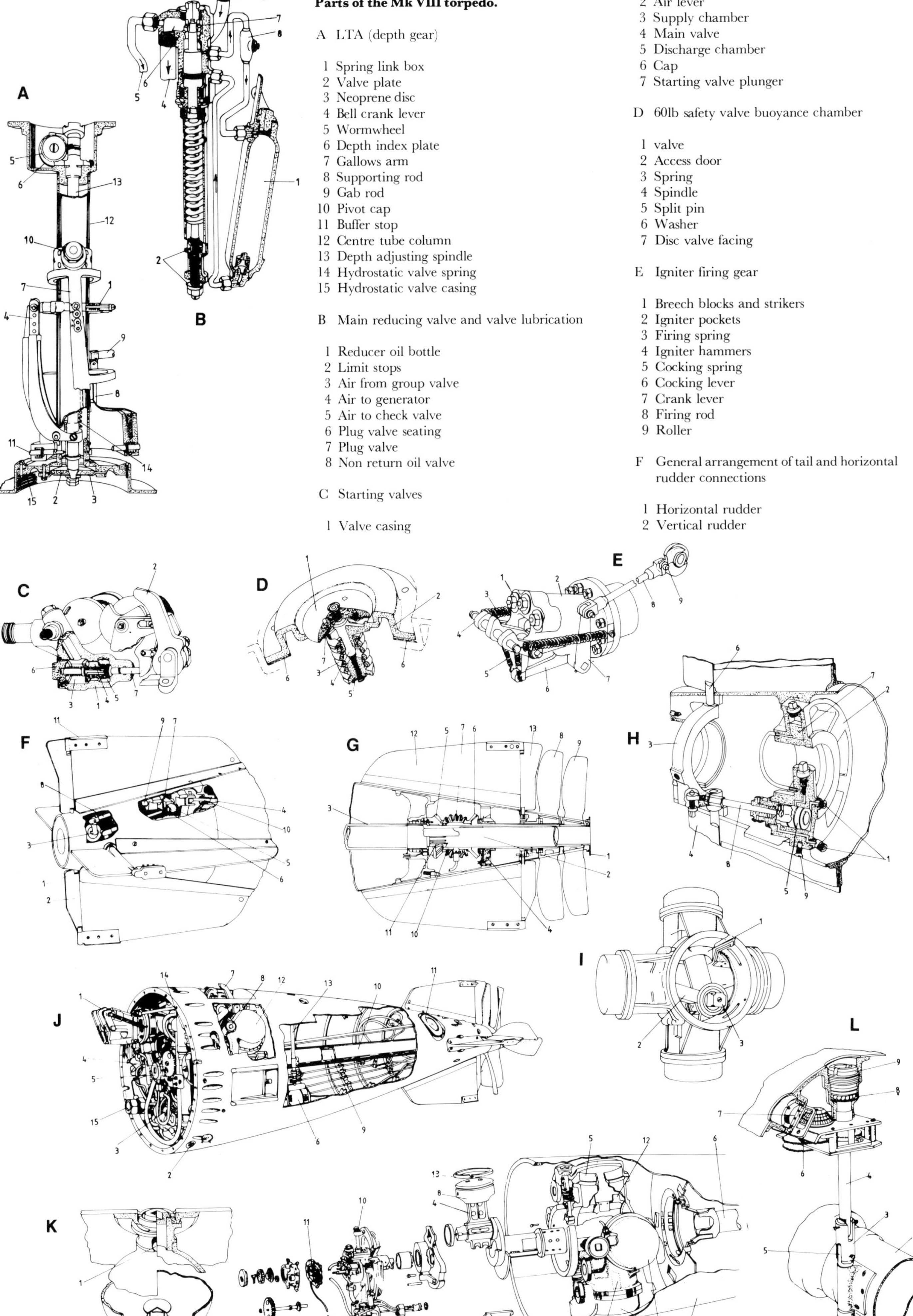

Parts of the Mk VIII torpedo.

A LTA (depth gear)

1 Spring link box
2 Valve plate
3 Neoprene disc
4 Bell crank lever
5 Wormwheel
6 Depth index plate
7 Gallows arm
8 Supporting rod
9 Gab rod
10 Pivot cap
11 Buffer stop
12 Centre tube column
13 Depth adjusting spindle
14 Hydrostatic valve spring
15 Hydrostatic valve casing

B Main reducing valve and valve lubrication

1 Reducer oil bottle
2 Limit stops
3 Air from group valve
4 Air to generator
5 Air to check valve
6 Plug valve seating
7 Plug valve
8 Non return oil valve

C Starting valves

1 Valve casing
2 Air lever
3 Supply chamber
4 Main valve
5 Discharge chamber
6 Cap
7 Starting valve plunger

D 60lb safety valve buoyance chamber

1 valve
2 Access door
3 Spring
4 Spindle
5 Split pin
6 Washer
7 Disc valve facing

E Igniter firing gear

1 Breech blocks and strikers
2 Igniter pockets
3 Firing spring
4 Igniter hammers
5 Cocking spring
6 Cocking lever
7 Crank lever
8 Firing rod
9 Roller

F General arrangement of tail and horizontal rudder connections

1 Horizontal rudder
2 Vertical rudder

3 Crank
4 Diving rod tube
5 Crosshead pivot
6 Rudder adjustment
7 Rudder crosshead
8 Connecting rod
9 Horizontal slider
10 Diving rod
11 Vertical rudder bearer

G Propeller shafts and tail gearing

1 Baffle plate
2 Main propeller shaft
3 Centre tube
4 Guard ring
5 Forward crown wheel
6 After crown wheel
7 Intermediate wheel
8 Forward propeller
9 After propeller
10 Crosshead
11 6 spline coupling
12 Vertical stabilising fin
13 Vertical rudder

H Steering engine and vertical rudder connections

1 Air leads from gyro
2 Guard ring
3 Crosshead
4 Vertical rudder
5 Piston
6 Inner pintle
7 Oil bottle
8 Distance rod
9 Securing screw

I Engine detail, cooling water system (water passes through channels in engine casing and is sprayed on to crank and connecting rod)

1 Piston
2 Connecting rod
3 Crank pin and bush

J Torpedo afterbody

1 Hammers
2 Speed setting location
3 Oil distributor
4 Water pump
5 Fuel timing valve
6 Air blast gyro
7 Air lever
8 Valve cap
9 Main propeller shaft
10 Centre tube
11 60lb safety valve
12 Cylinder head
13 Gyro angling spindle
14 Main reducer
15 Multiple pipe coupling

K Fuel bottle

1 Air inlet
2 Injection fuel to strainer in engine room
3 Pilot fuel to strainer in engine room

L External gyro angling gear

1 Forked clutch
2 Centre tube buoyance chamber
3 Jaw coupling
4 Angling spindle
5 Intermediate spindle
6 Sighting frame
7 Window disc
8 Single thrust bearing
9 Retaining nut

M Engine, general construction

1 Afterbody shell
2 Detachable cylinder head
3 Cylinder
4 Connecting rod
5 Cylinder liner
6 Tail shaft
7 Rotor geared to engine
8 Piston
9 Oil distributor
10 Counter gear drive
11 Water pump drive
12 Exhaust
13 Piston ring
14 Water strainer

John Lambert

design team for use against submarines was joined with Bowler under the name Joker. It was proposed to use the airborne 18in Mk XV, but reverberation, self noise and water entry shock caused much trouble. Joker was succeeded in 1943 by Dealer, which was an electric passive homer designed for surface launching or airborne with parachute retardation. Most of the design and the first prototypes were RAF. It was a very odd weapon, with depth control provided by motoring the main battery to and fro to alter the centre of gravity, and had no rudders for steering. Instead, two propellors were set in tandem on each side of a fixed fin, both propellers driven by an independently energised motor, and steering in azimuth was achieved by varying the relative voltage. The RNTF produced 100 in 1945 but they were never used in action and were quickly scrapped. For some reason this weapon was renamed Bidder A after the war – to add to the confusion of that period when several other homing torpedoes were under development.

Although airborne torpedoes were a very important weapon of carrier aircraft, they were not much favoured initially by the RAF, and it took a considerable time before adequate provision was made. Burner-cycle 18in (*17.7in, 45cm*) torpedoes were common to both services, and the main developments were in increased strength for greater dropping heights and speeds, and in larger warheads. The prewar staff requirements were for 150kts at 30–100ft (*9–30m*), which the first Mk XIIs could barely stand, but recommended figures for the Mk XV were 240kts at 400ft (*120m*), and Mk XVII (in production at the end of the war) was designed for 350kts. Larger warheads were limited to shore based aircraft as they made the torpedo too heavy for wartime British carrier aircraft, the Firebrand, which could take them, being too late for war service. The advantage of large explosive charges was less than might be thought, the amount of damage to the target varying at between the ⅓ and ⅔ powers of the charge weight ratios for a given explosive.

The standard explosive charge was initially TNT, but from 1943 the more powerful Torpex, 37–41% TNT, 41–45% RDX (cyclonite, cyclomethylene trinitramine), 18% aluminium replaced it, with 18in torpedoes having the higher priority.

As mentioned above, the magnetic part of the original Duplex CR (coil rod) pistol, in service only in 18in (*45cm*) torpedoes, was unreliable and it was finally abandoned at the end of 1943. A current was produced in a coil on a mu-metal rod as the torpedo passed under a ship and fired the warhead. It was tried successfully against the old flotilla leader *Bruce* in November 1939 and put the *Cavour* and *Duilio* out of action at Taranto, though the *Littorio* was hit by torpedoes with contact exploders. However it was not difficult to degauss so that it only operated 2–3ft (*60–90cm*) below the hull and, if the torpedo was deviated sharply, prematures were caused by the earth's magnetic field.

Its replacement, the CCR (compensated coil rod) with amplifier, was much better, as the compensated coils caused sudden movements to give equal and opposite effects, but under the target's hull the effects were not equal and, even if degaussed, the warhead was fired since the CCR was considerably more sensitive than the CR and functioned at 6–10ft (*180–300cm*) below the hull. The new pistol was liable to microphony from a nearby explosion or vibration if the torpedo broke surface violently, and was seriously affected by heat in the Far East. War Trials were begun in 1942 by submarines in British waters and in the Mediterranean, but were stopped as they coincided with a bad outbreak of gyro circling trouble and *Vernon*'s trials officer was lost with all his records in an air crash. Trials were resumed in December 1943 by the 1st Submarine Flotilla and later by other Submarine Flotillas and MTBs. It appears that in the following year over 250 CCR were expended with estimated results of 35.7% hits and probable hits by submarines and 40.5% by MTBs, compared with 22.6% and 28.2% for the previous year with contact exploders only.

By January 1945 CCR was standard for all submarines and MTB with 21in (*53.3cm*) torpedoes if the maintenance facilities were good. It was approved for cruisers (though not issued), but not for destroyers on account of 'counter-mining' and maintenance problems. The 18in (*45cm*) version was never sufficiently developed for war service.

PRE-WAR TORPEDOES STILL IN SERVICE

24.5in (*62.2cm*) Mk I

Two were fired by *Rodney* at *Bismarck* and this torpedo was otherwise carried only by *Nelson*. It was an oxygen-enriched air torpedo and was still unconverted to natural air when the TT were removed from *Nelson* in 1941-42 and blanked off in *Rodney* in 1943-44. Length overall 26ft 7in (*8103mm*), total weight 5700lb (*2585kg*), negative buoyancy 1229lb (*557kg*), explosive charge 743lb (*337kg*) TNT, range 15,000yd (*13,700m*)/35kts, 20,000yd (*18,300m*)/30kts. With shale oil and natural air the range would have been 7000yd (*6400m*)/35kts.

21in (*53.3cm*) Mk II

A wet-heater torpedo, the earlier versions dating to before the First World War. It was carried by some of the oldest destroyers and as a replacement for the Bliss-Leavitt in the former USN ones as well as in some submarines in the absence of anything better. Up to September 1944, 21 were expended. The explosive charge was 400lb (*181kg*) TNT, though torpedoes for internal TT in submarines and at first for former USN destroyers, had Mk IV or V warheads with 515lb (*234kg*). A single speed setting of 5000yd (*4570m*)/35kts was used in submarines with 8000 yd (*7300m*)/29kts in the former USN destroyers.

21in (*53.3cm*) Mk IV

This was the principal British torpedo of the First World War and was of wet-heater type. It was still standard for most of the earlier warships and was also issued to later ships including MTBs in the absence of more modern torpedoes. Expenditure to September 1944 totalled 516. Length overall 22ft 7½in (*6896mm*), total weight 3206lb (*1454kg*, negative buoyancy 445lb (*202kg*), explosive charge 515lb (*234kg*) TNT, range 8000yd (*7300m*)/35kts, 10,000yd (*9150m*)/29kts, 13,500yd (*12,350m*)/25kts. This was altered in torpedoes for submarines to 6000yd (*5500m*)/40kts, 9500yd (*8700m*)/ 30kts. Some composites were used with Mk VIII warheads in the earlier part of the war in *Havant* class destroyers but did not run very satisfactorily, and 100 were allocated as the initial salvo from the internal TT of selected modern submarines, the latter with a range of 6000yd (*5500m*)/35kts.

21in (*53.3cm*) Mk V

A wet-heater torpedo which first appeared in 1918. Originally negative buoyancy was 960lb (*435kg*) with total weight 3828lb (*1736kg*), but it was never issued in this form. It was 7½in (*190mm*) longer than Mk IV and was much lightened when introduced to service with explosive charge and range similar to those of Mk IV. It was originally in 'A' and 'B' class destroyers but was replaced by Mk IX, and also with strengthened tail, in the five RN *Kent* class, though the torpedo equipment was placed in store on reconstruction. It was issued in the absence of Mark IX and also to MTBs, 198 being expended up to September 1944.

21in (*53.3cm*) Mk VII

This was originally an oxygen-enriched air torpedo but was converted to natural air early in the war. At that time it was carried by *Australia*, *Canberra*, the *London* class and subsequent 8in (*203mm*) cruisers, but was later replaced by Mk IX as opportunity offered. Only nine Mk VII were expended. Length overall 25ft 6in (*7772mm*), total weight 4106lb (*1862kg*), explosive charge 740lb (*336kg*) TNT, range 16,000yd (*14,600m*)/33kts. With shale oil and natural air it was known as Mk VIIC and had a range of 5700yd (*5200m*)/35kts.

18in (*45cm, 17.7in*) Mk VII

The first torpedo to be designed with a wet heater and dating from 1909. It was used in the late 1920s for dropping from flying boats. Only one was expended in the war. The latest version Mk VII***** had a 320lb (*145kg*) TNT charge and range 5000yd (*4570m*)/35kts, 7000yd (*6400m*)/29kts.

18in (*45cm, 17.7in*) Mk VIII

Another wet-heater torpedo of 1913 vintage, designed originally for submarines and used as an airborne weapon until the mid 1930s. Two were expended during the war by MTBs. The TNT charge was as in Mk VII, but range was 2500yd (*2300m*)/35kts, 4000yd (*3650m*)/29kts.

18in (*45cm, 17.7in*) Mk XI

An airborne burner-cycle torpedo of which 22 were expended in the war, as far as is known by MTBs. Mk XI was intended to meet staff requirements for weight not over 1500lb (*680kg*), explosive charge 465lb (*211kg*) TNT, range 1500yd (*1370m*)/40kts, 4000yd (*3660m*)/24-25kts. It was to stand dropping at 150kts from 30-100ft (*9-30m*), not to dive below 60ft (*18m*) and to recover within 400yd (*360m*). Mk XI went to sea in late 1936, but suffered from weakness due to the long balance chamber and was soon replaced by Mk XII. The air vessel was smaller than in Mk XII but pressure was higher at 2600lb/in² (*183kg/cm²*). The explosive charge was 440lb (*200kg*) TNT and ranges in MTBs 1500yd (*1370m*)/40kts and 3000yd (*2740m*)/27kts.

TORPEDOES MANUFACTURED 1939-1945

Mk VIII was the first burner-cycle torpedo in service, carried during the war by all British submarines from the 'O' class onwards when available, and also issued to MTBs. It was used far more than any other British torpedo, expenditure to September 1944 being 3732 - 56.4% of the total for all torpedoes. It may be noted that post-war versions are still in service in 1983, 56 years after the first appearance of the original Mk VIII. The principal war version Mk VIII** was a considerable improvement on the original as shown below. It had higher air pressure, larger propellers, and was just about to go into production at the outbreak of war. There were no sea acceptance trials and a number of minor troubles were prevalent initially. Modifications of Mk VIII** could run at 75ft (*23m*) instead of the usual limit of 44ft (*13.4m*) and were strengthened for launching at 300ft (*91m*).

21in (53.3cm) Mark VIII**

Length oa	21ft 7in	6579mm
Total weight	3452lb max	1566kg max
Negative buoyancy	804lb max	365kg max
Volume air vessel	15.64ft³	4431
Pressure	3000lb/in²	211kg/cm²
Weight air	253lb	115kg
Shale oil	30lb	13.6kg
HP 45kts	322	
Consumption expendables	9.7lb/HP/hr	4.4kg/HP/hr
Explosive charge	805lb Torpex (orig 722lb TNT)	365kg Torpex (orig 327kg TNT)
Range	5000yd/45.5kts 7000yds/41kts	4570m/45.5kts 6400m/41kts

Early Mk VIII torpedoes had air pressure 2500lb/in² (*176kg/cm²*), HP and range at 40kts, 230 and 5000yd (*4570m*), and explosive charge 750lb (*340kg*) TNT. Mk VIII*E, primarily used in the external TT of submarines and at sea at the start of the war, lacked the larger propellors and 45.5kt setting of Mk VIII**, but had a strengthened air vessel with a 40kt range greater than in Mk VIII, VIII*. Mk VIII** (40) was built with a Mk VIII** forebody and IX** depth gear, after body and tail in order to speed production. Range was 7000yd (*6400m*)/40kts.

21in Mk VIII torpedo showing layout of principal features and dimensions.
John Lambert

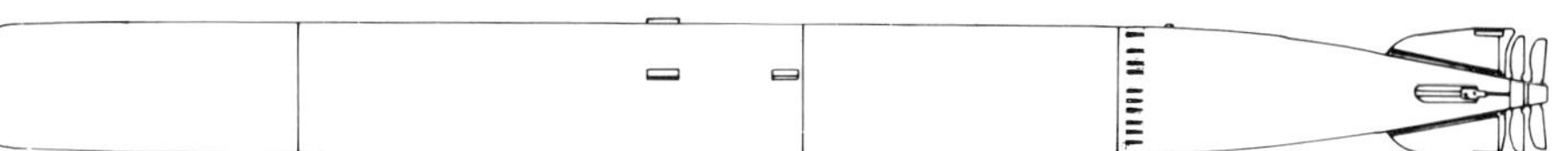

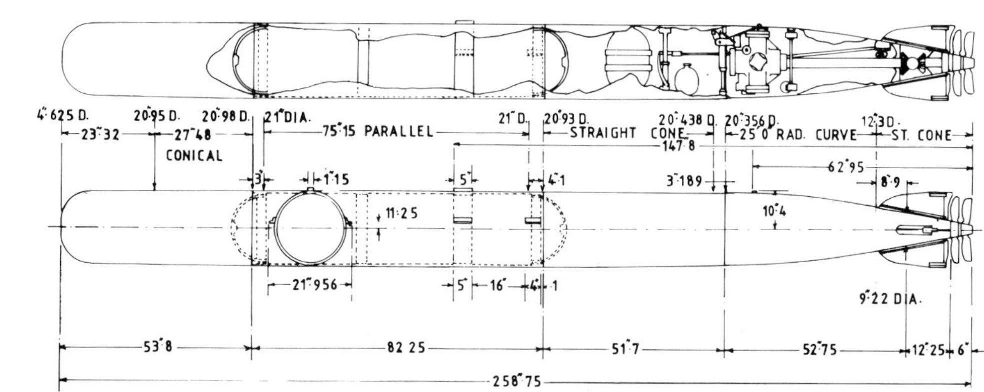

21in single TT mounted in MTB.
John Lambert

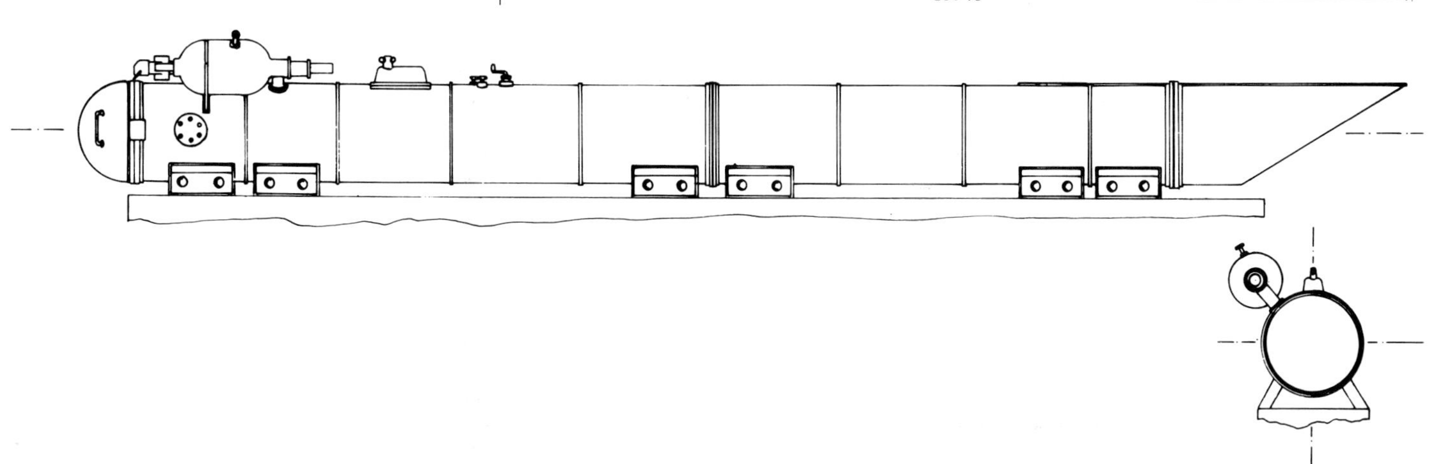

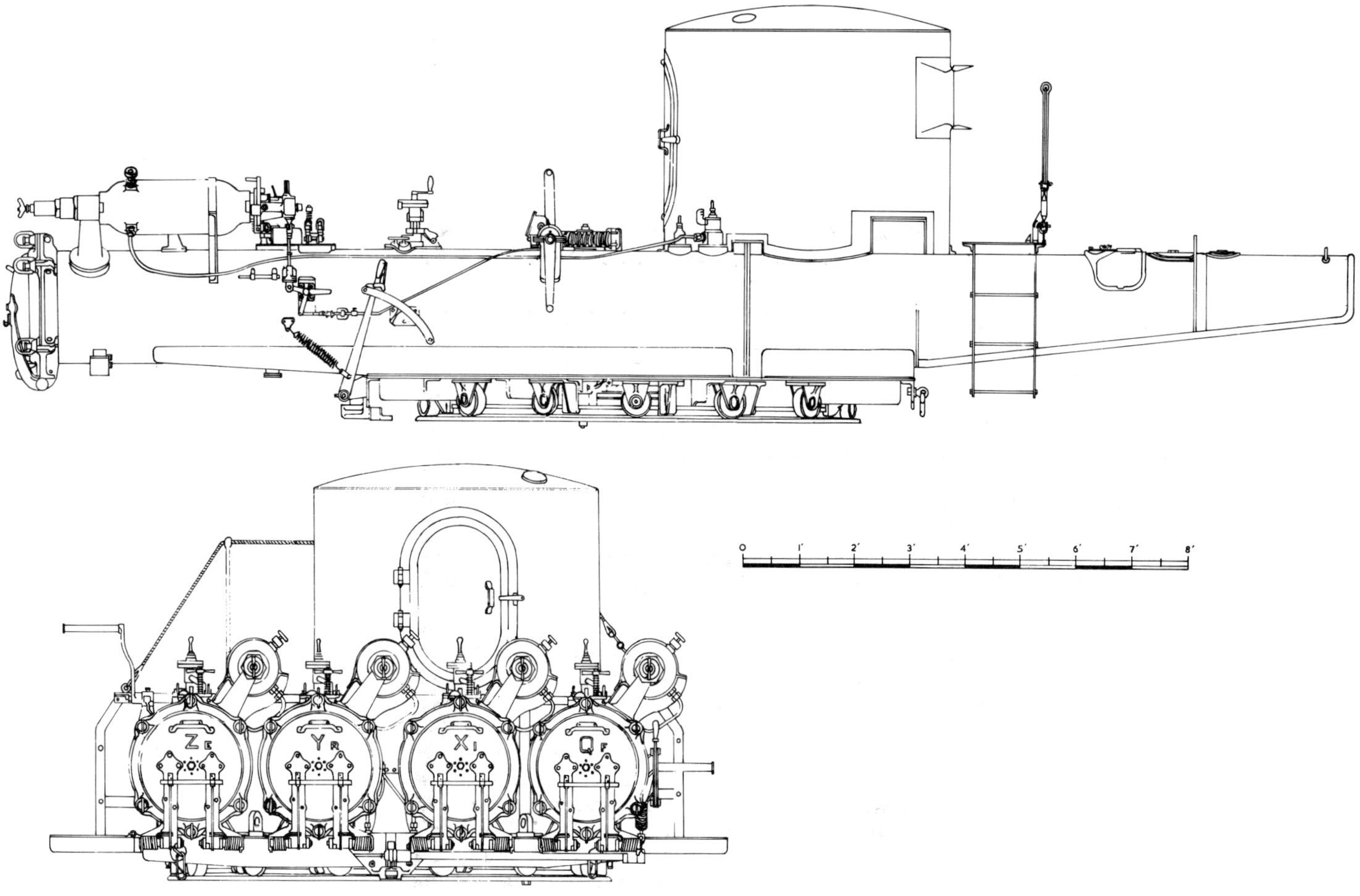

21in Mk VIII quadruple TT mounting for Mk IX torpedoes, in emergency programme fleet destroyers.
John Lambert

21in (53.3cm) Mark IX**

Length oa	23ft 10½in	7277mm
Total weight	3732lb	1693kg
Negative buoyancy	732lb	332kg
Volume air vessel	21.53ft³	610l
Pressure	3100lb/in²	218kg/cm²
Weight air	360lb	163kg
Shale oil	37.5lb	17kg
Hp at 41kts	264	
Consumption expendables	10.3lb/HP/hr	4.67kg/HP/hr
Explosive charge	810lb Torpex (orig. 727lb TNT)	367kg Torpex (orig. 330kg TNT)
Range	11,000yd/41kts 15,000yd/35kts	10050m/41kts 13700m/kts

This was another burner-cycle torpedo which first appeared in 1930, and it was considerably improved by 1939. If available it was issued to the *Leander* and later cruisers and to destroyers from the A class onwards, with a few exceptions. It also replaced Mk VII in some 8in (*203mm*) cruisers during the war. Expenditure to September 1944 was only 361. The principal war version was Mk IX**, first issued to 'J' and 'K' class destroyers in the summer of 1939. In 1943 it was decided to concentrate on the longest and heaviest torpedo that could be handled and fired by ships then under construction. Length could be increased by 12in (*305mm*) over that of Mk IX** and total weight raised to 4000lb (*1814kg*). Nitro fuels were considered, but required too many alterations and presented toxicity and ventilation problems. It was eventually decided to take up the 12in by increasing the explosive charge to 930lb (*422kg*) Torpex. None was in service during the war. Early Mk IX torpedoes had air pressure 2500lb/in² (*176kg/cm²*), HP at 35kts 170, explosive charge 750lb (*340kg*) TNT and range 10,500yd (*9600m*)/35kts, 13,500yd (*12,350m*)/30kts. In Mk IX* air pressure was 2650lb/in² (*186kg/cm²*) and range 500yds (*450m*) more at both speeds.

21in (53.3cm) Mark X*

Length oa	7200mm	23ft 7.5in
Total weight	1620kg	3571lb
Negative buoyancy	275kg	606lb
Volume air vessel	603 litres	21.3ft³
Pressure	200kg/cm²	2845lb/in²
Weight air	142kg	313lb
Explosive charge	300kg TNT	661 TNT
Range	3000m/47kts 5000m/43kts 8000m/36kts 12,000m/29kts	3280yd/47kts 5470yd/43kts 8750yd/36kts 13,120yd/29kts

This Mark covered a number of Whitehead wet-heater torpedoes for various foreign warships. Mk X was originally issued to Polish destroyers, and the small surplus later converted to Mk X* by altering the top lug. Mk X* was for Turkey but went to the six ex-Brazilian *Havant* class destroyers in place of their original Mk X** used in some MTB. Mk X*** was in some Dutch submarines and Mk X****, originally for Romania, was adapted for British warheads as none was available, and issued to some Greek submarines. The ex-Turkish *Inconstant* and *Ithuriel* had Mk IV, as did the *Havant* class eventually, while the ex-Turkish submarines *P614* and *P615* carried Mk X* for their external stern TT, with Mk VIII for the bow tubes. Expenditure of Mk X-X**** totalled 61. The engine was a Whitehead two-cylinder double acting. Mk X** was 200mm (*7.9in*) shorter than Mk X* with slightly reduced performance. Mk X*** is believed to be the torpedo described here under Other Countries, and Mk X**** was 6500mm (*21ft 4in*) long.

Triple torpedo tubes for Mk 10 torpedoes aboard the Polish destroyer *Blyskawica* in 1940
CPL

21in (53.3cm) Mark XI

Length oa	22ft 5in	6833mm
Total weight	3632lb	1647kg
Negative buoyancy	734lb	333kg
Explosive charge	710lb TNT	322kg TNT
Range	5500yd/28kts	5000m/28kts

This electric torpedo, based on the German G7e-T2, was never in service during the war as noted above. The two batteries each had 26 cells with a total weight of 1475lb (*669kg*) while the motor took 960 amps at 91 volts and 1755 rpm, the BHP being given as 98. The range given in the table is with the battery heated to 86°F (*30°C*). Otherwise it was 4500-5000yd (*4100-4570m*)/28kts.

Other 21in (53.3cm)

Type A, a project for the RAF, was abandoned in 1944. Weight was 2400lb (*1089kg*), explosive charge 700lb (*318kg*) range 4000yd (*3660m*)/40kts or 2000yd (*1830m*)/*c*49kts. A number of German G7a, also 21in (*53.3cm*), were captured in two supply ships and, converted to burn kerosene type fuel instead of Decalin, were issued to Dutch submarines as G7 AD. They were limited to 40kts because of breaking surface at higher speed and were later replaced by Mk VIII**.

18in (45cm, 17.7in) Mark XII

Length oa	16ft 3in	4953mm
Total weight	1548lb	702kg
Negative buoyancy	*c*230lb	*c*104kg
Volume air vessel	6.45ft^3	182.6l
Pressure	1600lb/in^2	112kg/cm^2
Weight air	52lb	23.6kg
Shale oil	7.5lb	3.4kg
HP 40kts	*c*140	
Consumption expendables	*c*10lb/HP/hr	*c*4.5kg/HP/hr
Explosive charge	388lb TNT	176kg TNT
Range	1500yd/40kts	1370m/40kts
	3500yd/27kts	3200m/27kts

Later versions had the shale oil increased to 10lb (*4.5kg*) and the air pressure in Mk XII** was 1900lb/in^2 (*134kg/cm^2*) giving 62lb air and a range of 2000yd (*1830m*)/40kts. Additional strengthening allowed dropping speeds of 250-270kts.

This burner-cycle airborne torpedo was an improved Mk XI and in production in 1937. It differed from Mk XI in a longer, lower pressure air vessel which slightly increased the low speed range and in a shorter, stronger balance chamber. Mk XII*, in service at the outbreak of war, was fitted with gyro angling and was strengthened with various small improvements. Flight in air was controlled by a monoplane tail, detached on striking the water, with two air rudders servo-operated from gyros, and roll by drum control gear in the aircraft with detachable wires to the torpedo. The wires were usually 18ft (*5.5m*) long and were intended to control the torpedo until it was clear of the aircraft's slipstream. Mk XII could almost meet staff requirements as given under Mk XI, but at 150kts control in air was unreliable and the torpedo tended to roll. Some later versions had a similar air-tail to that described under Mk XV.

Mk XII was the standard airborne torpedo for the first half of the war and was still in use later in aircraft and to a limited extent in MTBs. Altogether 1101 were expended to September 1944.

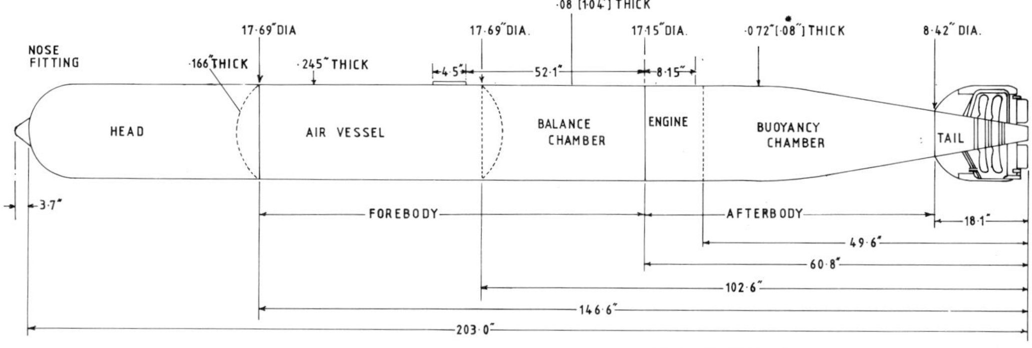

18in Mk XV and XVII torpedoes with principal dimensions (overall length was 207.4in for Mk XVII). *John Lambert*

18in single TT mounted in MTB. *John Lambert*

18in (45cm, 17.7in) Mark XV

Length oa	17ft 2¾in	5251mm
Total weight	1801lb	817kg
Negative buoyancy	*c*375lb	*c*170kg
Volume air vessel	6.45ft^3	182.6l
Pressure	2200lb/in^2	155kg/cm^2
Weight air	72lb	32.7kg
Shale oil	10lb	4.5kg
HP 40kts	*c*140	
Consumption expendables	*c*10lb/HP/hr	*c*4.5kg/HP/hr
Explosive charge	545lb Torpex	247kg Torpex
Range	2500yd/40kts	2290m/40kts
	3500yd/33kts	3200m/33kts

The 33kt setting was an alternative for MTBs only. The above explosive charge made the torpedo too heavy for wartime carrier aircraft which used 388lb (*176kg*) TNT or later 432.5lb (*196kg*) Torpex.

This was the standard airborne torpedo in the later years of the war, and was also used by MTBs. Total expenditure to September 1944 was 591. It generally resembled Mk XII and had the same burner cycle engine with higher air vessel pressure to give additional range at 40kts. The torpedo was strengthened for entry at up to 270kts, but because of weight limitations, the weakest parts had to be strengthened in succession. Thus, as one part was corrected, another failed and had to be strengthened in turn. A heavier Torpex warhead was available for land-based aircraft and MTBs, and an additional setting of 3500yd (*3200m*)/33kts was provided for the latter, while the anti-roll gear was much improved by replacing the wire drum by gyro controlled ailerons on the monoplane tail. These gyros were driven by the slipstream and venturis, and the aileron servo motors from air bottles. All this anti-roll gear was housed inside the air-tail. This type of tail could not be used with some of the older aircraft and, in these, the former type with drum gear was retained.

The above ranges were not long enough for MTB and a special torpedo could not be developed in time, though a longer air vessel in the Mk XII could have been produced fairly easily for *c*5000yd (4570m)/40kts. Mk XV* covered some torpedoes with air pressure reduced to 2000lb/in^2 (*141kg/cm^2*) because of possible cracks in the air vessels.

A strengthened Mk XV under test and in production at the end of the war. It was intended for dropping at 350kts and an increased explosive charge was provided for Firebrands and land-based aircraft, with a strengthened small warhead for others.

18in (45cm, 17.7in) Mark XVII

Length oa	17ft 3.4in	5268mm
Total weight	1874.5lb	850kg
Negative buoyancy	447lb	203kg
Volume air vessel	6.45ft³	182.6l
Pressure	2200lb/in²	155kg/cm²
Weight air	72lb	32.7kg
Shale oil	10lb	4.5kg
HP 40kts	*c*140	
Consumption expendables	*c*10lb/HP/hr	*c*4.5kg/HP/hr
Explosive charge	600lb Torpex	272kg Torpex
Range	2500yd/39-40kts	2290m/39-40kts

The alternative explosive charge was 432.5lb (*196kg*) Torpex.

Other **18in** (45cm, 17.7in)

Mark XIII. No details of this have been found and it may never have existed.

Mark XIV. Practically the whole stock of this was lost at Singapore. It was a Whitehead wet-heater torpedo with methylated spirits as fuel and air pressure 2420lb/in² (*170kg/cm²*). An eight-cylinder engine was used and the explosive charge was 375lb (*170kg*) TNT. Total weight was 1630lb (*739kg*). Ranges are given as 1650yd (*1500m*)/45kts and 2950yd (*2700m*)/41kts. It was used by the RAF but was less robust than Mk XII which replaced it.

Mark XVI. A proposed electric circling torpedo dropped by parachute, and with a speed of about 10kts for 30 minutes running. It was abandoned in 1943.

ANTI-SUBMARINE WEAPONS

Kempenfelt with Type D Depth Charges in the 1930s. *CPL*

In 1939 the only special A/S weapon for surface ships was the Mk VII depth-charge, in all essential particulars the same as the Type D of the First World War, and there was no satisfactory airborne weapon. To the middle of 1944 improved depth-charges remained the principal A/S weapon for surface ships, but from then on the ahead-throwing Hedgehog and Squid accounted for more U-boats and their ratio of successes to attacks was far better. The original A/S bombs were of very little use, and the far better airborne DC was not introduced until the summer of 1940 and then in totally inadequate quantities until the spring of 1941. It remained the principal airborne weapon though the homing Mk 24 torpedo, described with other US torpedoes, had a far higher success rate. There were restrictions on its use, so that airborne DCs accounted for more U-boats. A/S rockets, noted with other rockets, had some considerable successes and there was latterly a special projectile, known as Shark, for 4in (*101.6mm*) guns described below.

British forces accounted for the following German U-boats (allowing ½ for a shared kill):

Period	Surface ships	Shore based aircraft	Shipborne aircraft	Bombing raids
1939-42	72	31½	3	nil
1943-45	153	177	16½	22
Total	225	208½	19½	22

For surface ships the figures below indicate the relative success of DCs, Hedgehog and Squid.

Attacks and Successes Period	DC		Hedge-hog		Double Squid		Single Squid	
1st ½ 1943	554	27½	53	4½	—	—	—	—
2nd ½ 1943	4011	15	49	4	—	—	—	—
1st ½ 1944	404	30	70	10	—	—	3	0
2nd ½ 1944	98	5½	37	13	6	2½	17	4
1945	107	7½	59	15½	21	8½	3	2

For the last two periods these give a success rate of 6.34% for DC, 29.69% for Hedgehog, 40.74% for Double Squid and 30% for Single Squid.

SURFACE SHIP WEAPONS

DEPTH CHARGES

The main developments were to increase the speed of sinking and the maximum depth setting of the hydrostatic pistol from 300ft (*91m*) to twice that figure and eventually to 900ft (*274m*) or 1000ft (*305m*) in anticipation that U-boats might be able to sustain that depth. A pistol with a setting of 1450ft (*442m*) was developed during the war but did not enter service. It may be noted that the usual settings in late 1943 against a U-boat that had gone deep were between 500ft (*153m*) and 740ft (*226m*). More powerful explosives were introduced as available and the number was greatly increased, the original five-charge pattern being replaced by 10, 14 and ater 26 were often used in a single attack. Outfits originally 15–40 in most escorts, increased to 60–160, though if Squid was carried DCs were cut to 15, and 'Hunts' were limited to 30–70. Fleet destroyers later had 45–130.

Ship and Airborne DCs were numbered in one series, the latter including Mks VIII, XI, XIV, XV.

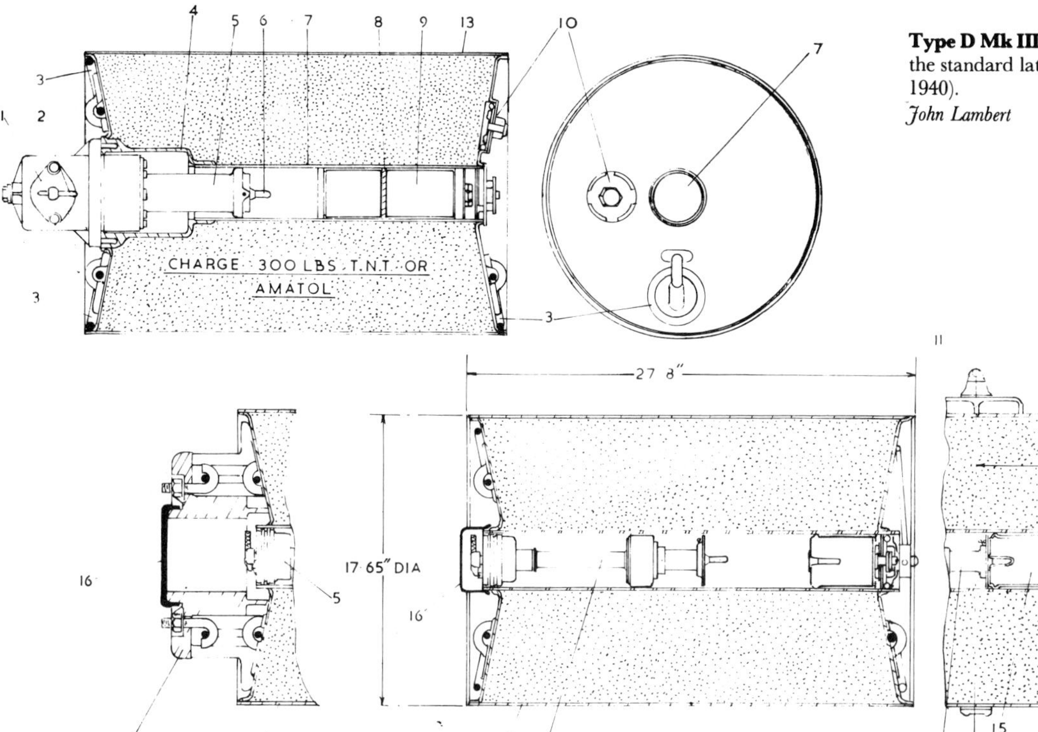

Type D Mk III Depth Charge in section. This was the standard late First World War DC (still in service 1940).
John Lambert

The MkVII Depth Charge developed from the Type D and standard in 1939/40. It is shown in section with part sections of the faster sinking Mk VII Heavy standard in 1941–45, and Mk VII Airborne DC.

1 Depth adjuster
2 Key
3 Lifting ring
4 Pistol chamber
5 Pistol
6 Detonator
7 Primer tube
8 Rolling rubber ring
9 Mark IV primer
10 Filling holes and bungs
11 Suspending band and pad
12 Double bung
13 Case
14 Buffer
15 Mark VIII primer
16 Rubber cover
17 Ballast weight

John Lambert

Mark VII

The 1939 standard with 290lb (*132kg*) amatol charge and total weight *c*420lb (*191kg*). The initial sinking speed was 7f/s (*2.1m/s*) with terminal velocity 9.9f/s (*3.0m/s*) reached at 250ft (*76m*) or almost at once from a DC thrower.

Mark VII Heavy

Introduced at the end of 1940, this had a 150lb (*68kg*) cast-iron weight attached, which increased the terminal velocity to 16.8f/s (*5.1m/s*), and was the standard ship DC until the end of the war. The 290lb (*132kg*) amatol charge would split a ⅞in (*22mm*) hull at 20ft (*6.1m*), and probably cause the submarine to surface at twice this distance. A minol charge introduced in December 1942 increased these distances to 26ft (*7.9m*) and 52ft (*15.8m*).

Mark IX

In this the fuze was actuated by the U-boat's magnetic field, but there was insufficient development effort for it to be introduced to service. The explosive charge was 300lb (*136kg*).

Type L

Another proximity fuzed DC depending on increasing UEP as it approached the U-boat. The explosive charge was *c*250lb (*113kg*) minol, and like MK IX it was never in service.

Mark X

A very large DC weighing 3050lb (*1383kg*) with 2000lb (*907kg*) charge. It was intended for launching from 21in (*53.3cm*) aw TT and was 10ft (*304.8cm*) long with in addition buoyancy chambers (*45.7cm*) diameter x 48 in (*121.9cm*) at either end. The purpose of these was to reduce the sinking speed to 6f/s (*1.8m/s*), the DC sinking with axis horizontal, so that the launching ship could get clear of the explosion, set at 220ft (*67m*), at a minimum of 11kts. It entered service in March 1942, and was first in *Chesterfield, Ambuscade, Boadicea, Buxton* and *Newmarket* but was rarely used. In July 1942 it was found that removal of the forward buoyancy chamber increased sinking speed to 21f/s (*6.4m/s*) and with the pistol setting at 640ft (*195m*) the launching ship was safe at 11kts. This DC known as Mk X*, was introduced in April 1943 and one or two of both Mk X and X* were carried in ships so equipped. It was found that the sea-keeping of certain turbo-electric 'Captain' class frigates was improved by added top weight and in December 1944 it was approved to equip all 'Captains' with two Mk X* launching axially over the stern from rails. In turbo-electric ships this was additional weight but in diesel-electric 16 Mk VII DC were landed to compensate. No damage was caused to these ships at 6kts.

In January 1945 it was agreed to proceed with Mk X** which had a faired nose and drum and fin tail, with the conical part buoyant, and was intended to sink at *c*50f/s (*15.2m/s*). It was intended for use down to 1500ft (*457m*) and at 900ft (*274m*) setting was safe from a stationary ship. Like other advanced DCs it was never in service, being superseded by ahead-throwing weapons.

Mark XII

A small DC with 55lb (*25kg*) minol charge for use against midget submarines and similar devices.

Mark XIII

A large version of the above with 124lb (*56kg*) minol charge used by coastal forces and also intended to deter pursuers, a tactic used by the Italians in the First World War.

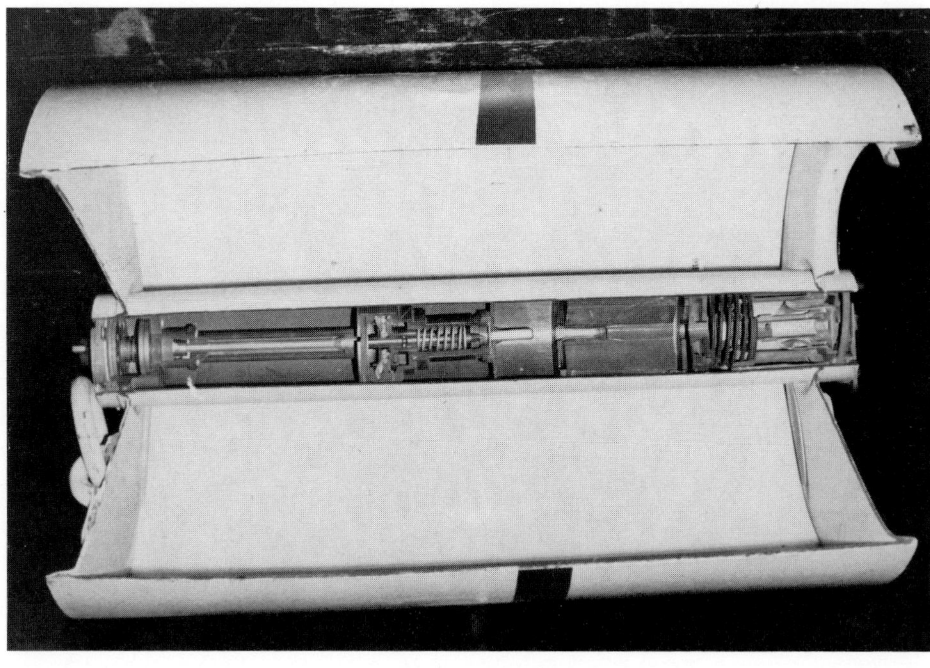

Above: Depth Charge of Mk VII type in section. *By courtesy of John Lambert*

Below: **Details of DC launching rails as fitted to 'Flower' class corvettes.**

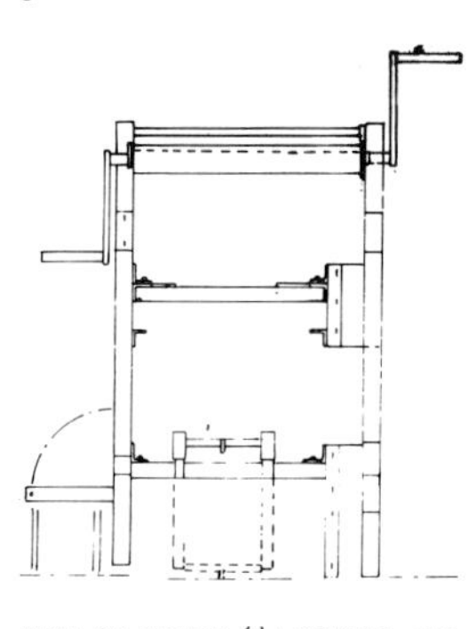

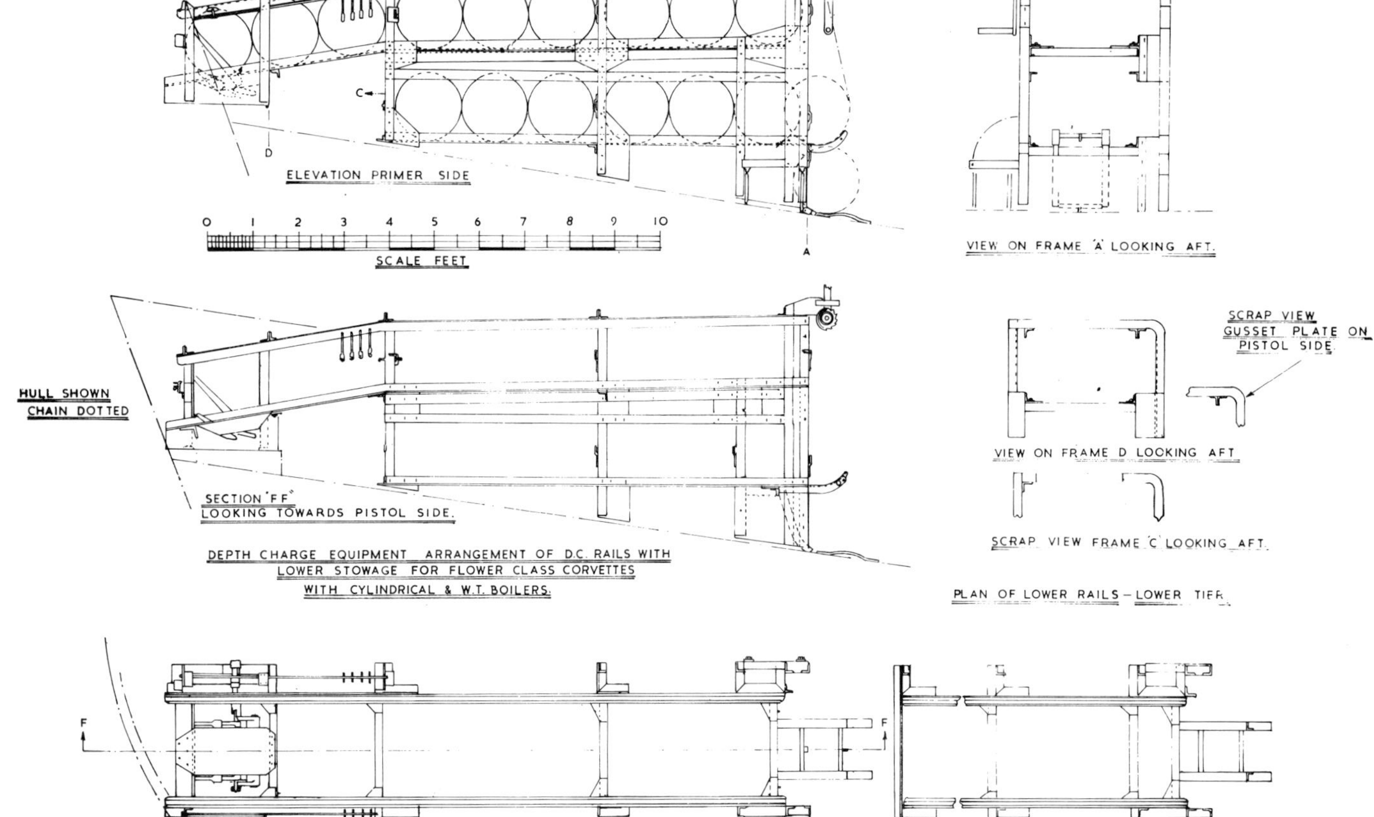

1 Rocking lever
2 Actuating lever
3 Resetting lever
4 Adjusting lever
5 Hydraulic receiver

John Lambert

Mark II Thrower

The Mk II Thornycroft depth charge thrower with a nominal range of 40yds (*37m*) was supplemented by the Mk IV DCT which had a piston type non-expendable arbor and a range of 67yds (*61m*) for the Mk VII DC and 51yd (*47m*) for the Mk VII Heavy. It was apparently first carried in *Winchelsea* in September 1941 and was succeeded in 1945 by the Mk V, first tried in *Highlander* in May 1944, with increased ranges of up to 78yd (*71m*) and 62yd (*57m*). Mks II and IV are often listed as ML 9.5in (*241.3mm*) DCLT IV and Mk V as ML 6in (*152.4mm*) DCT Mk V. The US 'K' gun, Mk VI DCT in the RN, was in Lend-Lease ships, but with altered ranges of 68yd (*62m*) and 55yd (*50m*) for Mk VII and VII Heavy DCs to suit British patterns. Some use was also made of 'Y' guns known as DCT Mk III.

Above: **Mk IV Thornycroft DC thrower often listed as ML 9.5in DCT Mk IV, with stowage rack.**
Below: **Mk V Thornycroft DC thrower often listed as ML 6in DCT Mk V, with stowage rack.**

1 Ramp
2 Hinged stool
3 Parbuckling hoist gear
4 Roller wheels
5 Wire stop
6 DC tray
7 Surge tank
8 Tumbler hook
9 Pipe to arrestor cylinder
10 Exhaust ports
11 Carrier piston
12 Barrel
13 Drain
14 ¼in bore copper vent pipe
15 1in bore copper vent pipe
16 Left arrestor
17 Right arrestor
18 Arrestor rod
19 Arrestor piston
John Lambert

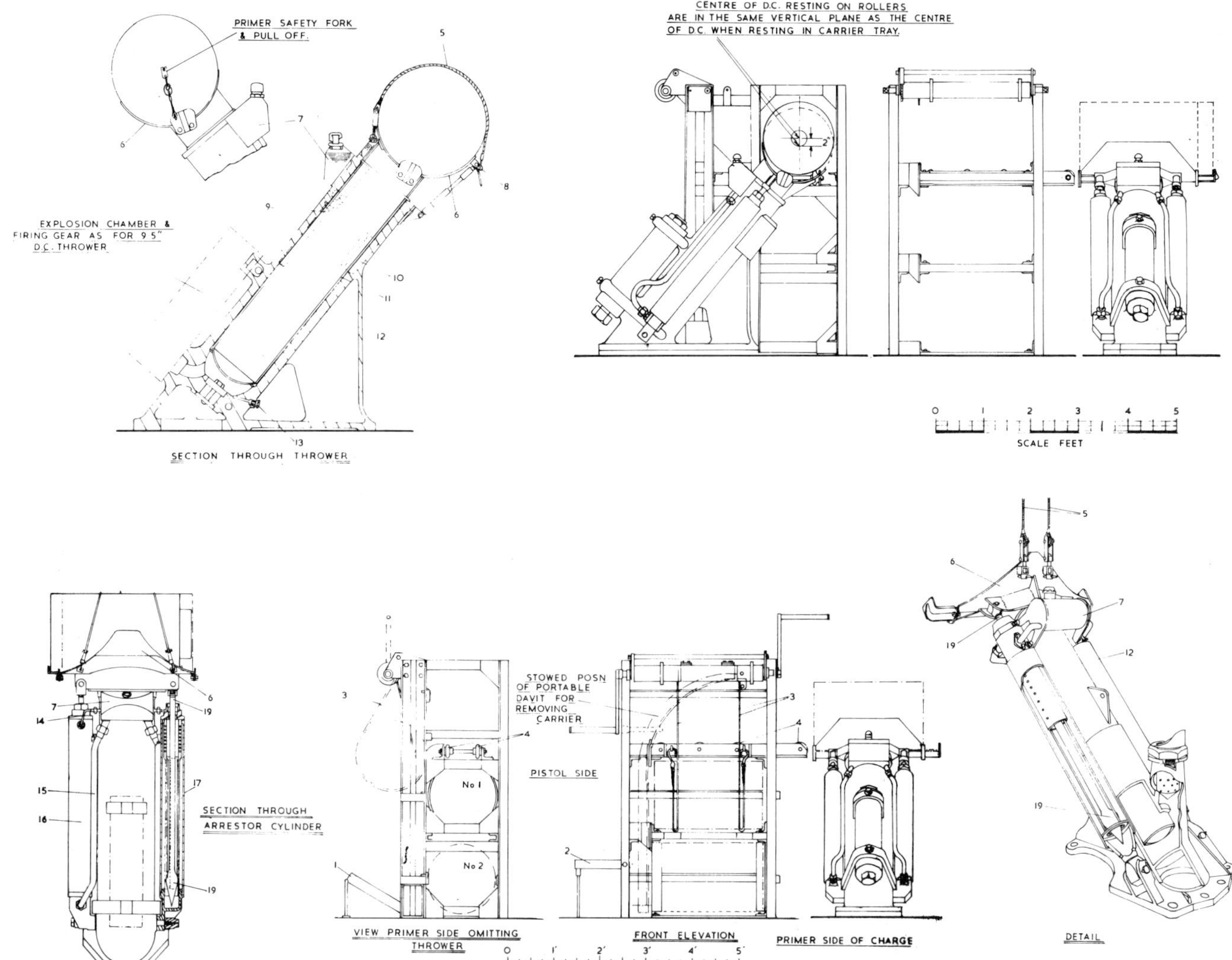

AHEAD-THROWING WEAPONS

Hedgehog

This was a 24-spigot mortar firing 7in (*177.8mm*) diameter contact-fuzed projectiles weighing 65lb (*29.5kg*) with a 35lb (*15.9kg*) torpex charge. Sinking speed was 22–23.5f/s (*6.7–7.2m/s*) and the spigots which were arranged with six in each of four vertical rows were angled to give a 40yd (*37m*) diameter circle at *c*200yd (*183m*) ahead of a stationary ship. Hedgehog was intended to be fired dead ahead, but the rows of spigots could be moved by electric motors to give *c*20° effective training and in later versions to compensate for roll. It was not very successful against deep targets, and eventually was not to be used if sonar contact was lost at over 400yd (*366m*) indicating that the target was probably below 400ft (*122m*). DCs were preferred if sonar conditions were bad. Hedgehog was usually fired with a total blind time of 16sec, corresponding to 175ft (*53m*) depth, and as a rule did not give an obvious kill.

A pilot model of the mounting with dummy ammunition was installed in B position in *Westcott* in May 1941 and sea trials took place at the end of the year in the same ship with Hedgehog in A position. Over 100 ships by the end of 1942 and eventually over 500 had been fitted, but there were no kills until November 1942 and it was not until 1944 with improved techniques that Hedgehog was really successful.

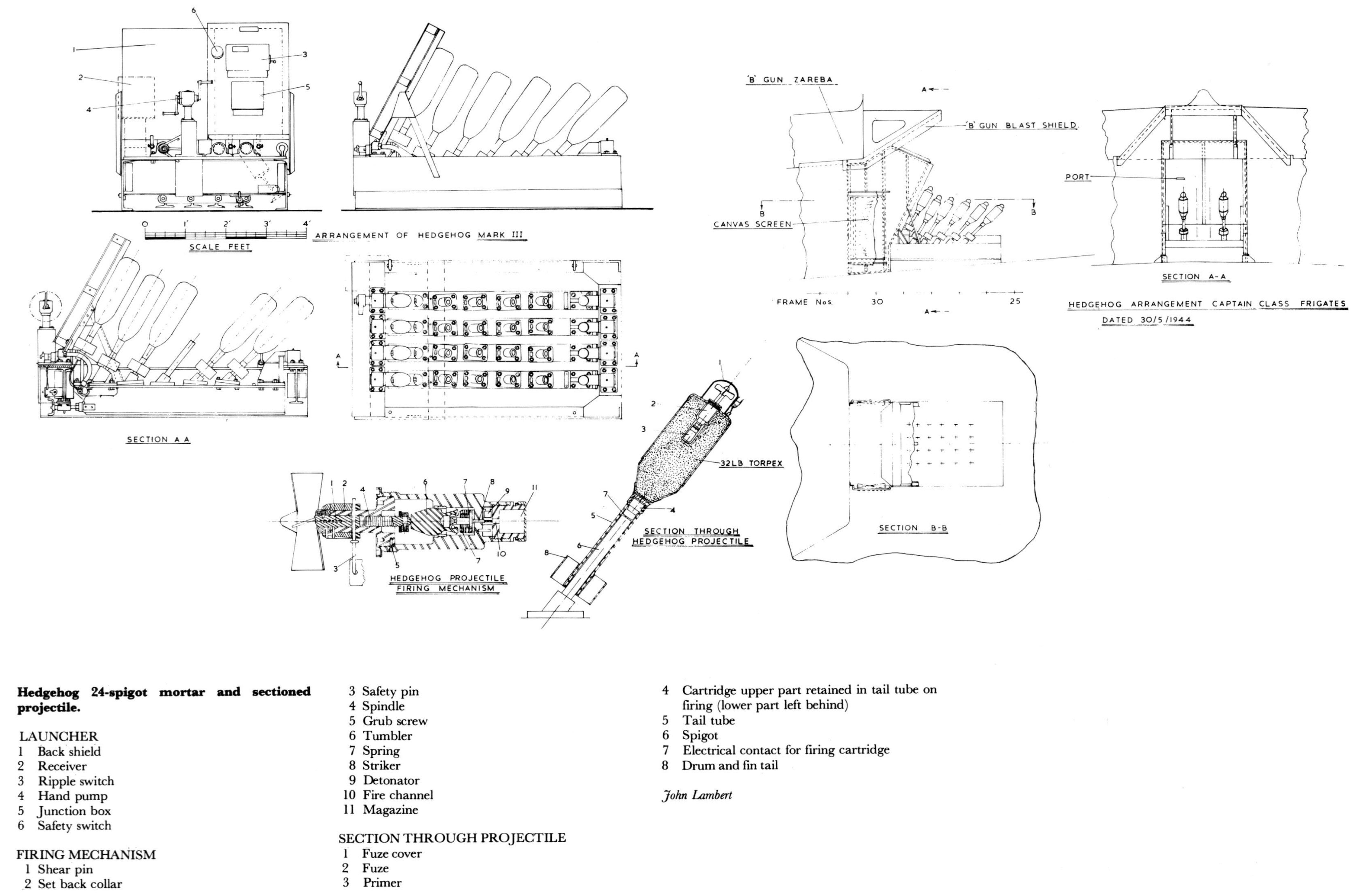

Hedgehog 24-spigot mortar and sectioned projectile.

LAUNCHER
1 Back shield
2 Receiver
3 Ripple switch
4 Hand pump
5 Junction box
6 Safety switch

FIRING MECHANISM
1 Shear pin
2 Set back collar
3 Safety pin
4 Spindle
5 Grub screw
6 Tumbler
7 Spring
8 Striker
9 Detonator
10 Fire channel
11 Magazine

SECTION THROUGH PROJECTILE
1 Fuze cover
2 Fuze
3 Primer
4 Cartridge upper part retained in tail tube on firing (lower part left behind)
5 Tail tube
6 Spigot
7 Electrical contact for firing cartridge
8 Drum and fin tail

John Lambert

Split Hedgehog

This was used in some sloops and other ships where it was important to retain the forward gun. The port and starboard halves were originally coupled together for tilt correction by wire cables which were not satisfactory, and later hydraulic jacks were used. About 35 ships were fitted, *Enchantress* being the first in July 1942, while *Fowey* first had the later type in April 1943.

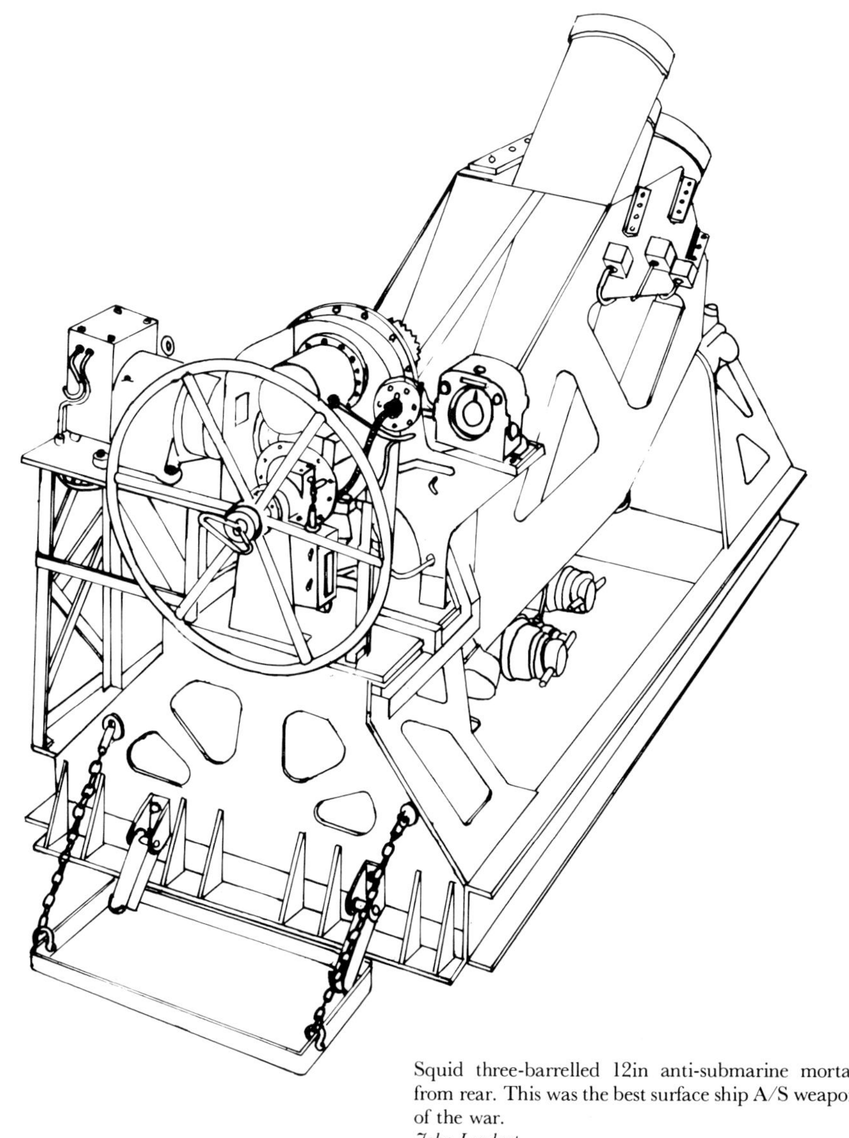

Squid three-barrelled 12in anti-submarine mortar from rear. This was the best surface ship A/S weapon of the war.
John Lambert

Parsnip

This comprised two ten-barrel units each firing a semicircular pattern with a common centre 250yd (*229m*) ahead of the mounting. The barrels were 7.5in (*190.5mm*) diameter with a simple screw breech, and the projectile weighed 120lb (*54kg*) with a 65lb (*29kg*) minol 2 burster. The design was sealed after sea trials in *Ambuscade* were completed in February 1943, but Parsnip was not used.

Squid

Ordered from the drawing board in 1942, this was a three-barrel 12in (*304.8mm*) mortar with the barrels fixed one behind the other in a frame which could be rotated through 90° to bring the barrels horizontal for loading. The projectiles weighed 390lb (*177kg*) with a 207lb (*94kg*) minol charge. Sinking speed was 43.5f/s (*13.3m/s*) and clockwork time fuzes were used, set automatically from the depth recorder to a maximum of 900ft (*274m*), and all three to the same setting. Each ship usually had two Squids but sometimes there was only one. Training was possible to *c*30° but the pattern was intended to be fired dead ahead. It was automatically fired from the Asdic (sonar) range recorder and comprised a triangle with 40yd (*37m*) sides at a mean range of *c*275yd (*250m*) ahead of the ship. If two Squids were carried, the patterns were usually set with 60ft (*18m*) differerence in depth, It should be noted that Squid depended on the contemporary development of the Q attachment and the later Type 147 Asdic which gave a measure of the target's depth.

Sea trials were held in *Ambuscade* in May 1943 and the first production Squid was in the corvette *Hadleigh Castle* in September 1943. The first frigate was *Loch Fada* in April 1944 and in general Squid was restricted to new construction, though one escort destroyer, *Escapade*, had two fitted in January 1945. By the end of the war only 60 to 70 ships had been equipped. The first successful use was by *Loch Killin* 31 July 1944.

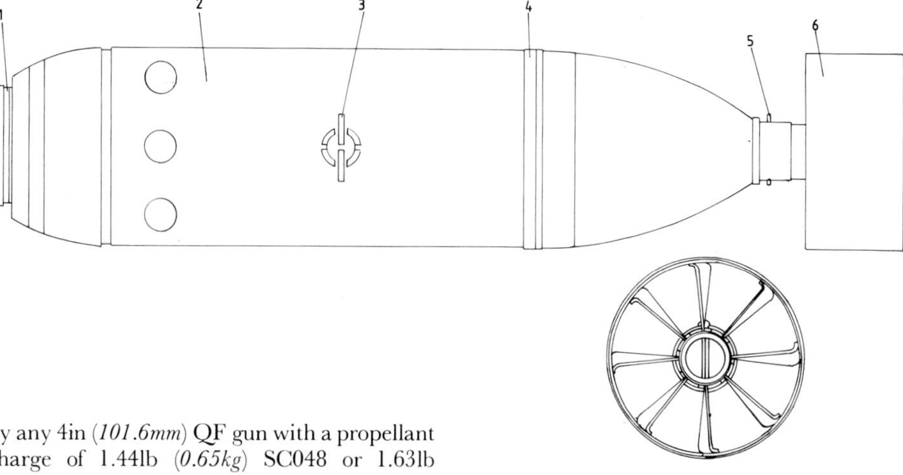

Squid projectile, longitudinal and tail views.

1 Fuze
2 Explosive filling
3 Centre of gravity
4 Gas check ring
5 Split pin
6 Tail

John Lambert

Other Ahead-Throwing Weapons

These included the Thornycroft long range DCT firing on a fixed-ahead bearing to over 300yd (*274m*). It was tried in *Whitehall* in January 1942 and was also fitted to the corvette *Dianella*, but was replaced in both by Hedgehog.

Development of the Vickers Type O thrower, a 13.5in (*343mm*) mortar firing a 900lb (*408kg*) projectile was stopped.

Shark

This projectile, of which the fuze drawings were not sealed until February 1945, could be fired by any 4in (*101.6mm*) QF gun with a propellant charge of 1.44lb (*0.65kg*) SC048 or 1.63lb (*0.74kg*) in Mk XVI*. It weighed 96.25lb (*43.66kg*) with 24lb (*10.9kg*) Torpex filling and overall length was 73.66in (*187.1cm*) maximum of which 53.5in (*135.9cm*) comprised the body and the rest the finned tail. There were two anti-ricochet nose rings and a base percussion fuze. It was to be fired at up to 800yd (*730m*) against surfaced submarines, striking the water *c*20yd (*18m*) short and continuing its trajectory underwater. It would pierce any tanks and detonate in contact with the pressure hull. The outfit is given as 12–22 per ship but it is not clear if it was ever used with success though trials were highly satisfactory.

AIRBORNE WEAPONS

The original 100lb (*45kg*) A/S bomb dated back to 1926 and eventually two versions, Mk I with 52% TNT and a steel tail, and Mk II with 62% TNT and a duralumin tail, entered service in March 1931. Both had a complicated nose fuze and were never properly tested. In August 1936 a new tail fuze was introduced with a fixed one-second delay and no action, which would operate on water if dropped from 200-400ft (*60-1220m*) and in October 1938 a pilot order was placed for 50 bombs each in 100lb (*45kg*), 250lb (*113kg*) and 500lb (*237kg*) sizes, to be known as Mk IV. None of these was satisfactory in service and after 1940 the A/S bomb was virtually abandoned in favour of the airborne DC with hydrostatic pistol, though the 100lb (*45kg*) remained a priority weapon for TNT/cyclonite charges until at least late 1942.

A new 600lb (*272kg*) A/S bomb was introduced in June 1943 subject to further development, apparently because the Mk VII Airborne DC had height and speed limitations and the 250lb (*113kg*) Mk VIII and XI were too small. The nose and tail fairings of the new bomb, which had a hydrostatic fuze and minol 2 filling, were intended to leave the body on entry. Countermining was initially troublesome and in the last two years of the war Coastal Command dropped only 97 in 28 attacks compared with 5790 of the 250lb (*113kg*) DC in 1170 attacks in the last 48 months. December 1944 conditions, with an improved fuze, were a minimum spacing of 80ft (*24m*) and dropping 50-5000ft (*15-1524m*) at 250kts. The mean firing depth was 32ft (*9.75m*).

A 35lb (*16kg*) shaped-charge A/S bomb, apparently backed by Lord Cherwell, was not successful and very little used, though production continued.

Mark VII Airborne DC

This conversion of the standard MK VII DC had nose and tail fairings provided by the Air Ministry, which broke off on striking the water, and a total weight of *c*450lb (*204kg*). The original pistol setting of 50ft (*15m*) was too deep for aircraft attack on a surfaced U-boat and it was reduced to 25ft (*7.6m*) in 1942. The Air Ministry had decided not to pursue DCs further on 17 April 1940 in spite of the unsatisfactory performance of A/S bombs, but pressure from RAF Coastal Command reversed this, though quantities were at first far too small, and it was not until the spring of 1941 that it was in general use. Objections were that it would not fit the internal stowage of the Hudson and that in 1940 it was not certain to function at over 100ft (*30m*) and 100kts. This was improved but it was still not cleared for over 150ft (*46m*) and 150kts in March 1942, though it remained in service in quantity until the end of the war.

Mark VIII DC

This was designed in 1941 to fit 250lb (*113kg*) bomb racks, and had an actual weight of 246lb (*111.6kg*) with 170lb (*77kg*) torpex, originally amatol, charge. It was one of the highest priority items for explosives containing cyclonite. The nose was dome shaped and dimensions were 11in (*27.94cm*) diameter x 16 39in (*99cm*) or 56in (*142cm*) over the tail. August 1943 limits were 750ft (*229m*) and 173kts and terminal velocity 600f/s (*183m/s*).

Mark XI DC

An improved Mk VIII with a concave nose to reduce liability to ricochet. It was the standard airborne DC from 1942 and eventual limits were apparently 1250ft (*381m*) and 250kts.

Mark XIV DC

A further improvement of the 250lb (*113kg*) DC with better low-depth detonation at a mean of 19ft (*5.8m*) instead of the previous 25ft (*7.6m*). This new depth held for 50-1500ft (*15-460m*) and 120 to 250kts. Mk XIV was not accepted by the RAF and was cancelled in 1945.

Mark XV DC

This was intended for use against U boats with Schnorkels and had one pistol set at 20ft (*6.1m*) and a second at 50ft (*15m*). Again it was not accepted by the RAF.

MINES

The position of the Royal Navy with regard to mines was far better in 1939 than it had been in 1914, and among other types an airborne magnetic mine had been developed, as well as a moored magnetic mine. Development of the former had been authorised in May 1936, a trial order for a small number was placed in July 1939, and in April 1940 when the first were laid, 200 were available. Production appears to have risen from 200 to 1600 a month in 1942 with plans to reach 4000 a month in mid-1943. The mines, which had coil-rod (CR) detectors, were fired by the rate of change of magnetism in the horizontal component of the field, and several different delay and anti-sweeping devices were in use by mid 1941. These included a not entirely reliable mechanical delay which gave a six-second period before detonation to allow the target to reach a position for maximum damage, and a double contact system in which the relay made contact first on one side and then on the other, being actuated by the change of polarity of the passing ship. The mine fired on the second contact to obtain a similar result to that given by the mechanical delay. There was, also a period delay mechanism which could not be used with the double contact system and allowed the relay to function a predetermined number of times before firing. Long-delay clocks could deactivate a mine for up to 40 days, and sterilisers could be fitted to run down the mine firing batteries and render it inert after a period of time depending on the resistance of the steriliser coils. An acoustic mechanism was ready in July 1942, and mines with this were first laid in September as it was rightly considered necessary to have an adequate stock before first use. Combined magnetic/acoustic mechanisms were first used late in April 1943. A small number of magnetic/pressure mines, (the latter a firing mechanism that was triggered by a magnetic impulse depending on the reduction in water pressure caused by the passage of a ship) were ready in the spring of 1945 but never used.

Although these types of mine were mainly laid by aircraft, others on similar principles were designed for laying by surface vessels or submarines, and it may be noted that the 'M' sinker magnetic mine had been laid by destroyers in August 1918, though this not very successful mine was long obsolete by 1939. Numerous types of moored mines were also developed as described below.

Originally aircraft-laid mines were dropped from low altitude, but this could lead to serious losses and in January 1944 laying by 10cm H_2S radar control from 10,000-15,000ft (*3000-4500m*) with parachutes was introduced. There were inaccuracies to begin with, some mines falling in Sweden 30m (*48km*) off position, but in May 1944 more than two-thirds were laid from a great height. It was impossible to prevent many from falling on land, which enabled German technicians to examine the firing mechanisms.

A summary written in March 1945 notes that aircraft could lay parachute ground mines from 15,000ft (*4500m*) in a minimum water depth of 30ft (*9m*) and non-parachute ones from 200ft (*60m*) in 12ft (*3.7m*) minimum. It also notes that moored mines could be laid by ships down to 300ft (*90m*) below the surface and in water up to 1000 fathoms (*1830m*), though at this depth the mooring wire rope was thin and its endurance low, and few mines were laid in half that depth, the majority being laid in under 100 fathoms (*180m*). Mines were laid from Bayonne to Hong Kong and from North Cape to Kerguelen. The summary gives the totals in enemy waters as over

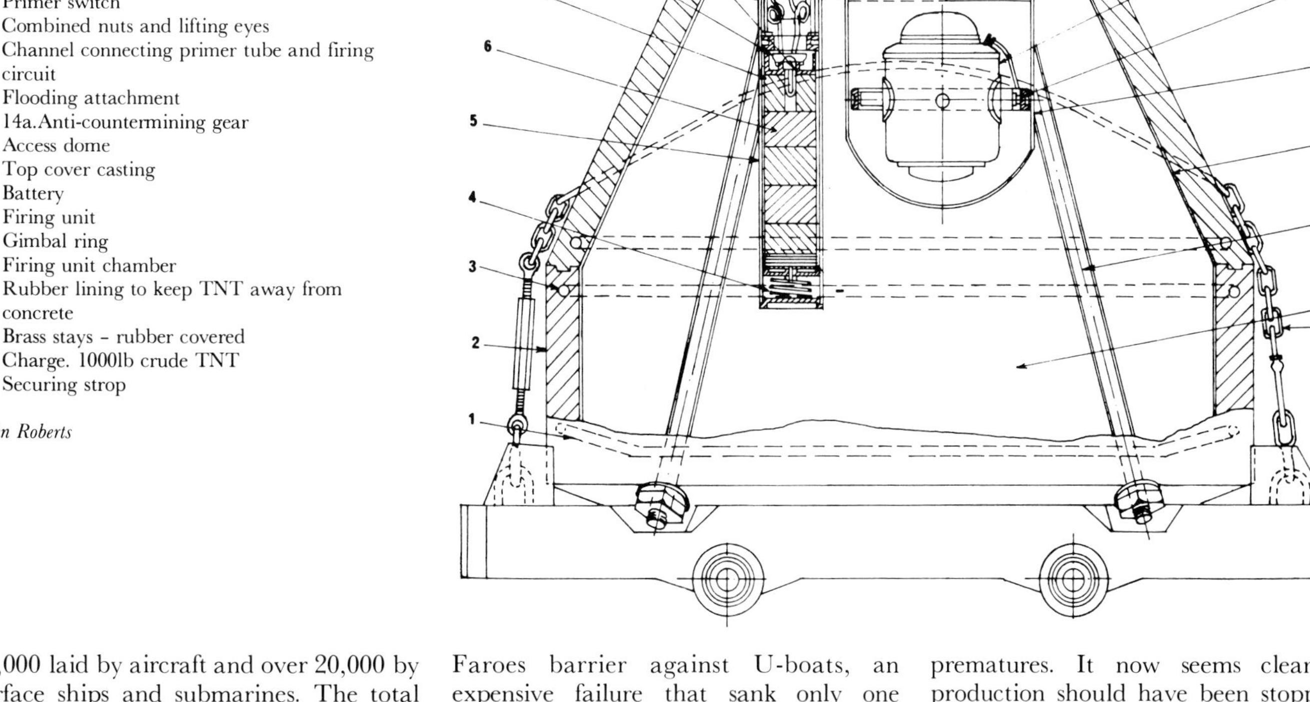

Sinker Mk I (M), the first magnetic mine, laid in August 1918 but long obsolete by 1939.

1 Brass wire reinforcement to base
2 Body of mine - concrete
3 Brass ring to reinforce body
4 Spiral spring to absorb shock on bottoming
5 Primer tube
6 Primer
7 Detonator adaptor
8 Screwed cap to keep detonator in place
9 Detonator
10 Primer switch
11 Combined nuts and lifting eyes
12 Channel connecting primer tube and firing circuit
13 Flooding attachment
14, 14a. Anti-countermining gear
15 Access dome
16 Top cover casting
17 Battery
18 Firing unit
19 Gimbal ring
20 Firing unit chamber
21 Rubber lining to keep TNT away from concrete
22 Brass stays - rubber covered
23 Charge. 1000lb crude TNT
24 Securing strop

John Roberts

40,000 laid by aircraft and over 20,000 by surface ships and submarines. The total laid by the RAF Home Commands during the whole war was 48,158 and these sank 545 merchant ships totalling 591,143 tons gross and 217 assorted warships of 147,264 tons displacement.

The March 1945 summary notes that, in addition, over 170,000 mines were laid by surface craft in protective fields. The majority of these were laid in the Iceland to Faroes barrier against U-boats, an expensive failure that sank only one submarine (*U 647*), as might have been forecast from a study of the 1918 Orkney to Norway barrier. Most of the mines were of antenna type, as in the 1918 barrier, and laying began in July 1940, being completed in early 1942, apart from later supplementary layings. In the early stages congestion in the depots was great and unstable mines had to be laid giving rise to prematures. It now seems clear that production should have been stopped in mid-1940.

Owing to shortages of TNT and RDX (cyclonite) most mines had 50/50 ammonium nitrate/TNT (amatol) explosive charges. This rather low quality explosive was later improved by adding *c*20% aluminium to produce minol.

The principal Second World War mines are listed under types below.

CONTACT MINES

HII

Old First World War stock used early in the war 320lb (*145kg*) charge. Hertz (acid filled) horns.

Mark XIV

A 1920s design with 320lb (*145kg*) or 500lb (*227kg*) charge and Hertz horns. When switch horns were developed it became Mark XVII.

Mark XV

This was constructed from 2-40in (*102cm*) diameter hemispheres with a 13½in (*34cm*) belt between. There were 11 switch horns and buoyancy was 840lb (*381kg*) with a 320lb (*145kg*) charge and 650lb (*295kg*) with a 500lb (*227kg*) one. It was originally designed for laying in 200-1000 fathoms (*365-1830m*) but the high buoyancy was valuable in tidal currents and it became a general-purpose mine.

Express and *Esk* as minelayers in early 1940. The mines on *Esk* are probably Mk XIV of the moored contact type.
CPL

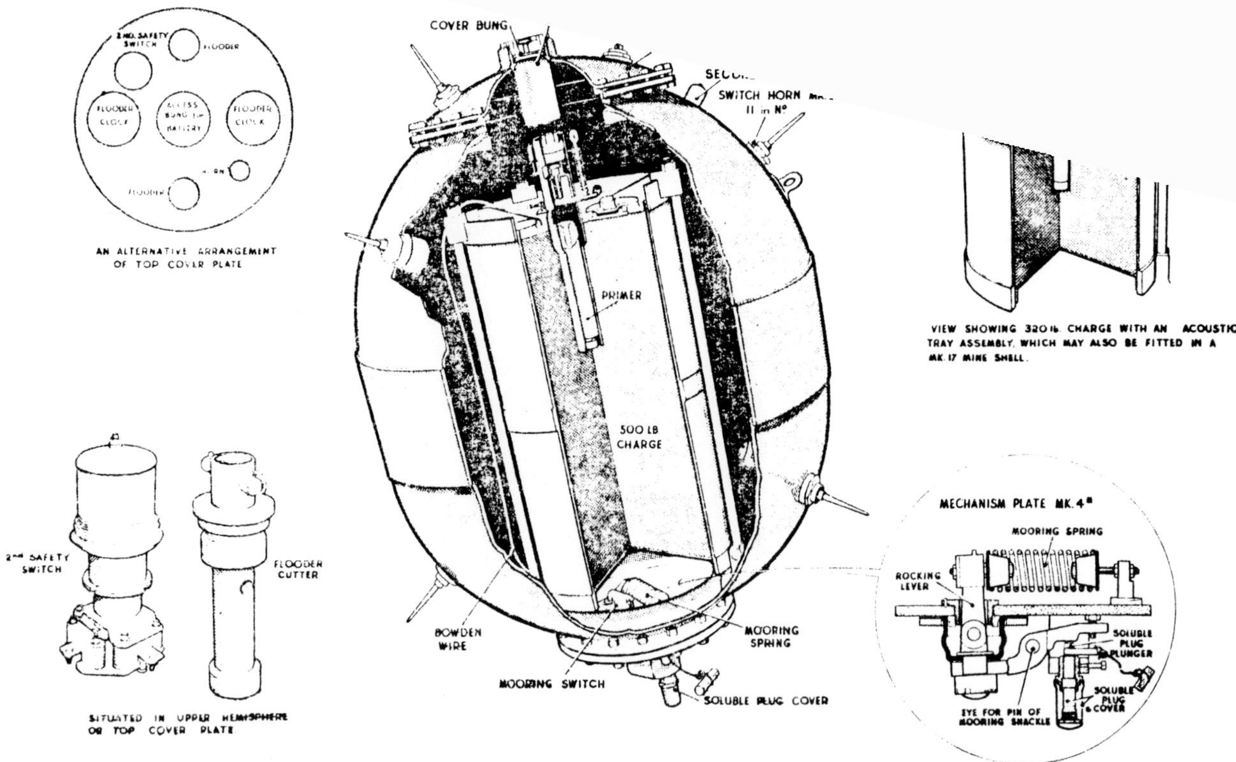

Mk XVII contact mine shown in section with details, including the acoustic version of Mk XVII. The former was the wartime standard contact mine. *MoD*

Mk XVII* sinker married to Mk XV mine. *MoD*

For 1000 fathoms the higher buoyancy was used with a ¾in (*19mm*) wire rope.

Mark XVI

Construction was similar to Mk XV except that the shell was thicker and the belt 4½in (*11.5cm*). It was for laying in 100 fathoms (*180m*) or less and, with 320lb (*145kg*) charge, buoyancy was *c*440lb (*200kg*). Hertz horns were retained. It was used in the *Porpoise* class submarines but was obsolete and replaced by various Mk XVII assemblies by the end of the war.

Mark XVII

Similar in construction to Mk XV but with an 8in (*20cm*) belt. There were 11 switch horns and it could be laid in 500 fathoms (*915m*). With a 320lb (*145kg*) charge, buoyancy was 640lb (*290kg*) and 450 lb (*204kg*) with a 500lb (*227kg*) one. It could be described as the standard contact mine.

Mark XIX

A small 31in (*79cm*) spherical mine with eight switch horns and a 100lb (*45kg*) charge. It could be laid in 200 fathoms (*365m*) and was intended for anti-submarine barrages at 35ft (*10.7m*) minimum below surface. The parts were mainly used to build up Mk XIXS and Mk XXVII, and the rest were scrapped at the end of 1944. Mk XIXS was similar but was for use against shallow-draught ships.

SNAGLINE MINES

Mark XXV

This had a standard 40in (*102cm*) diameter, 8in (*20cm*) belt, shell, basically that of Mk XII*. There were four switch horns with codline and bottle corks attached to one horn for use against E-boats. The charge was 500lb (*227kg*) and the mine was laid 15ft (*4.6cm*) below low water datum. It was approved in November 1943 but was replaced by the snagline version of Mk XVII shortly after the war.

Mark XXVII

A snagline version of the Mk XIX in service in June 1942 but obsolete in 1944-45.

MOORED MAGNETIC MINES

M Mark I

This mine had a mild-steel shell as in Mk XV with a 320lb (*145kg*) or 500lb charge (*227kg*). The mine shell was to stand a depth of 80 fathoms (*146m*).

MOORED ACOUSTIC MINES

Mark XVII

Primarily intended against E and R boats, and laid in 7-40 fathoms (*13-73m*). The charge was 320lb (*145kg*) but later apparently 500lb (*227kg*) in some.

MOORED ANTENNA MINES

Mark XX

This mine had a shell as in Mk XVII with 320lb (*145kg*) or 500lb (*227kg*) charge. The upper antenna was 60ft (*18m*) and the lower 74ft (*22.5m*) long. Mk XX* had the lower antenna only.

Mark XXII, Mk XXII*

These were like the above but had floating 60ft (*18m*) tubular antennae instead of solid ones supported by floats. Mines of this type depended on the UEP (underwater electric potential) effect; the near approach of a steel hull formed a battery with the copper antenna, sea water acting as the electrolyte.

AIRBORNE MOORED MINES

A Mark X

This mine was designed to the limits of the 1000lb (*454kg*) GP bomb and had a welded cylindrical case with parachute and *c*100lb (*45kg*) charge. Inertia switches were used for firing, and it could be moored in 40 fathoms (*73m*) maximum with a minimum laying depth of 60ft (*18m*). There was little demand and it was not in service.

SUBMARINE TT-LAID MOORED MINES

S Mark VI

This was based on US mines and no serious production design work was done until January 1945. It apparently reached the stage of discharge trials in late 1945. There was too much mine movement for CR magnetic mechanisms and the first were acoustic. Depth taking was hydrostatic. Total weight was *c*3400lb (*c1540kg*), length 21-22ft (*6.4-6.7m*) and charge 830-850lb (*376-385kg*).

AIRBORNE GROUND MINES

A Mark I

Originally designed to fit the same dropping gear as the 18in (*45cm*) Mark XI torpedo and for laying without parachute in a minimum depth of 30ft (*9m*). It was later adapted for parachute dropping and also for use by MTBs. The firing mechanism was originally magnetic but acoustic and magnetic/acoustic versions were developed as were magnetic/pressure though the last were never used. Weight was originally *c*1500lb (*680kg*), dimensions *c*18in (*45cm*) × 113in (*287cm*), charge 750lb (*340kg*).

A Mark II

Similar to the A Mk I but less use of scarce material.

A Mark III

Less use of scarce material. Some had impact firing as well. Mark III** was for dropping by Mosquitoes at 260kts from 300ft (*90m*) into inland waterways. It fitted the 4000lb (*1814kg*) bomb gear.

A Mark IV

Similar to Mk III but altered to suit manufacture by Pressed Steel Co.

A Mark V

A parachute mine with magnetic firing only, dating from August 1940 and designed to fit 1000lb bomb racks. Weight 1080lb (*490kg*), dimensions 15¾in (*40cm*) × 89in (*226cm*), charge 700lb (*318kg*) minol.

A Mark VI

This was approved in March 1944, superseding A Mks I-IV. It was a parachute mine with magnetic and acoustic firing, and was to the dimensions of the 2000lb (*907kg*) blast bomb. The charge was 1000lb (*454kg*) amatol or 1100lb (*499kg*) minol and the mine was 18.45in (*46.9cm*) × 109in (*277cm*) with a 7ft (*2.1m*) diameter parachute. Without the latter it could be dropped from low altitude or by MTBs.

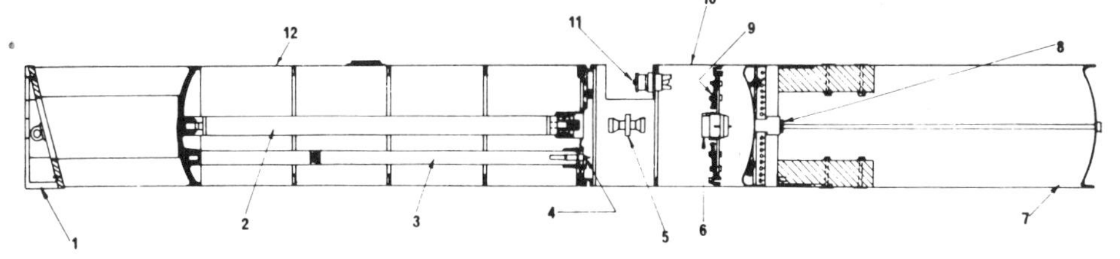

Early version of A Mk I airborne magnetic ground mine shown in section.

1 Nose fairing
2 CR unit
3 Primer
4 Detonator holder
5 AC switch
6 Relay
7 Detachable tail
8 Release mechanism
9 Rubber diaphragm
10 Rear section
11 Hydrostatic switch
12 Forward section

John Roberts

A Mark VII

An improved version of A Mk V available from the spring of 1944. It had magnetic firing only and including parachute was 15¾ (*40cm*) × 92in (*234cm*).

A Mark VIII

A mine for dropping in rivers and designed to fit 500lb (*227kg*) GP bomb gear. Bulk orders were placed in January 1944. It had magnetic firing, the acoustic version Mk VIII* being apparently not used in the war. Weight 500lb (*227kg*), dimensions 13in (*33cm*) × 57in (*145cm*), charge 180lb (*82kg*) amatol or 200lb (*91kg*) minol.

A Mark IX

Similar to A Mk VI but for later Fleet Air Arm aircraft. It was designed to accommodate a pressure firing unit. Weight 1775-1845lb (*805-837kg*), dimensions 18.5in (*47cm*) × 103.5in (*263cm*) plus 10in (*25cm*) for parachute, charge 1045lb (*474kg*) minol.

A Mark XI

Intended for underwater attack on capital ships, particularly in protected anchorages where torpedoes and B bombs were not usable. Maximum weight and diameter were to be 1850lb (*839kg*) and 22.4in (*56.9cm*) with 200-400kt dropping seed. 400 mines, converted A Mk III with special concrete-filled noses and inertia switches, were completed in March 1945 but the requirement was cancelled in July.

A Mark XXX

This project, cancelled in July 1942, was for a sinker with 300lb (*136kg*) amatol charge and a float that exploded the sinker if the former struck a vessel.

A Type J

A 1941 requirement for an aimable magnetic mine without parachute. Weight was to be 2000lb (*907kg*), minimum charge 630lb (*286kg*) and it was to be capable of being dropped from 10,000ft (*3000m*) into 4 fathoms (*7.3m*) with a minimum terminal velocity of 750f/s (*229m/s*). The requirement was cancelled in July 1944.

A Type S

A December 1944 requirement, under design at the end of the war to fit the space for a 1000lb (*454kg*) MC short-tail bomb. It was to have a high average velocity with dimensions 18in (*46cm*) x 71.5in (*182cm*).

IMPS, TIMS

An August 1940 requirement for an A Mk I mine with parachute, to fire instantaneously on impact (IMPS) or with six seconds' delay (TIMS). 30 of each were issued 26 September 1940. Large IMPS was a September 1940 requirement with 1100lb (*499kg*) amatol charge.

AIRBORNE DRIFTING MINES

O Mark I

An oscillating mine, somewhat like the old Leon, travelling from bottom to surface with impact firing. It was originally called Dogfish and 5000 were ordered in August 1944. The charge was apparently 200-400lb (*91-181kg*).

'R' MINES FOR RIVERS

R Type 1

This mine was a 15in (*38cm*) sphere with 25lb (*11kg*) TNT charge and a total weight of *c*70lb (*32kg*). About 24,000 were made in three different versions 'Floater' contact, 'Hopper' contact (trailing a slipper sinker) and 'Slug' (rolling along the river bed and then rising). There was a minimum arming delay of three hours.

R Type 2

This covered another 4000 from a different contractor.

B Types A and B

Spherical mines made from the lower hemispheres of Mk XIX with a 380lb (*172kg*) charge and a negative buoyancy of 4lb (*2kg*). Type A was a 'Slug' detonated only by clock and Type B a 'Hopper'. A small number were needed in 1940.

R Type 3

A quick-arming conversion of the R 'Floater' with two, three or four floats joined together. 4000 were converted in the 1940 emergency. Type 3* of February 1941 had a five-minute delay in arming.

SHIP-LAID GROUND MINES

M Type H

A CR (coil-rod) magnetic mine with 1200lb (*544kg*) amatol charge. The shell was a 24in (*61cm*) cylinder made of asbestos cement with rubber lining. Only the early stages were completed and it was abandoned.

M Mark III (formerly Type J)

A CR magnetic mine with steel case and 1500lb (*680kg*) amatol charge for laying from wide track mine-layer rails in 6-20 fathoms (*11-37m*). The revised requirement of 9 January 1942 increased the charge to 1600lb (*726kg*) amatol or 1750lb (*794kg*) minol. The first bulk delivery was in April 1941, and acoustic mechanisms were added from February 1943. The magnetic firing equipment had such devices as second look and sterilisers.

M Type P

A redesign of M Mark III with similar charge to the revised version but greater sensitivity. It had a steel case and was 26in (*66cm*) in diameter, standing *c*79in (*200cm*) above the laying rails. Total weight was about 2500lb (*1134kg*). Magnetic, acoustic or pressure firing was to be provided and the laying depth widened to 3-30 fathoms (*5.5-55m*). Pressure firing was deleted in March 1944 and the mine cancelled at the end of that month.

SUBMARINE TT-LAID GROUND MINES

M Mark II (originally Type G)

This mine, two of which occupied the space of one torpedo, was a CR magnetic mine with steriliser but without acoustic firing gear. It had a cylindrical steel shell and weighed 1760lb (*798kg*) with dimensions 21in (*53cm*) × 91in (*231cm*) and 1000lb (*454kg*) minol charge. It was to be laid at 8kts in 5-60 fathoms (*9-110m*) and was carried by 'T' and a few 'S' class submarines. A modified Mk IID was for Dutch submarines. A version could also be laid from coastal craft at 14kts. A contract for 2000 was placed in August 1940 but production was apparently stopped in November 1942.

M Mark V (originally Type Q)

The requirement for this was dated 24 April 1942. It was for 'A' class submarines and had increased sensitivity and also acoustic firing. Weight was *c*1880lb (*853kg*), charge *c*1100lb (*499kg*) minol and negative buoyancy 920lb (*417kg*). Production was apparently stopped in November 1942 but later resumed for delivery from September 1945.

CONTROLLED MINES

L Mark II

Design began in 1937 to replace L Mk I, and bulk contracts were placed in December 1939. It could be moored in 25 fathoms (*46m*) maximum and consisted of two 40in (*102cm*) hemispheres. Weight was 1180lb (*535kg*), buoyancy 468lb (*212kg*) and charge 500lb (*227kg*) amatol.

L Mark III

A cylindrical ground mine for a February 1940 requirement. Charges were 700lb (*318kg*), 1400lb (*635kg*) or 2000lb (*907kg*) and, with the heaviest charge, weight was 3503lb (*1589kg*).

L Mark IV

A ground mine for laying in shallow water by auxiliary local craft. The spherical shell was permanently fixed to a precast concrete sinker box and total weight was 1400lb (*635kg*) with 500lb (*227kg*) charge. 1000 were required by early September 1940, and another 4000 as soon as possible.

L Mark V

A ground mine with 500lb (*227kg*) charge, designed June 1941 but never made.

L Mark VI

This covered 200 converted 300lb (*136kg*) Mk VIII DCs needed for a specific operation in April 1943. The charge was 180lb (*82kg*) torpex.

M Mark IV

A modified M Mk III with 1900lb (*862kg*) charge. It was to remain safe until enemy shipping was in a captured harbour, and then be activated from a concealed position ashore.

Improvised Observation 'O'

Converted 21in (*53cm*) Mk II or Mk IV torpedo warheads. The total was 474.

CHARGES FOR X-CRAFT, CHARIOTS AND WELMAN CRAFT

The first and last of these were midget submarines with crews of four and one respectively, while the Chariot was designed from a recovered Italian two-man slow course torpedo (*Maiale*). All were intended for placing time-fuzed charges of near zero buoyancy below the hulls of moored ships.

In Chariots the charge case formed the nose and measured 22.2in (*56.4cm*) × 75in (*190cm*) with a weight of *c*965lb (*438kg*) including 590lb (*268kg*) torpex. A variant with the charge case divided into two, each containing 200lb (*91kg*) torpex, was cancelled, as was a larger Chariot with *c*1140lb (*517kg*) torpex, in September 1944.

The Welman craft was less successful and contracts were cancelled in March 1944. The filling was 425lb (*193kg*) torpex.

In the X-craft a large charge case was carried on each side of the submarine's hull. Tests showed that the original *c*4000lb (*1814kg*) amatol charge did not detonate completely though amatex (51% ammonium nitrate, 40% TNT, 9% cyclonite) did so. The original cases leaked at 200ft (*61m*) and had to be rectified to stand 300ft (*91m*).

In the final Mk XX charge case total weight was 5½ tons (*5.59t*) and the charge 3700lb (*1678kg*) minol with the addition of 5-10% cyclonite. The overall length of the charge case was 30ft (*9.14m*) with a 10ft 6in (*3.2m*) explosive chamber in the middle and buoyancy chambers at each end, these being adjusted to zero buoyancy.

BOMBS, ROCKETS AND MISSILES

BOMBS

No attempt will be made to describe all the bombs which could be effective against warships, and only AP and large bombs of other types will be noted. It should be remembered however that 500lb (*227kg*) or even 250lb (*113kg*) bombs could often cause most serious damage. A/S bombs are noted with other anti-submarine weapons.

AP Bombs

2000lb bombs

Nominal diameter	13.5in	342.9mm
Length oa	*c*112in	285cm
Weight (less tail and fuze)	1896lb	860kg
Bursting charge (shellite, originally 50/50, later 70/30)	166lb	75kg

The 2000lb (*907kg*) bomb was tried in 1929-31, being fired from a 13.5in (*342.9mm*) gun. The Air Staff July 1932 limit of 500lb (*227kg*) bomb weight stopped development for four years and also ensured that there was no other heavy bomb available at the outbreak of war. The nose was *c*2½ crh and Mk I had an aluminium tail, replaced by a steel one in Mk II (introduced in February 1942). Mk III with a modified cavity and base adapter followed in October 1943 but production was stopped in July 1944, and an improved design of 15in (*381mm*) diameter with more uniform stress in the walls and a larger burster was never in service.

Proof conditions were 7in (*17.8cm*) NC at 10° and 808f/s (*246m/s*), which the bomb would easily pass, and in trials in 1945-46 it had a considerable reserve of strength against reinforced concrete at 1140f/s (*347m/s*) and 15°. Terminal velocity was variously estimated at 2710-2920f/s (*826-890m/s*) and it was considered that 8in (*20.3cm*) C armour was needed to break up the bomb. In July 1941 three went right through the *Scharnhorst* at La Pallice but only one burst on exit.

No British carrier aircraft could take this bomb but the Avenger could have been adapted to do so. If a smaller AP bomb was required, the US 1600lb (*726kg*), which could be carried by the Barracuda, was used.

The 4500lb (*2040kg*) CP/RA rocket-assisted bomb designed for attacking heavy concrete structures had a 500lb (*227kg*) burster, and in tests in 1945–46 on reinforced concrete was sufficiently strong to stand impact at 1440f/s (*439m/s*) and 15°. Most failures were due to incipient heat treatment cracks near the lug holes. This weapon apparently originated in Admiralty proposals passed to the Air Ministry in December 1943. Much effort was expended in development and many of these bombs were made, but they were used only in limited quantities against U-boat pens late in the war, without any notable success as the rocket acceleration did not make for accuracy. The 'Disney' bomb used by the US 8th AAF in the latter months of the war was based on the above.

B Bombs

These were intended to be dropped near a ship and come up under the hull as the buoyancy chamber was sufficient to reduce the specific gravity of the bomb to below unity. Work on the problem began seriously in 1923, and originally a bomb of at least 2000lb (*907kg*) was wanted. This was reduced to 1100lb (*499kg*) and then after 1933 to 250lb (*113kg*). This last was available from 1939 but was never used against ships and proposals in late 1940 to convert it to a floating mine came to nothing. The later JW bomb, developed during the war, had an oscillating compressed-air/water mechanism and originally at least a 4ft (*1.2m*) parachute. The 400lb (*181kg*) Mk II was dropped without success by some of the Lancasters in the September 1944 attack on the *Tirpitz*.

CS (Capital Ship) Bombs

These were of large diameter, 45in (*114cm*), 38in (*96.5cm*) or 30in (*76cm*) and had a steel disc with a ring round the edge in front of the explosive. The idea was that the disc would be driven through the ship by the explosion, the ring acting as strengthening to the disc. In another version there was no disc, it being hoped that the explosion would cut a sufficiently thick disc out of the ship's structure, and there was also a hollow charge version. None was practicable as these bombs had to hit at a particular angle. However 50 of each size were made with discs and a few of 38in (*96.5cm*) diameter were dropped on ships at Gotenhafen in 1942 with unknown results.

SAP, GP, MC, HC Bombs

These series had approximate bursting charge weights of 18, 30, 50 and 75% respectively, though variations were quite large. They were mostly used and designed against land targets but as the 12,000lb (*5443kg*) MC sank the *Tirpitz* and irreparably damaged the *Lützow*, all the larger sizes are included. British-designed carrier aircraft were limited to 500lb (*227kg*) or 1000lb (*454kg*) bombs, though the Avenger could have taken up to 2000lb (*907kg*). All weights are nominal.

SAP. 500lb (*227kg*), block TNT filling, diameter 11.5in (*29.2cm*), wall 0.8in (*20mm*). RAF expenditure was 8348 in 1941 and 11612 during World War II.

GP. 500lb (*227kg*), diameter 12.8in (32.5cm), wall 0.7in (*18mm*); 1000lb (*454kg*), diameter 17.3in (*44cm*), wall 0.77in (*19.6mm*); 1900lb (*862kg*), diameter 18.7in (*47.5cm*), wall 1.2in (*30mm*); 4000lb (*1814kg*), wall 1.5in (*38mm*), filling amatex (51 ammonium nitrate, 40 TNT, 9 cyclonite). The 4000lb little used.

MC. 500lb (*227kg*), standard filling later amatex, diameter 13in (*33cm*), 1000lb (*454kg*), mostly filled minol 2, diameter 22in (*55.9cm*), later 20in (*50.8cm*) wall 0.55in (*14mm*). It had been intended to rely on the US M44.
4000lb (*1814kg*), mostly filled minol 2, wall 0.75in (*19mm*). An improved Mk II was introduced in September 1944.
12,000lb (*5443kg*), filled 5100lb (*2313kg*) torpex. Preferably cast in 3% chrome-molybdenum steel but some were in much inferior pearlitic manganese steel. The fins were off set to spin the bomb and thus maintain stability. It was not designed for 'hard' targets and against reinforced concrete would explode at 6–8ft (*1.8–2.4m*) though the explosion blast would penetrate such targets 18½ft (*5.6m*) thick. In all 76 were dropped in attacks on the *Tirpitz* from 11,350–17,500ft (*3460–5330m*), and 29 in the final attack from 12,500ft (*3810m*) or 16,500ft (*5030m*). Fuze delays on this occasion were 0.07 sec. The total dropped on all targets was 854.
22,000lb (*9979kg*), filled torpex. The original trial order for this and for the above was placed in July 1943 but work on the larger bomb was stopped from September 1943 to July 1944. Heat treatment difficulties meant that the wall had to be increased from 1.5in (*38mm*) to 1.75in (*44.5mm*). One was dropped on 14 March 1945 but the total was only 41.

HC. 2000lb (*907kg*), amatol filling, introduced after the 4000lb (*1814kg*). 4000lb (*1814kg*), diameter 30in (*76cm*), wall 0.31in (*8mm*). Later versions with 0.125in (*3.2mm*) steel or 0.31in (*8mm*) aluminium cases and respective charges of 86% and 89% were apparently never in production. 8000lb (*3629kg*), diameter 38in (*96.5cm*), filling amatex as amatol would not detonate properly. The number dropped was 1088 compared with nearly 68000 of the 4000lb (*1814kg*) HC. 12,000lb (*5443kg*), consisted of 3 × 4000lb (*1814kg*) sections. When dropped in water it broke up near the surface and detonation was incomplete. In all 186 were dropped.

AA ROCKETS

The first rockets to enter naval service in the war as weapons were for close range AA defence. None were of much efficacy, the most notorious being the 7in (*177.8mm*) parachute and cable rocket. Later in the war, rockets achieved notable success as airborne weapons against U-boats and other enemy craft, and in support of landings (as also noted in the USA section).

7in (177.8mm) UP Mark I

This comprised a 3in (*76.2mm*) rocket motor and 7in diameter projectile containing parachutes of *c*80in (*2m*) 40in (*1m*) and 8in (*20cm*) diameter and *c*900ft (*270m*) of 0.040in (*1mm*) wire with a small aerial mine charge of 8.4oz (*238gm*). The round was 32in (*81.3cm*) long and weighed 35lb (*15.9kg*). The effective range was 3000ft (*910m*) and sinking speed 16–23f/s (*5–7m/s*). The mounting had 20 barrels, usually fired in groups of 10 and weighed *c*4 tons.

The wire was intended to catch the wing of an attacking aircraft which would be destroyed by the aerial mine, but in fact the wire barrage took too long to establish and was easily avoided, while reloading was slow. The mines also tended to drift back on the firing ship and serious propellant fires could be caused by the ready-use lockers, as happened in *Hood*. It appears that 60 mountings were made, the last major ships with them apparently being *Newcastle* and *Birmingham*.

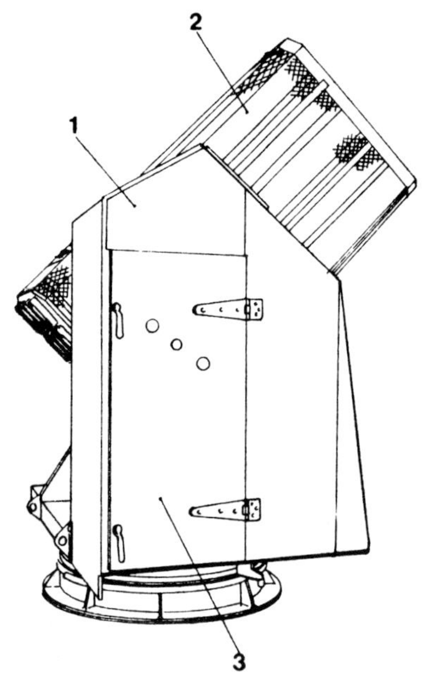

7in UP Mk I parachute and cable rocket in 20-barrel mounting.

1 Layer's cabinet
2 Mesh frame around tubes
3 Door to layer's cabinet

John Roberts

3in (76.2mm) UP Mk I

Developed from a weapon originally intended for the army, this rocket had a conventional bursting charge and time fuze. The round was 76in (*193cm*) long and weighed 56lb (*25.4kg*). It was launched singly from a mounting known as the Harvey projector and had an effective range of 4500ft (*1370m*) but lacked accuracy. There were 537 mountings in all, the only major ship with them being apparently the *Erebus*.

Other AA Weapons

Such devices as the PAC (parachute and cable) rocket, and the Holman projector for Mills bombs powered by compressed air or steam, or in Mk III by propellant, were not serious weapons of war except as morale boosters though on 1 March 1941 605 PAC and 1051 Holman projectors had been supplied to merchant ships. They were also in some minor warships and the Holman projector is credited with a few successes.

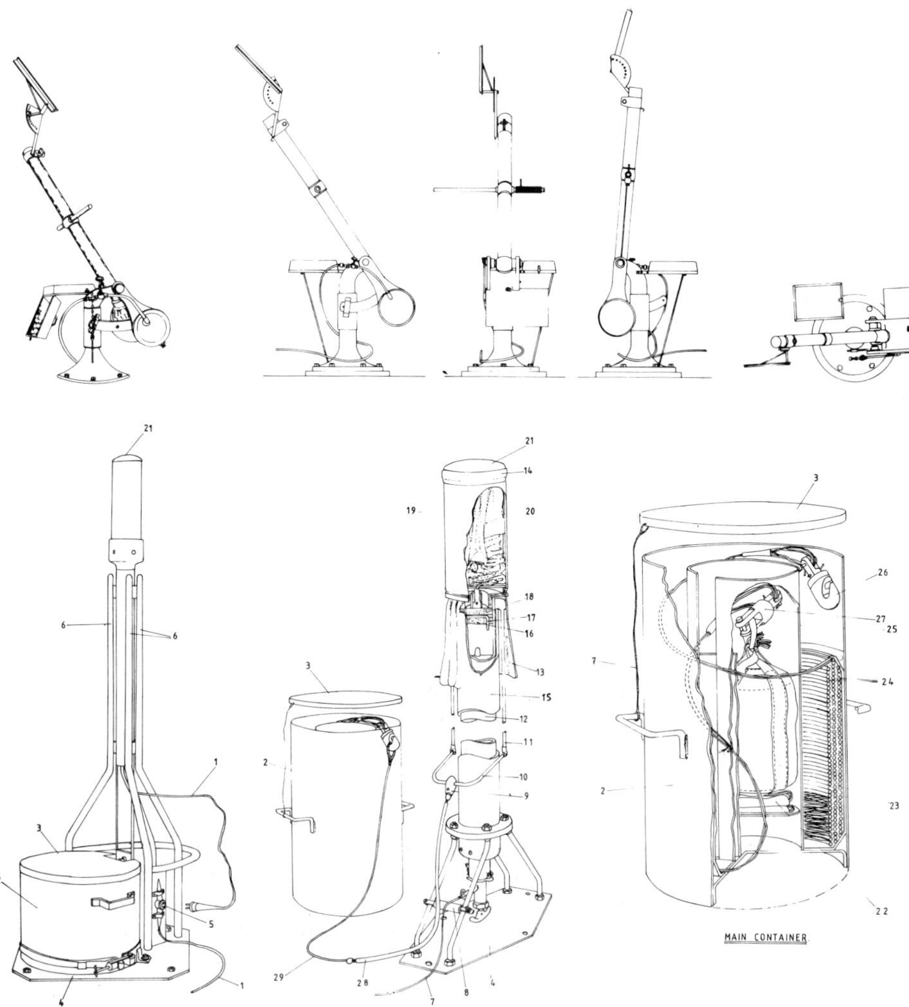

Holman projectors for Mills Grenades: (from left to right) early Mk I, general view, Mk IIA left side view, Mk IIA rear view, right side view at elevation 85°, and plan view.
John Lambert

PAC, Parachute and Cable, rocket device.

1 Firing lead
2 Main container
3 Lid
4 Base plate
5 Projector socket
6 Projector rails
7 Lanyard
8 Lanyard roller
9 Cone
10 Stirrup
11 Bridle
12 Rocket
13 Canvas gaiter
14 Sealing band
15 Barrel
16 Clay
17 Quickmatch
18 Burster
19 Parachute head
20 Parachute
21 Cap
22 Trail parachute
23 Lower parachute contained in fabric bag
24 Coils of KBID wire
25 Centre tube
26 Swivel at top of wire
27 Swivel at bottom of wire
28 Asbestos sleeve
29 Flexible tail

John Lambert

AIRBORNE AND SHORE BOMBARDMENT ROCKETS

The first success of airborne rockets against U-boats was on 23 May 1943 when a Swordfish from the escort carrier *Archer* sank *U752*. The rocket used was fin-stabilised with a 3in (*76.2mm*) motor and 25lb (*11.3kg*) AP shot as head. This measured 3.5in (*88.9mm*) in diameter and 12.4in (*31.5cm*) in length and would easily hole the pressure hull of a submarine. Total weight was *c*47lb (*21.3kg*) and velocity *c*1175f/s (*358m/s*). Later airborne rockets had the same motor but the head was a 60lb (*27.2kg*) SAP or HE shell of 5in (*127mm*) diameter. Total weight was 81.6lb (*37kg*), overall length 74.8in (*190cm*) and velocity 886f/s (*270m/s*). Photographs of these two rockets can be misleading as the concrete practice heads were respectively 5in (*127mm*) and 6in (*152mm*) diameter. A different rocket was used in the 'mattress' launchers of converted LCT (2) or LCT (3) which had a false deck with 792 to 1044 rockets electrically fired in salvos at a fixed range of 3500yd (*3200m*). The diameter of the rocket was 5in (*127mm*) and overall length 36.5in (*92.7cm*).

A 620lb (*281kg*), 10in (*254mm*) airborne rocket did not enter service.

GUIDED MISSILES

No guided missiles entered service with the RN but two projects were under development as a possible defence against kamikazes. The first of these, known as 'Breakmine', had been originally developed at Walton as a private venture by technicians from AA Command in conjunction with a radar developed by Cossor. It was later taken over by the Admiralty but World War II ended before guidance using a polarised radar beam had been satisfactorily achieved, though a few missiles had been flown. The other known as 'Stooge' did not make much progress. It was essentially a small model aircraft controlled from the ground by an operator using a joystick.

CV14 *Ticonderoga.* The radar and electronic communication equipment fitted to the island in the latter part of the war is shown, as is a Grumman Hellcat F6F-5 preparing to take off. The fast aircraft cariers, their aircraft (particularly the Hellcat), and the development of electronics were three of the most important factors in the victory of the USN in the Pacific.
USN

UNITED STATES OF AMERICA

This was the only country able to develop a wartime production that was sufficient to satisfy the reasonable demands of its own services and in addition provide many items for allies and co-belligerents. Development and subsequent rapid production of naval weapons were in the main linked to the immediate needs of the war and in particular to the fight with Japan. The USN (like the Japanese Navy) had the advantage of its own airforce, and this achieved a definite superiority by early 1943, but it was not until the end of that year that Japanese skills in night actions were overcome by improved radar and tactics based on its use.

AA defence was perhaps the field in which the USN was most clearly superior to other navies, and it should be noted that the best foreign designs of light AA, the Bofors and Oerlikon, were adopted and produced in huge quantities, rather than an equivalent developed in the US. In surface actions the excellent shooting of the *Washington* at the Battle of Guadalcanal should be set against the low percentage of hits obtained in several actions by 6in (*152mm*) cruisers, and there were similar variations in shore bombardment, though this could be attributed to prolonged practice or the lack of it.

The major weakness in USN weapons was the very bad performance of torpedoes in depth taking in the earlier part of the war and, at the same time, failures of their magnetic exploders and contact pistols were frequent.

NAVAL GUNS

The various types of each calibre of USN guns were identified by a mark and modification number, the original mark being mod O. For convenience in this book, mark and modification are presented, for example, as Mk 9/3. In contrast with British practice, BL and QF (bag and case guns) were in a single Mark series which did not include army guns. The USN was somewhat more prone to create new marks than the British, and there were many times as many modifications as British starred marks. The use of a letter for mark or mod indicated an experimental or prototype gun, though some curious items, such as 8in (*203mm*) anti-submarine howitzers Mks 7 and 8 and 105-calibre 3in (*76mm*) Mk 16, had found their way into the main series.

Although descriptions of the construction of all guns have been available, few drawings have been seen, and this has led to the use of US terms, as 'hoop' may refer to what might be a short hoop or a long tube in British descriptions. 'Jacket' is used for the innermost rear hoop and not for the outermost, as in Britain, and 'screw box liner' takes the place of breech bush. The length in calibres usually, but by no means always, indicates the bore length, which is otherwise rarely given in USN data. In BL guns, however, this is measured from the inner breech face and not as usual from the top of the mushroom head of the vent axial. A deduction of 0.3–0.4 calibres is thus made in the relevant gun data tables for bore length in BL guns. Chamber length is taken from the top of the mushroom head in BL and from the inner breech face in QF (case) guns to the base of the seated shot in both types. In the absence of many drawings and shot travel data, there is some uncertainty over the distance between the start of the rifling which is given in USN lists, and the base of the seated shot.

USN guns had low working pressures by British or German standards, even though data was taken at 90°F (*32.2°C*) charge temperature, and this latter must be borne in mind in comparing USN guns with those of other navies. The 3150f/s (*960m/s*) muzzle velocity of 5in (*127mm*)/51 guns reduced to 3120f/s (*951m/s*) at 80°F (*26.7°C*). Ranges are generally given for 90°F new gun muzzle velocity.

At one time, high MV was much sought after, but its importance lessened after the 6in (*152mm*)/53 introduced to service in the early 1920s and the most recent guns of 6in (*152mm*) and over had MVs of 2500f/s (*762m/s*) with APC shell, though the great weight of the latter meant that muzzle energies were higher than might at first appear. None of the wartime AA guns had very high velocities; the 3400f/s (*1036m/s*) 3in (*76mm*)/70 belongs to the post-war period.

The length and twist of the rifling are given for all the most important guns but very little data has been found on details of grooves and lands, and the following may not apply to all guns. The number of grooves was 6 × calibre in inches for heavy guns, increasing to 8 × or 9 × in lighter ones. The groove depth was ½–1% of the calibre in inches, and in most of the more recent guns grooves and lands were of approximately equal width at the muzzle, though in some the grooves were twice the lands. In guns of 5in (*127mm*) and over with uniform rifling it was usual to widen the land from origin to muzzle by 0.08in (*2mm*) in 1000in (*25,400mm*), though a much greater rate of increase had been tried. With increasing twist of semi-cubic parabola type, it was usual to keep the widths of groove and land constant, though lands of increasing width had formerly been favoured, but this type of rifling had been superseded by uniform twist in recent designs.

The built-up construction of many of the older guns could be criticised on the grounds that they contained too many component parts and even the latest 16in (*406mm*) Mks 6 and 7 and 12in (*305mm*) Mk 8 had more than would have been the case with British designs. The 8in (*203mm*) Mks 12 and 15 had, however, a simple structure of A tube (with or without liner) and jacket, while the 6in (*152mm*)/47 case gun and the more recent 5in (*127mm*) had a monobloc removable barrel and breech housing, as did the 8in (*203mm*) Mk 16 with the addition of a loose liner. Much use was made of autofretted forgings, but the most distinctive feature of later USN guns was the chromium plating of the bore to a depth of 0.0005in (*0.013mm*), with considerable improvement in gun life. The chromium plating normally extended over the length of the rifling and shot seating.

Gun mountings for 8in (*203mm*) guns and over, and also 6in (*152mm*) turrets, were described as Two or Three Gun (or Twin or Triple, if the guns were in a common cradle) for particular ships. Other mountings, including twin base ring mountings for 6in (*152mm*) and 5in (*127mm*), were numbered in a mark and modification series for each calibre of gun. Compared with British practice the numbers were many, as with guns. It should be remembered that US roller path diameters were measured from the outside of the path and not the mid-point, so that the rotating structures were even more compact than might seem. There is no doubt that 14in (*356mm*) triple and three-gun turrets were too small, which caused difficulties in ammunition supply and interference between guns when the three were fired together. The only real cure for the latter was to space the guns further apart, as in the later 16in (*406mm*) and 12in (*305mm*) three-gun turrets. The history of 8in (*203mm*) mountings was similar.

USN turrets were electrically powered, and except for a few items in the older installations the power was transmitted through hydraulic variable-speed drive gear. This system seems to have worked well. Remote power control (RPC), known as auto control, was much more widely fitted than in British ships. As in most navies, powder hoists were single stage in some turrets and two stage in others, but the practice of stowing the main shell supply on the fixed structure round the turret trunk, instead of in a shell room, was a particular USN feature.

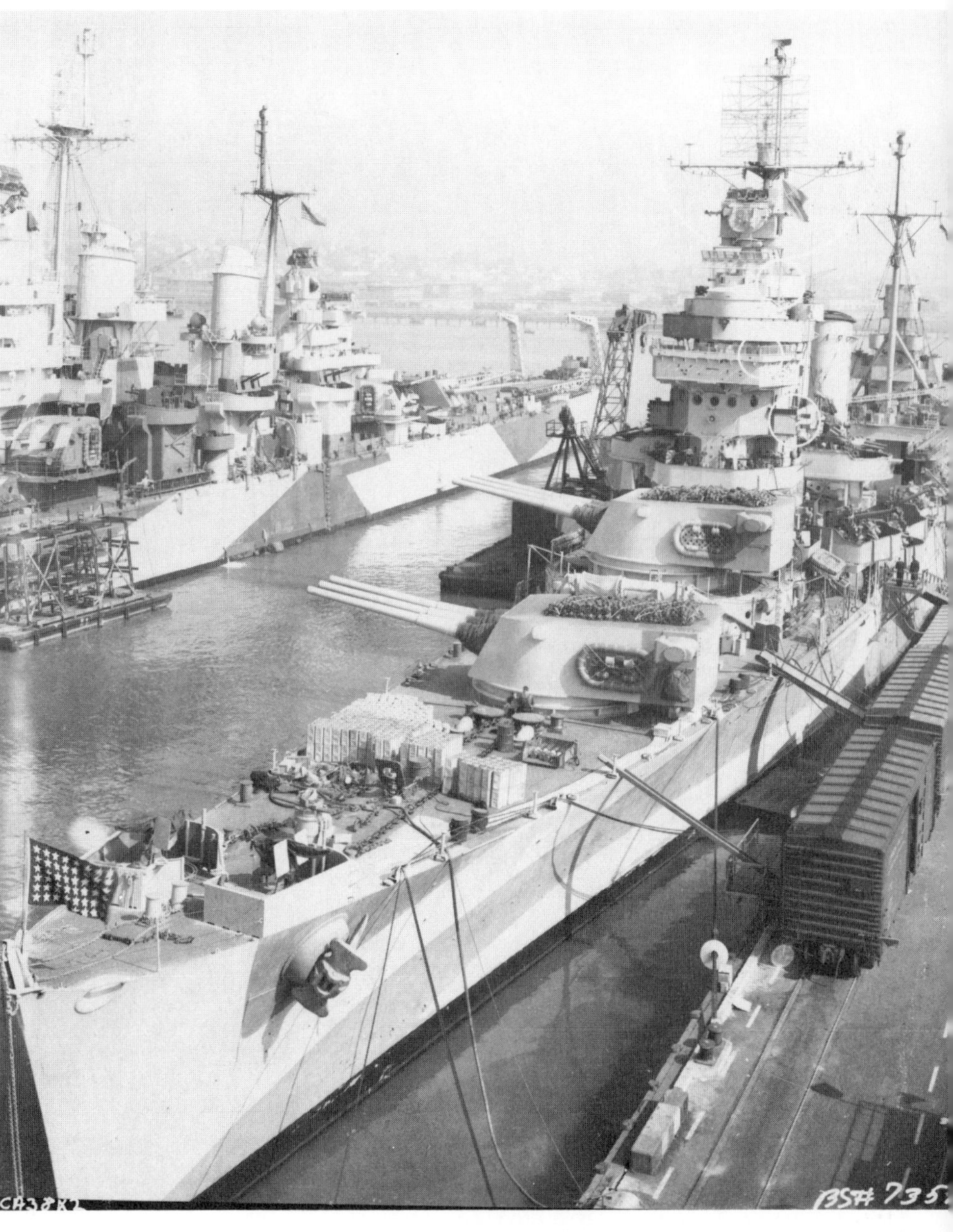

CA38 *San Francisco* as refitted in 1944, showing the forward triple 8in turrets, main battery director with Mk 3 radar and Mk 33 DP director with Mk 28 radar. *USN*

PROPELLANTS

The standard USN propellant was still nitrocellulose in multi-tube form. The composition was 99.5% NC(12.6% N), 0.5% diphenylamine, and the short grain usually had seven perforations, the web size varying from 0.023in (*0.58mm*) in short 3in (*76mm*) to about 0.174in (*4.42mm*) in 16in (*406mm*)/50. Other grain shapes were used, such as single tube in Oerlikons. Although this was a cooler propellant than the standard British SC at 865 calories and 3015°K compared with 970 and 3090°K, it was not flashless, and there was a requirement for such a propellant by the end of 1942. The immediate solution would be one of the British type nitroguanidine propellants, but these contained nitroglycerin and the USN had a rooted objection to this, as vapour might evolve and spread through the ship. This was an uncommon, but by no means unknown, event if the charges were overheated, and there was an instance in HMS *Glorious* in 1938, where pom-pom charges kept in the loading racks got very hot in the sun and the NG condensed on the ammunition as the temperature fell, which gave rise to the incorrect term 'exudation'.

In the event, a considerable quantity of Cordite N was obtained from Canada in mid 1944 and issued as an interim measure. This was an Army version of the Navy's NF, differing in its composition of 18.7%NG, 19%NC (13.1% N), and 7.3% centralite, instead of 21%, 16.5% (12.2% N) and 7.5%. With $1\frac{1}{2}$% incorporated potassium sulphate it was consistently flashless in 6in (152mm)/47 and 8in (*203mm*)/55, and with 5% in 16in (*406mm*)/45.

US developments involved fundamental changes replacing NG by solid explosive gelatinisers such as DINA (bis-nitroxyethylnitramine) or Fivonite (tetramethylolcyclopentanone tetranitrate), the former being preferred. Large orders for the Du Pont propellant Albanite were placed just before the end of the war. Albanite had the composition 19.5% DINA, 20.0% NC (12.6% N), 55.0% nitroguanidine, 4.0% dibutyl phthalate, 1.5% centralite No 1, to which potassium sulphate and lead, as a decoppering agent, were added in quantities for an 8in (*203mm*) gun of 1.5% and 1%. Results appear to have resembled those for the British type flashless, and propellant charges were increased by about 10% over those for NC.

The advantages of flashlessness had to be balanced against increased smoke, and at the end of the war the USN seem to have been moving towards accepting the latter, and to flashless outfits of around 50% for 5in (*127mm*), 25% for 6in (*152mm*), and 15% for heavier guns.

Since the loss of the *Maine* in 1898, of which the initial cause is sometimes attributed to smouldering bituminous coal and not decomposing NC, USN propellants had a good safety record, doubtless due to care in manufacture. There were, however, more cases of back-flame due to inadequate clearing of gases from gun bores than should have occurred. The cruiser *Boise* survived a Japanese 8in (*203mm*) shell bursting in her largest forward magazine, and her sister ship *Savannah* a German FX 1400kg (*3090lb*) guided SAP bomb which burst in No 3 turret handling room. In both cases sea water flooded in quickly enough to prevent a disastrous gas pressure rise from the ignited propellant. The principal charges concerned were separate 6in (*152mm*) QF (semi-fixed case) but in *Savannah* 5in (*127mm*) fixed illuminating and AA Common were involved as well as Bofors. On the other hand, a Japanese 800kg (*1760lb*) AP bomb exploded forward 14in (*356mm*) magazines in the *Arizona* at Pearl Harbor.

PROJECTILES

Major calibre APC shell was manufactured for the USN by Bethlehem, Midvale and Crucible Steel, and although as usual practices differed between the firms, certain features were constant. Like German but unlike British shells, the heads were 'sheath hardened', that is the centre part of the head, nearest the apex of the cavity, was not fully hardened, and burster charges of ammonium picrate (Explosive D) accounted for only 1.5% of the total weight. Although APC shell for 14in (*356mm*) and the older 16in (*406mm*) guns was by no means exceptionally heavy at 1500lb (*680kg*) and 2240lb (*1016kg*), that for the 16in (*406mm*) Mk 6 and 7 and for the 12in (*305mm*) Mk 8 was proportionately much heavier than in other navies, the weights being 2700lb (*1225kg*) and 1140lb (*517kg*). Both the extra-heavy APC and those of normal weight had a shell head radius of about 1.1 to 1.45 calibres as a rule, though a few had less, and in some there was a blunt point to the elliptical head. Cap weights averaged about 10% and overall lengths were 4.5 calibres for extra-heavy shells and about 4.0 for others. Ballistic caps (windshields) were usually 9 crh. The standard detonating base fuze had a delay of 0.035 seconds. K devices were generally fitted.

By the end of the war the emphasis was on as few types of shell as possible, and there seems to have been no attempt to develop separate shells for the attack of side and deck armour as was desired in Britain. USN APC does not appear to have particularly favoured, either.

Tests of Midvale 14in (*356mm*) 1500lb (*680kg*) shell in England in 1943 against Hadfield 1590lb (*721kg*) of the same calibre were not flattering to the US shell. At that date the specification velocities against 12in (*30cm*) C plates (USN class A) at 30° to the plate normal were 1820f/s (*555m/s*) and 1750f/s (*533m/s*) for US and British respectively. In the tests the Hadfield shell passed at only 1475f/s (*450m/s*) while the Midvale failed at 1528f/s (*466m/s*), though the higher velocity should have compensated for the weight difference, quite apart from a cavity for a 1.5% burster in the US shell and for 2.5% in the British. On the other hand, with the angle to the plate normal raised to 40°, a Midvale shell at 2046f/s (*624m/s*) was nearer to success than any British 14in (*356mm*).

Against the *Jean Bart* at Casablanca on 8 November 1942 a 2700lb (*1225kg*) 16in (*406mm*) shell from the *Massachusetts* went through decks of 5, 22, 150, 40, 7mm (*0.2, 0.87, 5.9, 1.58, 0.27in*), totalling 224mm (*8.82in*), before bursting in an empty 6in (*152mm*) magazine having travelled 34ft (*10.4m*) beyond the heavy deck. The approximate angle of descent was 64° to the vertical and striking velocity 1520f/s (*463m/s*).

In 1941 major calibre guns had an outfit of APC only, but HC shells were introduced in October 1942, and by 1944-45 ships on bombardment duty (except the oldest) had most of their outfit HC. This was lighter than APC, all 16in (*406mm*) being 1900lb (*862kg*), 14in (*356mm*) 1275lb (*578kg*) and for 12in (*305mm*) Mk 8, 940lb (*426kg*). Bursting charges, usually TNT, were 8-8.5% in weight. There were nose and base fuzes, the former being replaced by a steel plug against ship targets, and also an auxiliary detonating fuze between the nose fuze and gaine (booster). This was intended as an additonal safety device for the nose fuze and was not removable. Unfortunately it was liable to explode the shell on striking steel plate, thus nullifying the slight delay of the base fuze.

For 8in (*203mm*) guns there were 335lb (*152kg*) and 260lb (*118kg*) APC on the general lines of major calibre shell, but with heavier caps of 12.2-17.3% and, for the 260lb (*118kg*) shell, bursters of only 1.3-1.4%. A variable delay fuze was originally fitted, but proved unreliable and was replaced by the fixed delay type. Other shells in the 260lb (*118kg*) range included HC with 8.2% burster, AA Common with similar burster weight and nose and base fuzes (the former being of mechanical time type), and Special Common. This was a SAP shell with 4% ammonium picrate burster and a thin sheath cap or hood of about 4-4.5% weight which, unlike APC caps, was not hardened. The shell proper had a 1.75-2crh.

The 6in (*152mm*) APC of 130lb (*59kg*) resembled the heavy 8in (*203mm*), but the cap was relatively larger at 15.6-20.8% weight. The 105lb (*47.6kg*) range included HC and AA Common with bursters of 13% and Special Common. This had a hood of 4 to 6.5% and an ammonium picrate burster of only 2.1-2.4%. Illuminating (star) shell weighed 95-116lb (*43-52.6kg*), but it is not certain if it was in wartime service.

Explosive shell for the 5in (*127mm*)/38 Mk 12 gun was usually 4.15 calibre long and was 5¼ crh externally, whereas most USN shell was at least 7 crh, and in later designs 9. From photographs some 5in/38 shell appears to have been slightly boat-tailed. A variety of shells were available. Special Common weighed 55.18lb (*25.0kg*) and had a 3.7% ammonium picrate burster with a 5-7% hood. AA Common in its later forms weighted 54.15lb (*24.56kg*) and had a 14.3% burster. As usual, this had a mechanical time-fuze at the nose, as well as a base fuze. HC, white phosphorus smoke and illuminating shell were also available and, most importantly, AA shell with VT (Variable Time-Fuze). This weighed 54.61lb (*24.77kg*) and had a 14.4% burster. The VT fuze was in effect a very small and rugged continuous-wave radar which functioned when the reflections from the target, interfering with the outgoing pulses, set up a ripple pulse sufficient to trip an amplifying firing circuit. This Doppler effect method of bursting shells was understood by January 1941, but adequate ruggedness and reliability took some time to achieve. The first fully successful test firing was in June 1941, quantity production began in November 1942 and the first use in action was by *Helena* on 4 January 1943. Shells burst up to about 70ft (*21m*) from the target with the cone of fragments inclined at *c*55° back from the shell nose. The worst defect was that shells would burst on account of reflections from sea waves if fired at low elevation. This was partly overcome in fuzes issued from June 1944, but there was no complete solution.

In 1943, of 36,370 5in (*127mm*) shells 25% had VT fuzes, and these were credited with 51% of aircraft shot down. Later figures for October 1944 to January 1945 are given separately. VT fuzes could be made for 3in (*76mm*) shells, but the 40mm Bofors was far too small for 1945 techniques. Of other guns 5in (*127mm*)/51 had Common and from August 1942 HC, while 4in (*102mm*)/50 also had Special Common, HC being supplied from November 1942. USN Bofors and Oerlikon shells were generally similar to British, but Oerlikon HE had tetryl or TNT/PETN (Pentolite) bursters instead of the usual TNT.

With improvements in blind-fire equipment, tracer lost its popularity, and policy at the end of the war was to eliminate it for 3in (*76mm*) and larger guns. For 20mm and 40mm guns without blind-fire capability, it was to be retained largely for the morale of the gun crew, and with blind-fire, it was retained for day firing but not for night.

The USN in general favoured single driving bands of copper or cupro-nickel. Pronounced boat-tailing appears to have been limited to Bofors. Bourrelets were standard in USN shell designs.

Ammunition Performance, Kamikaze Actions, 1 October 1944–31 January 1945

Expenditure	**5in (127mm) Com**	**5in VT**	**3in/50 (76mm)**	**40mm**	**1.1in (28mm)**	**20mm**	**0.5in (12.7mm)**
Oct	2218	1575	88	51,729	—	109,813	8193
Nov	6064	1942	392	65,025	61	113,814	14,704
Dec	440	870	194	33,235	—	92,433	12,471
Jan	9363	3216	3943	109,068	2170	244,693	34,804
Total	22,085	7603	4617	259,057	2231	560,753	70,172
Planes destroyed							
Oct	1.5	6.5	1.5	23.5	—	11	—
Nov	5	6	1	27	—	13	—
Dec	9	4	—	33	—	23.5	0.5
Jan	3.5	8	4	30.5	1	15	2
Total	19	24.5	6.5	114	1	62.5	2.5
Rounds per plane							
Oct	1479	242	59	2201	—	9983	—
Nov	1213	324	392	2408	—	8755	—
Dec	493	218	—	1007	—	3933	24,942
Jan	2675	402	986	3576	2170	16,313	17,402
Average	1162	310	710	2272	2231	8972	28,069

Ammunition Performance, Non-Kamikaze Actions, 1 October 1944–31 January 1945

Expenditure	**5in (127mm) Com**	**5in VT**	**3in/50 (76mm)**	**40mm**	**1.1in (28mm)**	**20mm**	**0.5in (12.7mm)**
Oct	17,213	7265	1176	84,449	2278	210,660	19,993
Nov	3902	798	216	7496	693	17,359	875
Dec	3975	1164	251	20,431	—	53,834	9655
Jan	7058	3249	1367	42,251	1793	79,347	14,893
Total	32,148	12,476	3010	154,627	4764	361,200	45,416
Planes destroyed							
Oct	23	9.5	4	23	—	27	0.5
Nov	1.5	1	—	6.5	—	5.5	1
Dec	5	6.5	—	9.5	—	8	—
Jan	4	3	—	7.5	—	10	1.5
Total	33.5	20	4	46	—	50.5	3
Rounds per plane							
Oct	748	65	294	3672	—	7802	39,986
Nov	2601	798	—	1249	—	3156	875
Dec	795	179	—	2151	—	6729	—
Jan	1765	1083	—	5633	—	7935	9929
Average	960	624	752	3361	—	7152	15,139

FIRE-CONTROL

Only a brief outline of USN systems can be given here. Those for the main armament of battleships had been evolved in a different way from that favoured by Britain, as emphasis was placed on the plotting room or 'central' (transmitting station) rather than on the director. It may be remarked that British opinion after both world wars was inclined to favour the American view. In the later US battleships the range-keeper or computer of electro-mechanical type, corresponding to the British fire-control table, drove the director through RPC, and the correct solution of the target bearing kept the director telescopes on. Corrections were transmitted back by the director crew manually keeping on target. Similarly the gyroscopic stable vertical in the central provided an artificial horizon for level and cross-level determinations, which could again be corrected by manual adjustments from the director crew. The stable vertical had been introduced in the *Maryland* class as a not very successful aid to optical level and cross-level methods, but it had been greatly improved so that the main and auxiliary roles were reversed.

Pending radar developments, ranges were determined by the turret range-finders. Stereoscopic, instead of coincidence, instruments had been introduced in 1940 and those in the three-gun 16in (*406mm*) turrets were of about 44ft (*13.5m*) base. As spray would handicap these severely in rough seas, 26.5ft (*8m*) RFs were mounted on the Mk 38 directors carried high up in the ship. The USN had always attached great importance to accurate spotting, and a spotting glass (actually a 15ft (*4.5m*) stereo RF) was mounted on the CT roof until replaced by radar. This in addition enabled the fire control officer, located in part of the CT, to explore targets other than that being engaged. It should be noted that spotting seaplanes were retained throughout the war for use in bombardment or other indirect fire.

In the later ships all turrets had RPC from the central, working via servos on the variable speed elevating and training hydraulic drives. This enabled the stable vertical to maintain continuous aim except in very rough seas, when it would be necessary to fire at a constant point in the roll. An important difference from British practice was that the USN did not fire all guns simultaneously from the director, but used independent firing so that the various shots of a salvo were seldom fired at quite the same instant. In the three-gun 16in (*406mm*) turrets the sights for pointer and trainer had horizontal periscopes through the sides of the gunhouse, and this system was used in the *Arkansas*, but in intervening classes from the *New York* to the *Maryland* the sight periscopes looked through the gun ports below the guns.

The above notes mainly apply to the *North Carolina, South Dakota* and *Iowa* classes, but the systems in older battleships were modernised as opportunity offered, particularly in the rebuilt *West Virginia, California* and *Tennessee* which had Mk 34 directors and RPC for their turrets, both it would seem originally intended for the 6in (*152mm*) cruisers converted to the *Independence* class aircraft carriers, and capable of modification to suit the heavy guns. In the absence of RPC, follow-the-pointer gear was used. Data transmission was by selsyns (synchros) introduced originally in the *Maryland* class.

The Mk 3 surface fire-control radar introduced in late 1941 had, as used in battleships, an oblong 12 × 3ft (*3.66 ×*

Top: BB43 *Tennessee* laid up post war. The Mk 34 main battery director with Mk 8 radar and Mk 37 DP with Mk 12 radar and Mk 22 height finder are well shown. *USN*

BB42 *Idaho* 3 January 1942, with Mk 28 DP director, Mk 3 radar and Mk 31 main and secondary battery director on tower mast. *USN*

0.91m) antenna and worked at 40cm with 1.5 microsecond pulses and PRF of 1640. Power was 15–20kW and the beam 6° × 30°. Lobing was introduced with this set. Accuracy is given as 40yd (*37m*) and 2 mils, with resolution 400yd (*370m*) and 10°. Maximum range was at least 40,000yd (*37,000m*), and 16in (*406mm*) splashes could be ranged at half this distance.

Its successor the 10cm Mk 8, had a 10ft 2in × 3ft 4in (*3.1 × 1.0m*) antenna containing 42 polyrods scanned by phase-switching. Power was 15–20kW, later 20–30, pulse length 0.4 microseconds and PRF 1500. The beam was 2° × 3°, accuracies 15yd (*5m*) and 2 mils, and reliable range on a battleship target 40,000yd (*37,000m*). This set was introduced in late 1942–43 and many were later converted to mod 3 which was very similar to Mk 13. This last worked at 3cm and had a 8ft × 2ft (*2.44 × 0.61m*)

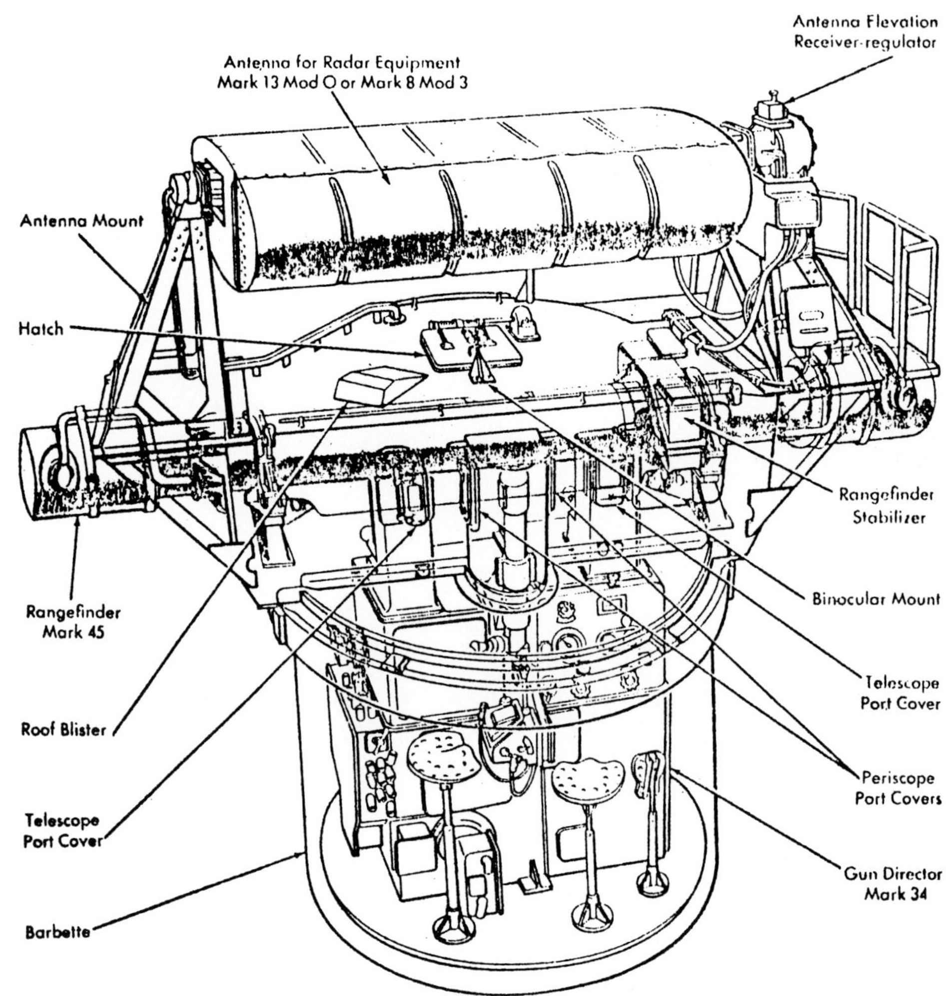

Mk 34 main battery director, front view, showing principal features.
USN

Lower left: CL48 *Honolulu* 30 January 1942. The after directors have not yet had radar installed, but Mk 3 has been fitted to the forward 6in director.
USN

CL48 *Honolulu* 24 October 1942. The after 6in director has a Mk 3 radar with 6 × 6ft antenna, and the Mk 33 DP director a Mk 4.
USN

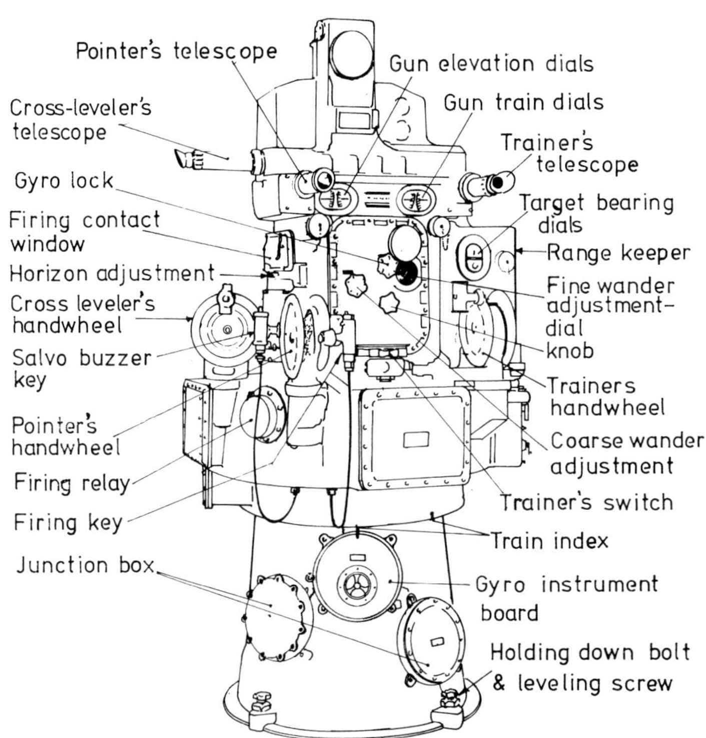

Mk 18 director, pointer and trainer side, originally fitted for 8in guns in *Lexington* and *Pensacola* classes.
CPL

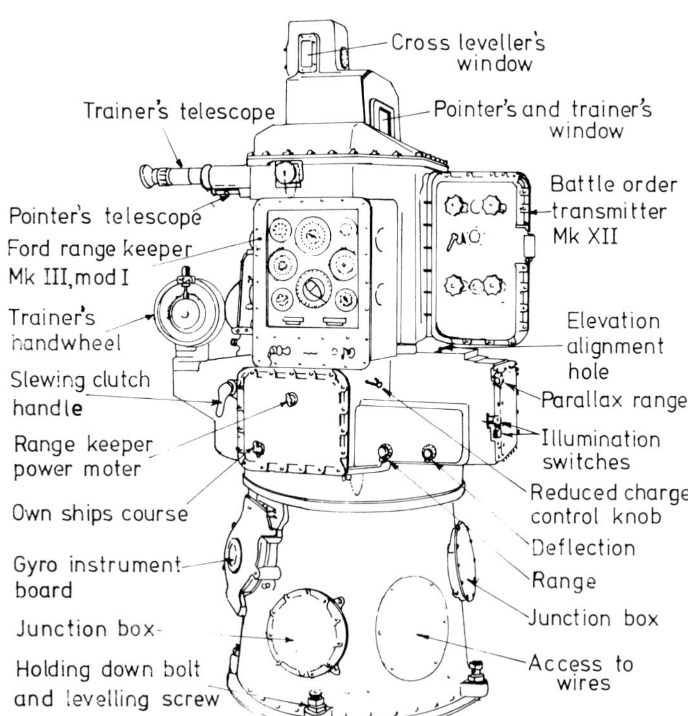

Mk 18/1 director, rangekeeper side.
CPL

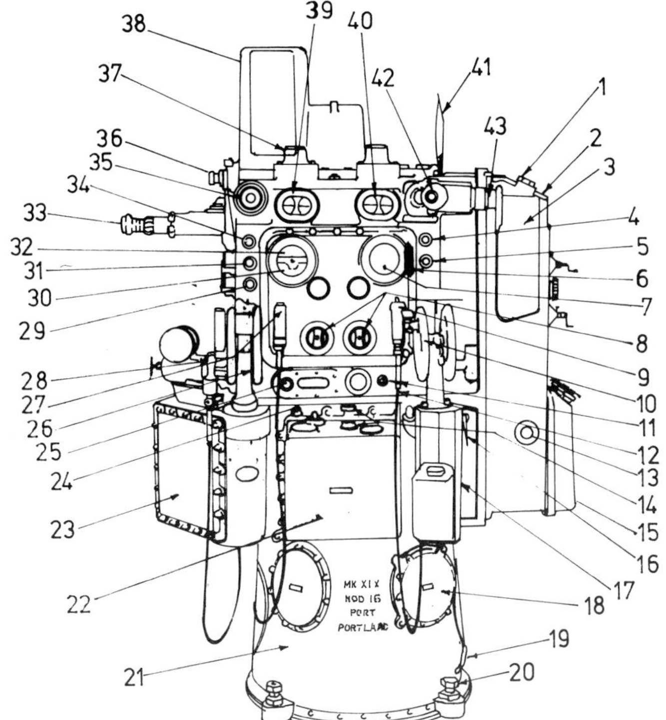

Mk 19/16, 17 director for 5in/25 guns, target and leveller side, and pointer and trainer side.

1 Ford Rangekeeper Mk IV Mod 6
2 Access to rangekeeper mechanism
3 Access to range motor
4 Power motor switch
5 Dynamotor switch
6 Gyro wattmeter
7 Target bearing designator
8 Rate dial windows, elevation and bearing
9 Trainer's rate key
10 Trainer's handwheels
11 Fuze control switch
12 Rate control switch
13 Time of flight dial
14 Initial velocity switch and dial
15 Access to rangekeeper, clutches, follow-ups, switches, etc
16 Quick-acting clamp
17 Access to fuzes
18 Junction box
19 Lifting hook
20 Levelling and holding-down bolt
21 Pedestal
22 Access to ballistic computer
23 Access to sight deflection, sight angle and fuze-setting transmitters
24 Pointer's and trainer's control knob
25 Pointer's altitude lock
26 Pointer's handwheels
27 Pointer's firing key
28 Pointer's rate key
29 Interior illumination switch
30 Target elevation designator
31 Dial illumination switch
32 Voltmeter, 22V circuit
33 Leveller's telescope
34 Cross-wire illumination control
35 Pointer's telescope
36 Pointer's collimator sight
37 Light well
38 Optical cap
39 Sight elevation dial
40 Sight train dial
41 Trainer's open sight
42 Trainer's telescope
43 Check sight
44 Cross-levelling window
45 Pipe connection
46 Leveller's window
47 Cross-levelling handwheel
48 Levelling handwheel
49 Leveller's control knob
50 Transmitter belt
51 Access to dynamotor
52 Access to dynamotor regulator
53 Access to gun elevation and train transmitters
54 Access to sight train and elevation transmitters
55 Access to compass receiver, 'B' and 'C' clutches, power motor
56 Gun elevation and train dials
57 Case
58 Access to stabilizer unit, train integrator
59 Access to stabilizer unit, elevation integrator, clutches
60 Pointer's and trainer's window
61 Levelling window
CPL

Mk 33 DP director in CV4 *Ranger*.
USN

paraboloid antenna scanned by rocking about its vertical axis within a radome. Power was 50kW, pulse length 0.3 microseconds and PRF 1800. The beam was 0.9° × 3.5° and range and accuracy similar to those of Mk 8.

Mk 27 was a standby radar mounted on CT and sometimes turret tops. It was a 10cm 50kW set with an 8° × 8° beam and resolution of 160yd (*146m*) and 6.5°.

The advantages of improved fire-control were well shown in the last of all battleship encounters in the Surigao Strait. In this night action at around 20,000yd (*18,300m*), the ships with Mk 8 radar and RPC, *West Virginia, California* and *Tennessee*, had little difficulty, while of those with older equipment *Maryland* picked up a target by ranging on *West Virginia*'s splashes, *Mississippi* fired only one salvo and *Pennsylvania* none.

The fire-control system for the main armament in later cruisers was generally similar to that in battleships, a below-deck plotting room or central dating back to the *Augusta* class. The Mk 34 director with 15ft (*4.6m*) stereo RF was introduced in *Wichita, Helena* and *St Louis*, and retrospectively fitted to older ships back to the survivors of the *Augusta* class, though the *New Orleans* class retained their older ones from considerations of weight and stability. *Pensacola* later had Mk 35 directors from destroyers with single purpose 5in (*127mm*) guns, and the *Alaska* class battleship type Mk 38. The dual purpose Mk 54 did not enter service until after the war in the *Des Moines* class. Turret range-finders were mostly of about 30ft (*9m*) base. RPC was fitted in all later ships and, as opportunity occurred, to surviving older ones back to *Pensacola*, but not *Salt Lake City*. Sights in the *Pensacola, Augusta* and *Portland* classes looked through ports in the gunhouse face, but later ships had horizontal periscopes through the sides. The principal fire-control radars, Mks 3, 8 and 13, were as in battleships.

The USN control systems for 5in (*127mm*) AA guns were all of the tachymetric linear rate type and were also dual purpose. The Mk 19 director for 5in/25 guns was, in its original form, first at sea in 1928 and was by some years the first effective heavy AA director in any navy. In 1939 it was still in the *Oklahoma, Pennsylvania, California, Maryland, Lexington, Pensacola* and *Augusta* classes, being retained in some cruisers until 1943. The director was manually trained and had a separate RF, though in late 1940 15ft (*4.6m*) stereo instruments were added.

The initial figures for target speed and altitude, taken from the RF, were fed into the mechanical computer (range-keeper) which predicted the future target position. One set of predictions enabled the pointer and trainer to check the range-keeper output and in effect spot, while a later prediction was used to aim the guns so that they led the target correctly, and there were also predictions for fuze setting. Gyro and optical stabilisation were included. There were several major modifications but none very successful, and shields were also added.

The Mk 28 director mounted in the *New Mexico* class and first five *New Orleans* class was also manually driven and incorporated stereo RF, stable element and computer on a single pedestal. It was too heavy even without radar, for hand training, and was succeeded by the power driven Mk 33 for both 5in (*127mm*)/25 and /38 guns. This was mounted in *Ranger, Quincy, Vincennes*, the *Farragut* class and many other ships, often replacing Mk 19 or Mk 28. It was designed for target speeds up to 275kts, later increased to 320 with some capability against diving targets at up to 400kts also added. Early directors were open topped but shields and radar were later fitted with some difficulty in balancing. It was not practicable to advance much further with relatively light self-contained directors, and in the Mk 37, on which work began in 1936, the computer and stable vertical were moved below decks. The first tests were in 1939 and it was adopted for all new major ships and for destroyers from the *Sims* class onwards, though retrospective fitting was restricted by the need to find space below decks.

The director, which had a crew of seven, was a compact turret-like structure on a high 'barbette' and was designed to accommodate radar, while a 15ft (*4.6m*) stereo RF was incorporated. It is sometimes described as triaxial but that applied to the sights, and strictly to the sight prisms as the body was fixed to the director. A slewing sight, so that the Director Officer could get on to a target quickly and track it until the pointer and trainer took over, was an important war

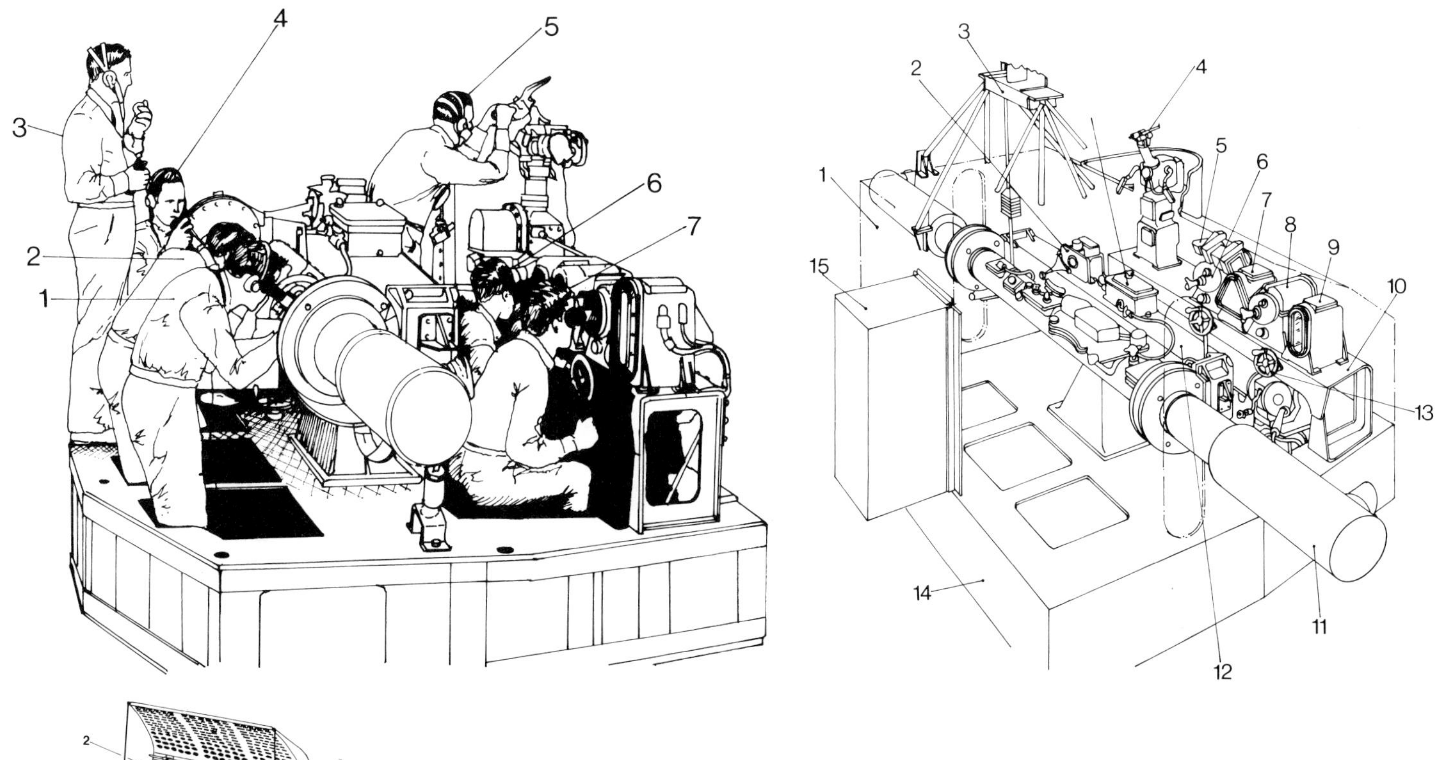

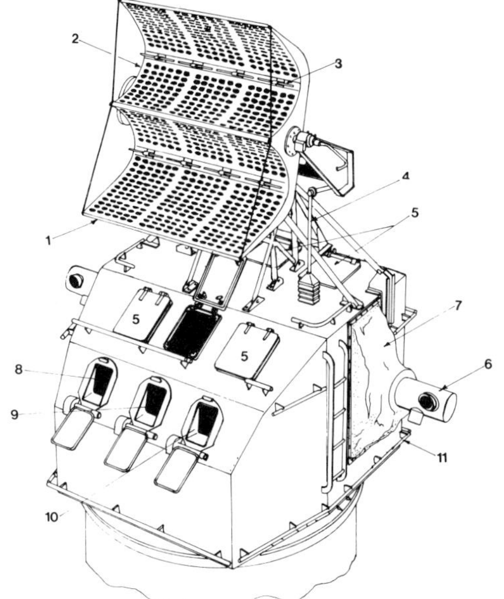

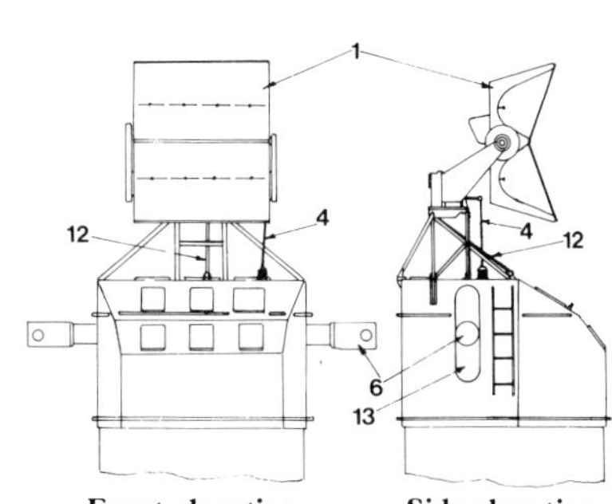

Mk 37 DP director with crew positions and internal details.

THE DIRECTOR MARK 37 (CREW POSITIONS)

1 Range talker
2 Range-finder operator
3 Illumination control officer
4 Talker
5 Control officer
6 Pointer
7 Trainer

THE DIRECTOR MARK 37 (INTERNAL DETAILS)

1 Shield
2 Range spot transmitter
3 Radar antenna mount
4 Slewing sight
5 Radar elevation indicator
6 Telescope
7 Elevation indicator
8 Telescope
9 Train indicator
10 Optical box shelf
11 Range-finder
12 Range-finder beam
13 Port closure handwheel
14 Carriage weldment
15 Blister for amplifier power assembly

THE DIRECTOR MARK 37

1 Mk 4 radar antenna
2 Reflector
3 Dipoles
4 Cross-level connecting rod to radar antenna
5 Observation hatches
6 15ft range-finder
7 Canvas weather cover over range-finder slot
8 Trainer's telescope port
9 Pointer's telescope port
10 Control officer's sight port
11 Handrail
12 Elevation connecting rod to radar antenna
13 Range-finder slot, allowing clearance for cross-level movement

CPL

addition. The electro-mechanical computer was designed for 400kts level and 250kts vertical target speed, which was adequate except for the not very successful Oka (Baka) of 1945. It incorporated fully automatic rate control and, unlike the British FKC, could take zero dead time. Director and computer represented a closed control loop which caused development problems due to the effects of servos in the system. By the end of the war the fitting of RPC was standard.

The Mk 37 was considered the best heavy AA system of the war, and was acknowledged by the British to be far better than any of their own contemporaries. Like all such systems it was inadequate against kamikazes, particularly when they were performing aerobatics, and the practice was to use the slew sight and VT shells, or the directors for the 40mm guns to which the 5in (*127mm*) were linked in increasing numbers.

The first fire-control radar for 5in (*127mm*)/38 DP guns was Mk 4 used with Mk 37 and 33 directors, and initially installed in September 1941. It was a 40cm set, in effect two half-Mk 3s stacked vertically. The antenna was 6 x 6ft (*1.83 x 1.83m*) and lobing was used with a 12° x 12° beam. It lacked blind-fire capacity and failed against low-flying aircraft, but otherwise ranges were 40,000yd (*37,000m*) for bombers and 30,000yd (*27,000m*) for large ships. Accuracies are given as 40yd (*37m*) and 4 mils, and resolution 400yd (*370m*) and 10°.

It was replaced from 1944 for most Mk 37 directors by the Mk 12 combined with the Mk 22 height finder. Mk 12 differed from Mk 4 in working at 33cm with automatic tracking in range and automatic measurement of range rate. The antenna was much the same size and the beam 10° x 10°. Power was 100-110kW with 0.5 microsecond pulses and PRF 480. Ranges were 45,000yd (*41,000m*) on aircraft and 40,000yd (*37,000m*) on ships. Accuracies were 20yd (*18m*) and 3 mils, and resolution 300yd (*270m*) and 7°. Mk 22 had a narrow parabolic antenna 1.5 x 6ft (*0.46 x 1.83m*)

DD364 *Mahan*, showing Mk 33 DP director and Mk 28 radar.
USN

and worked at 3cm and 25-35kW. The beam was 5° × 1.3° and the set was designed to detect low flying aircraft, at only 0.8° above the horizon. At over 1° the accuracy was 3 mils, and aircraft could be resolved 1.5° apart. Ranges were much as for Mk 12.

The other important set was Mk 28 introduced in 1944-45 for Mk 33 directors and for those Mk 37 that had insufficient room for Mk 12 radar. In the latter case, Mk 28 was usually associated with Mk 22. It was a 10cm set of 3kW with 0.5 microsecond pulses and PRF 1800. The antenna was a 3ft 9in (*1.14m*) paraboloid with conical scanning and a 6.5 × 6.5° beam. Range was about 45% of that of Mk 12, and accuracy is given as 15yd (*14m*) + 0.1% range and 4 mils. It was considered inferior to Mk 12 but much better than Mk 4.

Prior to 1940 close range AA guns were aimed by ring sights and tracer, and of several systems the Mk 14 gyrosight developed at MIT, and ordered in quantity in October 1941, was the first to be successful. Like subsequent close range types it was a relative rate system, with the angular rate in horizontal and vertical directions measured by two damped, constrained gyros. As ranges were short, a single estimated figure was taken for present and future ranges which simplified the computing part of the sight. As the gunner tracked the target, the optical line of sight for the correct lead angle was shifted by the gyros, and the gunner had to

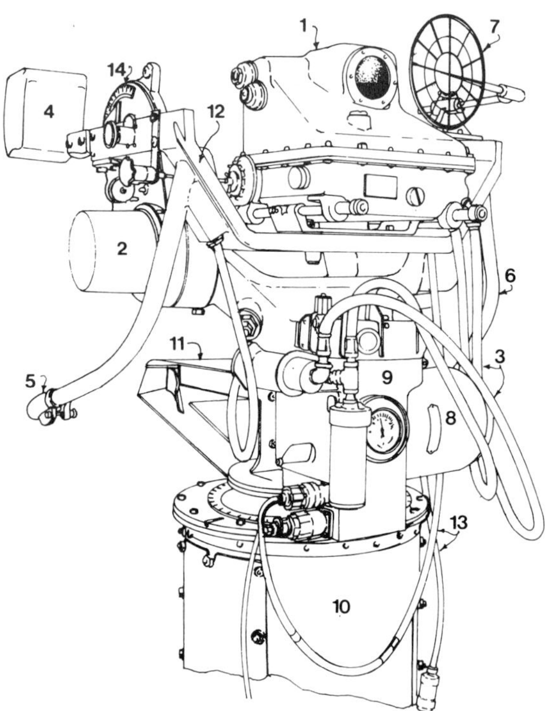

Mk 51 director, a simple one-man instrument for 40mm Bofors guns and also for 5in at close-range targets.

1 Mk 14 gyro gun sight
2 Elevation synchro unit
3 Air hoses
4 Counterbalance weights
5 Right handle with firing key
6 Left handlebar
7 Open ring sight
8 Power unit motor
9 Air power unit
10 Pedestal
11 Body rest
12 Sight bracket
13 Electricity cables
14 Elevation scale

CPL

move his gun to compensate, so that when aiming at the target he was applying the correct lead angle. The Mk 14 sight was principally used on Oerlikons, and for Bofors it was incorporated in the Mk 51 director. This was a simple one-man instrument with handlebar control and synchro transmission to the gun mounting. As noted above, many 5in (*127mm*) guns were cross-connected to the Mk 51 for close range targets, and it was also adapted for such weapons in ships too small to take a heavy director.

The Mk 15 gyrosight with improved optics was in the Mk 51 Mod 3 Director and also in the Mk 52 Director which included a range-only radar Mk 26. This worked at 10cm with a 9° x 9° beam and the main problem was for the operator below deck to gate the signal corresponding to the target tracked by the optical sight. The Mk 52 Director was chiefly used in destroyer escorts for 5in (*127mm*) and 3in (*76mm*) guns.

Full radar control and blind-fire capability were introduced with the Mk 63 Director tested in June 1944 and first installed in the aircraft carrier *Bon Homme Richard* in November 1944. A unique wartime feature was that the radar display was projected into the sight's field of view to ensure that they were on the same target. Chances of hitting with 40mm guns were considered to be two to four times greater than with the Mk 51 Director. As the antenna was too heavy for the director, it was located on the associated gun mounting. The usual radar was Mk 34 working at 3cm and 25-35kW with 0.3 microsecond pulses and PRF 1800. The antenna was a 30in (*0.76m*) dish and the beam 3° x 3°. Resolution was 200yd (*180m*) and 2.25° in bearing and elevation. Various methods of target acquisition were later incorporated.

The other blind-fire director was the group concentration Mk 57 developed by the Johns Hopkins APL and ordered in March 1944. It was supplied from October 1944 and first fitted in *Missouri*, *Alaska* and *Guam*. The rate gyros resembled those of the MIT systems but the director had an undisturbed line of sight, and the gyro data was fed to a computer below decks which controlled the guns, and was large enough to include ballistics for both 40mm and 5in (*127mm*)/38. The director was sufficiently strong to take radar, usually Mk 34, and the system's performance was considered to be about that of Mk 63, though target acquisition development appears to have been less advanced.

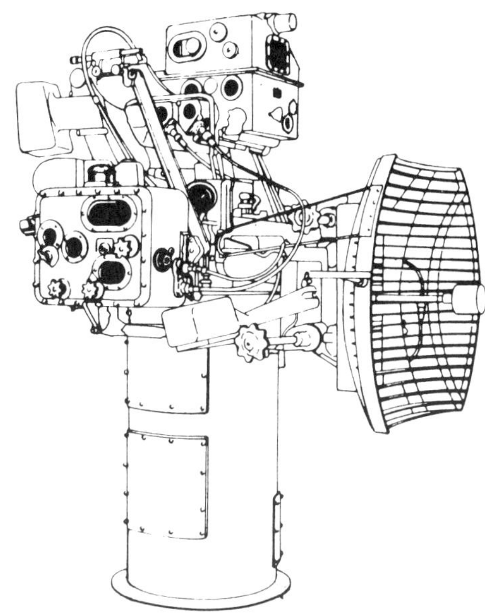

Mk 52 director with Mk 26 radar, mainly used in DEs for 5in and 3in guns.
CPL

HEAVY CALIBRE GUNS

18in (457mm) Mk 1/0

Gun Data

Bore	18.0in	457.2mm	
Weight incl BM	177.8 tons	180.7t	
Length oa	884in	22,453.6mm	49.11cal
Length bore	*c*859.6in	*c*21834mm	*c*47.75cal
Length chamber	*c*115.5in	*c*2934mm	
Volume chamber	36,900in³	604.7dm³	
Length rifling	737.263in	18,726.48mm	
Grooves			
Lands			
Twist	1 in 32		
Weight projectile	2900lb projected	1315kg	
Propellant charge	not determined		
Muzzle velocity	2700f/s projected	823m/s	
Working pressure	18tons/in²	2835kg/cm²	
Approx life	not determined		
Max range	not determined		

Design work on this, the largest rifled gun ever made for the USN, was begun in early 1919. The 18in (*457mm*) Mk 1/0 was to be a 48-calibre gun intended as a possible main armament for future battleships. The construction comprised liner, A tube which was hooped to the muzzle, jacket, nine hoops, six locking rings, a separate yoke ring and screw box liner. The breech mechanism was of down-swing type with Welin block and vertical lever operating gear. The slide surface began 135in (*3429mm*) from the breech face and extended for 177in (*4496mm*) with a diameter of 62.0in (*1575mm*) which was also the diameter over the chamber. Diameter at the muzzle was 29.7in (*754.4mm*).

The gun was about half finished at the time of the Washington Conference in 1921-22, and it was decided to convert it to a 16in (*406mm*) 56-calibre gun, known as Mk 4/0, for the study of the effects of high velocities in a heavy gun. A 31in (*787mm*) extension was fixed to the muzzle by a collar fitting, and separate bore and chamber liners replaced the original single one. The slide surface was moved 20in (*508mm*) forward and the new muzzle diameter was 28.5in (*724mm*). Proofing began at the Dahlgren ground in July 1927 and the gun was fired on occasion throughout the 1930s in various tests.

It was considered in a study of 1926-28 and again in 1938 as a possible battleship gun, but was rejected on the grounds of weight and of very short life and also because a sufficient angle of descent for the attack of decks would occur only at excessive ranges. A gun on the lines of the 18in (*457mm*)/48 was a much more inviting choice in 1938, but its weight, the size and cost of a suitable ship to mount a sufficient number, and above all the international reaction to a larger gun than 16in (*406mm*) ruled it out. Its performance would have been better than that of any 16in, as with a 3850lb (*1746kg*) shell, equivalent to the 16in (*406mm*) 2700lb (*1225kg*), a ship with 16in (*406mm*) side and 6¼in (*159mm*) deck, would have had no immune zone at all, and both side and deck would have been vulnerable at 25,000-30,500yd (*22900-27900m*).

As a result of continued interest in the performance of the 3850lb (*1746kg*) 18in (*457mm*) projectile against armour, it was decided to reconvert the 16in (*406mm*) Mk 4/0 and this was done in 1941, the gun being installed at Dahlgren on a special proof mounting and first fired in February 1942. The original 18in Mk 1/0 unfinished liner was still in existence, but to eliminate the shoulders and threads cut for the 31in (*787mm*) extension, the muzzle was cut back and the relined gun, now known as Mk A/O, was 47 calibres. Proposed chromium plating of the bore was cancelled.

16in (406mm) Mk 4/0

Gun Data

Bore	16.0in	406.4mm	
Weight incl BM	185.2 tons	188.2t	
Length oa	915in	23,241mm	57.19cal
Length bore	*c*891.2in	*c*22636.5mm	*c*55.7cal
Length chamber	*c*119.5in	*c*3035mm	
Volume chamber	34,000in^3	557.2dm^3	
Length rifling	765.712in	19,449.08mm	
Grooves			
Lands			
Twist	1 in 35		
Weight projectile	2240lb	1016kg	
Propellant charge	810lb NC	367.4kg NC	
Muzzle velocity	2960f/s	902m/s	
Working pressure	17.5t/in^2	2760kg/cm^2	
Approx life	45 EFC		
Max range	49,383yds/40° (longest recorded)	45,156m/40°	

18in (457mm) Mk A/O

Gun Data

Bore	18.0in	457.2mm	
Weight incl BM	177.0 tons	179.8t	
Length oa	865in	21,971mm	48.06cal
Length bore	*c*840.6in	*c*21351mm	*c*46.7cal
Length chamber	*c*114in	*c*2895.5mm	
Volume chamber	36,900in^3	604.7dm^3	
Length rifling	718.965in	18,261.71mm	
Grooves			
Lands			
Twist	1 in 25		
Weight projectile	3848lb	1745kg	
Propellant charge	890lb NC	403.7kg	
Muzzle velocity	2400f/s	731.5m/s	
Working pressure	?18tons/in^2	?2835kg/cm^2	
Approx life	not determined		
Max range	43,453yds/40° (longest recorded)	39,734m/40°	

16in (406mm) Mark 1/0–1/10 Mark 5/0–5/3 Mark 8/0–8/2

These 45-calibre guns were mounted in two gun turrets in *Maryland*, *Colorado* and *West Virginia* and would also have been in the uncompleted *Washington*, sunk as a gunnery target in November 1924. The prototype, known as the 16in (*406mm*) Type Gun was designed in August 1913 and proof fired in July 1914, 30 months before the first production orders. Brief details of the various marks and modifications were:

Mk 1/10. Liner, A tube, jacket, seven hoops, four hoop-locking rings, screw box liner. As with all USN 16in (*406mm*) the A tube was hooped to the muzzle. The slide surface started 131in (*3327mm*) from breech face and extended for 150in (*3810mm*) with diameter 49in (*1245mm*). Diameter over the chamber was 53.5in (*1359mm*) and at the muzzle 26.5in (*673mm*). Breech mechanism was of down-swing type with Welin block and vertical lever operation.

Mk 1/1. As 1/0 but uniform rifling.

Mk 1/2. 1/0 relined with liner-locking ring and locking collar and clearance between liner and tube shoulders.

Mk 1/3. 1/1 relined as in 1/2.

Mk 1/4. 1/0 with liner-locking ring and screw-box liner centring ring added.

Mk 1/5. 1/0 relined with heavier taper carbon steel liner, liner-locking ring and locking collar, clearances between liner and tube shoulders.

Mk 1/6. 1/0 relined as in 1/2 but with modified chamber band slope.

Mk 1/7. As 1/6 but tube and liner-locking ring instead of liner-locking ring and collar.

Gun Data Mk 8/0

Bore	16.0in	406.4mm	
Weight incl BM	105.3 tons	107.0t	
Length oa	736.0in	18,694mm	46.0 cal
Length bore	*c*715.2in	*c*18,166mm	*c*44.7 cal
Length chamber	*c*92.3in	*c*2344mm	
Volume chamber	23,195in^3	380.1dm^3	
Length rifling	616.86in	15,668.2mm	
Grooves	96		
Lands			
Twist	1 in 25		
Weight projectile	2240lb APC	1016kg APC	
Propellant charge	556lb NC	252kg NC	
Muzzle velocity	2520f/s	768m/s	
Working pressure	18 tons/in^2	2835kg/cm^2	
Approx life	395 EFC		
Max range	35,000yd/30°	32,000m/30°	

A muzzle velocity of 2635f/s (*803m/s*) and range of 34,900yd/30° (*31,910m*) are given for the 1900lb (*862kg*) HC shell.

Mk 5/1 differed from Mk 8/0 in chamber volume 23,506in^3 (*385.2dm*^{3}), rifling twist increasing 1 in 50 to 1 in 32, propellant charge 562lb (*255kg*) and life about 320 EFC as the bore was not chromium plated.

Mk 1/8. As 1/2 but tube and liner-locking ring.

Mk 1/9. As 1/4 but tube and liner-locking ring.

Mk 1/10. As 1/5 but tube and liner-locking ring.

Mk 5/0. Mk 1/2 relined. Main modification was design of chamber with different front slope and band seat.

Mk 5/1. 5/0 relined with tube and liner-locking ring replacing liner-locking ring.

Mk 5/2. Mks 1/7–10 or 5/0, 1 relined with one step taper alloy steel liner having heavy liner shrinkages. Tube and liner-locking ring. Chamber and rifling as in 5/0.

Mk 5/3. Experimental design for three-gun turrets originally known as MkC/O. Chamber identical to that of MK 6/0.

Mk 8/0. Mks 1/0, 1/7–10 or 5/0, 1 relined as in 5/2 but chamber identical to that of Mk 6/0.

Mk 8/1. Mk 1/10 relined. Differs from 8/0 in liner having taper forward of shoulder.

Mk 8/2. Mk 5/3 relined as 8/0.

Rifling was 1 in 50 to 1 in 32, except in Mks 1/1, 3 with 1 in 32 and Mks 8/0–2 with 1 in 25. The bores of Mks 8/0–2 were chromium plated 0.0005in (*0.013mm*) deep for 625.0in (*15,875mm*) from the muzzle. Originally the shells were 2100lb (*952.5kg*) and MV 2600f/s (*792m/s*), but later APC were 2240lb (*1016kg*) and HC 1900lb (*862kg*). It was not possible to accommodate 2700lb (*1225kg*) APC in the turret fittings. The propellant charge was divided into fifths.

A list of April 1944 shows the rebuilt *West Virginia* with Mk 8/0 and *Maryland* and *Colorado* with Mk 5/1, except that one gun in the last named was Mk 1/7. Altogether about 40 guns were made.

The two gun turrets were electrically powered and through hydraulic drive gear, except for the lower powder hoists. The training motor was 50HP, and each gun had a 50HP motor for elevation, 90HP for ramming and upper powder hoist, 35HP for shell hoist and 7.5HP for lower powder hoist. Elevation limits were +30° -4° and loading was at +1°.

RPC was fitted in the rebuilt *West Virginia* and was requested for the other two. The guns were in separate slides (cradles) with flame-proof bulkheads between, but they could be coupled together to allow elevation as a unit from either or both motors. The elevating lead screw was connected to the rear of the slide. Run-out was at least originally by a combination of springs and compressed air with hydraulic buffers, and as usual the breech was closed by compressed air from the gas ejector system.

The majority of the shells were stowed vertically on the fixed structure round the turret and parbuckled through openings to a stowage ring on the rotating structure and thence to the two pusher hoists which ran from forward of the turret axis to near the gun loading positions, where they were fed into trays and rolled to the ramming positions. The lower powder hoists were axial and of enclosed endless chain type. They fed the enclosed powder handling room below the gunhouse to which a full charge for each gun was raised in enclosed powder cars, one to each gun, by the ram operated upper powder hoists. This occurred while the shells were being rammed and the charges were unloaded onto the spanning tray for ramming.

Range and Elevation Data for APC shell, 2520f/s (768m/s) MV

Range (yd)	(m)	Elevation	Descent	Time of flight (sec)	Striking V (f/s)	(m/s)
6000	5490	2°52′	3°07′	7.66	2200	671
10,000	9140	5°06′	5°55′	13.40	2007	612
16,000	14,630	9°06′	11°32′	23.19	1758	536
20,000	18,290	12°18′	16°20′	30.58	1629	497
26,000	23,770	18°03′	25°07′	43.30	1507	459
30,000	27,430	22°44′	31°41′	53.07	1472	449
36,000	32,920	31°40′	42°24′	70.62	1496	456

Gun Mounting Data

Revolving Weight (less shells)	880 to 920 tons	894 to 935t
Roller path diameter (od)	27ft 7¼in	8.41m
Barbette int diameter	31ft	9.45m
Distance apart gun axes	*c*104in	*c*2.64m
Recoil distance	48in	122cm
Max elevating speed	*c*8°/sec	
Max training speed	*c*2°/sec	
Firing cycle	*c*40 secs	
Turret shield	face 18in; sides 10in; rear 9in; roof 5in (as rebuilt ?6¾in)	457mm; 254mm; 229mm; 127mm (?171mm)

Top: The three ships of the BB45 class firing 16in salvos before World War II.
CPL

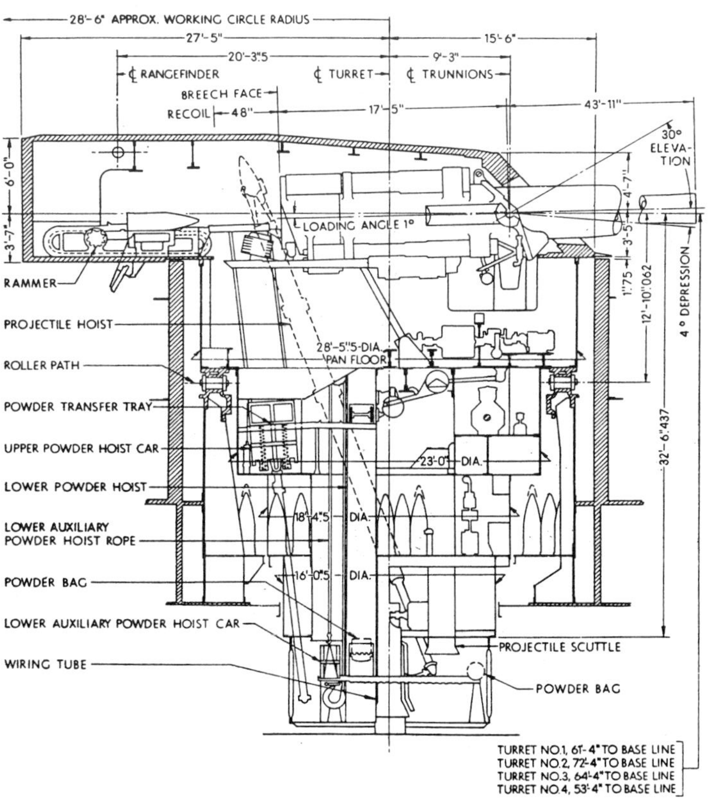

Two-gun turret for 16in/45 Mk 1, 5 or 8 guns BB45, 46, 48, *Colorado, Maryland, West Virginia.*
USN

These 50-calibre guns were intended for the 6 *South Dakota* class battleships and 6 *Lexington* class battlecruisers cancelled under the Washington Treaty. They were never mounted afloat though for a time in 1938 they were strongly favoured for the *Iowa* and *New Jersey*, and they also became the standard US heavy coast gun. The prototype was first fired in April 1918 and 150 production guns were ordered in 1918–21. When these were cancelled in February 1922, 71 including the prototype, were complete and 44 in progress. Brief details were:

Mark 2/0. Liner, A tube, jacket, seven hoops, four hoop-locking rings, screw box liner. Slide surface starts 143in (*3632mm*) from breech face and extends for 159in (*4039mm*) with diameter 52in (*1321mm*). Diameter over the chamber was 56.5in (*1435mm*) and 26.5in (*673mm*) at the muzzle. Breech mechanism similar to that of Mk 1.

Mark 2/1. Similar to 2/0 but uniform rifling of different groove profile.

Mark 3/0. Similar to Mk 2/0 but one step taper liner. Doubtful if any guns completed.

Mark 3/1. As 3/0 but uniform rifling. One gun converted to Mk D/O, pilot gun for Mk 7.

In British terms, the tubes and hoops were arranged as follows; tapered inner A tube/A tube/B1, B2, B3 tubes to muzzle 1/C, C2 tubes for about ⅔ of length/jacket and D tube/breech ring. The breech bush screwed into B1 which was the jacket in US terminology.

A total of 20 guns were transferred to the US Army in 1922–24, but the rest remained as naval stock and, in 1938, the Mk 2 appeared to be the obvious choice for *Iowa* and *New Jersey*, particularly as the Army had found it to be an excellent coast-defence gun, and the new 16in (*406mm*)/50 with a maximum diameter of 49in (*1245mm*) was still at the design stage. Unfortunately the Mk 2 needed a barbette of at least 39ft (*11.9m*) internal diameter, and the Bureau of Ordnance worked on this size, while the Bureau of Construction and Repair failed to appreciate it, and designed the ships for a 37ft 3in (*11.35m*) barbette, which was a tight fit for the new gun. It was five months before this discrepancy was realised, and the only solution was to abandon the Mk 2. The entire stock, except for three guns, was transferred to the Army for coast defence in January 1941.

By August 1945 there were 23 two-gun 16in (*406mm*) coast defence batteries of which 20 had Mk 2 guns and three the Army M1919, a ponderous weapon of higher performance and of wire-wound construction, though not at all the latest by British standards. External diameters were 62in (*1575mm*) over the chamber and 29.5in (*749mm*) at the muzzle.

16in (406mm) Marks 2/0, 2/1, 3/0, 3/1

Gun Data (performance as coast-defence gun)

Bore	16.0in	406.4mm	
Weight incl BM	128.15 tons	130.2t	
Length oa	816.0in	20,726mm	51.0cal
Length bore	*c*795.2in	*c*20,198mm	*c*49.7cal
Length chamber	*c*.113.2in	*c*2875mm	
Volume chamber	30,000in^3	491.6dm^3	
Length rifling	675.992in	17,170.2mm	
Grooves	(96)		
Lands			
Twist	1 in 50 to 1 in 32 or 1 in 32		
Weight projectile	2240lb	1016kg	
Propellant charge	648lb NC	294kg NC	
Muzzle velocity	2650f/s	808m/s	
Working pressure	18t/in^2	2835kg/cm^2	
Approx life	?200 EFC		
Max range	45,100yd/46°	41,240m/46°	

Gun Data Army M1919

Bore	16.0in	406.4mm	
Weight incl BM	152.05 tons	154.5t	
Length oa	824in	20,930mm	51.5cal
Length bore	*c*800in	*c*20,320mm	*c*50.0cal
Length chamber	*c*124.8in	*c*3170mm	
Volume chamber	40,900in^3	670.2dm^3	
Length rifling	*c*669in	*c*16,993mm	
Grooves	(144) 0.12in deep × 0.2091in	3.05 × 5.311mm	
Lands	0.14in	3.56mm	
Twist	1 in 30		
Weight projectile	2340lb	1061kg	
Propellant charge	832lb NC	377kg NC	
Muzzle velocity	2700f/s	823m/s	
Working pressure	17t/in^2	2690kg/cm^2	
Approx life	?150 EFC		
Max range	49,140yd/48°	44,930m/48°	

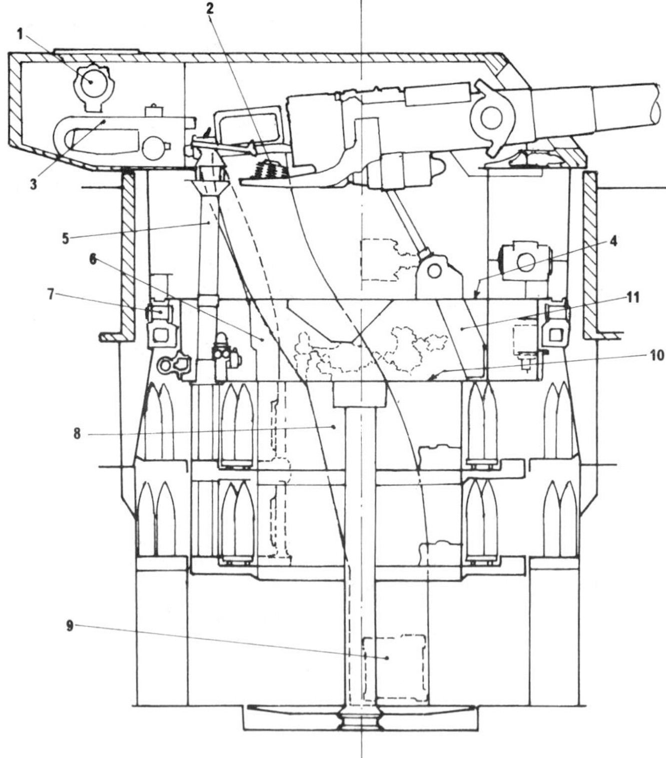

Opposite: 16in/45 Mk 6 guns in BB55 *North Carolina* on trials 1941.
CPL

Three-gun turret for 16in/45 Mk 6 guns. BB55–60 *North Carolina* and *South Dakota* classes.

1 Range-finder
2 Breech block (open)
3 Chain rammer
4 Pan floor
5 Centre projectile hoist
6 Left projectile hoist
7 Roller path
8 Powder hoist
9 Powder car
10 Electric deck
11 Elevating cylinder

CPL

Lightweight 45-calibre guns mounted in three-gun turrets in *North Carolina, Washington, South Dakota, Indiana, Massachusetts* and *Alabama*. Internally they were similar to the previous 45-calibre guns and in fact identical with the Mk 8. There was however the important difference that the mountings allowed 2700lb (*1225kg*) APC to be used though there were objections to the resultant low MV of 2300f/s (*701m/s*). The prototype gun Mk E/O was actually the old 16in (*406mm*) Type gun relined.

Brief details of the modifications were:

Mark 6/0. Liner, A tube, jacket, three hoops, two locking rings, liner-locking ring, yoke ring and screw box liner. The principal components were autofretted. The slide surface diameter and that over the chamber were 46in (*1168mm*), and at the muzzle 23.5in (*597mm*). Rifling was 1 in 50 to 1 in 32 in some and 1 in 25 in others. Guns were removable from the turret ports without dismantling the turret. The breech mechanism was of similar type to that of previous 16in (*406mm*).

Mark 6/1. As 6/0 but with tapped holes at breech end for securing the hinge lug to the gun. Rifling in all 1 in 25.

Mark 6/2. As 6/1 with set of adapter sleeves as wartime measure for re-gunning *Maryland* class. Doubtful if mounted.

The bores of all were chromium plated 0.0005in (*0.013mm*) deep for 625.0in (*15,875mm*) from the muzzle. HC shells were 1900lb (*862kg*) and the propellant charge was divided into sixths, not fifths as in the previous 45-calibre guns.

About 120 guns were made. A list of April 1944 shows Mk 6/1 in all six ships.

The three-gun turrets were electrically powered through hydraulic gear. There was a 300HP training motor and each gun had a 60HP motor for elevation, 60HP for ramming, 60HP for shell hoist and 75HP for powder hoist. In addition each of the two shell rings in the revolving structure was powered by a 40HP motor. Elevation limits were +45° to -2°, 0° in the superfiring turret, and loading was at +5°. RPC was fitted.

16in (406mm) Marks 6/0-6/2

Gun Data Mk 6/1

Bore	16.0in	406.4mm	
Weight	85.85 tons	87.2t	
Length oa	736.0in	18,694mm	46.0cal
Length bore	*c*715.2in	*c*18,166mm	*c*44.7cal
Length chamber	*c*92.3in	*c*2344mm	
Volume chamber	23,195in³	380.1dm³	
Length rifling	616.86in	15,668.2mm	
Grooves	(96)		
Lands			
Twist	1 in 25		
Weight projectile	2700lb	1225kg	
Propellant charge	540lb NC	245kg NC	
Muzzle velocity	2300f/s	701m/s	
Working pressure	18 tons/in²	2835kg/cm²	
Approx life	395 EFC		
Max range	36,900yd/45°	33,740m/45°	

Weight is for gun with solid breech without mechanism. With 1900lb (*862kg*) HC ranges were 40,180yd/45° (*36,740m*) with 2635f/s (*803m/s*) MV and 37,100yd/45° (*33,920m*) with 2525f/s (*770mls*).

Range and Elevation Data for APC shell, 2300f/s (701m/s) MV

Range (yd)	**(m)**	**Elevation**	**Descent**	**Time of flight (sec)**	**Striking V (f/s)**	**(m/s)**
6000	5490	3°23′	3°38′	8.28	2050	625
10,000	9140	5°59′	6°48′	14.45	1900	579
16,000	14,630	10°33′	12°51′	24.76	1704	519
20,000	18,290	14°09′	17°56′	32.55	1604	489
26,000	23,770	20°43′	27°01′	46.03	1509	460
30,000	27,430	26°14′	34°04′	56.64	1490	454
36,000	32,920	39°25′	47°54′	79.80	1551	473

Gun Mounting Data

Revolving weight (less shells)	1403-1437 tons	1426-1460t
Roller path diameter (od)	34ft 5in	10.49m
Barbette int diameter	37ft 3in	11.35m
Distance apart gun axes	117in	2.97m
Recoil distance	48in	122cm
Max elevating speed	12°/sec	
Max training speed	4°/sec	
Firing cycle	30 secs	
Turret shield (*N Carolina* class)	face 16in; sides 9.8in; rear 11.8in, roof 7in	406mm; 249mm; 300mm; 178mm
(*S Dakota* class)	face 18in; sides 9.5in; rear 12in; roof 7.25in	457mm; 241mm; 305mm; 184mm

The guns were in separate slides (cradles) but could be coupled together. The elevating lead screw was connected to the slide and run-out was by compressed air, while the breech was closed by compressed air from the gas ejector system. The construction of the turret was improved by the use of box girders instead of plate, and the removal of turret stool stiffeners provided space for a much improved shell supply. Shells were stowed vertically on two deck levels in the fixed structure and were parbuckled to two corresponding live-shell rings on the revolving structure. These rings rotated independently of the main revolving structure and brought shells close to the hoists which could be loaded from either deck level. The base of the pusher hoists was between the fixed and live rings, and the hoist for the centre gun ran straight to a position to the side and rear of the gun while those for the wing guns were curved to bring the top of the hoist to the desired position. The enclosed powder hoists ran from the hoist loading space, fed from the magazines by flame-proof scuttles, to the gunhouse where the powder cars were unloaded into the spanning trays.

The turrets were fast firing and the troubles of interference from shell wave if the guns were too close together were recognised, and the gun axes spaced 117in (*2.97m*) apart, in notable contrast to USN practice with previous 14in (*356mm*) three gun turrets. Doubts were expressed over the unbroken powder hoists but as far as is known no dangerous incidents attributable to these occurred, though it should be noted that no turret or barbette was holed by enemy projectiles.

16in (406mm) Mark 7/0

This lightweight 50-calibre gun was mounted in three gun turrets in *Iowa, New Jersey, Missouri* and *Wisconsin*, and was to be mounted in the unfinished *Illinois* and *Kentucky*, as well as in *Montana, Ohio, Maine, New Hampshire* and *Louisiana*, which were never laid down. Internally it differed from the previous 50-calibre Mks 2 and 3 in having a shorter chamber of 27,000in^3 (*442.5dm^3*) instead of 30,000in^3 (*491.6dm^3*). The pilot or prototype gun Mk D/O was a relined Mk 3/1, while Mk 7/A was a later experimental version of Mk 7/0, differing in having a loose liner. Mk 7/0 was similar to Mk 6 in construction, as shown below:

Mk 7/0. Liner, A tube, jacket, three hoops, two locking rings, tube and liner locking ring, yoke ring and screw box liner. The principal components were autofretted. The slide surface diameter and that over the chamber were 49in (*1245mm*) and over the muzzle 23.5in (*597mm*). The yoke stop was 53.5in (*1359mm*) from the breech face, 9.5in (*241mm*) more than in Mk 6/1, and guns were removable from the turret ports without dismantling the turret. The bore was chromium plated 0.0005in (*0.013mm*) deep for 690in (*17,526mm*) from the muzzle and the down-swing breech mechanism was of similar type to that in previous 16in (*406mm*) guns. HC shells were 1900lb (*862kg*) and the propellant charge was divided into sixths.

The three-gun turrets were generally similar to those for the Mk 6 gun and roller path, and barbette dimensions were the same, so that the problem of accommodating the 50-calibre gun was not easy. It was eventually solved at the price of crowding the turret training pinions and making them difficult of access. Elevation limits and loading angle were as for the Mk 6 gun, and RPC was fitted. Motor powers were similar except that each shell hoist motor was 75HP and each powder hoist 100HP. Recoiling weights per gun increased to 130.4 tons (*132.5t*) from 101.6 tons (*103.2t*) and oscillating weights per gun to 173.2 tons (*176.0t*) from 137.1 tons (*139.3t*). The gunhouse overall length was 50ft 7.5in (*15.43m*), compared with 47ft 7.5in-47ft 10.36in (*14.52-14.59m*). Accuracy suffered initially from poor gun alignment, which was not rectified until after the Battle of Leyte.

Gun Data Mk 7/0

Bore	16.0in	406.4mm	
Weight	106.8 tons	108.5t	
Length oa	816.0in	20,726mm	51.0cal
Length bore	*c*795.2in	*c*20,198mm	*c*49.7cal
Length chamber	*c*106.7in	*c*2710mm	
Volume chamber	27,000in^3	442.5dm^3	
Length rifling	682.46in	17,334.5mm	
Grooves	(96)		
Lands			
Twist	1 in 25		
Weight projectile	2700lb	1225kg	
Propellant charge	655lb NC	297kg NC	
Muzzle velocity	2500f/s	762m/s	
Working pressure	18.5 tons/in^2	2910kg/cm^2	
Approx life	290 EFC		
Max range	42,345yd/45°	38,720m/45°	

Weight is for gun without BM. With 1900lb (*862kg*) HC, MV is given as 2690f/s (*820m/s*) and range as 41,604yd/45° (*38,040m*).

Range and Elevation Data for APC shell, 2500f/s (762m/s) MV

Range (yd)	(m)	Elevation	Descent	Time of flight (sec)	Striking V (f/s)	(m/s)
6000	5490	2°52′	3°05′	7.62	2237	682
10,000	9140	5°03′	5°42′	13.24	2074	632
16,000	14,630	8°50′	10°43′	22.63	1859	567
20,000	18,290	11°47′	14°55′	29.59	1740	530
26,000	23,770	16°58′	22°28′	41.39	1615	492
30,000	27,430	21°07′	28°15′	50.32	1567	478
36,000	32,920	28°51′	38°00′	66.13	1560	475
40,000	36,580	36°05′	45°28′	79.96	1607	490

Gun Mounting Data for *Iowa* class

Revolving weight (less shells)	1701-1708 tons	1728-1735t
Roller path diameter (od)	34ft 5in	10.49m
Barbette int diameter	37ft 3in	11.35m
Distance apart gun axes	117in	2.97m
Recoil distance	48in	122cm
Max elevating speed	12°/sec	
Max training speed	4°/sec	
Firing cycle	30sec	
Turret shield	face 19.7in (17+2.7); sides 9.5in; rear 12in; roof 7.25in	500 (432+68)mm; 241mm; 305mm; 184mm
(in projected *Montana* class)	face 22.5in (18+4.5); sides 10in; rear 12in; roof 9.15in	572 (457+115)mm; 254mm; 305mm; 232mm

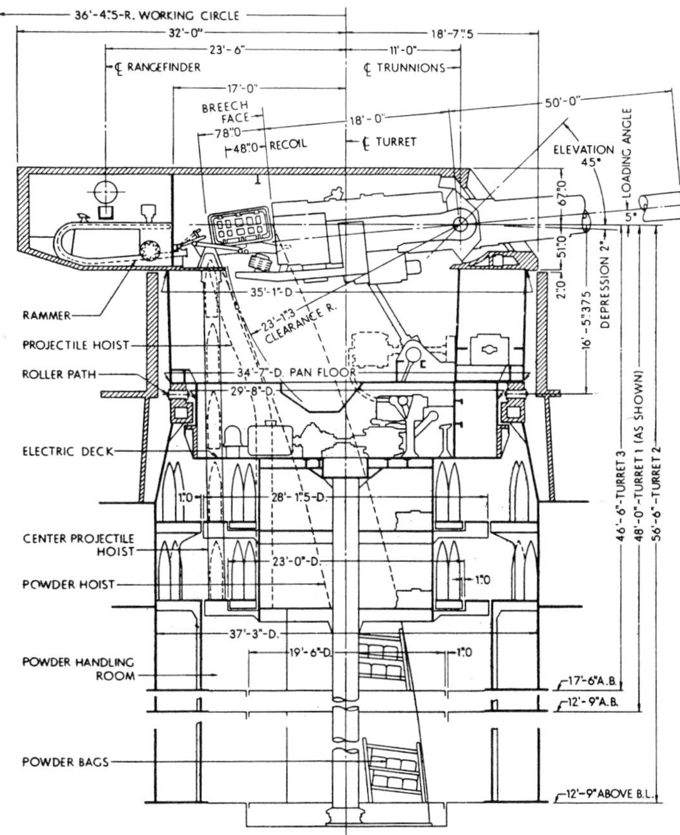

Three-gun turret for 16in/50 Mk 7 guns in longitudinal axial section.
USN

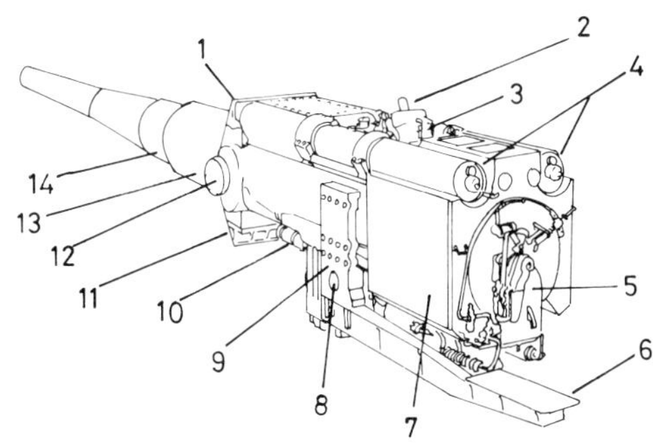

16in/50 Mk 7 gun with slide or cradle.

1 Upper shield plate
2 Depression buffer
3 Yoke locking link
4 Counter-recoil (run-out) cylinders
5 Downward opening breech
6 Loader's platform
7 Yoke
8 Slide locking pin
9 Rear end bracket
10 Recoil system expansion tank
11 Lower shield plate
12 Slide trunnion
13 Neoprene gun cover
14 Gun slide cylinder

Peter Hodges

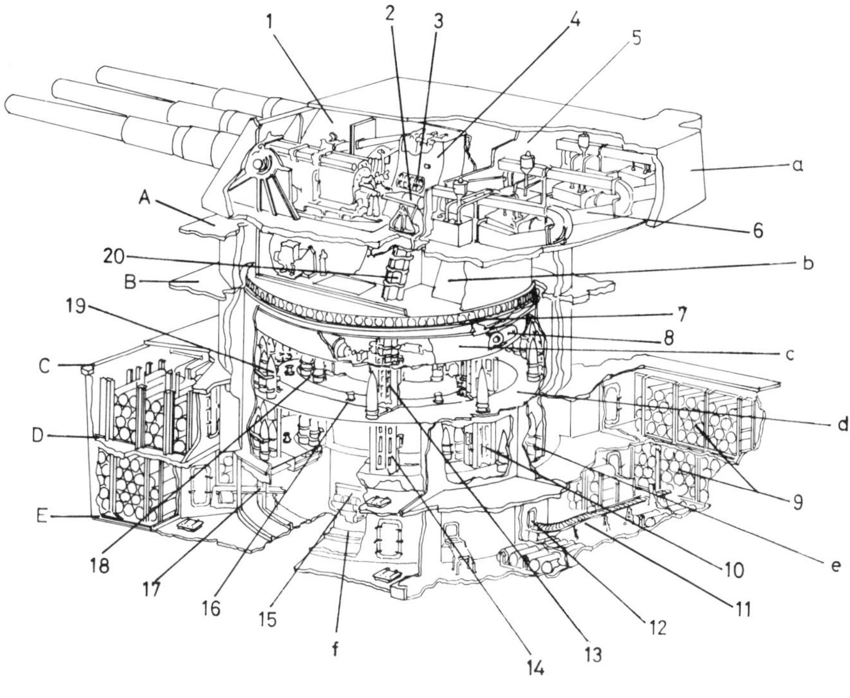

Three-gun turret for 16in/50 Mk 7 guns BB61-64 *Iowa* class.

1 Longitudinal flashtight bulkhead
2 Shell cradle
3 Powder charge door
4 Powder trunk
5 Lateral flashtight bulkhead
6 Rammer casing
7 Turret rollers
8 Training buffer
9 Upper and lower powder stowages
10 Centre gun lower shell hoist shutter casing
11 Roller conveyor
12 Powder scuttle
13 Left gun upper shell hoist shutter casing
14 Left gun lower shell hoist shutter casing
15 Powder hopper
16 Shell transfer capstan
17 Powder transfer tray
18 Upper revolving shell-ring
19 Upper fixed shell stowages
20 Shell hoist trunking
A Main deck
B Second deck
C Third deck
D First platform
E Second platform
a Gunhouse
b Pan floor
c Machinery floor
d Upper projectile handling floor
e Lower projectile handling floor
f Powder handling floor

Peter Hodges

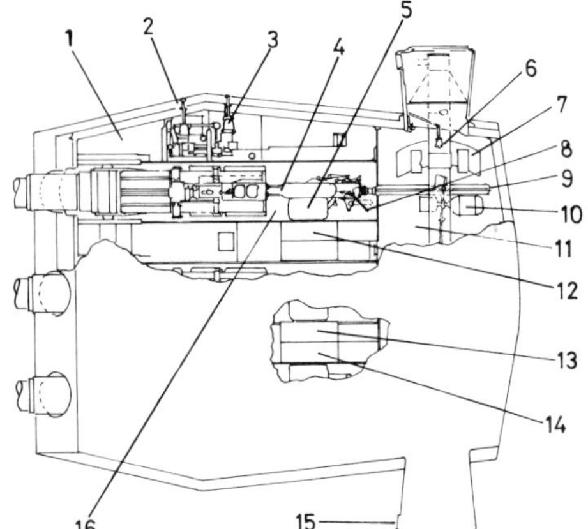

Three-gun turret for 16in/50 Mk 7 guns, gunhouse part plan.

1 Sight-setter's compartment
2 Trainer's telescope
3 Pointer's telescope
4 Spanning tray
5 Right gun powder hoist door
6 Range-finder
7 Range-finder traversing support platform
8 Right gun projectile cradle
9 Chain rammer casing
10 Rammer A and electric drive motor
11 Flashtight rammer compartment
12 Right gun powder trunk
13 Centre gun powder trunk
14 Left gun powder trunk
15 Range-finder hood shutter
16 Flashtight gun compartment

Note: apart from powder trunks, turret is symmetrical about the centreline

Peter Hodges

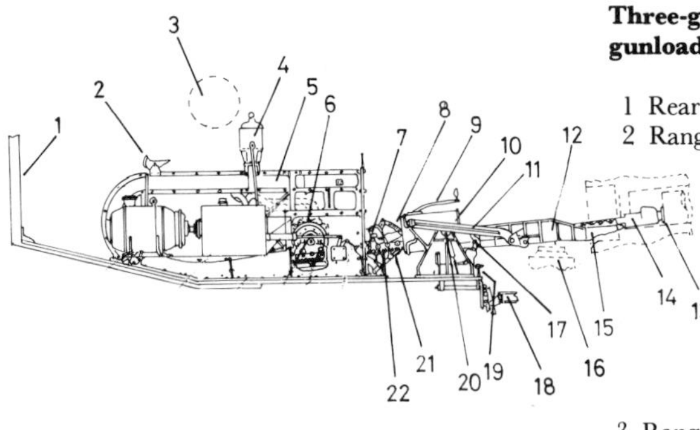

Three-gun turret for 16in/50 Mk 7 guns, gunloading arrangements.

1 Rear bulkhead
2 Range-finder operator's seat
3 Range-finder
4 Header tank
5 Chain rammer casing
6 B end
7 Rammer withdraw buffer
8 Control lever bracket
9 Projectile latch release lever
10 Projectile cradle
11 Control link
12 Spanning tray
13 Rammer head buffer
14 Rammer head link
15 Folding breech protection tray
16 Breech, opening downwards
17 Cradle opening buffer
18 Loading platform
19 Cradle release foot-pedal
20 Cradle axis
21 Control lever
22 Rammer tray

Peter Hodges

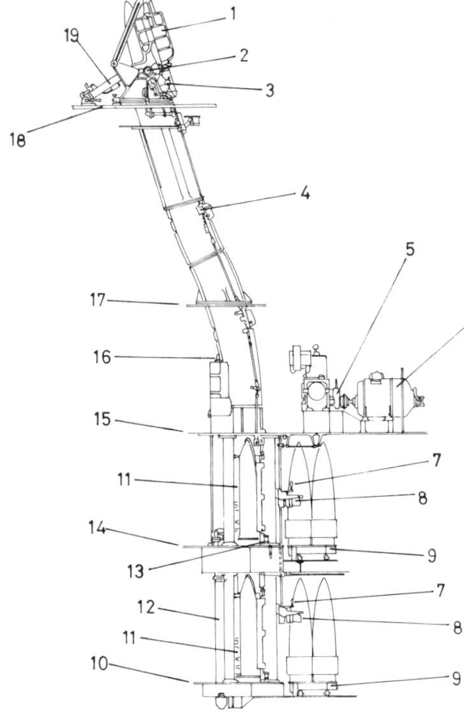

Three-gun turret for 16in/50 Mk 7 guns, outer gun projectile hoist.

1 Spanning tray
2 Cradle axis
3 Cradle buffer
4 Hoist pawl operating cylinder
5 Solenoid brake
6 Hoist A end electric drive motor
7 Hoist control handle
8 Hoist/projectile ring interlock solenoid
9 Projectile ring
10 Lower projectile handling floor
11 Hoist shutters
12 Shutter operating cylinder
13 'Parbuckling' roller
14 Upper projectile handling floor
15 Machinery floor
16 Shutter cylinder indicator
17 Pan floor
18 Gunhouse floor
19 Cradle operating cylinder

Peter Hodges

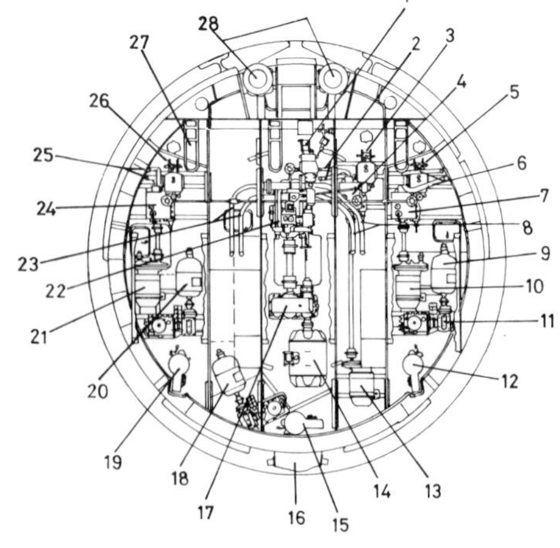

Three-gun turret for 16in/50 Mk 7 guns, machinery floor.

1 Trainer's handwheels
2 Pipework up to centre gun elevating B end
3 Centre gunlayer's handwheels
4 Centre gun elevation A end
5 Right gunlayer's handwheels
6 Pipework up to right gun elevating B end
7 Right gun elevating A end
8 Pipework up to training B end
9 Right gun projectile hoist electric motor
10 Right gun elevating A end electric drive motor
11 Reduction gear box
12 Right gun projectile hoist
13 Centre gun elevating A and electric drive motor
14 Training A end electric drive motor
15 Centre gun projectile hoist
16 Training limit buffer
17 Training gear reduction gearbox
18 Centre gun projectile hoist electric motor
19 Left gun projectile hoist
20 Left gun projectile hoist electric motor
21 Left gun elevating A end electric drive motor
22 Training gear A end
23 Pipework up to training B end
24 Left gun elevating A end
25 Pipework up to left gun elevating B end
26 Left gunlayer's handwheels
27 Pocket for elevating screw
28 Training pinions

Peter Hodges

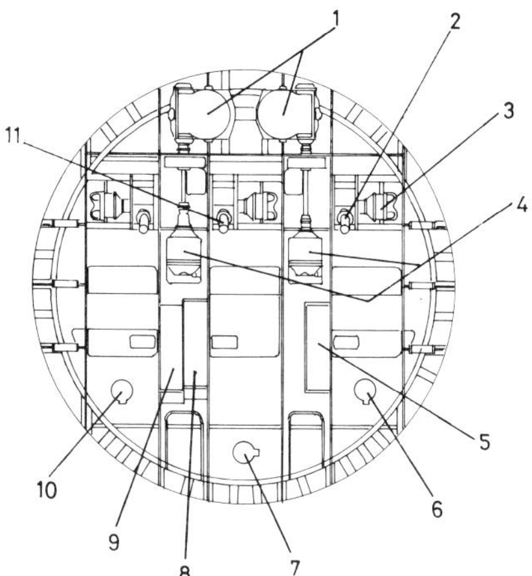

Three-gun turret for 16in/50 Mk 7 guns, turret pan floor.

1 Training gear worm and wormwheel gear boxes
2 Right gun elevating screw
3 Right gun elevating B end
4 Training gear B ends
5 Right gun powder trunk
6 Right gun projectile hoist
7 Centre gun projectile hoist
8 Centre powder trunk
9 Left gun powder trunk
10 Left gun projectile hoist
11 Centre gun elevating screw (offset to the left)

Peter Hodges

Three-gun turret for 16in/50 Mk 7 guns - upper and lower projectile stowage and handling room.

1 Fixed circumferential projectile stowages
2 Rotating circumferential projectile stowages on powered projectile ring
3 Projectile ring drive gear box
4 Hydraulic unit
5 Projectile ring electric motor
6 Right gun powder cage trunk
7 Projectile capstan, used to transfer projectiles by 'parbuckle' cables from fixed to moving stowages
8 Right gun projectile hoist
9 Electric capstan motor
10 Centre gun projectile hoist
11 Left gun projectile hoist
12 Left gun powder cage trunk
13 Centre gun powder cage trunk
14 Shaft drive to transfer capstans

Peter Hodges

These 45-calibre guns were mounted in two-gun turrets in *New York* and *Texas*, in two-gun and triple turrets in *Oklahoma* and *Nevada*, and in triple turrets in *Pennsylvania* and *Arizona*. Mks 8, 9 and 10 were conversions from Mks 1, 3 and 5 respectively, while Mk 12 was a further conversion from Mks 8, 9 and 10. Apart from constructional improvements, the main feature of these later marks was the enlarged chamber, also present in Mks 1/9, 1/12-1/14, 3/2-3/5, 5/1, 5/2, which permitted an increase in MV of 100f/s (*30m/s*) or alternatively of 100lb (*45kg*) in the shell weight.

The original prototype was known as Mk 2 and the first production gun was Mk 1/0 followed by 1/1 and 1/2 which differed in breech mechanism details. The construction comprised an A tube without liner, jacket eight hoops and a screw box liner with a flange 4in (*102mm*) thick and the full gun diameter of 46in (*1168mm*). The hoops were not adequately locked together and droop was excessive so that in Mk 1/3-1/14 four hoop-locking rings were added and the foremost hoop of the outer layer replaced by a longer one. All these except Mk 1/3 and 1/10 were also lined or relined.

Mk 3/0 resembled the modified Mk 1 except that there were three hoop locking rings. There was no liner but Mks 3/1-3/5 were lined or relined. Mk 5/0 was of improved construction with liner, A tube, jacket, five hoops, three hoop-locking rings and the screw box liner which had no large flange, screwed into the jacket (rear inner hoop in British terminology) instead of into the rear hoops of the two outer layers. Mks 5/1-5/3 differed mainly in liner or breech mechanism details.

Guns of these earlier marks with enlarged chambers are listed in the first paragraph. The prototypes for Mk 8 were known as 8/A and 8/B and the later marks were:

14in (356mm) Marks 8/0-8/7, 9/0-9/2, 10/0-10/2, 12/0-12/10

Gun Data Mk 12/0-/2, 12/4-/10

Bore	14in	355.6mm	
Weight incl BM	61.6-62.6 tons	62.6-63.6t	
Length oa	642.45in	16,318.2mm	45.89cal
Length bore	*c*624.2in	*c*15,855mm	*c*44.6cal
Length chamber	*c*86.2in	*c*2189mm	
Volume chamber	17,943in^3	294.0dm^3	
Length rifling	532.66in	13,529.6mm	
Grooves	(84)		
Lands			
Twist	1 in 25		
Weight projectile	1500lb	680kg	
Propellant charge NC	420lb	190.5kg NC	
Muzzle velocity	2600f/s	792m/s	
Working pressure	18 tons/in^2	2835kg/cm^2	
Approx life	250 EFC		
Max range	34,300yd/30° 23,000yd/15°	31,360m/30° 21,030m/15°	

The performance of Mks 8, 9 and 10 was as above except that life was about 200 EFC as they were not chromium plated in the bore. With 1275lb (*578kg*) HC and MV 2735f/s (*834m/s*), ranges were 34,700yd (*31,730m*) at 30° and 23,500yd (*21,490m*) at 15°.

Gun Mounting Data for *Pennsylvania* class

Revolving weight (less shells)	714-724 tons	725-736t
Roller path diameter (od)	27ft 1¼in	8.26m
Barbette int diameter	29ft	8.84m
Distance apart gun axes	*c*59in	*c*1.50m
Recoil distance	40in	102cm
Max elevating speed	*c*4°/sec	
Max training speed	*c*2°/sec	
Firing cycle	*c*50 sec	
Turret shield	face 18in; sides 10in; rear 9in; roof 5in	457mm; 254mm; 229mm; 127mm

The triple turrets in the *Oklahoma* class differed in a revolving weight of 748 tons (*760t*) and a barbette interior diameter of 30ft (*9.14m*).

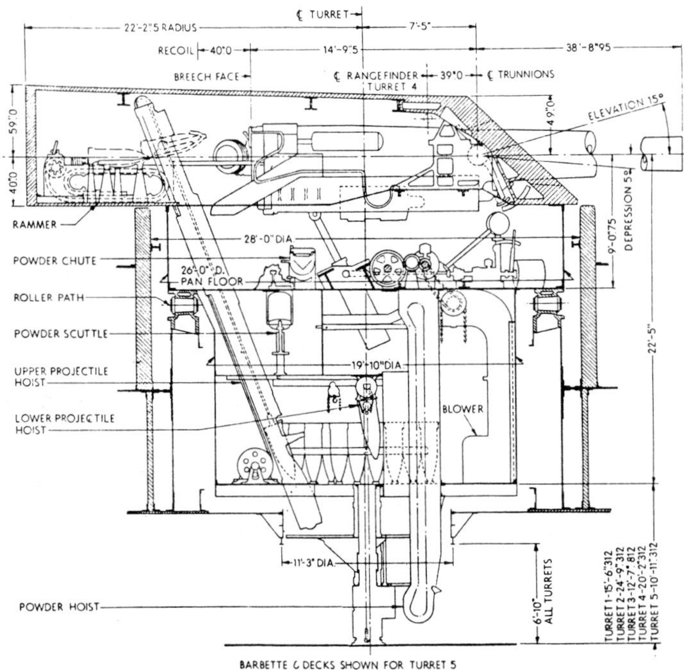

Two-gun turret for 14in/45 guns, BB34, 35, *New York*, *Texas*.
USN

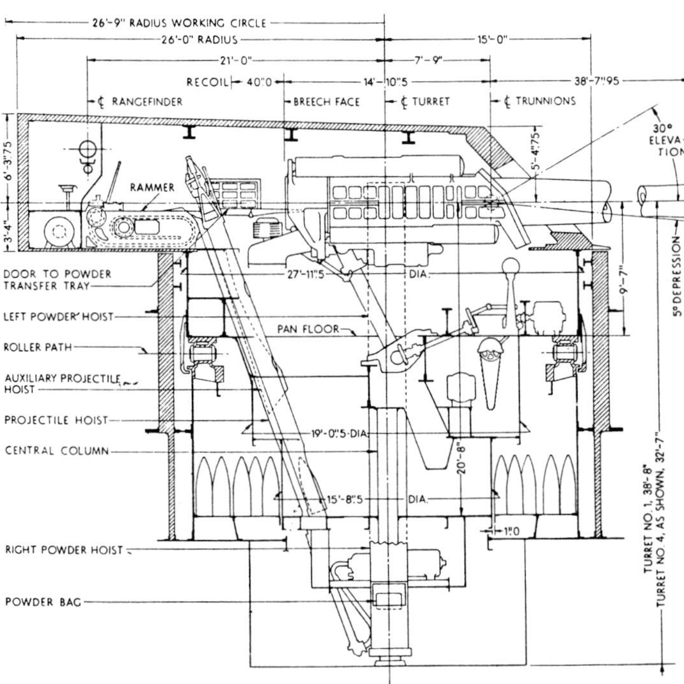

Triple turret for 14in/45 guns, BB36, 37, *Nevada*, *Oklahoma*.
Note: the two-gun turret in these ships is not shown.
USN

Mk 8/0. Mks 1/1, 1/3, 1/7-1/9, 1/11 lined or relined with one step taper liner with liner collar and tube and liner-locking ring at breech end. Band slope was 3½°, rifling uniform twist and breech mechanism down-swing with Welin block and Smith-Asbury mechanism. When converted from Mk 1/1, a longer foremost outer layer hoop and four hoop locking rings were added. The slide surface began 105.5in (*2680mm*) from the breech end and was 109.7 × 42in (*2786 × 1067mm*). Diameter over the chamber was 46in (*1168mm*).

Mk 8/1. As 8/0 but side swing BM.

Mk 8/2. As 8/0 but converted from Mk 1/4, 1/5.

Mk 8/3. As 8/1 but converted from Mk 1/4, 1/5.

Mk 8/4. 8/0 relined, chamber modified with projectile centering cylinder and 4° band seating slope.

Mk 8/5. Mk 1/7 relined, similar to 8/4 but slightly different band slope. Down swing BM. One gun only.

Mk 8/6. Mk 8/0 with additional hoop and hoop-locking ring. Chamber as in 8/4.

Mk 8/7. Mk 8/0 altered as 8/6 but different chamber design. One gun only.

Mk 9/0. Mk 3/2, 3/4 relined with one step taper liner with liner collar and tube and liner-locking ring at breech end. Rifling uniform twist. Down swing BM. The slide surface differed from that of Mk 8 in being 115in (*2921mm*) long.

Mk 9/1. As 9/0 but side swing BM.

Mk 9/2. Mk 3/1 relined as 9/0 but apparently two step liner. Down swing BM.

Mk 10/0. Mk 5/0, ?5/3 relined with apparently two step liner. Liner collar and locking ring at breech end. Rifling uniform twist. Down swing BM. Slide surface as in Mk 8/0.

Mk 10/1. As 10/0 but side swing BM.

Mk 10/2. Mk 5/2 relined with one step conical liner and chamber modified to 3½° band slope.

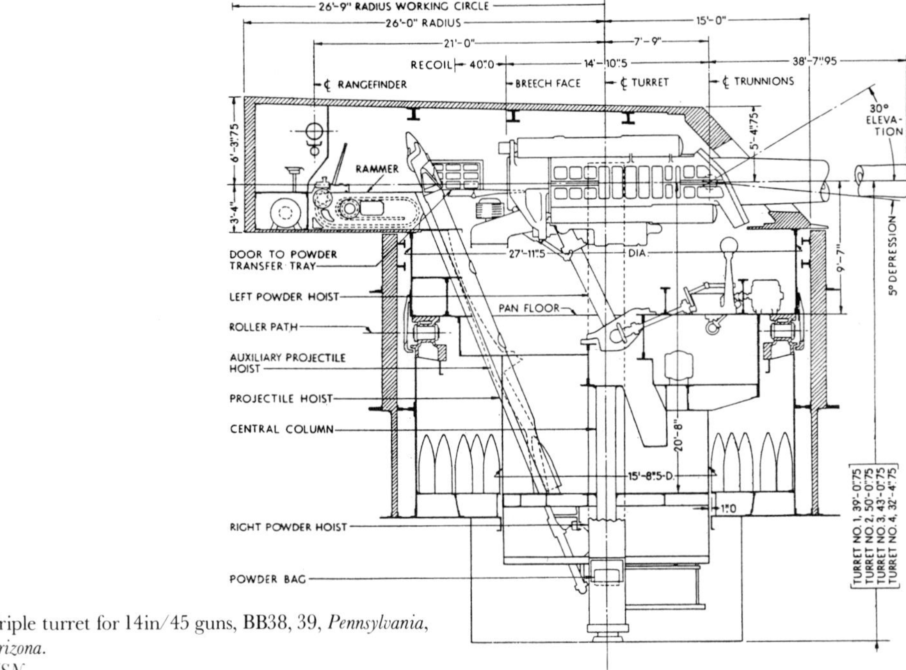

Triple turret for 14in/45 guns, BB38, 39, *Pennsylvania*, *Arizona*.
USN

Gun Mounting Data for two-gun turrets *Oklahoma* class

Revolving weight (less shells)	618 tons	628t
Roller path diameter (od)	25ft 1¼in	7.65m
Barbette int diameter	28ft	8.53m
Distance apart gun axes	88in	2.24m
Recoil distance	40in	102cm
Max elevating speed	*c*8°/sec	
Max training speed	*c*2°/sec	
Firing cycle	*c*45sec	
Turret shield	face 16in; sides 10in rear 9in roof 5in	406mm; 254mm; 229mm; 127mm

Differences in *New York* class

Revolving weight (less shells)	532 tons	541t
Max elevating speed	4°/sec	
Max training speed	100°/min	
Turret shield	face 14in; sides 9in; rear 8in; roof 5¾in	356mm; 229mm; 203mm; 146mm

Down swing BM. No mention of liner collar and locking ring but said to have four hoop-locking rings. The original Mk 5/2 had the jacket changed to provide a shoulder 24in (*610mm*) from the breech face to lock the A tube against rearward movement.

Mk 12/0. Mk 8/0, 8/1, 8/4, 8/5 if not converted from Mk 1/3, relined with heavy liner shrinkage. Chamber with projectile centering cylinder and 4° band seating slope. Down swing BM.

Mk 12/1. As 12/0 but from Mk 8/3.

Mk 12/2. As 12/0 but from Mk 8/0 and other modifications previously converted from Mk 1/3 having short foremost outer hoop. This last feature is not noted in the official description of Mk 1/3. Apparently five hoop locking rings.

Mk 12/3. As 12/0 but from Mk 8/B. Side swing BM.

Mk 12/4. As 12/0 but from Mk 9/0.

Mk 12/5. As 12/0 but from Mk 9/2.

Mk 12/6. As 12/0 but from Mk 10/0, 10/1.

Mk 12/7. As 12/0 but from Mk 10/2.

Mk 12/8. 12/1 with liner shoulder 330.15in (*8385.8mm*) from muzzle removed or Mk 8/3 relined with heavy liner shrinkage and chamber as in 12/0.

Mk 12/9. 12/5 or Mk 9/2 relined as in 12/8.

Mk 12/10. 12/6 or Mk 10/0, 10/1 relined as in 12/8.

Rifling was uniform 1 in 25 in Mk 12 and in Mk 8/A, and 1 in 32 in other Mk 8s, 9s and 10s. The Mk 12 series were chromium plated 0.0005in (*0.013mm*) deep in the bore for 540.0in (*13,716mm*) from the muzzle. APC shells weighed 1500lb (*680kg*) and HC 1275lb (*578kg*). Propellant charges were in quarters.

When lost *Arizona* had eleven Mk 8/4 and one Mk 8/5 while *Oklahoma* had two Mk 8/0, five Mk 9/0, one Mk 9/2 and two Mk 10/0. In April 1944 *Pennsylvania* had nine Mk 8/4 and three Mk 8/6; *Nevada* nine Mk 12/0 and one Mk 12/7; *New York* ten Mk 8/1 and *Texas* five Mk 8/1, three Mk 8/3, two Mk 10/1. By January 1945 *Nevada* is listed with a mixture of Mk 12/0, 12/2, 12/4 and 12/7 and *Texas* with Mk 12/0 and 12/1, though these are given as having down-swing BM. Two turrets were salved from *Arizona* and mounted in Oahu, but were apparently not ready until the last days of the war. The only other heavy gun coast defence turrets were the two gun turrets in Fort Drum at the entrance to Manila Bay but these had the Army 40-calibre wire-wound 14in (*356mm*) M1909.

There were considerable differences in the ships' turrets, but all were electrically powered with hydraulic drive gears for elevation and training in the *New York* class and for all but powder hoists in the *Oklahoma* and *Pennsylvania* classes. In the *New York* class the training motor was 25HP, increased in the later ships to 50HP for all turrets. Similarly each gun had a 15HP motor for elevation in the *New York* class, increased to 30HP per gun in the *Oklahoma* class two-gun turrets, while the triple turrets in this and the *Pennsylvania* class had a single 40HP elevating motor. Elevation limits were +15° to -5° in the *New York* class but in the others they were increased from this original figure to +30° -5°. Loading in all was at 0°. In the two-gun turrets there were separate slides (cradles) which could be coupled together, but the triple turrets had the guns in a single slide. Breech blocks opened sideways in the *New York* class and downwards in the others. Rammers were powered from 2-10HP motors in the two-gun turrets and from 2-30HP in the triples.

In the *New York* class shells were hoisted point downwards in 'buckets'. The upper hoists each driven by a 40HP motor, ran from the shell handling room in the rotating structure to the loading position, while the lower hoists, each 10HP, fed the stock in the shell handling room from the shell room. It appears that the hoists would not accommodate HC shell, at least without modification, and that the 1500lb (*680kg*) APC had a shorter ballistic cap than in other ships. The endless chain enclosed powder hoists, apparently both driven from an 11HP motor, and supplied the powder handling room whence the charges were passed through hand-ups to the guns. This seemingly dangerous system was tested in 1918 in the RN monitor *Raglan* which had Bethlehem turrets of similar type. An 11.1in (*283mm*) shell from the *Goeben* holed the barbette armour and ignited charges in the hand-ups but the flash did not spread below.

The two-gun turrets in the *Oklahoma* class had pusher shell hoists each with a 30HP motor, from the shell handling room to the loading position. The shells were stowed on their bases and parbuckled from the fixed structure to the handling room. The lower powder hoists were driven from a 10HP motor and charges transferred to the two upper hoists each 7½HP.

In the triple turrets the guns were supplied by two shell and three powder hoists. The shell hoists resembled those in the *Oklahoma*'s two-gun turrets except that in the *Pennsylvania* class they were powered from a single 60HP motor, but the powder hoists powered from 2-10HP motors, ran direct to the gunhouse where the charges were transferred to enclosed powder trays. There were obvious disadvantages in this method of supply and matters were not improved by the guns' being very close together, which also meant that serious shell interference had to be overcome.

14in (356mm) Marks 7/0-7/2, 11/0-11/5

Gun Data Mk 11/0-/3, 11/5

Bore	14in	355.6mm	
Weight incl BM	79.6 to 80.2 tons	80.9 to 81.5t	
Length oa	714.0in	18,136mm	51.0 cal
Length bore	*c*695.8in	*c*17673mm	*c*49.7cal
Length chamber	*c*83.1in	*c*2111mm	
Volume chamber	16,982in³	278.3dm³	
Length rifling	607.358in	15,426.9mm	
Grooves	(84)		
Lands			
Twist	1 in 25		
Weight projectile	1500lb	680kg	
Propellant charge	420lb NC	190.5kg NC	
Muzzle velocity	2700f/s	823m/s	
Working pressure	18t/in²	2835kg/cm²	
Approx life	250 EFC		
Max range	36,300yd/30°	33,190m/30°	

The performance of Mark 7 was as above except that life was about 200 EFC as the bore was not chromium plated. With 1275lb (*578kg*) HC and MV 2825f/s (*861m/s*) range was 36,600yd (*33,470m*) at 30°.

The serious constructional defects of the first 14in (*356mm*) were remedied in these 50-calibre guns which were mounted in three-gun turrets in *New Mexico, Mississippi, Idaho, Tennessee* and *California*. Mk 7 was a conversion of the earlier Mk 4 as were some Mk 11s, others being further conversions of Mk 7. The principal difference in these later Marks was that the chamber size was reduced without reduction in performance, though the propellant charge weight was 50lb (*22.7kg*) less and the same as in the later 45-calibre guns. Originally accuracy was poor with high dispersion, but it seems to have been much improved by alterations to the shot seating as detailed below.

There was no prototype and the first production guns, Mk 4/0, were built with a liner, A tube, jacket, three hoops, two locking rings and a screw box liner with a separate screwed on flange 4in (*102mm*) thick and the maximum gun diameter of 48in (*1219mm*). The breech was down swing with Welin block and Smith-Asbury mechanism. Mk 4/1 differed in having no flange on the screw box liner, with the jacket and rear hoop lengthened accordingly. Later modifications ran up to Mk 4/11 and the most important were:

Mk 4/3. Mk 4/0 relined with foremost step eliminated and uniform twist rifling.

Mk 4/8. Mk 4/3 with band seat of chamber modified.

Mk 4/4. Mk 4/1 relined as in 4/3.

Mk 4/9. Mk 4/4 with band seat of chamber modified.

Mk 4/11. 4/1 with band seat modified to 3½° slope by grinding while gun mounted aboard ship.

Mk 4/10 was an experimental gun with chamber as in Mk 7/0 and subsequently included with the latter.

Mk 4 guns were still mounted in *Tennessee* when Pearl Harbor was attacked, but were replaced in early 1942.

Mk 6/0 was almost identical with Mk 4/1 but had a single step taper liner and uniform twist rifling.

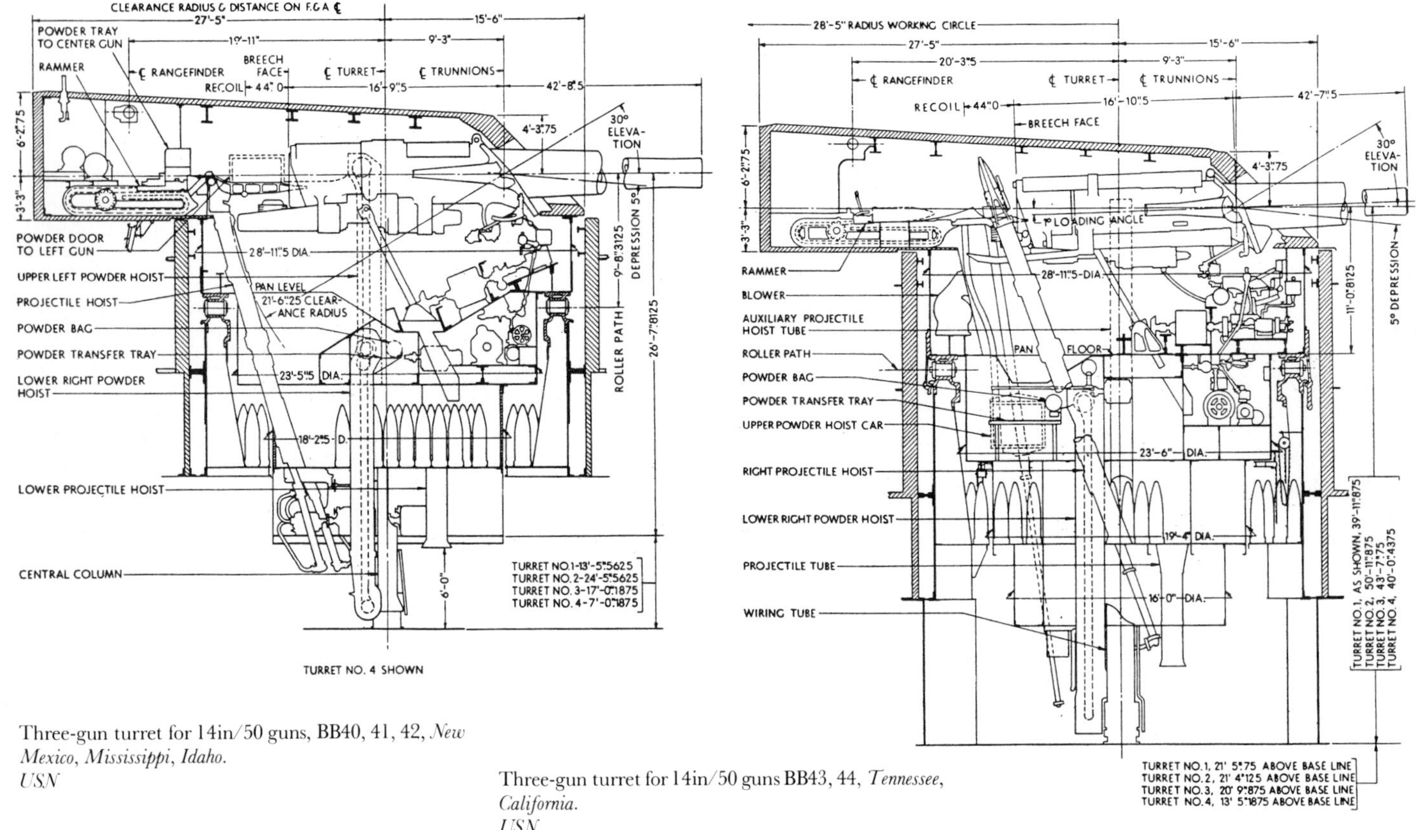

Three-gun turret for 14in/50 guns, BB40, 41, 42, *New Mexico*, *Mississippi*, *Idaho*.
USN

Three-gun turret for 14in/50 guns BB43, 44, *Tennessee*, *California*.
USN

The later marks with smaller chambers were:

Mk 7/0. Mks 4/0, 4/3, 4/8 relined with small chamber, single slope band seat and uniform rifling. The foremost liner step was eliminated. The slide surface began 120in (*3048mm*) from the breech face and was 132 × 44in (*3353* × 1118mm).

Mk 7/1. Mks 4/1, 4/4, 4/9 relined as in 7/0.

Mk 7/2. Data lacking but thought to be Mk 4/5 relined. One gun was again relined as Mk C/O, the prototype for Mk 11.

Mk 11/0. Mk 4/8, C/O, 7/0 relined. Alloy steel liner, small chamber, shell centering cone, single slope band seat, uniform rifling, chromium plated bore; also tube locking ring.

Mk 11/1. Mk 4/1, 4/4, 4/9, 4/11, 7/1 relined as in 11/0. Guns converted from Mk 4/1 had the foremost step on the liner removed.

Mk 11/2. Mk 11/0 with shoulder 340in (*8636mm*) from muzzle removed and forward section of liner and A tube machined to diametral taper of 1 in 250.

Mk 11/3. Mk 11/1 altered as in 11/2.

Mk 11/4. Not hooped to muzzle and 4in (*102mm*) shorter overall. The slide surface started 4in (*102mm*) nearer the breech face and was 152.5in (*3874mm*) long.

Mk 11/5. One Mk 7/1 with shoulder 340in (*8636mm*) from muzzle removed and A tube bore machined oversize for 590in (*14,986mm*) from muzzle with diametral taper 1 in 250.

Rifling was uniform 1 in 25 in Mk 11 and Mk C/O, but uniform 1 in 32 in Mk 7 and most of the earlier guns, though Mk 4/0, 4/1, 4/11 had increasing twist 1 in 50 to 1 in 32. The Mk 11 series and Mk C/O were chromium plated 0.0005in (*0.013mm*) deep in the bore for 613.0in (*15,570mm*) from the muzzle. APC and HC shells were as in the 45-calibre guns and propellant charges were in quarters.

In April 1944 *Tennessee* had one Mk 11/0 and eleven Mk 11/1. *California* and *New Mexico* each had twelve Mk 7/1. *Mississippi* had six Mk 7/0 and six Mk 7/1 and *Idaho* seven Mk 11/0 and five Mk 11/1, though by January 1945 *New Mexico* and *Mississippi* had Mk 11.

Range and Elevation Data for APC shell, 2625f/s (800m/s) MV

Range (yd)	(m)	Elevation	Descent	Time of flight (sec)	Striking V (f/s)	(m/s)
6000	5490	2°49′	2°55′	7.39	2267	691
10,000	9140	4°56′	5°37′	12.99	2040	622
16,000	14,630	8°46′	11°18′	22.71	1743	531
20,000	18,290	11°54′	16°20′	30.23	1588	484
26,000	23,770	17°39′	25°46′	43.25	1435	437
30,000	27,430	22°24′	33°00′	53.31	1390	424
36,000	32,920	31°34′	44°26′	71.56	1413	431

Gun Mounting Data for *Tennessee* class

Revolving weight (less shells)	958 tons	973t
Roller path diameter (od)	28ft $1\frac{1}{4}$in	8.57m
Barbette int diameter	31ft	9.45m
Distance apart gun axes	71in	1.80m
Recoil distance	44in	112cm
Max elevating speed	*c*9°/sec	
Max training speed	*c*2°/sec	
Firing cycle	*c*45sec	
Turret shield	face 18in; sides 10in; rear 9in; roof ?$6\frac{3}{4}$in	457mm; 254mm; 229mm; ?171mm

The turrets in the *New Mexico* class differed in a revolving weight of 897 tons (*911t*) and a 5in (*127mm*) roof.

An interesting variant was Mk B/O which, though it was never made, would have been useful if the *North Carolina* and *Washington* had had four-gun 14in (*356mm*) turrets as originally intended. The design was not hooped to the muzzle and was to be only 41in (*1041mm*) diameter over the chamber instead of 48in (*1219mm*), the weight with solid breech being 65.6 tons (*66.7t*).

The three-gun turrets were a considerable improvement on the previous triple as the guns were in separate slides and, though they were normally clutched together, the risk of all three guns being put out of action by a single shell was greatly reduced. The gun axes were still too close together but further apart than in the triple turret. As previously the mountings were electrically powered with hydraulic gear except for the powder hoists in the *New Mexico* class and for the lower ones in the *Tennessee* class. In the *California* and *Tennessee* there were a 50HP training motor and 50HP elevating motor for each gun, while ramming and the upper powder hoists were powered from two 90HP motors, the lower powder hoists from two $7\frac{1}{2}$HP and the shell hoists from two 35HP. Elevation was +30° to -5° and loading at +1°. RPC was fitted in both ships as rebuilt. There were flame proof bulkheads between the guns.

Most shells were stowed vertically on the fixed structure round the turret and parbuckled through openings to a stowage ring on the rotating structure and from there to the two pusher hoists which fed them to a position near the wing guns' loading gear. The centre gun had to be supplied from the wing hoists. The two lower enclosed endless chain powder hoists supplied the enclosed powder handling room, from which three ram-operated upper powder hoists raised the enclosed powder cars to each gun.

The mountings in the *New Mexico* class originally allowed +15° to -5° but this was altered to +30° -5°. Loading was at 0° and there were some differences in the electric motors. Thus the two 90HP units only powered the rammers, the upper powder hoists being powered from two 7½HP and the lower from two 10HP. According to a 1945 list there were three 35HP motors powering the shell hoists which indicates that space had been found for a hoist to the centre gun when the mountings were modernised in the 1930s. RPC was not fitted.

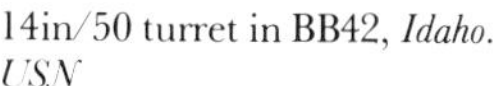
14in/50 turret in BB42, *Idaho*.
USN

12in (305mm) Marks 7/0-7/19

Known as 50-calibre, but actually 49.5 USN notation, these guns were mounted in two-gun turrets in the *Arkansas* and in the earlier part of the war in her demilitarised sister-ship *Wyoming*. The typical construction comprised liner, A tube, jacket, eight hoops and screw box liner with various locking hoops and rings. Apart from various liners, the principal differences were that Mk 7/3 had no liner, Mks 7/3, 7/7, 7/11, 7/15 had five hoops instead of eight and the chamber size was slightly increased in Mk 7/11 to 7/19; Mk 7/5 was never made. The only marks with original construction were 7/0 and 7/3, all others being lined or relined. The breech mechanism was side swing and hand operated, except that Mks 7/11 to 7/14 are given as having down swing.

Rifling was uniform 1 in 25 in Mk 7/0, increasing 1 in 50 to 1 in 32 in 7/1 to 7/3 and 7/19 with uniform 1 in 32 in the others. All were 44in (*1118mm*) diameter over the chamber. APC shells weighed 870lb (*395kg*) and HC 740lb (*336kg*). Propellant charges were in quarters.

Wyoming is listed as having Mk 7/2 and *Arkansas* Mks 7/4 and 7/6, altered to Mks 7/15 to 7/18 by January 1945.

The mountings resembled those in the *New York* and *Texas* and had the same +15° to -5° elevation with loading at 0°. Shells were however stowed on their sides and the lower shell hoists were not powered. Revolving weight (less shells) was 491 tons (*499t*) and roller path outer diameter 24ft 11in (*7.59m*), while the turret shields differed in having 12in (*305mm*) faces and 11in (*279mm*) rears.

12in (305mm) Mark 8/0

A new lightweight 50-calibre gun mounted in three-gun turrets in *Alaska* and *Guam* and intended for the unfinished *Hawaii* and the cancelled *Philippines*, *Puerto Rico* and *Samoa*. The prototype gun Mk A/O was a relined Mk 7/2.

Mk 8/0 was built with a liner, A tube, jacket, three hoops, two locking rings and a screw box liner with down swing breech mechanism. The diameter over the chamber and that of the slide surface were both 38in (*965mm*) and the latter

12in (305mm) Marks 7/0-7/19, 8/0

Gun Data for Marks 7/15-7/18

Bore	12in	304.8mm	
Weight incl BM	55.4 tons	56.3t	
Length oa	607.25in	15424mm	50.6cal
Length bore	*c*589.5in	*c*14973mm	*c*49.1cal
Length chamber	*c*83.7in	*c*2126mm	
Volume chamber	14,871in³	243.7dm³	
Weight projectile	870lb	395kg	
Propellant charge	337lb NC	153kg NC	
Muzzle velocity	2900f/s	884m/s	
Range	23,500yd/15°	21,490m/15°	

The original designed MV with APC of 2950f/s (*899m/s*) was reduced because of excessive wear. With 740lb (*336kg*) HC, MV was 3000f/s (*914m/s*) and range 23,900yd (*21,850m*) at 15°.

Gun Data for Mk 8/0

Bore	12in	304.8mm	
Weight less BM	48.6 tons	49.4t	
Length oa	612.0in	15,545mm	51.0cal
Length bore	*c*596.4in	*c*15,149mm	*c*49.7cal
Length chamber	*c*79.9in	*c*2029mm	
Volume chamber	11,863in³	194.4dm³	
Length rifling	511.96in	13,004mm	
Grooves	(72)		
Lands			
Twist	1 in 25		
Weight projectile	1140lb	517kg	
Propellant charge	270lb NC	122.5kg NC	
Muzzle velocity	2500f/s	762m/s	
Working pressure	19 tons/in²	2990kg/cm²	
Approx life	344 EFC		
Max range	38,573yd/45°	35,271m/45°	

With 940lb (*426kg*) HC and MV 2650f/s (*808m/s*), range was 38,021yd (*34,767m*).

Range and Elevation Data for APC shell, 2500f/s (762m/s) MV

Range (yd)	**(m)**	**Elevation**	**Descent**	**Time of flight (sec)**	**Striking V (f/s)**	**(m/s)**
6000	5490	3°02′	3°13′	7.74	2167	661
10,000	9140	5°21′	6°09′	13.60	1960	597
16,000	14,630	9°32′	12°12′	23.76	1691	515
20,000	18,290	12°56′	17°30′	31.51	1554	474
26,000	23,770	19°11′	27°16′	45.04	1427	435
30,000	27,430	24°21′	34°36′	55.55	1399	426
36,000	32,920	34°58′	46°48′	75.63	1443	440

began 39in (*991mm*) from the breech face and extended for 216in (*5486mm*). The bore was chromium plated 0.0005in (*0.013mm*) deep for 518in (*13,157mm*) from the muzzle.

APC shell corresponded to that of the later 16in (*406mm*) at 1140lb (*517kg*), but HC was relatively heavier at 940lb (*426kg*). Propellant charges were in quarters.

The three-gun turrets were on the lines of the 16in (*406mm*) but with alterations to the ammunition supply which it was hoped would increase speed and safety, but as was often the case, lack of development time led to trouble.

As usual the turrets were electrically powered through hydraulic gear. The training motor was 150HP and each gun had a 35HP elevating motor, though the slides (cradles) were normally coupled together, and a 40HP ramming motor. RPC was fitted, and elevation was +45° to -3° with loading at +7°. The shells were stowed vertically on two decks and transferred to two corresponding live shell rings each driven by a 40HP motor and indexed to position the shell at the base of the three pusher hoists, each 50HP, which led to the gun loading positions. A new feature was a shell handling room between the shell stowage and the live ring and equipped with transfer rammers. This was not liked and some at least of the transfer rammers were removed in favour of the usual parbuckling. In the superfiring turrets there was additional shell stowage and a third 40HP live shell ring at the base of the turret which supplied axial lower hoists driven from two 50HP motors.

The enclosed powder hoists were broken at the powder transfer room which provided the interlocking controls worked satisfactorily, reduced the firing cycle by 5 or 6 seconds, and increased safety. Each gun had a 35HP lower and 25HP upper hoist of ram type.

Below: BB32 *Wyoming* on 6 June 1942, partly de-militarised but still carrying 6-12in/50 Mk 7 guns.
USN

Right: Three-gun turret for 12in/50 Mk 8 guns, CB1, 2, *Alaska, Guam.*
USN

Gun Mounting Data

Revolving weight (less shells)	922 to 934 tons	937 to 949t
Roller path diameter (od)	26ft 10.984in	8.204m
Barbette int diameter	30ft	9.14m
Distance apart gun axes	*c*98in	*c*2.49m
Recoil distance	36in	91cm
Max elevating speed	11.97°/sec	
Max training speed	5°/sec	
Firing cycle	20-25sec	
Turret shield	face 12.8in sides 6-5.25in; rear 5.25in; roof 5in	325mm; 152-133mm; 133mm; 127mm

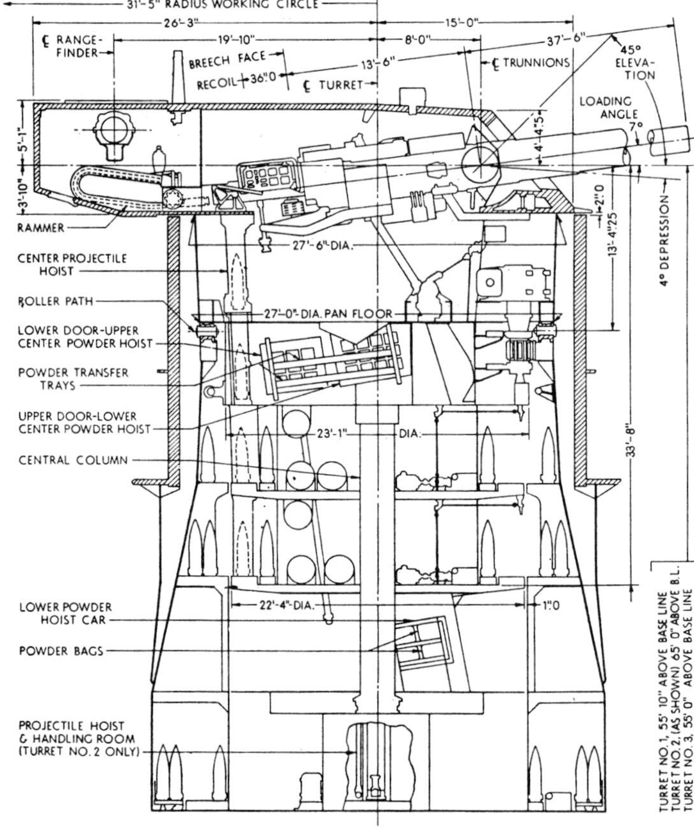

Right: Triple mount for 8in/55 guns, CA24,25, *Pensacola*, *Salt Lake City*.
Note: the twin mount is not shown.
USN

Far right: Triple mount for 8in/55 guns, CA26-31 *Northampton* class; similar in CA33, 35, *Portland*, *Indianapolis*.
USN

MEDIUM CALIBRE GUNS

Compared with most contemporary guns of similar bore, these 55-calibre weapons were very heavy, though the reasons for this are not clear. Not all the Marks mentioned entered service but those that did were in twin mountings in *Lexington* and *Saratoga*, *Pensacola* and *Salt Lake City*, and in triple mountings in the two last named as well as *Northampton, Chester, Louisville, Chicago, Houston, Augusta, Portland, Indianapolis, New Orleans, Astoria* and *Minneapolis*. It should be noted that the guns and mountings were removed from *Lexington* and *Saratoga* in early 1942 and added to the Oahu coast defences, while later in the war *Minneapolis* had Mk 15/1 described in the next section.

The differences between the various Marks were:

Mk 9/0. Liner, A tube, jacket, five hoops, three locking rings, screw box liner. Yoke ring in halves and set in annular groove. Down-swing breech mechanism with Welin block closed by compressed air from the gas ejector system. The diameter over the chamber was 33.5in (*851mm*) and the slide surface, which began 30.0in (*762mm*) from the breech face, was 160 × 33.5in (*4064 × 851mm*). The gun could be removed through the turret ports without dismantling the mounting.

Mk 9/1. Differed only in shorter jacket put on from breech end, thus locking A tube.

Mk 9/2. Like 9/1 but differing in front end of chamber and band seat.

Mk 9/3. Mk 9/0 with new liner and chamber as in 9/2.

Mk 9/4. Mk 9/2 relined with 1 in 30 rifling instead of 1 in 35.

Mk 9/5. One gun redesignated Mk 14/B before alteration.

Mk 10/0. Never built. Like Mk 9/0 but three hoops, two locking rings, integral yoke shoulder and slide surface diameter 29.5in (*749mm*).

Mk 11/0. A tube, jacket, one hoop, screw box liner, yoke ring in halves. Slide surface as in Mk 9/0. Assembled with zero shrinkage and autofretted as one piece forging.

Mk 13/0. Mk 9/2 with bore chromium plated 0.001in (*0.025mm*) deep for 84in (*2134mm*) from

8in (203mm) Marks 9/0-9/5, 10/0, 11/0, 13/0, 14/0-14/2

Gun Data for Mk 14/0

Bore	8in	203.2mm	
Weight incl BM	30.0 tons	30.48t	
Length oa	449.0in	11,405mm	56.13cal
Length bore	*c*437.6in	*c*11,115mm	*c*54.7cal
Length chamber	*c*60.0in	*c*1524mm	
Volume chamber	4860in^3	79.6dm^3	
Length rifling	373.65in	9490.7mm	
Grooves			
Lands			
Twist	1 in 25		
Weight projectile	260lb	118kg	
Propellant charge	90lb NC	40.8kg NC	
Muzzle velocity	2800f/s	853m/s	
Working pressure	17 tons/in^2	2680kg/cm^2	
Approx life	?715 EFC		
Max range	31,860yd/41°	29,130m/41°	

Mk 9/2 differed in weight including BM 29.78 tons (*30.26t*), volume chamber 5300in^3 (*86.9dm*^{3}), twist 1 in 35. Performance was the same but life ?550 EFC. The originally intended MV was 3000f/s (*914m/s*) but wear was too great and accuracy poor.

Range and Elevation Data for APC shell, 2800f/s (853m/s) MV

Range (yd)	(m)	Elevation	Descent	Time of flight (sec)	Striking V (f/s)	(m/s)
6000	5490	2°30′	2°59′	7.32	2166	660
10,000	9140	4°47′	6°25′	13.43	1800	549
16,000	14,630	9°39′	15°25′	25.25	1381	421
20,000	18,290	14°14′	24°23′	35.23	1227	374
26,000	23,770	24°06′	40°24′	53.92	1177	359
30,000	27,430	33°50′	51°22′	70.60	1226	374

Gun Mounting Data *New Orleans* class

Revolving weight	294 tons	299t
Roller path diameter (od)	18ft 11in	5.77m
Barbette int diameter	21ft	6.40m
Distance apart gun axes	?46in	?1.17m
Recoil distance	29.65in	75.3cm
Max elevating speed	*c*6°/sec	
Max training speed	*c*3.5°/sec	
Firing cycle	*c*18 secs	
Turret shield	face 6in; sides 1.5in; rear 1.5in; roof 2.25in	152mm; 38mm; 38mm; 57mm

The earlier triple mountings weighed 247-250 tons (*251-254t*) and twins 187 tons (*190t*). Shields had 2.5in (*63mm*) faces, 0.75in (*19mm*) sides and rears, 2in (*51mm*) roofs. The triple roller path outer diameter was 19ft 1¼in (*5.82m*).

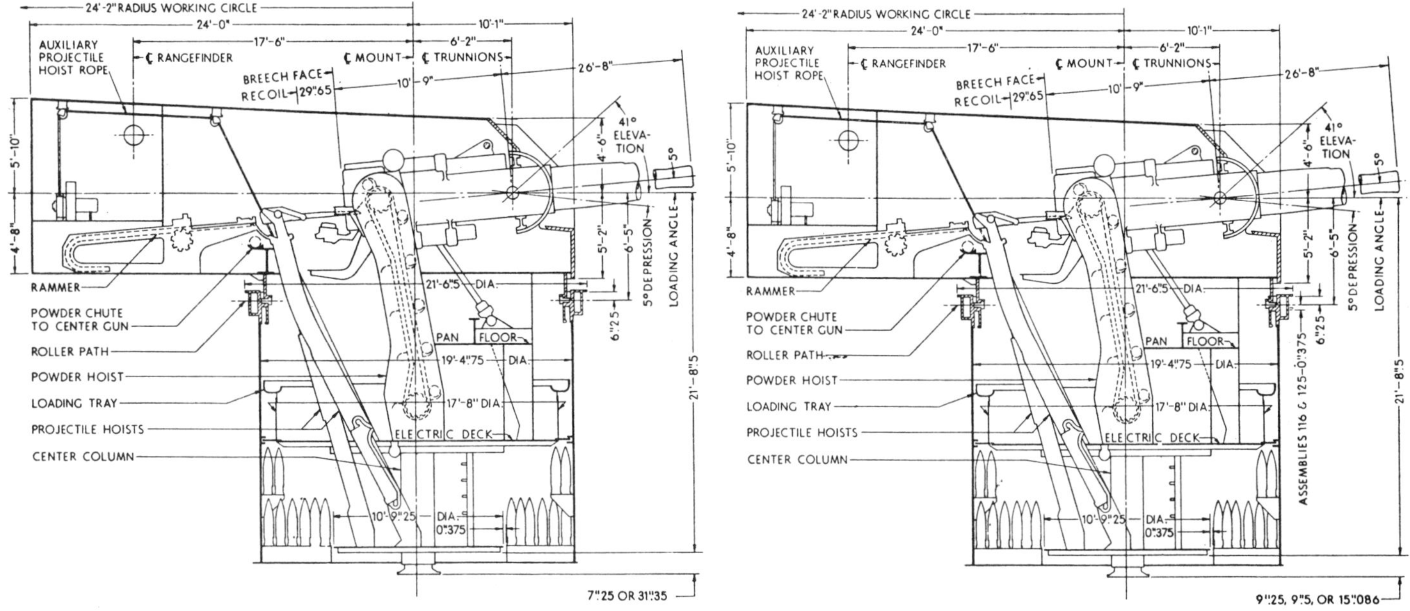

muzzle and for same distance forward from band seat. Locking rings given as four.

Mk 14/0,/1,/2 differed in having a smaller chamber, 1 in 25 rifling and in the bore being chromium plated 0.0005in (*0.013mm*) deep for 381.0in (*9677mm*) from the muzzle. The prototypes were 14/A, 14/B and 14/C, which was never made.

Mk 14/0. Mk 9/1 or 9/2 relined. Locking rings given as four.

Mk 14/1. Mk 14/B relined as in 14/0. 14/B was originally as Mk 9/3 but 14/1 is given as having four hoops instead of five.

Mk 14/2. Mk 11/0 with tapered liner.

It does not appear that any ships had the heavy 335lb (*152kg*) APC, all shells being 260lb (*118kg*). Propellant charges were in halves.

Mk 9/2 was in *Lexington* and *Saratoga* and the lost *Houston, Chicago* and *Astoria*, though *Northampton* had Mk 14/0. In April 1944 *Portland* and *Indianapolis* are listed with Mk 9/2, *Pensacola, Salt Lake City, Louisville, Augusta* and *New Orleans* with Mk 14/0, *Chester* with eight Mk 14/0 and one Mk 14/1 and *Minneapolis* with Mk 15/1. By January 1945 *Portland* and *Indianapolis* had Mk 14/0 with the rest unchanged.

There were two distinct types of triple mounting, both electrically powered through hydraulic gear. Those in the *New Orleans, Astoria* and *Minneapolis* had a 30HP training motor and an 18HP elevating one, the three guns being in a common cradle. There were 3-7½HP motors for ramming and 3-7HP for the pusher shell hoists, while the powder hoists were broken at the upper powder handling room, the upper hoists being powered from 6-1½HP motors and the lower from 2-15HP. Shells were stowed vertically on the fixed structure round the turret. Elevation limits were +41° to -5° and loading at +9°. RPC was fitted but possibly not to *Astoria*.

The earlier type, officially described as a mount and not a turret, differed in having no lower powder hoists in the rotating structure, the supply to the guns coming from the powder handling room, one deck below the turret floor. In *Pensacola* and *Salt Lake City* the elevating motor was 15HP and in all the powder hoists which did not have hydraulic drive gear, were powered from 2-3½HP motors. In addition 2-5HP motors are listed for lower powder hoists, presumably in the fixed structure. Loading was at +5° and RPC was eventually fitted to all that survived to 1945 except *Salt Lake City*. The twin turrets in this ship and *Pensacola* were similar but had a 20HP training and 10HP elevating motor with two ramming and two shell hoist motors. Details of the mountings in *Lexington* and *Saratoga* have not been found. They are believed to have been similar to the twin cruiser mountings.

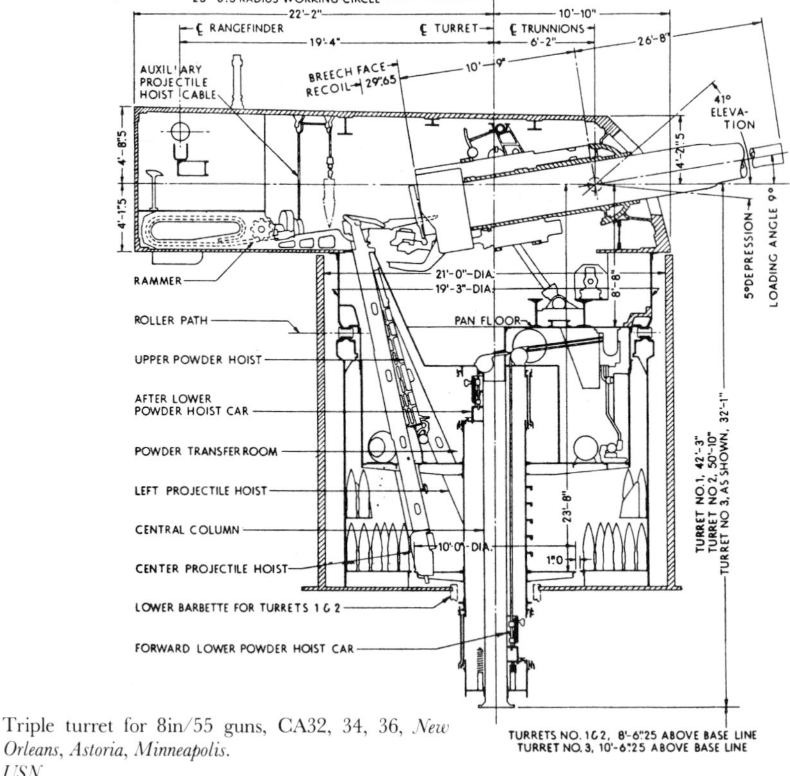

Triple turret for 8in/55 guns, CA32, 34, 36, *New Orleans, Astoria, Minneapolis*.
USN

After 8in/55 twin mounts in CV2 *Lexington* on firing trials 27 January 1928.
USN

8in (203mm) Marks 12/0-12/2, 15/0-15/2

These 55-calibre guns were similar to Mk 14 but were of much lighter construction and only 26in (*660mm*) diameter over the chamber and slide surface, except for Mk 12/2 and Mk 15/1, which had an adapter sleeve of 33.5in (*851mm*) diameter so that they could be used in mountings for the earlier type as noted for *Minneapolis*. Otherwise these lighter guns were in triple mountings in *Tuscaloosa, San Francisco, Quincy, Vincennes* and in three gun mountings in *Wichita* and the *Baltimore* and *Oregon City* classes. Twelve ships of the *Baltimore* class were commissioned during the war - *Baltimore, Boston, Canberra, Quincy, Pittsburgh, St Paul, Columbus, Bremerton, Fall River, Macon, Los Angeles, Chicago*. It will be noted that the names of some lost ships were quickly re-used.

The differences between the various Marks were:

Mk 12/0. Autofretted A tube and shrunk on jacket. Screw box liner and yoke ring in halves in annular groove. The slide surface began 30in (*762mm*) from the breech face and was 160 × 26in (*4064 × 660mm*). Breech mechanism similar to that of previous guns. Rifling was 1 in 35 and the bore was chromium plated 0.0005in (*0.013mm*) deep for 84in (*2134mm*) from the muzzle and from the chamber band seat forward. Guns could be removed from the turret ports without dismantling the turret.

Mk 12/1. As 12/0 but rifled 1 in 25 and with the bore chromium plated to the above depth for 381in (*9677mm*) from the muzzle.

Mk 12/2. Mk 12/1 with adapter sleeve increasing slide diameter to 33.5in (*851mm*).
Mk 15/0. As Mk 12/1 but form of chamber altered and identical to that of Mk 14/0.

Mk 15/1. Mk 15/0 with adapter sleeve as in Mk 12/2.

Mk 15/2. Mks 12/0-12/2, 15/0, 15/1 bored

Gun Data Mk 12/0, 12/1, 15/0, 15/2 (only differences from Mk 14/0 listed)

Weight incl BM	17.11 to 17.17 tons	17.38-17.45t
Twist	1in 35in Mk 12/0, rest 1in 25	
Weight projectile	335lb	152kg
Propellant charge	86lb NC	39kg NC
Muzzle Velocity	2500f/s	762m/s
Working pressure	18.2tons/in^2	2870kg/cm^2
Approx Life	715 EFC	
Max range	30,050yd/41°	27,480m/41°

With 260lb (*118kg*) HC and MV 2700f/s (*823m/s*) range was 29,800yd (*27,250m*) at 41°. Mks 12/2 and 15/1 weighed with BM 29.39 tons (*29.86t*). *With 260lb (118kg)* APC data was as for Mk 14/0.

Range and Elevation Data for 335lb (152kg) APC shell, 2500f/s (762m/s) MV

Range (yd)	**(m)**	**Elevation**	**Descent**	**Time of flight (sec)**	**Striking V (f/s)**	**(m/s)**
6000	5490	3°06′	3°35′	8.07	1995	608
10,000	9140	5°49′	7°31′	14.65	1702	519
16,000	14,630	11°21′	16°51′	26.99	1371	418
20,000	18,290	16°27′	25°44′	37.22	1248	380
26,000	23,770	27°25′	41°35′	56.81	1219	372
30,000	27,430	40°43′	54°27′	77.79	1294	394

Gun Mounting Data, *Baltimore* class

Revolving weight	297-304 tons	302-309t
Roller path diameter (od)	19ft 9in	6.02m
Barbette int diameter	22ft 6in max	6.86m max
Distance apart gun axes	*c*67in	*c*1.70m
Recoil distance	32in	81cm
Max elevating speed	10° 36′/sec	
Max training speed	5° 18′/sec	
Firing cycle	*c*15sec	
Turret shield	face 8in; sides 3.75-2in; rear 1.5in; roof 3in	203mm; 95-51mm; 38mm; 76mm

In *Wichita* the revolving weight was 314 tons (*319t*), elevating speed 10°8′/sec and the shield had 3.75in (*95mm*) sides and 2.75in (*70mm*) roof. In this ship and in the *Baltimore* class the barbettes were in the form of an inverted truncated cone.

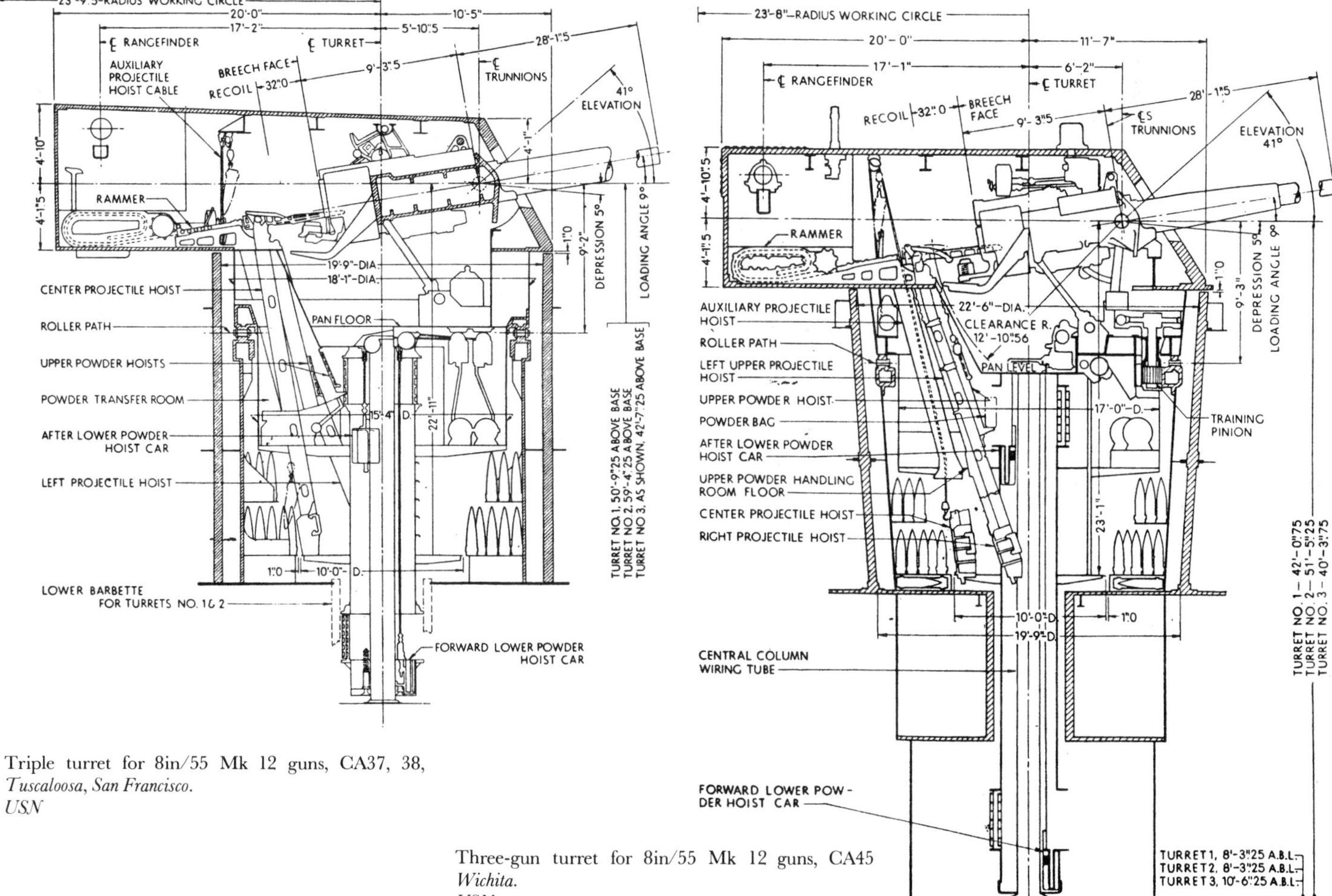

Triple turret for 8in/55 Mk 12 guns, CA37, 38, *Tuscaloosa, San Francisco.*
USN

Three-gun turret for 8in/55 Mk 12 guns, CA45 *Wichita.*
USN

Three-gun turret for 8in/55 Mk 12 or 15 guns, CA68 *Baltimore* class.
USN

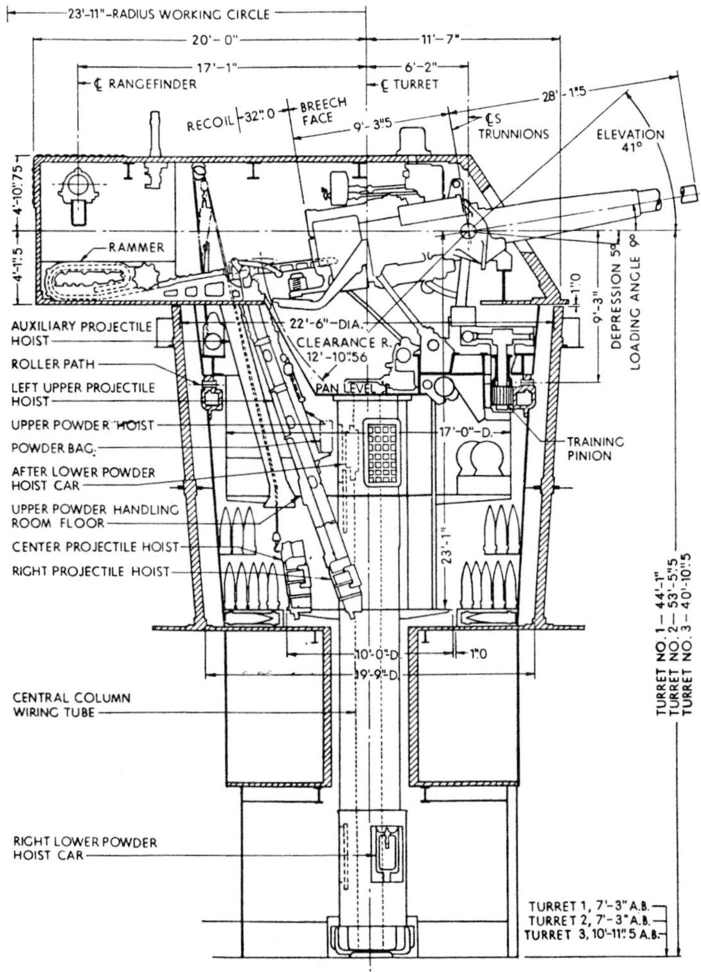

out and relined with liner having chamber, rifling and chromium plating as in 15/0. Adapter sleeves removed from Mks 12/2 and 15/1.

The *Baltimore* class had 335lb (*152kg*) APC and 260lb (*118kg*) HC, but earlier ships appear to have had all 260lb (*118kg*). Propellant charges were in halves. The *Tuscaloosa* class had Mk 12/0, *Wichita* and *Baltimore* Mk 12/1 and the rest of the latter class Mk 15/0.

The two experimental marks were 12/A, which was very like 12/0, but had a muzzle swell and 1 in 25 rifling, and 12/B which was a 12/0 with a muzzle liner and used on the proving ground only.

The mountings in the *Tuscaloosa* class resembled those in *New Orleans* (with some dimensional and weight differences listed in the table of data); the gunhouse was 30ft 5in (*9.27m*) in length instead of 33ft (*10.06m*). In *Wichita* and the *Baltimore* class, the guns were in individual cradles and further apart, though they were usually coupled together. The ammunition supply was generally similar with the same elevation limits and loading at +9°. The training motor was increased to 75HP with a 15HP elevating motor for each gun, the ramming motors were increased to 3-15HP and in the *Baltimore* class the shell hoist motors to 3-10HP (*Wichita* 3 × 7.5HP). The powder hoist motors were unchanged in the latter but in the *Baltimore* class the upper hoists were powered from 6-2HP motors and the lower from 3-25HP. All motors had hydraulic drive.

All were fitted with RPC except possibly *Quincy* and *Vincennes*, sunk at Savo Island in 1942.

Gun Mounting Data, *Tuscaloosa* class (where different from *New Orleans* class)

Revolving weight	250 tons	254t
Roller path diameter (od)	17ft 8in	5.38m
Barbette int diameter	19ft 9in	6.02m
	32in	81cm

The mountings in *Quincy* and *Vincennes*, lost in 1942, may have had further differences, but details have not been found. It is believed that turret stool stiffeners were eliminated and that the barbettes were coned as in *Wichita*.

8in/55 Mk 12 guns in after turret CA38 *San Francisco*.
USN

This 55-calibre SA gun firing semi-fixed, in British terms separate, ammunition, was a wartime development combining the power of the 8inch (*203mm*) with the firing speed of the 6inch (*152mm*)/47-calibre. It was mounted in three-gun turrets in the *Des Moines*, *Newport News* and *Salem*, but the first of these was not commissioned until November 1948. The class was originally to have totalled 12 ships and then eight.

The prototype guns were Mk B/O, a Mk 9/2 with a chamber liner, which with a different chamber liner became Mk C/O, and Mk E/O incorporating a modified Mk 15/0 tube with a 15/0 jacket, but having a housing and vertical sliding breech block. Mk 16/A was identical with 16/0 and was so designated before proof.

In Mk 16/0 there was a monobloc autofretted barrel with a loose liner held by a liner-locking ring. The barrel bore except for threaded areas, was chromium plated 0.0002in (*0.005mm*) deep and the outside of the liner was covered with flake graphite before assembly. The liner bore was chromium plated 0.0005in (*0.013mm*) deep for 392in (*9957mm*) from the muzzle. The barrel screwed into the housing which contained the vertical sliding breech block. The slide surface began 18.25in (*464mm*) from the barrel breech end and was 131.75 × 26.0in (*3346 × 660mm*) while the diameter over the chamber is given as 26.60in (*676mm*). Shells were as in the *Baltimore* class with the propellant charge in a single metal case.

The mounting was trained by a 125HP motor and there were 3–25HP elevating motors but instead of the usual lead screws, arcs and pinions were used. The rammers on the rear end of the slides, were powered from three 35HP motors, the shell hoists by three 20HP, the cartridge hoists by three 15HP and each of the four live shell rings by a 20HP motor. All these motors had hydraulic drive gear. Elevation limits were still +41° to -5° but in contrast with other 8in (*203mm*) mountings loading was at any angle.

Shells were stowed in the rotating structure on inner and outer live rings, both on two deck levels. The wing pusher hoists began between the inner and outer shell rings, while the centre one was inside the inner ring starting on the axis. The shells were delivered to trays attached to arms pivoted on the cradle trunnions and thence to transfer trays which moved into position for ramming. The cartridges were similarly raised by three hoists from a deck level below the shells to pivoted trays and placed behind the shells. Shell and cartridge case were rammed together. After firing, the empty case was extracted and ejected by a chute running forward under the guns. The whole loading system was automatic inasmuch as the gun continued firing as long as the trigger was pressed. RPC was fitted. It may be noted that pivoted trays for conveying shells and cartridges from hoist to gun were to be found in some Skoda designs for heavy calibre turrets before World War I.

Although the *Des Moines* class were around 21,000 tons full load, their maximum fire power of 90 335lb (*152kg*) shells per minute was formidable. The mountings appear to have worked well, though No 2 turret in *Newport News* was wrecked by a premature shell explosion in 1972.

8in (203mm) Mark 16/0

Gun Data for Mk 16/0

Bore	8in	203.2mm	
Weight barrel and liner	16.68 tons	16.95t	
Weight incl housing	*c*20 tons	*c*20.3t	
Length barrel and bore	440.10in	11,178.5mm	55.01cal
Length chamber	*c*51.3in	*c*1303mm	
Volume chamber	3367in³	55.2dm³	
Length rifling	383.495in	9740.77mm	
Grooves			
Lands			
Twist	1 in 25		
Weight projectile	335lb	152kg	
Propellant charge	78lb NC	35.4kg NC	
Muzzle velocity	2500f/s	762m/s	
Working pressure	18.2tons/in²	2870kg/cm²	
Approx life	780 EFC		
Max Range	30,050yd/41°	27,480m/41°	

With 260lb (*118kg*) HC and MV 2700f/s (*823m/s*), range was 29,800yd (*27,250m*) at 41°. The weight and size including the slide were much greater than indicated above as the oscillating weight per gun was 51.6 tons (*52.4t*) compared with 29.0 tons (*29.5t*) for Mks 12 and 15. The overall length from muzzle to the rammer at the rear of the slide was 588.5in (*14,948mm*).

Gun Mounting Data, *Des Moines* class

Revolving weight (less shells)	451 tons	458t
Roller path diameter (od)	24ft 4in	7.42m
Barbette int diameter	26ft	7.92m
Distance apart gun axes	?84in	?2.13m
Recoil distance	28in	71cm
Max elevating speed	8.2°/sec	
Max training speed	5°/sec	
Firing cycle	6secs	
Turret shield	face 8in; sides 3.75–2in; rear 1.5in; roof 4in	203mm; 95–51mm; 38mm; 102mm

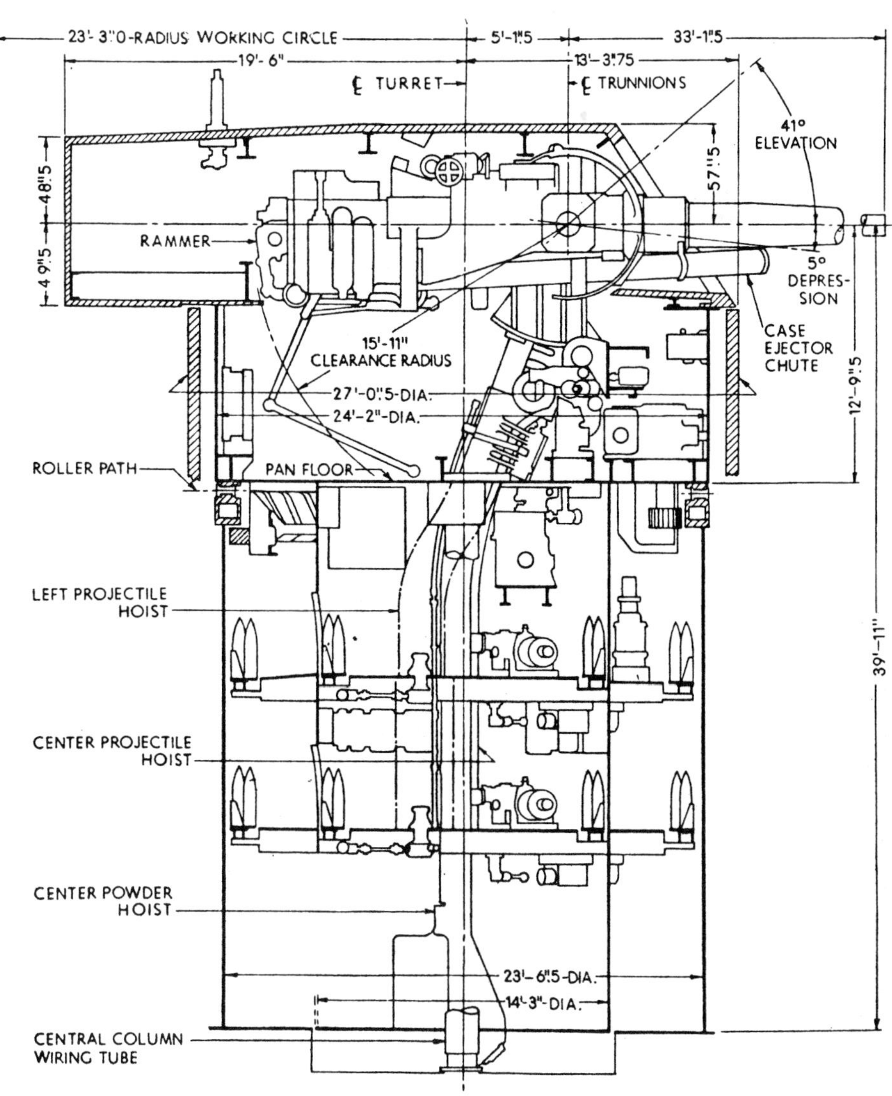

Three-gun turret for 8in/55 Mk 16 guns, CA134 *Des Moines* class.
USN

8in (203.2mm) Mark 6

A reserve stock of this 45-calibre BL gun, originally mounted in twin turrets in pre-dreadnoughts and armoured cruisers, was still maintained by the USN, though many had been transferred to the War Department in the 1920s. In the Second World War, 11 two-gun coast defence batteries were authorised, though not all were completed, the guns coming from naval stocks and originally from *New Jersey*, *Kansas*, *Minnesota* and *New Hampshire*.

The Mk 6 was a built-up gun with Welin breech block and existed in eight modifications, 6/0 to 6/7, with differences in liners, BM, chambers and rifling. The coast defence single mountings were of army type. Gun weight including breech mechanism 18.74-18.93 tons (*19.04-19.23t*), length overall 368.0in (*9372.6mm*) and the naval shell 260lb (*118kg*) with muzzle velocity 2750f/s (*838m/s*) and range 22500yd (*20575m*) at 20° 4′. The coast defence shell was of better shape and weighed 240lb (*109kg*) with MV 2850f/s (*869m/s*) and maximum range 35000yd (*32000m*).

7in (177.8mm) Mark 2

A 45-calibre BL gun originally mounted as the tertiary battery in the last classes of pre-dreadnoughts. A reserve stock was maintained by the USN and a number were used in emergency coast-defence batteries.

The Mk 2/0 was a built-up gun with Welin breech block, and relined with a taper liner became Mk 2/1. The naval P mountings, allowing +15° -7°, were retained for coast defence. Gun weight including BM was 12.81 tons (*13.02t*), length overall 323.0in (*8204.2mm*), shell 165lb (*74.8kg*), muzzle velocity 2700f/s (*823m/s*) and range at 15°, 16,500yd (*15,090m*).

6in (152.4mm) Marks 6 and 8

These 50-calibre guns were unique among USN BLs in that the nominal calibre length was overall. They were originally mounted as secondary or tertiary armament in pre-dreadnoughts and as main or secondary in armoured cruisers. Mk 6/0 was not hooped to the muzzle but Mks 6/1 and 6/2 were generally similar to Mks 8/0 to /4. All were built up guns with Welin breech blocks and Smith-Asbury BM. There were differences in details of construction, liners, rifling and chambers, but apart from Mk 6/0 which had a muzzle velocity of 2600f/s (*792m/s*) performance was identical.

In the Second World War they were used for emergency coast-defence batteries and were mounted in some ships, though the only two identified are the transport (AP) *Wharton* and the old harbour-based unclassified auxiliary (IX) *Seattle*, formerly an armoured cruiser. The particular Mks were 6/2 and 8/2.

Gun Data for Mk 6/2, Mk 8/2

Bore	6.0in	152.4mm	
Weight incl BM	8.43-8.55 tons	8.57-8.69t	
Length oa	300.2in	7625mm	50.03cal
Length bore	*c*291.5in	*c*7404mm	*c*48.6cal
Length chamber	*c*42.7in	*c*1085mm	
Volume chamber	2084in³	34.15dm³	
Weight projectile	105lb	47.6kg	
Propellant charge	37lb NC	16.8kg	
Muzzle velocity	2800f/s	853m/s	
Range	16,000yd/15°	14,630m/15°	

The hand-worked open P Mk 10 mountings allowed +15° -10° and weighed with gun 14.4-16.5 tons (*14.6-16.8t*).

6in (152.4mm) Marks 12/0-12/7, 14/0, 14/1, 15/0, 18/0-18/2

Heavy 53-calibre guns except for the lightweight Mk 15/0 which was never made, but relatively lighter than the 8in (*203mm*) Mk 9. They were originally intended for the anti-torpedo battery in the *South Dakota* and *Lexington* classes, cancelled under the Washington Treaty, and were in twin and single mountings in the ten *Omaha* class light cruisers and in single mountings in the large submarines *Argonaut*, *Narwhal* and *Nautilus*.

Mk 12/0. Liner, A tube, full length jacket, two hoops, locking ring and screw box liner. The taper liner was inserted after the gun had been built up. The breech had a side swing Welin block with Smith-Asbury mechanism.
Mk 12/1. As Mk 12/0 but 48 grooves, 1 in 35 instead of 36, zero to 1 in 25.
Mk 12/2. 12/1 modified for submarines with two aluminium bronze locking rings, slide surface with two aluminium bronze hoops and clamp ring at muzzle for watertight cover. BM made watertight.
Mk 12/3. Mks 12/0, 12/1 relined. Liner had collar at breech end, clearance at forward shoulder and liner locking ring. Chamber form altered.
Mk 12/4. Mk 12/2 relined as in 12/3.
Mk 12/5. Mk 12/0 with modified band seat and liner locking ring. One gun only.
Mk 12/6. Mk 12/2 with tube and liner locking ring.
Mk 12/7. Mk 12/1 with tube and liner locking ring.
Mk 14/0. Autofretted monobloc with screw box liner. Otherwise as Mk 12/1.
Mk 14/1. Mk 14/0 with taper liner, liner locking ring, breech end liner collar and clearance at forward shoulder.
Mk 18/0. Mks 12/0, 12/1, 12/3 relined with taper liner and tube and liner locking ring added. Bore chromium plated 0.0005in (*0.013mm*) deep for 270in (*6858mm*) from muzzle.
Mk 18/1. Mks 12/2, 12/4 relined and tube and liner locking ring added. Bore chromium plated as in 18/0.
Mk 18/2. Mk 14/0 with liner and bore chromium plated as in 18/0.

Gun Data for Mk 18/0, 18/2

Bore	6in	152.4mm	
Weight incl BM	10.11 tons	10.27t	
Length oa	325.0in	8255mm	54.17cal
Length bore	*c*315.6in	*c*8016mm	*c*52.6cal
Length chamber	*c*48.3	*c*1227mm	
Volume chamber	2100in³	34.4dm³	
Length rifling	264.27in	6712.5mm	
Grooves			
Lands			
Twist	1 in 35		
Weight projectile	105lb	47.6kg	
Propellant charge	44lb NC	19.96kg NC	
Muzzle velocity	3000f/s	914m/s	
Working pressure	17.5 tons/in²	2760kg/cm²	
Approx life	700 EFC		
Range	21,100yd/20°	19,290m/20°	
	23,300yd/25°	21,300m/25°	
	25,300yd/30°	23,130m/30°	

Mk 18/1 for submarines weighed, incl BM, 10.20 tons (*10.36t*).

The experimental Mks F/0 and F/1 were like Mk 18/0 and 18/2 but had 1 in 20 rifling and no chromium plating. All service marks except 12/0 were rifled 1 in 35. Mk 15/0 would have resembled Mk 14/0 but was much lighter at 5.85 tons (*5.94t*) including BM and only 19in (*483mm*) diameter over the chamber, while all the rest were 24.5in (*622mm*). The propellant charge was in a bag.

The twin Mk 16/1 mounting had a 10ft (*3.05m*) diameter base ring and weighed 51.8 tons (*52.6t*) with enclosed 0.25in (*6.4mm*) shield. It was trained by a 7.5HP motor and the guns with axes 28in (*71cm*) apart, were elevated by one of 3.5HP between +30° and -10°.

The single hand-worked P mountings Mk 13/1 to 13/3 in the *Omaha* class weighed up to 19.1 tons (*19.4t*) with circular 0.25in (*6.4mm*) shield and allowed +20° to -10°. In the three large submarines, the Mk 17/1 wet P mountings had no shield and weighed 16.83 tons (*17.10t*). Elevation was +25° to -10°.

Twin Mk 16/1 mounting for 6in/53 guns, CL6 *Cincinnati*. The Mk 35 director for the 6in and Mk 44 for the 1.1in quad are also shown.
USN

Two single 6in/53 guns in SS167 *Narwhal*.
CPL

These 47-calibre SA guns with semi-fixed ammunition bore little resemblance to the 53-calibre BL. They were in triple turrets in the seven ships of the *Brooklyn* class, the *Helena* and *St Louis* and the *Cleveland* and *Fargo* classes. No fewer than 25 of the *Cleveland* class were commissioned during the war. They were also in two-gun dual purpose turrets in the *Worcester* and *Roanoke*, not completed until 1948–49.

The prototype guns, Mks A/0, B/0, D/0, D/1 and E/0 were conversions from Mk 8 guns while Mk 16/A and 16/B closely resembled the production guns.

In Mk 16/0 there was a monobloc autofretted barrel secured to the housing by a bayonet type joint with interrupted threads. The vertical sliding block was accommodated in the housing. There was a 0.50in (*12.7mm*) ring attachment at the muzzle and the barrel was zinc sprayed externally for 25.5in (*648mm*) starting 20.25in (*514mm*) from the breech end.

Mk 16/1 was 16/0 with a taper liner. Both were chromium plated 0.0005in (*0.013mm*) deep in the bore for 246.0in (*6248mm*) from the muzzle. Diameter over the chamber was 17.40in (*442mm*). APC shell weighed 130lb (*59kg*) but HC and Common 105lb (*47.6kg*) as in previous 6in (*152.4mm*) guns. The propellant charge was in a single metal case weighing 28.2lb (*12.8kg*) empty.

The triple mountings were generally similar in all ships, and like the later 16in (*406mm*) and 8in (*203mm*) mountings benefited from the absence of turret stool stiffeners. As usual they were powered by electric motors with hydraulic drive gear and elevation was through a lead screw. The training motor was 50HP and the single elevating 25HP. The breech mechanisms and rammers located on the end of the slides, were operated from three 7.5HP motors in the *Cleveland* and *Fargo* classes and from one 20HP in the earlier ships. Each gun had unbroken shell and cartridge hoists, all six being powered from three 20HP motors or three 15HP in *Helena* and *St Louis*. Shell stowage was on the fixed structure.

Elevation was originally +40° to -5° but was increased to +60° to -5° as opportunity occurred. Loading was at any angle up to +20°. All eventually had RPC fitted. Cartridge cases were ejected through a port in the rear floor of the turret. In general the triple mounting with the guns elevating as one seems to have worked well in this instance.

The two-gun mounting was an earlier design than the three-gun 8in (*203mm*) in the *Des Moines* class and was not considered as satisfactory, so that a new 'automatic' three-gun dual purpose 6in (*152mm*) turret, on the lines of the above 8in (*203mm*), was intended to replace it. This new project, cancelled after the war, was expected to fire 20–25 rounds per gun per minute as compared with 12 in the two gun.

The latter had a 200HP training motor to allow the high performance needed for AA uses, and each gun a 15HP elevating, 30HP rammer, 10HP cartridge hoist and two 5HP shell hoists as AA and other projectiles had separate hoists. The live shell ring was driven by a 10HP motor. Hydraulic drive gear was fitted to all these motors. At the top of the unbroken hoists shells and cartridges were transferred mechanically to the loading trays, the rammers being on the rear end of the slides. Shells were stowed on three decks of the rotating structure with the hoists running from the two upper, and the live shell ring on the uppermost. Elevation was by arc and pinion with limits of +78° to -5° and loading at any angle. RPC was fitted.

6in (152.4mm) Marks 16/0, 16/1

Gun Data for Mk 16/0, 16/1

Bore	6in	152.4mm	
Weight barrel	4.30–4.31 tons	4.37–4.38t	
Weight with housing	6.49–6.50 tons	6.59–6.60t	
Length barrel and bore	282.25in	7169.2mm	47.04cal
Length chamber	*c*39.5in	*c*1003mm	
Volume chamber	1470in³	24.1dm³	
Length rifling	238.29in	6052.57mm	
Grooves			
Lands			
Twist	1 in 25		
Weight projectile	130lb	59kg	
Propellant charge	32lb NC	14.5kg NC	
Muzzle velocity	2500f/s	762m/s	
Working pressure	18.5 tons/in²	2910kg/cm²	
Approx Life	1500 EFC		
Max Range	26,118yd/47° 29′	23,882m/47° 29′	

With 105lb (*47.6kg*) HC and MV 2665f/s (*812m/s*) maximum range was 23,483yd (*21,473m*) at 46° 36′ and ceiling at 78° has 48,000ft (*14630m*). Length from muzzle to the end of the rammer on the slide was 369.45in (*9384mm*) in the triple mountings and 396.25in (*10,065mm*) in the two gun.

Range and Elevation Data for APC, 2500f/s (762m/s) MV

Range (yd)	**(m)**	**Elevation**	**Descent**	**Time of flight (sec)**	**Striking V (f/s)**	**(m/s)**
6000	5490	3°20′	4°09′	8.51	1799	548
10,000	9140	6°39′	9°40′	16.15	1428	435
16,000	14,630	14°29′	24°18′	31.62	1129	344
20,000	18,290	22°20′	36°38′	44.86	1102	336
26,000	23,770	44°24′	58°07′	77.27	1209	369
26,000	23,770	50°22′	62°11′	84.9	1235	376

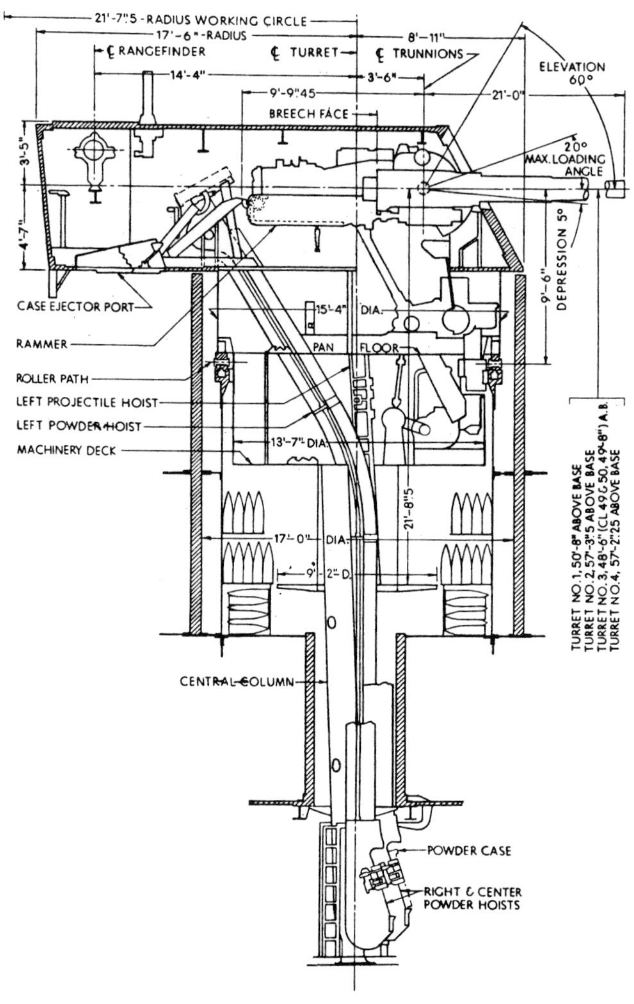

Triple turret for 6in/47 guns CL40–43, 46–48 *Brooklyn* class, CL49, 50 *St Louis* class.
USN

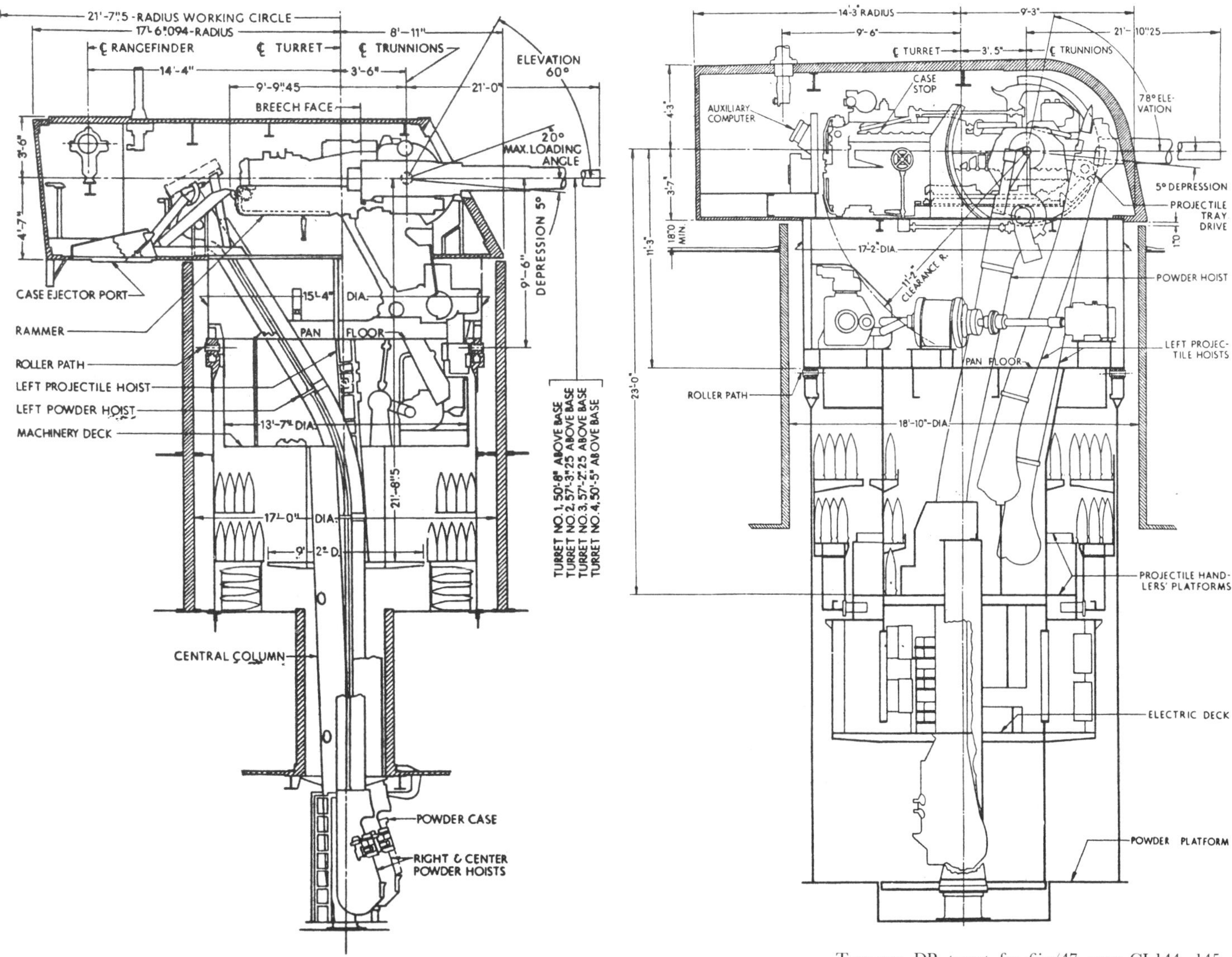

Triple turret for 6in/47 guns CL55 *Cleveland* class.
USN

Two-gun DP turret for 6in/47 guns CL144, 145, *Worcester*, *Roanoke*.
USN

Gun Mounting Data, *Cleveland*, *Fargo* classes

Revolving weight (less shells)	165 to 173 tons	168 to 176t
Roller path diameter (od)	15ft 3in	4.65m
Barbette int diameter	17ft	5.18m
Distance apart gun axes	*c*55in	*c*1.40m
Recoil distance	21in	53cm
Max elevating speed	11°/sec	
Max training speed	10°/sec	
Firing cycle	6-8sec	
Turret shield	face 6.5in; sides 3in; rear 1.5in; roof 3in	165mm; 76mm; 38mm; 76mm

The triples in the *Brooklyn* and *Helena* classes differed in revolving weight 154-167 tons (*156-170t*), elevating speed 10°/sec, turret sides and rear 1.25in (*32mm*), roof 2in (*51mm*).

Gun Mounting Data, *Worcester* class

Revolving weight (less shells)	208.5 tons	212t
Roller path diameter (od)	17ft	5.18m
Barbette int diameter	18ft 10in	5.74m
Distance apart gun axes	?105in	?2.67m
Recoil distance	21in	53cm
Max elevating speed	14.8°/sec	
Max training speed	25°/sec	
Firing cycle	5sec	
Turret shield	face 6.5in; sides 3in; rear 2in; roof 4in	165mm; 76mm; 51mm; 102mm

6in (152.4mm) Mark 17/0

A 47-calibre BL version of the Mk 16, only carried by the patrol gunboats *Charleston* and *Erie* in single-shielded P mountings with power training and elevation. The prototype Mk C/0 was a conversion from Mk 8, while the service Mk 17/0 had an autofretted monobloc barrel attached to a breech housing with side swing screw BM. There was a muzzle ring as in Mk 16 and the bore was chromium plated as in this gun. Diameter over the chamber was 24.8in (*630mm*) and shells weighed 105lb (*47.6kg*). Rifling was 1 in 30.

The Mk 18/0-18/2 P mountings had a 0.86in (*22mm*) open-back shield and a total weight of 15.4 tons (*15.65t*). There were 3.5HP motors for elevating and training, and elevation limits were +20° to -10°.

Gun Data

Bore	6in	152.4mm	
Weight incl solid breech	5.24 tons	5.32t	
Length oa	289in	7341mm	48.17cal
Length bore	*c*279.6in	*c*7102mm	*c*46.6cal
Length chamber	*c*36.3in	*c*922mm	
Volume chamber	1478in³	24.22dm³	
Weight projectile	105lb	47.6kg	
Propellant charge	34.5lb NC	15.65kg	
Muzzle velocity	2800f/s	853m/s	
Range	19,800yd/20°	18,100m/20°	

5in (127mm) Marks 7/2-7/10, 8/0-8/10, 15/0-15/4

This series of 51-calibre guns comprised BL versions of the Mk 7/0 separate ammunition QF originally mounted as anti-torpedo guns in the battleships of the *Utah* and *Arkansas* classes. The BL version was mounted in the *New York* to *Maryland* classes inclusive, and retrospectively in the *Utah* and *Arkansas* classes and also in the *Delaware* class. All those in service in 1941 still had the BL guns, and they were retained throughout the war in *Colorado*, *New Mexico*, *New York*, *Texas* and *Arkansas*. Other ships with them, at least in the earlier part of the war, included *Langley*, some escort carriers, five flush-deck destroyers and various Coast Guard cutters, auxiliaries and armed merchant ships. They were also mounted in some emergency coast defence batteries.

Gun Data Mk 15/0

Bore	5in	127mm	
Weight incl BM	5.05 tons	5.13t	
Length oa	261.25in	6635.75mm	52.25cal
Length bore	*c*253in	*c*6426mm	*c*50.6cal
Length chamber	*c*38.9in	*c*988mm	
Volume chamber	1202in³	19.7dm³	
Length rifling	212.09in	5387.09mm	
Grooves			
Lands			
Twist	1 in 35		
Weight projectile	50lb	22.7kg	
Propellant charge	24.5lb NC	11.1kg NC	
Muzzle velocity	3150f/s	960m/s	
Working pressure	17 tons/in²	2680kg/cm²	
Approx life	900 EFC		
Range	14,050yd/15° 15,850yd/20°	12,850m/15° 14,490m/20°	

5in/51 on single P mounting in DD233 *Gilmer* *c*1921.
USN

Only 11 of the above 25 modifications are listed as mounted in 1944-45, and descriptions are limited to these. There were also three experimental marks, 8/A, 15/A and 14/0, the latter having a smaller chamber.

Mk 7/2. Mk 7/0 with obturator seat bushing to convert to BL. A tube, jacket to muzzle, hoop, locking ring, screw box liner. BM side-swing Smith-Asbury, Welin block.
Mk 7/3. Mk 7/0 or 7/2 with taper liner.
Mk 7/4. The Mk 7/0 Type gun which differed in detail from 7/0 lined as in 7/3.
Mk 8/0. Like Mk 7/0 but modified chamber, and jacket and hoop extended 0.6in (*15mm*) at rear, altering screw box liner arrangements.
Mk 8/1. Mk 8/0 with taper liner and modified chamber.
Mk 8/4. Mk 8/0 lined or 8/1-8/3 relined. Taper liner with clearance at forward shoulder, modified chamber.
Mk 8/5. Mk 8/0 lined or 8/1, 8/2, 8/4 relined, as in 8/4 but liner collar added.
Mk 8/6. Mk 8/0 lined or 8/1, 8/2, 8/4, 8/5 relined, as in 8/5 but liner locking ring added.
Mk 8/7. Mk 8/4 with obturator seat and liner locking ring bushing.
Mk 8/10. Mk 8/5 with tube and liner locking ring added.
Mk 15/0. Mk 8/0 lined or Mk 8/1-8/7 relined, as in Mk 8/10. Bore chromium plated 0.0005in (*0.013mm*) for 220.0in (*5588mm*) from muzzle.

Mks 8/2, 8/3 mentioned above were lined 8/0s.

Diameter over the chamber was 21.0in (*533mm*). Rifling was 0 to 1 in 25 in Mks 7/3, 7/4, 8/0, 8/1, 1 in 25 in Mk 7/2, and 1 in 35 in the others.

The mountings were all P type, Mks 13/0-13/3 having +15° to -10° elevation, 13/4-13/7, 13/9, 13/11 +20° to -10° and 15/0-15/5 +20° to -15°. Some Mk 13/7 and a few Mk 15/1-15/5 had open-back 0.25in (*6.4mm*) shields. The total weight varied from 10.0 tons (*10.2t*) to 11.9 tons (*12.1t*). In battleships mountings were Mks 13/5-13/7, 13/9 or 13/11. The firing cycle was about 7sec.

5in (127mm) Marks 9/0-9/8

These 51-calibre separate ammunition QF guns were intended for submarines and originally mounted in the three boats of the *Barracuda* (VI) class, though removed in about 1928. From the *Tambor* class onwards, the design was adapted to take a 5in (*127mm*)/51, but it is only known to have been mounted in *Thresher*, *Tambor*, *Tautog*, *Tuna*, *Gar*, *Grayling* and *Hake*.

Mk 9/0 resembled Mk 8/0 with different screw box liner arrangement, the chamber modified for the cartridge case and BM adapted for submarines. The various modifications were Mk 9/0 lined or relined with variations in liner design, chamber details and rifling. None was chromium plated in the bore.

Gun Data for Mk 9/8 (differences from Mk 15/0)

Weight incl BM	5.08 tons	5.16t	
Length bore	255in	6477mm	51.0cal
Volume chamber	1200in^3	19.66dm^3	
Length rifling	214.10in	5438.1mm	
Approx life	?700 EFC		
Range	17,300yd/25°	15,820m/25°	

The wet P mounting Mk 18/0 allowed +25° to -8½° or 10° and had a total weight of 10.7 tons (*10.9t*).

5in (127mm) Marks 10/0-10/6, 11/0-11/10, 13/0

These 25-calibre fixed ammunition AA guns were very distinct from the above 51-calibre. Instead of being designed for the highest practicable muzzle velocity, they had one adequate for the AA role in the 1920s combined with the lowest possible moment of inertia to allow high training and elevation speeds in a hand-worked mounting.

In 1941 the 5in (*127mm*) 25-calibre gun was carried in battleships from the *Oklahoma* and *Nevada* to the *Maryland* class, in the carriers *Lexington*, *Saratoga* and *Ranger* and in cruisers from the *Pensacola* class to the *Quincy*, *Vincennes* and *Brooklyn* class. By the end of the war it was still in the survivors of the above cruisers except *Savannah* and *Honolulu*, but otherwise only in *Colorado*, *New Mexico* and *Mississippi*, the last named having no 5in/51s.

The experimental work was begun on a converted 5in (*127mm*) Mk 3/0 known as Mk 3/3 and other such guns were Mk 10A, the prototype for Mk 11/0, and Mk C/0 a slightly shortened Mk 13/0. The Marks listed as in service in 1944-45, were 10/1-10/3, 11/0-11/3, 11/7 and 13/0. Details of these and other Marks were:

Gun Data for Mk 13/0

Bore	5in	127mm	
Weight barrel	2105lb	955kg	
Weight with housing	*c*4270lb	*c*1937kg	
Length oa incl housing	142.25in	3613mm	
Length barrel and bore	125.0in	3175mm	25.0cal
Length chamber	*c*22.4in	*c*569mm	
Volume chamber	431in^3	7.06dm^3	
Length rifling	98.113in	2492.07mm	
Grooves			
Lands			
Twist	1 in 25		
Weight projectile	53.85lb	24.43kg	
Propellant charge	9.6lb NC	4.35kg	
Muzzle velocity	2110f/s	643m/s	
Working pressure	16.7 tons/in^2	2630kg/cm^2	
Approx life	4260 EFC		
Max Range	14,500yd/45°	13,260m/45°	
Ceiling	27,400ft/85°	8350m/85°	

Length oa incl housing was 142.25in (*3613mm*)

Mk 10/0. Autofretted monobloc barrel threaded and shrunk on housing. SA vertical sliding wedge BM. One gun later altered to Mk 10/A.
Mk 10/1. As 10/0 but barrel threaded and keyed to housing.
Mk 10/2. As 10/1 but part of housing left cheek cut away to ease loading.
Mk 10/3. Existing Mk 10/1 with housing modified to near that of 10/2.
Mk 10/4. Mk 10/2 with liner in differential cylinder in housing.
Mk 10/5. As 10/4 but different cylinder liner.
Mk 10/6. Mk 10/1 with cylinder liner as in 10/5.
Mk 11/0. Mk 10/2 with bore chromium plated 0.0005in (*0.013mm*) deep for 102in (*2591mm*) from muzzle.
Mk 11/1. Mk 10/3 chromium plated as 11/0.
Mk 11/2. Mk 11/0 with alterations to shell centring cylinder and band slope.
Mk 11/3. Mk 11/1 altered as in 11/2.
Mk 11/4. Originally intended for Army manufacture. None made.
Mk 11/5. Mk 11/0 with monel metal liner in differential cylinder in housing.
Mk 11/6. Mk 11/2 with cylinder liner as in 11/5.
Mk 11/7. Mk 11/3 with cylinder liner as in 11/5.
Mk 11/8. Mk 11/0 with monel metal cylinder liner to the design of steel liner in Mk 10/5.
Mk 11/9. Mk 11/7 with longer band slope, chamber being identical to that of Mk 13/0.
Mk 11/10. 11/6 with chamber as in 11/9.
Mk 13/0. Like Mk 11/0 but barrel and housing joined by interrupted threads (bayonet joint). Chamber as in Mk 11/9 and 11/10.

Rifling in all was 1 in 25 and diameter over the chamber 11.0in (*279mm*) except in Mk 13/0, where it was 11.497in (*292mm*). All Mk 11 modifications and Mk 13 had chromium plated bores, as in Mk 11/0.

Mountings were all P type. Of those listed in

early 1945 Mks 19/1, 19/2, 19/4, 19/6-19/9, 23/1 and 27/2-27/5 allowed +85° ;to -15°, and Mks 19/24-19/26 +85° to -10°. Weights varied from 9.02 to 10.67 tons (*9.16, 10.84t*) Mks 27/2-27/5 in some of the *Brooklyn* class had 3HP elevating and training motors and a hydraulic rammer driven from a 5HP motor. Elevating and training speeds were 20 and 30°/sec with RPC and *c*9% higher in local control. Mks 19/4, 19/6, 19/24-26 and 23/1 in other cruisers had 1HP elevating and 1HP or $1\frac{1}{2}$HP training motors with pneumatic rammers which were also in the remaining hand elevated and trained marks. Light shields were added to many and the firing cycle was 3-4sec.

5in/25 AA gun still in BB40 *New Mexico* July 1944. The fuze-setting machine with three fixed rounds is on the left.
USN

Adaptations of the 25-calibre AA gun for submarines, and in Mk 17/1 firing semi-fixed ammunition. They are recorded in 40° mountings in the following: (numbers being given instead of names for reasons of space) SS 292-352, 365-378, 381-426, 435, 475-490, 522-525. They also replaced other guns in some earlier boats such as SS 213, 214, 229, 234. Details were:

Mk 17/0. Tube of higher strength steel than in Mk 13/0 with shrunk forged copper-nickel alloy liner. Housing as in Mk 13/0, BM adapted for submarines. Bore chromium plated as in Mk 11/0.

5in (127mm) Marks 17/0, 17/1

Gun Data (differences from Mk 13/0)

Weight barrel	2163lb	981kg
Weight with housing	?	?
Approx life	2300 EFC	
Max range	14,500yd/40°	13,260m/40°

Mk 17/1. Mk 13/0 bored out and fitted with taper copper-nickel alloy liner. Shorter housing. Semi-fixed ammunition for easier handling in submarines. Bore chromium plated as in 17/0.

The wet P type Mk 40/0 mounting allowed +40° to -10° and weighed 6.25 tons (*6.35t*). There was no pneumatic rammer.

This famous 38-calibre SA gun firing semi-fixed ammunition was not only by far the most numerous of dual purpose guns, but was also perhaps the best of the Second World War. Although neither shell weight nor muzzle velocity was particularly great, rate of fire, reliability, accuracy life and rates of training and elevation in the power-worked mountings were all satisfactorily high. It was mounted in many different types of ship; the most important are given below. Some ships had more than one type of mounting and these are listed under each type.

In twin enclosed HA base ring mountings: aircraft carriers, *Essex* class, *Saratoga* as rearmed; battleships, *N Carolina, S Dakota* and *Iowa* classes, and as rearmed *W Virginia, Maryland, California, Tennessee, Pennsylvania, Nevada*; cruisers, *Alaska, Des Moines, Oregon City, Baltimore, Fargo, Cleveland, Helena, Atlanta* classes and as rearmed *Honolulu, Savannah*; destroyers *Gearing, Sumner* classes and rearmed units of *Somers* and *Porter* classes. Also in some landing ships and Coast Guard cutters.

In twin enclosed LA base ring mountings: destroyers, unrearmed units of *Somers* and *Porter* classes.

In single enclosed HA base ring mountings: battleship, *Idaho* as rearmed; cruiser, *Wichita*; destroyers, rearmed units of *Somers* and *Porter* classes and all others from *Dunlap* and *Fanning* to *Fletcher* class. Also in destroyer escorts and many other ships. Partially shielded mountings with canvas weather-resistant roofs were to be found in the after raised mountings of *Sims, Benson* and *Gleaves* classes and some *Benham* class.

In single open HA base ring mountings: aircraft carriers, *Essex* class, *Wasp, Hornet, Saratoga* as rearmed; cruiser, *Wichita*; destroyers *Benham* and *Sims* classes and originally some of *Benson* and *Gleaves*. In many other ships including merchant ships.

In single open LA base ring mountings: escort aircraft carriers.

In single open HA P mountings: aircraft carriers, *Yorktown* and *Enterprise*; destroyers, *Farragut, Mahan, Dunlap, Gridley* and *Bagley* classes. In the first two classes, forward P mountings had open back shields.

The prototype gun Mk A/O was a shortened Mk 9/0 with modified chamber, chamber liner and chromium plated bore. On relining it became Mk B/O. The service guns were mostly Mk 12/1 and details were:

Mk 12/0. Autofretted monobloc barrel secured to housing by interrupted threads (bayonet joint). BM. SA vertical sliding wedge. Bore chromium plated 0.0005in (*0.013mm*) deep for 164.5in (*4178mm*) from muzzle.

Mk 12/1. Differs from Mk 12/0 in longer keyway for barrel locking key, slightly modified chamber and bore chromium plated 162.25in (*4121.2mm*) from muzzle.

Mk 12/2. Like Mk 12/0 but barrel of higher strength steel, not autofretted.

All were 12.945in (*328.80mm*) diameter over the chamber and were rifled 1 in 30. The metal cartridge case weighed 13.25lb (*6.01kg*) empty.

There were ten mounting Marks, and a total of 133 modifications were listed in January 1945, so that considerable generalisations are necessary. The twin HA mountings comprised Mks 28, 29, 32 and 38. They were powered by electric motors through hydraulic gear, and the guns were elevated together by arcs and pinions on a common shaft. There were axial shell and cartridge hoists for each gun, incorporating fuze setters, and fed from a fixed handling room below the mounting. Hoists in the ships' structure supplied the handling room. Elevation was +85° to -15° with loading at any angle. There was a 4HP training and a 7.5 or 10HP elevating motor, while each gun had a 7.5 or 10HP motor for the hoists and a 5 or 7HP one for the rammer on the end of the slide. RPC was fitted in all.

The Mark 22 twin LA mounting was lighter and as lower elevation and training speeds were acceptable the power requirements were lower, with 5HP elevating and 15HP training motors. The elevation limits were +35° to -10°.

Of the single mountings, Mk 21 was basically a hand-worked P mounting allowing +85° to -15°, with open-back shields in some. RPC was added with 1.5HP elevation and 2HP training supplementary motors, and ramming was pneumatic or by a 5HP motor with hydraulic drive. It was a destroyer mounting, as was the power worked P Mk 24 except that 24/11 was for aircraft carriers. None had shields. Hoists were in the ships' structure and elevation was +85° to -15° (-10° in 24/11). A single 5 or 10HP motor powered training and elevation and a 5 or 7.5HP ramming. RPC was fitted.

Mk 25 was an enclosed single +85° -15° base ring mounting for destroyers, but the important series of this type was Mk 30 of which 79 modifications were listed in January 1945 with

5in (127mm) Marks 12/0-12/2

Gun Data for Mk 12/1

Bore	5in	127mm	
Weight barrel	1.783 tons	1.812t	
Weight with housing	3.200 tons	3.251t	
Length oa incl housing	223.75in	5683.3mm	
Length barrel and bore	190.0in	4826mm	38.0cal
Length chamber	28.66in	727.96mm	
Volume chamber	654in^3	10.72dm^3	
Length rifling	157.225in	3993.52mm	
Grooves	(45)		
Lands			
Twist	1 in 30		
Weight projectile	55lb	24.95kg	
Propellant charge	15.2lb NC	6.89kg NC	
Muzzle velocity	2600f/s	792m/s	
Working pressure	18 tons/in^2	2835kg/cm^2	
Approx life	4600 EFC		
Max range	15,892yd/27°	14,532m/27°	
	17,414yd/35°	15,923m/35°	
	18,200yd/45°	16,640m/45°	
Ceiling	37,200ft/85°	11,340m/85°	

Gun Mounting Data, Mk 28/3, twin in battleships

Weight	75.7 tons	76.9t
Distance apart gun axes	84in	2.13m
Recoil distance	15in	38cm
Max elevating speed	15°/sec	
Max training speed	25°/sec	
Firing cycle	3 sec	
Shield	2.50in	63.5mm

This was the heaviest mounting because of the thick shield which in most other twin HA was between 2.0in (*51mm*) and 0.75in (*19mm*) or only 0.5in (*13mm*) to 0.125in (*3.18mm*) in Mk 38 destroyer mountings which weighed 42.7-47.1 tons (*43.4-47.9t*), other details being the same).

The LA twin Mk 22 mounting with 0.125in (*3.18mm*) shield, weighed 28.9-35.4 tons (*29.4-36.0t*), had the gun axes 72in (*1.83m*) apart and elevating and training speeds of 11.6 and 14.7°/sec.

Gun Mounting Data, Mk 30/0, single enclosed in *Wichita*, destroyers

Weight	18.26-18.48 tons	18.55-18.78t
Recoil distance	15in	38cm
Max elevating speed	18°/sec	
Max training speed	34°/speed	
Firing cycle	2.7 sec	
Shield	0.125in	3.18mm

Gun Mounting Data, Mk 24/11, single P in aircraft carriers

Weight	14.78 tons	15.02t
Recoil distance	15in	38cm
Max elevating speed	15°/sec	
Max training speed	28.75°/sec	
Firing	*c*4 sec	
Shield	None	None

Hand-worked P mountings were lighter; the unshielded Mk 21/0 in destroyers weighed 13.06 tons (*13.27t*).

numbers up to Mk 30/85. The most complete mountings resembled single versions of the twin HA with enclosed shields, axial hoists, RPC and elevation +85° to -15°. A single 10HP motor powered training and elevation, a 7.5HP one the hoists and 7.5HP or 5HP the rammer. A few mountings of this type are listed without shields, but the principal open mountings were those for aircraft carriers which differed in having no axial hoists, the latter being part of the ships' structure.

Many other modifications, with or without shields and usually without axial hoists, were for lesser warships, auxiliaries and some merchant ships. A few were hand worked. Elevation was usually +85° to -15° though in some to -5°, -8.75° or -10°. The important exception was Mk 30/80 in escort aircraft carriers with elevation limited to +27° to -15° as the mountings were in the shadow of the overhanging flight decks. Shields, axial hoists and RPC were lacking.

Mk 37 which resembled the less complete Mk 30s with a simpler sighting system, had +85° to -15° elevation and was restricted to some auxiliaries and many merchant ships. It was power worked.

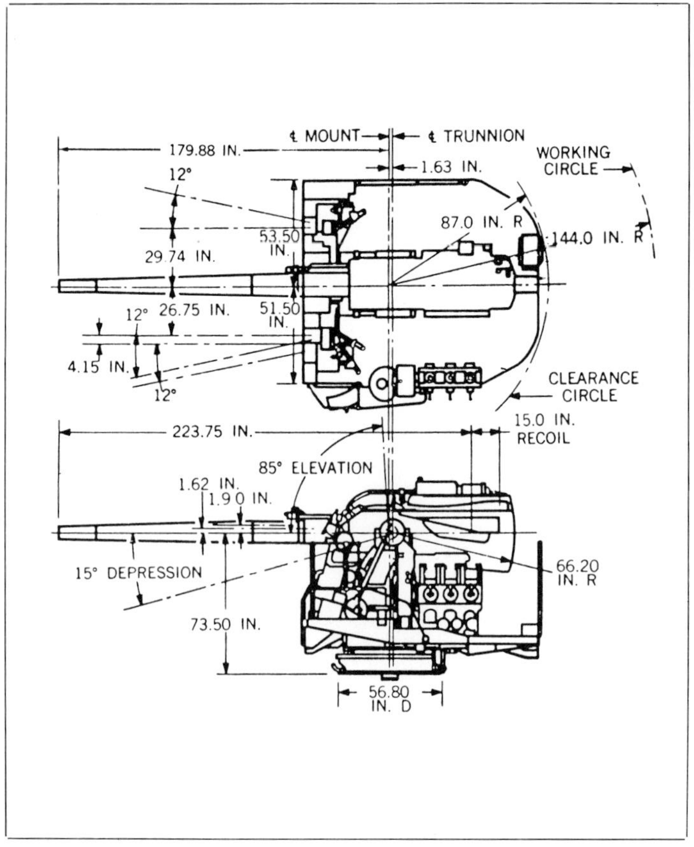

5in/38 mount Mk 24/6, a power worked single P mounting in destroyers.
USN

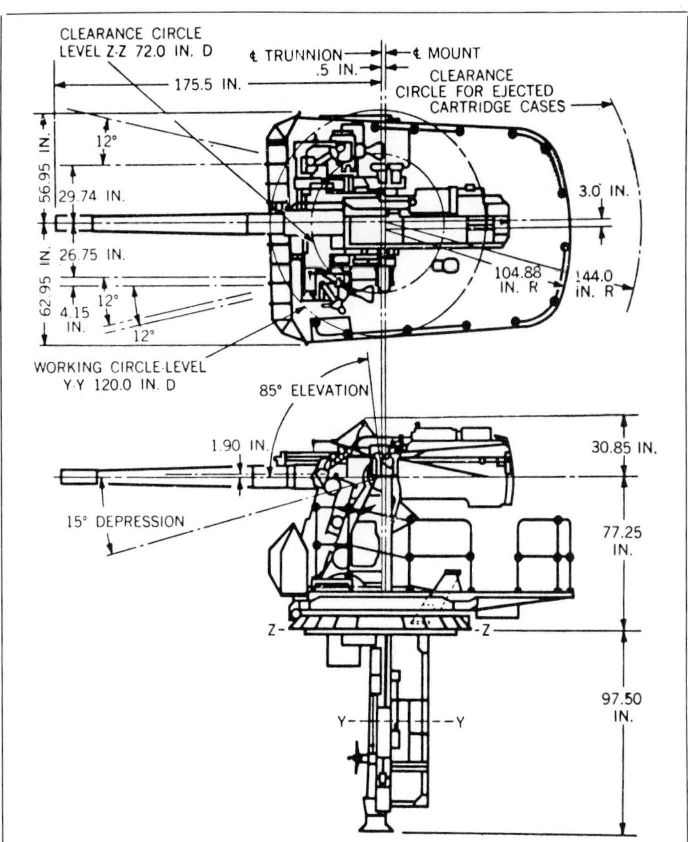

5in/38 mount Mk 30/8, a power worked single base ring mounting in destroyers and auxiliaries.
USN

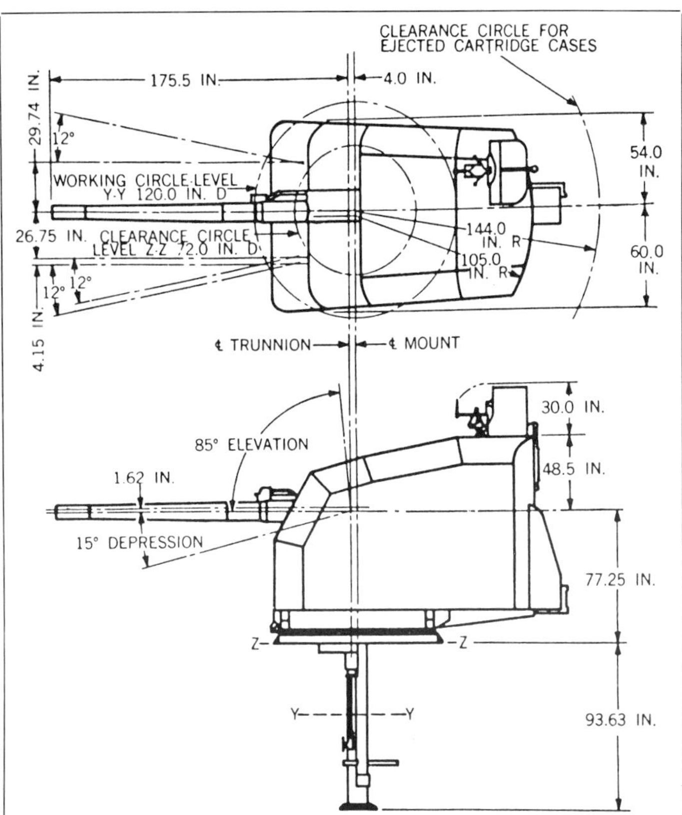

5in/38 mount Mk 30/18, a shielded power worked single base ring mounting in destroyers and some auxiliaries.
USN

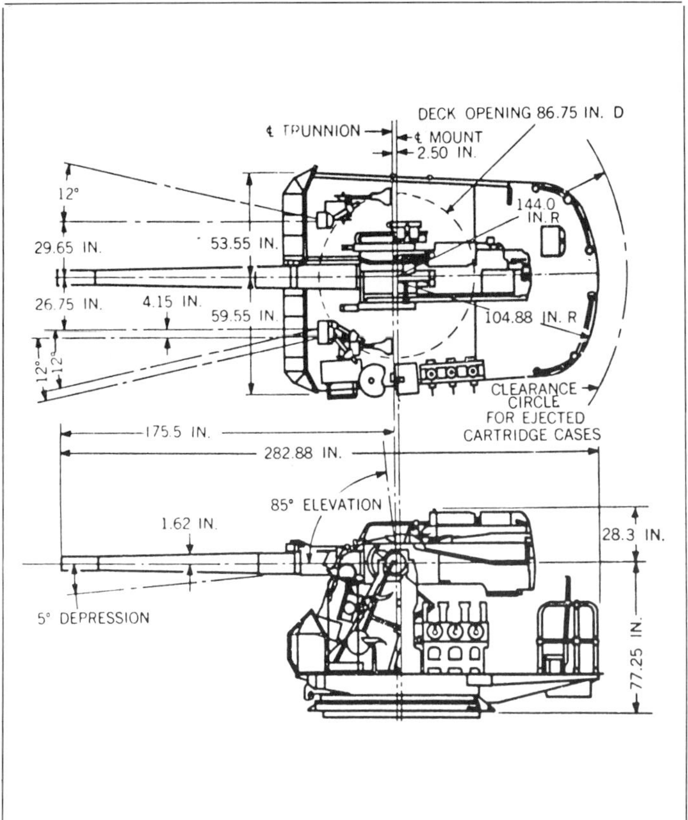

5in/38 mount Mk 30/51, a power worked single base ring mounting without integral hoists in some auxiliaries.
USN

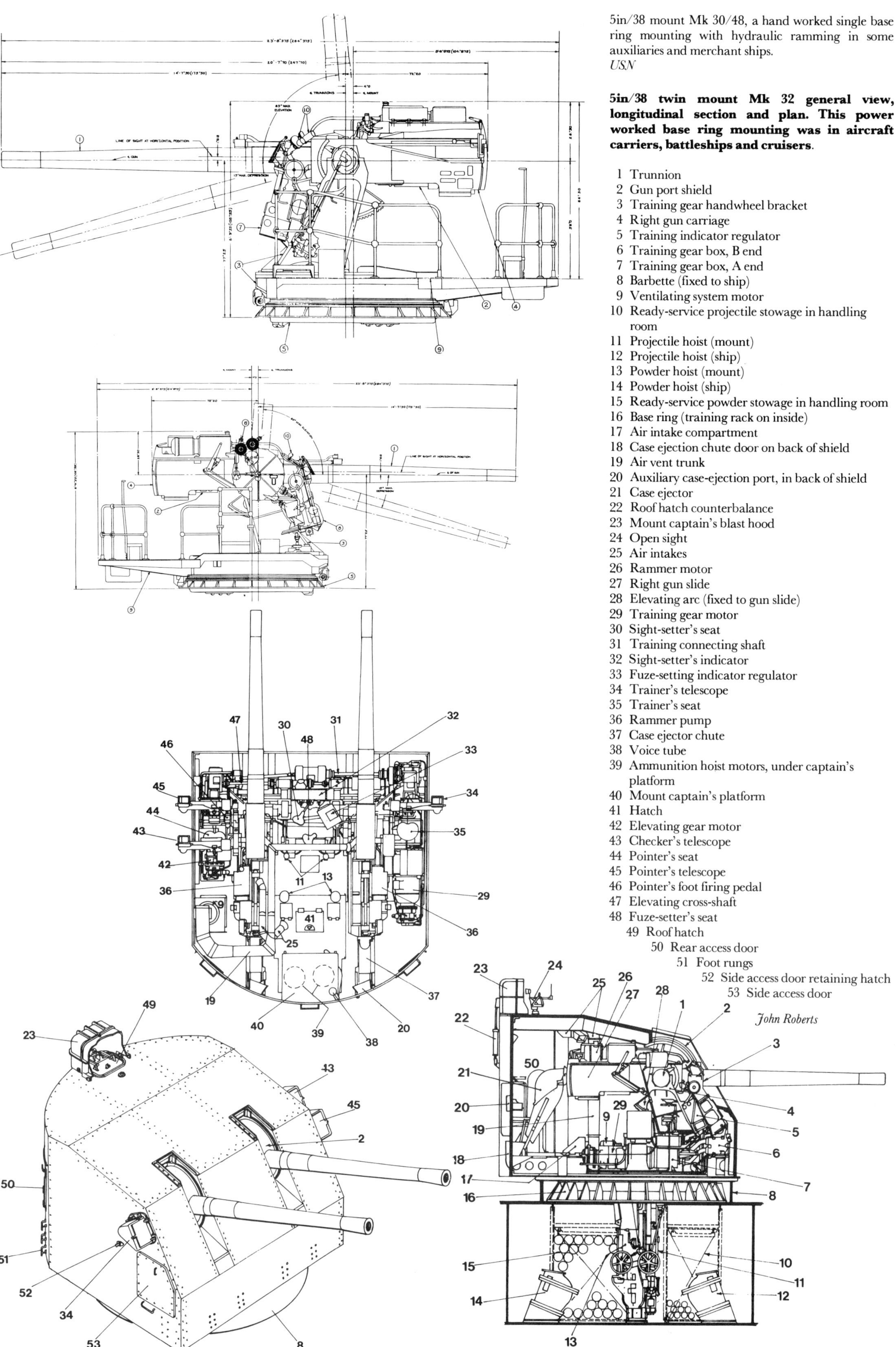

5in/38 mount Mk 30/48, a hand worked single base ring mounting with hydraulic ramming in some auxiliaries and merchant ships.
USN

5in/38 twin mount Mk 32 general view, longitudinal section and plan. This power worked base ring mounting was in aircraft carriers, battleships and cruisers.

1 Trunnion
2 Gun port shield
3 Training gear handwheel bracket
4 Right gun carriage
5 Training indicator regulator
6 Training gear box, B end
7 Training gear box, A end
8 Barbette (fixed to ship)
9 Ventilating system motor
10 Ready-service projectile stowage in handling room
11 Projectile hoist (mount)
12 Projectile hoist (ship)
13 Powder hoist (mount)
14 Powder hoist (ship)
15 Ready-service powder stowage in handling room
16 Base ring (training rack on inside)
17 Air intake compartment
18 Case ejection chute door on back of shield
19 Air vent trunk
20 Auxiliary case-ejection port, in back of shield
21 Case ejector
22 Roof hatch counterbalance
23 Mount captain's blast hood
24 Open sight
25 Air intakes
26 Rammer motor
27 Right gun slide
28 Elevating arc (fixed to gun slide)
29 Training gear motor
30 Sight-setter's seat
31 Training connecting shaft
32 Sight-setter's indicator
33 Fuze-setting indicator regulator
34 Trainer's telescope
35 Trainer's seat
36 Rammer pump
37 Case ejector chute
38 Voice tube
39 Ammunition hoist motors, under captain's platform
40 Mount captain's platform
41 Hatch
42 Elevating gear motor
43 Checker's telescope
44 Pointer's seat
45 Pointer's telescope
46 Pointer's foot firing pedal
47 Elevating cross-shaft
48 Fuze-setter's seat
49 Roof hatch
50 Rear access door
51 Foot rungs
52 Side access door retaining hatch
53 Side access door

John Roberts

5in/54 mount Mk 39/0 longitudinal section and plan. This was originally mounted in CVB41, 42, 43, *Midway*, *Franklin D Roosevelt*, *Coral Sea*. *USN*

Right side, longitudinal section

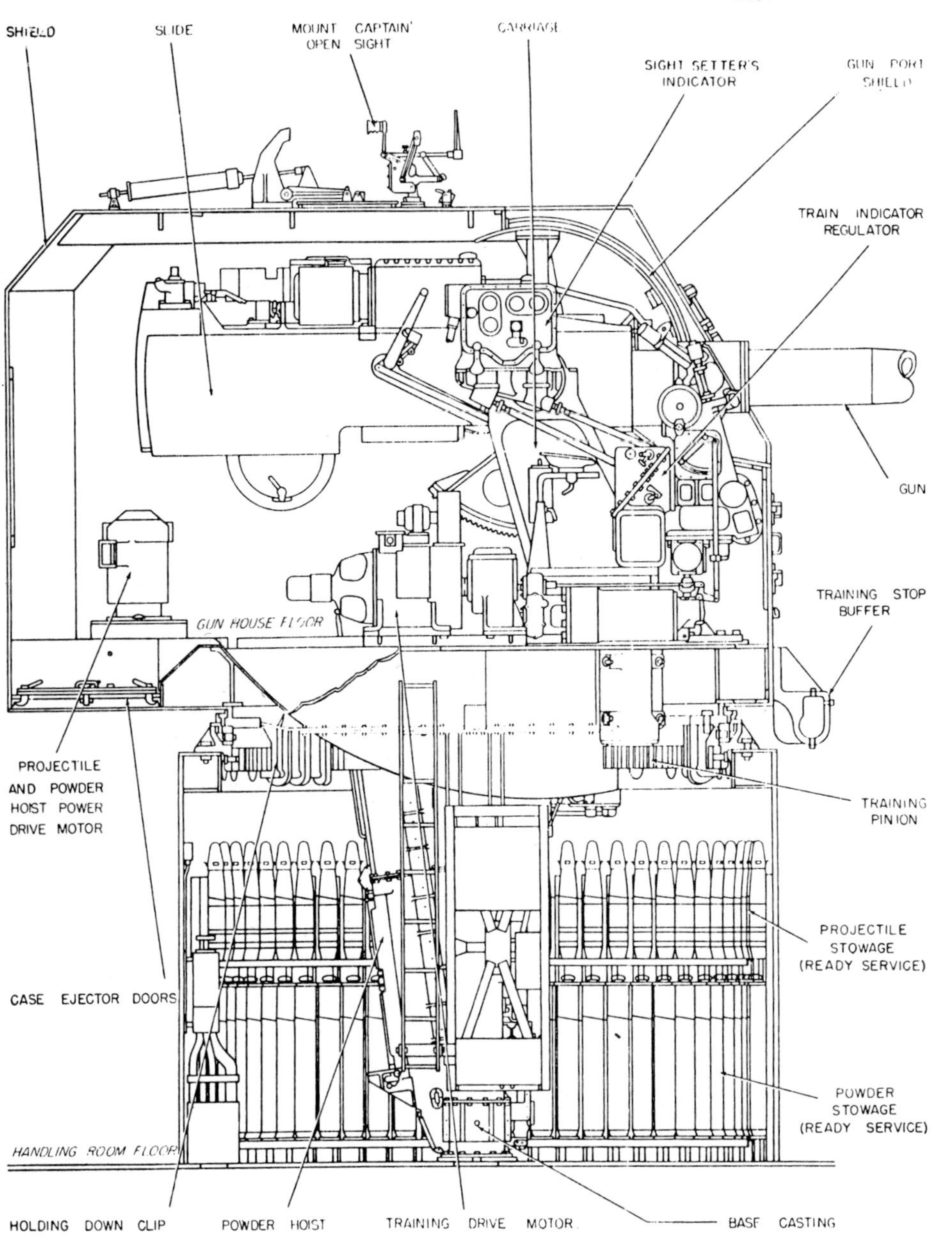

Plan view

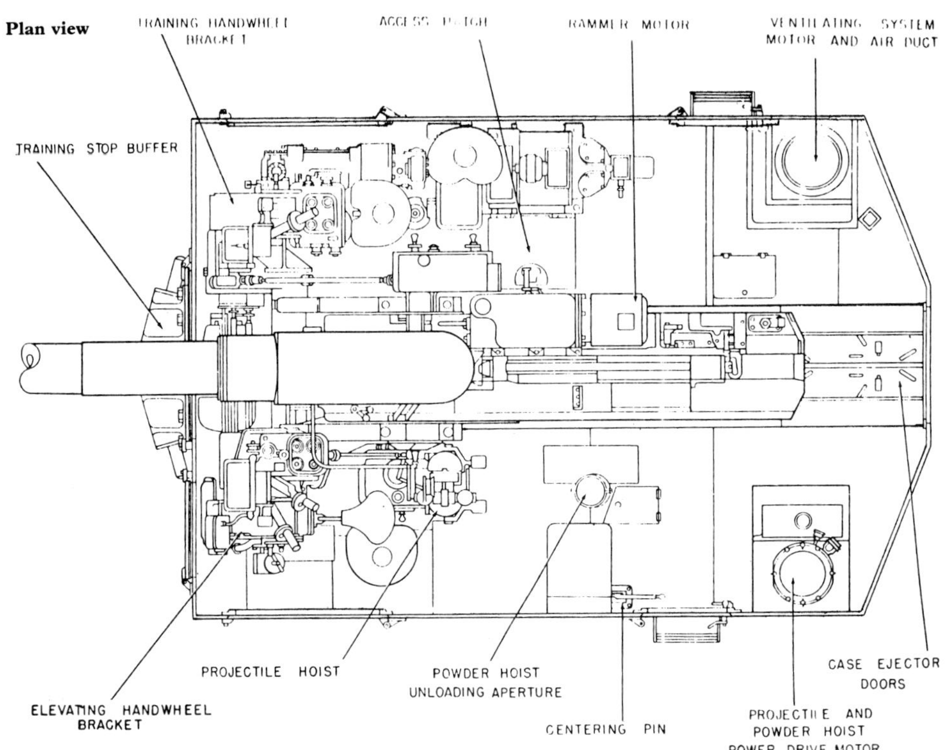

5in (127mm) Mark 16/0

A 54-calibre SA gun firing semi-fixed ammunition and intended as a longer range version of the Mk 12. It must not be confused with the fast firing Mk 18 gun in Mk 42 mounting carried by many ships postwar. The Mk 16 was originally to have been in twin Mk 41 mountings in the cancelled *Montana* class, and was not in service until shortly after the war in single mountings in the large aircraft carriers *Midway, Franklin D Roosevelt* and *Coral Sea*.

The prototype guns were 5in Mk D/O and E/O adapted from a cut-back 6in (*152mm*) Mk 8/0 and a 6in Mk 16/0 respectively. 5in (*127mm*) Mk 16/0 had a monobloc autofretted barrel secured to the housing by interrupted threads (bayonet joint). The SA breech mechanism was of vertical sliding wedge type. The bore was chromium plated 0.0005in (*0.013mm*) deep for 233.0in (*5918.2mm*) from the muzzle and diameter over the chamber was 13.495in (*342.77mm*). The empty cartridge case weighed *c*15lb (*6.8kg*).

The single Mk 39/0 mounting was of the power worked enclosed base ring type. Elevation was +85° to -10° with loading at any angle. The base ring diameter at deck level was 118in (*2.997m*).

This gun does not appear to have been liked as much as the Mk 12.

Gun Data

Bore	5in	127mm	
Weight barrel	2.483 tons	2.523t	
Length barrel and bore	270.0in	6858mm	54.0cal
Length chamber	*c*36.8in	*c*935mm	
Volume chamber	825.4in^3	13.526dm^3	
Length rifling	229.07in	5818.4mm	
Grooves			
Lands			
Twist	1 in 25		
Weight projectile	70lb	31.75kg	
Propellant charge	18.25lb NC	8.28kg NC	
Muzzle velocity	2650f/s	808m/s	
Working pressure	18.5tons/in^2	2915kg/cm^2	
Approx life	?3070 EFC		
Max range	25,909yd/47°24′	23,691m/47°24′	
Ceiling	51,600ft/85°	15,730m/85°	

Gun Mounting Data

Weight	33.0tons	33.5t
Recoil distance	19in	48cm
Max elevating speed	15°/sec	
Max training speed	30°/sec	
Firing cycle	4 sec	
Shield	0.75in	19mm

5in (127mm) Marks 5 and 6

These 50-calibre BL guns were originally mounted in cruisers and as the anti-torpedo battery in the *Delaware* and *North Dakota*, though later replaced in these two by 5in/51s. Mk 5/0 was not fully chase hooped but Mks 5/1, 6/0, 6/1 and 6/2 were generally similar to each other although they differed in details of construction, rifling and chamber design. All were built-up guns with Welin breech blocks and Vickers type BM.

In the Second World War they were used for emergency coast-defence batteries, and were mounted afloat in some Cargo ships (AK), Store ships (AF) and unclassified auxiliaries (IX). The Mk 12 25° mounting was apparently limited to Store ships, others having the 15° Mk 9. Both were open P type.

Gun Data for Marks 5/0 to 6/2

Bore	5.0in	127mm	
Weight incl BM	4.57–4.71 tons	4.64–4.79t	
Length oa	255.65in	6493.5mm	51.13cal
Length bore	*c*.248in	*c*6299mm	*c*49.6cal
Length chamber	*c*33in	*c*838mm	
Volume chamber	1208in^3	19.80dm^3	
Weight projectile	50lb	22.7kg	
Propellant charge	21lb NC	9.5kg	
Muzzle velocity	3000f/s	914m/s	
Range	13,500yd/15°	12,340m/15°	
	16,600yd/25°	15,180m/25°	

LIGHT CALIBRE GUNS

4in (101.6mm) Mark 9/0–9/24

At one time these 50-calibre QF fixed amunition guns were of great importance in the USN as they armed nearly all the destroyers completed during the 1914–18 war and from 1919 to 1922, as well as the 'S' class submarines. They were still carried by the survivors of the above that had not been rearmed, as well as by some armed yachts, patrol gunboats, surviving Eagle boats, various auxiliaries and many armed merchant ships. The guns also acquired a new importance as an armament for fleet submarines prior to the introduction of the 5in (*127mm*) Mk 17, and are known to have been mounted in *Dolphin* and the first seven *Balao* class (SS 285–291) as well as in rearmed boats as *Salmon, Seadragon, Gato* and *Robalo*.

Mk 9/0. Built with an A tube and full length jacket with muzzle swell. There was a screw box liner and Smith-Asbury Type side swing BM with Welin block.

Gun Data for Mk 9/23

Bore	4in	101.6mm	
Weight incl BM	2.725 tons	2.769t	
Length oa	206.53 tons	5245.9mm	51.63cal
Length bore	200.0in	5080mm	
Length chamber	*c*31.65in	*c*804mm	
Volume chamber	654.5in^3	10.73dm^3	
Length rifling	164.955in	4189.86mm	
Grooves			
Lands			
Twist	1 in 32		
Weight projectile	33lb	14.97kg	
Propellant charge	14.5lb NC 058	6.58kg NC	
Muzzle velocity	2900f/s	884m/s	
Working pressure	17 tons/in^2	2680kg/cm^2	
Approx life	500 EFC		
Range	15,920yd/20°	14,560m/20°	

Mk 9/2. Differed in a slightly thicker A tube to improve the lined design.

Mk 9/4. Mk 9/0 with deeper rifling grooves.

Mk 9/5. Mk 9/2 with deeper grooves and modified chamber centering cylinder.

Mk 9/8. Mk 9/0 or 9/4 modified as in 9/5.

Mk 9/20. Mk 9/5 with slide surface chromium plated.

Mk 9/22. Autofretted monobloc barrel with screw box liner. Slide surface chromium plated.

Mk 9/23. As 9/22, but with strengthening band at muzzle.

The remaining modifications listed in January 1945 - 9/6, 9/7, 9/15, 9/16, 9/18, 9/19, 9/21, 9/24 - were 9/0, 9/2, 9/4, 9/5 or 9/8 lined or relined with various differences in detail. Mks 9/18 to 9/24 had the slide surface chromium plated, but no Mk 9 had a chromium-plated bore. Diameter over the chamber was 16in (*406mm*) or 16.375in (*416mm*) in 9/24. Originally Mk 9 suffered from driving band troubles and excessive coppering. Rifling was usually 1 in 32 in later modifications and otherwise 0 to 1 in 25 or 0 to 1 in 31.17. The groove depth of 0.025in (*0.64mm*) in 9/0 was increased to 0.0375in (*0.95mm*) in 9/4 and to 0.05in (*1.27mm*) in 9/5 to 9/24. The fixed round weighed 62.4-64.75lb (*28.3-29.4kg*).

Of the single P mountings, Mks 12/6, 12/11, 12/21, 12/38, 12/40, 12/41, 12/43 and 12/44 are listed as 'wet', and others in January 1945 were 12/0 to 12/3, 12/10, 12/13 and 12/18. Some of these could have a small shield, 0.187-0.196in (*4.75-4.98mm*). All were hand worked and allowed +20° to -15° elevation. Weights were 4.53-5.63 tons (*4.60-5.72t*) and firing cycle about 7sec.

The twin Mk 14 mountings weighing 9.41 tons (*9.56t*) in the destroyers *Hovey* and *Long* were replaced by singles in 1940 on conversion to minesweepers.

4in (101.6mm) Mark 6

This 40-cal QF gun was of built-up type with screw BM and fired fixed ammunition. It dated back to the 1890s when it and other 4in/40 QFs were mounted as secondary armament in such ships as *Puritan, New York, Columbia* and *Minneapolis* and as main armament in patrol gunboats. Mk 6/0 is included in a list of April 1944, but it is not known in what ships it was mounted. The shell weighed 33lb (*14.97kg*) and muzzle velocity was 2000f/s (*610m/s*). Gun weight including BM, was 1.575 tons (*1.600t*).

4in (101.6mm) Mark 7

A 50-cal QF gun firing fixed ammunition, of built-up construction with screw BM, introduced in 1899 for secondary armament in the *Ozark* (ex-*Arkansas*) class monitors. Mk 7/1 was Mk 7/0 with a taper liner. Both occur in a list of April 1944 and are believed to have been mounted in some auxiliaries.

Gun Data

Bore	4.0in	101.6mm	
Weight incl BM	2.63 tons	2.67t	
Length oa	204.5in	5194.3mm	51.13cal
Length bore	200in	5080mm	50.0cal
Length chamber	*c*31.8in	*c*807.7mm	
Volume chamber	644.2in^3	10.56dm^3	
Weight projectile	33lb	14.97kg	
Propellant charge	9lb NC 040	4.08kg	
Muzzle velocity	2500f/s	762m/s	
Range			

4in (101.6mm) Mark 10

A 50-calibre QF gun firing fixed ammunition, of built-up construction with vertical sliding breech block and developed in 1914-15 as an AA gun. Ballistically it resembled the well known Mk 9. It was never put into production, though listed in April 1944.

Gun Data

Bore	4.0in	101.6mm	
Weight incl BM	3.06 tons	3.11t	
Length oa	211.0in	5359.4mm	52.75cal
Length bore	200in	5080mm	50.0cal
Length chamber	*c*31.8in	*c*.807.7mm	
Volume chamber	644in^3	10.55dm^3	
Weight projectile	33lb	14.97kg	
Propellant charge	14.0lb NC	6.35kg	
Muzzle velocity	2900f/s	884m/s	
Range	20,720yd/45°	18,950yd/45°	

Close-up of stern of a flush-deck destroyer as transferred to Britain in 1940, showing 4in/50 Mk 9 gun and, on the quarterdeck, a 3in/23.5 Mk 14.
CPL

These Marks were all 50-calibre guns, mostly SA, firing fixed ammunition, and mounted in various single HA hand-worked mountings. Later modifications of Mk 22 in powered twin or single mountings with loading equipment giving 45 to 50 rounds per gun per minute did not enter service until 1948, and the water-cooled 70-calibre gun with twice that rate of fire and firing a 15lb (*6.8kg*) shell at 3400f/s (*1036m/s*) was eight years later, though both had their origins in the Second World War.

The many older Marks were usually mounted in ships too overloaded, too small or lacking in priority for 5in (*127mm*) AA. Some were mounted pending the availability of automatic close range AA guns, and they were intially carried by many fleet submarines from the *Cachalot* to the *Gato* class. Other ships included the *New York* class, *Arkansas, Omaha* class, re-armed and converted flush-deck destroyers, destroyer escorts and very many lesser warships, auxiliaries and merchant ships.

Mks 10, 17 and 20 were built up guns with A tube, jacket and hoop not extending to muzzle. The housing for the vertical sliding breech block was separate from the jacket in Mk 10/2 (as lined 10/3), 10/5, 17/0 (as lined 17/1) and integral in the rest. Mk 10/5 not listed in 1944-45, was 10/2 with a copper-nickel alloy liner, 17/0 originally designated 10/4, was 10/2 with the bore and external working surfaces chromium plated for wet mountings and the chase red-lead painted, while some 17/1s were similarly converted from 10/3. Of the guns with integral housings 10/1 was 10/0 lined, 20/0 was the LA 6/0 converted to AA as was 20/1 with different rifling, while 20/2 was 20/0, 20/1 or 6/0 or 6/4 lined and in the last two converted to AA.

Mk 18/0 was made from copper-nickel alloy for wet mountings with A tube, jacket, screwed and shrunk breech housing and SA vertical sliding block. The bore was chromium plated.

Mks 21 and 22 were very similar apart from a collar on the chase in 22, intended for a concentric counter-recoil spring fitted only in Mk 24/0-/2 among wartime mountings. Both had chromium plated bores. Mks 21/0 and 22/0 had autofretted monobloc barrels secured to the breech housing by bayonet joints. Mk 22/2 differed only in a modified collar, while 21/2, 22/1 and 22/3 (modified collar) had barrels of higher-strength steel, not autofretted. Mk 21/1 was 21/0 modified for wet mountings with the chamber and external working surfaces chromium plated.

Internal chromium plating was 0.0005in (*0.013mm*) thick for 128in (*3251mm*) from the muzzle except in 21/1 and apparently 17/0, 17/1, where it covered the whole bore. Rifling was 1 in 32 in Mk 10/5, 18, 21 and 22, 0 to 1 in 25 in Mk 10/0-10/3, 17, 20/0 and 20/2 and 1 in 25 with hook section in 20/1. Diameter over the chamber was 11.0in (*279mm*) except in Mks 21 and 22 with 8.625in (*219mm*). The fixed round weighed 24lb (*10.9kg*) in all.

3in (76.2mm) Marks 10/0-10/5, 17/0, 17/1, 18/0, 20/0-20/2, 21/0-21/2, 22/0-22/3

Gun Data Mk 21/0

Bore	3in	76.2mm	
Weight barrel	1240lb	562kg	
Weight with housing	1760lb	798kg	
Length barrel and bore	150.25in	3816mm	50.08cal
Length oa with housing	159.65in	4055mm	53.22cal
Length chamber	22.07in	560.6mm	
Volume chamber	217in^3	3.56dm^3	
Length rifling	126.13in	3203.7mm	
Grooves	(24) 0.03in deep	0.76mm deep	
Lands			
Twist	1 in 32		
Weight projectile	13lb	5.9kg	
Propellant charge	3.7lb NC 033	1.68kg NC	
Muzzle velocity	2700f/s	823m/s	
Working pressure	17 tons/in^2	2680kg/cm^2	
Approx life	4300 EFC		
Max range	14,590yd/43° 02′	13,340m/43° 02′	
Ceiling	29,800ft/85°	9080m/85°	

The chief difference in other Marks was the weight with housing and BM which reached 2547lb (*1155kg*) in Mks 10 and 17 and 2830lb (*1284kg*) in Mk 18. Life was considerably less in wet guns and in those without chromium plating.

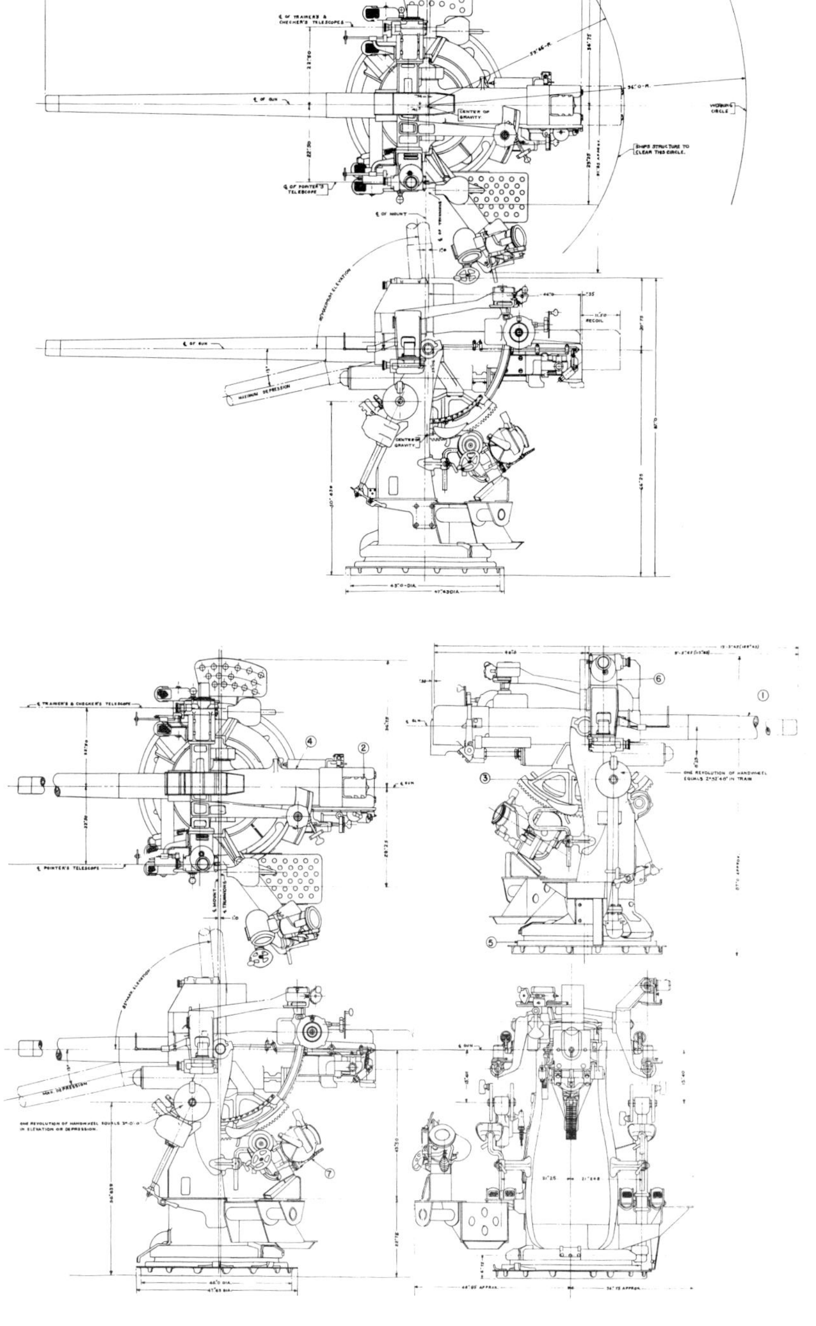

3in/50 Mk 21 gun in Mk 22 mount, typical of 3in/50 AA.

1 Mk 21 gun
2 Housing
3 Carriage
4 Slide
5 Stand
6 Sight
7 Fuze-setter

USN

3in/50 AA gun in old DD223 *McCormick* converted to DMS.
USN

In January 1945 wet mountings listed were Mk 11/8, 11/9, 11/11 for Mk 17 guns, Mk 19/0 for Mk 18 guns and Mk 21/0, 21/1 for Mk 21/1 gungs, while dry mountings were Mk 11/0-11/2, 11/5, 11/6, 11/10 for Mk 10 guns, Mk 20/1, 20/3 for Mk 20 guns and Mk 22/0-22/4, 22/6, 22/16, 22/17, 24/0-24/2 for Mk 21 and 22 guns. Spray shields were fitted to Mk 11/5, 11/6 and larger ones to Mk 22/2 and 22/3 supplied to Britain.

Weights varied 3-4.18 tons (*3.05-4.25t*), elevation from 84° to 90° and depression 10° to 15°. The firing cycle was 3-4 sec in favourable conditions.

3in (76.2mm) Marks 3/4-3/9, 5/0, 5/3, 6/0 6/2, 6/4, 6/7, 19/0

These were the 50-calibre low-angle guns with MV as in the AA, still listed in January 1945. Mk 19/0 was carried in some fleet submarines instead of the HA gun and the others in 'R' class submarines, various patrol craft, auxiliaries, coast guard vessels and merchant ships.

Mk 19/0 was a modern gun with chromium-plated bore and made from copper nickel alloy with an autofretted monobloc barrel secured to the housing by a bayonet joint, and SA vertical sliding BM, while the rest were built up guns, lined except for 3/4, 3/6, 5/0, 6/0 and 6/4. Mks 6/4 and 6/7 were for wet mountings, the latter with some external chromium plating. The Mk 3 series had side-swing screw BM.

Chromium plating in Mk 19/0 was as in 18/0 and diameters over the chamber as in monobloc and built-up AA guns. Rifling was 1 in 32 in 19/0, 1 in 25 in 5/0 and some 6/0 and 0 to 1 in 25 in other marks. The weights of shell and fixed round and the muzzle velocity were as in the AA guns.

The Mk 18/0 wet mounting for the Mk 19/0 gun weighed 2.90 tons (*2.95t*) and allowed +40° to -15° elevation. Mountings for the other guns allowed +15° to -10° or in Mk 7/10 and the wet 7/19 +30° to -20°. Respective ranges were 10,300yd (*9420m*) and 13,600yd (*12440m*).

The Mk 19/0 gun had a barrel weight of 1423lb (*645kg*) and weight with housing of 2162lb (*981kg*).

Other 3in (76.2mm) guns

Mks 2/1, 2/2 were 50-calibre built-up screw breech guns firing fixed ammunition, but with the muzzle velocity reduced to 2100f/s (*640m/s*) and the working pressure to 13 tons/in^2 (*2050kg/cm^2*) because of weakness. They were mounted in some Coast Guard vessels and merchant ships in 15° mountings giving a range of 7000yd (*6400m*).

Mk 9/0 was a 23-calibre built-up gun with a bronze sleeve and SA vertical sliding block. Fixed ammunition was fired with 13lb (*5.9kg*) shell and MV 1650f/s (*503m/s*). The gun was designed for retractable mountings in submarines and was last in the '0' class. The gun weight with BM was 749lb (*340kg*).

Mk 13/0 was a 23-calibre monobloc gun with SA horizontal sliding block. It was originally a boat gun and performance was as in 9/0, but gun weight with BM 531lb (*241kg*).

Mk 14/0 was generally similar to 13/0 but was 23.5 calibres. Mk 14/1 differed in having a muzzle blast reducer and balancing counterweight. Performance was as in 9/0 and weight with BM 593lb (*269kg*) in 14/0 and 658lb (*298kg*) in 14/1.

These were the most important of the short 3in (*76.2mm*) and were carried in 65° or 75° mountings by old destroyers, submarine chasers, armed yachts and various auxiliaries. They were also mounted in some major warships pending supply of 1.1in (*28mm*) quads. Range was 10,100yd (*9235m*) at 45° and ceiling 18,000ft (*5490m*) at 75°.

6pdr (57mm)

These guns dated back to the 1890s and early 1900s, when they were mounted as the anti-torpedo battery in battleships and cruisers and also as part of the armament of destroyers and other ships. A list of 1901 gives 735 guns as allocated. In the Second World War the surviving guns were in the three *Hawk* class minesweepers and in such vessels as former Coast Guard cutters, converted yachts and Coastal Picket patrol craft. The following marks are recorded in a list of April 1944.

Mk 1/0. 60cal. Hotchkiss with trunnions, manufacture in US and overseas.

Mk 1/1. As 1/0 but differences in BM, French manufacture.

Mk 1/2. As 1/1 but differences in BM.

Mk 1/3. Hotchkiss-EOC, differences in BM.

Mk 2/0. Hotchkiss, no trunnions, BM as 1/0 or 1/1.

Mk 3/0. 45cal. Hotchkiss, otherwise like 2/0, BM as 1/0.

Mk 6/0. 45cal. Driggs Schroeder, no trunnions.

Mk 6/1. 6/0 retubed with alloy steel tube.

Mk 7/0. Hotchkiss, almost as 3/0 but BM as 1/1.

Mk 7/1. As 7/0 but differences in balancing.

Mk 7/2. As 7/0 but alloy steel tube.

Mk 7/3. Ex-Coast Guard, like 7/0 but muzzle swell.

Mk 7/4. 7/0 retubed with alloy steel tube, differences from 7/2 in balancing.

Mk 8/0. 50cal. Driggs Schroeder, like 6/0 but 50cal, muzzle swell, differences in BM.

Mk 8/1. 8/0 retubed with alloy steel tube.

Mk 9/0. 42.3cal. SA. Maxim-Nordenfelt, monobloc, no trunnions.

Mk 9/1. As 9/0 but nickel steel and muzzle swell.

Mk 9/2. Like 9/0 but differences in BM, manufacture outside US.

Mk 10/0. 42.3cal. Nordenfelt with trunnions, monobloc.

Mk 11/0. 50cal. SA. Driggs Seabury, no trunnions.

Mk 11/1. 11/0 rebuilt, new tube and locking hoop.

In all the bore was 2.244in (*57mm*), weight incl BM 712-950lb (*323-431kg*), shell 6.03lb (*2.735kg*), MV 2240f/s (*683m/s*) or in 50cal guns 2303f/s (*702m/s*). Range is given as 8000yd (*7315m*) at 22° and 2240f/s (*683m/s*).

3pdr (47mm)

Generally contemporary with the 6pdr (*57mm*), this gun was mainly used where the larger gun was considered too heavy. The 1901 list of allocations gives 328 guns but 118 were also mounted in later pre-dreadnoughts and armoured cruisers as a secondary anti-torpedo battery to the principal one of 3in (*76mm*)/50 cal. The surviving guns were used in the Second World War for Coastal Picket and similar craft. According to a list of April 1944, the following marks were extant.

Mk 1/0. 40cal. Hotchkiss, with trunnions.

Mk 1/1. Like 1/0, made in France.

Mk 2/0. 45 cal. Driggs Schroeder, with trunnions.

Mk 3/0. Driggs Schroeder, like 2/0 but no trunnions and differences in BM.

Mk 4/0. 50cal. SA. Hotchkiss, no trunnions, muzzle swell.

Mk 4/1. 4/0 modified for different sight.

Mk 4/2. 4/0 retubed with alloy steel tube.

Mk 4/3. 4/1 retubed with alloy steel tube.

Mk 5/0. 50cal. SA. Maxim-Nordenfelt. Three guns purchased.

Mk 7/0. 45 cal. SA. Vickers, no trunnions. Only ten guns. Possibly Maxim-Nordenfelt.

Mk 8/0. 40cal. Hotchkiss-EOC, with trunnions.

Mk 9/0. 50cal. SA. Nordenfelt, no trunnions.

Mk 10/0. 50cal. SA. Hotchkiss, no trunnions.

Mk 10/1. Like 10/0 but longer slide, muzzle swell.

Mk 10/2. Like 10/1, constructional differences.

Mk 10/3. 10/0 retubed with alloy steel tube.

Mk 10/4. 10/1 retubed with alloy steel tube.

Mk 10/5. 10/2 retubed with alloy steel tube.

Mk 11/0. 50cal. SA. US RF Gun and Power, no trunnions, muzzle swell.

Mk 11/1. As 11/0 but no balancing hoop.

Mk 14/0. 50cal. SA. Driggs Seabury, no trunnions, muzzle swell, two chamber liners.

The bore was 1.85in (*47mm*) in all, weight incl BM 484-604lb (*220-274kg*), shell 3.30lb (*1.497kg*), MV 2026-2200f/s (*618-671m/s*). Range is given as 6800yd (*6220m*) at 20° and 2200f/s (*671m/s*).

AUTOMATIC GUNS

40mm (1.575in) Bofors

This famous 56-calibre gun in water-cooled form was the principal close range AA armament for USN ships in the Second World War. On 28 August 1940 a twin air-cooled sample arrived in New York from Sweden via Finland, and in that month guns in the Dutch escort vessel *van Kinsbergen* were successfully demonstrated off Trinidad. Manufacture was undertaken by the York Lock and Safe Company using drawings procured from the Dutch East Indies and Britain, and well in advance of obtaining Swedish permission in June 1941, when Bofors supplied additional drawings. The original intention was to use the twin Bofors to replace the quadruple 1.1in (*28mm*), but the quadruple Bofors was soon standard for large ships. The first pilot twin was produced in January 1942 and the first pilot quadruple in April 1942, but the latter was mounted afloat in the *Wyoming*, at that time a gunnery training ship, on 22 June 1942 followed by the twin in the destroyer *Coghlan* (*Benson* class) on 1 July. It was however mid 1944 before the demand was satisfied, and defence against

Gun Data Mk1, Mk2

Bore	1.575in	40mm	
Weight of gun	*c*1150lb	*c*522kg	
Weight of barrel	202lb	91.6kg	
Length gun	148.8in	3779.5mm	
Length bore	88.583in	2250mm	56.25cal
Length chamber	10.30in	261.6mm	
Volume chamber	28.3in^3	0.464dm^3	
Length rifling	75.85in	1926.6mm	
Grooves	(16) 0.0225in deep × 0.22	0.57 × 5.59mm	
Lands	0.0892in	2.266mm	
Twist	1 in 45 to 1 in 30		
Weight projectile	1.985lb	0.900kg	
Propellant charge	0.694lb NC 025	0.315kg	
Muzzle velocity	2890f/s	881m/s	
Working pressure	19.5 tons/in^2	3070kg/cm^2	
Approx life	9500 EFC		
Max range	11,000yd/42°	10,060m/42°	
Ceiling	22,800ft/90°	6950m/90°	

AP shot weight 1.96lb (*0.889kg*) and its blunter shape made the range about 9620yd (*8800m*).

Elevation, right side

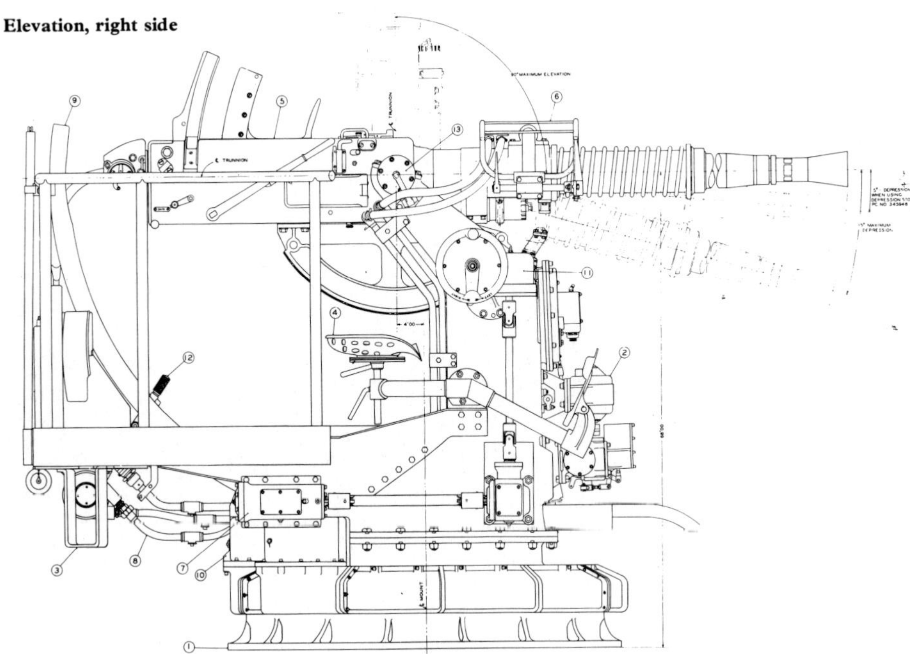

40mm Bofors twin mount Mk 1, elevation right side.

1 Stand and base ring
2 Firing mechanism
3 Platform
4 Seat and foot rest
5 Gun
6 Sight
7 Training gear worm
8 Cooling system
9 Case chute
10 Training buffer
11 Training gear manual drive
12 Training centering
13 Carriage

USN

Elevation, left side

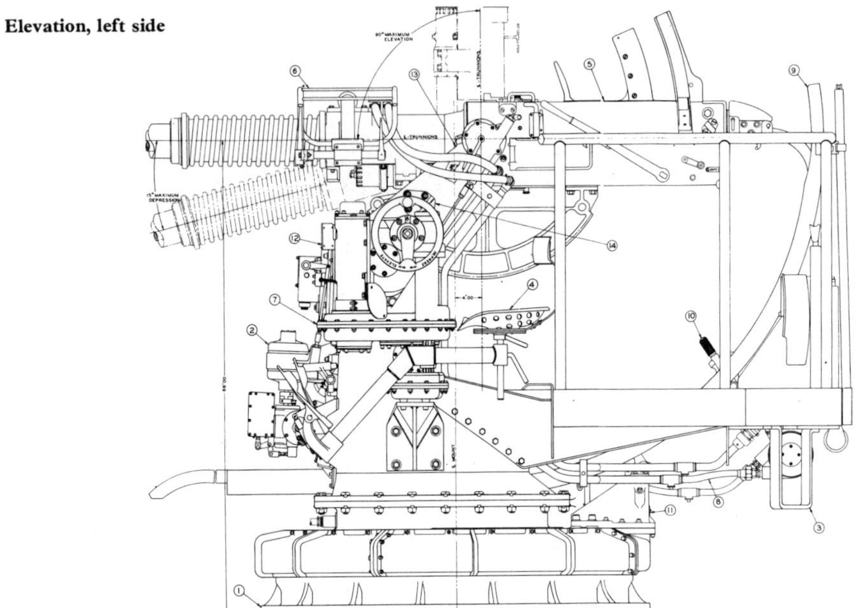

40mm Bofors twin mount Mk 1, elevation left side.

1 Stand and base ring
2 Firing mechanism
3 Platform
4 Seat and foot rest
5 Machine gun mechanism
6 Sight
7 Elevating gear manual drive
8 Cooling system
9 Case chutes
10 Training centering
11 Training buffer
12 Elevating gear worm
13 Carriage
14 Elevating centering

USN

Plan view

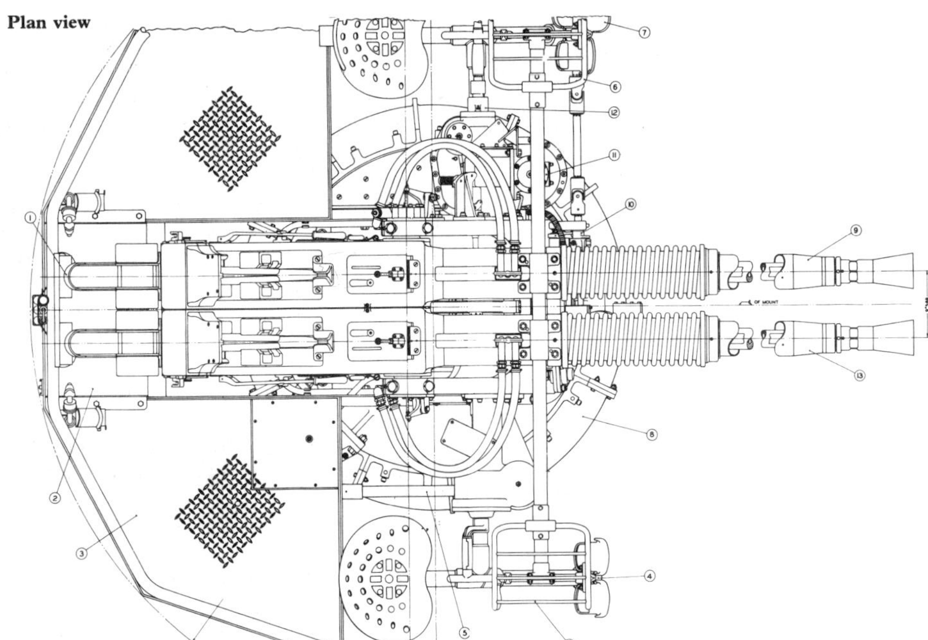

40mm Bofors twin mount Mk 1, plan view.

1 Case chutes
2 Cooling system
3 Platform
4 Seat and foot rest, right side
5 Training gear manual drive
6 Sights
7 Seat and foot rest, left side
8 Stand and base ring
9 Left machine gun
10 Firing mechanism
11 Elevation gear worm
12 Elevation gear worm
13 Right machine gun

USN

40mm Bofors twin mount Mk 1, front elevation.

1 Stand and base ring
2 Firing mechanism
3 Platform
4 Seat and foot rest, right side
5 Seat and foot rest, left side
6 Machine gun mechanism Mk 1
7 Machine gun mechanism Mk 2
8 Training gear manual drive
9 Elevation gear manual drive
10 Cooling system
11 Case chute
12 Elevation gear worm
13 Carriage
14 Sight
15 Training gear worm

USN

Front elevation

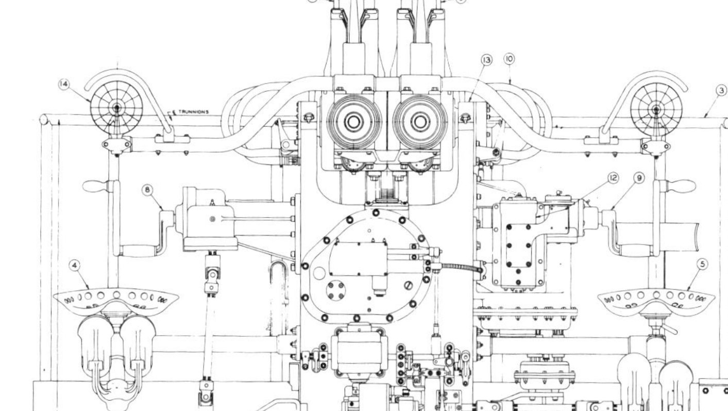

kamikaze attacks led to further large increases in the numbers mounted. The Bofors was the best available gun for this latter purpose, but the shell was too small for existing VT fuzes, and also too small to disintegrate a kamikaze so thoroughly that its ballistic trajectory would not carry it into its target at short range. If it had been ready in time, the 3in (*76.2mm*) with loading gear to give 45-50 rounds per gun per minute would have been preferred.

1945 figures show 25 quadruple Bofors in *Saratoga*, 10 to 18 in the *Essex* class, 12 to 20 in modern battleships, 8 to 14 in older and up to 12 or 14 in large cruisers. Mixed armaments of quadruple and twin were in many ships such as *Enterprise* with 11 quads and 8 twins, *Commencement Bay* class 3 and 12, some *Cleveland* class 4 and 6, *Gearing* class 3 and 2. Others with less space or weight-carrying ability had twins only though quads might also be found.

The US Army had tested a single air-cooled Bofors in 1937, and in 1940 Chrysler agreed to manufacture using British drawings. The USN acquired a number of these, and in addition to supplementing water cooled guns as in some destroyers, they were mounted in submarines, motor torpedo boats, some destroyer escorts and landing craft as well as in other ships.

Of surviving first line surface ships at the end of the war, the four *Gridley* class destroyers were probably unique in never having had Bofors guns.

The USN water-cooled guns were in matched pairs, the left-hand gun being Mk 1 and the right Mk 2. Apart from the barrel assemblies they were not interchangeable. In general they resembled British guns and the auto-loaders were similar to Types D and E in left and right British Mk IV guns. Single shots could be fired and the maximum rate was 160 per minute in automatic fire. Barrel diameter over the chamber was 5.59in (*142mm*) and weight and length of complete round about 4.75lb (*2.15kg*) and 17.62in (*447.5mm*). HE, Incendiary and AP shot were provided. Tracer burnt for 8.5-10.5 sec, and rounds were self destructing at 4000-5000yd (*3700m-4600m*). The bore was not chromium plated.

The single army gun was known as M1. It was generally similar to British and Canadian guns, with which the barrels were interchangeable. Most of the single guns were in hand-worked army type mountings known as Mk 3 and weighing 1.09 tons (*1.11t*), but some were in Mk 3/4 which had a navy modification of an earlier army power drive giving 24°/sec maximum elevating speed and 30°/sec training. Single hand-worked wet mountings were Mks 3/5 and 3/6. Mk 3/4 weighed 1.88 tons (*1.91t*) and like other Mk 3s allowed +90° to -6° elevation. It differed in having RPC and 1HP elevating and training motors.

The water-cooled guns were in biaxial twin and quadruple mountings, known as Mk 1 and Mk 2. There were many modifications mainly differing in details of the electrical and RPC systems. An asterisk indicated that the modifications *2/21 - *2/32 and *1/9 - *1/14 were limited to the Mk 63 Director which had the radar antenna on the gun mounting. Maximum elevating and training speeds were 24°/sec and 30°/sec in both Marks and elevation +90° to -15°. The recoil distance was 7.5-8in (*19-20cm*). The gun axes were 9.568in (*243mm*) apart in the twin, while the quadruple had two pairs of twins with the pair axes 60.0in (*1.524m*) apart. Both pairs elevated together but in some at least they could be uncoupled in case of damage. Elevating motors were 5HP in quad mountings and 3HP or 5HP in twins, while training motors were respectively 7.5HP or 5HP and 5HP or 3HP. Hydraulic driving gear was fitted to quadruple mountings and to some twins. Weights were: Mk 1, 5.80-6.65 tons (*5.89-6.76t*); Mk 2, 10.36-11.12 tons (*10.53-11.30t*), and with 0.375in (*9.5mm*) shield 11.12-11.88 tons (*11.30-12.07t*).

The Mk 4 quadruple mounting was a lightened version with a lighter amplidyne generator below decks and a GE RPC system. Elevation and training maximum speeds were 55°/sec and 50°/sec but only 100 had been made by the end of the war.

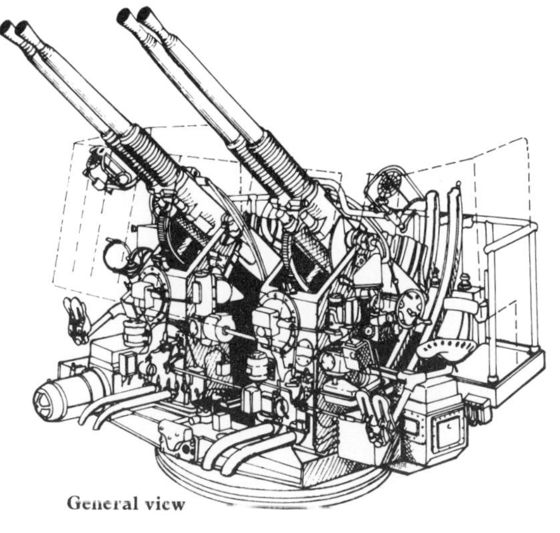

General view

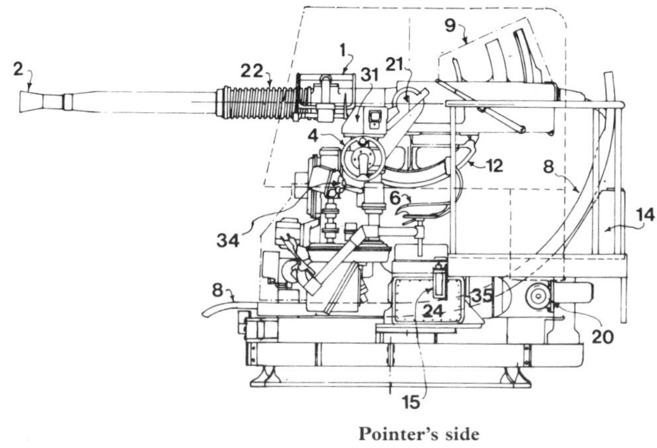

Pointer's side

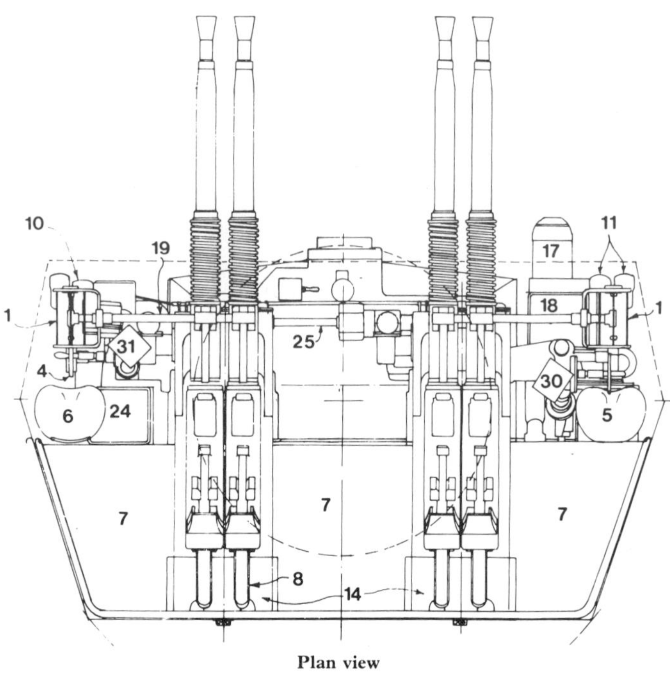

Plan view

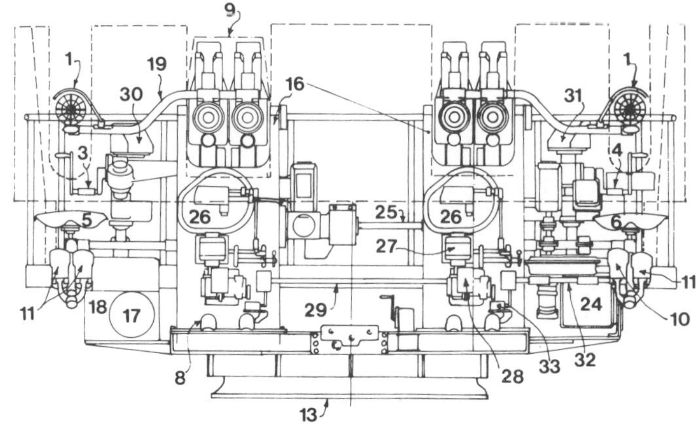

Front elevation

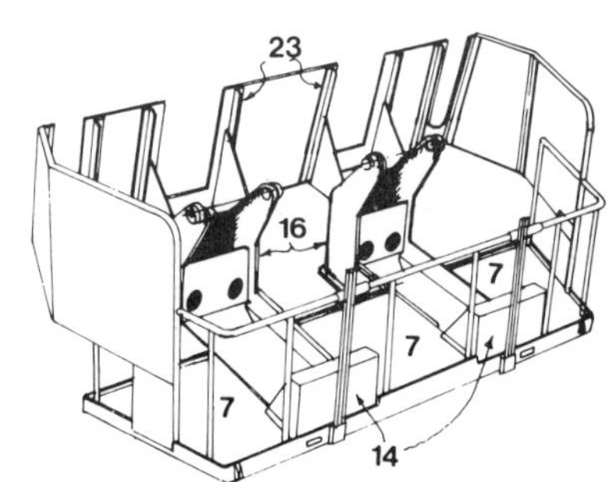

General view of shield and platform

40mm Bofors M1 guns in Mk 3 mounts as additional AA armament in DD419 *Wainwright.*
USN

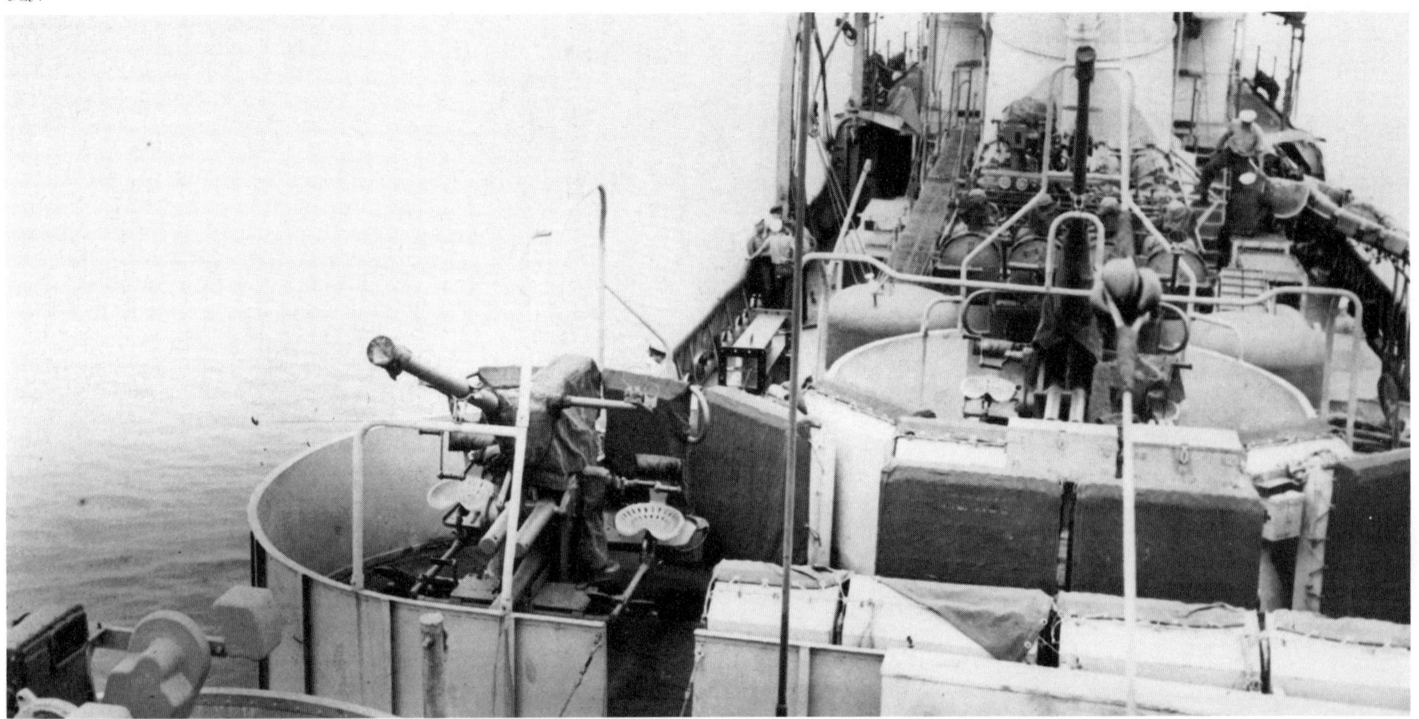

40mm Bofors quadruple mount Mk 2, the most formidable of the USN close range AA, general view, left side, plan view, front elevation, shield and platform.

1 Open sight
2 Flash guards
3 Training crank
4 Elevating crank
5 Trainer's seat
6 Pointer's seat
7 Loading platform
8 Case discharge chutes
9 Outline of loader hood
10 Firing pedal
11 Foot rest
12 Elevation arc
13 Stand
14 Coolant water tanks
15 Firing motor starters
16 Carriage
17 Train power motor
18 Power unit for train power drive
19 Sight bar
20 Cooling motor and pump
21 Trunnion
22 Recoil springs
23 Stiffening angle bars
24 Power unit elevation power drive
25 Cross-connection elevation drive
26 Firing stop-cam housing
27 Firing motor
28 Firing solenoid
29 Cross-connecting firing shaft
30 Train lag meter
31 Elevation lag meter
32 Firing pedal shaft
33 Firing switch
34 Local power joystick control
35 Elevation power motor

John Roberts

37mm (1.457in) guns

These included single-shot one pounders dating from the 1890s, still used as subcalibre guns and as the armament of some minor vessels. There were also the 1pdr Mk 16 used as an AA gun by the Marines, and various Army 37mm. The former was a 56-calibre water-cooled automatic firing a 1.25lb (*0.567kg*) shell at 3000f/s (*914m/s*), and the most interesting of the latter was the M9 removed from P39 Airacobra aircraft, and mounted in motor torpedo boats on adapted 3pdr (*47mm*) mountings. In its aircraft form this gun was 104in (*2642mm*) long, weighed 365lb (*166kg*) and fired a 1.34lb (*0.608kg*) projectile at 2900f/s (*884m/s*). There was a 30-round magazine and rate of fire is given as 125 per minute with a maximum range of 8875yd (*8115m*).

1.1in (27.9mm) Mark 1/1

Gun Data for Mark 1/1

Bore	1.10in	27.94mm	
Weight of barrel	108lb	49kg	
Length oa	119.58in	3037.3mm	
Length bore	82.0in	2082.8mm	74.55cal
Length chamber	*c*7.1in	*c*180mm	
Volume chamber	10.5in^3	0.172dm^3	
Weight projectile	*c*917lb	0.416kg	
Propellant charge	0.265lb NC	0.120kg NC	
Muzzle velocity	2700f/s	823m/s	
Range	7400yd/40° 53′/2600f/s	6770m/40° 53′/792m/s	
Ceiling	19,000ft/90°/2600f/s	5790m/90°/792m/s	

This 75-calibre recoil-operated water cooled automatic was for a time the standard USN close range AA weapon until superseded by the Bofors. Production orders had been placed with the Naval Gun Factory in 1934, but there were teething troubles and it was not available in quantity until 1940. It was always in quadruple mountings and in 1941-42 the normal allocation was four mountings in the larger modern ships though *Lexington* had 12, and one or two in some destroyers. It was retained in a few smaller ships until 1945, when it was ordered to be scrapped. The barrel was chromium plated internally and externally, the former 0.0005in (*0.013mm*) deep for 74.5in (*1892mm*) from the muzzle. The ammunition was fed from eight-round clips and the maximum rate of fire per gun was 150 per minute. The complete round weighed about 1.9lb (*862gm*). Tracer burnt for *c*3000yd (*2750m*) and shells were not self destructing. Mk 1/0 differed in having no muzzle flash hider and Mk 2/0 was an experimental gas operated conversion.

Elevation was +110° to -15°, and in the earlier mountings traversing to 30° on either side of the mounting centreline in the plane formed by guns and trunnions was allowed, though this feature was later abandoned. The various powered Mk 2 mountings weighed from 4.7-6.25 tons (*4.78-6.35t*) and maximum elevating and training speeds were 24° and 30°/sec. RPC was fitted and elevating and training motors were 3HP, except that the latter was 5HP in Mk 2/3, which retained traversing. Hydraulic drive gear was not used.

1.1in AA guns in quadruple mounting.
USN

1.1in in quadruple mounting with 20mm Oerlikons beyond.
USN

The adoption of this famous 70-calibre air cooled blow-back gun by the USN was approved in November 1940 after the British had decided in June to establish manufacture in the USA subject to the consent of the latter. The first US made gun was test-fired in June 1941 and and 379 were delivered up to the US entry into the war. It was mounted in almost every USN ship and, prior to the supply of the Bofors in quantity, had a very high reputation as a free-swinging gun. The heavier, power operated Bofors showed its superiority once it was generally available, and against kamikazes the Oerlikon shell was too small and its effective range too low to disintegrate the target in time. The well known saying, 'When the 20mm opens fire it's time to hit the deck', expressed a very general opinion.

In spite of this the numbers of Oerlikons remained very high in 1945. Figures indicate that the battleship *Washington* had 63 singles, eight twins and one quad, totalling 83 guns, and the carrier *Shangri La* seven singles and 53 twins for 113 guns. Average figures for the ten modern battleships were 55 guns and for the *Essex* class carriers 64.

US guns were generally very similar to British and from the users' point of view Mks 2/0 and 4/0 were identical to the RN Mk II. The American Marks were:

Mk 1/0. Developed from original Swiss.

Mk 2/0. Like 1/0 but cooling ribs and 2 locking slots.

Mk 3/0. Like 2/0 but some without cooling ribs and 1 locking slot.

Mk 4/0. Like 2/0 but different manufacturing tolerances when converted from metric to British units.

Mk 4/1. Like 4/0 but parkerised externally; adapter for modified lower double-loading stop plunger.

Mk 4/2. Like 4/1 but no cooling ribs and no provision for modified stop plunger.

Mk 4/3. Experimental for submarines; like 4/2 with chromium plated bore.

Mk 4/4. Like 4/2 but fluted chamber to allow ungreased brass cartridge cases; steel cases must be greased.

The most common appear to have been Mk 4/0 and 4/1. Rate of fire is given as about 450rpm, and the complete round weighed about 8.5oz (*241gm*). HE with and without tracer, HE incendiary and AP tracer were available.

Of the single mountings Mks 2 and 4 had the trunnion height adjustable by handwheel, gearing and screw jack, while in Mk 6 it was adjusted hydraulically by 3 pedals. Mks 5, mostly for Britain and 10 had fixed trunnion

20mm (0.7874in) Oerlikon

Gun Data (where different from details given under Great Britain)

Length rifling	48.728-49.061in	1237.69-1246.15mm
Weight projectile	0.2714lb	0.1231kg
Propellant charge	0.0631lb NC tube	0.0286kg NC tube
Muzzle velocity	2740-2770f/s	835-844m/s
Working pressure	19.6 tons/in^2	3090kg/cm^2

Weights and Elevation Data

	Approx wt with shield		**Elevation**
	lb	**kg**	
Mks 2 and 4	1695	769	+87° to -5° (+90° to -5° in Mk 4/3)
Mk 5	1540	699	+87° to -5°
Mk 6	1691	767	+90° to -15°
Mk 10	950-1100	431-499	+90° to -15°

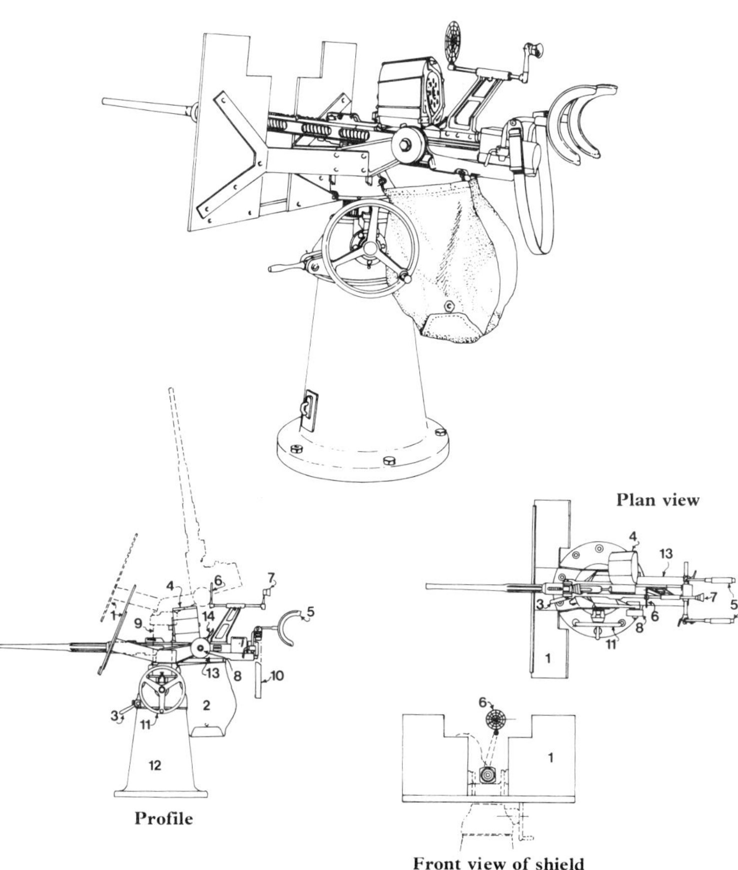

20mm Oerlikon single mount Mk 4, general view, left side, plan view and front view of shield.

1 Shield
2 Cartridge bag
3 Clamping lever
4 Magazine
5 Shoulder rests
6 Fore sight
7 Back sight
8 Elevation counterbalance spring case
9 Column
10 Back strap
11 Column raising handwheel
12 Pedestal
13 Cradle
14 Magazine catch

John Roberts

20mm Oerlikon quadruple Mk 15 power worked mounting. Magazine feed is retained in this.
USN

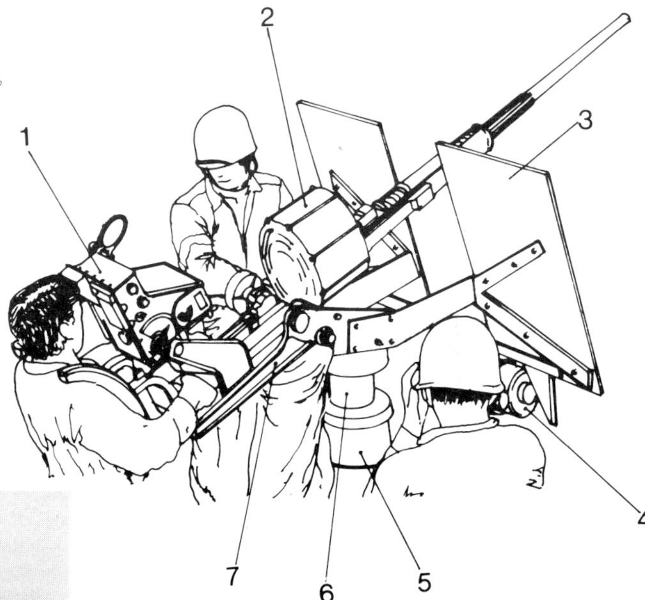

20mm Oerlikon with Mk 14 gyro sight, general view, with crew.

1 Mk 14 gun sight
2 Magazine
3 Shield
4 Power unit
5 Pedestal
6 Raising column
7 Cradle

CPL

height with cast iron and fabricated steel pedestals respectively. All were manually operated with free swinging. Shields 0.5in (*13mm*) thick and weighing 250lb (*113kg*) were fitted except to some Mk 5 and 10 mountings. There were many modifications running to at least 45 in Mk 10, but these are not further noted except that Mk 5/4 was a wet mounting.

The first twin mounting was completed in September 1944, and the most usual in service appears to have been Mk 24/5. This was manually operated and free swinging, some having a shield as in single mountings. Trunnion height was fixed and the pedestal fabricated steel. The gun axes were 6.5in (*165mm*) apart, and elevation +90° to -15°. The approximate weight with shield was only 1400lb (*635kg*).

Other mountings included the power worked quadruple Mk 15, originally intended for motor torpedo boats, and then fitted in *Massachusetts* and *Maryland*, followed by *Washington*, *Colorado* and *West Virginia*. Each ship had only one, and its purpose would seem to have been for firing at the less rugged suicide devices.

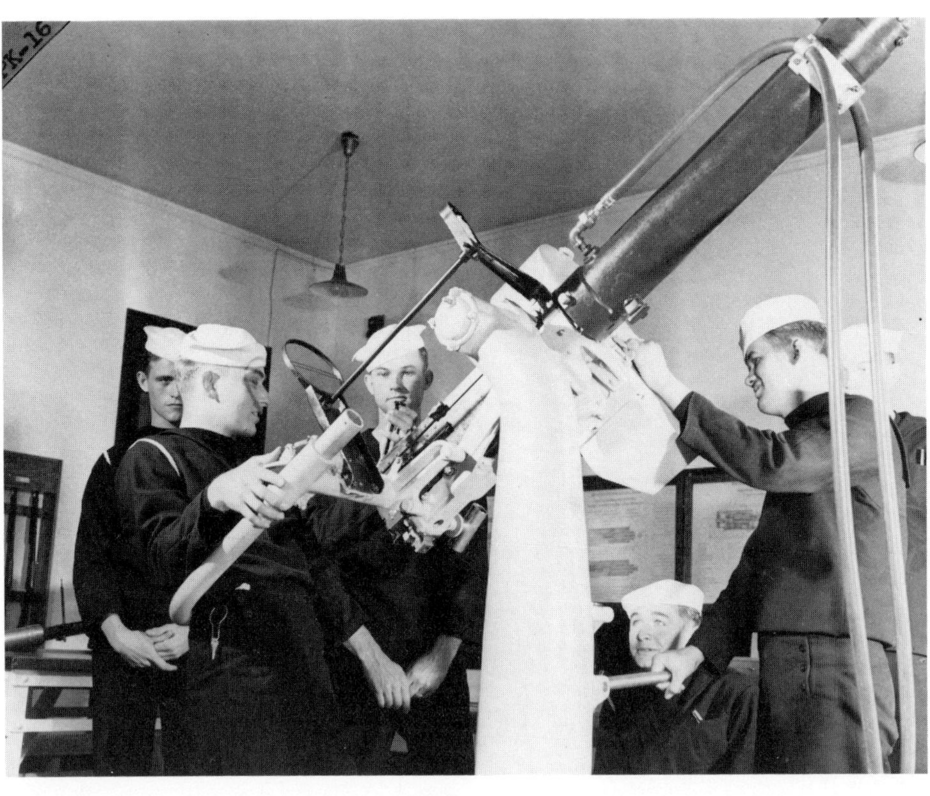

0.50in Browning M2 water cooled machine gun *c*1940. *USN*

This recoil operated machine gun with 110-round metal link belt, was the standard light close range AA weapon until the Oerlikon began to enter service in 1941. It was usually in single Mk 3 mountings and at one time *Lexington* and *Saratoga* had 48 each, apparently more than in any other ship. Late in the war the standard Army quadruple mounting was adapted as Mk 31 and six were installed in the *Essex* class carriers *Wasp* and *Lexington* and four in the escort carrier *Cape Gloucester* in place of Oerlikons. It is difficult to understand the reasoning behind this.

Rate of fire was 550-700 per minute and ammunition comprised AP, ball, incendiary and tracer, none having any bursting charge. Tracer burnt to 1600yd (*1460m*) maximum. The round weighed up to 0.255lb (*0.116kg*) and was 5.45in (*138.4mm*) maximum in length. Unlike aircraft versions the bore was not chromium plated. An air cooled Heavy-Barrel version differed from the data in the table in having a weight 84lb (*38.1kg*), barrel weight 27.4lb (*12.43kg*) and overall length 65.125in (*1654mm*). Rate of fire was 450-500rpm and unlike other versions, single shots could be fired.

In some craft particularly motor torpedo boats, aircraft type air cooled guns were twin mounted on Scarff rings. These guns weighed 61lb (*27.7kg*) and the barrels were 9in (*229mm*) shorter and weighed 9.81lb (*4.45kg*). Ammunition was as in the heavier guns and MV 2840f/s (*866m/s*). In aircraft at least the rate of fire was 750-850rpm.

0.50in (12.7mm) Browning M2 water cooled

Gun Data

Bore	0.50in	12.7mm	
Weight of gun	100.5lb (with water 121)	45.6kg (with water 54.9)	
Weight of barrel	15.2lb	6.89kg	
Length oa	66in	1676mm	
Length bore	45.0in	1143mm	90.0cal
Length chamber	2.78in	70.6mm	
Volume chamber	1.5in^3	24.6cm^3	
Weight projectile	1.6oz	45.4grams	
Propellant charge	0.54oz NC tube	15.3gm NC tube	
Muzzle velocity	2930f/s	893m/s	
Range	7400yd	6770m	
Ceiling	*c*15,000ft	4570m	

0.30in (7.62mm) machine guns

The AA capabilities of these were minimal, but they were carried by many submarines and other vessels, particularly in the earlier part of the war as emergency armament in merchant ships and auxiliaries. The guns included water and air cooled recoil operated Browning with belt feed, air cooled gas operated Lewis with magazine feed and air cooled gas operated Marlin with belt feed. Typical bullet weight was 151 grains (*9.8gm*) and MV 2700-2800f/s (*823-853m/s*). Rates of fire were usually 400-700rpm.

US NAVAL GUNS SUPPLIED TO BRITAIN

Although many of these were supplied as the armament of Lend-Lease ships, this was by no means always the case. Nothing over 5in (*127mm*) was delivered, but most calibres between that and 0.30in (*7.62mm*) were represented. Marks of guns and mountings are usually recorded but not modifications as a rule.

5in (127mm) 51-calibre Mark 8

This type of gun was not new to the British navy as three Bethlehem guns were mounted in the Scapa Flow defences during the First World War and a further 150 of an improved pattern were ordered for DAMS in 1918 but cancelled. The British designations of these were BL Mk VI and Mk VII. In World War II, 22 guns were supplied with the ten former Coast Guard cutters in mid 1941, but later mostly replaced by 4in (*102mm*) QF Mk V and other AA guns. Some of the 5in (*127mm*) went to New Zealand for coast defence.

Where given, the mod is Mk 8/7 but the two guns originally in *Sennen* were listed as Mk 7. Mountings were apparently all Mk 15.

5in (127mm) 38-calibre Mark 12

It seems that if supplies had been sufficient, much greater use would have been made of this gun, as is shown by the 1944 proposal to mount six twins in *Nelson*. In the event, only the light cruiser *Delhi*, of British-built ships, had the 5in/38 with five single mountings. Of Lend-Lease ships, the 23 escort carriers of the *Ameer* class each had two single mountings and the repair ships *Assistance* and *Diligence* one. The total number of guns is given as the 53 needed by the above, with a highest total of 24 in the loose-barrel summary as spares.

Guns were Mk 12/1 but there is some doubt over mountings. Those in *Delhi* were listed as Mk 30 without any mod number, which may indicate Mk 30/0, while the escort carriers mostly had Mk 37/2, but *Ameer, Atheling, Begum, Emperor, Empress, Slinger* and *Trumpeter* had Mk 30/50, and *Shah* was recorded with one Mk 37/2 and one Mk 35/2, the latter not found in the US January 1945 catalogue of mountings. This work lists Mk 30/80 as the escort carrier mounting, and Mks 30/50 and 37/2 were similar, but with 85° elevation instead of 27°, though the flight-deck edge would restrict AA capability.

4in Mk 9 guns in shielded Mk 12 P mountings on board lend-lease flush-decker DD in 1940.
CPL

4in (101.6mm) 50-calibre Mark 9

This type was, again, not new to the British Navy, three Bethlehem guns being mounted at Scapa Flow during the First World War and 150 of an improved pattern ordered in 1918 for DAMS but cancelled. These were known as QF Mk VIII and XIII. In the Second World War the US 4in Mk 9 was carried by the 50 destroyers, 6 'S' class submarines and first 15 escort carriers supplied under Lend-Lease, while 50 spare guns and 137 for DEMS were also sent, giving a total to the British Empire of 424 with, in addition, 60 for Dutch DEMS and 21 for Norwegian. Later in the war most of the destroyers retained only one 4in (*101.6mm*) and in four of the escort carriers the guns were replaced by 4in QF Mk V.

The US gun had a bad reputation for coppering and was also liable to steel choke. Vickers were asked in 1941 to prepare liner designs for US ammunition and for that used by the QF Mk XVI*, but the latter gave too-high pressures. A British round with 32lb (*14.5kg*) 6 crh shell and 14.4lb (*6.53kg*) NF/S 198-054 charge was designed, and was to give 14,194yd (*12,979m*) at 20° and 2760f/s (*841m/s*) but it is doubtful if it entered service.

As far as the surviving records show, the most common gun was Mk 9/5 and mounting Mk 12/1.

3in (76.2mm) 50-calibre HA Marks 10, 20, 21, 22

The two latest Marks were in many Lend-Lease ships, including all 'Captain' and 'Colony' class frigates, 'Kil' class corvettes and *Gazelle* class fleet mine-sweepers. Mk 20 was generally limited to minor warships, though the small Dutch cruiser *Tromp* had four, while Mk 10 was in the former Coast Guard cutters and three of the 50 destroyers. There were few Mk 10 in DEMS but the others were more common and were also to be found in the fast Cunard liners *Queen Mary, Queen Elizabeth* and *Aquitania*.

Originally 1000 were to be supplied by the USN, but the highest total in the summaries is 732 with, in addition, 128 spare barrels for Mks 21 and 22. The gun registers, which are usually the most reliable source, give 558 for Mks 21 and 22 combined, 64 Mk 20, and 49 Mk 10, a total of 671. It should be noted that by the end of 1942 sufficient 12pdrs (*76.2mm*) were available, and requirements for the 3in/50 were only for US built ships in spite of the low performance of the 12pdr. A British round with 16lb (*7.26kg*) or 17lb (*7.71kg*) 6crh shell and 4.91lb (*2.23kg*) NF/S 164-048 charge for a muzzle velocity of about 2400f/s (*732m/s*) was designed, but it is doubtful if it was issued.

Mountings were Mks 11, 20 and 22, as in the USN.

3in (72.6mm) 50-calibre LA Marks 2, 3, 5, 6

The screw breech variety of the above was used in the First World War, Bethlehem supplying 12 known as 3in/8cwt and 6 known as 3in/17cwt. They were mostly used in armed yachts. In the Second World War they were used in DEMS, apart from the three 'R' class submarines supplied under Lend-Lease, which apparently had Mk 3 guns. Register totals are 14 for the low velocity Mk 2, 337 for Mk 3, 4 for Mk 5 and 3 for Mk 6. Mountings were Mk 4 with a few Mk 7.

3in (76.2mm) 23.5-calibre Marks 4, 14

There is only one record of Mk 4, a Bethlehem landing gun, removed from a DEMS at Sydney, but Mk 14 was originally in 47 of the Lend-Lease destroyers and four of the Coast Guard cutters. On removal, some were transferred to DEMS. The summaries give a highest total of 81 guns, but the Register has 66. All Mk 14 guns were in the Mk 14 HA mounting.

6pdr (57mm)

Two Mk 3/1, a retubed Mk 3/0, and three Mk 9 are recorded in DEMS.

40mm Bofors and smaller guns

American versions of these mounted in British ships, are noted in the section dealing with the Royal Navy.

TORPEDOES

American torpedoes were found to be highly unsatisfactory in the earlier part of World War II, following insufficient testing, particularly with live warheads. Much of this was due to peacetime economies, but excessive secrecy over the details of the magnetic exploder and far too little liaison between the Naval Torpedo Station and the fleet were also to blame – as also the reluctance of the Bureau of Ordnance to accept good evidence of defects. Thus it was not officially announced until August 1942 that the standard Mk 14 submarine torpedo ran 10ft (*3m*) below its depth setting, and this was as a result of tests in June and July by Southwest Pacific Command in Australia.

The defects of the magnetic exploder are described below. It was ordered to be deactivated in the Pacific Fleet in June 1943, while the associated contact exploder which was highly unreliable at normal impact, was put right in September 1943 as a result of work at Pearl Harbor. In view of the above it is not surprising that such incidents occurred as the destroyers *Mustin* and *Anderson* failing to scuttle the carrier *Hornet* with a total of 16 torpedoes in October 1942 after the Battle of the Santa Cruz Islands, and the submarine *Tinosa* failing to sink the tanker *Tonan Maru No 3* in July 1943 with a total of 15.

In the latter part of the war matters were much improved and in addition to surface ship, submarine and airborne wet-heaters, electric torpedoes were developed and produced in quantity and homing torpedoes entered service with success, while development items included workable hydrogen peroxide weapons as well as a considerable number of improved homers.

Production in peacetime had been at the Naval Torpedo Station, Rhode Island, who were also responsible for design, and attempts to reopen the First World War Station at Alexandria, Virginia, were frustrated by the activities of certain politicians for 11 years until July 1941. In addition to these two, Bliss and the Pontiac Division of General Motors made torpedoes during the war and Westinghouse were responsible for the electric Mk 18 torpedo. At the outbreak of war in December 1941 production was as low as 60 per month with reserve stocks of modern torpedoes at a few hundreds. The bombing of the Cavite Navy Yard on 10 December 1941 destroyed 233 torpedoes. However, by the end of 1942, production had overtaken expenditure with 2382 against 2010 and in 1943 the production crisis was over, though difficulties of distribution meant that the obsolescent torpedoes brought back into service had not yet disappeared. Altogether US submarines fired 14,748 torpedoes against Japanese ships, while aircraft apparently dropped 1287.

Unlike other Navies the United States had standardised on turbine propulsion as long before as November 1905. Considerable development occurred but the alcohol-fuelled freshwater wet-heater system kept inlet temperatures fairly low, 840°F (*449°C*) and 395lb/in^2 (*27.8kg/cm^2*) in the airborne Mk 13 with the turbine at 11,000 rpm, and spectacular HP/weight or consumption figures were not aimed at. The turbine was of two-stage impulse type with contra-rotating rotors, no stator and three nozzles. More energetic fuel systems were considered and a torpedo using pure oxygen instead of air was run in 1931, but it seems that difficulties of oxygen supply to ships stopped this development. Hydrogen peroxide, known as 'Navol', originally at 50% strength, was investigated in the 1930s and development of submarine and destroyer torpedoes was well under way in 1940–41. It then lapsed for three years and although both torpedoes eventually reached limited production, neither was used in action.

Newport had worked intermittently on an electric torpedo between the World Wars but it was not until a captured German G7e was obtained from the RN in 1941 that interest was aroused. The contract for the US version, known as Mk 18, was assigned to Westinghouse, but Newport personnel, who were developing their own electric Mk 20, were not initially cooperative and the Mk 18 did not come into service until September 1943. There were a number of teething troubles, and a lack of purging of hydrogen evolved on standing resulted in some fires, one in *Flying Fish* causing the Torpex in the warhead to melt and run out. The Mk 18 became very popular with submarine commanders and comprised 30% of all torpedoes fired in 1944 and 65% of those in the last six months of the war. Post-war studies, however, revealed that few Japanese merchant ships spotted torpedo tracks, and that the low speed of the Mk 18 resulted in wet-heater torpedoes having a 17% better hit rate against merchant ships and 250% better against escorts.

The airborne Mk 13 and the various homing torpedoes are considered under the individual descriptions.

Warheads originally had TNT explosive charges but Torpex replaced this from 1943. Work on magnetic exploders was proposed in 1922 and progressed rapidly so that in May 1926 the old submarine *L 8* was destroyed in a test. The new dual Mk 6 exploder was developed at Newport and manufactured by General Electric, but secrecy was obsessive, the complete exploder was never tested against a live target and was stored until issued with the minimum of information in the summer of 1941. Only commanders and torpedo officers were told about the details. The torpedo was intended to run 10ft (*3m*) below a battleship and half that distance below smaller vessels. As with other magnetic exploders it was found to premature from sudden movements of the torpedo in the earth's field and it could also function short of the target from the horizontal complonent of the latter's field. The inertia impact part of the Mk 6 was so designed that at normal impact frictional forces on the firing pin were excessive, and it struck too weakly though functioning at oblique impact.

There was also an anti-countermining device which prevented functioning at a pressure greater than 50ft (*15m*) of water. Erratic behaviour of this was reported in April 1942 and inactivation at discretion authorised in June 1942.

The varied armament of *PT131* preparing for the Battle of Surigao Strait in October 1944. A single 20mm Oerlikon, 0.30in MGs, 22.4in Mk 13 torpedoes and Mk 8 rocket launchers are shown with an Army mortar on the bridge. Part of an Army 37mm can be seen to the right.
USN

OBSOLESCENT TORPEDOES STILL IN USE

Mark 7 18in (45cm, 17.7in)

A Bliss-Leavitt torpedo first issued in 1912 when it introduced wet heaters to the USN. It was still used by 'O' and 'R' class submarines. Length 17ft 0in (*5182mm*), weight 1628lb (*738kg*), explosive charge 326lb (*148kg*) TNT, range 6000yd (*5500m*)/35kts.

Mark 8 21in (53.3cm)

This was another Bliss-Leavitt torpedo and the first USN long 21in for destroyers. It was first at sea in 1914 and improved modifications were carried by old destroyers and MTBs in the war. Length 21ft 4.3in (*6510m*), weight 3050lb (*1383kg*), explosive charge 466lb (*211kg*) TNT, range 16,000yd (*14,600m*)/26kts. A higher speed setting was presumably available for MTBs. Figures of 380lb (*172kg*) TNT and 14,000yd (*12,800m*)/27kts are given for torpedoes supplied to Britain.

Mark 9 21in (53.3cm)

A short torpedo originally for the submerged TT of battleships and issued to 'S' class submarines in the war emergency. It was the last Bliss-Leavitt torpedo. Length 16ft 5in (*5004m*), weight 2015lb (*914kg*), explosive charge 210lb (*95kg*), range 7000yd (*6400m*)/27 kts.

Mark 10 21in (53.3cm)

A torpedo for submarines developed by Bliss and the Newport Torpedo Station during the First World War. It was used by 'S' class submarines. Length 16ft 3in (*4953mm*), weight 2215lb (*1005kg*), explosive charge 497lb (*225kg*) TNT, range 3500yd (*3200m*)/36kts.

Earlier US destroyers had a heavy torpedo armament as shown by the four 21in triple TT in these flush-deckers.
USN

WET-HEATER TORPEDOES FOR DESTROYERS

Mark 11 21in (53.3cm)

The first torpedo developed entirely by the Newport Station and dating to 1926. It appears to have been of heavier construction than previous torpedoes. Length 22ft 7in (*6883mm*), weight 3511lb (*1593kg*), explosive charge 500lb (*227kg*) TNT, range 6000yd (*5500m*)/46kts, 10,000yd (*9150m*)/34kts, 15,000yd (*13,700m*)/27kts.

Mark 12 21in (53.3cm)

A modified Mk 11 differing principally in a reduction of 2kts in the high-speed setting to achieve greater reliability. Length and charge were unchanged, weight 3505lb (*1590kg*), high-speed range 7000yd (*6400m*)/44kts.

Mark 15 21in (53.3cm)

The successor to Mks 11 and 12 and dated to 1935. It was the standard USN destroyer torpedo during the war, and had a much heavier warhead than the earlier marks. Length 24ft 0in (*7315mm*), weight 3841lb (*1742kg*), explosive charge 825lb (*374kg*) Torpex, range 6000yd (*5500m*)/45kts, 10,000yd (*9150m*)/33.5kts, 15,000yd (*13,700m*)/26.5kts.

WET-HEATER TORPEDOES FOR SUBMARINES

Mk 14 was the standard USN thermal torpedo for submarines and was a development of Mk 10, the first version dated to 1931. As with the British Mk VIII, later modifications continued in service for many years after the war, until at least the late 1970s.

Mark 14 21in (53.3cm)

Length oa	20ft 6in	6248mm
Total weight	3280lb	1488kg
Weight air	256lb	116kg
Alcohol	28lb	12.7kg
Fresh water	83lb	37.6kg
Consumption expendables	19.5lb/HP/hr	8.85kg/HP/hr
Explosive charge	643lb Torpex	292kg Torpex
Range	4500yd/46kts	4100m/46kts
	9000yd/31kt	8200m/31kt

The 31kt setting was rarely used during the war.

Mark 23 21in (53.3cm)

Virtually Mk 14 without the 31kt setting. It differed in a weight of 3259lb (*1478kg*) and was in service 1943–46.

Top: 21in Mk 14 torpedo which, with the almost identical Mk 23, was the standard wet-heater torpedo for submarines during the war. *Centre:* 22.4in Mk 13 airborne wet-heater torpedo, also wartime standard.

USN

Bottom: 21in Mk 15/3 wet-heater torpedo, wartime standard for destroyers.

USN

AIRBORNE WET-HEATER TORPEDOES

The origins of this date back to the 1920s but development was interrupted. It differed from the airborne torpedoes of other navies, which were usually 18in - actually 17.7in (*45cm*) - in its large diameter and short length and also in its relatively low speed and long range. The Japanese, who salvaged a considerable number, were critical (*see* Japanese section), but the British later thought it a good torpedo, though it had originally been far from satisfactory. Postwar figures quote 514 hits from 1287 torpedoes, a percentage of 39.9. It was subsequently also used by MTBs with a simple side launcher.

Originally dropping conditions were 110kts at 50ft (*15m*) which explains, at least in part, the near annihilation of the US torpedo planes at Midway. Improvements were made in the box type detachable wooden air tails, and drag rings and 'pickle barrel' false heads allowed high speed drops at 1000ft (*300m*) from the attack on Truk in February 1944 onwards. At the end of the war air stabilisation and deceleration had improved sufficiently to permit drops at 410kts from 2400ft (*730m*).

Mark 13 22.4in (56.9cm)

Length oa	13ft 5in	4089mm
Total weight	2216lb	1005kg
Negative buoyancy	523lb	237kg
Weight air	130lb	59kg
Alcohol	17lb	7.7kg
Fresh water	48lb	22kg
HP 33kts	98	
Consumption expendables	17.3lb/HP/hr	7.85kg/HP/hr
Explosive charge	600lb Torpex	262kg
Range	6300yd/33.5kts	5760m/33.5kts

Early torpedoes in service weighed 1927lb (*874kg*) and had 401lb (*182kg*) TNT explosive charges.

Mark 25 22.4in (56.9cm)

An intended replacement for Mk 13 under development in 1945 but never mass produced on account of large postwar stocks. It differed from Mk 13 in weight 2306lb (*1046kg*), explosive charge 725lb (*329kg*) and range 2500yd (*2300m*)/40kts.

22.4in Mk 13 torpedo with false head and detachable air tail on CVL 30 *San Jacinto* at Leyte 25 October 1944. *USN*

ELECTRIC NON-HOMING TORPEDOES FOR SUBMARINES

Mark 18 21in (53.3cm)

This was the Westinghouse torpedo based on the German G7e. It had the advantage of being trackless and of needing only *c*70% of the labour required to produce a wet-heater torpedo, but though many had been fired in the war, its low performance led to it being discarded in 1950 in favour of Mk 14 and the peroxide Mk 16. Mk 18 was not a very quiet torpedo, and teething troubles included lack of hydrogen purging, as noted previously, cold batteries, weak tail vanes and warping of the thin battery compartment shell. Length 20ft 5in (*6223mm*) weight 3154lb (*1431kg*), explosive charge 575lb (*261kg*) Torpex, range 4000yd (*3650m*)/29kts. A proposed anti-ship active homing version was never tested.

Mark 19 21in/53.3cm

An improved Mk 18 under development in 1945 but abandoned for Mk 26. It had the same range as Mk 18 but was 1in (*25mm*) longer, weighed 86lb (*39kg*) more and had an 800lb (*363kg*) Torpex explosive charge.

Mark 20 21in (53.3cm)

This was a Newport Torpedo Station design and was still under development in 1945. Length 20ft 6in (*6248mm*), weight 3100lb (*1406kg*), explosive charge 500lb (*227kg*) Torpex, range 3500yd (*3200m*)/33kts. It could be made much quieter than Mk 18, and a passive homing version was apparently ready in October 1945. A new light weight high-speed electric motor gave it a top speed of 39kts, and it could acquire a destroyer target at 200yd (*180m*) and 37kts. It is not known why it was not adopted post war, presumably the drastic change of priorities was responsible.

Mark 26 21in (53.3cm)

Under development in 1945 and dating from 1944, this was passed over in favour of the peroxide Mk 16. Length 20ft 6in (*6248mm*), weight 3200lb (*1451kg*), explosive charge 900lb (*408kg*) Torpex, range 6000yd (*5500m*)/40kts. It is not known how this high performance for an electric torpedo of that date was attained or whether it could in fact regularly achieve it.

HYDROGEN PEROXIDE TORPEDOES

A high-performance but very expensive torpedo for submarines. It was the descendent of a peroxide version of Mk 14, of which production had begun in 1940, but a new hydrogen peroxide plant was needed and the project was postponed until 1943. Mk 16 dated from 1944 and a limited number were made in 1945 but it was never used during the war, though it remained in service for a further 30 years.

Mark 16 21in (53.3cm)

Data Mark 16 Mod 3

Length	**20ft 6in**	6248mm
Total weight	4000lb	1814kg
Negative buoyancy	1260lb	572kg
Hydrogen peroxide	390lb	177kg
HP 46kts	*c*350	
Explosive charge	943lb Torpex	428kg
Range	13,700yd/46kts	12500m/46kts

Mark 16 Mod 1 weighed 3922lb (*1779kg*), explosive charge 920lb (*417kg*), range 11,000yd (*10,000m*)/46kts.

Mk 17/1 21in hydrogen peroxide torpedo, in limited service post war.
USN

Mark 17 21in (53.3cm)

A long range edition of Mk 16 for destroyers. Development was halted in 1941 but started again in 1944 in view of the Japanese 'long lance'. Mk 17 was never used in the war but a limited number were made and remained in service until 1950. Length 24ft 0in (*7315mm*), weight 4600lb (*2087kg*), explosive charge 880lb (*399kg*) Torpex, range 18,000yd (*16,500m*)/46kts.

HOMING TORPEDOES FOR SURFACE SHIPS AND SUBMARINES

Homing versions of Mks 18 and 20, which were not allocated a new mark, are noted under the parent non-homing torpedoes.

Mark 22 21in (53.3cm)

A Bell/Westinghouse electric homing torpedo for the attack of surface ships. Work was started in 1944 but discontinued in the following year in favour of Mk 35. Length 20ft 6in (*6248mm*), weight 3060lb (*1388kg*), explosive charge 500lb (*227kg*) Torpex, range 4000yd (*3660m*)/29kts.

Mark 27 19in (48.3cm)

A development of the airborne Mk 24 for submarines and fitted with 21in (*53.3cm*) guide rails to suit torpedo tubes. It was a passive homer intended for self-defence against escorts and, though slow and equipped with a small explosive charge, achieved considerable success in 1944-45, 106 being fired for 33 hits, of which 24 were fatal. It was used only against the Japanese. Length 7ft 6in (*2286mm*), weight 720lb (*327kg*), explosive charge 95lb (*43kg*) Torpex, range 5000yd (*4570m*)/12kts.

The larger 15.9kt Mk 27 Mod 4 was in service from 1946 to 1960.

Mark 28 21in (53.3cm)

A passive homer developed from Mk 18 and intended for submarine attack on ships. The USN considered motor and gear noises the most troublesome, unlike the Germans who regarded propeller noise the worst problem. As previously noted, Mk 18 was not a very quiet torpedo and Mk 28 had only one propellor, the tail gearing being eliminated. There were four hydrophones on the curved part of the nose. The project apparently dated to early 1943 and Mk 28 was ready for combat tests in 1945, making 5 hits from 16 fired. It was in production 1944-52, with 1750 made, and remained in service until 1960. Length 20ft 6in (*6248mm*), weight 2800lb (*1270kg*), explosive charge 585lb (*265kg*) Torpex, range 4000yd (*3660m*)/19.6kts.

Mark 29 21in (53.3cm)

Another passive homer developed from Mk 18 with a contra-rotating motor directly driving the propellors. It could operate with or without homing and was apparently not very successful, as redesign was called for in 1945 when it was still under development. Length 20ft 6in (*6248mm*), weight 3200lb (*1451kg*), explosive charge 550lb (*249kg*) Torpex, range 4000yd (*3660m*)/25kts, 12,000yd (*11,000m*)/21kts.

Mark 30 21in (53.3cm)

A wake following project of 1944-46. Length 20ft 6in (*6248mm*), explosive charge 600lb (*272kg*) Torpex, range 4000yd (*3660m*)/29kts.

There was also a Mark 30 mine, actually a small, surface ship-launched torpedo, intended as an alternative to the airborne Mk 24 mine or torpedo. It was originated by Brush Development in 1942 but cancelled. Details are given as diameter 10in (*25.4cm*), length 8ft 0in (*2438mm*), weight 265lb (*120kg*), explosive charge 50lb (*23kg*), range 3000yd (*2740m*)/12kts.

Mark 31 21in (53.3cm)

A further passive homing development of Mk 18 with acquisition on a 15kt destroyer at 200yd (*180m*) at 28kts. It was apparently not very satisfactory with greater self noise at 28kts than the homing version of Mk 20 had at 37kts. Redesign was needed in 1945 during development. Length 20ft 6in (*6248mm*), weight 2800lb (*1270kg*), explosive charge 500lb (*227kg*) Torpex, range 4000yd (*3660m*)/28kts, 12,000yd (*11,000m*)/20kts.

Mark 32 19in (48.3cm)

This, originally known as the Mk 32 mine, was the first USN active homing torpedo and was for use by surface ships against submarines. The project dated from 1942, and the Mk 32 was to steer downwards at a small fixed angle in a tight circle. It was thought to be fast enough to attack 'slow' submarines down to 400ft (*120m*), but could not deal with Type XXI U boats. The torpedo had fins 25.4in (*64.5cm*) diameter so that it had to be launched over the side, but it was also envisaged as a possible airborne weapon. Running time was 24min. Tests in 1944 unfortunately showed that within 50ft (*15m*) of the target there was insufficient time for the torpedo to receive its own echoes and it could turn away before hitting. It was however put into production before circuit modifications had been made, but only ten were completed before work was stopped in 1945, resuming six years later when about 330 were made. It remained in service until 1955. Length 6ft 11in (*2108mm*), weight 700lb (*318kg*), explosive charge 107lb (*49kg*) Torpex, range 9600yd (*8800m*)/12kts.

Mark 33 21in (53.3cm)

A passive homer, originally the Mk 33 mine, intended for use by submarines or aircraft against surface ships or submarines. It was the first torpedo to have a cast aluminium alloy shell and was tested in 1943–46, some of its features being used in the Mk 35 of the immediate postwar years. Length 13ft 0in (*3962mm*), weight 1795lb (*814kg*), explosive charge 550lb (*249kg*) Torpex, range 5000yd (*4570m*)/18.5kts, 19,000yd (*17,400m*)/12.5kts.

AIRBORNE HOMING TORPEDOES

Mark 33 is noted under homing torpedoes for surface ships and submarines.

Mark 21 22.4in (56.9cm)

This was originally a 25kt electric anti-ship torpedo and successful dropping trials were carried out in 1943, but it was soon abandoned in favour of Mod 2 which was turbine powered unlike other US homing torpedoes of the period, and was in fact a passive homing version of Mk 13. The turbine was very noisy at homing frequencies, and work was due to be cancelled in the spring of 1944 when it was found that the use of Neoprene gaskets and rubber mountings gave adequate homing at 33kts. Few hits were however made in tests due to poor manoeuvrability in the final attack, which was caused by the shroud ring on the tail, and was not overcome until after the war, when 312 were made as the payload of the Petrel missile introduced in 1955. Length 13ft 5in (*4089mm*), weight 2130lb (*966kg*), explosive charge 350lb (*159kg*) Torpex, range 6000yd (*5500m*)/33.5kts.

Mark 24 19in (48.3cm)

This anti-submarine passive homer was originally known as the Mk 24 mine and also as 'Fido'. Work began in the autumn of 1941 and it was first used in summer 1943. It appears that 346 were dropped and 68 submarines sunk and 33 damaged. Of these figures the US totals were 142, 31, 15, the rest being mostly dropped by the British. The success rate was about three times that of airborne depth charges. Running time was 10min and the specified dropping conditions 125kts from 250ft (*76m*). Homing was by four crystal hydrophones round the body with simple steering towards the noise. It was normally used against submarines that had just dived or were schnorkelling. It would have been too slow for Type XXI U-boats, and could be avoided by going very deep. Its use was somewhat restricted by possible risk to own ships and by security troubles. It should be noted that its service debut antedated that of Zaunkönig though not that of the ineffective Falke. Length 7ft 0in (*2134mm*), weight 680lb (*308kg*), explosive charge 92lb (*42kg*) Torpex range 4000yd (*3660m*)/12kts.

Mark 34 19in (48.3cm)

Initially known as the Mk 44 mine, this was an improved Mk 24 with magnetostrictive hydrophones and two batteries connected in series or parallel to allow 30min search at 11kts and then 6–8min attack at 17kts. Diameter over the fins was 26.4in (*67.1cm*). It was developed in 1944–45 and was eventually in service from 1948 to 1958, about 4050 being made. Length 10ft 5in (*3175mm*), weight 1150lb (*522kg*), explosive charge 116lb (*53kg*) Torpex, range 3600yd (*3300m*)/17kts, 12,000yd (*11,000m*)/11kts.

ANTI-SUBMARINE WEAPONS

Measured by the relative numbers of German U-boats destroyed, aircraft played an even greater part than in the British anti-submarine forces. Allowing half for a shared sinking, US surface ships accounted for 45 submarines, shore-based aircraft for 54 and shipborne aircraft for 32 while in addition 40 were destroyed in bombing raids on yards and bases. In the Pacific, because of geographical and different operational conditions, matters were not the same and, of Japanese submarines, surface ships accounted for 60, shore based aircraft for 3½ and shipborne for 9½. The depth charge was still the basic surface ship weapon and the USN soon learnt that far greater numbers had to be used in a single attack than had been originally thought. Of ahead throwing weapons the British Hedgehog was adopted in quantity, but Squid, which the Royal Navy considered far superior, was not favoured.

The most advanced aircraft weapon, the successful Mk 24 torpedo or mine, has been described under torpedoes, and others included various anti-submarine bombs or airborne depth charges and also rockets. The retrobomb for use with magnetic anomaly detectors (MAD), which were effective only to 600ft (*180m*) range, had a rocket charge to compensate for the aircraft's forward motion, so that the bomb could be dropped exactly over the contact.

Depth charges, probably Mk 6, and K gun on *PC548* in 1942.
USN

DEPTH CHARGES

Mark 3

A First World War DC with fuzing to a greater depth than the similar Mk 2 which was a British type with US hydrostatic pistol. Total weight 420lb (*191kg*), charge 300lb (*136kg*), sinking speed 6f/s (*1.8m/s*), depth 50-300ft (*15-91m*).

Mark 4

A larger First World War DC, with sinking speed and depth as for Mk 3, but with total weight 745lb (*338kg*) and charge 600lb (*272kg*).

Mark 6

This was a redesigned Mk 3 and standard in the earlier part of the war. Weight and charge were as in Mk 3 but sinking speed 8f/s (*2.4m/s*) and depth 30-300ft (*9-91m*). A later version with lead weights had a sinking speed of about 12f/s (*3.7m/s*), and maximum depth was increased to 600ft (*183m*).

Mark 7

A redesigned Mk 4 and standard in the earlier part of the war. Total weight was 768lb (*348kg*), charge 600lb (*272kg*), sinking speed 9f/s (*2.7m/s*) and depth 30-300ft (*9-91m*) increased in Mod 1 (issued in August 1942) to 600ft (*183m*). Versions with lead weights had a sinking speed of about 13f/s (*4m/s*).

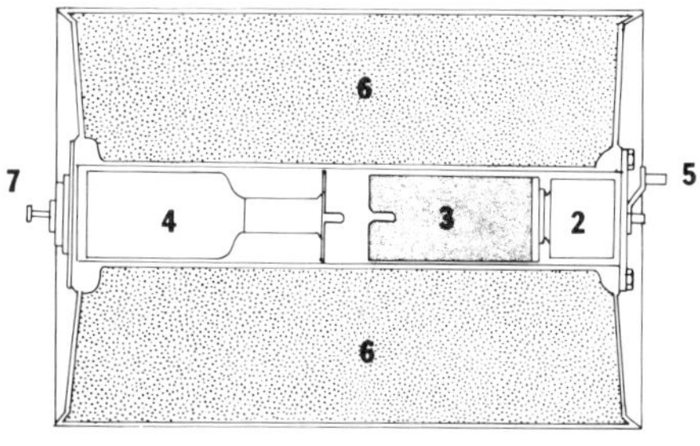

Mk 6 DC in section.

1 Shell
2 Booster extender
3 Booster
4 Pistol and detonator
5 Safety fork
6 Cast TNT
7 Inlet valve

Al Ross

Mark 8

This DC had a magnetic pistol and work on the project began in the autumn of 1941 with high hopes of its effectiveness. It was first issued in spring 1943 but was found to be unreliable and was not issued in quantity to Atlantic destroyer escorts until 1944, and was never available in very large numbers. Considerable maintenance, beyond peacetime navy capacities, was needed aboard ship, and the magnetic pistols were all deactivated at the end of the war. The magnetic pistol was armed at 35ft (*11m*) or 200ft (*61m*) and set to explode about 20-25ft (*6-7.5m*) from the submarine. There was also a hydrostatic pistol in case the DC did not go close enough to activate the magnetic pistol. The case was aluminium and there was a 150lb (*68kg*) lead weight. Total weight 525lb (*238kg*), charge 270lb (*122kg*), sinking speed 11.5f/s (*3.5m/s*), depth 50-500ft (*15-152m*).

Mark 9

This DC of 'teardrop' shape was standard in the latter part of the war. The tail fins were set to make it spin and thus stabilise the underwater trajectory, but in order to fit existing tracks the space for the explosive charge had to be reduced. Development began in early 1941 and it entered service in spring 1943. The charge was *c*200lb (*91kg*) Torpex and sinking speed originally 14.5f/s (*4.4m/s*) with the hydrostatic pistol having depth settings of 30-300 or 600ft (*9-91 or 183m*). In some later versions the depth limit was increased to 1000ft (*305m*) and sinking speed to 22.7f/s (*6.9m/s*) by means of a finer setting of the tail fins and added lead. Some were also strengthened because of stowage and launching damage.

Mark 10

A small DC with 25lb charge, of which limited numbers were issued in 1944 against frogmen, midget submarines and similar devices.

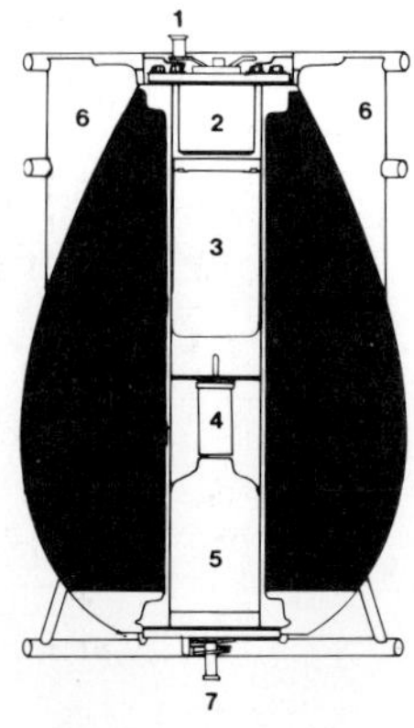

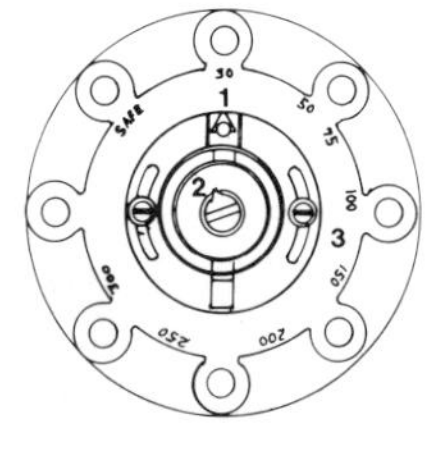

Mk 9 DC of teardrop form, standard in the latter part of the war. Internal and external views and depth setting index dials are shown.

1 Safety fork
2 Booster extender
3 Booster
4 Detonator
5 Pistol
6 Fins
7 Inlet valve cover

1 Index pointer
2 Deep firing pointer
3 Index plate

Stern rack for Mk 9 DCs. Side elevation, loading tray and release trap are shown.

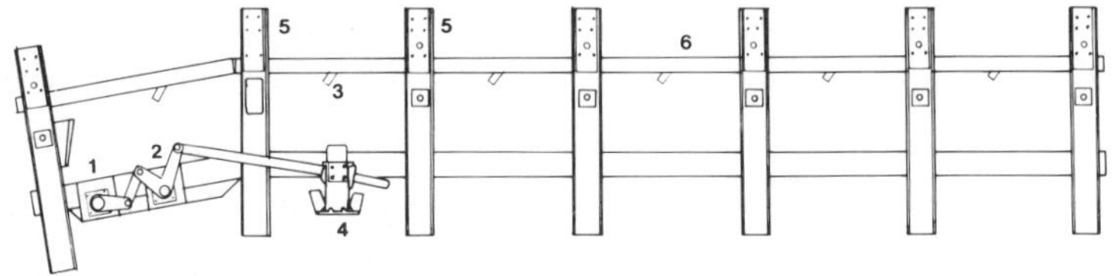

SIDE ELEVATION

1 Aft detent
2 Forward detent
3 Pawls
4 Detent release control
5 Stanchion
6 Track

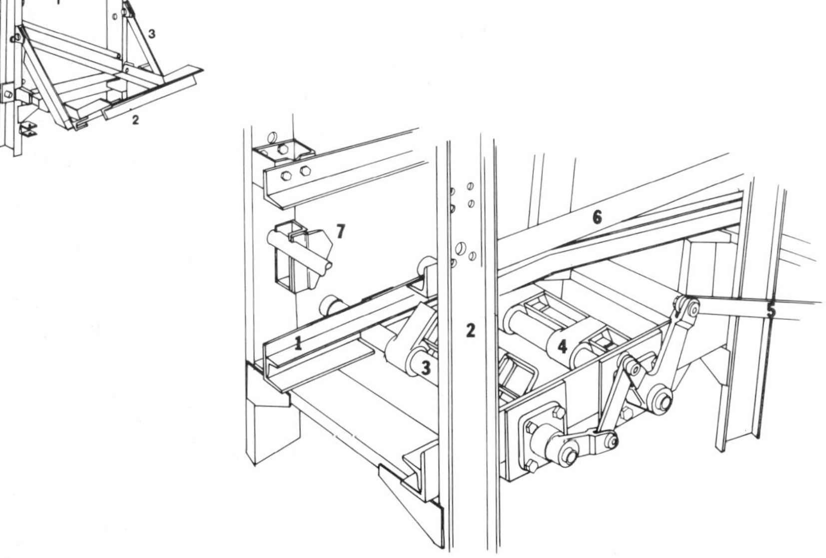

LOADING TRAY

1 Pawl
2 Loading tray
3 Angle support

Mk 9 RELEASE TRAP

1 Lower track
2 Stanchion
3 Aft detent
4 Forward detent
5 Lever to detent control
6 Upper track
7 Wiping plate

Al Ross

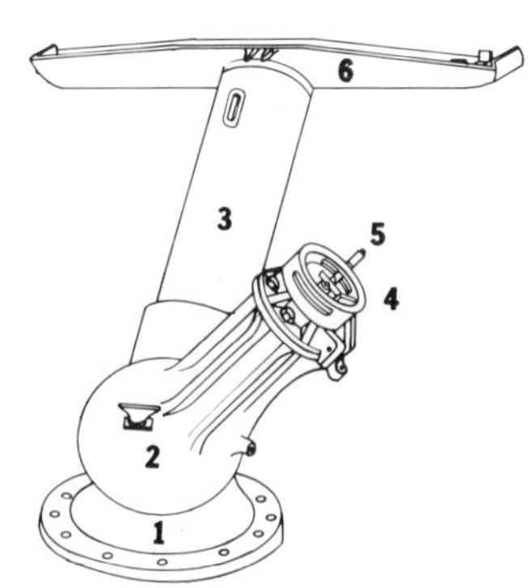

K gun or Mk 6 DC projector.

1 Base
2 Expansion chamber
3 Tube
4 Breech mechanism
5 Percussion igniter
6 Arbor with tray

Al Ross

Mark 11

A teardrop magnetic depth charge with total weight 480lb (*218kg*), charge 230lb (*104kg*) and, it is said, a sinking speed of 35f/s (*10.7m/s*). Probably not in service.

Mark 12

A fast-sinking torpedo-shaped DC with 45lb (*20kg*) charge and contact firing. Probably not in service.

Mark 14

An acoustic DC with an RCA Doppler acoustic pistol. The preliminary acoustic specification was determined in October 1943, and sea trials were held about a year later, but the war ended before it was issued to the fleet. It was apparently much more effective than the magnetic Mk 8. The DC was of teardrop shape with stable under-water trajectory. Total weight 340lb (*154kg*), charge 200lb (*91kg*), sinking speed 23f/s (*7.0m/s*).

Cluster Charge

Some use was apparently made of six Mousetrap warheads fired together from a K gun with dispersal in the air. (For Mousetrap and K gun, see below.)

Tracks and Projectors

The traditional way of launching DCs over the stern from tracks was the only available method for Mk 4 and 7 charges, but the smaller ones could be thrown by arbor type projectors. The Y gun (Projector Mk 1 with modified versions Mk 5 and 7) dated from the First World War and fired a DC simultaneously to port and starboard. It took up scarce centreline space and in mid 1941 the K gun (Projector Mk 6) was introduced. This could be mounted at the side as it fired a single DC. Originally loading davits were needed and the ready charges were stowed on their arbors, but later a roller rack holding three or four DCs was used with the arbors loaded separately. The K gun weighed 310lb (*142kg*) and fired a Mk 6, 9 or 14 DC to 60-150yd (*55-137m*) with time of flight 3.4-5.1sec. Typically four or six were mounted in destroyers with eight in destroyer escorts.

With six K guns the usual pattern was 9 charges or with eight, 14. There were normally two tracks at the stern as well, each with a maximum of 12 Mk 7 charges, though old and small ships had the smaller types. The total carried by destroyer escorts was generally at least 100. Both K guns and stern tracks made up the pattern. The Mk 6 depth charge was credited with a 21ft (*6.4m*) lethal radius and the Mk 7 with 29-35ft (*8.8-10.7m*) -which figures were probably too optimistic.

AIRBORNE ANTI-SUBMARINE BOMBS AND DEPTH CHARGES

Initially a standard Mk 6 DC was used with flight adapters but a number of special airborne weapons were soon in existence. The Mark numbers were allocated in the bomb series.

Mark 17

This was available in quantity by April 1942 and had a total weight of 325lb (*147kg*) with 234lb (*106kg*) TNT charge. Dimensions were 15in dia x 52.5in (*38 x 133.4cm*) and there was an impact nose fuze and a hydrostatic one athwartships which gave considerable trouble. The bomb had a round nose, which made it liable to ricochet, and a flat nosed attachment was added to cure this.

Mark 41

A successful flat-nosed version of Mk 17. Total weight 347lb (*157kg*), charge 227lb (*103kg*), dimensions 15 x 49.9in (*38 x 126.7cm*).

Mark 44

Similar to Mk 17 but with 249lb (*113kg*) Torpex charge. Total weight 330lb (*150kg*).

Mark 47

A flat-nosed version of Mk44 and similar to Mk 41, but with 252lb (*114kg*) Torpex charge. Total weight 355lb (*161kg*).

Mark 53

This was introduced late in the war and had the hydrostatic fuze located in the tail. Total weight 330lb (*150kg*), charge 225lb (*102kg*) TNT, dimensions 13.8 x 52.5in (*35 x 133.4cm*).

Mark 54

Similar to Mk 53 but with 250lb (*113kg*) Torpex charge and total weight 354lb (*161kg*). In service for over 30 years after the war.

Mk 17 anti-submarine bomb being removed from SOC-3 seaplane on CL41 *Philadelphia*, July 1942. *USN*

Mark 75

A redesigned Mk 53 with a thicker case and smooth interior to avoid prematures caused by cracks. Total weight 375lb (*170kg*). Doubtful if in service in the war.

There was also a series of larger bombs of which one at least was withdrawn because the explosion sometimes destroyed the aircraft using it.

Mark 29

Introduced in May 1942, this had a weak tail and unstable underwater trajectory. The round nose tended to cause ricochets, cured by a flat nose attachment. Total weight 650lb (*295kg*).

Mark 35

Details not known except total weight as above and dimensions 17.7 × 67.2in (*45 × 170.1cm*).

Mark 37

Dating from late 1942, this had the body of Mk 29 with a new tail. It was withdrawn as noted above. Total weight 658.5lb (*299kg*), dimensions as Mk 35.

Mark 38

This DC was shorter than the above at 61.1in (*155.2cm*) with total weight 629lb (*285kg*) and charge 425lb (*193kg*) TNT.

Mark 49

Dating from 1943, this had the dimensions of Mk 38 with total weight 668lb (*303kg*) and charge 472lb (*214kg*) Torpex.

Other A/S bombs were:

Mark 48

This had no athwartships hydrostatic fuze. Total weight 850lb (*386kg*), dimensions 18.6 × 68in (*47.2 × 172.7cm*).

Mark 71

A M64A1 GP bomb modified in 1944 to take an athwartships hydrostatic fuze. Total weight 525lb (*238kg*).

Retrobombs

These were modified Mousetrap 7in (*178mm*) diameter projectiles with a more powerful rocket motor.

The filling was originally TNT and later Torpex, and there were various modifications for firing speeds of 174-347kts. They were, at least originally, fired in groups of eight and were the first USN airborne rocket propelled weapon, undergoing service tests at the end of 1942. In the first half of 1944, two or three U-boats were sunk in the Straits of Gibraltar area in conjunction with surface ships, but there appears to be only one sinking due to MAD and retrobombs alone off Ushant in 1945. In all these Catalina flying boats of VP63 were responsible.

The Mk 24 torpedo or mine is described under Torpedoes, and other airborne A/S weapons under Rockets.

AHEAD-THROWING WEAPONS

Hedgehog

This British 24-spigot mortar was adopted by the USN and production began in late 1942. It was more popular and generally more successful than in the RN. There were two US versions: Projector Mk 10, firing an elliptical pattern, and Projector Mk11 firing a circular one. In both, electric motors at the front of the mount could tilt the spigots to compensate for roll and also to give up to 25° effective training. Total weight with rounds for six patterns was about 12.8 tons (*13,000kg*) and the recoil load of 40 tons was too much for small craft, so that Hedgehog was limited to all destroyer escorts and frigates as well as many 'flush deck' destroyers. It was not mounted in fleet destroyers.

The elliptical pattern allowed for 195ft (*59m*) error in deflection and 168ft (*51m*) in range and the circular pattern was of 134ft (*41m*) radius. Range could be adjusted but was usually about 250-270yd (*230-250m*) and time of flight about 10sec with sinking speed about 25f/s (*7.6m/s*). Reloading time was 3min. The bombs were contact fuzed, 7in (*178mm*) dia and weighed about 65lb (*29.5kg*) with about 35lb (*15.9kg*) Torpex charge, initially 30lb (*13.6kg*) TNT.

Mousetrap

A rocket launcher intended to take the place of Hedgehog in the smaller anti-submarine craft. Projector Mk 20 had four launching rails and Mk 22 eight. Neither could be compensated for roll and there was no range adjustment. The pattern from Mk 22 was about 240ft (*73m*) at

Mousetrap with four launching rails, known also as projector Mk 20, in *SC724*
USN

about 300yd (*274m*). At first an 85lb (*39kg*) bomb was intended, but it was difficult to handle in a seaway and it was replaced by the Hedgehog bomb. The rocket was 2.25in (*57mm*) diameter.

In addition to smaller craft, 12 *Benson* class destroyers had three Mk 22 for a time, and one of these, *Turner*, blew up and sank off the Ambrose Light in January 1944, the disaster being attributed to the contact fuzed projectiles, so that a Hedgehog equipped ship could be as liable.

Squid

This triple 12in (*304.8mm*) mortar was much preferred by the RN to Hedgehog but was not adopted by the USN, though it was tried in the frigate *Asheville* in 1944.

MINES

For geographical reasons mines were less important to the USN than to some other navies, but a large effort went into the development and production of new types. In addition to defensive fields, minelaying by surface ships had some success in the Solomon Islands, and from October 1942 laying by submarines was of increasing importance against Japanese shipping. It should be noted that the first batches of the submarine laid Mk 12 magnetic ground mine were delivered to Manila in late 1941, just before the war against Japan, but they had to be dumped in deep water to avoid their compromise. Carrier-borne Avengers first laid mines in March 1943, but the principal effort was by land based aircraft. The first appear to have been laid in February 1943 and in all 13,000 were dropped in Japanese occupied harbour areas, while from 27 March 1945 12,135 were laid in Japanese and Korean waters. These were dropped by about 100 B29s based at Tinian in the Marianas, and each aircraft could carry 12 of *c*1000lb (*454kg*) or 7 of *c*2000lb (*907kg*). Radar aiming from 5000-8000ft (*1500-2400m*) with parachutes was generally used, and the Japanese stated that at least 1000 fell on land, and about 1500 prematured after laying and particularly after storms. Upon sweeping a mine, chain countermining often occurred, sometimes for up to 16,000yd (*15km*). It was thought that this occurred with 200/800 cycle acoustic mines. On one occasion nine mines, including the one swept, exploded simultaneously.

In spite of these failings, the minelaying campaign was highly successful in supplementing the devastation of Japanese shipping caused by the torpedoes of US submarines. A variety of different influence mines were used, magnetic, acoustic and pressure, though the last were not used until May 1945 to avoid compromising them. A complete list of US firing mechanisms has not been found, but M3 and M5 were of magnetic needle type, the latter being used in moored mines. M4 was a single random look coil rod type while M9 and M11 had reverse look firing with varied interlook periods of 0.5 to over 10.5 seconds in the latter. An important advantage of reverse look firing was that it prevented chain countermining. A3 was acoustic working at 200-800 cycles, while A5 worked at subsonic frequencies. A6 was used in pressure mines and had magnetic triggering to prevent detonation by sea waves.

There were less restrictions on high quality explosives than in Britain and TNT fillings were generally replaced by Torpex in the latter part of the war.

MOORED MINES

Mark 5

A First World War mine with Hertz horns. Weight 1700lb (*771kg*), charge 500lb (*227kg*).

Mark 6

An antenna mine developed for the North Sea barrage in the First World War. It was spherical, 34in (*86cm*) diameter, with a weight of 1400lb (*635kg*) and charge 300lb (*136kg*) TNT and could be moored in up to 500 fathoms (*900m*). Mod 2 was of rising type, Mod 3 had 100ft (*30m*) and Mod 4 50ft (*15m*) lower copper antennae.

Mark 10

A horned contact mine for laying from the 21in (*53.3cm*) TT of submarines. The project was begun in about 1921 but was then dropped for a time. Weight 1760lb (*798kg*), charge 300lb (*136kg*). Later developments included Mod 1 (contact for submarines), Mod 3 (magnetic), Mod 5 (airborne contact), Mod 6 (parachute version of Mod 3), Mod 7 (Mod 3 altered for laying by MTB), Mod 8 (similar to Mod 6), Mod 9 (replacement for Mods 6 and 8). These all had 420lb (*190kg*) charges, while Mod 11 intended for the *Argonaut* was a contact mine with 500lb (*227kg*) charge. Weights were between 1800lb (*816kg*) and 1918lb (*870kg*).

Mark 11

An antenna mine for laying by the large submarine *Argonaut* and of the same diameter as her 40in (*102cm*) stern mine tubes. Weight 1875lb (*850kg*), charge 500lb (*227kg*). The *Argonaut* was in fact never used as a minelayer during the war.

Mark 16

An antenna mine replacing Mk 6 in part. Mod 1 weighed 2040lb (*925kg*) with a 600lb (*272kg*) charge and Mod 2 had acoustic firing.

GROUND MINES

A cylindrical, aluminium case, magnetic mine for laying from the TT of submarines and based on the German S-type of the 1920s. Dimensions were 20.8in dia x 94.25in (*52.8 x 239.4cm*) and weight 1445lb (*655kg*) with 1100lb (*499kg*) TNT charge or 1595lb (*723kg*) with 1250lb (*567kg*) Torpex.

Of the modifications, 1 was a parachute mine for aircraft, 3 a redesign for submarines and 4 a replacement of Mod 1 for aircraft.

Mark 12

	Weight	Charge
Mod 3 (TNT)	1390lb (630kg)	1060lb (481kg)
Mod 3 (Torpex)	1500lb (680kg)	1200lb (544kg)
Mod 4 (TNT)	1560lb (708kg)	1060lb (481kg)
Mod 4 (Torpex)	1700lb (771kg)	1200lb (544kg)

Mark 13

An airborne magnetic mine for laying without parachute. It could also be used as a bomb. Mods 1 and 2 became Mk 26 and 26 Mod 1, Mod 4 was for dropping in shallow water, Mod 5 was fitted with an acoustic exploder as was Mod 6 which also had a parachute. The weight was 990-1118lb (*449-507kg*) and the charge 640lb (*290kg*) TNT or 710lb (*322kg*) Torpex.

Mark 17

A magnetic mine laid from the TT of submarines. It is not clear how far this was used in the war. Weight 1825lb (*828kg*), charge 1375lb (*624kg*). Mod 1 became Mk 25.

Mark 18

A high-sensitivity magnetic mine laid by surface craft. Weight 2040lb (*925kg*), charge 1350lb (*612kg*).

Mark 25

An airborne magnetic mine. Mod 1 had A5 acoustic mechanism. Mod 2 had A6 pressure and Mod 3 was also acoustic. Depending on the flight gear, dimensions were 22.4in x 87.2-93in (*56.9cm x 221.5-236cm*) and weight 1950-2000lb (*885-907kg*). The charge was 1274lb (*578kg*) Torpex.

Mark 26

It is not clear to what extent Mk 26 and 26 Mod 1 airborne magnetic mines were used. The explosive charge was 465lb (*211kg*) TNT or 520lb (*236kg*) Torpex and weight 1000-1072lb (*454-486kg*).

Mark 26

Similar to Mk 26 Mod 1 but with a heavier charge and slanted nose for a better underwater trajectory. It was an acoustic mine but Mod 1 was magnetic, Mod 2 had A5 acoustic mechanism and Mod 3 A6 pressure. The charge was 570lb (*259kg*) TNT or 638lb (*289kg*) Torpex and weight 940-1082lb (*426-491kg*).

Mark 39

An airborne magnetic mine for dropping from high altitude without a parachute. Weight 2000lb (*907kg*), charge 800lb (*363kg*). It is not clear if it entered service during the war.

MOBILE GROUND MINES

Mark 27

This was launched from the TT of submarines and measured 21in x 20ft 6in (*53.3cm x 6.25m*). It could travel 4500yd (*4100m*)/10.5kts and had a charge of 877lb (*398kg*). It is not known whether this was used in the war.

DRIFTING MINES

These were numbered in a different series up to Mk 7; the following may have been in service during the war:

Mark 2

This apparently had a case like the Mk 6 mine of the other series with antenna and magnetic firing. It was suspended 15ft (*4.6m*) below a buoyant float.

Mark 3

Apparently similar but without magnetic firing and suspended 35ft (*10.7m*) below the surface.

Mark 4

These were for launching from 21in (*53.3cm*) TT by submarines. They were 9ft 3in (*2.82m*) long and apparently had antenna and acoustic firing. About 100 were made.

Mark 5

Intended for the 40in (*102cm*) minelaying tubes of the *Argonaut* and with a modified Mk 5 case of the other series.

Mark 6

This was shaped like a DC and had a 362lb (*164kg*) charge and apparently antenna firing.

Mark 7

Another mine with antenna firing, the charge being 523lb (*237kg*). Mod 1 was an oscillating mine and was replaced by Mk 19.

Mark 19

An oscillating mine laid by army aircraft. Weight is given as 550lb (*249kg*) and the charge was 190lb (*86kg*). Mod 2 was a Navy version.

CONTROLLED MINES

Mark 20

The weight is given as 435lb (*197kg*) and the charge as 300lb (*136kg*).

Mark 37

This had the case of a Mk 7/0 DC and weighed 738lb (*335kg*) with a 600lb (*272kg*) TNT charge.

BOMBS, ROCKETS AND GUIDED MISSILES

In the latter part of the war rockets were important USN weapons both for aircraft against surfaced submarines and other point targets, and also for modified landing craft in shore bombardment.

AIRBORNE ROCKETS

These were first developed in 1943 after British success against U-boats earlier in the year. As work had been proceeding on other rockets, matters moved quickly and the first two types were in service by the end of 1943.

3.5 in (88.9mm) ASW Rocket

This had a solid steel 20lb (*9.07kg*) head and a 3.5in (*88.9mm*) rocket motor with total weight of about 55lb (*24.95kg*) and overall length 55in (*1397mm*). It was fin stabilised and had a velocity of 1175f/s (*358m/s*). Against surfaced U-boats it could reach the target far sooner than normal bombs, and could penetrate the pressure hull through 50ft (*15m*) water, later extended to 130ft (*40m*). If damage was not fatal it would probably prevent the U-boat diving. It was initially issued to Avenger torpedo-bombers in escort carriers, and first used from *Block Island* in January 1944. Each aircraft carried eight on slotted 72in (*183cm*) launching rails, but the drag of these cut 17kts off the Avenger's speed, and in 1944 it was found that a pair of fixing posts gave sufficient accuracy so that the rocket's use could be extended to all carrier aircraft.

5in (127mm) Rocket

For use against ship and land targets, this rocket had the same motor as the above but the head was a modified 5in (*127mm*) AA shell. Total weight was *c*90lb (*40.8kg*) and velocity *c*875f/s (*267m/s*). This rocket was in service in the Pacific until the end of the war.

5in (127mm) HVAR

This rocket, also known as 'Holy Moses', had a new 5in (*127mm*) motor and was intended to replace the above, but supplies were not adequate until spring 1945. It was first used by the USAAF in the St Lo fighting in 1944. The head was either a base fuzed SAP or a nose and base fuzed HE, and total weight was 140lb (*63.5kg*), overall length 72in (*1829mm*) and velocity 1375f/s (*419m/s*). It was highly successful against point targets in the Pacific in late 1944 and 1945.

Top: 11.75in rocket known as Tiny Tim fired from Grumman Hellcat F6F-5.
USN

11.75in (298.5mm) Rocket

Known as 'Tiny Tim', this was developed as an anti-shipping rocket in 1944. The diameter was that of commercially available oil-well casing steel tubing which was used for the motor, and also that of the 500lb (*227 kg*) SAP bomb used as the warhead. It was fin stabilised and had to be dropped freely and fired with a lanyard that unreeled to avoid damaging the launching aircraft. It was accurate to *c*4000yd (*3650m*) and could penetrate 3-4ft (*0.9-1.2m*) reinforced concrete. Weight was 1280lb (*581kg*), length 123in (*3124m*) and velocity 810f/s (*247m/s*) above that of the launching aircraft. It was issued to *Franklin* and *Intrepid* in 1945 for service trials, and when the former was very severely damaged in March by two bombs, 12 'Tiny Tims', which armed fighter-bombers on the flight deck, caused a spectacular display as the fires ignited the rocket motors. They were apparently used at Okinawa by *Intrepid*'s aircraft but results have not been found.

SHORE BOMBARDMENT ROCKETS

The main purpose of these was to fill the gap between the lifting of ships' gunfire and the establishment of artillery ashore in an invasion landing. As rockets could be fired from relatively light launchers they were also used in motor torpedo boats and a few submarines to increase fire power.

4.5in (114.3mm) Rocket

This was originally an anti-personnel weapon comprising a 20lb (9kg) GP bomb with about 6.5lb (*2.95kg*) TNT charge, and a 2.25in (*57mm*) Mousetrap rocket with fin stabilisation. Range was *c*1100 yds (*1000m*), and it was first tested in June 1942 and used in the North African landings later that year. Fragmentation and smoke heads were developed. The original crate type Mk 1 launcher held 12 and elevation could be varied which was abandoned as unnecessary in Mk 8 of 1943. LCS (S) carried two launchers and larger support craft up to 40, while MTB had two modified Mk 8 with blast shields. The Mk 7 launcher, dating from late 1943, had a single rail with a gravity magazine and could fire 12 rockets in 4sec from about one-third the deck space of Mk 8. By the end of the war it was the most common launcher. Mk 11 was an improved version with jettisoning of dud rockets.

7.2in (183mm) Rocket

Known as 'Woofus', this had a demolition head for clearing underwater obstacles with a 2.25 (*57mm*) or 3.25 (*82.5mm*) motor giving ranges of 280yd (*256m*) or 420yd (*384m*). The Mk 24 launcher with 120 rails filled the well of LCMs. It was first in action in the 1944 landings in southern France but was apparently not entirely satisfactory.

LSM(R) showing six-rail Mk 30 and four-rail Mk 36 launchers for 5in fin stabilised rockets. A 40mm Bofors M1 with pipe frame to prevent firing into the bridge can be seen and also a 5in/38 in the LSM (R) in the distance.
USN

5in (127mm) Fin-stabilised Rocket

These weapons originally developed for and much used by aircraft, were carried by the earlier LSM (R) of the latter part of 1944. There were 30 six-rail Mk 30 launchers and 75 4-rail Mk 36, and the 480 rockets could be fired in 30 sec, but the first reloading took 2½ hours and additional ones 4½ hours each. Rockets of this type were adapted for 'window' for anti-radar purposes with two and four rail launchers, Mk 32 and 31.

5in (127mm) Spin-stabilised Rocket (SSR)

Previous US rockets described were all fixed fin, and the spin-stabilised type seems to have originated in a May 1943 proposal for a rocket with 10,000yd (9140m) range. This called for greatly improved dispersion and a 3.5in (*88.9mm*) SSR failed on this count. The 5in (*127mm*) SSR and launcher had sea trials in an MTB in August 1944 and boats in the Philippines were armed in March and April 1945. The Mk 50 launcher had eight rockets in two tiers of tubes, and two were fitted replacing a torpedo rach on each side. They were usually interconnected to the forward 20mm Oerlikon which had a similar trajectory.

A 5000yd (*4570m*) bombardment equivalent with HC head and a Mk 51 launcher on the lines of Mk 7 was also developed, and was expected to make 80% hits in a 500 × 500yd (*457m²*) area. They were first used in action by LCI (R) with six launchers each, in February 1945 at Iwo Jima and by LSM (R) at Okinawa. These had 20 launchers each and could fire 1020 rockets in the first minute, with 45 minutes for the first reloading and 1½ - 2 hours for each additional one. The was a considerable improvement on ships with finned rockets as the SSR was easier to load. The final LSM (R), which apparently missed the war, had 10 Mk 102 launchers. This was a twin mounting based on the twin 40mm Bofors and was trained and operated by remote control. It was continuously loaded in a vertical position from below decks by pusher hoist and depressed to fire.

The submarine *Barb* had a baseplate for a Mk 51 launcher welded to the deck forward, and launcher and rockets were added after surfacing. Shore bombardments were carried out on three occasions in 1945, ranges of 4000yd (*3660m*) and 5250yd (*4800m*) being quoted. Similar installations were added to *Chivo, Chopper* and *Requin* but were not in action.

GUIDED MISSILES

It is only possible to consider missiles that were actualy in combat service during the war, which restricts the USN to the air-to-surface Bat also known as Bomb Mk 57, SWOD Mk 9 and as ASMN-2 post-war. Bat was a low angle of glide weapon with a Mk 15 Mod 2 Radar Bombsight working in the X-band (*3cm*) for active homing. It was fairly successful in tests in late 1944, and in January 1945 it was decided to equip three squadrons of Privateer patrol bombers, each aircraft being able to carry two. The first squadron was originally based on Palawan and two Bats were first used at Balikpapan 23 April 1945. Later all three squadrons were based on Okinawa. Results were far from satisfactory, and at the end of the war 7000 of the 10,000 ordered were cancelled. Bat was much improved after the war, but the programme was abandoned in 1948.

The warhead was apparently a 1000lb (*454kg*) bomb and other details were total weight 1880lb (*853kg*), wing span 120in (*305cm*), tail span 143in (*363cm*) maximum glide range 30,000-40,000yd (*27,400-36,600m*).

Air-to-surface active homing missile known as Bat, first used 23 April 1945.
Norman Friedman

ATTACK DRONES

At one time it was thought that these might play an important part in the Pacific War and 2000 were on order in 1943. Nine drone squadrons were formed, reduced to four in March 1944. The TDR-1 drone was a small twin-engined monoplane with TV guidance from an Avenger, the original specification calling for a 2000lb (*907kg*) payload, a speed of 150kts and range of 600nm. The first combat operation was an attack on a beached AA ship in southern Bougainville 27 September 1944 which was apparently successful, but the programme was soon abandoned.

Another type of drone was a no longer combat standard heavy bomber packed with explosive, the pilot bailing out after take off. This was mainly a USAAF program but a navy Liberator loaded with Torpex successfully attacked an airfield on Heligoland on 3 September 1944 with TV guidance from a PV-1 Ventura.

BOMBS

As with other countries only AP and large bombs of other types are noted. Anti-submarine bombs are described with other anti-submarine weapons. USN bombs were numbers in a Mark series and USAAF in a M series though some, particularly older bombs, were numbered under their type. The prefix AN was sometimes used for bombs common to both services, though by no means always.

AP BOMBS

In 1941 these comprised a number of converted shells with down to 5% by weight of ammonium picrate as burster. M numbers and nominal weights were: M52, 1000lb (*454kg*); M60, 900lb (*408kg*); M61, 800lb (*363kg*); M62, 600lb (*272kg*); M63, 1400lb (*635kg*). From May 1942 they were replaced by AP Mk 1 of 1600lb (*726kg*) nominal weight with 209lb (*95kg*) ammonium picrate burster (13%). This could defeat 7in (*18cm*) Class B armour and would go through a 5in (*13.7cm*) deck from 7500ft (*2900m*) or from 4500ft (*1370m*) in a 300kt 60° dive. It could however only be used by the Avenger and Helldiver among carrier aircraft and it was rare for wartime carriers to have more than 20 of these bombs in their magazines.

The similar 1000lb (*454kg*) Mk 33 introduced in October 1942 was far more widely used. This could defeat 5.8in (*14.7cm*) Class B and would penetrate a 5in (*12.7cm*) deck from 10,000ft (*3050m*) or from 6500ft (*1980m*) in a 300kt 60° dive. The ammonium picrate content is usually given as 15%.

A rocket-assisted 1250lb (567kg) Mk 50 is dated 1943. This was originally intended for dive bombers but it is not known how often it was used if at all. Much larger AP bombs were developed in 1945 but missed the war. The Mk 63 of a nominal 4000lb (*1814kg*) had a 325lb (*147kg*) ammonium picrate burster and was to penetrate 12in (*30.5cm*) Class B armour from 20000ft (*6100m*). It was intended for dive or level bombing by the immediate postwar heavy load carrier aircraft, and the authorisation of a 24in (*609.6mm*) smooth bore bomb testing gun shows that 8000lb (*3629kg*) AP bombs were under serious consideration.

Bomb	**Actual wt**		**Diameter**		**Length oa**	
	(lb)	**(kg)**	**(in)**	**(mm)**	**(in)**	**(mm)**
AP Mk1	1590	721	14	355.6	83.5	2121
Mk33	1008	457	12	304.8	73	1854
Mk50	1269	576	12	304.8	85.24	2165
Mk63	3876	1758	18	457.2	82.5	2096

SAP, GP AND LIGHT CASE BOMBS

The largest standard SAP seems to have been the 1000lb (*454kg*) M59 with a 30% burster, a diameter of about 15in (*381mm*) and overall length about 71in (*1803mm*). GP bombs of this weight are usually credited with 50-52% TNT bursters, though a figure of 595lb (*270kg*) is given for M44. Mk 36 was a modified version of M44 and weighed 1028lb (*466kg*), with diameter 18.6in (*472.4mm*) and overall length 71.6in (*1819mm*). The larger 2000lb (*907kg*) M34 and M66 were only used by the Avenger among wartime carrier aircraft and magazine stowage was usually 20 or less. M34 had a burster of 1113lb (*505kg*) TNT and weighed 2050lb (*930kg*) with diameter 23in (*584.2mm*) and overall length about 92in (*2337mm*).

There was also a 4000lb (*1814kg*) M56 light case bomb about 33in (*838mm*) in diameter and *c*116in (*2946mm*) long which could be carried by postwar heavy load carrier aircraft.

JAPAN

Although the Japanese Navy was by far the most formidable opponent of Britain and the USA both on and over (although not under) the sea, its weapons are less well known than those of most other fleets. Because of Japan's acceptance of the risks of compressed pure oxygen, her later torpedoes for surface vessels and submarines had a better performance than those of any other country. Her more conventional aircraft torpedoes were also of high quality, as were the heavy armour-piercing bombs. Though variable in effectiveness, Japanese guns, mountings and projectiles showed much of interest, and while mines and anti-submarine weapons were generally backward the Japanese were unique in the development and large scale use of suicide weapons – even if the most common was simply a bomb-laden aircraft.

NAVAL GUNS

All the more important of these are described individually, with briefer notes on obsolescent guns as well as on the larger coast defence and land-based AA guns, and this introduction is concerned with general features and with ammunition and fire-control.

IDENTIFICATION

Japanese guns were usually distinguished by the year in which the design of the type of breech mechanism fitted was begun, 3rd Year Type or Type 89, for example. There are two Japanese chronological systems, based on the year of the regnal era, or on a supposed founding of the Empire in 660BC:

AD	Era	Year from 660BC
1900	Meiji 33	2560
1912	Meiji 45, Taisho 1	2572
1926	Taisho 15, Showa 1	2586
1945	Showa 20	2605

Dates of the earlier designs most commonly give the year of the era, and those of the more recent the last two digits of the continuous calendar year (or only the second, if the first of these digits was a zero). In the descriptive tables, bore and chamber dimensions are measured in BL guns from the top of the mushroom head to the muzzle and base of seated shot respectively, and in QF guns from the breech block inner face. Rifling lengths are for the full depth of the groove. Muzzle velocities are 'new gun' with charge temperature 21°C (*69.8°F*).

In many cases two figures are quoted, the lower being the average 'new gun' figure used for range tables, and the higher the maximum for the same charge and temperature, guns of the same pattern always showing an appreciable spread in muzzle velocity between one another, even when new.

Mutsu at Yokosuka 20 May 1936 in final stages of reconstruction.
Aldo Fraccaroli Collection

Furutaka as reconstructed with twin 20.3cm (*8in*) turrets and masthead range-finder.
Aldo Fraccaroli Collection

DESIGN OF GUNS AND MOUNTINGS

The Japanese guns and mountings in use until the First World War had been made by Elswick and Vickers, or copied from their designs, and certain features were still retained, notably the use of cord propellant and of wire winding in the construction of the heaviest guns. On the other hand there were wide divergences from British practice, as in the triple 46cm (*18.1in*) turret. Gun chambers were smaller in heavy guns with a higher density of loading than would have been the case in British guns of similar calibre, but differences in these matters were not otherwise great. Heavy-gun projectiles were relatively lighter than those of then-recent British designs, and the 12.7cm (*5in*) and 12cm (*4.7in*) guns also used light shells. Very high performance was avoided in Britain for naval guns, and only the Japanese 15.5cm (*6.1in*) and 10cm (*3.9in*) Type 98 fall in this category. Rifling grooves were deeper and lands wider than in normal British practice, and in the 46cm (*18.1in*) the number of grooves was considerably reduced from the usual figure for such a gun. The rifling twist was nearly always 1 in 28 instead of 1 in 30. Autofrettage treatment of liner and barrel forgings was frequent in later guns from 20.3cm (*8in*) downwards, and the inner A tubes of the 46cm (*18.1in*) were radially expanded into position.

CLOSE-RANGE AA ARMAMENT

As with other navies, close-range AA armament was neglected prior to the war, and large numbers of 25mm Hotchkiss-designed guns were added during 1942–45, particularly from 1944. A larger gun like the 40mm Bofors was badly needed, but attempts to copy the Bofors were not successful. Triaxial mountings were not used, nor was local 'joystick' control. Ward Leonard system RPC was used only on triple 25mm mountings.

PROPELLANTS

The most usual Japanese gun propellants were as follows:

	NG	NC	MJ	JJ	CL	OTU	MM
C_2	30	65	3	2			
C_3	26.5	68.5		5			
DC	30	64.8			4.5		0.7
DC_1	41	51.8			4.5	2	0.7
DC_2	27	64.3			5	3	0.7

NG = nitroglycerin, NC = nitrocellulose (13.15%N in C series, 11.85%N in DC series), MJ = mineral jelly, JJ = 'jala-jala' or 'jara-jara', beta naphthol methyl ether introduced as a stabiliser in 1912, CL = Centralite, symmetrical diphenyl diethyl urea, OTU = ortho tolyl urethane, introduced in 1933 and considered an improvement on Centralite, MM = mineral matter.

Nominal diameters of cord were given in units of 0.1mm. Fairly reliable flashless propellant containing additions of 8% hydrocellulose and 4–8% potassium sulphate was developed for guns up to 14cm (*5.5in*), but gave increased smoke and needed an increase of about 30% in the weight of charge. The 25mm Hotchkiss used a single tube grain, 2mm outer diameter, 0.5mm inner diameter, of 95.6%NC (13%N), 2.8% dinitrotoluene, 1.6% Centralite. BL charges were in shalloon bags, with the ignition ends sometimes silk, until the unavailability of Australian wool caused a change to all silk. Some progress had been made by 1945 in replacing brass QF cases by steel.

PROJECTILES

Major calibre Type 91 (1931) APC shell used by 46cm (*18.1in*), 41cm (*16.1in*) and 35.6cm (*14in*) guns was of unusual design and was intended to give an undisturbed underwater trajectory if the shell struck short but near the target. Clearly the very damaging effect of a 41cm underwater hit in the *Tosa* trials of June 1924 was much in mind. The cap - lapped to fit an individual shell, as well as being soldered and crimped - had a flat top on which a small, flat-bottomed, shallow domed cap head was located by screw threads ground on it and on the cap, meeting with threads on the inside of the windshield (ballistic cap). If the shell struck water, the windshield and cap head would be removed and the flat nose of the cap proper would give a stable course to the target. It was also thought that the sharp, flat shoulder of the cap gave some advantage in 'biting' armour plate at oblique impact. The base fuze had a 0.4sec delay to allow for underwater penetration by a near miss. The shell cavity had an aluminium block at the head and a cork lining, while the preformed TNA (trinitroanisole) explosive filling was wool wrapped. The explosive amounted to 1.46-1.65% of the total shell weight. Otherwise the shells, which were all made at Kure, were 4.35 calibres in overall length and had a 6/∞ head with boat tail and two copper bands. The base was not recessed. 'K' type shells giving dyed splashes were used off Samar.

In tests the shells were required to give complete penetration with cavity intact, that is capable of detonation, as follows:

Shell	Plate	Angle to normal	Striking Velocity
46cm-18.1in	410mm-16.1in VH	30°	525m/s 1722f/s
41cm-16.1in	380mm-15in VH	20°	480m/s 1575f/s
35.6cm-14in	330mm-13in VH	20°	485m/s 1591f/s

VH (Vickers hardened) armour was face hardened but not carburised. It was used in the *Yamato* class, and had been adopted for production, not ballistic, reasons. Apparently failures with 41cm and 35.6cm shells were very rare, but originally the 46cm had been tested at 37° to the normal and at about 465-470m/s (*1526-1542f/s*) when failures were more frequent than passes because the nose had become 'chewed' or broken, or because severe base slap had ruptured the cavity at the after edge of the rear band groove. These failures were respectively remedied by increasing the striking velocity and reducing the angle to 33° and then to 30°. Heavy Japanese APC never made any hits on a battleship in the war.

20.3cm (*8in*) Type 91 AP differed in having no cap, but the principle was similar: the shell body had a flat top with the cap head fixed to it by the windshield's screw threads. The shell noses and capheads were slightly softer than the larger ones, and the explosive content was 2.47% with an overall length of 4.46cal. Other details were similar including, it appears, the long delay fuze. Tests required complete penetration with intact cavity of 100mm (*3.9in*) NVNC homogeneous nickel-chromium-steel armour at 30°, 350m/s (*1148f/s*).

15.5cm (*6.1in*) Type 91 AP resembled the above but had a 2.06% explosive content and apparently a short delay fuze. Since the rearming of the *Mogami* class it had little application however.

Though 20.3cm shells caused much damage to cruisers during the war, a considerable number failed to detonate. 'K' type shells were used in daylight actions.

Base-fuzed HE was fired by 15.2cm (*6in*) and 14cm (*5.5in*) guns, and some for 14cm/50 guns had a small soft cap. Bursters were picric acid and 5.3-6.8% of the total weight, except in shells for 14cm/40 guns at 8.75%. Nose-fuzed HE was fired by nearly all guns, that for the larger being known as Common Type 0 (1940). Such shells with time fuzes were even supplied to 46cm (*18.1in*) guns for AA barrage purposes, and also to 41cm (*16.1in*) and 35.6cm (*14in*) guns. The different types of nose-fuzed HE can be summarised as follows:

Gun	% Weight of burster	Approx length oa in cal
46cm (*18.1in*), 41cm (*16.1in*), 35.6cm (*14in*)	4.54-4.73 TNA	3.4-3.5
20.3cm (*8in*)	6.49 TNA	4.3
15.5cm (*6.1in*)	5.52 picric acid	4.2
15.2cm (*6in*), 14cm (*5.5in*)/50	6.35-7.53 picric acid	3.8-4.0
15.2 (*6in*)/40	11.4 picric acid	3.5
12.7cm (*5in*), 12cm (*4.7in*)	9.11-9.72 TNA	3.4
	8.30-8.36 picric acid	3.4
10cm (*3.9in*)/65	7.32 TNT	4.1
10cm (*3.9in*)/50	7.32 picric acid	3.8
7.6cm (*3in*)/60	6.36 TNT	4.3
7.6cm (*3in*)/40	8.0 picric acid	3.7
20.3cm (*8in*) short	29 TNA	2.8
12cm (*4.7in*) short	19.4 TNA	2.8

The small bursters of the heaviest shells are to be noted, and were presumably intended to produce the best AA splinter effect. The only major-calibre shell hit on a US battleship in the Pacific war was by a 35.6cm of this type fired by *Kirishima*, which struck the after barbette in *South Dakota* at the Battle of Guadalcanal, and most if not all of the 15 or so 35.6cm shells that hit the cruiser *San Francisco* earlier in the same battle were also of this type.

In their efforts to improve the efficacy of long-range AA barrages, the Japanese introduced incendiary shrapnel known as Common Type 3 (1943), for 46cm (*18.1in*), 41cm (*16.1in*), 35.6cm (*14in*), 20.3cm (*8in*), 12.7cm (*5in*)/50 and 12.7cm (*5in*)/40 guns and containing respectively 996, 735, 480, 198 and 43 incendiary tubes 25 × 90mm (*1 × 3½in*) in the larger shells, and 20 × 50 (*0.8 × 2in*) in the 12.7cm. The incendiary mixture was 45% magnesium alloy, 40% barium nitrate, 9.3% polysulphide synthetic rubber, 5% natural rubber, 0.5% sulphur, 0.2% stearic acid, and the tubes were steel with a piece of quickmatch in the centre of the filling. The burst was initiated by mechanical time fuze, the incendiary tube ignited about 0.5sec later and burnt for 5sec at 3000°C with a flame about 5m (*16-17ft*) long. In the words of a Japanese officer who had imperfect but expressive English, 'The shell is bursted at the optimum points of the trajectory by fuze, and after that the energetic splinters sprint about igniferously.' The effective radius of the burst was 121m (*397ft*) in the 46cm, and 27m (*89ft*) in the 12.7cm with dispersion angles of 15° and 10° respectively. For comparison, the effective radius of the 46cm HE was 68m (*223ft*) and of the 12.7cm, 18.8m (*62ft*). The bursts were very spectacular but it is doubtful if they were high enough above the line of sight, as shrapnel drops towards the earth and requires to be burst higher than HE. In the heaviest Japanese shore bombardment, that of Henderson Field, Guadalcanal, in October 1942, *Kongo* fired 104 of these shells and *Haruna* 189 HE, out of a total of 918 35.6cm (*14in*) projectiles (the balance, 331 by *Kongo* and 294 by *Haruna*, being APC).

Common Type 4 (1944), similar in purpose but with the tubes filled with phosphorus, was made for 20.3cm (*8in*) short, 12.7cm (*5in*)/50 and 12cm (*4.7in*)/45 guns and incendiary projectiles with Thermite included in the Type 3 filling, for 20.3cm (*8in*) short, 14cm (*5.5in*)/50 and 12cm (*4.7in*)/45 guns.

Anti-submarine projectiles for 15.2cm (*6in*) or 14cm (*5.5in*) guns were Common Type 0 with a cylindrical head over the nose, but special flat-headed shell were made for 12.7cm (*5in*), 12cm (*4.7in*) and 7.6cm (*3in*)/40 guns with larger bursters for 12.7cm and 12cm. They were introduced in 1943 and when fired at 250m/s (*820f/s*) had a range of up to 4000-4300m (*4370-4700yd*) at 40° with a minimum of 750-800m (*820-875yd*), except for the 7.6cm, where the figures were 3200m (*3500yd*) and 700m (*765yd*).

Illuminating shells were originally simple star shells, without parachutes, but later types, said to be copied from a 5in US shell, had them. These shells were supplied for guns from 20.3cm (*8in*) to 12cm (*4.7in*) and, fired at muzzle velocity 750-700m/s (*2460-2300f/s*), had maximum ranges of 22,600-13,900m (*24,700-15,400yd*). Major calibre shell was designed to overcome the lack of adequate radar, and some 41cm (*16.1in*) was in service, but seems to have suffered from inadequate stability in flight. Maximum range was 22,100m (*24,200yd*), with 700m/s (*2300f/s*) muzzle velocity and candle power 5,300,000 compared with 1,700,000 for 20.3cm (*8in*).

HE ammunition for 25mm (*1in*) Hotchkiss guns had, according to postwar reports, a bursting charge of 6.8% reduced to 3.5% in HE tracer, the explosive being 60% TNT, 40% aluminium powder. Earlier reports on captured ammunition give 5.4% tetryl in HE, and 4.5% TNT/aluminium in HE tracer. Cyclonite or PETN-based compositions were used in some 13.2mm incendiary as well as the usual white phosphorus.

Whether the Japanese Navy had entirely overcome ammunition stability problems cannot be determined in the absence of a detailed report on why the *Mutsu* blew up at anchor in June 1943, but the implications of this event are sinister.

SURFACE FIRE-CONTROL

Japanese fire-control was much handicapped by inadequate radar. The design of the first type was not completed until early in 1942, and there was never a specialised fire-control radar, though the 10cm Mk 2, Model 2, Modification 45 was used as a combined surface-search and fire-control set. Peak output was 2kW and maximum range with a battleship target 25,000m (*27,300yd*), optimum accuracies being stated as ± 100m (*110yd*) in range and ± 2-3° in bearing. Ships were usually well supplied with optical range-finders, the largest sizes carried for the main armament being 15m (*49ft*) in the *Yamato* class, 10m (*33ft*) or 8m (*26ft*) in other battleships, 8m (*26ft*) in the *Tone* class and 6m (*20ft*) in other large cruisers. Many were combined coincidence and stereoscopic units. The standard HA range finder was a 4.5m (*15ft*) stereoscopic instrument. Details of the fire-control systems were often not up to the latest British or US practice. Switchboards were not arranged for ease in locating a particular circuit, and switching from forward to after main directors took at least a minute, as most used single selsyn circuits and turrets, guns, directors and computer dials had to be trained, elevated and set to particular values. Development of gyros for stable verticals and horizons was backward, and selsyn transmission systems were elementary. Many servo-mechanisms were copies of British and American designs, but the Aichi Clock Company's Electro-mechanical follow-up gear used in the later ships was original. Target indication was not well developed except perhaps in the Type 94 (1934) HA Director, where a pointer driven by a selsyn motor receiving signals from the control officer was seen against a small illuminated scale in the layer's and the trainer's telescopes. Japanese gunnery methods required that the target should be followed all the time and there was no time-interval compensating gear, though in certain conditions of cross-roll the training speed of heavy turrets was inadequate for continuous following.

The Japanese favoured very small salvo spreads, and to prevent interference when guns in a turret were fired together delays of 80 milliseconds were given to the centre gun in the 46cm (*18.1in*) triples, and of 40-60 milliseconds to one gun in twin turrets from 41cm (*16.1in*) to 20.3cm (*8in*). This was introduced in the *Yamato* class and fitted to older ships as opportunity occurred. Two devices were used, that in the transmitting station referred to as a 'trigger time-limiting device' and that in the turret as a 'firing-time separator', and both depending on rotation of a motor and on solenoids.

The most advanced surface-target fire-control system was that used for the main and secondary armament in the *Yamato* class and comprised Type 98 (1938) Director, Computer and Sokutekiban (a word for which there is no equivalent in English, indicating a device for calculating target speed and inclination). The director was completely enclosed, with the telescopes rigidly fixed to the tower, and only the prisms moved. It accommodated control officer, layer, trainer and cross-leveller and allowed +45° to -12° elevation. The computer was in three parts. The first contained own-ship and target speed resolvers and bearing rate calculator, the second wind speed resolver and deflection and range difference calculator, and the third tangent elevation parallax correction calculator, range and bearing plots, and training and quadrant elevation transmissions to the guns' follow-the-pointer dials. The sokutekiban was an appendage to the computer receiving data

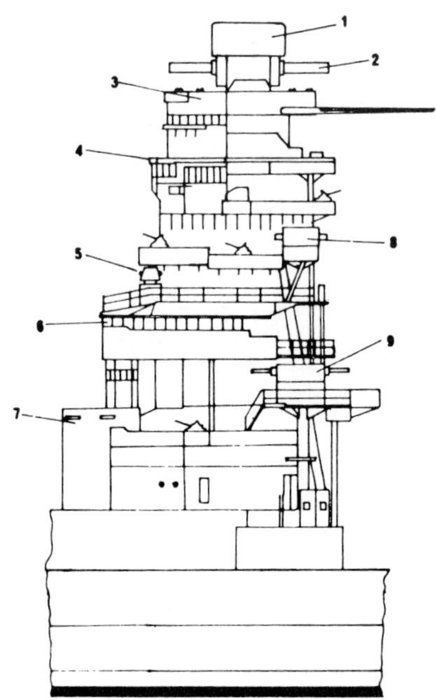

Forward control tower of *Hiei* as reconstructed 1940. The masthead director (hoiban) is a Type 94, as is the secondary armament one. The AA Director (koshaki) is a Type 94 (it should have a 4.5m RF).

1 Main armament director
2 10m range-finder
3 Air defence command post
4 Fighting bridge
5 Searchlight director
6 Compass platform
7 Conning tower
8 AA director
9 Secondary armament director

John Roberts

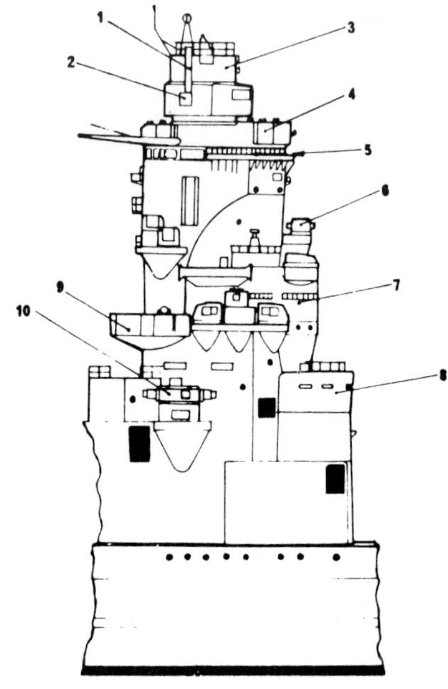

Forward control tower of *Yamato*, 1945. The masthead Director (hoiban) is a Type 98, which was fixed (only the prisms of the telescope moving).

1 Aerials for air/surface search radar Type 21
2 15m range-finder
3 Main armament director tower
4 Air defence command post
5 Fighting bridge
6 2.5m range-finder
7 Compass platform
8 Conning tower
9 Flag deck
10 4.5m range-finder

John Roberts

Takao at Yokosuka 1 May 1938 before reconstruction showing single 12cm (*4.7in*) HA and twin 61cm (*24in*) TT. The layout of the forward tower structure was simplified to some extent on reconstruction.
Aldo Fraccaroli Collection

from the director and transmitting target speed and inclination to the computer. Limits were measured range 50,000m (*54,680yd*), gun range 41,300m (*45,170yd*) deflection 130mils R, 160L, deflection in azimuth 500mils, own speed 35kts, target speed 40kts, wind speed 40m/s (*77.7kts*). Allowance was made for rotation of the earth.

Other battleships and 20.3cm (*8in*) cruisers had the Type 94 (1934) Director with Type 92 (1932) Computer and Sokutekiban. A different system was used, the computer supplying super-elevation and lateral deflection to the director where they were added differentially to the director setting and training. After parallax, roll and cross-roll corrections were added, quadrant elevation and training were supplied by the director to the gun's follow-the-pointer dials. The director was of normal biaxial type with telescopes for control officer, layer, trainer and cross-leveller and had calculating devices for roll in line of sight, cross-roll and parallax corrections. Director limits were +45° to -12° elevation and 10° maximum roll, while the Type 92 Computer limits were measured range 40,000m (*43,740yd*), gun range 39,800m (*43,520yd*), deflection 130 milsR, 160L, enemy course 90° R or L, own speed 30kts, target speed 40kts, wind speed 20m/s (*38.9kts*). The Type 92 sokutekiban supplied target speed and course to the computer and needed laying and training, like a director.

In later units roll and cross-roll were transmitted to the director from a gyro stable vertical in the transmitting station, parallax was calculated by the computer, and some computers had mechanisms for target speed and target angle and required input only of inclinometer angle.

Secondary guns in battleships and main armament in light cruisers had simplified Type 94 Directors without parallax correction or telescope for the control officer, and cross-roll corrections were added differentially in the Type 94 Computer which transmitted data direct to the guns and not via the director. This computer was similar in system to the British Admiralty Fire-Control Clock but was semi-tachymetric in principle and had a range plot. Its limits were measured range 20,000m (*21,870yd*), gun range 15,000m (*16,400yd*), deflection 90 milsR, 120L, own and target speeds 40kts. A conversion of the Type 94 Director for HA use in the *Isuzu*, when she was rearmed with 12.7cm (*5in*)/40 AA guns, was called the Type 94 Mod 5 or 6 and then the Type 2 (1942). This was also used for HA/LA fire in some destroyers with 12.7cm/50 guns. Otherwise these destroyers had the simplified Type 94 Director with a tachymetric or rate-measuring device known as the Type 94 Biodoban, the limits of which were: range 20,000m (*21,870yd*), gun range 19,800m (*21,650yd*), range rate 80kts (300kts for crude HA use), own and target speeds 40kts.

During World War II instances of very good and very bad Japanese gunnery against surface targets were to be found, but such variations occur in all navies and Japanese shooting was on the whole not much inferior to British and American against ships.

ANTI-AIRCRAFT FIRE-CONTROL

AA fire was less satisfactory. Supplementary deflection calculators were added to the main LA computer in battleships for main armament barrage fire, and some use was made of pre-calculated cards giving deflection for various ranges and rates. The principal system for AA guns was however the Type 94 (1934) HA Director and Computer. The Japanese term for HA director was 'koshaki' and for LA 'hoiban', which avoided some confusion. The Type 94 system was used for 12.7cm (*5in*), 12cm (*4.7in*) and 10cm (*3.9in*) AA guns in battleships, cruisers and aircraft carriers, and also for 10cm guns in *Akizuki* class destroyers and apparently for 7.6cm (*3in*)/60 guns.

The system was fully tachymetric with a triaxial director and a computer in the transmitting station incorporating a spherical resolver for deck tilt. In later units optical levelling and cross-levelling in the director was replaced by a gyro stable vertical in the transmitting station. Polar coordinates and slant ranges were used, and solutions were given for diving and climbing targets. The director was trained by electric-powered hydraulic gear, not rate aided, and incorporated an optical RF but no radar antennae. A range plot was provided in the computer, mainly to obtain a reliable rate, but this was replaced in the latest units by rate integrators. As was often the case, errors could be appreciable at long range as the calculating methods included some assumptions for convenience. Range, present elevation and training and inclination were transmitted from director to computer, and lateral and vertical deflection and fuze setting from computer to guns, the first two via the director. Limits were:

Director elevation 8°/sec
training 16°/sec
Accuracy elevation and training 12min, later 10min
Fuze setting 0.02sec
Average time, smooth tracking 20sec
Solution time 10–20sec
Present range 1500–20,000m (*1640–21,870yd*)
Present height zero–10,000m (*0–32,800ft*)
Future range (12.7cm, 12cm) 700–12,500m (*765–13,670yd*)
(**10cm**) 750–15,000m (*820–16,400yd*)
(**7.6cm**) 850–12,000m (*930–13,120yd*)
Elevation –15 +105°
Training ±220°
Cross-roll ±10°
Roll ±15°
Range rate ±500kts
Computer outputs –
Lateral deflection ± 45°
Vertical deflection ± 30°
Fuze 1 to 43sec

It is obvious that this system, production of which began in mid-1937, was much too slow. A modification enabled fire to be opened on estimated target course and speed, but after the disaster of the Battle of Midway in June 1942, work began on the Type 3 (1943) system. This was based on rectangular coordinates and needed nine men on the director and nine on the computer, but the prototype was never finished. The old Type 91 (1931) system which had director and computer on one manually worked pedestal mounting and the rangefinder separate, was still in some ships including the battleship *Haruna* at the end of the war, but was much inferior to the Type 94.

The previously noted HA modification of the Type 94 LA Director known as the Type 2 (1942) LA Director (hoiban, not koshaki) was combined with a computer known as the Type 2 Biodoban working on angular rate multiplied by time, to provide an HA/LA system for 12.7cm (*5in*)/50 guns in destroyers. Incidentally the usual term for fire control computers was 'shagekiban', or 'kosha shagekiban' if HA. The director was heavy, the computer exceedingly complicated, and the system does not seem to have been very satisfactory. A further development designed in 1944 and intended for cruisers and destroyers was to couple the above computer with a Type 5 (1945) Radar Director ('dentan hoiban'), but this did not reach completion.

The standard close-range HA director was the Type 95 (1935) 'shageki sochi' based on course and speed principles and originally copied from the French Le Prieur sight. It was combined with Ward Leonard RPC drive and scooter control and was used for triple 25mm mountings. The maximum target speed was 324kts but etched ring sights in the control officer's telescope increased this to 486kts, though the mounting drives were inadequate to follow this. There were production difficulties, and a simplified Type 4 (1944) Mod 3 unit was developed without RPC; this was used for 12.7cm (*5in*)/40 guns in escort destroyers, as well as for 25mm. A local director sight and computer for 10cm (*3.9in*)/65 and 7.6cm (*3in*)/60 guns based on Le Prieur sights was also made but had to be simplified for production reasons. Le Prieur computing sights, originally obtained from France for 25mm guns, resolved target speed, course and range to give vertical and lateral deflection, and a linkage automatically maintained the course arrow parallel with the target's course. Super elevation was mechanically varied with angular height. Supply was limited by manufacturing difficulties and they were mostly kept for manual triple 25mm mountings. Open ring sights and a few not very satisfactory etched-glass ring sights were used for 25mm single mountings, and for the 40mm Type 5 (1945) Bofors copy.

Maya as completed at Kobe, June 1932, showing forward single 12cm (*4.7in*) HA and twin 61cm (*24in*) TT.
Aldo Fraccaroli Collection

HEAVY CALIBRE GUNS

51cm (20.1in)/45

This design, which was never made, was intended for the projected sixth and seventh ships of the *Yamato* type, Battleships 48 and 49. Its construction was similar to that of the 46cm described below, and it seems to have been an enlarged version of this gun. None of the component tubes was heavy for so large a gun, the inner A weighing 21,700kg (*21.4 tons*), the A 30,000kg (*29.5 tons*) and the heaviest of the outer tubes 33,700kg (*33.2 tons*), respectively.

The projected ships were to have three twin turrets which would have permitted some simplification of the 46cm triple, but the weight was apparently even greater than that of the latter, the figure quoted being 2780t (*2736 tons*).

Gun Data

Bore	510mm	20.08in	
Weight incl BM	227,000kg	223.4 tons	
Length oa	23,560mm	927.56in	46.2cal
Length bore	*c*22,840mm	*c*899.2in	44.8cal
Projectile	2000kg	4409lb	
Propellant charge	480kg	1058lb	

48cm (18.9in)/45 5th Year Type (1916)

Work on this gun, which was apparently referred to as 36cm 5th Year Type, began shortly after World War I. The first gun split in test firing, but the second was fired satisfactorily and was still at Kamegakubi proving ground in December 1945, together with cradle and slide which were enlarged copies of those for the British 15in. The gun was wire wound for only part of its length, and judging from photographs the chase was slim, with a diameter at the muzzle of 29in (*73.7cm*). This size of gun was apparently considered too large for ships in 1921-22, as the projected Battleships 39-42 (also known as Battlecruisers 13-16) were to have eight 46cm/45 5th Year Type, while nine of the 46cm Type 94 were later mounted in *Yamato* and *Musashi*.

Apart from the bore of 480mm (*18.9in*) and nominal length of 45cal, data are lacking, but some Type 91 AP shells were made. These differed from the usual Japanese design in having only one driving band, were estimated to weigh 3800-3900lb (*c1750kg*) and were 81in (*c206cm*) long.

46cm (18.1in)/45 Type 94 (1934)

These guns, the largest ever mounted afloat, were in triple turrets in the *Yamato* and *Musashi* and were intended for the *Shinano* (completed as an aircraft carrier), the cancelled Battleship 46 and the projected 47. The gun design dated from 1939 and for reasons of secrecy it was referred to as the 40cm Type 94. Altogether 27 guns were made at Kure - nine each for *Yamato* and *Musashi*, two proof and experimental guns and seven others. The construction was unusual. The A tube, known as 2A and weighing 22,500kg (*22.1 tons*) had the 3A tube of 24,700kg (*24.3 tons*) shrunk on for somewhat over half the length from the breech end. This assembly was then wire wound and had a layer of two tubes shrunk on for the whole length, followed by a two-part jacket at the breech end. The various tube shoulders were fitted with Belleville spring washers, presumably to lessen stress concentration and 'steel choke', and this recalls the former use of cannelured rings in many Vickers designs. The inner A tube, known as 1A, of 15,900kg (*15.6 tons*) was radially expanded into place by hydraulic pressure of 110,000-120,000psi (*c7750-c8450kg/cm²*). The bore was divided into three parts and the highest expansion given to the third at the breech end. The inner A tube was rifled after in was in place. In addition, there were a short breech ring, and a breech bush screwed into the 3A tube. The breech mechanism is believed to have been a Japanese version of the Asbury type with the usual Welin screw block. It is not known whether there were any small circumferential serrations on the compression slope of the shot seating to prevent slip back at high elevation. The great disadvantage of this construction was that relining was possible only if the worn inner A was completely bored out.

Some accounts give the length overall as 21,300mm (*838.6in*) or 21,329mm (*839.7in*) which would increase the bore and chamber length by the same amount as the increase in length overall. The chamber volume is usually given as 480dm^3 which is impossible and is thought to be a mistake for 680. The charge which is sometimes given as 330kg (*728lb*) was in six bags, each with a 500gm (*17.6oz*) black powder igniter. In addition to the Type 91 AP shell, which had a nominal length of 1953.5mm (*76.9in*), time-fuzed HE and incendiary shrapnel shells were provided for AA use. These weighed 1360kg (*2998lb*) and are described in the section concerning Japanese ammunition. Muzzle velocity is given as 805m/s (*2641f/s*).

The triple turrets were a complete break with the older heavy gun mountings which had followed British practice in many ways. They were built at Kure, and only the six lost in *Yamato* and *Musashi* were completed, though one of *Shinano*'s was partly finished, much of the machinery for her other turrets was in existence and there was an incomplete structure for pit trials. The guns were in individual cradles, assembled from two semi-cylindrical steel castings with integral housings for the two recoil, the two compressed air run-out cylinders and the run-out control cylinder. The turret was powered from a hydraulic ring main using water plus soluble oil, and there was no local pump in the turret. Elevation was by cylinder and piston gear working on the rear end of the cradle, but it was possible to vary the length of the elevating arm by means of a crosshead and slipper worked by a small hand-controlled hydraulic cylinder. The object of this was to do away with slide locking at the loading angle of +3°, as the elevating arm was normally adjusted to give +41° to +3° (though this could be increased to +45° -5° if needed). Hand-operated bolts locked the guns at +1° when secured for sea. There were two independent sets of training gear, only one being used at a time. Each was powered by a 500HP vertical swashplate motor driving a train of straight-toothed pinions through a cone clutch and coaster gear. The latter closely resembled the ordinary bicycle drive in action. The designers had objected to a worm drive as requiring too much horizontal space and also because high loading caused severe pitting on the worm, but as fitted the training gear was not non-reversing and, if the direction of training was suddenly reversed at full speed, there was about half a degree of slip. Troubles seem to have occurred from overloading of the coaster-gear outer drum and rollers, and extra lubrication had to be provided.

Shells were stowed vertically and moved by push-pull gear. Of the total of 100 per gun, 60

Gun Data

Bore	460mm	18.11in	
Weight incl BM	165,000kg	162.4 tons	
Length oa	21,130mm	831.9in	45.9cal
Length bore	*c*20,480mm	*c*806.3in	44.5cal
Length chamber	*c*2890mm	*c*113.8in	
Volume chamber	?680dm^3	?41,496in^3	
Rifling grooves	(72) 4.6mm deep × *c*12.14mm	0.181 × *c*0.478in	
lands	*c*7.93mm	*c*0.312in	
twist	Uniform 1 in 28		
Weight Type 91 AP	1460Kg	3219lb	
Propellant charge	360kg 110DC$_1$	794lb	
Muzzle velocity	780-785m/s	2559/2575f/s	
Working pressure	3000-3200kg/cm^2	19/20.3 tons/in^2	
Approx life	200-250 EFC		
Max range	42,030m at 45°	45,960yd	

were stowed in the shell handling rooms in the revolving structure, and 40 in the shell room on the same level as the lower handling room, that is immediately below the main armour deck in 'B' and 'Y' and a deck lower in 'A'. In action, the guns would be supplied from the lower handling room and then from the upper one. Transfer from the shell room by push-pull gear and shell bogie was slower than supply by the hoists so that the handling rooms would be replenished between actions. It may be noted that the upper handling room could be filled only via the lower room and auxiliary or main hoists. There does not appear to have been any rapid method of changing the type of shell being fired. The upper and lower magazines were located one and two decks below the shell rooms and fed propellant handling rooms on the same levels, the lower one supplying the centre gun and the upper the two wing guns. Charges were stowed in sixths horizontally in cases. On removal from the cases they were manhandled to a roller chute, end to end, and pushed by hand to a power-driven revolving flashtight scuttle and thence to a power-driven transfer bogie with a pivoted tray that swung into line with the hoist flashdoor, so that the charge could be power rammed into the hoist cage. In all these operations the six parts of the charge were kept end to end.

Each gun had one hoist for shell and one for charge. The former were of normal pusher type and had openings without scuttles at both shell handling rooms, while the latter were in flashtight trunks of internal dimensions 94 x 287cm (*37 x 113in*). There was a cage of open framework running on rails with a cylindrical container holding the charge, made flashtight by end doors fitted to the cage frame, while there were top and bottom flashtight doors on the hoist trunk. The cage was driven by a hydraulic cylinder and rack, a train of pinions and a wire-winch drum. This gear was extremely heavy and used much lubricant.

On arrival at the gunhouse, the shell entered a tilting bucket in which it was set at 8° above horizontal, then rolled to a waiting tray and again to the loading tray of a combined shell bogie and chain rammer at the rear of the gunhouse in line with the gun. Without the shell this was 6.43m (*21ft*) long to the end of the thread-protecting tray and 1.42m (*4ft 8in*) high and was estimated to weigh about 3 tons. It ran forward about 4m (*13ft*) on rails to the loading position, as it did so, the front wheels ran down a decline reducing the shell angle to the gun-loading angle of +3°. The reason for the original 8° tilt was to allow the separate charge loading gear to swing into line below the shell loading tray when the bogie was in its rear position. With the charge-hoist cage the end doors of the cylindrical container were opened sufficiently to allow the charge to move sideways out of the cage into line with the gun. It was then moved forward to cover the breech threads, the charge chain rammer on the other side of the gunwell was brought into line, and all six parts of the charge loaded with one stroke of the rammer. The complete loading operation took about 23sec.

There were two auxiliary hoists driven by gear similar to, but smaller than, that of the main charge hoist, supplying shells and charges stowed vertically in suitable containers. Shells were transferred in the gunhouse manually by overhead travellers and chain purchase.

These turrets were heavy and flashtightness does not seem to have been up to British standards, while safety interlocks were few. The Japanese appear to have been well satisfied, except with the consumption of lubricant by the training gear and charge-hoist mechanism, the noise of the coaster gear, and difficulties with the shell hoists if the ship was rolling over 5°. As would be expected, muzzle blast was very great.

With Type 91 AP ranges and times of flight for 780m/s (*2559f/s*) MV

Elevation	Range (yd)	(m)	(sec)	
10°	18,410	16,830	26.05	
20°	30,530	27,920	49.21	
30°	39,180	35,830	70.27	
40°	44,510	40,700	89.42	
45°	45,960	42,030	98.6	Max elevation of mounting
48°	46,050	42,110	104	Max range of gun
50°	45,790	41,870	106.66	

It will be seen that in action against other ships 20° elevation would seldom be exceeded.

Other figures for the same MV

Range (m)	Range (yd)	Elevation	Remain V (m/s)	Remain V (f/s)	Descent
5000	5470	2.4°	690	2264	3.3°
10,000	10,940	5.4°	620	2034	7.2°
15,000	16,400	8.6°	562	1844	11.5°
20,000	21,870	12.6°	521	1709	16.5°
25,000	27,340	17.2°	490	1608	23.0°
30,000	32,810	23.2°	475	1558	31.4°

The elevations for 25,000 and 30,000m are slightly greater than those deduced from the previous figures.

Gun Mounting Weights

Weight of revolving parts	tonnes	tons
3 guns + BMs	495	487
Other elevating parts	228	225
Turntable + above	350	345
Below turntable	647	637
Gunhouse armour	790	776
Total	2510	2470

Gun Mounting Data

Roller path outer dia	13.05m	42.81ft
Roller path int dia	11.50m	37.73ft
Distance between gun axes	3.50m	137.8in
Recoil	1.43m	56.3in
Elevating speed max	8°/sec	
Training speed max	2°/sec	

Firing cycle at +3° elevation (approx times)

Open breech	2.0–2.5sec	**Ram charge**	3sec
Move shell loading bogie forward	3sec	**Withdraw rammer**	3sec
Ram shell	3sec	**Return charge cylinder + rammer**	3sec
Withdraw rammer + return bogie	5sec	**Close breech**	2sec
Moving charge cylinder + rammer load position	3sec	**Recoil and run-out**	2.5–3sec
		Total	29.5–30.5sec

At 41° elevation this would be increased by about 11 sec to cover depression and elevation of the gun with allowance for cut-off. There was a firing delay of 80 milliseconds on the centre gun to reduce interference when all three guns in a turret were fired together. The salvo spread was given as 500–600yd (*c500m*) at maximum range for 4 or 5 gun salvos and rather more for 9-gun. If the actual maximum range of over 40,000m is meant, the above figures are good, as is the rate of fire for so large a gun.

The turret shield had 650mm (*25.6*) face, 250mm (*9.8in*) sides, 190mm (*7.5in*) rear, 270mm (*10.6in*) roof. The face and, according to some accounts, the roof were face hardened.

Top right: 46cm (*18.1in*) guns in *Yamato* after turret. These, also in *Musashi*, were the heaviest guns ever mounted afloat.
CPL

About 40 of these guns, which dated from 1918, were made at Kure or at Muroran Ironworks. They were always known as 40cm or 16in. They were mounted in twin turrets in *Nagato* and *Mutsu* and were also intended for the *Kaga, Tosa, Amagi, Akagi, Takao, Atago, Kii, Owari, Suruga,* and *Omi,* all cancelled under the Washington treaty. A number were available for coast defence and six guns were mounted in twin turrets to cover the southern entrance to the Sea of Japan, the three turrets being located on Iki, Tsushima and at Pusan in Korea.

The construction of the guns was in general of the normal wire wound type, but they were lighter than would be expected, and the external diameter at the muzzle of about 26½in was an inch less than that of the British 15in Mk I, indicating that they may not have been wire wound for their full length. As usual in later Japanese guns, there were Belleville spring washers at the tube shoulders, and small circumferential serrations on the compression slope of the shot seating to prevent slip back. The usual Welin breech block was used but the Elswick 3-motion short-arm mechanism was employed with a 'slow cone' obturator seating, the guns resembling the British First World War 18in in these features.

Besides AP, time-fuzed HE and incendiary shrapnel were provided for AA use. These

41cm (16.1in)/45 3rd Year Type (1914)

Gun Data

Bore	410mm	16.14in	
Weight incl BM	102,000kg	100 tons	
Length oa	18,840mm	741.73in	45.95cal
Length bore	18,294mm	720.24in	44.62cal
Length chamber	2320.4mm	91.35in	
Volume chamber	467.11dm³	28,505in³	
Length rifling	15,629mm	615.31in	
Grooves	(84) 4.1mm deep × 8.754mm	0.161 × 0.345in	
Lands	6.58mm	0.259in	
Twist	Uniform 1 in 28		
Weight Type 91 AP	1020kg	2249lb	
Propellant charge	219kg 102 DC_1 or 110 C_2	483lb	
Muzzle velocity	780/785m/s	2559-2575f/s	
Working pressure	3000/3070kg/cm²	19-19.5tons/in²	
Approx life	250 EFC		
Max range	38,400m	42,000yd	

Range and Elevation Data for Type 91 AP and 780m/s MV

Range (m)	(yd)	**Elevation**	**Remain V** (m/s)	(f/s)	**Descent**
5000	5470	2.5°	685	2247	3.4°
10,000	10,940	5.7°	610	2001	7.5°
15,000	16,400	9.2°	539	1768	11.8°
20,000	21,870	13.5°	495	1624	17.5°
25,000	27,340	18.8°	465	1526	24.5°
30,000	32,810	25.5°	462	1516	34°

41cm (*16.1in*) guns in *Mutsu* forward turrets, taken in 1936.
CPL

weighed 936kg (*2064lb*) and the muzzle velocity is given as 805m/s (*2641f/s*). The propellant charge was in four bags, each with a 250gm (*8.8oz*) black powder igniter. Illuminating shell fired with reduced charges to give 700m/s (*2297f/s*) could also be carried. The older Type 88AP of 1000kg (*2205lb*) fired with a propellant charge of 224kg (*494lb*) at 790m/s (*2592f/s*) was probably still used by the coast defence guns. This shell was not boat tailed, and the chamber became 2431.9mm (*95.74in*) long and 480.30dm³ (*29,310in³*) in volume.

The turrets in some ways resembled the British 15in Mark I mountings and were powered from a hydraulic ring main. The training gear included a worm drive which suffered from wear. Elevation was by cylinder and piston attached to the rear of the slide. The rammers were mounted on a continuation of the gun slides and loading was possible at any elevation up to 20°. Originally the elevation range was +30° to -5° but this was altered to +43° to -3° by deepening the gun wells and lowering the revolving structure bodily towards the ship's bottom. The guns were run out by compressed air. A double longitudinal bulkhead separated the two guns and also the right and left sides in the working chamber, where shells and charges were transferred from lower to upper hoists. The shell rooms were located above the magazines. The gun-loading cage was offset from the gun bore and a container pivoted about a horizontal axis carried the shell and charge, the latter in a flash-tight compartment. Shell and charge could thus be rammed without moving the case in the hoist, the container being turned to bring each into line. All four quarter-charges were located end to end and were rammed at one stroke.

The coast-defence mountings are believed to have been originally intended for *Kaga* or *Tosa*. The turrets were more rectangular in appearance and were powered by individual oil hydraulic units. Elevation was +35° -2°.

Data for the turrets in *Nagato* and *Mutsu* as altered

Weight of revolving parts	1020t	1004 tons
Roller path dia	9.0m	29.5ft
Distance between gun axes	2.44m	8.0ft
Elevating speed max	5°/sec	
Training speed max	3°/sec	
Firing cycle	21.5sec at low elevation	
Turret shield	460mm (*18.1in*) face; 280mm (*11in*) side; 190mm (*7.5in*) rear; 250-230mm (*9.8-9in*) roof	

36cm (14in)/45 Vickers and 41st Year Types (1908)

The design for the first of these guns, which were all exactly 14in bore (*355.6mm*), was submitted by Vickers in November 1910, and was originally known as 12in Vickers Mk 'J' or 12in Meiji 43 Type (the 43rd year of the Meiji era being 1910). It later became known as 14in Vickers Mk 'A' or as 14in 43rd Year Type. The later, similar, Japanese design was known as 41st Year Type, as Japanese guns were usually dated by the beginning of design work on the type of breech mechanism. Such are the pitfalls of Japanese ordnance. Altogether about 100 guns were made, the Japanese built some at Kure or Muroran Ironworks, but a number of guns of the 41st Year Type and more forgings were supplied from England. There were several versions of the Japanese type, but they and the Vickers guns can be considered together. The latter were originally mounted in *Kongo* and *Hiei*, and the former in *Haruna*, *Kirishima*, *Fuso*, *Yamashiro*, *Ise* and *Hyuga*, all in twin turrets.

The Vickers guns were of normal, full-length-wire type with cannelured rings at the tube shoulders, and the earlier 41st Year Type guns were similar, though some of the later ones are believed to have had the inner A tube radially expanded into position. Circumferential serrations as in the 41cm were later added. Vickers 'pure couple' breech mechanism was used with a Welin block.

Gun Data

Bore	355.6mm	14in	
Weight incl BM	84,690-86,000kg	83.3-84.6 tons	
Length oa	16,469mm	648.4in	46.3cal
Length bore	16,002mm	630in	45cal
Length chamber	2006.7-2007.7mm	79.0-79.04in	
Volume chamber	294.9dm³	17,996 in³	
Length rifling	13,737-13,706mm	540.82-539.61in	
Grooves	(84) 3.048mm deep × 8.865mm	0.12 × 0.349in	
Lands	4.435mm	0.175in	
Twist	Uniform 1 in 28		
Weight Type 91 AP	673.5kg	1485lb	
Propellant charge	142.3kg 85 DC	313.8lb	
Muzzle velocity	770-775m/s	2526-2543f/s	
Working pressure	3000-3020kg/cm²	19-19.2tons/in²	
Approx life	250-280 EFC		
Max range	35,450m	38,770yd	

Time-fuzed HE and incendiary shrapnel weighed 625kg (*1,378lb*) and their MV was 805m/s (*2641f/s*). The propellant charge was in four bags with a 225gm (*7.9oz*) black powder igniter on each one.

Range and Elevation Data for Type 91 AP and 770m/s MV

Range		Elevation	Remain V		Descent
(m)	(yd)		(m/s)	(f/s)	
5000	5470	2.6°	670	2198	3.5°
10,000	10,940	6.1°	576	1890	7.5°
15,000	16,400	9.9°	510	1673	12.4°
20,000	21,870	14.4°	459	1506	18.9°
25,000	27,340	20°	420	1378	27.5°
30,000	32,810	28.7°	414	1358	35.9°

Gun Mounting Data

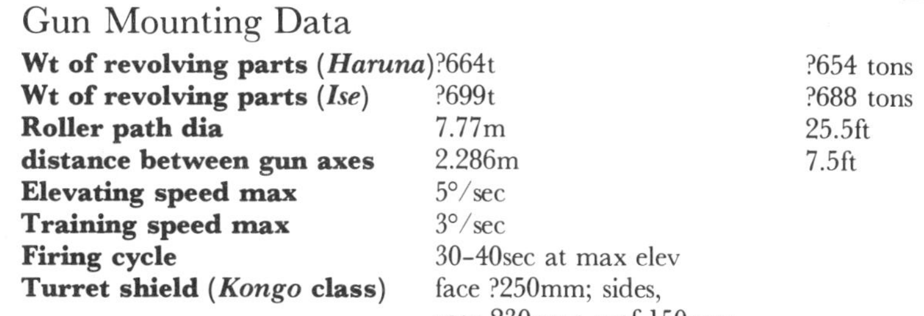

Wt of revolving parts (*Haruna*)	?664t	?654 tons
Wt of revolving parts (*Ise*)	?699t	?688 tons
Roller path dia	7.77m	25.5ft
distance between gun axes	2.286m	7.5ft
Elevating speed max	5°/sec	
Training speed max	3°/sec	
Firing cycle	30-40sec at max elev	
Turret shield (*Kongo* class)	face ?250mm; sides, rear 230mm; roof 150mm	9.8in; 9in; 5.9in
(*Fuso, Ise* classes)	face ?300mm; sides 250mm	11.8in; 9.8in

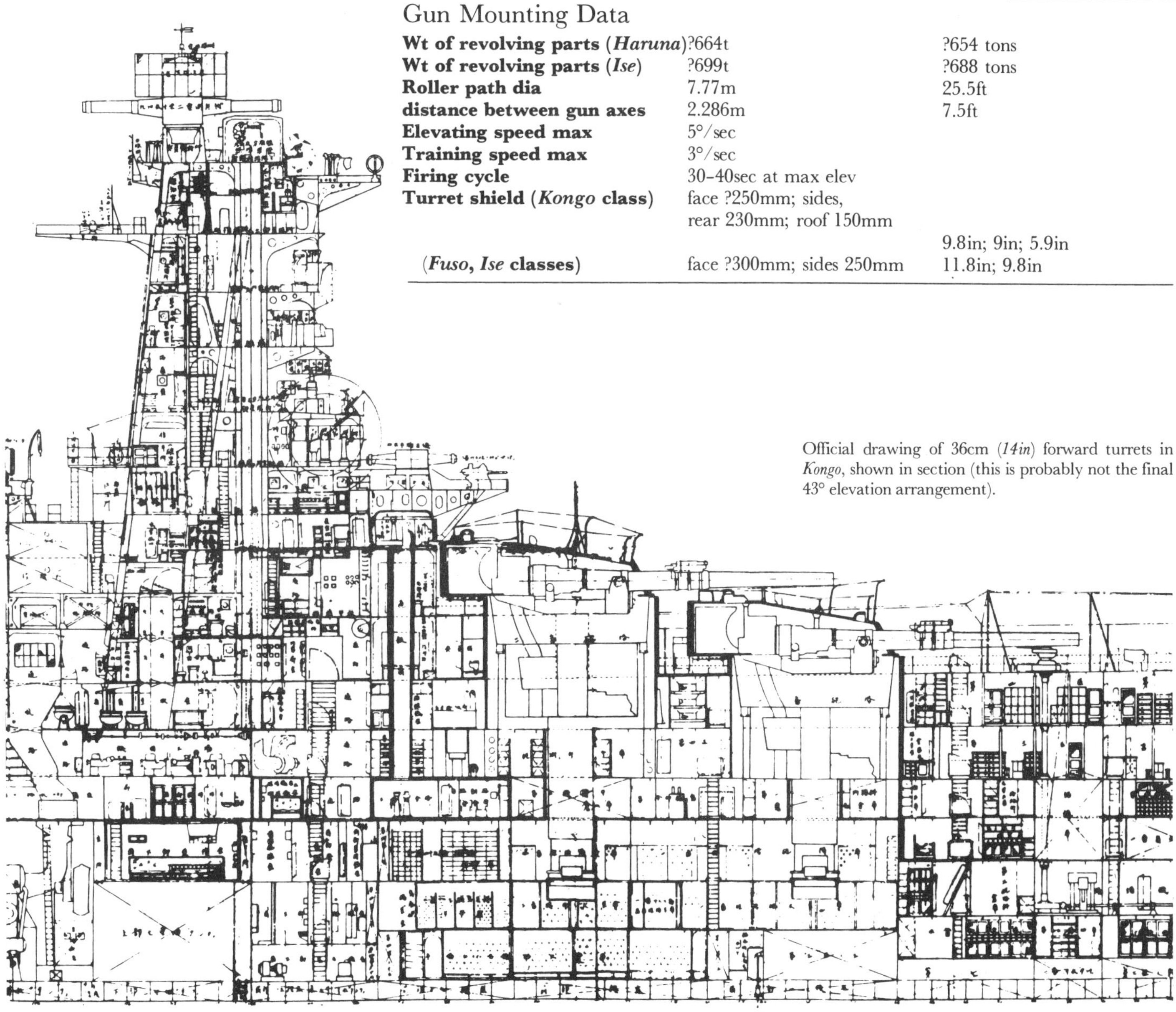

Official drawing of 36cm (*14in*) forward turrets in *Kongo*, shown in section (this is probably not the final 43° elevation arrangement).

The original mountings for *Kongo* were of the usual British type, except that auxiliary electric drive was provided. Elevation was +25° -5°, and shell rooms are shown below the magazines, though this was later changed. Elevation was increased to +33° and compressed air run-out provided in the 1920s, and later the mountings were altered to give +43° -3° and to resemble the 41cm mountings in the *Nagato* class except in some of the loading arrangements described below. There was however insufficient room in *Ise* and *Hyuga* to lower the revolving part of the two after turrets so that elevation could be increased only in the other four turrets. The precise loading arrangements are not known in every ship, but there were three types of gun-loading cage. The *Haruna* type resembled that in the 41cm, but the charge was in two compartments, each holding two quarters, so that it had to be rammed in two strokes. In the *Kongo* type the shell was on an extension to the main cage and the charge in two compartments in the cage proper, from which it rolled down into line with the gun and was rammed in two strokes. Lastly the *Ise* type was conventional and similar to the British 15in. Loading was possible up to 20° elevation, except in the *Fuso* type turret where it was at a fixed angle of +5°.

36cm (*14in*) guns in *Hyuga* amidships turrets prior to reconstruction.
CPL

36cm (*14in*) turrets in *Yamashiro* in course of alterations 1932. In Nos 2 and 4 only the barbette is in position, while No 3 has the roof removed.
CPL

No details have been found of the 50cal gun intended for triple turrets in the projected battlecruisers 795 and 796. It seems most likely that it would have been 310mm (*12.2in*) bore rather than 304.8mm (*12in*). A number of the latter guns in twin turrets removed from ships scrapped under the Washington treaty were mounted for coast defence. Altogether there were six turrets, two on Tsushima, one on Iki, two at Tokyo Bay and one at Tsugaru Straits. Two turrets had 50cal guns, two 45cal, and two 45cal small chamber, but their location has not been found, except that we know the 50cal guns were not on Tsushima. The original 23-25° elevation was increased to 33-35°:

30cm (12in) guns

Gun	Projectile	Charge	MV	Approx Range
304.8mm (*12in*)/50	400kg (*883lb*)	133.5kg (*294lb*) 110C_2	853-860m/s (2800-2820f/s)	29,500m (*32,300yd*)
304.8mm (*12in*)/45	400kg (*883lb*)	113.4kg (*250lb*) 80C_2	810m/s (*2657f/s*)	27,400m (*30,000yd*)
304.8mm (*12in*)/45 small chamber	400kg (*883lb*)	103kg (*227lb*) 80C_2	810m/s (*2657f/s*)	27,400m (*30,000yd*)

MEDIUM CALIBRE GUNS

These were actually 254mm (*10.0in*) bore. At the beginning of the war, one old 40.3cal gun Elswick Pattern 'R' was still mounted in the armoured cruiser *Kasuga*, and four 45cal guns in twin turrets taken from the *Aki*, were in the Tokyo Bay defences with elevation increased to 35°.

25cm (10in) guns

Gun	Projectile	Charge	MV	Approx Range
254mm)*10in*)/45	235kg (*518lb*)	69kg (*152lb*) 80C_2	810m/s (*2657f/s*)	24,600m (*26,900yd*)
254mm (*10in*)/40.3	227kg (*500lb*)	40kg (*88.5lb*)C_2	700m/s (*2297 f/s*)	18,000m (*19,700yd*)

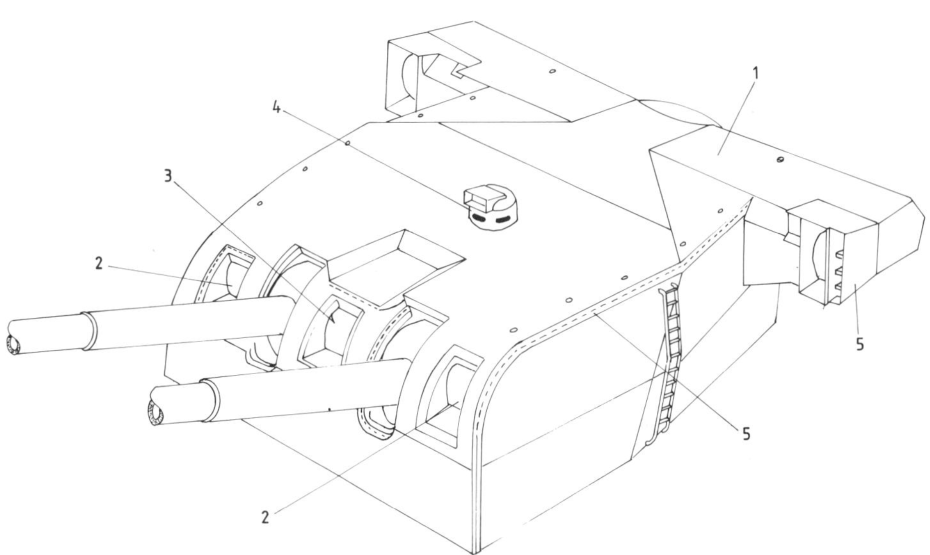

Details of twin 20.3cm (*8in*) turret as mounted in *Atago* class

1 Eight-meter range-finder
2 Layer's aperture
3 Trainer's aperture
4 Turret officer's scope
5 Sheet steel lagging for heat protection

John Lambert

There is much confusion about these. Neglecting the 203.2mm (*8.0in*) short gun, which is described later, there were three main groups: 20cm/50 II 3rd Year Type (1914), actually 203.2mm (*8.0in*); 20cm/50 I 3rd Year Type, 200mm (*7.874in*); 20cm/45 41st Year Type (1908) and Elswick Patterns S, U, U[1], W, all 203.2mm (*8.0in*), and all 45cal though often erroneously given as 40cal.

By the time Japan entered the war 20cm/50 II guns were mounted in twin turrets in all cruisers of the *Kako*, *Aoba*, *Nachi*, *Atago*, *Mogami* and *Tone* classes. They replaced 20cm/50 I singles in the *Kako* class, twins in the *Aoba* and *Nachi* classes, and 15.5cm triples in the *Mogami* class. They were also to be carried by the two *Ibuki* class which were cancelled as cruisers. The earlier guns were wire wound for part of their length and otherwise comprised an inner A tube, A tube, full-length jacket, breech ring and breech bush. The fore part of the inner A had a taper fit in the A tube with shoulders only at the rear. Later guns dispensed with wire winding, and all had Welin screw breech blocks operated by hydraulic power or by hand. It is said that about 300 guns were made, construction being shared between Kure and Muroran Ironworks. They appear to have been in short supply on

20cm (8in) guns

Gun Data 20cm/50 II

Bore	203.2mm	8.0in	
Weight incl BM	17,742-?19,000kg	17.46-?18.7 tons	
Length oa	10,310mm	405.91in	50.74cal
Length bore	10,000mm	393.70in	49.21cal
Length chamber	1348mm	53.07in	
Volume chamber	68dm^3	4150in^3	
Length rifling	8480.9mm	333.89in	
Grooves	(48) 2.28mm deep × 8.299mm	0.090 × 0.327in	
Lands	5.00mm	0.197in	
Twist	Uniform 1 in 27.56 (?28)		
Weight projectile	125.85kg	277.45lb	
Propellant charge	33.8kg 53DC	73.6lb	
Muzzle velocity	840m/s	2756f/s	
Working pressure	3130kg/cm^2	19.9tons/in^2	
Approx life	320-400EFC		
Max range	28,900m/40°; 29,400m/45°	31,600yd/40°;32,150yd/45°	

HE and incendiary shrapnel were of similar weight, but not illuminating shell, which was fired with a reduced charge at 710m/s (*2330f/s*). The full charge was in two bags each with an 85gm (*3oz*) black powder igniter. Other propellants were apparently used (80C_2, 70C_2, 60DC_1). The grain size of these seems large for the gun and their use may account for the discrepancies in salvo spread reported.

Foremost 20.3cm (*8in*) turrets in *Takao* taken in 1932. *CPL*

occasion as the *Kako* class had 20cm (*7.874in*) guns from *Ashigara* and *Haguro* with new 20.32cm (*8in*) inner A tubes and presumably a muzzle hoop.

The mountings varied in detail from class to class and, in some cases, from ship to ship, but many features were the same. They were individually powered by electrically driven oil-hydraulic pumps located in the revolving structure and found to be very noisy. Damage to rubber covered cables by leaking oil was another complaint. Run-out was by compressed air. There was one set of worm and worm-wheel training gear, and elevation in the type C, D and E mountings was by arc or rack and pinion but in later mountings by a cylinder and piston connected to the cradle. The *Aoba* class retained Type C mountings and the *Nachi* class Type D with sufficient modification to take the 20cm/50 II gun, and elevation in these was +40° -5°, though possibly later increased to 50° in *Aoba*. The *Atago* class had Type E mountings which allowed 70°, except *Maya*, which had 55° Type E, while the *Mogami* Type in that class, Type E_2 in the rearmed *Kako* class, and Type E_3 in the *Tone* class all allowed +55° -5°. The *Mogami* Type mountings differed in having a larger-diameter roller path to suit the former 15.5cm (*6.1in*) triple installation.

Magazines were located one deck below the shell rooms except in the *Kako* and *Aoba* classes where they were on the same deck. There were the usual flashtight drum scuttles between magazines and handing rooms and double flashdoors at the bottom of the charge hoists. In Type C and D mountings these were originally of pusher type but were replaced by cage-type hoists as in later mountings. Charges were delivered direct to the outside of the breech end of each gun. The shell rooms were usually located round the turret trunk and shells were transferred by shell bogie or circular roller track. Pusher hoists came up between and in rear of the guns, whence shells were moved via tilting buckets worked by handwheel and quadrant to the loading tray. Charges were loaded by hand, and they and shells separately power rammed at the loading angle of +5 or +7°. Some shell for AA use were often stowed between the guns, and time fuzes were set by hand in the loading tray.

Salvo spread was stated to be too large at 400m, range not given, but it was reported as very small in the action off Samar and the *Nachi* class achieved 280-330m firing at 20,000-22,000m in 1936. Possibly the grain size of the propellant caused the discrepancies noted above.

Range and Elevation Data for Type 91 AP at 835m/s (*2740f/s*) MV

Range (m)	Range (yd)	Elevation	Remain V (m/s)	Remain V (f/s)	Descent
5000	5470	2.4°	650	2133	3.0°
10,000	10,940	5.3°	498	1634	7.5°
15,000	16,400	10.5°	396	1299	15.8°
20,000	21,870	18.0°	364	1194	29.0°
25,000	27,340	30.0°	380	1247	47.0°

Gun Mounting Data

Wt (of revolving parts?)	166-175t	163-172 tons
Roller path outer dia	5.029m (*Mogami* Type 5.71m)	16.5ft (18.75ft)
Distance between gun axes	1.90m	74.8in
Elevating speed max	6-12°/sec	
Training speed max	4°/sec	
Firing cycle	12-15sec; 20-30sec at max elev	
Turret shield	25mm	1in

The design for the first of these guns, which were all exactly 14in bore (*355.6mm*), was submitted by Vickers in November 1910, and was originally known as 12in Vickers Mk 'J' or 12in Meiji 43 Type (the 43rd year of the Meiji era being 1910). It later became known as 14in Vickers Mk 'A' or as 14in 43rd Year Type. The later, similar, Japanese design was known as 41st Year Type, as Japanese guns were usually dated by the beginning of design work on the type of breech mechanism. Such are the pitfalls of Japanese ordnance. Altogether about 100 guns were made, the Japanese built some at Kure or Muroran Ironworks, but a number of guns of the 41st Year Type and more forgings were supplied from England. There were several versions of the Japanese type, but they and the Vickers guns can be considered together. The latter were originally mounted in *Kongo* and *Hiei*, and the former in *Haruna*, *Kirishima*, *Fuso*, *Yamashiro*, *Ise* and *Hyuga*, all in twin turrets.

The Vickers guns were of normal, full-length-wire type with cannelured rings at the tube shoulders, and the earlier 41st Year Type guns were similar, though some of the later ones are believed to have had the inner A tube radially expanded into position. Circumferential serrations as in the 41cm were later added. Vickers 'pure couple' breech mechanism was used with a Welin block.

36cm (14in)/45 Vickers and 41st Year Types (1908)

Gun Data

Bore	355.6mm	14in	
Weight incl BM	84,690-86,000kg	83.3-84.6 tons	
Length oa	16,469mm	648.4in	46.3cal
Length bore	16,002mm	630in	45cal
Length chamber	2006.7-2007.7mm	79.0-79.04in	
Volume chamber	294.9dm^3	17,996 in^3	
Length rifling	13,737-13,706mm	540.82-539.61in	
Grooves	(84) 3.048mm deep × 8.865mm	0.12 × 0.349in	
Lands	4.435mm	0.175in	
Twist	Uniform 1 in 28		
Weight Type 91 AP	673.5kg	1485lb	
Propellant charge	142.3kg 85 DC	313.8lb	
Muzzle velocity	770-775m/s	2526-2543f/s	
Working pressure	3000-3020kg/cm^2	19-19.2tons/in^2	
Approx life	250-280 EFC		
Max range	35,450m	38,770yd	

Time-fuzed HE and incendiary shrapnel weighed 625kg (*1,378lb*) and their MV was 805m/s (*2641f/s*). The propellant charge was in four bags with a 225gm (*7.9oz*) black powder igniter on each one.

Range and Elevation Data for Type 91 AP and 770m/s MV

Range		Elevation	Remain V		Descent
(m)	**(yd)**		**(m/s)**	**(f/s)**	
5000	5470	2.6°	670	2198	3.5°
10,000	10,940	6.1°	576	1890	7.5°
15,000	16,400	9.9°	510	1673	12.4°
20,000	21,870	14.4°	459	1506	18.9°
25,000	27,340	20°	420	1378	27.5°
30,000	32,810	28.7°	414	1358	35.9°

Gun Mounting Data

Wt of revolving parts (*Haruna*)	?664t	?654 tons
Wt of revolving parts (*Ise*)	?699t	?688 tons
Roller path dia	7.77m	25.5ft
distance between gun axes	2.286m	7.5ft
Elevating speed max	5°/sec	
Training speed max	3°/sec	
Firing cycle	30-40sec at max elev	
Turret shield (*Kongo* class)	face ?250mm; sides, rear 230mm; roof 150mm	9.8in; 9in; 5.9in
(***Fuso*, *Ise* classes**)	face ?300mm; sides 250mm	11.8in; 9.8in

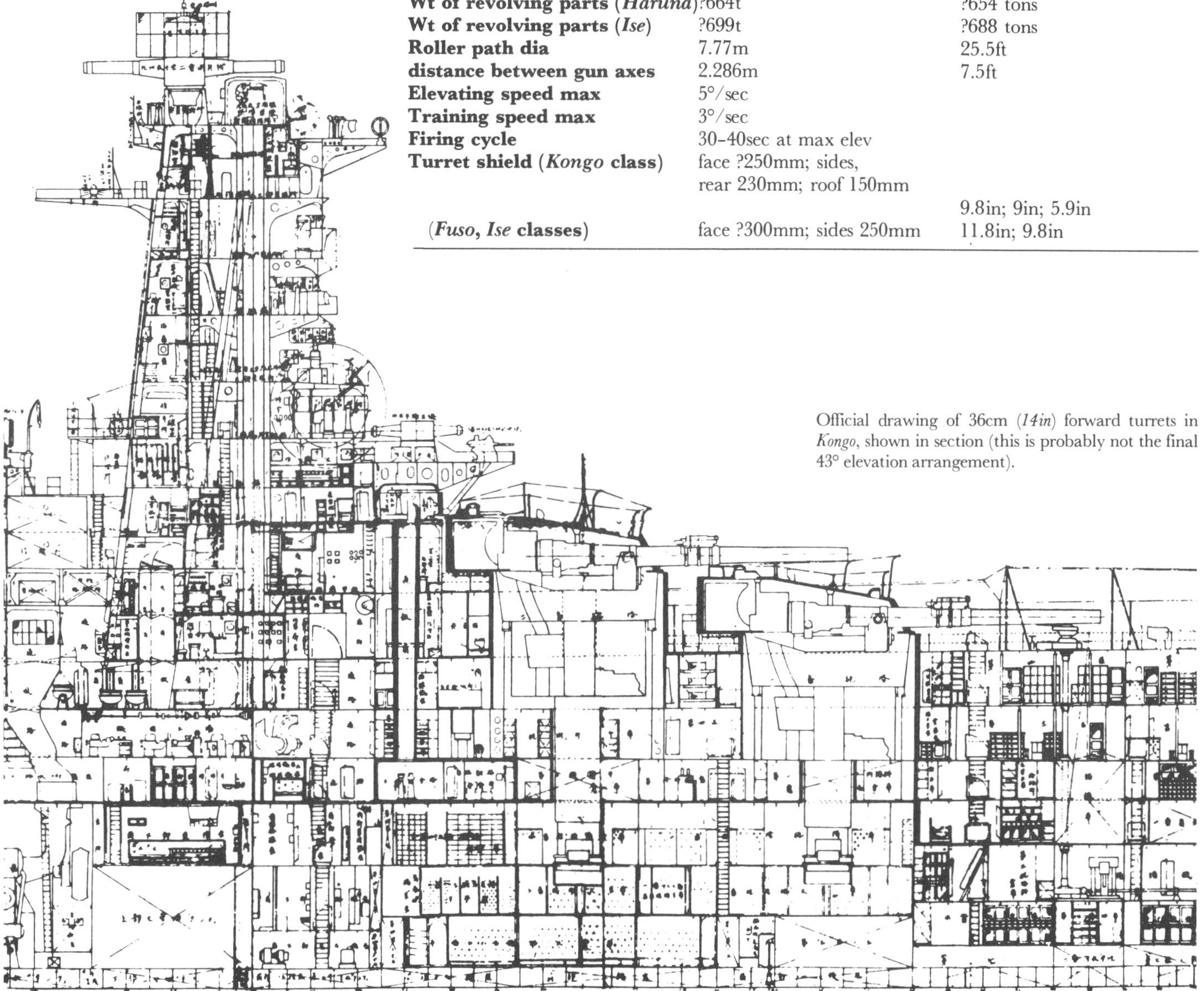

Official drawing of 36cm (*14in*) forward turrets in *Kongo*, shown in section (this is probably not the final 43° elevation arrangement).

The original mountings for *Kongo* were of the usual British type, except that auxiliary electric drive was provided. Elevation was +25° -5°, and shell rooms are shown below the magazines, though this was later changed. Elevation was increased to +33° and compressed air run-out provided in the 1920s, and later the mountings were altered to give +43° -3° and to resemble the 41cm mountings in the *Nagato* class except in some of the loading arrangements described below. There was however insufficient room in *Ise* and *Hyuga* to lower the revolving part of the two after turrets so that elevation could be increased only in the other four turrets. The precise loading arrangements are not known in every ship, but there were three types of gun-loading cage. The *Haruna* type resembled that in the 41cm, but the charge was in two compartments, each holding two quarters, so that it had to be rammed in two strokes. In the *Kongo* type the shell was on an extension to the main cage and the charge in two compartments in the cage proper, from which it rolled down into line with the gun and was rammed in two strokes. Lastly the *Ise* type was conventional and similar to the British 15in. Loading was possible up to 20° elevation, except in the *Fuso* type turret where it was at a fixed angle of +5°.

36cm (*14in*) guns in *Hyuga* amidships turrets prior to reconstruction.
CPL

36cm (*14in*) turrets in *Yamashiro* in course of alterations 1932. In Nos 2 and 4 only the barbette is in position, while No 3 has the roof removed.
CPL

20cm (*7.9in*) gun and cradle being hoisted into port turret of *Kaga*, 1929. On reconstruction the turrets were removed and the guns added to the casemate battery.
CPL

20cm/50 I guns were still mounted in the aircraft carriers *Akagi* and *Kaga* only. The twin Type B turrets which allowed 70° elevation, had been removed when the ships were modernised and only the single Type A[1] mountings remained. These allowed 25° elevation though blast effects limited this to 20-23° for much of the training arc. The guns were wire wound for part of their length and had screw breech blocks. They can be distinguished from II guns by the marked step in the chase diameter.

Gun Data 20cm/50 I

Bore	200mm	7.874in	
Weight incl BM	17,900kg	17.6 tons	
Length oa	10,000mm	393.70in	50.0cal
Length bore	*c*9690mm	*c*381.50in	*c*48.45cal
Weight projectile	110kg	242.5lb	
Propellant charge	32.55kg 53 DC	71.76lb	
Muzzle velocity	870m/s	2854f/s	
Working pressure	3000kg/cm^2	19tons/in^2	
Approx life	300 EFC		
Max range	22,600m/25°	24,700yd/25°	

20cm/45 guns were still mounted at the beginning of the war in those of the old armoured cruisers that retained their twin turrets. The guns were wire wound for part of their length and had screw breech blocks.

20cm/45 guns were mounted in some of the Japanese coast defences. There were two twin turrets at Tokyo Bay with 30° elevation, and some guns on various islands in the Pacific, including four on Wake and four on Tarawa in single P mountings giving 24° elevation. There was also a 20cm/50 on a 60° mounting in the Tokyo Bay area and ten further guns at Matsu Bay, some of which were probably 50 calibre.

Gun Data 20cm/45

Bore	203.2mm	8.0in	
Weight incl BM	18,750-19,400kg	18.45-19.1 tons	
Length oa	9487mm	373.5in	46.7cal
Length bore	9144mm	360in	45cal
Length chamber	1228-1291.6mm	48.355-50.85in	
Volume chamber	53.23-55.04dm^3	3248-3358.7in^3	
Weight projectile	113.4kg	250lb	
Propellant charge	25.85kg 70C$_2$	57lb	
Muzzle velocity	760m/s	2493f/s	
Max range	18,000m/30°	19,700yd/30°	

15.5cm (6.1in)/60 3rd Year Type (1914)

These guns, of which about 80 were made at Kure, were designed in 1933 and were originally mounted in triple turrets in the *Mogami* class cruisers. This class was rearmed with twin 20.3cm/50 guns, and the only ships that carried the 15.5cm triple in the war were *Yamato, Musashi* and the cruiser *Oyodo*, though it was intended for the other three *Yamato*s and the *Niyodo*, that were cancelled, or in the case of *Shinano* converted to an aircraft carrier. A triple turret was mounted on land for AA purposes at Sasebo and another at Kure, while there were two guns on single 60° mountings for coast defence in the Tokyo Bay area. Construction was simple, comprising principally an A tube, part-length jacket, breech ring and breech bush, though there were at least three versions differing in detail. The Welin block was operated hydraulically or by hand.

The propellant charge was in one bag with a 75gm (*2.6oz*) black powder igniter. AP and HE

Gun Data

Bore	155mm	6.10in	
Weight incl BM	12,700kg	12.50 tons	
Length oa	9615mm	378.54in	62.03cal
Length bore	9300mm	366.14in	60.0cal
Length chamber	1128mm	44.41in	
Volume chamber	38dm^3	2319in^3	
Length rifling	8025mm	315.94in	
Grooves	(40) 1.80mm deep × 7.514mm	0.71 × 0.296in	
Lands	4.66mm	0.183in	
Twist	Uniform 1 in 28		
Weight projectile	55.87kg	123.2lb	
Propellant charge	19.50kg 36 DC$_2$	43.0lb	
Muzzle velocity	920-925m/s	3018/3035f/s	
Working pressure	3390-3400kg/cm^2	21.5 tons/in^2	
Approx life	250-300 EFC		
Max range	27,400m/45°	29,960yd/45°	

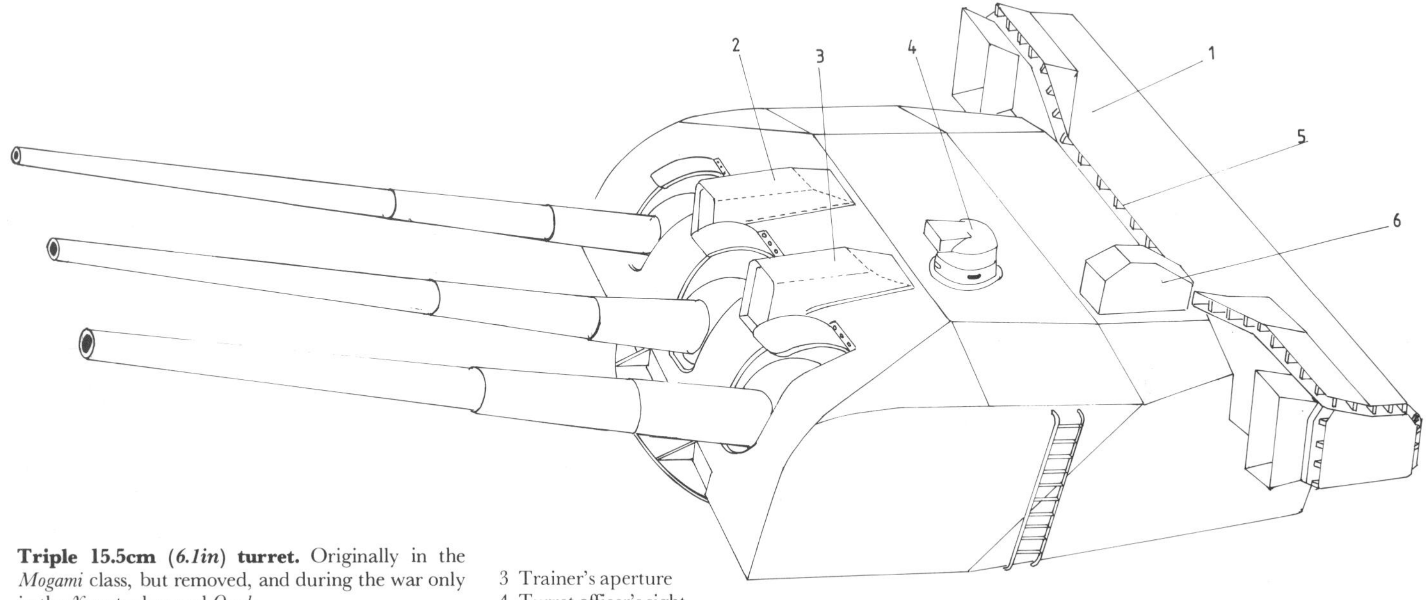

Triple 15.5cm (*6.1in*) turret. Originally in the *Mogami* class, but removed, and during the war only in the *Yamato* class and *Oyodo*.

1 Eight-meter range-finder
2 Gunlayer's aperture
3 Trainer's aperture
4 Turret officer's sight
5 Sheet steel lagging for heat protection
6 Exercise aiming device

John Lambert

shells were carried, but not incendiary shrapnel. Illuminating shell was fired with a reduced charge at 750m/s (*2461f/s*). The muzzle velocity is usually quoted as 950m/s (*3117f/s*), or even 980m/s (*3215f/s*), but reliable Japanese sources give the lower figure. Also the higher values do not agree with the maximum range. Even at 920-925m/s the performance was very high, with the usual result of limited life.

The mountings resembled the later 20cm adapted for three guns. To save space the breech mechanism of the centre gun was angled and opened upwards at 45°, the weight being balanced by springs. The pusher shell-hoists came up in rear of the guns, to the right of the left gun and to the left of the other two, while the charge hoists were just in rear of the breech, to the right of the right gun and to the left of the others. Other differences were the operation of the tilting shell buckets by handle and lever, the hand ramming of charges, and stowage of AA shell at the rear of the gunhouse. The elevating cylinder was connected to the cradle in front of the trunnions - this may have been done in some 20cm turrets - and in the *Yamato* class the main hydraulic pumps were located outside the turret to reduce noise. A single additional hoist for AA shell was fitted to only one trial turret which was never used afloat. Elevation was +55° to -7° and loading at +7°, while the rate of fire did not exceed five rounds a minute.

Range and Elevation Data for Type 91 AP at 920m/s MV

Range		**Elevation**	**Remain V**		**Descent**
(m)	**(yd)**		**(m/s)**	**f/s**	
5000	5470	2.3°	663	2175	3.0°
10,000	10,940	5.4°	465	1526	7.7°
15,000	16,400	11.2°	340	1115	16.5°
20,000	21,870	20.0°	320	1050	33.0°
25,000	27,340	35.0°	350	1148	56.0°

Gun Mounting Data

Wt (of revolving parts?)	180t	177 tons
Roller path outer dia	5.71m	18ft 9in
Distance between gun axes	1.55mm	61in
Elevating speed max	10°/sec	
Training speed max	6°/sec	
Firing cycle	12sec	
Turret shield	25mm	1in

Forward 15.5cm (*6.1in*) turrets in *Mikuma*, 1939.
CPL

15.2cm (*6in*) secondary battery, *Kongo* in 1931 during first reconstruction.
CPL

These were entirely distinct from the 15.5cm (*6.1in*) above, and none in the Japanese Navy was new. They were of 152.4mm (*6.0in*) bore, but it should be noted that Japanese Army 15cm guns were almost always 149.1mm (*5.87in*). Inter-service standardisation was not popular in Japan.

Of the naval guns, only the 15cm/50 Vickers and 41st Year (1908) Types need be considered in detail. These were introduced as secondary armament in the *Kongo* and *Fuso* classes, the *Kongo* having Vickers Mk 'M' guns and the other five ships the 41st Year Type of which there were a number of variants. Some guns were also made for stock and were used to arm the four *Agano* class light cruisers which had twin mountings. They were also intended for the projected light cruisers Nos 810 to 814, 5037, 5038. Coast-defence guns of these types were recorded only on Guam. The Vickers guns were wire wound for their full length, but the others were of three-layer built up type. All had screw breech blocks.

The *Kongo* and *Fuso* classes had P mountings with elevation increased to 30°, but the twin mountings made at Sasebo for the *Agano* class allowed +55° -7°. They were powered by electrically driven oil-hydraulic gear or could be operated by hand. Worm gears were used for training and elevation and there were shell hoists for each gun but charges were apparently passed up by hand. Loading was at +7° with hand ramming and AA fuzes were set before the shell was placed on the loading tray.

In addition to the 152.4mm (*6in*)/50, there were 45cal BL guns of various types and a smaller number of 40cal BL, as well as many 40cal QF. The latter, which was mostly of various Elswick patterns, were still mounted in some of the old armoured cruisers as well as in auxiliary ships or coast defence with the 45cal

15cm (6in) guns

Gun Data

Bore	152.4mm	6.0in	
Weight incl BM	8130-8360kg	8.0-8.23 tons	
Length oa	7770.8-7875.8mm	305.94-310.07in	50.99-51.68cal
Length bore	7515-7620mm	295.87-300.0in	49.31-50.0cal
Length chamber	949.36mm	37.376in	
Volume chamber	26.14dm^3	1595in^3	
Length rifling	6479.4-6584.4mm	255.09-259.23in	
Grooves	(42) 1.27mm deep x 7.62	0.050 × 0.300in	
Lands	3.78mm	0.1488in	
Twist	Uniform 1 in 30		
Weight projectile	45.36kg	100lb	
Propellant charge	12.4kg 37 DC	27.34lb	
Muzzle velocity	850-855m/s	2789-2805f/s	
Working pressure	2870-2900kg/cm^2	18.2-18.4 tons/in^2	
Approx life	500-600 EFC		
Max range	21,000m/45°	22,970yd/45°	

Type 4 Common and HE shell were supplied as well as illuminating and anti-submarine projectiles. The charge was in one bag with a 60 gram (2.1oz) black powder igniter.

Range and Elevation Data for Type 4 Common at 850m/s

Range		**Elevation**	**Remain V**		**Descent**
(m)	**(yd)**		**(m/s)**	**(f/s)**	
5000	5470	2.7°	530	1739	3.8°
10,000	10,940	8.0°	350	1148	12.5°
15,000	16,400	17.5°	320	1050	28.0°
20,000	21,870	34.0°	320	1050	52.0°

Gun Mounting Data

Total weight	73t	72 tons
Distance between gun axes	1.55m	61in
Elevating speed max	10°/sec	
Training speed max	6°/sec	
Firing cycle	10-15sec	
Turret shield	20mm	0.8in

and 40cal BL guns. These BL guns fired the same projectiles as the 50cal, with muzzle velocity of 825m/s (*2707f/s*) for the 45cal and probably about 750m/s (*2460f/s*) for the 40cal. The 40cal QF had HE shells of the same weight but with larger bursters, separate cartridge cases and MV of 700m/s (*2297f/s*).

The Japanese Army 149.1mm/50cal coast-defence guns fired a 40kg (*88.2lb*) shell with muzzle velocity of 875m/s (*2871f/s*) or one of 45kg (*99.2lb*) at 845m/s (*2772f/s*). They were of Krupp type but with tapered screw breech blocks and separate loading cartridge cases 1220mm (*48in*) long.

A more interesting Army gun was the 149.1mm/60cal Type 5 (1945) AA gun, of which two were emplaced in power-worked single mountings to defend the Imperial Palace in July 1945. These had horizontal sliding block SA breech mechanism and could attain 8-10 rounds a minute. Maximum elevating speed is given as 6°/sec and training as 9°/sec, both of which seem inadequate. The gun weighed *c*9980kg (*9.82 tons*) and fired a 44.4kg (*97.9lb*) shell at 930m/s (*3050f/s*). Fixed ammunition was used, the complete round being 1636mm (*64.4in*) long and weighing 84.5kg (*186.3lb*). The ceiling at 85° elevation was 19,050m (*62,500ft*), and the total weight including shield 55,000kg (*54 tons*).

14cm/50 (*5.5in*) BL guns in *Sendai*, 1939. *CPL*

14cm (5.51in) guns

This is another calibre which has caused some confusion. There were two quite distinct guns, the 14cm/50 3rd Year Type (1914) BL in surface ships only, and the 14cm/40 11th Year Type (1922) QF in submarines. The former fulfilled a similar role to the 6in Mark XII in the Royal Navy, and was carried in single mountings by the *Ise* class (until final reconstruction), *Nagato* class, *Hosho, Tatsuta* class, *Kuma, Nagara* and *Naka* classes (removed later from *Kitakami, Isuzu*), – the minelayer *Itsukushima* and some auxiliary ships. The *Yubari* had both single and twin mountings, and the latter were also in the *Kashima* class, *Nisshin, Okinoshima* and *Jingei* class. On single mountings it was the most common coast-defence gun in the Pacific Islands. The earlier guns were wire wound but later wire was omitted. Welin screw breech blocks were fitted.

Common and HE shells were carried and incendiary, illuminating and anti-submarine were also provided. The charge was in one bag with a 60gm (*2.1oz*) black powder igniter.

The single P mountings allowed +25° or +30° to -7° elevation except in the *Nagato* class with +35° -7°. The twin mountings were driven by self-contained oil-hydraulic gear or else by hand. The dredger hoists were independent of the mounting but there was an upper hoist tube below it. Elevation was +30° -7° except in the *Kashima* class with +35° -5°. Maximum elevating speed was 6°/sec, training 4°/sec, and loading was at any angle with hand ramming. The firing cycle was about 10sec. Total weight was 36,500-37,500kg (*35.9-36.9 tons*) with a 10mm (*0.4in*) shield except in the *Kashima* class – 49,000kg (*48.2 tons*) and 50mm (*2in*) shield.

Gun Data 14cm/50 3rd Year Type (1914)

Bore	140mm	5.512in	
Weight incl BM	5600-5700kg	5.5-5.6 tons	
Length oa	7235mm	284.84in	51.68cal
Length bore	7000mm	275.59in	50.0cal
Length chamber	942.4mm	37.10in	
Volume chamber	23dm³	1404in³	
Length rifling	5968.4mm	234.98in	
Grooves	(42) 1.40mm deep × 6.40mm	0.055 × 0.252in	
Lands	4.07mm	0.160in	
Twist	Uniform 1 in 28		
Weight projectile	38.0kg	83.8lb	
Propellant charge	10.97kg 37 DC	24.18lb	
Muzzle velocity	850-855m/s	2789-2805f/s	
Working pressure	2900-2910kg/cm²	18.4-18.5 tons/in²	
Approx life	500-600 EFC		
Max range	19,750m/35°	21,600yd/35°	

I 1 with 14cm/40 (*5.5in*) QF guns.
CPL

The 14cm/40 QF was in single P mountings in *I 1-4, I 9-48, I 52-56, I 58, I 121-124, I 361-373, I 400-402* and in twin P mountings in *I 7* and *I 8*. It was not in *I 5* and *I 6*. The earlier guns were built up but later ones had a monobloc barrel and breech ring. There was a horizontal sliding breech block, and separate loading ammunition was used with a brass case. The gun is said to have been mainly intended for use against destroyers.

The single mountings had a total weight of 8600kg (*8.46 tons*), were hand operated with a pneumatic hoist and elevated to +30° -5°. The firing cycle was 12sec. The twin mountings differed in a total weight of 18,300kg (*18 tons*) and elevation of +40° -7°, but were otherwise similar.

Gun Data 14cm/40 11th Year Type (1922)

Bore	140mm	5.512in	
Weight incl BM	3900kg	3.84 tons	
Length oa	5900mm	232.28in	42.14cal
Length bore	5600mm	220.47in	40.0cal
Length chamber	831.5mm	32.736in	
Volume chamber	$15dm^3$	$915in^3$	
Length rifling	4668mm	183.78in	
Grooves	(38) 1.65mm deep × 7.024mm	0.065 × 0.2765in	
Lands	4.55mm	0.179in	
Twist	Uniform 1 in 28		
Weight projectile	38.0kg	83.8lb	
Propellant charge	6.86kg 30 DC	15.12lb	
Muzzle velocity	700-705m/s	2297-2313f/s	
Working pressure	$2500kg/cm^2$	$15.9\ tons/in^2$	
Approx life	800-1000 EFC		
Max range	16,000m	17,500yd	

Base-fuzed shell was fired with a larger burster than in the 14cm/50.

14cm/50 (*5.5in*) BL as a coast-defence gun.
USN

12.7cm (5in)/50 Type 1 (1941)

This gun, also known as Type 5 (1945), was originally intended for twin mountings in ships, but the project was changed to single land mountings, the Japanese Navy being responsible for the AA defence of bases such as Kure. In the event only one prototype gun and mounting were completed. The gun was built with a monobloc barrel and breech ring and had SA horizontal sliding breech mechanism. Fixed ammunition was used with long nose shells.

Although the performance was less spectacular than that of the Army 149.1mm/60, elevation and training max speeds were 18°/sec and rate of fire 13-18 rounds per minute, compared with 6 and 9°/sec and 8-10rpm. The total weight less shield was 18,900kg (*18.6 tons*).

Gun Data

Bore	127mm	5.0 in
Weight incl BM	4665kg	4.59 tons
Rifling	36 grooves, Uniform 1 in 28	
Weight projectile	27kg	59.5lb
Propellant charge	9.8kg	21.6lb
Weight round	48.1kg	106.0lb
Muzzle velocity	880-910m/s	2887-2986f/s
Working pressure	$2800kg/cm^2$	$17.8\ tons/in^2$
Max range	22,400-23,600m	24,500-25,800yd
Ceiling	15,200-16,200m/85°	49,900-53,150ft/85°

12.7cm/50 (*5in*) BL in after twin mountings, *Ayanami*. *CPL*

12.7cm (5in)/50 3rd Year (1914)

Gun Data

Bore	127mm	5.0in	
Weight incl BM	4245kg	4.18 tons	
Length oa	6483mm	255.24in	51.05cal
Length bore	6265mm	246.65in	49.33cal
Length chamber	822.5mm	32.38in	
Volume chamber	16dm³	976in³	
Length rifling	5350.5mm	210.65in	
Grooves	(36) 1.52mm deep × 6.63mm	0.060 × 0.261in	
Lands	4.45mm	0.175in	
Twist	Uniform 1 in 28		
Weight projectile	23kg	50.7lb	
Propellant charge	7.7kg 30 DC	17.0lb	
Muzzle velocity	910-915m/s	2986-3002f/s	
Working pressure	2840kg/cm²	18 tons/in²	
Approx life	550-700 EFC		
Max range	18,400m	20,100yd	

This BL gun was the standard Japanese destroyer armament and was mounted as follows: first ten *Fubuki* class, Type A twin 40° elevation; other *Fubuki* and *Akatsuki* classes, Type B twin 75° elevation; *Hatsuharu* class, Type B twin 55° elevation and Type A single 55° elevation; *Shiratsuyu* class, Type C twin 55° elevation and Type B single 55° elevation; *Asashio, Kagero* classes, Type C twin 55° elevation; *Yugumo* class, *Shimakaze*, Type D twin 75° elevation. The guns, of which about 700 were made, were of built-up construction, originally three and later two layers with the usual breech ring and breech bush. Welin type blocks were fitted.

Nose-fuzed HE of two different types was carried and there were also two types of incendiary shrapnel as well as illuminating and anti-submarine shells. The charge was in one bag with a 50gm (*1.75oz*) black powder igniter.

There are discrepancies in the various lists of ships and mounting types, but those given above are believed to be correct, as are the maximum elevation figures. Depression was usually -7°, though drawings of *Nowaki* of the *Kagero* class show -1½°. In the twin mountings the guns were in separate cradles and could elevate separately. Loading was by hand, with hand ramming at +10° to +5°. There were pusher shell-hoists for each gun but charges were passed by hand. Fuzes were set by hand on the loading tray. Elevation and training were powered by electrically driven oil-hydraulic gear with hand operation in reserve. Maximum training speed was 4-6°/sec, which made the mountings almost useless for AA, while elevating, which was through a pinion and arc, is believed to have had a maximum speed of 6-12°/sec, though nearly 24° to 27° has been reported. The firing cycle is variously given as 6-12sec, and the total weight as 18,700kg (*18.4 tons*) for single mountings and 32,500kg (*32.0 tons*) for twins. Shields were 3mm (*0.12in*) thick. The mountings appear to have been liked but were considered to need strengthening, which may have accounted in part for the large dispersion noted.

12.7cm (5in)/40 Types 88 and 89 (1928, 1929)

Gun Data Type 89 (1929)

Bore	127mm	5.0in	
Weight incl BM	3100kg	3.05 tons	
Length oa	5284mm	208.03in	41.61cal
Length bore	5080mm (Type 88, 5096)	200.0in (200.63)	40.0 (40.13cal)
Length chamber	534.4mm	21.04in	
Volume chamber	9dm³	549in³	
Length rifling	4450.1mm	175.20in	
Grooves	(36) 1.52mm deep × 6.63	0.060 × 0.261in	
Lands	4.45mm	0.175in	
Twist	Uniform 1 in 28		
Weight projectile	23kg	50.7lb	
Propellant charge	3.98kg 21 DC	8.77lb	
Muzzle velocity	720-725m/s	2362/2379f/s	
Working pressure	2500-2530kg/cm²	15.9-16.1t/in²	
Approx life	800-1500 EFC		
Max range	14,700m	16,075yd	
Ceiling	9440m/90°	30,970ft/90°	

Type 88 was carried only in single mountings by *I5* and *I6*, but the very similar Type 89 in twin mountings was the standard naval heavy AA. Of ships in service during the war, all battleships, all large aircraft carriers except *Akagi* and *Taiho*, all small fleet aircraft carriers except *Hosho* and all the later heavy cruisers except the *Kako* and *Aoba* classes, the unreconstructed *Chokai* and *Maya* (until 1944), carried this AA armament, as did many other ships, while the *Matsu* and *Tachibana* class escort destroyers had a twin and a single mounting. About 1500 guns were made - about 900 between 1941 and 1945 - and a total of 362 were mounted ashore, including 96 in the Yokosuka and 54 in the Kure areas. The gun was of simple construction with monobloc barrel and breech ring and horizontal sliding breech block. Its main fault was the low muzzle velocity.

Nose-fuzed HE and incendiary shrapnel were fired against aircraft, and illuminating and anti-submarine shells were also provided. Fixed ammunition was fired with a brass or mild steel case and the AA round was 970.8mm (*38.22in*) long and weighed 34.3-35kg (*75.6-77.2lb*).

There were several variants of the twin AA mounting but most features were common to all. Elevating and training were by electrically driven oil hydraulic gear with hand operation in reserve. Loading was at any angle of elevation with a spring rammer cocked by the recoil. Fuze-setting machines were fixed to the breech faces of the guns and there was a loader's platform suspended from the rear end of the cradle to ease the working of the hand operated loading trays as the trunnions were 2.49m (*98in*) above the roller path. There were one or two hoists per mounting, and it was noted in the aircraft carrier *Katsuragi* that supply was by one electric dredger hoist that came up about 32m (*35yd*) and at least two bulkheads from the mounting. The elevation range was usually +90° -8° and a 2mm (*0.08in*) spray shield was supplied. Japanese opinion of the mounting was apparently very favourable.

The single mountings in *15* and *16* were hand worked with training and elevation rates of about 4°/sec, and a rate of fire of 8 rounds per minute. Supply was by penumatic hoist, elevation +75° -7° and total weight 8800kg - (*8.66 tons*).

Gun Mounting Data

Total weight, average	29,000kg	28.5 tons
Mean roller path dia	2.28m	7.48ft
Distance between gun axes	0.680m	26.77in
Elevating speed max	12°, later 16°	
Training speed max	6 to 7° later 16°	
Rate of fire	14 rounds/min, sustained 8	

12.7cm/40 (*5in*) QF Type 89 in twin HA mounting as a DP coast-defence gun.
USN

12.7cm/40 (*5in*) QF Type 89 in typical twin HA mounting, the standard naval heavy AA.
John Lambert

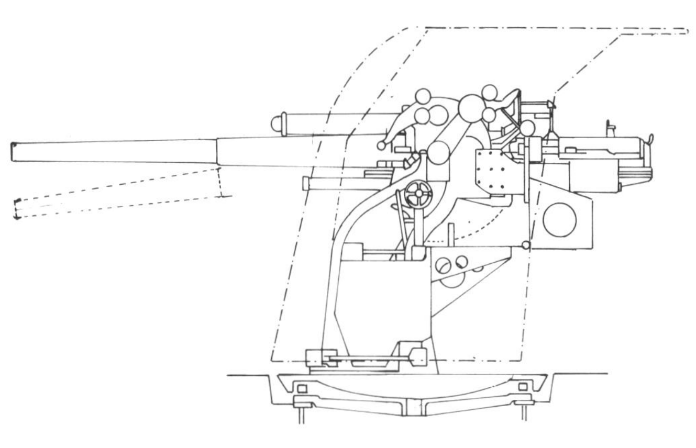

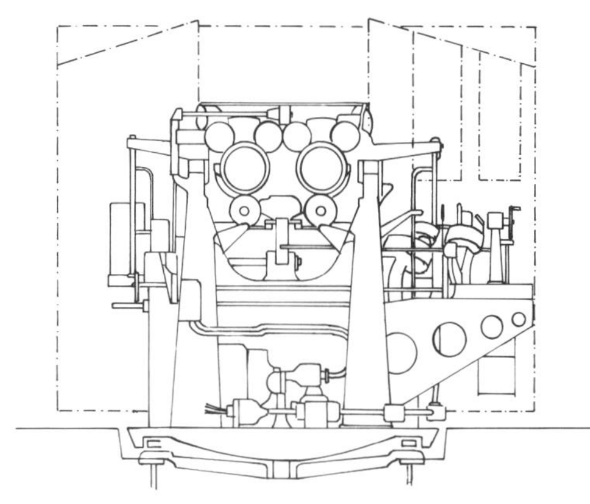

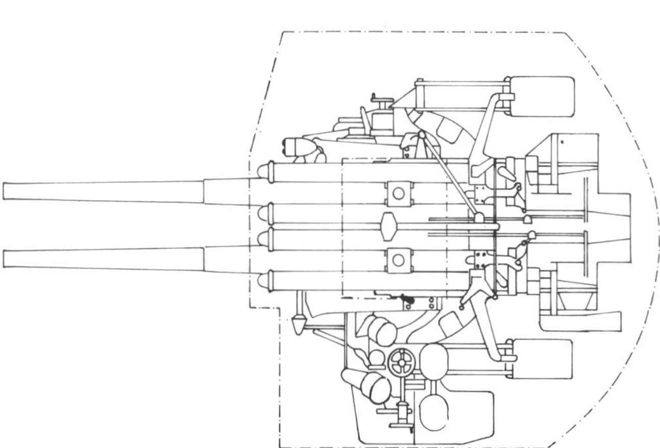

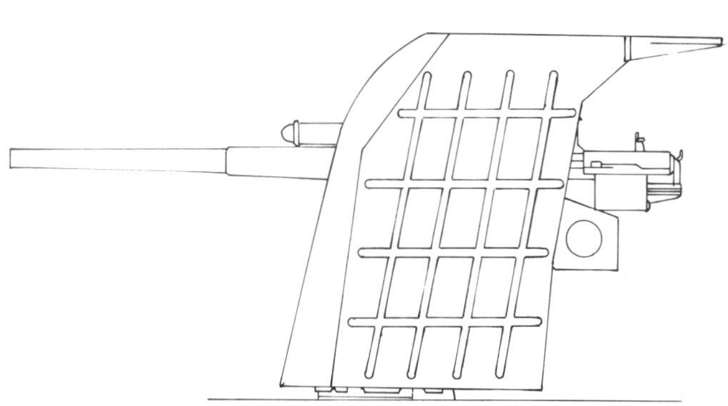

This is another calibre where there is considerable confusion, ships being credited with imaginary 50cal weapons, whereas the only 12cm in service that was longer than 45cal was the Army Type 3 (1943)AA. Like all Japanese 12cm guns this was of 120mm (*4.724in*) bore and was 56cal in length firing a 23.3kg (*51.4lb*) shell at *c*853m/s (*2800f/s*). It was used in fixed power-trained mountings, but only 154 guns were made and it was far outnumbered by the 405 Naval 45cal AA mounted on land.

The 12cm/45 10th Year Type (1921) gun was in twin mountings in the *Akagi* and in some escorts and auxiliaries, and in singles in the escort aircraft carriers *Taiyo* and *Unyo*, in cruisers of the *Kako* and *Aoba* classes, as well as in *Chokai*, which was never reconstructed, and in *Maya* until 1944. Latterly in *Yubari* and the *Ioshima* class, single mountings were also in many escorts and auxiliary vessels as well as on land (as noted above). Altogether about 3000 guns were made, 2320 of them in 1942 to 1945. The earlier guns were of built-up construction but later a monobloc barrel and breech ring were favoured. All had SA horizontal sliding block breech mechanism.

Some guns were rifled with 36 grooves. Fixed ammunition was fired with a brass or mild steel case, and base and nose-fuzed HE and also two kinds of incendiary shrapnel are listed, as well as illuminating and anti-submarine projectiles. The complete round weighed round 34kg (*75lb*) maximum and was *c*94cm (*37in*) long. A serious fault was that the 30 DC charge had too large a grain size for the gun, and unburnt propellant was present at the muzzle, leading to irregularity. Late in the war tubular grain charges were introduced, and also a 13crh shell weighing 22.5kg (*49.6lb*). This combination gave a range of 20,000m (*21,870yd*) and a ceiling at 75° elevation of 12,500m (*41,000ft*) without increasing muzzle velocity or working pressure.

There were various mountings and, in all of them, loading was by hand at any angle and fuze setting also by hand. Ammunition supply was by dredger hoists serving either one or two mountings. Elevation was +75° to -10° and rate of fire 10-11 rounds per minute. The twin mountings in *Akagi* and the singles in the cruisers had electrically powered oil-hydraulic gear for elevating and training with respective total weights of 20,300kg (*20 tons*) and 10,000kg (*9.8 tons*). There was also a powered mounting for escorts. Older mountings and those on land were manual with reported training rates of 10°/sec and elevating of 6.5°/sec. Spray shields with a thickness of 1.6-3.2mm (*0.06-0.12in*) were fitted to some single mountings.

12cm (4.7in) guns

Gun Data 12cm/45 10th Year Type (1921)

Bore	120mm	4.724in	
Weight incl BM	2900-2980kg	2.85-2.93 tons	
Length oa	5604mm	220.63in	46.7cal
Length bore	5400mm	212.60in	45.0cal
Length chamber	656mm	25.83in	
Volume chamber	10.774dm^3	657.5in^3	
Length rifling	4649.3mm	183.04in	
Grooves	(34) 1.45mm deep × 6.688	0.057 × 0.263in	
Lands	4.40mm	0.173in	
Twist	Uniform 1 in 28		
Weight projectile	20.41kg	45.0lb	
Propellant charge	5.50kg 30 DC	12.13lb	
Muzzle velocity	825-830m/s	2707-2723f/s	
Working pressure	2640-2650kg/cm^2	16.8 tons/in^2	
Approx life	700-1000 EFC		
Max range	16,000m	17,500yd	
Ceiling	10,000m/75°	32,800ft/75°	

12cm/45 (*4.7in*) QF 10th Year Type in single HA mountings as originally in *Nachi*.
CPL

12cm/45 (*4.7in*) QF 10th Year Type as a DP coast-defence gun.
USN

12cm/45 (*4.7in*) QF 3rd Year Type in the small destroyer *Kuri*.
CPL

These were in hand-worked single mountings, the 3rd Year Type in older destroyers up to and including the *Mutsuki* class and also in a few old submarines, the 11th Year Mk 'M' in the *Otori* and rearmed *Tomozuru* class torpedo boats, and Mks 'J' and 'L', both of which differed in having horizontal sliding breech blocks instead of screw, in *I 153-I 164* and *I 171-I 185* respectively. Both the screw breech types were also in some lesser warships, and the 3rd Year Type was a frequent coast-defence gun in the Pacific Islands. Most guns were of built-up construction but some had monobloc barrels and breech rings and a few may have been wire wound. All fired separate QF ammunition with brass cases.

Some of the older 3rd Year Type guns had 36 grooves, 1.02mm deep × 6.43mm (*0.040* × 0.253in), lands 4.04mm (*0.159in*), and 11th Year Mk 'J' and 'L' guns had a bore length of 5270mm (*207.48in*), 43.92cal, and rifling length 4470.8mm (*176.02in*). Some accounts give this bore and rifling length for the Mk 'M' gun with an overall length of 5400mm (*212.60in*), 45.0cal. Projectiles included base and nose fuzed HE, illuminating and anti-submarine.

Most mountings allowed +33° to -7° elevation but those in *I 171-185* went to -10° and the torpedo boat mountings gave +55° -10°. Loading was at 10° to 15° by hand, and firing cycle about 12sec with maximum elevating and training speeds of 5° and 4°/sec also by hand. There were pneumatic hoists in the submarines and otherwise a dredger hoist for every one or two mountings. Total weight was about 8900kg (*8.76 tons*), and 3mm (*0.12in*) shields were fitted on the torpedo boats and destroyers.

12cm (4.7in)/45 3rd Year Type (1914) and 11th Year Type (1922)

Gun Data 3rd Year Type

Bore	120mm	4.724in	
Weight incl BM	2616-3240kg	2.57-3.19 tons	
Length oa	5550mm	218.50in	46.25cal
Length bore	5400mm	212.60in	45.0cal
Length chamber	722.7mm	28.45in	
Volume chamber	10.44dm^3	637in^3	
Length rifling	4600.8mm	181.13in	
Grooves	(34) 1.45mm deep × 0.263in	0.057 × 0.263in	
Lands	4.40mm	0.173in	
Twist	Uniform 1 in 28		
Weight projectile	20.41kg	45.0lb	
Propellant charge	5.27kg	11.62lb	
Muzzle velocity	825m/s	2707f/s	
Working pressure	2700-2750kg/cm^2	17.1-17.5 tons/in^2	
Approx life	700-1000 EFC		
Max range	16,000m, 15,000m/33°	17,500yd, 16,400yd/33°	

Old 12cm/40 41st Year or Elswick Type guns were still in existence. These were similar to the British 4.7in QF Mks I - IV and fired a 20.4kg (*45lb*) shell at *c*660m/s (*2182f/s*).

LIGHT CALIBRE GUNS

This was another group where Army and Navy guns had different bores, respectively 105mm (*4.134in*) and 100mm (*3.937in*) though all known as 10cm. The only Army gun that needs to be noted was the 45cal 7th Year Type (1918), which was a QF coast defence gun with vertical sliding breech block firing separate ammunition. The shell and muzzle velocity were 15.9kg (*35.1lb*), 700m/s (*2297f/s*).

The 10cm/65 gun, considered by the Japanese to be the best that they had, was in twin mountings in the *Taiho* and *Oyodo*, and in the *Akizuki* class destroyers. It was also intended for many cancelled ships. A total of 169 guns were completed and after early 1945 installation on land had priority, so that 68 guns were located ashore in their twin mountings. Some guns had liners and others monobloc barrels, both with the usual breech ring, and with horizontal sliding breech blocks. Fixed ammunition was fired with brass cases.

Nose-fuzed HE shells were fired and the complete round was 1118mm (*44in*) long and weighed 28kg (*61.7lb*). The effect of high muzzle velocity in limiting barrel life is well shown and was the only Japanese complaint.

The mountings which were in closed shields in the *Akizuki* class were powered by electrically driven hydraulic gear with worm training and elevation, and could be hand worked in emergency. The elevation range was +90° -10° with loading at any angle by means of spring rammers cocked by the recoil. In the *Akizuki* class two dredger hoists supplied ammunition from the magazine to the working chamber in the fixed structure at 20-22 rounds per minute each. In the working chamber the rounds were manhandled to waiting positions at the entrances to the two upper pusher hoists. These were built as a unit and could not work independently, though the rate of supply could be varied. At the top of these hoists the round rolled automatically into one of the waiting positions from where it was passed to loaders standing on platforms which moved with the guns as in the 12.7cm Type 89. Fuze-setting machines were fixed to the breech faces of the guns and loading trays were hand operated.

10cm (4in) guns

Gun Data 10cm (3.9in)/65 Type 98 (1938)

Bore	100mm	3.937in	
Weight incl BM	3053kg	3.005 tons	
Length oa	6730mm	264.96in	67.3cal
Length bore	6500mm	255.91in	65.0cal
Length chamber	750mm	29.53in	
Volume chamber	10.5cm^3	641in^3	
Length rifling	5631mm	221.69in	
Grooves	(32) 1.25mm deep × 5.565mm	0.049 × 0.219in	
Lands	4.252mm	0.167in	
Twist	Uniform 1 in 28		
Weight projectile	13kg	28.7lb	
Propellant charge	6kg	13.23lb	
Muzzle velocity	1010m/s	3314f/s	
Working pressure	3050kg/cm^2	19.4 tons/in^2	
Approx life	350-400 EFC		
Max range	19,500m	21,300yd	
Ceiling	13,000m/90°	42,650ft/90°	

Mounting Data Type 98 (1938)

Total weight (*Akizuki*)	34,500kg	34 tons
Mean roller path dia	2.280m	7.48ft
Distance between gun axes	0.660m	25.98in
Elevating speed max	16°/sec	
Training speed max	12-16°/sec	
Rate of fire	15-21 rounds/min	
Shield	*c*3mm	*c*0.12in

Right: 10cm/65 (*3.9in*) Type 98 guns in twin HA mounting on land.
USN

Below: 10cm/65 (*3.9in*) Type 98 guns in twin power worked HA mountings in *Hatsuzuki* 11 June 1944.
Aldo Fraccaroli Collection

The 10cm/50 gun occurs only in hand worked single HA mountings in *I 165–I 170*. It had a monobloc barrel and breech ring with horizontal sliding breech block and fired fixed ammunition with a brass case. As in the 12cm 10th Year Type unburnt propellant was present at the muzzle.

The mounting allowed +90° -7° and could be hand loaded at any angle. The firing cycle was 5sec but the pneumatic hoist took 10sec to deliver a round.

Above: I 165, originally numbered *165*, with 10cm/50 (*3.9in*) Type 88 gun.
CPL

Gun Data 10cm (3.9in)/50 Type 88 (1928)

Bore	100mm	3.937in	
Weight incl BM	2830kg	2.79 tons	
Length oa	5300mm	208.66in	53.0cal
Length bore	5000mm	196.85in	50.0cal
Length chamber	625mm	24.61in	
Volume chamber	8dm^3	488in^3	
Length rifling	4295mm	169.09in	
Grooves	(32) 1.25mm deep × 5.565mm	0.049 × 0.219in	
Lands	4.252mm	0.167in	
Twist	Uniform 1 in 28		
Weight projectile	13kg	28.7lb	
Propellant charge	4.13kg 30 DC	9.11lb	
Muzzle velocity	885–895m/s	2904–2936f/s	
Working pressure	2820kg/cm^2	17.9 tons/in^2	
Approx life	400–700 EFC		
Max range	16,200m	17,700yd	
Ceiling	11,200m/90°	36,750ft/90°	

Nose-fuzed HE shell was fired and the round weighed 24kg (*52.9lb*).

8cm (3in) guns

All Navy guns under this classification were actually 76.2mm (*3.0in*) bore, but the Army 88mm AA gun was sometimes listed as 8cm. Incidentally this had no connection with any German 8.8cm (*3.465in*) gun.

The 8cm/60 was only in service afloat in the *Agano* class light cruisers, though four guns were at Maizuru. All were in twin mountings. the barrels were of linered or monobloc construction with breech rings and horizontal sliding blocks.

Fixed ammunition was fired with brass cases and nose-fuzed HE shells, the complete round weighing 12kg (*26.5lb*). The twin mountings were reduced editions of the 10cm Type 98 with +90° -10° elevation, a total weight of 12,500kg (*12.3 tons*) maximum elevating and training rates of about 16°/sec and a rate of fire of 25 rounds per minute.

The 8cm/30 3rd Year Type (1914), 11th Year Type (1922), Type 88 (1928) were all fixed ammunition guns and were in single HA mountings in many lesser warships, while the Type 88 was in submarines of the *Ro 33* and *Ro 35* classes. A considerable number of the 3rd Year Type were also mounted ashore. Older guns were built up but the more recent had monobloc barrels. The sliding breech blocks were inclined upwards at 45° to the right in the 3rd Year Type but were horizontal in the others.

Cartridge cases were brass or mild steel and shells included nose-fuzed HE and common, as well as shrapnel, tracer and anti-submarine. The complete round weighed about 9.25kg (*20.4lb*).

The single mountings were entirely hand worked with elevation +75° to -7° and a total weight of about 3350kg (*3.3 tons*). Maximum

Gun Data 8cm (3in)/60 Type 98 (1938)

Bore	76.2mm	3.0in	
Weight incl BM	1320kg	1.30 tons	
Length oa	4777m	188.07in	62.69cal
Length bore	4566.5mm	179.78in	59.93cal
Length chamber	440mm	17.32in	
Volume chamber	3.5dm^3	213.6in^3	
Length rifling	4036.5mm	158.92in	
Grooves	(24) 1.02mm deep × 6.12	0.040 × 0.241in	
Lands	3.85mm	0.152in	
Twist	Uniform 1 in 28		
Weight projectile	5.99kg	13.2lb	
Propellant charge	1.91kg	4.21lb	
Muzzle velocity	900–920m/s	2953–3018f/s	
Working pressure	2800–2900kg/cm^2	17.8–18.4 tons/in^2	
Approx life	Not determined		
Max range	13,600m	14,870yd	
Ceiling	9100m/90°	29,850ft/90°	

Gun Data 8cm (3in)/40 3rd Year Type (1914), 11th Year Type (1922), Type 88 (1928)

Bore	76.2mm	3.0in	
Weight incl BM	600kg	0.59 tons	
Length oa	3203mm	126.10in	42.03cal
Length bore	3048mm	120.0in	40.0cal
Length chamber	390mm	15.35in	
Volume chamber	2.057-2.1dm^3	125.5-128in^3	
Length rifling	2608.5mm	102.70in	
Grooves	(24) 1.00mm deep × 5.905	0.039 × 0.232in	
Lands	4.07mm	0.160in	
Twist	Uniform 1 in 28		
Weight projectile	5.67-5.99kg	12.5-13.2lb	
Propellant charge	0.89-0.93kg 20 C_3	1.96-2.05lb	
Muzzle velocity	680-685m/s	2231-2247f/s	
Working pressure	2220-2300kg/cm^2	14-14.6 tons/in^2	
Approx life	1200-2000 EFC		
Max range	10,800m	11,800yd	
Ceiling	7200m/75°	23,600ft/75°	

elevating speed was 7-10°/sec, training 10-11°/sec and rate of fire 13-20 rounds per minute.

The 8cm/40 41st Year Type (1908), Elswick Pattern 'N' and Vickers Mk 'Z' guns were similar or virtually identical to the British 12pdr/12cwt. They used separate ammunition with a 5.67kg (*12.5lb*) shell and muzzle velocity 680m/s (*2231f/s*). There were also various types of 23.4cal guns, usually known as 25cal, and firing 5.67-5.79kg (*12.5-12.8lb*) shells at 450-455m/s (*1476-1493f/s*).

Top right: 7.6cm/40 (*3in*) 3rd Year Type in 75° HA mounting.
USN

Above: 7.6cm/40 (*3in*) 11th Year Type in Submarine Chaser *No 25*, 31 January 1941.
CPL

7.5cm (2.953in)/44 Type 88 (1928)

This standard 75mm Army AA gun was used to some extent by the Navy. It fired a 6.5kg (*14.3lb*) shell at 720m/s (*2362f/s*). It is sometimes listed as 7cm which adds to the confusion as the Army also had guns of 70mm bore.

6cm and **5cm** guns

These included the almost universal Hotchkiss 57mm (6pdr) and 47mm (3pdr) and the similar Yamanouchi guns. The short 47mm/30 (2½pdr) was less well known. In both Hotchkiss and Yamanouchi versions the muzzle velocity was 455m/s (*1493f/s*).

This was intended for AA and anti-submarine use on merchant ships of over 5000 tons gross, and was also used in the Marianas for defence against landing craft. It was of monobloc construction with a screw breech and fired separate QF ammunition with brass or mild steel cases. About 250 guns were made from 1943.

Large capacity HE and two kinds of incendiary shrapnel were provided. The single mountings were hand operated and had a total weight of 4100kg (*4 tons*) with elevation of +75°-15°. It is said that maximum elevation and training speeds were 8°/sec with rate of fire of 4.5 rounds per minute, though the mountings were described as heavy and slow. Loading was at about +10° by hand and ammunition supply relied on the ships' cargo hoists and simple derricks.

20cm (8in) Short gun

Gun Data

Bore	203.2mm	8.0in	
Weight incl BM	630kg	0.62 tons	
Length oa	2520mm	99.21in	12.40cal
Length bore	2438.4mm	96.0in	12.0cal
Length chamber	395.4mm	15.57in	
Volume chamber	14.6dm^3	891in^2	
Length rifling	1984.4mm	78.13in	
Grooves	(32) 1.5mm deep × 16.61mm	0.059 × 0.654in	
Lands	3.34mm	0.131in	
Twist	Increasing 1 in 30 to 1 in 13		
Weight projectile	47kg	103.6lb	
Propellant charge	2kg	4.41lb	
Muzzle velocity	305m/s	1001f/s	
Working pressure	650-700kg/cm^2	4.1-4.4 tons/in^2	
Approx life	2000 EFC		
Max range	6300m	6890yd	
Ceiling	3300m/75°	10,830ft/75°	

Above: 20.3cm Short gun mounted ashore for defence against landing craft.
USN

Right: 12cm (*4.7in*) Short gun mounted ashore.
USN

This was the companion gun to the short 20cm, intended for merchant ships of under 5000 tons gross. Construction was similar, but some guns at least appear to have fired fixed ammunition. Cases were brass or mild steel. About 550 guns were made from 1941.

Large capacity HE shells were fired. The elevation of the single hand-worked mountings was +75° -15° and the total weight 1890kg (*1.86 tons*). Maximum elevation and training rates were said to be 12-13°/sec and rate of fire eight rounds per minute. Hand loading was at any elevation, but there were no hoists.

12cm (4.7in) Short gun

Gun Data

Bore	120mm	4.724in	
Weight incl BM	218kg	0.215tons	
Length oa	1510mm	59.45in	12.58cal
Length bore	1440mm	56.69in	12.0cal
Length chamber	240mm	9.45in	
Volume chamber	3dm^3	183in^3	
Length rifling	1127mm	44.37in	
Grooves	(24) 1.0mm deep × 11.78mm	0.039 × 0.464in	
Lands	3.93mm	0.155in	
Twist	Increasing 1 in 30 to 1 in 13		
Weight projectile	13kg	28.7lb	
Propellant charge	0.49kg	1.08lb	
Muzzle velocity	290m/s	951f/s	
Working pressure	700kg/cm^2	4.4 tons/in^2	
Approx life	Not determined		
Max range	5300m	5800yd	
Ceiling	2800/75°	9190ft/75°	

CLOSE-RANGE AA GUNS

40mm (1.575in) Type 5 (1945)

This gun originated in a British Army type Bofors and single hand-worked mounting captured at Singapore in 1942. A Japanese prototype underwent firing trials in the spring of 1943 and limited production began in that year, but the operation of the gun was never perfected, and it was not in service, though 5 to 10 per month were being produced in late 1944. The main Japanese alteration was to increase the barrel length from 2250mm (*88.58in*) to 2400mm (*94.49in*), the weight of barrel and mechanism being 516kg (*1138lb*) and that of the single hand-worked mounting 850kg (*1874lb*). Elevation was +95° -10° and rate of fire 110-130 per minute. Projectile, charge and muzzle velocity were 1000gm (*2.2lb*), 280-300gm (*9.88-10.58oz*), 900m/s (*2953f/s*).

40mm (1.575in) Vickers

About 500 guns and 200 mountings, single or twin, were imported from 1925 to 1935 when they began to be superseded by the 25mm Hotchkiss. The gun was very similar to the British 2pdr pom-pom but used a 50-round belt though attempts to increase this still further to 100 rounds were not successful. A 907gm (*2lb*) shell and 96gm (*3.39oz*) charge gave a muzzle velocity of 600m/s (*1969f/s*) and maximum rate of fire was 200 per minute. The single mounting weighed 660kg (*1455lb*) and the twin 2354kg (*5190lb*), both being hand worked and allowing +85° -5° elevation.

25mm (0.984in) Type 96 (1936)

Gun Data

Bore	25mm	0.984in	
Weight barrel	43kg	94.8lb	
Total weight less mag	115kg	253.5lb	
Length oa	2296mm	90.39in	
Length barrel	1500mm	59.06in	60cal
Length rifling	1350mm	53.15in	
Grooves	(12) 0.25mm deep × 3.58	0.0098 × 0.141 in	
Lands	2.96mm	0.117in	
Twist	Uniform 1 in 25.2		
Weight projectile	250gm	8.82oz	
Propellant charge	102-110gm Special	3.60-3.88oz	
Muzzle velocity	900m/s	2953f/s	
Working pressure	2700kg/cm^2	17.1 tons/in^2	
Approx life	12,000 EFC		
Max range	7500m	8200yd	
Ceiling	5500m/85°	18,040ft/85°	

This gas-operated gun, the standard close-range AA weapon of the Japanese Navy, was adopted in 1935 after previous study at the Hotchkiss works in France. A few guns and mountings were ordered from this company and, after firing trials at Yokosuka in 1935, quantity production started there. In 1936 numbers were mounted afloat in twin mountings of French and Japanese manufacture. Altogether 33,000 guns were made in Japan and 20,000 mountings of various single, twin and triple types. Japanese modifications to the original Hotchkiss Type 'J' gun included many stainless steel parts for use in submarines, the replacement of some parts by castings and the use of Rheinmetall type flash eliminators which had a slight muzzle brake action. The barrel was air cooled and not strictly monobloc as the cooling fin jacket strengthened the breech end. It screwed to the breech mechanism assembly but gas cylinder connections caused the barrel change time to be at least 5 minutes' work for two men. The rate of fire could be varied by a gas control valve and single shots were possible. The main troubles were broken firing pins and insufficient recoil, particularly in submarines, while if the breech bolt locking mechanism was worn it was possible for the gun to start firing when a new magazine was fitted. The latter held 15 rounds and fed downwards from the top of the gun, its empty weight being 6.35kg (*14lb*).

The projectile weight given in the Gun Data table is nominal, actual weights varying from 243gm (*8.57oz*) to 252gm (*8.89oz*) except for AP, which was 282gm (*9.95oz*). In addition to this HE, HE tracer, HE incendiary and several types of tracer were fired, some HE Tracer being self destroying. The complete rounds which had brass or steel cases weighed about 680gm (*1.5lb*) and were about 233mm (*9.17in*) long. Maximum effective range was about 1500-3000m (*4900-9800ft*) depending on target course, and rate of fire could be adjusted from 200 to 260 per minute, 220 being standard, though the practical rate was about half this, through magazine changes. Barrel life was limited by sights and directors which allowed only for 100m/s (328f/s) velocity loss, and projectiles were stable after over 20,000 rounds.

Single mountings were normally free swinging except for Model 10, designed for MTB, where training was by body movement inside the mounting ring and elevation by manual gear drive. Some submarine mountings could be lowered into the boat by hand or by mechanical drive from a distance. Twin and triple mountings had manual gear drive for training and elevation, but ships with the Type 95 (1935) Director had Ward-Leonard RPC for their triple mountings. This gave maximum training rates of 18°/sec and elevating of 12°/sec. Elevation in all was +85° -10° and the guns were in a horizontal line in twins and triples. Weights averaged 185kg (*408lb*), 1100kg (*2425lb*), and 1800kg (*3970lb*) for single, twin and triple mountings. Shields were not normally fitted but some triples in the *Yamato* class had them, principally for blast protection. Some mobile two-wheeled carriages were made for use on land, but most such guns, of which 3487 were recorded in Japan, were on naval mountings.

Japanese criticisms were as follows (the most important first):

1. Twin and triple mountings could not be trained and elevated fast enough either by hand or power.
2. Sights were inadequate for high speed targets.
3. Excessive vibration.
4. Magazines held too few rounds.
5. Muzzle blast.

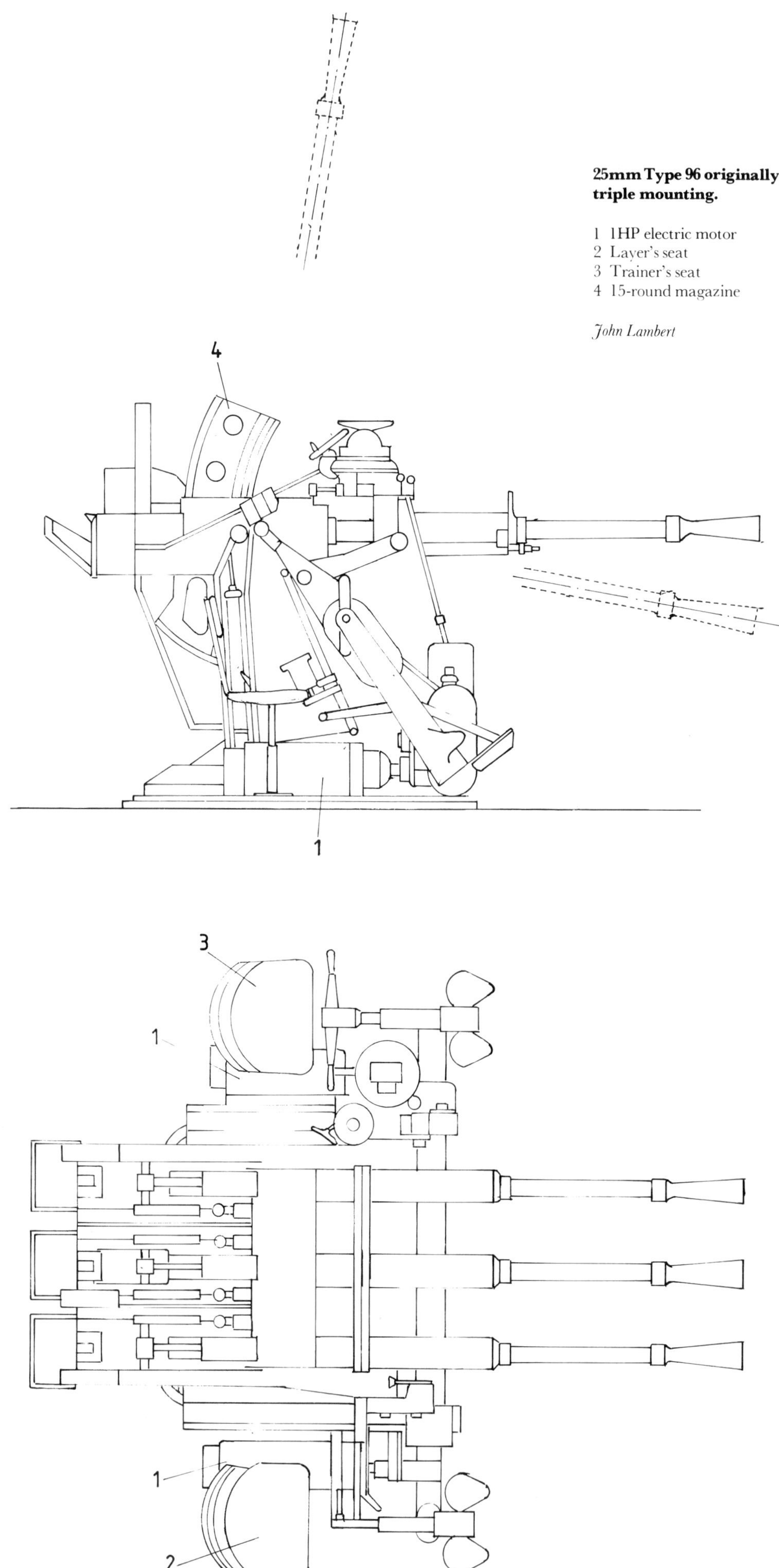

25mm Type 96 originally of Hotchkiss design, in triple mounting.

1 1HP electric motor
2 Layer's seat
3 Trainer's seat
4 15-round magazine

John Lambert

25mm Type 96 in single mountings, outboard of stowage for kaitens in *Kitakami* February 1945.
CPL

This was another air-cooled, gas-operated Hotchkiss gun, mostly imported pre-war but latterly made in Japan, production reaching 1200 a month late in the war. Because of gas cylinder connections, barrel changes took as long as in the 25mm, and the magazine resembled that of the larger gun but held 30 rounds. It was used in single, twin and quadruple manual mountings.

Ball, AP, tracer, white-phosphorus incendiary and HE incendiary were fired, the complete round weighing 112.6–118.5gm (*3.97–4.18oz*) with a length of 134.4–136.6mm (*5.29–5.38in*). The rate of fire could be adjusted between 425 and 475 per minute and was usually set at 450 but magazine changes reduced the practical rate to 250. Maximum effective range was about 700–1500m (*2300–4900ft*). The mountings which allowed +85° -15° were heavy, singles weighing 113–213kg (*249–470lb*), twins 314kg (*692lb*) and quadruples 1163kg (*2565lb*). The gun was also used on land, the total in Japan being 1494 towards the end of the war.

13.2mm (0.520in) Type 93 (1933)

Gun Data

Bore	13.2mm	0.520in	
Weight barrel	19.8kg	43.7lb	
Total weight less mag	41.8kg	92.2lb	
Length oa	1410mm	55.5in	
Length barrel	1003mm	39.5in	76cal
Grooves	(8) 0.15mm deep	0.006in deep	
Twist	Uniform 1 in 32		
Weight projectile	44.5–51.8gm	1.57–1.83oz	
Propellant charge	15gm	0.53oz	
Muzzle velocity	805m/s	2641f/s	
Working pressure	3000kg/cm^2	19 tons/in^2	
Max range	6000m	6560yd	
Ceiling	3980m/85°	13,060ft/85°	

Other Machine Guns

There were probably a few 12.7mm (*0.5in*) Vickers still in use, while 7.7mm (*0.303in*) Lewis were imported before the war as were 7.7mm recoil-operated water-cooled Vickers, the latter being also made in small quantities in Japan.

TORPEDOES

The excellence of Japanese torpedoes was due to the use of pure oxygen instead of air in the later types for surface ships and submarines, and that reliability of the whole torpedo, including the explosive charge system, had been attained by sinking many old ships as targets in live-practice runs. The latter was an obvious if costly precaution which was skimped or neglected by many navies, however. The advantage of pure oxygen lay in eliminating the 77% content of nitrogen in air, which was useless in the combustion process but served to form a conspicuous bubble track. The pure oxygen torpedo left a scarcely visible wake in addition to its far higher performance.

Like most navies, the Japanese had investigated the use of oxygen long before World War II, but this work had been abandoned in 1917, after about a year, because explosions in the generator occurred at ignition of the fuel. In 1927 Oyagi, later an Admiral, heard while studying torpedo design at Whitehead's Weymouth establishment that *Nelson* and *Rodney* had 24.5in (*62.2cm*) oxygen torpedoes. This was not strictly true, as the torpedoes used enriched air and not pure oxygen, but the report caused work to be restarted in 1928 at Kure under Rear-Admiral Kaneji Kishimoto and Captain Toshida Asakuma. A successful torpedo using about 50% oxygen was built in 1930 and the first Japanese pure oxygen torpedo was designed in 1933. This, the 61cm (*24in*) Type 93 Model 1, was the forerunner of the later versions of the Type 93, under the name of 'Long Lance', the most famous of all torpedoes.

The main problems to be solved were: (1) preventing explosion on ignition; (2) controlling temperature in the generator; (3) the use of sea water as diluent; (4) increase in engine strength and life; (5) improvements in the gyro for better direction keeping at the increased range. The initial solution to the first problem was to use a small 'first air vessel' with a pressure 5–10kg/cm^2 (*70–140lb/in^2*) above that of the oxygen vessel. The Kerosene fuel was ignited by air from the first air vessel and no oxygen was delivered until the pressure in the first air vessel fell below that of the oxygen. Detail engineering was not good and air leaks occurred. The air could be topped up in cruisers and destroyers and, with difficulty, in submarines which fired 53.3cm (*21in*) torpedoes of the same general design (though it was usual in this case to replace the torpedo by a spare), but in midget submarines, which originally had 45cm (*17.7in*) oxygen torpedoes muzzle-loaded in the TT, nothing could be done to prevent oxygen flowing if the air pressure fell below that of the oxygen, and on firing the torpedo would explode and the midget be destroyed. A better system used air from the steering air vessels for starting: as the engine revolved, the main oxygen delivery stop valve was opened fully in 60 revolutions, and the air valve from the steering vessels closed suddenly after 40. A third method proposed in 1943 was to introduce carbon tetrachloride to slow down the Kerosene/oxygen reaction. This seems to have worked well but hydrochloric acid was formed, which caused corrosion. Trichlorethylene was tried, but failed to prevent starting explosions.

The use of sea water in the combustion system eliminated the usual freshwater vessel, but salt deposits in the engine inlet slide valves and in the cylinders were troublesome and the valves had to be replaced after every three test or tuning runs, while an overhaul of engine, generator and reducing valve was required after each run. The correct generator design was the most difficult of the development problems and took a year to solve.

Heat losses were low, because of the relatively stagnant films of water on the inside and outside of the generator and an approximate calculation gave only 0.17% as against 16% based on the conduction of the metal alone. The gas from the generator had a composition of 16% CO_2, 6.6% CO, 77% H_2O and 0.4% O_2, H_2, N_2, etc. The outlet temperature was 660°C and reducer pressure at full power 38kg/cm^2 (*540lb/in^2*). As usual the engine room was open to sea-water flooding. The high pressure sea-water pumps were driven

Triple 61cm (*24in*) TT in *Hatsushimo* 15 March 1939. *Aldo Fraccaroli Collection*

from the engine and delivered to a buffer chamber which damped out the pump pressure fluctuations, a most important requirement. At high speed, 60% of the pump supply went to the generator and to pressurising the Kerosene bottle, 40% to cooling the engine crankcase and valves. At medium speed these figures altered to 40% and 60%, and at low speed to 30% and 70%. The engine cylinders were cooled by sea water flowing through the engine room. A separator to prevent water from being carried over with Kerosene on the initial dive and at the end of the run was fitted to the 61cm (*24in*) only.

The engine was a modified double-acting Whitehead with two horizontal cylinders in line, the bore and stroke being 142 × 180mm (*5.591 × 7.087in*) in the 61cm (*24in*) torpedo, and 130 × 160mm (*5.118 × 6.299in*) in the 53.3cm (*21in*).

It was found necessary to increase the clearance at top dead centre from 1mm (*0.040in*) to 3mm (*0.120in*), because of salt deposits, and accept the loss of efficiency. No attempt was made to attain very high outputs per unit of swept volume or engine weight, the engine in the 61cm (*24in*) developing 520HP with a weight (less generator) of 349kg (*770lb*) and a swept volume of 11,402cm^3 (*696in*^{3}).

With a maximum range of 40,000m (*43,700yd*), improvement in direction keeping was necessary, and a balanced differential air pressure unit was introduced between gyro and steering engine slide valve to eliminate sluggish operation of the link mechanism. The gyro was also mounted on rubber.

Torpedoes were mostly filled ashore, but small oxygen plants were fitted in cruisers and destroyers, the output of the former being 30m^3 (*1060ft*^{3}) of free oxygen per hour and of the latter half that figure. In heavy weather, purity deteriorated but 93% oxygen was acceptable if the Captain agreed.

Except in midget submarines, the safety record appears to have been good. The most feared risk seems to have been that splinters might pierce the torpedo oxygen vessel, and the local heat of impact be sufficient to ignite the steel and in this way detonate the warhead. In surface ships, four or five men were detailed for water hoses and an emergency tank by the TT mounting, and if the situation appeared critical the damaged torpedoes were fired. To slow down splinters the sides of TT were extended with 5mm (*0.2in*) protective plate.

It should be noted that not all Japanese 61cm (*24in*) torpedoes used oxygen, the earlier ones being of the conventional wet-heater air type. Pure oxygen torpedoes of this size were carried by the 18 heavy cruisers (though *Chokai, Maya* and apparently *Tone* and *Chikuma* did not have them in 1941), the *Agano* class light cruisers, and destroyers from the *Hatsuharu* class onwards. The four heavy cruisers mentioned had them later and the light cruisers *Kitakami* and *Oi* were reconstructed with 10 quadruple TT each and an outfit of 40 oxygen 61cm (*24in*) torpedoes each. Otherwise it is not known if they were issued to other older ships, but the light cruiser *Nagara* and destroyers *Shirayuki* and *Hatsuyuki* of the *Fubuki* class did not have them at the Battle of Guadalcanal.

Production of oxygen torpedoes was at Kure Arsenal, and it would seem that about 2600 Type 93 torpedoes were made, 1350 of them by the end of 1941. This was barely adequate, as use was lavish and the outfit in most destroyers was 16, with 16 or 24 in cruisers. Production of 53.3cm (*21in*) torpedoes used by submarines was about 3300 from 1938 when that of the oxygen Type 95 began, but this includes the enriched air Type 96 and the electric Type 92, both produced from 1942, and it would seem that about 2200 Type 95 were made. Earlier wet-heater air torpedoes were also used in the war.

The standard explosive charge was 60% TNT, 40% hexanitrodiphenylamine in blocks, known as Type 97. This had been introduced in 1907 by the German navy and had proved to be very stable to shock in the 1914-18 war. An aluminised version (60 TNT, 24 HND, 16 Al powder) is mentioned, but it is not known if it was used. Type 94 (60 TNA, 40 cyclonite) is also mentioned, and old torpedoes probably still had picric acid (shimose).

Later versions of Type 93 and 95 torpedoes had the round-nosed head modified to a more pointed form with a gain of 2kts in top speed. This was the result of tests on an Italian 53.3cm (*21in*) 50kt torpedo imported in 1939-40, but in tail form and other matters the Japanese torpedo was better.

Inertia pistols were used, though the oldest torpedoes had the whisker type. A new Type 2 exploder was designed to replace the older Type 90 which could premature from torpedo engine vibrations. The arming range of the Type 2 could be selected between 200m (*220yd*) and 400m (*440yd*) for surface ships and 300m (*330yd*) and 1600m (*1750yd*) for submarines. Magnetic pistols were developed for use in conjunction with the standard inertia type and accepted for service in July 1944. 80 were made for Type 95 torpedoes but results, if any, are not known.

Homing gear based on the comparison of sound intensity was also developed for the electric Type 92 torpedo, but here again it is not known if there were any successes. It appears that the Type 92 torpedo was itself too noisy.

Special heads (described under airborne torpedoes) were the Kite attachment used in some Type 92 and popular with a few submarine captains, and the shaped charge 'V' head apparently adopted for service in Types 93 and 95 in 1944.

Although pure-oxygen airborne torpedoes had been developed as Type 94, development was stopped in 1935, though about 100-120 are thought to have been made after this date, as the improved performance was not worth the complications of the oxygen system in a short range torpedo. Japanese 45cm (*17.7in*) airborne torpedoes, whether modifications of Type 91 or the later Type 4, which did not become fully operational, were of the wet-heater air pattern using eight-cylinder, two-row radial engines with poppet valves and cylinder bore and stroke 90 × 85mm (*3.543 x 3.346in*). There was only one speed setting. The various Type 91 torpedoes were considered very dependable, the weak points at water entry being the warhead joint and in the shell over the engine room and buoyancy chamber. With too low an entry angle (too high speed and too low altitude) the torpedo was liable to buckle in the vicinity of the buoyancy chamber. The optimum entry angle was 17-20° and the best combination for dropping 180kts at 100m (*330ft*), which gave a torpedo entrance speed of 103m (*338ft*)/sec. The earlier Type 91 could stand 250-260kts at 300m (*1000*ft) with a 50% higher entrance speed, and later versions 300 and finally 350kts while Type 4 withstood 400kts. The depth of dive by the torpedo was never specified, but dropping in 12m (*40ft*) depth of water was satisfactory. The favoured combination for this was 140kts at 30m (*100ft*) with an entry speed of about 80m (*260ft*)/sec.

To prevent impact damage to the warhead, a rubber sheath about 10mm (*0.4in*) thick which shattered on the water was used to cover about 60cm (*24in*) of the nose. Box-type wooden tail frames similar to the US were used for stability in the air, or a slightly less effective X-type if the bomb bay would not take the former. A feature which the Japanese considered very important was the anti-roll stabiliser. This consisted of small gyro-controlled flippers on each side of the torpedo with wooden frames attached for air travel which like the wooden tails broke off on striking the water. If rolling was allowed to occur, the horizontal rudders acted as steering rudders and could produce a sharp 'hook' on water entry. This device was introduced in Type 91 Mod 2 whereas in Mod 1 rolling had been prevented by partial filling of the warhead to lower the centre of gravity which tended to be high in all Japanese torpedoes.

Many experiments were made with net cutters, but all were unsatisfactory as rudder disturbance was caused by excessive cavitation from the cutters. The number of tail fins was increased from four to eight in some, and though the torpedoes were steadier in the water, recovery from the initial dive was too slow, taking 730m (*800yd*) instead of 350m (*380yd*). Many USN 22.4in (*56.9cm*) Mk 13 torpedoes were examined and the Japanese thought they were too short for a good underwater trajectory, and also disliked the shroud rings present in some, as previous Japanese work had shown increased resistance and interference with the propellers.

Inertia pistols were standard with a modified Type 90 exploder, though the Type 4 torpedo had a new Type 4. The main explosive charge was 60 TNT, 40 HND as in ship torpedoes. The Kite head mentioned above was introduced in 1944 as a substitute for a magnetic influence exploder. A small hydroplane was towed above and slightly abaft the warhead, and as the torpedo passed under the ship, the hydroplane struck the hull and broke away, firing the exploder. The success rate is not known.

The shaped charge head, also mentioned above, was known as Type 6 warhead in Type 93 and 95 torpedoes but as Type 4 in airborne, where it was apparently first used in March or April 1945. The V fitting consisted of a funnel-shaped steel liner with an external cone angle of 45° and an internal of *c*34°. Its weight was 83kg (*183lb*) and that of the explosive charge 305kg (*672lb*). On tests at Kure it penetrated a target of three 10mm (*0.4in*), three 19mm (*0.75in*) and one 10mm (*0.4in*) bulkheads, with spaces 2 × 1200mm (*47in*) air, 3 x 900mm (*35in*) water and 1 × 1000mm (*39in*) air. It appears that three were actually used off Kyushu but results are not known.

Research into airborne torpedoes was concentrated at Kanazawa near Yokosuka with production at Kure pre-war, but later at Nagasaki and Hikari Arsenals. Production of Type 91 Mod 1 was only pre-war and the total is given as 2092, while figures for later Mods of Type 91 from April 1941 to July 1945 total 7572, with 880 Type 4 in addition.

SHIP, SUBMARINE AND MTB TORPEDOES

53.3cm (21in) 6th Year Type (1917)

This was a conventional Kerosene-air wet-heater torpedo designed in 1917 and still in service in some of the older RO submarines. The engine was a four-cylinder radial of Schwarzkopf pattern, or in some apparently a two-cylinder double-acting Whitehead. Air consumption was 6kg (*13.2lb*)/BHP hour and the explosive charge 200kg (*441lb*). Ranges were 7000m (*7650yd*)/36kts, 10,000m (*10,900yd*)/32kts and 15,000m (*16,400yd*)/26kts. Length overall was 6840mm (*22ft 5.3in*) and total weight 1432kg (*3157lb*).

61cm (24in) 8th Year Type (1919)

Another conventional wet-heater torpedo adopted in 1920-21, and still used in old destroyers and light cruisers, the *Nagara* having examples at the Battle of Guadalcanal. The engine was a four-cylinder Schwarzkopf pattern radial, and air consumption 6kg (*13.2lb*)/BHP hour. Surviving torpedoes were probably Model 2 with a 345kg (*761lb*) shimose charge and ranges 10,000m (*10,900yd*)/38kts, 15,000m (*16,400yd*)/32kts, 20,000m (*21,900yd*)/28kts. Length overall was 8415mm (*27ft 7.3in*) and total weight 2362kg (*5207lb*).

53.3cm (21in) Type 89 (1929)

Developed for submarines, this was another Kerosene-air wet-heater torpedo introduced in 1931 and widely used in the earlier part of the war. The engine was a two-cylinder double-acting of Whitehead pattern and air consumption was improved to 5.1kg (*11.3lb*)/BHP hour. The explosive charge was 300kg (*661lb*) and ranges 5500m (*6000yd*)/45kts, 6000m (*6550yd*)/43kts, 10,000m (*10,900yd*)/35kts. Length overall was 7163mm (*23ft 6in*) and total weight 1668kg (*3677lb*).

53cm (*21in*) 6th Year Type torpedoes in twin TT in *Ohi*.
CPL

61cm (*24in*) 8th year Type torpedoes fired by the famous light cruiser *Jintsu*, 1927.
CPL

61cm (24in) Type 90 (1930)

Introduced in 1931 this was carried by the *Fubuki* class and by some heavy cruisers early in the war. The engine was a more powerful version of that in the Type 89 and air consumption was similar. The explosive charge was 375kg (*827lb*) and ranges 7000m (*7650yd*)/46kts, 10,000m (*10,900yd*)/43kts, 15,000m (*16,400yd*)/35kts. Length overall is believed to have been 8485mm (*27ft 10in*) and total weight 2605kg (*5743lb*).

53.3cm (21in) Type 92 (1932)

Data

Length oa	7150mm	23ft 5.5in
Length battery chamber	3539mm	11ft 7.3in
Total weight	1720kg	3792lb
Negative buoyancy	300kg	661lb
Explosive charge	300kg Type 97	661lb Type 97
Range	7000m/28-30kts	7650yd/28-30kts
Wander L or R (max)	120m/7000m	130yd/7650yd

This was an electric torpedo with a long history, as the Japanese began work in 1921 in the knowledge that the German Navy had produced a workable one three years previously. The Japanese design was completed in 1925 and in that year 3000m (*3300yd*)/30kts was achieved. Work continued and in 1934 the design of the Type 92 Modification 1 was completed but few were made, as the design was put on one side, ready for quantity production in war. In the event, production began in 1942 and at least 650 were made to supplement the main Type 95 submarine torpedo.

The Type 92 Mod 1 was powered by two 54-cell lead-acid batteries preheated from the submarine by six 250W metal-enclosed heaters to give maximum output, which was rated at 150amp/hr. The motor was a six-pole, compound interpole design rated at 95HP at 1250rpm and operating at 200V. Compressed air was carried for steering. The torpedo was slow compared with Type 95 but had even less track and was easier to produce. Its main defect was leakage between the battery chamber and after body.

The Type 92 Model 2 was to have been designed after the German G7e, 10 torpedoes and drawings have been delivered to the Japanese in 1942. They also examined torpedoes at the Penang U-boat base, but lack of manpower killed the project.

Top: 61cm (*24in*) quadruple TT for Type 93 Long Lance torpedoes in reconstructed *Takao*, 21 December 1939. Note that single 12cm (*4.7in*) AA guns are still mounted. *CPL*

Above: 61cm (*24in*) shielded quadruple TT for Type 93 torpedoes in *Shiranui*. *CPL*

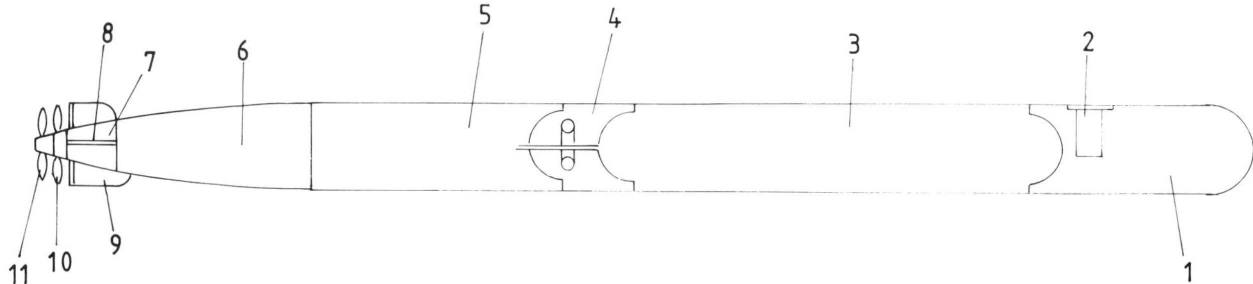

61cm (*24in*) Type 93 Model 1 Mod 2 Long Lance torpedo in schematic section (not to scale).

1 Explosive warhead, 610kg (*1345lb*) filled with 490kg (*1080.5lb*) of 97 shiki explosive
2 Fuze with 90 shiki firing pistol
3 Oxygen chamber, 980 litres at 225kg/cm^2 (*3200lb/in^2*)
4 Fuel chamber, 12.8 litres Kerosene
5 Midship section: lubricating oil container (67 litres); two steering air bottles (13.5 litres each). Centre section forms the forward buoyancy chamber containing No 3 steering air bottle (13.5 litres) first air vessel (13.5 litres), depth gear and circuit-valve. After section, forming engine room, middle-locking gear, combustion chamber, etc.
6 After body, forming after buoyancy chamber, gyroscope steering engine, etc.
7 Tail-housing bearing of shafts
8 Horizontal rudder
9 Vertical rudder
10 Forward propeller - 568mm (*22.4in*) diameter 4 bladed
11 After propeller - 530mm (*20.9in*) diameter 4 bladed

John Lambert

Model 1 was the experimental 'Long Lance' prototype, of which the features have been described above. The production torpedoes, dating from 1935, were Model 1 Mod 1. The main differences were that the strength of the bracing ribs in the fore body and rear buoyancy chamber was increased, more cooling water was supplied to the piston rod to prevent cracking, and the slide-valve gearing was improved.

Model 1 Mod 2 dated from 1936 and differed in many details. The oxygen vessel was made as a deep pressing with one integral end, as in all later types, instead of as a hollow forging. The bracing ribs of the rear buoyancy chamber were further strengthened, and cooling water to the slide valves increased with modifications to the buffer chamber, lubrication of the cross-head and group valve gearing.

Model 1 Mod 3, designed in 1944, started production in 1945 but was never in service. It combined the oxygen vessel and warhead of Mod 1 with the propulsion system of Model 3 described below.

Model 2 was an experimental torpedo designed in 1935 to meet a staff requirement for a higher speed torpedo in destroyers. Only two were built and experiments were discontinued in favour of research on turbines. When the latter ran into trouble, work on Model 2 began again in 1941. There were two engine designs, both essentially modifications of the two-cylinder double-acting Whitehead type. In the first the bore was increased with a rise in top speed to 51kts. The second was more successful and involved thicker cylinder walls and heads and stronger piston rods to stand the increased inlet pressure of 45kg/cm^2 (*640lb/in^2*), giving 850HP. A finer head after the Italian design was used and propeller pitch was reduced and revolutions increased. Three runs were made and gave 56kts over 5000m (*5500yd*).

Model 3, designed in 1943, had a longer, heavier warhead and a shorter oxygen vessel, and the first air vessel was replaced by carbon tetrachloride to prevent explosion on ignition.

61cm (24in) Type 93 (1933)

Data Model 1, Modifications 1, 2

Length oa	9000m	29ft 6.3in
Total weight	2700kg	5952lb
Negative buoyancy	480kg	1058lb
Volume oxygen vessel	980 litres	34.6ft^3
Pressure	225kg/cm^2	3200lb/in^2
Weight oxygen 15°C	299kg	659lb
Kerosene	106kg	233lb
HP (36-38kt)	200	
(40-42kt)	300	
(48-50kt)	520	
Consumption expendables	2.65kg/hp/hr	5.84lb/HP/hr
Explosive charge	490kg Type 97	1080lb Type 97
Range	20,000m/48-50kts	21,900yd/48-50kts
	32,000m/40-42kts	35,000yd/40-42kts
	40,000m/36-38kts	43,700yd/36-38kts
Wander L or R (max)	500m/20000m	550yd/21,900yd
	1000m/32000m	1100yd/35,000yd
	1500m/40000m	1640yd/43,700yd

Data Model 3, differences

Total weight	2800kg	6173lb
Negative buoyancy	580kg	1279lb
Volume oxygen vessel	750 litres	26.5ft^3
Pressure	200kg/cm^2	2850lb/in^2
Weight oxygen 15°C	204kg	450lb
Kerosene	78.4kg	173lb
Explosive charge	780kg Type 97	1720lb Type 97
Range	15,000m/48-50kts	16,400yd/48-50kts
	25,000m/40-42kts	27,300yd/40-42kts
	30,000m/36-38kts	32,800yd/36-38kts
Wander L or R (max)	350m/15,000m	380yd/16,400yd
	700m/25,000m	760yd/27,300yd
	1000m/30,000m	1100yd/32,800yd

This was a smaller version of the Type 93 intended for submarines, and designed in 1935.

Mod 1, of which production began in 1938, had first air vessel starting and resembled Type 93 Model 1 Mods 1 and 2, while Type 95 Model 2, designed in 1943, started with air from the steering air vessel which seems to have been preferred to the use of carbon tetrachloride. It also differed in a longer warhead and shorter oxygen vessel.

53.3cm (21in) Type 95 (1935)

Data Modification 1

Length oa	7150mm	23ft 5.5in
Total weight	1665kg	3671lb
Negative buoyancy	320kg	705lb
Volume oxygen vessel	386 litres	13.63ft^3
Pressure	215kg/cm^2	3050lb/in^2
Weight oxygen 15°C	113kg	
		249lb
Kerosene	41.3kg	91lb
HP (45–47kt)	330	
(49–51kt)	430	
Consumption expendables	2.65kg/HP/hr	5.84lb/HP/hr
Explosive charge	405kg Type 97	893lb Type 97
Range	9000m/49–51kts	9850yd/49–51kts
	12,000m/45–47kts	13,100yd/45–47kts
Wander L or R (max)	170m/9000m	185yd/9850yd
	250m/12,000m	270yd/13,100yd

Data Model 2, differences

Total weight	1730kg	3814lb
Negative buoyancy	385kg	849lb
Volume oxygen vessel	220 litres	7.77ft^3
Pressure	200kg/cm^2	2850lb/in^2
Weight oxygen 15°C	60kg	132lb
Explosive charge	550kg Type 97	1213lb Type 97
Range	5500m/49–51kts	6000yd/49–51kts
	7500m/45–47kts	8200yd/45–47kts
Wander L or R (max)	90m/5500m	100yd/6000yd
	130m/7500m	140yd/8200yd

This was a modified Type 95 Mod 1 torpedo, of which about 300 were made in 1942–43 because of troubles with the 'first air vessel' in the former. The Type 96 used air enriched to 38% oxygen, which gave safe starting with Kerosene and sea water, and was also used in the steering air vessel. A thin coating of lubricating oil could be used on valves between the oxygen vessel and the reducer, whereas with pure oxygen they had to be completely oil free which often caused corrosion and irregular functioning. The title of Type 96 appears to have been given to fill a gap in the series.

53.3cm (21in) Type 96 (1936)

Data Type 96, differences from Type 95 Modification 1

Weight enriched air 15°C	106kg	234lb
HP (48–50kt)	400	
Consumption expendables	4.03kg/HP/hr	8.88lb/HP/hr
Range	4500m/48–50kts	4900yd/48–50kts
Wander L or R (max)	70m/4500m	76yd/4900yd

This was designed for midget submarines and was essentially a smaller version of Types 93 and 95 with the same type of two-cylinder double-acting engine but reduced in size. It went into production in early 1939 but trouble with the first air vessel, as noted previously, caused its withdrawal after about 100 had been made, and it was used operationally only at Pearl Harbor.

45cm (17.7in) Type 97 (1937)

Data

Length oa	5600mm	18ft 4.5in
Total weight	980kg	2161lb
Negative buoyancy	251kg	553lb
Volume oxygen vessel	156 littes	5.51ft^3
Pressure	200kg/cm^2	2850lb/in^2
Weight oxygen 15°C	41kg	90.4lb
Kerosene	16.5kg	36.4lb
HP (44–46kt)	205	
Consumption expendables	3.03kg/HP/hr	6.68lb/HP/hr
Explosive charge	350kg Type 97	772lb Type 97
Range	5500m/44–46kts	6000yd/44–46kts
Wander L or R (max)	80m/5500m	90yd/6000yd

This torpedo, also known as Type 97 Special, worked on air enriched to 38% oxygen, Kerosene and sea water, and bore the same relationship to Type 97 as Type 96 did to Type 95. It was apparently called Type 98 to fill a gap in the series. About 130 were made from 1942.

45cm (17.7in) Type 98 (1938)

Data Type 98, differences from Type 97

Total weight	950kg	2094lb
Negative buoyancy	221kg	487lb
Pressure enriched air	175kg/cm^2	2500lb/in^2
Weight enriched air 15°C	35.8kg	78.9lb
HP (40–42kt)	152	
Consumption expendables	?4.6kg/HP/hr	?10.1lb/HP/hr
Range	3200m/40–42kts	3500yd/40–42kts
Wander L or R (max)	40m/3200m	45yd/3500yd

45cm (17.7in) Type 02 (1942)

This was a modification of the airborne Type 91 Mod 3 with a larger air vessel and different rear buoyancy chamber. The engine was an eight-cylinder two-row radial working on Kerosene, air and fresh water as in Type 91. About 800 were made in 1943–45 for midget submarines and MTBs.

Type 02 Special of which about 100 were made in 1944, had the same explosive charge but not the enlarged air vessel, so that range was reduced to 2000m *(2200yd)*/38–40kts. It was 10mm *(0.4in)* longer and weighed 975kg *(2150lb)*.

Data

Length oa	5600mm	18ft 4.5in
Total weight	1000kg	2205lb
Negative buoyancy	265kg	584lb
Volume air vessel	220 litres	7.77ft^3
Pressure	200kg/cm^2	2850lb/in^2
Weight air 15°C	54kg	119lb
Kerosene	5.94kg	13.1lb
Fresh water	20kg	44.1lb
HP (39–41kt)	150	
Consumption expendables	10.2kg/HP/hr	22.5lb/HP/hr
Explosive charge	350kg Type 97	772lb Type 97
Range	3000m/39–41kts	3300yd/39–41kts
Wander L or R (max)	45m/3000m	50yd/3300yd

28cm (11in) Type 05 (1945)

This was intended for small MTBs but only two prototypes were ever completed. It worked on Kerosene, air, fresh water, and had a 10HP five-cylinder swash plate engine. The explosive charge was 60kg *(132lb)*, length overall 3800mm *(12ft 5.6in)*, total weight 230kg *(507lb)* and range 1500m *(1640yd)*/17–23kts.

Experimental Turbine Torpedoes

Development began in 1934 to meet a staff requirement for 8000m *(8750yd)* at 60kt. Three designs known as F1, F2, F3 were worked on, but because of staff shortage only F3 seems to have been completed, though the others were run. It was found very difficult to prevent the torpedo breaking surface, and when a requirement for an additional 30,000m *(32,800yd)*/40kt setting was added, development was dropped.

The usual Kerosene, oxygen, sea-water system was used with the addition of zinc chloride solution to prevent blockage of the turbine nozzles with salt. This seems to have worked, but zinc oxide deposits of under 1mm *(0.040in)* thick had to be removed from the nozzles after every run. The turbine was of velocity compound three-stage Curtis type with two rows of blades on the rotor and a fixed row in between. There were seven nozzles 10.5mm *(0.413in)* diameter at a 20° angle and the rotor diameter was 220mm *(8.66in)* with 80 blades per row, and gas-inlet pressure was 40kg/cm^2 *(570lb/in^2)* and temperature 550°C. Turbine speed was 17,500rpm geared down to 1650 at the propellers, and the weight of turbine and gear box about 400kg *(880lb)*.

Data for 61cm (24in) F3 experimental

Length oa	8550mm	28ft 0.6in
Total weight	2700kg	5952lb
Volume oxygen vessel	750 litres	26.5ft^3
Pressure	215kg/cm^2	3060lb/in^2
Weight oxygen 15°C	219kg	483lb
Kerosene	49.5kg	109lb
HP (60kt)	1000	
Consumption expendables	3.19kg/HP/hr	7.03lb/HP/hr
Explosive charge	500kg	1102lb
Designed range	8000m/60kts	8750yd/60kts

AIRBORNE TORPEDOES

45cm (17.7in) Type 91 (1931)

The general features of this torpedo have been previously described. Mod 1, first manufactured in November 1931, was still in service ten years later and was carried by the 'Nell' torpedo bombers against the *Prince of Wales* and *Repulse*. Mod 2 had a heavier charge, a thinner air vessel, and anti-roll stabilisers. It was first delivered in April 1941 and was carried by 'Betty' bombers against the above British ships and by 'Kates' at Pearl Harbor. Mod 3 dated from October 1941 but does not seem to have entered service until the latter part of 1942. The charge was again increased, the air vessel thickened for increased pressure, and a heavier depth-keeping pendulum fitted. Bronze parts were replaced by steel where possible and eight tail fins were tried in some.

Mod 3 Improved of 1943 had the top side of the afterbody and engine room strengthened with longitudinal T bars to permit 300kts launching speed. This was followed in 1944 by Mod 3 Strong, which had I instead of T bars for strengthening the top side of the afterbody and

Data Modification 1

Length oa	5275mm	17ft 3.7in
Total weight	784kg	1728lb
Negative buoyancy	103kg	227lb
HP (41–43kt)	140	
Explosive charge	150kg Type 97	331lb Type 97
Range	2000m/41–43kts	2200yd/41–43kts
Max launch speed	260kts	

Data Modification 2, differences

Length oa	5486mm	18ft 0in
Total weight	935kg	1841lb
Negative buoyancy	123kg	271lb
Explosive charge	205kg Type 97	452lb Type 97

Data Modification 3, differences

Total weight	849kg	1872lb
Negative buoyancy	172kg	379lb
Explosive charge	240kg Type 97	529lb Type 97

Overall length as Mod 1.

also the underside of the warhead nose. The air vessel was thinned with reduced pressure and range, and maximum launching speed raised to 350kt.

Mod 4 Strong was the same torpedo with a heavier charge, and Mod 7 Strong differed in having a longer warhead for a still heavier explosive charge. Both these date from 1944.

Data Modification 3 Improved

Length oa	5275mm	17ft 3.7in
Total weight	857kg	1889lb
Negative buoyancy	180kg	397lb
Volume air vessel	182.6 litres	6.45ft^3
Pressure	180kg/cm^2	2560lb/in^2
Weight air 15°C	38kg	83.8lb
Kerosene	4.04kg	8.91lb
Fresh water	17kg	37.5lb
HP (41-43kt)	140	
Consumption expendables	7.92kg/HP/hr	17.46lb/HP/hr
Explosive charge	240kg Type 97	529lb Type 97
Range	2000m/41-43kts	2200yd/41-43kts
Max launch speed	300kts	

Data Modification 3 Strong, differences from 3 Improved

Volume air vessel	183.2 litres	6.47ft^3
Pressure	160kg/cm^2	2275lb/in^2
Weight air 15°C	33kg	72.8lb
Range	1500m/41-43kts	1640yd/41-43kts
Max launch speed	350kts	

Data Modification 4 Strong, differences from 3 Strong

Total weight	921kg	2030lb
Negative buoyancy	244kg	538lb
Explosive charge	308kg Type 97	679lb Type 97

Data Modification 7 Strong, differences from 3 Strong

Length oa	5715mm	18ft 9in
Total weight	1052kg	2319lb
Negative buoyancy	301kg	664lb
Explosive charge	420kg Type 97	926lb Type 97
Max speed of torpedo	40-42kts	

53.3cm (21in) Type 94 (1934) Model 1

This experimental Kerosene, oxygen, sea-water torpedo was apparently never made and reliable details are lacking.

45cm (17.7in) Type 94 (1934) Model 2

A limited number of these Kerosene, oxygen, sea-water torpedoes were made but were not in war service. Unlike others using this system, the engine was an eight-cylinder, two-row radial with poppet valves, as the range was too short for salt deposits to clog up the valve guides. Starting was by first air vessel, and anti-roll stabilisers were not fitted. Length overall was 5283mm (*17ft 4in*), total weight 848kg (*1870lb*), explosive charge 150kg (*331lb*) Type 97 and range, doubtfully, 3000m (*3300yd*)/48kts.

45cm (17.7in) Type 4 (1944)

This was a further strengthened Type 91 Mod 3 Strong for launch speeds of up to 400kts. All possible components were simplified for easier production with further replacement of bronze by steel. The weight of the depth-keeping pendulum was again increased and an improved free-wheeling gear fitted for the propellers. The first production deliveries were apparently in December 1944. There were two Marks, 2 and 4, differing in the size of the warhead.

Mk 4 differed in length overall 5715mm (*18ft 9in*), total weight 1104kg (*2434lb*), negative buoyancy 362kg (*798lb*), explosive charge 417kg (*919lb*) Type 97 and speed 40-42kts.

Data Mark 2

Length oa	5275mm	17ft 3.7in
Total weight	984kg	2169lb
Negative buoyancy	313kg	690lb
Volume air vessel	183.2 litres	6.47ft^3
Pressure	160kg/cm^2	2275lb/in^2
Weight air 15°C	33kg	72.8lb
Kerosene	3.47kg	7.64lb
Fresh water	17kg	37.5lb
HP (41-43kt)	140	
Consumption expendables	7.92kg/HP/hr	17.46lb/HP/hr
Explosive charge	304kg Type 97	670lb Type 97
Range	1500m/41-43kts	1640yd/41-43kts
Max launching speed	400kts	

Some experiments were made in 1944 with Kerosene, hydrazine hydrate, hydrogen peroxide systems, but were discontinued after a few months because of to difficulties in handling hydrogen peroxide. Various very short range unpropelled torpedoes, depending solely on the launching speed, were tested with little success. The QR spiralling torpedo seems to have been more successful. This was for use against submarines and consisted of a Type 91 Mod 2 arranged to run in a descending spiral of about 270m (*300yd*) diameter to a depth of 95-100m (c*320ft*). The distance run was *c*3700m (*400yd*)/26kts. About 50 were made in early 1945 and some were in service, but results are not known.

The Type M torpedo was a 58cm (*22.8in*) under development in 1942-44 for a new large seaplane, of which the design was never completed. Unlike other Japanese torpedoes it was to have a 'burner cycle' engine but this gave much trouble and the three made did not get past bench tests.

Experimental Airborne Torpedoes

Design Data Type M

Length oa	7100mm	23ft 3.5in
Total weight	2070kg	4564lb
Negative buoyancy	514kg	1133lb
Volume air vessel	380 litres	13.4ft^3
Pressure	220kg/cm^2	3130lb/in^2
Weight air 15°C	102kg	225lb
Kerosene	21.5kg	47.3lb
HP (50kt)	470	
Explosive charge	750kg Type 97	1653lb Type 97
Range	2500m/50kts	2730yd/50kts
Max launch speed	300kts	

MANNED SUICIDE TORPEDOES

Research into these manned suicide torpedoes began in January 1944 and the first prototype was built in June 1944. It was essentially a Type 93 Model 3 torpedo less warhead, fitted into a 1m (*39.4in*) diameter shell with superstructure, cockpit, controls and forebody added. The positive buoyancy was originally 37.5% of the weight, but this was reduced to 1.25%. They were carried by a few surface warships, including the light cruiser *Kitakami*, but actually used only by submarines. A tube connected the submarine with a hatch in the bottom of the kaiten and the latter was released 6000-7000m (*6600-7700yd*) from the target. It ran on a gyro course set by the submarine's navigator at 6m (*20ft*) for the calculated time and then surfaced. The target should have been approximately 1000m (*1100yd*) off and the kaiten pilot adjusted course and dived to the most suitable depth for the particular target. If he failed to hit, the pilot surfaced, changed course and tried again. There were two detonators, an electric one with two fuzes operated by the pilot, and an inertia impact type.

Altogether 330 Type 1 as described above entered service, 230 of these being the slightly longer and heavier Mod 1. There appears however to have been only one success, the sinking of the fleet oil tanker *Mississinewa* at Ulithi 20 November 1944. The worst defect was water leaking into the control compartment when the parent submarine ran submerged, as this caused the power unit to become waterlogged, and leaking oil caused starting explosions, it is said in two out of five fired.

Type 2 was larger, with an eight-cylinder (2 × 4 in line) engine intended to develop 1500HP running on a Kerosene, sea water, hydrogen peroxide, hydrazine hydrate system. Originally 1000 engines were ordered, but only two kaitens of this type were made, and production stopped in March 1945.

Type 4 was similar to Type 2 but the engine was converted to run on the usual oxygen system. About 50 were made, but much development was needed and this type was written off as a failure.

Type 10 was a slow 7kt kaiten converted from the Type 92 electric torpedo. It was intended for the defence of the coastal waters of Kyushu and Shikoku and would have been launched from the shore. Fewer than six were made.

Kaitens

Data Type 1 Modification 1

Diameter	100cm	39.4in
Length oa	1474cm	48ft 4.3in
Total weight	8300kg	18,300lb
Explosive charge	1550kg	3420lb
Performance	23,000m/30kts	25,000yd/30kts
	43,000m/20kts	47,000yd/20kts
	78,000m/12kts	85,000yd/12kts

Design Data Type 2

Diameter	135cm	53.1in
Length oa	1650cm	54ft 1.6in
Total weight	18370kg	40,500lb
Explosive charge	1550kg	3420lb
Performance	25,000m/40kts	27,300yd/40kts
	50,000m/30kts	54,700yd/30kts
	83,000m/20kts	90,700yd/20kts

Kaiten Type 1 ready for practice launch from *Kitakami*.
Aldo Fraccaroli Collection

ANTI-SUBMARINE WEAPONS

One of the worst failings of the Japanese navy was that insufficient attention was paid to the defence of merchant shipping against submarines until it was too late. In all, surface ships can be credited with 17 US submarines, aircraft with eight, and there was one shared sinking. In addition, surface ships and aircraft each sank one British submarine. As usual, the principal weapons were the depth charge and the A/S bomb.

A/S shells are noted in the Japanese gun section, as are the 20cm (*203.2mm, 8in*) and 12cm (*4.724in*) short guns. A 15cm A/S mortar intended for transports and merchant ships, was in a cradle mounting with all round training and recoil and run-out cylinders. This fired a projectile of about 27kg (*60lb*) projectile to a maximum range of 4100m (*4500yd*). A single navy type 81mm mortar was carried by many escorts, and there was also a 15cm diameter rocket propelled DC with a range of 3000m (*3280yd*) developed in April 1945 but not used. Early in the war, some use was made of an explosive sweep with contact fuze and 25kg (*55lb*) charge, but this had no success. The various DC explosives were Types 88, 97, 98, 1 (of which the composition is given under Mines) and Type 4, containing 79.2% ammonium perchlorate, 16.4% silicon, 0.3% iron, 0.7% aluminium, 2.5% oil.

15cm (*7.9in*) A/S Mortar and shipboard cradle mounting.
USN

DEPTH CHARGES

These were usually of obsolescent design, the standard dimensions being 77.5cm × 45cm diameter (*30.5 × 17.7in*). Trials had not been completed on a magnetic influence DC which weighed 264kg (*582lb*) with 100kg (*220lb*). Type 88 or 1 charge, and acoustic DC were still in the early stages of research.

Type 88

Doubtful if still in service. Charge 148kg (*326lb*) picric acid with hydrostatic pistol. Depth settings 25m (*82ft*) or 45m (*148ft*).

Type 91 Model 1 Mod 1

Apparently obsolete, with 100kg (*220lb*) Type 88 charge, hydrostatic pistol and settings 25m (*82ft*) or 50m (*164ft*).

Type 95

This was standard until the introduction of Type 2 and had a 100kg (*220lb*) Type 88 charge. Slow ships dropped it with an attached parachute so that they could escape the danger area of the explosion (as could the target). The pistol depended on the time for a certain amount of water to enter and operate the firing mechanism, the setting being controlled by varying the size of the water inlet. Depths were 30m (*98ft*) with and without parachute and 60m (*197ft*). Type 95 Model 1 Mod 1 had a 147kg (*324lb*) Type 97 or 98 charge, and Mod 2, 110kg (*243lb*) Type 1. Both apparently had a new pistol with additional 90m (*295ft*) setting.

Type 2

An almost direct copy of British types. The filling was apparently 105kg (*231lb*) Type 88, and the pistol on the same principles as in Type 95 with settings of 30m (*98ft*), 60m (*197ft*), 90m (*295ft*), 120m (*394ft*) and 145m (*476ft*). Type 2 Mod 1 had a 162kg (*357lb*) Type 97 or usually 98 charge and Type 2 Mod 2 110kg (*243lb*) Type 1 or 4.

There was also a 120kg (*265lb*) army DC which was mostly rigged on suicide motor boats, and a smaller one with approximately 34kg (*75lb*) charge.

Japanese DC attacks were usually broken off too soon and the settings were too shallow. There were no ahead-throwing weapons such as Hedgehog or Squid but the usual stern racks, broadside DCTs and some Y guns were fitted. The normal fleet destroyer outfit was 30 DCs in the latter part of the war, but most escorts (kaibokan) had 120 including those stowed below deck. In these last there were six, or sometimes eight DCTs a side with a single stern rack and a dumb-waiter hoist to raise DCs stowed below. The DC installation occupied about 16m (*52ft*) of the stern.

ANTI-SUBMARINE BOMBS

The numbering of these was as given for other Japanese naval bombs. Fuze settings are given as 25m (*82ft*), 45m (*148ft*) or 75m (*246ft*) and bursting charges were 70 TNA, 30 HND.

Type 99 No 6 Mark 2

One of the first A/S bombs, this had a nose fuze and strengthened tail. Total weight 63.6kg (*140lb*), diameter 240mm (*9.45in*), overall length 1073mm (*42.24in*), bursting charge *c*59.7%.

Type 99 No 6 Mark 2 Mod 1

Adopted in 1940, this was similar to the above but had an anti-ricochet ring tack welded to the nose. Dimensions were unchanged with total weight 67.9kg (*149.7lb*) and 55.9% bursting charge. The effective range is given as 4-5m (*13-16ft*).

Type 1 No 25 Mark 2 Model 1

Adopted in 1941, this had nose and tail fuzes with light sheet-metal fins to which plywood extensions were bolted. Total weight 266kg (*586lb*), diameter 357mm (*14.06in*), overall length 1910mm (*75.2in*). The bursting charge was 54% and effective range is given as 10m (*33ft*).
Model 1 had an anti-ricochet nose ring.

Exp 19 No 25 Mark 2

This bomb was for use with a magnetic airborne detector (jikitanchiki) which had a range of about 140m (*153yd*). The nose was made of wood with fibre case and fins, and there were nose and tail fuzes. Total weight 180kg (*397lb*), diameter 357mm (*14.06in*), bursting charge 77.8% and effective range about 8m (*26ft*).

Army A/S bombs were of ordinary GP pattern with the nose fuze plugged and a 3.5sec delay tail-fuze. The usual sizes were 50kg (*c110lb*), 100kg (*220lb*) and 250kg (*550lb*) but one of 500kg (*c1100lb*) with a heavy nose ring may have been used. Bursting charges were picric acid, and usually *c*45-48%.

MINES

As will be seen from the lists given below, these were one of the Japanese Navy's weaknesses, and no influence mines of Japanese manufacture were used, though the controlled Type 92 did have an acoustic detector. 93 magnetic mines were laid off Balikpapan in 1945, but these were of Allied origin. A number of British A Mk 1-IV magnetic mines had been captured at Singapore.

Japanese explosives used in mines were varied and comprised:

Shimose. Picric acid.

Type 88. 66% ammonium perchlorate, 16% ferro-silicon, 12% wood pulp, 6% oil. It was believed that silicon carbide assisted in the uniform propagation of a detonation wave through loosely packed powder.

Type 97. 60% TNT, 40% hexanitrodiphenylamine. An explosive known as 'B' with 16% aluminium replacing that amount of HND, is mentioned.

Type 98. 70% trinitroanisole, 30% hexanitrodiphenylamine. Used as an alternative to Type 97.

Type 1. 81% ammonium picrate, 16% aluminium, 2% wood pulp, 1% oil.

MINES IN SERVICE

The mines in the data table were laid by surface craft, except that Type 88, a copy of the old German U-mine, was laid by the *I121* class submarines, and that Aircraft Type 3 and a special version of Type 93 Model 1 were airborne. Of the mines laid by surface craft, the Type 93 series were most commonly used (particularly Model 1). Mark 6 Model 2 Mod 1 could be laid in water 1020m (*558 fathoms*) deep and the Type 93 series, if thin mooring cables were used, in 1072m (*586 fathoms*). Type 88 and Aircraft Type 3 had hydrostatic depth setting.

Moored Contact Mines

Mine	Total Weight kg	(lb)	Buoyancy (kg)	(lb)	Explosive Charge (kg)	(lb)	Hertz horns
Shimose 5 Mod 1	520	1146	100	220	83	183 Mk	4
Mk 6 Model 1	1156	2549	195	430	215	474 Mk	4
Mk 6 Model 2 and Mod 1	1080	2381	200	441	200	441 Mk	4
Mk 6 Model 3	900	1984	205	452	200	441 Mk	6
Type 88 Mod 1	960	2116	150	331	180	397 Mk	4
Type 93 Model 1	700	1543	120	265	100	220 Type 88	4
Type 93 Model 2	700	1543	120	265	100	220 Type 88	7
Type 93 Model 3	700	1543	120	265	100	220 Type 88	9
Type 93 Model 4	710	1565	110	243	110	243 Type 1	4
Type 4		?	?100	220	40	88 Type 88 or 1	3
Type 5		?	100	220	40	88 Type 1	3
Small Beach		?	50	110	40	88 Type 88 or 1	4
Aircraft Type 3 Mk 1 Model 1 (Parachute)	640	1411	98	216	80	176 Type 97	4

The *Yaeyama* with a load of moored mines, probably Type 93 Model 1, in about 1935. The main HA guns are 12cm (*4.7in*) 10th Year Type.
CPL

There is no record of any Type 92 being fired operationally, 144 were laid across the entrance to Tokyo Bay.

Other Mines

Mine	Total Weight (kg)	(lb)	Buoyancy (kg)	(lb)	Explosive Charge (kg)	(lb)	Notes
Aircraft Type 3 Mk 2 Model 1 (Parachute)	135	298	5	11	50	110 Type 97	Drifting, 3 switch-horn
Type 96 Mod 1	108	238	0 to -4	0-9	55	121 Type 88	Net, tension firing
Type 92	1300	2866	150	331	500	1102 Type 88	Controlled, acoustic detector

Type 92 Model 1 differed in having no acoustic detector.

MINES UNDER MANUFACTURE, NOT IN REGULAR SERVICE

Type 1

A drifting mine with 75kg (*165lb*) Type 88 charge and four Hertz horns, designed for use in enemy harbours. It had a propeller driven by a small electric motor, with hydrostatic control to maintain a depth of about 3m (*10ft*). It was intended for laying from I type submarines, two mines being carried in the marker buoy locker, but on the first operational trip the submarine was lost due to failure of the safety gear.

Type 2

A contact moored mine for laying from the TT of submarines and copied from the US Mk 10 Mod 1. The charge was 130kg (*287lb*) Type 97. About 600 were made, but the hydrostatic depth taker had been made in steel instead of the original brass and gave considerable trouble. This and the few submarines available prevented its use.

Type 3 Model 1

A copy of the German submarine laid TMC mine and magnetic circuit of 20 milligauss sensitivity. The charge was 890kg (*1962lb*) Type 97. Japanese workmanship was poor.

Type 3 Model 2

As Model 1 but with a copy of a German 100/350 cycle acoustic circuit. Workmanship, particularly of relays, was poor.

Aircraft Type 3 Mk 3 Model 1

An acoustic ground mine with parachute and working at 30–40kc. It weighed 850kg (*1874lb*), had a 400kg (*882lb*) Type 97 charge and could be laid by any torpedo plane with the proper racks. Some were at an airfield for laying when the war ended.

EXPERIMENTAL MINES

The most interesting of these was Type O, a controlled mine with coil-rod magnetic detector. It could be fired individually from the shore, and had wheels to fit the rails of a mine-layer. The case was bell shaped and apparently bronze, the total weight being given as 2000kg (*4409lb*) and the charge as 1000kg (*2205lb*) Type 88. Two fields of six mines each were laid at Truk in 1942 but never fired as water damaged the insulation of the coil rod unit, and no further use seems to have been made of this mine.

CHARGES FOR SUICIDE CRAFT

Of these, the various kaiten manned torpedoes are noted under conventional torpedoes, and others included the suicide midget submarines, known as kairyu, with a 600kg (*1323lb*) charge and various explosive motor boats.

The navy boats had a 290kg (*640lb*) Type 98 charge built into the bows and fired electrically on impact or from the cockpit, while army boats had a 120kg (*265lb*) DC in a rack on each side with mechanical release on impact and sometimes a third DC rolled over the stern.

There was also a 50kg (*110lb*) 'A' mine under manufacture for suicide swimmers.

BOMBS, ROCKETS AND GUIDED MISSILES

BOMBS

Only AP and large SAP and other bombs are noted, while A/S bombs are described with other anti-submarine weapons. In the nomenclature of Japanese naval bombs, Type = year of adoption, Number = approximate weight in units of 10kg, Model = major change, Modification = minor change, Land = land use, Ordinary = GP, Mks 1 to 33 = special bombs.

Type 99 No 80 Mk 5. Adopted in 1941, this bomb was intended for use against armoured capital ships and blew up the *Arizona* at Pearl Harbor. It was converted from a 41cm (*16.14in*) AP shell and the Japanese rated it as penetrating 150mm (*5.9in*) armour plate. The nose was 486.8mm (*19.165in*) thick, the bursting charge 2.8% TNA and the tail fuze was duplicated to insure detonation. An aluminium shock absorbing plug was placed ahead of the charge to protect it from impact detonation.

Type 2 No 80 Mk 5 Model 1. This was adopted in 1942 and still in production at the end of the war. It was very similar to the above and was also converted from a 41cm (*16.14in*) AP shell, but the nose was 304mm (*11.97in*) thick and the bursting charge 4.4% TNA.

Type 3 No. 150 Mk 5. A much larger bomb which could not be used by carrier aircraft unlike the number 80s. Otherwise the 1942 design was generally similar and the bomb was in experimental production at the end of the war. Its armour piercing properties were not determined. The nose was 475mm (*18.70in*) thick and the bursting charge 3.3% TNA.

Type 3 No 25 Model 1 Mk 4. A rocket accelerated bomb with side fuze adopted in 1944; no facts have been found on its use. The rocket, with 15kg (*33lb*) propellant, increased the bomb speed by 90m/s (*295f/s*) and it could penetrate 125–150mm (*4.9–5.9in*) armour plate. Nose thickness was 239.3mm (*9.42in*) and bursting charge 1.26% TNA.

AP Bombs

Bomb	Actual weight (kg)	(lb)	Diam (mm)	(in)	Length oa (mm)	(in)
Type 99 No 80 Mk 5	796.8	1757	409	16.10	2351	92.56
Type 2 No 80 Mk 5 Mod 1	811.2	1788	404	15.91	2330	91.73
Type 3 No 150 Mk 5	1498.6	3304	500	19.69	2740	107.87
Type 3 No 25 Mod 1 Mk 4	315.0	694	300	11.81	1884	74.17

SAP Bombs

Type 2 No 50 Model 1. Adopted in 1942, this was of forged steel with nose and tail fuzes, and would penetrate 80mm (*3.15in*) armour plate. The nose thickness was 197mm (*7.756in*) and bursting charge 12.5% TNA or 70 TNA, 30 HND. Actual weight 491.0kg (*1082lb*), diameter 396mm (*15.59in*), length overall 2000mm (*78.74in*).

The largest bombs with thinner walls were the navy No 100, which was probably never in production, and an army bomb of 989kg (*2180lb*) with 42.4% bursting charge, which does not appear to have been used. No 80 and No 50 bombs were in service in the navy. No 80, of which there were several variants, had a typical weight of 807.5kg (*1780lb*) and *c*40% bursting charge. It was first adopted in 1938. No 80 Mk 8 was a skip bomb with strengthened tail. It weighed 850kg (*1874lb*), had a skip distance of 150–300m (*165–330yd*) and was adopted in 1944. The usual No 50, first adopted in 1930, weighed 507kg (*1118lb*) and had a 43.58% burster. It had the same 450mm (*17.72in*) diameter as the No 80, but was shorter. The later bursting charges in all these were 70 TNA, 30 HND.

The army had a 500kg (c*1100lb*) bomb with 41.8% burster, a skip bomb of the same weight and about 380mm (*15in*) diameter; and possibly an 800kg (c*1760lb*) skip bomb.

ROCKETS

The Japanese navy developed and produced a number of spin-stabilised rockets of which only the 12cm (*4.724in*) was in service afloat. This is described below but it should be noted that the 45cm (*17.72in*) rocket dating from April 1944 and used on land in limited numbers in the Philippines, was the largest solid-fuel rocket in service in any country during the war. It was 1809mm (*71.22in*) in overall length, weighed 670kg (*1477lb*) and had a 167.2kg (*368.6lb*) TNA burster and 59.5kg (*131lb*) propellant charge with range 1600m (*1750yd*). The usual Japanese rocket propellant was Special DT6 - 30% NG, 60% NC, 3% Centralite, 7% mononitronaphthalene.

Airborne rockets were developed but production had only just begun at the end of the war. The navy favoured fin stabilisation for these and were some way ahead of the army's spin-stabilised development. The navy rocket was intended for use against surfaced submarines and landing craft. It could penetrate 25mm (*1in*) steel and weighed 13kg (*28.7lb*) with overall length 723mm (*28.46in*) and maximum velocity 230m/s (*755f/s*). The burster was 0.9kg (2lb) TNA and the propellant weighed 2kg (*4.4lb*).

12cm (4.724in) AA Rocket and Type 5 Launcher

Rocket Data		
Firing rails	1083mm	42.65in
Weight rocket	22.5kg	49.6lb
Length rocket	730mm	28.74in
Propellant	3.4kg	7.5lb
Max velocity	200m/s	656f/s
Max range	4800m	5250yd
Mounting Data		
Total weight	1597kg	3521lb
Elevating speed	18°/sec	
Training Speed	22°/sec	

This rocket, and a similar one with HE Head, were carried by some explosive motor boats fitted with a simple launching trough.

These were introduced to service in July 1944 and were installed in such carriers as had survived the Battle of the Philippine Sea and in those under construction. The usual number was six 28-rocket launchers but the *Shinano* was to have 12. The rocket had an incendiary shrapnel head with time fuzing preset at 5.5 or 8.5 secs corresponding to 1000m (*1100yd*) or 1500m (*1640yd*). They were electrically fired in single pairs or automatically in 14, the latter taking 10sec. Reloading of the launcher was by hand. The rocket had six 11.5mm (*0.453in*) diameter nozzles with 25° inclination and 10° divergence, and the propellant burnt for 1.6sec with maximum pressure 196kg/cm^2 (*2790lb/in^2*). The launcher was apparently developed from the 25mm triple and could be controlled by Ward-Leonard RPC or by two men in protected cabs. Elevation was +80° to +5°.

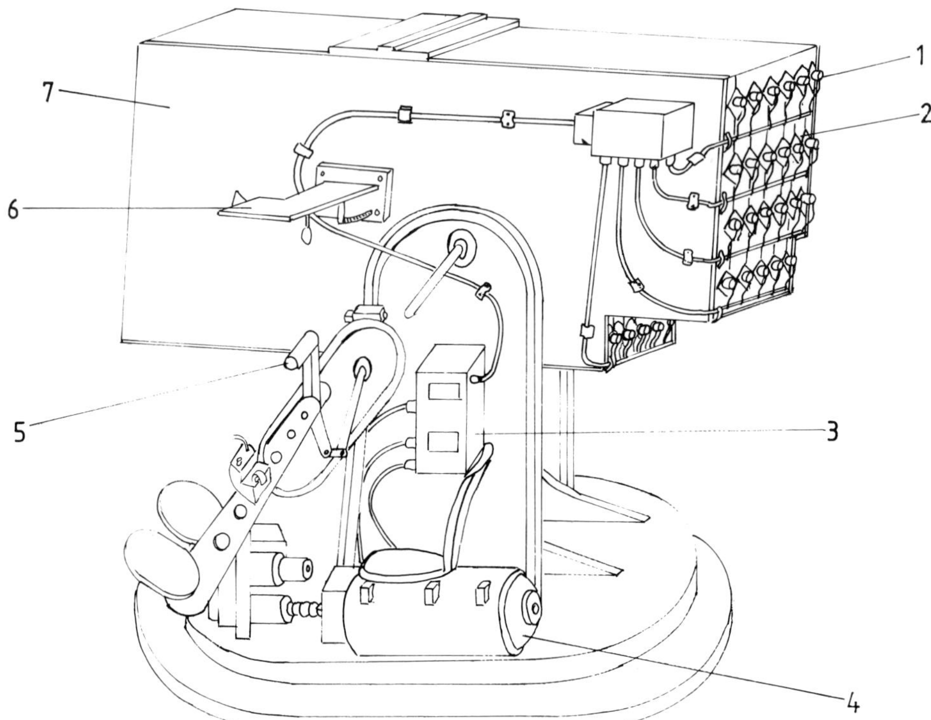

12cm (*4.7in*) 28-tube AA rocket launcher introduced to service July 1944.

1 Firing pin
2 Rocket igniting mechanism
3 Combination breech cut off and selection switch
4 1HP electric drive motor
5 Elevating handle
6 Sight rest
7 Side plate

John Lambert

GUIDED MISSILES

Kamikazes were only used from October 1944 when their country's situation had become hopeless, and such a weapon was possible only for a nation holding the Japanese philosophy of war. The missile was an aeroplane, the warhead a bomb (sometimes released before crashing) and the fuel in the petrol tanks, and the guidance system a pilot bent on suicide. Almost any type of aircraft was used, the Zero with 250kg (*551lb*) bomb being the most frequent, and Frances, which could take an 800kg (*1764lb*) bomb, heading the list of twin-engined aircraft. Old twin-float biplanes of fabric and wood, against which proximity fuzes were not effective, sank one destroyer and shared in the loss of another. It is thought that 2550 kamikazes were expended, and the most important warships sunk were the escort carriers *St Lo*, *Ommaney Bay* and *Bismarck Sea*, and 13 destroyers. The Allied fleet aircraft carriers were the prime target and, though many were damaged, some severely, all survived. Thanks to their armoured flight decks, the British aircraft carriers came through very well.

Major modifications to the kamikaze aircraft were rare, but Judy 43, a single seat version, had accelerating rockets to give an extra 35kts speed. The Japanese army developed the Sakura bomb, a hollow charge device with cyclonite type explosive, to go in the nose of a Peggy bomber. Type 1, which was probably too large to fit, weighed 2900kg (*6393lb*) and would penetrate a total of 253mm (*10in*) steel spaced over 12.5m (*41ft*) at 45°. Type 2, which weighed 1300kg (*2866lb*) with a 900kg (*1984lb*) charge, was fitted to a few aircraft, but none were used.

Oka 11, known to the US as Baka, was a rocket-propelled piloted glider bomb, developed by the Japanese navy, with production starting in September 1944. It is believed that 755 were made but relatively few were used. It was a midwing monoplane with span 5.0m (*16ft 5in*), length 6.066m (*19ft 11in*) and all-up weight 2140kg (*4718lb*). The warhead had a total weight of 1200kg (*2646lb*) with 515kg (*1135lb*) cast TNA burster and one nose and four base fuzes. The nose was 138mm (*5.43in*) thick and there was a 35mm (*1.38in*) aluminium plate in front of the charge, it is believed to cushion the filling against impact detonation. Each of the three solid fuel rockets in the tail contained 14.7kg (*32.4lb*) propellant. The usual parent aircraft was Betty, which was extremely vulnerable when carrying Oka as manoeuvrability was greatly reduced by the load.

Launching was usually at approximately 1400m (*4600ft*) and 170kts, 4–7nm from the target, Oka's glide speed was 200kts and for the last 3nm the rockets increased speed to 465kts in level flight and 540kts in a dive. This high speed made it a potentially very effective weapon but manoeuvrability was poor. In the first attempt to use it on 21 March 1945, the overloaded Bettys were intercepted and destroyed, and the only notable success was to sink the destroyer *Mannert L Abele*, already hit by a kamikaze, on 12 April 1945. Later jet-propelled versions were never operational, nor were the unmanned I-GO radio-controlled guided bombs. A further heat-homing bomb had not undergone final tests by the end of the war.

The battleship *Tirpitz* calibrating 38cm SKC/34 guns off Norway in 1942.
Aldo Fraccaroli Collection

GERMANY

The high reputation of German naval weapons in both the First and Second World Wars was in general well deserved, though the poor functioning of German torpedoes was a serious failing in the earlier part of World War II. Once this had been corrected, the electric torpedo proved a formidable weapon in attacks by U-boats, and the German Navy led the way in the use of homing and pattern-running torpedoes and also with magnetic, acoustic and pressure or 'oyster' mines. Relations between the highest echelons in navy and airforce were often difficult, and the latter were slow to realise the value of aircraft torpedoes (though they subsequently led in the introduction of guided bombs and missiles).

Gun and gun-mounting developments were often highly advanced, but some were more relevant to the navy Germany was hoping to build than to the wartime one that existed.

NAVAL GUNS

The more important guns and mountings are described in some detail, with briefer accounts of the less important. German coast defence was shared between the army and navy, the heavier batteries being almost always a naval responsibility, and a number of guns no longer used afloat are included.

IDENTIFICATION

Up to the end of the First World War naval guns were known as SK (*Schiffskanone*, ship's gun, or previously *Schnelladekanone*, QF gun) followed by the nominal overall length in calibres, eg 28cm SKL/50, but from then until 1939 the length was replaced in new types by the nominal date, expressed by the last two figures of the year, as in 28cm SKC/34. It should be noted that this had for many years been the method for classifying gun mountings, propellant charges and other such items. Guns intended principally for submarines and destroyers were known as Ubts K or Tbts K (*U-boots* or *Torpedo-boots Kanone*) and AA guns as *Flak*, though this term was not always included. Combinations of these terms occur in a few instances. From about 1940 new types were known as KM (*Kanone Marine*, navy gun) or as *Flak* M, followed by the date, as in the C system, eg 10.5cm KM44. Army types of gun kept their original designation, and experimental designs were sometimes known as *Gerät* (equipment), with an identifying number.

Mountings were known as DrhL (*Drehscheiben-lafette*, turntable mounting) in the case of turrets, and MPL (*mittel-pivot-lafette*, central pivot mounting) for many singles, though such terms as Tbts L, Ubts L and Flak L are frequent. M (for *Marine*) occurs in the latest mountings, as in guns. Most heavy coast defence guns were in BSG (*Bettungschiess-Gerüst*, platform firing framework) mountings, which resembled a railway mounting without the rail bogies and were supported on a concrete platform by a central pivot and ball race and a roller or bogie at the rear running on a circular arc.

GUN DESIGN

All German naval guns used a metal cartridge case with a sliding block breech, so that in the descriptive tables bore and chamber dimensions are measured from the breech-block inner face to the muzzle and base of seated shot respectively. Rifling lengths are usually given from the beginning of the groove in a new gun. Muzzle velocities are 'new gun' with charge temperature 15°C (*59°F*) and range tables were drawn up for this velocity.

Recent guns of 20.3cm (*8in*) and over were Krupp designs, while most of the smaller were Rheinmetall. In general they were much heavier than would be expected considering the lightness of Krupp guns of the First World War. This was due in the main to an increase in the weight of the breech end in order to move the centre of gravity in that direction and so reduce the size of the mounting, and also the overall weight, including guns, of the latter. In addition the heavier gun reduced the violence of recoil. In construction the main advances were in the provision of loose liners and barrels, reduction in number and increase in size of the outer component parts, and improvements in the securing of the breech end-piece and in the operation of the sliding breech block. Autofrettage does not appear to have been used in production naval guns. German guns tended to be considerably longer than corresponding British designs and to fire lighter shells at higher, and sometimes much higher, muzzle velocities. Chambers were smaller and of relatively small diameter (though exceptions to the latter can be found), and densities of loading much higher as 'cool' tubular propellant was used. Rifling grooves were deeper and the width ratio of groove to land much smaller than was usual in British guns. Increasing twist was nearly always used, the best form being found to be a cubic parabola.

GUN MOUNTINGS

German turret mountings were, with few exceptions, trained electrically but otherwise for the most part hydraulically powered, each turret having its own electrically driven pumps. Hoists were not broken and the revolving weight was taken by a ball and not a roller race. RPC for elevation was fitted in 20.3cm (*8in*) and over. The usual Siemens system had a tacho-generator/thyratron controlled motor operating four hydraulic control valves but was not entirely satisfactory, control being non-linear and depending on acceleration and on the pressure drop in the accumulator. In the *Admiral Hipper* an Askania system was used with induction motors fed by two phase-displaced currents and hydraulic jet tube amplification, which seems to have been at least as good a system.

Unlike others, the German Navy used triaxial mountings for the heaviest AA guns. The original idea, tested in *Schlesien* in 1929, was to have biaxial mountings on a stabilised platform but this was not satisfactory. Next, twin triaxial mountings

Superfiring 20.3cm twin Drh LC/34 turret in *Prinz Eugen*. Many features were similar to those in the 38cm twin and 28cm triple turrets.

1 Ball track
2 Machinery space
3 Charge handing room
4 Shell handing room
5 Ready use shells
(Note. Depression was actually 10°)

John Lambert

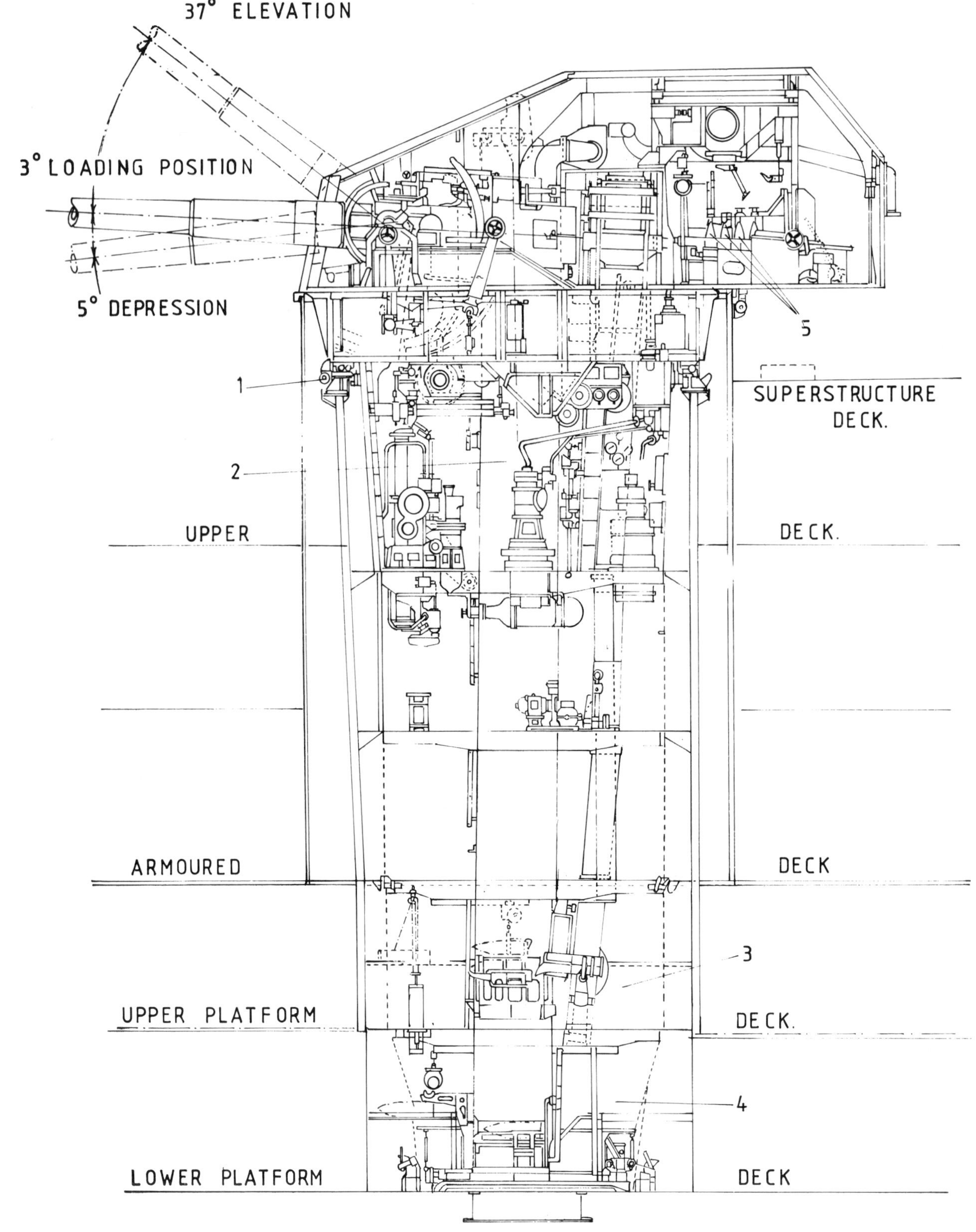

for the heavy 8.8cm (*3.4in*) SKC/25 were tried in *Köln* in 1930-31. The third axis in these was a cross-trunnion and not a cross-levelling axis, which was found to be unsuitable, and the latter axis was used in the twin 3.7cm LC/30, 8.8cm LC/31 and LC/32 mountings. In these, each gun had its own cross-levelling axis linked to a centre one by parallelogram rods. An arm with toothed arc and pinion driven by a motor and turning about the centre axis operated the system. The 3.7cm was directly stabilised by a gyro and support motor, but in the others RPC electric motors were used. Later mountings such as the twin 10.5cm (*4.1in*) LC/37 had only one cross-levelling axis as it was found that the motors could absorb the firing torque. The RPC system was all electric, as was the RPC elevation in these mountings, but the latter was not satisfactory and was only used for the roll angle, the remainder being superimposed by hand.

CLOSE-RANGE AA ARMAMENT

This was neglected before the war, the above 3.7cm LC/30 mounting having 'single shot' and not automatic guns and, until later 3.7cm guns were introduced, the largest automatic was 2cm.

PROPELLANTS

German naval guns used propellants of single tube-grain form known as RP (*Rohr-Pulver*, tube powder). There were several compositions, and in the individual gun descriptions the most recent generally used in a particular gun is given with the external and internal diameters of the grain in millimetres. To save nitroglycerin, the more recent propellants contained di-ethylene glycol dinitrate instead, which was also convenient for lowering the propellant's energy and erosive properties.

Propellant	**NC(%N)**	**NG**	**DGN**	**Akar**	**Centr**	**Mn**	**MgO**	**Graph**	**CV**	**Tok°**
RPC/12	64.13(11.9)	29.77	-	-	5.75	-	0.25	0.10	950	2975
RPC/32	66.6(11.5)	25.9	-	-	7.25	-	0.15	0.10	830	2630
RPC/38	69.45(12.2)	-	25.3	-	5.0	-	0.15	0.10	810	2495
RPC/38N	68.72(12.2)	-	25.03	-	1.5	4.5	0.15	0.10	810	2545
RPC/40	67.55(11.45)	-	24.6	-	7.5	-	0.25	0.10	720	2040
RPC/40N	64.87(12.2)	-	23.63	0.5	-	7.0	0.15	0.10	730	2185

NC (%N) = nitrocellulose (% Nitrogen), NG = Nitroglycerin, DGN = diethylene glycol dinitrate, Akar = Akardite, unsymmetrical diphenyl urea, probably n.propyl, Centr = Centralite, symmetrical diphenyl diethyl urea, Mn = Methyl Centralite, MgO = magnesium oxide, Graph = graphite, CV = calorific value, Tok° = uncooled explosion temperature, degrees, Kelvin.

Fixed ammunition was used from 10.5cm (*4.1cm*) downwards and also in the latest 12.8cm (*5in*) which were not in service afloat. Other guns of the latter size, 17cm (*6.7in*) and 15cm (*5.9in*) and the old 28cm SKL/40 (*11in*) were separate loading QF, but apart from this exception, guns from 20.3cm (*8in*) upwards had the rear part of the charge in a metal case, and the fore part in a double silk bag. It was normal to have a central tube of propellant in both parts of the charge of much greater diameter than the grain, and with very large fore charges such as those for the 40.6cm (*16in*) 'Adolf' coast defence gun, the whole fore charge was contained in an outer shell of propellant inside the silk bags for reasons of strength. The previous method of using brass bands to strengthen the fore charge was abandoned, as it was suspected that metallic deposits in the bore caused several split liners. The cooler propellants were more difficult to ignite than RPC/12 and the size and number of coarse-grained black powder igniters had to be increased. Brass cartridge cases were replaced to a great extent by steel during the war.

The reputation for not exploding in a serious fire which German propellant had gained in 1914-18 was maintained. When the *Gneisenau* was hit at Kiel during the night of 26/27 February 1942, the bomb burst on the hatch cover of the extraction duct from A turret magazine where there was an opening of about 5 x 15cm (*2 x 6in*) in the armour deck. Over 23 tons of RPC/32 propellant ignited, but there was no explosion, though the triple turret was lifted at least 50cm (*20in*) by the gas pressure.

PROJECTILES

The following notes on German naval shells concern for the most part those fired by the more modern guns mounted afloat, and the numerous and varied types used by the older guns are omitted. Armour piercing shell provided for guns from 15cm (*5.9in*) upwards was the responsibility of Krupp, and the design had been standardized in 1936. The last production was in 1943. The shell head had an ogive of 1.3cal radius, the cap resembled the Firth-Brown knob and wide ring type and the ballistic cap was of 10cal radius except in 28cm SKC/28 (*11in*) guns mounted in the 'pocket battleships', and in 15cm (*5.9in*), where it was 8.5cal. In the latter shells, the tangent to the beginning of the ballistic cap arc was inclined at 5°, whereas in 10crh shells it was not inclined, so that the nominal total length of 8.5crh APC was only 3.7-3.8cal and that of 10crh 4.4cal. The bursting charge was TNT desensitized with beeswax, the amount of the latter decreasing from head to base of the cavity. The weight of the bursting charge was 2-2.5% except in the 28cm SKC/28 where it was a little higher. Like USN, but unlike British shells, German APC were 'sheath hardened', that is the part surrounding the cavity head was not hardened.

Base-fuzed HE was fired by 12.7cm (*5in*) guns upwards and was intended for use against light armour and to penetrate far inside unarmoured targets. Armour piercing caps were limited to 38cm (*15in*) and 40.6cm (*16in*) shells and ballistic caps resembled those for APC, the 12.7cm having an 8.6crh head. Overall lengths were 4.2-4.7cal. The 40kg (*88lb*) shell fired by 15cm Tbts KC/36 guns in destroyers was exceptional in being boat-tailed. Bursting charges were TNT as in APC with a weight of 4.4-6.7%, later designs usually having the smaller bursters, though the 40kg 15cm was again an exception with 9.3%.

Omitting close range AA for the present, all guns fired nose-fuzed HE. From 12.7cm upwards ballistic caps of the same radius as in other shells were fitted, while 10.5cm (*4.1in*) and 8.8cm (*3.4in*) shells had 10crh without ballistic caps or 13crh in those for the 8.8cm SKC/31. Overall length varied from 4.2 to 4.8cal and bursters were usually

TNT and 6.3-8.6% by weight. Once again the boat-tailed 40kg 15cm was an exception with 13.4%, and similar percentages occur in the 12.8cm (*5in*) KM40 and KM41 which were not in service afloat. The last of these had a 20crh nose and a length of 5cal overall as did one of the shells for the 10.5cm KM44, also not in service, while in a further shell for the latter gun these figures were 40crh and 5.7cal. A proportion of nose-fuzed HE from 15cm (*5.9in*) downwards had tracers, and many 10.5 and 8.8cm outfits had shells with additional incendiary bodies. Illuminating shell was carried for 20.3-8.8cm (*8-3.4in*).

APC base-fuzed and nose-fuzed HE were designed to range together and had a single range table. Two driving bands were usual, with three on major calibre shells, and on those for such high performance guns as the 15cm (*5.9in*) SKC/25 and 8.8cm (*3.4in*) SKC/31. With copper bands there was often a lead decoppering band below them, but the tendency was to replace copper by sintered electrolytic iron powder in shells of 15cm and below. According to some views, it was superior to copper as a band material, but this opinion does not seem to have been widely held outside Germany. Welded soft iron rings were also used, though these were more advantageous at higher velocities than those of naval guns.

For close range, AA shell fillings included nitropenta (pentaerythritol tetranitrate), cyclonite and other explosives with or without aluminium powder. For AP tracer, the weight of the burster was about 2% and for HE incendiary tracer about 5 to 7½%. The earlier HE tracer for the 3.7cm SKC/30 gun had a 3.7% TNT burster. 'Mine shell' with at least 15% burster was developed for later 3.7cm and 3cm guns.

PERFORMANCE

German naval guns had a high reputation in Britain but it is not certain that this was entirely deserved. It was thought on examination after the war that shot-seating and driving-band details in the 40.6cm (*16in*) were at fault and that German heavy guns were overworked. Certainly, regularity of muzzle velocity was generally inferior, and range table 50% zones were appreciably longer than in equivalent British guns, though they were considerably narrower.

EXPERIMENTAL DESIGNS

Although to a lesser extent than the army, the German Navy had its share of unconventional and extreme designs. Thus there was preliminary design work on the coastal 24cm Flak 85 (*9.4in*) of 73cal overall and intended to fire a 180kg (*397lb*) shell at 1000m/s (*3281f/s*) using fixed ammunition and a round weighing 320kg (*705lb*). More complete designs were prepared for the 15cm Flak 65 (*5.9in*) of 103cal overall which was to fire a 48kg (*106lb*) shell at 1230m/s (*4035f/s*), the round weighing 100kg (*220lb*). Trials were carried out with taper bore, and also with recoilless guns. Of the latter, the 8.8cm DKM43 (*3.4in*) was intended for small warships and fired an 9kg (*19.8lb*) shell at 600m/s (*1969f/s*). The rear blast was, however, very troublesome and the mounting not rigid enough. The much larger 28cm DKM44 (*11in*) was intended for coast defence and fired a 315kg (*694lb*) shell at 750m/s (*2461f/s*). One gun was built and proved.

LA FIRE-CONTROL

The German low-angle fire-control installation, type 1935, was fitted in the *Bismarck*, *Scharnhorst* and *Hipper* classes, and was used for the main armament and for the 15cm (*5.9in*) guns. There were director positions fore and aft and at the fore top, and each comprised a rotating hood and several low-angle directors. The rotating hood had a stereoscopic range-finder of up to 10.5m (*35ft*) or 7m (*23ft*) in the *Hipper* class. There were also 10.5m RF in the main turrets of the *Bismarck* and *Scharnhorst* classes, later removed from A, and 7m in the superfiring turrets of the *Hipper* class. The hood was stabilised in the lateral plane by the central A-Gyro (own ship's course) and the level stabilised by local D-Gyro. The directors were placed somewhat lower than the hood and could be rotated independently, the target bearing angle being transmitted between them by follow the pointer gear. The low-angle directors were shaped like a column with telescopes for gunnery officer, trainer and layer and each director could be used for main or 15cm armament. Weight and space occupied were both small. The output value were true-level angle and target-bearing angle in ship's system. The director telescopes were stabilised by lateral and vertical motors controlled by thyratron RPC. In the lateral plane, the main A-Gyro was the source, small errors being corrected by the director trainer, while in the vertical plane either a local DE Gyro system or the transmitting station's target-angle converter could be used. The latter was mainly used for blind firing and had the exact artificial horizon of the BC-Gyro system (roll and pitch angle), but the local system, independent of the transmitting station, was usually preferred, as the RPC chain was very short and 'hunting' very small and, though the DE-Gyro artificial horizon could be in error by ½°, the error altered slowly and could be compensated easily by the director layer.

There were fore and aft transmitting stations each with computers for main and 15cm guns, if mounted. The geometric computer had input of target bearing angle in the horizon plane, course angle of own ship referred to horizon plane, own ship's speed and range. The output comprised target speed, target inclination relative to line of sight, target course and range obtained from the mean values of the turret and director RFs or by Radar. The ballistic computer took over the range rate and cross-range rate by cross wires and also allowed for wear, muzzle velocity, twist, air density and wind. The output of lateral deflection and tangent elevation, both referred to the horizon system, were passed to the transmitting units, of which there were four (one for main and 15cm guns in each transmitting station) or two in the *Hipper* class. Each transmitting unit had two spherical angular converters. The target-angle converter's input comprised target bearing in ship's system from the director, roll angle and pitch angle, both in ship's system from B and C Gyros, and the output consisted of the target-bearing angle in the horizon system (fed to geometric computer) and the artificial-level angle relative to the artificial horizon, measured vertically to the ship's plane. The gun-angle converter's input consisted of the gun-training angle in the horizon system, the gun-elevation angle referred to the artificial horizon, and the roll and pitch angles in the ship's system, and the output comprised the gun training and elevation in the ship's system. Individual convergence was added in differential gear and corrections to level angle were computed in an internal-level angle circuit. Remote power control (RPC) was only fitted for gun elevation, and training motors were hand controlled via follow-the-pointer (ftp) gear as was the elevation driving cylinder if RPC was not in use. If

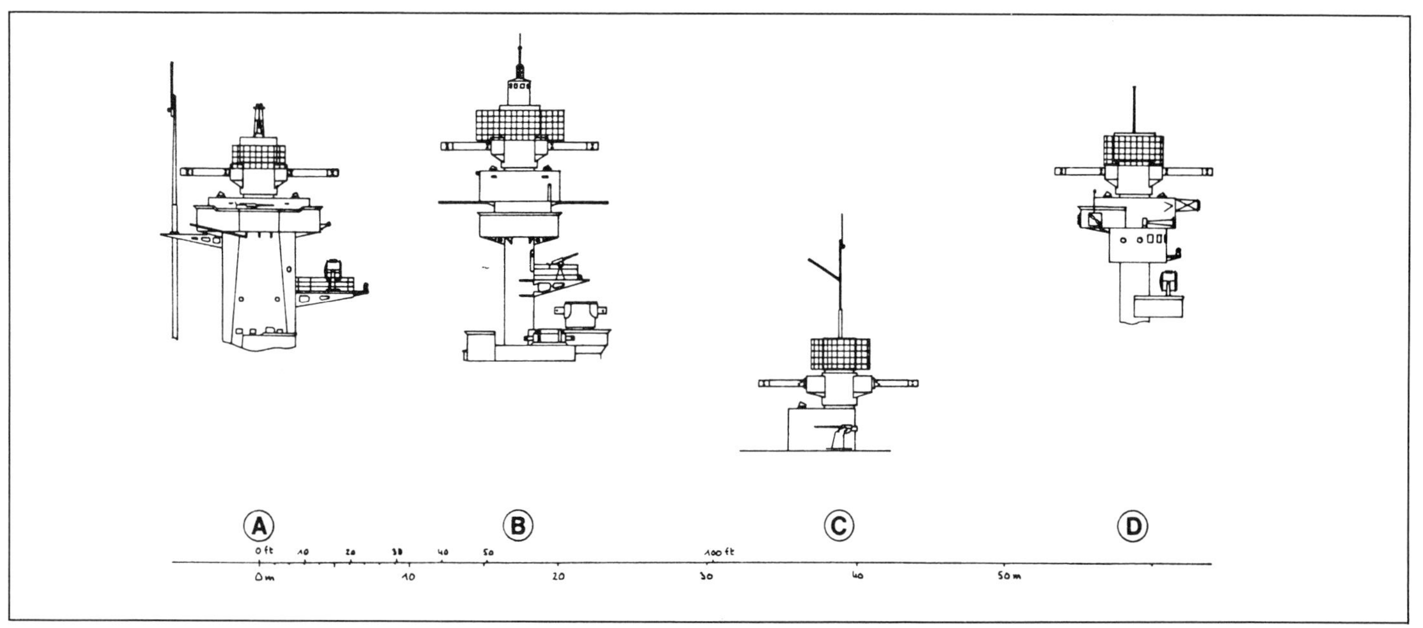

Radar antennae and RFs in *Lützow* (ex-*Deutschland*) class.

A *Graf Spee* in 1939 with 10.5m RF and 1.8 × 0.8m antenna for FuMO 22 on foretop hood

B *Lützow* in 1939 with similar equipment but the more usual 6 × 2m antenna

C *Scheer* in 1941 showing after 10.5m RF and 4 × 2m antenna for FuMO 27

D *Scheer* in 1940 with 10.5m RF and 4 × 2m antenna for FuMO 27 on foretop hood

Erwin Sieche

Radar antennae and RFs in *Scharnhorst* class.

A The after 10.5m RF with 4 × 2m antenna for FuMO 27 as fitted in summer 1941

B Foretop in November 1939 with 10.5m RF and 6 × 2m antenna for FuMO 22

C Foretop in February 1942 with 4 × 2m antenna for FuMO 27

Erwin Sieche

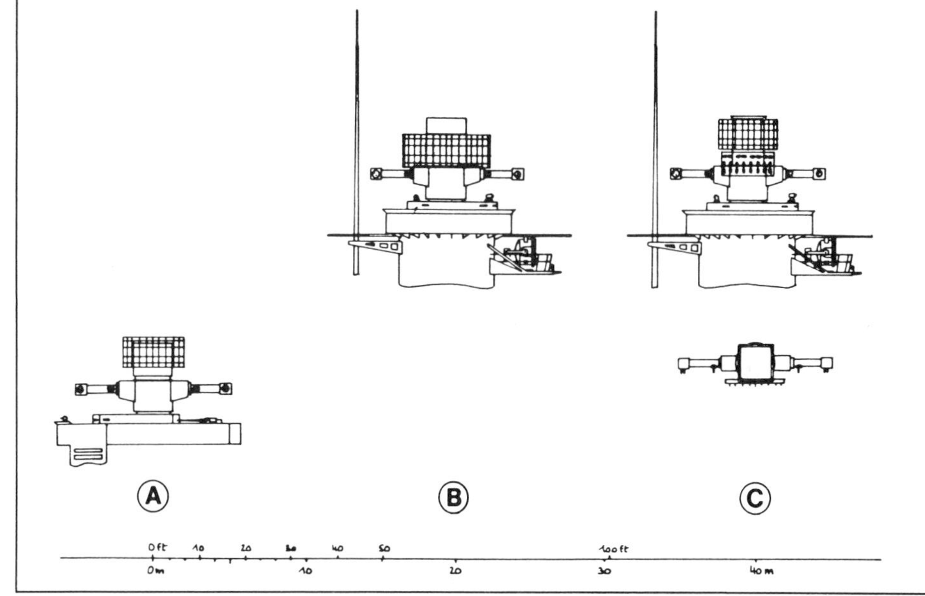

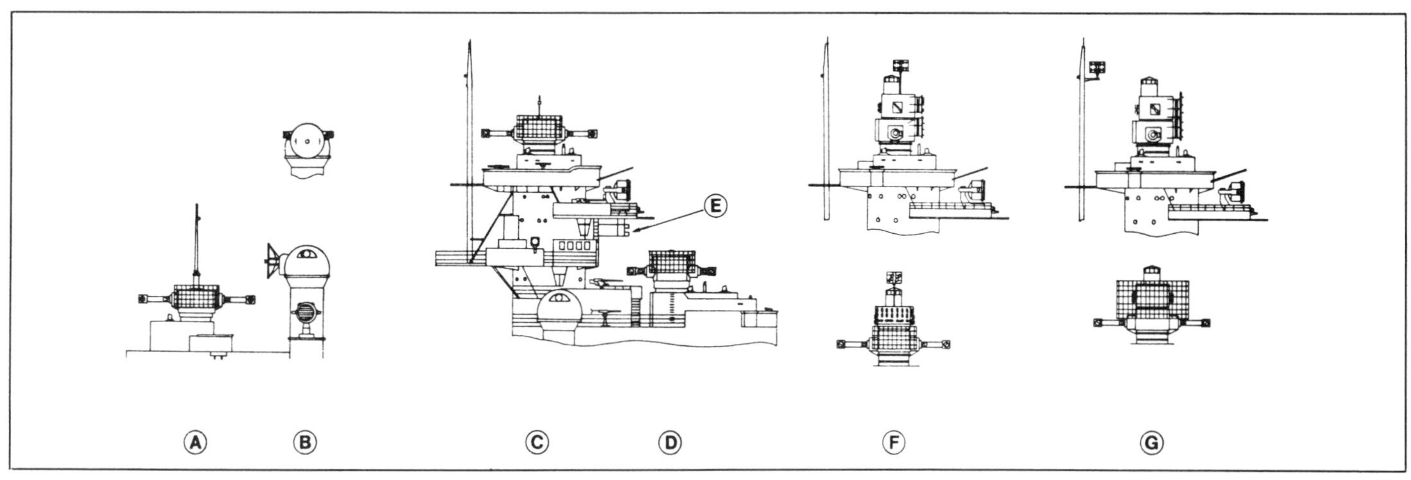

Radar antennae and RFs in *Bismarck* class.

A The after 10.5m RF in *Tirpitz* with 4 × 2m antenna for FuMO 23

B Type 1937 triaxial AA director in *Tirpitz* with 3m diameter antenna for FuMO 213 (Würzburg D) as fitted in 1944

C Foretop 10.5m RF with 4 × 2m antenna for FuMO 23

D Forward 7m RF with antenna for FuMO 23

E Possibly FuMo 21 dipoles in *Bismarck*

F Foretop in *Tirpitz* 1942–1944 with additional 4 × 2m antenna for FuMO 27

G The final foretop layout in *Tirpitz* with 6.6 × 3.2m antenna for FuMO 26

Erwin Sieche

Radar antennae and RFs in *Hipper* class.

A The after 7m RF with 4 × 2m antenna for FuMO 27 in *Hipper* from 1941-2
B Mainmast in *Hipper* with 6 × 2m antenna for FuMO 25 probably added in 1945. A Type 33 triaxial AA director is shown below
C Foretop 7m RF with 4 × 2m antenna for FuMO 27 in *Hipper* from 1941-2

Erwin Sieche

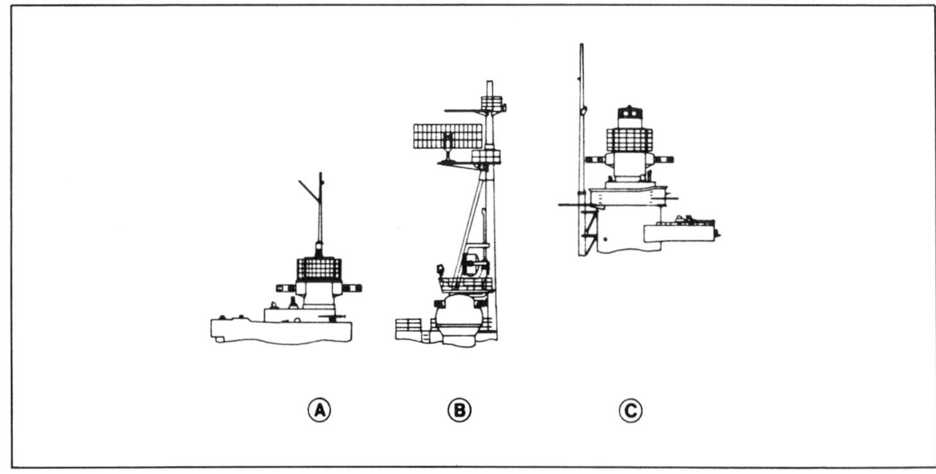

Radar antennae and RFs in *Prinz Eugen*.

A The after 7m RF with 4 × 2m antenna for FuMO 27
B Mainmast with 6 × 2m antenna for FuMO 25 as fitted August 1944. A Type 37 triaxial AA director is shown below
C Foretop 7m RF with 4 × 2m antenna for FuMO 27 removed in September 1942
D The foretop as modified with antenna for FuMO 26 and sided additions for height-finding. The lower radar is a FuMB 4 'Samos' search set. This layout was altered in August 1944
E The final foretop layout with 6.6 × 3.2m antenna for the boosted FuMO 26 and FuMO 81 'Berlin-S' search set at the foremast head

Erwin Sieche

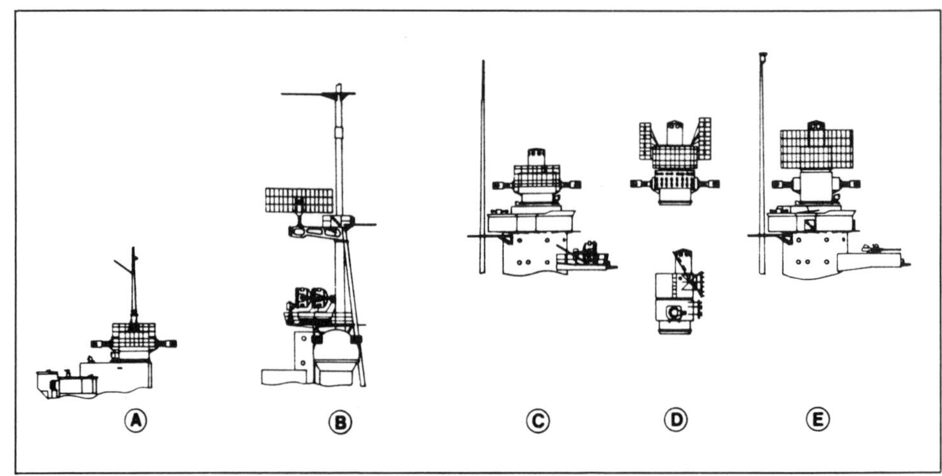

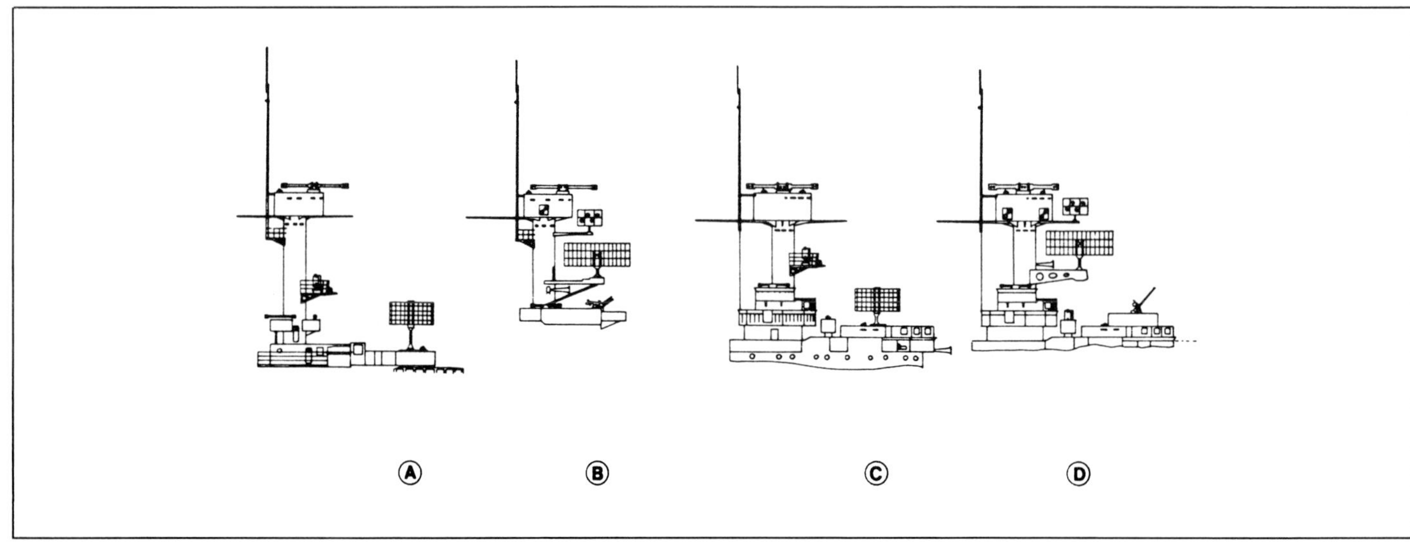

Radar antennae and RFs in light cruisers.

A *Köln* in 1941-2 with foretop RF retained but the forward one replaced by 4 × 2m antenna for FuMO 21
B *Leipzig* in August 1943 with 6 × 2m antenna for FuMO 25 on bracket.
C *Nürnberg* in summer 1941 with forward RF replaced by 4 × 2m antenna for FuMO 21
D *Nürnberg* with 6 × 2m antenna for FuMO 25 fitted in summer 1944

Erwin Sieche

the ship's motion was too violent for ftp alignment, time interval compensating (TIC) gear was used. In this the guns were trained and/or elevated at arbitrary speed, and when they were passing the firing position the firing circuit was automatically operated considering the pre-firing angle. TIC gear was fitted for training and elevation in 28cm (*11in*) and 20.3cm (*8in*) ships but only for training in 38cm (*15in*).

The Type 1930 installation in the 15cm cruisers and the *Lützow* class was as modified, similar to the Type 1935, and there were other similar but simplified director systems for destroyers and for illuminating shell and optical or infra-red searchlights. The *Lützow* class had a similar RF distribution to the battleships but retained that in A turret. There were no turret RF in the 15cm cruisers.

In triple turrets the centre gun was fired 10-20 milliseconds in advance of the others to lessen interference, and firing delays were relatively long with the standard solenoid-operated striker, the time from firing contact to striker impact varying from 200 milliseconds with 38cm (*15in*) to 80 with 12.7cm (*5in*).

The German navy was among the first to appreciate the possibilities of radar as a range finding method, and a Seetakt (*Seetaktische Geräte*) set was installed in the *Graf Spee* in 1936, the first naval radar in the world. At the outbreak of war the *Graf Spee* had a FuMO 22 set located on the foretop RF hood and training with it, and the same set was fitted to *Lützow, Scheer, Scharnhorst, Gneisenau, Hipper* and *Blücher*. It should be noted that radar nomenclature was altered during the war, and for convenience the later system is used here. FuMO 22 worked at *c*368 MHz (*82cm*) with maximum power 8kW, PRF 500 and 5-microsecond pulses. The antenna mattress which was split with the lower part for transmission, was usually 6 × 2m (*19.7 × 6.6ft*), though a 1939 photograph of *Graf Spee* shows 1.8 × 0.8m (*71 × 31in*). Range against a battleship target was 25,000m (*27,300yd*) and bearing accuracy ± 5°. The sets were not very satisfactory, being highly susceptible to moisture and shock from gunfire while the antenna distorted in heavy seas. FuMO 23 was similar but had an improved installation on a large RF hood. It was on the foretop, forward and after RF in *Bismarck, Tirpitz* and briefly in *Prinz Eugen*, and some antennae were apparently 4 × 2m (*13.1 × 6.6ft*).

Improved sets were introduced from 1940 with the reception part of the antenna divided in two and considerably better bearing accuracy at ±0.25/0.3°. FuMO 27 with a 4 × 2m (*13.1 × 6.6ft*) antenna had a combined RF and radar mount and was installed in one or more positions in *Tirpitz, Scharnhorst, Gneisenau, Scheer, Prinz Eugen* and *Hipper*, but apparently not in *Lützow*. FuMO 26 differed in having a new horizontally polarised antenna measuring 6.6 × 3.2m (*21.7 × 10.5ft*). This gave less reflection from waves and better resolution of *c*300m (*330yd*). Peak power was originally unaltered and range is given as 20,000-25,000m (*22,000*-27,300yd) with the same accuracy of ± 70m (*77yd*) as in previous sets and bearing accuracy of ± 0.25°. Single sets were in *Tirpitz* and *Prinz Eugen* and possibly in the other ships noted as having FuMO 27. By 1945 the set in *Prinz Eugen* was raised to 60kW peak power with 4-microsecond pulses and an improved accuracy of ± 50m (*55yd*). In FuMO 34 the peak power was increased to 125kW giving a range of 40,000-50,000m (*43,700- 54,700yd*), but it is thought that none was in service afloat. There were no shorter wavelength German surface fire-control radars in service, although 9cm and 3cm sets were planned.

Nürnberg from forward showing triple turret for 15cm SKC/25 guns, antenna (apparently 4.5 × 2m, for FuMO 25) and foretop RF.
Aldo Fraccaroli Collection

In light cruisers, destroyers and large torpedo boats FuMO 21, similar to 22 or 23, with a 4 × 2m (*13.1 × 6.6ft*) antenna was mounted on a pedestal, as was FuMO 24, while FuMO 25 was on a mast bracket. These were similar to 27, the former having a 6 × 2m (*19.7 × 6.6ft*) antenna, and the latter either this or the 4 × 2m size. From 1943 FuMO 25 appeared on larger ships as its training was not limited by that of the RF. FuMO 32 and 33 were 24 and 25 with peak power increased to 125kW but it is doubtful if any were in service afloat.

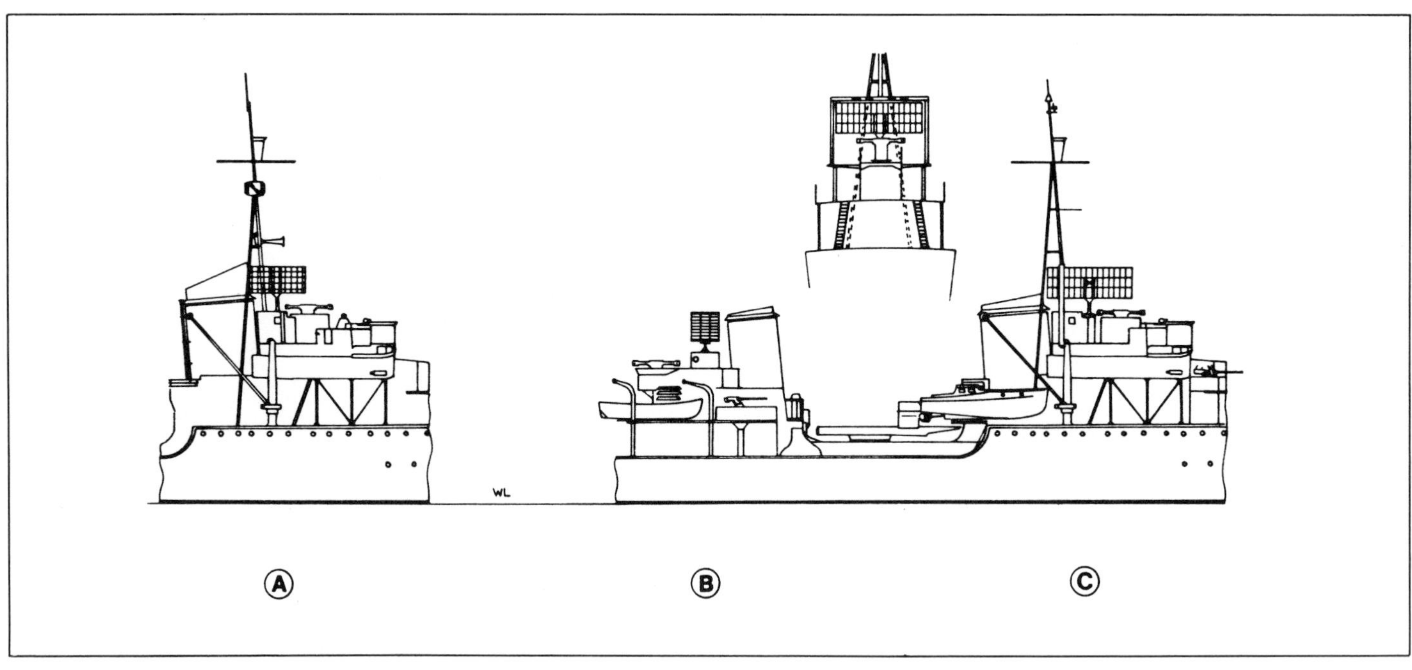

Radar antennae in *Paul Jacobi* (Z 5).

A 4 x 2m antenna for FuMO 21 on bridge with training hindered by mast, 1941
B (FuMO 63 search radar)
C Transverse view shows 'goal-post' mast and 6 x 2m antenna for FuMO 24

Erwin Sieche

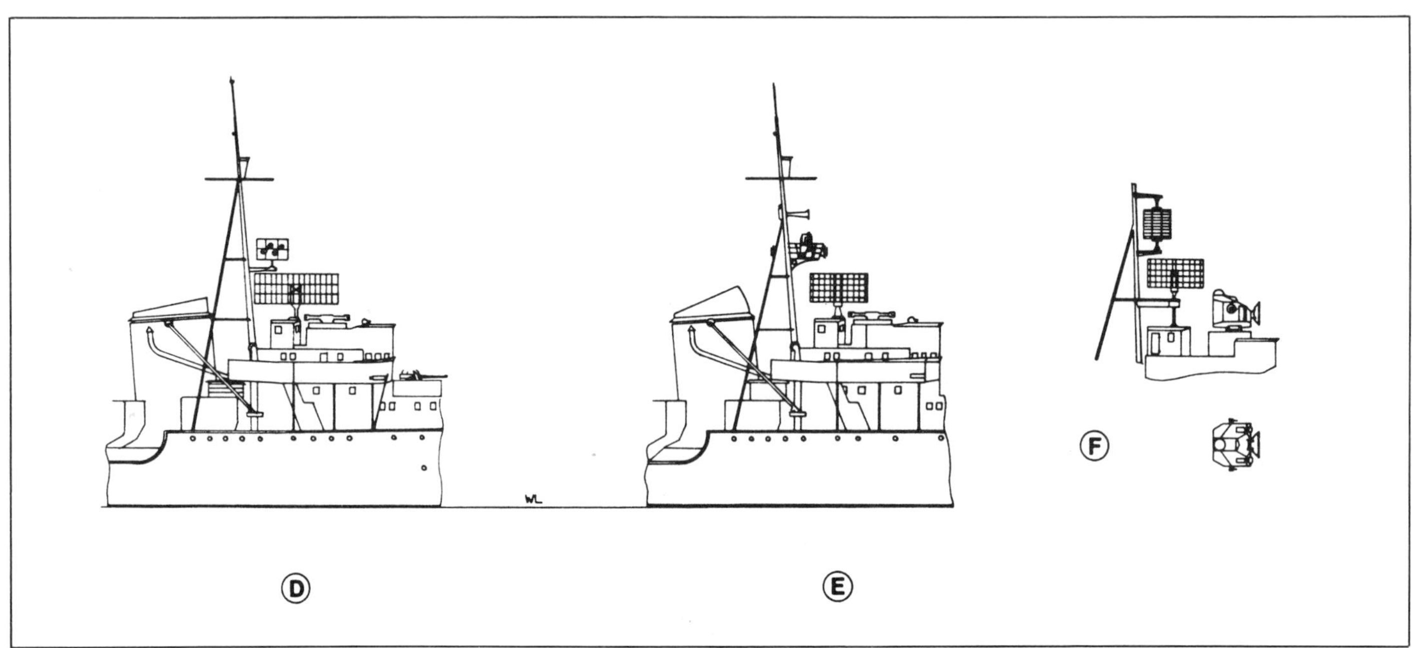

Radar antennae in *Z 25*, *Z 38* and *Z 52*.

D 6 x 2m antenna for FuMO 24 on bridge of *Z 25* with sufficient clearance from mast. This was replaced in 1944 by a 4 x 2m antenna for FuMO 21
E 4 x 2m antenna for FuMO 21 in *Z 38*
F Equipment intended for the uncompleted *Z 52*. The Type 1934B triaxial director for the twin 12.8cm KM41 guns has a 1.5m diameter antenna for FuMO 231 (Euklid). A 4 x 2m antenna is also shown and a search radar antenna on the foremast.

Erwin Sieche

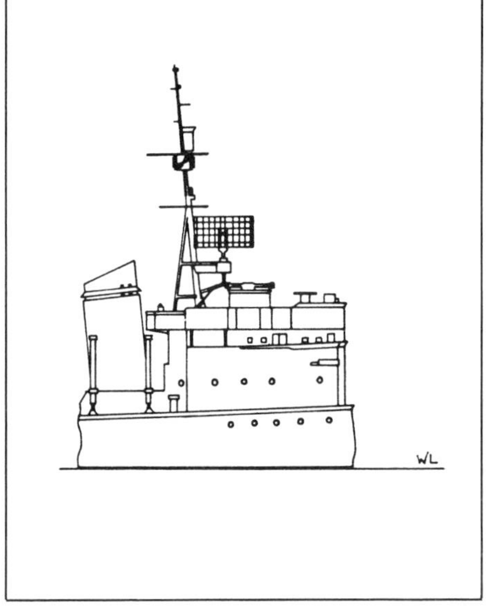

Radar antennae in torpedo-boats.

4 x 2m antenna for FuMO 21 on foremast projection in *T 22* class torpedo-boat.
Erwin Sieche

HA FIRE-CONTROL

For twin 10.5cm (*4.1in*) or 8.8cm (*3.4in*) guns there were three types of high-angle fire-control installation. Type 1931 was in the light cruisers and *Lützow* class. The director with biaxial sights and 1.5m (*5ft*) and 2m (*7ft*) range-finders was on a platform directly stabilised by three big gyros without servomotors. A target-angle converter was superfluous and the big gyros had the advantage of providing a good steady artificial horizon. Correcting pendulums were installed in 1933. There were several defects however. If in a heavy roll the director platform contacted the fixed structure of the ship at the limit positions, the gyro stabilisation became useless, while with servomotors it was possible to disconnect. It took 20 minutes to start the big gyros and it was possible to replace a damaged one only in a dockyard. The gimbal rings formed the gun-angle converter and also carried the heavy weight of the director. This was not a suitable combination and it was difficult to damp vibrations from underwater hits. Suggestions for small gyros and a cross-level axis were made in 1932, but not accepted for 10 years. The tachymetric predictor was located in the transmitting station below deck.

The Type 1933 director in the *Scharnhorst* class, *Blücher* and *Hipper* had a spherical shield which improved protection but the director weight, less amplifiers and generators, was increased from 21,000kg (*20.7 tons*) to 41,000kg (*40.4 tons*). It may be noted that the big gyro rotors each weighed 260kg (*573lb*).

The Type 1937 in *Bismarck, Tirpitz* and *Prinz Eugen* had small gyros and servomotors for yaw, level and cross-level but had similar mechanical structure and gimbal rings. The director weight was reduced to 36,000kg (*35.4 tons*) including 5000kg (*4.9 tons*) ballast to maintain the centre of gravity after the big gyros were omitted. The defects of gimbal rings, vibration and weight remained. Only one prototype of the Type 1942 director which weighed about 6000kg (*5.9 tons*) was completed.

This was designed for 10.5cm (*4.1in*) and larger AA, and had gyros with servo motors for the three director axes. The director platform was supported on the strong cross-level axis which had limits of ±25° with errors of ± 4 to 6′, instead of on gimbal rings so that it was much better able to resist underwater hits. Radar was fitted and the gunnery officer's long-base telescope was combined with a 3m (*9.8ft*) RF. There were two types, 1942 A with predictor and gun-angle converter inside the director and supplied with data by shafts, and 1942 B intended for the 10.5cm twin KM44, with the above two items in the transmitting station. Weights were similar as 1942 B had a smaller but thicker shield than the 13mm (*0.5in*) of 1942 A.

The Type 1943 A and B directors resembled the above but were combined LA/HA with triaxial/biaxial angular converters and TIC gear. Type 1943 B was intended for the twin 12.8cm (*5.04in*) Drh LM41 biaxial mountings (52° elevation) in Type 42C and possibly 36C destroyers.

A modified Type 1942 A with the *Luftwaffe* fully-automatic KORE predictor, was considered for the 5.5cm (*2.165in*) Gerät 58 on single triaxial mountings in Type 42C destroyers, but no director was in service afloat for close range AA, and sights with estimated target course, speed and range set to give the lead single, or optical ring sights were used.

The radar intended for the above directors was FuMO 231, also known as 'Euklid'. This was to work at 1035/1200MHz (*29/25cm*) with 50kW peak power, PRF 750 and range of 20,000-30,000m (*22,000-33,000yd*) against aircraft with accuracy limits of ±30m, ±0.2° horizontally and ±0.3° vertically. The parabolic antenna was 1.5m (*59in*) diameter and was stabilised with the director. A further development FuMO 232, known as 'Kassel', had a 4.5m (*14.8ft*) antenna which improved accuracy. Prototypes of both were completed and there was also a planned Euklid Z to work at 3cm.

However, the only AA fire-control sets afloat were some of the *Luftwaffe* Würzburg series, too massive for most warships, though they were in some AA ships converted from captured coast defence ships or old cruisers, and in 1944 one was fitted on an AA director in *Tirpitz*. Würzburg D, known as FuMO 213 in the navy, worked at *c*560 MHz (*54cm*) and 8 kW peak power, the range with a 3m (*9.8ft*) diameter antenna being as in Euklid but accuracy was less.

Würzburg-Riese (giant), FuMO 214, differed in the 7.5m (*24.6ft*) diameter antenna which gave a range of 40,000-60,000m (*43,700-65,600yd*) with bearing limits of ± 0.15° on both axes. The *Luftwaffe* Fighter Direction ship *Togo* had one on a stabilised mounting but it was otherwise far too bulky.

HEAVY CALIBRE GUNS

The largest naval gun ever constructed, though of far smaller bore than the 80cm (*31.5in*) railway guns. It is doubtful whether it was envisaged as the armament of a ship or more probably only for experimental work, and for even the distant projected battleships of over 100,000 tons a 50.8cm (*20in*) gun was proposed. It is curious that the actual bore of 533.4mm is exactly 21in and one may wonder if Sir Robert Hadfield's statement after the First World War, that he was ready to make 21in AP shells, had been remembered, though there was never the slightest chance of Britain's making a gun of this size. Gerät 36 was ordered in 1938, and the gun and cradle sufficiently near completion to allow firing, though the proof mounting was apparently unfinished. The gun was of four-layer built-up construction with shrunk liner, A tube and two outer tube layers. It had the usual Krupp horizontal sliding breech block.

53cm (21in) Gerät 36

Gun Data

Bore	533.4mm	21in	
Weight incl BM	335,100kg	329.8 tons	
Length oa	27,700mm	1090.55in	51.93cal
Length bore	26,040mm	1025.20in	48.82cal
Length chamber	4366mm	171.89in	
Volume chamber	1250dm^3	76,280in^3	
Length rifling	21,417mm	843.19in	
Grooves	(110) 6mm deep × 8.2	0.236 × 0.323in	
Lands	7.03mm	0.277in	
Twist	1 in 35.9 to 1 in 29.9		
Weight projectile	2200kg	4850lb	
Propellant charge	800kg Gu RP	1764lb	
Muzzle velocity	820m/s	2690f/s	
Working pressure	3000kg/cm^2	19t/in^2	
Max range	?47,500m/50°	?51,950yd/50°	

The charge was in three parts, the rear one in a metal case, and the shells had three driving bands. Details were:
APC. Length oa 2621mm (*103.19in*), burster 45.45kg (*100.2lb*).
Nose-fuzed HE. Length oa 2636mm (*103.78in*), burster 220kg (*485lb*).
Cartridge case. Dimensions 135 × 625mm max (*53.15 × 24.61in*), flange 655mm (*25.79in*), weight 157kg (*346lb*).
Rear cartridge incl case. 460kg (*1014lb*).
Fore and middle cartridges. Each 1150mm (*45.28in*), 250kg (*551lb*).

As indicated above, Gu RP, a nitroguanidine propellant, was to be used.

There were three versions of this gun: the original, for proof and experimental work; the naval, intended for twin turrets in the abortive battleships 'H', 'J', 'K', 'L', 'M', 'N'; the coast defence also known as *Adolf*, which was a conversion of the naval gun with larger chamber. The latter were mounted singly in BSG (*Bettungschiess-Gerüst*) mountings allowing 52° elevation. The best known battery was the three-gun *Lindemann* near Sangatte which fired at Dover, and others were in Norway and at Gotenhafen. Incidentally, of the *Lindemann* guns, one was left hand and two right, indicating their naval turret origin, and only one had power ramming. The unusual construction of the guns included both a loose barrel, which was universally interchangeable between production guns, and a loose liner which only fitted a particular barrel. Both barrel and liner could be changed from either end but more easily from the muzzle. The B tube into which the barrel fitted did not extend to the muzzle, and there was a jacket over the rear end of the B tube, a breech end-piece thrust over the jacket and kept in place by a threaded ring, and a breech block supporting piece inserted in the breech end-piece and secured by a threaded ring. A retaining ring with two fittings for transmitting rotation forces was screwed on to the rear of the barrel. The horizontal sliding breech block weighed 3600kg (*3.54 tons*) and the production guns had a heavy barrel and liner, respectively 41,600kg (*40.94 tons*) and 20,800kg (*20.47 tons*), while those in the proof gun weighed 37,700kg (*37.1 tons*) and 17,400kg (*17.13 tons*). The latter figures resembled those for a scaled-up loose barrel 38cm (*15in*), but those for the production guns indicate that conversion to 42cm (*16.5in*) may have been in view, though no guns were so altered.

The propellant charge for naval guns was to be in two parts, a main charge of 128kg (*282.2lb*) in a brass case weighing 91kg (*201lb*) and a fore charge of 134kg (*295.4lb*). The main charge had a bottom igniter of 800gm (*28oz*) coarse-grained black powder and a top one of 1000gm (*35oz*), while the fore charge had a bottom igniter of 1200gm (*42oz*). Projectiles comprised APC, base-fuzed HE and nose-fuzed HE all ranging alike. Coast-defence guns had these and also a 600kg (*1323lb*) HE with fuzes at nose and base, and a muzzle velocity of 1050m/s (*3445f/s*). The maximum range with this shell was 56,000m (*61,240yd*) compared with about 43,100m (*47,100yd*) for the heavier shells, and life was increased to 290–300 EFC. With RPC/40 (*12.5/4.2*) propellant, the main charge was 130kg (*286.6lb*) in a brass, later mild steel, case and the fore charge 164kg (*361.6lb*) for the heavier shells and 205kg (*452lb*) for the light. The problems raised by such large cartridges are noted in the introduction.

The cradle for a single gun weighed 59,000kg (*58 tons*) and the twin turret for the 'H' class battleships 1475t (*1452 tons*), of which the shield

40cm (16in) SKC/34

Gun Data for Naval version

Bore	406.4mm	16in	
Weight incl BM	159,900kg	157.4 tons	
Length oa	21,130mm	831.89in	52cal
Length bore	19,750mm	777.56in	48.6cal
Length chamber	2481mm	97.677in	
Volume chamber	420dm^3	25,630in^3	
Length rifling	17,066mm	671.89in	
Grooves	(90) 4.8mm deep × 7.98	0.189 × 0.314in	
Lands	6.2mm	0.244in	
Twist	Increasing 1 in 40 to 1 in 32		
Weight projectile	1030kg	2271lb	
Propellant charge	262kg RPC/38 (22/11)	578lb	
Muzzle velocity	810m/s	2657f/s	
Working pressure	3200kg/cm^2	20.3 tons/in^2	
Approx life	180–210 EFC		
Max range	*c*36,400m/30°	*c*39,800yd/30°	

The figure for gun weight includes the Hornrings to which the piston rods of the recoil and run-out cylinders were attached. Without these it becomes 152,700kg (*150.3 tons*). The original gun differed in weight, 150,400kg (*148 tons*) or 142,710kg (*140.46 tons*) less Hornrings, while the coast defence guns had chamber length 2676mm (*105.354in*) volume 460dm^3 (*28,071in^3*) and rifling length 16,871mm (*664.21in*).

armour accounted for 513t (*505 tons*). The thickness of this is given as face 385mm (*15.2in*), sides 240mm (*9.4in*), roof 130mm (*5.1in*) minimum. The internal diameter of the barbette was to be 11m (*36ft*) and the mounting which would generally have resembled that for the 38cm (*15in*), allowed +30° -5½° elevation.

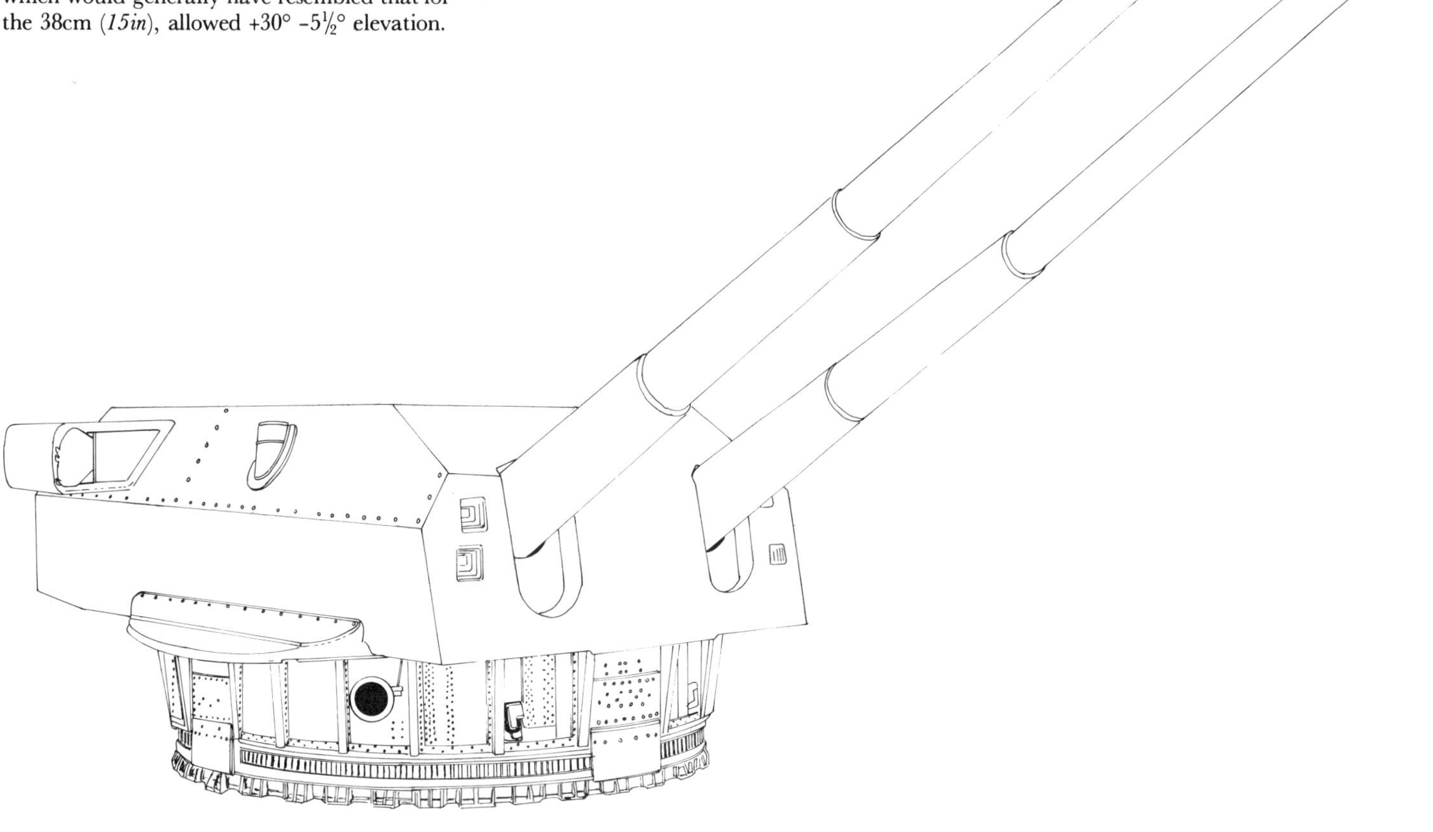

Twin turret for 40.6cm SKC/34 guns as intended for the cancelled 'H' class battleships. The turret was never made, but several guns, often known as *Adolf*, were modified for coast defence and emplaced in single BSG mountings.
John Lambert

Mounted in twin Drh LC/34 turrets in *Bismarck* and *Tirpitz* and intended for the projected battlecruisers 'O', 'P', 'Q'. It was also to be carried by the rearmed *Gneisenau* and work was begun on three twin turrets for this ship, while a further twin turret ordered by Russia was also incomplete. It was intended to emplace two of these turrets at Cap de la Hague and two at Paimpol in France but this was never done, though at the end of the war work was well advanced on emplacing two of the four at Oxsby in Denmark. The 38cm was also widely used as a coast-defence gun on single BSG mountings allowing 55° elevation or more, the best-known battery being the four-gun *Todt* near Haringzelles which fired across the Straits of Dover. The coast defence guns, which were also known as *Siegfried*, had larger chambers than those in *Bismarck* and *Tirpitz* and there were also differences in construction, the later guns being built with loose barrels and loose liners as in the 40.6cm (*16in*) while those in *Bismarck* and *Tirpitz* had a loose liner removed from the breech end; as in the later guns this was not universally exchangeable. Otherwise, these earlier guns had an A tube with four rings shrunk over it for about two-thirds of the length from the breech, a jacket shrunk over about two-thirds of the ring layer and a breech end-piece, breech block supporting piece, and breech block, as in the 40.6cm. The block weighed 2800kg (*2.76 tons*), the liner 14,300kg (*14.1 tons*) in both versions, the earlier A tube 22,670kg (*22.3 tons*) and the later loose barrel 32,300kg (*31.8 tons*).

For naval guns, the main charge of 112.5kg (*248lb*) was in a brass case weighing 70kg (*154lb*)

38cm (15in) SKC/34

Gun Data for earlier version

Bore	380mm	14.96in	
Weight incl BM	111,000kg	109.2 tons	
Length oa	19,630mm	772.83in	51.66cal
Length bore	18,405mm	724.61in	48.43cal
Length chamber	2230mm	87.795in	
Volume chamber	319dm^3	19,467in^3	
Length rifling	15,982mm	629.21in	
Grooves	(90) 4.5mm deep × 7.76	0.177 × 0.306in	
Lands	5.5mm	0.217in	
Twist	Increasing 1 in 36 to 1 in 30		
Weight projectile	800kg	1764lb	
Propellant charge	212kg RPC/38(17/7)	467lb	
Muzzle velocity	820m/s	2690f/s	
Working pressure	3200kg/cm^2	20.3 tons/in^2	
Approx life	250 EFC		
Max range	35,550m/30°	38,880yd/30°	

Without Hornrings the weight becomes 101,000kg (*99.4 tons*). Later guns were 300kg lighter and, for coast-defence guns, chamber length was 2479mm (*97.598in*), volume 361.7dm^3 (*22,072in^3*) and rifling length 15,748mm (*620.0in*).

Range and Elevation Data for 800kg (1764lb) shell

Range (m)	**(yd)**	**Elevation**	**Descent**	**Time of flight (sec)**	**Striking V (m/s)**	**(f/s)**
5000	5470	2.2°	2.4°	6.5	727	2385
10,000	10,940	4.9°	5.8°	13.9	641	2103
15,000	16,400	8.1°	10.4°	22.3	568	1864
20,000	21,870	12.1°	16.4°	32.0	511	1677
25,000	27,340	16.8°	23.8°	43.0	473	1552
30,000	32,810	22.4°	31.9°	55.5	457	1499
35,000	38,280	29.1°	40.3°	69.9	462	1516

Gun Mounting Data

Revolving weight	1064t	1047 tons
Ball track diameter	8.75m	28.71ft
Barbette int diameter	10.00m	32.81ft
Distance apart gun axes	3.75m	147.6in
Recoil distance	1050mm	41.3in
Max elevating speed	6°/sec	
Max training speed	5.4°/sec	
Firing cycle at 4° elev	26sec	
Turret shield		
(*Bismarck* class)	face 360mm; sides 220mm; rear 320	14.2in; 8.7in; 12.6in
	front and rear sloping roof 180mm;	7.1in;
	side sloping roof 150mm;	5.9in;
	flat roof 130	5.1in

38cm SKC/34 guns in *Bismarck* when fitting out. *Aldo Fraccaroli Collection*

and the fore charge weighed 99.5kg (*219lb*). Coarse-grained black powder igniters comprised 500 gm (*17.6oz*) at the bottom and 750gm (*26.4oz*) at the top of the main charge with 1000gm (*35.2oz*) at the bottom of the fore charge. APC, base-fuzed HE and nose-fuzed HE shells were carried. Coast-defence guns also had a 495kg (*1091lb*) HE shell with nose and base fuzes. The muzzle velocity with this was 1050m/s (*3445f/s*) giving a maximum range of 54,900m (*60,000yd*) compared with 42,100m (*46,040yd*) for the heavier shells. Life was also increased to nearly 350 EFC. Firing RPC/40 (13/4.3) the main charge was 115kg (*253.5lb*), and the fore charge 143kg (*315lb*) with the heavier shells and 180kg (*397lb*) with the light.

The twin turrets had electric training, auxiliary elevation, auxiliary hoists and reserve power for some of the loading gear, but otherwise they were hydraulically powered by two electrically driven pumps in each turret using water/glycerine as the pressure medium. The guns were in individual cylindrical cradles but were normally coupled together. Hydro-pneumatic run-out was employed with one recuperator and two recoil cylinders per gun. Elevation was by means of a hydraulic cylinder driving the elevating arc by rack and pinion. An electro-hydraulic RPC system was fitted but was apparently not very satisfactory. The auxiliary gear comprised a motor with worm drive of the arc. Elevation limits were +30° -5½°. The main and auxiliary training motors drove through a worm and gear train and there was also a transportable emergency motor with chain drive of the worm shaft.

The shell rooms were below the magazines and there were shell and cartridge ring cars in the respective handing rooms. The main hoists were driven by hydraulic cylinders with rack and pinion drive of a wire drum. They ran direct to the gunhouse, the shell cage picking up the charge cage on ascent. The main and fore charges were end to end on one tray. The two hoists came up between the guns, and the shells were transferred by rammers to the pivoted loading trays which moved into position behind the respective gun. The charges were transferred to waiting cages and after the shell was loaded the waiting cage moved down to the level of the pivoted loading tray. The space between them was bridged by a ramp, and the charges rolled into the loading tray. Fore and main charges were rammed together. The loading angle was +2½° and a telescopic, chain-operated rammer was used. A spent-cartridge tray was moved in and out from the side of the gun. The auxiliary hoists transported shells and charges one after another in a vertical position and came up in rear of the guns, where the ammunition was transferred to a tiltable cage and could be loaded by the main rammer. The auxiliary loading rammer was hand worked by between 10 and 14 men. As usual in German turrets, safety precautions were sketchy by British standards.

Twin 38cm Drh LC/34 turret as mounted in *Bismarck* class.

1 Local gunsight telescope
2 Main cage cable sheaves
3 Breech slot
4 Exhaust fan trunking
5 Range-finder
6 Rammer
7 Shell on shell tray
8 Armoured barbette
9 Training base support trunk
10 Machinery space
11 Auxiliary ammunition hoist trunk
12 Overhead charge rail
13 Overhead shell rail
14 Shell handing room
15 Shell ring rollers
16 Revolving shell ring
17 Cartridge ring rollers
18 Revolving cartridge ring
19 Charge handing room
20 Main ammunition trunk
21 High pressure air cylinder
22 Hydraulic pump unit
23 Elevating gear
24 Training base ball bearing
25 Toothed elevating arc

Peter Hodges

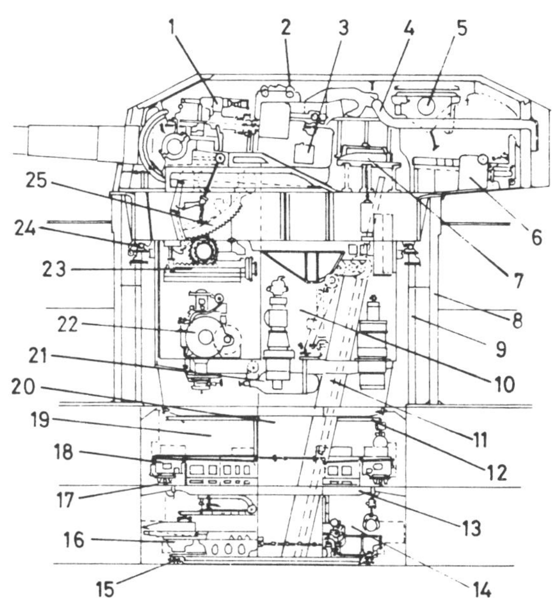

These guns, which like all German 28cm were actually 283mm (*11.14in*) bore, were mounted in triple Drh LC/28 turrets in *Scharnhorst* and *Gneisenau*. The turrets differed from the earlier ones of the same type in having heavier shields and are sometimes referred to as Drh LC/34. When the *Gneisenau* was disarmed in 1943, B and C turrets were prepared for emplacement in Norway, and it was intended to mount the three guns from the burnt out A turret at Rosenburg in Holland in singe Drh LC/37 coast-defence turrets. The construction included an A tube and loose liner which only fitted a particular A tube and was changed from the breech end. A two-part jacket was shrunk over the A tube for about two-thirds of its length, a breech end-piece was screwed hot on to the jacket, and a breech block supporting piece screwed into the breech end-piece. The breech block was of the usual horizontal sliding type and weighed *c*1000kg (*0.98 tons*), while the A tube was 13,700kg (*13.5 tons*) and the loose liner 6700kg (*6.6 tons*).

The main charge of 76.5kg (*168.6lb*) was in a brass case weighing 47.5kg (*104.7lb*) and the fore charge weighed 42.5kg (*93.7lb*). Coarse-grain black powder igniters of 360gm (*12.7oz*) each were at either end of the main charge and at the base of the fore charge. APC, base-fuzed HE and nose-fuzed HE were carried, and the two latter weighed 315kg (*694.5lb*) and had MVs of 900m/s (*2953f/s*) though they ranged similarly to the APC of 330kg (*727.5lb*) and 890m/s (*2920f/s*).

In many particulars the triple turrets resembled the 38cm twin, the main differences being in the ammunition supply and loading. There were no cartridge ring cars, since sliding channels and traversing tongs were used for the main charge while the fore charge was passed by hand. The hoist for the left gun came up between it and the centre gun, and those for the other two between the centre and right. In the charge cage, the main charge was on a tray above the fore charge, and the latter was loaded by hand. The centre-gun auxiliary hoist came up behind the gun and there was a tiltable cage as in the 38cm, but the wing auxiliary hoists were behind and to the side of the guns, shells and main charges being transported by overhead gear. The elevation range was +40° to -8° for A and C turrets and +40° to -9° for B , and loading was at +2°.

28cm (11in) SKC/34

Gun Data

Bore	283mm	11.14in	
Weight incl BM	53,250kg	52.4 tons	
Length oa	15,415mm	606.89in	54.47cal
Length bore	14,505mm	571.06in	51.25cal
Length chamber	2619mm	103.11in	
Volume chamber	180dm³	10,984in³	
Length rifling	11,725mm	461.61in	
Grooves	(80) 3.25mm deep × 6.72	0.128 × 0.265in	
Lands	4.4mm	0.173in	
Twist	Increasing 1 in 50 to 1 in 35		
Weight projectile (APC)	330kg	727.5lb	
Propellant charge	119kg RPC/38(15/4.9)	262.3lb	
Muzzle velocity	890m/s	2920f/s	
Working pressure	3200kg/cm²	20.3 tons/in²	
Approx life	300 EFC		
Max range	40,930m/40°	44,760yd/40°	

Without Hornrings the above weight is reduced to 50,100kg (*49.3 tons*).

Range and Elevation Data for APC shells

Range (m)	(yds)	Elevation	Descent	Striking V (m/s)	(f/s)
5000	5470	2.0°	2.5°	766	2513
10,000	10,940	4.3°	5.7°	652	2139
15,000	16,400	7.4°	10.3°	556	1824
20,000	21,870	11.3°	17.2°	481	1578
25,000	27,340	16.2°	25.7°	436	1430
30,000	32,810	22.0°	35.3°	418	1371
35,000	38,280	29.2°	44.0°	428	1404
40,000	43,740	38.2°	52.0°	460	1509

Gun Mounting Data

Revolving Weight	750t	738 tons
Ball track diameter	9.00m	29.53ft
Barbette int diameter	10.20m	33.46ft
Distance apart gun axes	2.75m	108.3in
Recoil distance	1200mm	47.2in
Max elevating speed	8°/sec	
Max training speed	7.2°/sec	
Firing cycle (min)	17sec	
Turret shield	face 360mm;	14.2in
	sides 200m;	7.9in
	sloping roof 150mm	5.9in

Mounted in triple Drh LC/28 turrets in *Lützow* ex-*Deutschland*, *Admiral Scheer* and *Admiral Graf Spee*. The gun construction was similar to that of the 28cm SKC/34, but the jacket was in one piece. The A tube weighed 13,800kg (*13.6 tons*) and the loose liner 5650kg (*5.56 tons*).

The main charge weighed 71.0kg (*156.5lb*) with a brass case, as in the SKC/34, and the fore charge 36.0kg (*79.4lb*). Igniters were as in the SKC/34 and APC, base-fuzed HE and nose-fuzed HE shells were carried. Their aerodynamic shape was not as good as that of the later 28cm shells, and their ballistics were inferior.

Apart from the lighter shield and guns, the turret resembled those in *Scharnhorst* and *Gneisenau*. The revolving weight is given as 600t (*590 tons*) and the shield as face 140mm (*5.5in*), sides 85mm (*3.4in*), roof 105-85mm (*4.1-3.4in*).

28cm (11in) SKC/28

Gun Data

Bore	283mm	11.14in	
Weight incl BM	48,200kg	47.4 tons	
Length oa	14,815mm	583.27in	52.35cal
Length bore	13,905mm	547.44in	49.13cal
Length chamber	2333mm	91.85in	
Volume chamber	160dm^3	9764in^3	
Length rifling	11411mm	449.25in	
Grooves	(80) 3.25mm deep × 6.72	0.128 × 0.265in	
Lands	4.4mm	0.173in	
Twist	Increasing 1 in 50 to 1 in 35		
Weight projectile	300kg	661.4lb	
Propellant charge	107kg RPC/38 (16/7.2)	235.9lb	
Muzzle velocity	910m/s	2986f/s	
Working pressure	3200kg/cm^2	20.3 tons/in^2	
Approx life	340 EFC		
Max range	36,475m/40°	39,890yd/40°	

Without Hornrings the gun weighed 46,850kg (*46.1tons*).

Range and Elevation Data

Range (m)	(yd)	Elevation	Descent	Striking V (m/s)	(f/s)
5000	5470	1.9°	2.4°	752	2467
10,000	10,940	4.5°	6.0°	611	2005
15,000	16,400	8.0°	11.8°	493	1617
20,000	21,870	12.5°	21.4°	407	1335
25,000	27,340	18.6°	34.2°	360	1181
30,000	32,810	26.3°	46.4°	353	1158
35,000	38,280	36.4°	56.0°	380	1247

28cm SKC/28 guns in triple Drh LC/28 turret *Graf Spee* 1939.
Aldo Fraccaroli Collection

28cm SKL/40 guns in twin Drh LC/01 turret. The AA guns are 8.8cm Flak L/45. The ship is probably *Schlesien* c1930.
CPL

This obsolescent gun was mounted in twin Drh LC/01 turrets in the old battleships *Schlesien* and *Schleswig-Holstein*, and as a coast-defence gun in the four-gun *Graf Spee* battery originally at Wangerooge and later at Brest.

28cm (11in) SKL/40

Gun Data

Bore	283mm	11.14in	
Weight incl BM	45,300kg	44.6 tons	
Length oa	11,200mm	440.94in	39.58cal
Length bore	10,401mm	409.49in	36.75cal
Length chamber	1847mm	72.72in	
Volume chamber	123.1dm³	7512in³	
Weight projectile	240kg	529lb	
Propellant charge	70.0kg RPC/38(11/5.1)	154.3lb	
Muzzle velocity	820m/s	2690f/s	
Max range	18,830m/30°	20,590yd/30°	
With longer shell	25,640m/30°	28,040yd/30°	

Coast-defence guns were in old BSG mountings and with 284kg (*626lb*) shells and MV 740m/s (*2428f/s*) had a range of 27,750m/45° (*30,350yd*).

HEAVY COAST-DEFENCE GUNS

Brief details of the most important of these are given (not mounted afloat, but manned by Navy). Foreign guns taken over in World War Two are not included.

A new design of gun which is believed to have been intended originally for possible commerce-raiding heavy cruisers as well as for coast defence. As far as is known, it did not enter service.

30.5cm (12in) SKC/39

Gun Data

Bore	305mm	12.01in	
Weight incl BM	66,800kg	65.7 tons	
Length oa	17,000mm	669.29in	55.74cal
Length bore	15,925mm	626.97in	52.21cal
Length chamber	3077mm	121.14in	
Volume chamber	290dm³	17,697in³	
Length rifling	12,725mm	500.98in	
Grooves	(72) 3.6mm deep × 8.11 to 8.70 at muzzle	0.142 × 0.319 - 0.3425in	
Lands	5.20mm to 4.61 to muzzle	0.205-0.1815in	
Twist	Increasing 1 in 32.6 to 1 in 27.6		
Weight projectile	415kg	915lb	
Propellant charge	172kg RPC/40N	379lb	
Muzzle velocity	865m/s	2880f/s	
Working pressure	3000kg/cm²	19 tons/in²	
Max range	*c*42,800m/49°	*c*46,800yd/49°	

With a 250kg (*551lb*) shell and 200kg (*441lb*) charge MV was 1120m/s (*3675f/s*) and maximum range 51,400m (*56,200yd*). Working pressure increased to 3300kg/cm² (*21 tons/in²*).

This gun was the principal armament of German First World War battleships and some battlecruisers and its particulars are in marked contrast to those of the SKC/39. The best known battery was the six-gun *Friedrich August* at Wangerooge, from which three guns on BSG mountings were moved to near Wimille on the Channel coast.

30.5cm (12in) SKL/50

Gun Data

Bore	305mm	12.01in	
Weight incl BM	51,850kg	51.03 tons	
Length oa	15,250mm	600.39in	50.0cal
Length bore	14,461mm	569.33in	47.41cal
Length chamber	2493mm	98.15in	
Volume chamber	197.5dm^3	12,052in^3	
Weight projectile	415kg	915lb	
Propellant charge	121.5kg RPC/38(18/8)	268lb	
Muzzle velocity	850m/s	2789f/s	
Max range	41,300m/47°46′		

The above shell was of much better shape and longer range than those used afloat in 1914–18, shooting 9300m (*10,170yd*) further at maximum elevation. With a 250kg (*551lb*) shell and 143kg (*315lb*) charge performance was as for the SKC/39.

Mounted in *Moltke*, *Goeben* and *Seydlitz* in the 1914–18 War. The *Grosser Kurfürst* battery at Framzelle, previously at Pillau, was part of the Channel defences and had four guns in single Drh LC/37 coast turrets.

28cm (11in) SKL/50

Gun Data

Bore	283mm	11.14in	
Weight incl BM	41,500kg	40.8 tons	
Length oa	14,150mm	557.09in	50.0cal
Length bore	13,421mm	528.39in	47.42cal
Length chamber	2192mm	86.30in	
Volume chamber	150dm^3	9154in^3	
Weight projectile	284kg	626lb	
Propellant charge	114.0/119.1kg RPC/38(16/6)	251.3/262.6lb	
Muzzle velocity	895m/s	2936f/s	
Max range	38,600m/49.5°	42,400yd/49.5°	

The above shell ranged 7900m (*8640yd*) further at maximum elevation than the 302kg (*666lb*) used at sea in 1914–18.

This was mounted in the *Nassau* class and in *Von der Tann* in the First World War. It was in several coast defence batteries and differed from the SKL/50 in the details given in the table.

28cm (11in) SKL/45

Gun Data

Weight incl BM	39,800kg	39.2 tons	
Length oa	12,735mm	501.38in	45.0cal
Length bore	12,006mm	472.68in	42.42cal
Muzzle velocity	875m/s	2871f/s	
Max range	36,900m/49.2°	40,350yd/49.2°	

There is often some confusion over these guns. They were originally two Russian 25.4cm (*10in*) guns captured in 1915 and converted to 24cm with horizontal sliding breech blocks. They were mounted in old type coast defence mountings in the *Oldenburg* battery originally at Borkum and later moved to the Channel.

24cm (9.4in) SKL/50

Gun Data

Bore	238mm	9.37in	
Weight incl BM	30,700kg	30.2 tons	
Length oa	11,777–11,796mm	463.66–464.41in	49.48–49.56cal
Length bore	11,118mm	437.72in	46.71cal
Length chamber	1830mm	72.05in	
Volume chamber	90dm^3	5492in^3	
Weight projectile	148.5kg	327.4lb	
Propellant charge	48kg RPC/12 (12/5)	105.8lb	
Muzzle velocity	900m/s	2953f/s	
Max range	26,700m/30°	29,200yd/30°	

This obsolescent gun, originally mounted in battleships and in two armoured cruisers laid down in the 1890s, for the most part, was on old BSG mountings in several batteries, the best known being *Hamburg* moved from Nordeney to Cherbourg.

24cm (9.4in) SKL/40

Gun Data

Bore	238mm	9.37in	
Weight incl BM	24,040–25,640kg	23.66–25.24 tons	
Length oa	9550mm	375.98in	40.13cal
Length bore	8866mm	349.06in	37.25cal
Length chamber	1467mm	57.76in	
Volume chamber	72.2dm^3	4406in^3	
Weight projectile	148.5–151kg	327.4–332.9lb	
Propellant	46.8kg RPC/38(12/6.6)	103.2lb	
Muzzle velocity	810m/s	2657f/s	
Max range	26,600m/45.8°	29,090yd/45.8°	

The shells given above ranged 7520m (*8220yd*) further than the original 140kg (*308.6lb*) at maximum elevation.

MEDIUM CALIBRE GUNS

This gun was mounted in twin Drh LC/34 turrets in the cruisers *Admiral Hipper, Blücher* and *Prinz Eugen* as well as being intended for the uncompleted *Seydlitz* and *Lützow*, the last of which was sold to the Soviet Union in 1940. Two of the turrets from *Seydlitz* were mounted on Ile de Croix and the other two were intended for Ile de Ré. The gun had a loose barrel, which would fit any gun and was exchangeable from the rear, an inner and outer jacket, a breech end-piece screwed hot on to the outer jacket, and a breech-block supporting piece pushed into the breech end-piece and held by a threaded ring. The breech block was of the usual horizontal sliding type, hydraulically worked, and weighed 450kg (*992lb*) while the loose barrel weighed 5580kg (*5.49 tons*).

20.3cm (8in) SKC/34

Gun Data

Bore	203mm	7.99in	
Weight incl BM	20,700kg	20.4 tons	
Length oa	12,150mm	478.35in	59.85cal
Length bore	11,518mm	453.46in	56.74cal
Length chamber	1873mm	73.74in	
Volume chamber	70.0dm^3	4272in^3	
Length rifling	9527mm	375.08in	
Grooves	(64) 2.4mm deep × 5.76	0.094 × 0.227in	
Lands	4.2mm	0.165in	
Twist	Increasing 1 in 40 to 1 in 35		
Weight projectile	122kg	269lb	
Propellant charge	50.8kg RPC/38(11/4.3)	112lb	
Muzzle velocity	925m/s	3035f/s	
Working pressure	3200kg/cm^2	20.3 tons/in^2	
Approx life	510 EFC		
Max range	33,540m/37°	36,680yd/37°	

The weight less Hornrings was 19,550kg (*19.24tons*).

After 20.3cm SKC/34 guns in twin Drh LC/34 turrets, in *Prinz Eugen*. Note that only the superfiring turret has a 7m RF, and to accommodate it, the front slope of the roof is lengthened and the flat part raised. *CPL*

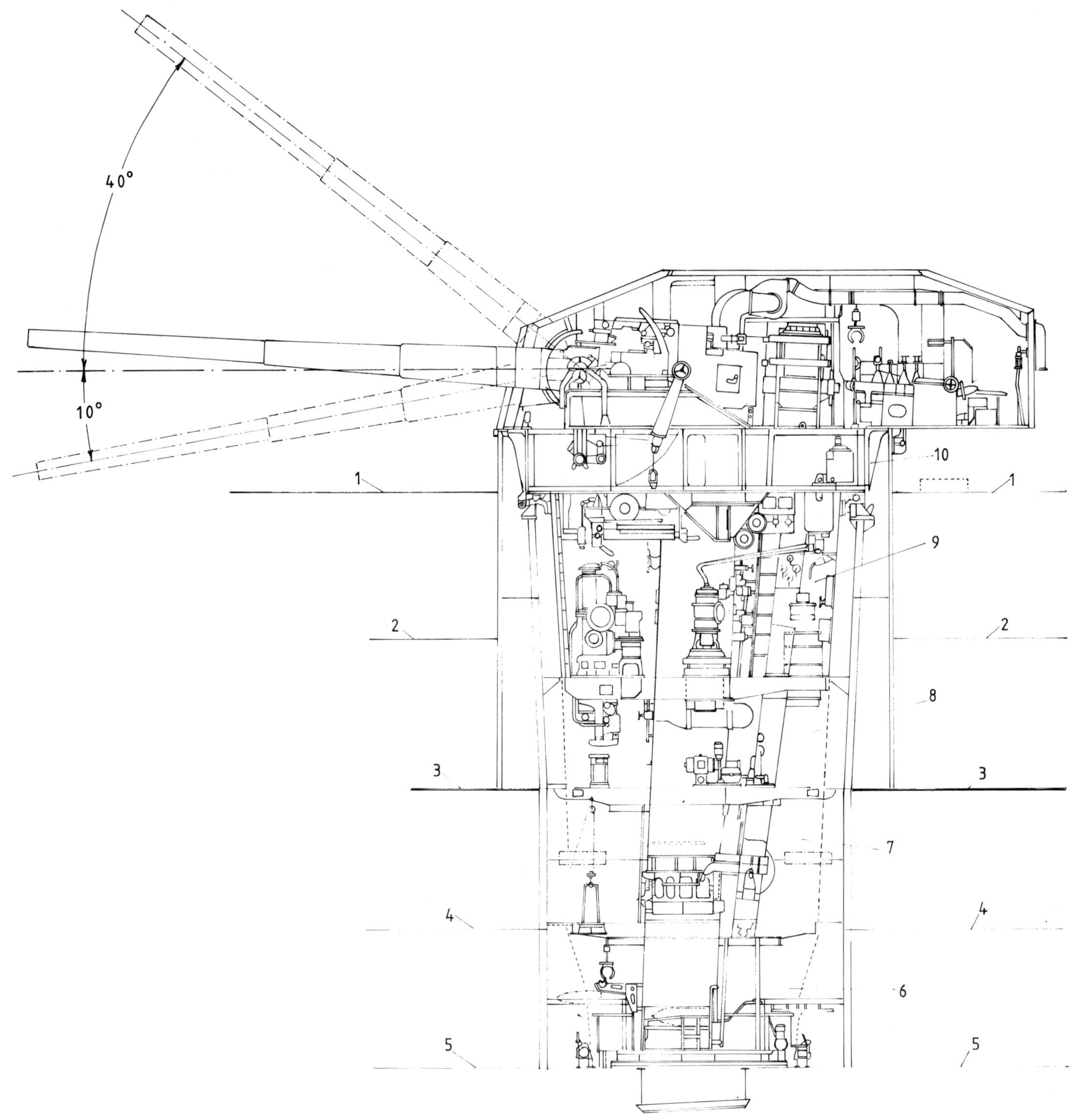

The after non-superfiring 20.3cm turret in *Prinz Eugen* shown in longitudinal section. (As built elevation was 37° not 40°)

1 Upper deck
2 Battery deck
3 Armoured deck
4 Upper platform deck
5 Lower platform deck
6 Shell platform
7 Cartridge platform
8 Work space
9 Machinery space
10 Turret ring

John Lambert

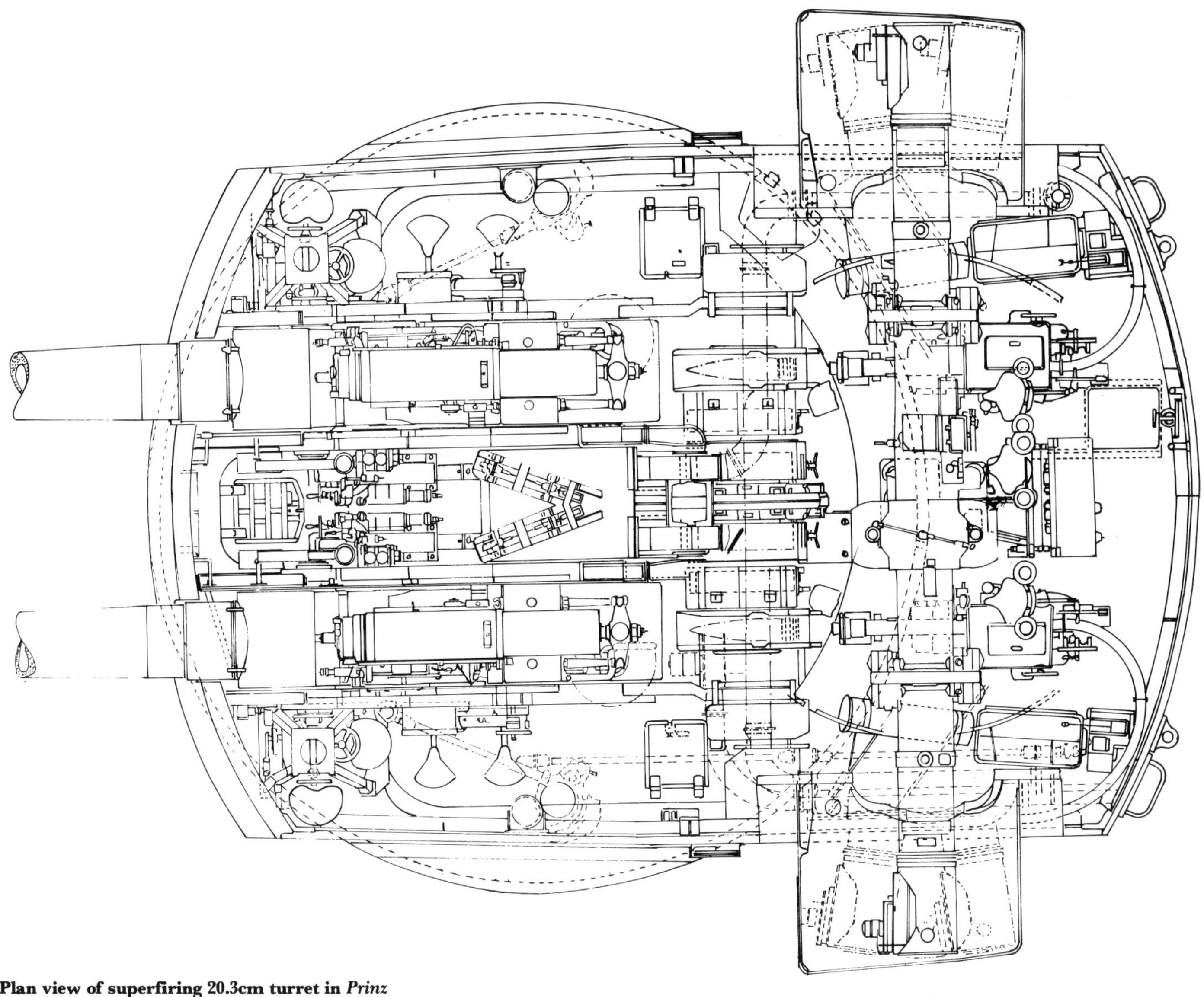

Plan view of superfiring 20.3cm turret in *Prinz Eugen*.

John Lambert

The main charge of 29.7kg (*65.5lb*) was in a brass case weighing 18.2kg (*40.1lb*) and the fore charge weighed 21.1kg (*46.5lb*). Coarse-grain black powder igniters amounted to 160gm (*5.6oz*) at the base of the main charge, 180gm (*6.3oz*) at the top and 200gm (*7oz*) at the base of the fore charge. Projectiles comprised APC, base-fuzed HE and nose-fuzed HE and 40 illuminating shell per ship were also provided. These weighed 103kg (*227lb*) and had a MV of 700m/s (*2297f/s*).

The twin turrets which allowed +37° to -10°, elevation, -9° in 'A', generally resembled the 38cm (*15in*). Loading was at +3°. The main differences were the use of electrically driven Pittler-Thoma hydraulic gear for auxiliary training, the absence of cartridge-ring cars, both fore and main charges being passed by hand, and the presence of two trays in the charge hoist cage with the main charge above the fore. The latter were loaded by hand, but shells and main charges were loaded as in the 38cm. Auxiliary hoists were similar but electric reserve power for the main loading gear was replaced by hand.

Range and Elevation Data

Range (m)	(yd)	Elevation	Descent	Time of flight (sec)	Striking V (m/s)	(f/s)
5000	5470	1.9°	2.1°	6.0	744	2441
10,000	10,940	4.4°	6.1°	13.6	587	1926
15,000	16,400	8.1°	12.8°	23.4	463	1519
20,000	21,870	13.3°	23.6°	35.9	382	1253
25,000	27,340	20.3°	36.8°	51.1	353	1158
30,000	32,810	29.1°	48.8°	69.0	363	1191

Gun Mounting Data

Revolving weight	248t	244 tons
Ball track diameter	5.33m	17.49ft
Barbette int diameter	6.40m	21.0ft
Distance apart gun axes	2.16m	85.0in
Recoil distance	625mm	24.6in
Max elevating speed	8°/sec	
Max training speed	8°/sec	
Firing cycle (min)	12sec	
Turret shield	face 160mm	6.3in

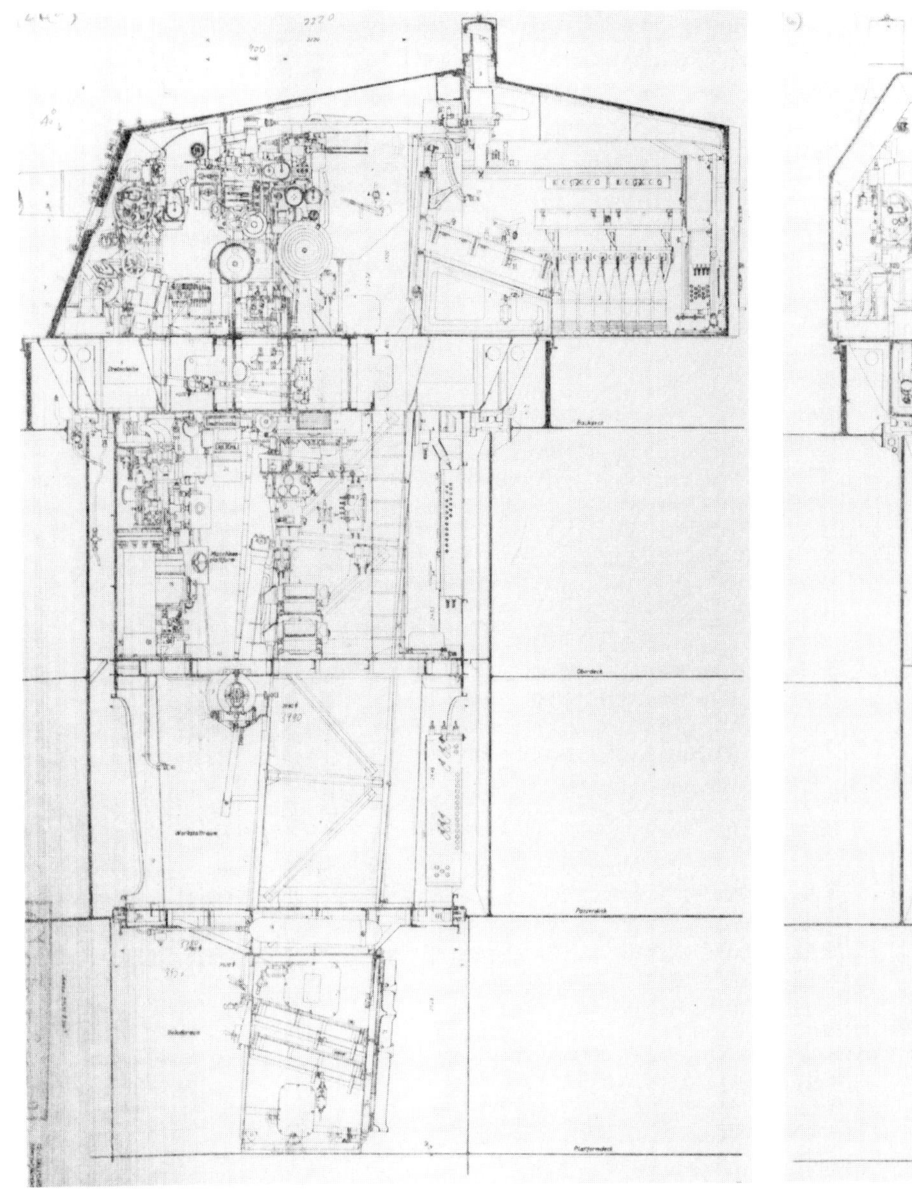

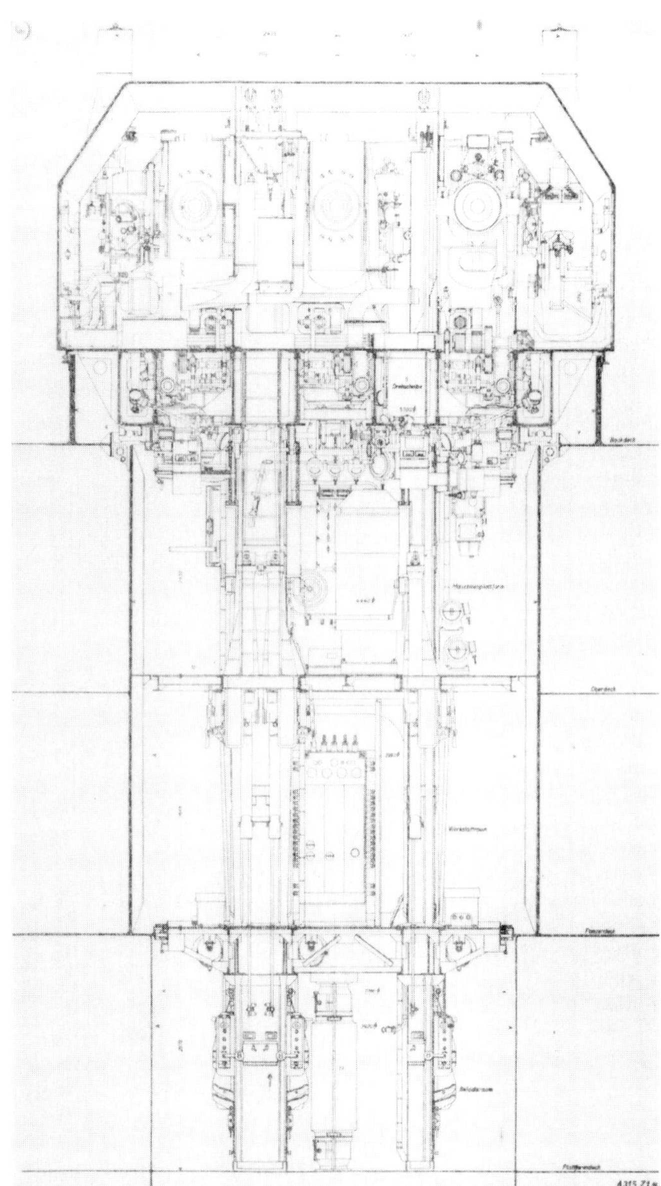

Triple 15cm Drh LC/25 turret in *Nürnberg* in longitudinal and transverse sections. The guns were 15cm SKC/25.
Official drawing, by courtesy of Mike whitley

The after triple 15cm Drh LC/25 turrets in *Köln*. The offsetting of superfiring turrets was in this class only, though some projected Vickers designs of *c*1920 incorporated it.
Aldo Fraccaroli Collection

This, the most powerful of the German naval 15cm guns, was mounted in triple Drh LC/25 turrets in the *Köln* class, the *Leipzig* and *Nürnberg*. The main components of the gun were a loose barrel weighing 3250kg (*3.2 tons*), a jacket and a breech end-piece with a vertical sliding breech block weighing 150kg (*330lb*). As with all German 15cm guns, the actual bore was 149.1mm. It was considered to be too heavy and powerful for other 15cm gun applications.

There were no fore charges and the propellant was in a brass case weighing 13.5kg (*29.8lb*) as normal for separate ammunition QF guns. APC, base-fuzed HE and nose-fuzed HE, with and without tracer, were carried with 120 illuminating shell per ship, the latter weighing 41kg (*90.4lb*) and having a muzzle velocity of 650m/s (*2133f/s*).

The guns were in individual cradles, each with separate elevating gear, but were normally coupled and fired together. Training was electric, the type of motor having very high inertia, and elevation hydraulic, the turret being provided with self-contained electrically driven pumps. In this, unlike larger-calibre turrets, the elevating cylinder and not the piston was moved. The elevation limits were +40° to -10°. Magazines and shell rooms were on the same deck, and projectiles and charges were passed to the hoists by hand. There were no breaks in the hoists, one of which came up between the left and centre guns, and two between centre and right, and in the gunhouse shells and charges were transferred from inclined hoist cages to inclined ready trays and loaded and rammed by hand. The breech mechanism was also hand worked. The turrets in *Nürnberg* had heavier shields than the others.

15cm (5.9in) SKC/25

Gun Data

Bore	149.1mm	5.87in	
Weight incl BM	11,970kg	11.78tons	
Length oa	9080mm	357.48in	60.90cal
Length bore	8570mm	337.40in	57.48cal
Length chamber	1396mm	54.96in	
Volume chamber	27.7dm^3	1690in^3	
Length rifling	7067mm	278.23in	
Grooves	(44) 1.75mm deep × 6.14mm	0.069 × 0.242in	
Lands	4.5mm	0.177in	
Twist	Increasing 1 in 45 to 1 in 30		
Weight projectile	45.5kg	100.3lb	
Propellant charge	20.4kg RPC/38(10/4.4)	45lb	
Muzzle velocity	960m/s	3150f/s	
Working pressure	3000kg/cm^2	19.0 tons/in^2	
Approx life	500 EFC		
Max range	25,700m/40°	28,100yd/40°	

Range and Elevation Data

Range (m)	**(yd)**	**Elevation**	**Descent**	**Striking V (m/s)**	**(f/s)**
5000	5470	1.7°	2.2°	673	2208
10,000	10,940	5.3°	8.8°	445	1460
15,000	16,400	11.5°	23.5°	318	1043
20,000	21,870	21.4°	42°	314	1030
25,000	27,340	36.3°	59.5°	332	1089

Gun Mounting Data

Revolving Weight	136,910kg	134.75 tons
(in *Nürnberg*)	147,150kg	144.83 tons
Ball track dia	4.50m	14.76ft
Barbette int dia	5.7m	18.7ft
Distance apart gun axes	1.55m	61.0in
Recoil distance	370mm	14.6in
Max elevating speed	8°/sec	
Max training speed	6-8°/sec	
Firing cycle (min)	7.5sec	
Turret shield	30-20mm	1.2-0.8in
(in *Nürnberg*)	80-20mm	3.15-0.8in

Graf Spee showing 15cm SKC/28 guns in MPLC/28 mountings.
CPL

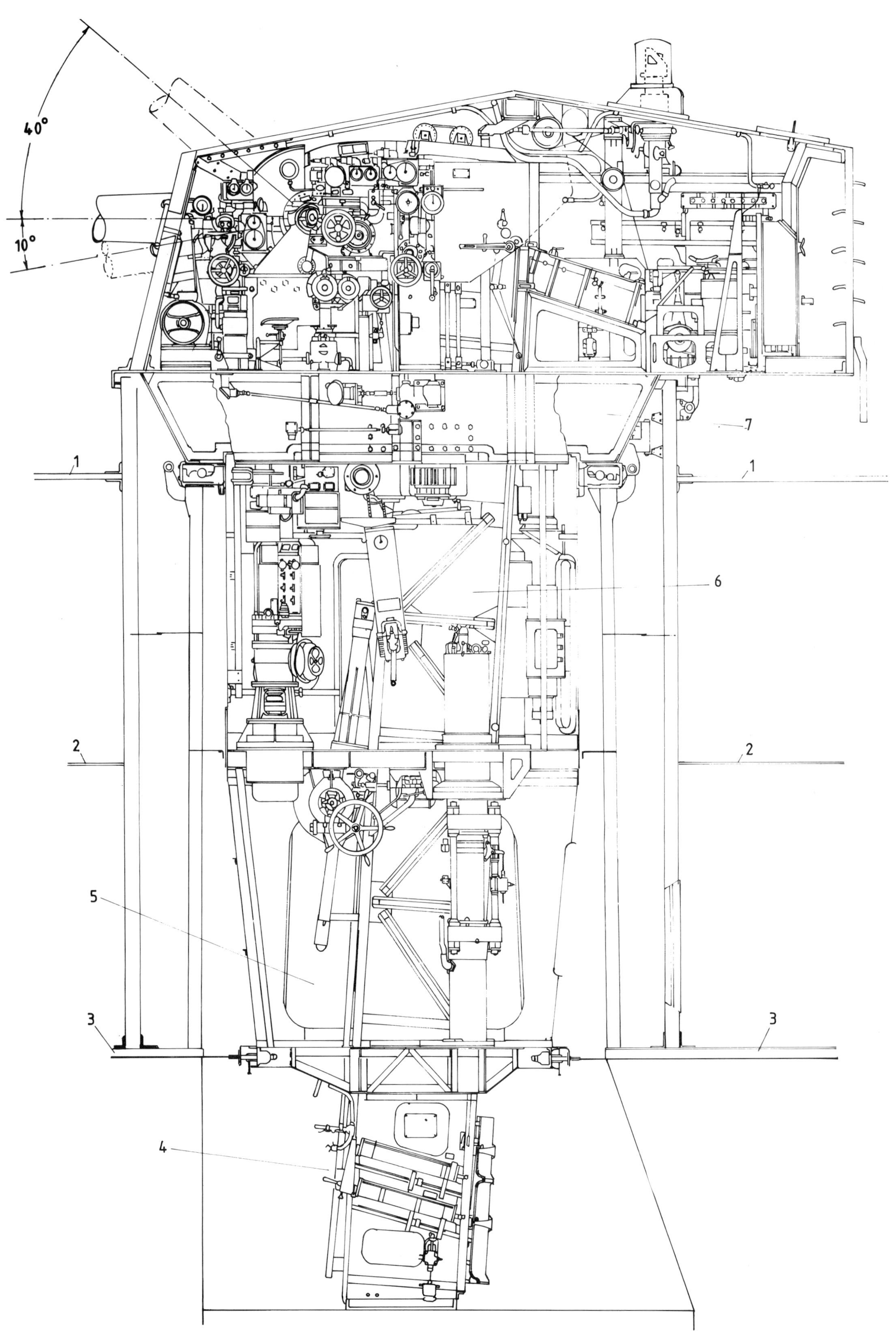
40°
10°
1
1
2
2
3
3
4
5
6
7

This gun was mounted in twin Drh LC/34 turrets in the *Bismarck* and *Scharnhorst* classes and these were also intended for battleships 'H', 'L', 'K', 'L', 'M', 'N' and, in a lighter version, for cruisers 'M', 'N', 'O', 'P', 'Q', 'R'. The single guns in the *Scharnhorst* class were in MPLC/35 mountings while the *Lützow* ex-*Deutschland* class had MPLC/28, and twin Dopp MPLC/36 were intended for the *Graf Zeppelin*. A number of spare twin turrets were also mounted for coast defence and there were some single guns in KstMPLC/36 mountings. There were slight variations between the guns in the above mountings, but they resembled the 15cm SKC/25 in construction with a loose barrel weight of 2680-2710kg (*2.64-2.67 tons*). The barrels fitted any gun and were changed from the breech end. In all naval mountings the breech block moved vertically.

The cartridge case weighed 8.54kg (*18.83lb*). APC shell was available but the outfit usually comprised base-fuzed HE, nose-fuzed HE with and without tracer and illuminating shell as for the SKC/25.

The twin Drh LC/34 turrets generally resembled the triple C/25 but there was a double hoist between and in rear of the guns which delivered two shells and two charges simultaneously. Elevation was +40° to -10°.

The MPL mountings allowed +35° -10° elevation and the shields were 60-20mm (*2.36-0.8in*) in the C/28 and C/35. The latter's shield was larger, giving a total weight of 26,710kg (*26.29 tons*) compared with 24,830kg (*24.44 tons*). The Dopp MPLC/36 weighed 47,600kg (*46.85 tons*) and had the two guns in a common cradle with axes 800mm (*31.5in*) apart. The shield was 30mm (*1.2in*) and power elevation and training gave maximum speeds of 6° and 8°/sec.

Twin 15cm Drh LC/34 turret with 15cm SKC/28 guns as mounted in *Bismarck* and *Scharnhorst* classes in longitudinal section.

1 Upper deck
2 Battery deck
3 Armoured deck
4 Ammunition input
5 Work space
6 Machinery space
7 Turntable

John Lambert

15cm (5.9in) SKC/28

Gun Data

Bore	149.1mm	5.87in	
Weight incl BM	9026/9080kg	8.88/8.94 tons	
Length oa	8200mm	322.83in	55.0cal
Length bore	7816mm	307.72in	52.42cal
Length chamber	1152mm	45.35in	
Volume chamber	21.7dm^3	1324in^3	
Length rifling	6588mm	259.37in	
Grooves	(44) 1.75mm deep x 6.14	0.069 x 0.242in	
Lands	4.5mm	0.177in	
Twist	Increasing 1 in 50 to 1 in 30		
Weight projectile	45.3kg	99.87lb	
Propellant charge	14.15kg RPC/38(7.5/3)	31.195lb	
Muzzle velocity	875m/s	2871f/s	
Working pressure	3000kg/cm^2	19.0 tons/in^2	
Approx life	1100 EFC		
Max range	22,000m/35°	24,060yd/35°	
	23,000m/40°	25,150yd/40°	

Gun Mounting Data Drh LC/34

Revolving weight	114,000/120,000kg	112/118 tons
Ball track diameter	3.63m	11.91ft
Barbette int diameter	4.8in	15.75ft
Recoil distance	370mm	14.6in
Max elevating speed	8°/sec	
Max training speed	9°/sec	
Firing cycle (min)	7.5sec	
Turret shield (*Scharnhorst*)	140-30mm	5.5-1.2in
(*Bismarck*)	100-20mm	3.9-0.8in

The turret for the proposed light cruisers 'M' to 'R' was to have a thinner shield and weigh *c*102,000kg (*100 tons*).

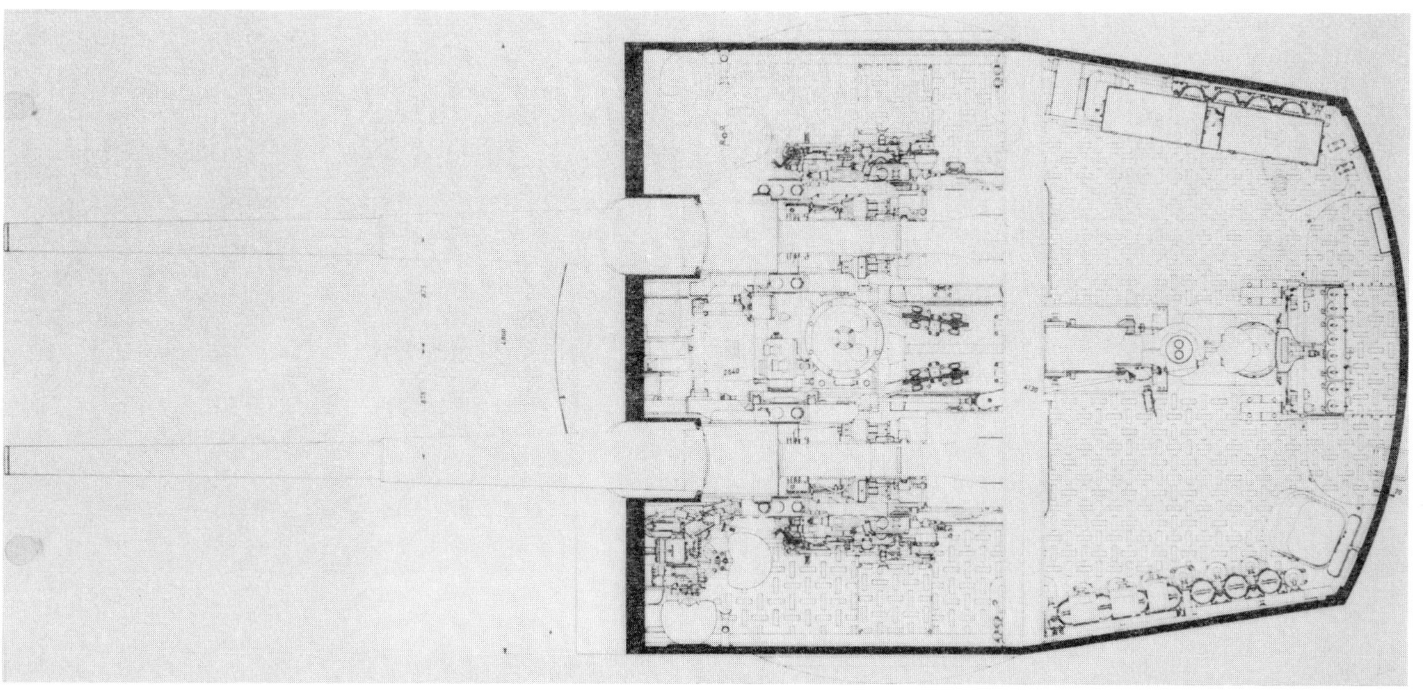

Twin 15cm Drh LC/34 turret with 15cm SKC/28 guns in plan.
Official drawing, by courtesy of Mike Whitley

Twin 15cm Drh LC/34 turret with 15cm SKC/28 guns in transverse section.
Official drawing, by courtesy of Mike Whitley

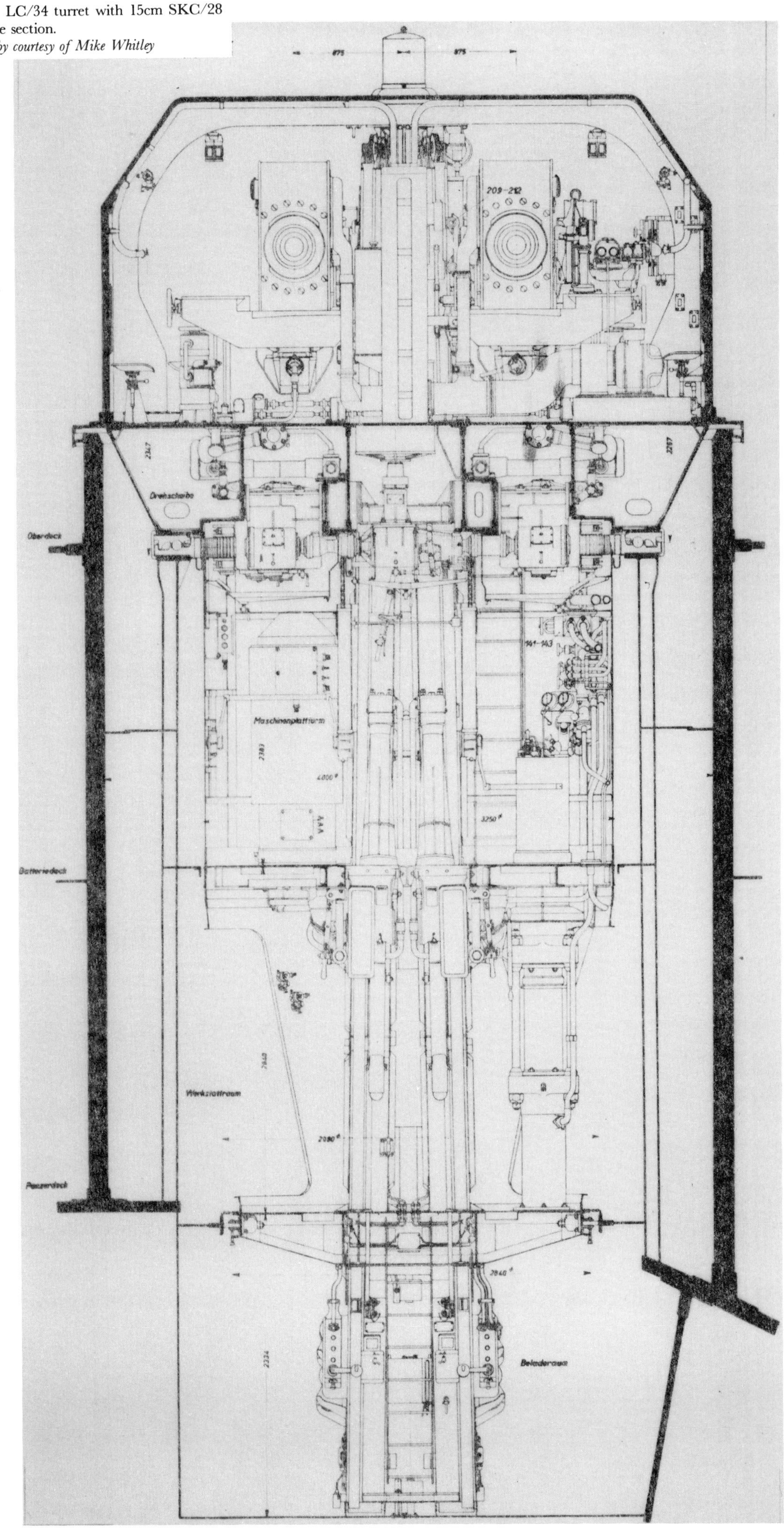

As indicated by its title, this gun was primarily for destroyers and was carried in twin Drh LC/38 and single Tbts LC/36 mountings in Type 36A, though several did not have a twin mounting initially, and it was not until June 1942 that this entered service in *Z 23*. It was never in *Z 26–Z 28* and *Z 30*. The Type 34 destroyer *Bruno Heinemann* temporarily mounted four single guns for trials in April 1938, and twin mountings were intended for the projected battlecruisers 'O', 'P', 'Q' and scouting cruisers Sp 1-3, while single ones were in the re-armed *Emden* and in some converted merchant ship raiders and supply ships. The construction differed from that of the SKC/25 and C/28 in that the loose barrel, which weighed 2370kg (*2.33 tons*), could be changed from the muzzle end and that the breech block was horizontal. There were two types, Tbts KC/36 for single mountings and Tbts KC/36T for twins. The latter was considerably heavier at the breech end to move the centre of gravity in that direction.

The cartridge case was as in the SKC/28. 40kg (*88.2lb*) shells, which were boat tailed, were carried by destroyers and base-fuzed HE and nose-fuzed HE with and without tracer were provided with 80 illuminating shell per ship of the same type as in the SKC/25. Originally the same 45.3kg (*99.87lb*) shells as in the SKC/28 were to be used with muzzle velocity of 835m/s (*2740f/s*) and maximum range 21,950 (*24,000yd*) but they were found to be too heavy for ease of handling in destroyers, though still issued to the *Emden*.

The twin Drh LC/38 mountings had a single common cradle and an elevation range of +65° -10°, which gave some AA capacity, though training and elevation were too slow. These were powered by electrically driven Pittler-Thoma hydraulic gear, or alternatively by hand, and as non-reversible worms made the hand drive too heavy for one man, not very satisfactory brakes were used to check movement. The hoists were electric with belt drive on the Ardelt system.

There were two types of Tbts LC/36 mounting, one with hand elevation and training and the other with alternative Pittler-Thoma gear. Both elevated to +30° -10° and had a recoil of 425mm (*16.7in*). The former with a 10-6mm shield weighed 16,100kg (*15.85 tons*), and the latter with a 40-20mm shield 19,540kg (*19.23 tons*).

15cm (5.9in) Tbts KC/36

Gun Data

Bore	149.1mm	5.87in	
Weight incl BM	7200kg-T 8564kg	7.09 tons-T 8.43 tons	
Length oa	7165mm	282.09in	48.05cal
Length bore	6815mm	268.31in	45.71cal
Length chamber	1088mm	42.83in	
Volume chamber	21.2dm^3	1294in^3	
Length rifling	5587mm	219.96in	
Grooves	(44) 1.75mm deep × 6.14	0.069 × 0.242in	
Lands	4.5mm	0.177in	
Twist	Increasing 1 in 45 to 1 in 30		
Weight projectile	40kg	88.2lb	
Propellant charge	13.5kg RPC/38(7.5/3)	29.76lb	
Muzzle velocity	875m/s	2871f/s	
Working pressure	3000kg/cm^2	19.0 tons/in^2	
Approx life	1600 EFC		
Max range	23,500m/47°	25,700yd/47°	

Gun Mounting Data Drh LC/38

Revolving Weight	62,500kg	61.5 tons
Ball track diameter	2.80m	9.19ft
Recoil distance	440mm	17.3in
Max elevating speed	8°/sec	
Max training speed	8°/sec	
Firing cycle min	7.5sec	
Turret shield	30-15mm	1.2-0.6in

Above: Twin 15cm Drh LC/38 mounting with 15cm Tbts KC/36 guns in *Z 24* in 1943.
Aldo Fraccaroli Collection

Right: The after 12.7cm SKC/34 guns in *Z 11* (*Bernd von Arnim*) in 1938.
Aldo Fraccaroli Collection

Brief details are given of this gun, which formed the secondary armament of all First World War German dreadnoughts and battlecruisers as well as the main armament of all the later light cruisers of that period. In the Second World War it was initially in the *Schlesien, Schleswig-Holstein* and *Emden*, and later in some converted merchant ship raiders, including the *Kormoran*, and in some supply ships, as well as being used for coast defence.

15cm (5.9in) SKL/45

Gun Data

Bore	149.1mm	5.87in	
Weight incl BM	5730/6102kg	5.64/6.00 tons	
Length oa	6710mm	264.17in	45.0cal
Length bore	6326mm	249.06in	42.43cal
Length chamber	1150mm	45.28in	
Volume chamber	21.7dm^3	1324in^3	
Weight projectile	45.3kg	99.87lb	
Propellant charge	14.35kg RPC/38 (7.5/3)	31.64lb	
Muzzle velocity	835m/s	2740f/s	
Max range	19,400m/30°	21,220yd/30°	

The range given is for the same shells as in SKC/28.

These guns differed only in their mountings and were in the *S 113* class destroyers and the larger U-boats of the First World War. In 1939–45 they were mounted in several converted merchant ship raiders, some supply ships and for coast defence.

15cm (5.9in) Tbts KL/45 and Ubts + Tbts KL/45

Gun Data

Bore	149.1mm	5.87in	
Weight incl BM	3990kg	3.93 tons	
Length oa	6675mm	262.80in	44.77cal
Length bore	6291mm	247.68in	42.19cal
Length chamber	749mm	29.49in	
Volume chamber	14.06dm^3	858in^3	
Weight projectile	45.3kg	99.87lb	
Propellant charge	8.32kg RPC/38(6.5/2.8)	18.34lb	
Muzzle velocity	680m/s	2231f/s	
Max range	14,500m/30°	15,860yd/30°	
	15,900m/40°	17,390yd/40°	

An older type of shell was used by these guns.

Former medium calibre German naval guns used for coast defence include the 21cm SKL/45 in BSG mountings and the 17cm SKL/40 and 15cm SKL/40 in centre-pivot (MPL) mountings. The last named was also in some transports and supply ships. Ranges are for the latest type of projectile issued.

Medium Calibre Coast-Defence Guns

Gun Data

Gun	**Bore**	**Projectile**	**Muzzle Velocity**	**Max range**
21cm SKL/45	209.3mm	113.5kg	900m/s	29,000m/45°
(*8.2in*)	(*8.24in*)	(*250.2lb*)	(*2953f/s*)	(*31,700yd*)
17cm SKL/40	172.6mm	62.8kg	875m/s	20,100m/22°
(*6.7in*)	(*6.795in*)	(*138.5lb*)	(*2871f/s*)	(*21,980yd*)
15cm SKL/40	149.1mm	40.0kg	800m/s	14,300m/30°
(*5.9in*)	(*5.87in*)	(*88.2lb*)	(*2625f/s*)	(*15,640yd*)

The above 17cm gun was entirely distinct from the 17cm K18 Army heavy field gun which was also used for coast defence, and ranged to 29,600m (*32,370yd*).

Intended for twin LDrh LM41 mountings in Type 36C and 42C destroyers and not in service. Fixed ammunition was used.

12.8cm (5in) KM41

Gun Data

Bore	128mm	5.04in	
Weight incl BM	4250kg	4.18 tons	
Length oa	5807mm	228.62in	45.37cal
Length bore	5400mm	212.60in	42.19cal
Length chamber	689mm	27.126in	
Volume chamber	14.37dm^3	877in^3	
Length rifling	4537.4mm	178.64in	
Grooves	(40) 1.7mm deep × 5.05	0.067 × 0.199in	
Lands	5.0mm	0.197in	
Twist	Increasing 1 in 35.9 to 1 in 29.9		
Weight projectile	28kg	61.73lb	
Propellant charge	10.0kg RPC/40N	22.05lb	
Muzzle velocity	830m/s	2723f/s	
Working pressure	2950kg/cm^2	18.7 tons/in^2	
Approx life	Not determined		
Max range	22,000m	24,060yd	

The chamber was much shorter and of larger diameter than usual in German guns. With a 20crh shell the complete round weighed 49kg (*108lb*) and was 1346.1mm (*53in*) long.

The twin mounting generally resembled the 15cm DrhLC/38 and allowed +52° to -15° elevation. Total weight was 40,500kg (*39.9 tons*).

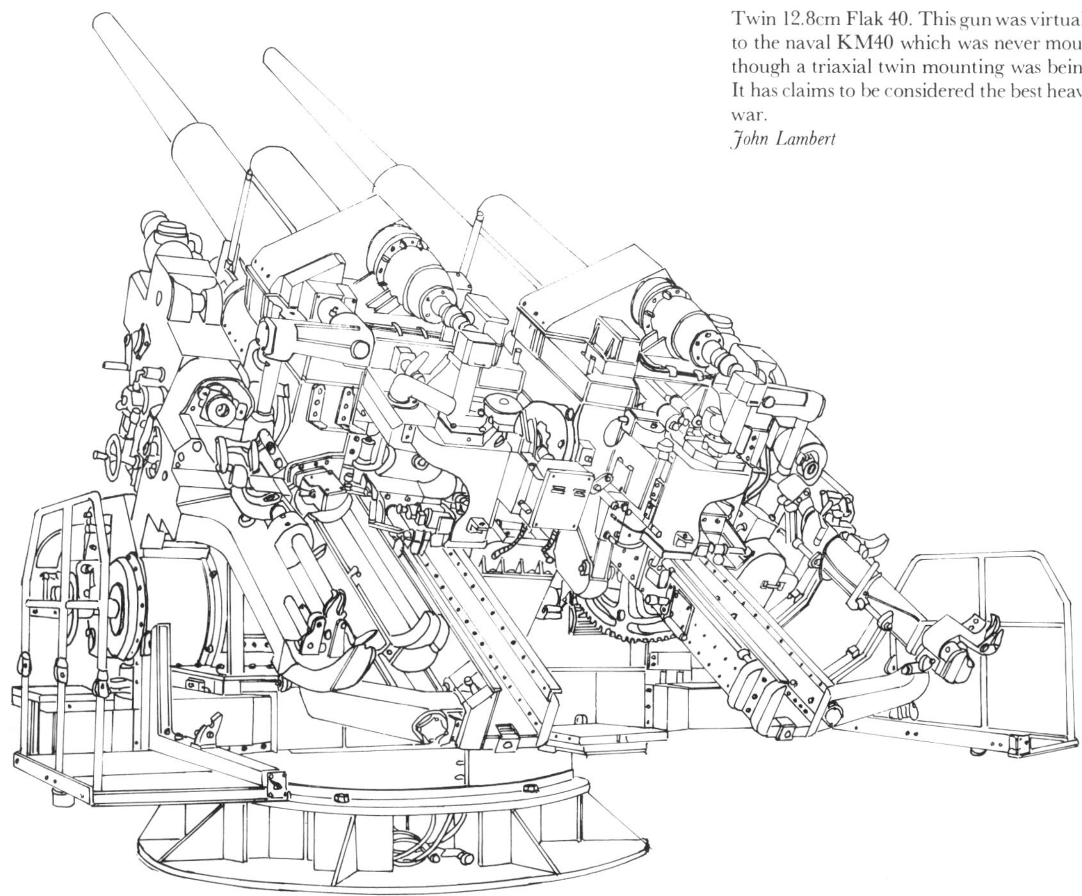

Twin 12.8cm Flak 40. This gun was virtually identical to the naval KM40 which was never mounted afloat, though a triaxial twin mounting was being designed. It has claims to be considered the best heavy AA of the war.
John Lambert

This was the naval version of the well-known 12.8cm Flak 40. It was never mounted afloat, though the design for the twin triaxial Dopp Flak LM44 turret with full RPC was in progress. There were a number of naval batteries at the most exposed ports with twin Dopp Flak LM40 mountings and one near Kiel had the Dopp L (Pzk) C/40 turret which was armoured and had 'funnel' shields to catch fragments from a burst barrel outside, but near to, the turret. Later guns incorporated a three-piece loose barrel so that alloy steel could be saved by changing only the most worn section.

Fixed ammunition was fired.

12.8cm (5in) KM40

Gun Data

Bore	128mm	5.04in	
Weight incl BM	*c*4800kg	*c*4.72 tons	
Length oa	7835mm	308.46in	61.21cal
Length bore	7490.4mm	294.90in	58.52cal
Length chamber	906mm	35.67in	
Volume chamber	14.37dm^3	877in^3	
Length rifling	6478mm	255.04in	
Grooves	(40) 1.7mm deep × 6.55	0.067 × 0.258in	
Lands	3.5mm	0.138in	
Twist	Increasing 1 in 53.9 to 1 in 32.6		
Weight projectile	26.0kg	57.32lb	
Propellant charge	10.1kg RPC/40N (6.5/2.5)	22.27lb	
Muzzle velocity	900m/s	2953f/s	
Working pressure	2850kg/cm^2	18 tons/in^2	
Approx life	*c*1400/1500 EFC		
Max range	20,600m/45°	22,530yd/45°	
Ceiling	14,800m/85°	48,560ft/85°	

With a 10/2crh shell, the complete round weighed 47.4kg (*104.5lb*) and was 1487.7mm (*58.57in*) long.

Some of the earlier guns were bored out 10.5cm SKC/28 and all were actually 128mm (*5.04in*) bore. They were mounted in single hand worked 12.7cm MPLC/34 or 10.5cm MPLC/28 mountings in Type 34, 36 and 36B destroyers, the sloop *Grille*, gunnery training ship *Bremse*, and torpedo-boats *Leopard* and *Luchs*, and were also intended for the Type 38B and 40 destroyers, the Type 40 torpedo-boats and in twin Drh LC/38 apt mountings for the Type XI U-boats. The construction principally comprised a loose barrel, jacket and breech end-piece with vertical sliding breech block. The loose barrel weighed 1260kg (*1.24 tons*) or 1180kg (*1.16 tons*) in the converted 10.5cm. Separate ammunition was fired, and the cartridge case weighed 7.2kg (*15.9lb*). The outfit for destroyers comprised base-fuzed HE and nose-fuzed HE with and without tracer, each ship also having 80 illuminating shell weighing 27.4kg (*60.4lb*) with MV 650m/s (*2133f/s*).

The 12.7cm MPL mountings had a total weight of 10,220kg (*10.06tons*) with an 8mm (*0.3in*) shield, and the converted 10.5cm mountings 7960kg (*7.83 tons*) or 8010kg (*7.88 tons*) with 3mm (*0.12in*) or 5mm (*0.2in*) shields. Both allowed +30° to -10° elevation. The intended twin U-boat mounting was of turret type with 30-20mm (*1.2-0.8in*) shield, elevated to +40° and had a total weight of 42,200kg (*41.5 tons*).

12.7cm (5in) SKC/34

Gun Data

Bore	128mm	5.04in	
Weight incl BM	3645kg	3.59tons	
Length oa	5760mm	226.77in	45.0cal
Length bore	5430mm	213.78in	42.42cal
Length chamber	825mm	32.48in	
Volume chamber	12.19dm³	744in³	
Length rifling	4536mm	178.58in	
Grooves	(40) 1.5mm deep × 6.0	0.059 × 0.236in	
Lands	4.0mm	0.157in	
Twist	Increasing 1 in 35 to 1 in 30		
Weight projectile	28.0kg	61.73lb	
Propellant charge	8.7kg RPC/38(6.4/2.6)	19.18lb	
Muzzle velocity	830m/s	2723f/s	
Working pressure	2950kg/cm²	18.7 tons/in²	
Approx life	1950 EFC		
Max range	17,400m/30°	19,030yd/30°	

Converted 10.5cm SKC/28 guns weighed 3450kg (*3.395 tons*) and those intended for Type XI U-boats 4625kg (*4.55 tons*) due to increased breech end weight.

12.7cm SKC/34 guns in converted 10.5cm MPLC/28 mountings in the torpedo-boat *Luchs*. *CPL*

LIGHT CALIBRE GUNS

10.5cm (*4.1in*) are unusually confusing for German naval guns. The most important are described below with briefer notes on the rest.

This gun was never in service but it and its twin Dopp Flak LM44 mounting are of much interest. The gun included a divided loose barrel so that only the most worn section need be changed, and a muzzle brake was fitted, while projectiles had 20 or 40crh heads thus attaining good performance without high muzzle velocity. The twin triaxial mounting had RPC for training, elevation and cross-levelling, but a projected single mounting was cancelled.

The Dopp Flak LM44 mounting was intended for large torpedo-boats or escorts and was on a turntable with a relatively small-diameter ball race and the training rack outside this. The guns were in a twin cradle and recoil was long. Power was from an electrically driven pump with hydraulic motors for training, elevation and cross-levelling. There was a small, open-back shield. Ammunition was passed through vertical revolving scuttles to men standing in the hollow fixed pedestal support and from there passed through a tube to the

10.5cm (4.1in) KM44

Gun Data

Bore	105mm	4.134in	
Weight incl BM	*c*1850kg	*c*1.82 tons	
Length oa	5023mm	197.76in	47.84cal
Length bore	4715mm	185.63in	44.90cal
Length chamber	*c*680mm	*c*26.8in	
Volume chamber	7.16dm³	437in³	
Length rifling	3898mm	153.46in	
Grooves	(24) 1.25mm deep × 5.70	0.049 × 0.224in	
Lands	8.04mm	0.317in	
Twist	Increasing 1 in 29.9 to 1 in 25.6		
Weight projectile	15.5kg (40crh), 17kg (20crh)	34.17, 37.5lb	
Propellant charge	6.1kg RPC/40 N	13.45lb	
Muzzle velocity	835m/s (15.5kg), 785m/s (17kg)	2740, 2575f/s	
Working pressure	3000kg/cm²	19 tons/in²	
Approx life	Not determined		
Max range	19,000m/48° (17kg)	20,780yd/48°	
Ceiling	*c*13,000m/75° (17kg)	*c*42,650ft/75°	

revolving part on the upper deck. It was then placed in the loading mechanism which was automatically driven via hydraulic accumulators by the recoil and set the fuze and loaded the round. Elevation was +75° to -15° and cross-levelling ±17°.

With a 17kg shell the complete round weighed 28.8kg (*63.5lb*) and was 1189.7mm (*46.84in*) long while with the 15.5kg shell these figures were 27.3kg (*60.2lb*), 1272mm (*50.08in*).

Gun Mounting Data

Weight	18,600kg	18.3 tons
Recoil distance	800mm	31.5in
Max elevating speed	16°/sec	
Max training speed	12°/sec (slew 20°/sec)	
Max cross-levelling speed	12°/sec	
Rate of fire per gun	12-14 rounds/min	
Shield	18mm max	0.7in max

It is clear that this mounting required more speed, but that would probably have meant increased weight.

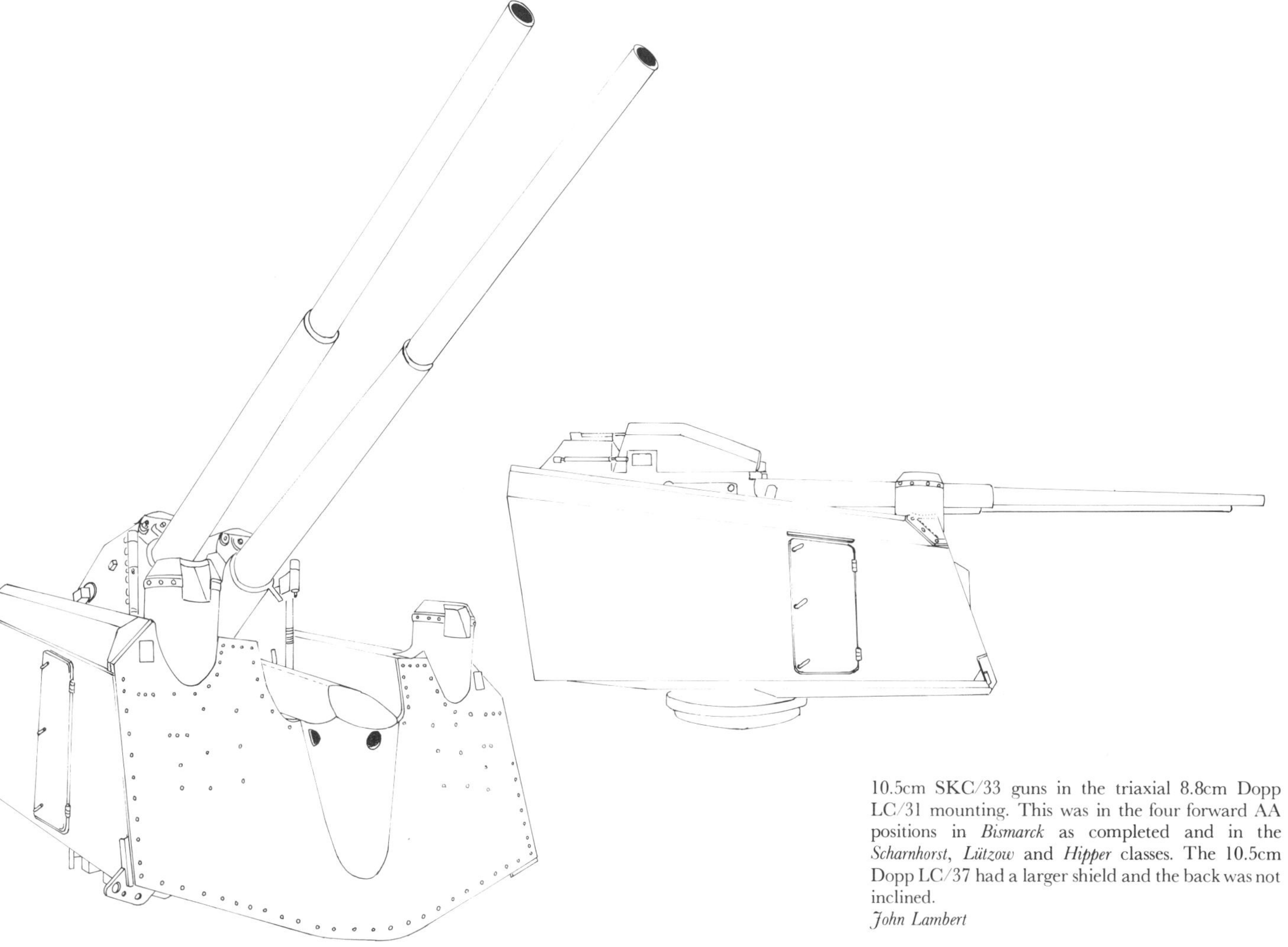

10.5cm SKC/33 guns in the triaxial 8.8cm Dopp LC/31 mounting. This was in the four forward AA positions in *Bismarck* as completed and in the *Scharnhorst*, *Lützow* and *Hipper* classes. The 10.5cm Dopp LC/37 had a larger shield and the back was not inclined.
John Lambert

10.5cm (4.1in) SKC/33

This was the standard AA gun for the larger German warships, superseding the 8.8cm SKC/31. In 8.8cm Dopp LC/31 twin mountings it was in the *Scharnhorst, Lützow* and *Hipper* classes as well as the *Bauer* class of U-boat depot ships, while in 10.5cm Dopp LC/37 twins it was in the *Bismarck* class, though the four forward mountings in *Bismarck* as completed were actually LC/31, was intended for the *Seydlitz* and *Graf Zeppelin*, and was used to rearm S-boat depot ships of the *Lüderitz* and *Nachtigal* classes. A twin turret mounting, Drh LC/38, had been designed for the 'H' class battleships. All mountings were triaxial. The earlier guns principally comprised a loose barrel weighing 1075kg (*1.058 tons*) jacket and breech end-piece, with a vertical sliding block. Later a lighter, two-part loose barrel of 750kg (*0.738 tons*) was introduced with a heavier jacket, and the final version for the twin turrets had the fore part of the bore as a loose muzzle piece and the rear part as a short loose liner. These guns were known as SKC/33 na and SKC/33 nT respectively.

Gun Data

Bore	105mm	4.134in	
Weight incl BM	4560kg; na 4695; nT 4300	4.49; 4.62; 4.23 tons	
Length oa	6840mm	269.29in	65.14cal
Length bore	6348mm	249.92in	60.46cal
Length chamber	698mm	27.48in	
Volume chamber	7.31dm³	446in³	
Length rifling	5531mm	217.76in	
Grooves	(36) 1.3mm deep × 5.5	0.051 × 0.2165in	
Lands	3.66mm	0.144in	
Twist	Increasing 1 in 55 to 1 in 35		
Weight projectile	15.1kg	33.3lb	
Propellant charge	6.05kg RPC/40N (5.5/2.1)	13.34lb	
Muzzle velocity	900m/s	2953f/s	
Working pressure	2850kg/cm²	18 tons/in²	
Approx life	2950 EFC		
Max range	17,700m	19,360yd	
Ceiling	12,500m/80°	41,000ft/80°	

The complete round weighed 27.35kg (*60.3lb*) and was 1164mm (*45.83in*) long.

Prinz Eugen showing twin 10.5cm SKC/33 guns in 8.8cm Dopp LC/31 mounting and Type 37 triaxial AA director.
Aldo Fraccaroli Collection

Fixed ammunition was fired and the outfit comprised HE and HE incendiary, both nose fuzed and with or without tracer. Depot ships also carried some AP, and this and HE incendiary weighed 15.8kg (*34.8lb*) instead of 15.1kg (*33.3lb*). Illuminating shell weighed 14.7kg (*32.4lb*) with MV of 650m/s (*2133f/s*).

The 8.8cm Dopp LC/31 mounting could take the 10.5cm SKC/33, and both it and the 10.5cm Dopp LC/37 mounting were of twin centre pivot type. The latter could be distinguished by the larger shield. Both mountings had separate cradles and were trained by electrically driven hydraulic gear with electric elevation and cross-levelling. Elevation had partial and cross-levelling full RPC. The loading gear made use of transport rollers. An electric motor on the cradle drove a continuously running roller above the bore, and there was a lower spring-loaded roller, which was not driven, in the breech block. When the breech opened, the upper roller remained raised so that the cartridge case could be extracted. Up to 18 rounds a minute could be attained in the C/37 mounting. Elevation was +80° to -9°, or to -8° in C/31, and cross-levelling ±17° in both.

The proposed Drh LC/38 twin turret mounting was electrically powered with full RPC, and had hoists coming up on the outside of each gun, the ammunition being horizontal in the hoist cages. There were to be short and long trunk versions. Elevation was +80° to -8° and cross-levelling ±17°.

Gun Mounting Data Dopp LC/31

Total Weight	27,805kg	27.366 tons
Distance apart gun axes	680mm	26.8in
Max recoil	410mm	16.1in
Max elevation speed	10°/sec	
Max training speed	8°/sec	
Max cross-levelling speed	5°sec	
Shield	15-10mm	0.6-0.4in

Gun Mounting Data Dopp LC/37

Total Weight	27,055kg	26.628 tons
Distance apart gun axes	660mm	26in
Max recoil	380mm	15in
Max elevation speed	12°/sec	
Max training speed	8.5°/sec	
Max cross-levelling speed	8°/sec	
Shield	20-8mm	0.8-0.3in

Gun Mounting Data Drh LC/38

Total Weight	43,500-45,000kg	42.8-44.3 tons
Ball track diameter	3.70m	12.14ft
Distance apart gun axes	970mm	38.2in
Max recoil	400mm	15.7in
Max elevation speed	12°/sec	
Max training speed	10°/sec (slew 20°/sec)	
Max cross-levelling speed	10°/sec	
Shield	20mm	0.8in

None of these mountings had sufficiently fast elevation or training.

10.5cm (4.1in) SKC/32

This was a widely used gun of moderate performance and always mounted singly. In MPLC/32 mountings it was in Type 35 and 37 torpedo-boats, some F-boats and some Type 40 minesweepers as well as other vessels. The higher-angle MPLC/32 gE was later in the *Schlesien* class and *Emden* and also in Type 39 torpedo-boats, Type 35 and some Type 35 and 43 minesweepers among the more important ships. Ubts LC/32 mountings were in Type I and early Type IX U-boats, and Ubts LC/36 in Type IX and X U-boats until removed and mounted in some Type 40 minesweepers. Some guns were also in 8.8cm MPLC/30 AA mountings, and a triaxial Flak LC/35 mounting was proposed. The earlier SKC/32 guns were built with a barrel, jacket and breech-end piece, as were the SKC/32 U in Ubts LC/36 mountings, but SKC/32 nS in MPLC/32 gE had a lighter two part loose barrel. Fixed ammunition was fired.

Outfits were similar to those for the SKC/33 but not all ships had HE incendiary and AP was

Gun Data

Bore	105mm	4.134in	
Weight incl BM	1585kg, U 1785, nS 1765	1.560, 1.757, 1.737 tons	
Length oa	4740mm, U 4860	186.61, 191.34in	45.14, 46.29cal
Length bore	4400mm	173.23in	41.90cal
Length chamber	586.5mm	23.09in	
Volume chamber	5.38dm³	328in³	
Length rifling	3694mm	145.43in	
Grooves	(32) 1.25mm deep × 6.8	0.049 × 0.268in	
Lands	3.5mm	0.138in	
Twist	Increasing 1 in 45 to 1 in 30		
Weight projectile	15.1kg	33.3lb	
Propellant charge	4.08kg RPC/40N(4.4/1.7)	8.995lb	
Muzzle velocity	785m/s	2575f/s	
Working pressure	2850kg/cm²	18 tons/in²	
Approx life	4100 EFC		
Max range	15,175m/44.4°	16,595yd/44.4°	
Ceiling	10,300m/80°	33,800ft/80°	

The complete round weighed 24.2kg (*53.35lb*) with a length of 1051.7mm (*41.4in*).

carried by torpedo-boats, F-boats and minesweepers as well as by some other vessels.

Gun Mounting Data for Hand-worked Mountings

Mounting	Elevation	Total Weight (kg)	(tons)	Shield (mm)	(in)
MPLC/32	+50° -10°	6485	6.38	8 or 5-4	0.3 or 0.2-0.15
MPLC/32 gE	+70° -10°	6750	6.64	12-18	0.47-0.3
Ubts LC/32	+35° -10°	4970	4.89		
Ubts LC/36	+30° -10°	4600	4.53		
8.8cm MPLC/30	+80° -9°	6910	6.80	15-10	0.6-0.4

Fleet escort *F 6*. The forward gun is a 10.5cm, probably SKC/32 in MPLC/32. *CPL*

As noted above some guns were later converted to 12.7cm SKC/34. It was originally in the *Bremse* and was mounted in some of the *Wolf* class torpedo-boats, being still in *Jaguar* in 1944. The MPLC/28 mounting allowed +30° to -10°, and fixed ammunition was fired.

10.5cm (4.1in) SKC/28

Gun Data

Bore	105mm	4.134in	
Weight incl BM	3660kg	3.60tons	
Length oa	5760mm	226.77in	54.86cal
Length bore	5430.5mm	213.80in	51.72cal
Length chamber	814mm	32.05in	
Volume chamber	8.4dm³	513in³	
Weight projectile	14.7kg	32.4lb	
Propellant charge	5.37kg RPC/32(6.5/3.5)	11.84lb	
Muzzle velocity	925m/s	3035f/s	
Max range	17,250m/30°	18,860yd/30°	

Other 10.5cm (4.1in) guns

The 10.5cm Ubts KL/45 was mounted only in submarine *U A*, ex-Turkish *Batiray*. It fired the same ammunition as the SKC/28 but the gun was shorter, 48.5cal overall, 45cal bore, and lighter at 2135kg (*2.10 tons*). Muzzle velocity was 890m/s (*2920f/s*) and the mounting allowed +45° to -10° elevation.

Of First World War guns, many 10.5cm Ubts and Tbts Flak L/45 were altered to take the same ammunition as the SKC/32 and had the same performance. They were mounted in Ubts and Tbts LC/16 which gave +50° to -10° elevation, and were in the *Möwe* class torpedo-boats, some F-boats, and some Type 40 and older minesweepers among the more important vessels. Some guns were to be found in 8.8cm MPLC/30 mountings which allowed +80° to -9°. Some 10.5cm SKL/45 and Flak L/45 were altered in the same way, the mountings giving +30° to -10° and +70° to -5° respectively.

Unaltered guns were mostly used for coast defence, though altered guns and SKC/32s were also to be found. The unaltered guns fired a 17.4kg (*38.4lb*) shell at 710m/s (*2329f/s*) or 690m/s (*2264f/s*) in the case of the older SKL/40.

UA (ex-Turkish *Batiray*) with 10.5cm Ubts KL/45, only carried by this submarine in the German navy. *Aldo Fraccaroli Collection*

8.8cm (3.4in)

This was another confusing calibre, particularly in view of its use for Army AA, anti-tank and tank guns. Only naval weapons are described here.

8.8cm (3.4in) SKC/31

Gun Data

Bore	88mm	3.465in	
Weight incl BM	4255kg	4.188 tons	
Length oa	6870mm	270.47in	78.07cal
Length bore	6340mm	249.61in	72.05cal
Length chamber	838.5mm	33.01in	
Volume chamber	6.4dm³	391in³	
Length rifling	5421.5mm	213.44in	
Grooves	(28) 1.2mm deep × 5.97	0.047 × 0.235in	
Lands	3.9mm	0.154in	
Twist	Increasing 1 in 55 to 1 in 35		
Weight projectile	9.0kg	19.84lb	
Propellant charge	4.53kg RPC/32 (5.5/2)	9.99lb	
Muzzle velocity	1060m/s	3478f/s	
Working pressure	3100kg/cm²	19.7 tons/in²	
Approx life	?1500 EFC		
Max range	17,800m	19,470yd	
Ceiling	13,300m/80°	43,640ft/80°	

The complete round weighed 18.5kg (*40.8lb*) and was 1227.5mm (*48.3in*) long.

This was superseded by the 10.5cm SKC/33 as the standard large ship AA gun, but was still in the *Lützow*, ex-*Deutschland* at the beginning of the war. The twin Dopp LC/31 mountings were adapted for the 10.5cm. The gun was of loose barrel type, this item weighing 915kg (*0.90 tons*) with vertical sliding block. Muzzle droop was 2.6mm (*0.102in*).

Fixed ammunition with nose-fuzed HE with and without tracer was fired. Illuminating shell of 9.4kg (*20.7lb*) and 650m/s (*2133f/s*) was also carried.

The mounting was as described for the 10.5cm SKC/33 except that the total weight was 27,300kg (*26.87 tons*) and elevation +80° to -10°.

An earlier gun of the same performance and bore length, but 75.28cal overall and weighing 5980kg (*5.89 tons*) was known as the SKC/25 and was tried in *Köln* in 1930-31 but not introduced.

8.8cm SKC/32 guns in triaxial Dopp LC/32 mountings for *Köln* on the proving ground. *Aldo Fraccaroli Collection*

A gun of less extreme performance with a much smaller chamber, carried in twin triaxial Dopp LC/32 mountings by the *Köln* class, *Leipzig* and *Nürnberg*. It was of loose barrel type with vertical sliding block, the barrel weighing 925kg (*0.91 tons*). A version with a two-part loose barrel, known as SKC/32in, in 10.5cm Dopp LC/37 mountings was intended for the 'M' class light cruisers.

Fixed ammunition was fired, and the outfit comprised nose-fuzed HE with and without tracer and with a larger burster than in the SKC/31. 120 rounds of illuminating shell were carried per ship.

The Dopp LC/32 mounting resembled the LC/31 but was lighter, the total weight being 23,650kg (*23.28 tons*) and the shield thinner at 12-10mm (*0.47-0.4in*).

8.8cm (3.4in) SKC/32

Gun Data

Bore	88mm	3.465in	
Weight incl BM	3640kg	3.58 tons	
Length oa	6690mm	263.39in	76.02cal
Length bore	6340.5mm	249.63in	72.05cal
Length chamber	530.7mm	20.89in	
Volume chamber	3.67dm³	224in³	
Length rifling	5745.5mm	226.20in	
Grooves	(28) 1.2mm deep × 6.4	0.047 × 0.252in	
Lands	3.47mm	0.137in	
Twist	Increasing 1 in 60 to 1 in 35		
Weight projectile	9.0kg	19.84lb	
Propellant charge	2.93kg RPC/38(4.5/1.5)	6.46lb	
Muzzle velocity	950m/s	3117f/s	
Working pressure	3150kg/cm²	20 tons/in²	
Approx life	3200 EFC		
Max range	17,200m	18,800yd	
Ceiling	12,400m/80°	40,680ft/80°	

The complete round weighed 15.2kg (*33.5lb*) and was 932mm (*36.69in*) long.

Both these guns were intended for smaller warships such as submarine-chasers or Flak-corvettes. The SKC/30 was in single biaxial MPLC/30 AA mountings, and a U-boat version, SKC/30U, in Ubts Flak LC/41 is mentioned. It is believed that the KM41 was not actually in service. It was intended for the Flak LM41 single triaxial turntable mounting. The SKC/30 gun had a barrel and breech end-piece with a half-length loose liner and vertical sliding-block, while the KM41 had a monobloc barrel easily removable from the breech end-piece and a horizontal sliding block. It was also fitted with a muzzle brake.

Fixed ammunition was fired with nose-fuzed HE shells with and without tracer, some ships also having HE incendiary which weighed 9.5kg (*20.94lb*) and most if not all some AP of 10.2kg (*22.5lb*) and also illuminating shell.

The hand-worked MPLC/30 mounting allowed +80° to -10° elevation and had a total weight of 5760kg (*5.67 tons*) with a 15-10mm (*0.6-0.4in*) shield and a fuze-setting machine. In the Flak LM41 elevation was +75° to -10° and cross-levelling ± 15°. There were no integral hoists and total weight was 4750kg (*4.675 tons*) but with a lighter shield than in the MPLC/30.

8.8cm (3.4in) SKC/30 and KM41

Gun Data

Bore	88mm	3.465in	
Weight incl BM	1230kg	1.21 tons	
Length oa	3960mm	155.91in	45cal
Length bore	3706mm	145.91in	42.11cal
Length chamber	530mm	20.87in	
Volume chamber	3.67dm³	224in³	
Length rifling	3109.5mm	122.42in	
Grooves	(32) 1.05mm deep × 5.4	0.041 × 0.213in	
Lands	3.2mm	0.126in	
Twist	Increasing 1 in 45 to 1 in 31		
Weight projectile	9.0kg	19.84lb	
Propellant charge	2.82kg	6.22lb	
Muzzle velocity	790m/s	2592f/s	
Working pressure	2750kg/cm²	17.5 tons/in²	
Approx life	7000 EFC		
Max range	14,175m/43.5°	15,500yd/43.5°	
Ceiling	9700m/80°	31,820ft/80°	

The KM41 was identical internally and had the same performance but only weighed 960kg (*0.945 tons*).

This gun in the Ubts LC/35 mounting was originally in early Type VII U-boats and later in some Type 40 minesweepers and submarine chasers. It was built with a barrel, small jacket and breech end-piece, and had a vertical sliding block.

Fixed ammunition was fired and outfits for minesweepers and subchasers include nose-fuzed HE and HE incendiary both with and without tracer, AP and illuminating shell. Weights for HE incendiary and AP were as in the SKC/30 and the illuminating shell was the usual 9.4kg (*20.7lb*) but with muzzle velocity of 600m/s (*1969f/s*).

The Ubts LC/35 mounting was hand worked, allowed +30 to -10° elevation and weighed 2425kg (*2.387 tons*) without shield.

8.8cm (3.4in) SKC/35

Gun Data

Bore	88mm	3.465in	
Weight incl BM	776kg	0.764 tons	
Length oa	3985mm	156.89in	45.28cal
Length bore	3731mm	146.89in	42.40cal
Length chamber	348.7mm	13.73in	
Volume chamber	2.49dm³	152in³	
Length rifling	3313.5mm	130.45in	
Rifling	As 8.8cm SKC/30 but final twist 1 in 30		
Weight projectile	9.0kg	19.84lb	
Propellant charge	2.1kg RPC/40N (3.6/1.07)	4.63lb	
Muzzle velocity	700m/s	2297f/s	
Working pressure	2400kg/cm²	15.2 tons/in²	
Approx life	12,000 EFC		
Max range	11,950m/30°	13,070yd/30°	

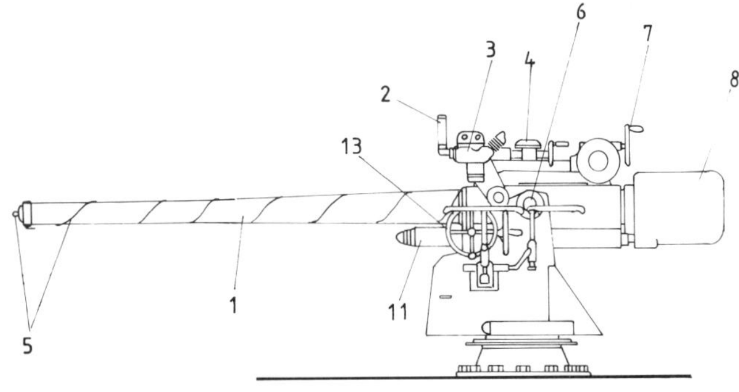

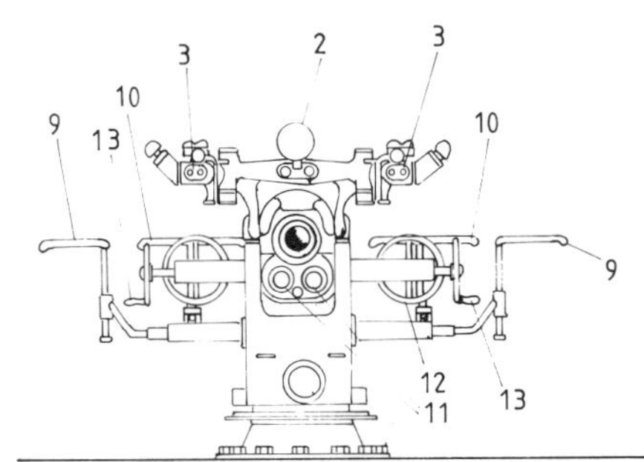

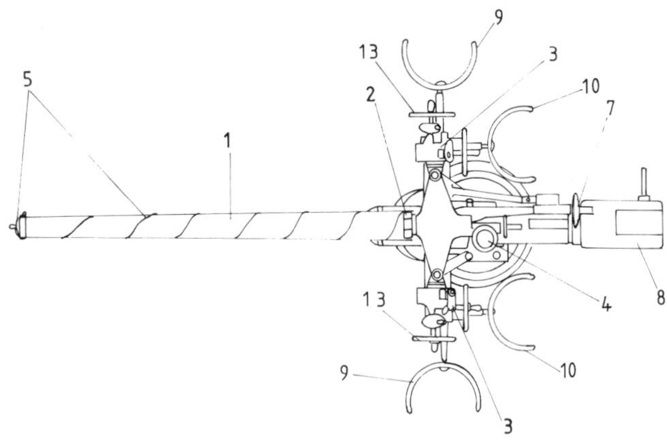

8.8cm SKC/35 in Ubts LC/35 mounting, originally in early Type VII U-boats.

1 Barrel
2 Fore sight
3 Combination rear sight
4 Deflection dial
5 Tompion and wire
6 Gun trunnion
7 Deflection handwheel
8 Breech block
9 Elevator's harness
10 Trainer's harness
11 Recoil cylinders
12 Training handwheel
13 Elevating handwheel

John Lambert

8.8cm gun in *U212* in 1942. It is probably SKC/35.
Aldo Fraccaroli Collection

Other 8.8cm (3.4in) guns

First World War 8.8cm SKL/45 and Flak L/45 guns had been altered to take the same ammunition as the SKC/30 and had the same performance. They were in MPLC/13 mountings allowing +70° to -10° elevation, and early in the war Flak L/45 guns were in the *Schlesien* class and *Emden*, and subsequently in Flak-corvettes and other small warships, together with SKL/45.

8.8cm Tbts KL/45 firing the older 9.75kg (*21.5lb*) or 10kg (*22.05lb*) shells at 650m/s (*2133f/s*) were in Tbts LC/13 mountings with +25° to -10° elevation in some of the oldest torpedo-boats.

7.5-5cm (2.95-1.97in) guns excluding close-range AA

Gun Data 6cm and 5cm

Gun	Bore	Weight Projectile	Muzzle velocity
6cm S-Bts KL/21 } 6cm Bts KL/21 }	60mm (*2.36in*)	3.0kg (*6.61lb*)	345m/s (*1132f/s*)
5cm SKL/55	50mm (*1.97in*)	1.75kg (*3.86lb*)	746m/s (*2448f/s*)
5cm SKL/40 } 5cm Tbts KL/40 }	50mm (*1.97in*)	1.75kg (*3.86lb*)	656m/s (*2152f/s*)

Both 6cm fired separate ammunition.

Of the naval guns, only the 7.5cm SKC/34 (*2.95in*) was recent and this was 36.2cal overall, 33.4cal bore and fired a 5.8kg (*12.8lb*) shell at 6.16m/s (*2021f/s*). The Ein LC/34 mounting allowed +80° to -10° elevation. Some use was also made of the 7.5cm Pak 40M in LM43 or BordL39/43 mountings. This former anti-tank gun was 46cal overall and fired a 6.8kg (*15lb*) AP projectile at 792m/s (*2598f/s*). The rest are listed in the table.

AUTOMATIC GUNS

This gas-operated air-cooled automatic gun was intended for land and sea service, but only two prototypes were made. It was envisaged for the Type 42C destroyers, and various single triaxial mountings as well as a quadraxial design, and the possibility of using the Army biaxial mounting, were under investigation. The ammunition clip held five rounds and the gun fired with the breech locked as it moved forward from recoil. The rate of fire was 120/150 per minute and single shots could be fired. No alloy steels were to be used in construction.

5.5cm (2.165in) Gerät 58

Approximate Gun Data

Bore	55mm	2.165in	
Weight of gun	650kg	1430lb	
Weight of barrel	350kg	770lb	
Length oa	6000mm	236in	
Length barrel	4220mm	166in	76.7cal
Length rifling	3750mm	148in	
Grooves	(20) 0.75mm deep × 4.34	0.030 × 0.171in	
Lands	4.3mm	0.169in	
Twist	Increasing 1 in 90 to 1 in 25.6		
Weight projectile	2kg	4.4lb	
Propellant charge	1.1kg	2.4lb	
Muzzle velocity	1020m/s	3350f/s	

The shell was to have a 23% bursting charge and the complete round weighed 5.3kg (*11.8lb*) and was 665mm (*26.2in*) long.

Range/Time Data

Range (m)	**(yd)**	**Time (sec)**
1000	1090	1.10
2000	2190	2.50
3000	3280	4.34
4000	4370	6.75

Schematic layout of modified hydraulic biaxial mounting for 5.5cm Gerät 58.

1 Mounting
2 Intermediate pedestal
3 Pump
4 Gyro-sights
5 Gyro rotary converter
6 Seat for layer
7 Seat for trainer

Official drawing, by courtesy of Mike Whitley

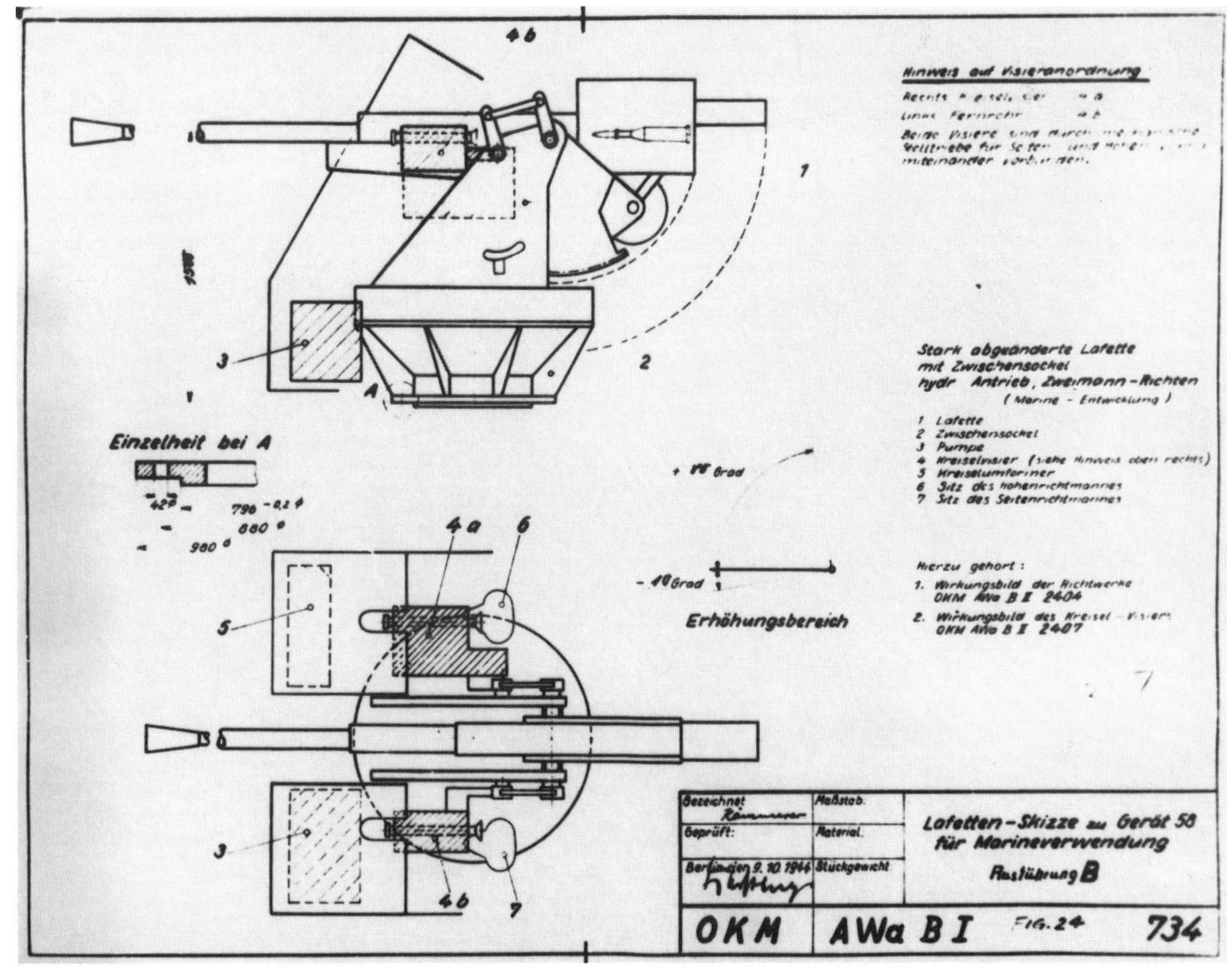

One of the two 5.5cm Gerät 58 prototypes.
By courtesy of Mike Whitley

Single 40mm Bofors (4cm Flak 28) in *Prinz Eugen* 1945.
Aldo Fraccaroli Collection

4cm (1.575in) Flak 28

This was the well known Bofors, to be found in single mountings towards the end of the war in several ships including the *Admiral Hipper* and *Prinz Eugen*. The shell weighed 955gm (*2.105lb*) and with a charge of 303gm (*0.668lb*) Str PC/38N the muzzle velocity was 850m/s (*2789f/s*). Only HE tracer was fired.

3.7cm SKC/30 single shot gun in Ein LC/34 mounting.
Aldo Fraccaroli Collection

A gas-operated air-cooled automatic gun designed for easy production and in service in the Army and Navy. The ammunition strip held eight rounds, and the gun fired with the breech locked. The maximum rate of fire was 250 rounds per minute. Late in the war it was carried by the *Admiral Scheer, Lützow, Nürnberg* and *Köln* as well as by Type 35 and 37 torpedo-boats and some Type 40 minesweepers. Tests in sea water for U-boats were apparently satisfactory.

The single Flak LM43 mounting was trained by shoulder stirrup and elevated by hand wheel and gear train. Total weight including shield, was 1350kg (*1.33 tons*) and elevation +90° to -10°. The Flak LM44 mounting was the LM42 for the M42 gun modified to take the M43. It differed from the LM43 mounting in having hand wheel training and a total weight of 1400kg (*1.38 tons*).

3.7cm (1.457in) Flak M43

Gun Data

Bore	37mm	1.457in	
Weight of gun	355kg	783lb	
Weight of barrel	50kg	110lb	
Length oa	3300mm	129.92in	
Length barrel	2106mm	82.91in	56.92cal
Length chamber	241.2mm	9.496in	
Volume chamber	0.227dm^3	13.85in^3	
Length rifling	1838.4mm	72.38in	
Grooves	(20) 0.5mm deep × 3.6mm	0.0217 × 0.142in	
Lands	2.2mm	0.087in	
Twist	Increasing 1 in 60 to 1 in 35.9		
Weight projectile	0.644kg	1.420lb	
Propellant charge	0.190kg Digl RP-8-2 (2.2/0.85)	0.419lb	
Muzzle velocity	820m/s	2690f/s	
Working pressure	2600kg/cm^2	16.5 tons/in^2	
Max range	6500m	7100yd	
Ceiling	4800m/90°	15,750ft/90°	

The above projectile weight is for HE incendiary tracer but a limited amount of AP tracer was also issued and an outfit of one third of the latter was intended but supplies were never sufficient. The AP tracer weighed 0.700kg (*1.54lb*) and with a charge of 0.185kg (*0.408lb*) Digl RP-8-2, MV was 790m/s (*2592f/s*). The HE incendiary tracer round weighed 1.49kg (*3.28lb*) and was 368mm (*14.49in*) long.

This was a recoil-operated, air-cooled automatic gun and was essentially a longer-barrel improvement of the Army Flak 36. The ammunition strip held six rounds, and maximum rate of fire was 160-180 rounds per minute. Late in the war it was mounted in U-boats, the *Emden*, destroyers and minesweepers.

The Flak LM42 and twin Dopp Flak LM42 mountings both had hand wheel training and elevation, allowed +90° to -10° elevation and with shield weighed respectively 1350kg (*1.33 tons*) and 1750kg (*1.72 tons*).

3.7in (1.457cm) Flak M42

Gun Data

Bore	37mm	1.457in	
Weight of gun	300kg	660lb	
Weight of barrel	100.8kg	222lb	
Length oa	-	-	
Length barrel	2560mm	100.79in	69.19cal
Length chamber	223mm	8.78in	
Volume chamber	0.270dm^3	16.48in^3	
Length rifling	2289mm	90.12in	
Grooves	(20) 0.55mm deep × 3.81	0.0217 × 0.150in	
Lands	2.0mm	0.079in	
Twist	Uniform 1 in 25.6		
Weight projectile	0.644kg	1.420lb	
Propellant charge	0.175kg RPC/38N (1.8/0.8)	0.386lb	
Muzzle velocity	845m/s	2772f/s	
Working pressure	2950kg/cm^2	18.7 tons/in^2	
Approx life	7000 EFC		
Max range	*c*6600m	*c*7200yd	
Ceiling	*c*4900m/90°	*c*16,000ft/90°	

Notes on projectiles for the Flak M43 apply here except that the charge for AP was as given above and muzzle velocity 815m/s (*2674f/s*). In minesweepers half the allowance was to be AP and half HE tracer, not incendiary. This weighed 0.635kg (*1.400lb*) and had a muzzle velocity of 865m/s (*2838f/s*). The HE incendiary tracer round weighed 1.37kg (*3.02lb*) and was 355mm (*13.98in*) long.

This was a high-velocity single-shot gun, with a vertical sliding block and, in the earlier part of the war, the only German naval close-range AA heavier than 20mm. It was mounted in twin triaxial Dopp LC/30, single Ein LC/34 and in U-boats single Ubts LC/39 mountings, the last having the SKC/30U gun. The *Tirpitz* and *Scharnhorst* were carrying the SKC/30 when lost, and late in the war it was still in Type 39 torpedo-boats and many lesser warships. The rate of fire was about 30 rounds per minute.

The Dopp LC/30 mounting had the guns in separate cradles and was trained and elevated by hand with direct gyro cross-levelling over ± 19.5°. Elevation was +85° to -9° and total weight 3670kg (*3.61 tons*). The Ein LC/34 mounting had an 8mm (*0.3in*) shield, elevated from +80° to -10° and had a total weight of 1860-2020kg (*1.83-1.99 tons*), while the Ubts LC/39 was trained by shoulder stirrup with hand wheel and gear train elevation from +90° to -10°, and weighed 1450kg (*1.43 tons*).

3.7cm (1.457in) SKC/30

Gun Data

Bore	37mm	1.457in	
Weight incl BM	243kg	536lb	
Length oa	3074mm	121.02in	83.08cal
Length bore	2960mm	116.54in	80.0cal
Length chamber	357mm	14.055in	
Volume chamber	0.5dm^3	30.5in^3	
Length rifling	2554mm	100.55	
Grooves	(16) 0.55mm deep × 4.76mm	0.0217 × 0.187in	
Lands	2.5mm	0.098in	
Twist	Increasing 1 in 50 to 1 in 35		
Weight projectile	0.748kg	1.649lb	
Propellant charge	0.365kg RPC/38N (2.8/0.8)	0.805lb	
Muzzle velocity	1000m/s	3281f/s	
Working pressure	2950kg/cm^2	18.7 tons/in^2	
Approx life	7500 EFC		
Max range	8500m/35.7°	9300yd/35.7°	
Ceiling	6800m/85°	22,300ft/85°	

The usual projectile was HE tracer, and the complete round weighed 2.1kg (*4.63lb*) and was 516mm (*20.3in*) long.

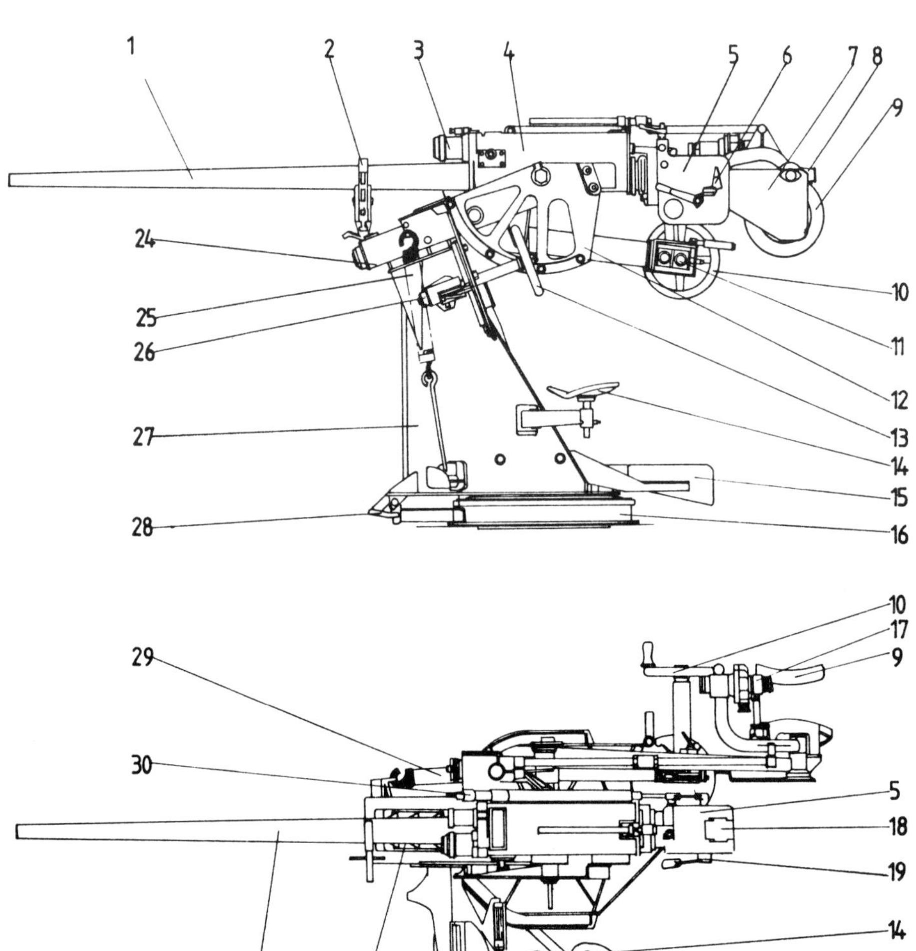

3.7cm SKC/30U gun in Ubts LC/39 mounting.

1 Gun barrel
2 Travelling lock
3 Recuperator cylinder
4 Gun body
5 Breech housing
6 Ready-to-fire indicator
7 Shield for elevation number
8 Elevation number shoulder piece mounting bar
9 Left shoulder piece for elevation number
10 Elevation control wheel
11 Fuze setter
12 Gun cradle
13 Traverse control handle
14 Traverse number seat
15 Pedestal
16 Gun mounting base
17 Elevation optical sight
18 Breech block
19 Breech operating lever
20 Traverse sight
21 Lead indicator
22 Mounting bar and transmission shaft for traverse controls
23 Barrel slide
24 Stabilising buffer
25 Mounting piston
26 Traverse gearing
27 Gun mount
28 Traverse lock
29 Mounting piston
30 Breech automatic opening linkage (on recoil)

David Westwood

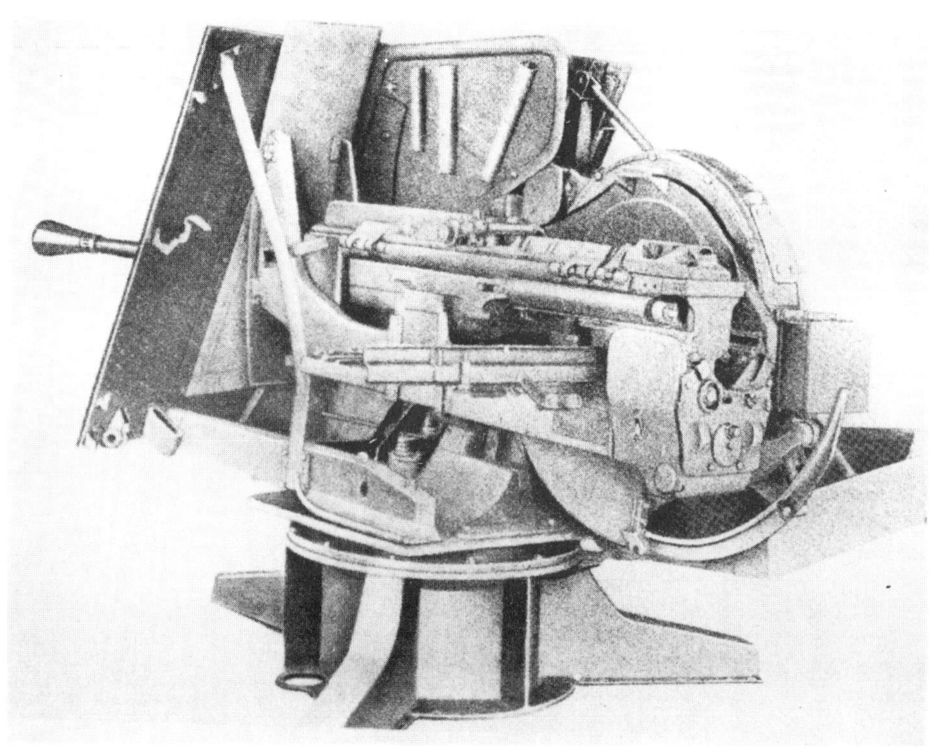
3.7cm Flak M43 automatic gun on test mounting. *Author's Collection*

Other 3.7cm (1.457in) guns

The Army Flak 36 was occasionally to be found in some smaller vessels. This resembled the Flak M42 with a shorter 57cal barrel and fired the same ammunition, but the muzzle velocity was 25m/s (*82f/s*) lower. The raider *Kormoran* had 2-3.7cm PaK apt, a converted anti-tank gun firing 0.685kg (*1.51lb*) projectiles at 745m/s (*2444f/s*) in a mounting allowing +25° elevation. There was also still some 3.7cmMK, a version of the 1pdr pom-pom, which fired 0.5kg (*1.1lb*) shells at 540m/s (*1772f/s*).

3cm (1.18in)

Several gas-operated automatic guns of this calibre were under development, and in various mountings were intended for Type 42C destroyers, Type XXI U-boats and the latest S-boats, but none was in service, though the twin U-boat mounting was in production with 2cm guns replacing the 3cm. High capacity HE 'mine' shell weighing 0.330kg (*0.73lb*) and AP weighing 0.500kg (*1.1lb*) would be fired, both with tracer, and with respective muzzle velocities of 900m/s (*2953f/s*) and 725m/s (*2379f/s*) except in the Brunner design, which had a 73cal instead of a 53cal barrel and muzzle velocities of 1100m/s (*3609f/s*) and 900m/s (*2953f/s*). Rate of fire was 400-420 rounds a minute.

2cm Flak 38 in quadruple mounting. As adapted for the Navy it was known as Vierlings L38/43, and was probably the best of such weapons.
John Lambert

One of the most widely used German guns, this recoil-operated air-cooled automatic was to be found in single, twin or quadruple mountings in warships of all sizes and was also standard in the German Army. The magazine held 20 or 40 rounds and rate of fire was 450-500 rounds a minute. The principal defect was that a single hit was not likely to destroy an aircraft, and this led to the development of the 3cm.

The majority of single and twin pedestal (Sockel) mountings had free training and elevation by shoulder piece with total weights of 400-450kg (*0.39-0.44 tons*) for singles and 1000kg (*0.98 tons*) for twins, the latter including shield. Elevation was +78° or 85° to -10° or 11°. A Ubts single made in limited numbers had a pressure-tight cover and could be brought out by two men. The L41 single mounting for S-boats worked in a well of 1700mm (*66.9in*) diameter, and had elevation by handwheel with free training. Total weight was 500kg (*0.54 tons*) and elevation +85° to -10°. The Army quadruple mounting was adapted for the Navy as Vierlings L38/43 and had hand wheels for training and elevation, the limits of the latter being +90° to -10°. The shield was 12mm (*0.47in*) but the total weight was 2200kg (*2.165 tons*).

The twin turntable LM44U, intended to take 3cm guns in Type XXI U-boats but adapted for the 2cm, was a far more advanced mounting able to stand 200m (*650ft*) diving depth and with hydraulic training and elevation joy-stick controlled, and foot-pedal operation of the triggers. Surprisingly the mounting was biaxial. The guns were mounted above one another and ammunition was fed from left and right through hollow trunnions 615mm (*24.2in*) diameter. On each side of the turret ring, pressure tight holders held 11-20 round magazines, spring pressure bringing the next magazine forward after one was removed. An armoured cupola 17mm (*0.7in*) thick protected the crew of three. The total weight of the mounting with ammunition was 3600kg (*3.54 tons*), the turret ring was 1700mm (*66.9in*) diameter and elevation was +78° to -10°. Training speed is given as 60°/sec (also as 30°) and elevating as 30°/sec.

2cm Flak 38 (0.787in)

Gun Data

Bore	20mm	0.787in	
Weight of gun	57.5-71kg	126.8-156.5lb	
Weight of barrel	18kg	39.7lb	
Length oa	2252.5mm	88.68in	
Length barrel	1300mm	51.18in	65.0cal
Length chamber	121.5mm	4.783in	
Volume chamber	0.048dm³	2.93in³	
Length rifling	1159.4mm	45.65in	
Grooves	(8) 0.325mm deep × 5.2	0.0128 × 0.205in	
Lands	2.65mm	0.104in	
Twist	Uniform 1 in 36		
Weight projectile	0.120kg	0.265lb	
Propellant charge	0.415kg NzRP (3/0.5)	0.0915lb	
Muzzle velocity	875m/s	2871f/s	
Working pressure	2800kg/cm²	17.8 tons/in²	
Approx life	20,000 EFC		
Max range	4800m	5250yd	
Ceiling	3700m	12,100ft	

The above projectile and MV figures are for HE incendiary tracer, the standard ammunition. It was intended to replace half the outfit of this by AP tracer but shortage of the latter limited the amount to a quarter of the total. The heaviest AP tracer weighed 0.148kg (*0.326lb*) and MV was 800m/s (*2625f/s*). The complete round weighed 0.312-0.340kg (*0.688-0.750lb*) and was 203mm (*8in*) long.

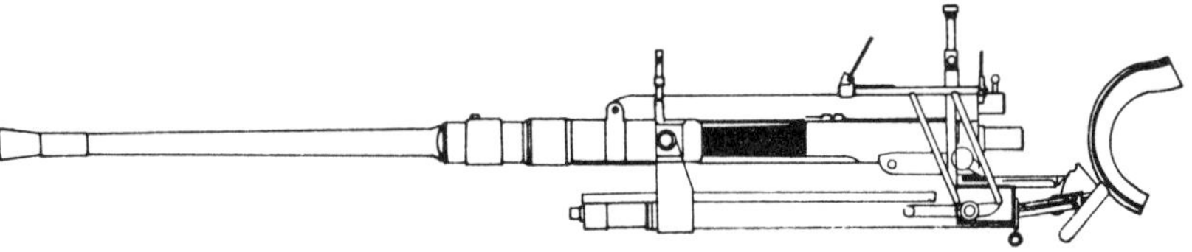

2cm Flak 38. This widely used magazine-fed gun performed similar functions to the Oerlikon in the allied navies.
David Westwood

2cm Flak 38 Vierling from forward.
Przemysław Budzbon Collection

Other 2cm (0.787in) and smaller guns

The predecessor of the Flak 38 was the Flak 30, which took the same ammunition and had the same muzzle velocity, but differed in a rate of fire of only 280-300 rounds a minute. It was mounted in single or twin pedestal mountings with free training and elevation similar or identical to those for the Flak 38. Examples of the 2cm Madsen and of Flak 28 and 29 of Oerlikon pattern were in use, and the 15mm (*0.59in*) MG 151 was in some S-boats. This last was a recoil operated gun weighing 36kg (*79.4lb*) and with an 83.6cal barrel. Muzzle velocity varied from 960m/s (*3150f/s*) with a 57gm (*2.01oz*) shell to 850m/s (*2789f/s*) with 72gm (*2.54oz*), and rate of fire was 700 rounds per minute. Of small-arms calibre guns the recoil operated 7.92mm (*0.3118in*) MG81 had a 60cal barrel and muzzle velocity of 705m/s (*2313f/s*) with a rate of fire of 1400-1600 rounds per minute. This was mainly an aircraft gun, developed from the more common MG34 which had a 79cal barrel and muzzle velocity of about 760m/s (*2493f/s*). The rate of fire was 800-900 rounds per minute and single shots could be fired, which was not the case with the MG81. The MG34 was air cooled and fed by 50-250 round belts or by 75-round saddle drums. The older MG15, fed by a 25-round box magazine, had a rate of fire of 450-500 rounds per minute.

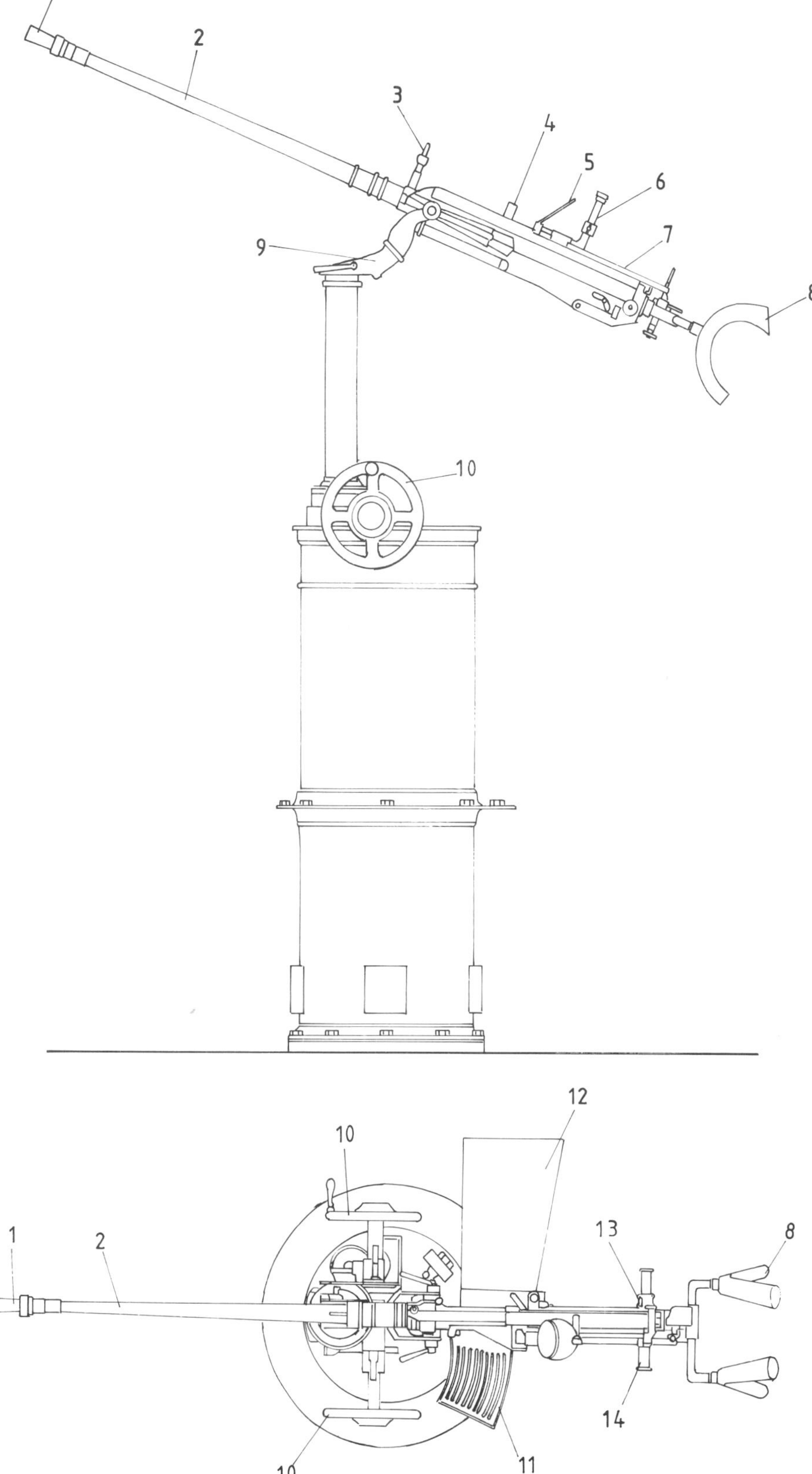

2cm Flak 30 on single U-boat mounting in AA position.

1 Flash guard
2 Barrel
3 Fore sight - surface action
4 Cocking handle
5 Ring sight for anti-aircraft targets
6 Rear sight post for surface targets
7 Breech cover
8 Gunner's shoulder rest
9 Free rotating arm
10 Elevating handwheel
11 20-round magazine
12 Receiver for empty cartridge cases
13 Firing trigger
14 Gunner's hand grip

John Lambert

Twin 3.7cm (probably Flak M42), and single 2cm Flak 38 in *U 190* and *U 889* at Halifax 24 September 1945.
Aldo Fraccaroli Collection

TORPEDOES

The importance of reliable torpedoes was very great in view of the German navy's dependence on the U-boat, particularly as a destroyer of merchant shipping, and it is remarkable that very soon after the outbreak of war serious defects were found to be present. The worst of these was the liability of the magnetic pistol to fire prematurely, and as an immediate measure the pistols were desensitized and torpedoes set to hit. It was then found that depth keeping was faulty and that the rather crude striker gear was liable to blinds. These two last defects were soon remedied but magnetic pistols were withdrawn in early 1940 and did not reappear until late 1943. More thorough testing of live service torpedoes would have prevented much of the above.

Another item on the debit side was the relative scarcity of new types of torpedoes, ready for service, that came from the very large experimental works. Eckenförde had a staff of about 5000 with a workshop area more than five times that of the entire RNTF in Greenock, while Gotenhafen, completed during the war and the site of most of the homing torpedo work, had a staff of 2500. There was a smaller establishment at Neu Brandenburg on the Tollense See where private firms, who carried out much research and development work, could experiment. It may be noted that the RN Experimental Establishment at Greenock had a wartime staff of 500. Over 60 different torpedo designs were tried by the Germans, 16 using hydrogen peroxide as the oxidant. This system is described below, but no torpedo so powered was ready for service.

A third weakness, dating back to before the war, was in airborne torpedoes. Responsibility for these was taken over by the *Luftwaffe* in mid 1942 and from 1943 there was a *Luftwaffe* torpedo establishment at Hexengrund near Gotenhafen. Details of airborne torpedo development are given below.

On the credit side the principal item was the development and eventual production in large numbers of the 53.3cm (*21in*) G7e later known as T2, electric torpedo. A successful electric torpedo (but capable of only *c*2000m (*2200yd*)/28kts) had been issued in 1918, though it was never used. Development was carried on from 1923 in Germany and, for reasons of secrecy, in Sweden, where torpedoes were built and tested. In 1929 there were successful trials at Karlskrona, and the main features of the design were frozen to await eventual quantity production. The British had no knowledge of this work until parts were recovered from the bottom of Scapa Flow when the sunken *Royal Oak* was examined in 1939, and it was not until 27 August 1941, when *U 570* was captured with 12 G7e torpedoes, that complete samples were available.

The great disadvantage of electric torpedoes was their poor range and speed. 1939 figures for T2 were only 5000m (*5470yd*)/30kts and this was not improved beyond 7500m (*8200yd*)/30kts at the end of the war. On the other hand they were trackless, relatively quiet (though this was chiefly due to the low speed), and easier to build than the wet heater type. The standard German 53.3cm (*21in*) G7a (T1) of the latter type, took 3730 man hours per torpedo in 1939, which was reduced to 1707 by 1943, but was still well above the 1255 per G7e (T2). Total German production of 53.3cm torpedoes, mostly electric, rose from 70 per month before the war to 1000 a month by the spring of 1941 and to a peak of 1700 in 1943, falling to 1400 a month in 1944, with a probable war total of *c*70,000. Expenditure neglecting torpedoes lost in sunken ships and depots was nothing like this, the total fired up to the end of January 1945 being just over 10,000, of which *c*7000 were electric G7e, 2300 wet-heater G7a, and 640 electric acoustic homing T5 (Zaunkönig 1). About 5%, mostly G7a, were pattern runners, which, with the homing torpedoes, are described later. Production was at Deutsche Werke Kiel, with in addition Julius Pintsche Berlin, Auto-Union Zwickau, Borgward Bremen, and Planeta Dresden. In U-boats the proportion of electric to wet-heater was always at least 4 to 1 and increased as the war progressed, but surface ships used wet-heater with electric also in E-boats.

The G7a torpedo was the result of step-by-step development of the First World War 50cm (*19.7in*) G7 and differed from most heater torpedoes in using Decalin (decahydronaphthalene) instead of Kerosene as fuel. The 60cm (*23.6in*) H8 and proposed 70cm (*27.6in*) J9 of First World War vintage do not seem to have had any descendants except the experimental Junkers 75cm (*29.5in*) M5.

German research into high-performance fuel systems was on a very large scale. Pure high-pressure oxygen on the Japanese system was rejected because of the risk of

Striking down a G7e (T2) electric torpedo in *U 55*. *Aldo Fraccaroli Collection*

explosion on starting. Hydrogen and oxygen failed because of the rapid diffusion of high pressure hydrogen, 25% being lost in three days, which might well have been foreseen. A system using liquid ammonia and oxygen was promising, but was rejected in 1938 because of the track from dissociation of excess ammonia. A fuel and oxygen system with carbon dioxide as the diluent was given up because of the risk that carbon dioxide might leak into a submarine's crew space. Magnesium or aluminium with oxygen was impossible to control, and eventually hydrogen peroxide was selected as the oxidant. Work on this had been started in the early 1930s by Dr Walter, and an 80–85% solution stabilised by phosphoric acid or oxyquinoline was soon available from German industry. This was highly dangerous in contact with most materials, though compatible with aluminium and some stainless steels, ceramics and plastics. The ideal reputed life was six months at 50°C (*122°F*).

The safest method of use was to decompose the hydrogen peroxide with sodium or calcium permanganate. This released steam, oxygen and manganese dioxide, which catalysed the decomposition of more hydrogen peroxide to steam and oxygen. However, finely divided manganese dioxide was carried over, and proved objectionable in the turbine of the torpedo. It should be mentioned that reciprocating radial engines used in the earlier hydrogen peroxide torpedoes had been given up, primarily because oil from the engine was present in the exhaust, so that the torpedo was not completely trackless. The problems of fine manganese dioxide were overcome by using a liquid known as Helman (80% hydrazine hydrate, 20% methyl alcohol) to decompose the peroxide, 0.05% of potassium cuprocyanide or other copper compound being added just in advance of the hydrogen peroxide. Helman and Decalin fuel were admitted to the combustion pot, followed almost immediately by the water or sea-water diluent, and about a second later by the hydrogen peroxide. Once combustion started the Helman was cut off. Design of the combustion pot was very difficult as the reaction temperature was about 2300°C (*4170°F*). The various experimental torpedoes differed considerably but turbines all seem to have been of single stage axial flow impulse type.

Many German scientists favoured oxygen instead of hydrogen peroxide, but work on this was abandoned in 1943. This decision may well have been influenced by Dr Walter, and one cannot help feeling that it was mistaken, except insofar as hydrogen peroxide developments were more advanced. The oxygen system favoured was the Kreislauf closed cycle using the exhaust gas as a diluent, and the engine was an internal combustion Junkers with carburettor and spark ignition.

The most important of these experimental torpedoes are described individually, as are the various homing torpedo systems, but some notes are given here on pattern running which could apply to more than one type of torpedo.

The demand for pattern running arose with the need to increase the firing range of U-boats which had been usually under 1000m (*1100yd*) in 1939, but was two or three times as much in 1943 and steadily increasing. The first system, 'Fat' (*Federapparat*), had an adjustable straight run, followed by a 180° turn and repeated legs of 800m (*870yd*) or 1500m (*1640yd*). The turning radius was 170m (*186yd*) and, as the torpedo only advanced up the pattern during turns, the speed of advance was $7\frac{1}{2}$kts with short legs and 5kts with long. The pattern was set 90° to left or right as desired, and the U-boat had to attack the convoy from more or less abeam. This system, which was first responsible for sinking a ship 29 December 1942, was applied to G7a torpedoes but 'Fat 2' was also fitted to the improved electric T3a. It was intended for use against escorts and attacks could be made from ahead. There were no short legs and at the end of the fore run the torpedo either circled or ran long legs.

'Lut' (*Lage unabhängiger Torpedo*) was more complicated. The fore course was variable from the gyro angle and the range at which the pattern began could also be varied, as could the angle of the pattern relative to the fore course. The speed of advance was varied by control of the angle of each leg on either side of the pattern centre line. The maximum was 20kts to avoid very small track angles at which the pistol might fail to fire, and the minimum for a 30kt torpedo 10kts with *c*500m (*550yd*) legs and 5kts with *c*1500m (*1640yd*). In order to centre the pattern, the initial leg was half that of the succeeding ones. The pattern settings were made from tables based on theoretical solutions to various situations with adjustments fed to the torpedo up to the moment of firing. Very great tactical skill was needed with 'Lut' which was only used operationally by U-boats in the last months of the war, about 70 torpedoes with it being fired, though it was also used in the very long range and slow T3d (Dackel) in the Seine Bay in 1944. The heavy battery and increased negative buoyancy in T3a caused them to roll very heavily on 'Fat' and 'Lut' turns so that they sometimes broke surface.

The standard explosive charges were SW18, SW36 and SW39 (S1, S2, S3). An improved SW39a was developed and there were various substitute explosives.

Explosive	TNT	HND	Am nitrate	Aluminium
SW18	60	24	-	16
SW36	67	8	-	25
SW39	45	5	30	20
SW39a	50	10	5	35

HND=Hexanitrodiphenylamine.

As noted above, the original magnetic pistol was a failure. It depended on a duplex coil rod and was not difficult to degauss so that it only operated 60-90cm (*2-3ft*) below the hull. It was also too sensitive to the earth's field if deviated sharply, which gave rise to perturbation failures. The best of the German magnetic pistols was TZ5 used in the T5 (Zaunkönig) torpedo. It was basically a metal detector with two coils, one providing an alternating magnetic field at 50-200 cycles, while the coils were balanced so that there was no induced field in the second coil. In the presence of a mass of metal, even if it had no magnetic field, there was an induced current in the second coil which detonated the warhead at up to 6m (*13ft*) below the keel. It was sensitive to metal above the torpedo only so that the firing U-boat could escape possible self-destruction by diving. TZ6, designed to fit any 53.3cm (*21in*) torpedo, was cleared for production as the war ended. The usual nose whisker impact pistol could not be fitted in homing torpedoes with acoustic gear in the nose, and was replaced by an inertia pistol in rear of the warhead.

Airborne 45cm (*17.7in*) torpedoes had been used to a limited extent by the German Navy in the First World War and had sunk three merchant ships off the English coast, but it was manifestly impossible to develop them in secret. It was considered that the Norwegians at Horten were somewhat ahead of other countries in the problems of torpedo attitude and roll during air flight, and a contract was placed in March 1934. After fairly good interim trials, Schwarzkopf, who had not touched torpedo work since 1918, undertook the development with redesign to suit their manufacturing methods. The target was 160 by 1936 and 600 by 1939, but there were serious troubles. Production at the outbreak of war was about five per month, and as late as October 1939 there were 26 failures from 52 drops in a practice exercise, though it is not clear how far this could have been improved in deeper water. Attempts had been made in 1938 to buy Italian Fiume torpedoes, but there were difficulties over the supply of scarce materials and the contract was not signed until the end of March 1939. Eventually about 1000 were supplied. At the beginning of the war there was thus only the modified Horten torpedo F5 carried by the slow Heinkel 115 seaplane, and neither inspired much confidence. In the spring of 1940 the Naval Staff agreed to stop development and production during the war. At about this time a few were used operationa ly and the *Luftwaffe* began to show interest. Development thus continued slowly, resulting in late 1941 in the faster F5b, which with some modifications remained in service to the end of the war. The F5b was a compromise solution, as tests on the navy designed F5a were too long and extensive.

In April 1942 Hitler ordered that the development of airborne torpedoes be stepped up by all possible means, and a few months later the *Luftwaffe* took this over from the navy. A production target of 3000 a month at the end of 1943 was set, but the highest attained was 700-900 a month in the first half of 1944. Even so, the total production of about 10,000 was well in excess of expenditure, as *c*4000 were used from 1942 to the autumn of 1944, and at one time several thousand were in stock, which did not encourage new improvements.

Towards the end of the war the *Luftwaffe* began to lose interest as increasing air speeds required more and more strengthening of the torpedo, and better AA defence made attack very hazardous. The usual torpedo planes were various modifications of the Heinkel 111 or Junkers 88, but finally emergency adaptations of the Fw 190 or Me 410 were tried, the former with better results than expected. The Heinkel 177 A5 was intended to carry four torpedoes to be fired in a salvo with up to 13° spread to left and right, but fuel shortage apparently prevented this.

NON-HOMING SHIP, SUBMARINE AND MTB TORPEDOES

All were 53.3cm (21in).

G7a (T1) 53.3cm wet-heater torpedo.
David Westwood

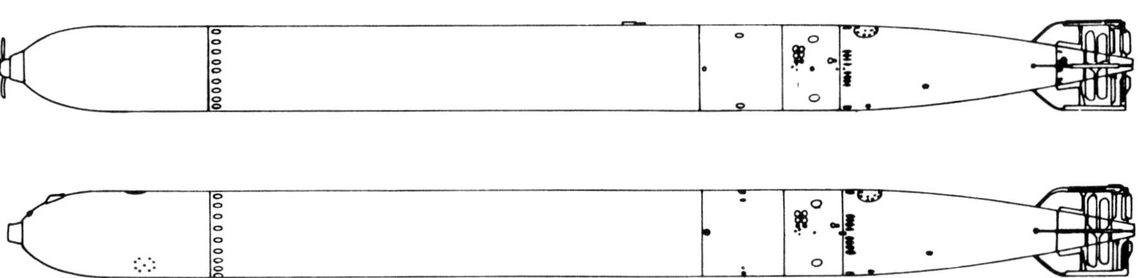

G7a T1

A conventional wet-heater compressed-air torpedo with three speed settings, though the four-cylinder radial engine was found to be overloaded at 44kts and this setting was cancelled for the early years of the war, being later reintroduced after engine modifications. Engine and combustion chamber weighed 137.5kg (*303lb*) and gear box and shafting 23kg (*51lb*). Cylinder dimensions were 125 x 110mm with swept volume 5.4 litres. 1939 performance figures were lower than those given below at 5000m (*5500yd*)/44kts, 7500m (*8200yd*)/40kts, 12,500m (*13,700yd*)/30kts.

Data

Length oa	7186mm	23ft 7in
Total weight	1528kg	3369lb
Negative buoyancy	274kg	604lb
Volume air vessel	676 litres	23.87ft^3
Pressure	2000kg/cm^2	2850lb/in^2
Weight air	161kg	355lb
Decalin	12.9kg	28.4lb
Water	57kg	126lb
HP (44kts)	320	
Consumption expendables	8.5kg/HP/hr	18.7lb/HP/hr
Explosive charge	300kg	661lb
Range	6000m/44kts	6560yd/44kts
	8000m/40kts	8750yd/40kts
	14,000m/30kts	15,300yd/30kts

G7e T2

An electric torpedo using lead/acid accumulators. There were two batteries, each having 26 cells with 13 positive and 14 negative plates. The weight of the batteries was 665kg (*1466lb*) and length *c*4.8m (*c16ft*). There were heating elements in the battery cases which warmed the batteries to 30°C (*86°F*) when in a target area. The motor was of eight-pole series wound type with no interpoles, and could develop 96HP for 5min 40sec. With this short running time, it was possible to reduce the motor weight to *c*113kg (*c250lb*). The batteries were rated at 93 amp hours and running current was 950 amps at 1755rpm. There was no starter in the usual sense, an air operated main switch connecting the batteries directly with a momentary current of 4000 amps.

This torpedo was mainly used by submarines but was fired by E-boats from 1942.

Data

Length oa	7186mm	23ft 7in
Total weight	1603kg	3534lb
Negative buoyancy	271kg	597lb
Explosive charge	300kg	661lb
Range	5000m/30kts	5470yd/30kts

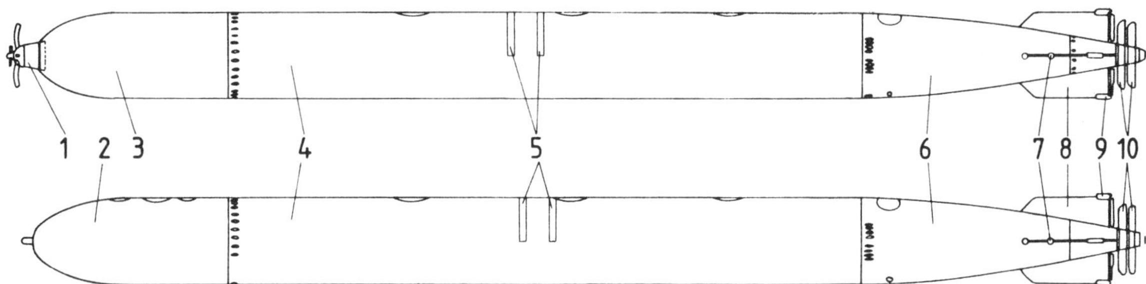

G7e (T2) 53.3cm electric torpedo.

1. Firing pistol (here the G7H is shown)
2. Practice warhead
3. Warhead
4. Main body and battery container
5. Green torpedo-type markings (positions varied)
6. Rear body and electric motor housing
7. Depth keeping fins (both sides)
8. Attitude fins
9. Attitude adjusters (controlled by internal gyro-compass)
10. Contra-rotating propellers

David Westwood

T3

As T2 but with influence fuze.

T3a

T2 modified by fitting a redesigned battery of 125 amp hour capacity with 17 positive and 18 negative plates per cell. This increased the range to 7500m (*8200yd*)/29-30kts but total weight also increased to 1755kg (*3869lb*) and negative buoyancy to 426kg (*939lb*). Further attempts to increase the positive plates to 19 caused too great a negative buoyancy.

Earlier work had shown that T2 could be redesigned to give 3000m (*3300yd*)/35kts, but only at the cost of battery reliability. The limits of the lead-acid accumulator had clearly been reached and research concentrated on primary batteries with anticipated advantages of lighter weight, no self discharge and no maintenance in the submarine, as well as reduced use of lead. A contract was placed with IG Farben for a magnesium-carbon battery with nitric acid and sodium bichromate electrolyte added at the moment of firing, and then circulated by a pump which kept adding fresh acid during the run. Difficulties in the production of high current carbon electrodes and in circulating the electrolyte were unsolved at the end of the war. The projected primary battery torpedo was apparently known as G7p and had an intended range of 9000m (*9840yd*)/30kts.

T3b

The propulsive part of the small battle unit Marder. The pilot occupied the forward battery section and released an electric torpedo strapped to the propulsive part when within range. As the speed of the combined unit was only 2.5kt, buoyancy of both parts had to be neutral. Marder was an extreme case of the midget submarine concept and not a manned torpedo like the Kaiten where the pilot had no chance of survival.

T3c

This was fired from midget submarines and, like Marder, had to be of neutral buoyancy to avoid upsetting the trim of these very small craft. The forward battery was omitted and weight was 1332kg (*2937lb*) with range 4000m (*4370yd*)/18.5kt.

T3d Dackel

A very long-range, slow pattern runner, improvised from a normal electric torpedo and intended for use in harbour or restricted areas. About 300 were adapted and issued from July 1944. About 80 or 90 were fired largely against shipping in the Seine Bay. The range was 57,000m (*62,300yd*)/9kts, the low speed being very favourable for the accumulators, though negative buoyancy had to be virtually zero. The main difficulty was to supply enough compressed air for over three hours running of depth gear and gyro, and an empty battery chamber containing various existing air bottles was added behind the warhead. The explosive charge was apparently reduced to 281kg (*620lb*) with a whisker impact pistol. Total weight was 2216kg (*4885lb*) and length overall about 11m (*36ft*).

Dackel, which was fired from rafts or from E-boats, had special 'Lut' gear allowing a straight run of up to 34,600m (*37,800yd*) followed by circling or legs of up to 2650m (*2900yd*). Very detailed firing programmes bearing in mind tidal currents were prepared. On direction trials to 19,000m (*20,800yd*), 80% of the runs were within 2000m (*2200yd*) of the intended line of fire, but spread was increasing rapidly with range and would probably have been very large indeed at 34,600m (*37,800yd*).

T3e Kreuzotter

Another electric torpedo for midget submarines with total weight 1343kg (*2961lb*) and range apparently 7500m (*8200yd*)/20kts.

T6

This, which did not enter service, was T2a with an improved warhead and the same total weight and range.

T12

This electric torpedo, intended for midget submarines, was 5500mm (*18ft*) long and had a total weight of 1261kg (*2780lb*) with range 3000m (*3280yd*)/30kts. It was apparently not in service.

HOMING TORPEDOES

All were 53.3cm (*21in*) except Pfau.

T4 Falke

The first passive homer, intended for use against merchant ships so that a 20kt torpedo was acceptable. Homing was by simple noise measurement, and about 100 T4s were made and about 30 used from January 1943, but it was obvious that a weapon to attack convoy escorts was essential. T4 had a total weight of 1937kg (*3080lb*) and range was 7500m (*8200yd*)/20kts.

Serious experiments on homing began in 1936 and it was decided to concentrate on electric torpedoes in 1940. The early records were lost when the Gotenhafen experimental works were demolished before the Russians overran the area.

T5 Zaunkönig 1

This passive homer, known to the British as GNAT, was intended to attack convoy escorts proceeding at 10–18kts. The torpedo speed was limited to 24–25kts for reasons of self noise so that it was unlikely to catch a ship doing over 18kts as the homing run was sinuous, and at below 10kts the target's noise would not be sufficient to activate the homing system. There were two varieties of T5, one with a flat and the other with a rounded nose. The first had four magnetostrictive hydrophones wired in pairs with a phase delay between pairs so that the maximum electrical output was for sound arriving at ± 25° to the torpedo axis. In the second a bakelite cap protected two hydrophones, each behind a funnel baffled to give maximum sensitivity at ± 25°. To give good acoustic transmission, cap and funnels were filled with glycerin and ethylene glycol. Both used an amplitude comparison system known as Amsel and the rudders steered to the noisier side.

The system was virtually deaf abaft *c*70°, and if the sound was straight ahead both receivers gave equal voltages, so that the torpedo would run straight until it was passing the target when a very sharp turn was called for. The torpedo could not comply and missed astern, running out of contact. Two programmes were devised to avoid this and could be selected by a switch. If the relative bearings of the U-boat from target were 0–110° the 'Ahead' programme was used, and if 110–180° the 'Astern'. In 'Ahead', the first signal caused the torpedo to circle until it picked up a counter command. This brought it abaft the beam of the target from where it was expected to home normally. The rudder was locked amidships for two seconds each time the signal was lost, but the gyro course which would take the torpedo away from the target was never switched in.

In 'Astern' after homing began, the rudder remained hard over as long as a signal was received. When the signal failed the rudder was locked amidships for about 2sec and then the original gyro course was held until a signal was again received.

For the first 400m (*400yd*) the homing was inoperative and the torpedo followed the gyro course to give the U-boat a chance to keep clear, and as previously noted the pistol only responded to targets above. The homing distance varied very much, but 450m (*500yd*) was reasonable for a 15kt ship. To reduce bottom reflections the minimum depth was originally 90m (*50 fathoms*), but this was later reduced to 18m (*10 fathoms*) when T5 was issued to E-boats. Total weight of the torpedo was 1497kg (*3300lb*) and range 5700m (*6230yd*)/24–25kts. Maintenance was a serious problem as torpedoes were damp and difficult of internal access, and a T5 had 11 electronic valves, 26 relays, 1760 soldered or screw connections, and 30,000m (*33,000yd*) of wire. Much effort went into the development of the T5 including over 2500 test runs.

U-boats initially carried two each, later four, and 640 were fired for 58 hits, whereas all other German torpedoes aggregated over 20% hits, though it must be noted that T5 was often fired at difficult targets, and that there were special allied countermeasures. When T5 was first used in September 1943, these were not in operation and three escorts were sunk and another damaged. It had been believed for a considerable time that acoustic torpedoes were on the way, and the design of a noise maker known as 'Foxer' was begun in late 1942. It began to be used after the above T5 attacks, but it was many months before all escorts had it. Foxer was a towed arrangement of metal rods which clanged together and, by German estimates, produced 10–100 times the noise of a ship. It was known to U-boat crews as the 'circular saw'. It spoilt the performance of the towing ship's sound gear, and the first models could not be towed at over 15kts, though this was increased to 20kts in later patterns.

In addition speeds of over 18kts and of 8kts or less provided a good measure of protection, as the Germans had expected, but they had not foreseen an effective tactical counter known as 'Step aside'. On locating the surfaced U-boat, by radar or other means, the escort would turn back to place the U-boat 60° on the opposite bow, and continue this course for a mile at 15kts, then turning to parallel the original bearing of the U-boat and covering a further mile before turning towards the U-boat and attacking.

T5a

A modified T5 used by E-boats with range 8000m (*8750yd*)/22kt.

T5b

This had the same range as T5a but was used by submarines.

T10 Spinne

A standard electric torpedo modified for wire guidance and developed from 1942 for coast defence. Total weight was 1620kg (*3571lb*) and range 5000m (*5470yd*)/30kts. Steel wire *c*0.25mm (*0.010in*) diameter, with insulation which reduced the specific gravity to a little over 1, was used with 5000m (*5470yd*) in a fixed coil, the lightly greased turns unwinding from the inside like a ball of string and paying out through a tube which kept the wire clear of the propellers. The torpedo started on gyro course and was fired with about half the estimated director angle. When the operator, usually located high on cliffs, took over, the gyro was permanently disconnected and the torpedo was kept on line between operator and target. Control was much easier than might be expected and one operator could handle three torpedoes. To check direction the torpedo could be instructed to surface briefly and at night a lamp covering 20° aft was flashed. T10 could also be fired from ships.

About 200 were made and first issued in the summer of 1944, but results were apparently dubious.

T11 Zaunkönig 2

Development of an improved T5, less influenced by Foxer, was put in hand at the beginning of 1944 but in view of the state of the war, only fairly quick modifications could be accepted. Trials in Danzig Bay showed that a towed noise maker was apparently effective in attacks from right ahead of the target. A receiver was designed with listening characteristics that were changed during the run. Initially there was no response at all between right ahead and 15° on either bow, and when the torpedo was fired at an escort towing a decoy the first sound heard was the escort as the bearing drew abaft 15°. At this signal the torpedo turned 180° with acoustics switched off and then followed ordinary homing procedure. The previous wide dead arc would result in increased weaving so that the circuit was arranged to give a very narrow dead angle after the 180° turn.

So that unimportant targets could be bypassed, the initial range for which homing was inoperative could be set at 300m (*330yd*), 600m (*660yd*), 1100m (*1200yd*), 1900m (*2080yd*). It was hoped to use battery cells with 17 positive plates to give a range of 9000m (*9850yd*), but this made the torpedo too heavy, and weight and range were as for T5. Quieter propellers and reduced weaving widened the target speed limits to 19-8kt, and as the idea of firing below periscope depth using acoustic data was gaining ground, T11 could be fired at 50m (*165ft*) depth. T11 was ready for issue at the end of the war but apparently only one U-boat had it and none was fired.

Other homing systems in alphabetical order:

Ackermann

This was intended to home along the wake by detecting turbulence at two pressure-tap points near the nose and tail, but the effects were too small. It may be noted that a similar system had been devised in Britain over 40 years previously.

Boje

An active homer developed from 1942 by Atlas Werke, Munich. Later versions were known as Geier. A very great amount of research into propeller noise and reverberation was stimulated by this project.

Fasan

A project at the discussion stage and apparently dropped for Geier. Acoustic detection of the target would trigger a 'Lut' type pattern, thus avoiding faulty positioning of the latter.

Geier

This active homer was the successor to Boje. Geier 1 was tried in March 1944. The improved Geier 2 began its test running in the autumn of 1944 and apparently had nearly reached the production stage at the end of the war. A further Geier 3 was planned.

A sharply beamed 80kc pulse was transmitted at the rate of 3/sec at 40° to port and starboard of the torpedo axis, and if the echo exceeded a set value the rudders were operated. The pulse rate was chosen arbitrarily and limited the range of the response to 250m (*275yd*) maximum. If a slower rate had been used, the interval could easily have been too long, especially in the important case of attack from ahead, where the torpedo had to turn quickly to avoid missing astern.

Reverberation, reflection by surface disturbances in a seaway, mainly due to layers of air bubbles drawn down by the water motion, reduced the response range to *c*50m (*55yd*) in force 5. The amplifiers in Geier were arranged so that the gain immediately after transmission was small and increased quickly to the end of the sounding period so that the useful echo and reverberation were at steady strength regardless of target distance. Even in the worst bearing when right ahead, the echo was greater than reverberation if the sea was below force 3, while abeam the ship target acted like a mirror.

In devising the steering procedure, it was necessary to consider: (1) Echoes were stronger, the nearer to perpendicular the target was to the beam; (2) The strong echo effect of the wake which, even in rough seas, persisted to several hundred metres astern; (3) In the vicinity of the propellers, the gear would become passive and respond to target sound. Procedures investigated were 'Single turn', 'Multiple turn' and 'Preferred side'.

Single turn. The torpedo approached on gyro course, which was permanently disconnected at the first acoustic signal. The torpedo turned towards the side from which the signal came and continued until a counter signal was received. This was simple, but any major interference would start the torpedo on a circle.

Multiple turn. Similar, with the rudder to starboard or port as long as signals arrive. If none was received for about a second, the torpedo returned to gyro course.

Preferred side. This was an attempt to exploit the wake. The torpedo was set to starboard or port priority, and if signals were received on both sides only the priority command was carried out, even if the other were louder. If the signal came from one side only it was obeyed, whether priority or not. As an example, suppose that the torpedo comes from starboard on a broad-track angle with starboard priority set. As it approaches the quarter of the target it picks up a starboard echo from the target and a port one from the wake. The starboard signal is obeyed, and the torpedo turns until it is lost and only the port echo from the wake is heard. This signal is in turn obeyed until the starboard echo is again received. The same procedure was repeated until the torpedo hit on one of its turns to port. The prepared side was always that on which the torpedo was fired, but a later refinement allowed the torpedo to choose the direction of the first echo as the preferred side.

Another later addition was to have two receiving circuits, one at the signal frequency of 80kc and the other at about 90kc. The signal echo was only received on the first circuit, but both received noises and reverberation, so that with suitable circuitry the echo/noise ratio could be much improved.

It was thought that Geier had a rather better chance than T11 against towed noise makers and also against DCs and isolated peaks of background noise.

Ibis

An active homer intended to weave along the wake. It was dropped in favour of Geier.

Lerche

A wire-controlled passive homer based on the human ear's ability to perceive the quality of sounds, even if the desired signal is the weakest of the sounds coming in. The operator could distinguish between a decoy and a ship's propellers by 'beats' in the latter at the shaft rate. A 35kc magnetostriction hydrophone in the nose of the torpedo was trained on command by a small electric motor to limits of ±60° and the amplified signals transmitted back. The orders for the movement of the hydrophone, disconnecting the torpedo gyro and port and starboard rudder for any length of time, were transmitted at different frequencies to frequency sensitive relays so that a single wire carried data from and orders to the torpedo. The wire was paid out from the torpedo and from the firing U-boat.

Development was begun by AEG in 1942 and experimental runs from a fixed firing point were made in 1944. It was apparently in one U-boat for tests at the end of the war, but its success was not certain. Much of the gear was captured by the Russians.

Märchen

A theoretical project homing on changes in the magnetic field, but compensation for movement of the torpedo in the earth's field was so difficult that it was impracticable.

Pfau

A passive homing system allied to Amsel as used in T5, but depending on phase, not amplitude, difference. The frequency range was wider, as was the bearing range for searching, and indication of the target bearing was quicker. Development started in the mid 1930s and test models were being run in 1939, but work was then dropped for about two years. When taken up again it was intended for a homing version of the 45cm (*17.7in*) wet-heater F5b which was an airborne weapon and was to have a range of 6000m (*6560yd*)/24kts as a homer. This torpedo, known as LT1B4, weighed 820kg (*1808lb*) and had a 165-175kg (*364-386lb*) explosive charge. It was ready in April 1944, but the acoustic gear could not stand the water impact and Pfau was abandoned.

Taube

A passive system working on a low frequency of 50-100 cycles and intended as a remedy for Foxer, as small towed decoys could not generate loud noises at low frequencies. It was abandoned because attenuation and disturbance noises made the target signal difficult to detect.

AIRBORNE TORPEDOES

F5 was the Norwegian torpedo as developed by Schwarzkopf, and not of very high performance with a range of 2200m (*2500yd*)/33kts. The usual wet heater system was used with a radial engine, the torpedo weighed 737kg (*1625lb*) and the explosive charge was 200kg (*441lb*). The original dropping speed was 75kts from 15-25m (*c50-80ft*).

F5b was a development of the above in service from late 1941 and until the end of the war with relatively minor modifications. The earliest versions were the 40kt LT1A1 and the 33kt LT1A2, the latter eventually for training only. In early 1944 LT1B1 and LT1B2 were introduced. These had the same speed as the above A1 and A2, and B2 was for training only, but they differed in having electrical setting of the gyro angling instead of mechanical as in the A series. The 24kt pattern-running LT1A3 and LT1B3 followed in mid 1944. All had a four-cylinder radial engine of 94 × 90mm and 2.5 litres swept volume, working on Decalin/air/70% water, 30% alcohol, the latter addition to prevent freezing. Initially the usual dropping speed was 120-130kts at 30-40m (*100-130ft*), but 150kts caused no serious difficulties. This torpedo was also used in some small craft from 1942.

To control flight in the air a wooden K3 tail which broke off on hitting the water was fitted. This was a fixed triplane of 50cm (*20in*) span and was replaced in 1944 by the L2 tail which was similar but had ailerons operated as an additional function by a very heavy gyro, started by a cartridge some milliseconds before release. At this time the previous anti-rolling KA ring was eliminated. This was a ring 20cm (*8in*) long located between the head and body with two gyro operated fins. The L2 tail permitted increased dropping speeds and heights, and various other devices were tried including a ricochet disc fixed to the nose to ensure that forces on the torpedo after entry (when the water was thrown clear, except at the extreme nose) were exactly normal to the axis. The disc was blown clear by a small charge *c*40m (*45yd*) from entry and was claimed to give satisfactory results at 250kts in 15m (*50ft*) of water, though the highest standard test speed appears to have been 183kts from 120m (*390ft*). The 24kt pattern runners were fitted with Gear 9a, an initial run of 1700-3000m (*1860-3280yd*) was set before take-off, and after completing this the torpedo ran in 300-500m (*330-550yd*) circles. An improved 9b which could be set in flight, and permitted the torpedo to circle or run legs, as in 'Fat', did not enter service.

45cm (17.7in) fuel/air not homing

Data F5b modifications

Length oa	4804-5160mm	15ft 9.1in-16ft 11.1in
Total weight	725-812kg	1598-1790lb
Negative buoyancy	147-202kg	324-445lb
Volume air vessel	163 litres	5.76ft^3
Pressure	200kg/cm^2	2850lb/in^2
Weight air	38.5kg	84.9lb
Decalin	2.75kg	6.06lb
70 water 30 alcohol	21.0kg	46.3lb
Hp (24kts)	38	
(40 kts)	168	
Explosive charge	180/250kg	397/551lb
Range	2000m/40kts	2200yd/40kts
	6000m/24kts	6560yd/24kts

Airborne torpedoes had only one speed setting. At 24kts the negative buoyancy was too great with 240kg (*529lb*) or 250kg (*551lb*) explosive charges, and these were limited to 200kg (*441lb*) max.

F5w

This was the German designation of the Italian Fiume torpedo used in considerable numbers pending large scale production of F5b. It is described in the Italian section and brief details were: length overall 5460mm (*17ft 11in*), total weight 869-905kg (*1916-1995lb*), explosive charge 170-200kg (*375-441lb*), range 3000m (*3300yd*)/40kt.

F5i

The German designation of the Naples torpedo described in the Italian section. It was not used in service by the Germans.

LT850

This was applied to 66 Japanese torpedoes, not apparently of the latest pattern. The Germans disapproved of the frequent Japanese maintenance schedules and they were not used.

LT900

A proposed development of the Italian torpedoes with heavier charge and longer range.

There was also a proposal to modify the standard 53.3cm (*21in*) G7a to give 50kts with increased power and a 1000mm (*39.4in*) reduction in length.

AIRBORNE ELECTRIC TORPEDOES

LT180 and 350

The German designations of the Italian 50cm (*19.7in*) circling torpedoes described in the latter section. Only the larger LT350 was in German service, about 1000 being supplied by Italy. These somewhat primitive weapons were parachute dropped and are believed to have been first used in June 1942, though there were no successes until nine months later. Length overall 2600mm (*8ft 6.4in*), total weight 350kg (*772lb*), explosive charge 120kg (*265lb*), range 15,000m (*16,400yd*)/13.5kts falling to 3.9kts.

EXPERIMENTAL HYDROGEN PEROXIDE TORPEDOES

All except F5u ran on concentrated hydrogen peroxide and were 53.3cm (*21in*) except F5u and LT1000.

F5u

A 45cm (*17.7in*) airborne torpedo developed from the standard F5b, and using 60% hydrogen peroxide, 60% hydrazine hydrate with a four-cylinder radial engine. There was some track as the exhaust contained 20% nitrogen, but this was permissible in airborne torpedoes. On trials 5000m (*5500yd*)/40kt and 12,000m (*13000yd*)/24kt were obtained. As with other German airborne torpedoes there was only one speed setting and the two versions were known as LTIIB1 and LTIIB3 respectively, the latter being a pattern runner. Dr Walter considered it the most successful peroxide torpedo, and it was apparently accepted by the *Luftwaffe*, but further development was abandoned in the project purge of mid 1944.

Goldbutt

A small turbine torpedo intended for midget submarines with range 3100m (*3390yd*)/50kts.

Goldfisch

Similar to Goldbutt but 3430m (*3750yd*)/45kts.

K-butt

Another turbine torpedo for midget submarines, launched from an external frame. The range was 3000m (*3280yd*)/45kt. At the end of the war, 60 had been produced for service but further development work was needed.

Klippfisch

Tested in 1942, this had the radial engine of the G7a (T1). Range was 6500m (*7100yd*)/40kts.

LT1000

An airborne turbine torpedo with range 5000m (*5500yd*)/50kts, but work was stopped in 1943. Weight was *c*1000kg (*2206lb*) and the cross section elliptical 1000 × 500mm (*39.4 × 19.7in*)

LT1200

An airborne jet propelled torpedo but the range of 900m (*1000yd*)/38kts was too short. Weight *c*1200kg (*2650lb*).

LT1500

Another airborne jet torpedo with range 2000m (*2200yd*)/38–40kts. This was considered inadequate for a torpedo of *c*1500kg (*3300lb*). Construction was of light alloy castings. Tests on LT1200 and LT1500 were broken off in mid 1943.

Mondfish

A jet torpedo for coast defence. Range was 1200m (*1310yd*)/40 or possibly 45kts.

Schildbutt

A turbine torpedo using sea water as the diluent. The intended range was 14,000m (*15300yd*)/45kt, but when tested after the war, only sufficient power for 40kts was developed on the brake, and tests were not satisfactory enough to attempt 40kt range runs. Design changes were needed before the pump could deliver the requirements for a 45kt output.

Steinbarsch

This turbine torpedo was intended for submarines and was to have 'Lut' pattern-running gear. It was the most advanced design that had reached full scale experiments, and 100 were produced for service, but further development work was still needed. The combustion chamber was bolted directly to the turbine inlet and the working liquids were pressurized by compressed air. The torpedo was capable of its intended 8000m (*8750yd*)/45kt.

Steinbutt

Another turbine torpedo of which 100 were produced for service, though further development work was needed. The intended range of 8000m (*8750yd*)/45kt could be attained, with the turbine giving 435BHP at 23,000rpm, reduced to 1550 at the propellers. Expendables were Decalin 16.8kg (*37lb*), hydrogen peroxide 129kg (*284lb*), water 171.5kg (*378lb*), Helman and air 26.8kg (*59lb*), and consumption 8kg (*17.7lb*)/HP/hr.

Steinfisch

An earlier version of Steinbutt with range 7000m (*7650yd*)/45kt.

Zaunbutt

A turbine torpedo with homing capability. All drawings were lost in air-raids.

Steinwal

The most advanced of the hydrogen peroxide torpedoes, but tests after the war gave no really satisfactory brake runs and the torpedo could not be run on the range. Sea water was used as the diluent and compressed air was abandoned for pressurizing the working liquids, which were all pumped. Changes that were shown to be required in pump design would have posed some formidable mechanical problems. The turbine was intended to give 500HP at 30,000rpm and the rotor was machined from a solid steel disc by a machine developed by Askania of Berlin. There was a cardan gear on the driving shaft which, with an internally toothed fly-wheel ring, revolved in the opposite direction to the rotor, thus preventing initial roll on firing. The exhaust bubbled out through a perforated ring round the engine compartment and quickly dissolved. The bubble screen was claimed to reduce radiated engine noise. Engine, combustion chamber and reducer weighed 224kg (*494lb*) and gear box and shafting 61kg (*134.5lb*). The long range was solely for pattern running and special 'Lut' equipment was fitted.

Designed Data

Length oa	7125mm	23ft 4½in
Total weight	1801kt	3970lb
Negative buoyance	463kg	1021lb
Weight H_2O_2	369kg	814lb
Decalin	50kg	110lb
Helman, air, water	48kg	106lb
Consumption expendables	3.85kg/HP/hr	8.5lb/HP/hr
Explosive charge	300kg	661lb
Range	*c*22,000m/45kt	*c*24,000yd/45kt

EXPERIMENTAL KREISLAUF CYCLE TORPEDOES

M5

A very large torpedo 75cm (*29.5in*) diameter and about 11m (*36ft*) long, which was under development prewar but was abandoned, apparently because every test model sank on trials. With a 600HP Junkers engined 23,800m (*26,000yd*)/40kt could have been achieved.

53.3cm (21in)

This was powered by a 4.3 litre (*262in³*) eight-cylinder V4-stroke water-cooled Junkers engine supercharged at 2.5 atmos, and developing 425HP at 4360rpm. The engine room was dry and the exhaust gases which left the engine at *c*1000°C (*1830°F*) were reduced to *c*60°C (*140°F*) in a seawater cooler and added to the aviation gasoline fuel and oxygen at the carburettor. As oxygen was added, part of the exhaust gases were eliminated via an excess pressure valve. 40 engines which had twice the efficiency of the Walter turbine were made, and range running had begun when the project was closed down. It was expected that 18,000m (*19,700yd*)/45kt and 27,000m (*29,500yd*)/40kt would be attained.

ANTI-SUBMARINE WEAPONS

The principal anti-submarine weapon remained the depth charge carried by surface vessels as, although airborne depth charges had been developed, few submarines were actually sunk by German aircraft when they were at sea. Of those belonging to the Western Allies, only one possible and another shared can be credited to German aircraft, apart from four sunk at Malta in 1942 (for some of which Italian bombers may have been responsible). Surface vessels accounted for 12 and the above shared sinking. Facts on Russian losses are even now unreliable but if we omit Soviet ships sunk in harbour or when stranded, it would seem that only five at most can be credited to aircraft, compared with 18 or so to surface vessels. It should be noted that the mine was the main killer of Russian submarines.

There were several more advanced anti-submarine weapons under design or development, such as long-range mortars or rockets, but none appear to have entered service.

Depth charges on board *UJ 2197* 25 August 1942. The gun is a 3.7cm SKC/30.
Aldo Fraccaroli Collection

Depth Charges standard type

Type	Total weight kg (lb)	Charge kg (lb)	Max depth setting m (ft)	Sinking speed m/s (f/s)
WBD	180 (397)	125 (276)	120 (394)	3.5 (11.5)
WBF	139 (306)	60 (132)	75 (246)	2.23 (7.3)
WBG	180 (397)	60 (132)	120 (394)	3.5 (11.5)
WBH	240 (529)	60 (132)	150 (492)	4.35 (14.3)

There were six depth settings for each type running from 15-25m (*49-82ft*) up to the above maximum. The charges had SW18 as the explosive filling, and maximum destructive ranges against a 12mm (*0.47in*) hull were 8m (*26ft*) for WBD and 5.6m (*18ft*) for the others. Time fuzes were used.

German thrower or mortar designs seem usually to have been single barrelled though an illustration of C/41, for which no data has been found, shows three barrels. A Rheinmetall drawing for a thrower gives the weight of the latter as 275 (*606lb*), initial velocity 35m/s (*115f/s*) and arbor 35kg (*77lb*). The DC is shown with its long axis horizontally across the trajectory and is given as 45cm (*17.7in*) diameter with total weight 186kg (*410lb*).

Other Rheinmetall designs, which as far as is known did not enter service, include mortars for an egg-shaped bomb 45cm (*17.7in*) diameter, and including arbor 150cm (*59in*) long and 195kg (*430lb*) in weight with 135kg (*298lb*) charge. The total weight of the mortar was 1230-1500kg (*2712-3307lb*), muzzle velocity 50m/s (*164f/s*) and range *c*200m (*210yd*). Longer range designs were to fire a 30.5cm (*12in*) diameter projectile weighing 226 kg (*498lb*). The heaviest version weighed 6800kg (*6.7 tons*) including mounting, with muzzle velocity 190m/s (*623f/s*) and range 3000m (*3280yd*). The ancestry of these may be found in the British 11in (*28cm*) howitzer of the First World War.

MINES

German mines had a high reputation in both World Wars, and in 1939-45 most attention was focused on the various ground influence mines, at first magnetic, then acoustic and magnetic/acoustic, and finally magnetic/pressure or acoustic/pressure. Satisfactory methods of dealing with the various magnetic and acoustic mines were devised, but the pressure mine was never surmounted during the war and could be destroyed only by countermining. Limiting the speed of a ship to 4kts in dangerous waters gave some protection. Moored mines were responsible for the loss of the cruiser *Neptune*, the only major allied warship sunk by a mine, and in this instance the German mines were laid by Italian cruisers. The field off Cape Juminda in the Gulf of Finland, which eventually comprised 2828 German and Finnish moored mines, mostly contact with some antenna, and in addition 1500 explosive anti-sweeping devices, devastated the Russian forces withdrawing from Tallinn (Reval) and with subsequent losses caused what remains the greatest disaster ever due to a minefield.

The peak of allied merchant ship losses from mines was in 1939-40, and altogether mines accounted for 534 ships of 1,406,037 gross tons, respectively 10.3% and 6.5% of the total.

The German navy set up a mine warfare research and development command in 1920 and the first experiments in the laying of airborne parachute mines began in 1931. These were successfully concluded but the project was turned over to the *Luftwaffe* in 1936 and no further interest was shown until 1938-39. Large numbers were to be ready for the spring of 1940, with an eventual target of 50,000, but at the outbreak of war only 1500 magnetic mines were in existence, with a stock of over 20,000 contact mines. Instead of waiting until a great number of magnetic mines were available (and their large scale introduction in the spring and summer of 1940 would have been devastating) the Germans began to lay them at once, at first by U-boat, then by seaplanes and also by destroyers. Only 470 were actually laid in the first three months of the war, though of the 1800 mines laid by destroyers in October 1939-February 1940 half were ground magnetic and half moored contact. A similar error was made with acoustic mines which were laid in August 1940 before an adequate stock was in existence.

With pressure mines the error was different. Dönitz wanted to lay them in large numbers from the end of August 1943, but the risk of their being recovered, quickly copied and dropped in the U-boat training areas in the Baltic was considered to be too great, and none was laid until the night of 6/7 June 1944 in the Normandy invasion area and, since the *Luftwaffe* stock was located at Magdeburg, no airborne mines until after 9 June. The fear of their recovery was well founded as one was collected close inshore at Luc-sur-Mer on 20 June. On the other hand, a large scale laying of pressure mines in the waters where the invasion forces were assembling, would in all probability have wrecked the operation before it began.

German contact mines usually had Hertz and not switch horns, although there were exceptions, and in moored fields use was made of EMR snag obstructors with chain moorings and EMC shells which, in addition to acting as deep-water sweep obstructors, filled in the gaps in the minefield to prevent their location by sonar. There were various other smaller sweep-obstructor floats with cutters or explosive charges.

Magnetic mines, unlike British ones, were fired by a change of magnetism in the vertical field and originally required the passage of a ship built in the northern hemisphere and thus with the N magnetic pole downwards. The polarity was later sometimes reversed, as ships with excessive degaussing behaved as if they had been built in the southern hemisphere. By 1941 most LMA and LMB mines had a firing unit activated by both polarities. The original sensitivity was 30 millioersteds, later improved to 10. Later acoustic and some pressure mines had magnetic triggering with 5 millioersteds sensitivity, while other pressure mines were triggered acoustically. The first magnetic/acoustic mine was recovered in September 1941. Improvements in acoustic mechanisms included a low-pass filter to reduce the operating frequency from *c*1000 to *c*250 cycles and in 1943 a firing unit working at 30 cycles was introduced. This last was triggered by medium frequencies and was never recovered during the war. The object of these reduced frequencies was to make sweeping more difficult.

Among the various devices fitted were 'Period Delay Mechanisms', which prevented the mine from detonating until after a predetermined number of actuations up to 9, 12 or 15, and 'Rendering Active Mechanisms' which delayed the mine's becoming active underwater for up to 6 hours, 6 days or 12 days. Another device rendered the mine alternately active and safe at regular daily intervals. Anti-stripping equipment was later discontinued as it was liable to cause German casualties.

The standard explosive fillings were SW18 and SW36, while S16, S18 and SW36 were used in airborne mines. An analysis of S16 gave 31.4% ammonium nitrate, 5.9% sodium nitrate, 2.3% potassium nitrate, 9.7% cyclonite, 10.1% ethylene diamine dinitrate, 0.6% TNT, 40% aluminium.

The most important German mines are described below. There were also a number of developments never operational during the war:

1. An improved pressure acoustic unit, protected against swell. The units were for BM 1000 mines and almost ready for service.
2. A series of pressure units not combined with acoustic or magnetic mechanisms, intended for use in a small form of BM mine.
3. A special bomb-mine fitted with an optical unit intended for use in rivers for destroying bridges.
5. Various magnetic units on the British coil-rod principle, some with valve amplifiers for increased sensitivity.
5. More advanced magnetic acoustic combinations to complicate sweeping.
6. An echo sounding unit, triggered acoustically and operating at the change of depth, due to the presence of a ship. There were two versions, one for a ground BM mine and the other for a deep laid spherical buoyant mine intended to part from its mooring on actuation and detonate after a short delay.

EM SERIES

'Standard' mines, nearly all moored and mostly contact.

EMA (British designation GU)

This mine was first washed ashore in January 1941 and was later obsolete. The shell was oval 1.6m × 0.8m diameter (*63 × 31.5in*) and there were five Hertz horns with 150kg (*331lb*) charge and mooring depths of 100m (*55 fathoms*) or 150m (*82 fathoms*).

EMB

Similar to EMA but the shell was 0.9m (*35.4in*) dia and charge 220kg (*485lb*).

EMC (British designation GY)

The basic version of this widely used mine was first washed ashore in October 1939. It had a spherical shell 1.12m (*44in*) diameter, with seven Hertz horns and a charge of 300kg (*661lb*). Alternative mooring depths were 100m (*55 fathoms*), 200m (*109 fathoms*), 300m (*164 fathoms*), 500m (*273 fathoms*).

EMC m KA

This mine differed in having a charge of 250kg (*551lb*) or 285kg (*628lb*) and mooring depths of 200m (*109 fathoms*), 300m (*164 fathoms*) or 400m (*219 fathoms*). The KA gear, introduced in 1940 and later discarded, comprised a 30m (*98ft*) Tombac tube over the upper part of the mooring wire. This tube when subject to an upward drag in sweeping, closed a switch and exploded the mine. The gear replaced the former KE switch which closed when the mooring was cut or the strain on it relieved.

EMC m Kette (chain)

This had a charge of 250kg (*551lb*) and mooring depths of 100m (*55 fathoms*) or 200m (*109 fathoms*). It was introduced in the first half of 1943, and the upper part of the mooring wire was protected by 6m (*20ft*) of chain to make sweeping difficult.

EMC m Kette u Reissleine (snagline)

This mine was similar to the above but had five Hertz horns. It was introduced in the first half of 1943. The snagline was copied from the British as an alternative to antennae and counteracted the rise of tide. It hung vertically over the mine and firing was effected by tearing off a horn.

EMC m An Z (antenna firing). British designation GV*

This mine, in service in 1939, had a charge of 285kg (*628lb*) or 300kg (*661lb*) and mooring depths of 200 (*109 fathoms*) or 350m (*191 fathoms*). The upper antennae was 20m (66ft) or 40m (*131ft*) long and was supported by a float 5m (*16ft*) below the surface, while the lower antenna ran below the mine for 15m (*49ft*) or 30m (*98ft*). The upper antennae was later removed, but in 1941 a version was introduced with a 20m (*66ft*) upper antenna only, the top being supported on the surface by corks. This mine could be moored in 100-300m (*55-164 fathoms*) and also in 500m (*273 fathoms*).

EMD (British designation GX)

This was first washed ashore in October 1939. The spherical shell was 1.0m (*39.4in*) diameter with five Hertz horns and a charge of 150kg (*331lb*). Mooring depths were 100m (*55 fathoms*) or 200m (*109 fathoms*).

An antenna version with four horns, known to the British as GV, was first washed ashore in September 1940.

EMF (British designation GO*

A moored magnetic mine for laying from surface craft. The aluminium alloy shell was 1.12m (*44in*) diameter and the charge 350kg (*772lb*) while mooring depths were 200m (*109 fathoms*), 300m (*164 fathoms*) or 500m (*273 fathoms*). It was in service in 1939, but was sensitive to rough seas and liable to prematures.

EMG

A moored surface mine developed from EMC and introduced in 1941 but later withdrawn as it was impossible to render it absolutely safe. The shell and charge were as in EMC but there were four Hertz horns and a 100kg (*220lb*) compensating weight below the mine to reduce buoyancy. Mooring depth was 180m (*98 fathoms*).

EMS

A drifting contact mine with periscope attachment and 14kg (*31lb*) charge. It was intended as a trap for anti-submarine vessels and was considered for small battle units. Although dating to 1941 it had not been used up to mid 1943.

? (British designation GL)

A moored contact mine with five Hertz horns and 110kg (*243lb*) charge, first washed ashore in July 1940.

FM SERIES

Small shallow water contact mines, usually moored.

FMA

Details not known, possibly obsolete.

FMB

20kg (*44lb*) charge.

FMC (British designation GQ)

A moored mine with five Hertz horns and 40kg (*88lb*) charge.

? (British designation GL)

This may belong here. It was a small spherical drifting river mine with a contact firing rod, electrical firing and 12kg (*26lb*) charge. GLP differed in percussion firing.

UM SERIES

Anti-submarine mines also used with shallow settings.

UMA (British designation GZ)

This mine was first washed ashore in November 1939. It was of moored contact type with five Hertz and three switch horns and 30kg (*66lb*) charge. The shell was 0.8m (*31.5in*) diameter and mooring depths were 50m (*27 fathoms*) or 100m (*55 fathoms*).

UMA (K)

Introduced in 1942, this was a surface version with only the five Hertz horns and a 48kg (*106lb*) weight below the mine.

UMB (British designation GR)

An improved UMA in service in 1939. It had five Hertz and three switch horns with the charge increased to 40kg (*88lb*) and the shell diameter to 0.84m (*33in*). Mooring depths were 65m (*36 fathoms*), 100m (*55 fathoms*), 150m (*82 fathoms*), 200m (*109 fathoms*) or 300m (*164 fathoms*). A hydrostatic flooder, known as HV, which acted if the mine rose above its set depth was introduced in 1940 so that German ships could pass over the minefield. This device could be disconnected by a screw.

UMB m KA

This had the same type of fitting as EMC m KA and there were other UMB versions with the upper part of the mooring protected by a chain and with or without various snaglines.

KM SERIES

Coastal mines.

KMA (British designation GK)

Also known as 'Katie'. A ground mine with 75kg (*165lb*) charge in a rectangular concrete box anchor surmounted by a tubular steel tripod frame to 2.7m (*8ft 10in*) above the base of the anchor. There was a single Hertz horn at the top with a snagline for 6-10m (*20-33ft*) water and no snagline for 0-5m (*0-16ft*). This mine was laid by surface craft and had a total weight of 1000kg (*2205lb*).

? (British designation GJ)

This may belong here. A spherical mine with one Hertz horn and 12kg (*26lb*) charge probably used as a beach mine.

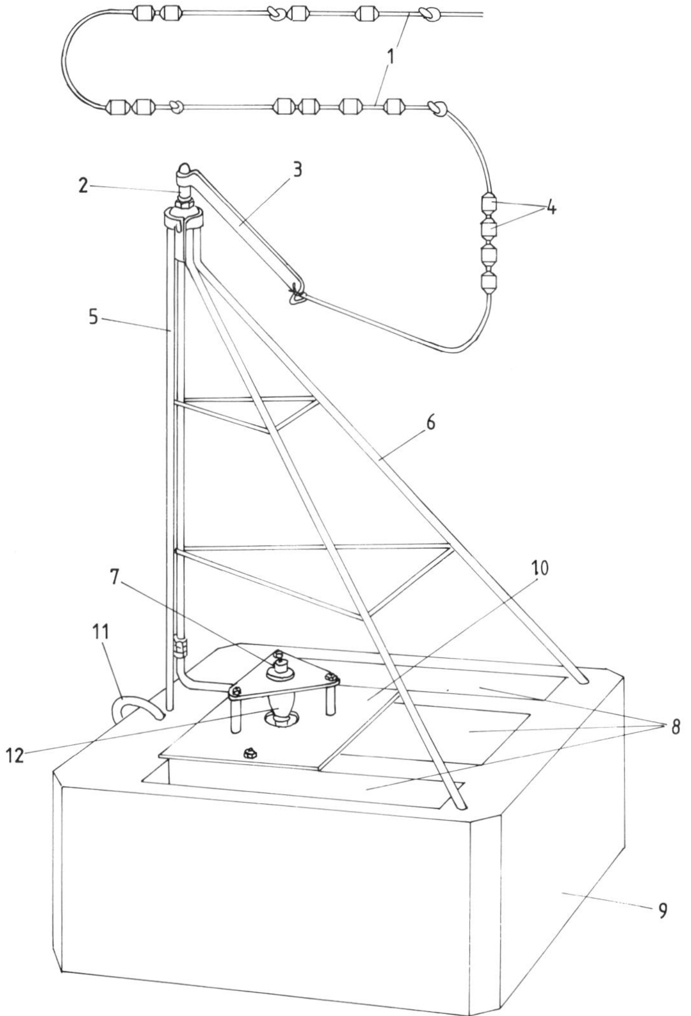

KMA ground contact anti-invasion mine with snagline for depths of 6m or over.

1 Snagline
2 Hertz horn
3 Swivel lever arm
4 Rubber floats
5 Detonator lead conduit
6 Tripod
7 Soluble plug and arming switch
8 Openings in concrete base
9 Concrete base
10 Charge case
11 Lifting eye
12 Detonator carrier

John Lambert

OM SERIES

Surface mines

OMA (K)

A mine of special shape, rather like a King Crab less its tail spike, for use in tidal waters up to 15m (*49ft*) depth against invasion craft. Its use was limited as it was visible on the surface. The shell was 1.06m (*41.7in*) diameter and 0.79m (*31in*) high and there were six Hertz horns with 30kg (*66lb*) charge. A flooder was fitted and the mooring wire was protected by 11m (*36ft*) of double chain and 11m (*36ft*) of single chain.

RM SERIES

These could be used as controlled or observation mines, as independent ground magnetic mines and probably as controlled magnetic mines. Details for some of the series have not been found.

RMA (British designation GH)

Also known as *Schildkröte* (turtle) mine. This was in service in 1939 as a hemispherical ground magnetic mine, laid by surface craft. The charge was apparently 800kg (*1764lb*).

RMB

Similar to RMA and also in service in 1939, but differing in a 460kg (*1014lb*) charge.

RMD

A ground mine for all types of influence mechanism, laid by surface craft and designed to use the smallet possible quantity of scarce materials. The charge was 450kg (*992lb*) and it is noted that the mine lay better on the seabed than the cylindrical type.

RMH (British designation GI)

A rectangular box shaped ground mine with wood casing. It was laid by surface craft, and had a 770kg (*1698lb*) charge.

SM SERIES

Moored influence mines for laying from the vertical mine tubes of Type V11D and XB U-boats.

SMA (British designation GO)

This was introduced in 1942 and had magnetic and apparently other types of influence firing. The aluminium alloy shell was 1.17m (*46in*) diameter, charge 350kg (*772lb*) and mooring depths 400m (*219 fathoms*) or 600m (*328 fathoms*).

TM SERIES

Influence mines laid from the TT of U boats.

TMA (British designation GT)

First washed ashore July 1941. A moored magnetic mine introduced in 1940 was known to have been laid by surface craft and seaplanes as well as by U-boats. It proved unsatisfactory and was withdrawn in 1941. The aluminium alloy shell was 0.53m (*21in*) diameter and 2.7m (*106in*) long and the charge was 230kg (*507lb*) with mooring depths 150m (*82 fathoms*) or 270m (*148 fathoms*).

TMB (British designation GS)

First recovered May 1940 (magnetic). A ground influence mine, the magnetic version in service in 1939, being followed by acoustic or magnetic/acoustic types. The cylindrical shell was aluminium alloy and said to lay badly on the seabed. The charge varied from 420-560kg (*926-1235lb*) and the mine was normally laid in 22-27m (*12-15 fathoms*). TMB/S, introduced in 1940, was for laying from the TT of E-boats.

TMA moored influence (magnetic) mine. Laid from TT of U-boats, also by surface craft and seaplanes (withdrawn in 1941).

1. Mooring rope
2. Buoyancy chamber
3. Charge
4. Bowden wire
5. Fins
6. Mooring shackle
7. Mechanism plate covered by light casing

John Lambert

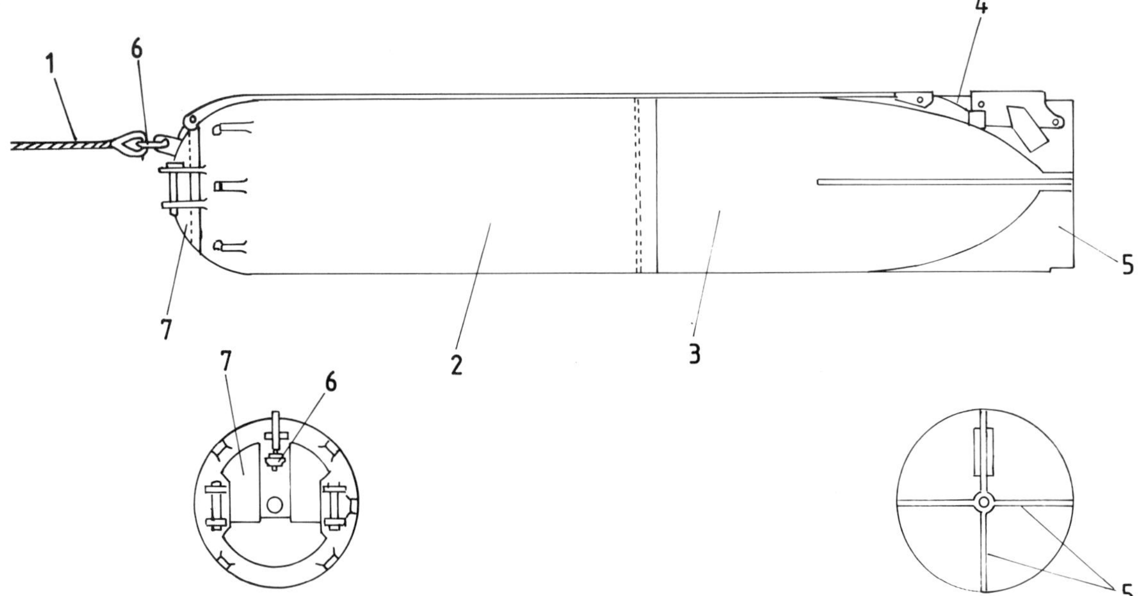

TMB ground influence mine laid from TT of U-boats.

1 Deflector plate
2 Arming clock starter
3 80-day clock cover
4 Mechanism cover
5 Primer placer

John Lambert

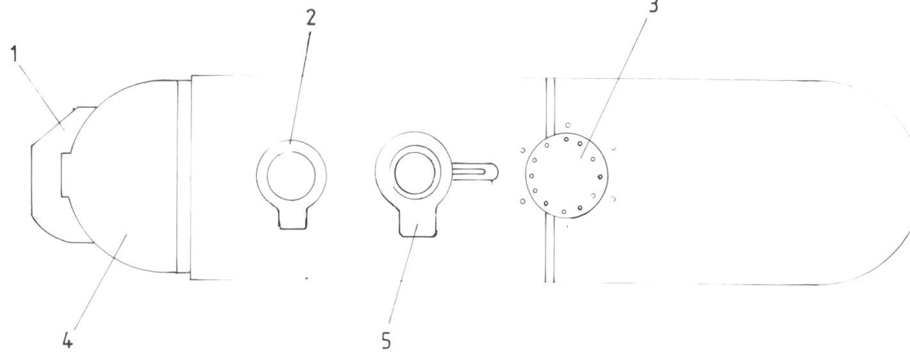

TMC (British designation GN)

Introduced in 1940, this ground influence mine was an enlarged TMB. Firing could be magnetic, acoustic or from 1942 magnetic/acoustic. The aluminium alloy shell was 0.53m (*21in*) diameter and 3.38m (*133in*) long. The charge was 860-930kg (*1896-2050lb*) and the mine was laid down to 37m (*20 fathoms*).

MT SERIES

Ground mine torpedoes laid from TT.

MTA

This apparently dated from 1942 but details have not been found.

LM SERIES

Airborne parachute mines.

LMA (British designation GD)

First recovered July 1940 (magnetic). This ground influence mine with aluminium alloy shell was in service in 1939 with magnetic firing and later with acoustic or magnetic/acoustic. The charge was 300kg (*661lb*), total weight 550kg (*1213lb*), and a 22sec delay impact fuze could be fitted, which exploded the mine if it fell on dry land or in water less than 3.7m (*12ft*) deep. A seldom-used setting would explode the mine if it was moved into shallow water.

An earlier version with British designation GA and later obsolete was first recovered 23 November 1939.

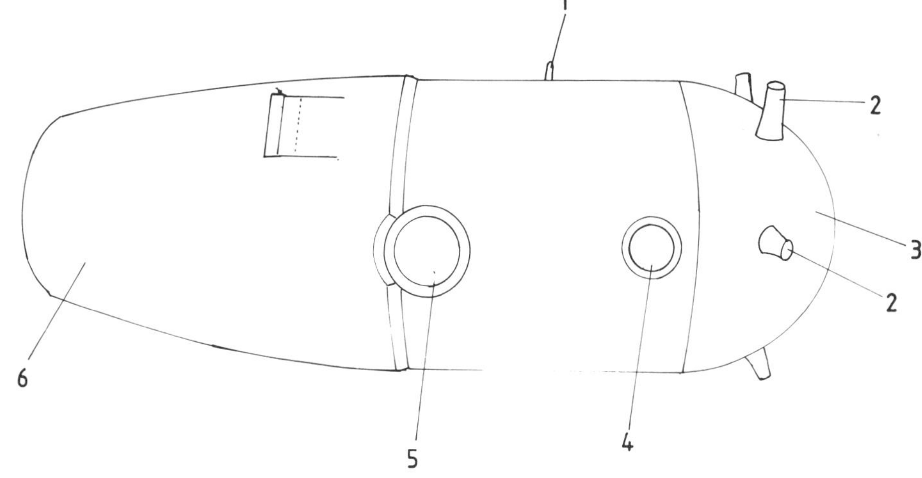

LMA early pattern airborne parachute ground influence (magnetic) mine. Obsolescent in 1940.

1 Lifting lug
2 Anti-roll bars
3 Filling plate
4 Detonator cover plate
5 Clock starter plate
6 Parachute housing

John Lambert

LMB (British designation GC)

First recovered May 1940 (magnetic), October 1940 (acoustic). A larger ground influence mine than LMA. It had an aluminium alloy shell and was in service in 1939 with magnetic firing and later with acoustic or magnetic/ acoustic while in 1944 some had magnetic/pressure firing. The charge was 705kg (*1554lb*), total weight 960kg (*2116lb*) and an impact fuze could be fitted as in LMA.

LMB/S introduced in the first half of 1943 was adapted for E boats but was liable to countermining, while LMB III introduced in July/August 1943 had an acoustic unit designed against ships with bow noise-making gear.

An early version later obsolete with British designation GB was first recovered in December 1939.

LMF (British designation GP)

A moored influence mine, generally magnetic, dating from 1942 and apparently first used by E-boats in the first half of 1943, this version being known as LMF/S. The airborne LMF had an aluminium alloy shell 0.65m (*25.6in*) diameter × 2.7m (*106in*) with 290kg (*639lb*) charge. Mooring depths were 150m (*82 fathoms*), 200m (*109 fathoms*), or 300m (*164 fathoms*), though 100m (*55 fathoms*) was quoted initially. Total weight was 1050kg (*2315lb*).

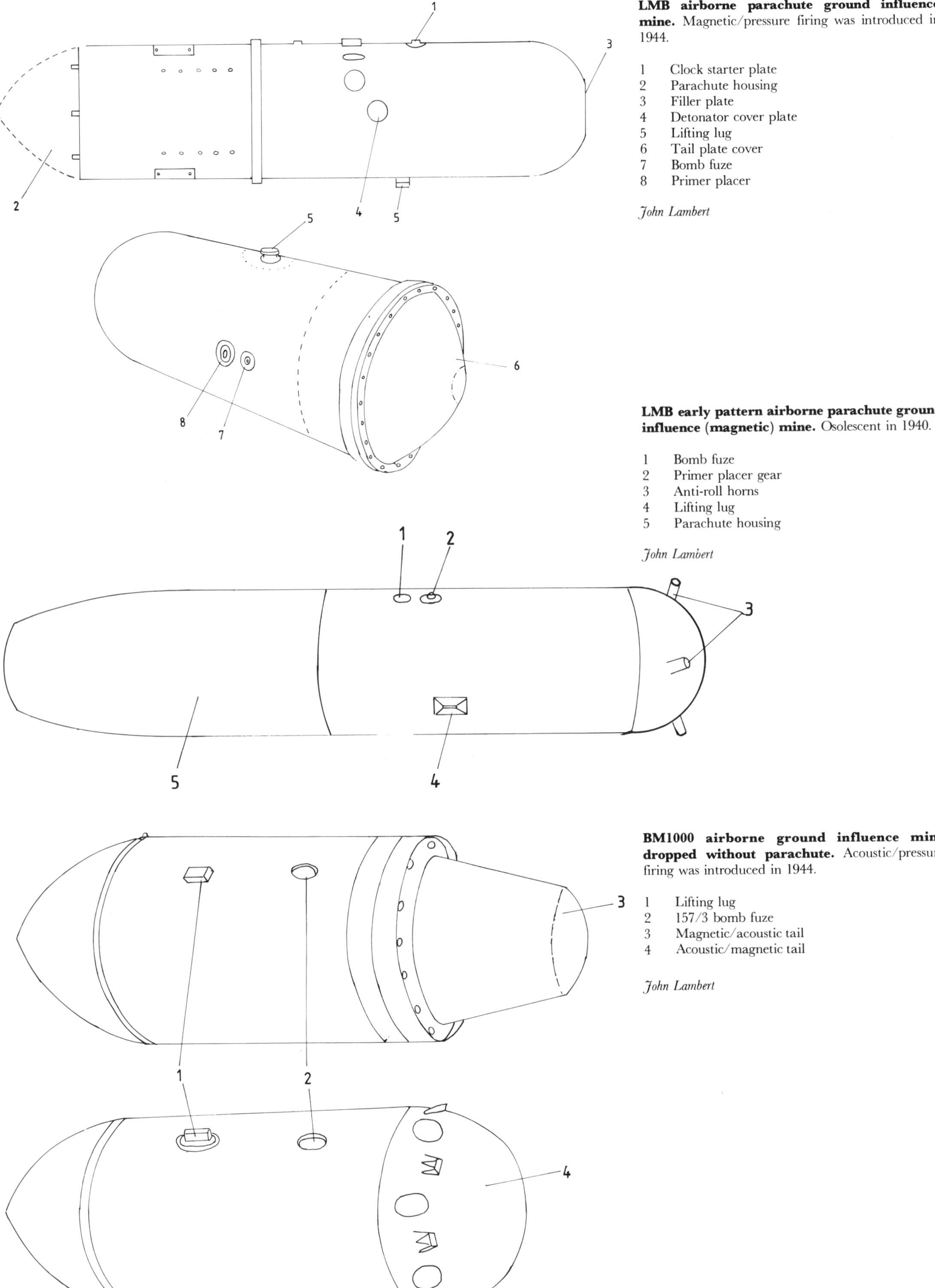

LMB airborne parachute ground influence mine. Magnetic/pressure firing was introduced in 1944.

1 Clock starter plate
2 Parachute housing
3 Filler plate
4 Detonator cover plate
5 Lifting lug
6 Tail plate cover
7 Bomb fuze
8 Primer placer

John Lambert

LMB early pattern airborne parachute ground influence (magnetic) mine. Osolescent in 1940.

1 Bomb fuze
2 Primer placer gear
3 Anti-roll horns
4 Lifting lug
5 Parachute housing

John Lambert

BM1000 airborne ground influence mine dropped without parachute. Acoustic/pressure firing was introduced in 1944.

1 Lifting lug
2 157/3 bomb fuze
3 Magnetic/acoustic tail
4 Acoustic/magnetic tail

John Lambert

BM SERIES

Airborne mines with no parachute.

BM 1000 (British designation GG)

First recovered May 1941 (magnetic). A ground influence mine with 680kg (*1499lb*) charge, total weight 1000kg (*2205lb*) and magnetic, acoustic, magnetic/acoustic firing or from 1944 acoustic/pressure. The shell was non-magnetic steel. An impact fuze could also be fitted which was designed to explode the mines instantaneously if they fell on hard ground or with a 90 second delay if they fell on soft ground or in the water less than 7.3m (*24ft*) deep. It would also explode the mines if they were subsequently moved into water of less than this depth. Without this impact fuze they could be dropped in 6m (*20ft*) water from 500m (*1640ft*) or less, in 9m (*30ft*) from 500–1000m (*1640–3280ft*) and in 11m (*36ft*) from over 1000m (*3280ft*). The maximum dropping height was 6000m (*19,700ft*), and it was apparently used in water up to 35m (*19 fathoms*).

BMA

Believed to have a charge of about 600kg (*1323lb*).

BMC (British designation GM)

A moored contact mine introduced in July/August 1943 with a shell 0.66m (*26in*) diameter × 1m (*39in*). The charge was 50kg (*110lb*) and there were four 'push-rod' horns with a seawater battery. Mooring depth was 150m (*82 fathoms*) and total weight 620kg (*1367lb*).

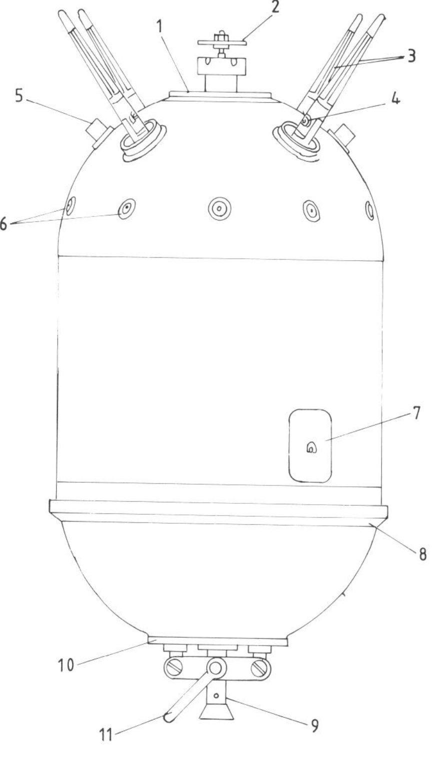

BMC airborne moored contact mine, no parachute.

1 Cover plate carrying master switch
2 Horn release plate
3 Four push-rod horns
4 Hinge
5 Tapped bosses
6 Welded projections
7 Plate covering detonator pocket
8 Seating band for sinker
9 Sinker securing spindle
10 Mechanism plate
11 Mooring shackle

John Lambert

CHARGES FOR EXPLOSIVE MOTOR BOATS

These boats, known as Linsen, were not suicide craft. They were used in groups of three, two being explosive boats and the other a control boat. The explosive boats each with a 300kg (*661lb*) charge, were steered to a suitable distance from the target when the control boat took over and the explosive boats' crew jumped overboard to be picked up by the control boat.

BOMBS, ROCKETS AND GUIDED MISSILES

BOMBS

No German aircraft carrier project was ever completed, and the *Luftwaffe* was not primarily geared to naval operations. None the less, several effective bombs for attacking warships and other vessels were developed.

The most important of these were of 500kg (*1100lb*) and 1000kg (*2200lb*) nominal weight. Rocket-accelerated versions designed to pierce 14cm ($5\frac{1}{2}$*in*) and 17cm ($6\frac{3}{4}$*in*) armour respectively, had fillings of desensitized TNT with base fuses and, in the case of the 1000kg, a shock-absorbing block at the head of the cavity.

AP Bombs

Data

Nominal weight	500kg (*1100lb*)	1000kg (*2200lb*)
Bursting charge	15kg (*33lb*)	55kg (*121lb*)
Max body dia	300mm (*11.81in*)	398mm (*15.67in*)
Tail dia	362mm (*14.25in*)	510mm (*20.08in*)
Length of body	856mm (*33.46in*)	1190mm (*46.85in*)
Length oa	2100mm (*82.68in*)	2220mm (*87.40in*)

These included bombs of 500kg (*1100lb*), 1000kg (*2200lb*) and 1400kg (*3090lb*) nominal weight. The fillings were of desensitized TNT, with side fuzes and apparently a shock absorbing block at the head of the cavity in all. The 1400kg known as 'Fritz' had a hardened head to 64cm (*25.2in*) from the nose, and a transitional zone of 15cm (*6in*). The guided version known as 'Fritz' X or FX-1400 is noted below. The designed piercing limits were respectively 8cm (*3.1in*), 10-14cm (*3.9-5.5in*), 11.5-16cm (*4.5-6.3in*) and dimensions were as shown in the table.

SAP Bombs

Data

Nominal weight	500kg (*1100lb*)	1000kg (*2200lb*)	1400kg (*3090lb*)
Bursting charge	*c*100kg (*c220lb*)	*c*160kg (*c353lb*)	*c*300kg (*c661lb*)
Dia	396mm (*15.59in*)	500m (*19.69in*)	562mm (*22.13in*)
Length of body	1370mm (*53.94in*)	1476mm (*58.11in*)	1932mm (*76.06in*)
Length oa	2007mm (*79.02in*)	2100mm (*82.68in*)	2836mm (*111.65in*)

FX-1400 Guided Bomb

The FX-1400 guided bomb had course correction by radio from the parent aircraft, usually a Do217, and a tail flare to aid visual steering. It was dropped from 3700-5800m (*12,000-19,000ft*), the bomb aimer having to keep a straight and level course, reducing speed after release, which apparently accounted for only 400-500 being made. Experiments were carried out from February 1942 to mid 1943 when it was used in a raid on Malta with little success. Attacks on shipping in the Sicilian landings also achieved little, but off Salerno it very seriously damaged *Warspite, Savannah* and *Uganda*. Its great success was however the fatal hit on the new Italian battleship *Roma* when steaming at 30kts and in the middle of a 90° turn. FX-1400 seems to have been last used in April 1944 in a raid on Plymouth, but caused little damage.

Other heavy bombs

Data

Nominal weight	1025kg (*2260lb*)	1700kg (*3750lb*)
Bursting charge	*c*520kg (*1146lb*)	*c*700kg (*1543lb*)
Dia	654mm (*25.75in*)	660m (*25.98in*)
Length of body	1885mm (*74.21in*)	2315mm (*91.14in*)
Length oa	2800mm (*110.24in*)	3300mm (*129.92in*)

These included 1025kg (*2260lb*) and 1700kg (*3750lb*) bombs known as 'Pandora' and 'Paul' and roughly equivalent to British MC bombs. The construction differed as the 1025kg had a thin body and base welded to a thicker head, and the 1700kg was of one-piece construction. The fillings were of amatol type, apparently with aluminium additions in the 1025kg, and side fuzes were used with a shock absorbing block at the end of the cavity in the 1700kg. The 1025kg would go through a 40-50mm (*1.6-2in*) deck, and the 1700kg one of 6-8cm (*2.4-3.1in*) but both would break up on greater thicknesses.

There were also 1800kg (*3970lb*) and 2500kg (*5510lb*) bombs but, unlike the 1700kg above, these were of welded construction with tube bodies and cast heads and bases. Details have not been found for the 2500kg, but the 1800kg known as 'Satan' had the same diameter as the 1700kg, with a longer body of about 2667mm (*105in*) and a bursting charge of 990kg (*2183lb*).

ROCKETS

For a country which brought the V2 into service, used a 21cm airborne rocket effectively against heavy bomber formations, and had several AA weapons in advanced development, as well as a project in the early design stages for a submersible towed vessel to carry and launch 3-V2 rockets, it is remarkable that the rockets in service in the German Navy comprised only the 7.3cm (*2.874in*) Föhn and another of 8.6cm (*3.386in*), known from the launcher mounting as R Ag M42/43.

Föhn was fired from racks containing 35 launching trays in five tiers and at 1400-1600m (*1530-1750yd*) the 35 rockets would cover an area of 90 × 120m (*100 × 130yd*), though they were sometimes fired in two salvos. The rocket head weighed 2.64kg (*5.82lb*) with an 11.4% burster and had a time and percussion fuze usually set to 6.5sec. Maximum velocity was 300m/s (*984f/s*) with range 4200m/45° (*4590yd*) and ceiling 2400m/90° (*7870ft*). The launching rack weighed 600kg (*1323lb*).

The low-velocity 8.6cm rocket was fired from single tubular launchers weighing about 36kg (*79lb*) at 2-2.5sec intervals. A number of different types were developed, limited in service to five. They were black powder propelled with 8-4.5mm (*0.177in*) nozzles at 9° angle, and spin stabilised. The HE versions weighed about 8.4kg (*18.5lb*) and had time and percussion fuzes set to 400m (*440yd*) or 800m (*870yd*). These were used with others containing parachutes and 100mm (*328ft*) of steel wire and opening at 300-400m (*330-440yd*) or at 800-1000m (*870-1090yd*). They were lighter than the HE versions at 5-5.3kg (*11-11.7lb*). An illuminating version weighing 4.3kg (*9.5lb*) was intended for use with HE at surface targets.

Against aircraft the rockets were used in barrage fire, each launcher firing five of the 1000m parachute and wire type followed by two five-round groups, the first of the short range parachute and wire or the 800m HE, and the second of the 400m HE. Each group was of a single type of rocket. It does not appear that either the 8.6 or 7.3cm rockets had any great success.

Among weapons in various stages of development were an anti-submarine rocket 28cm (*11in*) or 30.5cm (*12in*) diameter, with a fuze activated by water pressure on a rubber membrane and exploding on impact or at 10-12m (*33-39ft*), and a rocket propelled spherical skip bomb, known as 'Kurt'. The bomb was 75cm (*29.5in*) diameter and weighed about 300kg (*660lb*). It had impact and hydrostatic fuzes. On striking the water the rocket was blown off, and the bomb skimmed the water, until it hit the target where it sank and was detonated. It was not a success and only 40 to 50 were made.

GUIDED MISSILES

Germany was well ahead of other countries in the development of these at the end of the war, and 'Wasserfall', a command guidance supersonic land based AA weapon, was nearing completion of operational trials. There was no similar naval weapon in this advanced state, but airborne guided weapons had been used against ships with fair success since the second half of 1943. Of these the FX-1400 is noted with other heavy bombs, but the Hs293 was a true guided missile, and is described below. Mistel, a composite aircraft with a long fuselage Ju88H as the drone and a piloted Me109 or Fw190 temporarily fixed to it, was intended for attacks on large warships if fitted with a large hollow charge warhead, but it was apparently not so used.

Hs293

This was a small monoplane developed by Henschel with span 3.23m (*10ft 7in*), length 4.128m (*13ft 6½in*) and weight about 770kg (*1700lb*). The warhead weighed about 500kg (*1100lb*) with 310kg (*683lb*) explosive charge. A small rocket engine carried under the main body was started after release from the parent aircraft. The fuel was hydrogen peroxide decomposed by sudden admission to sodium permanganate to steam and oxygen. This was wasteful as 47% of the gas was free oxygen, but it was very simple and adequate for the short range Hs293. The usual parent aircraft were the Do217 and He177, each of which could carry two, and they were controlled by radio from the parent aircraft which had a special missile operator. There was a flare in the tail of the Hs293 to assist aiming, and operational range was apparently 4000–20,000m (*c4400–22,000yd*) with a speed of 300–400kts depending on flight angles.

The missile was first used successfully on 27 August 1943, when the sloop *Egret* was blown up, and it was effective against shipping, though other warships of escort vessel status and above lost due to it comprised only the cruiser *Spartan* which capsized in about 1¼ hours on 29 January 1944, the destroyer *Inglefield* and the 'Hunts' *Dulverton* and *Rockwood*, the last named being classed as not worth repair. It could usually be dealt with by concentrated close-range AA fire, and smoke screens could be effective, but the real counter was radio-jamming equipment with skilled operators, both of which took some time to procure.

Later members of the Hs293 series included at least one with a bomb-torpedo warhead but these do not appear to have reached operational service.

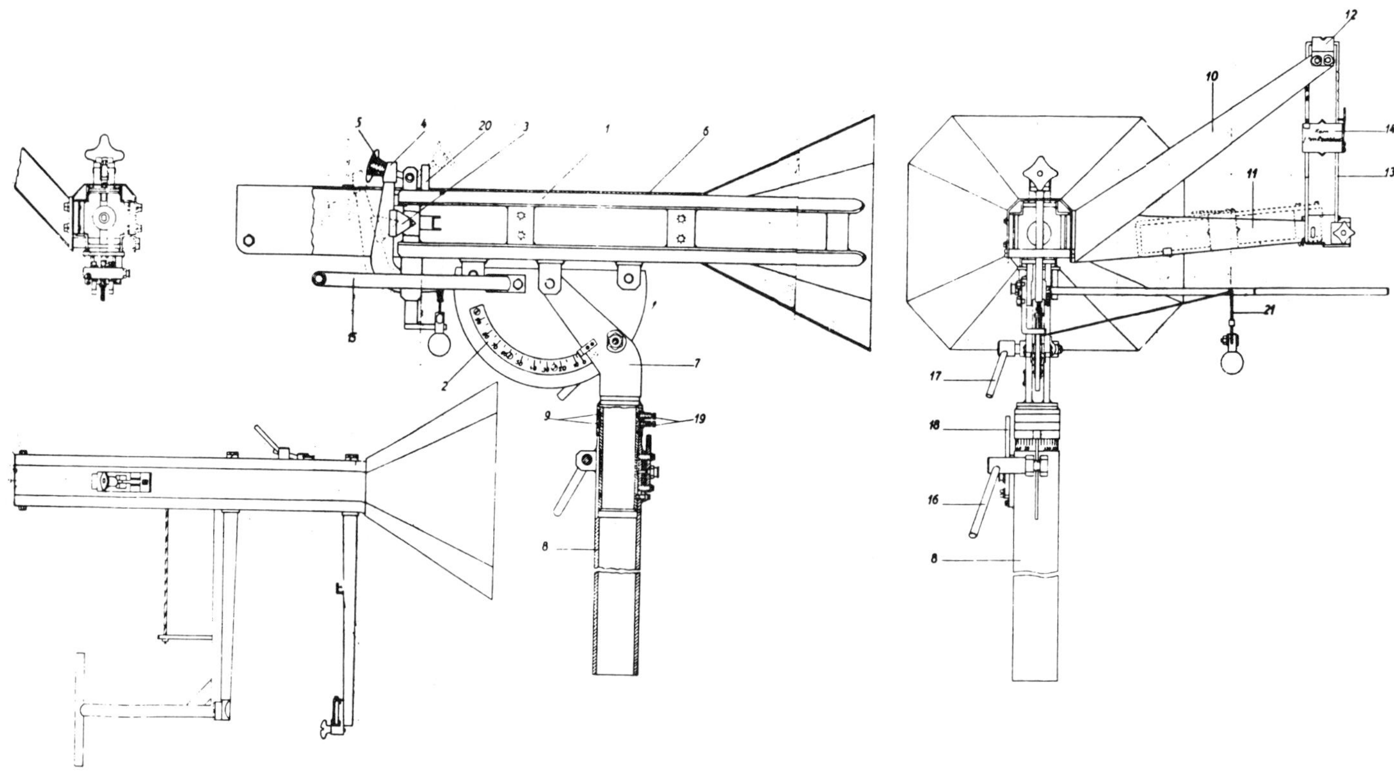

Rocket launcher M42 for 8.6cm rocket.

1 Launching trough
2 Elevation scale
3 Firing hammer
4 Striker
5 Striker screw
6 Protective steel sheet
7 Fork
8 Tubular column
9 Clampring
10 Arm
11 Arm
12 Back sight
13 Lever
14 Fore sight
15 Training arm
16 Clamp
17 Clamp
18 Stop
19 Screws
20 Holding ring
21 Wire cable

Official drawing, by courtesy of Mike Whitley

FRANCE

The relative strength and standing of the French navy have always been liable to wide fluctuations, but in the late 1930s both were increasing to a level not attained since the beginning of the century. Unfortunately, as a result of the disastrous defeat of the French armies in 1940, the navy was not able to operate as a united force. Its strongest feature was probably its gun armament for surface fire, though this was handicapped by lack of sufficient development effort on new items (such as some of the complicated mountings) before their introduction to service. On the other hand anti-aircraft defence was particularly weak, especially at close range, except for those ships rearmed in America. Underwater weapons do not appear to have had any outstanding features apart from the turbine in the 40cm (*15.75in*) torpedo, with higher gas temperatures than usual.

NAVAL GUNS

The French had pioneered the use of autofretted components, and their later medium and light naval guns were usually of advanced construction, as shown in the individual descriptions. Heavy guns, although fitted with loose liners in the more recent designs, were still of complicated assembly with very many component parts by British standards. Upward opening screw breech blocks were a French innovation in the heavier guns.

Muzzle velocities tended to be high for a given shell weight in the main armament of battleships and cruisers, though the French were too experienced to attempt to rival Italian figures, and in most destroyer and AA guns the muzzle velocities were lower than usual. The standard charge temperature for the determination of muzzle velocity was 20°C (*68*°F).

A remarkable collection of old, and sometimes very old, guns were used to arm merchant ships and auxiliaries, and in the 203mm (*7.992in*) M1931 A tubes from an obsolescent though still powerful 240mm (*9.449in*) are believed to have been re-used after suitable adaptation.

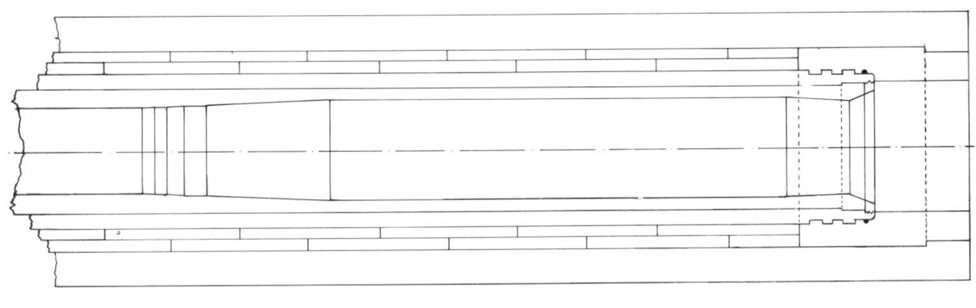

380mm/45 M1935, structure of breech end. This shows the two rows of short hoops, a traditional French method of construction, surprisingly retained in the 380mm.
John Lambert

GUN MOUNTINGS

As will be seen from the individual descriptions, French gun mountings varied considerably in design. They were usually powered electrically with RPC in the later installations, and the newer turrets and base ring mountings (except the 380mm) were supported on ball races, and not roller races as were the earlier. Quadruple mountings, which would have been a feature of the battleships whose construction was abandoned in the First World War, were present in the new capital ships for the main armament and, with less justification, for the DP secondary armament in the first two. Except perhaps for barrage fire, this limited their AA capabilities, and the same was the case with the heavier calibre triples in the next ships, where the AA role had to be virtually abandoned.

The main armament quadruple turrets differed from the British in the *King George V* class in being essentially two twins in a common barbette, as indeed were the DP quadruples. The disadvantage of quadruple mountings was shown in the action at Casablanca, where A turret in the *Jean Bart*, the only one then with guns, was jammed for 9¼ hours by a 16in (*406.4mm*) shell from the *Massachusetts* which ricocheted against the edge of the 150mm (*5.9in*) cap plate protecting the horizontal space between barbette and turret. A large piece of the cap plate was gouged up and jammed the turret in train. On the other hand, the two twin arrangement demonstrated its advantages at Mers El Kébir when a 15in (*381mm*) shell from the *Hood* struck the 150mm (*5.9in*) roof of B turret in the *Dunkerque* over the right outer gunport. Most of the shell bounced off, but the roof was holed and armour fragments, or perhaps part of the shell, entered and two quarter-charges caught fire, killing all the starboard gun crew. The port guns were however able to continue in action.

Dunkerque firing 330mm/50 M1931. The quadruple turrets are operating as double twins, the normal procedure.
Jacques Navarret

PROPELLANTS

The most widely used French propellant was still nitrocellulose, in strip form and known as BM. This had in earlier years an evil reputation for spontaneous ignition, as demonstrated in the *Iéna* and *Liberté* disasters, but manufacture had been much improved and up to 2% of diphenylamine incorporated as stabiliser. The calorific value is generally given as 870, with T_0 at around 3020-3030°K. The thickness of the strip was indicated by an arbitrary number, increasing with thickness, and it is believed that the actual figures were as given in the table.

	mm	in
BM5	1.6	0.063
BM7	1.7	0.067
BM9	1.85	0.073
BM11	2.3	0.091
BM13	2.95	0.116
BM15	3.6	0.142
BM16	3.95	0.156
BM17	4.3	0.169

A more modern, 'solventless' propellant known as SD was used in 380mm (*14.96in*), 330mm (*12.99in*) and as an alternative in a few other guns. It was in single tube grain form, and the composition was 64-65% nitrocellulose, 25% nitroglycerin and 8-9% centralite. The calorific value was about 800 and T_0 2600°K approximately. SD_{19} had apparently a grain 14mm (*0.55in*) external and 4mm (*0.157in*) internal diameter, but sizes for SD_{21} are not to hand though the difference between external and internal diameters was probably 11.4mm (*0.449in*).

BM reduced flash charges with KCl (potassium chloride) additions, were available for the later 138.6mm (*5.457in*) and many smaller guns. Igniters were black powder, but detailed arrangements are not known. The total for the 47kg (*103.6lb*) BM13 charge in the 203mm (*7.992in*) gun amounted to 0.80kg (*1.76lb*).

Except for older guns, fixed ammunition was used by 100mm (*3.937in*) and smaller, and also by the 130mm (*5.118in*) M1932 and M1935. Separate QF was fired by other 130mm, 138.6mm (*5.457in*) and 152.4mm (*6in*) guns as well as by older 100mm. Larger guns used bag charges. Cartridge cases were normally brass but some 152.4mm (*6in*) were aluminium bronze.

PROJECTILES

French shells probably exhibited more variety than those of any other navy, but certain features were general in the more recent. These were long heads, the total length of the ballistic cap approaching half the overall length of the shell, boat tails (streamlining) and the use of two, or often three, copper driving bands. Bourrelets were standard.

It would be unfair to judge heavy French APC by the 380mm (*14.96in*) prematures at Dakar. This shell was 5cal overall and had a 2.45% burster of picric acid/dinitronaphthalene. The usual proportion is given as 80/20, but an analysis gave 83.2/16.8. As in many piercing shell and base-fuzed HE, a 'K' device was fitted with a supplementary nose fuze for colouring shell splashes. The 330mm (*12.99in*) shell was similar except that the burster was 3.62% possibly in view of the German armoured ships ('pocket battleships') being the most likely target, though the 575kg (*1268lb*) L/4.4 shell for the older 340mm (*13.39in*) had a burster of 3.77%.

For the 330mm HE a burster of 11.5% picric acid (Mélinite) or possibly TNT is given.

Shells for 203mm (*7.992in*) guns were 4.78-5cal long, the latest 134kg (*295lb*) AP M1936 being the shortest. The burster for this is not known, but previous AP had 3.2% and HE *c*6.7%. The explosive was picric acid in the latter, and in some shells in pressed form with paraffin wax or stearine addition, instead of cast.

For 155mm (*6.102in*) guns shells were 5-5.2cal long, base-fuzed HE having a burster of 5.9% picric acid or later 5.2% cast TNT. The latest internally fuzed HE had 9.5% picric acid. 152.4mm (6in) shells are recorded from 4.8 to 5.4cal in length, the latter being an AP with 3.2% burster.

In destroyers, 138.6mm (*5.457in*) guns had L/4.9 base fuzed HE and L/5 internally fuzed HE with respective bursters of 5.95% pressed TNT and 10% cast picric acid. Separate ammunition 130mm (*5.118in*) guns had similar L/5 or L/5.1 shells with smaller bursters, 4.56% pressed TNT, 5.63% cast TNT and 8.3% cast picric acid. Fixed ammunition 130mm had base-fuzed HE with the same pressed TNT filling, but also nose-fuzed HE 4.5cal long with 11% cast TNT.

Star shell was apparently available for 152.4mm (*6in*) to 75mm (*2.953in*) guns.

FIRE-CONTROL

Except for such ships as were equipped with British or US sets in the latter part of the war, there was no fire-control radar, and only a few primitive search installations were fitted. For main armament range-finders it was usual to have two stereoscopic instruments in one housing in the latest ships. Thus the *Richelieu* had two 13.5m (*44.3ft*) RFs in each main turret and another two on the principal director tower. These last had also an additional stereoscopic system for determining small alterations of course by the target. In the *Dunkerque* the installations were similar except that the RFs were 12m (*39.4ft*). The after main armament director tower similarly had 2-8m (*26.2ft*) in both ships, with an additional small alteration of target course instrument in *Richelieu*. This size of stereoscopic RF was also used as a single instrument in the 152.4mm (*6in*) turrets and principal secondary armament director in *Richelieu*, as well as for the main armament in older battleships and the later cruisers, but *Dunkerque*'s secondary armament had 6m (*19.7ft*) instruments.

Precise details of director gyro sights, level and cross-level correctors and fire-control tables or computers are not to hand. The main calculating position was below both armour decks in *Richelieu* and *Dunkerque* with, in the latter at least, facilities for firing at a target over the horizon with data supplied from another ship. For the 130mm (*5.118in*) guns in *Dunkerque* there were two calculating positions with equipment for aircraft and surface fire-control (*conjugateur mécanique*), below both armour decks, and another position aft between the armour decks with graphical equipment (*conjugateur graphique*).

Centralised fire-control and follow-the-pointer equipment do not appear to have been introduced in destroyers until the *Fantasque* class with 138.6mm (*5.457in*)/50 M1929 guns.

RPC was fitted to many mountings as later described, but according to German opinion, satisfactory functioning was doubtful. *Dunkerque*'s main turrets had Sautter-Harlé-Blondel RPC for training. The training motors of director and turrets ran synchronously. A DC circuit also from the director, with voltage produced by hand-operated control and approximately proportional to the training velocity, was guided over a correction generator to the field windings of a Leonard generator, and thus the armature voltage of the Leonard generator was approximately proportional to the training velocity. This did not give exact synchronism for training angle, and

The tower foremast of *Strasbourg* with double 12m range-finders on the main armament director and secondary directors above this and to port of the foremast base.
Jacques Navarret

the training motor was wired so that additional synchronising was produced by an operator correcting any errors by hand control of additional DC excitation in the Ward-Leonard generator.

A similar method was used for elevation and also for the 130mm (*5.118in*), but German sources doubted that the above system could work satisfactorily.

In the cruiser *Foch* the turrets had RPC for training only. The electric motor drove through Janney gear with a constant speed hydraulic pump and hydraulic motor, and this was controlled according to training speed and displacement. Speed control was by hand operation in the director and there was no acceleration control. Errors were corrected by hand. German sources indicate that this worked better than the system in *Dunkerque*.

Jean Bart's A turret, Casablanca 1943. The 380mm guns are in process of removal.
Jacques Navarret

HEAVY CALIBRE GUNS

This was by far the most powerful gun ever mounted in French ships, though exceeded in calibre by the short 420mm (*16.54in*) M1875. It was in quadruple turrets in the *Richelieu* and *Jean Bart* and would also have been in the *Clemenceau*, which was not completed, and the *Gascogne* which was not laid down. The early history of the finished guns was eventful. The *Richelieu* had all her eight guns when she went to Dakar in June 1940, but during the British-Free French attack in September the two starboard guns of B turret, the only one immediately ready for action, both failed at the first salvo. The inner gun burst and the outer one bulged, with the rifling gashed for 8m (*26ft*). The cause was eventually considered to be defective shell. Meanwhile the *Jean Bart* had reached Casablanca in June with four guns in A turret, which was not completed until May 1942. Of the guns for B turret, two were loaded into a

380mm (14.96in)/45 M1935

Gun Data

Bore	380mm	14.96in	
Weight incl BM	94.13t	92.64 tons	
Length oa	17,882mm	704.02in	47.06cal
	17,257mm	679.41in	45.41cal
Length chamber	2830mm	111.42in	
Volume chamber	456.6dm^3	27,863in^3	
Length rifling	14,157mm	557.36in	
Grooves	(80) 3.7 × 8.9mm	0.146 × 0.350in	
Lands	6.0mm	0.236in	
Twist	1 in 25.57		
Weight projectile	884 kg AP	1949lb AP	
Propellant charge	288kg SD_{21}	635lb SD_{21}	
Muzzle velocity	830m/s	2723f/s	
Working pressure	3200kg/cm^2	20.3 tons/in^2	
Approx life	200 EFC		
Max range	41,700m/35°/830m/s	45,600yd/35°/2723f/s	

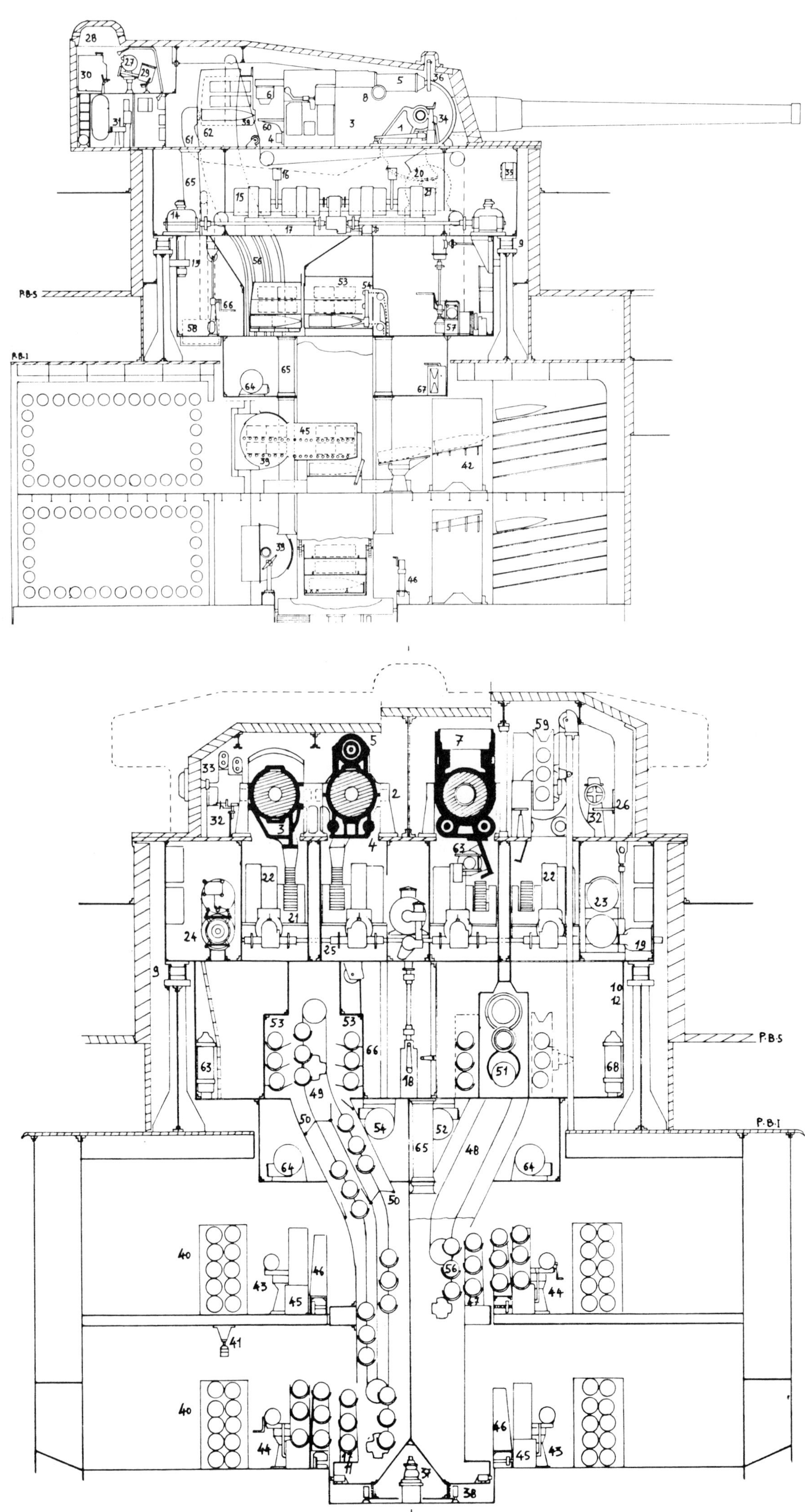
P.B.S
P.B.I

cargo ship at St Nazaire, but the crane then failed, so that the remaining two were mutilated at the yard, and the first two were lost when the cargo ship was sunk by German air attack.

In 1943 when the *Richelieu* was refitted in New York, the four guns from *Jean Bart*'s A turret were transferred to her as replacements and spares. The *Richelieu*'s guns were rebored to take British shell, apparently to 381mm (*15.00in*), though it had been determined before the war that the optimum for this shell was 14.985in (*380.62mm*). Meanwhile, the eight guns originally for *Clemenceau* were taken to Norway by the Germans, though it does not appear that they were actually mounted for coast defence, and it was these guns that were in the *Jean Bart* after the war.

The construction of the guns was a curious mixture of modern and traditional French methods. Drawings of a gun believed to be one of those intended for the *Clemenceau* show a loose liner with rotation prevented by a key in the muzzle bush, and an A tube, with over it a screwed on breech bush, ten hoops and three tubes to the muzzle ending in the muzzle bush. The outer layer comprised a jacket in two lengths. As often with French gun drawings, the breech ring is not shown. Another drawing of the breech end of an earlier gun differs in a double hoop layer, the inner of ten and the outer of nine plus two half-length hoops to break the joins. The liner is shown butting on a short ring screwed into the end of the A tube. External diameters over the chamber are shown in the table.

	mm	in
Chamber	457	17.99
Liner	562	22.13
A tube	697	27.44
First hoop layer	797	31.38
Second hoop layer	897	35.31
Jacket	1200	47.24

Range and Elevation Data for 830m/s (2723f/s) MV

Range (m)	**(yd)**	**Elevation°**	**Descent°**	**Striking V (m/s)**	**(f/s)**
10,000	10,936	4.4	5.2	675	2215
15,000	16,404	7.4	9.0	608	1995
20,000	21,872	10.9	14.0	544	1785
25,000	27,340	14.9	20.2	514	1686
30,000	32,808	19.8	27.2	490	1608
35,000	38,276	25.5	38.1	479	1572

Gun Mounting Data

Revolving weight	2476t	2437 tons
Roller path dia	12.0m	39ft 4in
Barbette int dia	13.3m	43ft 8in
Distance apart gun axes		
Nos 1-2, 3-4	1.95m	76.8in
Nos 2-3	2.95m	116.1in
Recoil	1.325m	52.2in
Max elevating speed	5.5°/sec	
Max training speed	5°/sec	
Firing cycle	25-40sec	
Turret shield	face 450mm; sides 300mm; rear 250mm; roof 195-170mm	face 16.9in; sides 11.8in; rear 9.8in; roof 7.7-6.7in

The Welin screw breech block opened upwards automatically as the gun ran out. It was hydro-pneumatically powered and was balanced by counterweights. The opening and closing times are both given as 3.5sec. An automatic lock with a magazine for ten electric tubes was fitted.

The propellant charges were in quarters, which was unusual with such a heavy charge, and it appears that only AP shell was originally supplied. The figures in the gun data table are for the original French charge, but after *Richelieu*'s 1943 refit, a muzzle velocity of 800m/s (2625f/s) was given for a multitube US charge. The figure of 785m/s (*2575f/s*) sometimes quoted was an arbitrary one for range tables.

The quadruple turret was a St Chamond design developed from the 330mm (*12.99in*). The guns were in two pairs with a 45mm (*1.8in*) bulkhead between them on the turret centre line. Each gun was in a separate cradle but according to some descriptions the relative movement of the guns in a pair was limited, presumably by the elevating gear.

Training and elevation were powered by Leonard circuit electric motors with hydraulic drive, each pair having a single elevating motor with individual drive gear. RPC was fitted for elevation and training and the main power supply to the turret was 460 volt DC. The elevation limits were +35° to -5°. The magazines and shell rooms for each pair were on the same deck at opposite sides of the barbette, with those for one pair on the strengthened inner bottom and for the other pair directly above. Ammunition was fed by a shell and cartridge ring to a dredger hoist, one for each pair, and transferred in the working chamber to the gun loading cages of the upper hoists of which there was one to each gun. The cages had three compartments, the lower for the shell and the other two for two quarter-charges each. An electric chain rammer was carried on an extension from each cradle and loading was at any elevation. A spanning tray to protect the screw threads of the breech cavity ran in and out automatically, and the complete ramming time was 13.5sec.

380mm quadruple turret in longitudinal and transverse sections.

1 Trunnion bearers
2 Trunnions
3 Cradles
4 Recoil cylinders
5 Run-out cylinders
6 Breech-blocks
7 Counterweights for breech-block
8 Flywheel for handworking breech
9 Roller path for conical rollers
10 Clamps
11 Centring rollers at base of trunk
12 Training ring-gear
13 Training pinions
14 Training drive gear
15 Training motors
16 Training motor brakes
17 Training transmission shaft
18 Hand training gear
19 Spring-loaded training stop
20 Elevation arcs
21 Elevation pinions
22 Elevation drive gear
23 Elevation motors
24 Elevation motor brakes
25 Elevation transmission shaft
26 Hand elevation gear
27 Range-finder training gear
28 Range-finder hood
29 Range-finder trainer
30 Range-finder stabilization
31 Auxiliary plotting table
32 Sight-setting, range and deflection
33 Layer's telescopes
34 Auxiliary training position
35 Auxiliary trainer
36 Trainer's periscope
37 Revolving pivot
38 Idler rollers
39 Upper and lower charge drums
40 Supplementary shell stowage
41 Overhead shell grab
42 Shell conveyors in shell rooms
43 Twin rotating waiting tray
44 Twin fixed waiting tray
45 Fixed ammunition ring
46 Revolving ammunition ring
47 Dredger hoist waiting position
48 Short dredger hoist
49 Long dredger hoist
50 Anti-flash flaps
51 Dredger hoist motors
52 Dredger hoist converters
53 Dredger hoist unloading positions
54 Transfer rammers
55 Dredger hoist cage
56 Gun-loading cage guide rails
57 Hand drive for upper hoists
58 Counterweight
59 Cage in shell-ramming position
60 Spanning trays
61 Rammer arm
62 Rammer head
63 Rammer motors and brakes
64 Converters for upper hoists and rammers
65 Trunks for auxiliary hoists
66 Winch for auxiliary hoists
67 Rectifiers
68 Compressed air bottles

Robert Dumas

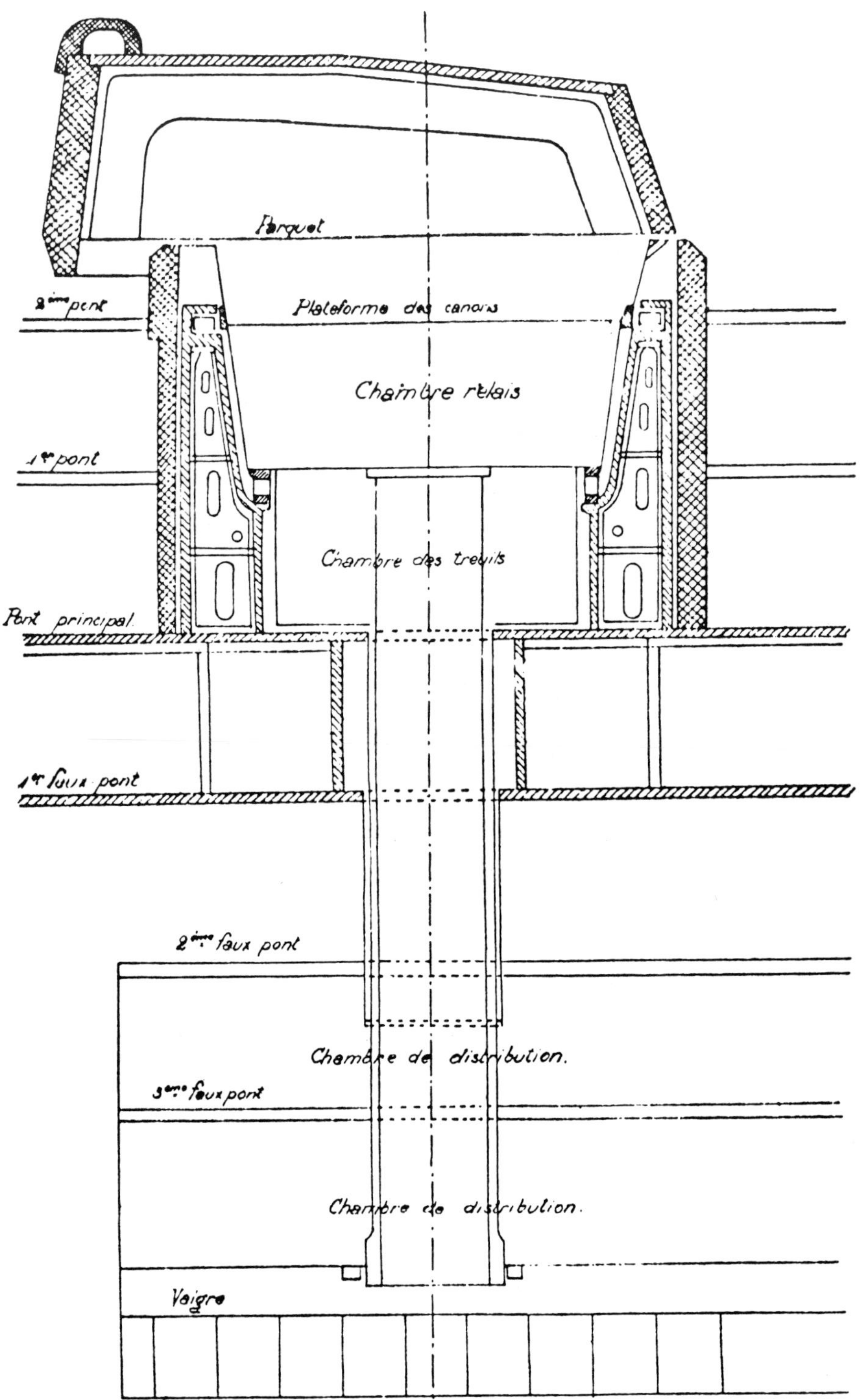

Left: Section of turret installation for 340mm and 305mm guns in *Bretagne* and *Courbet* classes.
Robert Dumas

Right: 340mm coast-defence turret M1924 as installed at Cap Cepet, longitudinal and (overleaf) transverse sections.
Official, by courtesy of Robert Dumas

This gun was in twin turrets in the *Bretagne*, *Lorraine*, and *Provence*, and was to have been in quadruple turrets in the five *Normandie* and four *Lille* class, respectively not completed and not laid down, of the First World War period. There were thus a number of spare guns, and they were mounted for coast defence in two twin turrets at Cap Cepet near Toulon and in four single French versions of the German BSG mounting at Plouharnel near Quiberon. It was also the most favoured French railway gun.

The construction was generally similar in principle to that of the 380mm (*14.96in*) but there was an additional C tube and no loose liner, and the Welin screw breech block is believed to have opened horizontally. The naval propellant charge was in quarters and there were a number of different shells, as listed with the gun data.

The mountings which were modernised to some extent before the war, allowed +23° to -5° elevation with loading at +2°. The guns were in separate cradles and training and elevation were electrically powered with hydraulic drive

340mm (13.39in)/45 M1912

Gun Data (with APC M1924 shell of 4.4 calibre length)

Bore	340mm	13.39in	
Weight incl BM	66.95t	65.89 tons	
Length oa	16,115mm	634.45in	47.40cal
Length bore	15,580mm	613.39in	45.82cal
Length chamber	2055mm	80.91in	
Volume chamber	256.4dm^3	15,646in^3	
Length rifling	13,250mm	521.65in	
Grooves	(102) 1.9 × 7.5mm	0.075 × 0.295in	
Lands	3.0mm	0.118in	
	1 in 29.89		
Weight projectile	575kg AP	1268lb	
Propellant charge	153.5kg BM 16	338.4lb BM 16	
Muzzle velocity	780m/s	2559f/s	
Working pressure	2800kg/cm^2	17.8 tons/in^2	
Approx life	?350 EFC		
Max range	26,600m/23°/780m/s	29,090yd/23°/2559f/s	

The coast defence turret allowed 50° elevation, giving a max range with the above shell of 35,432m (*38749yd*) at 47½°. It is not known how many ships' turrets had been altered to take L/4.4 shell.

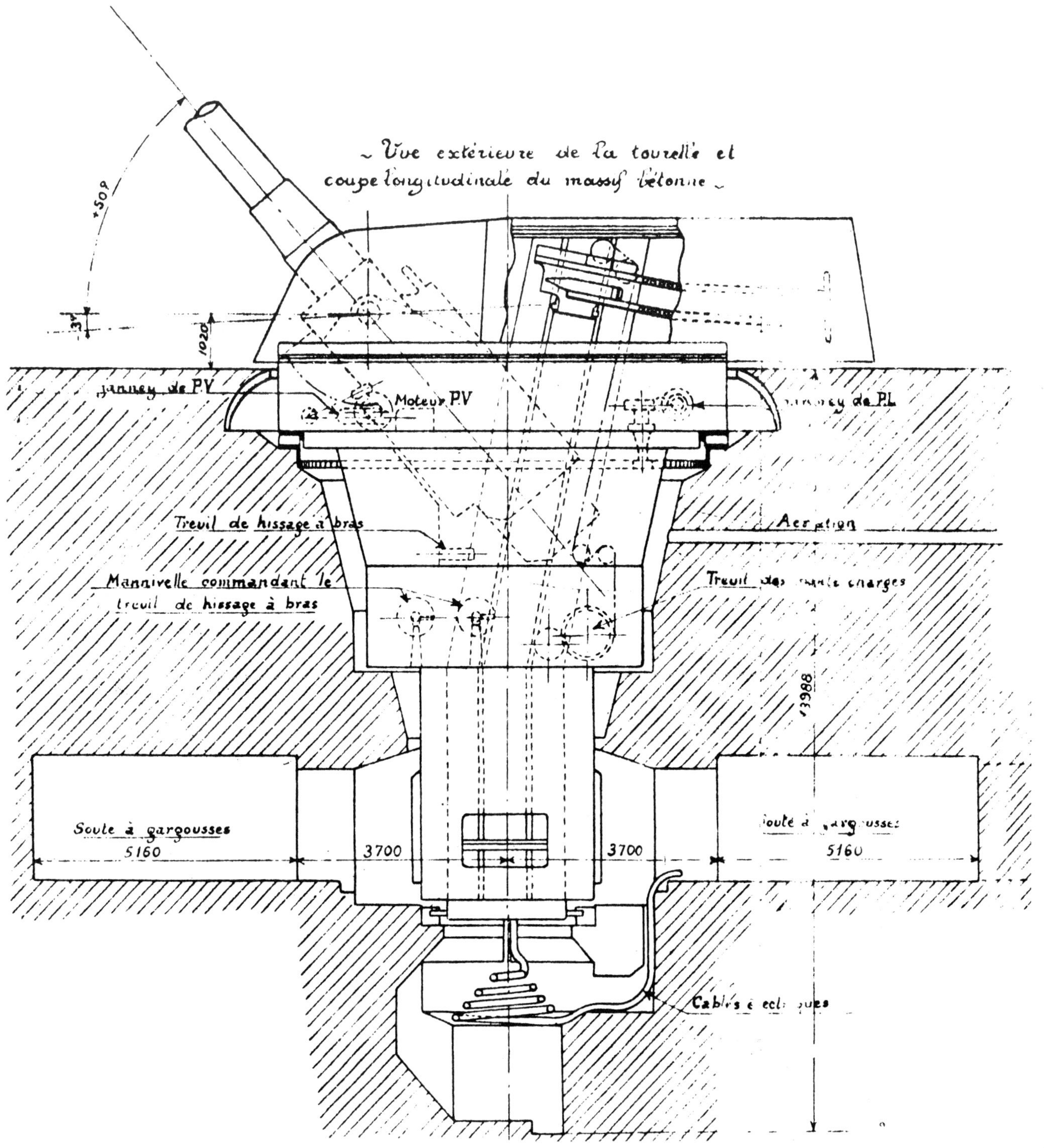

gear. The chain rammers were also electric and the hoists were broken at the working chamber. The gun loading cages had three compartments, the lower for the shell and the others for two quarter-charges each.

Data for Other Shells

Shell	Weight	Propellant charge	MV	Notes
APC M1912 L/3.7	555kg (1224lb)	153.5kg (338.4lb) BM16	794m/s (2605f/s)	K version as L/3.8, 558kg (1230lb)
HE M1926 L/3.1	382kg (842lb)	140kg (308.6lb) BM15	885m/s (2904f/s)	
HE 15A	465kg (1025lb)	153.5kg (338.4lb) BM16	893m/s (2930f/s)	Railway guns
HE17 FATO	445kg (981lb)	177kg (390lb) SD19G	916m/s (3005f/s)	Railway guns
HE FATO 32-6°	431.8kg (952lb)	177kg (390lb) SD19G	921m/s (3022f/s)	Railway guns

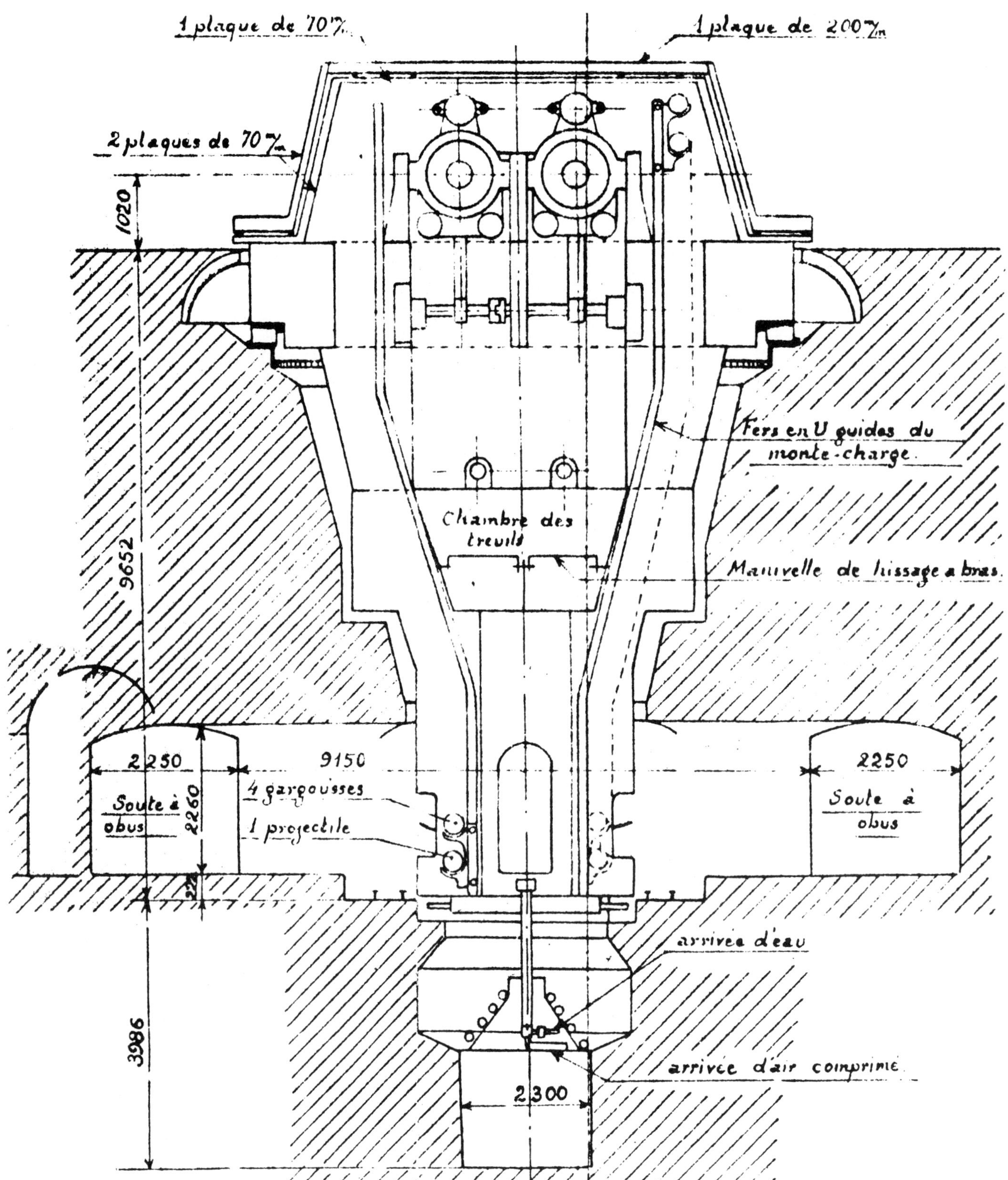
1 plaque de 70%
1 plaque de 200%
2 plaques de 70%
1020
9652
Fers en U guides du monte-charge
Chambre des treuils
Manivelle de hissage à bras
2250
9150
2250
Soute à obus
2260
4 gargousses
1 projectile
Soute à obus
arrivée d'eau
3986
arrivée d'air comprimé
2300

330mm A turret in *Strasbourg* October 1941.
Jacques Navarret

This gun was mounted in quadruple turrets in the *Dunkerque* and *Strasbourg*. Drawings have not been found, but the construction is believed to have been very similar to that of the 380mm (*14.96in*). There was a loose autofretted liner and it is probable that there was only a single row of hoops over the breech end of the A tube. Breech mechanism details were as in the 380mm, but opening and closing times slightly faster at 3sec. Propellant charges were in quarters and AP and HE shells were available.

The turrets, developed by St Chamond, were in many respects smaller versions of the 380mm, and the description of the latter applies to the 330mm, except that the ramming time was probably a little less than 13.5sec and that the bulkhead between gun pairs was 40mm (*1.6in*) and, as may have been the case in the larger turret, extended to the working chamber where it was apparently 25mm (*1in*). Additional items of information were that the 100HP training motor was duplicated as was the Leonard generator, to give 100% reserve, that the elevating motors were both 75HP and that the supporting ball race contained 152 balls of 182mm (*7.17in*) diameter. The Sautter-Harlé-Blondel RPC gear was apparently far from satisfactory.

330mm (12.99in)/50 M1931

Gun Data

Bore	330mm	12.99in	
Weight incl BM	70.535t	69.42 tons	
Length oa	17,170mm	675.98in	52.03cal
Length bore	16,645mm	655.31in	50.44cal
Length chamber	2470mm	97.24in	
Volume chamber	293dm^3	17,880in^3	
Length rifling	13,940mm	548.82in	
Grooves	(80) 3.2 × 7.73m?	0.126 × 0.304in?	
Lands	5.2mm?	0.205in?	
Twist	1 in 25.57		
Weight projectile	560kg AP	1235lb AP	
Propellant charge	192kg SD_{19}	423lb SD_{19}	
Muzzle velocity	870m/s	2854f/s	
Working pressure	3200kg/cm^2	20.3 tons/in^2	
Approx life	250 EFC		
Max range	41,700m/35°/870m/s	45,600yd/35°/2854f/s	

The HE shell weighed 522kg (*1151lb*) and with the above charge MV was 885m/s (*2904f/s*) and 35° range 40,600m (*44,400yd*).

Range and Elevation Data for 870m/s (2854f/s) MV

Range (m)	**(yd)**	**Elevation °**	**Descent°**	**Striking V (m/s)**	**(f/s)**
10,000	10,936	4.3	5.2	689	2261
15,000	16,404	7.2	9.1	611	2005
20,000	21,872	10.2	14.2	535	1755
25,000	27,340	14.8	21.3	492	1614
30,000	32,808	19.6	28.8	466	1529
35,000	38,276	25.4	36.8	461	1512

Gun Mounting Data

Revolving weight	1497t	1473 tons
Ball track dia	10.4m	34ft 1in
Barbette int dia	11.5m	37ft 9in
Distance apart gun axes		
Nos 1-2, 3-4	1.69m	66.5in
Nos 2-3	2.54m	100in
Recoil	1.15m	45.3in
Max elevating speed	6°/sec	
Max training speed	5°/sec	
Firing cycle	22-40sec	
Turret shield	face 330mm; sides 250mm; rear (A) 345mm, (B) 335mm; roof 150mm	face 13in; sides 9.8in; rear (A) 13.6m, (B) 13.2in; roof 5.9in
Strasbourg differs in	face 360mm; rear (A,B) 355mm; roof 160mm	face 14.2in, rear (A,B) 14in; roof 6.3in

330mm quadruple turret in longitudinal and transverse sections.

1 Superstructure deck
2 Upper deck
3 Upper armour deck
4 Lower armour deck
5 Armoured barbette base
6 Upper hoist
7 Lower hoist
8 Turret roof
9 Side glacis, 50mm + 100mm
10 Turret floor, 50mm
11 Turret pan floor
12 Working chamber floor
13 Working chamber lower platform
14 Trunk
15 Ring bulkhead
16 Supports for ball track
17 Ball track
18 Clamps
19 Training motors
20 Training transmission shaft
21 Training drive gear
22 Training pinion
23 Training converter
24 Elevation converter
25 Elevation motor
26 Elevation transmission shaft
27 Elevation clutch for one gun
28 Elevation gear-case
29 Elevation drive gear
30 Elevation arc
31 Cradle
32 Recoil cylinders
33 Run-out cylinders
34 Centring rollers for trunk
35 Revolving pivot
36 Compressed air bottles

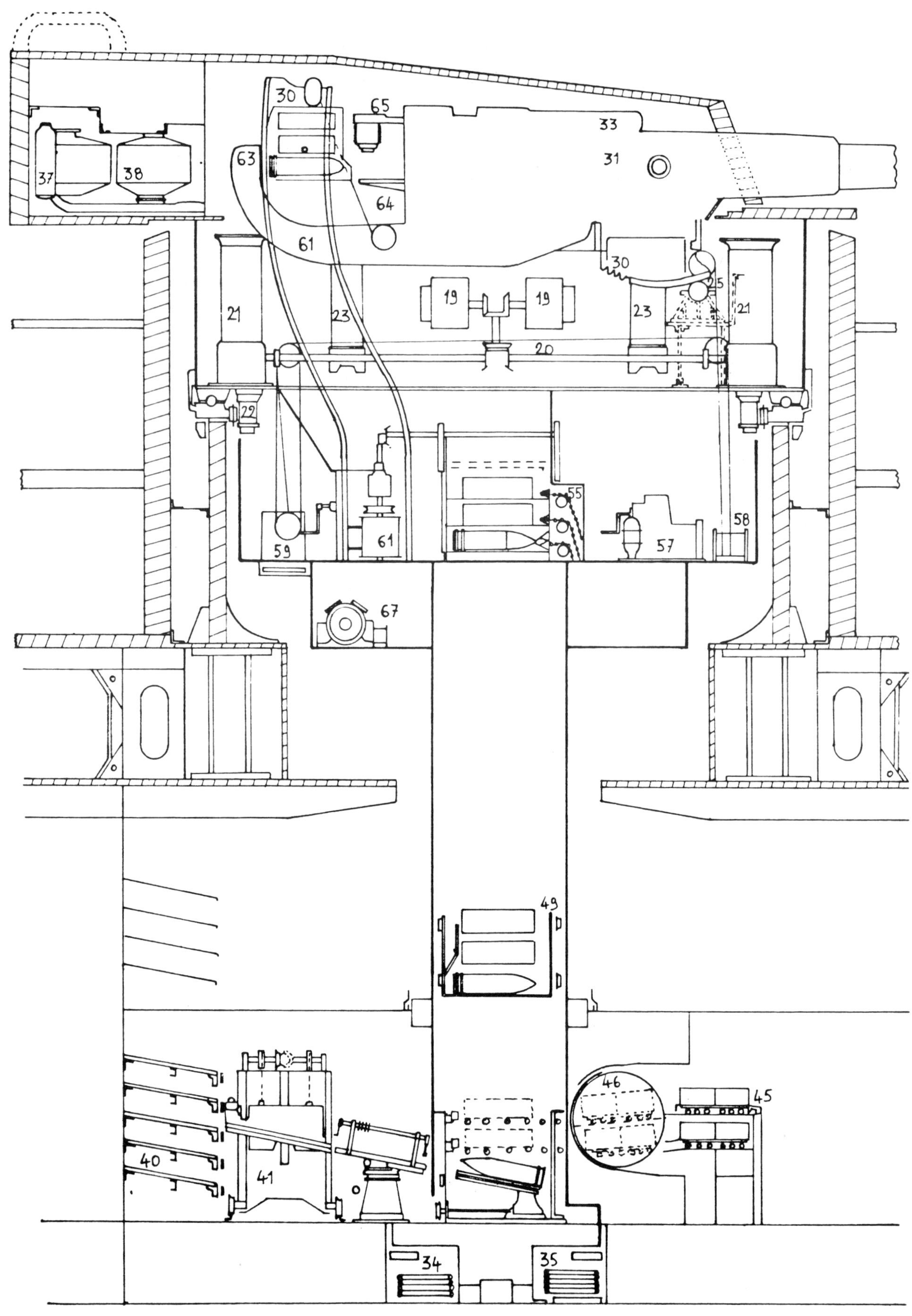

37 Water containers
38 Air filters
39 [Omitted]
40 Shell stowage
41 Shell bogie
42 Twin rotating waiting tray
43 Twin fixed waiting tray
44 Fixed ammunition ring
45 Charge waiting position
46 Charge drum
47 Revolving ammunition ring
48 Dredger hoist waiting position
49 Dredger hoist cage
50 Anti-flash flaps
51 Dredger hoist motor
52 Upper chain sprocket wheel
53 Lower chain sprocket wheel
54 Dredger hoist unloading positions
55 Transfer rammers
56 Gun-loading cage
57 Hand drive for upper hoists
58 Drum for hand drive
59 Counterweight
60 Cage in shell-ramming position
61 Rammer arm
62 Rammer motor
63 Rammer head
64 Spanning-tray
65 Breech-block
66 Converters for upper hoists and rammers
67 Auxiliary converters for upper hoists and rammers

Robert Dumas

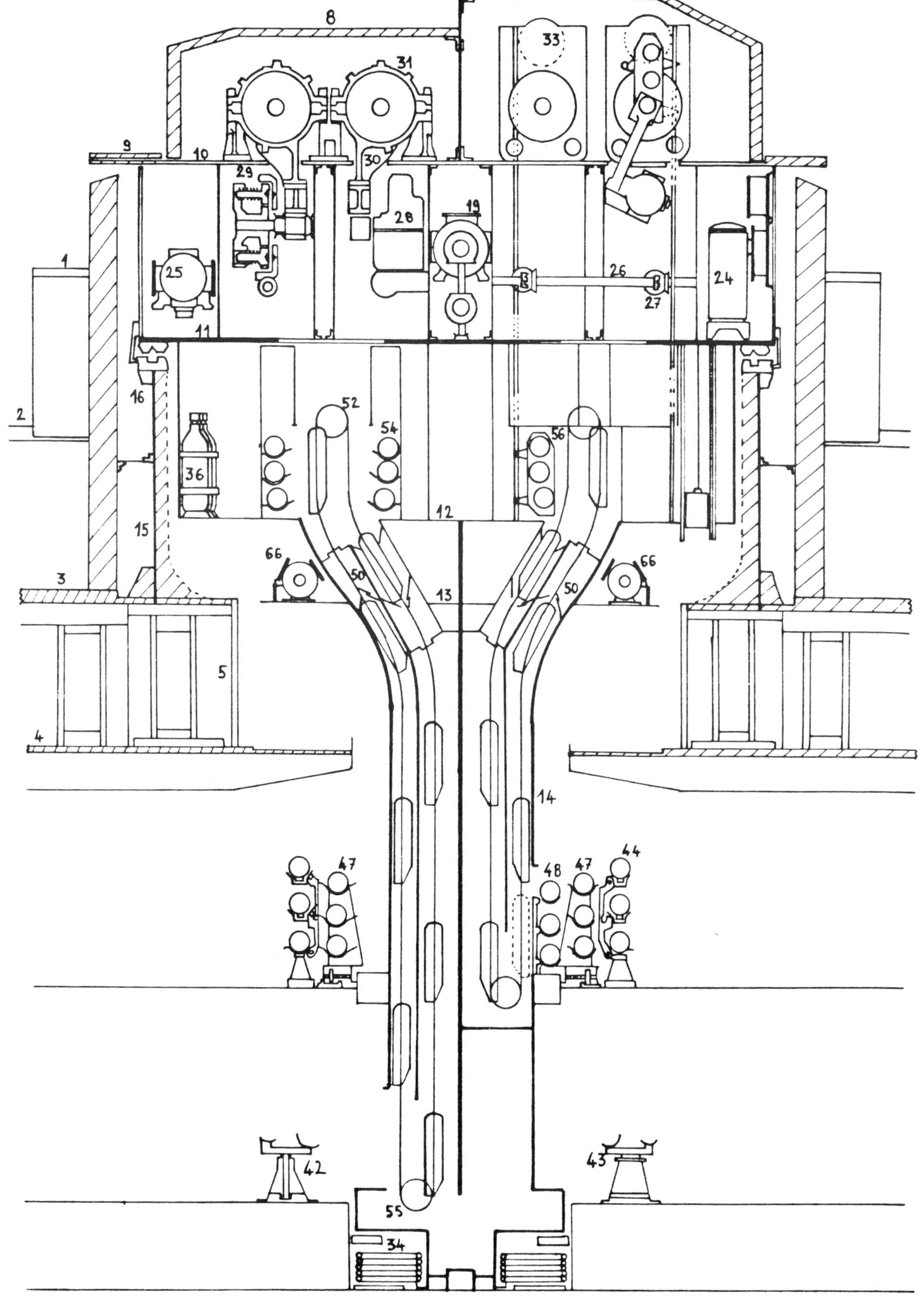

305mm (12.008in)/45 M1906-10

Of normal French heavy gun construction, this was mounted in twin turrets in the old dreadnoughts of the *Courbet* class. The weight including BM was 54t (*53.15 tons*), the actual bore 44.55cal and the 432kg (*952lb*) AP shell had a muzzle velocity of 783m/s (*2569f/s*) with 124.3kg (*274lb*) BM17 propellant. Long shells could not be fired as the rifling was 1 in 43, and the HE was 308kg (*679lb*), a 117.1kg (*258.2lb*) BM15 propellant charge giving 905m/s (*2969f/s*).

The turret mountings were of barbette type, the traditional French centre pivot turret being abandoned for heavy guns in the *Courbet* class, and as modified allowed 23° elevation. The gun is included in a list of French railway ordnance.

305mm (12.008in)/45 M1906

Similar to M1906-10 but differing in constructional details, this was only in the *Condorcet*, the last survivor of the *Danton* class. The twin turrets were of the French centre pivot type and are said to have allowed 18° elevation.

The gun is included in a list of railway ordnance.

MEDIUM CALIBRE GUNS

240mm (9.449in)/50 M1902-06

This gun, of complicated built-up construction, was still mounted in twin barbette type turrets in the *Condorcet*. It appears in a list of French coast-defence guns and was reported on by Krupp, but all French 240mm coast-defence guns that have been identified were the 40cal M1893-96. It is believed that A tubes from the M1902-06 were used in the construction of the 203mm (*7.992in*) M1931.

Weight including BM was 29.4t (*28.94 tons*), bore length 48.92cal and with 220kg (*485lb*) shell and 67kg (*147.7lb*) BM15 charge, muzzle velocity was 800m/s (*2625f/s*). As rifling was 1 in 57, long-nosed shell could not be fired, and even at 45° range was only 23812m (*26041yd*).

203mm (7.992in)/50 M1924

Gun Data

Bore	203mm	7.992in	
Weight incl BM	20.716t	20.389 tons	
Length oa	10,500m	413.39in	51.72cal
Length bore	10,149.5mm	399.59in	49.998cal
Length chamber	1855.5mm	73.05in	
Volume chamber	91.682dm³	5594.8in³	
Length rifling	8122mm	319.76in	
Grooves	(60) 1.9 × 7.5mm	0.075 × 0.295in	
Lands	3.0mm	0.118in	
Twist	1 in 25.59		
Weight projectile	134kg AP	295lb AP	
Propellant charge	47kg BM13	103.6lb BM13	
Muzzle velocity	820m/s	2690f/s	
Working pressure	*c*3000kg/cm²	*c*19.0 tons/in²	
Approx life	?600 EFC		
Max range	?30,000m/45°/820m/s	?32,800yd/45°/2690f/s	

The range with the above M1936 APC shell is not known. With 123.1kg (*271.4lb*) shell and MV 850m/s (*2789f/s*), range was 31,400m (*34,340yd*)/45° and 28,000m (30,620yd)/30°. With this latter shell, the originally intended MV was 895m/s (*2936f/s*) with 53kg (*117lb*) charge and working pressure 3200kg/cm² (*20.3 tons/in²*).

Gun Mounting Data, Cruisers

Revolving Weight	180t	177 tons
Roller path dia	5.05m	16ft 7in
Barbette int dia	5.9m	19ft 4in
Distance apart gun axes	1.88m	74in
Recoil	70cm	27.5in
Max elevating speed	*c*10°/sec	
Max training speed	6°/sec	
Firing cycle	12-15sec (in *Surcouf* 20sec)	
Turret shield	30mm	1.2in

This gun was mounted in twin turrets in the cruisers *Duquesne, Tourville, Suffren, Colbert, Foch, Dupleix* and in a special twin mounting in the large submarine *Surcouf*. It was of simple construction with a thick autofretted A tube, shrunk jacket and breech ring. The Welin type breech block opened upwards and screwed into the A tube. The maximum diameter of the chamber was 250mm (*9.84in*) and that of the A tube 510mm (*20.08in*) over it, with a maximum jacket diameter of 750mm (*29.53in*). The propellant charge was in halves and there were AP and HE shells of several types. Originally these weighed 123.1-123.82kg (*271.4-272.98lb*), but the next series, which had longer bases, were lighter at 119.07-119.72kg (*262.5-263.94lb*) and the latest M1936 AP considerably heavier at 134kg (*295lb*).

In the twin turrets the guns were in separate cradles with individual toothed elevating arcs. There was a 22.5HP electric training motor with hydraulic drive, and RPC was fitted - but not for elevation, where each gun had a 30HP motor also with hydraulic drive. The guns could however be coupled together. Elevation was +45° to -5° with loading at +10° to -5°. Catapult rammers cocked by the recoil were used for projectiles. The shell rooms were below the magazines, except that some of the forward magazine stowage was on the same deck as the shell rooms. A short hoist raised the shells one deck to the loading position for the lower dredger hoists. These were apparently supplied from a shell and cartridge ring and ran to the working chamber where ammunition was transferred to the upper cage hoists. These had two cages, one ascending while the other descended, with a by-pass so that the cages could pass one another. The hoists came up at the outside of the guns and shells were transferred to swinging arms which locked to the guns for loading.

Details of the *Surcouf*'s mounting are lacking, but it is known to have been trainable with 30° maximum elevation and hoists running direct to the gun floor. Fire could be opened 2½min after surfacing, and with its cylindrical shield the turret was more spacious than those in cruisers. The gun axes were approximately 2.64m (*104in*) apart.

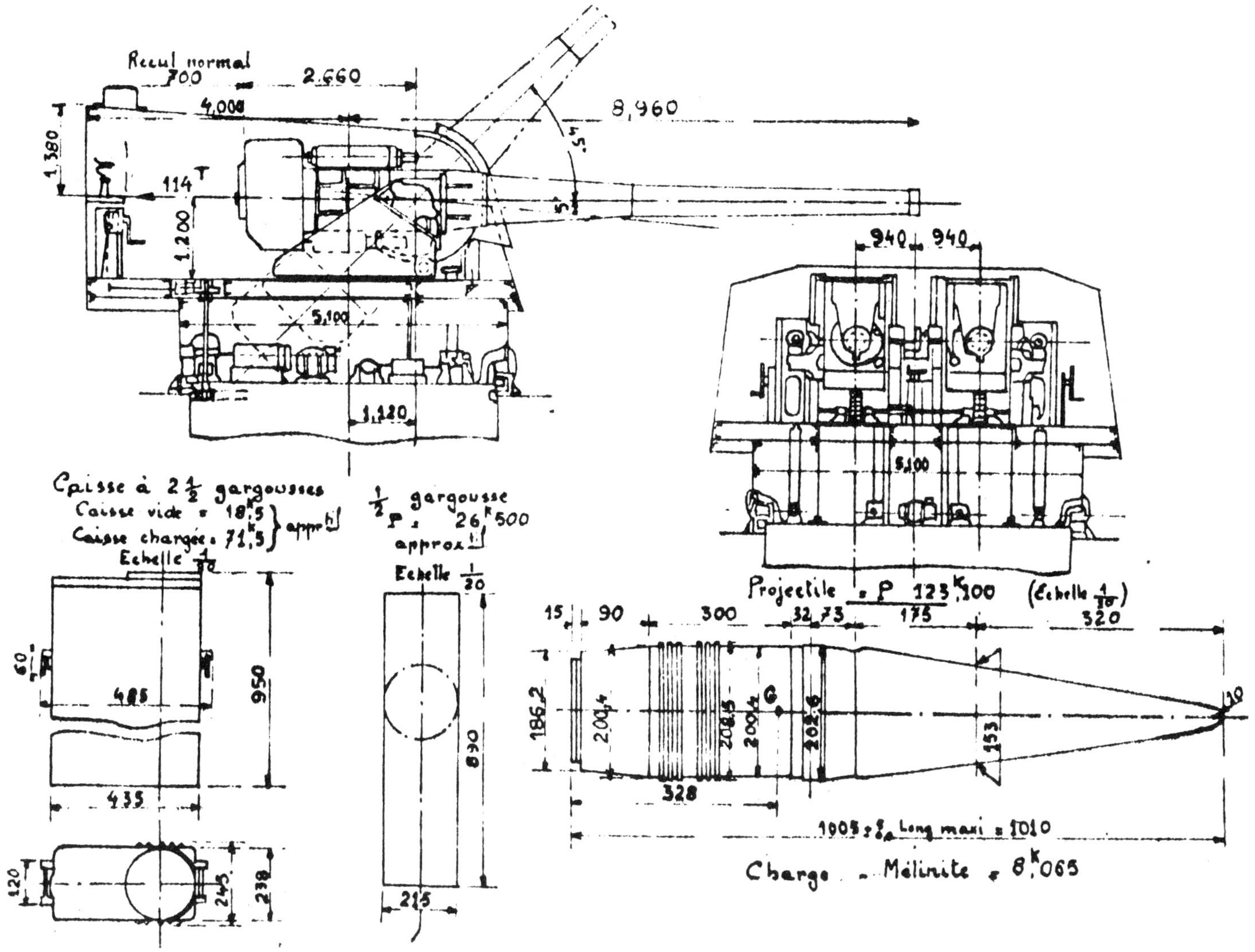

Above: 203mm M1924 guns in twin M1924 mounting. These were in the *Duquesne* and *Suffren* classes.
Official, by courtesy of Robert Dumas

Right: 203mm M1924 guns in twin mounting in *Surcouf* 1940. These were the largest guns in any Second World War submarine.
CPL

203mm (7.992in)/55 M1931

This gun was mounted only in the twin turrets of the cruiser *Algérie*. Except for the longer bore, it was identical internally to M1924 and used the same ammunition, but the construction differed. There were an A tube and jacket, both with the same external diameter over the chamber as in M1924, but the internal diameter of the A tube was here 324mm (*12.76in*) to accommodate a liner. A small ring at the breech end of the liner with a taper seating on it, screwed into the A tube, and there was a breech ring but no breech bush, the Welin block screwing into the A tube.

It is believed that the A tubes, which were not autofretted, came from 240mm (*9.449in*)/50 M1902-06 guns.

Drawings of the turret mounting have not been seen, but it is thought to have resembled those in other 203mm cruisers except for the heavier shield.

Gun Data differences from 203mm M1924

Weight incl BM	22.04t	21.69 tons	
Length oa	11,650mm	458.66in	57.39cal
Length bore	11,299.5mm	444.86in	55.66cal
Length rifling	9272mm	365.04in	
Muzzle velocity	c840m/s	c2756f/s	
Max range	?31,000m/45°/840m/s	?33,000yd/45°/2756f/s	

Muzzle velocity and range are estimated for 134kg (*295lb*) APC M1936.

Gun Mounting Data

Turret shield	face 100mm; sides 70mm; rear 40mm; roof 70mm	face 3.9in; sides 2.76in; rear 1.6in; roof 2.76in

194mm (7.638in)/50 M1902

Originally in the battleships of the *Démocratie* class and in the armoured cruisers *Waldeck Rousseau, Edgar Quinet, Ernest Renan* and *Jules Michelet*, this gun was no longer mounted afloat, but occurs in German lists of naval ammunition and in a list of French coast-defence guns. All 194mm guns that have been identified were, however, of earlier models. The M1902 was a powerful gun, the muzzle velocity, with an 89.5kg (*197.3lb*) AP shell and 38.4kg (*84.7lb*) BM13 charge, being 945m/s (*3100f/s*) and, with an 91.8kg (*202.4lb*) HE and 39.18kg (*86.4lb*) charge, 940m/s (*3084f/s*). The AP shells were not long nosed as 45° range was 25,960m (*28,390yd*).

The training cruiser *Jeanne d'Arc* on 28 April 1937 showing forward 155mm mountings.
CPL

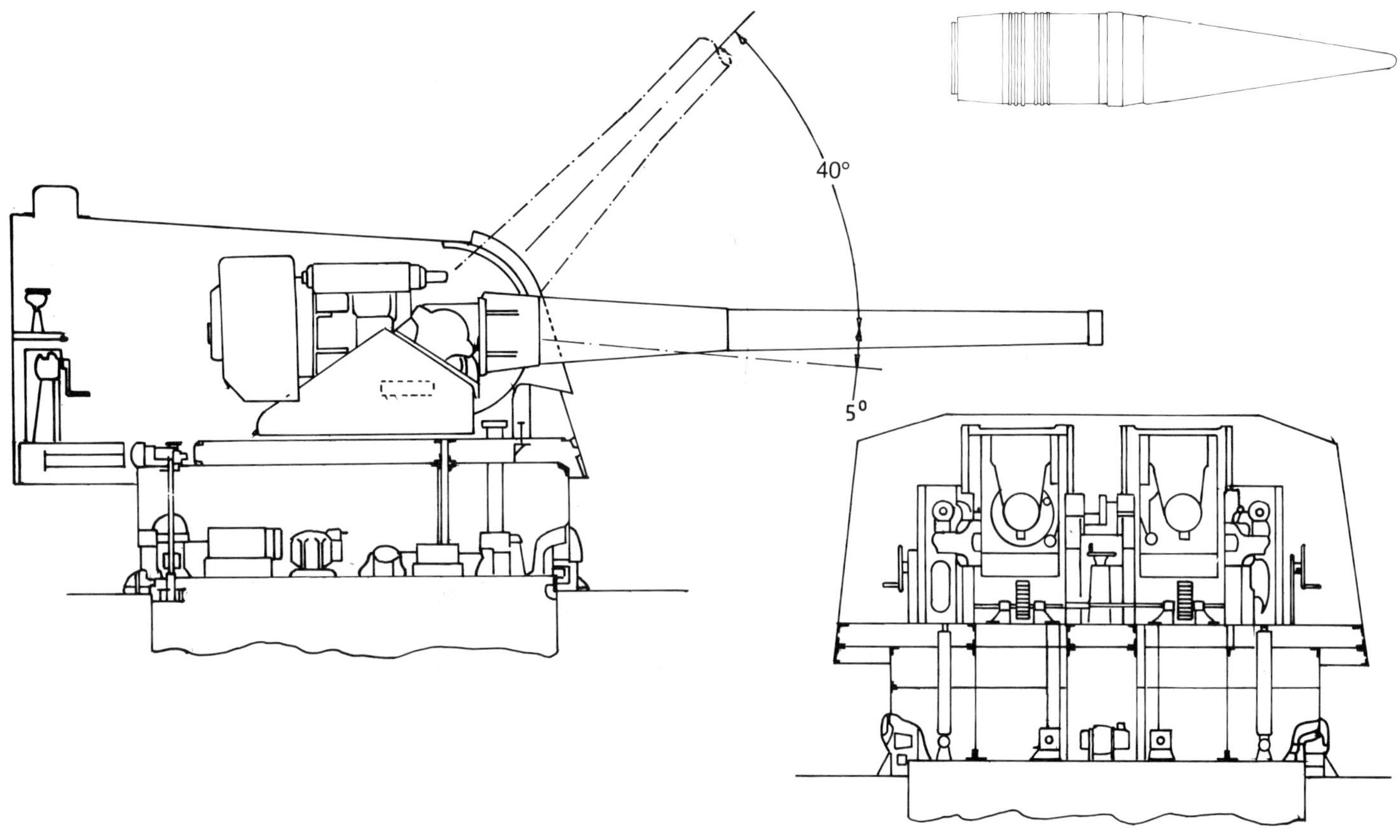

155mm M1920 guns in twin M1920 mounting as in *Duguay-Trouin* class and *Jeanne d'Arc*.
John Lambert

A BL gun carried in twin turrets by the *Duguay-Trouin* class and the training cruiser *Jeanne d'Arc*, as well as in single casemate mountings in the aircraft carrier *Béarn.* The gun was built with a liner, autofretted A tube, jacket in two lengths and breech ring. There was a short collar at the breech end of the liner screwing into the A tube, but no breech bush, the Welin screw block, which opened upwards, being taken by the A tube. The propellant charge was in halves and SAP and HE shell were provided, some of the latter with internal fuze weighing 59.0kg (*130.1lb*) instead of the usual 56.5kg (*124.6lb*).

Details are lacking of the single mounting, except that the shield was 70mm (*2.76in*), the total weight of 36.8t (*36.2 tons*) apparently including items not usually so treated. The twin turrets had the guns in separate cradles each with a toothed elevating arc. Training and elevation were electrically powered with hydraulic drive and RPC was later to be fitted for training. The elevation range was +40° to -5°. Shells and charges were hoisted together with the shell in the upper compartment. The lower hoists were of dredger type with transfer in the working chamber to upper cage hoists. Shells were moved by tongs to loading trays which traversed into position for loading by spring rammers. Charges were apparently hand rammed.

155mm (6.102in)/50 M1920

Gun Data

Bore	155mm	6.102in	
Weight incl BM	8.87t	8.73 tons	
Length oa	8050mm	316.93in	51.94cal
Length bore	7750mm	305.12in	50.0cal
Length chamber	1240mm	48.82in	
Volume chamber	36.67dm³	2238in³	
Length rifling	6362mm	250.47mm	
Grooves	(?46) 1.5 x 7.5mm?	?0.059 x 0.295in	
Lands	?3mm	?0.12in	
Twist	1 in 22.35		
Weight projectile	56.5kg	124.6lb	
Propellant charge	19.81kg BM11	43.67lb BM11	
Muzzle velocity	850m/s	2789f/s	
Working pressure	3050kg/cm²	19.4 tons/in²	
Approx life	?700 EFC		
Max range	26,100m/40°/850m/s	28,540yd/40°/2789f/s	

Gun Mounting Data

Revolving weight	*c*80t	*c*78.7 tons
Roller path dia	4.05m	13ft 3in
Barbette int dia	4.85m	15ft 11in
Distance apart gun axes	1.50m	59in
Recoil	55cm	21.7in
Max elevating speed	*c*6°/sec	
Max training speed	6.4°/sec	
Firing cycle	12-20sec	
Turret shield	25mm	1.0in

This gun was introduced in the light cruiser *Émile Bertin* and was mounted in triple turrets in this ship and in the succeeding *La Galissonnière* class. It was next to be in the *Richelieu* class in a new M1936 DP triple turret and was to combine the functions of secondary armament against surface targets with that of the principal AA gun. The turret was a failure in this dual role and two of the five were removed from the *Richelieu* before completion and replaced with 100mm (*3.94in*) AA guns. The *Jean Bart*, completed after the war, likewise had only three of these turrets.

The gun was built with an autofretted jacket, breech ring and loose barrel, and the SA breech mechanism had a vertical sliding block. Separate QF ammunition was fired and the cartridge case was 1006mm (*39.6in*) overall and weighed 17.1kg (*37.7lb*). Piercing and HE shells were supplied, and as often with French ammunition there were several patterns varying in weight from 54.17-57.15kg (*119.4-126.0lb*). A later 58.8kg (*129.6lb*) shell was an adapted USN 130lb (*59kg*).

The triple cruiser mounting seems to have been highly satisfactory. The guns were in individual cradles and training and elevation were each powered by a 60HP Leonard electric motor with hydraulic drive. The guns were driven together by the elevating gear with differentials for individual correction between the hydraulic drive and the elevating worms. RPC was fitted for training and elevation. Limits for the latter were +45° -10° with loading at +15° -5°. The BM was arranged to operate automatically and a catapult rammer was used for shells, with a chain rammer for cartridges. Shell rooms and magazines were separate, and each turret had three shell and four cartridge hoists, all of pusher type. Shells were tipped by hand into a slide which transferred them to the power operated loading gear. Ready stowage in the handing room totalled 25 shells, of which 17 were for aircraft targets, and 21 cartridges.

The triple mountings in the *Richelieu* were intended to elevate to 90° with loading over the full +90° to -10°. In fact loading was difficult or impossible at beyond 45° and the maximum elevation was reduced to 75°, increased to 85° after the war. The guns were in separate cradles and RPC was fitted, but the mountings differed from the above in having hydro-pneumatic chain rammers on extensions from the cradles. There were separate pusher hoists for AA and surface shells which came up to the left of the gun, while the pusher cartridge hoists came up to the right. For reasons of alignment the hoists were broken between the armour decks where rotating transfer mechanisms were installed. The two forward turrets, which were removed, would have been 28m (*92ft*) from their magazine and would have required a long horizontal transfer between the armoured decks.

152.4mm (6in)/55 M1930

Gun Data

Bore	152.4mm	6.0in	
Weight incl BM	7.780t	7.657 tons	
Length oa	8860mm	348.82in	58.14cal
Length bore	8390mm	330.315in	55.05cal
Length chamber	1059.5mm	41.71in	
Volume chamber	29.089dm^3	1775.1in^3	
Length rifling	7165.5mm	282.11in	
Grooves	(46) 1.5 × 7.37mm	0.059 × 0.290in	
Lands	3.0mm	0.118in	
Twist	1 in 25.59		
Weight projectile	54.17kg	119.4lb	
Propellant charge	17.3kg BM11	38.1lb BM11	
Muzzle velocity	870m/s	2854f/s	
Working pressure	3200kg/cm^2	20.3 tons/in^2	
Approx life	?700 EFC		
Max range	26,474m/45°/870m/s	28,952yd/45°/2854f/s	

Gun Mounting Data, *La Galissonnière* class

Revolving weight	172t	169.3 tons
Ball track dia	4.64m	15ft 3in
Barbette int dia	5.81m	19ft 1in
Distance apart gun axes	1.65m	65in
Recoil	50cm	20in
Max elevating speed	8°/sec	
Max training speed	12°/sec	
Firing cycle	7-8sec	
Turret shield	face 100mm; sides 50mm; rear 40mm; roof 45mm	face 3.9in; sides 2in; rear 1.6in; roof 1.8in

Mountings in *Richelieu*, differences

Revolving weight	228t	224.4 tons
Ball track dia	6.62m	21ft 8.6in
Barbette int dia	7.3m	23ft 11in
Recoil	75cm	29.5in
Distance apart gun axes	1.85m	72.8in
Turret shield	face 115mm; rest 70mm	face 4.5in; rest 2.75in

Left: The cruiser *Georges Leygues* in 1949 showing the forward triple 152mm turrets. Unlike the DP mounting these were highly satisfactory.
CPL

Below: 152mm M1936/C1930 triple DP mounting with loading at 90° elevation. This version was originally intended for the *Richelieu* class but was too ambitious.
Official, by courtesy of Robert Dumas

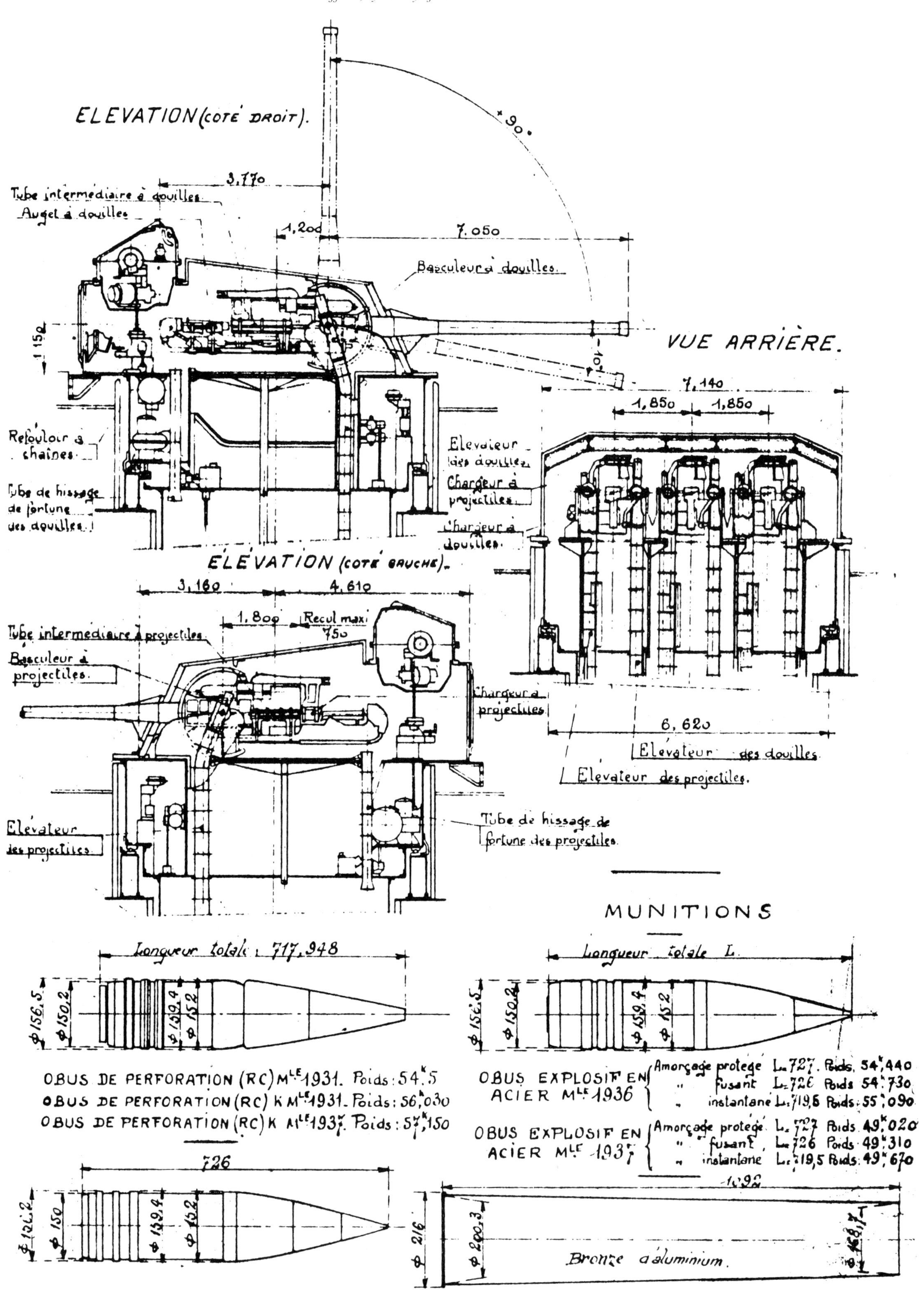

155mm (6.102in)/38.2 GPF

Some of these First World War heavy field guns were adapted for mounting in large auxiliaries and armed merchant ships. The shell weighed 43.1kg (*95lb*) and MV was 735m/s (*2411f/s*) with a 40° range of 16,270m (*17,790yd*).

149.1mm (5.87in) SKL/45, Tbts KL/45, Ubts u Tbts KL/45

These former German guns were carried in ships taken over by the French after the First World War. They were mounted in armed merchant cruisers, *Barfleur* and *Charles Plumier*. Details will be found under Germany.

145mm (5.709in)/45 M1910

Originally a First World War army conversion of the 138.6mm (*5.457in*)/55 M1910, the guns being rebored and shortened. It is not known how many ships carried it, but it was in the old sloop *Epinal* on single mountings. Separate QF ammunition was fired with the same case as in the 138.6mm M1910. With a 36kg (*79.4lb*) HE shell and 10.38kg (*22.88lb*) BM9 charge, MV was 755m/s (*2477f/s*) and range 14,810m (*16,200yd*) at 36°.

It appears that older M1887, M1891^2, and M1893 guns were also rebored to take the same shell, but details are lacking except that the cartridge case was 340mm (*13.4in*) overall instead of 900mm (*35.4in*).

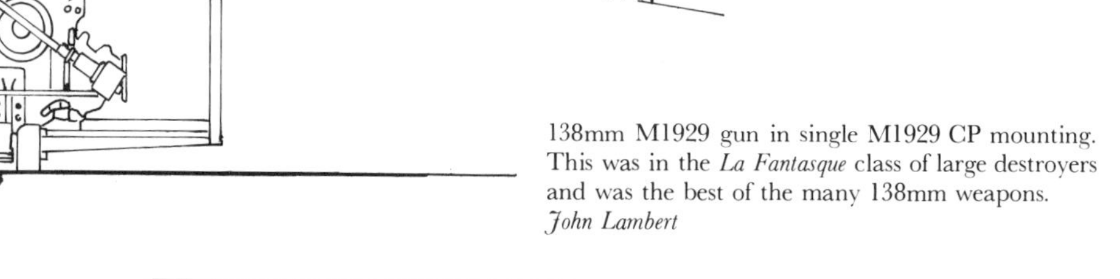

138mm M1929 gun in single M1929 CP mounting. This was in the *La Fantasque* class of large destroyers and was the best of the many 138mm weapons. *John Lambert*

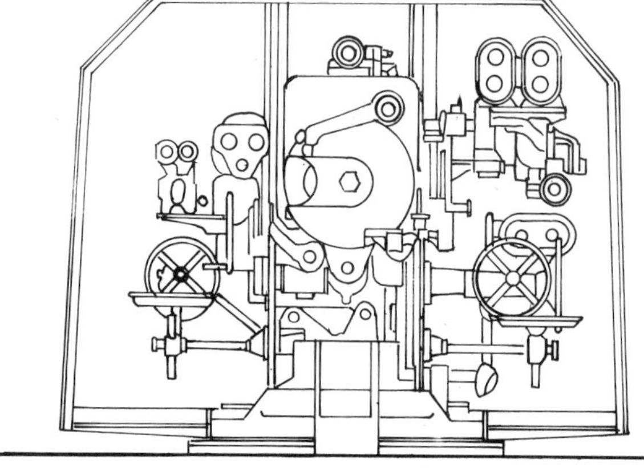

138.6mm (5.457in)/50 M1929, M1934

Gun Data M1929

Bore	138.6mm	5.457in	
Weight incl BM	4.275t (M1934 4.650t)	4.207 (4.577) tons	
Length oa	7280mm	286.61in	52.53cal
Length bore	6927mm	272.72in	49.98cal
Length chamber	939.8mm	37.00in	
Volume chamber	20.359dm^3	1242.4in^3	
Length rifling	5835.5mm	229.74in	
Grooves	(42) 1.22 × 7.35mm?	0.048 × 0.289mm?	
Lands	3mm?	0.118in?	
Twist	1 in 22.35		
Weight projectile	40.6kg	89.5lb	
Propellant charge	12.09kg BM11	26.65lb BM11	
Muzzle velocity	800m/s	2625f/s	
Working pressure	2500kg/cm^2	15.9 tons/in^2	
Approx life	?900 EFC		
Max range	20,000m/30°/800m/s	21,870yd/30°/2625f/s	

M1929 was introduced in *Le Fantasque* class large destroyers, where it was in single mountings, and M1934 was in twin mountings in the later *Mogador* and *Volta*. The gun was built with a monobloc autofretted barrel and breech ring screwed on cold. The SA breech mechanism had a horizontal sliding block. Separate QF ammunition was fired, the cartridge case being that used in 138.6mm guns from M1910 onwards. It was 900mm (*35.4in*) overall and weighed 12.96kg (*28.57lb*) empty. SAP and HE shells were carried.

The single CP mountings were hand trained and elevated and weighed only 11.57t (*11.39 tons*) complete. Elevation was +30° to -10°, recoil 43cm (*17in*) and the shield 5mm (*0.2in*) thick. There were four shell and four cartridge dredger hoists, guns Nos 3 and 4 sharing the same, and ammunition slides ran from hoists to guns which had automatic spring rammers. The firing cycle is given as 5sec but 8 or 9sec was more practicable.

The twin M1934 mountings were of base-ring 'turret' type with the guns in separate cradles which could be coupled together. Training and elevation were powered by 3HP Leonard electric motors with RPC, and each gun had individual worm gear elevation drive from a common motor. The limits were +30° to -10°, which would have been increased to +35°-10° in later ships of the *Mogador* type if these had been built (*Kléber* class). Each gun had pusher shell and cartridge hoists in a fixed shaft on the mounting axis. Ammunition was transferred to a rotatable tipping drum from which it slid out into the loading mechanism. A catapult rammer was used for shells, but cartridges were rammed by hand. Loading was at any elevation, but the mechanism was liable to defects and failure, and the intended rate of fire was not attained.

Mounting Data *Mogador* class

Revolving Weight	34.6t	34.05 tons
Ball track dia	1.59m	62.6in
Distance apart gun axes	1.33m	52.4in
Recoil	50cm	20in
Max elevating speed	14°/sec	
Max training speed	10°/sec	
Firing cycle	8-10sec	
Shield	10mm	0.4in

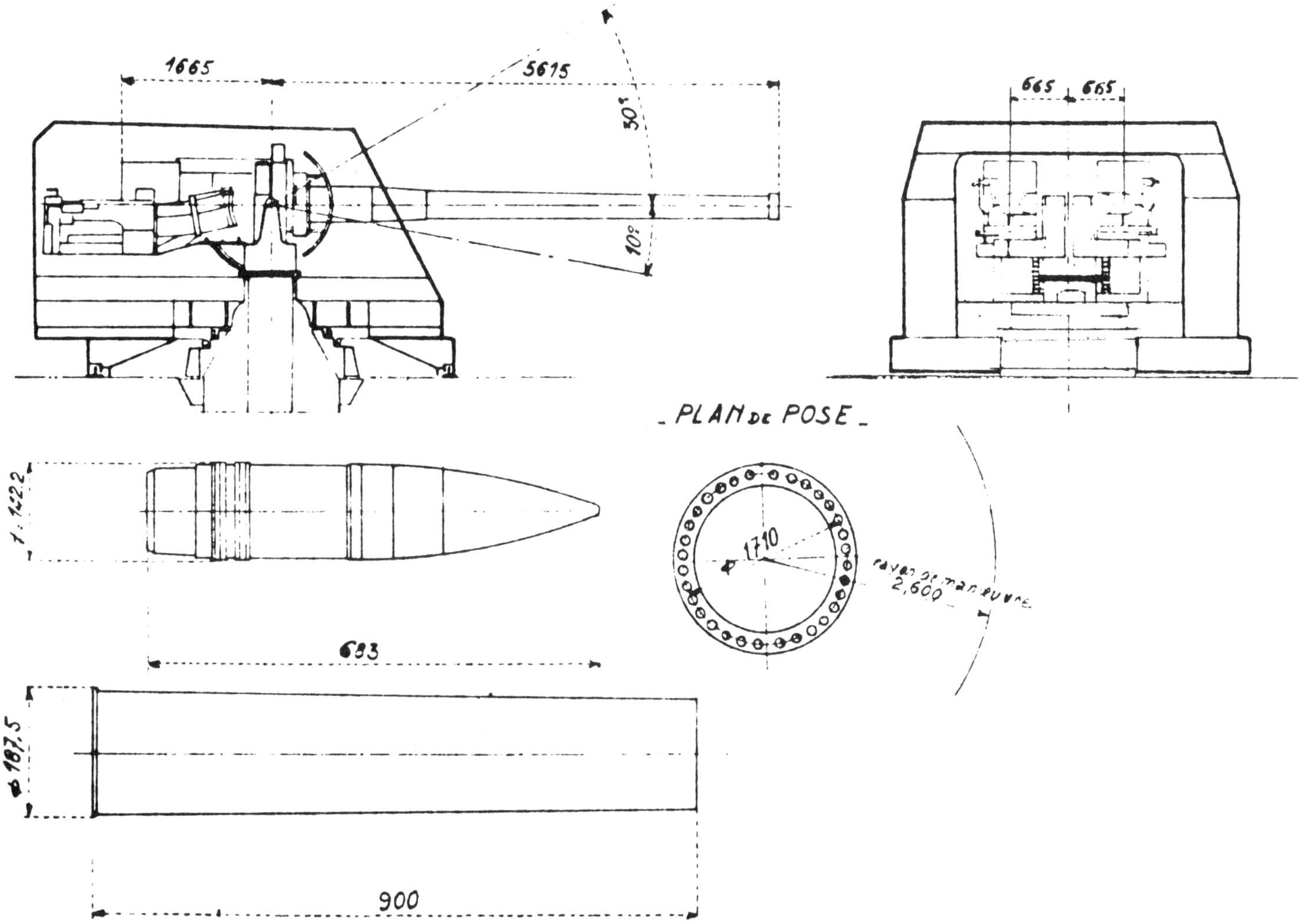

1665 5615 30° 10°
665 665
- PLAN DE POSE -
1710
rayon de manœuvre 2,600
1 : 122,2
633
⌀ 187,5
900

Above: 138mm M1934 guns in twin PSD M1934 mounting as in *Mogador* and *Volta*. Defects in the loading gear limited the rate of fire.
Official, by courtesy of Robert Dumas

Right: The forward 138mm M1929 guns in a destroyer of the *Le Fantasque* class.
Jacques Navarret

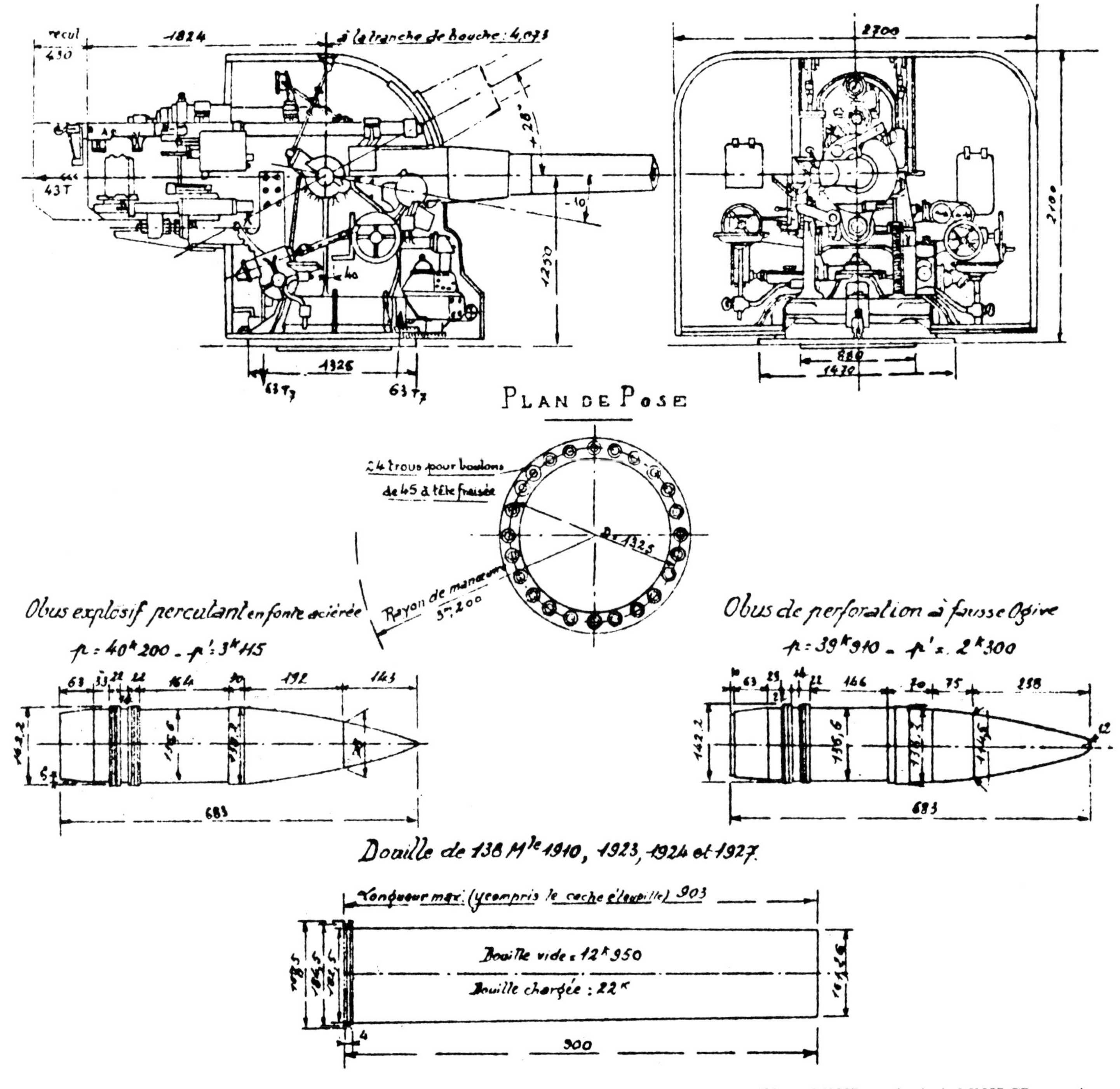

138mm M1927 gun in single M1927 CP mounting. This was in many ships and was the first French 138mm gun with a sliding breech-block.
Official, by courtesy of Robert Dumas

138.6mm (5.457in)/40 M1927

Gun Data

Weight incl BM	4.1t	4.04 tons
Weight projectile	40.6kg	89.5lb
Propellant charge	8.967kg BM7	19.77lb BM7
Muzzle velocity	700m/s	2297f/s
Working pressure	2500kg/cm^2	15.9 tons/in^2
Max range	16,600m/28°/700m/s	18,150yd/28°/2297f/s

This gun was in single mountings in the *Aigle* and *Cassard* classes of large destroyers, the *Bougainville* class of sloops and in the minelayer *La Tour d'Auvergne* (ex-*Pluton*). It had an autofretted barrel and SA horizontal sliding block BM. Separate QF ammunition was fired with the same shells and cartridge case as in M1929, but the propellant charge was smaller. The mounting had an automatic spring rammer and allowed +28° -10° elevation. The total weight with gun is given as 13t (*12.8 tons*). The shield was 3mm (*0.12in*) and recoil distance 36cm (*14in*). The firing cycle of the gun was 4 or 5sec but the dredger hoists doubled this.

138.6mm (5.457in)/40 M1923

Carried in single mountings by the large destroyers of the *Vauban* and *Guépard* classes, this gun differed from the M1927 in construction and in being fitted with a Welin screw breech block. Ballistics were similar, but the mounting which had higher trunnions, allowed +35° -10° elevation for a range of 18,200m (*19,900yd*). There was an automatic spring rammer for shells, cartridges being loaded by hand, but it was difficult to load at over 15° elevation and the practical firing cycle was 10–12sec.

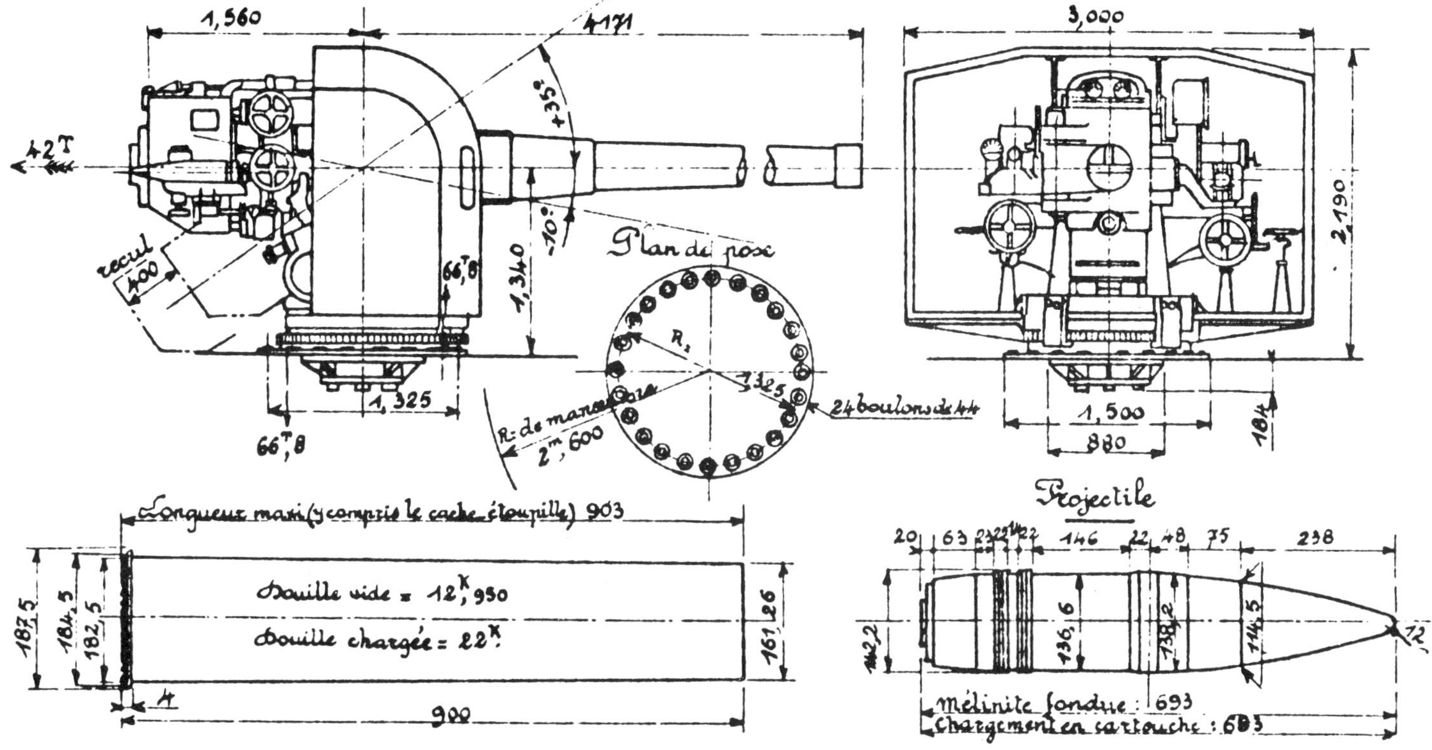

Above: 138mm M1923 gun in single M1924 CP mounting. In the *Vauban* and *Guépard* classes. This had a Welin breech-block.
Official, by courtesy of Robert Dumas

Below: 138mm M1910 gun in *Bretagne* type mounting, modified for First World War sloops still in service.
Official, by courtesy of Robert Dumas

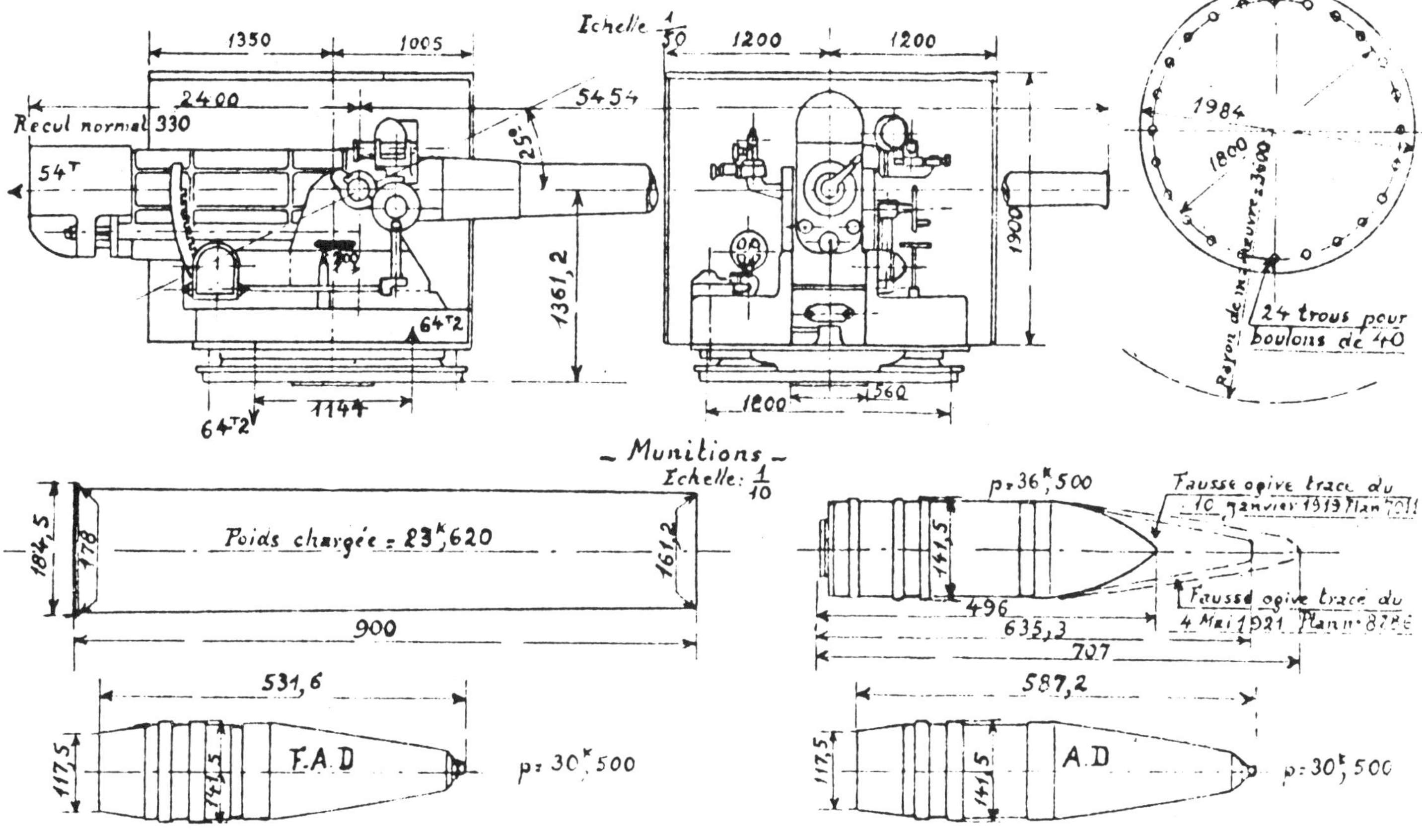

This was in single mountings as an anti-torpedo craft battery in the *Bretagne* and *Courbet* classes, and was also mounted in old sloops of the *Arras* class as well as in coast defence. It was of built up construction with a screw breech and fired separate QF ammunition. The cartridge case was as in later 138.6mm guns but shells were different, the length being limited by the 1in 36 rifling, so that SAP weighed 39.5kg (*87.1lb*) and HE 31.5kg (*69.4lb*). The mountings originally allowed +15° -10° elevation but this was altered to +25° -7°. The firing cycle was 10-12sec.

138.6mm (5.457in)/55 M1910

Gun Data

Weight incl BM	5.32t	5.24 tons
Weight projectile	39.5kg SAP	87.1lb
Propellant charge	10.44kg BM9	23.02lb BM9
Muzzle velocity	790m/s	2592f/s
Working pressure	2380kg/cm^2	15.1 tons/in^2
Max range	16,100m/25°/790m/s	17,600yd/25°/2592f/s

With 31.5kg (*69.4lb*) HE, MV was 840m/s (*2756f/s*), working pressure 2000kg/cm^2 (*12.7 tons/in^2*) and range about 1000m (*1100yd*) down.

138.6mm (5.457in)/45 M1891[2], M1893

These were built-up screw-breech guns removed from scrapped warships and mounted in auxiliaries. Separate QF ammunition was fired and with a 36.5kg (*80.5lb*) shell MV was 725m/s (*2379f/s*), or with 31.5kg (*69.4lb*) 765m/s (*2510f/s*).

130mm (5.118in)/45 M1932,M1935

Gun Data M1932

Bore	130mm	5.118in	
Weight incl BM	3.70t	3.64 tons	
Length oa	6245mm	245.87in	48.04cal
Length bore	5899mm	232.24in	45.38cal
Length chamber	707.4mm	27.85in	
Volume chamber	13.292dm^3	811.1in^3	
Length rifling	5049mm	198.78in	
Twist	1 in 25.59		
Weight projectile	32.11kg SAP	70.79lb SAP	
Propellant charge	8.76kg BM9	19.29lb BM9	
Muzzle velocity	800m/s	2625f/s	
Working pressure	2700kg/cm^2	17.1 tons/in^2	
Approx life	?900 EFC		
Max range	20,870m/45°/800m/s	22,820yd/45°/2625f/s	

With 29.515kg (*65.07lb*) HE, MV was 840m/s (*2756f/s*).

Mounting Data, quadruple turret

Revolving Weight	200t	197 tons
Ball track dia	5.9m	19ft 4in
Barbette int dia	7.0m	23ft
Distance apart gun axes		
Nos 1-2, 3-4	0.55m	21.7in
Nos 2-3	2.45m	96.5in
Recoil	42cm	16.5in
Max elevating speed	8°/sec	
Max training speed	12°/sec	
Firing cycle	5-6sec	
Turret shield	face 135mm; sides 90mm; rear 80mm; roof 90mm	face 5.3in; sides 3.5in; rear 3.1in; roof 3.5in

Mounting Data, twin DP

Revolving weight	81.2t	79.9 tons
Ball track	3.5m	11ft 6in
Ring bulkhead dia	4.6m	15ft 1in
Shield	20mm	0.8in

M1932 was carried in twin and quadruple DP mountings by the *Dunkerque* and *Strasbourg* and the very similar M1935 in twin LA mountings by the *Le Hardi* class destroyers. M1932 was also intended for the *Joffre* class aircraft carriers in twin DP mountings. The gun was built with an autofretted barrel and a breech ring. The breech block was of vertical-sliding type in DP, but horizontal in LA mountings. Fixed ammunition was fired with either 32.11kg (*70.79lb*) or 33.4kg (*73.6lb*) SAP or 29.515kg (*65.07lb*) HE. The SAP round was 1349.4mm (*53.126in*) overall, and the HE one 1284.4mm (*50.567in*), the cartridge case being 800m (*31.5in*) overall with a base flange diameter of 183mm (*7.205in*). As the round weighed up to 53.0kg (*116.8lb*) it was near the limit for naval fixed ammunition of the Second World War.

The quadruple mountings were developed by St Chamond and do not seem to have been very successful, the loading system in particular being liable to defects. The guns were in cast steel cradles and fixed together in pairs with a 20mm (*0.8in*) bulkhead extending for two-thirds of the turret length between pairs. Training was by a 35HP electric motor with hydraulic drive gear and elevation similarly by a 15HP motor, each pair of guns having a toothed arc. The motor circuits were of Leonard pattern with Sautter-Harlé RPC. Elevation limits were +75° to -10° with loading at any angle. Rounds were passed by hand to the base of the pusher hoists. Each gun had a double hoist, one for AA and one for surface rounds, and those for the after turret ran direct from the handing room, but for the other two the hoists were broken between the armour decks because of the location of turrets and magazine. The hoists came up by the outer cradle trunnions of each pair and the rounds were passed to the loading tray by a combination of hydraulically powered tilting and rotating trays and slide tracks. Rammers were pneumatic with the breech closing automatically after ramming, and the spent case was ejected onto the loading tray which turned so that the case could be thrown by hand on to a conveyor. Ready stowage in the rotating structure amounted to 32 AA and 16 surface rounds.

The twin DP mountings resembled one half of a quadruple, but the guns were further apart than in the pairs of the latter, the shield was thin, and training and elevating motors both 10HP. The mountings were located about 23m (*75ft*) abaft the forward magazines so that ammunition had to be transferred horizontally between the armour decks.

The LA mountings were of base-ring type with a revolving weight of 32.6t (*32.1 tons*) and were trained and elevated by electric power as the other mountings. The guns were in separate cradles with axes 1.3m (*51in*) apart, recoil distance was 50cm (*20in*) and elevation +35° -10°. The pusher hoists were in a fixed shaft and delivered two rounds per gun at a time into drums pivoting on the trunnion axis. Springs projected the rounds for each gun into upper and lower loading-trays from where they were power-rammed alternately. Loading was possible to +30° and the firing cycle is quoted as 4sec, though 6sec seems more realistic.

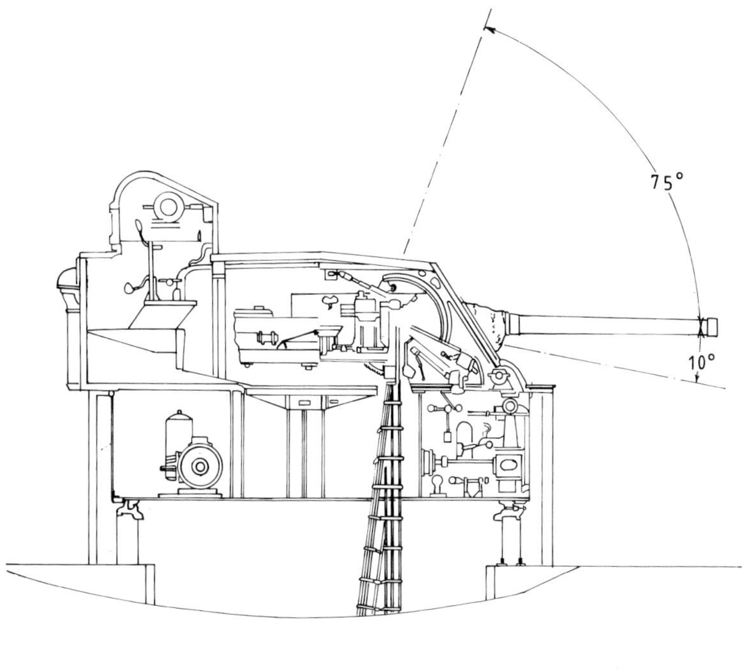

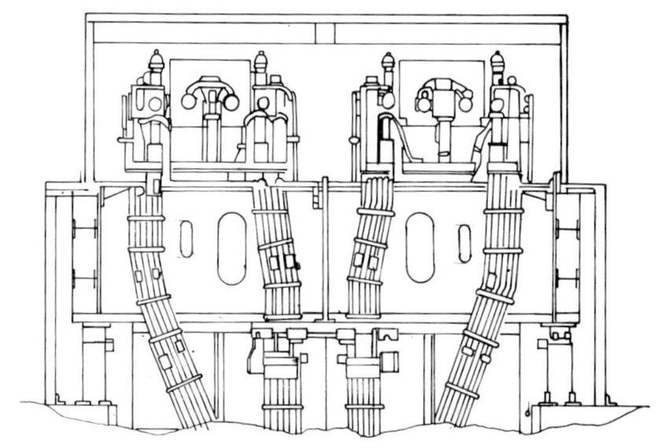

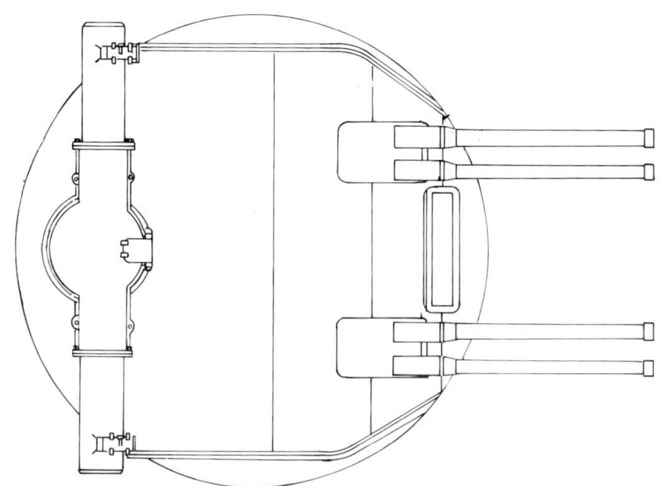

130mm M1932 guns in quadruple M1932 DP mounting. This was in *Dunkerque* and *Strasbourg* and was not entirely satisfactory.
John Lambert

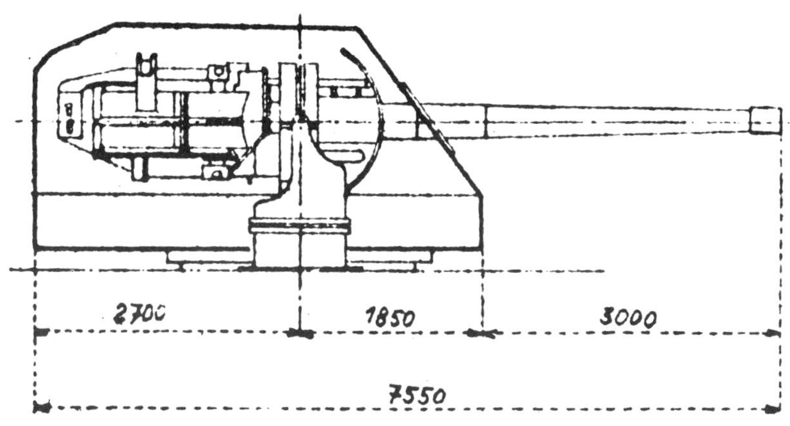

130mm M1935 guns in twin M1935 mounting for *Le Hardi* class destroyers.
Official, by courtesy of Robert Dumas

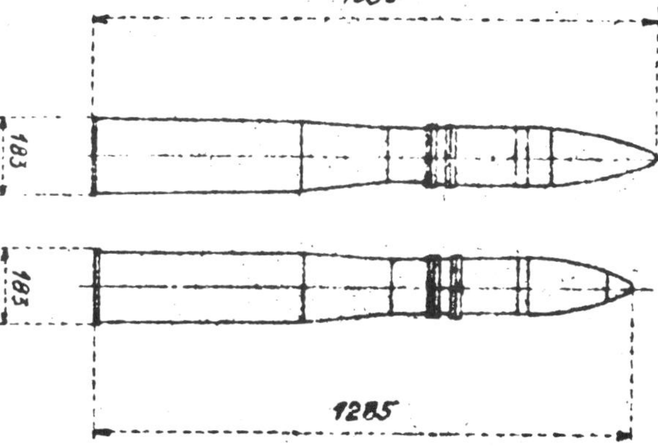

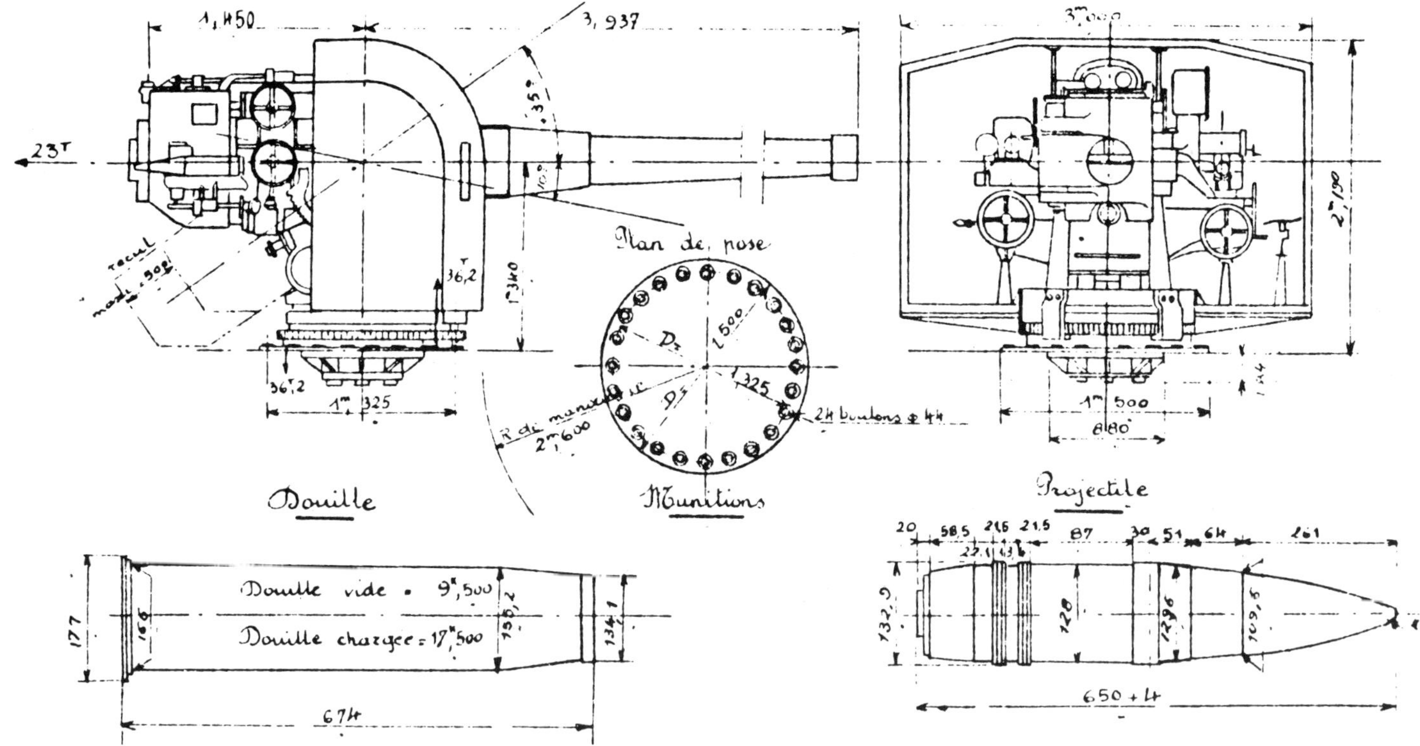

130mm M1924 gun in single M1924 CP mounting in the *La Fortuné* class destroyers.
Official, by courtesy of Robert Dumas

This gun, carried in single mountings by the *Le Fortuné* class destroyers fired separate QF ammunition and was of autofretted built-up construction with a Welin screw breech block. SAP shell, of which there were several types, averaged 33.74kg (*74.38lb*) and internally fuzed HE weighed 34.85kg (*76.83lb*). The cartridge case was 674mm (*26.54in*) overall and with propellant charge weighed 17.5kg (*38.6lb*). The mountings allowed +35° -10° elevation and had an automatic spring rammer, but loading was difficult at over 15° and the practical firing cycle was 10-12sec. The total weight with gun is given as 12.7t (*12.5 tons*).

130mm (5.118in)/40 M1924

Gun Data

Weight incl BM	3.814t	3.75 tons
Weight projectile	34.85kg	76.83lb
Propellant charge	7.73kg BM9	17.04lb BM9
Muzzle velocity	725m/s	2379f/s
Working pressure	2570kg/cm^2	16.3 tons/in^2
Max range	18,700m/35°/725m/s	20,450yd/35°/2379f/s

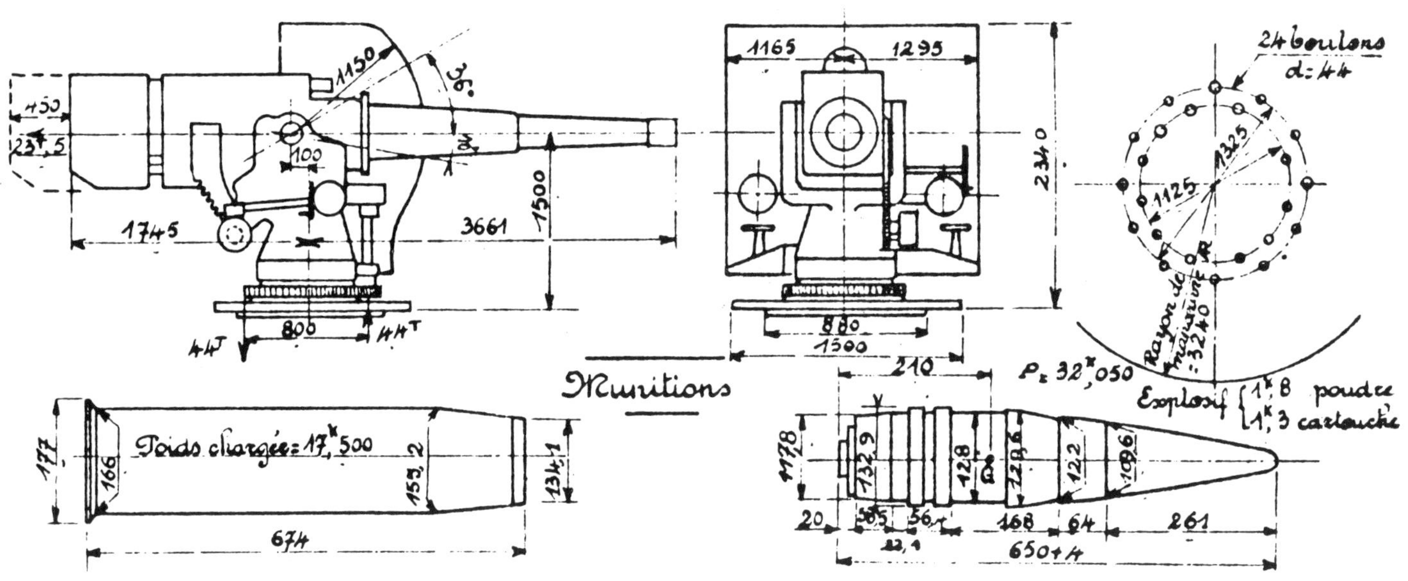

130mm M1919 gun in single M1919 CP mounting. This was hand loaded and had higher trunnions than M1924. It was in the *Jaguar* and *Bourrasque* classes.
Official, by courtesy of Robert Dumas

130mm (5.118in)/40 M1919

In single mountings in the destroyers of the *Jaguar* and *Bourrasque* classes, this gun differed from M1924, in not being autofretted, and in weighing with BM 4.05t (*3.35 tons*). Ammunition was the same. The mounting had higher trunnions and allowed +36° -10° elevation which increased range to 18,900m (*20,670yd*), but loading was by hand and the actual firing cycle was apparently 12-15sec. Recoil was given as 45cm (*18in*) and total weight as 12.5-12.75t (*12.3-12.55 tons*).

LIGHT CALIBRE GUNS

100mm (3.937in) guns

These are confusing particularly as they were often of similarly moderate performance.

M1936. A 34-calibre gun with eccentric screw block mounted in the submarine *Aurore*, and intended for the rest of her class and for the *Roland Morillot* and *Emeraude* classes. The gun weighed 1.00t (*0.98 tons*) and gun and mounting 3.05t (*3.0 tons*). Recoil was 57cm (*22.4in*) and elevation +30° -5°. The fixed round was 802.5mm (*31.59in*) long.

M1933. This 45-calibre gun was to be in twin-base ring AA mountings intended for the cruiser *De Grasse* as originally designed, and for the torpedo boats of the *Agile* class. M1933 weighed 1.5t (*1.48 tons*) and fired a 14.9kg (*32.8lb*) shell at 760m/s (*2493f/s*). The mounting in *Agile* was to weigh 29.8t (*29.3 tons*), with a ball track diameter of 1.9m (*6ft 3in*) and +90° -10° elevation. The guns were 65cm (*25.6in*) apart in individual cradles and each had pusher hoists with mechanical loading.

M1932. A 45-calibre gun with horizontal sliding block carried in single mountings by the *Melpomène* class torpedo boats, and recorded in the escorts *Chevreuil* and *La Capricieuse*. SAP shell weighed 14.95kg (*32.96lb*) and, with a 4.025kg (*8.87lb*) BM7 charge, MV was 755m/s (*2477f/s*), but HE was lighter at 13.47kg (*29.7lb*) and MV was 785m/s (*2575f/s*). The fixed round weighed up to 24.15kg (*53.24lb*) and was 1010mm (*39.8in*) long with the cartridge case 617mm (*24.29in*). The mountings allowed +34° -10° and range is quoted as 15,000m (*16,400yd*) with SAP. The firing cycle is given as 6sec.

M1930. A 45-calibre gun carried in twin shielded AA mountings by the *Algérie*, and the *Lorraine* as originally altered, but wartime photos show single 75mm (*2.95in*) guns in the latter. In the *Richelieu*, two of the 152.4mm (*6in*) triples were replaced in 1939 by six twin 100mm M1930 when it was realised that the former would not be a satisfactory AA weapon, and some came from the *Lorraine*.

The gun had an autofretted barrel and SA concentric ring BM. It weighed 1.65t (*1.62 tons*) and fired similar ammunition to the M1932 at the same muzzle velocity. Loading was by spring rammers, the guns were in a common cradle and the mounting, which weighed 13.5t (*13.3 tons*) allowed +80°-10° elevation. The firing cycle is given as 6sec and maximum range as 15,800m (*17,280yd*) with ceiling about 10,000m (*32,280ft*).

M1927. Similar to M1932 and firing the same ammunition with identical MV. It was in single mountings allowing +85°-10° in the seaplane tender *Commandant Teste*.

M1925. This 45-calibre gun was introduced in the *Redoutable* class submarines in a mounting with +70°-10° elevation. It had concentric ring BM and fired *c*14.5kg (*32lb*) shells at 760m/s (*2493fs*).

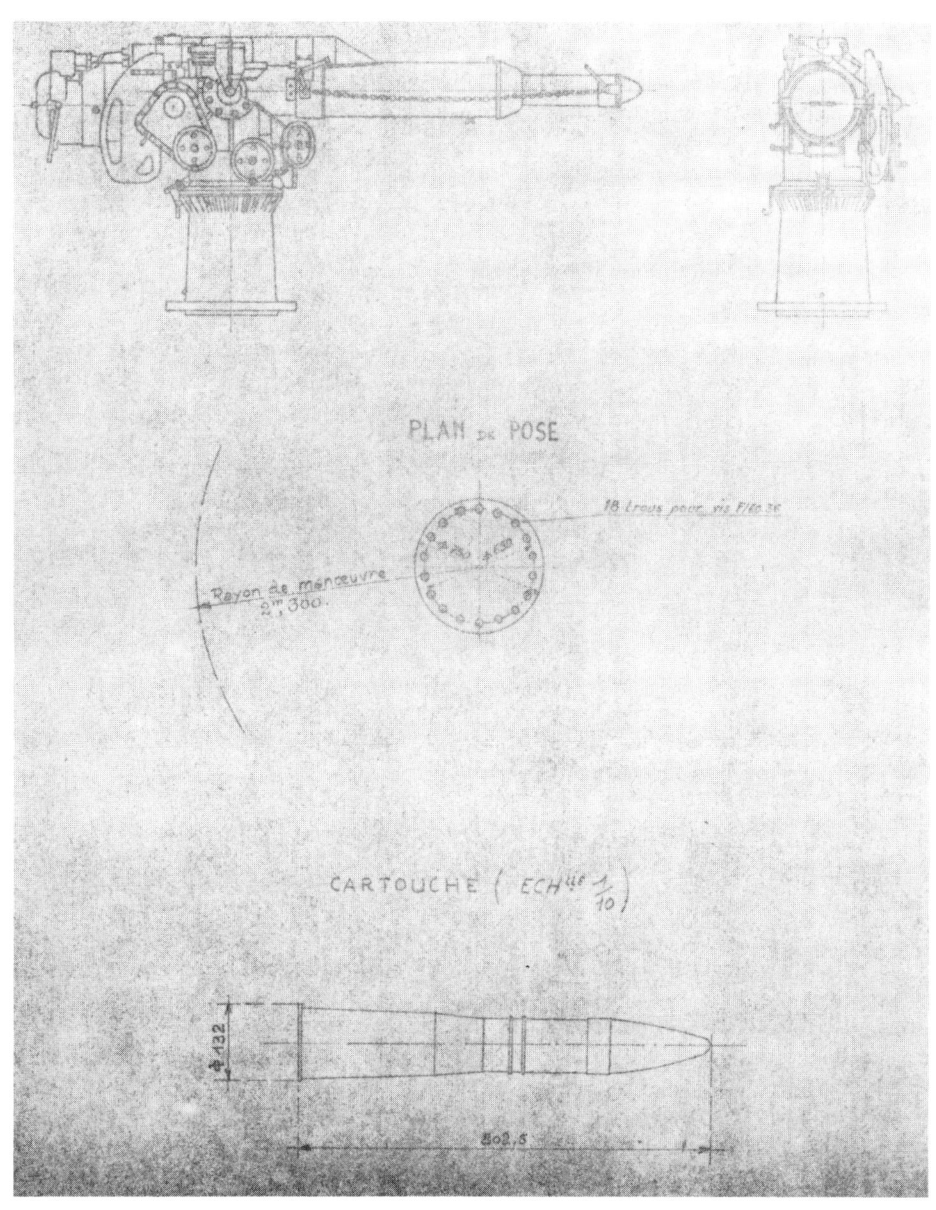

100mm M1936 gun in SM M1936 mounting, intended for future French submarines.
Official, by courtesy of Robert Dumas

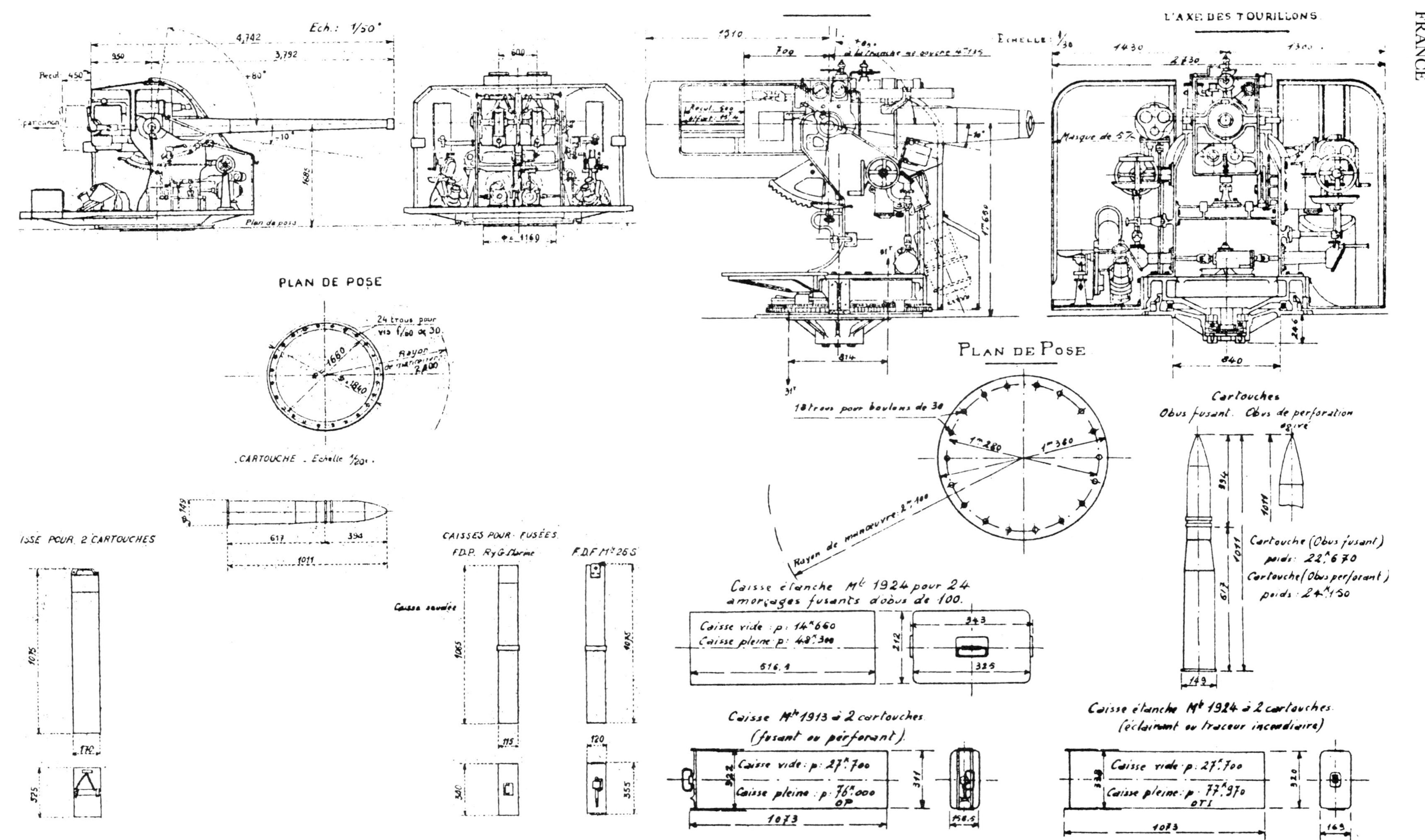

100mm M1930 guns in twin CAD M1931 mounting. This was introduced as the AA armament of the *Algérie* and was then for a time in the reconstructed *Lorraine* and in 1939 in the *Richelieu*.
Official, by courtesy of Robert Dumas

100mm M1927 gun in CA M1927 mounting only in the *Commandant Teste*.
Official, by courtesy of Robert Dumas

100mm M1925 gun in SMCA/CA M1925 mounting in *Redoutable* class submarines and some oil tankers.
Official, by courtesy of Robert Dumas

90mm M1926 gun in twin CAD M1930 mounting. In several ships including *Dupleix*, *Emile Bertin* and the *La Galissonière* class.
Official, by courtesy of Robert Dumas

Older Models. 45-calibre guns included M1891[2], 1892, 1893, 1897 T[e] 1917 and 1917. They were in older warships and auxiliaries, and differed from later guns in firing separate and not fixed ammunition. A gun similar, if not identical, to M1917 is believed to have been in the *Requin* class, and this version may have fired fixed rounds. With a 16.0kg (*35.3lb*) SAP shell MV was 703m/s (*2306f/s*). Guns of 26.2 calibre were QFC and included M1881 TR and TR T[e] 1891-92. They were limited to minor armed ships and auxiliaries, and with the above SAP shell MV was 510m/s (*1673f/s*).

90mm (3.543in)/50 M1926

This AA gun was carried in single CA M1926 or twin CA M1930 mountings by the *Colbert, Foch, Dupleix, Émile Bertin* and the *La Galissonnière* class. It was also in the *Jean Bart* as an emergency armament and in various other warships, such as the net-layer *Gladiateur* and some escorts of the *Élan* and *Chamois* classes. The gun had an autofretted barrel with SA Schneider concentric ring BM and weighed 1.60t (*1.57 tons*). The HE shell was 9.505kg (*20.955lb*) and with a 3.1kg (*6.83lb*) BM5 charge MV was 850m/s (*2789f/s*). The fixed round weighed 18kg (*39.7lb*) and range was 15,440m (*16,885 yd*) at 40° with ceiling 10,600m (*34,800ft*) at 80°.

The mountings allowed +80° -10°, and the twin appears to have had the guns in a common cradle. There were automatic rammers, but loading was difficult at over 60° and the firing cycle is given as 6sec. Recoil was 50cm (*19.7in*) and the weight of the mounting 13.7t (*13.5 tons*) for the twin and 7t (*6.7 tons*) for the single.

90mm (3.543in)/24 M1877, 1891

An old BL field gun mounted on Elswick shoulder-piece mountings, and used in the First World War for minor armed merchant vessels. Some survived and were used by the French for the same purpose in the Second World War. The shell weighed 8.3kg (*18.3lb*) and MV was 490m/s (*1608f/s*).

75mm (2.953in)/50 M1922, 1924, 1927

These AA guns were in single mountings in many ships including the *Bretagne* class, *Béarn, Suffren* and *Duquesne* and *Duguay Trouin* classes. The gun weighed 1.070t (*1.053 tons*) and had Schneider concentric ring BM. The shell weighed 5.93kg (*13.07lb*) and with 2.18kg (*4.81lb*) BM5 charge MV was 850m/s (*2789f/s*). The fixed round weighed 12kg (*26.5lb*) and was 966.7mm (*38.06in*) long. Range at 40° was 14,100m (*15,420yd*) and ceiling at 90° about 10,000m (*32,800ft*). The firing cycle is variously given as 7.5sec and 4sec.

Other **75mm** (2.953in) guns

34.5-calibre guns included M1925 and M1928, AA in many of the smaller submarines, and M1897 and M1915-18 adapted versions of the famous field gun, mostly in minor ships. HE

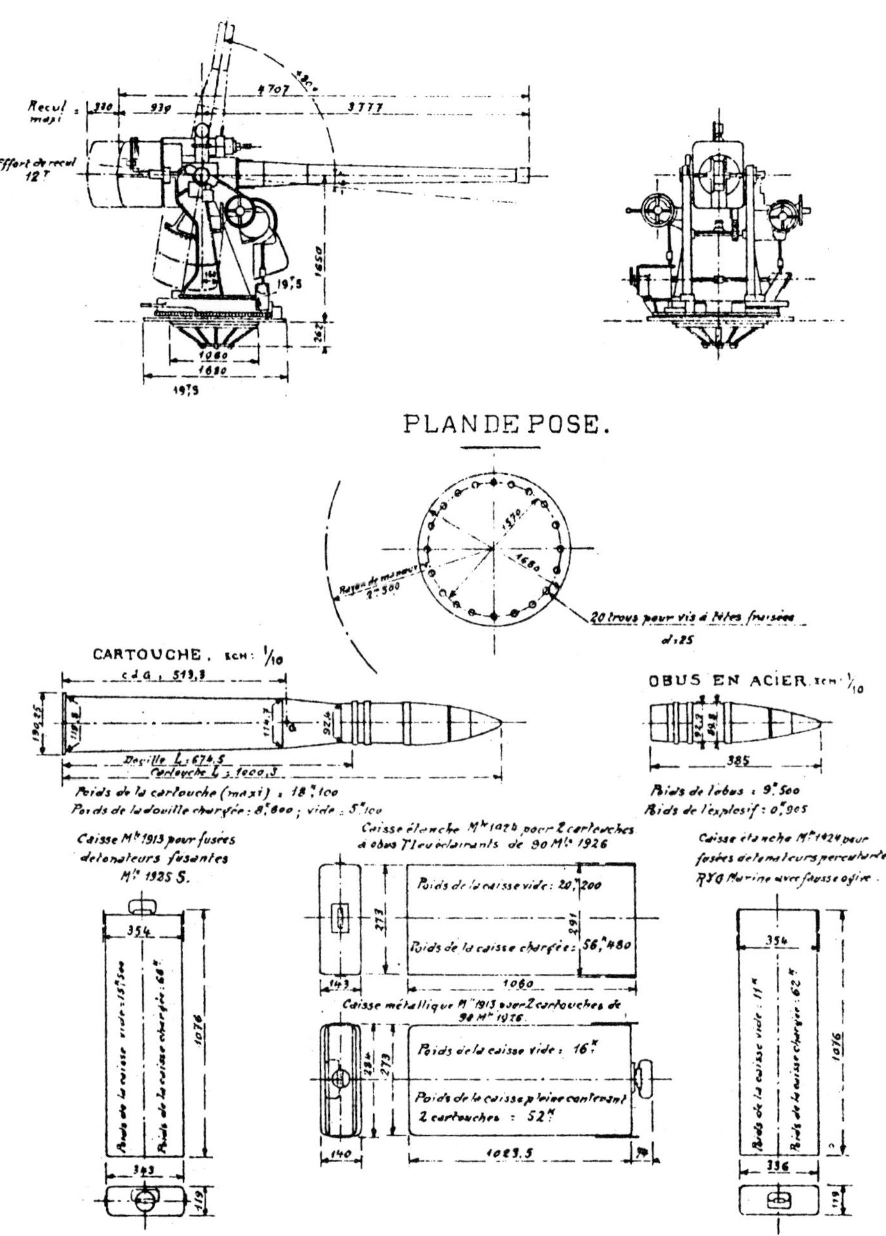

Above: 90mm M1926 gun in CA M1926 mounting. This was in a number of ships including *Colbert* and *Foch*.
Official, by courtesy of Robert Dumas

Below: 75mm M1922 gun in CA M1922 mounting. In many ships but superseded in the more recent by 90mm or larger guns.
Robert Dumas

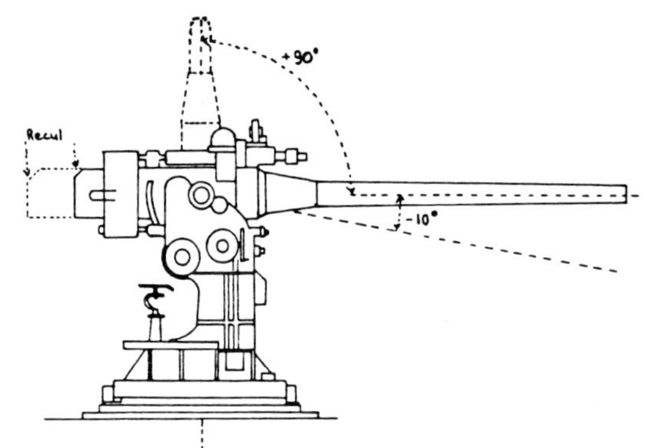

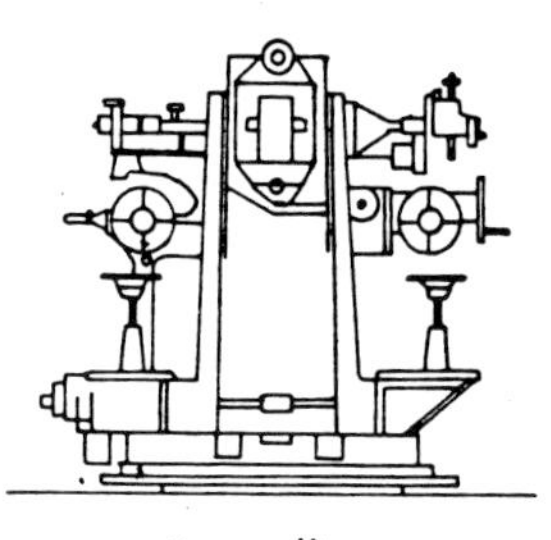

shells weighed 6.175kg (*13.6lb*) and MV was 570m/s (*1870f/s*) while SAP, for use against surfaced submarines, was 7.98kg (*17.6lb*) with MV 505m/s (*1657f/s*).

The 62.5-calibre M1908 originally mounted as the anti-torpedo craft battery in the *Danton* class still occurred in a list of range tables. With the same HE shell weight as above, MV was 860m/s (*2822f/s*), though it was originally given as 930m/s (*3051f/s*) with a 6.4kg (*14.1lb*) shell.

65mm (2.559in) guns

The 50-calibre M1902 firing a 4.17kg (*9.19lb*) shell at 800m/s (*2625f/s*) was still listed, as was the older 50-calibre M1888-91 with MV 715m/s (*2346f/s*).

47mm (1.850in) guns

These comprised the 40-calibre Hotchkiss M1885 and the 50-calibre M1902.

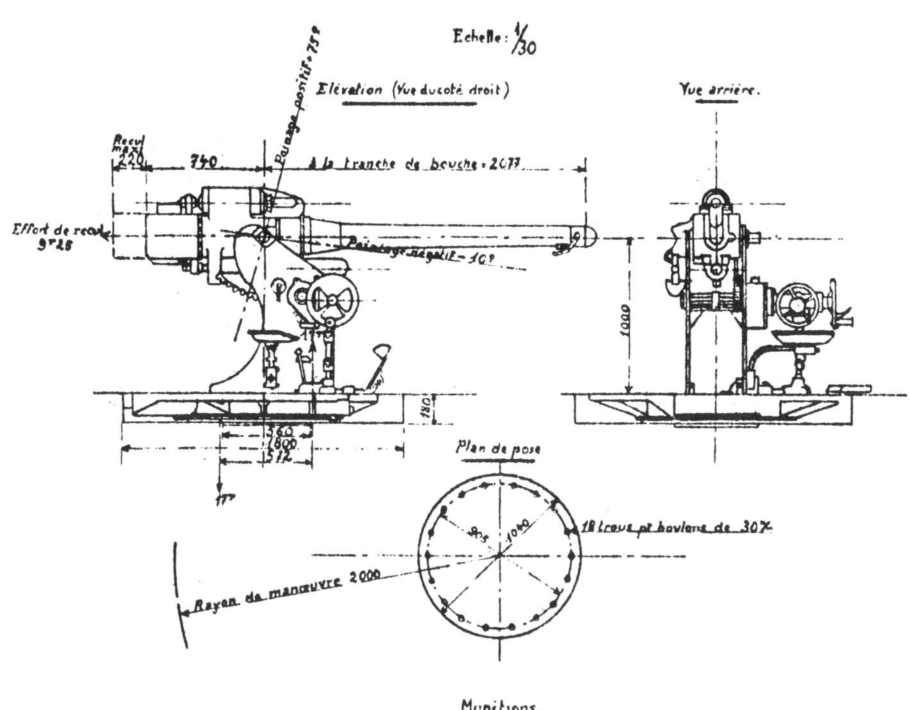

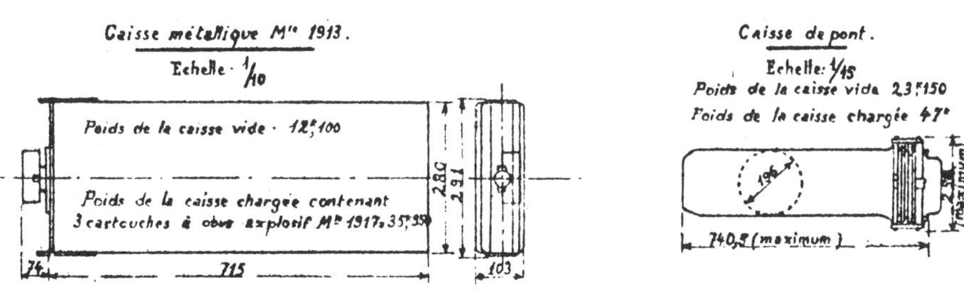

Left: 75mm M1928 gun in SMCA M1928 mounting, carried by many smaller submarines.
Official, by courtesy of Robert Dumas

Below: 75mm M1897-15 gun in CA M1925 mounting. A modification of the famous field-gun; in some smaller submarines and other vessels.
Official, by courtesy of Robert Dumas

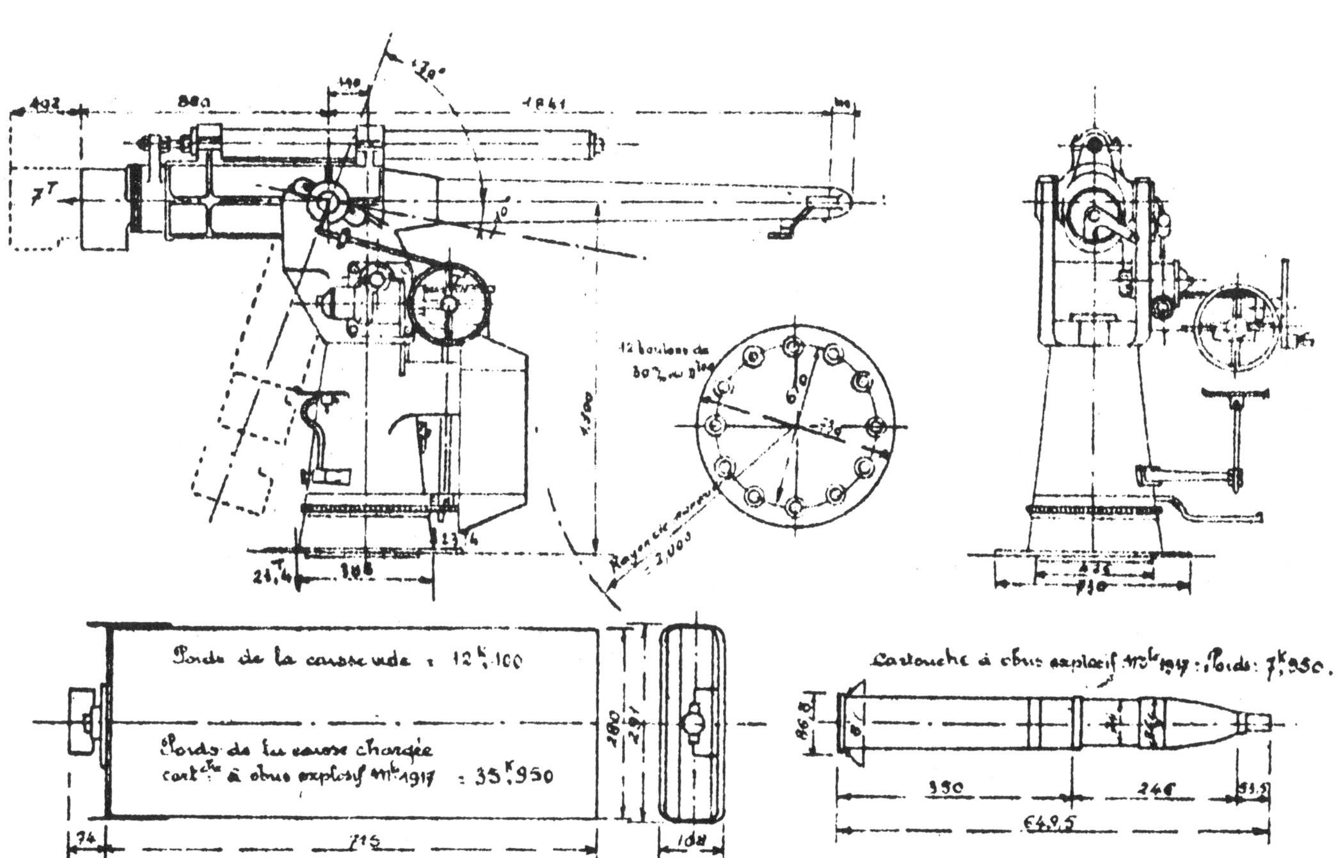

AUTOMATIC GUNS

37mm (1.457in) guns

These were the principal light AA guns in French ships, except for those fortunate enough to acquire the Bofors from Allied sources.

M1935. A 48-calibre fully automatic gun intended for the most important and most recent ships in quadruple or twin mountings. Development was not completed, but a prototype twin base-ring mounting was tried in the old sloop *Amiens*, apparently with success. Each gun had a pusher hoist for six-round magazines and the mounting was electrically powered with Sautter-Harlé RPC for training but not for elevation. The rate of fire per gun was 165 per minute, and with a 0.831kg (*1.83lb*) shell and 0.21kg (*0.46lb*) special Hotchkiss charge MV was 825m/s (*2707f/s*). Elevation was given as +85° -10° and range as 8000m (*8750yd*).

M1925 and M1933. 50-calibre SA guns in single and twin mountings respectively. The rate of fire was given as 30–42 rounds per minute and the highest quoted MV 850m/s (*2789f/s*) with a 0.725kg (*1.598lb*) shell.

They were not adequate AA guns, particularly as the initial number of barrels per ship never exceeded 12 and rarely 8. It may be noted that when the *Richelieu* was refitted at New York Navy Yard in 1943, her 37mm were replaced by 14 quadruple Bofors.

Twin 37mm M1933 guns in *Le Triomphant* 1941. *CPL*

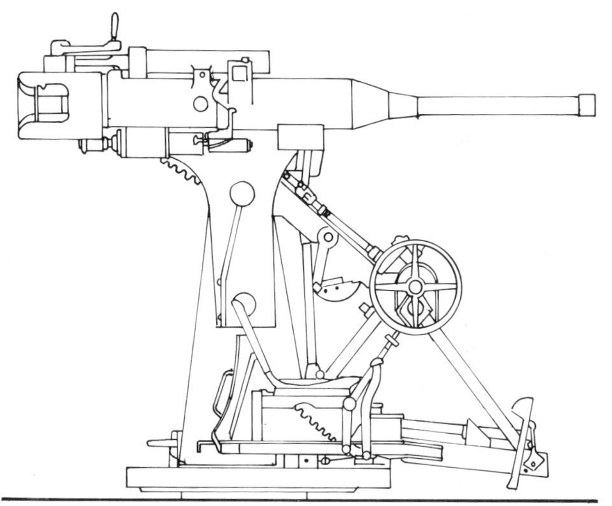

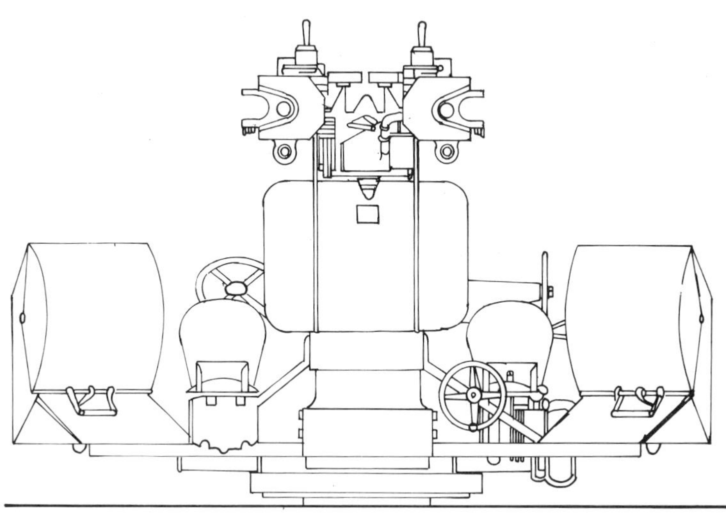

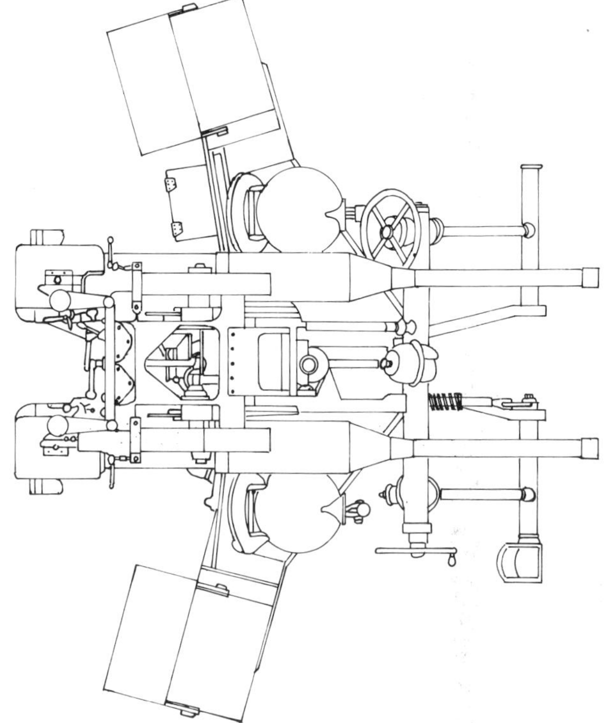

37mm M1933 guns in twin CAD M1933 mounting. One of the standard French AA weapons but not automatic firing and therefore inadequate.
John Lambert

37mm M1925 gun in CA/SMCA M1925 mounting. Of similar performance to the M1933 gun.
Official, by courtesy of Robert Dumas

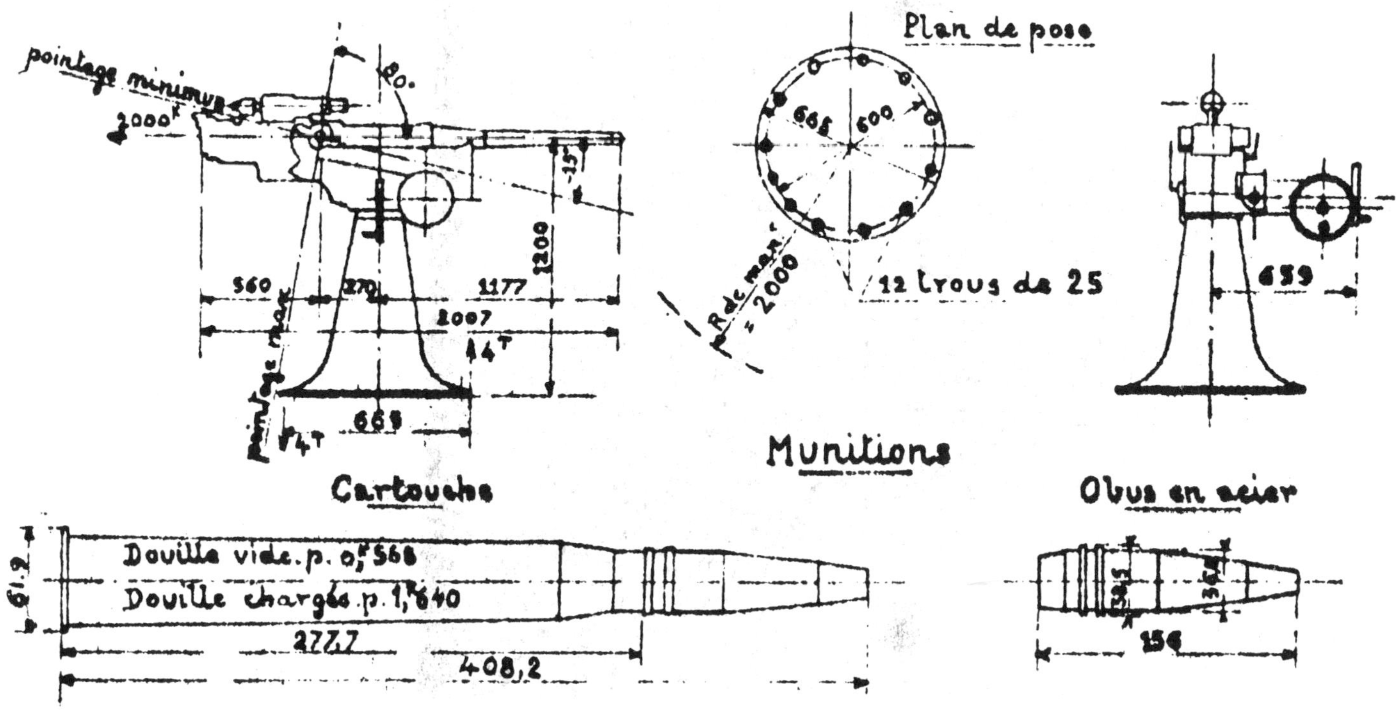

Lighter guns

Included in these were 25mm (*0.984in*), 13.2mm *(0.520in)* and 8mm (*0.315in*) Hotchkiss and 7.5mm (*0.295in*) MAC and Darne. The most interesting were the 25mm M1938 and the 13.2mm. The former was a water-cooled 60-calibre gun firing a 0.25–0.30kg (*0.55–0.66lb*) projectile at 900–875m/s (*2953–2871f/s*). The magazine held 15 rounds and rate of fire was given at 250–300 rounds per minute. Mountings were mostly twin. Few, if any, reached service.

The 13.2mm 76-calibre gun was widely used in twin and quadruple mountings. The projectile was 50–52gm (*1.76–1.83ozs*) and MV 800m/s (*2625f/s*). There was a 30-round magazine and rate of fire was 450 rounds per minute. In ships rearmed from allied sources this gun was largely replaced by the 20mm (*0.787in*) Oerlikon.

Below: 13.2mm Hotchkiss machine gun with magazine feed, shown in section.
Official, by courtesy of Robert Dumas

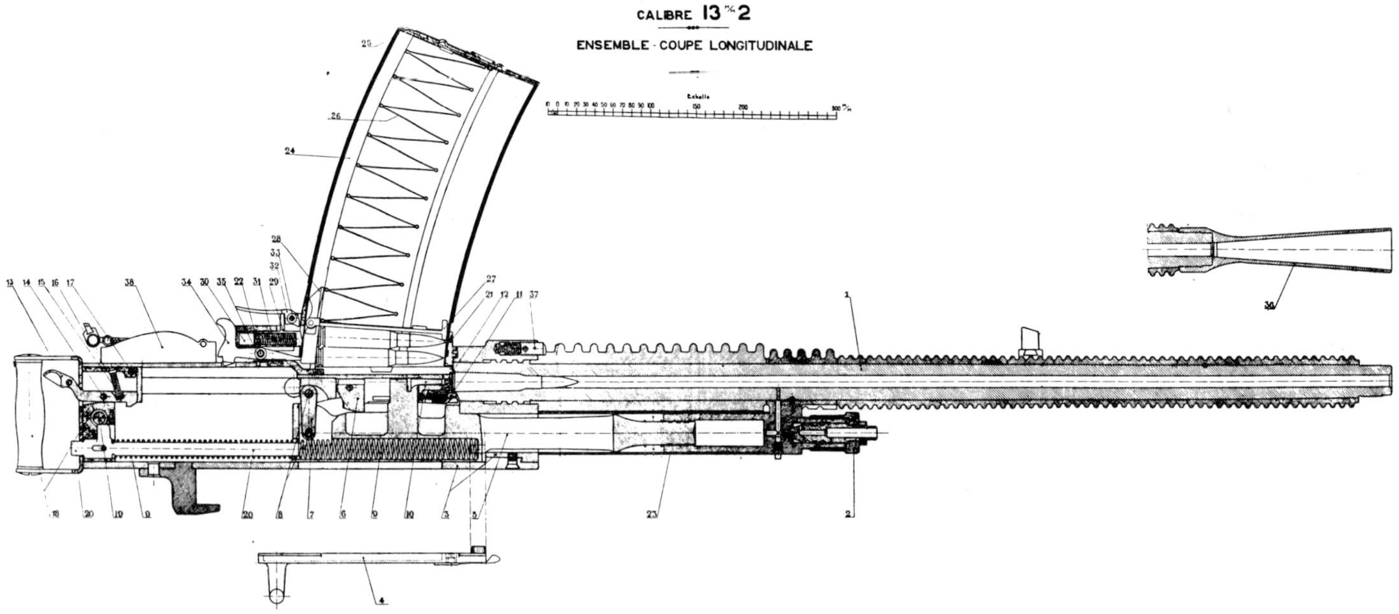

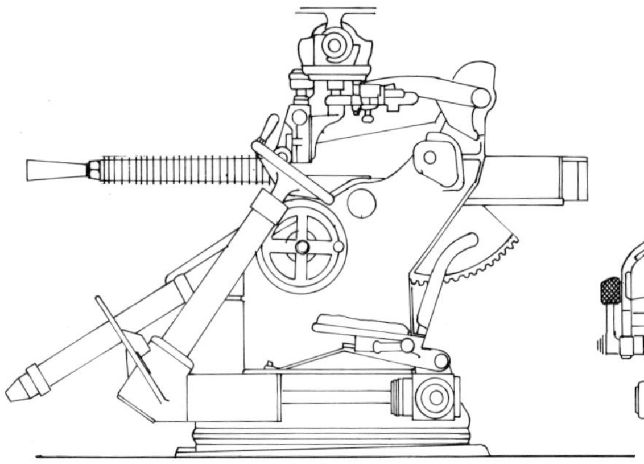

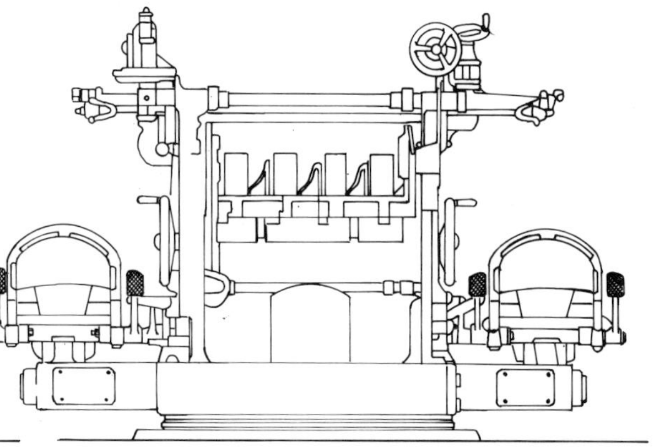

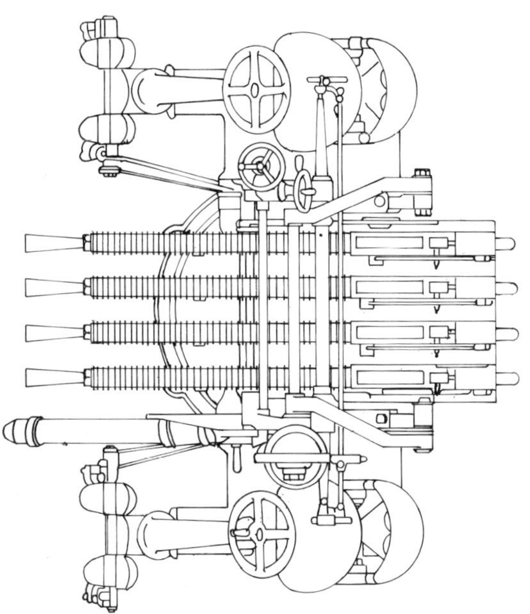

Left: General arrangement of 13.2mm Hotchkiss in quadruple mounting.
John Lambert

Right: 13.2mm Hotchkiss in twin Type R4 mounting.
Official, by courtesy of Robert Dumas

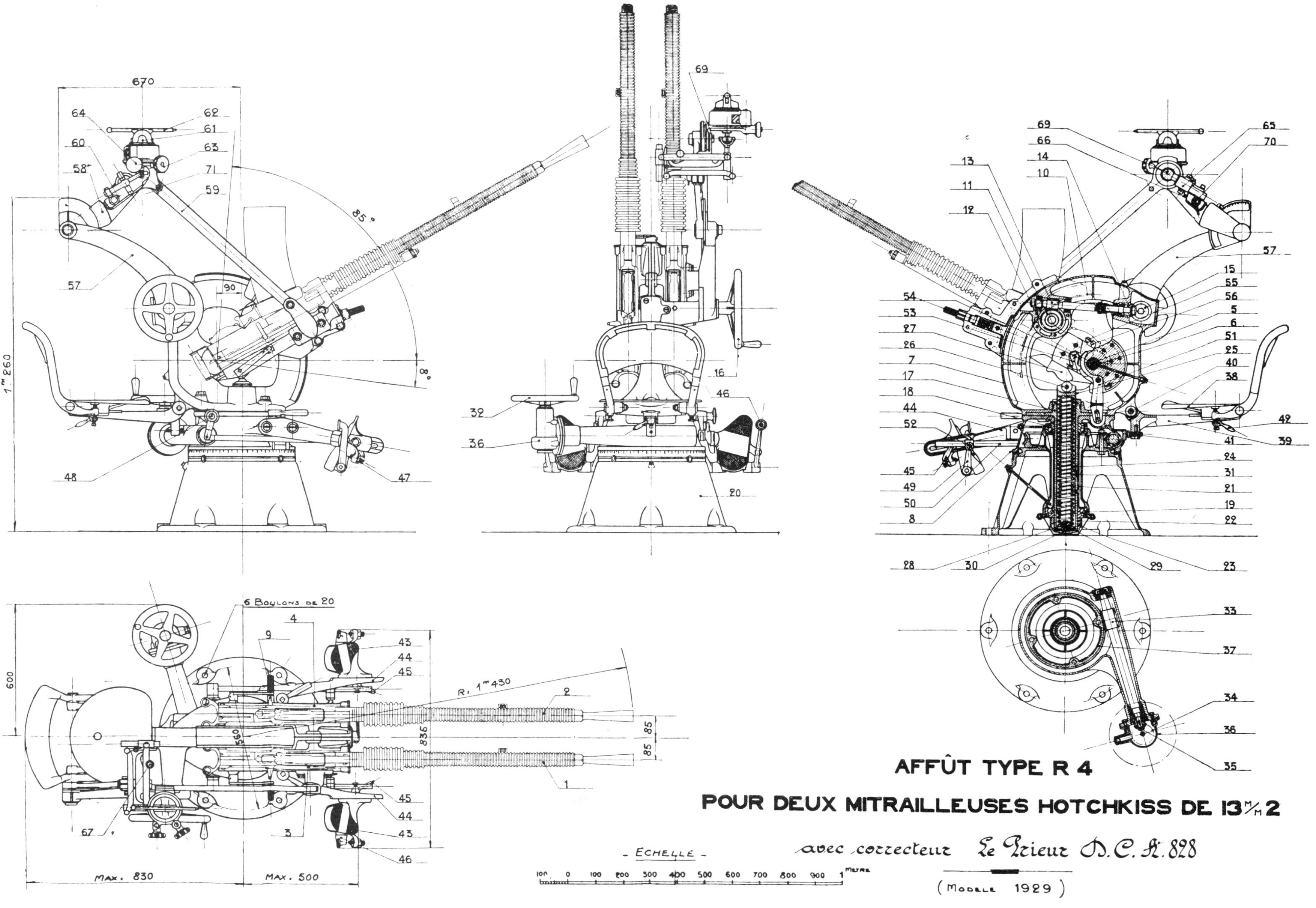
AFFÛT TYPE R 4
POUR DEUX MITRAILLEUSES HOTCHKISS DE 13 M/M 2
avec correcteur Le Prieur D.C.A. 828
(Modèle 1929)
- ECHELLE -
100 0 100 200 300 400 500 600 700 800 900 1 MÈTRE
6 Boulons de 20
Max. 830
Max. 500
R. 1 m 430
1 m 260
670
600
836
560
85
85
85°
8°
90

TORPEDOES

French torpedoes were generally designed at Toulon and made there or at St Tropez, in which works Schneider had an interest. The Toulon workshops were severely damaged in the war, and in 1945 production was centralised at St Tropez. The main wartime interest lies in the alcohol fuelled single-stage turbine system developed in 1926 and used in the 40cm (*15.75in*) torpedoes. This was one of the best turbine systems of the period between the World Wars, because of the high gas temperature of 1300°C at the nozzles. At 15,000rpm, 175HP was developed with a total weight of 190lb (*86kg*), also as 190HP, 175lb (*79kg*), and a consumption rate of 17.5lb (*7.94kg*)/HP/hr made up of 14.20lb (*6.44kg*) air, 1.60lb (*0.73kg*) fuel and 1.7lb (*0.77kg*) diluent.

Experiments made in 1913 with sea water as diluent in a turbine had been abandoned. Turbine work continued, however, after 1926 and culminated in an oxygen torpedo produced towards the end of the Second World War. The usual explosive charge was TNT but 85 per cent TNT, 15 per cent aluminium was also used.

Starboard triple TT for 55cm M1923DT torpedoes in *Le Triomphant* 1941.
CPL

A Kerosene wet-heater torpedo with four-cylinder radial engine.

55cm (21.65in) 19V, Toulon

Length oa	6.6m	21ft 8in
Total weight	1385kg	3053lb
Volume air vessel	486 litres	17.16ft^3
Pressure	150kg/cm^2	2130lb/in^2
Explosive charge	238kg picric acid	525lb picric acid
Range	2000m/43kts	2200yd/43kts
	4000m/35kts	4400yd/35kts

55cm (21.65in) 19D, Toulon

This was essentially an enlarged and longer range version of 19V.

Data

Length oa	8.2m	26ft 11in
Total weight	1830kg	4034lb
Volume air vessel	804 litres	28.4ft^3
Pressure	170kg/cm^2	2420lb/in^2
Explosive charge	238kg picric acid	525lb picric acid
Range	6000m/35kts	6560yd/35kts
	14,000m/25kts	15,300yd/25kts

55cm (21.65in) 23DT, Toulon

This was a much improved torpedo carried by flotilla leaders and destroyers. The engine was a four-cylinder radial working on the Schneider alcohol/air heater system with alcohol acting as fuel and diluent.

The ranges for 23D used in cruisers are given as 6000m (*6560yd*)/43kts, 14,000m (*15,300yd*)/35kts, 20,000m (*21,900yd*)/29kts.

Data

Length oa	8.28m	27ft 2in
Total weight	2068kg	4560lb
Volume air vessel	822 litres	29.03ft^3
Pressure	200kg/cm^2	2850lb/in^2
Explosive charge	310kg TNT	683lb TNT
Range	9000m/39kts	9840yd/39kts
	13,000m/35kts	14,200yd/35kts

55cm (21.65in) 24V, 24M, Toulon

These were also alcohol/air heater torpedoes but had two-cylinder horizontal engines. They were carried by submarines.

Data

Length oa	6.6m	21ft 8in
Total weight	1490kg	3285lb
Volume air vessel	460 litres	16.2ft^3
Pressure	194kg/cm^2	2760lb/in^2
Explosive charge	310kg TNT	683lb TNT
Range	3000m/45kts	3300yd/45kts
	7000m/35kts	7650yd/35kts

These figures are for an early version, as ranges are given later as 4000m (*4400yd*)/45kts, 8000m (*8750yd*)/35kts. There is also mention of a 415kg (*915lb*) TNT explosive charge.

55cm (21.65in) oxygen torpedo

Details of this turbine-driven torpedo produced in 1944-45 are not to hand. Various ranges have been quoted including 3000m (*3300yd*)/55kts to 8000m (*8750yd*)/50kts and 18,000m (*19,700yd*)/40kts to 9150m (*10,000yd*)/46kts.

45cm (17.7in) M12D, Toulon

A wet-heater torpedo of old design. Length 5.75m (*18ft 10in*), weight 1012kg (*2231lb*), explosive charge 145kg (*320lb*) TNT, range 8000m (*8750yd*)/28kts.

M18 was 5.88m (*19ft 3½in*) in length with top speed 3000m (*3300yd*)/34kts.

40cm (15.75in) 26V, W, DA, Toulon/St Tropez

A turbine engined torpedo as described above, 26V being used in submarines, 26W in MTB and 26DA in aircraft. Maximum dropping height in the last is said to have been 80m (*260ft*) and the propellers were surrounded by a shroud ring.

Data

Length oa	5.14m	16ft 10½in
Total weight	674kg	1486lb
Volume air vessel	120 litres	4.24ft^3
Pressure	200kg/cm^2	2850lb/in^2
Explosive charge	144kg TNT	317lb TNT
Range	2000m/44kts	2200yd/44kts
	3000m/35kts	3300yd/35kts

ANTI-SUBMARINE WEAPONS

For the most part these comprised depth charges carried by surface ships. An airborne depth charge was under trial. The Ginocchio anti-submarine towed torpedo was apparently carried by *Le Hardi* class destroyers and by torpedo boats, but details have not been found.

Depth charges

200kg (*441lb*) charge. The total weight was 260kg (*573lb*), dimensions 50 × 88cm (*19.7* × 34.6in), sinking speed 3m (*10ft*)/sec and depth settings 30m (*100ft*), 50m (*165ft*), 75m (*250ft*), 100m (*330ft*) or in an improved version 40m (*130ft*), 80m (*260ft*), 120m (*390ft*). Fuzing was hydrostatic.

100kg (*220lb*) charge. In this the total weight was 130kg (*287lb*), dimensions 35 × 84cm (*13.8* × 33in), sinking speed 2.2m (*7.2ft*)/sec and depth settings 30m (*100ft*), 50m (*165ft*), 75m (*250ft*), 100m (*330ft*).

35kg (*77lb*) charge. This small DC had total weight 52kg (*115lb*) and sinking speed and depth settings as above.

The 200kg charge was carried by destroyers and destroyer leaders and dropped at 30–50m (*100–165ft*) intervals from enclosed roller chain stowages which each held 12 DCs. The 100kg charge was carried by sloops and similar vessels and either dropped or thrown, while the 35kg charge was for small slow craft.

With the 100kg charge the 100/250 M1928 trainable mortar could reach 250m(273yd) in 5–6sec, while the Thornycroft 24cm (*9.45in*) mortar had a range of 60m (*66yd*) with 4sec flight time.

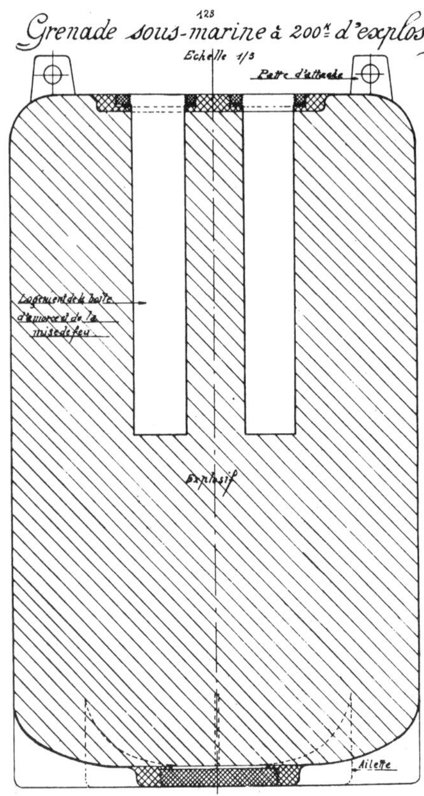

DC with 200kg charge carried by destroyers and dropped from enclosed roller-chain stowages.
Official, by courtesy of Robert Dumas

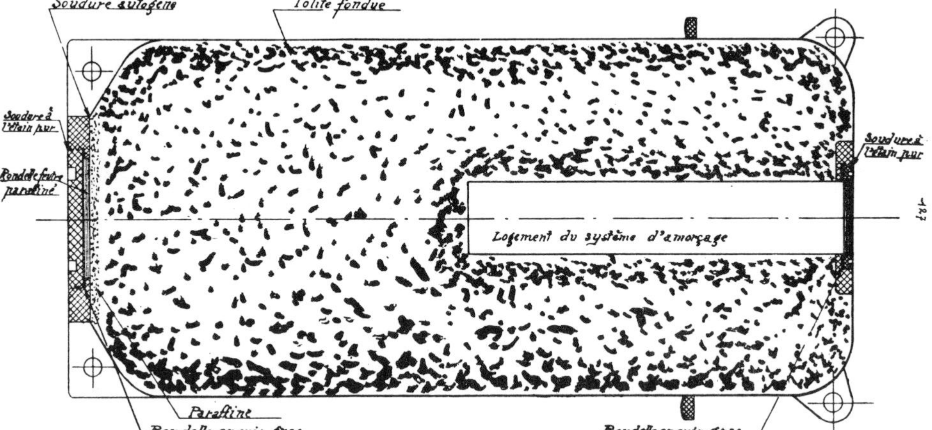

DC with 100kg charge. It could be fired from the 100/250 M1928 mortar and the 24cm Thornycroft mortar.
Official, by courtesy of Robert Dumas

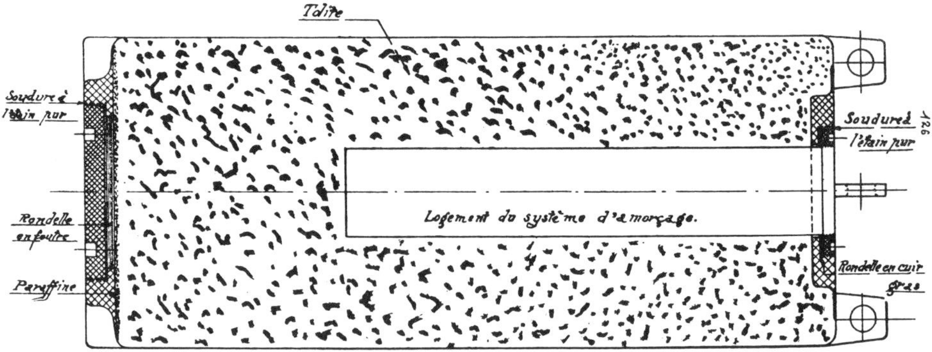

DC with 35kg charge carried by slow A/S vessels.
Official, by courtesy of Robert Dumas

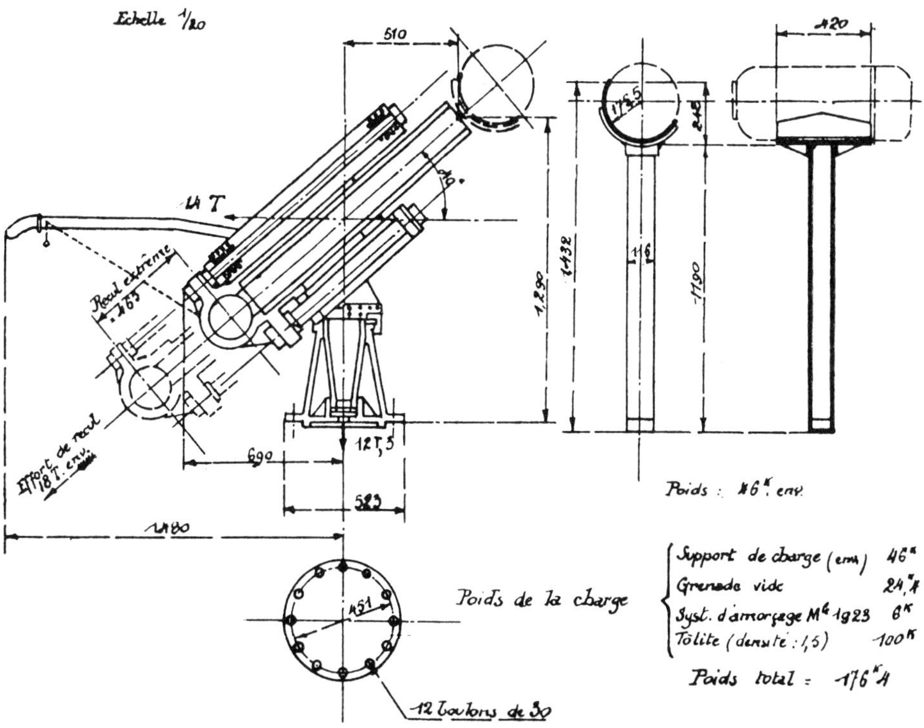

100/250 M1928 mortar on trainable mounting.
Official, by courtesy of Robert Dumas

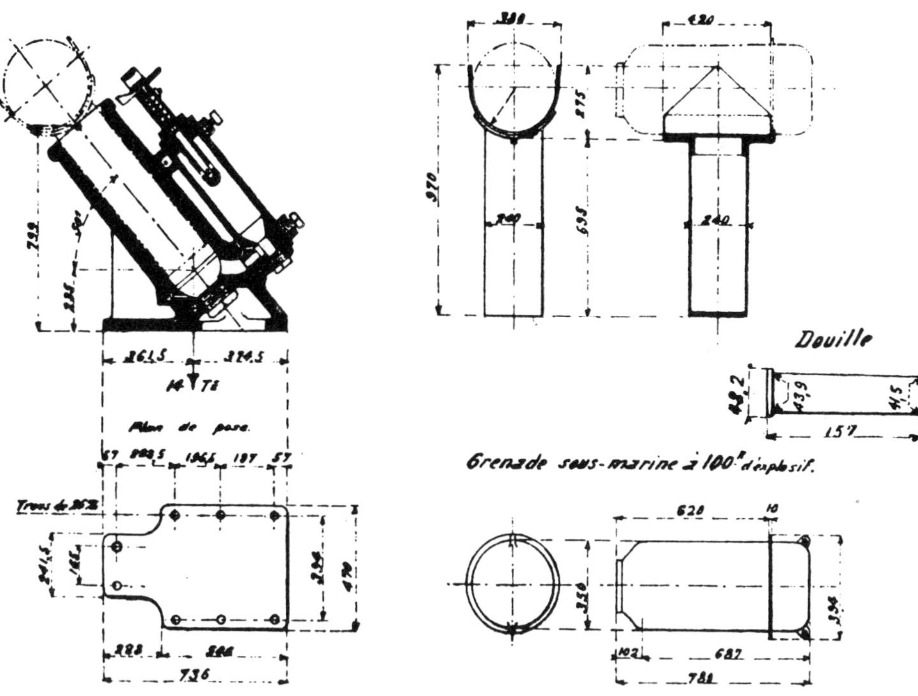

24cm Thornycroft mortar. This was on a fixed mounting.
Official, by courtesy of Robert Dumas

MINES

The development of new types of mine would doubtless have progressed if the whole French navy had remained as an active force in 1939–45. As it was the mines in service were mostly of moored contact type, generally with switch horns. Explosive charges were normally TNT or picric acid (Mélinite). A prefix B to the model number indicated Bréguet mines, H Sautter-Harlé, HS Sautter-Harlé for submarines. Other letters usually after the model number, included:

AR	(*Amorçage rapide*) rapid priming.
B	Brown type antennae.
G	Made at Guérigny to Harlé drawings.
M	Modified.
P	(*Profonde*), depth of mine increased from 40m (*22 fathoms*) to 90m (*49 fathoms*).
SM	Submarines.
U	(*Unifiée*), built with standardised parts.
UM	Mine deeper than P, at least 180m (*98 fathoms*).
Y	Hertz horns.
Z	Switch horns.

Of those without switch horns, B1, B2, B3 had lever firing, H1 pendulum and MC 38 induction. B5B and some H5 had antennae, the former mine having 25m (*82ft*) upper and 30m (*98ft*) lower. In addition to the above there is believed to have been a moored spherical mine with lever firing and 150-200kg (*331-441lb*) charge. Some other details were as follows:

B1 Spherical shell.
B2 In service 1916.
B3 In service 1922. Mooring wire 400m (*219 fathoms*).
B4, 4M In service 1936. Mooring wire 225m (*123 fathoms*), 300m (*164 fathoms*), 400m (*219 fathoms*), mine at 90m (*49 fathoms*).
B5B Mine at 90m (*49 fathoms*).
H3 In service 1916.
H4 In service 1924. Coast defence mine.
H4AR In service 1930.
H5 In service 1928.
H5AR In service 1930.
H5UM1, 2 In service 1935. Mooring wire 500m (*273 fathoms*), mine at 180m (*98 fathoms*).
H52M Experimental 1938, for great depths.
H7 Multiple mine for use against submarines - four auxiliary bombs, each with four Hertz horns. Mooring wire 300m (*164 fathoms*).
HS1M In service 1920.
HS2 In service 1920. Mooring wire 220m (*120 fathoms*).
HS4 In service 1928. Mooring wire 200m (*109 fathoms*).
HS4AR In service 1930. Spherical shell.
HS4P In service 1930. Spherical shell, mine at 90m (*94 fathoms*).
MC 38 Trials.

Mines

Mine	Total weight kg(lb)	Charge kg(lb)	Shell dia m(in)	Switch horns
B1	360 (*794*)	60 (*132*) g-c	0.77 (*30*)	None
B2	650 (*1433*)	100 (*220*) Mélin	0.865 (*34*)	None
B3	670 (*1477*)	110 (*243*) Mélin	0.865 (*34*)	None
B4, 4M	530 (*1168*)	80 (*176*) Mélin	0.785 (*31*)	6
B5B	1150 (*2535*)	220 (*485*)	—	4
H1	520 (1146)	80 (*176*) g-c	0.90 (*35*)	None
H3	452/502 (*996/1107*)	60 (*132*)g-c	0.75 (*29.5*)	5
H4, 4AR	1135 (*2502*)	220 (*485*) TNT	1.04 (*41*)	5; 4 in AR
H5, 5AR	1160 (*2557*)	220 (*485*) TNT	1.04 (*41*)	5; 4 in AR
H5UM1,2	1100 (*2425*)	220 (*485*) TNT	1.04 (*41*)	4
H5 2M	—	—	—	—
H6	—	330 (*661*)	1.15 (*45*)	4
H7	665 (*1446*)	100 (*220*)	0.83 (*33*)	6
HS1	488 (*1076*)	60 (*132*) g-c	0.77 (*30*)	5
HS1M	700 (*1543*)	113 (*249*) TNT	0.77 (*30*)	5
HS2	1090 (*2403*)	220 (*485*) TNT	1.04 (*41*)	5
HS4, 4U, 4UM 4AR, 4P	1150 (*2535*)	220 (*485*) TNT	1.04 (*41*)	5; 4 pushrod in AR, P
HS4V	1150 (*2535*)	200 (*441*)	1.04 (*41*)	4
HS4UM1,2	1150 (*2535*)	220 (*485*)	1.00 (*39*)	—
HS5	—	220 (*485*)	1.04 (*41*)	4
HS6	1150 (*2535*)	200 (*441*)	1.04 (*41*)	4
MC38	575 (*1268*)	80 (*176*)	0.60 (*23.6*)	None

There was also a mine for the TT of submarines under development, but work was apparently suspended in 1938, and airborne moored and drifting mines, both under development in 1938.

BOMBS

As with other countries, no attempt has been made to give a complete list. Special AP bombs included a 220kg (*485lb*) derived from a 24cm (*9.45in*) shell, and the 560kg (*1235lb*) M1939 derived from a 34cm (*13.4in*).

The largest HE bombs found are listed.

HE Bombs

Weight	Dimensions	Charge	Remarks
536kg (*1182lb*)	545 × 2230mm (*21.5 × 87.8in*)	300kg (*661lb*)	2 fuzes
570kg (*1257lb*)	490 × 2150mm (*19.3 × 84.6in*)	270kg (*595lb*)	2 fuzes, case 11mm (0.43in)

ITALY

Of all the major naval powers, Italy had the weakest industrial base, and although the navy was favoured more than the army and airforce in the provision of high-performance armament, there was no specialised naval airforce, and no aircraft carrier entered service, while many features of the AA gun armament needed attention, as did surface fire-control. The Italian Navy was backward in the development of radar, with on occasions disastrous results in night action. One development on the borders between weapons and warships was the 'slow-course torpedo', generally known as *Maiale* (pig), which achieved considerable success and, unlike the Japanese kaiten, offered its crew a fair chance of survival.

Littorio firing forward 381mm turrets with practice charges. The forward starboard 152mm turret is also shown.
Elio Ando'

NAVAL GUNS

Ansaldo and OTO, the main sources of Italian naval guns and mountings, at first developed their designs from Armstrong and Vickers originals, but later diverged to a considerable extent. For a time Schneider, too, had some influence on Ansaldo. The most original Italian constructional feature was the use of thin taper liners. They were sometimes of loose type (it is not known how far these had to be fitted to a particular A tube) and also of shrunk or tupped pattern. In addition some use was made of the Salerno process of expanding liners in position. The seating for the liner was machined oversize and the liner expanded by a series of drifts drawn through hydraulically. The chamber and rifling had to be finally machined.

The original muzzle velocity of many Italian guns was very high considering the shell weight, and in several cases had to be drastically reduced in the interests of accuracy and life. Muzzle velocities were determined at a charge temperature of 32°C (*89.6°F*).

Much ingenuity was shown in adapting old designs. The numerous guns of the 100mm (*3.937in*) series were developed from the Skoda gun of that calibre used by the Austro-Hungarian navy in the First World War, and the 320mm (*12.6in*) was a retubing of the 304.8mm (*12in*) Armstrong and Vickers guns in the Italian dreadnoughts of the same period. As far as is known, this increase in bore was unique in service heavy naval guns, though during the First World War the French produced 285mm (*11.22in*) railway guns from 274mm (*10.79in*), and 400mm (*15.75in*) and 370mm (*14.57in*) long howitzers from 340mm (*13.39in*) and 305mm (*12in*) guns.

GUN MOUNTINGS

Italian mountings were generally powered electrically, and the 381mm (*15in*) triple turret and the quadraxial 90mm (*3.543in*) AA mounting are described in some detail under their respective guns. The latter was not entirely successful and the same is true of the moving-trunnion twin Minisini 100mm (*3.937in*) AA which was widely used. A bad feature in many twin mountings from 203mm (*8in*) downwards was the coupling of the guns in a common cradle with the gun axes close together. This introduced serious inaccuracies from shell interference if the two guns were fired together as intended. Turrets were supported on roller paths, except for most 203mm (*8in*) and 152mm (*6in*) which were on ball tracks.

The most interesting feature of ammunition supply was the replacement of the upper part of the hoists by a swinging arm pivoted about the cradle trunnions. This was introduced in the twin mountings for the 203mm (*8in*)/53 and was also in 152mm (*6in*) twins. Its origins appear to have been in Skoda designs for projected heavy gun turrets.

PROPELLANTS

For many years the Italian navy had used a propellant, referred to as C, of typical composition 25.5% nitroglycerin, 68.5% nitrocellulose, 5% petroleum jelly, 1% sodium bicarbonate. This was similar to CSP_2, Chilworth Special 2, much favoured by Elswick before the First World War as an alternative to MD cordite, and also similar to the German RPC/06 which was their standard propellant until the introduction of the solventless RPC/12. It was not until 1936 that the Italian Navy introduced solventless propellants with NAC from Dinamite Nobel and FC_4 from Bombrini-Parodi-Delfino. NAC contained 27% nitroglycerin, 66% nitroacetylcellulose (NC mixed with a small amount of acetyl cellulose) and 7% centralite, while FC_4 had 28% nitroglycerin, 64% nitrocellulose, 4% phthalit, 3% centralite and 1% petroleum jelly.

Reduced flash was produced by the addition of KC1 (potassium chloride) but large scale use appears to have been delayed, though such propellants were supplied for guns from 203mm (*8in*) to 120mm (*4.7mm*).

The usual grain form was single tube, though it is interesting to note that charges for the 381mm (*15in*)/50 also had a disc of propellant at the end, possibly to spread the flash of igniter or tube. Sketch drawings show igniters at each end of part BL charges but it is not clear if this was normal practice.

Fixed ammunition was used in guns below 120mm (*4.7in*), separate QF in those from 152mm (*6in*) to 120mm (*4.7in*) inclusive, and bag ammunition in guns over 152mm (*6in*). Bags were made from calico or silk and cartridge cases normally from brass. Aluminium was tried but was not a success, though steel, suitably rustproofed, was adopted in the war, particularly for 102mm (*4in*) and below.

PROJECTILES

Major calibre Italian APC shell had a smaller burster than usual, the figure being about 2% and the standard explosive cast TNT. Sketch drawings show an AP cap resembling the knob and ring type, and the ballistic cap was cast in aluminium alloy. The 381mm (*15in*) shell was 4.46 calibres in overall length and had much the same relative air resistance as the British 6/12crh 14in (*356mm*), though the 320mm (*12.6in*) was inferior. Italian shells of almost all types suffered from over wide manufacturing tolerances, which increased the often high dispersion, but otherwise the quality of large APC was good. British tests in 1944 with filled and fuzed shell against 6in (*152mm*) NC plate at angles of 60° and 65° to the normal and striking velocities of 1444f/s (*440m/s*) and 1449f/s (*442m/s*) showed in both instances that the shell detonated after bouncing off the plate, which was holed and considerably damaged at 60° and less so at 65°, though the plate was also holed in this case. This performance appears to have been considered good at the time.

In 381mm (*15in*) ships about 74% of the outfit was APC and in 320mm (*12.6in*) about 68%, the balance in both being HE. This was approximately 87% of the APC in total weight and had a 10% TNT burster. The nose fuze, said to be too sensitive, was inside the ballistic cap.

For 203mm (*8in*) guns the AP was called 'piercing shell' (*granata perforante*) and not 'shot' (*projettile perforante* or *palla*). It was 4.17 calibres overall and at one time had a magnesium alloy ballistic cap. Sketch drawings show a rather thin sheath type AP cap. The burster was 2.7% TNT, and air resistance less than in the British 5/10crh shell, but considerably more than in the German 10crh. The HE shell was similar to that for major calibres but with a 7.4% burster.

In 152mm (*6in*) guns a return was made to 'shot' with a 1.86% burster. Length was 4.13 calibres overall and the ballistic cap an aluminium alloy casting. HE was similar to that for larger guns, except that the burster was 5.3%. 'Piercing shell' and HE of this type were supplied down to 100mm (*3.9in*) guns. There was also AA shell which differed in having a nose fuze with no ballistic cap and a burster of up to 15%. Fuzes were igniferous or mechanical time, or time and percussion. Fragmentation was apparently inadequate. These shells were made with a monobloc body from 203mm (*8in*) to 120mm (*4.7in*) and with a two-part body from 102mm (*4in*) down, but not for automatic guns which usually had monobloc shell bodies with percussion fuzes and relatively smaller bursters.

From 1936 there was some replacement of the cast TNT, particularly in 102mm (*4in*) and smaller guns by Antisanzionite (ASN). This was also cast, and contained 70% ammonium nitrate, 10% dicyandiamide, 20% pentaerythritol tetranitrate.

Star shell, derived from First World War German, was available for 120mm (*4.7in*), to 76mm (*3in*) guns in 1940, but was inadequate. Improved shell for calibres up to 152mm (*6in*) and apparently 203mm (*8in*), was under development, but it does not appear that any over 135mm (*5.3in*) was in service.

Most Italian shells and apparently all of 120mm (*4.7in*) and over, were not boat tailed, the 140mm (*5.5in*) which was, being captured from Yugoslavia. Bourrelets were usual, at least in larger shells, and copper driving bands single, though some 203mm (*8in*) and 152mm (*6in*) had two. A decoppering ring of lead-tin alloy was sometimes fitted in rear of the driving band.

FIRE-CONTROL

Italian fire-control equipment was mostly provided by Officine Galileo (OG) and San Giorgio (SG). For surface fire a director system with fire-control calculating machine or computer was used. The latest range-finders combined stereoscopic and coincidence instruments in one case, but the optical systems and rangetakers were separate. Those in the 381mm (*15in*) turrets in the *Littorio* class were of 12m (*39.4ft*) base, while the mast RFs in this class and the largest in cruisers were 7.2m (*23.6ft*). There was also an instrument of the latter size for measuring small alterations of course.

The first effective Italian radar EC-3 ter, generally known as 'Gufo', was installed in *Littorio* in September 1942 and a further 11 ships were equipped in 1943. In addition seven German sets, mostly FuMO 24/40G, were fitted between March 1942 and the late spring of 1943. Ranges could be determined but they were not specialised fire control radars in the British or US sense.

A gyro instrument, supplying the continuous variation of the target's bearing, was introduced in *Trieste* in 1927, and at about the same time this ship had the first inclinometer. The latter continued to be fitted but was in general unsatisfactory.

There were apparently four main types of electro-mechanical computer, and a simplified version for torpedo boats. A photograph of a San Giorgio instrument for battleships does not show any large scale plot. Sights were stabilised in the later directors though it appears that the stabilising equipment was inadequate. In the *Littorio* class, the principal director was at the masthead with an armoured installation lower down.

AA fire progressed gradually from barrage to director control but the electro-mechanical computer was too slow for AA use. Gyrosights and similar directors for close range guns were lacking.

In addition to these deficiencies, data transmission was not considered entirely satisfactory, and the follow-the-pointer system was criticised.

Forward tower mast in *Littorio* with 7.2m San Giorgio range-finder in the top, 3m range-finder in the 90mm director and EC-3 ter 'Gufo' radar on the second main director.
Elio Ando'

Forward tower mast in *Zara* with 5m range-finder in main and secondary directors for 203mm guns and sided directors for 100mm with 3m range-finder.
Elio Ando'

Andrea Doria showing director for 135mm guns with 5m range-finder.
Elio Ando'

Roma, the last Italian battleship, showing the forward 381mm triple turrets.
CPL

HEAVY CALIBRE GUNS

These very powerful guns were mounted in triple turrets in the *Littorio* class. Guns and mountings were all of Ansaldo design though the turrets for *Vittorio Veneto* and two of those in *Roma* were made by OTO. Most of the guns were built with an A tube which was in two layers over the chamber and part of the rifled bore, the outer layer continuing to the muzzle, a jacket for about 72% of the total length and a breech bush screwing into the jacket. There was also a loose liner apparently removable from the breech end. It seems however that the guns in *Littorio* were not of loose liner type, but built up from six major components, some at least being autofretted. Both types had a cylindrical muzzle swell 61cm (*24in*) in diameter. The breech block was of Welin type with three plain and six threaded sectors. It was hydro-pneumatically operated and opened to the left in the left gun and to the right in the other two. Cocking of the mechanism was semi-automatic. The theoretical time for opening or closing was 3.5sec, which was slightly exceeded in practice. Firing

381mm (15in)/50 Ansaldo 1934

Gun Data

Bore	381mm	15.0in	
Weight incl BM	102.4t	100.8 tons	
Weight loose liner			
Length oa	19,781mm	778.78in	51.92cal
Length bore	19,050mm	750.0in	50.0cal
Length chamber	3071mm	120.91in	
Volume chamber	456.216dm^3	27,840in^3	
Length rifling	15,850mm	624.0in	
Grooves	(96) 3.1 × 8.458mm	0.122 × 0.333in	
Lands	4.0mm	0.157in	
Twist	1 in 30		
Weight projectile	885kg AP	1951lb AP	
Propellant charge	271.7kg NAC	599lb NAC	
Muzzle velocity	870m/s	2854f/s	
Working pressure	3200kg/cm^2	20.3tons/in^2	
Approx life	110-130EFC		
Max range	42,260m/35°/850m/s	46,216yd/35°/2789f/s	

The range of 42,800m (*46,800yd*), sometimes quoted, is thought to be that for 36° elevation.

was electro-mechanical with solenoid and spring.

There was a considerable difference in weight between the 885kg (*1951lb*) APC and the 774kg (*1706lb*) HE, presumably because the length of a full-weight HE was too great. The propellant charge was in six bags. Gun life and dispersion suffered from the high muzzle velocity, which could have been reduced with advantage.

The guns were in individual cast steel cradles and separated by splinter bulkheads. There were four recoil-recuperator cylinders arranged symmetrically round the gun axis. Elevation is usually given as +35° -5° but the Ansaldo handbook says +36° -5½°. Each gun had two electric motors on a common shaft fed by a Ward-Leonard generator. Gearing from the motors drove a threaded screw engaging with an internal thread in a sleeve, of which the outside was provided with a rack meshing with a spur gear arc on the cradle. Loading was at +15° and a special mechanism referred to as 'reset-in-loading' disconnected the field Ward-Leonard dynamo from the aiming circuit. The switch time was at least 2sec and at worst, which was apparently rare, 8sec.

The turret was carried by 72 tapered rollers in groups of four, the lower roller path being flat and the upper tapered. Immediately below was a ring of 24 spring loaded vertical rollers and there were eight centring rollers at the lower end of the turret axis. A twin armature training motor was fed in series by two Ward-Leonard motor generators. There was a bevel wheel differential, two-speed gear and worm reduction gears with pinions engaging a rack on the turret structure. Training speeds were either 6°/sec or 2°/sec and if only half the training power was used speeds were not reduced, but acceleration was halved.

Aim in training was by follow-the-pointer gear, and in elevation by the same, or else controlled by the layer through 'stabilised aiming'. Power was supplied to the turrets by 3-450kW diesel dynamos.

Shell rooms were below magazines and the shells were moved, apparently by overhead gear, to a ring conveyor on rails in the shell handing room and from there to the waiting trays of the lower hoists. There was an anti-flash shield on the opening between shell room and shell handling room. A conveyor received charges from the magazine through anti-flash scuttles and fed them to the waiting trays. The slides on which the charges moved were double and arranged one above the other; this was repeated up the supply chain because of the length of the whole six-part charge. Shell and charge conveyors were electrically powered. For reasons of space, the arrangements for the centre gun differed in detail from those for the wing guns.

The upper hoists, one per gun, raised ammunition from the transfer trays in the working chamber to the gunhouse. Each hoist had two cages, one up and one down, and was in a completely enclosed shaft inclined at 14°. Power was supplied by electric winches. The cages consisted of an outer cage with no bottom, and an inner cage with three vertically arranged cylindrical compartments, the lower holding the shell and the middle and upper each three sixth-charges. The inner cage could slide down inside the outer until the upper charge compartment was in the former position of the shell compartment.

In the working chamber the three compartments of the cage were loaded together from vertically arranged transfer trays, but in the gunhouse the shell compartment was brought in line with the gun axis and the charge compartments were lowered in succession. The 1° divergence between the cage compartments, at 14°, and the gun axis, at 15°, was to ensure that the rammer chain was rigid along its whole run. The rammer was mounted behind the hoist shaft and was electrically powered from a continuously running motor. Charges were rammed at a slower speed than shells. The space between the cage and gun was filled by a loading tray hinged on the hoist shaft which uncovered an opening in the latter through which loading could take place. The loading tray joined a loading guide, which protected the breech threads. The outer cage had an opening for the rammer at the rear and three in front for the working chamber transfer trays.

Range and Elevation Data for 850m/s (2789f/s)

Range (m)	(yd)	Elevation°	Descent°	Striking V (m/s)	(f/s)
10,000	10,936	4.3	5.0	687	2254
15,000	16,404	7.2	8.65	620	2034
20,000	21,872	10.6	13.4	563	1847
25,000	27,340	14.45	19.3	524	1719
30,000	32,808	19.2	26.1	498	1634
35,000	38,276	24.65	37.6	483	1585

Gun Mounting Data

Revolving weight	1595t	1570 tons
Roller path dia (mean)	11.896m	39ft
Barbette int dia	13.19m	43ft 3in
Distance apart gun axes	2.63m	103.5in
Recoil	1.00m	39.4in
Max elevating speed	6°/sec	
Max training speed	6°/sec	
Firing cycle	45sec	
Turret shield	face 350mm; sides, roof 200mm	face 13.8in; sides, roof 7.9in

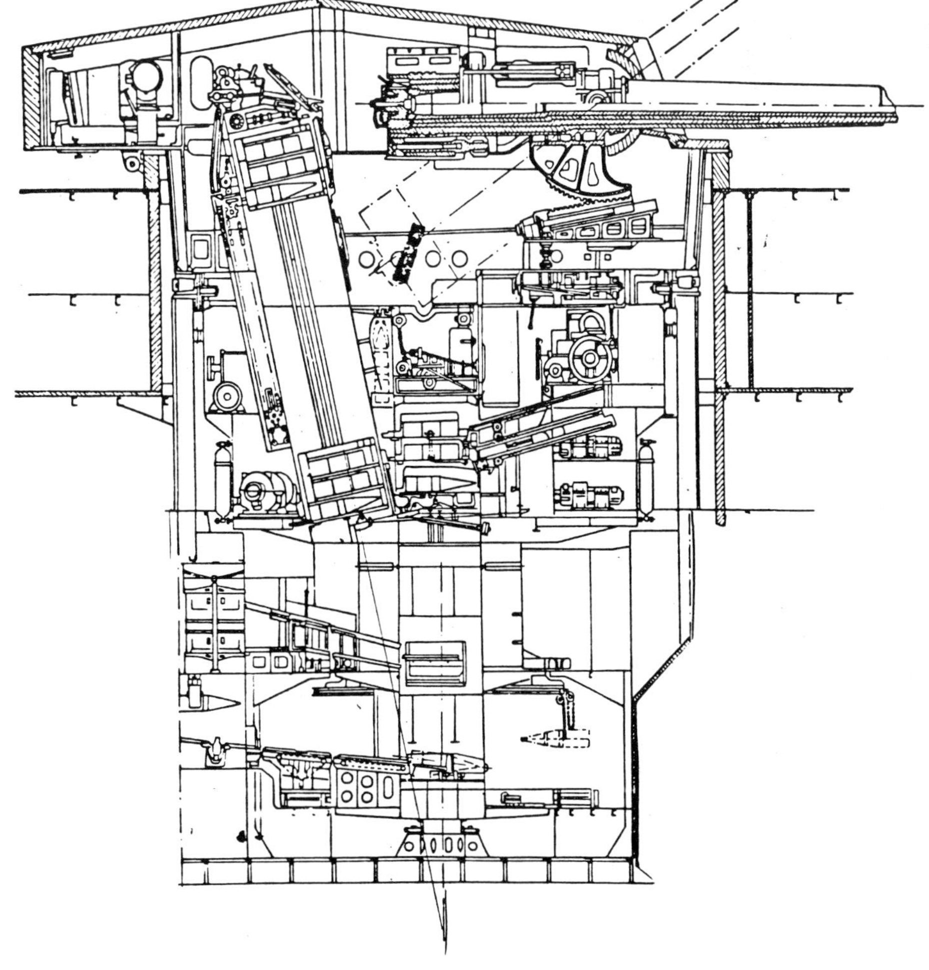

Longitudinal section of Ansaldo 381mm triple turret in all ships of the *Vittorio Veneto* class.
ANB

381mm (15in)/40

This was originally intended for the four ships of the cancelled *Caracciolo* class, and was used in the First World War in monitors and floating batteries and on land. There was still a twin mounting in the monitor *Faà di Bruno*, re-designated GM 194, and ten guns were mounted in Italian coast defences in June 1940. There were two types, Elswick Pattern 'A' and Vickers Mk 'A', weighing with BM 83.75t (*82.45 tons*). Shell weight was 884kg (*1949lb*) and MV 700m/s (*2297f/s*).

320mm guns converted by OTO, in forward turrets of *Andrea Doria*.
Elio Ando'

320mm (12.6in)/43.8 M1934, 1936

Converted 304.8mm (*12in*)/46-calibre guns mounted in M1934 triple and twin mountings in the *Cesare* class and in M1936 triple and twin in the *Duilio* class. There were two designs of gun involved, the originals having been Elswick Pattern 'T' in the *Cesare* and *Duilio*, and Vickers Mk 'G' in the *Cavour* and *Doria*. The structure of these guns differed, Mk 'G' being of normal fully wire-wound type with inner A, A, B tubes, jacket and breech ring, while Pattern 'T' had inner A tube, A tube in two parts joined by a screwed collar, B tube and half-length wire, jacket and short breech ring. The Elswick guns were converted by Ansaldo and the Vickers by OTO. In conversion the guns were bored out to remove the original A tube and apparently some of the wire, and the remainder was shrunk on a new A tube. It is not clear whether a shrunk or tupped inner A tube was also fitted. The breech mechanism was of normal swinging type with Welin block and was pneumatically operated.

The conversion was judged to be satisfactory as it was quick and cheap, and 13.4% more muzzle energy was obtained, but the longitudinal resistance to droop was slightly reduced, and accuracy suffered with increased dispersion. HE shell was considerably lighter than APC at 458kg (*1010lb*) as against 525kg (*1157lb*), in order to limit its length. Propellant charges were in quarters.

Gun Data

Bore	320mm	12.6in	
Weight incl BM	64.0t	63.0 tons	
Length oa	*c*14,500mm	*c*571in	*c*45.3cal
Length bore	14,000mm	551.2in	43.75cal
Length chamber	*c*2500mm	*c*98.4in	
Volume chamber	*c*350dm^3	*c*21,360in^3	
Length rifling	*c*11,320mm	*c*445.7in	
Grooves	?80		
Twist	1 in 30		
Weight projectile	525kg AP	1157lb AP	
Propellant charge	175kg	386lb	
Muzzle velocity	830m/s	2723f/s	
Working pressure	3100kg/cm^2	19.7tons/in^2	
Approx life	150 EFC		
Max range	28,600m/27°/800m/s	31,280yd/27°/2625f/s	

At 30° the range is given as 29,400m (*32,150yd*) which does not agree with the 27° figure. If this last is correct, the 30° range would be about 30,270m (*33,100yd*).

Gun Mountings Data

Revolving weight (triple)	745t	733 tons
(twin)	548t	539 tons
Roller path dia (triple)	8.53m	28ft 0in
(twin)	7.47m	24ft 6in
Barbette int dia (triple)	9.60m	31ft 6in
(twin)	8.53m	28ft 0in
Distance apart gun axes (both)	2.286m	90in
Recoil	1.05m	41in
Max elevating speed	6°/sec	
Max training speed	5°/sec	
Firng cycle	30sec	
Turret shield	280mm max	11in max

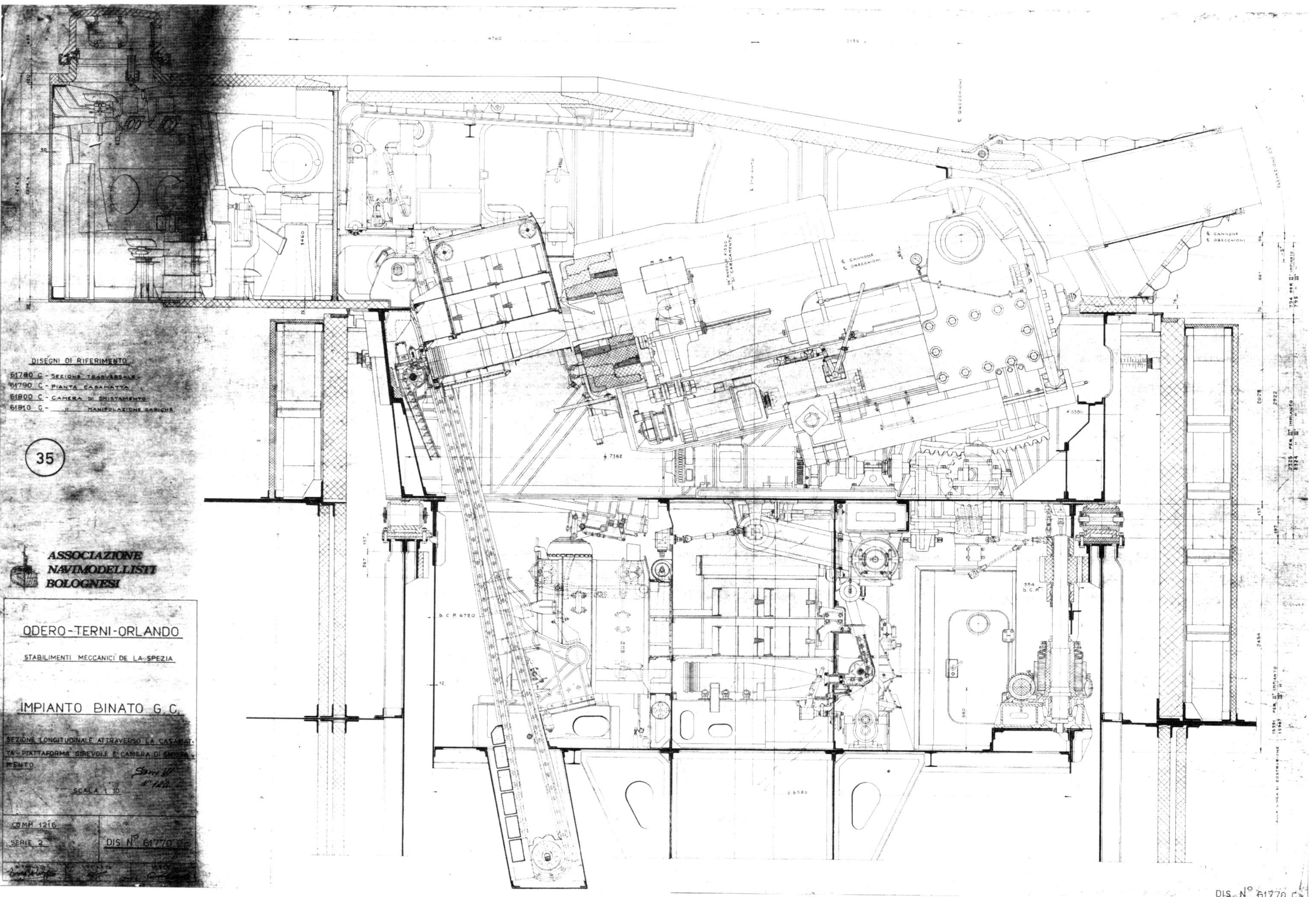

320mm twin M1934 mounting, longitudinal section.
ANB

The triple and twin turrets designed by Elswick or Vickers had originally been hydraulically powered with elevation of +20° -5° and loading at any angle. They were converted to electric power with loading at +12° and elevation +27° -5° in M1934, while +30° -5° is usually given for M1936, though a report on a gunnery visit to the *Duilio* in 1946 quotes +27° -5°. In this ship elevation was by screw jacks which were said to be very satisfactory, but in *Cavour* worm and wheel, pinion and arc trains were apparently used. The shell rooms were below the magazines, and each gun had an upper and lower hoist with the usual type of cage. There were power-driven shell and charge rings, and shells were moved to the lower hoists by hand-operated sprocket and chain gear while the quarter-charges were passed by hand. In the working chamber, shells and charges were automatically rolled to transfer trays which tilted 12° to bring them at right angles to the upper hoists, and then fed to the gun loading cages by hand operated chain rammers. The gun loading rammers were hydraulic or pneumatic. Ammunition supply was as above in both triple and twin turrets, and the guns were all in individual cradles. Antiflash precautions were simple and apparently not up to the latest requirements.

304.8mm (12in)

Guns Data

Gun	Weight incl BM	Shell	Muzzle Velocity
50-calibre	74.3t (*73.15 tons*)	445kg (*981lb*)	865m/s (2838f/s)
46-calibre	63.5t (*62.5 tons*)	452kg (*997lb*)	840m/s (2756f/s)
42-calibre	54.3t (*53.4 tons*)	450kg (*992lb*)	800m/s (2625f/s)

These are the usually quoted figures for the 42-calibre. A generally reliable wartime German list of Italian shells gives 452kg (*997lb*) and 765m/s (*2510f/s*)

40-calibre	51.6t (*50.8 tons*)	417kg (*919lb*)	780m/s(*2559f/s*)

A considerable number of guns were still in existence, 25 being mounted in Italian coast defences in June 1940.

50-calibre. This was never a naval gun, but six to Elswick Pattern 'Q' were supplied for coast defence. They were probably the heaviest 304.8mm (*12in*) guns ever in regular service.

46-calibre. Many of these were converted to 320mm (*12.6in*) for the reconstructed *Cesare* and *Duilio* classes, but there were still numerous unconverted guns including those from the scrapped *Dante* and salved *Leonardo de Vinci*. There were two types, Elswick Pattern 'T' and Vickers Mk 'G'.

42-calibre. Skoda guns of 45cal overall length and 305.0mm (*12.008in*) bore with horizontal wedge breech and the propellant charge in a brass case. They were originally in the Austro-Hungarian *Erzherzog Franz Ferdinand*, *Radetzky* and *Tegetthof*, ceded after the First World War.

40-calibre. Elswick Pattern 'I' originally in the *Brin* and *Vittorio Emanuele* classes. They were still mounted on pontoons GM 191 and 192.

254mm (10in)/45

Gun Data

Bore	254mm	10in	
Weight incl BM	35.0t	34.5 tons	
Length oa	11,908.5mm	468.84in	46.88cal
Length bore	11,430mm	450in	45.0cal
Length chamber	1903.7mm	74.95in	
Volume chamber	180.26dm^3	11,000in^3	
Weight projectile	227kg	500lb	
Propellant charge	84.2kg C	186lb C	
Muzzle velocity	870m/s	2854f/s	
Range	*c*25,000m/25°	*c*27,300yd/25°	

A gun of normal Elswick construction, wire-wound for 75% of its length, and mounted in twin turrets in the old armoured cruiser *San Giorgio*. The design Pattern was 'W'. The mountings allowed +25° to -5° and were electrically powered with loading at fixed elevation, though compensating gear for the rammers, to allow a restricted choice of angle, was apparently fitted originally. Roller path diameter was 5.41m (*17ft 9in*) and shields 20cm (*8in*) maximum.

The old *San Giorgio* with 254mm Elswick Pattern 'W' guns.
Elio Ando'

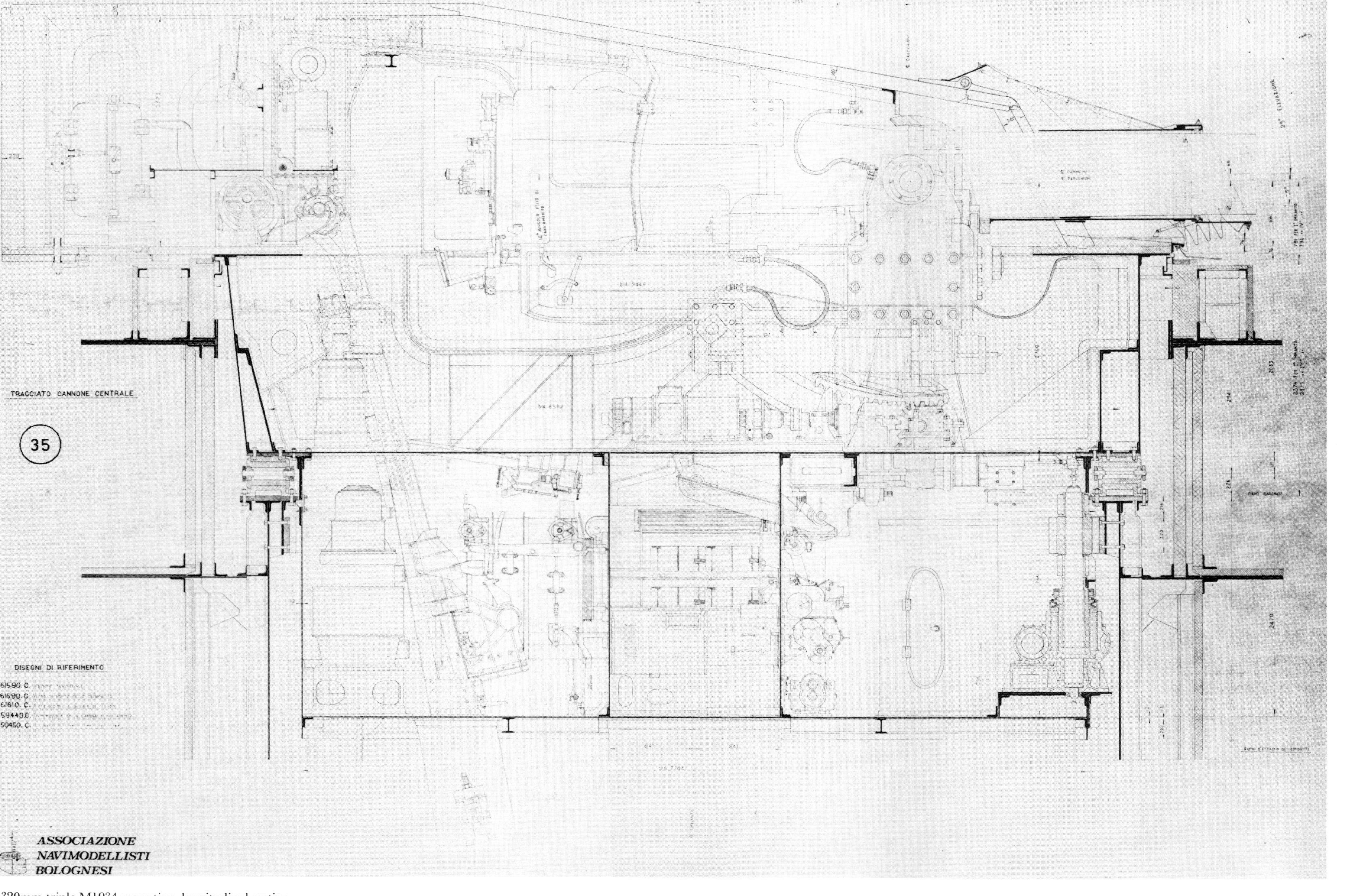

320mm triple M1934 mounting, longitudinal section.
ANB

203mm/53 guns in forward turrets of *Pola*. Note the small distance between the muzzles in each pair. *Elio Ando'*

MEDIUM CALIBRE GUNS

The guns in the above two types of mounting were the same, M1927 covering twin turrets in the *Zara*, *Fiume*, *Gorizia* and *Pola*, while M1929 was a lighter version in the *Bolzano*. The gun was built with A tube, full length jacket and breech ring, and had a loose liner which could be exchanged on board. The breech mechanism with Welin screw block was hydraulically operated and the bag charge was in two parts. The gun was an improvement on the 203.2mm (*8in*)/50 and worked at a higher pressure, though the muzzle velocity, which was originally as high as 960m/s (*3150f/s*) for a new gun with AP shell, was reduced to 900m/s (*2953f/s*).

The M1927 turret had electric training and elevation, the latter by means of a screw jack inclined backwards from near the front of the revolving structure to in rear of the cradle trunnions. Both guns were close together in a common cradle, and the rammers were carried on an extension from the cradle. They were hydraulically powered, possibly electrically in *Pola*, and loading was at any angle of elevation. For the first time in an Italian turret, a swinging arm pivoted about the cradle trunnions replaced the upper part of the hoists. There were apparently two cartridge hoists and one shell hoist, all of endless-chain type, and ammunition was conveyed from the top of the hoists to the loading trays by the swinging arm. Magazines were above the shell rooms and it appears that the bag charges were hoisted in protective cases, removed before loading.

The M1929 turret appears to have been similar, but lightened where possible, and with a thinner shield. Elevation in both was +45° -5°. The main defect was the use of a common cradle with the guns close together.

203.2mm (8in)/53 Ansaldo 1927, 1929

Gun Data

Bore	203.2mm	8.0in	
Weight incl BM	19.5t	19.2 tons	
Length oa	11,177mm	440.04in	55.00cal
Length bore	10,769.6mm	424.0in	53.0cal
Length chamber	*c*1640mm	*c*64.6in	
Volume chamber	79.158dm³	4830.5in³	
Length rifling	9031mm	355.55in	
Grooves	52		
Twist	1 in 30		
Weight projectile	125.3kg AP	276.2lb AP	
Propellant charge	50.8kg C 18.0/6.5, 7.5mm	112.0lb C 0.71/0.256, 0.295in	
Muzzle velocity	960m/s	3150f/s	
Working pressure	3360kg/cm²	21.3 tons/in²	
Max range	34,208m/45°/950m/s	37,410yd/45°/3117f/s	
Figures with HE shell, using a finer grain propellant.			
Weight projectile	110.57kg HE	243.77lb HE	
Propellant charge	41.8kg C 12.6/3.5mm	92.15lb C 0.496/0.138in	
Muzzle Velocity	940m/s	3084f/s	
Working pressure	3250kg/cm²	20.6tons/in²	
Max range	30,547m/45°/930m/s	33,407yd/45°/3051f/s	

With AP shell and the later MV of 900m/s (*2953f/s*), the propellant charge is thought to have been as above for HE, and range was 31,324m/45° (*34,256yd*).

Gun Mounting Data M1927

Revolving Weight	181.0t	178.1 tons
Ball track dia	5.0m	16ft 5in
Barbette int dia	6.1m	20ft 0in
Distance apart gun axes	1.0m	39.4in
Recoil	55cm	21.7in
Max elevating speed	5°/sec	
Max training speed	6°/sec	
Firing cycle	16sec	
Turret shield	150mm max	5.9in max
For M1929 in *Bolzano*	100mm max	3.9in max

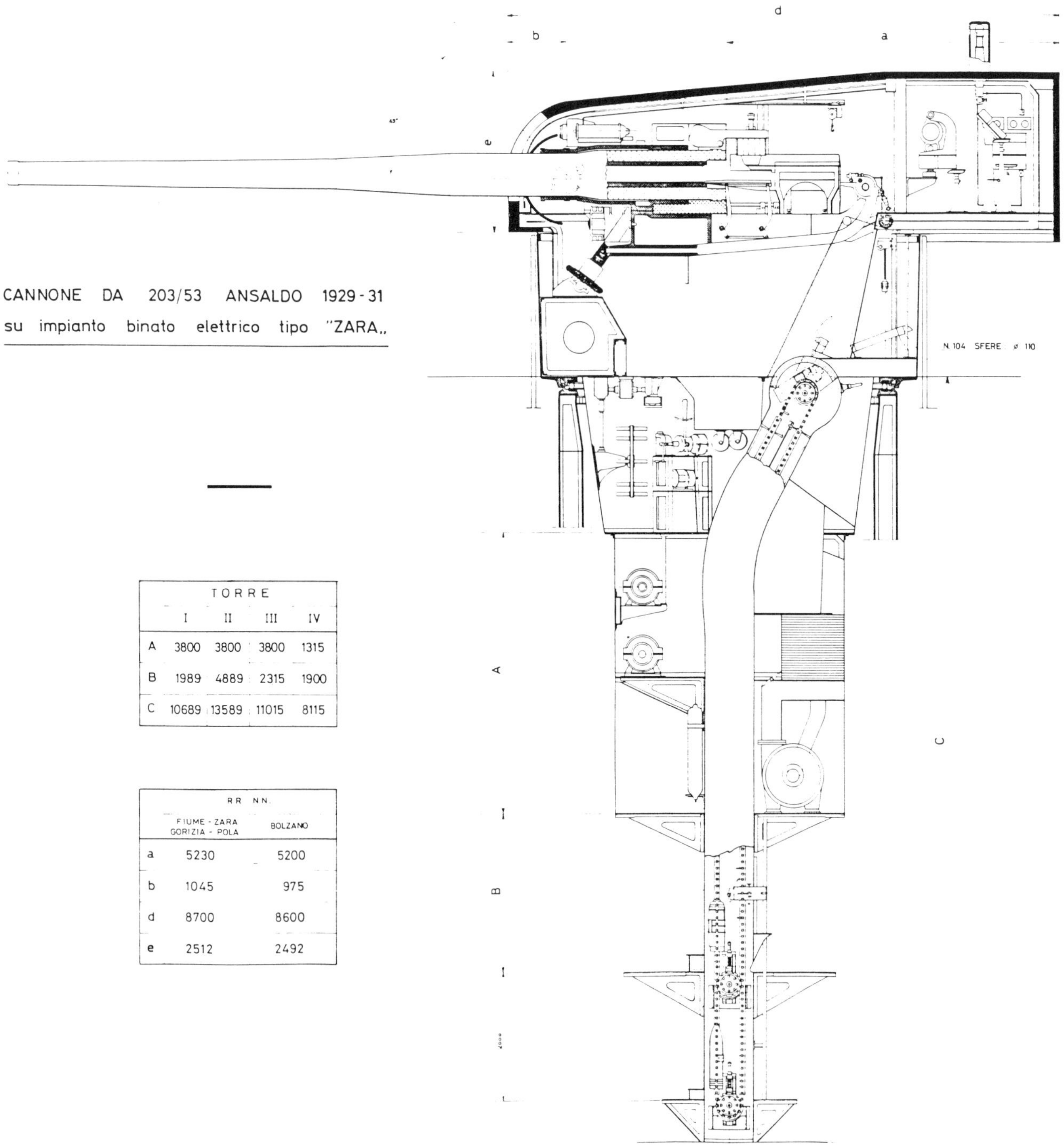

CANNONE DA 203/53 ANSALDO 1929-31
su impianto binato elettrico tipo "ZARA,,

N. 104 SFERE ø 110

	TORRE			
	I	II	III	IV
A	3800	3800	3800	1315
B	1989	4889	2315	1900
C	10689	13589	11015	8115

	RR NN.	
	FIUME - ZARA GORIZIA - POLA	BOLZANO
a	5230	5200
b	1045	975
d	8700	8600
e	2512	2492

Longitudinal section of M1927 twin mounting for 203mm/53 guns in *Zara* class.
ANB

Trento in 1941 showing after M1924 turrets for 203mm/50 guns. Note the small distance between muzzles.
Elio Ando'

This gun was limited to the twin turrets in the *Trento* and *Trieste*, apart from a spare turret later mounted for coast defence. It was of built-up construction with fixed liner and the main components were autofretted by the Schneider process. There was a Welin screw breech block and the propellant charge appears to have been in a single bag.

For reasons partly due to the mounting, dispersion was very high, and the original MV of 905m/s (*2969f/s*) with AP shell was reduced to 840m/s (*2756f/s*) with a lighter shell without, it seems, curing the defect.

The mounting which had electrically powered training, elevation, hoists and rammer, suffered from having both guns close together in a common cradle, and the ball track was only 4.52m (*14ft 10in*) in diameter. A small scale drawing has been seen, but this does not show the ammunition supply in any detail. There was no swinging arm, and shell hoists were of pusher type with loading at +15°. Elevation is usually given as +45° -1½°, but the drawing here shows +45° -7°.

203.2mm (8in)/50 Ansaldo 1924

Gun Data

Bore	203.2mm	8.0in	
Weight incl BM	21.4t	21.06 tons	
Length oa	10,537mm	414.84in	51.86cal
Length bore	10,160mm	400.0	50.0cal
Length chamber	*c*1560mm	*c*61.4in	
Volume chamber	75.028dm³	4578.5in³	
Length rifling	8505mm	334.8in	
Grooves	52		
Twist	1 in 30		
Weight projectile	125.3kg AP	276.2lb AP	
Propellant charge	47.3kg C	104.3lb C	
Muzzle velocity	905m/s	2969f/s	
Working pressure	2950kg/cm²	18.7 tons/in²	
Max range	31,324m/45°/900m/s	34,256yd/45°/2953f/s	

With 110.57kg (*243.77lb*) HE and the same propellant charge, MV was 940m/s (*3084f/s*) and maximum range 30,547m (*33,407yd*)/45°/930m/s (*3051f/s*).

With the later reduced performance, the projectile is given as 118kg (*260lb*), MV as 840m/s (*2756f/s*), working pressure as 2800kg/cm² (*17.8 tons/in²*) and range as 28,000m (*30,600yd*).

Gun Mounting Data

Ball track dia	4.52m	14ft 10in
Barbette int dia	*c*5.67m	*c*18ft 7in
Distance apart gun axes	1.0m	39.4in
Recoil distance	70cm	27½in
Firing cycle	18secs	
(at 45°)	40secs	
Turret shield	100mm max	3.9in max

203.2mm (8in)/45

Elswick Pattern 'W', originally mounted in the *Brin, Vittorio Emanuele* and *Garibaldi* classes, but limited in June 1940 to four coast-defence guns, though some others were later added. Weight with BM was 19.4t (*19.1 tons*), the shell 116kg (*256lb*) and MV 790m/s (*2592f/s*).

Elswick Pattern 'C' 190mm guns in twin turrets in *San Giorgio*. The 100mm/47 OTO M1928 AA guns are also shown and two 254mm are visible.
Elio Ando'

The *San Giorgio* mounted eight of these Elswick Pattern 'C' guns in twin turrets. The construction was of normal Elswick type, wire wound for 75% of the length, and the mountings allowed +25° -7°. Turret shields were 18cm (*7in*) maximum. This gun and/or Vickers Mk 'D', which had the same performance and was originally in the *Pisa*, were in GM216. It seems that some were also mounted in coast-defence batteries, as it is otherwise hard to account for the 24 listed in June 1940.

190.5mm (7.5in)/45

Gun Data 190.5mm (7.5in)/45 EOC Pattern 'C'

Bore	190.5mm	7.5in	
Weight incl BM	13.99t	13.77 tons	
Length oa	8905.2mm	350.6in	46.75cal
Length bore	8572.5mm	337.5in	45.0cal
Length chamber	1312.55mm	51.675in	
Volume chamber	69.24dm³	4225in³	
Weight projectile	90.9kg	200.4lb	
Propellant charge	*c*32.3kg C	*c*71.2lb C	
Muzzle velocity	864m/s	2835f/s	
Range	*c*22,000m/25°	*c*24,000yd/25°	

190mm (7.48in)/39

Former Austro-Hungarian Skoda guns of 42cal length overall. Weight with BM was 12.7t (*12.5 tons*) and original shell weight and MV, 47kg (*214lb*), 800m/s (*2625f/s*). There were two guns on GM269, and they were also mounted in coast-defence batteries in Italy and North Africa.

152.4mm (6in)/55 Ansaldo 1934, OTO 1936

There was very little difference between these. Ansaldo guns were mounted in triple turrets in the *Littorio*, and in triple and twin in the *Garibaldi* class, OTO guns in triples in the *Vittorio Veneto* and *Roma*. These guns were better than the 152.4mm (*6in*)/53, having a more reasonable muzzle velocity and being in individual cradles. Also the expansion ratio was higher, giving better thermodynamics in the internal ballistics. They are generally described as loose-liner guns with autofretted A tube and full-length jacket, but a drawing of a relined OTO gun shows a thin taper liner with retaining bush and forward shoulder, but no provision against rotation. The A tube, bored out to suit the liner, has a thin wall at the

Gun Data

Bore	152.4mm	6.0in	
Weight incl BM	8.9t	8.76 tons	
Length oa	*c*8840mm	*c*348in	*c*58cal
Length bore	8382mm	330.0in	55.0cal
Length chamber	*c*1005mm	*c*39.6in	
Volume chamber	25.190dm³	1537in³	
Length rifling oa	7300.5mm	287.42in	
Grooves	40		
Twist	1 in 30		
Weight projectile	50kg AP	110lb AP	
Propellant charge	16.35kg NAC	36.05lb NAC	
Muzzle velocity	910m/s	2986f/s	
Working pressure	3270kg/cm²	20.8 tons/in²	
Max range	25,740m/45°/900m/s	28,150yd/45°/2953f/s	

With 44.4kg (*97.9lb*) HE new gun MV was 995m/s (*3133f/s*), and maximum range 24,900m (*27,230yd*)/45°/945m/s (*3100f/s*).

The forward 152mm/55 Ansaldo M1934 guns in *Duca degli Abruzzi*.
Elio Ando'

muzzle, and it is probable that the liner was shrunk or tupped. The breech mechanism had a horizontal sliding block and was hand operated. Separate loading QF ammunition was fired.

The mountings were electrically powered with elevation by arc and worm. Each gun had a separate cradle and the pneumatic rammers were of telescopic type located on an extension from the cradles. In the twin mountings there were inclined endless chain hoists, each gun having separate shell and cartridge hoists. These did not reach the gunhouse, and ammunition was conveyed to the loading trays by swinging arms pivotted about the trunnions.

Arrangements were different in the triple turrets which had upper and lower endless chain shell and cartridge hoists, the upper hoists coming up to the left rear of the left and centre guns, and to the right rear of the right gun.

Gun Mounting Data

Weight less shield (triple)	135.4t	133.3 tons
Ball track dia (twin)	5m	16ft 5in
(triple)	*c*6m	*c*19ft 8in
Barbette int dia (twin)	5.8m	19ft 0in
(triple)	*c*7.0m	*c*23ft
Distance apart gun axes (twin and triple)	*c*1.26m	*c*50in
Firing cycle	13-15sec	
Turret shield (*Littorio* class)	face 280mm; sides 130-80mm; rear 80mm; roof 150-105mm	face 11in; sides 5.1-3.1in; rear 3.1in; roof 5.9-4.1in
(*Garibaldi* class)	face 145mm; sides 35mm; roof 60mm	face 5.7in; sides 1.4in; roof 2.4in

Elevation in both twin and triple turrets was +45° -5° with loading up to 20°.

Sectional elevation (below) and plan (right) of twin turret for 152mm/55 Ansaldo M1934 guns.
ANB

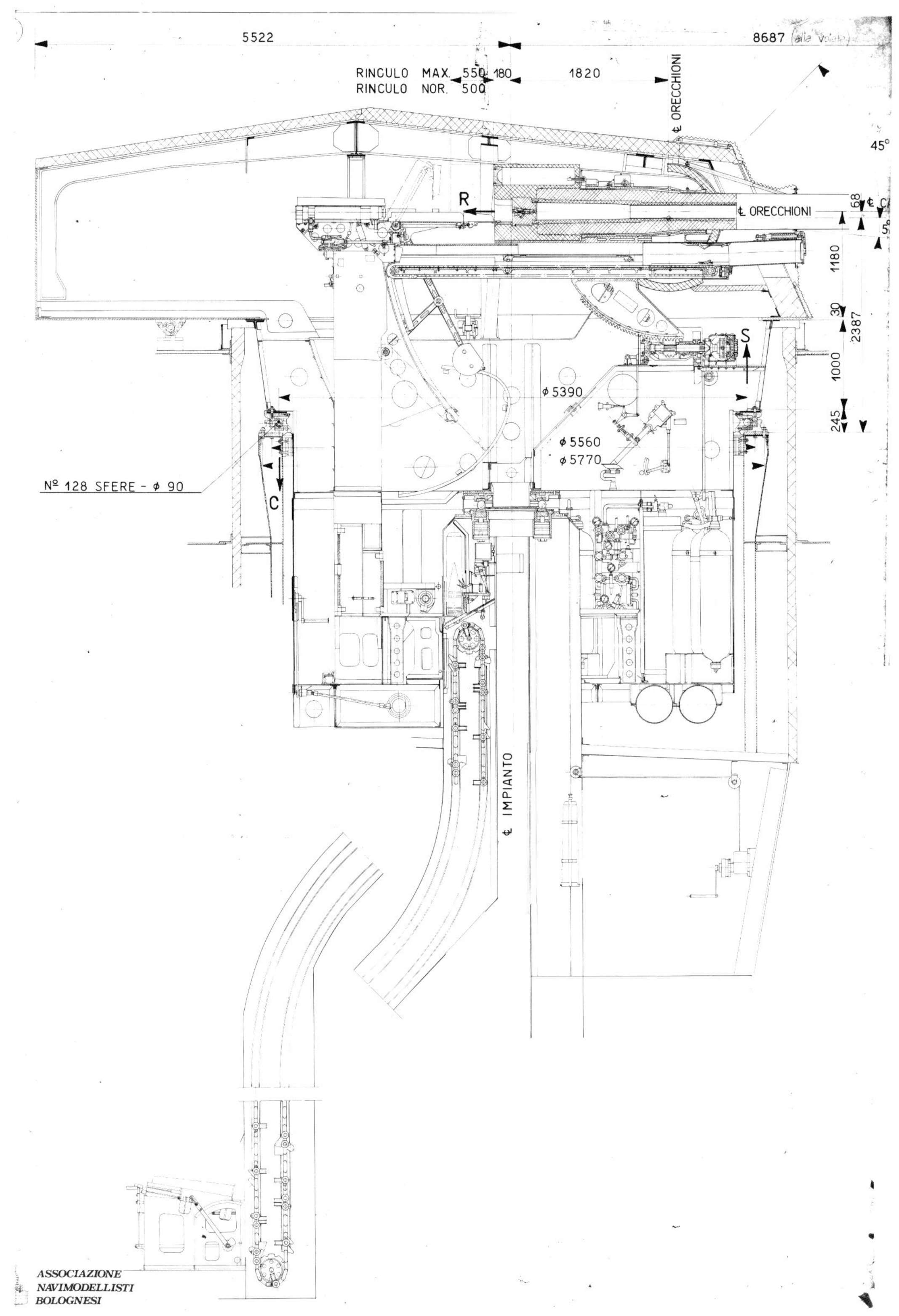

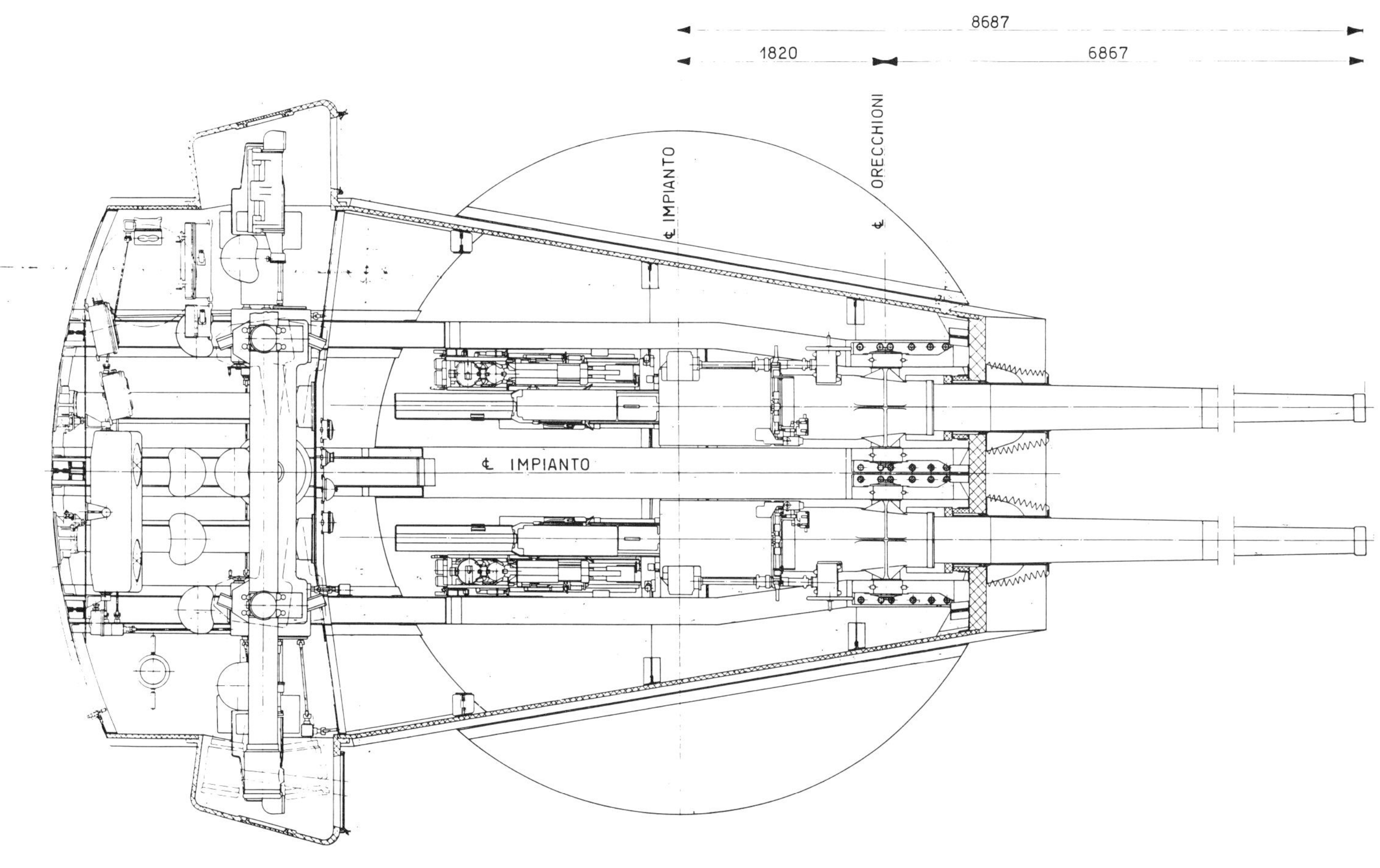

The Ansaldo guns were mounted in twin turrets in the *Giussano* class, and the OTO guns similarly in the *Diaz, Attendolo* and *Duca D'Aosta* classes. The performance specifications were unfortunate, with very high muzzle velocity, guns close together in common cradles and, at least in the *Giussano* and *Diaz* classes, structures that were too light. As related below, muzzle velocities had to be drastically reduced.

The construction of the Ansaldo guns seems to have varied. A drawing of a relined gun shows A tube, jacket and very heavy breech ring screwed to the jacket with a square thread, and a relatively thick taper liner with a retaining bush screwed into the rear end of the jacket. There was no positive forward stop, and no provision against rotation, indicating a shrunk or tupped liner. Another drawing shows a loose liner weighing 1374kg (*3030lb*). The rear shoulders were in contact, the liner secured longitudinally by plates in the breech ring with two other forward steps and another at the muzzle for a bush with two keys.

A drawing of an OTO gun shows a thin, loose liner of Pittoni type, A tube, full length jacket and breech ring. The liner which weighed 617kg (*1360lb*), had a forward shoulder just in front of the shot seating, a retaining bush and an interrupted screw collar at the muzzle end of the jacket with six keys.

It is doubtful if either loose liner was universally interchangeable. Breech mechanisms were of horizontal sliding block type and separate QF ammunition was fired. The original new gun MV of 1000m/s (*3281f/s*) with AP shell led to excessive dispersion which was not entirely remedied by a reduction to 850m/s (*2789f/s*).

The turrets were electrically powered with

152.4mm (6in)/53 Ansaldo 1926, OTO 1929

Gun Data

Bore	152.4mm	6.0in	
Weight incl BM (Ansaldo)	7.34t	7.22 tons	
(OTO)	7.69t	7.57 tons	
Length oa (Ansaldo)	8544mm	336.38in	56.06cal
(OTO)	8541mm	336.26in	56.04cal
Length bore	8077.2mm	318.0in	53.0cal
Length chamber	*c*1320mm	*c*52in	
Volume chamber	33.496dm^3	2044in^3	
Length rifling oa (Ansaldo)	6681.5mm	263.05in	
(OTO)	6678.5mm	262.93in	
Grooves	40		
Twist	1 in 30		
Weight projectile	50kg AP	110lb AP	
Propellant charge	21.425kg C	47.23lb C	
Muzzle velocity	1000m/s	3281f/s	
Working pressure	3300kg/cm^2	20.95 tons/in^2	
Max range	28,400m/45°/975m/s	31,060yd/45°/3199f/s	

With 44.3kg (*97.7lb*) HE, the original propellant charge was 19.5kg (*43lb*) C and new gun MV 950m/s (*3117f/s*), the range being 24,600m (*26,900yd*)/45°/935m/s (*3068f/s*).

Firing 47.5kg (*104.7lb*) shell at the later MV of 850m/s (*2789f/s*), working pressure was 3050kg/cm^2 (*19.4 tons/in^2*) and range 22,600m (*24,700yd*)/45°.

Gun Mounting Data

Total weight	*c*100t	*c*98 tons
Ball track dia	4.6m	15ft 1in
Barbette int dia	5.4m	17ft 9in
Distance apart gun axes	75cm	29½in
Max elevating speed	5°/sec	
Max training speed	6°/sec	
Firing cycle	12sec	
Turret shield, max		
(*Giussano, Diaz* classes)	23mm	0.9in
(*Attendolo* class)	70mm	2.76in
(*Aosta* class)	90mm	3.54in

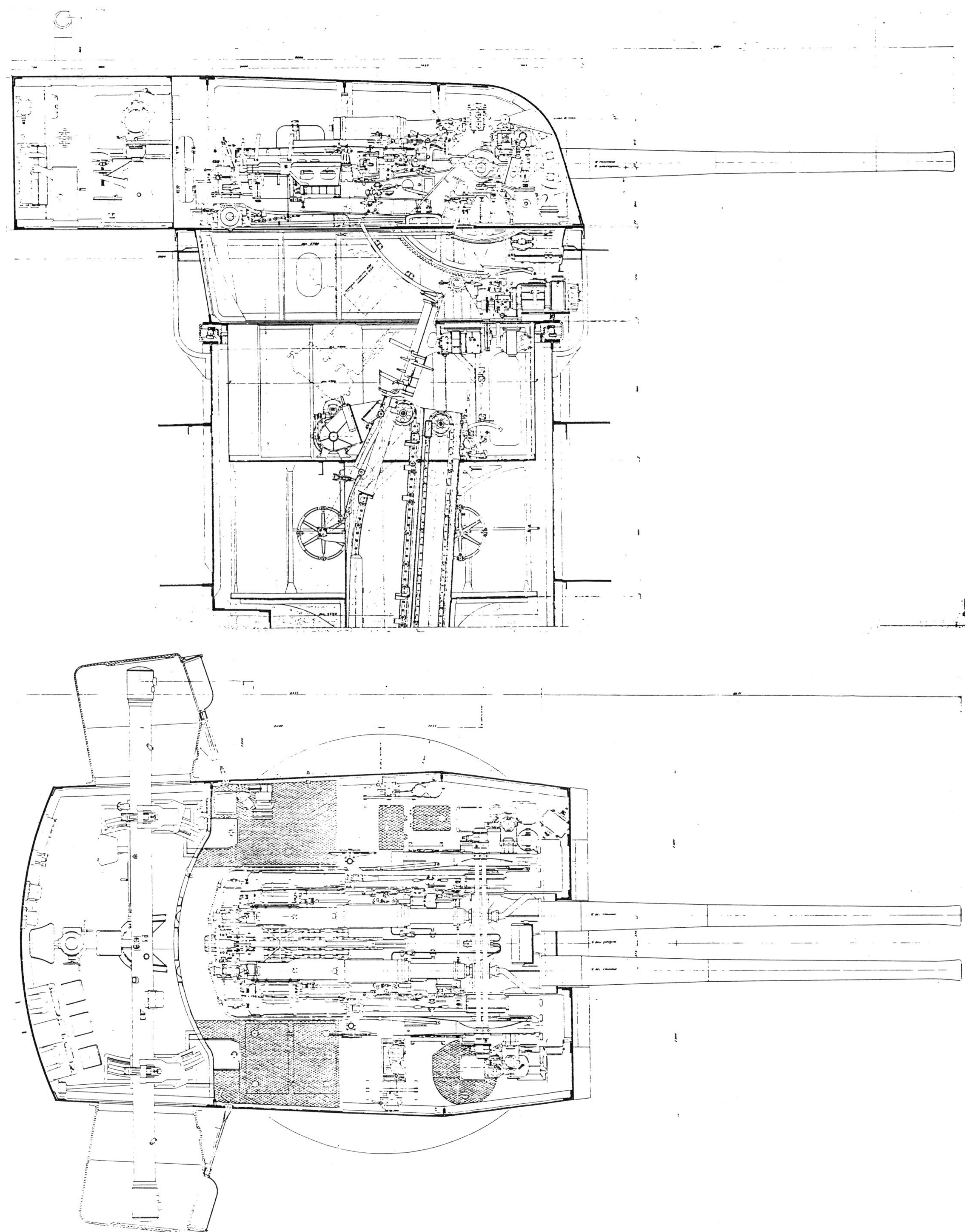

chain rammers, and the guns were close together in a common cradle. In the *Giussano* class there were inclined electric dredger hoists and a swinging arm pivoted at the trunnions, conveyed ammunition on a tilting tray to the loading tray. The loading angle was +20°. Arrangements in other ships are believed to have been similar, with some unspecified improvements in the *Attendolo* and *Aosta* classes (possibly the addition of separate cartridge pusher hoists shown in some drawings). Empty cases were transferred mechanically to a compartment below the turret floor, except in the *Aosta* class where a conveyor belt moved them forward to ports in the turret face.

Elevation was +45° -5° in the *Giussano* class and +45° -10° in the others.

Top: Longitudinal section of OTO twin turret for 152mm/53 M1929 guns.
ANB

Above: Plan of OTO twin turret for 152mm/53 M1929 guns. Note the small distance between the barrels.
ANB

152.4mm (6in) older types

These comprised 50-, 45- and 40-calibre guns, mostly from old ships and used for coast defence and for arming the larger merchant ships. The principal ex-naval guns were the Schneider 45cal formerly in the *Duilio* class, and various patterns of the old Elswick 40cal QF.

Gun	Weight incl BM	Shell	Muzzle velocity
45-calibre	7.14t (7.03 tons)	47kg (103.6lb)	830m/s (2723f/s)
40-calibre	6.7t (6.6 tons)	47kg (103.6lb)	695m/s (2280f/s)

Typical figures are given for 40-calibre guns.

149.1mm (5.87in) guns

These included the German SKL/45, called 43-calibre in the Italian navy, and still mounted in the *Bari* (ex-*Pillau*) and *Taranto* (ex-*Strassburg*), as well as former Austro-Hungarian 47 and 37cal guns of overall length 50 and 40cal. These two latter, and also SKL/45s from the scrapped *Ancona* (ex-*Graudenz*), were mounted in coast-defence batteries with two each on the pontoons GM239 and 240.

Details of the SKL/45 are given in the German section. Italian sources quote the MV as 890m/s (*2920f/s*), which appears impossibly high and is 10m/s (*33f/s*) more than that of the Austro-Hungarian 47cal gun.

135mm guns in triple OTO M1937 turrets in *Andrea Doria*. These were not AA guns.
Elio Ando'

135mm (5.315in)/45 OTO 1937, 1938, Ansaldo 1938

Mounted in triple M1937 turrets in the *Duilio* and *Doria* as secondary armament, and in M1938 twins in the *Regolo* ('Capitani Romani' class), these guns were designed to give about the same range as the 120mm (*4.7in*)/50 with a considerably lower MV and better dispersion. In fact, also because of the wider spacing between guns in the twin mountings, this was reduced to about a quarter of the 120mm figure. Single-shielded mountings, intended for the *Aquila*, re-armed *Premuda* and destroyers of the 'Comandanti Medaglie d'Oro' class, were never in service afloat, though some, as well as twins, were mounted in coast defences. A twin AA version, intended for the *Etna* and *Vesuvio* and also for a projected rebuilding of the badly damaged *Cavour*, was still far off.

Guns in the *Duilio* in 1946 had a loose barrel, jacket and breech ring with rotation of the

Gun Data

Bore	135mm	5.315in	
Weight incl BM	6.01t	5.915 tons	
Length bore	6075mm	239.17in	45.0cal
Length chamber	*c*850mm,	*c*33.46in	
Volume chamber	*c*16dm³	*c*976in³	
Length rifling	5142mm	202.44in	
Weight projectile	32.7kg	72.1lb	
Propellant charge	8.875kg NAC	19.57lb NAC	
Muzzle velocity	825m/s (?835)	2707f/s (?2740)	
Max range	19,600m/45°	21,430yd/45°	

Gun Mounting Data

Weight complete (twin)	42t	41.3 tons
(triple)	105t	103.3 tons
Distance apart axes (twin)	*c*140cm	*c*55in
(triple)	*c*74cm	*c*29in
Recoil	55cm	21.7in
Max training speed (triple)	10°/sec	
Firing cycle	8–10sec	
Shield (twin)	20mm max	0.8in max
(triple)	120mm max	4.7in max

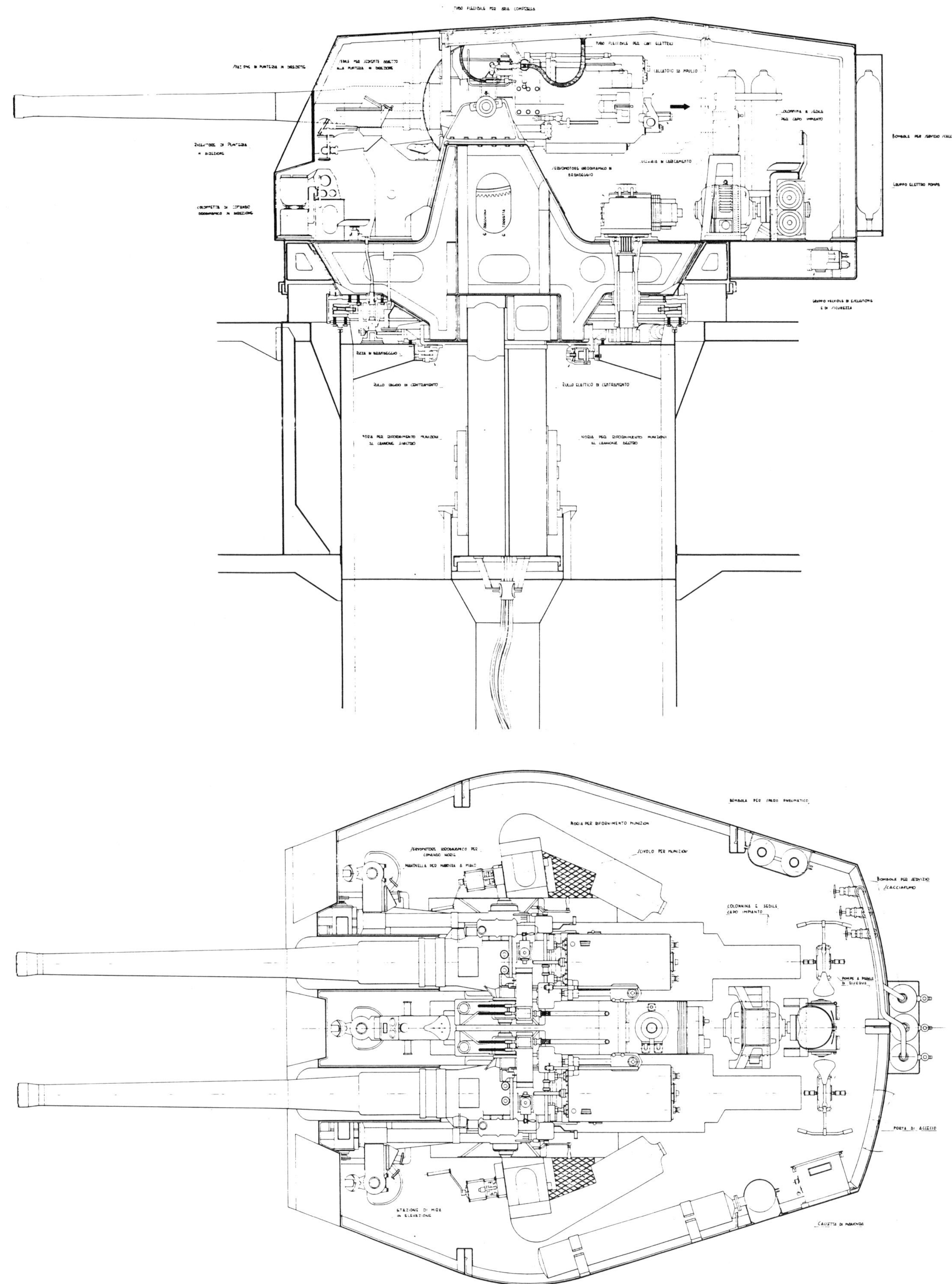

Top: Twin OTO M1938 turret in longitudinal section. These were mounted in the *Regolo* class. *ANB*

Above: Plan of OTO M1938 turret. The guns were further apart than in some previous designs. *ANB*

barrel prevented by two small keys in the breech ring which incorporated recoil and run-out cylinders. OTO drawings of about 1943, however, show a thin taper liner held by a retaining bush and forward shoulder. There were no muzzle keys and it is not clear if a bush adjacent to the retaining bush keyed the liner. It was thought that the liner was not of loose pattern. It was noted that the breech ring, which was screwed to the jacket by square threads, had an unusually long bearing length on the latter.

The breech mechanism was of horizontal sliding block type and hand operated. Separate QF ammunition was fired.

The triple mountings were of orthodox, electrically powered design with the guns in separate cradles. Rammers were recoil operated and apparently too weak to load shells effectively at beyond 30° elevation. Cartridges were loaded by hand, and spent cases discharged to the front by conveyors and chutes under each barrel. Shells and cartridges were stowed together in three magazines on different decks. They were placed by hand in vertical drums and raised alternately to the main deck by electric hoists, two to each magazine. At the top they were horizontally discharged to the deck, and shells separated from cartridges by automatic guide plates. Ammunition was manhandled through a door in the ring bulkhead and raised by short electric hoists to the gunhouse. It was placed by hand in the loading tray.

Training was by rack and pinion, and elevation by worm and arc on the centre line of the cradle. The guns could be elevated separately by hand but only together by power, though any one could be cut out from power operation.

The twin mounting was more spacious, with the cradles further apart. Ramming was similar, but each of the four turrets had its own magazine, from which two vertical hoists led to a handling room where ammunition was transferred to two inclined hoists in the revolving structure. Elevation in both mountings was +45° -5°, or possibly to -7° in twins.

120mm (4.724in)/50 Ansaldo 1926, 1936, 1937, 1940, OTO 1931, 1933, 1936

Typical Gun Data

Bore	120mm	4.724in	
Weight incl BM	3.36t	3.31 tons	
Length oa	6400mm	251.97in	53.55cal
Length bore	6000m	236.22in	50.0cal
Length chamber	938.5mm	36.95in	
Volume chamber	15.078dm^3	920.11in^3	
Length rifling	4958mm	195.20in	
Grooves	36?		
Twist	1 in 30?		
Weight projectile	23.49kg	51.79lb	
Propellant charge	9.7kg NAC	21.4lb NAC	
Muzzle velocity	950m/s	3117f/s	
Working pressure	3150kg/cm^2	20.0 tons/in^2	
Max range	19,600m/45°/920m/s	21,430yd/45°/3018f/s	
	18,200m/35°/920m/s	19,900yd/35°/3018f/s	

MV later reduced to 920m/s (*3018f/s*).

Gun Mountings Data

Weight complete (t/tons)		
Ans 1926	20.238	19.918
OTO 1931	17.65	17.37
OTO 1936	22.80	22.44
Ans 1936/37	21.60	21.26
Ans 1940	12.00	11.81
OTO 1933	34.00	33.46
Distance apart axes	56cm	22in
Firing cycle	9.5-10sec	
Shield usually	12mm	0.47in
in OTO 1933	120mm max	4.7in max

These separate ammunition QF guns were in twin mountings in destroyers from the 'Navigatori' to the 'Soldati' classes, except for the single Ansaldo 1940 in some of the later of the above, and the twin turret OTO 1933 as secondary armament in the *Cesare* class. There were differences between the various guns, sketch drawings showing OTO 1936 with a heavier breech end than 1931, and Ansaldo 1937 between the two. They are generally referred to as having loose liners, but drawings of a relined OTO 1931 indicate that there was originally an A tube without liner, and the new, relatively thick, taper liner, held by a retaining bush and forward shoulder, had been either shrunk or tupped in. The rebored A tube was left with a very thin wall at the muzzle. All had horizontal sliding breech blocks.

Originally the Ansaldo 1926 suffered from excessive dispersion and MV was reduced from 950m/s (*3117f/s*) to 920m/s (*3018f/s*) without curing the defect, which was largely due to the two guns being too close together in a common cradle. Later twin mountings also had this feature and appear to have had similar problems. Training and elevation by arc and pinion were electrically powered.

Ansaldo 1926. In 'Navigatori' class, *Dardo, Folgore* classes with elevation +45° -10°. The mounting was originally intended for hand training and elevation but came out too heavy, so that electric training and elevation had to be provided with added weight and complication.
OTO 1931, 1936. In *Maestrale, Oriani* and, doubtfully, in first units of 'Soldati' classes.

120mm/50 OTO 1933 guns in twin turrets in *Giulio Cesare*. Elevation was limited to 42°.
ANB

Elevation was +33° -7° in M1931 and +35° -10° in M1936. The former was lighter and less robust than M1926, but weight was increased in M1936 which had a larger shield.

Ansaldo 1936, 1937. In 'Soldati' class. Elevation was +40° -10° in M1936 and +42° -10° in M1937.

Ansaldo 1940. In *Lanciere, Camicia Nera, Geniere, Carabiniere, Bombardiere, Corsaro, Legionario, Mitragliere*; shielded single mountings with +45° -10° elevation. It had the additional function of a star shell gun and was added to *Maestrale* in replacement of a 120mm/15 howitzer.

OTO 1933. Twin turrets in *Cesare* and *Cavour*. Elevation was +42° -10° and the loading gear, with mechanical rammers, was fixed to the cradle, whereas destroyer mountings seem to have had no special loading equipment. Hoists ran from the magazines to the battery deck, ammunition then being passed by hand to the turret bases where there were ready racks. The sloping turret hoists ran to the outside of the guns. This differed from the supply to destroyer twin mountings, where it appears that there were twin dredger hoists in rear of the mounting.

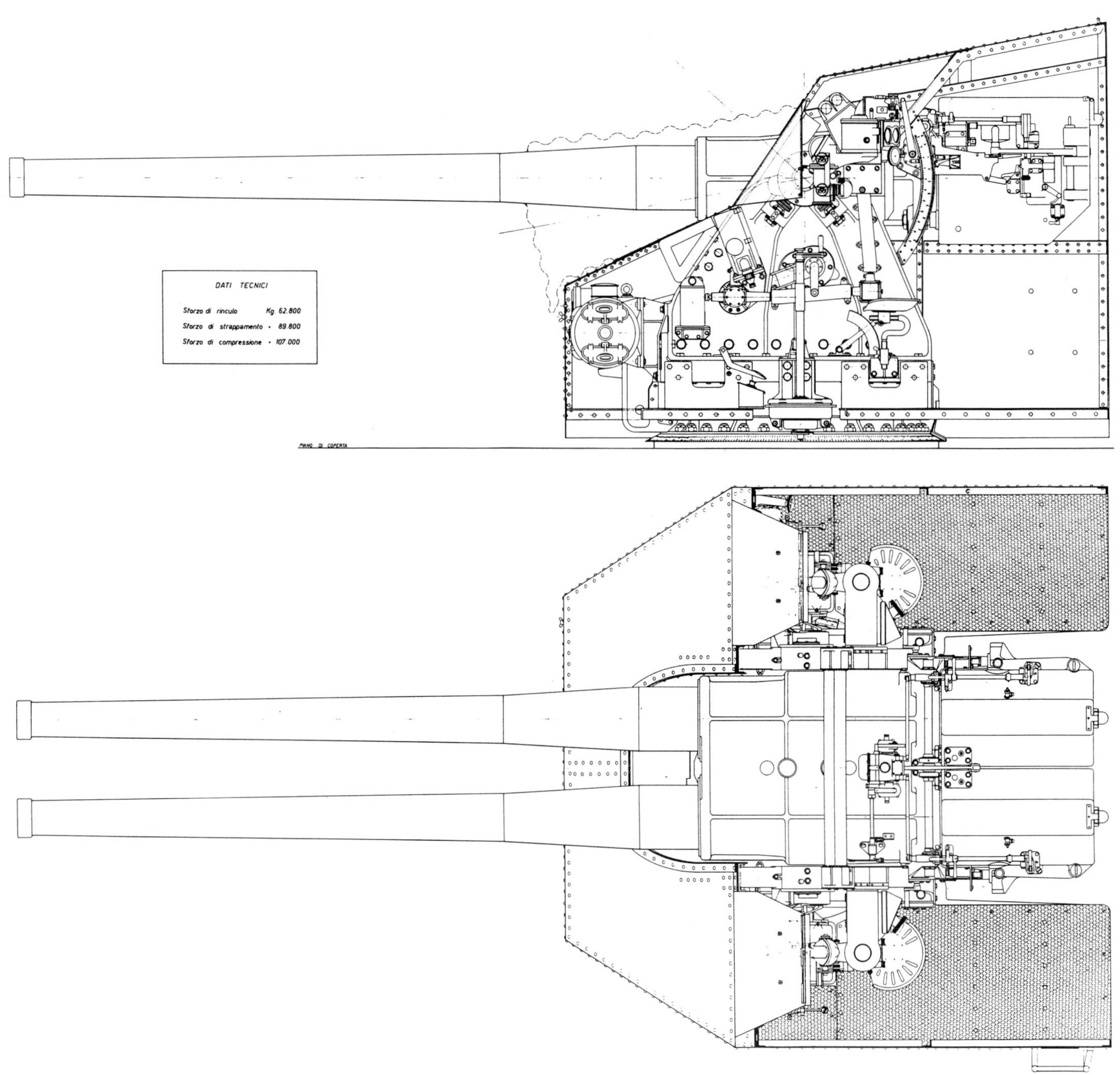

Top: Longitudinal drawing of 120mm/50 Ansaldo 1937 in twin mounting as in 'Soldati' class.
ANB

Above: Plan view of 120mm/50 Ansaldo 1937 in twin mounting. Note the closeness of the guns.
ANB

120mm (4.724in)

50-calibre M1909. Elswick BL guns, Pattern 'EE', originally in *Dante, Cesare, Quarto* and *Marsala* class, and similar Vickers design originally in *Leonardo da Vinci* and *Cavour*, but both later limited to coast defence. Weight with BM for Pattern 'EE', 3.42t (*3.365 tons*), shell 22.75kg (*50.15lb*) and MV 840m/s (*2756f/s*).

45-calibre OTO 1931. This was a separate ammunition QF with horizontal sliding block, on single P mountings in the submarines of the *Balilla* class, *Fieramosca, Micca* and the *Calvi* class. Weight is given as 3.2t (*3.15 tons*), and with 22kg (*48.5lb*) shell, MV was 730m/s (*2395f/s*). The mounting allowed +32° -4° elevation, and range is given as 14,000m (*15,300yd*) which seems too high.

45-calibre OTO 1926 and Vickers Terni 1924. These were similar and were in twin-shielded mountings in the *Turbine* and rearmed *Sella* classes (OTO) and *Sauro* class (VT). The guns had screw BM and appear in an ammunition list as BL, though separate loading QF seems more likely. Oscillating weight was about 4t (*3.94 tons*) and overall length is given as 5423mm (*213.5in*) for the VT gun, which indicates a bore length of 44cal if QF. With 23.15kg (*51.0lb*) shell and 7.6kg (*16.75lb*) NAC charge, MV is given as 850m/s (*2789f/s*).

The mountings had the guns in a common cradle with the axes 58cm (*22.8in*) apart, so that dispersion was considerable. The total mounting weight is given as 16.9t (*16.6 tons*) for OTO 1926, and elevation was +33° -10°, range being quoted as 15,500m (*16,950yd*).

45-calibre Schneider-Canet-Armstrong 1918 and 1918/19. M1918 was in single mountings, sometimes shielded, in various auxiliary ships and coast-defence installations, while M1918/19 was in twin mountings in the *Leone* class and the sloop *Eritrea.* Performance was similar to the above guns, but the twin mountings had +32° -10° and the single +30° -10° elevation.

45-calibre Armstrong 1918. Derived from the old 40cal gun, this was in AMCs, troop transports and coast-defence batteries. The open P mountings allowed +30° -10° elevation and with 23.15kg (*51.0lb*) shell, MV was 750m/s (*2461f/s*) and range 12,600m (*13,800yd*).

Right: 120mm/45 OTO 1931 in *Guiseppe Finzi.*
Elio Ando'

Below: 120mm/45 OTO 1926 guns in twin mounting in longitudinal and transverse sections as mounted in the *Turbine* class. The shield is not shown.
ANB

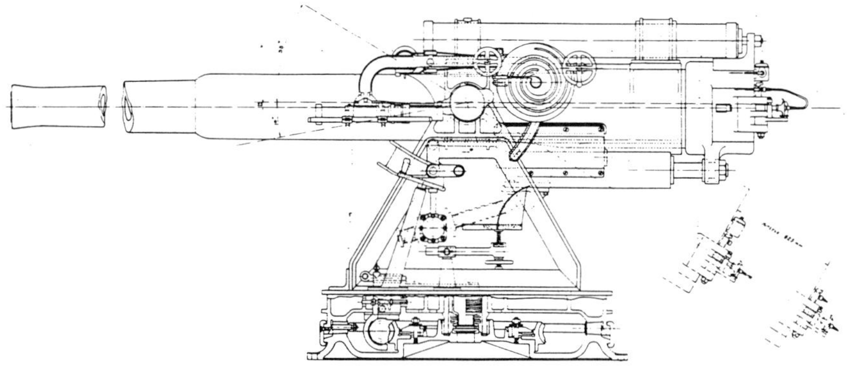

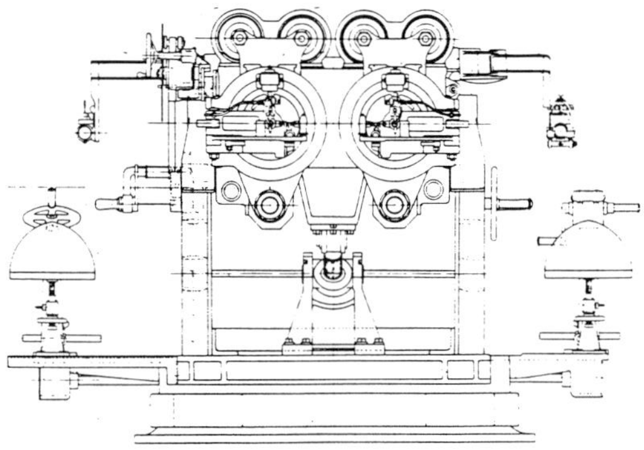

Bottom: Plan of 120mm/45 OTO 1926 guns in twin mounting.
ANB

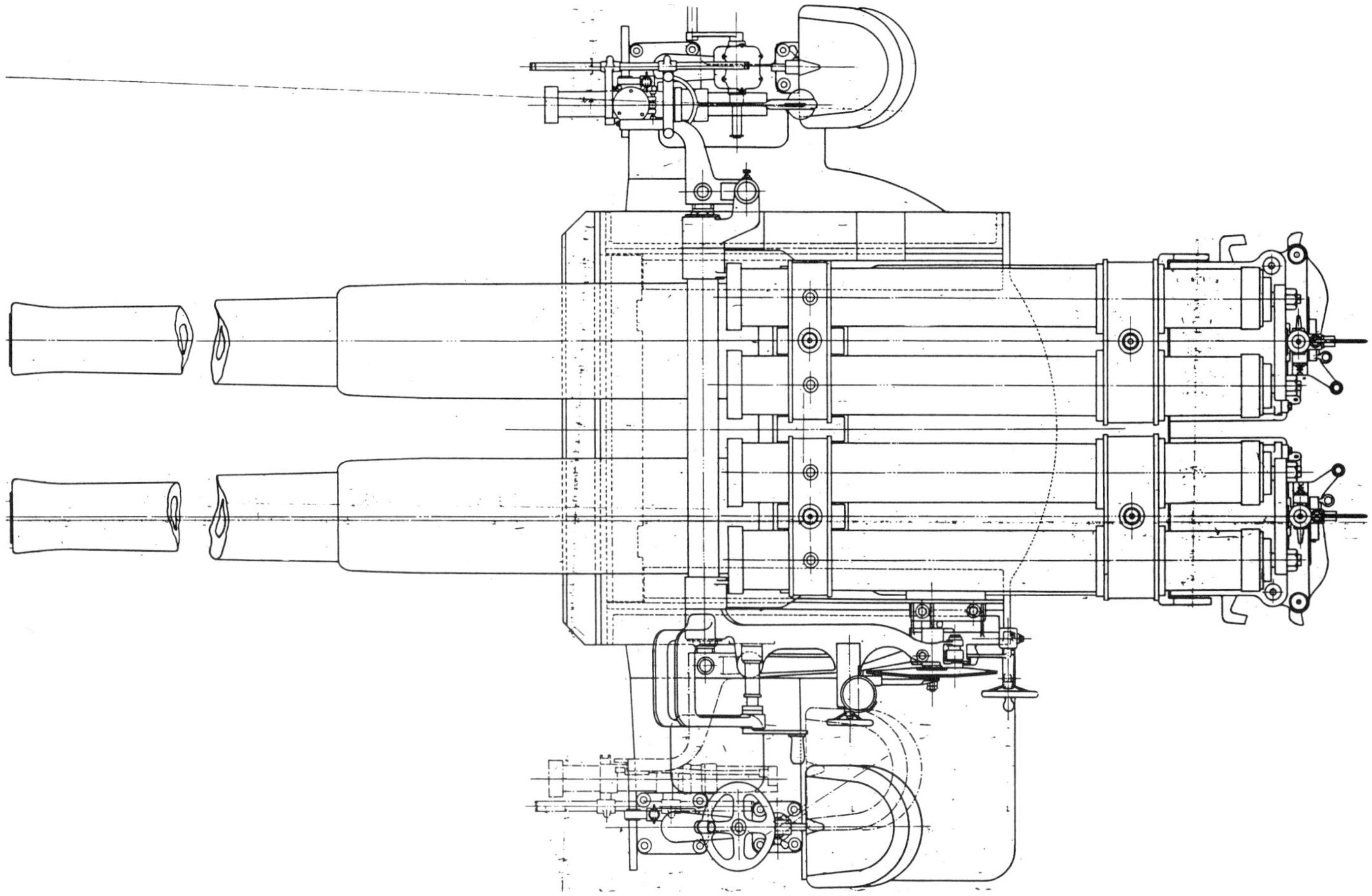

40-calibre Armstrong 1889, 1891. On single mountings with up to +32° -7° elevation, these guns (identical with the British QF Mk I and III) were in AMCs and troop transports as well as coast defence, while there were four in each of the *Littorio* class as star shell guns, which were at least better than the 15cal howitzer. With 19.75kg (*43.5lb*) shell, MV was about 700m/s (*2297f/s*).

27-calibre OTO 1924. Formerly in *Balilla* class and *Fieramosca* but removed before the war, and later used as AA guns at Messina. With 19.36kg (*42.7lb*) shell, MV is given as 730m/s (*2395f/s*) and ceiling as 7800m (*25600ft*).

15-calibre OTO 1933, 1934. Star shell howitzers in *Maestrale, Oriani* and some of 'Soldati' classes and also mounted for a time in the *Zara* class. Elevation was +50° -5°, star shell 19.8kg (*43.7lb*) MV 4000m/s (*1312f/s*) and effective range 4000m (*4400yd*) with maximum 6400m (*7000yd*).

120mm/40 Armstrong 1889 and 1891 as star shell guns, with 90mm/50, 37mm/54 and 20mm/65 Breda AA guns in *Littorio*.
Elio Ando'

LIGHT CALIBRE GUNS

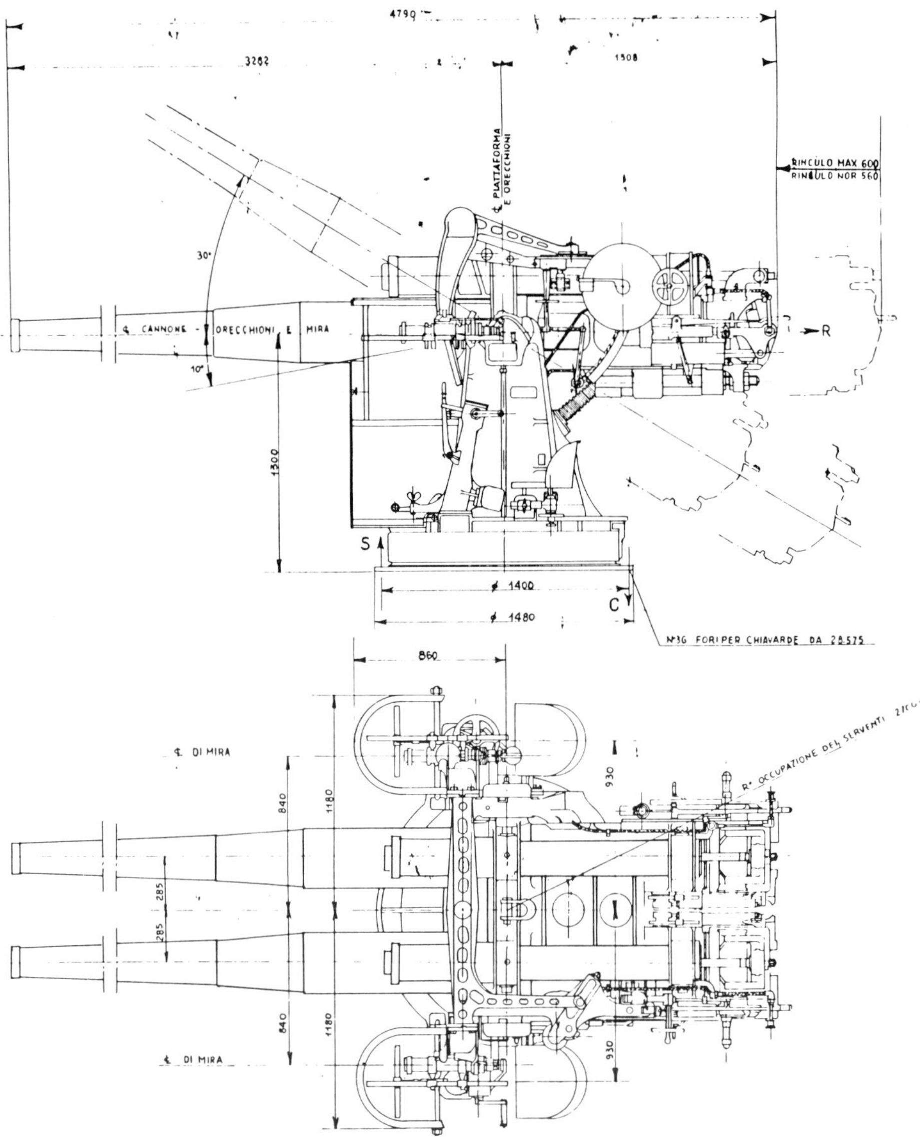

101.6mm/45 Schneider-Armstrong M1919 guns in twin mounting. Shown in side view and plan, this unsatisfactory mounting was limited to the *Curtatone* class.
ANB

45-calibre Schneider-Armstrong 1917, 1919. M1917 was virtually the British QF Mark V of which No 974 had been sent to Italy during the First World War as a pattern. It was made by Ansaldo under licence and proved a satisfactory gun in open single mountings allowing +35° -5° elevation. Some guns at least differed in having vertical sliding block BM instead of horizontal, and a higher performance was permitted than in British service. Fixed ammunition was fired. It was mounted in torpedo boats of the 'Generali', *Palestro*, *La Masa* and *Sirtori* classes as well as in auxiliary units and coast defence. The weight of the complete mounting was 4.6t (*4.53 tons*).

M1919 was in unsatisfactory twin mountings with both guns in a common cradle and was limited to the *Curtatone* class. Total weight was 10t (*9.84 tons*) and elevation +35° -5°. It was replaced by single mountings during the war.

45-calibre Schneider-Canet 1917. Similar to the above but the single open mountings allowed +30° -5°. It was mounted in the *Mirabello* class, various minor and auxiliary units and in coast defence.

35-calibre Schneider-Armstrong 1914-15, Terni 1914. There were of British type with sliding block BM, vertical in some at least, and were satisfactory within their limits. The open P mountings allowed +45° -5° and weighed complete about 5.0t (*4.92 tons*). They were mounted in torpedo boats of the *Pilo* class, *Audace*, *Diana* and various light units, auxiliaries and coast defence. They were also in submarines of the *Mameli*, *Pisani*, *Bandiera*, *Squalo*, *Bragadin*, *Argonauta* and *Settembrini* classes and many were mounted as improvised AA on platforms in Sicily and Southern Italy in 1942-43. Fixed ammunition was fired.

101.6mm (4in) guns

Gun Data

Gun	Weight incl BM	Shell	MV	Quoted range
45cal	2.364t (*2.327 tons*)	13.74kg (*30.3lb*)	850m/s (*2789f/s*)	15,000m/35° (*16,400yd*)
35cal	1.22t (*1.20 tons*)	13.74kg (*30.3lb*)	750m/s (*2461f/s*)	11,700m/45° (*12,800yd*)

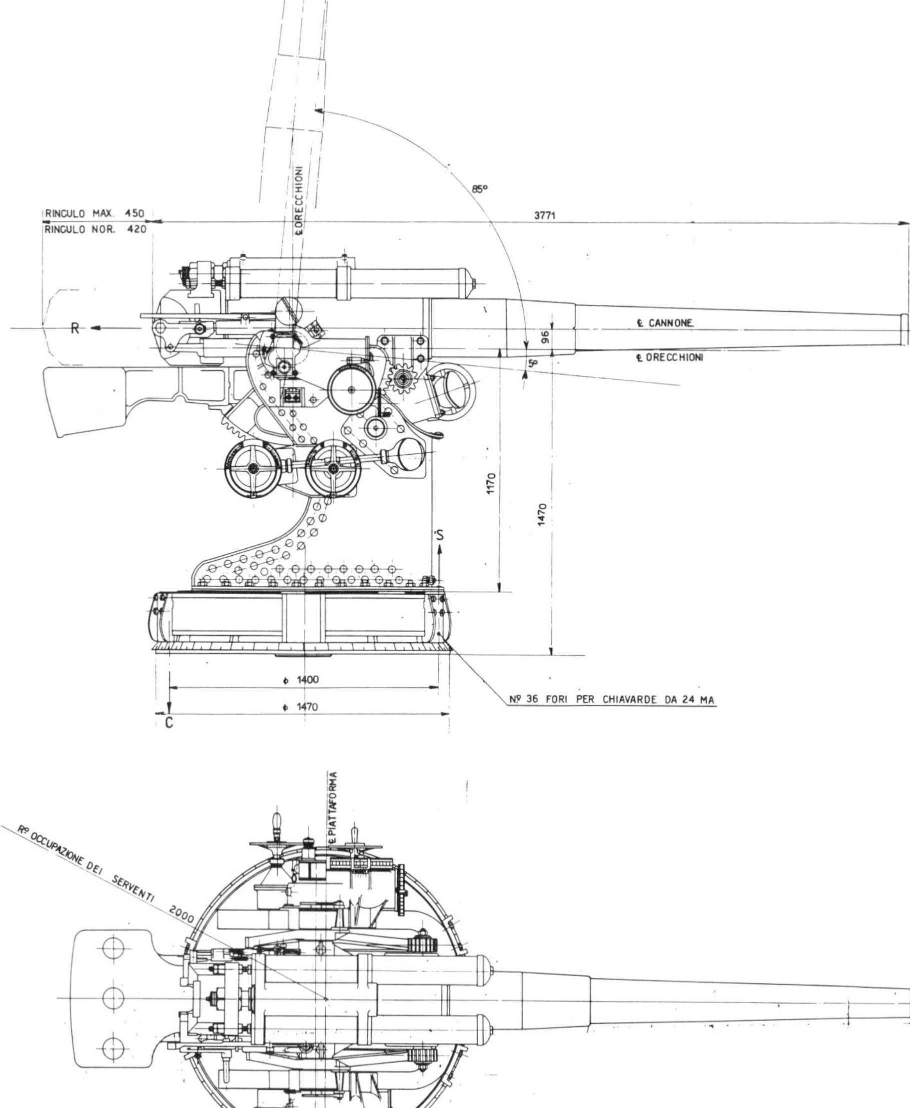

Above: Side view of 101.6mm/35 Schneider-Armstrong M1914-15 or Terni M1914 in AA mounting.
ANB

Right: Plan view of 101.6mm/35 in AA mounting.
ANB

100mm (3.937in)/47AA OTO 1924, 1927, 1928

Gun Data

	100mm	3.937in	
Weight incl BM	2.0t	1.97 tons	
Length oa	4985mm	196.26in	49.85cal
Length bore	4700mm	185.04in	47.0cal
Weight projectile	13.8kg	30.4lb	
Propellant charge	5.0kg NAC	11.0lb NAC	
Muzzle velocity	880m/s (? reduced to 850)	2887f/s (? reduced to 2789)	
Max range	15,240m	16,670yd	

Gun Mounting Data

Weight complete	15.033t	14.796 tons
Distance apart gun axes	44cm	17.3in
Firing cycle	7.5-6 sec	
Shield	usually 8-10mm	0.3-0.4in

These guns were virtually reproductions, but with loose liners, of the Skoda 10cm/50(oa) of 1910 which was in service in the Italian navy during the 1920s in the *Brindisi* (ex-*Helgoland*), *Venezia* (ex-*Saida*) and seven destroyers of the former *Tatra* class, known as the *Cortellazzo* (ex-*Lika*) class. The AA guns were mounted in the *Cesare* class, all 203mm (*8in*) and 152mm (*6in*) cruisers, and added to the old *San Giorgio*. All were in twin mountings with adjustable trunnions which were raised as the guns elevated. The most widely used model was the OTO M1928 gun in the RM (Italian Navy) M1927/28 mounting.

Drawings thought to refer to this gun show an A tube, jacket and thin taper loose liner with a breech ring screwed to both A tube and jacket. The liner, which had a wall thickness of approximately 12mm (*0.47in*) and weighed 159kg (*350lb*), was held by a shoulder just forward of the chamber and by an interrupted screw collar with six muzzle keys. The breech block was of horizontal sliding type and fixed ammunition was fired, the round weighing 26kg (*57.3lb*) with a length of 1.2m (*47.2in*).

The twin-shielded mountings had both guns in a common cradle and allowed 80° or 85° -5°. The older mountings were hand loaded, but later ones had mechanised arrangements with

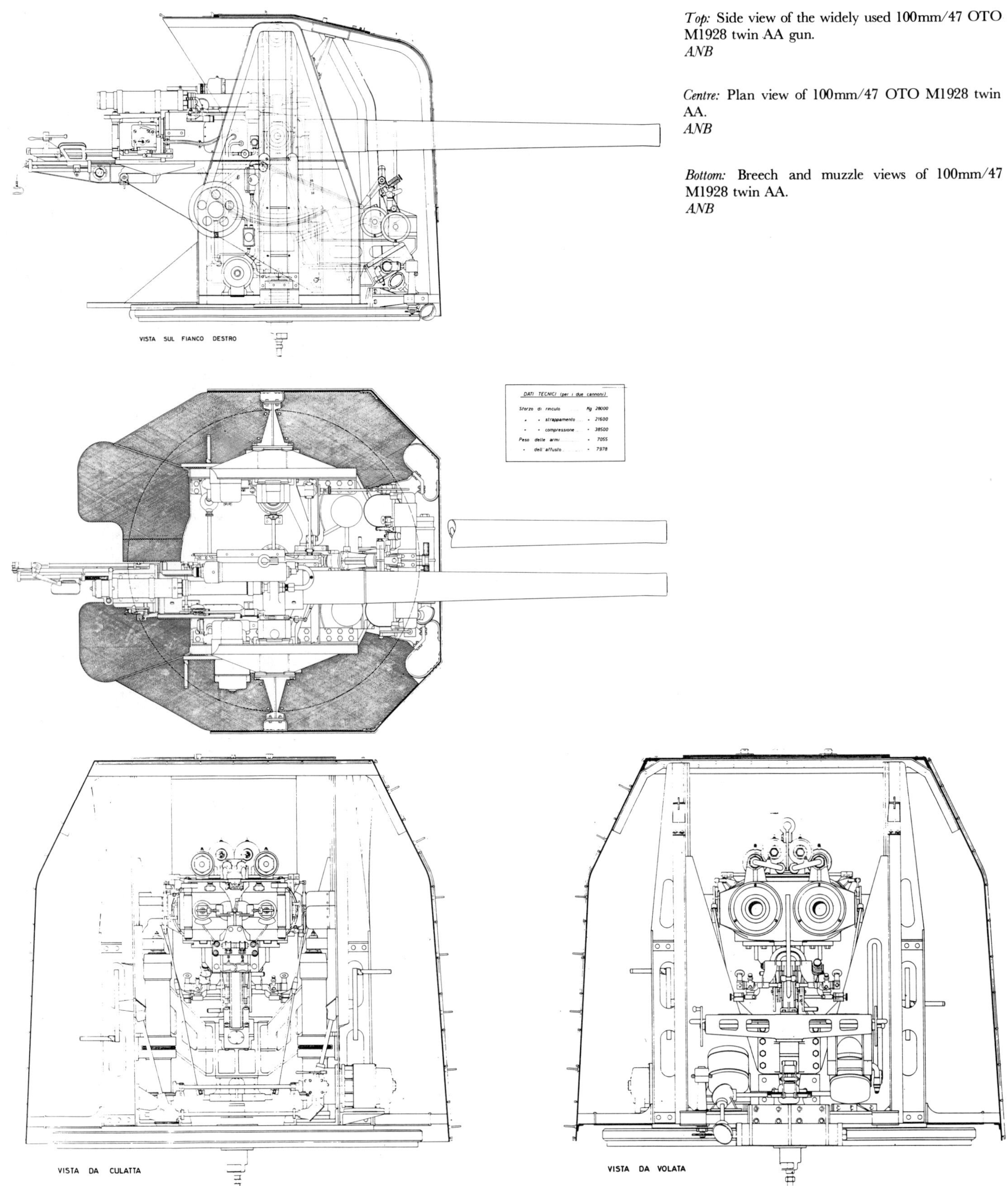

Top: Side view of the widely used 100mm/47 OTO M1928 twin AA gun.
ANB

Centre: Plan view of 100mm/47 OTO M1928 twin AA.
ANB

Bottom: Breech and muzzle views of 100mm/47 M1928 twin AA.
ANB

pneumatic rammers. The cradle trunnions were automatically raised by electric power to increase breech clearance above the base of the mounting as the guns elevated. The mechanism was devised by Comandante Minisini and the whole mounting was often named after him. The trunnion height was adjustable between 1.6 and 2.5m (*5ft 3in, 8ft 3in*). The speed of trunnion movement was found to be too slow to follow the necessary rapid variation in elevation, particularly if the ship was rolling, and the equipment was of limited efficiency. It was difficult to use in aimed fire against low flying torpedo planes, and more adapted for barrage fire.

100mm (3.937in)/47 OTO 1931 in OTO 1931, 1935, RM 1937, OTO 1937 in OTO 1937

These guns were further developments of the Skoda 1910 model, and were in single, usually shielded, hand-worked mountings in the torpedo boats of the *Spica* and *Ariete* classes, destroyer escorts of the *Orsa* and *Animoso* classes and corvettes of the *Gabbiano* class. The guns generally resembled the AA versions, and fired similar shells, though a muzzle velocity of approximately 900m/s (*2953f/s*) was originally intended, but reduced to 855m/s (*2805f/s*) to limit long-range dispersion.

The OTO 1931 mounting allowed +45° -6°, increased in the others to +60° -10°. The RM mounting was little used and, as opportunity occurred, OTO 1931 in the earlier units of the *Spica* class was replaced by OTO 1935 or 1937. The two latter weighed, with gun and shield, 6.315t (*6.215 tons*) and 6.765t (*6.658 tons*) respectively.

In general these guns seem to have been satisfactory within their limits, which were particularly apparent in AA fire.

100mm (3.937in)/47 OTO 1931, 1935, 1938 for submarines

Further guns of the same general type, developed from the earlier OTO 1928 for submarines, and mounted in single open P mountings in nearly all the more recent Italian boats, the principal exceptions being the *Micca* and *Calvi* class with 120mm (*4.7in*) and the *Romolo* class with 20mm. They were also in some auxiliary ships.

In general, the guns were similar to the AA type but overall length was 4940mm (*194.49in*) and MV 840m/s (*2756f/s*) with 13.8kg (*30.4lb*) shell. The mountings of which the most efficient was OTO 1938M weighing with gun 4.65t (*4.58 tons*), allowed +32° -5° and range is given as 12,600m (*13,800yd*).

100mm (3.937in)/43 OTO 1927 for submarines

Descended from OTO 1924, an unsuccessful attempt to reduce the Skoda 1910 to 43cal bore length. It was not very satisfactory and was only in CT mountings in the *Foca* and *Brin* classes, and later progressively replaced by deck mounted 100/47s. With the usual shell, MV was approximately 800m/s (*2625f/s*) and range approximately 11,000m (*12,000yd*). Elevation was +35° -5°.

90mm (3.543in)/53 Ansaldo 1939/41

A much-liked army AA gun, of which six were being installed at the armistice in pontoon GD32, the hull of the old cruiser *Puglia*, for the defence of Livorno. It was also extensively mounted on land for the defence of naval bases. The gun was derived from the naval 90/50 and had a monobloc barrel. The P mounting, which allowed 85° elevation, was not stabilised and had equilibriator cylinders. The shell weighed 10.07kg (*22.2lb*), and MV was 840m/s (*2756f/s*) with firing cycle 3-4sec.

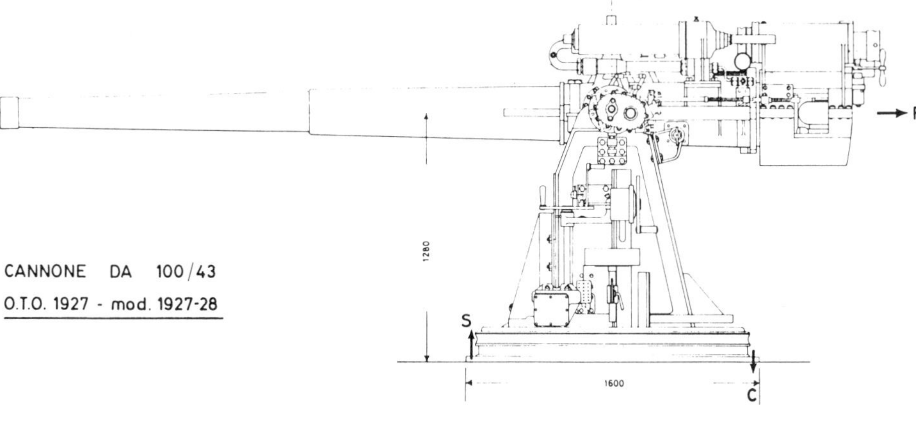

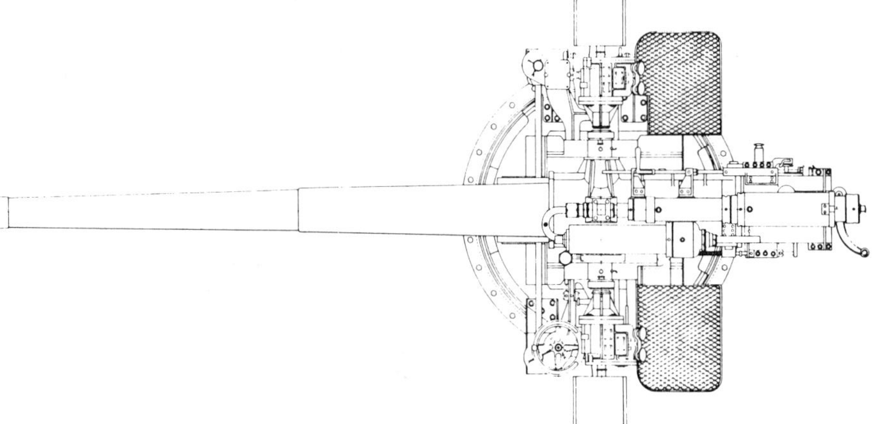

Top: Torpedo boat *Ariel* of the *Spica* class, showing the after 100mm/47 OTO 1937 guns. These were not AA.
Elio Ando'

Centre: Argo in 1942 with 100mm/47 OTO 1935 gun.
Elio Ando'

Bottom: The not very satisfactory 100mm/43 OTO 1927 gun in side and plan view.
ANB

These were similar and were based on development work at Ansaldo. The original prototypes were 48 calibres in length, and the 50-calibre guns were installed in the *Littorio* and *Duilio* classes on unique single quadraxial mountings which form the main interest. An unstabilised conventional mounting intended for the fast sloop *Diana* was cancelled. The gun had an autofretted monobloc barrel with a screwed-on breech ring containing the horizontal sliding breech block and seatings for the recoil and run-out cylinders. It appears to have been accurate and reliable, if not very spectacular in performance. The fixed round weighed approximately 18kg (*40lb*).

The four axes of the mounting were training, elevation, roll correction and pitch correction. Training and elevation were by hand only, the limits of the latter being +75° -3°. The gunhouse trained in the inner cast-steel frame of a gimbal system with axes fore and aft and athwartships. By means of a lead screw and nut, the outer cast-steel gimbal frame oscillated about the fore and aft axis to correct for roll, and with a similar screw and nut the inner gimbal frame oscillated about the athwartships axis to correct for pitch. Both lead screws were electrically powered with RPC as described below, and the screw helix angle was small so that the drive would not run back.

Ammunition was raised from magazines to main deck by electric hoists capable of 30 rounds per minute. It was then passed by hand to the lower compartment of the mountings, each having about 90 rounds stacked in spring clips round this compartment. A short hoist in the stabilised part of the mounting, powered by a 2HP motor and with speeds of 12, 16 or 30 rounds per minute, raised the round vertically to the gunhouse, where it was automatically turned to the horizontal and loaded by hand with a pantograph link rammer. An automatic fuze setter formed part of the top of the hoist.

There was an enclosed oval turret type shield with a barbette below, considerably higher in the *Littorio* class, and it appears that this type of shield was fitted mainly to protect the installation from the blast of the main armament on extreme bearings so that the AA guns could continue firing.

The stabilisation system, which was designed and manufactured by the San Giorgio company of Genoa, was as follows: the very complex stable element provided roll and pitch outputs in terms of displacement angle, angular velocity and angular acceleration. There were 11 gyros, and roll was transmitted to ±14½° and pitch to ±5°. The main gyro had a vertical spin axis and was driven from a 60V, three-phase, 120-cycle supply, the synchronous speed being 7200rpm. Weight was added at the base of the gyro to bring the centre of gravity below the gimbal axes, so that it functioned as a normal gyro pendulum. Rigidly fixed to the gimbal ring were two small gyros with horizontal spin axes. These worked off a special 90V, three-phase supply with the frequency varied by a hand-set control up to 250 cycles, when the synchronous speed was 15,000rpm. The frequency was adjusted to a function of the ship's speed through the water. When the ship turned in azimuth, these gyros exerted a torque about the outer gimbal axis of the main gyro and approximately neutralised the centrifugal force on it. As the ship turned, the fore and aft line was not tangential to the turning circle and this yaw produced a small centrifugal force component in a fore and aft direction on the main gyro. No attempt was made to correct for this. The angles transmitted to the RPC potentiometer were limited to the ±14½° and ±5° noted above.

To obtain the first and second derivatives of roll required four gyros, and another four needed for the derivatives of pitch were identical, except for being at right angles to the roll component, measured in the deck plane. There was thus, strictly, a geometrical error, but the errors in the two vertical planes were negligible, as the maximum values of roll and pitch were small. The first roll derivative was

90mm (3.543in)/50 Ansaldo 1938, OTO 1939

Gun Data

Bore	90mm	3.543in	
Weight incl BM	1.21t	1.19 tons	
Length bore	4500mm	177.17in	50.0cal
Weight projectile	10.1kg	22.3lb	
Propellant charge	3.4kg	7.5lb	
Muzzle velocity	860m/s	2822f/s	
Working pressure	3050kg/cm²	19.37 tons/in²	
Max range	*c*16,000m	*c*17,500yd	
Ceiling	*c*10,800m	*c*35,400ft	

Gun Mounting Data

Weight of complete 'turret'	19.072t	18.771 tons
Recoil	48.4cm	19in
Firing cycle (normal)	5sec	

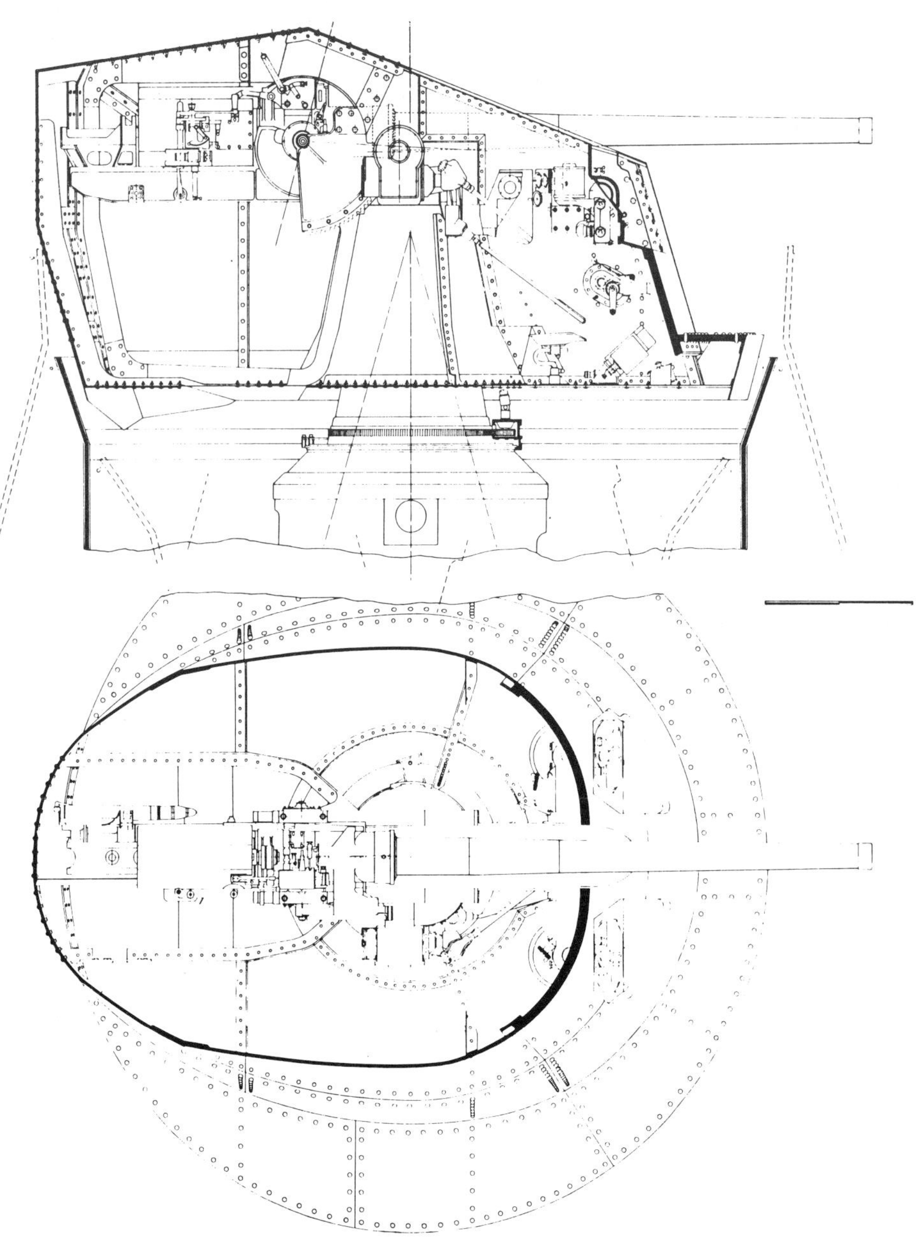

Side and plan view of the 90mm/50 AA gun in quadraxial mounting. Only the upper part of the installation is shown.
ANB

determined from two contra-rotating gyros with vertical spin axes, mounted side by side, each with freedom about a single gimbal axis in the athwartships direction. The single gimbal axes were coupled by toothed sectors and one axis carried an arm connected to centering springs. The contra-rotating gyros were free from the extraneous torque due to gimbal friction which would affect a single gyro if there were tilting due to roll rate and the ship turned in azimuth at the same time. These two gyros thus measured the rate of roll by the usual constrained-gyro technique.

Another two gyros were mounted vertically above the first pair, but in a common gimbal ring not constrained in the roll direction. The inner gimbal axes were connected by toothed sectors and constrained by springs. The movement of the first pair was transmitted by mechanical linkage, of which the ratio was altered by hand adjustment when first tried at sea. Thus, the second pair measured the derivative of motion of the first pair - that is the angular acceleration of roll.

The derivatives of pitch were determined in a similar way with the necessary 90° changes in horizontal directions.

To facilitate testing in harbour, the whole stable element was contained in a cradle with axis fore and aft and could be oscillated by a motor to test the roll side. The whole stable element could be turned 90° to test the pitch side.

Selsyn AC-type transmission brought resetting from electric motors at the gun to feed one side of a differential gear (one per circuit). Through a torque amplifier, the displacement gyro drove the other side of each of these six differential gears, and thus the centre member of a differential represented misalignment between gun and gyro. Since the power motors were also fed with velocity and acceleration signals, the displacement misalignment was expected to be small and deal only with wander due to lack of strict symmetry in velocity and acceleration parts of the control. For this reason, the displacement circuit had no compensation to remove lag in its contribution to the total problem. The differential gears thus drove rotary contacts on potentiometers of the type used in the constrained gyro units, and these controlled the second field windings of Ward-Leonard generators, the windings of the six generators being connected to the respective control circuits.

Littorio showing single 90mm/50 AA guns.
Elio Ando'

Owing to the construction of the constrained gyro assemblies, angular velocity and acceleration were produced as a combined motion which moved a roller contact on a commutator-type potentiometer. If the effect were applied direct to the first field windings of the six Ward-Leonard generators, all in series, out-of-balance would occur as the windings warmed up and increased in resistance, so that a metadyne generator was interposed between potentiometer and generator field. This kept the output current proportional to the input voltage if the second circuit changed in resistance.

Tests of two prototype mountings with 48-calibre guns were carried out in the old armoured cruiser *San Giorgio* in 1938 and were considered satisfactory, but the lead screw RPC motors were removed from the *Duilio* class in 1942, apparently because water entered through the gap needed to accommodate the roll and pitch motion of the mounting. In the *Littorio* class the mountings were much higher and stabilisation was retained. There seems no doubt that the stabilisation gear was not robust enough for a weight of around 20 tons, and that it was too advanced for its day.

76.2mm (3in) guns

Nearly all of these had been made by Ansaldo in 1914-19, either under licence or to their own modified design. The parent gun was the British 12pdr/12cwt (*610kg*) and the Italian versions were identical or similar, though fixed rather than separate ammunition appears to have been normal. The principal surviving types were as follows:

40-calibre Armstrong 1916, 1917. On single open P mountings allowing +42° -10°, in minor units and auxiliaries with a number in coast defence. With 6.5kg (*14.3lb*) shell, MV is given as 680m/s (*2231f/s*) and range as 10,000m (*10,900yd*).

40-calibre AA Ansaldo, Italian Navy, 1916. The AA shell weighed 6.0kg (*13.27lb*) MV rising to 690m/s (*2264f/s*). The mountings allowed +65° -10°.

40-calibre AA Ansaldo 1917. This differed in the mounting allowing +75° -10°. MV is quoted at 760m/s (*2493f/s*) which seems unlikely.

These AA guns were mounted in older warships, at least early in the war, and in minor and auxiliary vessels. As many as 730 were used for the AA defence of Italy, some of these being on pontoons.

76mm/40 Armstrong 1917 gun in the small minelayer *Fasana*.
Elio Ando'

Other 76.2mm (*3in*) guns surviving in small numbers were a 50-calibre Vickers, originally in *Pisa* and limited to coast defence, a 30-calibre Armstrong M1914, and a 23-calibre Ansaldo M1918. Both of these were in a few minor units. They fired a 4.28kg (*9.44lb*) shell at respective MVs of approximately 550m/s (*1804f/s*) and 420m/s (*1378f/s*).

65mm (2.559in)/64 Ansaldo-Terni M1939

A jointly developed medium-range AA gun which never entered service, though 12 in single shielded mountings were due for the *Aquila* in autumn 1943. It was originally 56 calibres in length, increased to 62 and then 64, and from an illustration of a 64-calibre prototype had a barrel, long jacket and vertical sliding breech block. The electrically powered loading equipment included dual loading trays and a pantograph linkage rammer fixed to the cradle, so that loading was at any elevation. The rammer gave much trouble which was not completely cured by summer 1943, and it was considered that hand loading would be much more reliable even if somewhat slower. The gun was never in series production, the programme for production was cancelled in the summer of 1943, and work ceased at the armistice.

The shell was about 4.08kg (*9lb*), MV 950m/s (*3117f/s*), and firing cycle approximately 3sec, presumably with hand ramming. Effective range is quoted as about 7500m (*8200yd*).

57mm (2.244in)/43 Nordenfelt 1887

Unlike most navies the Italian had preferred this gun to the equivalent Hotchkiss. It fired a 2.9kg (*6.4lb*) shell at 665m/s (*2182f/s*) and some were still in minor and auxiliary ships as well as in coast defence. The old type P mounting allowed +15° -10° and range was 7400m (*8090yd*).

40mm (1.575in)/39 Vickers-Terni 1915, 1917

The British 2pdr Mark II manufactured under licence by Terni until the early 1930s, after 50 had been transferred to Italy during the First World War. It was in single mountings, mostly in the older destroyers and torpedo boats, though some of the *Dardo, Folgore* and 'Navigatori' classes had it in the early part of the war. The commonest mounting, M1930 mod, weighed 852kg (*1878lb*) and had a crew of five. Elevation was +80° -5°, and the ammunition box held 50 rounds. Italian data gives MV approximately 610m/s (*2000f/s*) with 0.9kg (*2lb*) shell, which was self destroying at 4475m (*4900yd*).

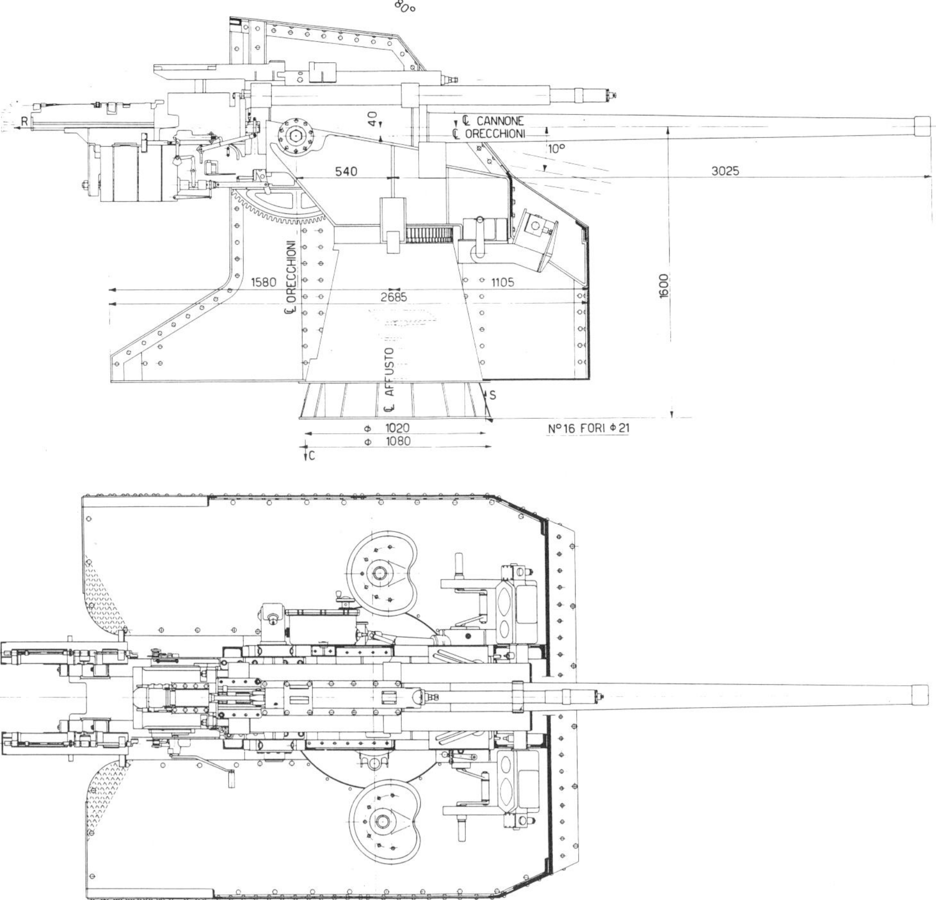

Top: 65mm/64 Ansaldo-Terni M1939 medium range AA gun in elevation and plan view. This never entered service.
ANB

Centre: 40mm/39 Vickers-Terni 1915 pom-pom in an unidentified torpedo boat.
Elio Ando'

Bottom: 37mm/54 Breda water-cooled automatic guns in twin M1932 mounting in a *Zara* class cruiser.
Elio Ando'

AUTOMATIC GUNS

This was the standard Italian close-range AA for larger ships, though the number of barrels only reached 20 in the *Littorio* class. Of the various mountings, M1932 was a twin with stabilised line of sight through ±10° roll, M1938 was another twin without the stabilisation and replaced M1932 in production from 1939, though M1932 continued in service throughout the war, while M1939 was a single collapsible mounting for installation on the forecastles of the *Littorio* and *Duilio* classes. There was also a RM (Navy) 1939 single mounting of more conventional type. Elevation was +80° -10° in twins and +90° -10° in singles.

The gun was water cooled with circulating pump in M1932, but otherwise air cooled. It was gas operated and the system was considered to limit performance on the grounds of rather low rate of fire and liability to damage. There was a simple flat magazine holding six rounds, which was vertical in the twin mountings and horizontal in the singles. It was possible to load the magazines one after another to maintain the rate of fire. This is given as 120 rounds per minute with alternative settings of 90 and 60. The HE self-destroying round weighed 1.63kg (*3.59lb*) and was 162.5mm (*6.398in*) long.

The twin mountings suffered from heavy vibration and required a strong supporting structure. Conditions were improved in the collapsible M1939, which had one man as layer and trainer, by the addition of an equilibriator linked to the cradle. The RM1939, with separate layer and trainer, apparently had a similar fitting.

37mm (1.457in)/54 Breda 1932, 1938, 1939

Gun Data

Bore	37mm	1.457in
Weight of gun (1938)	277kg	611lb
Weight projectile	0.823kg	1.814lb
Propellant charge	0.200kg NAC	0.44lb NAC
Muzzle velocity	800m/s	2625f/s
Working pressure	2800kg/cm^2	17.8 tons/in^2
Max range	7800m	8530yd
Ceiling	5000m	16,400ft
Effective range	4000m	4370yd

Approximate Total Weight of Mountings

M1932	5.0t	4.9 tons
M1938	4.3t	4.2 tons
M1939	1.5t	1.48 tons
RM1939	2.0t	1.97 tons

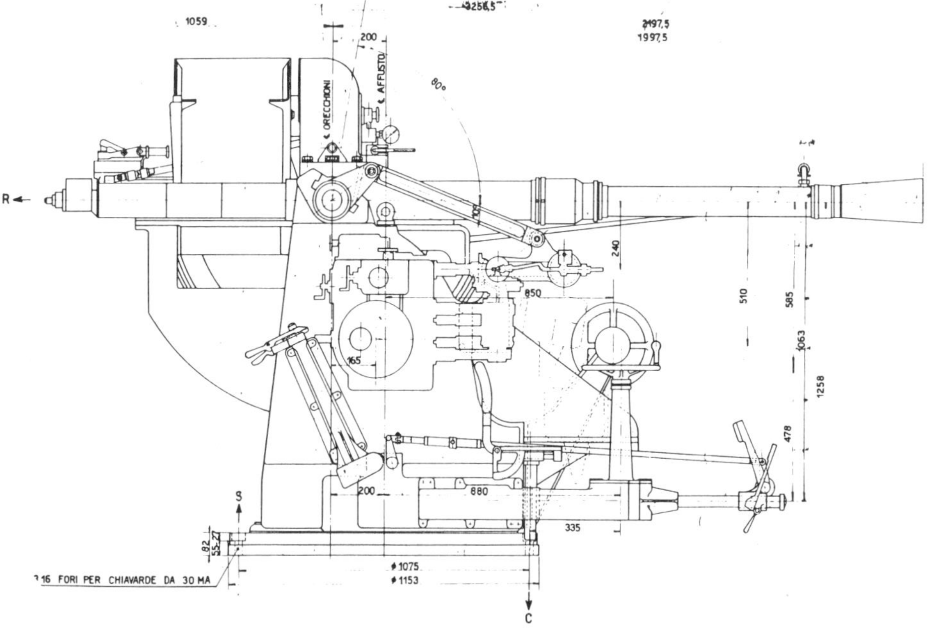

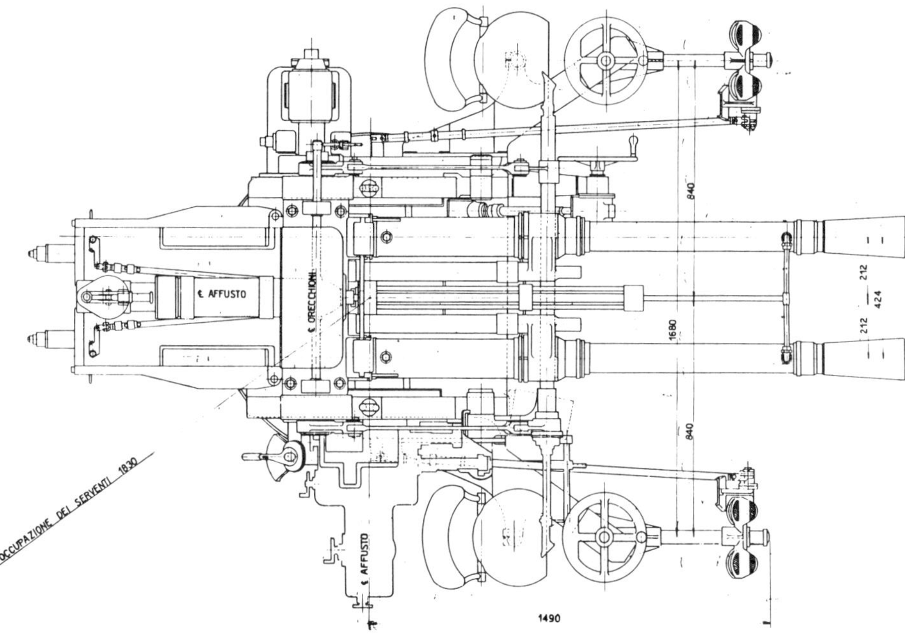

37mm/54 Breda water-cooled guns in twin mounting, side and plan view.
ANB

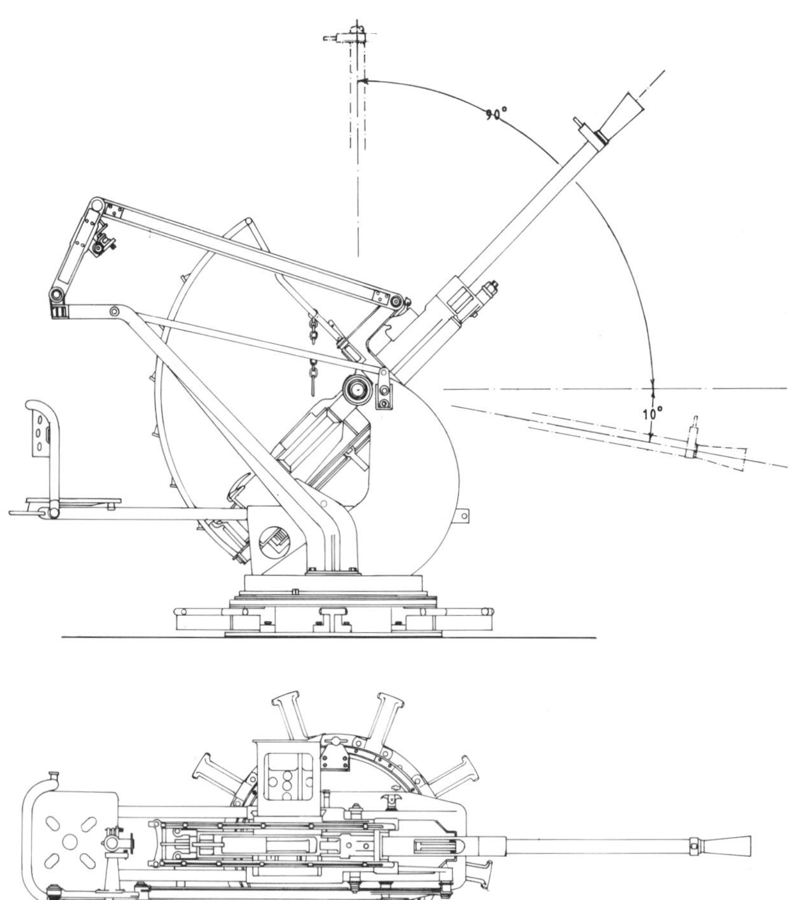

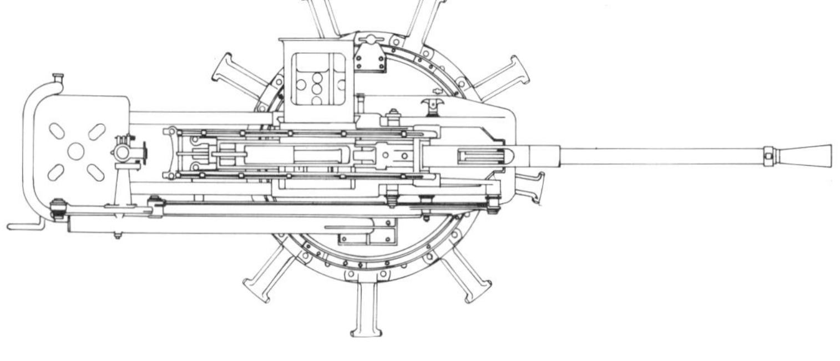

20mm/65 Breda automatic gun in single mounting in side and plan view.
ANB

20mm/65 Breda guns in twin RM1935 mounting in a torpedo boat.
Elio Ando'

20mm (0.787in)/65 Breda 1935, 1939, 1940

Gun Data

Bore	20mm	0.7874in
Weight of gun	72kg	159lb
Weight projectile	0.134kg	0.295lb
Propellant charge	0.038kg FC_4	1.34oz FC_4
Muzzle velocity	*c*840m/s	*c*2756f/s
Working pressure	2600kg/cm²	16.5 tons/in²
Max range	5500m	6000yd
Ceiling	2900m	9500ft
Effective range	2500m	2730yd

The standard Italian gun of the above calibre, mounted in most types of warship, though the number of barrels was low in comparison with US or British ships, the greatest number being 32 in the *Vittorio Veneto* (apart from a figure of 82 for the incomplete *Aquila*). The most common mounting, RM (Italian Navy) 1935, was a stabilised twin with the left gun diagonally above the right, and both mounted on an erect disc moving inside a fixed circular rim. One man acted as layer and trainer out of a crew of five, and the mounting was heavy at 2330kg (*5137lb*) complete. Elevation was +100° -10°. M1939 was a little used single mounting, but M1940, which was free swinging, was in many light units. It weighed 312.5kg (*689lb*) with gun, and elevation in both singles was +90° -10°.

The gun was air cooled and gas operated, and seems to have been considered fairly efficient, though with the disadvantages of the 37mm (*1.457in*) in its operating system. It was derived from the 13.2mm (*0.52in*) Breda M1931. The flat horizontal magazines held 12 rounds and an unusual feature was that the empty case was reinserted in its own compartment of the magazine.

The rate of fire was about 240 per minute, and the complete round weighed 0.320kg (*0.705lb*).

Other 20mm (0.787in) guns

20mm/70 Scotti-Isotta Fraschini M1939, Scotti-OM M1941. The Scotti gun, of similar performance to the Breda, was ordered in some quantity as supplies of the latter were inadequate. The most widely used mounting was a modified twin RM1935, but a single M1939 was also in many ships, and a disappearing mounting, apparently M1941, which was also single, was in the *Romolo* and some of the *Flutto* classes of submarines.

20mm/70 Oerlikon. Imported from Switzerland, and first in service in early 1941. It was apparently considered the best of the 20mm, but numbers were limited for financial reasons. There were two types, 1S with a 15-round strip magazine, on single hand-worked mountings allowing +90° -15°, and 3S with a 60-round drum magazine on free swinging mountings with adjustable trunnion height and elevation +87° -5°.

20mm/65 Flakvierling M38. The standard German gun on a quadruple mounting, and believed to have been in the destroyer escorts *Animoso, Ardente, Ardimentoso* and in some smaller units.

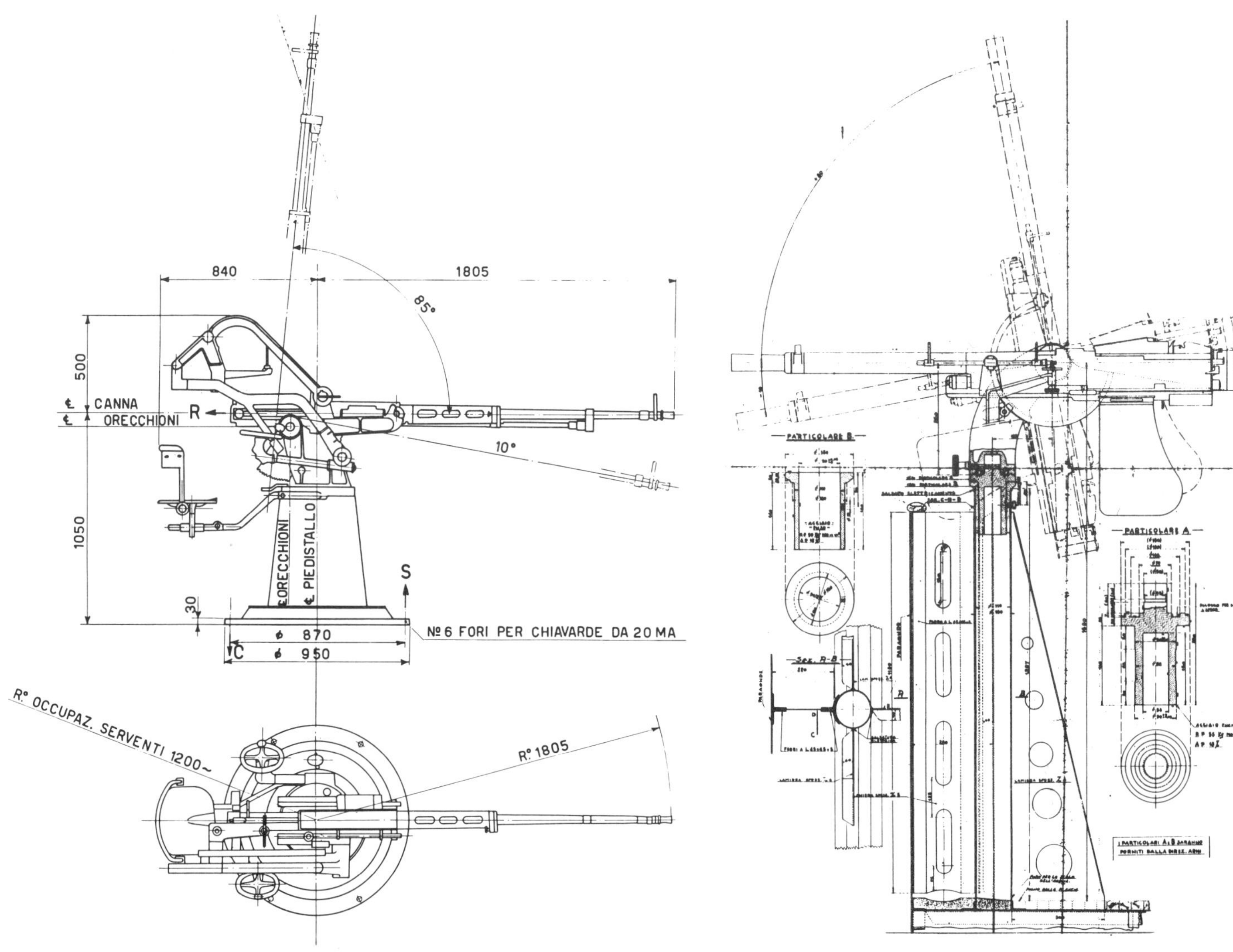

20mm/70 Scotti-Isotta Fraschini automatic gun in M1939 mounting.
ANB

13.2mm/75.7 Breda machine guns in twin mounting.
ANB

This was still retained in many submarines on twin, disappearing, free-swinging mountings allowing +90° -10°. A single free-swinging mounting with +80° -10° elevation was in light units, and a heavy - 695kg (*1532lb*) - hand-worked twin, allowing +85° -11°, in merchant ships and auxiliary cruisers. The gun was gas operated and air cooled with a 30-round vertical magazine. The complete round weighed 0.125kg (*0.276lb*) and was 136.5mm (*5.374in*) long. Maximum rate of fire is given as 500 per minute.

13.2mm (0.52in)/75.7 Breda M1931

Gun Data

Bore	13.2mm	0.52in
Weight of gun	47.5kg	104.7lb
Weight projectile	0.051kg	1.8oz
Weight propellant	0.0154kg	0.54oz
Muzzle velocity	790m/s	2592f/s
Max range	*c*6000m	*c*6600yd
Effective range	2000m	2200yd

Rifle-calibre Machine Guns.

These were either 8mm (*0.315in*) or 6.5mm (*0.256in*). The former included the gas operated, air-cooled Breda M1937 with a 20-round magazine, and the recoil operated, air-cooled Fiat M1914/35 which had a 50-round metal link belt. The smaller calibre guns were the recoil operated, air-cooled Breda 1930 with a 20-round magazine and the gas operated, water-cooled Colt M1915 with 250-round fabric belt. None was of particularly high performance.

Guns in former French and Yugoslavian ships

Few ex-French ships actually entered service in the Italian Navy. The heaviest guns were 138.6mm (*5.457in*)/40cal M1923 in FR21 (ex-*Lion*) and 130mm (*5.118in*)/40cal M1919 in FR23 (ex-*Tigre*) and FR31 (ex-*Trombe*). These and other guns are described in the French section.

The most important ex-Yugoslavian ships were the *Premuda* (ex-*Dubrovnik*), *Sebenico* (ex-*Beograd*) and *Lubiana* (ex-*Ljubljana*). The last two had 120mm (*4.724in*) Skoda guns, and the *Premuda* 140mm (*5.512in*), also Skoda. Both fired separate QF ammunition.

Gun Data Skoda 140mm and 120mm

Gun	140mm (*5.512in*)/56cal	120mm (*4.724in*)/46cal
Weight incl BM	6t (*5.9 tons*)	3.8t (*3.74 tons*)
Weight projectile	39.8kg (*87.7lb*)	24kg (*52.9lb*)
Propellant charge	15.5kg (*34.2lb*) NAC	7.85kg (*17.3lb*) C
Muzzle velocity	880m/s (*2887f/s*)	850m/s (*2789f/s*)
Weight with mounting	15.6t (*15.4 tons*)	-
Elevation	45°	35°

As usual with Skoda guns, the above calibre length is overall. The 140mm shells were boat tailed, and maximum range was 23,400m (*25,600yd*).

TORPEDOES

Triple TT for SI 270/533. 4 × 7.2 torpedoes in *Eugenio di Savoia*.
Elio Ando'

Italian torpedoes were initially rumoured in Britain to have a very high performance, but capture of a comprehensive list in 1940 showed that their range and speed, though high in the later weapons, were not exceptional except perhaps in the 50kt torpedoes for submarines. Another matter revealed by this list was that, including obsolescent designs, there were at least 36 different types or marks. No attempt will be made to describe all of these, and attention is concentrated on the later types. The principal makers were Whitehead at Fiume and Silurificio Italiano at Naples, the torpedoes being identified by the letters W or SI. The designation used was much fuller than usual, comprising maker's letter, charge weight in kg/diameter in mm × length in m, particular type or mark. Except for some special, circling, electric airborne torpedoes, wet-heater systems were used with natural air and Kerosene type fuel. In old torpedoes, the engine was a four-cylinder Brotherhood type radial, but later Fiume ones had a two-cylinder horizontal double-acting, while Naples torpedoes had a two-row eight-cylinder radial or, in the latest, an eight-cylinder vertical in line. It is believed that a V-12 was considered.

The Italian navy tried cyclonite on its own as a warhead explosive before the Second World War, but it was deficient in safety and TNT was used, and later also 60 TNT, 20 cyclonite, 20 aluminium, ASN (70 ammonium nitrate, 10 dicyandiamide, 20 PETN) and the German SW18 and SW36.

Whisker impact pistols were obsolescent and replaced by an inertia pendulum type, two being fitted in modern warheads. These would fire on impact, even at fine track angles, the limit claimed being 15° at 5kts. They were liable to fire when going through a ship's wake and occasionally if the torpedo rolled. A magnetic pistol based on a coil without the usual rod was developed. This was fired from distortion of the field from the torpedo air vessel, which was magnetised, but the pistol was later given up, though the German Navy used it to some extent in heater torpedoes where there was no electric supply. It was considered to be a little less liable to perturbations than their own coil rod and amplifier.

Airborne torpedoes were usually dropped at a range of about 2300m (*2500yd*) and, early in the war, from about 37m (*120ft*) on average, though up to twice this height on occasion. Later, 100m (*330ft*) at 160kts was standard. The usual Savoia S79 torpedo plane was intended to take two torpedoes though only one was often carried. A large monoplane air tail was fitted and aileron anti-roll gear was operated from inside the torpedo.

53.3cm (21in) FIUME TORPEDOES

(Some sources give the figures of the title as 250/533.4 × 7.5.) This high-speed torpedo for submarines had a slimmer head than usual which, according to the Japanese who acquired a torpedo in 1940, was worth about +2kts, though the Fiume tail was inferior to the Japanese type and cancelled the advantage. The Japanese also commented on the comparative thinness of the propeller blades. They thought well enough of the slim head to alter many of their own torpedoes accordingly. The engine was a two-cylinder horizontal double-acting.

W270/533.4 × 7.2 Veloce

Data

Length oa	7200mm	23ft 7in
Total weight	1700kg	3748lb
Volume air vessel	660 litres	23.3ft^3
Pressure	200kg/cm^2	2850lb/in^2
HP	450 at 50kt	
Explosive charge	270kg	595lb
Range	3000–4000m/50kt 12,000m/30kt	3300–4400yd/50kt 13,100yd/30kt

The length is also given as 7500m (*24ft 7in*) and charge 250kg (*551lb*).

This torpedo was apparently 7200mm (*23ft 7in*) long and had a 270kg (*595lb*) charge. The range is given as 4000m (*4400yd*)/48kts. German reports give a similar high speed range for a Weymouth Whitehead in Italian service for submarines.

W270/533.4 × 7.2 'F'

Data

Length oa	6840mm	22ft 5in
Total weight	1550kg	3417lb
Explosive charge	270kg	595lb
Range	4000m/48kt 8000m/36kt	4400yd/48kt 8750yd/36kt

W250/533.4 × 6.5

As indicated this was 6500mm (*21ft 4in*) with a 250kg (*551lb*) charge. The range is given as 3000m (*3300yd*)/43kts and 10,000m (*10,900yd*)/28kts.

These torpedoes were 6860mm (*22ft 6in*) and 7200mm (*23ft 7in*) long with 260kg (*573lb*) charge. Ranges are given for both as 4000m (*4400yd*)/43kts and 12,000m (*13,100yd*)/30kts. The longer may be the same as a torpedo given in German reports as follows.

W260/533.4 × 6.86 and 7.20

Data

Length oa	7200mm	23ft 7in
Total weight	1700kg	3748lb
Volume air vessel	660 litres	23.3ft^3
Pressure	175kg/cm^2	2490lb/in^2
Explosive charge	270kg	595lb
Range	3000m/42kts	3300yd/42kts
	7000m/32kts	7650yd/32kts
	9200m/30kts	10,060yd/30kts
	12,000m/26kts	13,100yd/26kts

53.3cm (21in) NAPLES TORPEDOES

SI 270/533.4 × 7.2 'I'

A torpedo for submarines with an eight-cylinder in-line engine. The charge was 270kg (*595lb*) and range 4000m (*4400yd*)/49kts, 8000m (*8750yd*)/38kts.

An older torpedo, 7500mm (*24ft 7in*) long with a 250kg (*551lb*) charge. The range was 3000m (*3300yd*)/40kts, 12,000m (*13,100yd*)/26kts.

SI 270/533.4 × 7.2

Data

Length oa	7200mm	23ft 7in
Total weight	1700kg	3748lb
Volume air vessel	?562 litres	19.85ft^3
Pressure	?180kg/cm^2	2560lb/in^2
Explosive charge	270kg	595lb
Range	4000m/46kts	4400yd/46kts
	8000m/35kts	8750yd/35kts
	12000m/29kts	13,100yd/29kts

Speeds are also given as 48kts, 38kts, 30kts for the above ranges. These may apply to a later version. The figures for volume and pressure of the air vessel seem to be low.

An unidentified torpedo, possibly SI 270/533. 4 × 7.2 'I', being struck down in a submarine *c*1942.
Aldo Fraccaroli Collection

SI 270/533. 4 × 7.2 torpedo being hoisted aboard *Pompeo Magno*, Ancona 1943.
Aldo Fraccaroli Collection

SI 270/533.4 × 7.2

This was apparently the usual torpedo for cruisers and destroyers. The engine was a two-row eight-cylinder radial.

45cm (17.7in) TORPEDOES

W200/450 × 5.75

This torpedo was carried by the *Cagni* class submarines and was also used with subcalibre fittings for 53.3cm (*21in*) above water and submerged TT. Length 5750mm (*18ft 10½in*), charge 200kg (*441lb*), range 3000m (*3300yd*)/44kts, 8000m (*8750yd*)/30kts.

SI 200/450 × 5.36

Carried by some MAS, this torpedo had a two-row eight-cylinder radial engine. Length 5360mm (*17ft 7in*), weight 930kg (*2050lb*), charge 200kg (*441lb*), range not accurately known, but probably at least 2000m (*2200yd*)/44kts.

SI 170/450 × 5.25

Another MAS torpedo with length 5250mm (*17ft 2½in*), weight 860kg (*1896lb*), charge 170kg (*375lb*), range 4000m (*4400yd*)/37kts.

W110/450 × 5.5

A lighter torpedo for MAS, length 5500mm (*18ft 0½in*), weight 770kg (*1698lb*), charge 110kg (*243lb*), range 2000m (*2200yd*)/43kts.

W170/450 × 5.75

A Weymouth torpedo apparently used by some MAS. Length 5750mm (*18ft 10½in*), weight 930kg (*2050lb*), charge 170kg (*375lb*), range 1000m (*1100yd*)/48kts, 2000m (*2200yd*)/42kts.

Triple TT probably for W200/450 × 5.75 torpedoes in the torpedo boat *Ariete*.
Elio Ando'

AIRBORNE TORPEDOES

The earlier 45cm (*17.7in*) torpedo which had a 130kg (*287lb*) charge with total weight 740kg (*1631lb*) and range 2000m (*2200yd*)/38kts, possibly also 3000m (*3300yd*)/36kts, was replaced by the two following.

W (also used by the Germans in quantity as F5w)

A 45cm (*17.7in*) Fiume torpedo with a horizontal two-cylinder double-acting engine, capable of 183HP and with cylinders 120 × 100mm (*4.72 × 3.94in*).

Data

Length oa	5460mm	17ft 11in
Total weight	905kg	1995lb
Volume air vessel	273 litres	9.64ft³
Pressure	200kg/cm²	2850lb/in²
Weight air	60kg	132lb
Kerosene	3.6kg	7.9lb
Water	21kg	46lb
HP at 40kts	*c*155	
Explosive charge	200kg	441lb
Range	3000m/40kts	3300yd/40kts

Early versions apparently had a 170kg (*375lb*) charge with total weight 869kg (*1916lb*).

SI (designated F5i by the Germans but not adopted)

A 45cm (*17.7in*) Naples torpedo with a two-row eight-cylinder radial engine developing 200HP maximum and with cylinders 80 × 75mm (*3.15 × 2.95in*).

Data

Length oa	5360mm	17ft 7in
Total weight	973kg	2145lb
Volume air vessel	232 litres	8.19ft³
Pressure	200kg/cm²	2850lb/in²
Weight air	54kg	119lb
Kerosene	3.6kg	7.9lb
Water	30kg	66lb
HP at 40kts	155	
Explosive charge	200kg	441lb
Range	3000m/40kts	3300yd/40kts

An earlier version had length 5250mm (*17ft 2½in*), total weight 885kg (*1951lb*), charge 175kg (*386lb*).

This was a short parachute-dropped 50cm (*19.7in*) electric torpedo. There was no depth control, each torpedo having its density balanced and running just below the surface oscillating considerably. The lateral control was primitive and the torpedo described irregular spirals and curves. Dropping conditions are quoted as 150kts from 60m (*200ft*) or 70m (*230ft*) minimum, but it appears that 180m (*600ft*) or more was usual.

Circling Torpedo (also used by the Germans in some quantity as LT350)

Data

Length oa	2600mm	8ft 6½in
Total weight	350kg	772lb
HP	3.5	
Explosive charge	120kg	265lb
Range	15,000m/13.5kts dropping to 3.9kts	16,400yd/13.5kts dropping to 3.9kts

There was another circling torpedo, known to the Germans at LT280, but not used by them. Full details have not been found but weight was 280kg (*617lb*), HP2.6, charge 90kg (*198lb*) and range 12,000m (*13,100yd*) at the above speeds. It was presumably 45cm (*17.7in*) diameter.

ANTI-SUBMARINE WEAPONS

As with most other navies, the principal weapon was the depth charge carried by surface ships. A towed torpedo was also in service. No allied submarine was sunk at sea in attacks by Italian aircraft, though three were sunk in Malta in 1942 by the bombs of German or Italian planes.

DEPTH CHARGES

B TG 100/1927

Made by Moncenisio, this had a 100kg (*220lb*) charge with hydrostatic fuzing. The depth settings were 25m (*80ft*), 50m (*165ft*), 75m (*250ft*), 100m (*330ft*).

B TG 50/1917, 1927

Also made by Moncenisio, the charge was 50kg (*110lb*) with hydrostatic fuzing and depth settings 20m (*65ft*), 40m (*130ft*), 70m (*230ft*), 100m (*330ft*). Earlier versions apparently had only one depth setting, and there are references to a later small DC with the above settings, but charge 35.5kg (*78lb*) and total weight 50kg (*110lb*).

The torpedo boat *Lupo*, 4 May 1942, showing DCs on launching racks and between them a towed torpedo, Type 1927-46T-BF.
Aldo Fraccaroli Collection

B TG 50/1936

Another Moncenisio DC intended for throwers with diameter 30cm (*11.8in*), total weight 64kg (*141lb*) and charge 50kg (*110lb*).

B TG 100/?

Made by Scotti and also intended for throwers, this had diameter 43cm (*16.9in*), total weight 128kg (*282lb*) and charge 100kg (*220lb*). Another Scotti DC had a 50kg (*110lb*) charge.

DC Thrower

A thrower or mortar with an arbor for DCs with 100kg (*220lb*) charge, was trainable and normally elevated to 45° though it could be loaded when horizontal. The barrel was 43.2cm (*17in*) diameter. Fixed DC throwers were also used.

A DC thrower in *Alvise da Mosto* c1941.
Aldo Fraccaroli Collection

MINES

The relative weaknesses of the Italian economy prevented a very large mining effort by the Italian Navy, but the considerable total of 54,457 were laid. As will be seen from the descriptions, a variety of different patterns of diverse origins were employed, but most were of moored contact type. Charges for special weapons, such as the slow-course torpedo, are noted, and the Italian navy exploited this device with a very fair measure of success. The favoured explosives were TNT or TNT with up to 50% cyclonite but, as in other navies, substitutes had to be used.

MOORED MINES

Bollo P125/1928, 1932, 1935

These mines, originally designed by Admiral Bollo and manufactured by Pignone, were Hertz-horned mines, though there were also antenna versions of M1932 and 1935. The charge was 125kg (*276lb*) and the mine shell was designed for 12m (*39ft*) maximum in M1928 and 30m (*98ft*) in the others.

It is thought that these were the mines with British designation II which had six Hertz horns.

Elia 145/1925

Of Vickers design, this had nine Hertz horns and 145kg (*320lb*) charge. The shell was spherical and 1.06m (*42in*) diameter.

Elia P145/1930

Of Vickers design, this was also manufactured by Pignone. There were seven Hertz horns, and there was apparently also an antenna version. The charge was 145kg (*320lb*) and the shell was egg-shaped with diameter 0.97m (*38in*). It was intended for use against submarines and the mooring wire, the upper part of which was protected by chain, had a length of 365m (*200 fathoms*) though 500m (*273 fathoms*) is also quoted. The maximum depth for the mine shell is given as 60m (*33 fathoms*) or 100m (55 fathoms). This is thought to be the mine with British designation IJ.

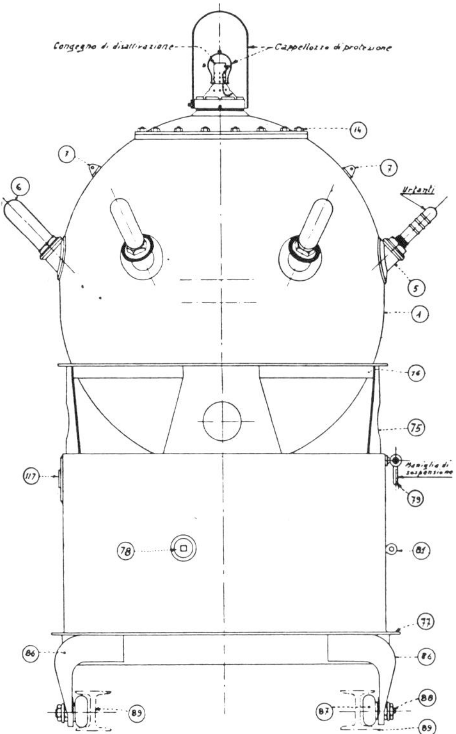

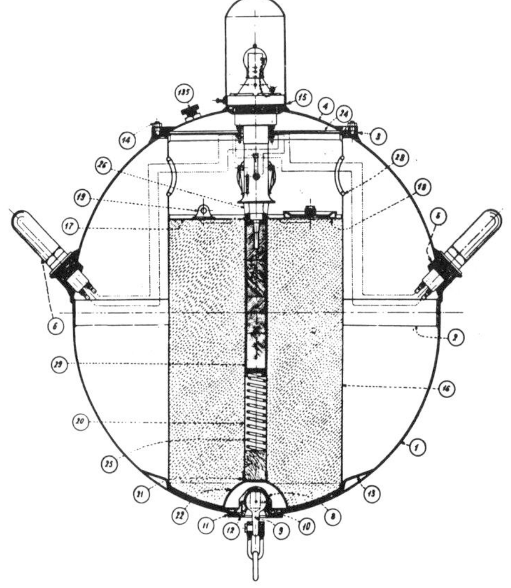

Bollo P125/1932 moored mine in section.
ANB

Bollo P125/1932 moored mine with anchor on launching rails.
ANB

P200 (P5)

British designation IK, built by Pignone from 1936, this mine had nine Hertz horns and a charge of 200kg (*441lb*). Total weight was 1150kg (*2535lb*) and buoyancy 225kg (*496lb*). The shell diameter was 1.17m (*46in*) and it could stand 100m (*55 fathoms*), as the mine was designed for use against submarines or surface vessels. The mooring wire was 120m (*60 fathoms*), 520m (*284 fathoms*) or 820m (*448 fathoms*).

There were another version with British designation IKA which had eight Hertz horns and an acoustic firing system, but it is not clear if there was also a magnetic version.

Coloniale P125

Derived from P200 and specially built by Pignone for tropical waters. The charge was 125kg (*276lb*) and mooring wire 200m (*109 fathoms*).

P4/150/1938 CR (Caratteristiche Ridotte)

Another Pignone mine derived from P200. Total weight was 825kg (*1819lb*), charge 150kg (*331lb*) and shell diameter 0.97m (*38in*). It was for use against surface vessels and the mooring wire was 210m (*115 fathoms*) with 20m (*66ft*) of protective chain.

P150, P150/1935

These were built by Pignone and were for minelaying submarines, the first for the *Foca* class and the second for the *Micca* and *Bragadin* class. Both had 150kg (*331lb*) or 120kg (*265lb*) charges and 300m (*164 fathom*) mooring wires.

Italia M 1932

This mine was also for submarines and had a total weight of 1100kg (*2425lb*) with a 150kg (*331lb*) charge. There were seven Hertz horns and the egg-shaped shell was 0.90m (*35in*) in diameter and could stand 100m (*55 fathoms*). The mooring wire was 520m (*284 fathoms*) with the upper part protected by a chain. This would seem to have been the mine with British designation IL.

P200(P5) moored mine and anchor. The Hertz horns are apparently blanked off.
Aldo Fraccaroli Collection

British designation IM

This mine had a 77kg (*170lb*) charge and four 'break-off' horns which admitted water to a hydrostatically operated firing device.

Italia Type A

An experimental antenna mine for deep waters. The total weight was 4500kg (*9921lb*) and there were two mine shells, the main one spherical and 2.0m (*79in*) in diameter with a 300kg (*661lb*) charge, and the other cylindrical with hemispherical ends, 0.5m diameter × 1.3m (*20 × 51in*) with a 100kg (*220lb*) charge. The upper antenna was 45m (*148ft*) and the lower 35m (*115ft*) while the mine was designed for 100m (*55 fathoms*) depth. The normal anchor depth is given as 1500m (*820 fathoms*) though a somewhat unlikely 4000m (*2187 fathoms*) is quoted for the mooring wire.

Italia Type B

This was another antenna mine, apparently based on a Vickers prototype. It was not ready for service. The shell was spherical of 1.30m (*51in*) diameter, with four Hertz horns and upper and lower antennae of 30m (*98ft*) and 35m (*115ft*). The charge was 250kg (*551lb*) and total weight 1545kg (*3406lb*). The mine was designed for 100m (*55 fathoms*) depth and the mooring wire was 1000m (*547 fathoms*).

GROUND MINES

Delta mine

This was an airborne parachute mine with magnetic firing. The total weight is given as 500kg (*1102lb*) and the charge as 380kg (*838lb*). It could also be laid by MTB.

British designation IP

An airborne antenna mine with 335kg (*739lb*) charge.

DRIFTING MINES

British designation IN

An oblong shaped contact mine with six horns and 70kg (*154lb*) charge. It was designed to flood and sink nine hours after laying.

British designation IO

A constant depth mine without horns and fired by impact. The charge was 195kg (*430lb*) and depth 3-7m (*10-23ft*).

FIRST WORLD WAR MINES STILL LISTED

VE (Vickers Elia)

This was manufactured before and during World War I and had a total weight of 760kg (*1676lb*) with 145kg (*320lb*) charge.

Harlé 75/M 1911

An old type Sautter-Harlé mine with 75kg (*165lb*) charge and 100m (*55 fathoms*) mooring wire.

Harlé 70/M 1916

Similar to the above with 70kg (*154lb*) charge.

Harlé 100/M 1916

Similar but with 100kg (*220lb*) charge.

SG 125/1916

Manufactured by San Giorgio for the minelaying submarines X2, X3 laid up in September 1940. Charge 125kg (*276lb*).

UC 200/1921

This was apparently a copy of the German mine developed for the later First World War minelaying U-boats. It is not clear whether any Italian submarines could accommodate it. The charge was 200kg (*441lb*).

All the above were of moored contact type.

MINES FROM OTHER NAVIES

The Germans supplied a number of mines, apparently UMA and UMB, moored contact anti-submarine mines, EMC a moored contact mine and EMF a moored magnetic mine. Details of these are given in the German section.

Some were captured from Yugoslavia and comprised sundry mines of British and French manufacture and also some Lindholmen-Motala mines from Sweden, described in the section dealing with the smaller navies. As far as is known all were of moored contact type.

There were also some Austro-Hungarian mines taken after the First World War. These had charges of 100kg (*220lb*) ammonal (ammonium nitrate/aluminium with charcoal additions and in some mixes TNT).

CHARGES FOR MANNED TORPEDOES, EXPLOSIVE MOTOR BOATS AND SWIMMERS

The Italian Navy had employed early versions of this type of device in the First World War, and they pioneered their use in the second. They were not suicide weapons in the Japanese sense, though two motor boats seem to have been so used in the attack on Malta in July 1941, which was a disastrous failure. The charge in the explosive motor boats was generally 300kg (*661lb*) located in the bows. The two-man slow-course torpedo, *Maiale*, resembled the British Chariot which was in fact derived from it, and had a neutral buoyancy head placed against the condenser inlet of the target, where it was retained by the suction, or else clamped to the bilge keel. The explosive charge was originally 220kg (*485lb*), later 250kg (*551lb*) and finally 300kg (*661lb*). The greatest success was the disabling of the *Queen Elizabeth* and *Valiant* in Alexandria harbour in December 1941.

The sabotage charges used by swimmers against merchant ships in neutral harbours, comprised at least three types. One had a 3kg (*6.6lb*) charge, the second two containers each with 15kg (*33lb*) and the third was a smaller version of the second.

BOMBS

An Italian list of late 1941 gives a 250kg (*551lb*) AP bomb which was 25.4cm (*10in*) in diameter and 122cm (*48in*) overall with 76cm (*30in*) body length. This was clearly adapted from a 25.4cm (*10in*) shell. The largest bomb listed was an 800kg (*1764lb*) MC with 357kg (*787lb*) charge, 45cm (*17.7in*) diameter and 330cm (*130in*) overall length.

SOVIET UNION

The Soviet Navy of the Second World War bore little resemblance to that of today. Its main function was to protect the seaward flanks of the Russian armies, to aid in the defence of Leningrad, Sevastopol and other coastal cities, and to control the inland waterways in the areas of fighting. These tasks were performed with great courage and often successfully, but strictly naval operations were far less successful, and the figures for enemy ships sunk which still persist in Russian histories are demonstrably exaggerated. It must be remembered that many senior naval officers were victims of the purges of Stalin's campaign of terror, and the survivors were likely to have their initiative diminished. Stalin's grandiose plans for large warships were beyond the then capabilities of Soviet industry and in any event the war would have forced their abandonment.

Neglecting those weapons supplied by Britain and America, the best actually in naval service were probably guns of 130mm (*5.118in*) and below, though fire-control seems to have been moderate and AA armaments were inadequate. Underwater weapons were not up to the best, and it is remarkable that the country's mining was relatively far inferior to that of the First World War.

The 305mm/52 guns in No 2 triple turret in *Sevastopol* late 1940. At that time the ship was still named *Parizhskaya Kommuna*.
J Micinski Collection

NAVAL GUNS

Older Russian guns were usually of rather complicated built-up construction but the more recent up to 181mm (*7.126in*), were apparently of loose-liner, loose-barrel or monobloc type. No new Russian heavy gun was mounted afloat though some were used in coast defence, and it is believed that these were of built-up construction. Lengths give in calibres in the gun's title are normally overall and not for the bore. Muzzle velocities were usually high for a given shell weight, but were excessive only in the 181mm, where Italian influence is clear. It must be noted that reliable muzzle velocity figures for the larger guns are rarely to be found, though apparently reliable maximum ranges occur in some lists. In most recent guns the muzzle velocity has been deduced from the latter assuming the long-nosed boat-tailed Russian M1928 pattern shell. For heavy guns more data was available for an 8/16crh shell without boat tail, and MV estimates have been based on this. They are thus on the high side of those for M1928 shell, and if this pattern was fired by recent heavy guns the actual MV may have been somewhat less than that given.

The standard charge temperature was 15°C (*59°F*) as in the German navy, though figures for a few of the oldest guns may have been at a higher temperature.

Little is known on Russian gun mountings, and what is available will be found in the notes under each type of gun.

PROPELLANTS

The standard Russian propellant was nitrocellulose with 1% diphenylamine, in multitube grain form, though heavy guns may have used single tube. Other propellants appear to have been a solventless nitrocellulose/nitroglycerin composition and a similar one with di- and trinitrotoluene additions.

Fixed ammunition was fired by guns of 101.6mm (*4in*) bore and below, while very old 152.4mm (*6in*) and 120mm (*4.724in*) guns used separate QF ammunition as did 130mm (*5.118in*)/50 guns and it is believed the most recent 152.4mm (*6in*).

PROJECTILES

Older Russian shells were usually of about 4crh form, occasionally up to 6crh, without boat tails, but the M1928 pattern had a 12.5/16cr head and boat tail. This and some of the earlier heavy shells had two driving bands instead of one. The band material was generally copper but cupro-nickel was also used.

The standard explosive filling was cast TNT with pressed TNT in the smaller AA shells, which also had cyclonite additions in some. The proportion of burster in APC shell was 2.7% for the 305mm (*12.01in*)/52, reduced to about 2% in 181mm (*7.126in*), while in HE figures of 10.5-13.5% have been found for earlier shells which were generally base fuzed, but 7.5% is given for the nose-fuzed 181mm.

Shrapnel was at one time carried for all guns but it is doubtful if this remained the case, and there is no data on star shell.

FIRE-CONTROL

Russian fire-control is not believed to have been particularly good but many details are lacking. The largest range-finders were of 8m (*26.25ft*) base and, according to German data, the *Gangut* class had a coincidence instrument in the fore and after main armament directors and a stereoscopic one in each turret, all being of this size. In the *Kirov* class of cruisers, the fore top director had three range-finders and it is thought that one was actually an instrument for detecting small alterations of the target's course, thus showing the Italian influence in these ships.

Radar sets were limited to those obtained from USA and Britain, though an experimental copy of a British 285 AA gunnery set, of which a number had been supplied, was made before the end of the war.

A German triaxial AA director was fitted to *Voroshilov* and possibly another to *Kirov* - and other equipment may also have been supplied. As far as is known RPC was not fitted in any Russian ships.

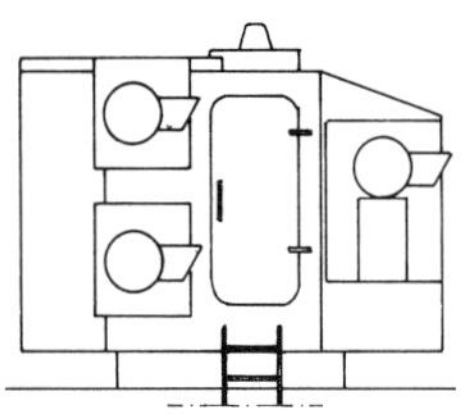

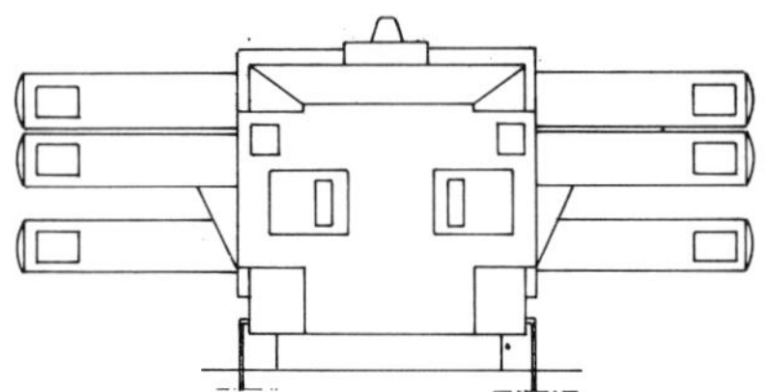

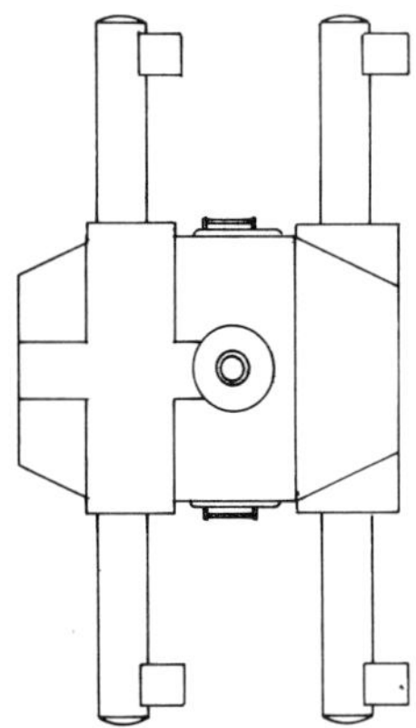

Top: Fore top main director in *Kirov* class with three range-finders or small alteration of target course instruments.
P Budzbon

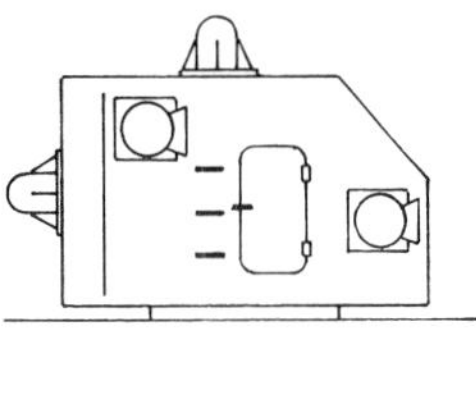

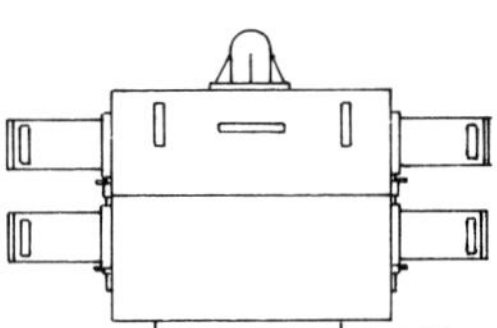

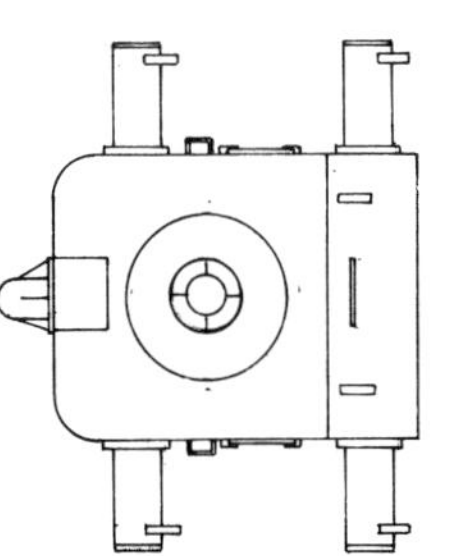

Right: Earlier type of director for destroyers fitted in *Leningrad*, *Gnevnyi* and *Storozhevoi* classes, *Opitnyi* and *Ognyevoi*.
P Budzbon

Director for 130mm/50 guns fitted in later destroyers of the *Ognyevoi* and post-war *Skory* classes.
P Budzbon

HEAVY CALIBRE GUNS

406.4mm (16in)/50

This guns was to have been mounted in triple turrets in the four very large battleships whose construction was abandoned in 1940-41, and which would have been named *Sovietsky Soyuz*, *Sovietskaya Ukraina*, *Sovietskaya Bielorossiya* and *Sovietskaya Rossiya*. It is not clear if the 50-calibre length was that of the bore or, as used to be the rule in the Russian navy, overall, in which case the bore would have been around 48.5 calibres. The construction, of built-up types probably employed more tubes and hoops than in contemporary British practice and the screw breech block would have been of Welin pattern. It is said that the prototype gun built by the Kirov (Putilov) works at Leningrad was tested in early 1940, with not very satisfactory results, but it was capable of firing on the Germans in August 1941 from the Leningrad naval proving ground.

Whether the Russians could have built the 36 guns plus spares needed for the above ships is doubtful, but it appears that four guns were, or were to be, mounted for coast defence during the war.

This was not the first time that the Russian navy had shown interest in guns of this size, as a 406.4mm (*16in*) of 45 calibres overall length was built for them by Vickers in the First World War but never delivered. Although it was not strictly relevant to the Second World War, some details are given below as it is the most recent Russian heavy gun for which much information is available.

The only reliable data for the 50-calibre gun that has been seen is in a coast-defence list giving a shell of 1108kg (*2443lb*) and range 45,500m (*49,760yd*). Assuming that this is at 50° elevation and that the shell was 8/16crh, not boat tailed, the muzzle velocity would be 810-815m/s (*2657-2674f/s*) which is high, but not excessive, for a shell of the above weight

Details of the triple mounting are not known except that the turret face was to be 495mm (*19.5in*).

406.4mm (16in)/45

Originally intended as the prototype gun for projected Black Sea battleships, this was known as 16in Mk A by Vickers and otherwise in England as the 15in A gun. It was proved in August 1917 and later converted to an experimental super-velocity 205mm (*8.071in*) known as 8in sub-calibre Mk I. It was built to a Vickers design, and as a 406.4mm (*16in*) had a tapered inner A tube, A tube, three B tubes to the muzzle, two C tubes for about two-thirds of the length, jacket and screwed collar. There was a short breech ring and the breech bush taking the Welin block screwed into the rear C tube. The diameter over the chamber was 1298.4mm (*51.2in*) and at 2cal from the muzzle 685.8mm (*27in*).

As will be seen from the data table below, this gun if lengthened 5cal would easily have attained the calculated performance of the later 50-calibre gun.

Gun Data

Bore	406.4mm	16in	
Weight incl BM	109.4t	107.7 tons	
Length oa	18,288mm	720in	45.0cal
Length bore	17,740.6mm	698.45in	43.65cal
Length chamber	3225.55mm	126.99in	
Volume chamber	540.77dm^3	33,000in^3	
Length rifling	14,363.7mm	565.5in	
Weight projectile	1116.3kg	2461lb	
Propellant charge	347kg NCT 20 × 7.2mm	765lb NCT 0.78 × 0.283in	
Muzzle velocity	792.5m/s	2600f/s	
Working pressure	2950kg/cm^2	18.7 tons/in^2	

380mm (14.96in)/51.66

A total of 16 of these German SKC/34 guns and eight twin Drh LC/34 mountings were ordered from Krupp but never delivered. Details will be found in the German section.

355.6mm (14in)/52

Gun Data

Bore	355.6mm	14in	
Weight incl BM	83.33t	82.01 tons	
Length oa	18,491.2mm	728in	52.0cal
Length bore	17,927.3mm	705.8in	50.41cal
Length chamber	2811.27mm	110.68in	
Volume chamber	359.5dm^3	21,940in^3	
Length rifling	14,954.25mm	588.75in	
Grooves	(84) 2.67 × 9.14mm	0.105 × 0.36in	
Lands	4.06mm	0.16in	
Twist	1 in 29.89		
Weight projectile	748kg	1649lb	
Propellant charge	245.7kg NCT	541.7lb NCT	
Muzzle velocity	823m/s	2700f/s	
Working pressure	2950kg/cm^2	18.7 tons/in^2	

355.6mm/52 gun on railway mounting. The original Vickers guns of this type intended for the uncompleted *Borodino* class launched in 1915/16 became the British 14in Mk VI.
M Twardowski Collection

According to a coast-defence list, the shell was 748kg (*1649lb*) and range 44,600m (*48,780yd*). Assuming 50° elevation and an 8/16crh shell, not boat tailed, the muzzle velocity would be approximately 830m/s (*2723f/s*). Between 1931 and 1941 a three-gun battery was added to the Baltic defences and another to those of the Far East. It was also used as a railway gun. German data give a muzzle velocity of 731.5m/s (*2400f/s*) with the above weight of shell and a charge of 207kg (*456lb*). With a shorter nose L/4 or L/4.7 shell maximum range is given as 31,000m (*33,900yd*).

This gun was originally intended for the four ships of the *Borodino* class of the First World War, which were never completed. Of the 48 guns plus spares required, 36 were ordered from Vickers in November 1913, but it is doubtful if any were delivered. The specified muzzle velocity was 823m/s (*2700f/s*) but, after the Russian Revolution when the guns were taken over for railway mountings as 14in Mk VI, it was found that they lacked strength, since out of 16 proved seven expanded, and the margin of longitudinal strength was also small. The low performance figures given in German data are thus understandable, and it seems likely that the high figures apply to selected, or perhaps strengthened, guns.

The gun was known to Vickers as 14in Mk B and was built with an A tube, four B tubes to the muzzle, three C tubes, two D tubes, jacket. There was a small breech ring and the breech bush screwed into the jacket with a small shrunk collar on the rear end of the bush. A Welin screw block with Vickers breech mechanism was fitted. It is thought that this construction was to a Russian design.

305mm (12.01in)/56

This gun was to have been mounted in triple turrets in the battle-cruisers *Kronshtadt* and *Sevastopol*, whose construction was abandoned in 1940-41. It is not certain if the 56 calibres is the length of the bore or overall. In the latter case, the bore would be about 54.5cal. Constructional details are not known, but a gun is said to have been tested at Leningrad in the autumn of 1940 with highly satisfactory results. It appears that 12 305mm guns were, or were to be, mounted for coast defence during the war, but it is not known how many were of this type.

The only reliable data is from a coast-defence list which gives a 479.9kg (*1058lb*) shell and 43,900m (*48,000yd*) range. Assuming 50° elevation and an 8/16crh shell, not boat tailed, the muzzle velocity would have been about 850m/s (*2789f/s*). This indicates a powerful gun, surpassing the German 30.5cm SKC/39. Some sources give a 380kg (*838lb*) shell, clearly HE, with a range of over 46,000m (*50,300yd*) which would be perfectly possible at a likely muzzle velocity of about 940m/s (*3084f/s*).

Details of the triple mounting are not known, though 305mm (*12in*) has been given for the turret face.

305mm (12.01in)/52 M1910-M1914

These were the most powerful guns ever mounted in a completed Russian-built ship. They were in triple turrets in the four ships of the *Gangut* class, the three of the *Imperatritsa Maria* class and the uncompleted *Imperator Nikolai I*. Of these, only three of the *Gangut* class survived to the Second World War – *Oktyabrskaya Revolutsia* (ex-*Gangut*), *Parizhskaya Kommuna* (ex-*Sevastopol*) and *Marat* (ex-*Petropavlovsk*). The last two of these reverted to their original names in 1943.

The construction was of Russian design with in M1910, A tube, two B tubes to the muzzle, two C tubes for 10,952.5mm (*431.2in*), two D tubes for 7152.6mm (*281.6in*) and jacket. The breech bush screwed into the jacket, locking the parts together, and a collar was shrunk on the breech bush and the end of the collar covered by a small ring with a shoulder. Both collar and ring were placed in position when 'white hot'. There was a filling piece, with copper sealing ring, between breech bush and A tube as in former 305mm guns. The screw breech block was of Welin pattern. It is possible that this construction was modified in M1914, but details are lacking.

Gun Data M1914

Bore	305mm	12.01in	
Weight incl BM	51.85t	51.03 tons	
Length oa	15,900mm	625.98in	52.13cal
Length bore	15,419.5mm	607.07in	50.56cal
Length chamber	2391.5mm	94.15in	
Volume chamber	224dm^3	13,669in^3	
Length rifling	12,912mm	508.35in	
Grooves	(72) 2.0 × 9.0mm	0.079 × 0.354in	
Lands	4.3mm	0.169in	
Twist	1in 30		
Weight projectile	470.9kg AP	1038lb AP	
Propellant charge	157kg NCT, 5mm wall	346lb NCT, 0.197in wall	
Muzzle velocity	762m/s	2500f/s	
Working pressure	2700kg/cm^2	17.1 tons/in^2	
Max range	24,620m/25°/762m/s	26,925yd/25°/2500f/s	

The above chamber dimensions are for a gun firing standard German 405kg (*893lb*) shell. A weight as low as 47.1t (*46.4 tons*) has been given for M1910. The Russian HE shell weighed 324kg (*714.3lb*) and MV was 925m/s (*3035f/s*).

APC and a much lighter high-capacity base-fuzed HE were carried and the bag charge was in halves. Both shells are believed to have been about 4crh. There may also have been shrapnel.

This gun was much used in coast-defence batteries, the total for 305mm in 1941 being four four-gun batteries for the Baltic, two four-gun for the Black Sea and two five-gun in the Far East. Most if not all had this gun, and it is thought that some of the 12 guns mentioned under the 305mm/56 were also of the earlier type. It was also used as a railway gun.

The mountings in the surviving ships were designed by Coventry Ordnance Works. The guns were elevated independently with limits of +25° -5° or, it is said, +24° -5° in *Oktyabrskaya Revolutsia*. Training and elevation were electrically powered with hydraulic drive gear, hoists were broken at the working chamber and loading limits are given as +15° -0°. Recoil was 1.27m (*50in*), firing cycle 40sec and total weight 720t (*709 tons*). The turret shield is given as face 203mm (*8in*), sides 150mm (*6in*), roof 76mm (*3in*), and rear 305mm (*12in*), probably in part as balancing.

Below: Triple 305mm/52 turret in *Sevastopol*, in side, plan and front view.
P Budzbon

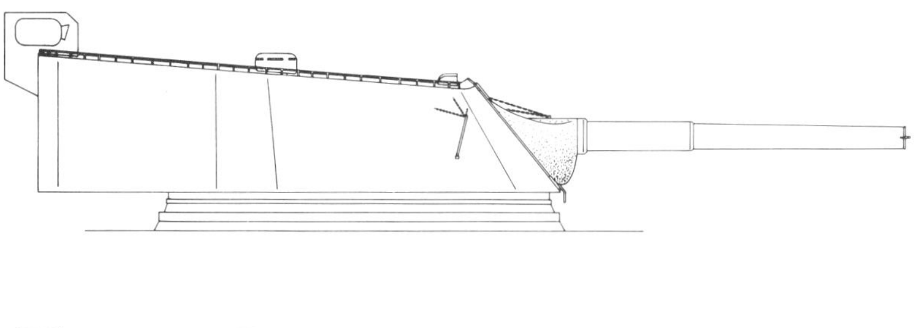

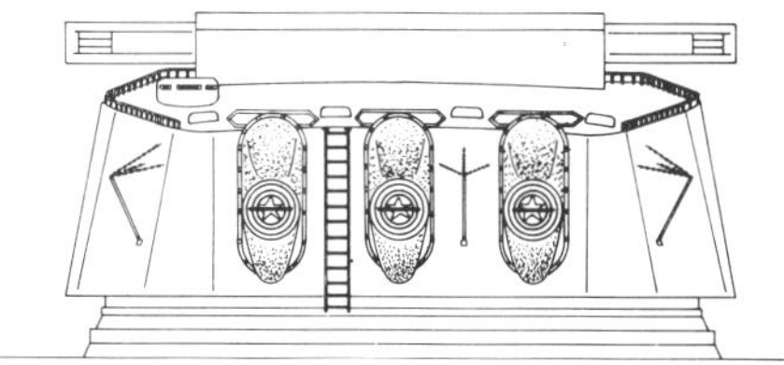

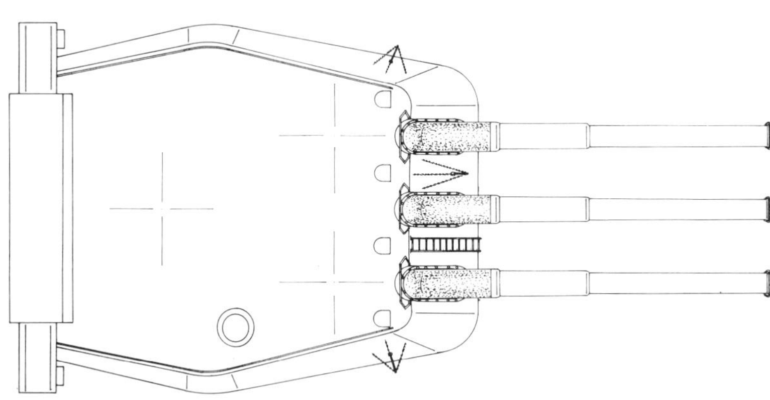

MEDIUM CALIBRE GUNS

203.2mm (8in) or 203mm (7.992in)

The floating battery *Tallinn*, formerly the German cruiser *Lützow* sold incomplete in 1940, had three such guns. Details are not known, but if the guns were not German 20.3cm SKC/34, they were probably not of unusually high performance.

181mm (7.126in)/57

A very high performance gun mounted in single turrets in the *Krasnyi Kavkaz* and in triples in the *Kirov, Maksim Gorky, Molotov, Voroshilov, Kalinin* and *Kaganovich*. The 57-calibre length may be overall, in which case the bore would be near 55.5cal. The gun was built with a loose liner, A tube, jacket and breech ring, and had a screw breech block probably of Welin type. AP and HE shells were of M1928 pattern with long heads and boat tails. They both weighed 97.5kg (*215lb*), equivalent to a 137.95kg (*304lb*) 203mm (*8in*). The propellant charge is given as 42kg (*92.6lb*) and was of bag type, probably in halves, while the normally quoted muzzle velocity was 920m/s (*3018f/s*). This is just possible for the maximum range of 37,800m (*41,340yd*), though a figure approaching 930m/s (*3051f/s*) would seem more likely.

The guns were in a common cradle in the triple mounting, which was electrically powered as was the breech mechanism. Elevation was +50° -5°, with loading at +5° and a firing cycle of 10-15sec depending on elevation. The turret shield was 76mm (*3in*)

Bottom: The *Krasnyi Kavkaz* post-war showing the after single 181mm turrets.
B Lemachko Collection

maximum. Photographs indicate that the gun axes were 83cm (*32.7in*) apart, which was too close to be satisfactory.

The single mounting was also electrically powered and probably allowed the same elevation. There was no break in the hoists, those for shells coming up to the right and for charges to the left. The latter were passed to the gun by hand but shells were pushed over rollers.

The gun was also used in coast defence and railway mountings. As with some Italian guns the performance was too high, and it is quite probable that it had to be reduced in service.

Below: Triple 181mm/57 turret in *Kirov* class. The closeness of the barrels indicates Italian influence and was particularly undesirable with such a high performance gun.
P Budzbon

Bottom: Triple 152mm/57 turrets as mounted in *Chapayev* class completed post-war.
P Budzbon

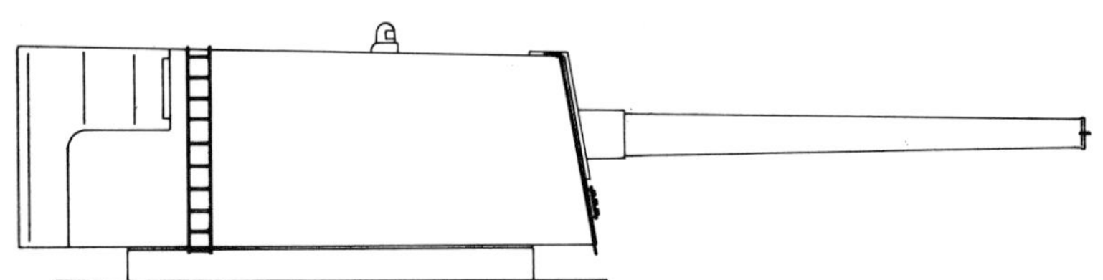

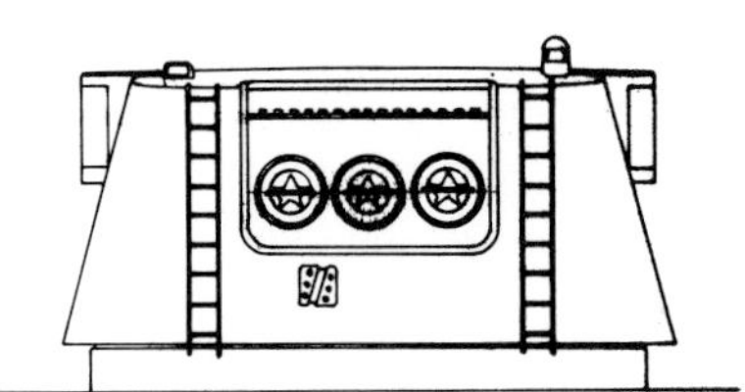

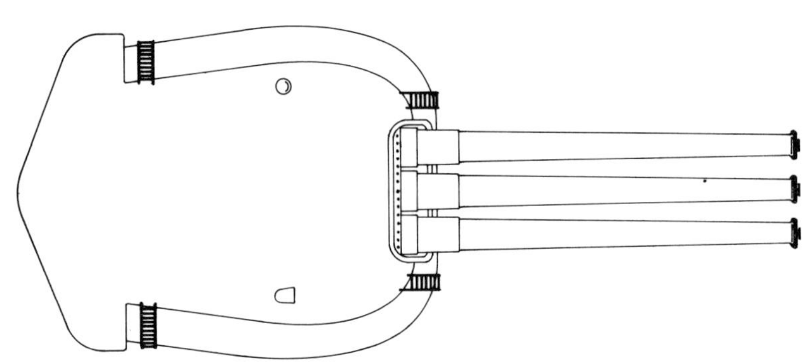

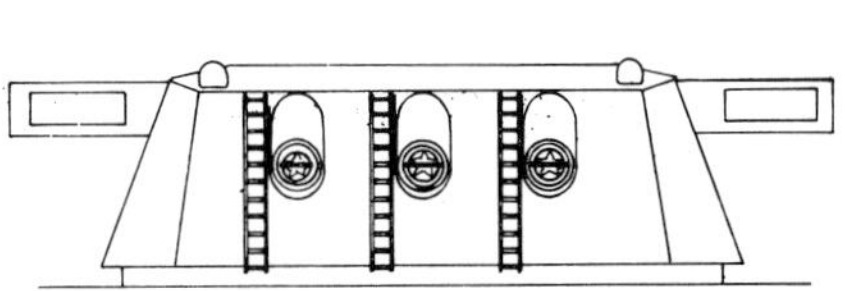

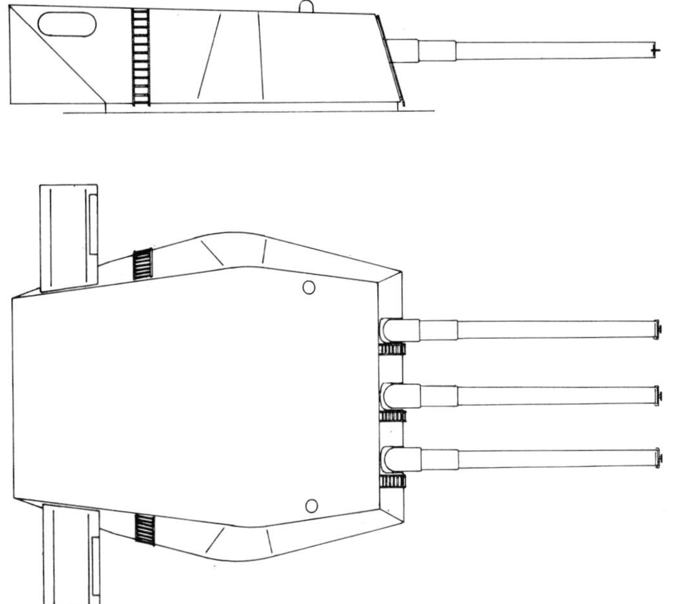

152.4mm (6in)/57

This was not in service afloat during the war, though mounted in some coast defence batteries. It would have been in twin turrets in the *Sovietskiy Soyuz* class and perhaps the *Kronshtadt* class, and was introduced in triple turrets in the *Chapayev* class cruisers completed after the war.

It is believed to have been a separate ammunition QF gun with sliding breech block and, if the 57-calibre length is overall, that of the bore would be about 54cal. A coast-defence list gives the shell as 55kg (*121lb*) and range as 29,000m (*31,700yd*). The muzzle velocity is usually given as 915m/s (*3002f/s*), but if the shell form was good this is too high and about 885m/s (*2904f/s*) more likely.

The triple turrets appear large and the guns were in separate cradles. It is thought that elevation was +50° -5°.

152.4mm (6in)/45

This old screw breech separate ammunition QF of 43.5cal bore length, may have been the gun mounted in some of the Amur river monitors. The shell weighed 41.4kg (*91.3lb*) and MV was 792.5m/s (*2600f/s*).

130mm (5.118in)/55

There were two patterns of this BL gun, one known to Vickers as Mk 'A' and introduced in 1914-18, and the other Mk 'B', of which 55 guns and as many spare barrels were delivered in the latter part of the Second World War.

The first and possibly the second pattern were also made in Russia. They were in single mountings in the *Chervonaya Ukraina*, *Krasnyi Krym*, the ancient cruisers *Aurora* and *Komintern*, and many lesser auxiliary warships, as well as in the large destroyers of the *Leningrad* class.

Mark 'A' was built with an A tube, three B tubes to the muzzle, jacket, and small breech ring. The breech bush taking the Welin block screwed into the jacket, with a gun ring for buffer connections screwed on to the jacket. Mk 'B' had a loose barrel, jacket and breech ring with breech bush and gun ring. The usual shell appears to have been base fuzed HE, and the charge was in a single bag.

The older mountings allowed 20° elevation with a firing cycle of 7.5sec, and Vickers also list one with a weight including gun and 38-25mm (*1.5-1in*) shield, of 17.95t (*17.67 tons*) and +30° -5° elevation.

Gun Data VSM Mk 'B'

Bore	130mm	5.118in	
Weight incl BM	5.258t	5.175 tons	
Weight loose barrel	2.515t	2.475 tons	
Length oa	7150.1mm	281.5in	55.00cal
Length bore	6939.8mm	273.22in	53.38cal
Length chamber	1033.86mm	40.703in	
Volume chamber	17.53dm³	1070in³	
Length rifling	5862.22mm	230.796in	
Grooves	(30) 1.00 × 9.14mm	0.0395 × 0.36in	
Lands	4.46mm	0.1756in	
Twist	1 in 29.89		
Weight projectile	36.86kg	81.26lb	
Propellant charge	10.83kg NCT	23.875lb NCT	
Muzzle velocity	823m/s	2700f/s	
Working pressure	3000kg/cm²	19 tons/in²	
Max range	16,500m/20°	18,045yd/20°	
	19,600m/30°	21,435yd/30°	

Mk 'A' had no loose barrel, otherwise figures were the same.

130mm (5.118in)/50

A separate ammunition SA gun in single mountings in destroyers of the *Gnevnyi* and *Storozhevoi* classes (the latter name ship subsequently had one twin) and the experimental *Opitnyi*. In twin mountings, it was in the *Tashkent* and the *Ognyevoi* class. It was also used in coast defence and may have been in various lesser warships. The gun had a loose liner and horizontal sliding breech block, and if the 50-calibre length is overall, the bore was near 47cal. The HE shell was apparently of M1928 pattern with long head and boat tail and weighed 33.4kg (*73.6lb*), though a coast-defence list gives 35.5kg (*78.3lb*). The latter gives the range as 25,400m (*27,780yd*), which does not demand a muzzle velocity greater than about 845m/s (*2772f/s*) if the shell was really of M1928 pattern, though 870m/s (*2854f/s*) is given in German lists.

These give a weight of 12t (*11.8 tons*) for the single mounting with 10mm (*0.4in*) shield, but figures for the twin mounting which had the guns in a common cradle are not listed. Elevation was probably +45° -10° and firing cycle 6-8sec.

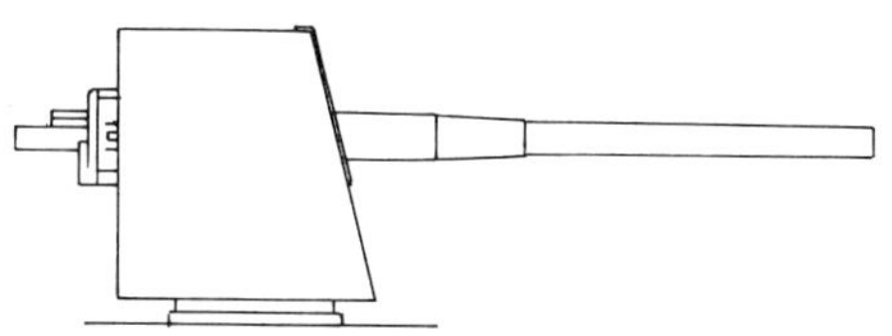

Top: 130mm/50 gun in single mounting as in many destroyers.
P Budzbon

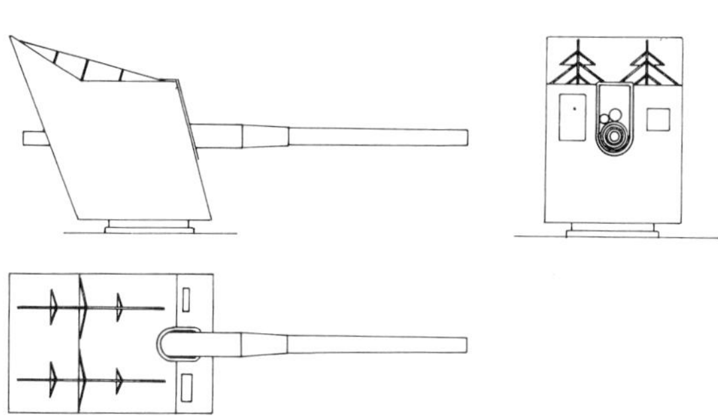

Right: 130mm/50 gun in single mounting with blast screen added.
P Budzbon

Above left: 130mm/50 gun in single mounting with modified shield.
P Budzbon

Above right: 130mm/50 gun in twin mounting carried by a few wartime destroyers.
P Budzbon

120mm (4.724in)/50

A gun of this description was mounted in the secondary battery of the *Gangut* class. That built by Vickers and mounted in the armoured cruiser *Rurik*, scrapped *c*1930, was a BL gun of 48.36cal bore, weighing 3.15t (*3.1 tons*) and firing a 20.5kg (*45.2lb*) shell at 930m/s (*3051f/s*) but it is not known if this was the gun in question. A range of 14,450m (*15,800yd*) at 20°, given for the *Marat*'s battery, agrees reasonably well with the above firing about 4crh shell. A coast-defence list gives the shell as 22.9kg (*50.5lb*) and a range, presumably at 45°, of 21,000m (*22,970yd*), but lack of data on the shell form prevents the muzzle velocity being estimated.

Below: The Amur river monitor *Lenin* after modernisation in the 1930s with 120mm/45 guns in twin turrets.
P Budzbon

120mm (4.724in)/45

An older screw breech QF gun which was carried in twin turrets in the Amur river monitors. With a 20.5kg (*45.2lb*) shell, MV was 823m/s (*2700f/s*).

LIGHT CALIBRE GUNS

101.6mm (4in)/60

In its day a famous Obuchov gun, first in service in 1913 in the *Novik* (later *Yakov Sverdlov*) and still in single mountings in the older Russian destroyers, the *Uragan* class escort vessels and some lesser warships. The gun fired fixed ammunition and had a horizontal sliding breech block, with a bore length of about 57cal and wieght 2.2t (*2.17 tons*). The base-fuzed HE shell weighed 17.7kg (*39lb*), the propellant charge 6kg (*13.2lb*) and the complete round 30kg (*66lb*) giving a muzzle velocity of 823m/s (*2700f/s*) and a range of 15,000m (*16,400yd*) at the maximum 20° elevation of the mounting. The firing cycle is given as 6sec. The mountings had a very small breast shield originally, but a larger one of conventional type was added to some.

The old Black Sea destroyer *Nezamozhnik* in 1942 showing 102mm/60 guns with two 76mm/30.5 M1915 AA guns in the foreground.
M Twardowski Collection

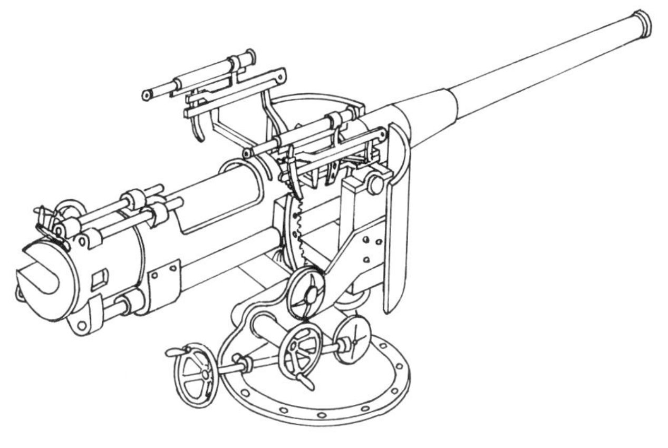

Above: 102mm/60 in single mounting with breast shield. A famous gun for destroyers in its day.
P Budzbon

Top right: 102mm/45 gun in CT mounting in submarine *D 4* (*Revolyutsioner*) in 1933.
B Lemachko Collection

101.6mm (4in)/45

A fixed ammunition gun in the 'D' and 'L 1' classes of submarines and possibly in *S 1* originally. The shell weighed 17.5kg (*38.6lb*), muzzle velocity was 755m/s (*2477f/s*) and maximum elevation is given as 60°.

100mm (3.937in)/56 B34

A fixed-ammunition AA gun carried in single mountings by cruisers of the *Kirov* and *Maksim Gorky* classes, and also by the *Yastreb* and some of the *Uragan* classes of escort vessels, as well as the *Polukhin* class of minesweepers and the gunboat, ex-destroyer, *Konstruktor*. It would have been in twin mountings in the cancelled *Sovietsky Soyuz* and *Kronshtadt* classes while the *Chapayev* class, when eventually completed, also carried it in postwar twin triaxial mountings. It may have been added during the war to the *Oktyabrskaya Revolutsia* and possibly to a few other ships.

Details of construction are not known, except that the sliding breech block moved horizontally. Assuming the 56-calibre length to be overall, the bore would be about 53cal. The fixed round weighed about 28kg (*61.7lb*) and was 133cm (*52.4in*) long. The shell accounted for 15.6kg (*34.4lb*) of this weight and the propellant charge 6kg (*13.2lb*) for a muzzle velocity of 900m/s (*2953f/s*). The single mounting allowed +85° -10°, and there was a pneumatic rammer with a probable firing cycle of 4sec. Maximum range was 22,400m (*24,500yd*) and ceiling approximately 15,000m (*49,200ft*).

100mm (3.937in)/52

Another fixed-ammunition gun in single mountings in submarines of the later 'L', 'P', 'S' and 'K' classes and in the *Tral* class minesweepers. Bore length was near 49cal, and a horizontally sliding breech block was used. The round weighed 25.6kg (*56.4lb*) and the shell 15.6kg (*34.4lb*). Muzzle velocity was probably about 800m/s (*2625f/s*) and the mountings allowed +45° -5° elevation.

Centre: 100mm/56 B34 gun in single unshielded AA mounting.
P Budzbon

Bottom: 100mm/56 B34 gun in single shielded AA mounting. This was the most powerful of wartime Russian naval AA.
P Budzbon

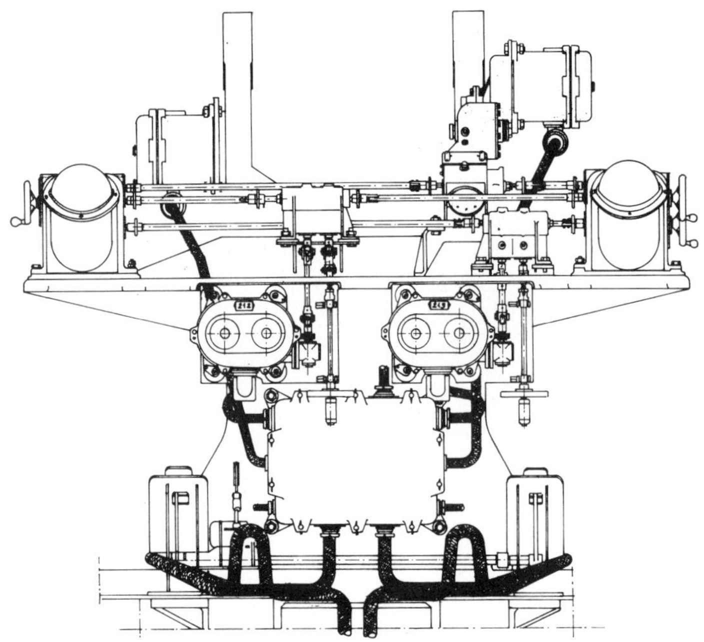

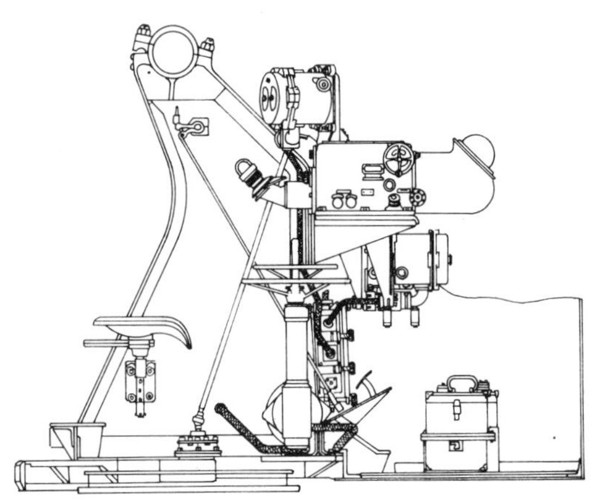

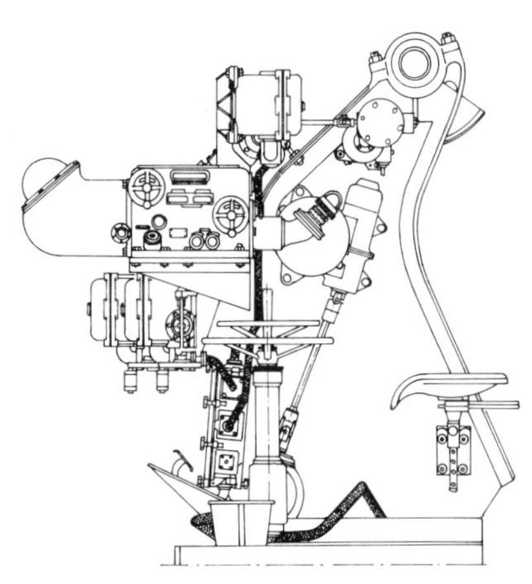

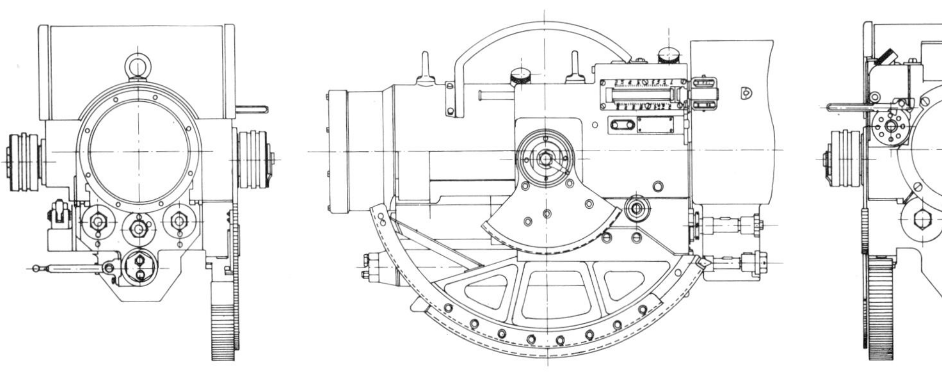

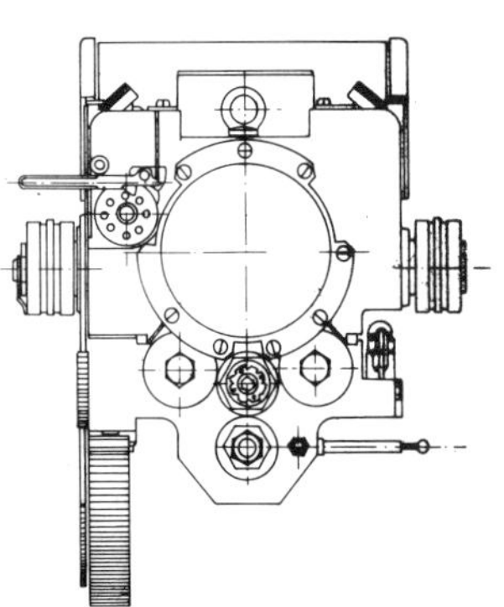

Top: 85mm/55 Mk 90K single mounting, looking aft showing reflector sights and transmitters.
P Budzbon

Centre left: 85mm/55 Mk 90K single mounting, right elevation showing reflector sights and transmitters.
P Budzbon

Centre right: 85mm/55 Mk 90K single mounting, left elevation showing reflector sights and transmitters.
P Budzbon

Bottom: 85mm/55 Mk 90K single mounting gun cradle.
P Budzbon

100mm (3.937in)/50

This, better known by its 47-calibre bore length, was the Italian AA gun described in that section. It was in the cruiser *Krasnyi Kavkaz* in twin Minisini mountings (originally single), and may have been added to a few other ships, including the *Krasnyi Krym*.

85mm (3.346in)/55

This AA gun, developed from an army weapon, was in a twin mounting in the *Ognyevoi* class destroyers and in singles in the escort vessel *Albatros* and perhaps a few other ships. The shell weighed 9.54kg (*21lb*) and muzzle velocity is given as 825m/s (*2707f/s*) with elevation as +70° or 75° -5°.

85mm (3.346in)/53

Another development of the army AA gun, mounted in the turret of the T34/85 tank. This turret was adapted for some of the later armoured motor gunboats, but details of the gun's performance in this role are lacking. The muzzle velocity in tanks with full-calibre projectile was about 795m/s (*2608f/s*).

76.2mm (3in)/55

An AA gun with vertical sliding block, carried by many ships including most of the later destroyers, in single-shielded mountings allowing +85° elevation. The firing cycle was about 3.5sec. The gun weight is given as only 0.7t (*0.69 tons*), and that of the fixed round was 11.2kg (*24.7lb*) with 6.6kg (*14.6lb*) shell. The muzzle velocity was 813m/s (*2667f/s*) and ceiling 9200m (*30,180ft*) indicating a range of about 13,500m (*14,760yd*).

76.2mm (3in)/41.5

Mounted in T34 tank turrets, which were adapted for armoured motor gunboats. With a 6.3kg (*13.9lb*) shell, muzzle velocity was 662m/s (*2172f/s*).

76.2mm (3in)/30.5

There were two guns of this length, but the relation, if any, between them is not known. One had a similar history to the above, but was in early T34 turrets. With the same shell, muzzle velocity was 612m/s (*2008f/s*).

The other, M1915, was an AA gun of First-World-War date, still in some older ships, and firing a 5.5kg (*12.1lb*) shell at 640m/s (*2100f/s*).

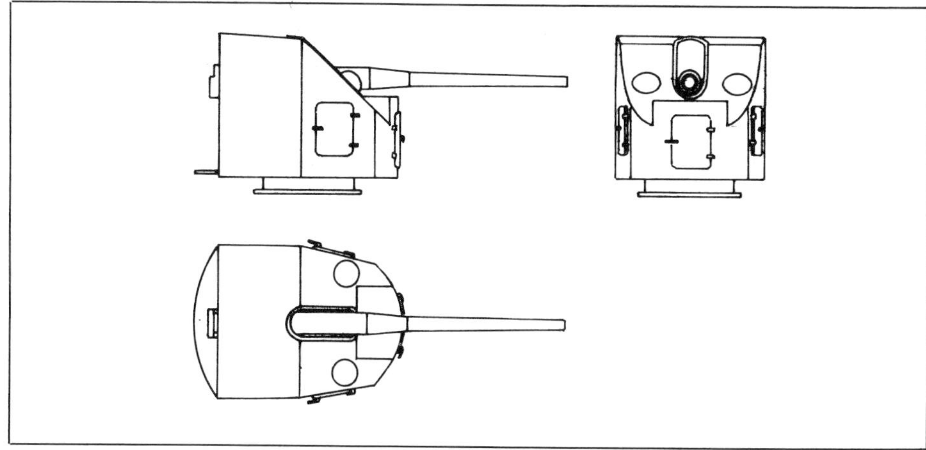

Top: 85mm/55 guns in twin HA M1944/39-3 mounting.
P Budzbon

Centre: 76mm/55 gun in single shielded AA mounting. This was widely used.
P Budzbon

Bottom: 76mm/41.5 gun in an adapted T34 tank turret in an armoured MGB.
P Budzbon Collection

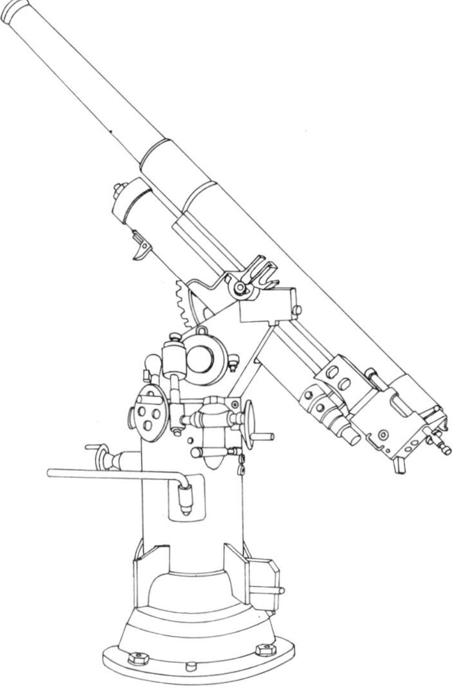

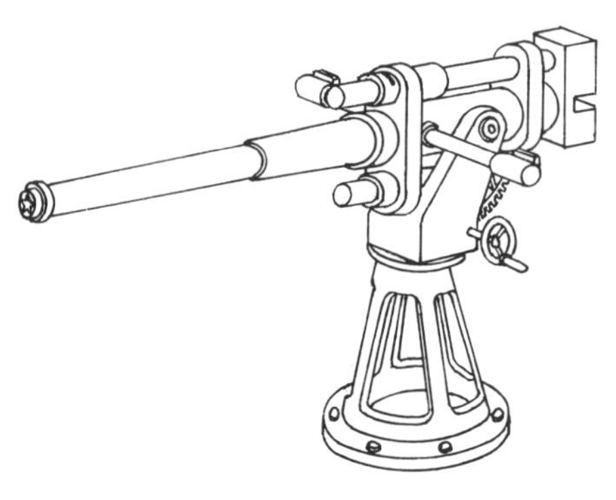

Top left: 76mm/30.5 M1915 gun in single AA mounting.
P Budzbon

Above left: 45mm/46 SA gun in AA mounting carried by the 'K' class and other submarines.
P Budzbon

Top right: 75mm/50 guns in submarine of *Bars* class in 1930s.
P Budzbon Collection

Above right: 45mm/46 SA gun in AA mounting in 'Mo-4' type sub-chaser.
J Micinski Collection

75mm (2.953in)/50

Here again there were two guns of this length. One, weighing 0.7t (*0.69 tons*), was on 60° mountings in the oldest submarines and probably other vessels, and fired a 6kg (*13.2lb*) shell at 750m/s (*2461f/s*), while the other was a screw breech LA gun dating from before World War I. This weighed 0.906t (*0.892 tons*) and fired a 4.9kg (*10.8lb*) shell at 823m/s (*2700f/s*).

45mm (1.772in)/46

A semi-automatic AA gun carried in single mountings by many ships including the smaller submarines. The fixed round weighed 3.45kg (*7.61lb*) and elevation was +85° -10°.

Gun Data

Weight of gun	?110kg	?243lb	
Total weight of mounting incl gun	510kg	1124lb	
Length bore	1975mm	77.76in	43.89cal
Length rifling	1650mm	64.96in	
Weight projectile	1.43kg	3.15lb	
Propellant charge	0.36kg	0.79lb	
Muzzle velocity	760m/s	2493f/s	
Max range	9500m	10,400yd	
Ceiling	6000m	19,700ft	
Recoil	32cm	12.6in	
Firing cycle	2sec		

AUTOMATIC GUNS

This air-cooled automatic AA gun in a hand-operated single mounting replaced the 45mm (*1.772in*) in the larger and in the later ships during the war. A twin mounting, also hand operated, does not appear to have been introduced until after the war. The gun had a five round (?) magazine, and barrels were apparently changed after 100 rounds to cool off. The rate of fire was about 160 per minute, and the round weighed about 1.75kg (*3.86lb*).

37mm (1.457in)/67 M39

Gun Data

Length bore	*c*2323.6mm	*c*91.48in	62.8cal
Length chamber	261mm	10.276in	
Volume chamber	0.265dm^3	16.17in^3	
Length rifling	2054mm	80.87in	
Weight projectile	0.775kg AP	1.709lb AP	
	0.732kg HE	1.614lb HE	
Muzzle velocity	880m/s AP	2887f/s AP	
	908m/s HE	2979f/s HE	
Max range	*c*8000m	*c*8750yd	
Ceiling	*c*6000m	*c*19,700ft	

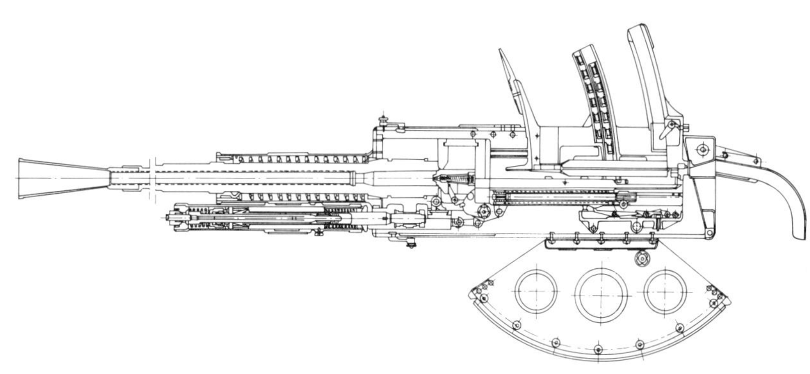

Right: 37mm/67 M39 automatic in longitudinal section. This was potentially the most effective of wartime Russian close-range naval AA.
P Budzbon

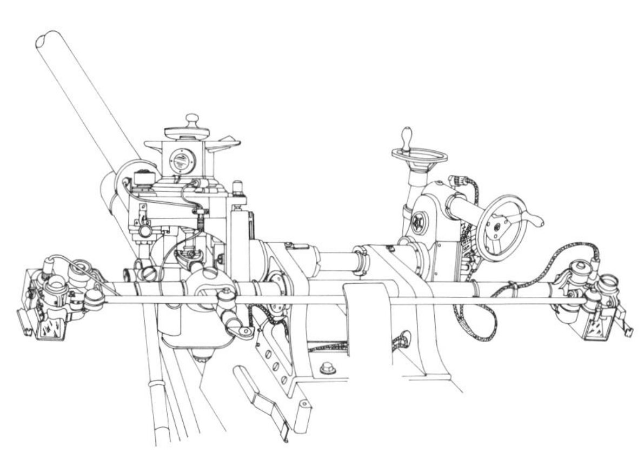

Below left: Predictor for 37mm/67 M39.
P Budzbon

Below right: 37mm/67 M39 in single partly shielded AA mounting.
P Budzbon

Smaller Guns

These included 20mm (*0.7874in*), 12.7mm (*0.5in*) and 7.62mm (*0.3in*) automatic guns of which by far the most important was the 12.7mm Degtjarev DSHK M38. This was very widely used in single and also quadruple mountings with the barrels side by side. A metal belt was fitted holding 50 rounds, and the rate of fire was 300–500 rounds per minute. The projectile weighed 43g (*1.52oz*) and muzzle velocity was 814m/s (*2671f/s*) with a maximum range of 5400m (*5900yd*).

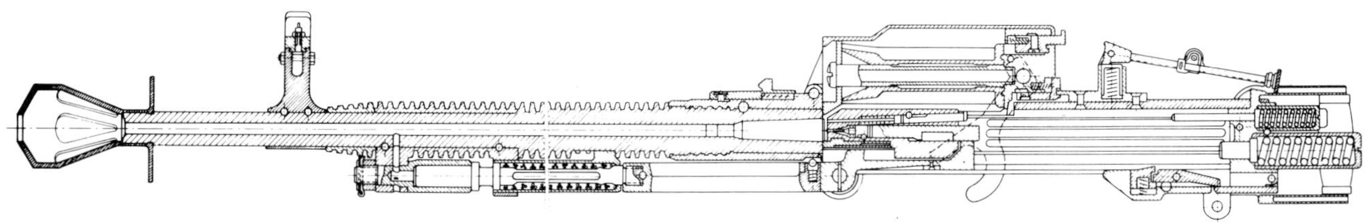

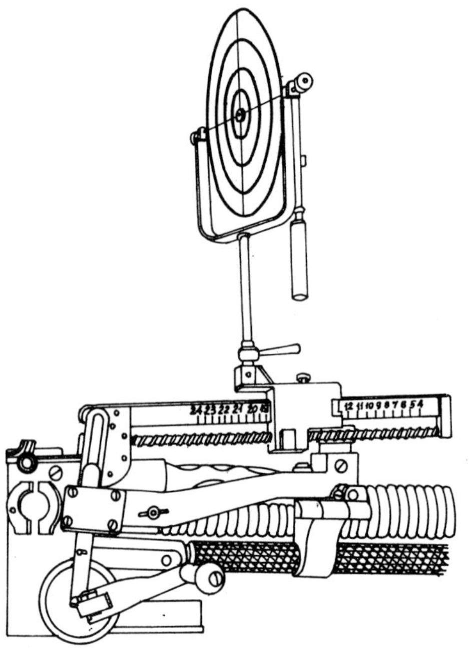

Above: 12.7mm Degtjarev DSHK M38 machine gun in longitudinal section.
P Budzbon

Far left: AA ring sight for 12.7mm DSHK M38 machine gun.
P Budzbon

Left: 12.7mm DSHK M38/46 machine guns in shielded twin mounting with the guns one above the other. This was probably post war.
P Budzbon

Centre: 7.62mm SHKAS machine gun, side view.
P Budzbon

Bottom: 7.62 Maxim machine guns in quadruple mounting with ring sight.
M Twardowski Collection

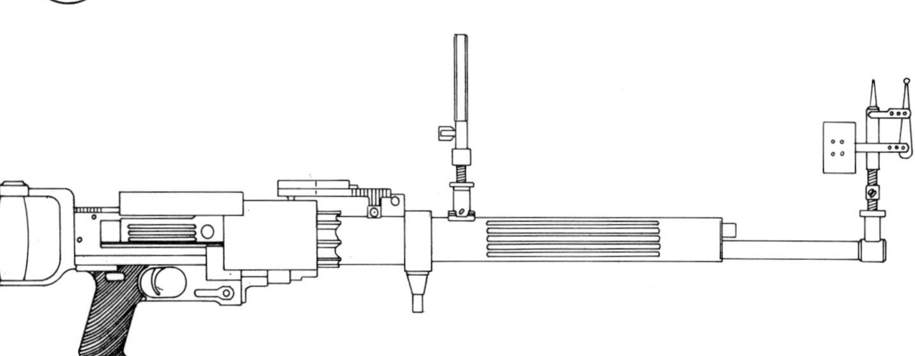

TORPEDOES

There is little available material on the above in the West, and this brief account is based on a German naval intelligence publication of 1944. So far as is known, Russian torpedoes had no particular features of merit.

The explosive charge was usually a mixture of TNT with hexanitrodiphenylamine or tetryl and inertia pistols were standard in all but the oldest.

60cm (23.6in)

Experimental. No data except length 8m (*26ft 3in*).

53.3cm (21in) 27K

A Fiume torpedo later made at Leningrad, with a two-cylinder horizontal engine and Kerosene wet heater. Spiral track gear was fitted. Length was 7.04m (*23ft 1in*), weight 1730kg (*3814lb*), explosive charge 250kg (*551lb*) or 275kg (*606lb*) TNT and range 4200m (*4600yd*)/43kts, 6000m (*6560yd*)/37kts, 15,000m (*16,400yd*)/25kts.

53.3cm (21in) 27P

This was apparently a version of the above for submarines and was made at Leningrad. The following figures are doubtful. Weight 1700kg (*3748lb*), explosive charge 290kg (*639lb*) TNT, range 4000m (*4400yd*)/43kts, 9000m (*9840yd*)/32kts.

Left: Hoisting a 53.3cm torpedo aboard *Shch 215* during the war. The torpedo is probably a 38 Type 3.
P Budzbon

Centre: 53.3cm Type 3 torpedo, standard for the more modern surface ships and submarines. It was made at Leningrad.
P Budzbon

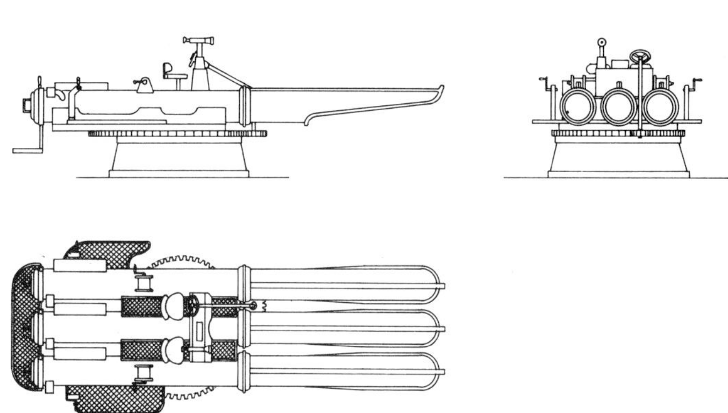

Bottom: Triple 53.3cm TT as fitted to the more modern destroyers.
P Budzbon

53.3cm (21in) 38 Type 3

Apparently the latest standard torpedo for surface ships and submarines. It was made at Leningrad and was of Kerosene wet-heater type. The engine was an eight-cylinder with two vertical banks of four, and the volume of air 669 litres (*23.6ft*^{3}) at 180kg/cm^2 (*2560lb/in*^{2}). Length 7.27m (*23ft 10in*), weight 1610kg (*3549lb*), explosive charge 300kg (*661lb*) TNT/tetryl, range 4000m (*4400yd*)/43.5kts, 8000m (*8750yd*)/34.5kts, 12,000m (*13,100yd*)/28.5kt. The speeds for the two shorter ranges are also given as 46kts and 36kts.

53.3cm (21in) d4

A Naples torpedo bought in Italy and carried by some at least of the Type 7 destroyers. Range is given as 4000m (*4400yd*)/50kts. If correctly identified in Italian lists, this had a two-row eight-cylinder radial engine with air volume 562 litres (*19.85ft*^{3}) and pressure 180kg/cm^2 (*2560lb/in*^{2}), length 7.2m (*23ft 7in*), weight 1700kg (*3748lb*) and explosive charge 270kg (*595lb*).

53.3cm (21in) Type 40 Weymouth

Apparently experimental with a two-cylinder horizontal engine and length 7m (*23ft*), weight 1560kg (*3439lb*), explosive charge 300kg (*661lb*), and range 4000m (*4400yd*)/43.5kts, 10,000m (*10,900yd*)/30kts, 15,000m (*16,400yd*)/23kts. The data given appears to be that for one of the normal Weymouth models.

53.3cm (21in) ? model

A Russian torpedo for MTBs. Available data is inconsistent and does not make sense.

53.3cm (21in) Airborne

Data is also inconsistent for this, but it appears to have had a 230kg (*507lb*) explosive charge and range 4000m (*4400yd*)/40kts. The dropping height is given as 10-25m (*30-80ft*).

45cm (17.7in) 12 F

A bronze Fiume torpedo built in Russia after the first 250 had been delivered in 1914. It was still used in some old torpedo boats and submarines and had a horizontal two-cylinder engine with alcohol heater. Length 5.7m (*18ft 8in*), weight 860kg (*1896lb*), explosive charge 140kg (*309lb*) TNT, range 3000m (*3300yd*)/38kts, 6000m (*6560yd*)29kts.

45cm (17.7in) 16

This was a Russian development of the above with zig-zag running gear and a higher speed. Length 6m (*19ft 8in*), weight 850kg (*1874lb*), explosive charge 170kg (*375lb*) TNT.

45cm (17.7in) 36

This was made at Leningrad. Length 5.7m (*18ft 8in*), weight 920kg (*2028lb*), explosive charge 200kg (*441lb*), range 3000m (*3300yd*)/41kts, 6000m (*6560yd*)/*31kts*.

45cm (17.7in) 36 AN

An airborne torpedo intended for dropping at 160kts from 30m (*100ft*). Weight 920kg (*2028lb*), explosive charge apparently 250kg (*551lb*) and range doubtfully 4000m (*4400yd*)/40kts.

45cm (17.7in) 36 AV

Another airborne torpedo for high dropping with a parachute, the figure quoted being 2000m (*6560ft*). The torpedo was intended for spiral running, and on dropping leapt high out of the water.

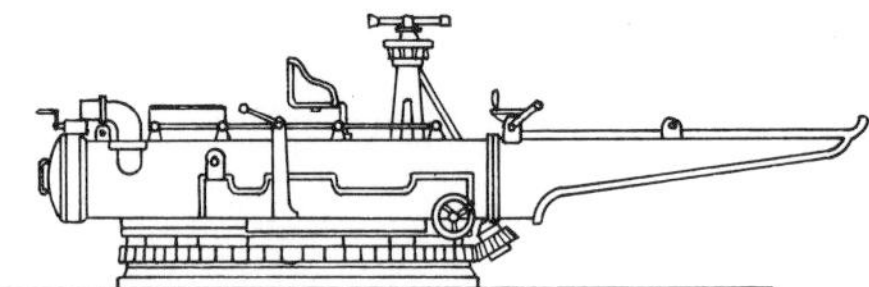

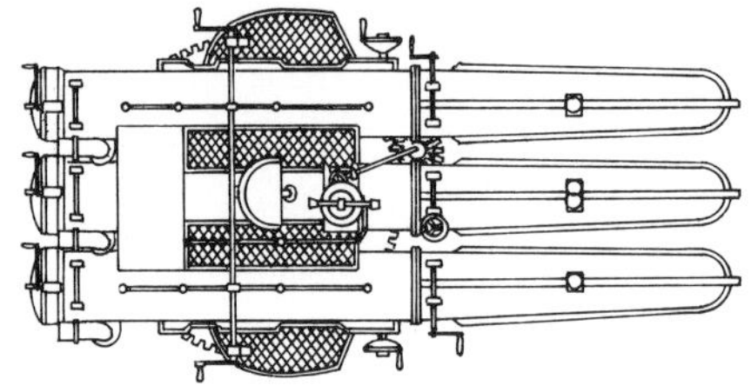

Above: 45cm 36 torpedo used in several modifications.
P Budzbon

Left: Triple 45cm TT as fitted in escorts of the *Uragan* class.
P Budzbon

45cm (17.7in) ? model

A St Tropez torpedo with horizontal two-cylinder engine, length 5.5m (*18ft*), weight 800kg (*1764lb*), explosive charge 165kg (*364lb*) TNT, range 2000m (*2200yd*)/45kts, 6000m (*6560yd*)/32kts.

45cm (17.7in) ? model

A Weymouth torpedo, apparently loot from Estonia, with a four-cylinder radial engine, length 5.5m (*18ft*), weight 890 kg (*1962lb*), explosive charge 170kg (*375lb*), range 3000m (*3300yd*)/42kts, 6000m (*6560yd*)/36kts, 9500m (*10,400yd*)/29kts.

Other torpedoes included BRJ with a 1-3m (*3-10ft*) antenna for radio control from aircraft, an experimental electric version of the same, and an airborne rocket torpedo.

ANTI-SUBMARINE WEAPONS

As usual available data is taken from German wartime sources. The principal weapon was the depth charge carried by surface vessels, with explosive charges of TNT or TNT with 15-30% hexanitrodiphenylamine, though substitute fillings were doubtless used.

DEPTH CHARGES

135kg (298lb) charge

Russian B1 with total weight 165kg (*364lb*), dimensions 43 × 71.2cm (*16.9 × 28in*), sinking speed 2.3-2.5m (*7.5-8.2ft*)/sec and depth settings in range 20-100m (*65-330ft*). Older versions had time fuzes, and later hydrostatic.

115kg (254lb) charge

Vickers 4 VB, total weight 162.5kg (*358lb*), dimensions 42 × 72.3cm (*16.5 × 28.5in*), sinking speed 2.3m (*7.5ft*)/sec and depth setting 12m (*40ft*), 24m (*80ft*), 37m (*120ft*), 49m (*160ft*). Fuzing was hydrostatic.

25kg (55lb) charge

Russian M1, total weight 36kg (*79.4lb*), dimensions 25.2 × 42cm (*9.9 × 16.5in*), sinking speed 2.1-2.2m (*6.9-7.2ft*)/sec and depth settings in range 15-100m (*50-330ft*). Fuzing was as in B1 versions.

16kg (35lb) charge

Vickers 4 VM, total weight 22kg (*49lb*), dimensions 15 × 52cm (*5.9 × 20.5in*), sinking speed 1.8m (*5.9ft*)/sec and depth settings 12m (*40ft*), 24m (*80ft*). Fuzing was hydrostatic.

Depth charge mortars are believed to have been mounted in some of the later escort vessels but details are lacking. A depth charge thrower, type BMB-1, is illustrated.

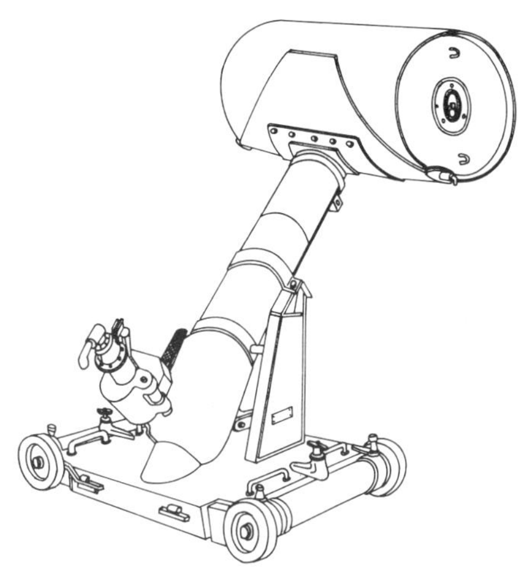

Above: BMB-1 type depth charge thrower.
P Budzbon

Right: Two depth charge throwers on stern of *Storozhevoi* class destroyer of Black Sea Fleet.
P Budzbon Collection

MINES

Very little is available on these and the list given below is from the same German intelligence publication as for torpedoes. It would seem that the Russians did not maintain the high position that their mining had held in 1914-17. Russian mines are believed to have sunk 38 merchant ships of 68,121 tons gross and 40 assorted surface warships of 26,803 tons in 1941-45, together with two confirmed U-boats.

The explosive charge was TNT, or the same with 15-30% hexanitrodiphenylamine or tetryl. Gun cotton was probably used in some of the older mines. Two devices were anti-sweeping gear, known as Tschaika, and in the newer mines Baltoschka, which was inserted between the mine body and mooring wire and was intended to free the mine if the mooring wire was caught by a paravane. Tschaika had a wooden body with a clamping device, and an explosive charge was hung on a 10m (*33ft*) wire below the mine body. The total weight was 16kg (*35lb*). A moored minefield protector, MZ-26, is illustrated.

M 1908

A mine with five lead horns, 100kg (*220lb*) charge and spherical shell 0.9m (*35.4in*) diameter. The mooring wire was 130m (*70 fathoms*).

M 1912

An inertia pendulum impact mine. The spherical shell was 0.9m (35.4in) diameter, charge 90kg (*198lb*) and mooring wire 120m (*65 fathoms*). The anchor was considered to be too light.

M 1908/39 moored mine with Hertz horns and spherical shell.

P Budzbon

M 1916

Another inertia pendulum impact mine, distinct from M 1912. Charge 116kg (*256lb*), mooring wire 400m (*220 fathoms*).

M 1926

An inertia pendulum impact mine with 240kg (*529lb*) TNT charge and 120m (*65 fathoms*) mooring wire. The oval shell was 0.9m (*35.4in*) diameter.

M 1926 inertia pendulum mine.
M Twardowski Collection

M 1931 KB1 horned mine with anchor.
P Budzbon

M 1931 (KB1)

An improved M 1908 with five lead horns, but antenna were fitted in some. Charge 200-250kg (*441-551lb*), mooring wire 146m (*80 fathoms*) or 238m (*130 fathoms*). The oval shell was 0.9m (*35.4in*) diameter.

MA 1939 (KB3)

A mine with horns and 35m (*115ft*) antenna, introduced in 1941-42. Charge 250kg (*551lb*).

System M 12, Type PLT-10

For submarines, this had inertia pendulum impact and was carried by 'L' and 'D' class boats. Charge 230kg (*507lb*), mooring wire 120m (*65 fathoms*). The shell was a truncated cone 0.8m (*31.5in*) diameter.

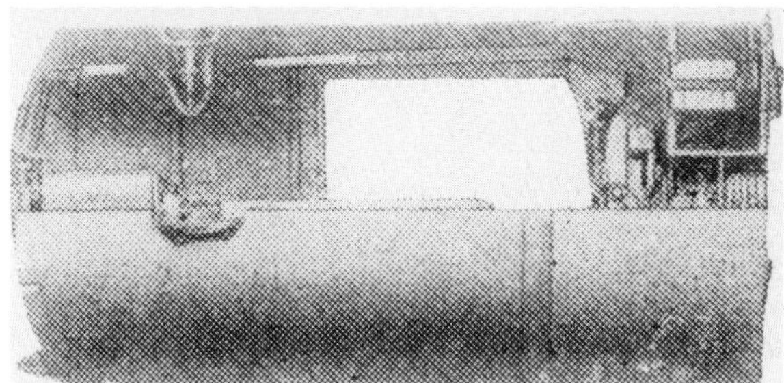

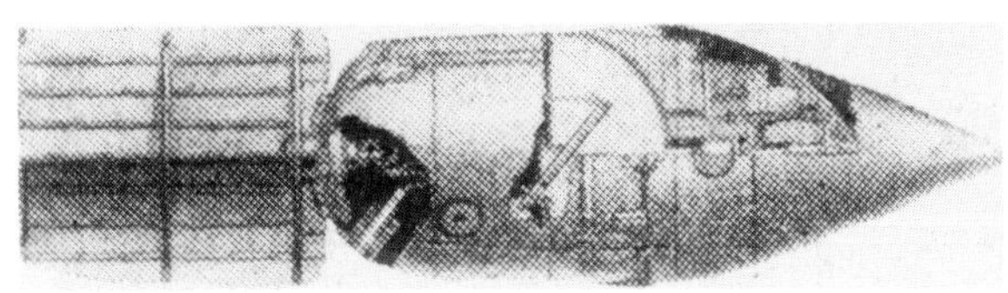

PLT-G mine for laying by submarines (top) and AMG airborne mine dropped without parachute.
M Twardowski Collection

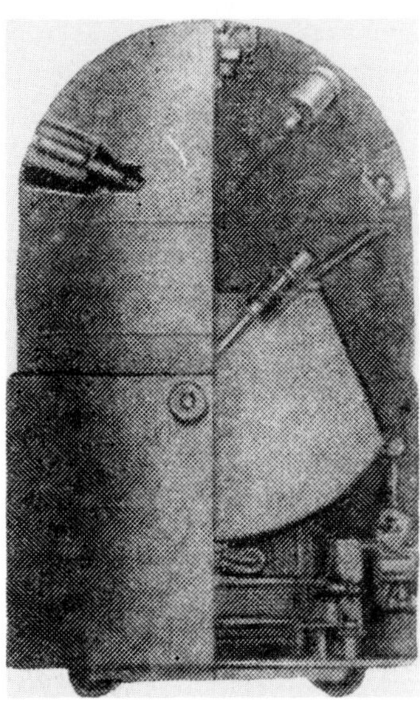

EP type mine laid by 'K' class submarines.
M Twardowski Collection

EP-SA

For submarines, a mine with five lead horns carried in 'K' class boats. Charge 200kg (*441lb*) or 300kg (*661lb*), mooring wire 130m (*70 fathoms*). The oval shell was 0.9m (*35.4in*) diameter.

German EMA

Modified as mine for submarines. Charge 150kg (*331lb*).

Airborne mine Type Geiro

This was developed from M 1926 and had no parachute. The horns were moved out by springs after dropping. Charge 235kg (*518lb*), mooring wire 145m (*80 fathoms*). This is probably the AMG type illustrated.

Parachute mine M 12

This had four parachutes with charge 90kg (*198lb*) and mooring wire 120m (*65 fathoms*). It appears that sulphuric acid equipment was carried to corrode a hole in the ice.

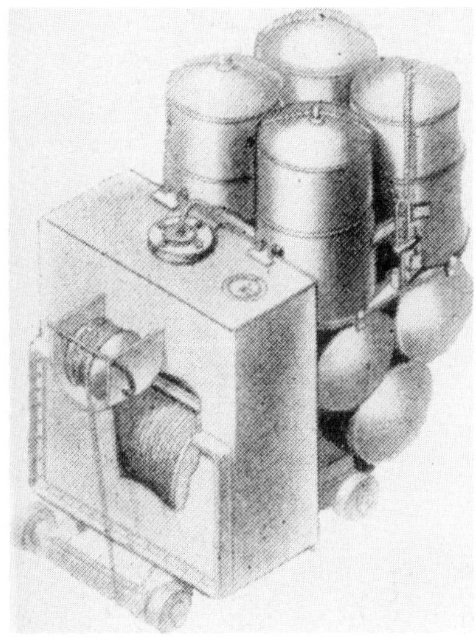

MZ-26 moored minefield protector.
M Twardowski Collection

Mirab type magnetic mine for use in rivers and harbours.
M Twardowski Collection

Airborne bomb mine PM

A parachute mine with five lead horns and a shell like that of M 1931. There were moored and drifting versions, the latter having accumulators for a propeller which presumably kept the mine at a constant depth. Charge 200-250kg (*441-551lb*) TNT-HND.

Others included controlled mines with charges of 65-250kg (*143-551lb*), a mine for laying from the TT of submarines, possibly PLT-G, which was not satisfactory, a tidal mine under trial and, possibly, a Type 23 magnetic ground mine, also under trial (though it is also stated that there was no Russian magnetic mine). Some British A Mk 1 were however used from 1943, and there was a turtle-shaped mine known as Mirab for use in rivers and harbours, but details are lacking.

BOMBS AND ROCKETS

BOMBS

The larger bombs listed by German sources were SAP of 502kg (*1107lb*) and 965kg (*2127lb*) with respective charges of 106kg (*234lb*) and 207kg (*456lb*), and HE of 500kg (*1102lb*) and 1000kg (*2205lb*) with respective charges of 215kg (*474lb*) and 475kg (*1047lb*).

ROCKETS

The RBS-132 rocket-bomb had a total weight of 51kg (*112lb*), dimensions 132 × 1510mm (*5.197 × 59.45in*) and an explosive charge of 4.6kg (*10.1lb*) TNT. The propellant weighed 7.2kg (*15.9lb*) and maximum velocity was 320m/s (*1050f/s*) with a maximum range of 2000m (*2200yd*) from the aircraft. The launching guides were 1434mm (*56.46in*) and the bomb could pierce 75mm (*3in*) armour.

Many armoured river gunboats had adapted army launchers for 82mm (*3.23in*) M8 and 130mm (*5.118in*) M13 rockets.

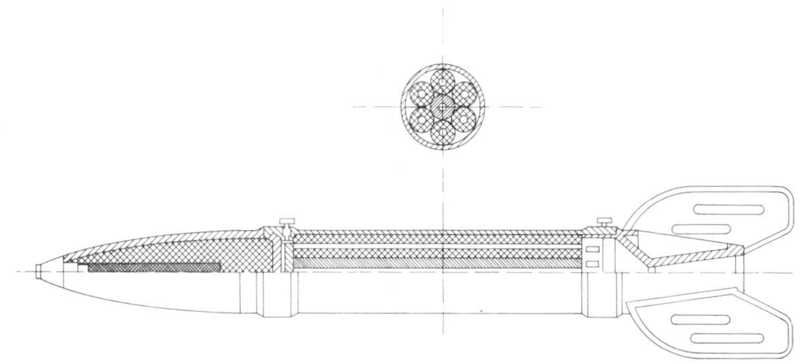

M13 type 130mm Army rocket fired by many armoured river gunboats.
P Budzbon

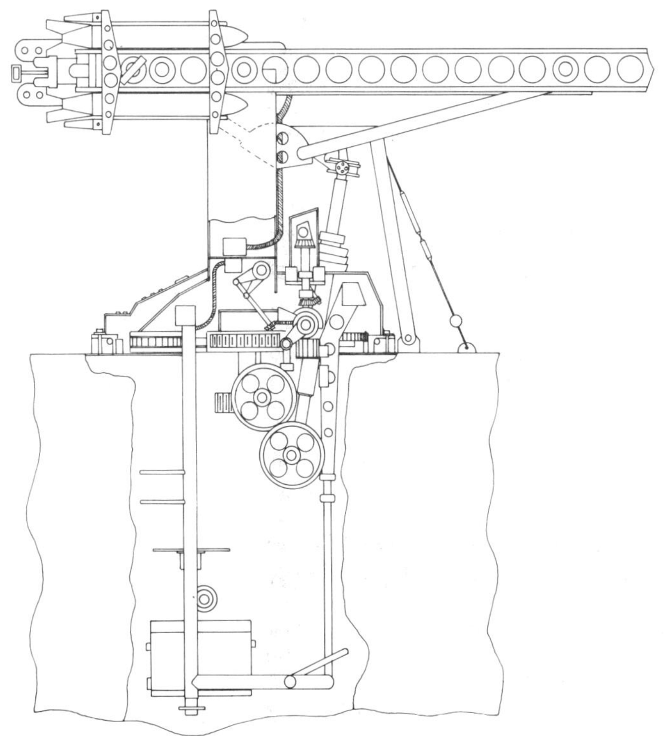

M8 type Army launcher for 82mm rockets as adapted for armoured river gunboats.
P Budzbon

OTHER COUNTRIES

This section is concerned with the guns carried in 1939-45 by the ships of the following navies, in alphabetical order: Argentina, Brazil, Chile, Denmark, Finland, Greece, Netherlands, Norway, Peru, Poland, Portugal, Romania, Spain, Sweden, Thailand, Turkey, Yugoslavia. Only guns of 100mm (*3.937in*) and over are listed comprehensively, and there are general notes on those of smaller calibre. This division has been chosen as it is also the boundary between guns that can be identified in most cases with a good degree of certainty, and those where identification is often doubtful. The details of guns of British and American manufacture and those of British design, but made in Spain, are given in Imperial units with metric conversion, but otherwise the opposite applies (though there are a few exceptions for various reasons).

Sweden was, with Bofors, self sufficient in guns and supplied them to other countries. In addition to their world famous close range AA, Bofors had pioneered the use of steel castings instead of forgings in gun construction. The first in service, a mobile naval coast-defence 84mm (*3.3in*) M81, was delivered in 1884. Spain had the Carraca works in which Vickers had an interest, and the Netherlands, and to a lesser extent Denmark, built some of their own guns, but otherwise all the above navies obtained their guns from other countries. It should be remembered that the triaxial Hazemeyer twin Bofors mounting was introduced to Britain from the Netherlands.

The Chinese navy is excluded, as it was devastated in 1937-38 during the war with Japan, and the heaviest surviving gun afloat appears to have been a single 6in (*152.4mm*)/40 EOC QF.

NAVAL GUNS

ARGENTINA

12in (304.8mm)/50 Bethlehem

These guns, mounted in twin turrets in the *Rivadavia* and *Moreno*, are generally thought to be the same as the USN Mk 7 described in that section. However contemporary Bethlehem tables list the 12in/50 as 66 tons (*67.06t*), the weight being increased at the breech end to move the centre of gravity in that direction. In either case the shell was 870lb (*394.6kg*) and MV 2900f/s (*884m/s*). From photographs, the barbette diameter is similar to that of the USN gun, and it is likely that the mounting was also similar except that the turret roof was probably not over 4in (*10cm*).

10in (254mm)/40 EOC

Pattern P[1] guns in single turrets in the *Belgrano* and *Pueyrredon*, weighing with BM 30.0 tons (*30.5t*) and firing a 500lb (*226.8kg*) shell at 2300f/s (*701m/s*).

238mm (9.37in)/35 Krupp

Mounted in single turrets in the *Independencia* and *Libertad*, this gun weighed with BM 21.9t (*21.6 tons*), and fired a 160kg (*353lb*) shell at 650 m/s (*2133f/s*).

The *Rivadavia* (Argentina) fitting out. The forward 12in/50 turrets are shown as are some of the 6in/50 secondary battery. Her sister-ship *Moreno* is in the background.
By courtesy of R L Scheina

Stern view of the *Pueyrredon* (Argentina) showing the after 10in/40 single turret.
By courtesy of R L Scheina

7.5in (190.5mm)/52

There are considerable doubts about this gun, which was in twin turrets in the *Almirante Brown* and *25 de Mayo*. Previous Elswick drawings of a BL gun give a weight with BM of 17.6 tons (*17.9t*) or 13.75 tons (*14t*) if made in higher strength alloy steel. Both fired a 200lb (*90.7kg*) shell at 3116f/s (*950m/s*). A later Vickers drawing of a twin turret has a lighter BL gun, not exceeding 13 tons (*13.2t*). This is shown with A tube, B tube to 96.25in (*2445mm*) from muzzle, jacket and breech ring. The breech opens upwards, and overall length is shown as 403.063in (*10,237.8mm*). On the other hand a Vickers-Armstrong copy of an Odero-Terni drawing has a separate ammunition QF gun with sliding breech block. There are a thin inner A tube, thick A tube, jacket and breech ring, and overall length is 410.63in (*10,430mm*). The chamber appears to be 58.86in (*1495mm*) long with a volume of *c*3826in^3 (*62.7dm^3*).

The above mentioned Vickers twin mounting has the guns in a common cradle with the axes only 31.875in (*81cm*) apart. The mean roller path diameter is 14ft 6in (*4.42m*) with the rotating structure angled outwards above, and the barbette internal diameter 17ft 8.6in (*5.40m*). The turret is powered by a self contained hydraulic unit and elevation is +45° -7° with loading at up to 12° as the rammer and shell tray move in an arc on curved vertical rails. The hoists come up on the outside of each gun and have a passing space for the up and down cages. The shell is nearly horizontal above the vertical containers for the two half charges.

The time of writing (1983) is not propitious for further investigation from Argentine sources.

6in (152.4mm)/50 QF Vickers Armstrong

This gun known as Mk W, and mounted in triple turrets in *La Argentina*, was an interesting comparison with the British Mk XXIII. It was built with an autofretted loose barrel, jacket and breech ring and had a horizontal sliding block with SA mechanism. Separate ammunition was fired, the cartridge weighing 69lb (*31.3kg*).

The turrets were powered by self contained electrically driven oil hydraulic equipment and elevation was +45° to -7° with loading at +5°. The guns were in separate cradles but all three could be coupled together, or the centre gun with left or right. There was no break in the hoists which came up to the right of the left gun and to the left of the other two. Shells and cartridges were apparently hoisted in the same cage and transferred to the loading cage in the gunhouse.

Gun Data

Bore	6in	152.4mm	
Weight incl BM	6.776 tons	6.885t	
Weight loose barrel	2.013 tons	2.045t	
Length overall	314.54in	7989.4mm	52.42cal
Length bore	300.0in	7620mm	50.0cal
Length chamber	43.126in	1095.4mm	
Volume chamber	1500in^3	24.58dm^3	
Length rifling (full depth)	253.70in	6443.9mm	
Grooves	(40) 0.05 × 0.315in	1.27 × 8.00mm	
Lands	0.156in	3.96mm	
Twist	1 in 30		
Weight projectile	100lb	45.4kg	
Muzzle velocity	2953f/s	900m/s	
Working pressure	19 tons/in^2	2990kg/cm^2	
Max range	25,700yd/45°	23,500m/45°	

Gun Mounting Data

Revolving weight (incl 60 ready shell)	132-139 tons	134-141t
Roller path dia	17ft 6in	5.33m
Barbette int dia	21ft	6.40m
Distance apart gun axes	48in	1.22m
Recoil distance	16.5in	42cm
Turret shield	face 3in; rest 1in	face 75mm; rest 25mm

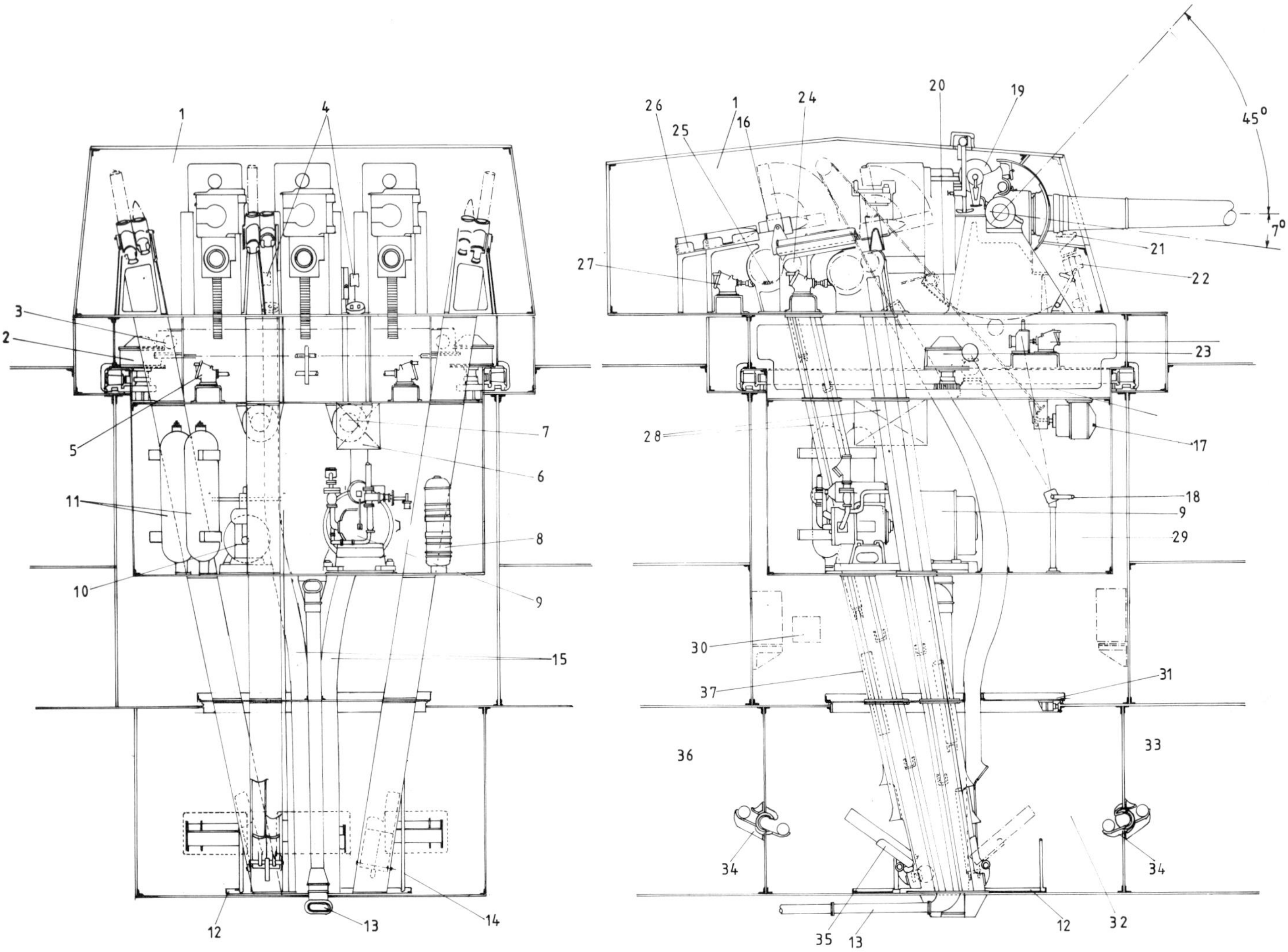

Triple 6in QF turret as mounted in *La Argentina* in longitudinal and transverse sections.

1 Gunhouse
2 Training gear
3 Elevating motor and gear
4 Auxiliary hoist bollards
5 Training motor
6 Hydraulic tank
7 Auxiliary bollard motor
8 Oil cooler
9 Pump and motor
10 Air compressor unit
11 Air flasks
12 Revolving platform
13 Power cables
14 Supports for revolving platform
15 Auxiliary hoists
16 Tilting buckets
17 Motors for bollards for auxiliary hoists
18 Hand elevating gear
19 Sighting gear
20 Elevating arc and pinion
21 Local director sight
22 Training receiver
23 Training gear
24 Chain wheel (driving)
25 Worm and spur gearing
26 Receiving trays
27 Hydraulic motor for hoist
28 Hoist casings
29 Working chamber
30 Charging panel
31 Trunk guide rollers
32 Handling room
33 Shell room
34 Flash tight scuttles for shells
35 Loading tray
36 Magazine
37 Main ammunition hoist (endless chain)

John Lambert

Left: La Argentina with superfiring 6in triple turret trained to starboard.
CPL

6in (152.4mm)/40 QF EOC

Of the many patterns of this type, the guns still mounted in the *Pueyrredon* were apparently the British QF Mk II. With 100lb (*45.4kg*) shells, MV was up to 2297f/s (*700m/s*) depending on the charge.

6in (152.4mm)/50 Bethlehem

Mounted in the secondary batteries of the *Rivadavia* and *Moreno*, this gun is believed to be similar to the USN Mk 8 noted in that section. With a 105lb (*47.6kg*) shell, MV was 2800f/s (*853m/s*).

4.724in (120mm)/45 QF

Of Argentine destroyers the *Corrientes* class had the British MK IX* and the *Mendoza* class Vickers Mk E. The latter differed in being wire wound for part of its length and in having an inner A tube as well as only 28 rifling grooves and slight differences in chamber and cartridge case. With a 48.5lb (*22kg*) shell and 13.5lb (*6.12kg*) CSP_2 charge, MV was 2789f/s (*850m/s*). Elevation was +35° -10°.

Other 4.724in (120mm)

The *Cervantes* class destroyers purchased from Spain had 45cal BL guns noted under that navy, the training ship *Sarmiento* an early Vickers 45cal QF and the *Belgrano, Independencia* and *Libertad* Elswick 40cal QF.

4in (101.6mm)/50 QF Vickers Armstrong

Gun Data

Bore	4in	101.6mm	
Weight incl BM	2.175 tons	2.210t	
Weight loose barrel	0.619 tons	0.629t	
Length oa	210.75in	5353mm	52.69cal
Length bore	200.0in	5080mm	50.0cal
Length chamber	29.976in	761.4mm	
Volume chamber	499.8in^3	8.19dm^3	
Length rifling	166.807in	4236.9mm	
Grooves	(32) 0.039 × 0.270in	1.00 × 6.86mm	
Lands	0.123in	3.12mm	
Twist	1 in 30		
Weight projectile	31lb	14.1kg	
Muzzle velocity	3000f/s	914m/s	
Working pressure	19 tons/in^2	2990kg/cm^2	
Max range	19,900yd/45°	18,200m/45°	
Ceiling	37,400ft/90°	11,400m/90°	

Known as Mk P this was a loose barrel gun with vertical sliding breech block carried by *La Argentina* in single AA mountings allowing +90° -5°. The fixed round weighed 57.75lb (*26.2kg*), and max training and elevating speeds were 16° and 14°/second with RPC, though it is not known if this was actually installed.

4in (101.6mm)/50 QF Bethlehem

Believed to be similar to the USN Mk 9 described in that section, this gun was mounted in the *Cordoba* and *Jujuy* classes of destroyers and from a photograph of the *Robinson*, it appears that it was also mounted in the *Bouchard* class minesweepers. The weight with BM is given as 2.6 tons (*2.64t*) and with a 30.8lb (*14kg*) shell, MV was 3000f/s (*914m/s*). Fixed ammunition was fired.

101.6mm (4in)/45 and /40 Odero-Terni

These guns, not 100mm (*3.937in*), were mounted respectively in single, not twin, AA mountings in the *Almirante Brown* and *25 de Mayo* and in deck mountings in the *Salta* class submarines. Both fired fixed ammunition with the same cartridge and a propellant charge of 4.77kg (*10.52lb*) probably CSP_2. MV for the 40cal gun is given as 875m/s (*2871f/s*) with a 13.75kg (*30.3lb*) shell.

BRAZIL

12in (304.8mm)/45 EOC

Gun Data

Bore	12in	304.8mm	
Weight incl BM	60.97 tons	61.95t	
Length oa	561.55in	14,263.4mm	46.796cal
Length bore	540in	13,716mm	45.0cal
Length chamber	82.71in	2100.83mm	
Volume chamber	18,000in^3	294.97dm^3	
Weight projectile	850lb	385.6kg	
Propellant charge	285lb CSP_2	129.3kg CSP_2	
Muzzle velocity	2800f/s	853m/s	

Gun Mounting Data

Roller path	22ft 6in	6.86m
Barbette int dia	26ft	7.92m
Distance apart gun axes	90in	2.286m
Turret shield	face 12in; sides, rear 8in; roof 3-2in originally	face 30cm; sides, rear 20cm; roof 75-50mm originally

The use of tubular instead of cord propellant grain made it possible to increase muzzle velocity from the 2725f/s (*831m/s*) of RN 12in/45 guns, and roller path and barbette were 12in (*30.5cm*) smaller than in the British B VIII series for 12in/45 Mk X.

This, known as Pattern L, was an earlier version of the British Mk XIII, Pattern W, mounted in *Agincourt* during the 1914-18 war. It was carried in twin turrets by the *Minas Gerais* and *Sao Paulo* and was of normal wire-wound construction, except that the outer of the two tubes under the wire, was in three pieces and that the wire extended for only three-quarters of the length. Elswick BM with an interrupted, but not stepped, screw block was fitted. The mounting originally allowed +13° to -5°, probably altered to +20° -5°, and loading was at +5°. It was hydraulically powered with the hoists broken at the working chamber.

6in (152.4mm)/50

This, mounted in the river monitor *Parnaiba*, may have been an EOC Pattern DD QF from the old cruiser *Barroso* firing a 100lb (*45.4kg*) shell at 2600f/s (*792m/s*).

5in (127mm)/38 Mk 12 USN

This gun which was in single mountings in the *Greenhalgh* class destroyers, is described in the US section.

4.724in (120mm)/50 EOC

Pattern CC, a BL gun, mounted in the secondary batteries of the *Minas Gerais* and *Sao Paulo* and also in the *Bahia*, *Rio Grande do Sul* and possibly the river monitor *Paraguacu*. Weight with BM was 3.316 tons (*3.369t*) and with a 45lb (*20.4kg*) shell and 15.1lb (*6.85kg*) CSP_2 charge MV was 3000f/s (*914m/s*).

Other 4.724in (120mm)

The submarine *Humaita* apparently had a 41-calibre Ansaldo QF and the river monitor *Pernambuco* Elswick 40-calibre QF. The latter had a larger chamber than usual and MV 2500f/s (*762m/s*) with 45lb (*20.4kg*) shell.

Top: The *Minas Gerais* (Brazil) on trials in September 1909. The centreline and port wing 12in/45 turrets are shown but most of the 4.7in/50 secondary battery is not yet mounted.
CPL

Above: 4in/45 Vickers Armstrong Mk N gun in the Brazilian minelayer *Carioca*.
By courtesy of R L Scheina

4in (101.6mm)/45 QF Vickers Armstrong

Mark N in the *Carioca* class minelayers fired a 31lb (*14.06kg*) shell at 2800f/s (*853m/s*).

Other 4in (101.6mm)

These included the British 40-calibre QF Mk IV in the old destroyer *Maranhao*, and the 40-calibre BL Elswick Pattern M in the *Mato Grosso* class.

100mm (3.937in)/47 OTO 1931-1938

Mounted in the *Tamoio* class submarines and described in the Italian section.

CHILE

Known as Pattern A or as Mk I in British service, this gun was mounted in twin turrets in the *Almirante Latorre* which served in the Grand Fleet as HMS *Canada*. The gun was of normal wire-wound construction with tapered inner A tube and Elswick three-motion short-arm breech mechanism with Welin block. It was of slightly higher performance than the Mk VII gun with which it forms an interesting comparison. Shells were approximately 4crh and propellant charges were in quarters. The mountings were powered from a hydraulic main and allowed +20° -5° elevation with loading at any angle. The elevating rams were connected to vertical arms fixed to the slide trunnions, and shell rooms were below magazines with hoists broken at the working chamber.

14in (355.6mm)/45 EOC

Gun Data

Bore	14in	355.6mm	
Weight incl BM	84.75 tons	86.11t	
Length oa	648.4in	16,469.4mm	46.31cal
length bore	630.0in	16,002mm	45.0cal
Length chamber	94.165in	2391.8mm	
Volume chamber	23,500in^3	385.1dm^3	
Length rifling	529.82in	13,457.4mm	
Grooves	(84) 0.12 × 0.349in	3.05 × 8.86mm	
Lands	0.174in	4.42mm	
Twist	1 in 30		
Weight projectile	1586lb	719.4kg	
Propellant charge	344lb MD 45	156kg MD 45	
Muzzle velocity	2507f/s	764m/s	
Working pressure	20 tons/in^2	3150kg/cm^2	
Approx life	350 EFC		
Max range	24,400yd/20°	22,310m/20°	

Gun Mounting Data

Revolving weight	660 tons	671t
Roller path dia	27ft	8.23m
Barbette int dia	31ft	9.45m
Distance apart gun axes	100in	2.54m
Recoil distance	45in	114cm
Max elevating speed	3°/sec	
Max training speed	3°/sec	
Firing cycle	30sec	
Turret shield	face, sides, rear 10in; roof 4-3in originally	face, sides, rear 25cm; roof 10-7.5cm originally

The *Almirante Latorre* (Chile) at the end of her career. In 1915-18 as HMS *Canada*, her ten 14in/45 guns made her a much valued unit of the Grand Fleet.
CPL

The Chilean destroyer *Serrano* with 4.7in/45 QF guns. The small shields, similar to those in early 4.7in British destroyers, are well shown.
CPL

8in (203.2mm)/40 EOC

Pattern T in single turrets in the old cruiser *O'Higgins*. The gun weighed 16.54 tons (*16.81t*) including BM and fired a 210lb (*95.3kg*) or 250lb (*113.4kg*) shell at 2575f/s (*785m/s*) or 2440f/s (*744m/s*).

Also Pattern P, actually 39.94cal, in shielded mountings in the older cruiser *Blanco Encalada*. With BM this weighed 15.39 tons (*15.64t*) and fired a 210lb (*95.3kg*) shell at 2242f/s (*683m/s*).

6in (152.4mm)/50 EOC

Pattern TT or in Britain Mk XVII, and noted in that section, was mounted as secondary armament in the *Almirante Latorre* and it is believed, was also in the rearmed *Chacabuco*. The mountings allowed 15°, at least originally, and not 20° as in HMS *Eagle*.

6in (152.4mm)/40 QF EOC

Patterns W^2, Z^3 and Z^4 in the *Blanco Encalada* and *O'Higgins* had larger chambers than usual in this type of gun, and fired a 100lb (*45.4kg*) shell at 2500f/s (*762m/s*).

4.724in (120mm)/45 QF Vickers Armstrong

Mk E noted under Argentina, was mounted in the *Serrano* class destroyers, the *O'Brien* class submarines and probably the depot ship *Araucano*. In Chilean service a 48.5lb (*22kg*) shell was fired with 11.75lb (*5.33kg*) MD 19 charge and MV 2658f/s (*810m/s*).

4in (101.6mm) guns

These included the British 45cal QF Mk V as AA in the *Almirante Latorre*, and EOC Pattern S, a 40cal gun known as QF Mk VI in Britain during the First World War. This was in the *Lynch* class destroyers, and had a slightly higher performance than QF Mk IV, from which it differed in a smaller chamber and screw BM.

DENMARK

240mm (9.449in)/43 Bofors M1906

A BL gun of 42cal bore length mounted in single turrets in the old coast defence ship *Peder Skram*. The gun weighed 24.5t (*24.1 tons*) including BM, and fired a 160kg (*353lb*) shell at 805m/s (*2641f/s*) or possibly 820m/s (*2690f/s*).

149.1mm (5.87in)/50 Bofors M1906

A BL gun of 48.8 cal bore length mounted in the *Peder Skram*, and after she was scuttled, in a German coast defence battery. MV was 830m/s (*2723f/s*) with a 51kg (*112.4lb*) shell.

149.1mm (5.87in)/45 Bofors M1922

Mounted in the coast defence ship *Niels Juel*, this QF gun of 45cal overall length, had a horizontal sliding breech block, weighed with BM 6.1t (*6.0 tons*), and fired a 46kg (*101lb*) shell at 835m/s (*2740f/s*). Elevation was +30° -10°.

149mm/45 Bofors M1922 gun and mounting for *Niels Juel* (Denmark) without shield.
Bofors, by courtesy of K-E Westerlund

120mm (4.724in)/40 Danish

Only in the fishery protection vessel *Ingolf*, this gun fired a 20kg (*44lb*) shell at 770m/s (*2526f/s*).

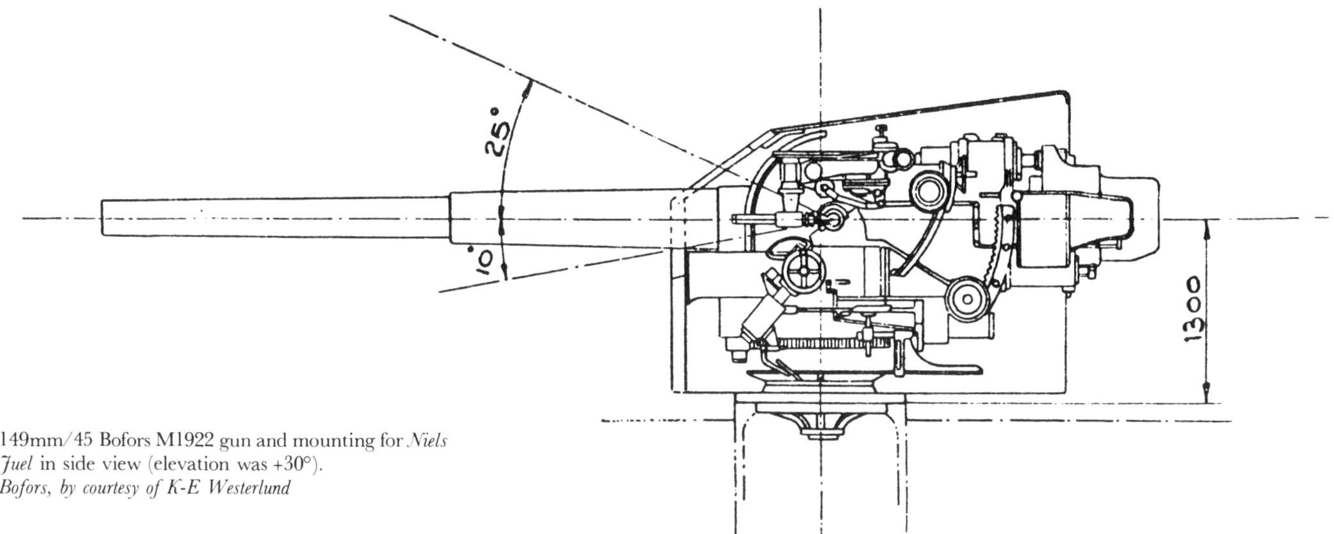

149mm/45 Bofors M1922 gun and mounting for *Niels Juel* in side view (elevation was +30°).
Bofors, by courtesy of K-E Westerlund

FINLAND

254mm (10in)/45 Bofors

This gun was in twin turrets in the *Väinämöinen* and *Ilmarinen.* It was built with an A tube, two part jacket and screwed-on breech piece, and had a horizontal sliding breech block though a screw block was eventually to be fitted. Weight with BM was 37.9t (*37.3 tons*) and overall length 46.26cal. The shell weighed 225kg (*496lb*), charge 70kg (*154lb*) and case 45kg (*99lb*) with MV 850m/s (*2789f/s*).

The turret was carried on a ball track and was electrically powered with hydraulic drive gear for training and elevation. The guns were in separate cradles, coupled together, and loading was at 0° with elevation +45° -10° giving a range of 30,300m (*33,140yd*). Recoil was 675mm (*26.6in*) and the turret revolving weight 256t (*252 tons*). The turret shields had 10cm (*4in*) faces, 5cm (*2in*) sides and 7.5cm (*3in*) roofs.

105mm (4.134in)/50 Bofors M1932

This AA gun was in twin shielded mountings in the above ships. It was 50cal in overall length, had a SA horizontal sliding breech block and with BM weighed 2.55t (*2.51 tons*). The 16kg (*35.3lb*) shell was fired at 800m/s (*2625f/s*) MV with a 4.1kg (*9.04lb*) charge, the fixed round weighing 25.2kg (*55.6lb*). The mounting allowed +85° -10° elevation and the guns were in a common cradle. Automatic rammers were powered from hydro-pneumatic accumulators and the firing cycle was 4sec. Total weight of gun, mounting and 15mm (*0.6in*) shield was 22.1t (*21.75 tons*), range 18,200m (*19,900yd*) and ceiling 12,000m (*39,400ft*).

Other guns

Russian 130mm (*5.118in*) and 101.6mm (*4in*) were mounted in various minor vessels.

Centre: 254mm/45 twin turret for the Finnish *Väinämöinen* in Bofors' erecting shop.
Bofors, by courtesy of K-E Westerlund

Bottom: The *Väinämöinen* in 1944 showing 254mm/45 turrets and 105mm/50 twin AA guns.
By courtesy of K-E Westerlund

GREECE

It is not known if the *Kilkis* (ex-*Idaho*) retained her original armament. This comprised USN 12in (*304.8mm*) Mk 5, 8in (*203.2mm*) Mk 6, and 7in (*177.8mm*) Mk 2. The two latter are noted under the US section, and the 12in weighed with BM 52.9 tons (*53.7t*), and fired an 870lb (*394.6kg*) shell at 2700f/s (*823m/s*) with 305lb (*138.3kg*) NC propellant charge. All three types were mounted in German coast-defence batteries including four 12in on Aegina.

9.2in (233.68mm)/45 EOC

A wire-wound gun known as Pattern H, mounted in twin turrets in the armoured cruiser *Averoff*. Weight with BM was 26.73 tons (*27.16t*) and with 380lb (*172.4kg*) shell and 117lb (*53kg*) SC 205 charge, MV was *c*2700f/s (*823m/s*).

7.5in (190.5mm)/45 EOC

Pattern B in twin turrets in the *Averoff* was also a wire-wound gun, weighing with BM 13.815 ton (*14.037t*) and firing a 200lb (*90.7kg*) shell with 61.9lb (*28.1kg*) SC 150 charge at 2770f/s (*844m/s*).

6in (152.4mm)/50 EOC

Mounted in the minelayer *Helle*, two guns being Pattern NN and one WW. Both generally resembled the British Mk XVII but had a smaller chamber. With 32.75lb (*14.86kg*) CSP$_2$ charge and 100lb (*45.4kg*) shell, MV was 3000f/s (*914m/s*).

128mm (5.04in)/45 QF Rheinmetall

This in the *Vasilevs Georgios* class destroyers, was the same as the German 12.7cm SKC/34, described in that section and actually of 128mm bore.

120mm (4.724in)/50 QF, OTO

Similar to the gun described in the Italian section, but in single mountings in the *Hydra* class destroyers. The recommended British charge was 8.39kg (*18.5lb*) SC 150 for 914m/s (*3000f/s*).

Other guns

These were a 4in (*101.6mm*)/50 QF Bethlehem, as noted under Argentina, in the *Aetos* class destroyers and a French 100mm (*3.937in*)/40 QF, for which details are lacking, in the *Glafkos* and *Katsonis* classes of submarines.

NETHERLANDS

283mm (11.14in)/42.5 QF Krupp

This gun was still mounted in single turrets in the partly disarmed coast defence ship *Soerabaja*. It is generally listed as weighing 31.0t (*30.5 tons*) and firing a 270kg (*595lb*) shell at 890m/s (*2920f/s*). The nearest that has been found in many reliable German lists, is the trunnioned Kst KL/45. This weighed with BM 34.0t (*33.5 tons*), was 42.16cal overall and 39.58cal bore length, and fired a 302kg (*666lb*) shell at 845m/s (*2772f/s*) which is compatible with the above performance figures.

The turret weight with shield is given as 197.4t (*194.3 tons*), elevation +15° -4° and max range 16,100m (*17,600yd*).

240mm (9.449in)/40 QF Krupp

This was in single turrets in the floating batteries *IJmuiden* (ex-*Heemskerck*) and *Vlieerede* (ex-*Hertog Hendrik*). Weight with BM was 24.5t (*24.1 tons*) and bore length 37.15cal. The shell weighed 170kg (*375lb*) and according to German lists MV was 780m/s (*2559f/s*). This figure applies to the guns as used in German coast defence, but higher MVs of 820m/s (*2690f/s*) for *Hendrik* and 850m/s (*2789f/s*) for *Heemskerck* occur in some lists. The latter seems unlikely. Elevation was +20° -4°.

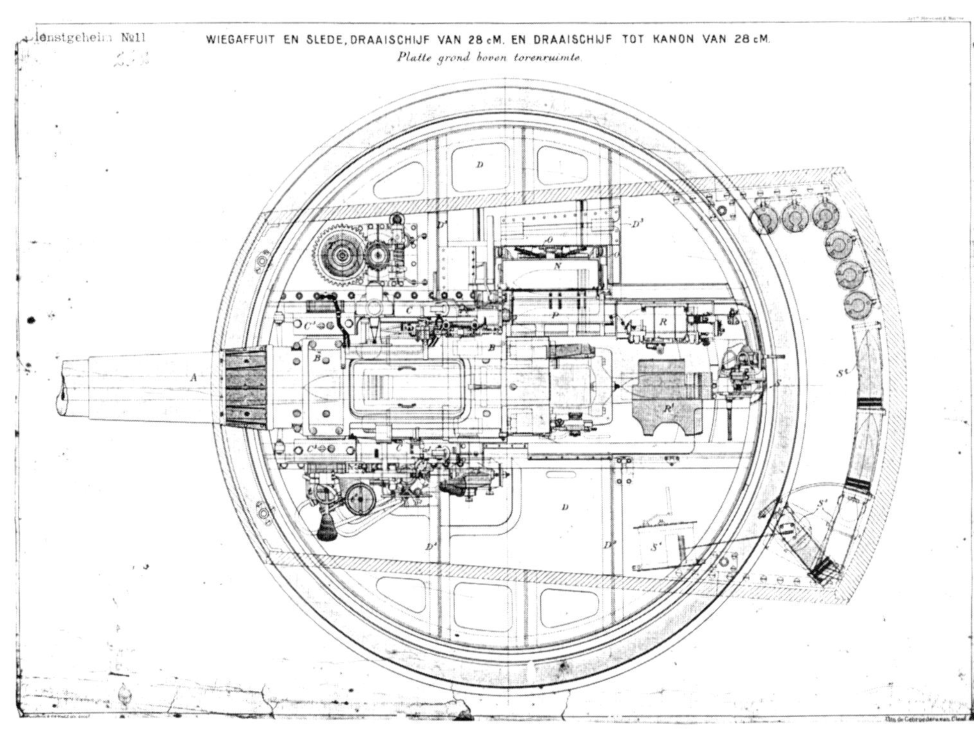

283mm/42.5 Krupp single turret in plan section. *Helders Marinemuseum*

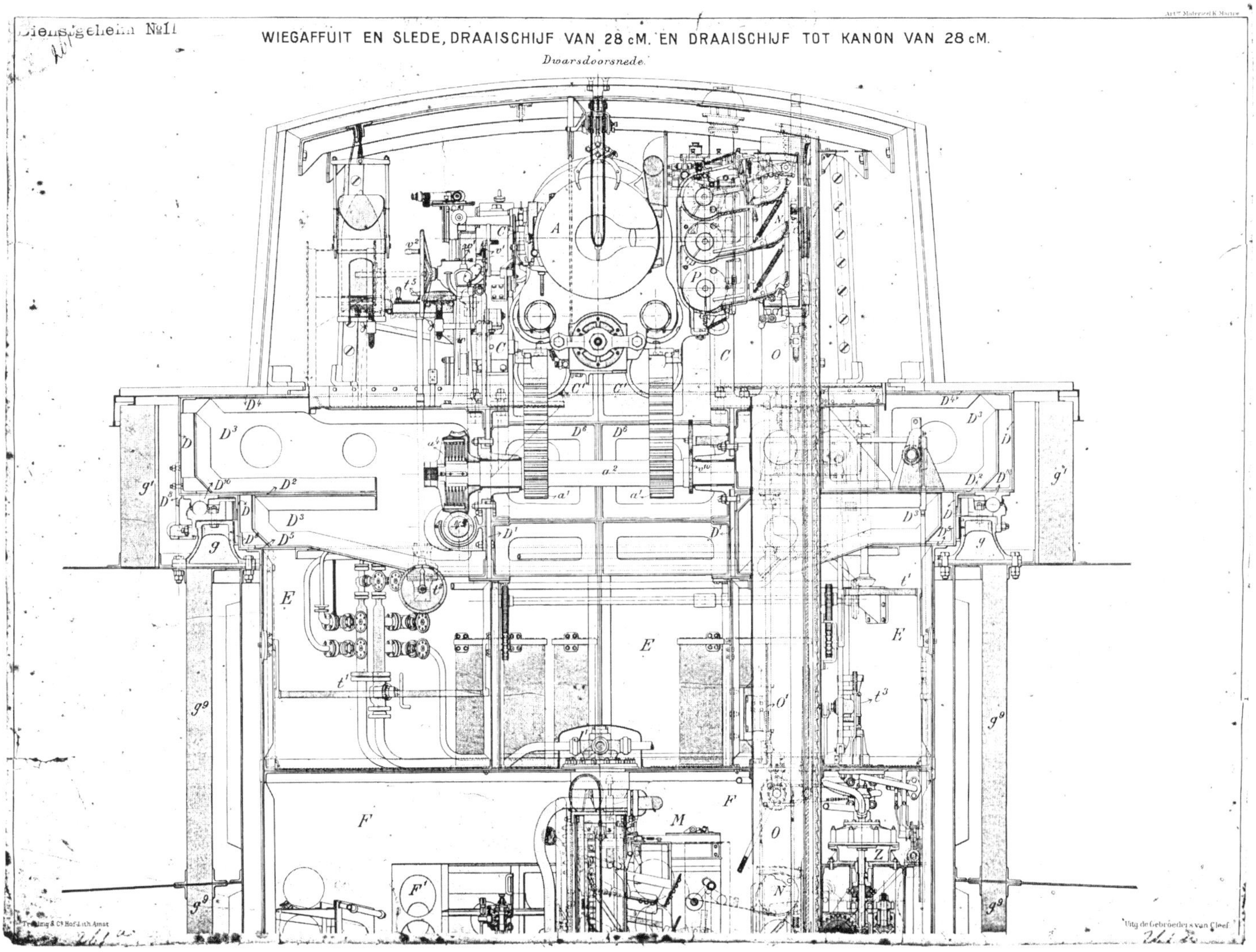

Dienstgeheim No 11

WIEGAFFUIT EN SLEDE, DRAAISCHIJF VAN 28 cM. EN DRAAISCHIJF TOT KANON VAN 28 cM.

Dwarsdoorsnede

283mm/42.5 Krupp single turret for the Dutch *Soerabaja* in transverse section.
Helders Marinemuseum

149.1mm (5.87in)/50 QF

There were several marks of these guns but the differences between them are not fully known. They comprised:

- Mk 6 Bofors M1924 - *Java, Sumatra* - Gun Nos 55-64, 45-54
- Mk 7 Bofors M1925 - *Flores, Soemba* - Gun Nos 65-67, 68-70
- Mk 8 Bofors - *JM van Nassau*
- Mk 9 Wilton-Fijenoord - *De Ruyter* twin
- Mk 10 Wilton-Fijenoord - *De Ruyter* single
- Mk 11 Wilton-Fijenoord - *Tromp* twin - Gun Nos 1-6

Flores and *Soemba* were regunned from *Sumatra* in 1944. It is not know why the series of gun numbers which went back to the *Evertsen* class, launched in 1894, was broken or whether *JM van Nassau* and *De Ruyter* were in the old or another new series. All the above had horizontal sliding breech blocks and similar ballistics firing a 46.7kg (*103lb*) AP or 46kg (*101.4lb*) HE at 900m/s (*2953f/s*). The original charge was 16.7kg (*36.8lb*) and cartridge case 9.5kg (*20.9lb*) while the replacement British propellant was 15.88kg (*35lb*) SC 205 or 17kg (*37.5lb*) NP/S 263-066. Gun weights were 7.24t (*7.13 tons*) to 7.5t (*7.38 tons*) and mountings allowed 60° elevation in the *De Ruyter* and *Tromp* and 29° or 30° in the others. Revolving weights in the *De Ruyter* were 25t (*24.6 tons*) for the single and 70.6 (*69.5 tons*) to 71.2t (*70.1 tons*) for the twins. Shields in this ship were 30mm (*1.2in*).

The Mk 6 gun had an overall length of 52.95 cal and the gun and mounting with 80mm (*3.15in*) maximum shield weighed 20.35t (*20.0 tons*). Range with original shells was 21,200in (*23,200yd*)/29°.

149mm/50 Mk 6, Bofors M1924 gun and mounting for the Dutch *Java* and *Sumatra*.
Bofors, by courtesy of K-E Westerlund

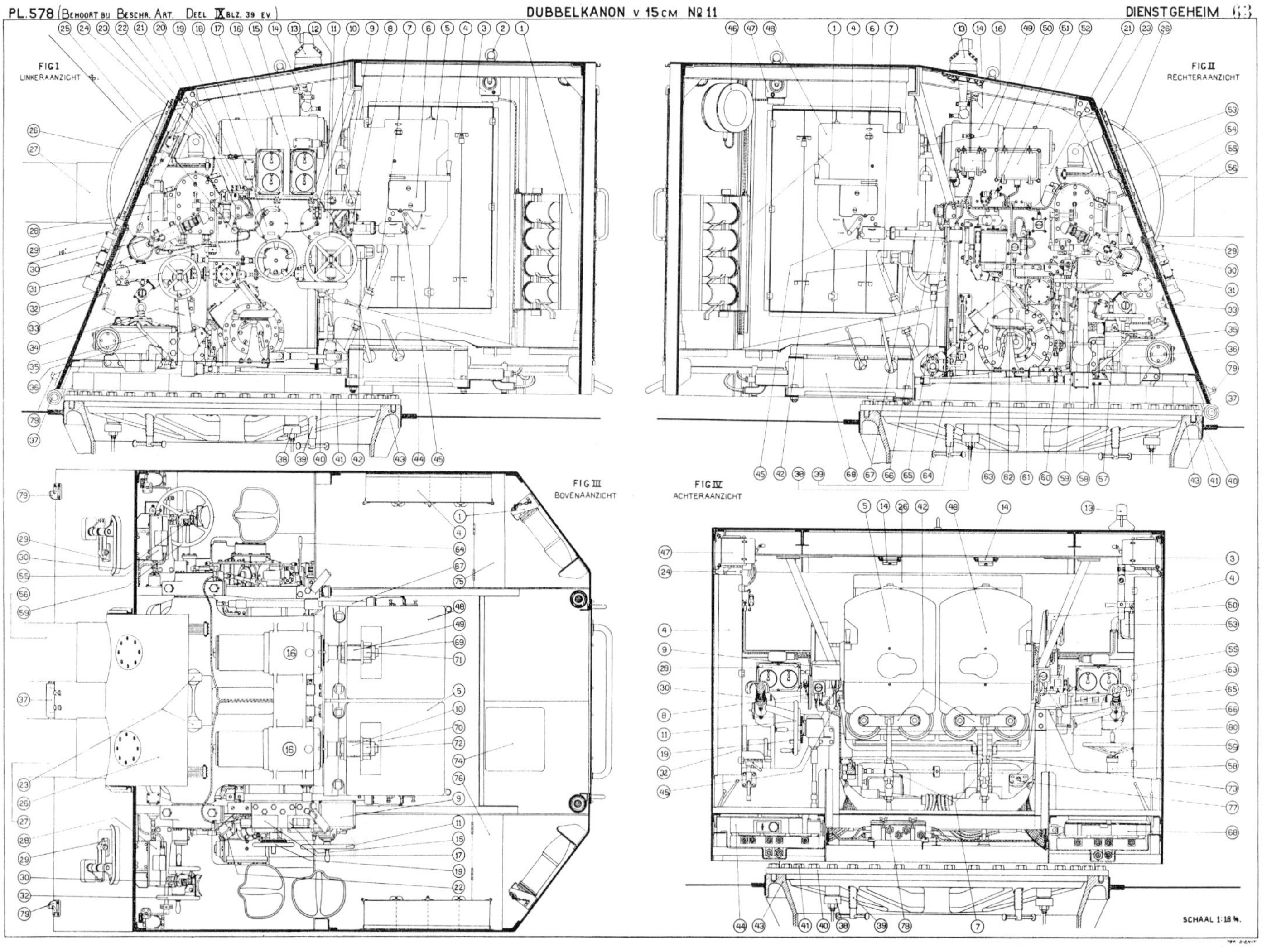

120mm (4.724in)/50 QF

This included the Bofors M1924 Mk 4 in the *Evertsen* class destroyers, the Wilton-Fijenoord Mk 5 and it is believed Mk 6 and 7 in the *Van Galen* class destroyers, the sloop *Van Kinsbergen* and the minelayer *Van der Zaan* respectively. All had horizontal sliding breech blocks and fired a 24kg (*52.9lb*) shell at 900m/s (*2953f/s*). The original charge was 8.8kg (*19.4lb*) and case 8.3kg (*18.3lb*). Gun weights were 3.96-4.27t (*3.90-4.20 tons*) and mountings allowed +30° to +35° max elevation with possibly about 45° in *Van Kinsbergen*.

The Mk 4 gun was 53.25cal overall with a total mounting weight of 10.0t (*9.84 tons*) and range 19,500m (*21,300yd*)/30°.

120mm (4.724in)/45 QF Wilton-Fijenoord

This AA gun, known as Mk 8, was mounted only in ships completed for the Germans, comprising twin and single in the destroyer *ZH1* (ex-*Gerard Callenburgh*) and twin in the gunboats *Z 1 - Z 3*. The gun, which weighed 3.4t (*3.35 tons*) was apparently built with a loose barrel, jacket and removable breech ring and had a vertical sliding breech block. The fixed round weighed 32kg (*70.5lb*) and MV was 800m/s (*2625f/s*) with a 20.5kg (*45.2lb*) shell and 5.0kg (*11lb*) charge.

An experimental twin triaxial mounting was built by Bofors. This weighed 58t (*57 tons*) and was criticised by the Germans as the cross-level axis carried not only most of the shield but also the very heavy casing for the dredger hoists.

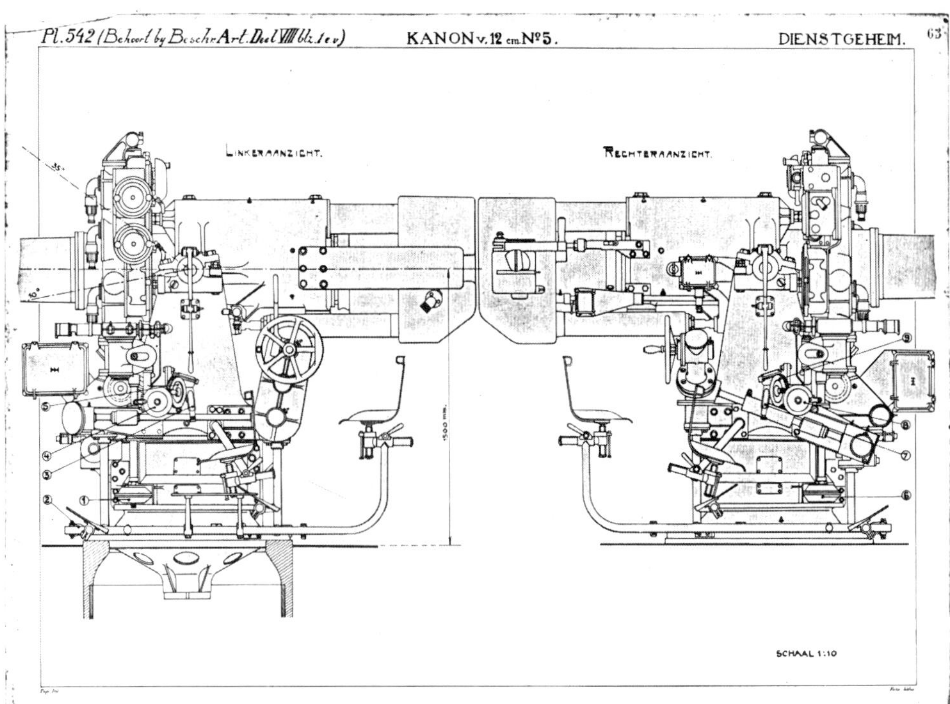

Top: 149mm/50 Mk 11 guns and twin shielded mounting in Dutch *Tromp*, shown in left and right side, plan and rear sections.
Helders Marinemuseum

Above: 120mm/50 Mk 5 gun and mounting for the Dutch *Van Galen* class destroyers, left and right views.
Helders Marinemuseum

Other 120mm (4.724in)

40-calibre QF Krupp guns were in a few old ships.

105mm (4.134in)/50 QF Krupp

Mounted in the *Brinio* class gunboats, this fired an 18kg (*39.7lb*) shell at 883m/s (*2897f/s*). Elevation was +20° -10°.

4in (101.6mm)/45 QF Mk XVI*

Fully described in the British section and in twin mountings in the *Heemskerck* and *Isaac Sweers* as armed in Britain.

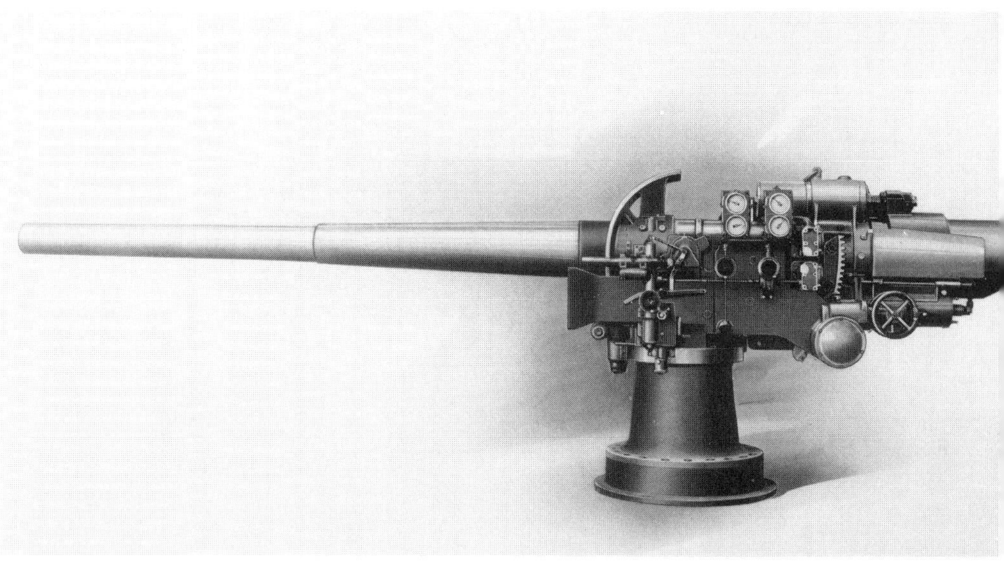

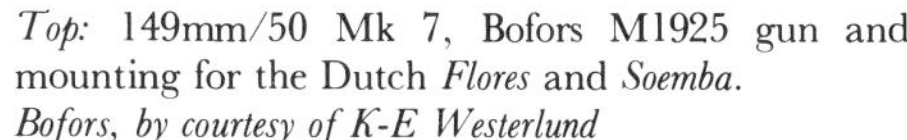

Top: 149mm/50 Mk 7, Bofors M1925 gun and mounting for the Dutch *Flores* and *Soemba*.
Bofors, by courtesy of K-E Westerlund

Centre: 120mm/50 Mk 4, Bofors M1924 gun and mounting for the Dutch *Evertsen* class destroyers.
Bofors, by courtesy of K-E Westerlund

Below: 105mm/50 Krupp gun and mounting for the Dutch *Brinio* class gunboats, side view and plan.
Helders Marinemuseum

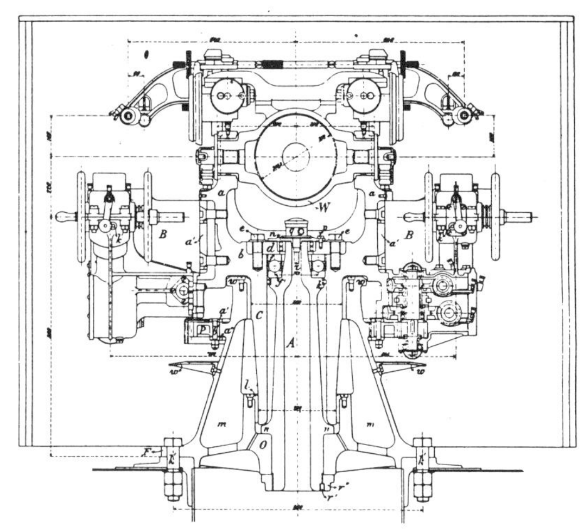

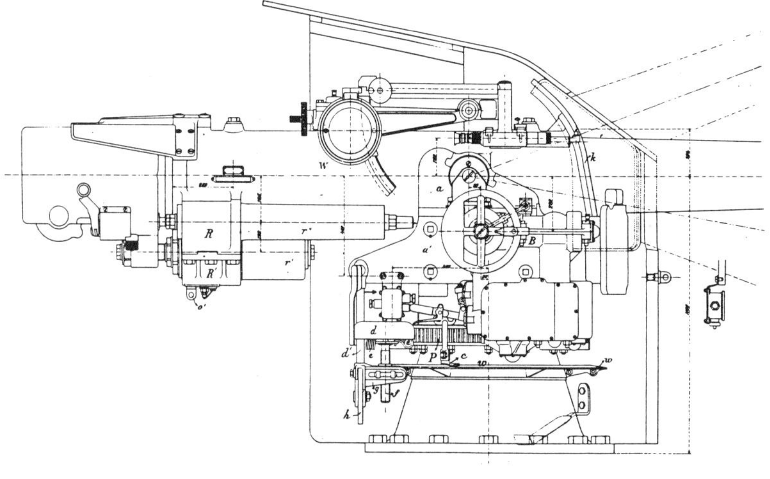

The *Eidsvold* (Norway) armed with 8.24in/43.8cal Elswick guns.
CPL

NORWAY

8.24in (209.3mm)/43.8 EOC

Partly wire-wound BL guns, Patterns B and C, respectively in the *Tordenskjold* and *Norge* class of coast defence ships, though the former are believed to have been disarmed. The guns were in single turrets and Pattern C, which was slightly the lighter, weighed with BM 18.5 tons (*18.8t*). Both fired a 313lb (*142kg*) shell at 2297f/s (*700m/s*). Elevation was apparently +15° -5°.

5.87in (149.1mm)/45.8 EOC

A BL gun, Pattern FF, mounted in the *Norge* class and firing a 99.3lb (*45kg*) shell at 2625f/s (*800m/s*).

120mm (4.724in)/44.1 QF Bofors

A separate ammunition gun in the minelayer *Olav Tryggvason*. With a 21kg (*46.3lb*) shell, MV was 800m/s (*2625f/s*). Elevation is believed to have been +45° -10°.

4.724in (120mm)/43.9 QF EOC

Formerly at least in the *Tordenskjold* class, this was the screw breech Pattern Y with a 45lb (*20.4kg*) shell and MV 2570f/s (*783m/s*).

4in (101.6mm)/45 QF Mk V

Described in the British section and mounted in the torpedo boat *Sleipner* as rearmed.

101.6mm (4in)/40 QF Bofors

There were two versions of this gun, the earlier in the minelayer *Fröya* and the other in the torpedo boats of the *Sleipner* and *Odin* classes. The latter at least fired fixed ammunition, and was retained in the vessels captured by the Germans or completed for them. Both versions fired a 14.1kg (*31.1lb*) shell at 775m/s (*2543f/s*).

PERU

6in (152.4mm)/50 Vickers

This gun, known as Mk J, was in single mountings in the old cruisers *Grau* and *Bolognesi*. It was of partly wire-wound construction and had a chamber of the same volume as in the British Mk XI but of increased length. Weight with BM was 8.01 tons (*8.14t*) and with a 100lb (*45.4kg*) shell MV was 2965f/s (*904m/s*).

101.6mm (4in)/60 QF Russian

Described in the Russian section, this was in the destroyers *Guise* and *Villar* purchased from Estonia. A gun of the same calibre, but of unknown origin and data, was mounted in the depot ship *Lima*.

The Polish destroyers *Blyskawica* and *Grom* in 1940 with 120mm/50 Bofors M34/36 guns.
CPL

POLAND

130mm (5.118in)/40 QF French

This gun was in single and twin mountings in the destroyers *Blyskawica* and *Grom* and the minelayer *Gryf*. It was of loose barrel QF not SA type with horizontal sliding breech block, and fired fixed ammunition, the round being 1.47m (*58in*) long and weighing 41kg (*90.4lb*). The twin mounting was carried on a turn-table and both guns were in a common cradle. As usual in Bofors mountings for medium guns run-out was by springs. Elevation was +30° -3°.

M1924 guns in the destroyers *Burza* and *Wicher* and described in the French section.

120mm (4.724in)/50 QF Bofors M34/36

Gun Data

Bore	120mm	4.724in	
Weight incl BM	4.115t	4.050 tons	
Length oa	6390mm	251.57in	53.25cal
Length bore	*c*6000mm	*c*236.22in	*c*50.0cal
Length chamber	*c*936mm	*c*36.85in	
Volume chamber	14.5dm^3	885in^3	
Rifling grooves	36, incr twist		
Weight projectile	24kg	52.9lb	
Propellant charge	9.4kg Swedish 868cal (WL)	20.7lb	
Muzzle velocity	900m/s	2953f/s	
Working pressure	3300kg/cm^2	20.95 tons/in^2	
Max range	19,500m/30°	21,300yd/30°	

Gun Mounting Data

Total weight incl guns, shield	20.5t	20.2 tons
Recoil distance	55cm	21.7in
Shield weight	2.85t	2.8 tons
Shield thickness	7mm	0.276in

105mm (4.134in)/41 QF Bofors

In the *Orzel* class submarines, this gun fired a 16kg (*35.3lb*) shell at 700m/s (*2297f/s*).

4in (101.6mm)/45 QF Mk XVI*

Fully described in the British section and in twin mountings in the rearmed *Blyskawica*.

100mm (3.937in)/40 QF French

In *Wilk* class submarines but details are lacking, though in appearance it resembles the 45cal gun in the French *Requin* class.

The Polish submarine *Orzel* with a 105mm/41 Bofors gun.
CPL

PORTUGAL

4.724in (120mm)/50 QF Vickers Armstrong

This gun known as Mk G, was in single mountings in the *Vouga* class destroyers and the *Albuquerque*, *Velho* and *Nunes* classes of sloops. It was built with inner A tube, A tube, jacket and breech ring and had a horizontal sliding breech block. It forms an interesting comparison with the British Mk XI.

Gun Data

Bore	4.724in	120mm	
Weight incl BM	3.342 tons	3.396t	
Length oa	247.7in	6291.5mm	52.43cal
Length bore	236.22in	6000mm	50.0cal
Length chamber	33.46in	850mm	
Volume chamber	$685in^3$	$11.225dm^3$	
Length rifling	199.59in	5069.5mm	
Weight projectile	48.5lb	22kg	
Propellant charge	15.78lb MDT 52/13	7.158kg MDT 52/13	
Muzzle velocity	3002f/s	915m/s	
Working pressure	19.5-20 tons/in^2	3070-3150kg/cm^2	
Max range	*c*21,300yd/45°	*c*19,500m/45°	

The *Vouga* (Portugal) showing 4.7in/50 Vickers Armstrong Mk G guns.
CPL

4in (101.6mm)/40 QF Vickers Armstrong

Mk M, mounted in the *Delfim* class submarines, was generally similar to the British Mk XII* but had A tube and jacket with SA BM. The chamber was slightly larger and, with a 31lb (*14.06kg*) shell and 5.344lb (*2.424kg*) MD 16 charge, MV was 2274f/s (*693m/s*).

Other guns

The sloops *Republica* and *Araujo* had British 4in (*101.6mm*) QF Mk IV and the old destroyer *Tamega* apparently still had the 3.937in (*100mm*)/41 QF EOC Pattern N firing a 28.66lb (*13kg*) shell at 2390f/s (*728m/s*).

ROMANIA

There is little data on the guns in Romanian ships, but it is believed that they are correctly identified in the following.

120mm (4.724in)/50 QF Bofors

In *Regele Ferdinand* class destroyers. Probably of similar performance to those in Netherlands navy.

120mm (4.724in)/45 Italian

In *Marasti* class destroyers and probably Schneider-Canet-Armstrong M1918 and 1918-19 noted in the Italian section.

120mm (4.724in)/40 QF Skoda

Former Austrian guns in river monitors *Basarabia* and *Bucovina* firing a 23.77kg (*52.4lb*) shell at 690m/s (*2264f/s*).

120mm (4.724in)/35 QF Krupp

In river monitors of the *Bratianu* class and also the *Ardeal*, firing a shell as above at 650m/s (*2132f/s*).

105mm (4.134in) Ubts KL/45

This gun in the submarine *Marsuinul* is noted in the German section.

105mm (4.134in) SKC/32

In the minelayer *Murgescu* and described in the German section.

101.6mm (4in)/35 QF Italian

Noted in the Italian section and believed to have been in the submarine *Delfinul*.

100mm (3.937in)/45 QF French

Of First World War or previous date, this gun was in the ex-French gunboats of the *Lt Remus* class and is noted in that section.

SPAIN

15in (381mm)/45 Vickers Mk B

Eighteen of these guns were supplied for coast defence between 1929 and 1935, to a design originally intended for the projected Brazilian battleship *Riachuelo* cancelled in 1914. It was built with an A tube, three B tubes, C tube and jacket with a short breech ring, shrunk collar and breech bush screwing into the jacket. Weight with BM was 86.9 tons (*88.3t*), length overall 695.7in (*17,670.8mm*), chamber volume 21,665in^3 (*355dm^3*) and working pressure 19 tons/in^2 (*3000kg/cm^2*). With a 1951lb (*885kg*) shell and 441lb (*200kg*) charge, MV was 2500f/s (*762m/s*). Range at 40° was 38,386yd (*35,100m*).

8in (203.2mm)/50 Vickers Armstrong

Known as Mk D this was mounted in twin turrets in the *Canarias*. The principal components of the gun were an A tube, B tube not extending to the muzzle, and jacket. It was lighter than the British Mk VIII, weighing 15.8 tons (*16.05t*) including BM. With a 256lb (*116.1kg*) shell and 80lb (*36.3kg*) propellant charge, MV was 2904f/s (*885m/s*) and maximum range 32,530yd (*29,750m*) at *c*49°.

The mountings generally resembled the British Mk II and had similar hollow rammers for holding the propellant charges, but the roller path diameter was reduced from 18ft (*5.49m*) to 15ft (*4.57m*) with the turret structure angled outwards above. The barbette internal diameter was 19ft (*5.79m*) instead of 20ft 6in (*6.25m*) and the gunhouse was also smaller with the gun axes 76in (*1.93m*) apart instead of 84in (*2.13m*). Elevation was +50° -3° with loading at 8°, and the turret shield was 1in (*25mm*) thick.

6in (152.4mm)/50 Vickers Carraca

Gun Data

Weight incl BM	8.6 tons	8.74t	
Length oa	309.728in	7867.1mm	51.62cal
Length bore	300in	7620mm	50.0cal
Length chamber	35.037in	889.94mm	
Volume chamber	1550in^3	25.40dm^3	
Length rifling	261.723in	6647.76mm	
Weight projectile	100lb	45.4kg	
Propellant charge	33lb	15kg	
Muzzle velocity	2953f/s	900m/s	
Range	*c*22,300yd/35°	*c*20,400m/35°	

Mk T and U BL guns carried in single and twin mountings in the *Cervera* class and in single in the *Mendez Nunez* and *Navarra*. The construction was of built up type with A tube, three B tubes, jacket and breech ring. Earlier mountings allowed 15° elevation, possibly later increased to the 35° of the *Cervera* class. The mean roller path diameter of the twin mounting was 10ft (*3.05m*).

Single mounted 6in/50 Vickers Carraca guns in the Spanish cruiser *Mendez Nunez*.
CPL

Known as Mk F, this was in single AA mountings in the *Canarias* and reconstructed *Mendez Nunez* though the latter was not in service again until 1947. The gun was built with an A tube, jacket, not to the muzzle, and breech ring. The SA BM had a horizontal sliding block and maximum elevation was 80°. The loading gear was powered by compressed air and the fixed round weighed 79.4lb (*36kg*).

4.724in (120mm)/45 QF Vickers Armstrong

Gun Data

Weight incl BM	2.95 tons	3.00t	
Length oa	224.08in	5691.6mm	47.43cal
Length bore	212.58in	5399.5mm	45.0cal
Chamber volume	630in^3	10.32dm^3	
Weight projectile	48.5lb	22.0kg	
Propellant charge	14.33lb CSP_2	6.5kg CSP_2	
Muzzle velocity	2800f/s	853m/s	
Working pressure	20 tons/in^2	3150kg/cm^2	

This or a similar gun was also in the *Antequera* class destroyers and *Jupiter* class minelayers on LA mountings, but precise data are lacking.

The Spanish destroyer *Almirante Antequera* in 1937 showing after 4.7in/45 guns.
CPL

4.724in (120mm)/45 Vickers Carraca

A BL gun mounted in the *Barcaiztegui* class destroyers and firing a 48.5lb (*22.0kg*) shell at 2789f/s (*850m/s*).

120mm (4.724in)/45 Italian

In the ex-Italian *Ceuta* class destroyers, and probably Schneider-Canet-Armstrong M 1918/19 noted in that section.

105mm (4.134in)/45 SKC 32

This is believed to have been mounted in the rearmed *Cervera* as an AA gun, and also in the *Eolo* class minelayers and the rearmed gunboat *Canalejas*. The gun is described in the German section.

4in (101.6mm)/45 and /40 QF Vickers Carraca

Respectively Mk L in the unrearmed *Cervera* class as AA and the *Alsedo* class destroyers as LA, and Mk K in the *Dato* class gunboats and *Sotelo*.

Both were built-up guns otherwise resembling the British QF Mk V and Mk IV, but with higher MV of 2700f/s (*823m/s*) and 2300f/s (*701m/s*).

Other Italian guns in ex-Italian ships

The *Huesca* class destroyers mounted 101.6mm (*4in*)/45 QF and the *Mola* class submarines 100mm (*3.937in*)/47 or possibly 43 QF. These are noted in the Italian section.

SWEDEN

Unless otherwise noted all Swedish guns were Bofors.

This gun was mounted in twin turrets in the *Sverige* class and was of built-up construction with a hand-operated screw breech block of the Bofors ogival type. Loading was at 0° and the electrically powered turrets had hoists broken at the working chamber. Elevation was originally +20° -5° and according to some reports later increased to +35° -5°, though there appears to be little space for this.

283mm (11.14in)/45 M12

Gun Data

Bore	283mm	11.14in	
Weight incl BM	44.1t	43.4 tons	
Length oa	12,735mm	501.38in	45.0cal
Length bore	*c*12,295mm	*c*484.06in	*c*43.45cal
Length chamber	1660mm	65.35in	
Length rifling	10,515mm	413.98in	
Grooves	80		
Twist	1 in 50 to 1 in 28		
Weight projectile	305kg	672.4lb	
Propellant charge	100kg	220.5lb	
Muzzle velocity	870m/s	2854f/s	
Working pressure	3000kg/cm^2	19 tons/in^2	
Max range	29,000m/35°	31,700yd/35°	

Gun Mounting Data

Revolving weight	353.7t	348.1 tons
Barbette int dia	*c*7.0m	*c*23ft
Distance apart gun axes	*c*2.1m	*c*83in
Recoil distance	73cm	28.7in
Max elevating speed	5°/sec	
Max training speed	4°/sec	
Firing cycle	20sec	
Turret shield	face 20cm	face 8in

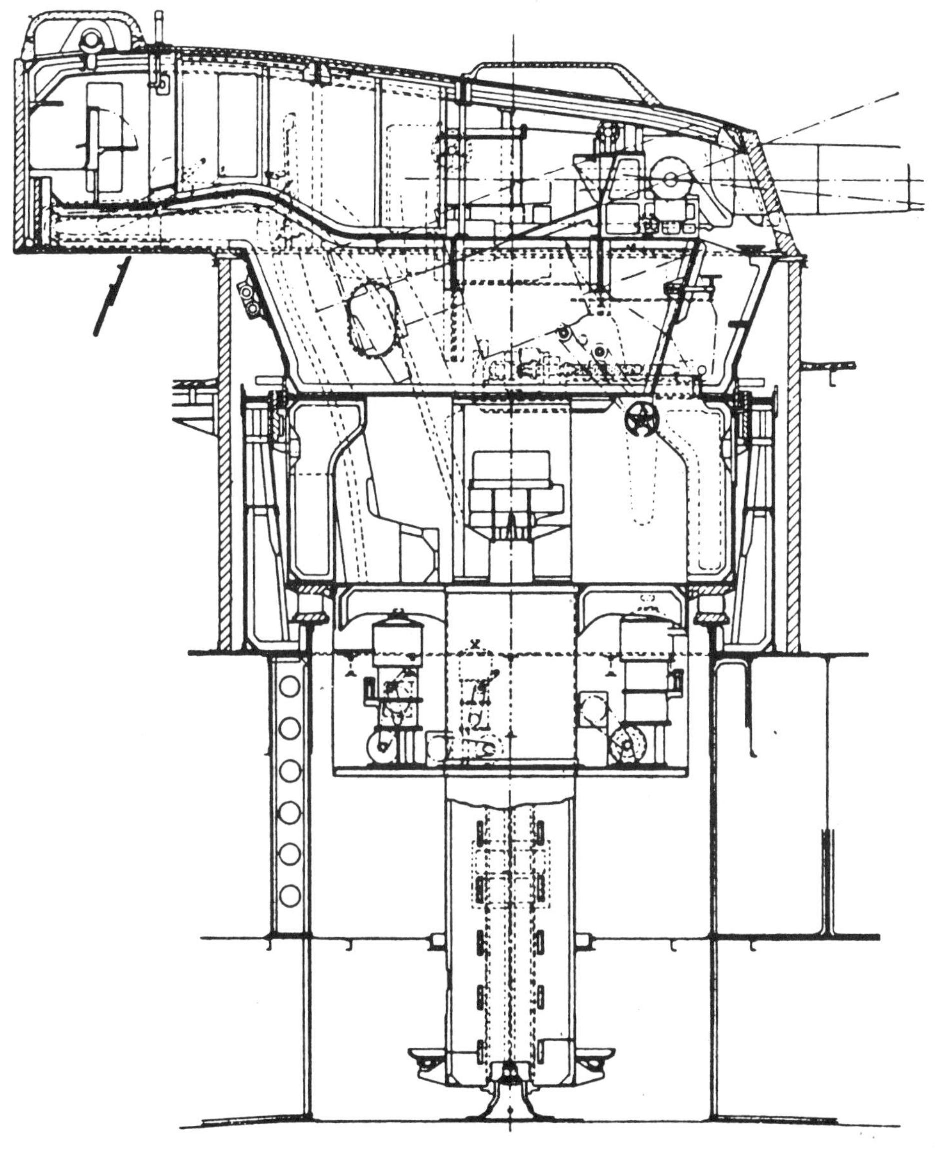

Bofors 283mm/45 M12 guns in twin turret in *Sverige* class (Sweden), longitudinal section.
Bofors, by courtesy of K-E Westerlund

Left: The first Bofors 283mm/45 M12 gun on the proving ground 1913.
Bofors, by courtesy of K-E Westerlund

Below: Interior of twin turret in Swedish cruiser *Gotland* showing breech end of 152mm/55 M30 gun.
Bofors, by courtesy of K-E Westerlund

210mm (8.268in)/44.4 M98

This BL gun was in single turrets in the *Oscar II* and the *Äran* class and fired at 125kg (*276lb*) shell at 750m/s (*2461f/s*), or a 120kg (*265lb*) at 775m/s (*2543f/s*).

152.4mm (6in)/55 M30

A built-up BL gun with ogival screw breech block mounted in twin turrets and single casemates in the *Gotland*. Length was 55.12cal overall, weight with BM 10.2t (*10.04 tons*) and MV 900m/s (*2953f/s*) with a 46kg (*101lb*) shell and 16.5kg (*36.4lb*) charge. The twin turrets were electrically powered with hydraulic drive gear, and the guns were in separate cradles, normally coupled together. Elevation was +60° -10° with loading at +20° -10° but the casemate mountings elevated to 30° only. The turret revolving weight with 20mm (*0.8in*) maximum shield was 72t (*70.9 tons*) and range 24,400m (*26,700yd*).

152.4mm (6in)/50 M12

Another BL gun in single and twin turrets in the *Sverige* class. Weight was 7.75t (*7.63 tons*) with BM and with a 46kg (*101lb*) shell MV was 850m/s (*2789f/s*).

152.4mm (6in)/50 M03

In twin turrets in the *Oscar II* and *Fylgia*, this gun was similar to M12 and had the same performance.

152.4mm (6in)/44.4 M98

A BL gun in single turrets in the *Äran* class and in single mountings in the minelayer *Älvsnabben*. Weight with BM was 5.91t (*5.82 tons*) and with a 45.4kg (*100lb*) shell MV was 750m/s (*2461f/s*).

120mm (4.724in)/45 M24-24C

These guns were in single mountings in the *Ehrensköld* class (M24), *Klas Horn* class (M24B) and *Göteborg* and *Visby* classes (M24C). The main difference was that M24C was of loose barrel type. All had horizontal sliding breech blocks, were 46cal overall length and fired a 21kg (*46.3lb*) shell at 800m/s (*2625f/s*) with 4.9kg (*10.8lb*) charge. Separate ammunition was used, the cartridge weighing 10.15kg (*22.4lb*) and elevation was +45° -10° giving a range of 19,300m (*21,100yd*). For M24C the gun and BM weighed 3.00t (*2.95 tons*) and the complete mounting with 5mm (*0.2in*) shield 8.7t (*8.56 tons*).

Above: Bofors 120mm/45 M24B gun and mounting for the Swedish *Klas Horn* class destroyers.
Bofors, by courtesy of K-E Westerlund

120mm (4.72in)/50 M11

Mounted in the minelayer *Clas Fleming*, this gun fired a 21kg (*46.3lb*) shell at 860m/s (*2822f/s*).

105mm (4.134in)/50 QF M42

Mounted as AA in the *Mode* class torpedo boats this gun fired a 16.5kg (*36.4lb*) shell at 830m/s (*2723f/s*). The fixed round weighed 26kg (*57lb*).

105mm (4.134in)/41 QF M40

As AA in the *Arholma* class minesweepers, this had the same weight of shell as in the above, but MV was 700m/s (*2297f/s*).

105mm (4.134in)/41 QF M25

Mounted in the *Draken* class submarines, this fired a 16kg (*35.3lb*) shell at 700m/s (*2297f/s*).

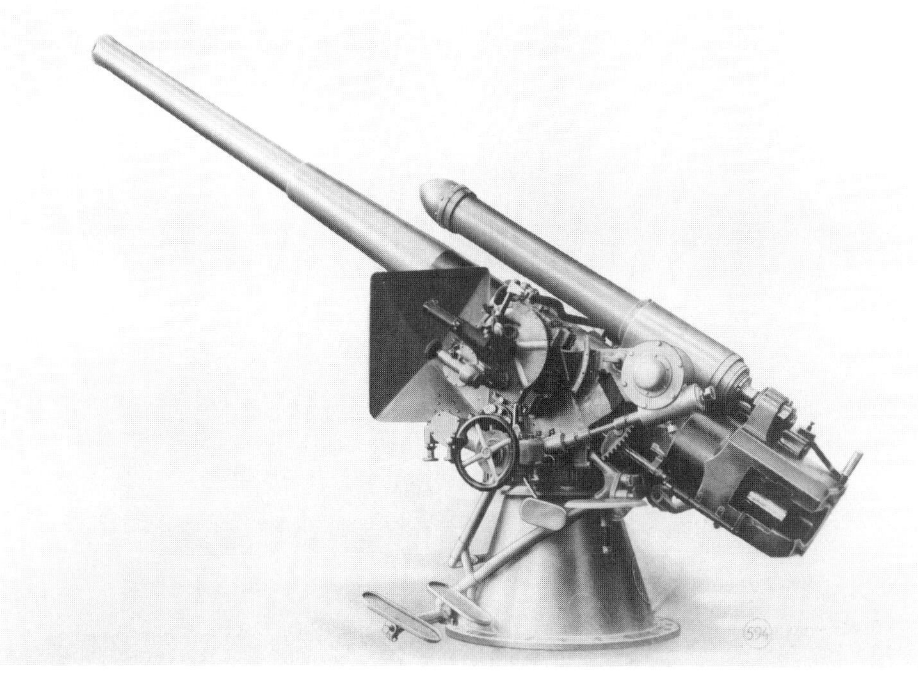

Bofors 105mm/41 M25 gun and mounting as in the Swedish *Draken* class submarines.
Bofors, by courtesy of K-E Westerlund

Italian guns in purchased Italian ships

These comprised 120mm (*4.724in*)/45 OTO 1926 in *Psilander* and *Puke* and 100mm (*3.937in*)/47, probably OTO 1931, in *Romulus* and *Remus*. Both are described in the Italian section.

THAILAND

203.2mm (8in)/50 Japanese

There is no definite information on this gun which was in twin turrets in the *Ayuthia* class coast-defence ships. It may be noted that Vickers-Armstrong designed a twin turret to take Mk D guns as in the *Canarias*. The roller path diameter was unchanged but the gunhouse was smaller and elevation +45° -3° with loading at +7°. Revolving weight with 3in (*75mm*) max shield, was 161 tons (*163.6t*).

6in (152.4mm)/50 EOC

It is not clear whether these guns, mounted in single turrets in the *Ratanokosindra* class gunboats, were Pattern TT, that is the British Mk VII, or Mk XXI, a coast-defence version of Mk XVII and differing only in a larger chamber of 1825in^3 (*29.91dm^3*). With a 100lb (*45.4kg*) shell MV was 3000f/s (*914m/s*) and range at the 30° maximum elevation of the mounting 20,430yd (*18,680m*).

Other guns

These comprised a Japanese 120mm (*4.724in*)/45 in the *Tachin* class sloops and the British 4in (*101.6mm*) QF Mk IV in the old destroyer *Phra Ruang*.

TURKEY

283mm (11.14in) SKL/50

This was mounted in twin turrets in the *Yavuz*, formerly the German battle-cruiser *Goeben*. The gun is noted in the German section but with different ammunition from that originally carried. This comprised a 302kg (*666lb*) shell and 106kg (*234lb*) RPC/12 charge giving a muzzle velocity of 880m/s (*2887f/s*). By 1918 elevation had been increased to 22½° from the original 13½° and range was 21,700m (*23,730yd*), the shell having a rather blunt head. It is not known whether ammunition and mountings had been altered by 1939. The latter

Gun Mounting Data, original

Weight (heaviest turret)	444.5t	437.5 tons
Ball track dia	6.92m	22ft 8½in
Barbette int dia	8.1m	26ft 7in
Max elevating speed	4°/sec	
Max training speed	3.3°/sec	
Turret shield	face 230mm; sides 180mm; rear 230mm; roof 90-60mm	face 9in; sides 7in; rear 9in; roof 3.5-2.4in

was originally electrically powered with elevation through hydraulic drive. The guns were in separate cradles but could be coupled together via the elevating gear. Loading and ramming as well as the BM were hand operated. Shell rooms were below magazines with separate lower hoists and transfer in the working chamber. The upper shell hoists came up between and in rear of the guns, with hand-worked trays moving sideways into the loading position, but the upper cartridge hoists came up near the turret centre on the outside of the guns with separate slides to the breech end for main and fore charges. The former were transferred by hand-worked cartridge trays, while the latter were picked up and placed in position for loading. The hoists could supply three rounds per gun in 51sec including loading and unloading the hoists, and the firing cycle with a strong and well trained crew was about 20sec.

The Turkish destroyer *Kocatepe* with 120mm/50 Ansaldo or OTO guns.
CPL

149.1mm (5.87in) SKL/45

This gun is noted in the German section and was mounted in the secondary battery of the *Yavuz* and also in the old cruiser *Hamidiye*. Elevation was originally 19° in the former.

130mm (5.118in)/55 Russian

Mounted in the old cruiser *Mecidiye*, this BL gun was Vickers Mk A.

120mm (4.724in)/50 QF Ansaldo, OTO

Similar to the gun described in the Italian section and carried in single mountings by the *Adatepe* class and in twins by the *Zafer* class of destroyers.

4.724in (120mm) QF Mk IX**

The well-known British gun mounted in destroyers of the *Demirhisar* class.

105mm (4.134in) Ubts KL/45

Noted in the German section and mounted in the *Atilay* class submarines and probably in the *Gur*.

4in (101.6mm) QF Mk XX

Noted in the British section, this was Vickers Armstrong Mk M* and mounted in the *Burac Reis* class submarines.

Other guns

The submarines *Sakarya* and *Dumlupynar* may have mounted 100mm (*3.937in*)/43 Italian guns and the old torpedo gunboats *Berk* and *Peyk* originally had 105mm (*4.134in*)/40 Krupp, but these may have been changed on reconstruction.

YUGOSLAVIA

140mm (5.512in)/56 Skoda

This gun was in single mountings in the *Dubrovnik*. Weight with BM was 6t (*5.9 tons*) and separate QF ammunition was fired. The shell weighed 39.8kg (*87.7lb*), MV was 880m/s (*2887f/s*), and as the shell was boat tailed, range at 45° was 23,400m (*25,600yd*).

120mm (4.724in)/46 Skoda

A separate ammunition QF gun in single mountings in the *Beograd* class destroyers. Weight with BM was 3.8t (*3.74 tons*), and a 24kg (*52.9lb*) shell was fired at 850m/s (*2789f/s*).

120mm (4.724in)/40 Skoda, /35 Krupp

Noted in the Romanian section. The first was in the river monitors *Vardar* and *Drava* and the second in *Sava* and *Morava*.

The *Dubrovnik* (Yugoslavia) showing 140mm/56 Skoda guns.
CPL

Other guns

The submarines of the *Hrabri* class are believed to have had British 4in (*101.6mm*) QF Mk IV, but the AA guns of about this calibre in the *Galeb* class minelayers and aircraft tender *Zmaj* have not been identified.

SMALLER GUNS

These fell into three groups, the first of 90mm (*3.543in*), 88mm (*3.465in*), 87mm (*3.425in*), 83mm (*3.268in*), 88mm being the most common, the second of 76.2mm (*3in*) and 75mm (*2.953in*) and the third of 40mm (*1.575in*), 37mm (*1.457in*), 25mm (*0.984in*), 20mm (*0.787in*) and smaller. In most cases guns of equivalent performance can be found in the major navies, but details of a few from the first two groups are given below.

Of automatic guns the most interesting was an experimental 57mm (*2.244in*)/60 Bofors firing a 2.7kg (*5.95lb*) shell at 900m/s (*2953f/s*), and tried in single mountings in the Swedish coast defence ships *Oscar II* and *Manligheten*.

Miscellaneous Small Guns

Gun	**Weight incl BM**	**Projectile**	**MV**	**Notes**
88mm (*3.543in*)/45 Bofors, Wilton-Fijenoord	1.665t (*1.639 tons*)	10kg (*22lb*)	800m/s (*2625f/s*)	Netherlands submarines
3in (*76.2mm*)/50 Vickers Armstrong Mk H, J	1.162 tons (*1.181t*)	14.3lb (*6.5kg*)	2559f/s (*780m/s*)	Argentina, Chile, Portugal, ? Spain
75mm (*2.952in*)/60 Bofors M1928	1.22t (*1.2 tons*)	6.8kg (*15lb*)	830m/s (*2723f/s*)	Sweden
75mm (*2.953in*)/55 Bofors, Wilton-Fijenoord	1.385t (*1.363 tons*)	5.9kg (*13lb*)	895m/s (*2936f/s*)	Netherlands

88mm/45 gun in the Dutch submarine *K VIII*.
By courtesy of F J IJselling

The prototype 40mm Bofors gun made for the Swedish Navy. It is shown on a wheeled carriage for transport between the factory and range. The first serviceable 40mm gun was completed in the late summer of 1930 and the first automatic shots were fired on 17 October. Much development work was still needed, and the first fully automatic salvo was not fired until 10 November 1931. Official trials took place on 21 March 1932. The further history of the gun is given in the British and USA sections.
Bofors, by courtesy of K-E Westerlund

TORPEDOES

Nearly all the minor navies relied on imported torpedoes, the principal exceptions being Sweden and Norway with manufacture at Karlskrona or from 1941 Motala and Horten respectively. As previously noted an airborne Horten 45cm (*17.7in*) was adopted by Germany, and a Swedish Lesto turbine was tested in Britain in 1936 with much interest. Unlike most torpedo turbines this ran at the very high speed of 60,100rpm at which 310 BHP was developed, but the power/weight ratio was less than in a burner cycle engine and unit consumption of expendables considerably higher.

Details are given of a few of the higher performance torpedoes used by Sweden and the Netherlands.

Swedish electric 53.3cm M27 UE torpedo being hoisted aboard a submarine.
By courtesy of K-E Westerlund

53.3cm (21in)

Swedish type M27 JA. A Karlskrona torpedo with nine-cylinder W engine, length 7.5m (*24ft 7in*), weight 1680kg (*3704lb*), volume air vessel 640 litres (*22.6ft*^{3}), pressure 170kg/cm^2 (*2420lb/in*^{2}), explosive charge 250kg (*551lb*) TNT/HND, 10,000m (*10,900yd*)/33kts, 20,000m (*21,900yd*)/26kts. The high-speed range is given as 2000m (*2200yd*)/40kts, which would seem to be an error for 5000m (*5470yd*).

53.3cm (21in)

Swedish electric M27 UE. This was intended for submarines and was also from Karlskrona. The range is quoted as 2000m (*2200yd*)/36kts, 3000m (*3300yd*)/33kts and shows unusually high speeds for an electric torpedo of the war period.

53.3cm (21in)

Weymouth for Netherlands. This appears to have had the highest performance of various Weymouth, Fiume and St Tropez torpedoes. The engine was a two-cylinder horizontal, length 7.2m (*23ft 7in*), weight 1650kg (*3638lb*), volume air vessel 583 litres (*20.6ft*^{3}), pressure 200kg/cm^2 (*2850lb/in*^{2}), explosive charge 350kg (*772lb*) TNT, range 4000m (*4400yd*)/45kts, 12,000m (*13,100yd*)/28kts. It is thought to be the torpedo known as Mk X*** in Britain.

45cm (17.7in)

Horten airborne for Netherlands. This was intended for dropping at 100kts and up to 80m (*260ft*). Details are not certain but it is believed, length 4.8m (*15ft 9in*), weight 740kg (*1631lb*), explosive charge 150kg (*331lb*), range 1500m (*1640yd*)/45 kts, 5000m (*5470yd*)/30kts.

Another 45cm (*17.7in*) Horten torpedo with four cylinder radial engine, but not certainly airborne, had length 5.43m (*17ft 10in*), weight 820kg (*1808lb*), explosive charge 180kg (*397lb*) TNT, range 2500m (*2730yd*)/40kts, 6700m (*7300yd*)/28 kts.

There was also a 53.3cm (*21in*) Horten airborne torpedo but it is not known if it was ever used. Length is given as 5.0m (*16ft 5in*), explosive charge 250kg (*551lb*), range 2000m (*2200yd*)/42kts.

Swedish 53.3cm M27 JA torpedo for destroyers.
By courtesy of K-E Westerlund

MINES

Many countries relied at least in part, on Vickers types. Swedish Lindholmen-Motala mines were also used by some navies as were Sautter-Harlé.

DENMARK

Lindholmen-Motala moored contact mine

Described under Sweden.

Vickers H3

A moored mine with seven Hertz horns and shell 1.04m (*41in*) diameter. Total weight was 960kg (*2116lb*), charge 140/200kg (*309/441lb*) and mooring wire 180m (*98 fathoms*) or 300m (*164 fathoms*).

Another moored mine had a charge of 60/70kg (*132/154lb*) and two push-rod horns. The firing battery was on land.

FINLAND

Lindholmen-Motala moored contact mine

Described under Sweden.

Vickers T2

An egg-shaped moored mine with Hertz horns and shell 0.89m (*35in*) in diameter. Total weight was 935kg (*2061lb*), charge 200kg (*441lb*) and mooring wire 150m (*82 fathoms*).

SII

A mine with Hertz horns which could be used for the vertical tubes of submarines. Other details not known.

NETHERLANDS

Vickers T2

Described under Finland.

Vickers H2

A moored mine with six Hertz horns and shell diameter 0.97m (*38in*). Total weight was 896kg (*1975lb*), charge 200kg (*441lb*) and mooring wire 110m (*60 fathoms*) or 365m (*200 fathoms*).

Vickers H5A

Apparently under trial, this moored mine had Hertz horns with a 21m (*69ft*) upper antenna. The shell was 1.00m (*39in*) diameter, total weight 964kg (*2125lb*), charge 250kg (*551lb*), mooring wire 180m (*98 fathoms*) or 300m (*164 fathoms*), and maximum depth of mine 100m (*55 fathoms*).

Sautter-Harlé H1

An old type of mine with 75kg (*165lb*) charge.

German U-boat mine of 1914–18

A moored contact mine of near spherical form with four or five Hertz horns and 116kg (*256lb*) charge.

Controlled ground mine

This was fired from land and weighed 636kg (*1402lb*) with 456kg (*1005lb*) charge.

NORWAY

Mine with pendulum firing

Data uncertain but of moored type with charge in range 40/90kg (*88/198lb*).

Tendapp-Mine HII/400

A moored mine with six Hertz horns and 150kg (*331lb*) charge.

POLAND

SM5

Carried in Polish submarines in 1939, this was the Sautter-Harlé HS4AR, described in the French section.

Polish SM5 mine for submarines, actually the Sautter-Harlé HS4AR.
P Budzbon

ROMANIA

The mines used were Vickers H3 and Sautter-Harlé HS1 and HS4, described under Denmark and France, but H3 is given with six Hertz horns and antenna.

SWEDEN

Vickers T2

Described under Finland.

Lindholmen-Motala M18

A moored mine with four Hertz horns and oblong shell. The total weight is given as 740kg (*1631lb*), charge 150/200kg (*331/441lb*) and mooring wire 200m (*109 fathoms*) or 1500m (*820 fathoms*). M24, F32 and F2 were for submarines, with charges of 100kg (*220lb*), 150kg (*331lb*) and 200kg (*441lb*) respectively.

Controlled magnetic mine

A moored mine with non-magnetic cylindrical shell and fired singly or in groups from land and also automatically. Total weight 740kg (*1631lb*) and charge 200kg (*441lb*).

Airborne magnetic mine

Copied and developed by Asea from British A Mk I-IV mines of which some had landed in Sweden. The main difference was that the charge was increased to 600kg (*1323lb*). It was known as F9.

Above: Swedish Lindholmen-Motala M18 moored mine being laid by an auxiliary minelayer during the war.
By courtesy of K-E Westerlund

Right: A Swedish moored mine, probably magnetic, being laid by the *Älvsnabben* in 1945.
By courtesy of K-E Westerlund

INDEX

Individual guns and weapons are not indexed, since they can be found easily by reference to the detailed list of contents. All named ships, classes and types are given below, with references in the captions printed in *italics*.